PRODUCT LIABILITY LAW IN TEXAS

PRODUCT LIABILITY LAW IN TEXAS

First Edition

JAMES B. SALES
B.S., LL.B., University of Texas
Attorney at Law, Houston, Texas

Coauthored by

Paul Cauley
Debbie Crupain
Catherine Graubart
Therese Hartwell
Dale Mellencamp
Barbara Paulissen
Adam Schiffer
Phyllis Schrader
Rhonda Rhodes Wile

Library of Congress Catalog Card Number: 85-018150

ISBN 0-913797-09-X

PREFACE

Like the legendary "Topsy," the law of product liability has grown and expanded in direction and magnitude unmatched in any other area of tort law. When the concept of strict tort liability for products was formulated by §402A of the *Restatement (Second) of Torts* in 1965, jurisdictions across the country began the tedious process of forging the rules and concepts that would define the scope and applicability of this unique doctrine. The Texas law of product liability, like its counterpart in the other jurisdictions, has literally exploded in the twenty years since its genesis in the *Restatement*. Despite the intensity and breadth of litigation which has spawned the myriad of decisions that has provided the contour to the doctrine of products liability, there continues to exist many unanswered issues, conceptual inconsistencies and even dichotomies within this state's decisional law.

An effort was mounted in 1977 to structure a treatise on the law of product liability as it existed ten years after its adoption by the Texas Supreme Court. The original work, entitled THE LAW OF STRICT TORT LIABILITY in Texas, endeavored to comprehensively summarize and provide an analysis of strict tort liability as articulated by §402 of the *Restatement*. Even before the treatise was published, several decisions modified and significantly altered the law as discussed in that treatise. Despite the 1977 treatise and its 1981 supplement, the law has, indeed, proceeded apace. With the thought in mind that the body of law defining the scope and applicability of product liability has grown immeasurably in the past eighteen years, the decision was made to totally rewrite the original treatise and to endeavor, to the extent possible, to provide a compact and definitive work on the entire spectrum of product liability law.

It has been my goal to produce a reference of the substantive law that governs all phases of product liability litigation in the state. Both state and federal decisions relating to the Texas law on product liability are the principal focus of this work. It should be noted that the subjects are treated in a substantive manner and no effort has been made to provide a "how to" book or a "book of forms." I hope that attorneys involved in this challenging area of tort jurisprudence will find this treatise a worthwhile reference that can be utilized both in the office and at the courthouse. As a word of caution, no treatise addressing product liability law in the state of Texas can ever be totally current and represent the last word. Development of the law in this area rarely stops long enough to be reported at rest and, even as this book is being published, judicial decisions are continuing to expand, alter and mold the rules that govern product liability in Texas. Because the law proceeds apace and the rules change as new problems are confronted, the reader is cautioned to view this treatise as primarily a reference work and a starting point in addressing the numerous problems implicit in any product liability lawsuit.

I wish to extend my grateful appreciation to the editors of the Houston Law Review without whose invaluable assistance, determined motivation, and enthusiastic effort an undertaking of this magnitude would not have been possible. I particularly wish to express my personal appreciation to Phyllis Schrader, Tim O'Neal, Debbie Crupain and Barbara Paulissen for the extra commitment that each made to insure that this work was completed in a timely manner and published on schedule.

JAMES B. SALES

Houston Texas
July 1, 1985

TABLE OF CONTENTS

CHAPTER II. PROOF OF CAUSES OF ACTION 129

CHAPTER V. INDUSTRY-WIDE STRICT TORT LIABILITY . . . 365

CHAPTER VI. PROSPECTIVE PLAINTIFFS . . . 425

CHAPTER VII. DAMAGES . . . 447

CHAPTER I. THEORIES OF LIABILITY FOR PRODUCT RELATED ACCIDENTS*

---

* Phyllis Schrader coauthored this chapter.

1.00 GENERALLY

The concept of strict tort liability for product related injuries was initially articulated in the *Restatement (Second) Of Torts* in 1965,[1] and was adopted by the Texas Supreme Court in 1967.[2] In the twenty years since the adoption of § 402A, the law has undergone an astonishing evolution of expansion. Texas has emerged as one of the most progressively liberal of all jurisdictions in products liability law. Current efforts for a national Product Liability Act to preempt the law of strict tort liability of individual jurisdictions has not yet been successful,[3] and judicially developed state law continues to govern Texas cases. This chapter reviews the historical evolution and development of strict tort liability, and focuses on and discusses the current theories of strict tort liability actions. It examines in detail each of the quintessential elements for asserting a cause of action in strict tort liability under § 402A.[4] The chapter also considers strict liability in tort under §402B (innocent misrepresentation), and recovery for a product-related accident under breach of the implied warranties prescribed by the Uniform Commercial Code.

---

1. RESTATEMENT (SECOND) OF TORTS § 402A (1965).
2. McKisson v. Sales Affiliates, Inc., 416 S.W.2d 787, 790 (Tex. 1967), *noted in* 19 BAYLOR L. REV. 510, (1967); Shamrock Fuel & Oil Sales Co. v. Tunks, 416 S.W.2d 779, 781 (Tex. 1967).
3. Refer to notes 65-69 *infra* and accompanying text.
4. Keeton, *Products Liability*, 50 F.R.D. 338, (1971) (article). *See generally* Sales, *An Overview of Strict Tort Liability in Texas*, 11 HOUS. L. REV. 1043 (1974).

A. *Historical Background*

The development of strict tort liability for physical injury presents a novel and unique creation of the common law. In the early years of the century, concurrent with development of an industrial based society and economy, a social policy gradually emerged that provided a basis for compensation to those who were injured as the result of a product-caused accident.[5] As technology developed and products became increasingly complex, and as marketing systems began extending from a regional to a national basis, the traditional theories of negligence and warranty were perceived inadequate to protect injured consumers.[6] In response to the evolution of a technically complex industrial society in place of the traditional rural oriented society, judicially fashioned remedies developed that significantly modified the common law negligence rule. Thus, negligence causes of action were restructured to abrogate the privity impediment when personal injury occurred as the result of an "inherently dangerous" and defective product.[7] For example, a consumer who sustained injury from contaminated food or drugs, or who was injured by inherently dangerous equipment, could institute a negligence action against the manufacturer even though he had not purchased the product directly from the manufacturer and, therefore, lacked privity.[8]

In 1916, the New York Court of Appeals in the seminal case of

---

5. Hill, *How Strict is Strict? Have the Walls of the Citadel Really Crumbled?*, 32 TEX. B.J. 759 (1969).

6. Professor S. Birnbaum has observed that "The doctrine of strict products liability is grounded in social and economic policy considerations that were inadequately served under traditional negligence concepts." Birnbaum, *Unmasking the Test for Design Defect: From Negligence [to Warranty] to Strict Liability to Negligence*, 33 VAND. L. REV. 593 (1980). *See also* Greenman v. Yuba Power Prod., Inc., 59 Cal.2d 57, 377 P.2d 897, 27 Cal.Rptr. 697 (1963); Henningsen v. Bloomfield Motors Inc., 32 N.J. 358, 161 A.2d 69 (1960); Prosser, *The Assault Upon the Citadel (Strict Liability to the Consumer)*, 69 YALE L.J. 1099 (1960); Wade, *On Product "Design Defects" and Their Actionability*, 33 VAND L. REV. 551, 552-3 (1980).

7. In 1916, Judge Cardozo rejected the "inherent danger" requirement in negligence actions in the landmark case of MacPherson v. Buick Motor Co., 217 N.Y. 382, 111 N.E. 1050 (1916).

8. Cushing v. Rodman, 82 F.2d 864, 868 (D.C. Cir. 1936) (plaintiff broke tooth on a roll containing a pebble and recovered under implied warranty that food is wholesome). Devlin v. Smith, 89 N.Y. 470 (1882) (plaintiff's decedent killed when defective scaffolding broke); *See, e.g.* Thomas v. Winchester, 6 N.Y. 397 (1852) (woman injured when she took a poison falsely labeled as a mild medicine succeeded in a negligence action against both the retail druggist and the chemist).

MacPherson v. Buick Motor Co. extended the manufacturer's duty of reasonable care beyond the purchaser to all foreseeable users.[9] Justice Cardozo declared that in negligence actions, privity of contract no longer represented a requirement for an action instituted by an injured user of a product against the manufacturer.[10] Negligence for a dangerously defective product was dramatically extended.

Following abrogation of the privity requirement for a negligence action, Texas extended the product supplier's liability even further through the vehicle of an implied warranty in tort. In 1942, in *Jacob E. Decker & Sons v. Capps*,[11] the Texas Supreme Court concluded that a manufacturer of contaminated pork sausage was liable to an injured consumer based on breach of a warranty implied by law and unencumbered by the traditional privity of contract.[12] The court predicated this newly formulated concept on considerations of public policy. In the case of food products that were contaminated and unfit for human consumption, the product so completely failed its purpose that the law implied a warranty of fitness benefiting the ultimate user.[13] Until the 1960's, Texas limited the concept of a warranty implied by law to food products.[14]

In 1960, a New Jersey court in *Henningsen v. Bloomfield Motors, Inc.*, abrogated the privity requirement in a breach of warranty case paralleling the *MacPherson* abrogation of the privity requirement for negligence actions forty-five years earlier.[15] In *Henningsen*, plaintiff was injured when a newly purchased vehicle that she was driving suddenly and unexpectedly veered from the

---

9. 111 N.E. at 1053.

10. *Id.*

11. 139 Tex. 609, 164 S.W.2d 828 (1942).

12. 139 Tex. at 612, 164 S.W.2d at 829.

13. *Id.*

14. Comment, *Strict Products Liability — Its Application and Meaning*, 21 Sw. L.J. 629, 630 (1967); *see, e.g.*, Capetillo v. Crosby County Fuel Ass'n, 407 S.W.2d 335, 335-37 (Tex. Civ. App.—Amarillo 1966, no writ); Cruz v. Ansul Chem. Co., 399 S.W.2d 944, 947-48 (Tex. Civ. App.—Corpus Christi 1966, writ ref'd n.r.e., *overruled on other grounds*); O.M. Franklin Serum Co. v. C.A. Hoover & Sun, 418 S.W.2d 482 (Tex. 1967); Anheuser-Busch, Inc. v. Butler, 180 S.W.2d 996, 997-98 (Tex. Civ. App.—Amarillo 1944, no writ); Latham v. Coca-Cola Bottling Co., 175 S.W.2d 426, 427 (Tex. Civ. App.—Fort Worth 1943, no writ); Jax Beer Co. v. Schaeffer, 173 S.W.2d 285, 287 (Tex. Civ. App.—El Paso 1943, writ ref'd w.o.m.). *Contra* Ford Motor Co. v. Grimes, 408 S.W.2d 313, 315 (Tex. Civ. App.—Eastland 1966, writ dism'd).

15. Henningsen v. Bloomfield Motors, Inc., 32 N.J. 358, 161 A.2d 69 (1960).

roadway and collided with a fixed object. Plaintiff contended that the steering wheel malfunctioned and froze. In imposing liability on the manufacturer based on a form of breach of warranty, the court painstakingly noted that the basis of the action rested not on traditional contractual remedies but, rather, was based solely on considerations of public policy.[16]

Theories of implied warranties thus were transformed into a vehicle to provide a remedy to consumers injured as the result of product related occurrences. Utilizing the vehicle of a warranty implied by law, however, created a plethora of problems. The application of an implied warranty remedy in the absence of privity conceptually violated the very essence of warranty theory; historically a purchaser was authorized to sue only his immediate seller.[17] Moreover, the warranty theory was subject to significant limitations. An appropriate written disclaimer nullified the warranty.[18] In a warranty action, prompt notice of a breach was required to be communicated to the seller.[19] The privity requirement continued to retain vitality in numerous jurisdictions.[20] The use of a warranty implied by law as the basis for recovery of damages for injuries inflicted in products related events was described as "a freak hybrid born of the illicit intercourse of tort and contract."[21]

Adoption of the theory of strict tort liability represented the ultimate response to the legally cumbersome theories of breach of warranty and negligence in product defect cases. In 1962, the Supreme Court of California formulated the concept of strict tort liability in the landmark decision of *Greenman v. Yuba Power Products, Inc.*[22] Plaintiff was injured when operating a defective lathe. Citing *Henningsen*, the California court declared that a manufacturer was strictly liable in tort for an injury caused by a defective

---

16. 32 N.J. at 384, 161 A.2d at 83 (quoting Mazetti v. Armour & Co., 75 Wash. 622, 135 P. 633 (1913)).

17. Hasbrouck v. Armour & Co., 139 Wis. 357, 121 N.W. 157 (1909); Lebourdais v. Vitrified Wheel Co., 194 Mass. 341, 80 N.E. 482 (1907); Liggett & Myers Tobacco Co. v. Cannon, 132 Tenn. 419, 178 S.W. 1009 (1915).

18. Prosser, *The Assault Upon the Citadel* (*Strict Liability to the Consumer*), 69 Yale L.J. 1099, 1131 (1960).

19. *Id.* at 1131.

20. *Id.* at 1129.

21. *Id.* at 1126.

22. Greenman v. Yuba Power Products, Inc., 59 Cal. 2d 57, 377 P.2d 897, 27 Cal. Rptr. 697 (1963).

product introduced into the marketplace.[23]

The authors of the *Restatement (Second) Of Torts* relying almost entirely on the astonishingly unique *Greenman* rationale for imposing liability on product sellers, formulated § 402A of the *Restatement.* Section 402A represents the linchpin of today's doctrine of strict tort liability or, as it is more commonly characterized, product liability.[24] Under the *Restatement* formulation of the strict tort liability doctrine, a party injured in connection with the use of any type of product may recover damages against any supplier in the distributive chain of that product upon proof that the product was defective, that it reached the consumer without substantial change from the time it left the hands of the manufacturer, that the defective condition rendered the product unreasonably dangerous, and that this unreasonably dangerous condition was a cause in fact of injury to the user.

Strict tort liability under § 402A differs noticeably from the concept of common law negligence. Negligence has represented the predominant tort remedy for compensation of personal injury damages since the genesis of the tort reparations system. Negligence evaluates the conduct of the product supplier while strict tort liability focuses entirely on the condition of the product.[25]

Texas adopted the strict tort liability doctrine in 1967 in the landmark case of *McKisson v. Sales Affiliates, Inc.*[26] Plaintiff sustained severe burns to her face and scalp accompanied by hair loss when a permanent wave solution manufactured by the defendant was applied to her hair.[27] The Texas Supreme Court, expressly adopting § 402A of the *Restatement* concluded that the *Decker* rule concerning impure foods should be extended to include all defective products that cause physical harm to persons.[28] In a com-

---

23. 57 Cal. 2d at 63, 377 P.2d at 901, 27 Cal. Rptr. at 701.

24. To Regulate Interstate Commerce by Providing for a Uniform Product Liability Law, and for Other Purposes, 1983: Hearings on S. 44 Before the Subcomm. on the Consumer of the Senate Comm. on Commerce, Science, and Transportation, 98th Cong., 1st Sess. 67 (1983) (statement of James B. Sales, Houston, Tex.) [hereinafter *Hearings on S. 44*]

25. *See* Scronce v. Howard Bros. Discount Stores, 679 F.2d 1204 (4th Cir. 1982) (applying Texas law); Fleishman v. Guadiano, 651 S.W.2d 730 (Tex. 1983); Turner v. General Motors, 584 S.W.2d 844 (Tex. 1979); Gonzales v. Caterpillar Tractor Co., 571 S.W.2d 867 (Tex. 1978); Bell Helicopter Co. v. Bradshaw, 594 S.W.2d 519 (Tex. Civ. App.—Corpus Christi 1979, writ ref'd n.r.e.).

26. 416 S.W.2d 787 (Tex. 1967).

27. *Id.* at 790.

28. *Id.* at 789.

panion case, *Shamrock Fuel and Oil Sales Co. v. Tunks*,[29] plaintiff, a small child, was severely burned after pouring kerosene adulterated with gasoline on a burning stick. The Texas Supreme Court, reaffirming its landmark decision in *McKisson*, concluded that the manufacturer was strictly liable in tort under § 402A for plaintiff's injuries.[30] These two decisions inaugurated the explosive era of strict tort liability for product related injuries in Texas. As adopted, the doctrine of strict tort liability authorizes the injured consumer to recover damages without the necessity of proving negligence or breach of implied warranty by the manufacturer or product supplier. Today, strict liability in tort has been expanded to encompass actions predicated not only on the traditional type of manufacturing defect, but to actions premised entirely on alleged defective design and defective marketing.

B. *Rationale for the Strict Tort Liability Doctrine*

The formulators of § 402A originally contemplated imposing strict tort liability upon suppliers of flawed products.[31] The rationale underlying this unique and far reaching doctrine is essentially socioeconomic in origin.[32] Basically, the doctrine of necessity, is totally dependent on the dubious "deep pocket" principle.[33] As be-

---

29. *Shamrock Fuel & Oil Sales, Inc. v. Tunks*, 416 S.W.2d 779 (Tex. 1967).

30. *Id.* at 779.

31. *Hearings on S. 44*, 98th Cong., 1st Sess. 66 (1983).

32. Comment c to RESTATEMENT § 402A provides:

> On whatever theory, the justification for strict liability has been said to be that the seller, by marketing his product for use and consumption, has undertaken and assumed a special responsibility toward any member of the consuming public who may be injured by it; that the public has the right to and does expect, in the case of products which it needs and for which it is forced to rely upon the seller, that reputable sellers will stand behind their goods; that public policy demands that the burden of accidental injuries caused by products intended for consumption be placed upon those who market them, and be treated as a cost of production against which liability insurance can be obtained; and that the consumer of such products is entitled to the maximum of protection at the hands of someone, and the proper persons to afford it are those who market the products. RESTATEMENT (SECOND) OF TORTS, § 402A comment c (1965).

33. *See* Greenman v. Yuba Power Prods. Inc., 59 Cal. 2d 57, 377 P.2d 897, 27 Cal. Rptr. 697, (1963); Beshada v. Johns-Manville Prod. Corp., 90 N.J. 191, 447 A.2d 539, (1982); Caterpillar Tractor Co. v. Beck, 593 P.2d 871, (Alaska 1979); Lewis v. Timco, Inc., 697 F.2d 1252, (5th Cir. 1983). *See also* Challoner v. Day & Zimmerman, Inc., 512 F.2d 77, 84 (5th Cir., *vacated*, 423 U.S. 3 (1975). *See generally*, Hill, *How Strict is Strict? Have The Walls of the Citadel Really Crumbled?*, 32 TEX. B.J. 59, 799 (1969).

tween an injured party and a product supplier who purportedly has made a profit either from the manufacture or the sale of a product, the product supplier is judicially declared to occupy a better position to absorb the cost of injury than the injured consumer. This socioeconomic rationale relies solely on the validity of the perception that the supplier is better able to withstand the economic impact of large jury awards than the injured consumer or user; the supplier purportedly can distribute the cost of these large damage awards to all consumers in the marketplace.[34] This cost is distributed either by raising the price of products distributed to the consumers in the marketplace or by purchasing appropriate insurance whose premium costs likewise, theoretically, are distributed to the innocent consumers of the product—a form of social redistribution of the costs.[35] In addition, strict tort liability satisfies society's interest in compensating injured parties.[36] Those who analyze legal problems from the perspective of economic efficiency argue that taxing the manufacturer with the costs of injuries caused by a product creates an optimal allocation of goods and resources. Under this rather arcane rationale, when each enterprise pays its own way, all of society benefits.[37]

An additional rationale articulated in support of the strict tort liability doctrine presumes an implied representation of quality and safety by product suppliers. This representational theorem presupposes that in marketing and selling products, the supplier impliedly represents to the public that the product introduced into the channels of commerce is safe for use.[38] Unfortunately, since the

---

34. Holford, *The Limits of Strict Liability for Product Design and Manufacture*, 52 TEXAS L. REV. 81, 82 (1973). Birnbaum notes that "Manufacturers . . . are thought to be in the best position to distribute the costs of product-related injuries by purchasing insurance or increasing prices of their products." Birnbaum, *supra* note 6, at 643.

35. The socioeconomic concept of placing the costs on the product supplier redistribution to consumers through increased prices of the products or purchase of additional insurance underlies the very essence of the doctrine of strict tort liability. See RESTATEMENT (SECOND) OF TORTS § 402A comment c (1965).

36. Professor Birnbaum observes that "If courts are going to apply strict liabilty as a purely compensatory device then they should be forthright in identifying it as such instead of covertly providing recovery under the rubric of a risk-spreading rationale." Birnbaum, *supra* note 6, at 643.

37. See, for example, R. POSNER, ECONOMIC ANALYSISIS OF LAW 3-4, 6, 9-10, 12-13 (2d ed. 1977); *Symposium: Products Liability: Economic Analysis and the Law*, 38 CHI. L. REV. 1 (1970).

38. The following cases recognize a warranty of fitness and safety implied in law: Higbee v. Giant Food Shopping Center, 106 F. Supp. 586 (E.D. Va. 1952); Vinyard v. Duck, 278

doctrine of strict tort liability is premised entirely on the condition of the product and not the conduct of the product supplier, the representational theorem rests on a questionable foundation.

Much criticism has developed in the last few years attributable primarily to the expansion of an already liberal concept.[39] Critics observe that the enormous increase in litigation and the mind boggling awards have imposed an intolerable burden on industry.[40] Perhaps one of the most significant difficulties is precipitated by the state of flux and unpredictable applications of the law in the various jurisdictions. Neither the manufacturers nor their insurers can predict and assess in a meaningful manner their potential liability under strict tort liability to allow for appropriate pricing and expensing.[41] Skyrocketing insurance rates and economically devas-

---

Ala. 687, 180 So.2d 522 (1965); Gonzales v. Safeway Stores, 147 Colo. 358, 363 P.2d 667 (1961); Sams v. Ezy-Way Foodliner Co., 157 Me. 10, 170 A.2d 160 (1961); John A. Brown Co. v. Shelton, 391 P.2d 259 (Okl. 1964).

39. *See* Henderson, *Renewed Judicial Controversy Over Defective Product Design: Toward the Preservation of an Emerging Consensus*, 63 MINN. L. REV. 773 (1979); Henderson, *Judicial Review of Manufacturers' Conscious Design Choices: The Limits of Adjudication* 73 COLUM. L. REV. 1531 (1973); Hoenig, *Product Designs and Strict Tort Liability: Is There a Better Approach?* 8 SW. REV. 109 (1976); Schwartz, *Comments to Model Uniform Prod. Liability Act*, 44 FED. REG. 62, 714 (1979); Birnbaum, *supra* n.6 at 593.

40. *Hearings on S. 44*, 98th Cong. 1st Sess. 258 (1983) (statement of Luke Rich, Chief of Staff for Senator Walter Floss): "Uncertainties in the products liability tort-litigation system have an adverse effect on international trade, a fact which affects the economy generally . . . . American manufacturers and product sellers generally pay products liability insurance rates which are 20 times higher than those in Europe." *See also* Henderson, *Products Liability and the Passage of Time: The Imprisonment of Corporate Rationality* (Symposium: The Passage of Time; the Implications for Product Liability) 58 N.Y.U.L. REV. 765 (Oct. 1983).

41. *Id.*: "Insurance rates reflect the fact that manufacturers and product sellers are unable to predict the legal standards which will apply in future claims." *See e.g.*, the testimony of the National Machine Tool Builders' Association before a House subcommittee: "The average machine tool builder has seen his product liability insurance costs rise from $10,000 in 1970 to $40,000 in 1975 to $71,000 in 1976 and then almost double again to $132,100 this year [1977]." *Product Liability Insurance, Hearings Before the Subcomittee on Capital, Investment and Business Opportunities of the House Committee on Small Businesses*, 95th Cong., 1st Sess. 287 (1977). Information from the metal cutting machinery builders reflects even more dramatic escalation: premiums increased from an average of $1,900 in 1970 to $126,800 in 1977 (an increase of 6,673 percent). *Id.* at 291. Professor Birnbaum has observed that, "While it is certainly true that not all industries have experienced such extravagant increases in product liability insurance premiums, it is nevertheless clear that in many instances premium increases have exceeded 200% and that increases of more than 1,000% over the last eight years are not uncommon." Birnbaum cites *Product Liability Insurance, A Report of the Subcommittee on Capital, Investment and Business Opportunities of the House Committee of Small Businesses*, H.R. REP. No. 95-997, 95th Cong. 2d Sess. 8-11 (1978). Birnbaum, *supra* note 6, at 644 nn.260-62 *passim*. *See also* Wade, *supra*

tating damage claims in some industries have annihilated product suppliers by forcing them into bankruptcies[42] and have seriously thwarted pioneering and development of new products.[43] It is thus the innocent consumer who ultimately bears the unintended side effects of the strict tort liability system.[44] Some have suggested that despite the growth of litigation, adequate compensation for injured parties has not necessarily occurred because funds are often diverted for extended legal battles.[45] For example, a recent study by the Rand Corporation purportedly demonstrated that for every dollar paid to claimants, fifty-eight cents is spent for legal defense; of the dollar the claimant is awarded, forty-one cents is allocated to the claimant's attorney.[46]

A significant portion of the criticism that has emerged focuses on the perceived unwarranted extension of the concept of strict tort liability beyond the literal parameters of the *Restatement*[47]

---

note 6, 576 n.119.

42. *Hearings on S. 44*, 98th Cong. 1st Sess. 258 (1983) (statement of Luke Rich, Chief of Staff for Senator Walter Floss).

43. *Id.*; *see also id.* at 171 (opening statement of Rep. James T. Broyhill).

44. *Id.* at 257: "Legal costs are generally passed on to consumers in the form of higher products process." *See also id.* at 67 (statement of James Sales): "The loss is then distributed to the entire consuming public, the innocent buyers and users of that product."

45. *Id.* at 257 (statement of Luke Rich, Chief of Staff for Senator Walter Floss):

> The testimony before the U.S. Senate Committee of a press brake manufacturer illustrates the magnitude of these legal and transaction costs:
>
> "During the most recent fiscal year, our small company and its insurers paid out $850,000 for products liability claims. But only 18 percent of that amount went to pay settlements to claimants. About $700,000 went for defense lawyers and other transaction costs. I firmly believe that a uniform set of balanced product liability rules would have saved our company and its insurers over 60 percent of the $700,000 we have expended."

46. *Hearings on S. 44*, 98th Cong. 2nd Sess. 376 (1984) (opening statement by Sen. Bob Kasten)

47. Courts have engaged in judicial redefinition of the RESTATEMENT and have liberalized the literal provisions of the RESTATEMENT to embrace, in addition to the flawed product, design defects. *See, e.g.*, Pike v. Frank G. Hough Co., 2 C.3d 440, 467 P.2d 229, 85 Cal. Rptr. 629 (1970); Rindlisbaker v. Wilson, 95 Idaho 752, 519 P.2d 421 (1974); Reid v. Spadone Mach. Co., 119 N.H. 457, 404 A.2d 1094 (1979); Bexiga v. Havir Mfg. Corp., 60 N.J. 402, 290 A.2d 281 (N.J. 1972); Rourke v. Garza, 530 S.W.2d 794 (Tex. 1975). Utilizing the rationale of social policy, courts have expanded the concept of strict tort liability to include products with marketing defects, e.g. failure to warn adequately and/or a failure to provide appropriate or adequate directions for efficient and/or safe use: Jahnig v. Coismann, 283 N.W.2d 557 (S.D. 1979); Williams v. Brown Mfg. Co., 93 Ill. App. 2d 334, 236 N.E.2d 125 (1968); *rev'd on other grounds*. 45 Ill. 2d 418, 261 N.E. 2d 305 (1970); Tucson Indus. Inc. v. Schwartz, 108 Ariz. 464 501 P.2d 936 (1972); Technical Chemical Co. v. Jacobs, 480 S.W.2d 602 (Tex. 1972); Freund v. Cellofilm Properties, Inc., 87 N.J. 229 432 A.2d 925 (1981); Borel v.

Initially, the *Restatement* was designed to provide injured parties with a relatively easy method for recovering damages for injuries caused by flawed products that failed to conform to the manufacturer's own specifications.[48] As initially formulated, the doctrine was never really intended to apply to products that were perfectly made in compliance with the specifications of the manufacturer but were deemed to be defective because of some design configuration or marketing defect.[49] Design and marketing defects, unlike manufacturing defects, do not have a clear and readily perceived standard against which to be judged, and as a result attempts by the courts to define standards have led to a confused and almost incoherent area of the law.[50]

Currently seventy per cent of America's products are distributed in states other than those in which they were manufactured. Coupled with this statistic is the well-recognized fact that each jurisdiction has formulated and applies differing standards governing acceptable design.[51] National manufacturers confront an erratic patchwork quilt of design and marketing lists that have been fashioned and, in many instances, refashioned by each jurisdiction to evaluate whether a particular product is defective.[52] A national manufacturer who introduces a product into various states experiences insoluble difficulty in designing a product that will satisfy the design standards of every jurisdiction. For example, in design defect cases, criteria or tests by which a trier of fact is obligated to evaluate the design differ vastly. In California[53] and Alaska[54] the test for a defective design provides alternatively that: (a) a product may be found defective in design if the plaintiff establishes that

---

Fibreboard Paper Prod. Corp. 493 F.2d 1076 (5th Cir. 1973), *cert. denied*, 419 U.S. 869 (1974); Needham v. White Laboratories, Inc., 639 F.2d 394 (7th Cir. 1981), *cert. denied* 454 U.S. 927 (1981); Gryc v. Dayton-Hudson Corp., 297 N.W.2d 727 (Minn. 1980), *cert. denied* 449 U.S. 921 (1980).

48. *Hearings on S. 44*, 98th Cong. 1st Sess. 68 (1983).

49. *Id.*

50. Refer to notes 53-58 *infra* and accompanying text.

51. *Hearings on S. 44*, 98th Cong. 1st Sess. 68 (1983). One commentator observes that, "[I]f, as a social matter one deems it desirable to hold manufacturers absolutely liable for product-related injuries, then a legislative approach to the problem is required so that limits can be reasonably placed upon recovery." Birnbaum, *supra* note 6, at 643-44.

52. *Hearings on S. 44*, 98th Cong., 1st Sess. 69 (1983).

53. Barker v. Lull Engineering Co., Inc., 20 Cal. 3d 413, 573 P.2d 443, 143 Cal. Rptr. 225 (1978).

54. Caterpillar Tractor Co. v. Beck, 593 P.2d 871 (Alaska 1979).

the product failed to perform as safely as an ordinary consumer would expect it to when used in an intended or reasonably foreseeable manner or (b) a product may be found defective in design if the plaintiff demonstrates that the product design proximately caused his injury and the defendant fails to establish in light of the relevant factors, that, on balance, the benefits of the challenged design outweigh the risk of danger inherent in such design. In Texas[55] and similar jurisdictions, a product is defective in design if it is unreasonably dangerous as designed, taking into consideration the utility of the product and the risk involved in its use. Other jurisdictions, such as New Jersey,[56] deem a product defective in design if it is established that the product fails to perform as safely as an ordinary consumer would expect when used in an intended or reasonably foreseeable manner. Some jurisdictions, such as Oregon,[57] deem a product defective when a reasonable person would not have put the product in the stream of commerce if he had had knowledge of its harmful character. Yet other jurisdictions, such as Pennsylvania, essentially transform the supplier of the product into an absolute insurer by declaring that a design is defective it it left the supplier's control lacking any element to make it safe for its intended use.[58] A manufacturer may have difficulty engineering a design that will satisfy the variety of tests and standards by which its product will be evaluated.

A problem unique to product liability involves the complex nature of the products and the technicality associated with evaluating the product.[59] Litigation too often devolves into a battle of expert witnesses. Serious concern has been expressed about the technical considerations that form the basis of a strict tort liability

---

55. Turner v. General Motors Corp., 584 S.W.2d 844, (Tex. 1979); Claytor v. General Motors Corp., 277 S.C. 259, 286 S.E.2d 129, (1982).

56. Suter v. San Angelo Foundry & Mach. Co., 81 N.J. 150, 406 A.2d 140, (1979); Vincer v. Esther Williams All-Aluminum Swimming Pool Co., 69 Wis. 2d 326, 230 N.W.2d 794, (1975); Brady v. Melody Homes Mfr., 121 Ariz. 253, 589 P.2d 896 (Ariz. Ct. App. 1979).

57. Phillips v. Kimwood Mach. Co., 269 Or. 485, 525 P.2d 1033 (1974); Wilson v. Piper Aircraft Corp., 282 Or. 61, 577 P.2d 1322, *reh'g denied with opinion*, 282 Or. 411, 579 P.2d 1287 (1978).

58. Azzarello v. Black Bros. Co., 480 Pa. 547, 391 A.2d 1020, (1978). Professor Wade, *supra* note 6, at 560 notes that *Azzarello* "is confusing and of uncertain significance."

59. *See, e.g.*, Heaton v. Ford Motor Co., 248 Or. 467, 435 P.2d 806, 809 (1967). *See* Wade, *supra* note 6, at 551, 569. *See also* Sales, *Automobile Design Sufficiency and Enhanced Injury: A New Concept for No-Fault Liability*, 38 INS. COUNS. J. 388, (1971).

action based on a design defect.[60] Others view strict tort liability based on defective design or marketing as involving matters no more complex or technical than areas such a medical malpractice. National legislation as a potential solution has been both praised and condemned. One witness appearing before a Senate subcommittee outlined opposition to national legislation on four specific bases: (1) national legislation would nationalize the judiciary and preempt present negligence and products laws;[61] (2) national legislation would tend to "freeze" the law in a particular pattern;[62] (3) national legislation as interpreted by the various states would not bring about national uniformity;[63] and (4) states have worked out reasonable standards for deciding cases presented to them in the products liability area and, therefore, national legislation is not needed.[64]

Efforts for national legislation were initiated in 1976 when President Gerald Ford appointed a task force to study the products liability area.[65] Under the administration of President Carter,[66] the Department of Commerce drafted a model Uniform Product Liability Act for voluntary consideration by the states. In

60. Quote from Henderson, *supra* note 39 at 1531; Hoenig, L. *supra* note 39, at 109; Schwartz, *supra* note 39 at 714.

61. Chief Justice Pope appeared on behalf of the Conference of Chief Justices and expressed concern for the impact the proposed federal legislation would have on the system. He commented, "The chief justices are just as concerned about a fair system as anybody. And left alone we will arrive at this favorable result. . . ." *Hearings on S. 44*, 98th Cong., 2nd Sess. 378 (1984) (statement of Hon. Jack Pope). *See also* Chief Justice Pope's statement in the first session of Congress, *Id.* at 235 (1983).

62. *Hearings on S. 44*, 98th Cong. 1st Sess. 235 (1983) (statement of Hon. Jack Pope). See also *id.*, p. 63 (statement of Prof. W. Page Keeton of the University of Texas School of Law in Austin). Professor Keeton testified: "I am opposed on principle to codification of tort law either at the Federal level or at the State level, because codification of the law in detail, as this bill would do, destroys the flexibility that the courts would otherwise have . . . . It leads to rigidity in the law."

63. *Hearings on S. 44*, 98th Cong. 2nd Sess. 377 (1984) (statement of Hon. Jack Pope) Pope commented, "It [the proposed bill] disturbes many settled practices . . . . There is being achieved through the common law the unformity that this bill, in our judgment, will destroy" *See also id.* (statement of Professor Keeton) at 65: "It is my opinion that the bill will not achieve uniformity and it will vastly increase the amount of uncertainty in the law in a particular state."

64. "[I]t will disrupt practices and procedures that many of us have worked for a lifetime in order to straighten out and to streamline." *Id.* at 377 (statement of Hon. Jack Pope). See also *id.* at 65 (statement of Professor Keeton): "While products liability law varies from state to state, the law of a particular state has become fairly well settled."

65. *Hearings on S. 44*, 98th Cong., 1st Sess. 112 (1983).

66. *Id.*

1982, Senate Bill 2631, which provides national standards in products liability, was introduced.[67] Its successor and counterpart, Senate Bill 44, was introduced in 1983 by Senator Bob Kasten of Wisconsin and co-sponsored by various other legislators.[68] At the close of the 98th Congress, the bill was favorably reported to the Senate by its Committee on Commerce, Science, and Transportation, but the Senate failed to act on the bill before the close of the session. The debate continues, however, and proposals for national products liability legislation undoubtedly will continue with a concomitant swirl of controversy and discussion.[69]

1.01 Strict Tort Liability Under § 402A of the Restatement

Texas early adopted strict tort liability as outlined in Section 402A of *Restatement (Second) Of Torts*. Consequently, any analysis of this doctrine in Texas must focus on the *Restatement*. The *Restatement* articulates the doctrine of strict tort liability as follows:

(1) One who sells any product in a defective condition unreasonably dangerous to the user or consumer, or to his property, is subject to liability for physical harm thereby caused to the ultimate user or consumer or to his property, if

(a) the seller is engaged in the business of selling such a product, and

(b) it is expected to and does reach the user or consumer without substantial change in the condition in which it is sold.

2. The rule stated in Subsection (1) applies although

(a) the seller has exercised all possible care in the preparation and sale of his product, and

(b) The user or consumer has not bought the product from or entered into any contractual relation with the seller.[70]

---

67. *Id.*

68. *Id.*

69. *Id.* The full Commerce Committee favorably reported on S. 44 to the Senate on May 23, 1984. The bill was referred to the Senate Labor Committee until September 12, 1984, but it did not reach consideration by the full Senate in 1984.

70. Restatement (Second) of Torts § 402A (1965). *See e.g.*, Syrie v. Knoll Int'l, 748 F.2d 304 (5th Cir. 1984).

A. Defective Condition

Product related injury cases based upon the strict tort liability doctrine require that the plaintiff prove the existence of a defect in the product.[71] In the absence of evidence of a defect, the concept of strict tort liability is inapplicable.[72] Though proof of a specific defect is not required, evidence of probative value indicating that a defect existed in the product at the time of the accident constitutes a prerequisite for a cause of action based on § 402A.[73] The mere occurrence of an accident involving a product, or the occurrence of a product failure or malfunction, does not constitute probative evidence that the product is defective.[74]

The introduction of a defective product into the channels of commerce is fundamental to the doctrine of strict tort liability.[75] The mere use of a product in the channels of commerce, however, does not satisfy the requirement that the product must be introduced into the channels of commerce for purposes of strict tort liability. For example, in *Thate v. Texas & Pac. Ry.*,[76] a railroad

71. *See, e.g.*, Bass v. General Motors Corp., 491 S.W.2d 941, 946 (Tex. Civ. App.—Corpus Christi 1973, writ ref'd n.r.e.). *See also* Annot., 51 A.L.R.3d 8 (1973) (proof of defect).

72. Revlon, Inc. v. Hampton, 551 S.W.2d 121 (Tex. Civ. App.—Beaumont 1977, no writ). Plaintiff's failure to establish that a hair dye was defective foreclosed recovery under strict tort liability. *Id.* at 123. *See also* Martin v. Chesebrough-Pond's, Inc., 614 F.2d 498 (5th Cir. 1980); Armstrong Rubber Co. v. Urquidez, 570 S.W.2d 374 (Tex. 1978); McCants v. Salameh, 608 S.W.2d 304 (Tex. Civ. App.—Waco 1980, writ ref'd n.r.e.); Caterpillar Tractor Co. v. Gonzales, 599 S.W.2d 633 (Tex. Civ. App.—El Paso 1980, writ ref'd n.r.e.).

73. Quinn v. Southwest Wood Prods. Inc., 597 F.2d 1018 (5th Cir. 1979); Franks v. Nat'l Dairy Prods. Corp., 414 F.2d 682 (5th Cir. 1969); V. Mueller & Co. v. Corley, 570 S.W.2d 140 (Tex. Civ. App.—Houston [1st Dist.] 1978, writ ref'd n.r.e.).

74. Hagans v. Oliver Mach. Co., 576 F.2d 97 (5th Cir. 1978); Simien v. S.S. Kresge Co., 566 F.2d 551 (5th Cir. 1978); Syrie v. Knoll Intern., 748 F.2d 304 (5th Cir. 1984); Henderson v. Ford Motor Co., 519 S.W.2d 87 (Tex. 1974), *overruled in part on other grounds*, Turner v. General Motors Corp., 584 S.W.2d 844, 847 (Tex. 1979); Acord v. General Motors Corp., 669 S.W.2d 111 (Tex. 1984); Bell Helicopter Co. v. Bradshaw, 594 S.W.2d 519 (Tex. Civ. App.—Corpus Christi 1979, writ ref'd n.r.e.).

75. Foster v. Ford Motor Co., 616 F.2d 1304 (5th Cir. 1980); Armstrong Rubber Co. v. Urquidez, 570 S.W.2d 374 (Tex. 1978); Thate v. Texas & Pac. Ry. Co., 595 S.W.2d 591 (Tex. Civ. App.—Dallas 1980, writ dism'd).

76. 595 S.W.2d 591 (Tex. Civ. App.—Dallas 1980, writ dism'd). *Accord*, Foster v. Ford Motor Co., 616 F.2d 1304 (5th Cir. 1980); Watson v. Alexander, 532 F. Supp. 1004 (E.D. Tex. 1982); Hernandez v. S. Pac. Transp. Co., 641 S.W.2d 947 (Tex. App.—Corpus Christi 1982, no writ). In Smith v. Borg-Warner Corp., 626 F.2d 384 (5th Cir. 1980), the Fifth Circuit noted that *Urquidez* and *Thate* were analogous but not squarely on point in connection with a product that was in the process of manufacture when it exploded and injured an employee of a company which had subcontracted the work that resulted in the accident.

company brakeman was injured while using a railroad car with a defective stanchion. Strict tort liability was deemed inapplicable because the railroad had not released the railroad car into the channels of commerce for use by or sale to the consuming public. Moreover, an occasional seller of a product is not encompassed within the ambit of section 402A.[77]

Though the term "defective condition" is not easily defined, a defective condition has been variously characterized a a "condition not contemplated by the ultimate consumer, which will be unreasonably dangerous to him,"[78] a condition that "exposes its user to an unreasonable risk of harm when used for the purpose for which it was intended,"[79] and a condition that "fails to match the average quality of like products."[80] The test of a defective condition in a product in Texas is dependent upon the type of defect that is asserted. Defective products are commonly categorized into three distinct types: manufacturing, design, and marketing defects. The standard for measuring whether the product is in a defective condition necessarily depends on consideration of the three types of defective conditions alleged to exists in the product involved in the litigation.

1. *Manufacturing Defect.* A manufacturing defect occurs when the finished product does not conform to the design standards and specifications of the manufacturer and usually involves deficiencies in the construction, assembly, or materials used in fabricating the product.[81] The manufacturing defects reflects a flaw in the product as manufactured.[82] To establish a cause of action for strict tort liability, it is incumbent on the plaintiff to establish the existence of a flaw in the product at the time it leaves the pos-

---

77. *See* Galindo v. Precision American Corp., 754 F.2d 1212, 1217 (5th Cir. 1985).

78. RESTATEMENT (SECOND) OF TORTS,, § 402A comment g (1965).

79. Rourke v. Garza, 530 S.W.2d 794, 798 (Tex. 1975).

80. Traynor, *The Ways and Meanings of Defective Products and Strict Liability*, 32 TENN. L. REV. 363, 367 (1965).

81. Miller v. Bock Laundry Machine Co., 568 S.W.2d 648 (Tex. 1977); Henderson v. Ford Motor Co., 519 S.W.2d 87 (Tex. 1974); Pittsburg Coca-Cola Bottling Works v. Ponder, 443 S.W.2d 546 (Tex. 1969); Jack Roach-Bissonnet Inc. v. Puskar, 417 S.W.2d 262 (Tex. 1967); Fitzgerald Marine Sales v. Le Unes, 659 S.W.2d 917 (Tex. App.—Ft. Worth 1983, writ dism'd).

82. A flawed product is one that is supplied in a condition that does not comport with its expected condition. Two Rivers Co. v. Curtiss Breeding Serv. 624 F.2d 1242, 1249 (5th Cir. 1980), *cert. denied*, 450 U.S. 920 (1981).

session of the seller.[83]

A manufacturing flaw is evaluated in comparison to the manufacturer's own specifications for the product.[84] Probably as a result of this comparative evaluation standard, the theory of manufacturing defect has not been extensively discussed in recent years. Though many of the earliest cases in strict tort liability involved the failure of a product to comply with the manufacturer's own specifications,[85] manufacturing defect cases represent a lesser number of litigated cases as compared to the more frequently-litigated areas of design and marketing defect. It is not essential that the ultimate defect as it developed prior to the accident exist in that precise from at the time the product left the possession of the manufacturer. A product that is assembled or manufactured in a manner that a change will occur or is reasonably expected to occur in its intended and reasonably foreseeable use or misuse satisfies the requirement of a defective condition.[86] For example, in *Sharp v. Chrysler Corp.*,[87] a rubber seal in a brake cylinder encased in the brake drum failed after a number of years' use. Concluding that circumstantial evidence established a defective condition the court noted that "if an assembler or a manufacturer places into the channels of trade a product so fragile that anticipated use is likely to create a dangerous condition, he has distributed a defective product."[88] The test for a defective condition involving a flawed product is the "reasonable consumer expectation." A defective condition is one that is dangerous to an extent beyond that which would be contemplated by the ordinary user of the product, with the ordinary knowledge common to the community as to the product's characteristics.[89] Essentially, a consumer expects a product to

---

83. Burleson v. Coastal Recreation, Inc., 572 F.2d 509 (5th Cir. 1978).

84. Holford, *supra* note 34, at 82-83.

85. Two landmark decisions in 1967 that adopted the doctrine of tort liability for Texas involved manufacturing defects: Shamrock Fuel and Oil Sales, Inc. v. Tunks, 416 S.W.2d 779, 782 (Tex. 1967) (kerosene adulterated with gasoline) and McKisson v. Sales Affiliates, Inc., 416 S.W.2d 787 (Tex. 1967) (permanent wave solution in which the constituent elements separated).

86. Miller v. Bock Laundry Mach. Co., 568 S.W.2d 648 (Tex. 1977); Bell Helicopter Co. v. Bradshaw 594 S.W.2d 519 (Tex. Civ. App.—Corpus Christi 1979, writ ref'd n.r.e.); Sharp v. Chrysler Corp., 432 S.W.2d 131 (Tex. Civ. App.—Houston [14th Dist.] 1968, writ ref.'d n.r.e.).

87. 432 S.W.2d 131 (Tex. Civ. App.—Houston [14th Dist.] 1968, writ ref.'d n.r.e.).

88. *Id.* at 136.

89. RESTATEMENT (SECOND) OF TORTS § 402A, comment i (1965). Daberko v. Heil Co.,

be properly assembled and free of defects. The presence of a flaw that renders the product unreasonably dangerous frustrates the consumer's expectations.

a. General Products. Manufacturing deficiencies or flaws vary in nature. For example, *Nugenet v. Utica Cutlery Co.* involved an allegedly defective knife blade that snapped back and hit the plaintiff in the eye because of a stress riser;[90] *Travenol Laboratories, Inc. v. Bandy Laboratories, Inc.* involved a defective surgeon's glove which purportedly allowed rabies vaccine to become contaminated;[91] *Fitzgerald Marine Sales v. LeUnes* involved a crack in the steering wheel installed on a bass boat;[92] *Messick v. General Motors Corp.* involved a warped rear axle and warped rear wheel suspension system which adversely affected the normal operation of the vehicle;[93] and *McNeese v. Reading & Bates Drilling Co.* involved a drilling rig monorail system which collapsed.[94]

Certain types of products present unique problems in the manufacturing defect area. For example, evidence relating to a product destroyed in the accident create difficulties in proof. As a consequence, proof of a defect causing a product-related accident based on circumstantial evidence of the facts surrounding the acci-

---

681 F.2d 445, 448 (5th Cir. 1982); Rourke v. Garza, 530 S.W.2d 794 (Tex. 1978). A defect is defined in terms of consumer expectations. Two Rivers Co. v. Curtiss Breeding Serv. 624 F.2d 1242, 1249 (5th Cir. 1980), *cert. denied*, 450 U.S. 920 (1981). A product that fails to satisfy reasonable consumer expectations is deemed defective. Metal Window Prod. Co. v. Magnusen, 485 S.W.2d 355 (Tex. Civ. App.—Houston [14th Dist.] 1972, writ ref.'d n.r.e.); Ford Motor Co. v. Pool, 688 S.W.2d 879 (Tex. App.—Texarkana 1985).

90. Nugent v. Utica Cutlery Co., 636 S.W.2d 805 (Tex. App.—San Antonio 1982, writ dism'd).

91. 608 S.W.2d 308 (Tex. Civ. App.—Waco 1980, writ ref'd n.r.e.).

92. 659 S.W.2d 917 (Tex. App.—Ft. Worth 1983, writ dism'd).

93. 460 F.2d 485 (5th Cir. 1972). Other examples of manufacturing defects include: Putnam v. Erie City Manufacturing Co., 338 F.2d 911 (5th Cir. 1964), (a fork stem on a wheelchair fractured because of a fatigue failure); Darryl v. Ford Motor Co., 440 S.W.2d 630 (Tex. 1969), (a push rod for a brake pedal bent when the brake was applied in a normal stopping configuration); Air & Pump Co. v. Almaquer, 609 S.W.2d 309 (Tex. Civ. App.—Corpus Christi 1980, no writ) (break in copper tubing of a compressor pressure control system); Shoppers World v. Villarreal, 518 S.W.2d 913 (Tex. App.—Corpus Christi 1975, writ ref'd n.r.e.), (a slit in a container of soap permitted soap to escape and invade the floor area where customer walked); Cosper v. General Motors Corp., 472 S.W.2d 552 (Tex. Civ. App.—Eastland 1971, writ ref'd n.r.e.), (a hole in an exhaust system allowed carbon monoxide to enter the occupant compartment of the vehicle); Waller v. Coca-Cola Bottlers Ass'n, 523 S.W.2d 306 (Tex. Civ. App.—Houston [1st Dist.] 1975, no writ), (a soft drink carton collapsed as it was being carried by a customer).

94. 749 F.2d 270 (5th Cir. 1985).

dent will suffice.[95] The mere occurrence of an accident or malfunction, however, does not per se demonstrate a defective condition.[96] Though abrogating the stringent requirement of establishing a precise defect by direct evidence, the courts mandate that the circumstantial evidence prove the probability of a defective condition by more than mere speculation, conjecture, or surmise.[97]

Manufacturing defects in high-precision instruments present unusual problems because such instruments may be unavoidably unsafe. In *Dreiling v. General Electric Co.*,[98] plaintiff underwent a surgical procedure to replace a defective heart pacemaker. The evidence demonstrated that once the pacemaker was assembled, it was impossible to inspect the internal mechanism for defects.[99] The trial court instructed the jury that the product was not defective if it was as safe as scientific knowledge could possibly make it.[100] In affirming judgment for defendant, the Fifth Circuit recognized that the "state of the art" that existed rendered impossible a further inspection of this product.[101] Thus, a highly beneficial product that is unavoidably unsafe may negate that it is in a defective condition that renders it unreasonably dangerous.[102]

---

95. Mahan Volkswagon, Inc. v. Hall, 648 S.W.2d 324 (Tex. App.—Houston [1st Dist.] 1982, writ ref'd n.r.e.); Thiele v. Chick, 631 S.W.2d 526 (Tex. App.—Houston [1st Dist.] 1982, writ ref'd n.r.e.); Rawlings Sporting Goods Co. v. Daniels, 619 S.W.2d 435 (Tex. Civ. App.—Waco 1981, writ ref'd n.r.e.); V. Muellar Co. v. Corley, 570 S.W.2d 140 (Tex. Civ. App.—Houston [1st Dist.] 1978, writ ref'd n.r.e.).

96. *See, e.g.*, Quinn v. Southwest Wood Prods., Inc., 597 F.2d 1018 (5th Cir. 1979); Hagans v. Oliver Mach. Co., 576 F.2d 97 (5th Cir. 1978); McCants v. Salameh, 608 S.W.2d 304 (Tex. Civ. App.—Waco 1980, writ ref'd n.r.e.). *See also*, Carroll v. Ford Motor Co., 462 S.W.2d 57 (Tex. Civ. App.—Houston [14th Dist.] 1970, no writ); *Henderson*, 519 S.W.2d 87 (Tex. 1975); Helene Curtis Indus., Inc. v. Pruitt, 385 F.2d 84 (5th cir. 1967); *Puskar*, 417 S.W.2d 262 (Tex. 1967).

The following articles survey the various jurisdictions in cases of products liability related to automobiles: Annot., 100 A.L.R.3d 158 (1980) (steering system); Annot., 100 A.L.R.3d 471 (1980) (drive train); Annot., 100 A.L.R.3d 912 (1980) (suspension system); Annot., 99 A.L.R.3d 179 (1980) (defective brakes); Annot., 96 A.L.R.3d 265 (1979) (gasoline tank); Annot., 84 A.L.R.3d 877 (1978) (door glass); Annot., 81 A.L.R.3d 318 (1977) (tires).

97. C. A. Hoover and Son v. O. M. Franklin Serum Co., 444 S.W.2d 596, 597 (Tex. 1967).

98. 511 F.2d 768 (5th Cir. 1975) (applying Louisiana law).

99. *Id.* at 776.

100. *Id.* at 776 n.9.

101. *Id.* at 776.

102. Generally, a manufacturer is liable irrespective of the exercise of due care. RESTATEMENT comment *a* provides that "[t]he rule is one of strict liability, making the seller subject to liability to the user or consumer even though he has exercised all possible care in the preparation and sale of the product." RESTATEMENT (SECOND) OF TORTS, Explanatory

b. Food Products. Manufacturing flaws that involve food products present additional unusual problems.[103] Generally, food products are viewed as defective if unwholesome, contaminated or unfit for human consumption.[104] One problem involves proving that the food is unwholesome or contaminated. Normally, the plaintiff has consumed the food and, therefore, the food product frequently is unavailable to be analyzed or tested to identify the specific defect. In *Hebert v. Loveless*[105] a number of patrons at a restaurant became ill after consuming food, ice, and beverages.[106] The food analyses, however, were insufficient to identify the precise defect.[107] The court concluded that when a large number of people become ill after consuming identical foods at the same time, the consumer is relieved of the obligation to establish the specific cause of his illness.[108] The burden is "discharged by circumstantial evidence that something ingested is unwholesome and unfit."[109]

The consumer expectation standard applies in an equally unusual manner in certain types of food cases. Many food products contain an unintended yet natural substance. Texas has adopted the "reasonable expectation" test in evaluating whether a particular food product is defective. If the consumer or user would not reasonably expect a particular foreign substance in a processed product, then the product is defective and unreasonably dangerous.[110] Some jurisdictions apply the "foreign -natural" test in evaluating whether a food product contains a defect. Under this test, if the foreign substance is natural to the product (such as a pit in a peach) and is reasonably anticipated, the product does not contain

---

Notes § 402A, comment a 348 (1965). State of the art, however, appears to limit the scope of liability. *See, e.g.*, Dreiling v. General Elec. Co., 511 F.2d 768 (5th Cir. 1975); Boatland of Houston Inc. v. Bailey, 609 S.W.2d 743 (Tex. 1980).

103. *Compare* Matthews v. Campbell Soup Co., 380 F. Supp. 1061 (S.D. Tex. 1974), *with* Jim Dandy Fast Foods, Inc. v. Carpenter, 535 S.W.2d 786 (Tex. Civ. App.—Houston [1st Dist.] 1976, no writ).

104. Matthews v. Campbell Soup Co., 380 F. Supp. 1061, 1063 (S.D. Tex. 1974); Jacob E. Decker & Sons, Inc. v. Capps, 139 Tex. 609, 164 S.W.2d 828, 829 (1942); Hebert v. Loveless, 474 S.W.2d 732, 737 (Tex. Civ. App.—Beaumont 1971, writ ref'd n.r.e.).

105. 474 S.W.2d 732 (Tex. Civ. App.—Beaumont 1971, writ ref'd n.r.e.).

106. *Id.* at 733.

107. *Id.* at 736.

108. *Id.* at 738.

109. *Id.* at 739. *See also* F. W. Woolworth Co. v. Garza, 390 S.W.2d 90 (Tex. Civ. App.—San Antonio 1965, writ ref'd n.r.e.).

110. Jim Dandy Fast Foods, Inc. v. Carpenter, 535 S.W.2d 786 (Tex. Civ. App.—Houston [1st Dist.] 1976, no writ) (chicken bone in a fried breast of chicken).

a defect. If the substance discovered in the food is foreign to the product, such as metal shavings in a can of peas, the product is deemed defective for purposes of strict tort liability.[111]

Another food area involves trichinae-infested pork. While the seller of raw pork possesses no effective method to detect trichinae, the consumer may completely eliminate the defect by heating the pork above a temperature of 137 F.[112] Though Texas has not determined whether trichinae-infested pork is inherently defective, other jurisdictions have developed differing standards.[113] All jurisdictions agree that the proper use of pork by the consumer presupposes proper cooking before consumption.[114] Some jurisdictions define "proper cooking" to be "ordinary household cooking,"[115] while other jurisdictions define proper cooking as heating the pork to the temperature of 137 F, which destroys the trichinae.[116] Understandably, disagreement exists among the jurisdictions whether strict tort liability applies when, irrespective of prior cooking, the pork contains trichinae.[117]

2. *Design Defects in Strict Tort Liability.* The doctrine of strict liability under Section 402A has also been extended to defectively designed products.[118] Design defects arise when the product

---

111. Hunt v. Ferguson-Paulus Enterprises, Inc., 243 Or. 546, 415 P.2d 13 (1966); Mix v. Ingersoll Candy Co., 6 Cal. 2d 674, 59 P.2d 144 (1936) (chicken bone is natural to chicken pie).

112. Hollinger v. Shoppers Paradise of New Jersey, Inc., 134 N.J. Super. 328, 340 A.2d 687, 691 (1975).

113. *Id.* at 694-95. *See also* Annot., 96 A.L.R.3d 451 (1979) (trichinosis).

114. See RESTATEMENT (SECOND) OF TORTS § 402A comment h at 351 (1965). Comment h provides in part:

> A product is not in a defective condition when it is safe for normal handling and consumption. If the injury results from abnormal handling, as where a bottled beverage is knocked against a radiator to remove the cap, or from abnormal preparation for use, as where too much salt is added to food, or from abnormal consumption, as where a child eats too much candy and is made ill, the seller is not liable.

115. Meyer v. Greenwood, 125 Ind. App. 288, 124 N.E.2d 870, 871 (1955); Holt v. Mann, 294 Mass. 21, 200 N.E. 403, 405 (Sup. Jud. Ct. 1936); Adams v. Scheib, 408 Pa. 452, 184 A.2d 700, 705 (1962).

116. Kobeckis v. Budzko, 225 A.2d 418, 424 (Me. 1967); Hollinger v. Shoppers Paradise, Inc., 134 N.J. Super. 328, 340 A.2d 687, 695 (L. Div. 1975).

117. *Compare* Holt v. Mann, 294 Mass. 21, 200 N.E. 403 (1936), *with* Kobeckis v. Budzko, 225 A.2d 418 (Me. 1967); *and* Scheller v. Wilson Certified Foods, Inc., 114 Az. 159, 559 P.2d 1074 (Ariz. Ct. App. 1976).

118. *See, e.g.*, Pizza Inn, Inc. v. Tiffany, 454 S.W.2d 420 (Tex. Civ. App.—Waco 1970,

is manufactured in exact conformity with the manufacturer's plans and specifications, but the product is considered defective because the design renders the product unreasonably dangerous.[119] Unlike manufacturing defects, there exists no definite objective standard to evaluate whether a design is defective.[120] The consequence, of course, has been a disconcerting ambiguity that jurisdictions have struggled to resolve, redefining and restructuring the standard for measuring a design defect case.[121] All jurisdictions acknowledge that a defectively designed product is one that is manufactured in strict compliance with the specifications of the manufacturer but is defective because some aspect of the design configuration makes the product *unreasonably dangerous* for its reasonably intended or expected use. The principal difficulty in assessing strict tort liability for a defective design involves articulation of an evaluative standard or comparative basis for defining the parameters of "unreasonably dangerous."[122]

---

no writ). *See also* Shelak v. White Motor Co., 581 F.2d 1155 (5th Cir. 1978); Hagans v. Oliver Mach. Co., 576 F.2d 97 (5th Cir. 1978); Mitchell v. Fruehauf Corp., 568 F.2d 1139 (5th Cir. 1978); Acord v. General Motors Corp., 669 S.W.2d 111 (Tex. 1984); Duncan v. Cessna Aircraft Corp., 665 S.W.2d 414 (Tex. 1984); Boatland of Houston, Inc. v. Bailey, 609 S.W.2d 743 (Tex. 1980); Rourke v. Garza, 530 S.W.2d 794 (Tex. 1975); Gonzales v. Caterpillar Tractor Co., 571 S.W.2d 867 (Tex. 1978); General Motors Corp. v. Hopkins, 548 S.W.2d 344 (Tex. 1977), *overruled in part on other grounds*; McCants v. Salameh, 608 S.W.2d 304 (Tex. Civ. App.—Waco 1980, writ ref'd n.r.e.); Wenzel v. Rollins Motor Co., 598 S.W.2d 895 (Tex. Civ. App.—El Paso 1980, writ ref'd n.r.e.); Lubbock Mfg. Co. v. Perez, 591 S.W.2d 907 (Tex. Civ. App.—Waco 1979, writ dism'd by agr.).

119. Webb v. Rodgers Machinery Mfg. Co., 750 F.2d 368 (5th Cir. 1985); Foster v. Ford Motor Co., 616 F.2d 1304 (5th Cir. 1980); Mitchell v. Freuhauf Corp., 568 F.2d 1139 (5th Cir. 1978); Fleishman v. Guadiano, 651 S.W.2d 730 (Tex. 1983); Turner v. General Motors Corp., 584 S.W.2d 844 (Tex. 1979); General Motors Corp. v. Hopkins, 548 S.W.2d 344 (Tex. 1977); Rourke v. Garza, 530 S.W.2d 794 (Tex. 1975); Bell Helicopter Co. v. Bradshaw, 594 S.W.2d 519 (Tex. Civ. App.—Corpus Christi 1979, writ ref'd n.r.e.). The manufacturer who produced a product in strict compliance with the specifications and plans furnished by another is not subject to strict tort liability unless the manufacturer clearly perceives a dangerous condition or hazard and possesses discretion to fabricate the product with a different and safer design. *See, e.g.*, Spangler v. Kranco, Inc., 481 F.2d 373 (4th Cir. 1973); Littlehale v. E. I. Dupont de Nemours & Co., 268 F. Supp. 791 (S.D.N.Y. 1966), *aff'd* 380 F.2d 274 (2d Cir. 1967); Moon v. Swinger Boss. Co., 205 Neb. 292, 287 N.W.2d 430 (1980).

120. Dean Wade notes that "Some courts are concerned that the phrase 'unreasonably dangerous', without more, does not put the issue meaningfully before the jury." Wade, *On Product Design Defects and Their Actionability*, 33 VAND L. REV. 551, 571 (1980).

121. Compare the plight of California in redefining defective design in Cronin v. J. B. Olson Corp., 8 Cal.3d, 121, 501 P.2d 1153, 104 Cal. Rptr. 433 (1972) with Barker v. Lull Eng'g. Co., 20 Cal. 3d 413, 573 P.2d 443, 143 Cal. Rptr. 225 (1978).

122. *See generally* Wade, *On Product Design Defects and Their Actionability*, 33 VAND L. REV. 551 (1980); Birnbaum, *Unmasking the Test for Design Defect, From Negli-*

a. General Legal Standard of Defective Design. The underlying standard for a design defect traces its origins to the *Restatement.* Under Section 402A, the *Restatement* defines a defective and unreasonably dangerous product as one not contemplated by the ordinary consumer possessing the ordinary knowledge common to the community as to its characteristics.[123] During the formative stages, the consumer expectation standard governed.[124]

Subsequently, in *Henderson v. Ford Motor Co.*[125] and in the later decision of *General Motors Corp. v. Hopkins*,[126] the Texas Supreme Court redefined "design defect" to mean a design that was "unreasonably dangerous." The court further defined "unreasonably dangerous" in terms of a disjunctive test: the product is "unreasonably dangerous" either if any product so designed would not be placed in the stream of commerce by a prudent manufacturer aware of the risk involved in its use, or if the product would not meet the reasonable safety expectations of the ordinary consumer.[127] In *Henderson*, plaintiff was injured when her vehicle suddenly accelerated out of control and crashed into a light standard. Plaintiff contended that a defectively designed carburetor system caused the unexpected acceleration. After reviewing the confusing ambiguity in the standard for evaluating a design defect, the Texas Supreme Court adopted the bifurcated test urged by Dean Keeton. This bifurcated test required either one of two circumstances to establish that the product was "unreasonably dangerous." Later in *General Motors Corp. v. Hopkins*,[128] the Supreme Court reaffirmed the disjunctive bifurcated test originally formulated in *Henderson*.

The Texas Supreme in *Turner v. General Motors Corp.* reexamined this bifurcated standard for evaluating a design defect.[129] *Turner* involved an accident in which the plaintiff sustained a quadriplegia when the 1969 Chevrolet he was operating overturned

---

gence [to Warranty] to Strict Liability to Negligence, 33 VAND L. REV. 593 (1980).

123. RESTATEMENT (SECOND) OF TORTS, § 402A comment i (1965).

124. Rourke v. Garza, 530 S.W.2d 794 (Tex. 1975). See also Pizza Inn v. Tiffany, 454 S.W.2d 420 (Tex. Civ. App.—Waco, 1970, no writ).

125. 519 S.W.2d 87 (Tex. 1974).

126. 548 S.W.2d 344 (Tex. 1977).

127. General Motors Corp. v. Hopkins, 548 S.W.2d 344 (Tex. 1977); Henderson v. Ford Motor Co., 519 S.W.2d 87, (Tex. 1974).

128. 548 S.W.2d 344 (Tex. 1977).

129. 584 S.W.2d 844 (Tex. 1979).

as he attempted to avoid colliding with another vehicle.[130] The injury allegedly occurred when the vehicle roof collapsed into the occupant compartment during the course of the overturn. The Texas Supreme Court reexamined the evolution of defective design in Texas. Concluding that the earlier bifurcated standard engendered confusion and misunderstanding without a concomitant meaningful test to evaluate an reasonably dangerous design, the Court expressly rejected the bifurcated test promulgated in *Henderson* and *Hopkins* and substituted a newly formulated balancing test. The Supreme Court redefined the term "defectively designed" to mean "a product that is unreasonably dangerous as designed, taking into consideration the utility of the product and the risk involved in its use."[131]

The Texas Supreme Court in *Turner* rejected as inappropriate any additional instruction to the jury to consider specific facts in balancing the utility of the design against its risk for harm. The court specifically rejected enumeration of the following factors previously approved by the intermediate appellate court as jury instruction: (1) the utility of the product versus the gravity and likelihood of injury; (2) the availability of a substitute design; (3) the ability of the manufacturer to eliminate the unsafe characteristic of the product without impairing its usefulness; and (4) the user's anticipated awareness of the danger of the product.[132] The court emphasized that though the listed factors may not be given as jury instructions, they should be advanced by both parties during the litigation.[133]

---

130. *Id.* at 845-46.

131. *Id.* at 849. *Accord* Carter v. Massey-Ferguson, Inc., 716 F.2d 344, 347 (5th Cir. 1984); Daberko v. Heil Co., 681 F.2d 445 (5th Cir. 1982); Hagan v. EZ Mfg. Co., 674 F.2d 1047 (5th Cir. 1982); Foster v. Ford Motor Co., 616 F.2d 1304 (5th Cir. 1980); Accord v. General Motors Corp., 669 S.W.2d 111 (Tex. 1984); Fleishman v. Guadiano, 651 S.W.2d 730 (Tex. 1984). Compare this standard with Sours v. General Motors Corp., 717 F.2d 1511 (6th Cir. 1983) (applying Ohio law). For an additional analysis of *Turner*, see Birnbaum, *supra* note 6, at 631-34.

132. *Id.* at 847, 849. The Fifth Circuit in Carter v. Massey-Ferguson, Inc., 716 F.2d 344, 348 (5th Cir. 1983) observes "The Texas Supreme Court has rejected the use of specific, enumerated guidelines in the jury instruction on the standard of unreasonable dangerousness." *Id.* at 348.

133. *Id. Accord*, Davidson v. Stanadyne Inc., 718 F.2d 1334 (5th Cir. 1983); Carter v. Massey-Ferguson, Inc., 716 F.2d 344 (5th Cir. 1983); Kindred v. Con/Chem, Inc., 650 S.W.2d 61 (Tex. 1983). *See generally* Edgar, Product Liability in Texas, 11 Tex. Tech L. Rev. 23, 29 (1979). Wade, *On Product "Design Defects and Their Actionability"*, 33 Vand L. Rev. 551, 572 (1980).

Various factors such as those stated above have been suggested by courts and legal commentators as an aid to the trier of fact in evaluating any design defect case.[134] Dean Wade, a recorder of the *Restatement* has written:

> Courts rightly have hesitated to provide juries with a list of policy factors to be balanced in reaching a value judgment. In a design case on the other hand, it seems appropriate to instruct a jury to consider the extent of the danger involved in the present design and the possibility of adopting an alternative, safer design. The instruction, of course, should state that the alternative design should not jeopardize other safety aspects of the product, and must be feasible from the standpoint of technology, cost and utility. The precise wording of the instruction is important and any list of abstract factors of different types is likely to confuse the jury. At the same time, an explanation of the need for considering whether the design could feasibly be made safer is quite helpful.[135]

All commentators agree that both parties should frame their evidence and arguments to incorporate these factors. The court's decision in *Turner* rejected efforts to provide more specific instructions to the jury because of a concern that an enumeration of abstract principles would merely confuse rather than aid the jury.[136] The standard for "unreasonably dangerous" poses the nature of the issue for the jury in a succinct and understandable fashion.[137] The risk versus utility standard established in *Turner* is

---

134. The Texas Supreme Court in *Turner* commented on factors which may be advanced during litigation:

> The majority of the Court of Civil Appeals enumerated four factors it would require to be balanced in determining the fact issue of defective design; the dissenting justice would require a fifth factor. These suggested factors were apparently derived from two cited law review articles: that of Dean Wade, *Strict Tort Liability of Manufacturers*, 19 Sw. L.J. 5, 17 (1965) suggesting seven factors; and that of Dean Keeton, *Manufacturer's Liability: The Meaning of "Defect" in the Manufacture and Design of Products*, 20 SYRACUSE L. REV. 559, 565 (1969), suggesting four factors. Dean Wade, in a later article, *On the Nature of Strict Tort Liability for Products*, 44 MISS. L.J. 825, 838, 840 (1973), offered a revised list of seven factors which seemed to him to be of significance in applying the unreasonably dangerous standard . . . . 584 S.W.2d at 849.

135. Wade, *supra* note 6 at 573.

136. *Id. See generally* Birnbaum, *supra* note 6, at 632; Wade, *supra* note 6, at 573; Edgar, *Products Liability in Texas*, 11 TEX. TECH L. REV. 23, 28 (1979).

137. 584 S.W.2d at 847. Refer to Chapter IX, SUBMISSION OF THE PRODUCTS CASE, *infra*.

now well entrenched in Texas.[138] Application of this balancing criteria requires the court to consider the interest of both parties, realizing that the user is entitled to expect that the product has been properly designed to meet its intended use but, at the same time, acknowledging that the manufacturer is not an insurer of the product and is not required to design a product to be the best that science can produce or to guarantee that no harm can come to the user of the product.[139]

Uncertainty in the manner of effectively evaluating the risk against the utility of a product as designed persisted despite the *Turner* decision. Amidst this confusion and uncertainty, *Boatland of Houston, Inc. v. Bailey*,[140] reached the court. *Boatland* involved a strict tort liability action based on defective design for the wrongful death of the operator of a bass boat. Plaintiff's decedent was fatally injured when the bass boat struck a partially submerged tree stump causing the plaintiff to be ejected from the boat into the water. The boat continued to circle and eventually struck the decedent who was struggling in the water. Plaintiffs alleged that the boat was defectively designed because of the absence of any device that would automatically kill the engine if the operator were ejected from the boat.[141] Plaintiff introduced evidence of the

---

138. *See, e.g.* Jett Edwards Patterson v. Rohm Gesellschaft, CA3-81-1006-R, Northern District Tex., Dallas (May 14, 1985). Shipp v. General Motors Corp., 750 F.2d 418 (5th Cir. 1985); Syrie v. Knoll Int'l 748 F.2d 304 (5th Cir. 1984); Davidson v. Stanadyne, Inc., 718 F.2d 1334 (5th Cir. 1983); Carter v. Massey Ferguson, Inc., 716 F.2d 344 (5th Cir. 1983); Daberko v. Heil Co., 681 F.2d 445 (5th Cir. 1982); Burks v. Firestone Tire & Rubber Co., 633 F.2d 1152 (5th Cir. 1981); Acord v. General Motors Corp., 669 S.W.2d 111, (Tex. 1984); Fleishman v. Guadiano, 651 S.W.2d 730 (Tex. 1984); Kindred v. Con/Chem, Inc., 650 S.W.2d 61 (Tex. 1983); Ford Motor Co. v. Pool, 688 S.W.2d 879 (Tex. App.—Texarkana 1985, no writ).

139. Daberko v. Heil Co., 681 F.2d 445 (5th Cir. 1982); Hagans v. Oliver Machinery Co., 576 F.2d 97 (5th Cir. 1978); Henderson v. Ford Motor Co., 519 S.W.2d 87 (Tex. 1974). Safety is not the sole criteria to be considered in the design of a product. Syrie v. Knoll Int'l 748 F.2d 304 (5th Cir. 1984); Hagan v. EZ Mfg. Co., 674 F.2d 1047 (5th Cir. 1982).

140. 609 S.W.2d 743 (Tex. 1980).

141. *Id.* at 746. The Supreme Court specifically noted:

> Whether a product was defectively designed must be judged against the technological contact existing at the time of its manufacture. Thus, when the plaintiff alleges that a product was defectively designed because it lacked a specific feature, attention may become focused on the feasibility of that feature—the capacity to provide the feature without greatly increasing the product's cost or impairing usefulness. This feasibility is a relative, not an absolute, concept; the more scientifically and economically feasible the alternative was, the more likely that a jury may find that the product was defectively designed. A plaintiff may advance the

economic feasibility of a kill switch device while the defendant introduced evidence rebutting plaintiff's evidence of feasibility of a kill switch. Defendant contended that the kill switch was neither commercially available at the time of manufacture and sale of the boat nor appropriate for installation on bass boats. The intermediate court of appeals rejected any evidence regarding the feasibility or economic advisability of alternative safety features. Reversing the intermediate appellate court, the Texas Supreme Court declared that defective design was determinable in relation to safer design alternatives. The court noted that "the fact that [the product's] risks could be diminished easily or cheaply may greatly influence the outcome of the case."[142] The court also emphatically noted that "whether a product was defectively designed must be adjudged against the technological context existing at the time of its manufacture."[143] Feasibility was defined by the court to mean the capacity of the manufacturer to provide an alternative design feature without greatly increasing the cost of the product or significantly impairing its usefulness for the purpose for which it was designed. In discussing feasible alternative designs, the court admonished the plaintiff to introduce evidence establishing a safer design alternative that was in actual use, that was available or that was known at the time that the defendant manufactured the product.[144] Additionally, the court noted that evidence demonstrating

---

argument that a safer alternative was feasible with evidence that it was in actual use or was available at the time of manufacture. Feasibility may also be shown with evidence of the scientific and economic capacity to develop the safer alternative. Thus, evidence of the actual use of, or capacity to use, safer alternatives is relevant insofar as it depicts the available scientific knowledge and the practicalities of applying that knowlege to a product's design. This method of presenting evidence of a defective design is not new to the Texas law of product liability. (citing Rourke v. Garza, 530 S.W.2d 794 (Tex. 1975); Henderson v. Ford Motor Co., 519 S.W.2d 87 (Tex. 1974); Williams v. General Motors Corp., 501 S.W.2d 930 (Tex. Civ. App.—Houston [1st Dist.] 1973, writ ref'd n.r.e.); Hartzell Propeller Co. v. Alexander, 485 S.W.2d 943 (Tex. Civ App.—Waco 1972, writ ref'd n.r.e.); and Pizza Inn, Inc. v. Tiffany, 454 S.W.2d 420 (Tex. Civ. App.—Waco 1970, no writ)).

142. *Id.*

143. *Id.*

144. Similarly, in Caterpillar Tractor Co. v. Boyett, 674 S.W.2d 782 (Tex. App.—Corpus Christi 1984, writ granted); plaintiff was injured when run over by an allegedly defectively design dirt loader. The court, following *Boatland*, declared that "Evidence of the actual use of or capacity to use safer alternatives is relevant insofar as it depicts the available scientific knowlege and practicability of applying that knowlege to a product design." *Id.* at 790.

both scientific and economic availability for a safer design advanced the feasibility factor. In contrast, the court noted that the manufacturer was entitled to submit evidence that a particular design alternative was impossible because of the existing state of the art or lack of feasibility, such as time constraints between development of a design alternative and production of the redesigned product.[145] Defendant was also urged to introduce evidence establishing the impracticability of an alternative design because of excessive cost or impairment of the product's utility. The *Boatland* court specifically declared that scientific knowledge, the practicalities and implementation of the proposed design alternatives, economic considerations and the potential impairment of the utility of the product constituted relevant evidence that should be advanced by both parties to demonstrate whether the risk of harm presented by the product as designed outweighed the utility of the product.[146]

The risk versus utility standard received further clarification in *Kindred v. Con/Chem, Inc.*[147] Plaintiffs were injured when a paint primer they were using to clean the inside of a cylindrical

---

145. *Id.* at 748. In fact, the court noted:

> In contrast, defendant's strongest rebuttal evidence is that a particular design alternative was impossible due to the state of the art. Yet the defendant's ability to rebut the plaintiff's evidence is not limited to showing that a particular alternative was impossible; it is entitled to rebut the plaintiff's evidence of feasibility with evidence of limitations on feasibility. A suggested alternative may be invested or discovered but not be feasible for use because of the time necessary for its application and implementation. Also a suggested alternative may be available, but impractical for reasons such as greatly increased costs or impairment of the product's usefulness. When the plaintiff has introduced evidence that a safer alternative was feasible because it was used, the defendant may then introduce contradictory evidence that it was not used.

146. *Id.* at 748. In arriving at its decision, the court alluded to the factors approved for advancing the risk versus utility balancing originally articulated by Wade, *Strict Tort Liability of Manufacturers*, 19 Sw. L.J. 5, 17 (1965). In a recent decision the Fifth Circuit concluded that a manufacturer's evidence that a design alternative proposed by the plaintiff was not used by other manufacturers is not necessarily determinative. In *Shipp v. General Motors Corp.* plaintiff was injured and suffered paralysis when the Pontiac TransAm she was driving overturned during an accident. Plaintiff alleged that the roof was defectively designed and its partial collapse caused her injury. Defendant urged that the defective nature of a product can only be determined by reference to a safer design alternative. The court concluded: "Holly Shipp offered evidence of the dangerousness of the TransAm roof and the feasibility and availability of a safer alternative. That no other passenger car employed this design will not alone defeat recovery." *Shipp v. General Motors Corp.*, 750 F.2d 418, (5th Cir. 1985).

147. 650 S.W.2d 61 (Tex. 1983).

beer storage tank ignited at a temperature of 50F. Plaintiffs were severely burned when they passed through the flames in an effort to reach the storage tank's only available exit. Plaintiffs instituted a strict tort liability action against the manufacturer based on a defective design in formulating the primer with a low flash point. Evidence was introduced that a safer alternative in the form of a water base rather than an isopropyl alcohol base would significantly reduce the flash point of the primer.[148] The trial court granted judgment for the manufacturer rejecting the allegation of defective design. In reversing the trial court, the Texas Supreme Court concluded that evidence of a feasible alternative safer design constituted sufficient probative evidence to raise a fact issue on defective design. Essentially, the Court declared that a plaintiff need only establish a safer design alternative that would have eliminated the risk presented by the existing product design.[149] The failure to establish that an alternative safer design was economically feasible or cost effective is not essential to satisfy the proof prescribed in *Boatland*.[150]

The *Kindred* court implied that evidence of alternative safer design satisfies the burden of the plaintiff to raise a fact issue for the jury.[151] Evidence of economic feasibility or impairment of product utility is not required.[152] As the court noted:

> Kurtz and Kindred do not have to prove the final cost of a safer alternative to get to the jury. They are only required to present some evidence of probative value. Expert testimony that water could have been substituted for ninety-five percent of the product is evidence of probative value . . . [T]here is some evidence, more than a scintilla, if the evidence furnishes some reasonable basis for differing conclusions by reasonable minds as to the existence of the vital fact.[153]

---

148. *Id.* at 62.

149. *Id.* at 63.

150. Addressing the manufactuer's argument that plaintiff failed to establish all of the factors discussed by the Supreme Court in *Boatland of Houston, Inc. v. Bailey*, 609 S.W.2d 743 (Tex. 1982), the court observed that: "Con/Chem was silent as to any expense in producing the safer alternative. The jury therefore could have inferred that Con/Primer X could have been made less flammable at a reasonable cost."

151. *Id.*

152. *Id.* As noted by the Fifth Circuit in Shipp v. General Motors Corp., 750 F.2d 418 (5th Cir. 1985), "The Texas Supreme Court has never explicitly made proof of each balancing factor a distinct element of a strict liability claim" *Id.* at 421-22.

153. *Id.*

Recent decisions reaffirm the viability of the *Turner* risk versus utility test for defective design. In 1983, the Texas Supreme Court considered the case of *Fleishman v. Guadiano*[154] in which the plaintiff sustained a severe injury when she fell from a ladder. The plaintiff instituted an action for strict tort liability based on defective design. The plaintiff requested but the trial court refused to instruct the jury that they could not consider any evidence of plaintiff's contributory negligence in determining whether the product was defectively designed.[155] The Supreme Court emphasized that a jury should be instructed to balance the risk associated with the product as designed against its utility and that no additional instruction or information was necessary or authorized.[156]

Further emphasis of the stringent parameters of the risk versus utility test was amplified in *Acord v. General Motors Corp.*[157] Plaintiff's wife was fatally injured and his minor son severely injured when their car was struck by a truck with allegedly defective brakes. The trial court instructed the jury that the manufacturer of a product is not an insurer and that the manufacturer need not manufacture the safest product possible.[158] Though the court acknowledged the statement reflected a correct pronouncement of the law governing product liability, the court concluded that the instruction to the jury was impermissible.[159] Any instruction other than the *Turner* instruction constitutes surplusage and an imper-

---

154. 651 S.W.2d 730 (Tex. 1983).

155. *Id.* at 731.

156. *Id.* Dean Wade has suggested that "If a court has not already held strict liability to apply to design and warning cases, it perhaps should consider treating these cases (as distinguished from manufacturing flaw cases) as negligence cases. Wade, *On The Effect on Product Liability of Knowledge Unavailable Prior to Marketing*, 58 N.Y.U. L. Rev. 734, 760 (1983).

157. 669 S.W.2d 111 (Tex. 1984).

158. *Id.* at 113. Endeavoring to put to final rest any attempt to extend or embellish the standard for design defect, the Supreme Court stated:

> If Turner was not sufficiently specific to advise the bench and bar that in strict liability cases the jury is not to be instructed with balancing factors, surely we have laid this matter to rest by our opinion in Fleishman v. Guadiano, 651 S.W.2d 730 (Tex. 1983), where we again endorsed the submission as approved by Turner and upheld the trial court's refusal to give any other instructions. The jury need not and should not be burdened with surplus instructions. . . . We explicitly approve the Pattern Jury Charges issue and instruction for design defect cases, and disapprove the addition of any other instructions in such cases, however correctly they may state the law under Section 402A of the Restatement (Second) of Torts.

159. *Id.* at 116.

missible diversion from the ultimate issues.[160]

The decisions of the Texas Supreme Court in *Boatland, Kindred* and *Acord* establish beyond peradventure the controlling effect of the risk versus utility standard. Though both sides are urged to introduce evidence advancing the various factors considered in weighing the risk against the utility of the product as designed, any instruction to the jury embellishing on the "unreasonably dangerous" standard constitutes reversible error.[161]

b. Application of the Standard to Design Defect and Safety Features. A significant factor in weighing the risk of harm presented by a particular design against the utility of the product as designed involves a consideration of whether safety guards or other appropriate protective devices are feasible and appropriate for incorporation in a product. A failure to incorporate such protective devices may constitute a design defect within the scope of strict tort liability in Texas.[162] The initial case that considered extension of strict tort liability to defective design involved a product

---

160. First International Bank in San Antonio v. Roper Corp., 686 S.W.2d 602 (Tex. 1985).

161. Acord v. General Motors Corp., 669 S.W.2d 111, 115 (Tex. 1984). In *Carter v. Massey Ferguson, Inc.*, 716 F.2d 344, 348 (5th Cir. 1983), the Fifth Circuit noted that:

> The Texas Supreme Court has rejected the use of specific, enumerated guidelines in the jury instruction on the standard of unreasonable dangerousness. (cites case). The supreme court, however, has suggested that evidence of certain factors would be useful to the fact finder in the risk-utility balance. These factors include the availability of substitute products, the manufacturer's ability to eliminate some of the risks associated with the product without adversely affecting the usefulness or cost of the product, and the expectations of the ordinary consumer.

See Davidson v. Stanadyne, Inc., 718 F.2d 1334, 1337-38 (5th Cir. 1983). For a novel approach to evaluating design defect cases, see Travershi, *Seizing the Middle Ground Between Rules and Standard in Design Defect Litigation; Advancing the Directed Verdict Practice in the Law of Torts*, 57 N.Y.U. L. Rev. 521 (1983).

162. Davidson v. Stanadyne, Inc., 718 F.2d 1334 (5th Cir. 1983) (failure to include a "scald guard" on a tub and shower faucet); Foster v. Ford Motor Co., 616 F.2d 1304 (5th Cir. 1980) (failure to employ a clamp to secure bales of hay on front end loader); Rourke v. Garza, 530 S.W.2d 794 (Tex. 1975) (failure to incorporate cleats on scaffolding board to prevent the board from rolling off the support structure); Bell Helicopter Co. v. Bradshaw, 594 S.W.2d 519 (Tex. Civ. App.—Corpus Christi 1979, writ ref'd n.r.e.) (failure to utilize a more durable and long-lasting rotor blade on a helicopter); Helicoid Gage Div. of Am. Chain & Cable Co. v. Howell, 511 S.W.2d 573 (Tex. Civ. App.—Houston [14th Dist.] 1974, writ ref'd n.r.e.) (failure to incorporate safety glass in a high pressure industrial system); Pizza Inn, Inc. v. Tiffany, 454 S.W.2d 420 (Tex. Civ. App—Waco 1970, no writ) (failure to incorporate safety guard on pizza dough machine). *See also* Annot., 95 A.L.R.3d 1066 (1979) (duty to equip with safety devices).

lacking a protective safety device. In *Pizza Inn, Inc. v. Tiffany*,[163] plaintiff sustained serious injuries to his fingers when he attempted to extricate a foreign object from some pizza dough that had migrated into the unprotected cutting blades of the dough making machine. The court concluded that failure to provide a protective handguard constituted a defective design that rendered the product unreasonably dangerous.[164]

Similarly, in *Carter v. Massey-Ferguson, Inc.*,[165] plaintiff, a woodcutter, sustained serious injuries when a skidder, which is a motorized log-moving device, backed into him. Evidence indicated that the skidder could have been equipped with a backup alarm which would have alerted anyone in the vicinity that the skidder was in a reverse travel mode. The court concluded that the failure to incorporate an available and effective backup alarm system rendered the skidder defective and unreasonably dangerous.[166]

A determination that the failure to incorporate a safety device constitutes a defective design depends on balancing the risk of harm against the utility of the product as designed. Normally, when the cost to incorporate an available safety device is miniscule, and the safety device neither adversely impairs the effectiveness of the product, nor increases the risk of harm, a manufacturer may be strictly liable in tort based on a defective design for a failure to incorporate available safety devices on the product.[167] Design of a product with protective safety devices is predicated not only on use of the product for its intended purpose, but for all

---

163. 454 S.W.2d 420 (Tex. Civ. App.—Waco 1970, no writ).

164. *Id.* at 422.

165. 716 F.2d 344, 349 (5th Cir. 1983). See also Webb v. Rodgers Machinery Mfg. Co., 750 F.2d 368 (5th Cir. 1985) (failure to incorporate an anti kickback device on an industrial wood shaper).

166. *Id.* at 350.

167. Davidson v. Stanadyne, Inc., 718 F.2d 1334 (5th Cir. 1983) (failure to include a "scald guard" on a tub or shower faucet); Foster v. Ford Motor Co., 616 F.2d 1304 (5th Cir. 1980) (failure to include grappling cables on front end hay loader device); Boatland of Houston, Inc. v. Bailey, 609 S.W.2d 743 (Tex. Civ. 1980) (failure to include kill switch on bass boat); Turner v. General Motors Corp., 584 S.W.2d 844 (Tex. 1979) (failure to design vehicle roof with roll bars); Gonzales v. Caterpillar Tractor Co., 571 S.W.2d 867 (Tex. 1978) (failure to locate stepdown away from tracks on a caterpillar tractor loader and failure to apply anti-skid material to the step); Helicoid Gage Div. of Am. Chain & Cable Co. v. Howell, 511 S.W.2d 573 (Tex. Civ. App.—Houston [14th Dist.] 1974, writ ref'd n.r.e.) (failure to utilize safety glass rather than other material that would fragment when subjected to elevated pressures).

foreseeable uses of that product.[168] In *Davidson v. Stanadyne, Inc.*,[169] for example, plaintiff instituted a strict tort liability action based on defective design against the manufacturer of a shower faucet. The plaintiff was badly scalded when she inadvertently brushed against the faucet while taking a shower. The plaintiff maintained that a "scald guard" was available and should have been installed on the shower faucet. The Fifth Circuit noted that "[m]erely because the need for the safety device would not arise when the product was used in its intended manner, does not necessarily mean that the absence of the safety device cannot render the product unreasonably dangerous."[170] Foreseeable use means that which is objectively reasonable to expect, not what might conceivably occur.[171] Neither irrational nor bizarre uses are contemplated. Otherwise, the manufacturer is metamorphized into an insurer.

A frequent question arises whether subsequent remedial design changes after an accident constitutes admissible evidence on defective design. Rule 407(a) of the newly codified Texas Rules of Evidence provides such information is admissible in strict tort liability cases.[172] With this codification, Texas joins a minority of jurisdictions that hold evidence of subsequent remedial measures is not admissible in negligence actions but is admissible in strict tort

---

168. The design must anticipate both the intended and reasonably foreseeable uses and misuses. Turner v. General Motors Corp., 584 S.W.2d 844 (Tex. 1979); General Motors Corp. v. Hopkins, 548 S.W.2d 344 (Tex. 1977). *See also* Gootee v. Colt Industries, Inc., 712 F.2d 1057 (6th Cir. 1983); DeMedeiros v. Koehring Co., 709 F.2d 734 (1st Cir. 1983); Branch v. Chevron Int'l Oil Co., 681 F.2d 426 (5th Cir. 1982); Schell v. AMF Inc., 567 F.2d 1259 (3d Cir. 1977).

169. 718 F.2d 1334 (5th Cir. 1983).

170. *Id.* at 1338.

171. Artis v. Fibre Metal Products, 115 Ill. App.3d 228, 450 N.E.2d 756 (1983). It is not reasonably foreseeable that a user would receive a fractured neck when a railroad tie fell on his hard hat.) Berg v. Underwood Hair Adaptions Process Inc., ____ F.2d ____ (2d Cir. 1984) (No. 84-7675; slip opinion at 1055) (no duty to warn of the bizarre or the deliberate abuse of a product); Laney v. Coleman Co. Inc., 758 F.2d 1299, 1302 (8th Cir. 1985) (the issue is the use of the product objectively foreseeable).

172. Rule 407(a) provides:

> When, after an event, measures are taken which, if taken previously, would have made the event less likely to occur, evidence of the subsequent remedial measures is not admissible to prove negligence of culpable conduct in connection with the event. This rule does not require the exclusion of evidence of subsequent remedial measures when offered for another purpose, such a proving ownership, control or feasibility of precautionary measures, if controverted, or impeachment. Nothing in this rule shall preclude admissibility in products liability cases based on strict liability. TEX. R. EVID. 407(a).

liability actions.[173] The adoption of Rule 407a, however, contradicts prior Texas decisional law that excluded evidence of subsequent remedial measures in actions based either on negligence or strict tort liability.[174] In view of the adoption of Rule 407a, it appears that subsequent design changes, subject to the state of the art limitation, is admissible in a strict liability action. A serious question exists, however, whether subsequent remedial measures are admissible in strict tort liability actions based on marketing defects.

A critical factor in evaluating whether a product is defectively designed, particularly in view of a weighing of the risk of harm against the utility of the product as designed and consistent with the newly codified Rule 407a of the Texas Rules of Evidence, is the technological availability of alternative safer designs at the time the product is designed, manufactured and marketed.[175] Adequacy of design is measured by the technology existing at the time the product is actually manufactured.[176] Thus, whether an alternative safer design is available which would render the product safer is measured solely by the scientific technology available at the time of the design and manufacture of the product. In *Boatland of Houston, Inc. v. Bailey*,[177] the operator of a bass boat was ejected from the boat when the boat struck a submerged log in the water. The boat continued to operate and circle and, eventually, the deceased was struck by the rotating propeller of the circling boat.

---

173. Refer to Chapter II, PROOF OF CAUSES OF ACTION. *See also* Annot., 74 A.L.R.3d 1001 (1976) (admissibility of evidence on subsequent remedial measures).

174. *See, e.g.*, McCants v. Salameh, 608 S.W.2d 304 (Tex. Civ. App.—Waco 1980, writ ref'd n.r.e.); Bell Helicopter Co. v. Bradshaw, 594 S.W.2d 519 (Tex. Civ. App.—Corpus Christi, 1979 writ ref'd n.r.e.); Simms v. Southwest Texas Methodist Hosp., 535 S.W.2d 192 (Tex. Civ. App.—San Antonio, 1976, writ ref'd n.r.e.).

175. Davidson v. Stanadyne, Inc., 718 F.2d 1334 (5th Cir. 1983); Kindred v. Con/Chem Inc., 650 S.W.2d 61 (Tex. 1983); Boatland of Houston, Inc. v. Bailey, 609 S.W.2d 743 (Tex. 1980).

176. Boatland of Houston, Inc. v. Bailey, 609 S.W.2d 743 (Tex. 1980); McCants v. Salameh, 608 S.W.2d 304 (Tex. Civ. App.—Waco 1980). But in *Carter v. Johns-Manville Sales Corp.*, 557 F. Supp. 1317 (E.D. Tex. 1983), the court, despite the Erie constraints posed by Boatland of Houston Inc. v. Bailey, and McCants v. Salameh, rejected the limitations of available technology, i.e., state of the art. The opinion not only ostensibly ignores the state of the art constraint but, by its language, impliedly assails the unreasonably dangerous requirement of a defective design which has been the established law of Texas since adoption of Section 402A in 1967. *See also* O'Brien v. Muskin Corp, 94 N.J. 169, 463 A.2d 298 (N.J. 1983); Appel v. Standex Int'l Corp., 62 Or. App. 208, 660 P.2d 686 (1983).

177. 609 S.W.2d 743 (Tex. 1980).

The plaintiff contended that the bass boat was defectively designed and unreasonably dangerous by reason of the absence of a kill switch that would disconnect operation of the boat upon ejection of the operator. The trial court permitted the manufacturer to introduce evidence that kill switches were neither technologically feasible nor commercially available at the time that the particular bass boat was designed, manufactured and sold. The intermediate court of appeals concluded that the trial court erred in permitting "state of the art" evidence.[178] The Texas Supreme Court reversed the intermediate appellate court, concluding that state of the art, as distinguished from industry practice or custom, constituted proper rebuttal to plaintiff's contention that a feasible alternative safer design was available.[179] The Supreme Court defined "state of the art" as the existing technological environment at the time of a product's manufacture and includes scientific knowledge, economic feasibility and practicability of implementation.[180]

The Texas Supreme Court further noted that evidence of feasibility of an alternative design could be established either by proof of the design alternatives used by other manufacturers or proof that an alternative safer design was known and technologically capable of being developed.[181] In contrast, the manufacturer may rebut design feasibility by establishing that the design alternative has not yet been invented or is not commercially available, that the design alternative is not feasible for use on the product because of time constraints or that the design is impracticable because it would either interfere with the usefulness of the product or substantially and significantly increase its cost.[182] Generally,

---

178. 585 S.W.2d 805 (Tex. Civ. App.—Houston [1st Dist.] 1979, *rev'd* 609 S.W.2d 743 (Tex. 1980)).

179. 609 S.W.2d at 749.

180. *Id.* at 748.

181. *Id.* at 748-49.

182. *Id. See also* Burks v. Firestone Tire & Rubber Co., 633 F.2d 1152 (5th Cir. 1981). A manufacturer is not obligated to eliminate or significantly impair the utility of a product to make it absolutely safe. Hagans v. Oliver Mach. Co., 576 F.2d 97 (5th Cir. 1978); Boatland of Houston, Inc. v. Bailey, 609 S.W.2d 743 (Tex. 1980). In *Hethcoat v. Chevron Oil Co.*, 364 So.2d 1243 (Fla. Dist. Ct. App. 1978) (*per curiam*), *remanded in part per curiam*, 380 So.2d 1035 (Fla. 1980), the plaintiff, a welder, was fatally injured when an acetylene and oxygen flame from his torch exploded oil vapors and volatile materials contained in a large tank assembly designed for heating asphalt by circulating hot oil in a coil and transporting it to a storage tank. Plaintiff was using a torch to remove a deteriorated inner lining of the

whether a feasible safer alternative design is technologically feasible and available and whether the failure to incorporate such alternative design renders a product unreasonably dangerous constitutes a jury issue.[183] The burden is imposed upon the plaintiff, however, to establish that a feasible safer design alternative is technologically available and that such alternative would have eliminated the risk of harm.[184]

Though strict tort liability does not impose on the manufacturer a duty to design an accident-proof product, the manufacturer may not escape liability merely by designing a product that conforms with the standards and customs of that particular industry. In *Garcia v. Sky Climber, Inc.*,[185] a cable separated inside a scaffold hoisting machine causing the scaffold to fall with the plaintiff. Other manufacturers did not include fail safe mechanisms on scaffolding hoist equipment.[186] The court emphasized that proof that the existing design complied with existing custom and practice in the industry does not preclude strict tort liability for a defective design.[187]

---

heating chamber which was the heart of the storage tank system when the vapors ignited and exploded. In rejecting, as a matter of law, plaintiff's contention that a design defect existed, the court observed:

> The mere fact that an injury occurs as the result of the use of, or being in the vicinity of, a machine does not render the manufacturer liable. Virtually every machine is capable of being the instrument of hurt. Automobiles run over people, guns discharge bullets into people and electrical appliances shock and kill people. A pencil sharpener will grind off a finger if placed into it. A dishwasher will sever fingers and hand if inserted while in operation. To design a machine incapable of doing injury would require the design of an apparatus having no use. The law will not require an absurdity.

Id. at 1244.

183. Mitchell v. Freuhauf Corp., 568 F.2d 1139 (5th Cir. 1978) (alternative design of trailer other than hanging meat from the trailer roof, when this caused the trailer to become unbalanced while negotiating sharp curves); Gonzales v. Caterpillar Tractor Co., 571 S.W.2d 867 (Tex. 1978) (relocating step on a caterpillar tractor excavator and using antiskid material on the step to protect operator from slipping while working in the muddy conditions).

184. In *Boatland of Houston, Inc v. Bailey*, 609 S.W.2d 743 (Tex. 1980), the Texas Supreme Court noted that the plaintiff may be required to advance the existence of a feasible design alternative in order to attack product design. The mere fact that a feasible design alternative is available does not eliminate the necessity for submitting the balancing test to the jury. Burks v. Firestone Tire & Rubber Co., 633 F.2d 1152 (5th Cir. 1981).

185. 470 S.W.2d 261 (Tex. Civ. App.—Houston [1st Dist.] 1971, writ ref'd n.r.e.).

186. *Id.* at 264.

187. *Id.* at 264, 268-69; *Accord*, Shipp v. General Motors Corp. 750 F.2d 418, 423 (5th Cir. 1985); Rivera v. Rockford Mach. & Tool Co., 1 Ill. App. 3d 641, 274 N.E.2d 828, 833 (1971). *See also* Turner v. General Motors Corp., 514 S.W.2d 497 (Tex. Civ. App.—Houston

A related issue involves the product supplier's duty to provide safety devices on complicated multifunctional products. Many jurisdictions distinguish between unifunctional and multifunctional products. If a product is unifunctional and unreasonably dangerous in the absence of appropriate safety devices, strict tort liability for defective design may ensue.[188] The manufacturer is obligated to adopt all technologically available alternative safety devices that render a product safe for its intended and reasonably foreseeable uses.[189] If the product is multifunctional in its operations, however, and multiple safety devices are required to insure safety in the performance of these various functions, the manufacturer is not obligated to provide protective safety devices.[190] To require multiple protective safety devices on a product that is multifaceted in its functions imposes an unreasonable obligation on the manufacturer.[191] Of course, a defect in a multifunctional product unrelated to the performance of its multifaceted functions does not relieve the product supplier of strict tort liability.[192]

Another issue involves the installation of protective safety devices on products that are ultimately modified or altered by third parties.[193] As a general principle, a product supplier is under no

---

[14th Dist.] 1974, writ ref'd n.r.e.).

188. Rios v. Niagara Mach. & Tool Works, 12 Ill. App. 3d 739, 299 N.E.2d 86, 90 (1973); *see* Bexiga v. Havir Mfg. Corp., 60 N.J. 402, 290 A.2d 281, 284 (1972).

189. *See generally*, Boatland of Houston, Inc. v. Bailey, 609 S.W.2d 743 (Tex. 1980).

190. In Hagans v. Oliver Mach. Co., 576 F.2d 97 (5th Cir. 1978); plaintiff was feeding a board into an industrial saw when the circular blade struck a knot in the wood, causing the board to jerk abruptly and pull plaintiff's hand into the rotating blade. Because certain operations could not be performed with a handguard over the blade, the saw was designed with a removable handguard. The particular handguard was not in use at the time of plaintiff's accident. Rejecting the contention that the design of the industrial saw was defective for failure to incorporate a permanently affixed handguard over the rotating blade, the Fifth Circuit observed that the saw was designed to perform a wider range of woodworking operations and that it was equipped with a blade guard to protect the operator in those operations which could be performed with a blade in place. *Id.* at 100. The court emphasized that by designing the industrial saw with a removable blade guard, the manufacturer struck an appropriate compromise, harmonizing the product's utility with safety to the user. *Id.* at 101. The court further observed that a permanently attached blade guard assembly would significantly impair the usefulness of the product and that the law would not require a manufacturer to destroy the utility of a product to make it absolutely safe. *Id.* A similar analysis was followed in Hagan v. EZ Mfg. Co., 674 F.2d 1047 (5th Cir. 1982). *Accord*, Curtis v. General Motors Corp., 649 F.2d 808 (10th Cir. 1981); Colson v. Allied Products Co., 640 F.2d 5 (5th Cir. 1981).

191. 576 F.2d 97, 101 (5th Cir. 1978).

192. Scott v. Dreis & Krump Mfg. Co., 26 Ill. App. 3d 971, 326 N.E.2d 74, 83 (1975).

193. A subsequent change or modification of the product after it leaves the manufac-

duty to provide protective safety devices on products that are ultimately converted and modified to perform functions totally different than intended and not reasonably foreseeable[194] or that are altered to operate in an unanticipated environment.[195] Reasonable foreseeability remains the outer parameter for designing for product safety.

---

turer's hands forecloses the imposition of strict tort liability. Hanlon v. Cyril Bath Co., 541 F.2d 343 (3d Cir. 1975) (manufacturer of press brake not liable for injuries to employee who accidently activated machine when attempting to remove piece of metal lodged therein because employer had substituted a more easily activated electrical starting device); C & S Fuel, Inc. v. Clark Equip. Co., 552 F. Supp. 340 (E.D. Ky. 1982) (manufacturer of tractor destroyed by fire not liable due to unforeseeable substantial change by cutting away a portion of a protective plate in the tractor); Ford v. International Harvester Co., 430 So.2d 912 (Fla. App. 1983) (manufacturer or truck chassis not liable for failure to install back-up warning signals where manufacturer knew truck would be substantially altered prior to delivery to ultimate consumer for use as a trash truck); Gasdiel v. Federal Press Co., 78 Ill. App. 3d 222, 396 N.E.2d 1241 (Ill. 1979) (manufacturer of punch press not liable due to substitution by purchaser of a significantly different starting mechanism on punch press); Rients v. International Harvestor Co., 346 N.W.2d 359 (Minn. App. 1984) (numerous modifications and repairs to the axle of tractor precluded recovery by plaintiff); King v. K. R. Wilson & Co., 8 Ohio St. 3d 9, 455 N.E.2d 1282 (1983) (manufacturer not liable when electrical activation system was modified resulting in change from two palm buttons to two pull-back safety handles and the spring in one of the handles broke); Stuckey v. Young Exploration Co., 586 P.2d 726 (Okla. 1978) (truck manufacturer not liable for failure of steering mechanism in eleven year old truck which had undergone two major modifications); Padron v. Goodyear Tire & Rubber Co., 34 Wash. App. 473, 662 P.2d 67 (1983) (where front wheels and tires of tractor were changed one year after purchase, tractor underwent substantial change in condition and manufacturer not strictly liable); Rooney v. Federal Press Co., 751 F.2d 140 (3d Cir. 1984) (employer who added a foot pedal to a power press that circumvented the safety of the two hand operated buttons designed into the press constituted a substantial alteration).

194. In other situations, subsequent alterations may not exempt the manufacturer from strict tort liability. Saupitty v. Yazoo Mfg. Co., 726 F.2d 657 (10th Cir. 1984) (manufacturer of riding lawnmower was not absolved of liability for injury to plaintiff because of the removal of scrubber brakes and belt guard from mower prior to the accident); Hollinger v. Wagner Mining Equip. Co., 667 F.2d 402 (3d Cir. 1981) (removal of manual horn from trackless diesel powered vehicle used in mine precluded summary judgment for manufacturer because the removal constituted a material fact issue whether a substantial change occurred on the vehicle); Bich v. General Electric Co., 27 Wash. App. 25, 614 P.2d 1323 (Wash. 1980) (in accident involving electrician the issues of whether a transformer was unreasonably dangerous because of inadequate warnings of the potential dangers involved in substituting a different brand of fuses incorporating different time-delay characteristics represented a question for the jury); Soler v. Castmaster Div. of H.P.M. Corp., 98 N.J. 137, 484 A.2d 1225 (1984).

195. Elliott v. Century Chevrolet Co., 597 S.W.2d 563 (Tex. Civ. App.—Fort Worth 1980, writ ref'd n.r.e.); Daberko v. Heil Co., 681 F.2d 445 (5th Cir. 1982). *See also* Shawyer v. Roberts Corp., 90 Wisc. 2d 72, 280 N.W.2d 226 (1979); Grover Hill Grain Co. v. Baughman Oster Inc., 728 F.2d 784 (6th Cir. 1984); Haupt v. Atwood Oceanics Inc., 681 F.2d 1058 (5th Cir. 1982).

Likewise, a dangerous condition that is open and obvious, and therefore unavoidable, may exonerate the manufacturer from utilizing an alternative safer design or protective device. Most jurisdictions recognize that no duty exists to design products in which the danger is open and apparent.[196] Of course, if the risk of harm is great and the cost of eliminating the danger is minimal, a duty to design the product with a safer design probably will result.[197]

c. *Crashworthiness and Design Defect.* The doctrine of strict tort liability includes design defects that neither cause nor contribute to cause the original accident but, because of some aspect of the design configuration, the user sustains an aggravation or enhancement of the injuries that would have been produced by the original accident.[198] In *Turner v. General Motors Corp.*,[199] plaintiff was injured when the 1969 Chevrolet he was operating overturned as he attempted to avoid colliding with another vehicle on the roadway. When the vehicle overturned, the roof collapsed into the passenger compartment allegedly causing the plaintiff to sustain quadriplegia. The plaintiff contended that the roof of the vehicle lacked strength sufficient to withstand collapse during a foreseeable rollover of the vehicle and, therefore, was defectively

---

196. *See, e.g.* Pressley v. Sears Roebuck & Co., 738 F.2d 1222 (11th cir. 1984); Estrada v. Schmutz Mfg. Co., 734 F.2d 1218 (7th cir. 1984); Miller v. Utica Mill Specialty Mach. Co., 731 F.2d 305 (6th Cir. 1984); Hagans v. Oliver Mach. Co., 576 F.2d 97 (5th Cir. 1978).

197. Helicoid Gage Div. of Am. Chain and Cable Co. v. Howell, 511 S.W.2d 573 (Tex. Civ. App.—Houston [14th Dist.] 1974, writ. ref'd n.r.e.).

198. Shipp v. General Motors Corp., 750 F.2d 418 (5th Cir. 1985) (roof crush on overturn); Maxey v. Freightliner Corp., 450 F. Supp. 955 (N.D. Tex. 1978), *aff'd*, 623 F.2d 395 (5th Cir. 1980), *rev'd on other grounds*, 665 F.2d 1367 (5th Cir. 1982) (en banc) (rupture of saddle tanks on a tractor after an overturn); Duncan v. Cessna Aircraft Co., 665 S.W.2d 414 (Tex. 1984) (inadequate leg supports for aircraft seat which caused seat to collapse upon impact of plane with a mountain); Boatland of Houston, Inc. v. Bailey, 609 S.W.2d 743 (Tex. 1980) (absence of "kill switch" to deactiviate motor and prevent bass boat propeller from injuring plaintiff after occurrence of the original accident when the boat hit a stump and ejected operator from the boat); Turner v. General Motors Corp., 584 S.W.2d 844 (Tex. 1979) (defectively designed roof of a vehicle which deformed during an overturn of the vehicle causing a spinal injury to the driver); Wenzel v. Rollins Motor co., 598 S.W.2d 895 (Tex. Civ. App.—El Paso 1980, writ ref'd n.r.e.) (vehicle overturn). *See also* Hoenig, *Resolution of Crashworthiness Design Claims*, 55 St. John's L. Rev. 633 (summer 1981). Hoenig argues that the "crashworthiness doctrine" allows for open-ended liability; he proposes that liability should depend upon a "reasonableness" standard. *Id.* at 634-35, 671.

199. 584 S.W.2d 844 (Tex. 1979).

designed.[200] The Texas Supreme Court repudiated any distinction in strict tort liability between a design defect causing the original accident and a design defect that enhances an injury after the original accident producing event. The court concluded that strict tort liability was applicable in the crashworthiness context.[201] The *Turner* court declared that the crashworthiness issue is evaluated by balancing the risk of harm caused by the product as designed against the utility of that product.[202] Notwithstanding adoption of the crashworthiness concept, the supreme court distinguished between a vehicle that must be designed to be crashworthy in its foreseeable environment of use and a crashproof vehicle. There is no duty to design a vehicle that is crashproof or foolproof.[203]

The crashworthiness doctrine was reconsidered and reaffirmed in *Duncan v. Cessna Aircraft Corp.*[204] Plaintiff, a passenger in an aircraft, was fatally injured when the leg supports on the seat on which he was located collapsed when the aircraft crashed into a mountain.[205] The court formulated the concept of comparative causation as the basis to assess the percentage of cause of the injuries sustained by the plaintiff attributable to the defective design in a crashworthiness context.[206]

The duty of a manufacturer to design a crashworthy vehicle has engendered much discussion in the various jurisdictions.[207]

---

200. *Id.* at 845-46.

201. *Id.* at 847; *Accord* Wenzel v. Rollins Motor Co., 598 S.W.2d 895 (Tex. Civ. App.—El Paso 1980, writ ref'd n.r.e.). Sales, *Automobile Design Sufficiency and Enhanced Injury; a New Concept for No-Fault Liability*, 38 INS. COUNSEL J. 388 (1971).

202. *Turner*, 584 S.W.2d at 847.

203. *Id.* at 847-49. Significantly, in *Roy v. Volkswagenwerk Aktiengesellschoft*, 600 F. Supp. 653 (C.D. Calif. 1985), the court declined to find a van that overturned after leaving the road at high speed was defectively designed when "the design has been in use for 25 years and has met with overwelming consumer acceptance throughout the entire world . . . defies common sense."

204. 665 S.W.2d 414 (Tex. 1984).

205. *Id.* at 418, 427-28, 435.

206. "We therefore hold that in products liability cases in which at least one defendant is found liable on a theory other than negligence, the plaintiff's damages shall be reduced only by the percentage of causation attributed to plaintiff, regardless of how large or small that percentage may be." *Id.* at 429.

207. Frericks v. General Motors Corp., 20 Md. App. 518, 317 A.2d 494, 502-04 (1974); A significant number of jurisdictions have imposed a duty to design a crashworthy vehicle. *See, e.g.*, Nanda v. Ford Motor Co., 509 F.2d 213 (7th Cir. 1974) (placement of fuel tank in floor of trunk); Passwaters v. General Motors Corp., 454 F.2d 1270 (8th Cir. 1972) (unshielded metal flanges on wheel cover); Dyson v. General Motor Corp., 298 F. Supp. 1064 (E.D. Pa. 1969) (roof collapsed); Badorek v. General Motors Corp., 11 Cal. App. 3d 902, 90

Larson v. General Motors Corp.,[208] represents the landmark decision that formulated the concept of liability for a design defect in a crashworthiness context. In *Larson*, plaintiff was injured in a head-on collision when the steering mechanism was thrust rearward upon impact with a fixed object. Plaintiff contended that placement of the steering shaft immediately behind the left front wheel constituted a defective design, since it was foreseeable that upon frontal impact the left front wheel would be forced rearward into the steering shaft which, in turn, would be forced upward into the area of the driver's position.[209] Though *Larson* was predicated on a negligence concept, jurisdictions quickly adopted the concept of design defect in crashworthiness based on the strict tort liability doctrine.[210]

The *Restatement* suggests that a product is not defective when it is safe for normal handling.[211] Jurisdictions adopting the *Larson* rationale perceive that "collisions are so frequent and common that they must be considered an unavoidable incidence of the normal and proper use of automobiles."[212] Since collisions are inherent in the normal use of a vehicle, the manufacturer is obligated to design the vehicle to prevent or ameliorate an unreasonable risk of injury to the user in the event of a foreseeable collision. The concept of reasonably foreseeable or intended use to include

---

Cal. Rptr. 305 (1970) (ruptured gasoline tank); Rutherford v. Chrysler Motor Corp., 60 Mich. App. 392, 231 N.W.2d 413 (1975) (front seat track assembly became disengaged); Ellithorpe v. Ford Motor Co., 503 S.W.2d 516 (Tenn. 1973) (three sharp prongs protruded from hub of steering wheel); Baumgardner v. American Motors Corp., 83 Wash. 2d 751, 522 P.2d 829 (1974) (front seat broke loose; seat belt remained attached); Arbet v. Gussarson, 66 Wis 2d 551, 225 N.W.2d 431 (1975) (four doors jammed; fire erupted from ruptured gas tank). Some jurisdictions reject any duty to design a crashworthy car. *See e.g.*, Frericks v. General Motors Corp., 20 Md. App. 518, 317 A.2d 494 (1974) (roof collapsed); Walton v. Chrysler Motor Corp., 229 So.2d 568 (Miss. 1969) (seat collapsed); Burkhard v. Short, 28 Ohio App. 2d 141, 275 N.E.2d 632 (1971) (unpadded dashboard). For an extended discussion of the liability of manufacturers, sellers, and distributors of motor vehicles involved in accidents in which a defective design merely enhances an injury otherwise caused by the original accident, see Annot., 42 A.L.R.3d 560 (1972 and Supp. 1984).

208. 391 F.2d 495 (8th Cir. 1968). *Accord*, Fox v. Ford Motor Co., 575 F.2d 774 (10th Cir. 1978); Knippen v. Ford Motor Co., 546 F.2d 993 (D.C. Cir. 1976).

209. 391 F.2d at 497, 502.

210. Refer to note 207 *supra*.

211. Restatement (Second) of Torts § 402A, comment h (1965).

212. Turner v. General Motors Corp., 514 S.W.2d 497, 503 (Tex. Civ. App.—Houston [14th Dist.] 1974, writ ref'd n.r.e.). Though *Larsen* is recognized by a majority of courts, it is not universally accepted. *See, e.g.*, Pattillo v. Cessna Aircraft Corp., 379 So.2d 1225 (Miss. 1980).

the "environment of use" constitutes a critical factor in defining the duty of design. Loosely translated, the manufacturer must anticipate the risk inherent in a product when used or involved in the environment which is anticipated by the nature of the product.[213] For vehicles, the foreseeable environment of use encompasses operation of vehicles on public roads and highways where accidents constitute a common occurrence.

Serious controversy exists whether jurors are adequately qualified to evaluate design defects in the context of crashworthiness. The inexperienced lay person lacks expertise to determine that a complicated and highly sophisticated design formulated by literally thousands of engineers based on a myriad of competing and crucial factors is defective.[214] In comparing the evaluation of design defects to the evaluation of medical malpractice, courts declare that no appreciable difference exists in the ability of lay persons to evaluate a defective engineering design that enhances an injury following an original accident.[215]

A significant factor in the imposition of a duty to design a vehicle so as to preclude or ameliorate enhancement of injury following an accident involves establishing that an alternative design would have eliminated or, at least, minimized the injury. Essentially, the manufacturer is not liable for injuries associated with the design of a vehicle in the absence of evidence which establishes that *but for* the existing design configuration the particular injuries or enhancement of injuries would not have occurred. This concept of duty was considered and frontally addressed by the Third Circuit in *Huddell v. Levin*,[216] The plaintiff allegedly sustained a skull

---

213. 514 S.W.2d at 504. Scholarly articles discussing various aspects of the crashworthiness doctrine include: Nader and Page, *Automobile Design and the Judicial Process*. 55 CALIF. L. REV. 645 (1967); Note, *Manufactuter's Liability for an "Uncrashworthy" Automobile*. 52 CORNELL L.Q. 444 (1967); Comment, *Auto Design: Manufacturers' Duty to Reasonably Protect Occupants against the Effects of Collision*. 1969 U. ILL. L. F. 396 (1969).

214. *See e.g.*, Heaton v. Ford Motor Co., 248 Ore. 467, 435 P.2d 806, 809 (1967). *See also* Korli v. Ford Motor Co., 69 Cal. App. 3d 115, 137 Cal. Rptr. 828 (1977); Sales, *Automobile Design Sufficiency and Enhanced Injury: A New Concept for No-Fault Liability*, 38 INS. COUNSEL J. 388 (1971); Wade, *supra* note 6, at 568-69.

215. Badorek v. General Motors Corp., 11 Cal. App. 3d 902, 924, 90 Cal. Rptr. 305, 320 (1970). Evaluation of medical malpractice, however, involves the specific conduct of a particular individual as distinguished from several million vehicles which operate in every jurisdiction.

216. 537 F.2d 726 (3d Cir. 1976).

fracture when struck from behind by a vehicle moving at a high speed. Plaintiff contended that the design of the headrest and header linings increased the magnitude of the injury sustained by the operator of the vehicle. The Third Circuit rejected any liability based on defective design. Addressing the duty concept in a crashworthiness context, the Third Circuit observed that to impose an obligation on the manufacturer to design against enhanced injuries resulting from a second impact, the plaintiff must establish (1) that a safer alternative design exists that is practicable under the circumstances, (2) that no injury or less injury would have resulted upon utilization of the design alternative and (3) a method exists that identifies the injuries actually enhanced by the defective design.[217]

Numerous jurisdictions adhere to the *Huddel* concept. This concept imposes on the plaintiff the burden to prove that he sustained an identifiable aggravation or enhancement of an injury directly attributable to the existing design configuration of the vehicle as a basis for imposing strict tort liability.[218]

Other jurisdictions, recognizing the difficulty presented to the plaintiff in establishing divisibility of injury and identifying that portion of the injury caused or enhanced by the design defect, alter the basis upon which a duty is imposed on the manufacturer. In a significant opinion, the Eighth Circuit in *Mitchell v. Volkswagenwerk, A.G.*,[219] rejected the *Huddell* rule and substituted, instead, the rule that the plaintiff is required only to prove that a defective design in the vehicle was a substantial factor in producing damages over and above the damages caused in the original impact.[220] Once the plaintiff establishes that a specific design defect, indeed, was a substantial factor in enhancing the nature and extent of the injuries suffered by the original accident, the manufacturer is deemed a joint tortfeasor and the burden of establishing divisibility of in-

---

217. *Id.* at 737-38. *Accord,* Polk v. Ford Motor Co., 529 F.2d 259, (8th Cir.), *cert. denied,* 426 U.S. 907 (1976); Jeng v. Witters, 452 F. Supp. 1349 (M.D. Pa. 1978), *aff'd* 591 F.2d 1335 (3d Cir. 1979); Stahl v. Ford Motor Co., 64 Ill. App. 3d 919, 381 N.E.2d 1211 (1978). *See generally* Sales, *Contribution and Indemnity Between Negligent and Strictly Liable Tortfeasors,* 12 St. Mary's L.J. 323 (1980); Sales, *Limitations on Recovery of Damages in Personal Injury Actions,* 18 S. Tex. L.J. 217, 265 (1977).

218. Sales, *Limitations on Recovery of Damages in Personal Injury Actions,* 18 S. Tex. L.J. 217, 263-65 (1977).

219. 669 F.2d 1199 (8th Cir. 1982).

220. *Id.* at 1206.

jury attributable to the defective design is transferred to the product supplier.[221]

The Texas Supreme Court decision in *Duncan v. Cessna Aircraft Corp.*,[222] which involved a design defect in a crashworthiness context, implicity focuses on this issue. The Texas Supreme Court concluded that defective design applied with equal force and effect to the crashworthiness concept after the original accident has occurred as it does in causing the original accident.[223] The court formulated the concept of comparative causation and declared that:

> Comparative causation is especially appropriate in crashworthiness cases where the product defect causes or enhances injuries but does not cause the accident. The conduct which actually caused the accident, . . . [then] could not cause the same degree of harm if there were no product defect. Rather, it is a combination of factors that causes plaintiff's injuries. The jury is asked to apportion responsibility between all whose actions or products combined to cause the entirety of the plaintiff's injuries.[224]

Under the comparative causation formula, the conduct and/or products of all parties is submitted to the jury for a percentage allocation that the conduct and/or products of each party causes or contributes to cause plaintiff's injuries.[225]

The Fifth Circuit recently considered the crashworthiness issue in *Shipp v. General Motors Corp.*[226] Plaintiff was injured when the Pontiac TransAm she was driving overturned. Plaintiff suffered a fractured back and permanent paralysis as a result of the rollover. The roof over the driver's seat partially collapsed; plaintiff asserted that the collapse occurred because the roof was defectively designed. She further asserted that the roof's impact upon her shoulder fractured her back. Affirming an award of $750,000 to the plaintiff, the Fifth Circuit commented:

> The courts of Texas, whose pronouncements we are here bound to follow, have not explicitly addressed the burden of proof in crashworthinesss cases. GM contends that Texas would adopt the burden outlined in *Huddell*. . . . GM would deduce that the

221. *Id.*
222. 665 S.W.2d 414 (Tex. 1984).
223. *Id.* at 418.
224. *Id.*
225. *Id.* at 429.
226. 750 F.2d 418 (5th Cir. 1985).

> adoption of comparative causation in *Duncan v. Cessna Aircraft Co.*, 665 S.W.2d 414 (Tex. 1984), signals the Texas view of the yet unfaced causation question. . . . We read a different signal. The Texas version of comparative fault does not increase a plaintiff's burden, but continues to require only that the plaintiff prove that a defect was a producing cause of the injury. . . . We see no retreat in Texas from its rule that a defect need only be a "producing cause" of injury and that there may be more than one such cause.[227]

The *Duncan* approach to the crashworthiness problem represents a hybrid approach between *Huddell* and *Mitchell.* It appears that the *Duncan* formula of comparative causation provides a mechanism for the jury to allocate percentage responsibility based on the conduct of the plaintiff and any third parties, as well as the product of the manufacturer. This undobutedly represents a more direct, and in the overall scheme of strict tort liability, a more equitable approach to resolving the allocation of responsibility in a crashworthiness context.

d. Limitations on Recovery for Defective Design. Manufacturers are not insurers of their products.[228] Moreover, manufacturers are neither obligated to design the best or the safest product possible,[229] nor are they compelled to manufacture products that are fail safe.[230] Though these principles govern strict tort liability in Texas, the courts are proscribed from instructing the jury on these principles of strict tort liability law.[231]

Generally, the manufacturer is not impressed with a continuing duty to upgrade the design of a product that has been mar-

---

227. *Id.* at 424-25.

228. Syrie v. Knoll Int'l, 748 F.2d 304 (5th Cir. 1984); Daberko v. Heil Co., 681 F.2d 445 (5th Cir. 1982); Hagans v. Oliver Machinery Co., 576 F.2d 97 (5th Cir. 1978); Weakley v. Fischback & Moore, Inc., 515 F.2d 1260 (5th Cir. 1975); Henderson v. Ford Motor Co., 519 S.W.2d 87 (Tex. 1974); McCants v. Salameh, 608 S.W.2d 304 (Tex. Civ. App.—Waco 1980, writ ref'd n.r.e.); Bell Helicopter Co. v. Bradshaw, 594 S.W.2d 519 (Tex. Civ. App—Corpus Christi 1979, writ ref'd n.r.e.).

229. *Bell Helicopter Co.*, 594 S.W.2d at 530.

230. Syrie v. Knoll Int'l., 748 F.2d 304 (5th Cir. 1984); Carter v. Massey Ferguson, 716 F.2d 344 (5th Cir. 1984); Davidson v. Stanadyne Inc., 718 F.2d 1334 (5th Cir. 1983); Daberko v. Heil Co., 681 F.2d 445 (5th Civ. 1983); Hagan v. EZ Mfg., Co., 674 F.2d 1047 (5th Cir. 1982); Acord v. General Motors Corp., 669 S.W.2d 111 (Tex.1984); Henderson v. Ford Motor Co., 519 S.W.2d 87 (Tex. 1974).

231. Acord v. General Motors Corp., 669 S.W.2d 111, (Tex. 1984); Fleishman v. Guadiano, 651 S.W.2d 730 (Tex. 1983).

keted and placed into the channels of commerce.[232] A possible exception may arise when the manufacturer possesses access to records that identify the owners of prior designed products. For example, an intermediary in the manufacturer's conduit of marketing and distribution may provide the manufacturer with easy identification of product owners. Under these circumstances, a duty may arise to upgrade or, at a minimun, provide an option to the owner to adapt the new and safer design to existing products. In *Bell Helicopter v. Bradshaw*,[233] the court concluded that a manufacturer and dealer with easy access to purchasers of helicopters were obligated to replace inadequately designed helicopter rotor blades on earlier designed and marketed helicopters.[234] The court noted that a manufacturer that voluntarily undertakes to upgrade its product must exercise that duty to furnish the latest safer design to products already in use. The duty to use reasonable means to insure replacement of safer components on a previously designed and marketed products is dependent on the continuing relationship between the product supplier and the user.[235]

Similarly, in *Miller Industries v. Caterpillar Tractor Co.*,[236] the court determined that the manufacturer inadequately warned shipowners of faulty sun gear and piston pins in a ship's engine.[237] The manufacturer discovered that the sun gear would fail within the first two hundred hours of use and that it was foreseeable that

---

232. Syrie v. Knoll Int'l, 748 F.2d 304 (5th Cir. 1984); Bell Helicopter Co. v. Bradshaw, 594 S.W.2d 519 (Tex. Civ. App.—Corpus Christi 1979, writ ref'd n.r.e.). *But cf.*, Miller Industries v. Caterpillar Tractor Co., 733 F.2d 813 (11th Cir. 1984) (inadequate warning of faulty sun gear which disabled vessel at sea.) Refer to notes 203-209 *infra* and accompanying text.

233. 594 S.W.2d 519 (Tex. Civ. App.—Corpus Christi 1979, writ ref'd n.r.e.).

234. *Id.* at 531. The 102 series tail rotor blades in use reflected a history of in-flight fatigue fracture failures in the absence of proper maintenance. The 117 series rotors provided a safer alternative for helicopters. The court concluded that although Bell lost control of the helocopter through sale to an unknown person in 1961, it regained substantial control of the helicopter when in 1969 it was acquired by a Bell service station. The helicopter remained with the Bell service station until 1973. It was at this time, the court speculated, that Bell should have employed more forceful measures to insure that the faulty 102 system was replaced by the superior 117 system. *Id.* at 530-31. In Syrie v. Knoll Int'l, 748 F.2d 304, 311-12 (5th Cir. 1984), the Fifth Circuit noted that, in the absence of regained control of the product, the manufacturer has no continuing duty to update and advance design or warnings.

235. 594 S.W.2d at 532.

236. 733 F.2d 813 (11th Cir. 1984).

237. *Id.* at 818.

the vessel would be disabled at sea and subject to unreasonable risks of danger. The manufacturer communicated this information by a form letter to its authorized dealers. The court concluded that the gravity of the danger required more than a form letter to the dealer; it required actual notice to the user and replacement of the less than safely designed components.[238] Because dealers are required to comply with manufacturer directives, the manufacturer was deemed to exercise sufficient control to insure that faulty parts were replaced on products previously marketed.[239]

Another limitation involves government contracts in which the design of a product has been contractually specified by the government. A design that conforms to the contractual specifications of a federal government contract, as a general principle, precludes application of strict tort liability.[240] The government contract defense limits the discretion of the manufacturer to select other design options that might conceivably be safer and equally utilitarian in use.[241] The concept of the government contract limitation arises

---

238. *Id.* at 821-22.

239. *Id.*

240. See McKay v. Rockwell Int'l Corp., Inc., 704 F.2d 444 (9th Cir. 1983), *cert. denied*, 104 U.S. 711 (1984); Brown v. Caterpillar Tractor Co., 696 F.2d 246 (3d Cir. 1982); Sanner v. Ford Motor Co., 144 N.J. Super. 1, 364 A.2d 43 (1976), *aff'd*, 154 N.J. Super. 407, 381 A.2d 805 (1977), *cert. denied*, 384 A.2d 846 1978); Hubbs v. United Technologies, 574 F. Supp. 96 (E.D. Pa. 1983); *In re* "Agent Orange" Prod. Liab. Litig. 534 F. Supp. 1046 (E.D. N.Y. 1982), *cert. denied*, 104 S.Ct. 1417 (1984).

241. The government contractor defense, first enunciated by the Supreme Court in *Yearsley v. W. A. Ross Construction Co.*, 309 U.S. 18 (1940), allows a government contractor to avoid liability for its actions when it complies with government specifications during the execution or performance of a contract with the United States. Generally the defense may be applied only when the government itself is immune. *See In re* "Agent Orange" Prod. Liab. Litig., 506 F. Supp. 762, 792 (E.D.N.Y. 1980), *reh'g denied*, 534 F. Supp. 1046 (E.D.N.Y. 1982), *cert. denied*, 104 S. Ct. 1417 (1984); Green v. ICI America, Inc., 362 F. Supp. 1263, 1266 (E.D. Tenn. 1973); Littlehale v. E. I duPont de Nemours & Co., 268 F. Supp. 791, 803 n. 17 (S.D.N.Y. 1966), *aff'd*, 380 F.2d 274 (2d Cir. 1967). *See also* Kontsanbos v. Boeing Co., 755 F.2d 352 (3d Cir. 1985); Lockheed Aircraft Corp. v. United States, 103 S. Ct. 1033 (1983); McKay v. Rockwell International Corp., Inc., 704 F.2d 444 (9th Cir. 1983), *cert. denied*, 104 U.S. 711 (1984); Brown v. Caterpillar Tractor Co., 696 F.2d (3d Cir. 1982); Merrit, Chapman & Scott Corp. v. Guy F. Atkinson Co., 295 F.2d 14 (9th Cir. 1961); Sanner v. Ford Motor Co., 144 N.J. Super. 1, 364 A.2d 43 (1976), *aff'd*, 154 N.J. Super. 407, 381 A.2d 805 (1977), *cert. denied*, 384 A.2d 846 (1978); Hubbs v. United Technologies, 574 F. Supp. 96 (E.D. Pa. 1983); Casabianca v. Casabianca, 104 Misc. 2d 348, 349, 428 N.Y.S. 2d 400, 402 (N.Y. Sup. Ct. 1980).

Recent scholarly articles dealing with the immunity of the government in strict tort liability incude: Sales, *Government Contract Defense: Sharing The Protective Cloak of Savings Immunity after Mckay v. Rockwell International Corp.* 37 BAYLOR L. REV. 181

from the government immunity from suit in connection with certain product related accidents. In this context, the manufacturer that supplies the product in strict compliance with government specifications actually acts as agent for and stands in the shoes of the federal government. The immunity of the federal government applies with equal force and effect to the product supplier.[242]

A further limitation on the design defect liability of a product supplier is the unforeseeable misuse of a product. The concept of strict tort liability contemplates a duty on the part of a product supplier to design its products to be safe for their intended and reasonably foreseeable use.[243] In *General Motors Corp. v. Hopkins*,[244] plaintiff lost control of his truck while negotiating a hairpin turn allegedly as a result of a lockup in components of the carburetor on the pickup truck. When the plaintiff purchased the pickup truck originally, he removed the original carburetor and replaced it with a Holley racing carburetor. After several weeks, the

---

(1985). Tobak, *A Case of Mistaken Liability: The Government Contractor's Liability for Injuries Incurred by Members of the Armed Forces*, 13 PUB. CONT. L.J. 74, 93-94 (1982); Note, *Liability of a Manufacturer for Products Defectively Designed by the Government*, 23 B.C.L. REV. 1025, 1050 n.132 (1982); Note, *The Government Contractor Defense and Manufacturers of Military Equipment: McKay v. Rockwell International Corporation*, 21 HOUS. L. REV. 855 (1984); Comment, *The Government Contract Defense in Strict Liability Suits for Defective Design*, 48 U. CHI. L. REV. 1030, 1045-46 (1981); Comment, *Agent Orange and the Government Contract Defense: Are Military Manufacturers Immune from Products Liability?*, 36 U. MIAMI L. REV. 489, 495 (1982).

242. *Id.*

243. Foster v. Ford Motor Co., 616 F.2d 1304 (5th Cir. 1980) (failure to use load levellers and clamps on front end loading device used with a tractor); Mitchell v. Fruehauf Corp., 568 F.2d 1139 (5th Cir. 1978) (use of hanging meat hooks in meat trailer which would cause the trailer to become overbalanced when negotiating sharp curves and turns); Gonzales v. Caterpillar Tractor Co., 571 S.W.2d 867 (Tex. 1978) (failure to place anti-skid material on a stepdown from a Caterpillar tractor loader and failure to locate the stepdown away from the tracks of the tractor when used in a muddy environment); Miller v. Boch Laundry Machinery Co., 568 S.W.2d 648 (Tex. 1977) (use of rubber pads to support a safety device when such pads were expected to deteriorate when used in an oily environment); General Motors Corp. v. Hopkins, 548 S.W.2d 344 (Tex. 1977) (design of carburetor that would cause the butterfly valves to stick in an open position and accelerate the vehicle out of control); Rawlings Sporting Goods Co., Inc. v. Daniels, 619 S.W.2d 435 (Tex. Civ. App.—Waco 1981, writ ref'd n.r.e.) (football helmet that deformed upon impact); Lubbock Mfg. Co. v. Perez, 591 S.W.2d 907 (Tex. Civ. App.—Waco 1979, no writ) (design of an LP transport trailer with too high center of gravity) Bell Helicopter Co. v. Bradshaw, 594 S.W.2d 519 (Tex. Civ. App.—Corpus Christi 1979, writ ref'd n.r.e.) (use of a helicopter rotor blade with a limited useful and safe life). *See* Holford, *The Limits of Strict Liability for Product Design and Manufacture*, 52 TEX. L. REV. 81 (1973).

244. 548 S.W.2d 344 (Tex. 1977).

plaintiff attempted to reinstall the original carburetor and, in the process, misinstalled the carburetor in eleven separate and distinct respects.[245] The issue of the change in the product was viewed as a misuse under defenses to strict tort liability and the Texas Supreme Court concluded that misuse constituted a partial defense only to the extent that the product supplier could not reasonably foresee the misuse of a product by the user.[246] Foreseeable misuse, declared the Supreme Court, merely constitutes a concurring cause of the accident and resulting injury. Unfortunately, the *Hopkins* opinion was presented to the Supreme Court as a misuse issue. In reality, the misinstallation of the carburetor constituted a substantial alteration rather than a misuse. Under the *Restatement*[247] the plaintiff is obligated to establish as an element of his strict tort liability action that the product was in *the same condition* at the time it left the possession and control of the manufacturer as existed at the time of the accident. Negating any substantial alteration is fundamental to a strict tort liability action and should not be confused with misuse. The term "misuse" is a shorthand method of stating that a product has been used in a manner neither intended nor objectively and reasonably foreseeable. Misuse, in legal effect, is an unforeseeable and an unintended use of a product.

In *Colvin v. Robert E. McKee, Inc.*,[248] misuse or alteration was further considered. Plaintiff was an ironworker who was injured when he grabbed an unsecured length of steel purlin on a construction job. Though the steel purlin was shorter than the manufacturer's specifications, the Texas Supreme Court concluded that misplacement of the purlin rather than its length caused the accident:

> An essential element of Colvin's strict liability cause of action is a finding that the product was not fit for its intended or reasonably foreseeable use at the time it left the manufacturer. The purlins

---

245. *Id.* at 348.

246. *Id.* at 349, 352. In order for a substantial alteration to insulate the product supplier from liability, the material change in design must directly alter the function of the product so that it directly creates the risk of danger to the ultimate user. *Soler v. Castmaster*, 98 N.J. 137, 484 A.2d 1225 (1984).

247. Restatement (Second) of Torts, § 402A comment g (1965) provides: "The seller is not liable when he delivers the product in a safe condition, and subsequent mishandling or other causes make it harmful by the time it is consumed."

248. 671 S.W.2d 556 (Tex. App.—Dallas), *aff'd*, 682 S.W.2d 243 (Tex. 1984).

> were intended to be welded to the top of the trusses and were to serve as spacers between the trusses and the roof material. The uncontroverted evidence proved that the purlins were fit for the intended purpose of providng a spacer between the trusses and the building roof when they left Red Steel. The question remaining is whether Red Steel reasonably could have foreseen that the purlins would be placed atop the trusses, left there unattached, violating the safety standards of the Associated General Contractors of America, Inc. and then used by a skilled ironworker to pull himself upright. Red Steel could not reasonably have foreseen such a use. The purlins were used for the intended purpose and there is no evidence of any other intended or foreseeable use. The dangerous condition which contributed to Colvin's fall was created on the jobsite not by Red Steel, but by Colvin, his fellow employees, and McKee.[249]

Essentially, a product supplier is obligated to design a product to be reasonably safe for the product's intended and reasonably foreseeable uses. A misuse constitutes nothing more than an unreasonable and unintended use of a product and, therefore, exceeds the product's design parameters. Virtually any product is capable of producing injury when misused. This is particularly true when injury results from bizarre and unforeseeable misuses. As an example, in *Artis v. Fibre Metal Products*,[250] plaintiff sustained a severe injury to his neck when a railroad tie fell and struck the side of his head. Plaintiff contended that the hard hat manufactured by the defendant was defectively designed because it failed to prevent injury to his neck from a large falling object. Rejecting any duty on the part of the manufacturer to design the hard hat to prevent such injury, the court observed:

> To allege, as plaintiff does, that the protection expected by the consumer, however unreasonable, determines the standard of foreseeable use is irrational; application of such a standard would make the manufacturer of a protective device worn by an injured person an absolute insurer of his product, a result that has been rejected repeatedly by Illinois courts. Foreseeability means that which is *objectively reasonable* to expect, not merely what might conceivably occur. Liability of a manufacturer properly encom-

---

249. 671 S.W.2d at 557. *See generally*, Rooney v. Federal Press Co., 751 F.2d 140 (3rd Cir. 1984); Thomas v. Munson Mach. Co., 463 So. 2d 1044 (Miss. 1985).

250. 115 Ill. App. 3d 228, 450 N.E.2d 756 (1983).

> passes. . . .only those situations where the product is being used for the purpose for which it was intended or for which it is reasonably foreseeable that it may be used. Any other approach to the problem results in making the manufacturer and those in the chain of product distribution virtual insurers of the product, a position rejected in *Suvada*.[251]

It is readily apparent that the duty to adopt a safer design alternative applies only when the product is utilized for its intended and objectively reasonable foreseeable uses. Reasonably foreseeable use means a use that is objectively reasonable to expect and not any use that might conceivably occur under any combination of circumstances. Uses that are irrational, bizarre, or aberrational simply do not warrant the imposition of strict tort liability for a design defect.

3. Marketing Defect (Failure to Warn and/or Instruct for Safe Use).

a. Basis for marketing defect and general legal standards. Under strict tort liability as articulated in Section 402A, a product that is properly manufactured and safely designed may nevertheless be defective and unreasonably dangerous in the absence of adequate warnings of the dangerous propensities inherent in or reasonably foreseeable in connection with the use of the product.[252] The genesis of strict tort liability for failure to provide adequate warnings of the dangerous characteristics and propensities of a

---

251. *Id.* at 759 (emphasis in original, citations omitted). *See also*, Gootee v. Colt Industries, Inc., 712 F.2d 105 (6th Cir. 1983); Mach v. General Motors Corp., 315 N.W.2d 561 (1982).

252. *See e.g.*, Fabian v. E. W. Bliss Co., 582 F.2d 1257, 1261 (10th Cir. 1978) (a defect necessarily includes a lack of adequate warnings); Ortho Pharmaceutical Corp. v. Chapman, 388 N.E.2d 541, 549 (Ind. App. 1979) ("An absence of proper warning . . . can range from a complete absence of any warning to a warning which is given but is inadequate"). Under Texas law, a product is unreasonably dangerous and, therefore, defective if the manufacturer markets the product without supplying adequate warnings of the dangers associated with using the product as well as failing to provide adequate instructions for avoiding such risks. Gross v. Black & Decker, Inc., 695 F.2d 858 (5th Cir. 1983). It has been stated that "under Section 402A a product that is safely designed and manufactured can nevertheless be 'dangerously defective' if the manufacturer has reason to know of the dangerous propensities of the product but fails adequately to warn purchasers or users. Bryant v. Technical Research Co., 654 F.2d 1337, 1344 (9th Cir. 1981). *See generally*, Keeton, *Products Liability -Inadequacy of Information*, 48 TEX. L. REV. 398, 398 (1970); Sales, *The Duty to Warn and Instruct for Safe Use in Strict Tort Liability*, 13 ST. MARY'S L. J. 521, 524 (1982); Annot., 53 A.L.R.3d 239 (1973).

product or the failure to provide directions for safe and effective use of a product is the *Restatement*.

The commentary to Section 402A of the *Restatement* specifically provides that "in order to prevent the product from being unreasonably dangerous, the seller may be required to give directions or warnings, on the container, as to its use."[253] A marketing defect, as distinguished from a manufacturing flaw or design defect involves: (1) the failure to provide any warning of the dangerous propensities or risks involved in the use of a product; (2) the failure to provide an adequate warning of the dangerous characteristics and risks of harm associated with use of a product; (3) the failure to provide any instructions for safe use to avoid the dangers and risks involved in the use of a product; and (4) the failure to provide adequate instructions for the safe and efficient use of the product so as to avoid the dangers associated with the product's use.[254] A marketing defect, therefore, can range from a complete absence of any warning or instruction to a warning or instruction that is inadequate to effectively communicate the warning or instruction to the product user.[255]

The rationale undergirding the marketing obligation imposed on a product supplier is predicated on furnishing the user sufficient information to make an informed choice to use a product that possesses certain potential dangers or risks of harm. Essentially, the product supplier is obligated to furnish the potential user all available relevant information regarding the characteristics and propensities of a product to enable the user to make a conscious choice whether the utility of the product outweighs the po-

---

253. RESTATEMENT (SECOND) OF TORTS, Section 402A, Comment j (1965).

254. *See generally*, Sales, *The Duty to Warn and Instruct for Safe Use in Strict Tort Liability*, 13 ST. MARY'S L. J. 521, 547 (1982).

255. *Compare* Technical Chemical Co. v. Jacobs, 480 S.W.2d 602 (Tex. 1972), involving the failure to provide any warning of the risk of danger or harm in applying a freon can to the high side of a compressor unit, *and* Borel v. Fibreboard Paper Products Corp., 493 F.2d 1076 (5th Cir. 1973), *cert. denied*, 419 U.S. 869 (1974), involving a failure to warn users of asbestos of the risk of contracting asbestosis from prolonged exposure to asbestos dust *with* Bristol-Myers Co. v. Gonzales, 561 S.W.2d 801 (Tex. 1978), involving a warning to doctors relating to the use of Kantrex but failing to warn that repeated irrigation of surgical wounds could cause an ototoxic condition in the patient *and* Kritser v. Beech Aircraft Corp., 479 F.2d 1089 (5th Cir. 1973), involving a warning to the operator of an aircraft to avoid prolonged operation of aircraft in a slip or slide condition under low fuel condition but failing to advise of the effects of failing to heed the instruction.

tential risks of harm or danger in its use.[256]

Strict tort liability based on a marketing defect requires five elements: (1) an unreasonably dangerous risk of harm from dangers inherent in the product or reasonably foreseeable in the product's use; (2) the dangerous propensity or risk of harm of a product must be known or knowable by the product supplier at the time the product is marketed; (3) a marketing defect must exist, i.e., the absence of a warning, the absence of an adequate warning or the absence of any or an adequate instruction for safe use; (4) the absence of a warning or instruction for use must render the product unreasonably dangerous; and (5) the failure to warn must be a producing cause of the accident and resulting injuries suffered by the user.[257]

The duty of a product supplier to provide warnings and instructions for safe use arises when the unreasonably dangerous characteristics and propensities of a product exceed the level of danger normally contemplated or reasonably anticipated by the ordinary consumer.[258] As announced in the *Restatement* an unreasonably dangerous condition contemplates that the product sold "must be dangerous to an extent beyond that which would be contemplated by the ordinary consumer who purchases it, with the ordinary knowledge common to the community as to its characteristics."[259] All products necessarily present some potential risk of

---

256. *See, e.g.*, Borel v. Fibreboard Paper Products Corp., 493 F.2d 1076, 1089 (5th Cir. 1973), *cert. denied*, 419 U.S. 869 (1974) (a warning must advise a reasonable person of the dangers so that the individual may elect not to purchase the product with knowledge of the danger); Rawlings Sporting Goods, Co. v. Daniels, 619 S.W.2d 435 (Tex. App.—Waco 1981, writ ref'd n.r.e.) (the manufacturer possesses a superior knowledge of the limitations of its product and, where it is foreseeable that a consumer will rely on the product and expose himself to risk he might avoid if aware of the risks of harm a duty to warn arises). Ragsdale Bros., Inc. v. Margo ___ S.W.2d ___ (Tex. App.—San Antonio 1985, no writ) (user entitled to information necessary to make an intelligent choice). This is contemplated by Restatement (Second) of Torts, §402A, comment i (1965) which specifically provides that "the article sold must be dangerous to an extent beyond that which would be contemplated by the ordinary consumer who purchases it with the ordinary knowledge common to the community as to its charateristics." Obviously, a purchaser-user cannot weigh the risk of harm against the utility of the product if the risk of harm and dangerous propensities of the product are unknown and the user has not been informed.

257. Reyes v. Wyeth Laboratories, 498 F.2d 1264, 1272 (5th Cir.), *cert. denied*, 419 U.S. 1096 (1974); Thomas v. St. Joseph's Hosp. 618 S.W.2d 791, 797 (Tex. App.—Houston [1st Dist.] 1981, writ ref'd n.r.e.); Gravis v. Parke-Davis & Co., 502 S.W.2d 863, 868 (Tex. Civ. App.—Corpus Christ 1973, writ ref'd n.r.e.).

258. Restatement (Second) of Torts, §402A, comment j (1965).

259. *Id.*, comment i.

danger either in the product's intended or reasonably foreseeable use or environment of use.[260] The mere fact that a product is dangerous or presents some risk of harm does not preclude the product from being marketed. Rather, the potential liability of a product supplier to warn of dangerous propensities and characteristics of a product depends on the reasonable expectation of the purchaser and foreseeable users of the product.[261] Antecedent to determining the reasonable expectation of the ordinary consumer, however, is a determination whether the product marketed is so unreasonably dangerous that no warning or instruction for use will ameliorate its unreasonably dangerous condition. Essentially, a two-prong test is applied by the court to ascertain whether a product as marketed, accompanied by the appropriate warnings and instructions for use, is unreasonably dangerous *per se*. Initially, it must be determined whether the product is unavoidably unsafe for its intended or reasonably foreseeable use. An unavoidably unsafe product, under the *Restatement*, contemplates that some products, in the present state of human knowledge, are quite incapable of being made safe for their intended and ordinary use.[262] Once it is determined that the product is unavoidably unsafe, and that the dangerous propensity or risk of harm has been warned against, the court in the first instance must determine whether the product is still so unsafe that marketing the product at all is unreasonably

---

260. *See* Annot., 53 A.L.R.3d 239, 251 (1973). The author notes: "Since the use of almost any product involves some degree of danger, the duty of the manufacturer to warn of danger must be related, or made dependent upon, the degree of danger involved in the use of the product." In Little, *Product Liability - The Growing Uncertainty About Warnings*, 12 FORUM 995, 997 (1977), the author states that, "it is fairly well settled that the manufacturer or seller need not give warning of such dangers or problems as present only a very slight risk of harm or from which the damage or injury would, at best, be minimal."

261. Jackson v. Johns-Manville Sales Corp., 727 F.2d 506 (5th Cir. 1984), *rev'd on other grounds*, ___ F.2d ___ (5th Cir. 1985) (en banc); Pavlides v. Galveston Yachet Basin, Inc., 727 F.2d 330 (5th Cir. 1984); Hagans v. Oliver Mach. Co., 576 F.2d 97 (5th Cir. 1978); Borel v. Fibreboard Paper Products Corp., 493 F.2d 1076 (5th Cir. 1973), *cert. denied*, 419 U.S. 869 (1974); Rawlings Sporting Goods Co., Inc v. Daniels, 619 S.W.2d 435 (Tex. App. - Waco 1981, writ ref'd n.r.e.).

262. RESTATEMENT (SECOND) OF TORTS, Section 402A, comment k (1965), defines unavoidably unsafe products as "products, which, in the present state of human knowledge, are quite incapable of being made safe for their intended and ordinary use. . . .[T]he seller of such products, again, with the qualification that they are properly prepared and marketed, and proper warning is given, where the situation calls for it, is not be held to strict liability for unfortunate consequences attending their use, merely because he has undertaken to supply the public with an apparently useful and desirable product, attendant with a known but apparently reasonable risk."

dangerous. To decide whether the product is unreasonably dangerous *per se*, the court must balance the utility of the product against its dangerous propensities. A product that is beneficial and for which there are no safer alternatives may be marketed with appropriate warnings. Other products that are deemed to be severely dangerous and possessing a high risk of danger that cannot be eliminated and for which safer alternatives are available may be regarded as unreasonably dangerous *per se*.[263] Under a characterization of unreasonably dangerous *per se*, the marketing of the product under any circumstances imposes strict tort liability on the product supplier, irrespective of the adequacy of the warning of the danger or the adequacy of instructions for use of the product in the least dangerous manner.[264] This balancing process necessarily involves an evaluation of the normal expectations of the consumer as to the manner in which the product will perform, the degree of simplicity or complexity involved in the product's use, the severity and magnitude of the dangerous potential or risk of harm to which the user is exposed, the likelihood of harm to the user in the environment of the product's use, and the fact that an

---

263. The adoption of a two step analysis in determining if a product is unreasonably dangerous per se was enunicated in Reyes v. Wyeth Labs, 498 F.2d 1264 (5th Cir.), *cert. denied*, 419 U.S. 1096 (1974) and in Needham v. White Laboratories, Inc., 639 F.2d 394, 401 (7th Cir. 1981):

> Once it is determined that the product is unavoidably unsafe and that the dangers warned against, it must be determined whether the product is so unsafe that marketing it at all is 'unreasonably dangerous per se.' In order to decide whether the product is unreasonably dangerous per se, a court must balance the utility of the product against its dangers.

264. Certain products are so unreasonably dangerous even when accompanied by a warning that marketing the product at all results in liability for a product that is unreasonably dangerous per se. This is particularly appropriate where a safer substitute product exists that accomplishes the the same result. *See e.g.*, d'Hedouville v. Pioneer Hotel Co., 552 F.2d 886 (9th Cir. 1977); Fowler v. General Electric Co. 40 N.C. App. 301, 252 S.E.2d 862 (1979); O'Brien v. Muskin Corp., 94 N.J. 169, 463 A.2d 298 (1983); Ruggeri v. Minnesota Mining & Mfg. Co., 63 Ill.App.3d 525, 380 N.E.2d 445 (1978); Strum, Ruger & Co. v. Day, 594 P.2d 38 (Alaska 1979); Uloth v. City Tank Corp., 376 Mass. 874, 384 N.E.2d 1188 (1978). As a practical matter, most products possess a utilitarian purpose despite the severe risks of harm. Consequently, the issue invariably involves a fact issue that must be ultimately resolved by the jury. *See e.g.*, Reyes v. Wyeth Laboratories, 498 F.2d 1264, 1277 (5th Cir.), *cert. denied*, 419 U.S. 1096 (1974); Dixon v. Van Waters & Rogers, 674 S.W.2d 479 (Tex. App.—Fort Worth 1984, writ ref'd n.r.e.), *per curiam*, 682 S.W.2d 533 (Tex. 1984); Ford Motor Co. v. Nowak, 638 S.W.2d 582 (Tex. App.—Corpus Christi 1982, writ ref'd n.r.e.); Pearson v. Hevi-Duty Electric, 618 S.W.2d 784 (Tex. App.—Houston [1st Dist.] 1981, writ ref'd n.r.e.); Rawlings Sporting Goods Co., Inc v. Daniels, 619 S.W.2d 435 (Tex. App.—Waco 1981, writ ref'd n.r.e.); Lopez v. Aro Corp., 584 S.W.2d 333 (Tex. App.—San Antonio 1979, writ ref'd n.r.e.).

adequate warning and instruction for safe use will significantly eliminate the dangerous potential of the product.[265] If the balance is not struck in favor of the utility of the product, then no warning or instructions for use will prevent the product from being characterized as unreasonably dangerous *per se*. As noted by the court in *Needham v. White Laboratories, Inc.*,[266] "a court will impose strict product liability even if a warning is given if the product remains unsafe when the warning is followed and the risk of danger outweighs any apparent usefulness of the product."

If the utility of the product outweighs its risk of harm and dangerous potential, the product is not unreasonably dangerous to market.[267] This means, of course, that the risk of harm or the dangerous potential of the product is outweighed by the beneficial purposes it serves.[268] Of course, this involves both a qualitative and quantitative weighing of the legitimate public interest in the particular product's availability.[269] When a product qualitatively and

---

265. RESTATEMENT (SECOND) OF TORTS, Section 402A, comments j and k (1965). Under these circumstances, liability for marketing a product may be avoided provided the product is accompanied by an adequate warning. Palvides v. Galveston Yacht Basin, Inc., 727 F.2d 330 (5th Cir. 1984); Gross v. Black & Decker Inc., 695 F.2d 858 (5th Cir. 1983); Reyes v. Wyeth Laboratories, 498 F.2d 1264, 1274 (5th Cir. 1974), *cert. denied*, 419 U.S. 1096 (1974). *See generally*, Sales, *The Duty to Warn and Instruct for Safe Use in Strict Tort Liability*, 13 ST. MARY'S L. J., 521 528-29 (1982).

266. 639 F.2d 394, 401 (7th Cir. 1981), *cert. denied*, 454 U.S. 927. Dean Keeton, *Products Liability - Inadequacy of Information*, 48 TEX. L. REV. 398, 404 (1970), suggests that an evaluation that a product is unreasonably dangerous per se can be made when there is an absence of an inadequate warning.

267. Obviously, if the benefits of a particular product are reasonably beneficial to the public, such product cannot be deemed to be unreasonably dangerous per se if accompanied by an appropriate warning and instructions for use. *See e.g.*, Brochu v. Ortho Pharmaceutical Corp., 642 F.2d 652 (1st Cir. 1981); Reyes v. Wyeth Labs, 498 F.2d 1264 (5th Cir. 1974), *cert. denied*, 419 U.S. 1096 (1974); Ortho Pharmaceutical Corp. v. Chapman, 388 N.E.2d 541 (Ind. App. 1979).

268. *See generally*, Sales, *The Duty to Warn and Instruct for Safe Use in Strict Tort Liability*, 13 ST MARY'S L. J. 521, 528 (1982).

269. As noted by the Fifth Circuit in Borel v. Fibreboard Papers Products Corp., 493 F.2d 1076, 1088-89 (5th Cir. 1973), *cert. denied*, 419 U.S. 869 (1974):

> Strict liability may not always be appropriate in such cases because of the important benefits derived from the use of the product. This is especially so with respect to new drugs that are essential in treating disease but involve a high degree of risk. It may also be so with respect to other commercial products possessing both unparalleled utility and unquestioned danger. As a practical matter, the decision to market such a product requires a balancing of the product's utility against its known or foreseeable danger. But, as comment k makes clear, even when such balancing leads to the conclusion that marketing is justified, the seller still has a responsibility to inform the user or consumer of the risk of harm. The

quantitatively serves a legitimate public purpose, then the product is not unreasonably dangerous as marketed provided the product is accompanied by adequate warnings of the risks of harm and instructions for safe use.[270]

The duty to provide adequate warnings and instructions for safe use is governed by the risks of harm involved in the intended and reasonably foreseeable uses of the product.[271] The product supplier is not obligated, however, to warn of every risk of harm, mishap or dangerous potential that may occur in the use of a product.[272] In particular, a product supplier is not obligated to provide warnings of unforeseeable dangers inherent in the use of a product.[273]

Reasonable foreseeability is limited to uses that are objectively

---

failure to give adequate warnings in these circumstances renders the product unreasonably dangerous.

270. Restatement (Second) of Torts, § 402A, comment j (1965).

271. As stated in Pearson v. Hevi-Duty Electric, 618 S.W.2d 784, 787 (Tex. Civ. App.—Houston [1st Dist.] 1981, writ ref'd n.r.e.), "The seller of a product is legally obligated to provide warnings of dangers that can arise in intended or foreseeable use of products." *See also*, Pittsburg Corning Corp. v. Thomas, ____ S.W.2d ____ (Tex. App.—Houston [14th Dist.] 1984, no writ); Ford Motor Co. v. Nowak, 638 S.W.2d 582 (Tex. App.—Corpus Christi 1982, writ ref'd n.r.e.); Bituminous Casualty Corp. v. Black & Decker Mfg. Co., 518 S.W.2d 868 (Tex. Civ. App.—Dallas 1974, writ ref'd n.r.e.); Ragsdale Bros., Inc. v. Margo, ___ S.W.2d ___ (Tex. App.—San Antonio 1985, no writ).

272. *See, e.g.*, Cruz v. Texaco, Inc., 589 F. Supp. 777 (S.D. Ill. 1984) (danger of operating a winch truck at highway speeds with a piece of heavy equipment hanging from the raised winch); Caplaco One, Inc. v. Amerex Corp., 435 F. Supp. 1116, 1119 (E.D. Mo. 1977) (when indicator on fire extinguisher read to recharge it was obvious to ordinary user that extinguisher contained an improper amount of pressure); McCaleb v. Mackey Paint Mfg. Co., 343 So. 2d 511, 514 (Ala. 1977) (a flammable chemical used as a painter thinner around an operation that introduced significant heat and sparks was not the type of use intended); Thibault v. Sears, Roebuck & Co., 118 N.H. 802, 806, 395 A.2d 843, 848 (1978) (product misuse and aberrational uses are not within the ambit of foreseeability requiring a warning).

273. For example, in Johnson v. Jones-Blair Paint Co., 607 S.W.2d 305 (Tex. Civ. App.—Eastland 1980, writ ref'd n.r.e.), the manufacturer is not required to foresee that a user of paint would employ gasoline near an open flame to remove paint spots from the floor. The basis of the duty to warn is the intended and foreseeable use and environment of use of a product. In Bridges v. Chemrex Specialty Coatings, Inc., 704 F.2d 175 (5th Cir. 1983), manufacturer not required to foresee children tossing firecrackers into empty and open drums that contained flammable chemicals. *See generally*, Gross v. Black & Decker, Inc., 695 F.2d 858 (5th Cir. 1983); Ionmar Compania Naviera S.A. v. Olin Corp., 666 F.2d 897 (5th Cir. 1982); Shop Rite Foods, Inc. v. Upjohn Co., 619 S.W.2d 574 (Tex. App.—Amarillo 1981, writ ref'd n.r.e.). Foreseeability, provided it is objectively reasonable, would include reasonably anticipated misuses. *See e.g.*, Temple v. Zimmer U.S.A., Inc., 678 S.W.2d 723 (Tex. App.—Houston [1st Dist.] 1984, no writ); Blackwell Burner Co. v. Cerda, 644 S.W.2d 512 (Tex. App.—San Antonio 1982, writ ref'd n.r.e.).

reasonable to expect and anticipate in the use of a product; it does not encompass uses that are totally bizarre, aberrational or which represent wholly unexpected product misuse.[274] This limitation is particularly important in the marketing area. Unless the duty to warn of the risks of dangers in the use of a product is limited to objectively foreseeable uses, the imposition of a duty to warn of the bizarre, aberrational and wholly unanticipated use transforms the product supplier to an insurer.[275] It is a well established principle in strict tort liability that a product supplier is not an insurer of the product. Strict tort liability ensues only if the product is unreasonably dangerous as marketed for its intended and reasonably foreseeable uses.[276] The product supplier is assumed to possess information regarding the latest research, reports of dangers, scientific developments and technical breakthroughs relating to its product.[277] In essence, a product supplier is deemed in law to be an expert on its product and is presumed to know all the dangers that exist in the product at the time it is marketed.[278] Excusable igno-

---

274. *See e.g.*, Martin v. Harrington & Richardson, Inc., 743 F.2d 1200 (7th Cir. 1984); Estrada v. Schmultz Mfg. Co., 734 F.2d 1218 (7th Cir. 1984); Hunt v. Blasius, 74 Ill. 2d 203, 384 N.E.2d 368, 372 (1978); Artis v. Fibre Metal Products, 115 Ill. App.3d 228, 450 N.E.2d 756 (1983). As noted by the court in Holecek v. E-Z Just, 124 Ill. App.3d 251, 252, 464 N.E.2d 696, 698 (1984), [i]n retrospect, almost nothing is entirely unforeseeable. Foreseeability means that which is objectively reasonable to expect, not merely what might conceivably occur." *Id.* at 698.

275. The concept of absolute liability for product related accident contravenes the purpose and intent of RESTATEMENT (SECOND) OF TORTS, §402A (1965).

276. Product suppliers are not regarded as insurers and are not required to insure that their product is fail safe or cannot cause injury. *See generally*, Daberko v. Heil Co., 681 F.2d 445 (5th Cir. 1982); Hagans v. Oliver Mach. Co., 576 F.2d 97 (5th Cir. 1978); Weakley v. Fischbach & Moore, Inc., 515 F.2d 1260 (5th Cir. 1975); Acord v. General Motors Corp., 669 S.W.2d 111 (Tex. 1984); Henderson v. Ford Motor Co., 519 S.W.2d 87 (Tex. 1974); McCants v. Salameh, 608 S.W.2d 304 (Tex. Civ. App.—Waco 1980, writ ref'd n.r.e.); Bell Helicopter Co. v. Bradshaw, 594 S.W.2d 519 (Tex. Civ. App.—Corpus Christi 1979, writ ref'd n.r.e.).

277. Reyes v. Wyeth Laboratories, 498 F.2d 1264, 1277 (5th Cir.), *cert. denied*, 419 U.S. 1096 (1974) (manufacturer held to the skill of an expert in its field and presumed to possess an expert's knowledge of arts, materials and processes of business); Borel v. Fibreboard Paper Products Corp., 493 F.2d 1076, 1089 (5th Cir. 1973), *cert. denied*, 419 U.S. 869 (1974) (manufacturer held to the knowledge and skill of an expert); Bristol-Myers Co. v. Gonzales, 561 S.W.2d 801, 804 (Tex. 1978) (manufacturer deemed to be an expert and to possess knowledge of all potential dangers associated with the product). *See generally*, Lindsay v. Ortho Pharmaceutical Corp., 637 F.2d 87, 91 (2d Cir. 1980); Karjala v. Johns-Manville Product Corp., 523 F.2d 155, 159 (8th Cir. 1975); Basko v. Sterling Drug, Inc., 416 F.2d 417, 426 (2d Cir. 1969); Dias v. Daisy-Heddon, 390 N.E.2d 222 (Ind. App. 1979); Seley v. G. D. Searle & Co., 67 Ohio 423, N.E.2d 831, 837 (Ohio 1981).

278. *Id.*

rance which is a relevant consideration in an action predicated on negligence is totally immaterial and irrelevant in strict tort liability. The quintessential element is the knowledge of an unreasonably dangerous condition or risk or harm associated with use of a product that is either known or reasonably knowable based on available scientific data.[279] Though this possesses connotations of negligence as many commentators have suggested,[280] it is not a negligence concept in any significant manner. The product supplier is deemed to know of any risk of harm or dangerous propensities of the product at the time it is marketed that is scientifically knowable at the time.[281] Whether the product supplier actually knew or, in the exercise of reasonable care, should have known of existing scientific data that disclosed a particular dangerous propensity of the product is wholly irrelevant.[282]

Under the *Restatement*, the product supplier is required to provide warnings against risks of harm or dangerous potential only if it has knowledge, or by the application of reasonably developed human skill and foresight should have knowledge, of the presence of the danger.[283] The Texas courts subscribe to the majority position that the product supplier is obligated only to warn of risks of harm or dangerous propensities associated with use of a product

---

279. Reyes v. Wyeth Laboratories, 498 F.2d 1264, 1277 (5th Cir.), *cert. denied*, 419 U.S. 1096 (1974). A manufacturer is deemed not only to be an expert in the field but is imputed with all of the knowledge that experts in the particular field possess. *See* Bristol-Myers Co. v. Gonzales, 561 S.W.2d 801, 804 (Tex. 1978).

280. Keeton, *Products Liability-Inadequacy of Information*, 48 TEX. L. REV. 398 (1970); Note, *Products Liability In Texas: Foreseeability and Warnings*, 58 TEX. L. REV. 1323, 1332 (1980); Kidwell, *The Duty to Warn: A Description of the Model of Decision*, 53 TEX. L. REV. 1375, 1377 (1975). *See generally*, Jones v. Meat Packers Equip. Co., 723 F.2d 370 (4th Cir. 1983), applying Virginia law which recognizes RESTATEMENT (SECOND) OF TORTS, § 388 (1965), a negligence standard.

281. *Id.*

282. *See, e.g.*, Karjala v. Johns-Manville Products Corp., 523 F.2d 155, 159 (8th Cir. 1975); Rawlings Sporting Goods Co. v. Daniels, 619 S.W.2d 435 (Tex. App.—Waco 1981, writ ref'd n.r.e.) (every manufacturer has a duty to warn of dangers in its of its product of which it knows or should know).

283. RESTATEMENT (SECOND) OF TORTS, § 402A, comment j (1965) provides: "In order to prevent the product from being unreasonably dangerous, the seller may be required to give directions or warning, on the container, as to its use. . . .Where, however, the product contains an ingredient. . . .whose danger is not generally known, or if known is one which the consumer would reasonably not expect to find in the product, the seller is required to give warning against it, if he has knowledge, or by the application of reasonable, developed human skill and foresight should have knowledge, of the presence of the ingredient and the danger."

that are either known or reasonably foreseeable and anticipated at the time the product is placed into the channels of commerce.[284] If the product supplier could not have reasonably foreseen by the application of reasonably developed human skill and foresight the dangers inherent in the product or its foreseeable use or environment of use, the supplier is relieved of the obligation to provide any warning or instruction for use. Conversely, however, where the risk of harm or dangerous potential of a product is known or reasonably foreseeable or knowable, the product is unreasonably dangerous when marketed in the absence of a warning of the particular risks of harm and instructions and directions for safe use.[285]

This issue was directly confronted by the Fifth Circuit in *Borel v. Fibreboard Paper Products Corp.*[286] Plaintiff contracted asbestosis and mesothelioma as a result of exposure to asbestos products over an extended period of time.[287] Though evidence at the trial conflicted a significant amount of evidence disclosed that medical literature and other data was available during the relevant period that plaintiff was exposed to asbestos products indicating that prolonged exposure to asbestos created a risk of contracting asbestosis. Concluding that the jury was justified in finding that the product supplier's failure to warn rendered the asbestos unreasonably dangerous, the Fifth Circuit observed:

> First, we approach the question whether the danger to Borel

---

284. Pavlides v. Galveston Yacht Basin, Inc., 727 F.2d 330 (5th Cir. 1984); Bridges v. Chemrex Specialty Coatings, Inc., 704 F.2d 175 (5th Cir. 1983); Hagans v. Oliver Mach. Co., 576 F.2d 97 (5th Cir. 1978); Inomar Compania Naviera S. A. v. Olin Corp., 666 F.2d 897 (5th Cir. 1982); Reyes v. Wyeth Laboratories, Inc., 498 F.2d 1264 (5th Cir.), *cert. denied*, 419 U.S. 1096 (1974); Borel v. Fibreboard Paper Products Co., 493 F.2d 1076 (5th Cir. 1973), *cert. denied*, 419 U.S. 869 (1974); Carter v. Johns-Manville Sales Corp., 557 F. Supp. 1317 (E.D. Tex. 1983); Bristol-Myers Co. v. Gonzales, 561 S.W.2d 801 (Tex. 1978); Crocker v. Winthrop Laboratories, 514 S.W.2d 429 (Tex. 1974); Pearson v. Hevi-Duty Elec. Co., 618 S.W.2d 784 (Tex. App.—Houston [1st Dist.] 1981, writ ref'd n.r.e.); Schering Corp. v. Giesecke, 589 S.W.2d 516 (Tex. Civ. App.—Eastland 1979, writ ref'd n.r.e.); Ethicon, Inc. v. Parten, 520 S.W.2d 527 (Tex. Civ. App.—Houston [14th Dist.] 1975, no writ).

285. Knowledge of the dangerous propensity or risk of harm posed by a product at the time of marketing rather than at the time of the accident producing event governs the manufacturer's obligation to warn of dangers involved in the intended and reasonably foreseeable uses of a product. Borel v. Fibreboard Paper Products Co., 493 F.2d 1076 (5th Cir. 1973), *cert. denied*, 419 U.S. 869 (1974); Reyes v. Wyeth Laboratories, Inc., 498 F.2d 1264 (5th Cir. 1974), *cert. denied*, 419 U.S. 1096 (1974); Crocker v. Winthrop Laboratories, 514 S.W.2d 429 (Tex. 1974); Bristol-Myers Co. v. Gonzales, 561 S.W.2d 801 (Tex. 1978).

286. 493 F.2d 1076, 1091 (5th Cir. 1973), *cert. denied*, 419 U.S. 869 (1974).

287. *Id.* at 1081.

> and other insulation workers was foreseeable at the time the products causing Borel's injury were sold. The defendants' position is that they did not breach their duty to warn because the danger from inhaling asbestos was not foreseeable until about 1968 and that, in view of the long latent period of the diease, Borel must have contracted asbestosis well before that date.
>
> To begin, we note the disease of asbestosis is cumulative. Thus, both Borel's earliest exposure to asbestos dust, occurring in the late 1930s and his most recent exposure, occurring in 1968, could have contributed to his overall condition. The defendant's failure to warn of the dangers of the exposures occurring in 1968 may have resulted in an actionable injury to Borel. But even if it is assumed that Borel's condition was attributable principally to his earlier exposures, the defendants' argument still fails since there is ample evidence in the record that the danger of inhaling asbestos, including the disease of asbestosis, was widely recognized at least as early as the 1930's.
>
> . . . As stated in our recital of the facts, several studies published during the 1930's and 1940's reported the danger to asbestos plant workers and others exposed to asbestos dust and urged precautionary measures to eliminate hazardous concentrations.[288]

In *Woodill v. Parke-Davis & Co.*,[289] plaintiff sustained fetal injuries caused by the drug Petocin administered to the mother during delivery. The manufacturer contended it did not and could not reasonably have foreseen the adverse side effects of the drug on the fetus. The Illinois Supreme Court, following the limitation articulated in comment *j* of the *Restatement*, and adopted in Texas, observed that the drug supplier was not strictly liable in tort for failure to warn of the adverse side effects of Petocin.[290] The court noted that at the time the drug was marketed the adverse side effects experienced by the plaintiff was neither a known or reasonably and scientifically knowable risk of harm.[291]

It is important to emphasize that knowledge or the reasonably developed foresight and scientific knowledge is measured by the information available at the time the product is marketed. For example, pre-existing government studies, medical journal articles and medical research on highly toxic characteristics of a particular

---

288. *Id.* at 1092-93.
289. 79 Ill. 2d 26, 31, 402 N.E.2d 194, 198 (1980).
290. *Id.* at 197-98.
291. *Id.*

chemical or drug is determinative of the scope of knowledge attributed to the product supplier. Whether the product supplier was aware of information of existing risk of danger or dangerous propensity of a product at the time of marketing is immaterial, since knowledge of the risk of harm or dangerous potential is imputed to the product supplier.[292] This limitation may be properly be characterized as a form of state of the art similar to that applied in design defect cases. To impose on the product supplier a duty to provide warnings of risks or dangerous propensities associated with a product, it is imperative that the risk of harm or dangerous propensity be known or scientifically knowable at the time that the product is marketed.[293] In the absence of actual knowledge or scientific knowledge that exists at the time of marketing, strict tort liability may not be imposed on a product supplier for failure to warn or provide instructions for use.[294]

A minority of jurisdictions reject the known or reasonably

---

292. Webb v. Rodgers Mach. Mfg. Co., 750 F.2d 368 (5th Cir. 1985); Harrison v. Flota Mercante Grancolumbiana S.A., 577 F.2d 968 (5th Cir. 1978); Hagans v. Oliver Mach. Co., 576 F.2d 97 (5th Cir. 1978); Borel v. Fibreboard Paper Products Corp., 493 F.2d 1076, 1088 (5th Cir. 1973), *cert. denied*, 419 U.S. 869 (1974); Bristol-Myers Co. v. Gonzales, 561 S.W.2d 801 (Tex. 1978); Rawlings Sporting Goods Co. v. Daniels, 619 S.W.2d 435 (Tex. App. - Waco 1981, writ ref'd n.r.e.); Lopez v. Aro Corp., 584 S.W.2d 333 (Tex. Civ. App.—San Antonio 1979, writ ref'd n.r.e.); Ethicon, Inc. v. Parten, 520 S.W.2d 527 (Tex. Civ. App.—Houston [14th Dist.] 1975, no writ). Other jursidictions likewise require that the danger be known or knowable at the time of marketing. *See e.g.*, Bryant v. Technical Research Co., 654 F.2d 1337 (9th Cir. 1981); Billiar v. Minnesota Mining & Mfg. Co., 623 F.2d 240 (2d Cir. 1980); Ezagui v. Dow Chemical Corp., 598 F.2d 727 (2d Cir. 1979); Wisconsin Elec. Power Co. v. Zallea Bros., Inc., 606 F.2d 697 (7th Cir. 1979); Barnes v. Litton Indus. Products, 555 F.2d 1184 (4th Cir. 1977); Stief v. J. A. Sexauer Mfg. Co., 380 F.2d 453 (2d Cir. 1967), *cert. denied*, 389 U.S. 897 (1967); Ferebee v. Chevron Chem. Co., 736 F.2d 1529 (D.C. Cir. 1984); Mico Mobile Sales & Leasing, Inc. v. Skyline Corp., 97 Idaho 408, 546 P.2d 54 (1975); Wooderson v. Ortho Pharmaceutical Corp., 235 Kan. 387, 681 P.2d 1038 (1984); Ford Motor Co. v. McCamish, 559 S.W.2d 507 (Ky. Ct. App. 1977).

293. *Id.*

294. Rawlings Sporting Goods Co., Inc. v. Daniels, 619 S.W.2d 435 (Tex. App.—Waco 1981, writ ref'd n.r.e.); Bristol-Myers Co. v. Gonzales, 561 S.W.2d 801 (Tex. 1978). A number of jurisdictions perceive that foreseeability of danger at the time of marketing really translates into a negligence concept. *See e.g.*, Jones v. Meat Packers Equip. Co., 723 F.2d 370 (4th Cir. 1983); Miller v. Caterpillar Tractor Co., 697 F.2d 141 (6th Cir. 1983); Leachman v. Beech Aircraft Corp., 694 F.2d 1301 (D.C. Cir. 1982); Brizendine v. Visador Co., 437 F.2d 822 (9th Cir. 1970); Sterling Drug, Inc. v. Yarrow, 408 F.2d 978 (8th Cir. 1969); In re Air Crash Disaster at Washington, D.C., 559 F. Supp. 333 (D.C. 1983); Chambers v. G. D. Searle & Co., 441 F. Supp. 377 (D. Md. 1975); Torsiello v. Whitehall Laboratories 165 N.J. Super. 311, 398 A.2d 132, *cert. denied*, 404 A.2d 1150 (N.J. 1979); Rainbow v. Albert Elia Bldg. Co. 490 A.D.2d 250, 373 N.Y.S.2d 928 (1975).

knowable requirement as a predicate to the imposition of strict tort liability for failure to warn or provide instructions for safe use.[295] In the rather startling decision of *Beshada v. Johns-Manville Product Corp.*,[296] the New Jersey Supreme Court concluded that in strict tort liability it is immaterial that the risk of harm or dangerous propensity of a product was neither known nor scientifically knowable at the time it was marketed.[297] Rather, the court indicated that since strict tort liability is predicated on the condition of the product and not the conduct of the product supplier, a determination of whether an adequate warning of the risks of danger or dangerous propensities was provided is gauged by information available at the time of trial. In essence, the *Beshada* court imputes to the manufacturer at the time of marketing any information that may be scientifically developed many years after the product has been introduced into the channels of commerce.[298] Only a very few jurisdictions have succumbed to the *Beshada* view of the marketing defect.[299] Interestingly, the New Jersey Supreme Court in the recent case of *Feldman v. Lederle Laboratories*[300] retreated from its *Beshada* ruling that knowledge of risks of harm knowable at the time of trial is imputed to the manufacturer. The *Feldman* court noted:

> If *Beshada* were deemed to hold generally or in all cases, par-

---

295. Hamilton v. Hardy, 37 Colo. App. 375, 549 P.2d 1099 (1976); DeBattista v. Argonaut Southwest Ins. Co., 403 So. 2d 26 (La. 1981); Berkebile v. Brantly Helicopter Corp., 462 Pa. 83, 337 A.2d 893 (1975); Beshada v. Johns-Manville Products Corp., 90, N.J. 191, 447 A.2d 539 (1982). These jurisdictions conclude that strict tort liability focuses on the condition of the product, not the conduct of the supplier. Under this rationale, these jurisdictions analyze that the ultimate issue is whether the product is defective and warrants a warning based on information relating to its risk of harm and dangers at the time of trial.

296. 91 N.J. 191 447 A.2d 539 (1982). Significantly, the New Jersey Supreme Court has essentially overruled *Beshada* in Feldman v. Lederle Labs, 97 N.J. 429, 479 A.2d 374 (1984), in which the court holds that the risk of harm of an ethical drug must be known or knowable to the manufacturer at the time of marketing.

297. 447 A.2d at 554. *See also* Schwartz, *The Post-Sale Duty to Warn: Two Unfortunate Forks in the Road to a Reasonable Doctrine*, 58 N.Y.U. L. Rev., 892 (1983) for a discussion of the *Beshada* decision.

298. 447 A. 2d at 545-46.

299. Halphen v. Johns-Manville Sales Corp., 737 F.2d 462 (5th Cir. 1984) (applying Louisiana law); Little v. P.D.G. Indust. Inc., 19 Wash. App. 812, 579 P.2d 940 (1978); Hamilton v. Hardy, 37 Colo. App. 375, 549 P.2d 1099, 1109 (Colo. App. 1976); Racer v. Johnson & Johnson, 629 S.W.2d 387 (Mo. App.) *cert. denied*, 103 S. Ct. 26 (1982); Berkebile v. Brantly Helicopter Corp., 462 Pa. 83, 337 A.2d 893 (1975).

300. 97 N.J. 429, 479 A.2d 374 (1984).

> ticularly with respect to a situation like the present one involving drugs vital to health, that in a warning context knowledge of the unknowable is relevant in determining the applicability of strict liability, we would not agree. . . We do not overrule *Beshada*, but restrict *Beshada* to the circumstances giving rise to its holding.[301]

Elimination of the foreseeability requirement of particular risks of harm or dangerous propensity associated with use of a product at the time it is marketed judicially metamorphosizes the product supplier into an insurer against any product related accident.[302] A product supplier, viewed as an expert in the field of the product, is expected to warn ultimate users of any risks of harm or dangers inherent in the foreseeable use of the product that is either known or scientifically and technically knowable at the time of the product's marketing. Conversely, it is an inanity in the extreme to impose strict tort liability on a product supplier for failure to warn of a risk of harm or danger that was neither known nor scientifically knowable at the time it was marketed. The consuming public would be deprived of valuable products because the failure to limit the scope of the duty to warn to the known or knowable risks and dangers would impose absolute liability and an insurer status on the supplier.

b. *Types of Risk that Mandate a Warning or Instruction for Safe Use.* A duty to warn and provide instructions for safe use is imposed as a matter of law based on the dangerous propensities of a particular product. Marketing defects encompass four specific type of conditions: (1) products that are inherently dangerous; (2) products that are dangerous and provide serious risk of harm for their intended and reasonably foreseeable use and environment of use; (3) products that are dangerous only to a few individuals who possess an idiosyncratic susceptibility; and (4) products that are unavoidably unsafe. Thus, the nature of the product itself determines the duty of the product supplier to provide a warning or instruction for safe use.[303]

---

301. *Id.* at 387-88.

302. Borel v. Fibreboard Paper Products Corp., 493 F.2d 1076, 1089 (5th Cir. 1973), *cert. denied*, 419 U.S. 869 (1974). *See generally*, Sales, *The Duty to Warn and Instruct for Safe Use in Strict Tort Liability*, 13 St. Mary's L. J. 521, 544-45 (1982).

303. Gross v. Black & Decker Inc., 695 F.2d 858 (5th Cir. 1983); Bristol-Myers Co. v. Gonzales, 561 S.W.2d 801 (Tex. 1978); Dixon v. Van Waters & Rogers, 674 S.W.2d 479 (Tex.

Numerous products, because of intrinsic propensities present the potential for serious harm to the user of the product. For example, certain chemicals are highly toxic to users, certain drugs possess severe side effects, industrial machinery is highly dangerous in its normal operation, and electrical appliances are extremely dangerous under circumstances of use.[304] The duty to warn of the risks of harm and dangerous propensities and to furnish instructions for safe use of these products is critical.[305] The duty, of course, is dictated to a significant degree by the type of product and environment of use that is objectively foreseeable. Though the product may be safely marketed with adequate warnings and instructions for safe use, marketing the product without an adequate warning or instruction for safe use renders it unreasonably dangerous. Product suppliers are generally deemed to know their product and, therefore, are perceived to know the risk of harm and dangerous potential posed by that product.[306] The failure to provide an

---

App.—Fort Worth 1984), writ ref'd n.r.e., *per curiam*, 682 S.W.2d 533 (Tex. 1984); Pearson v. Hevi-Duty Electric Co., 618 S.W.2d 784 (Tex. App.—Houston [1st Dist.] 1981, writ ref'd n.r.e.); Allied Industrial International Inc. v. Placencio, 685 S.W.2d 364 (Tex. App.—San Antonio 1985, no writ).

304. *See, e.g.*, Gross v. Black & Decker, 695 F.2d 858 (5th Cir. 1983) (danger of amputation of arms while operating an unprotected radial arms saw); Howard v. General Cable Corp., 674 F.2d 351 (5th Cir. 1982) (danger of electric arc from placing mounted aerial cable bucket in proximity to electrical wires); Page v. Barko Hydraulics, 673 F.2d 134 (5th Cir. 1982) (danger from spewing hydraulic fluid when pneumatic hose detached underneath operator's chair); Ionmar Compania Naviera S.A. v. Olin Corp., 666 F.2d 897 (5th Cir. 1982) (danger of stevedores exposure to chemical HTH in shipment); Borel v. Fibreboard Paper Products Corp., 493 F.2d 1076, 1089 (5th Cir. 1973), *cert. denied*, 419 U.S. 869 (1974) (dangers of asbestosis from inhaling asbestos dust); Technical Chemical Co. v. Jacobs, 480 S.W.2d 602 (Tex. 1972) (danger of connecting freon can to the high pressure side of a compressor); Dixon v. Van Waters & Rogers, 674 S.W.2d 479 (Tex. App.—Fort Worth 1984) writ ref'd n.r.e. per curiam, 682 S.W.2d 533 (Tex. 1984). (danger of toxicity from inhalation of hydrochloric acid fumes); Blackwell Burner Co. v. Cerda, 644 S.W.2d 512 (Tex. App.—San Antonio 1982, writ ref'd n.r.e.) (operating pressure burner hose connected to pressure vessel by bailing wire).

305. *See generally*, Keeton, *Product Liability - Inadequacy of Information*, 48 TEX. L. REV. 398 (1970); Little, *Products Liability—The Growing Uncertainty About Warnings*, 12 FORUM 995 (1977); Sales, *The Duty to Warn and Instruct for Safe Use in Strict Tort Liability*, 13 ST. MARY'S L. J. 521 (1982).

306. For example, in Air Shields, Inc. v. Spears, 590 S.W.2d 574 (Tex. Civ. App.—Waco 1979, writ ref'd n.r.e.), the manufacturer of an incubator was deemed to know the danger of prolonged use of oxygen in an incubator and was required to warn hospital and physician. Similarly, in E. R. Squibb & Sons, Inc. v. Heflin, 579 S.W.2d 19 (Tex. Civ. App.—Beaumont 1979, writ ref'd n.r.e.), the manufacturer of a substance used in performing a discogram was deemed to be aware of the danger of possible infiltration of the substance into the patient's subarachnoid space and to warn physician of the danger. In Hamil-

adequate warning of the danger and to furnish instructions for safe use of the product so as to avoid known dangerous propensities is critical. Failure to provide a warning and instruction for safe use will result in the imposition of strict tort liability on the product supplier.[307]

A second condition that mandates an adequate warning and instruction for safe use is a product that poses an unreasonable risk of harm and danger when used in an unintended but objectively foreseeable manner.[308] Extension of the duty to warn and to provide instruction for safe use when a product is used in an unintended but foreseeable manner is foreshadowed by the *Restatement*.[309] It is not dangers posed by the bizarre, the aberrational or the misuse of a product that dictates a duty to warn or instruct for safe use. Rather, it is the danger or risk or harm presented by the reasonably foreseeable use or foreseeable environment of use of the product.[310] For example, in *Byrd v. Hunt Tool Shipyards, Inc.*,[311] a

---

ton v. Motor Coach Indus. Inc., 569 S.W.2d 571 (Tex. Civ. App.—Texarkana 1978, no writ), the manufacturer of compression loaded spring incorporated into an air cylinder used on a bus was deemed to know the danger of opening the cylinder under spring load and to provide a warning to ultimate users.

307. Restatement (Second) of Torts, Section 402A, comment j (1965). *See generally*, Gross v. Black & Decker, 695 F.2d 858 (5th Cir. 1983); Borel v. Fibreboard Paper Products Corp., 493 F.2d 1076, 1088 (5th Cir. 1973), *cert. denied*, 419 U.S. 869 (1974); Bristol-Myers Co. v. Gonzales, 561 S.W.2d 801 (Tex. 1978); Dixon v. Van Waters & Rogers, 674 S.W.2d 479 (Tex. App.—Fort Worth 1984) writ ref'd n.r.e. per curiam, 682 S.W.2d 533 (Tex. 1984); Blackwell Burner Co. v. Cerda, 644 S.W.2d 512 (Tex. Civ. App.—San Antonio 1982, writ ref'd n.r.e.); Pearson v. Hevi-Duty Elec. 618 S.W.2d 784 (Tex. Civ. App.—Houston [1st Dist.] 1981, writ ref'd n.r.e.).

308. Technical Chemical Co. v. Jacobs, 480 S.W.2d 602 (Tex. 1972) (improper connection of freon can to high pressure side of a car compressor); Ethicon, Inc. v. Parten, 520 S.W.2d 527 (Tex. Civ. App.—Houston [14th Dist.] 1975, no writ) (use of a surgical needle by a physician by improperly handling the needle while performing abdominal surgery); Bituminous Casualty Corp. v. Black & Decker Mfg. Co., 518 S.W.2d 868 (Tex. Civ. App.—Dallas 1974, writ ref'd n.r.e.) (use of high speed cup rock grinder without protective shield); Ford Motor Co. v. Russell & Smith Ford Co., 474 S.W.2d 549 (Tex. Civ. App.—Houston [14th Dist] 1971, no writ) (installation of improper model air conditioner in van with inadequate cooling system). *See also* Kay v. Cessna Aircraft Co., 548 F.2d 1370 (9th Cir. 1977) (under California law, plaintiff may recover in products liability from manufacturer for absence of warning light indicating rear engine not operating, even if plaintiff is operating the aircraft in a manner not intended, if the unintended use is reasonably foreseeable to manufacturer); General Elec. Co. v. Schmal, 623 S.W.2d 482 (Tex. App.— Tyler 1981, writ ref'd n.r.e.).

309. Restatement (Second) of Torts, § 402A, comment j (1965) provides that "the seller is required to give warning . . . if he has knowledge, or by the application of reasonable, developed human skill and foresight should have knowledge, of the presence of the ingredient and the danger."

310. Foreseeable use is presumed to encompass knowable, or reasonably expected and

sandblaster-painter contracted silicosis from inhaling dust despite the use of a safety hood. The manufacturer designed the hood to protect against the hazard of silicosis, but the hood was ineffective even when used with a respirator. The failure to warn that the protective hood was ineffectual to protect the user in its foreseeable use and environment of use rendered the product unreasonably dangerous.[312] Similarly, in *Ethicon, Inc. v. Parten*,[313] a surgical needle fractured as a physician was performing abdominal surgery. Though the physician was manipulating the needle improperly, it was noted that the physician was using the needle for its intended purpose and in a reasonably foreseeable manner. The court noted that the fact that the physician may have grasped the needle improperly was clearly foreseeable under the circumstances.[314]

Foreseeable environment of use, like foreseeable use, determines the manufacturer's duty to warn of potential risks of harm and dangers and to instruct in the safe use of the product. In *Russell v. G.A.F. Corp.*,[315] plaintiff, a carpenter, was injured while installing sheets of corrugated asbestos cement in an interior ceiling when a sheet of cement upon which he stepped shattered, causing him to fall. Plaintiff contended that the product supplier should have placed a warning on each ceiling sheet that the sheet should not be walked upon by the installers. Evidence indicated that manufacturers were aware of the common practice in the industry for carpenters to walk on the materials without use of underlying support to distribute stress.[316] Though use of the ceiling sheets as a walking surface was not an intended use of the product, the manufacturer's knowledge that the product was customarily used in this manner in this type of environment imposed a duty to warn of the risk of harm associated with such use of the cement sheets.[317] Per-

---

anticipated use. *See e.g.*, LeBouef v. Goodyear Tire & Rubber Co., 451 F. Supp. 253 (W.D. La. 1978), *affirmed*, 623 F.2d 985 (5th Cir. 1980); Sturm, Ruger & Co. v. Day, 594 P.2d 38 (Alaska 1979); Russell v. G.A.F. Corp., 422 A.2d 989 (D.C. 1980); Moran v. Faberge, Inc., 273 Md. 538, 332 A.2d 11, 20 (1975). But it does not encompass unreasonable uses or not reasonably foreseeable misuses. *See, e.g.*, Bridges v. Chemrex Specialty Coatings, Inc., 704 F.2d 175 (5th Cir. 1983).

311. 650 F.2d 44 (5th Cir. 1981).

312. *Id.* at 48.

313. 520 S.W.2d 527 (Tex. Civ. App.—Houston [14th Dist.] 1975, no writ).

314. *Id. See also*, Webb v. Rodgers Mach. Mfg. Co., 750 F.2d 368, 372 (5th Cir. 1985).

315. 422 A.2d 989 (D.C. 1980).

316. *Id.* at 990.

317. *Id.* at 991-92.

haps the concept of foreseeable environment of a product's use is most graphically illustrated in *Conder v. Hull Lift Truck, Inc.*[318] Plaintiff was severely injured when a forklift truck he was riding accelerated out of control and overturned. Misadjustment in the governor linkage that was performed by a third party who serviced and maintained the truck caused the vehicle to accelerate out of control.[319] Since misadjustment was foreseeable by the manufacturer, the product was defective in the absence of warning that misadjustment of the linkage could produce uncontrolled acceleration. The court reasoned: "The environmental approach to product use assumes a manufacturer markets a product for an intended use. . . When product misuse and its intended risk is reasonably foreseeable, the manufacturer is in the best position to avoid product related injuries."[320]

The obligation to warn and provide directions for safe use are constrained by the limits of foreseeable use and the foreseeable environment of use.[321] This may include, under certain circumstances, objectively foreseeable misuse of the product.[322] A duty to warn, however, is not extended to uses of a product that are bizarre, aberrational or that are not reasonably foreseeable misuses.[323] This limitation insures that the product supplier is not

---

318. 405 N.E.2d 538 (Ind. App. 1980).

319. *Id.* at 541.

320. *Id.* at 546.

321. Foreseeable environment, like foreseeable use of the product, delineates the manufacturer's duty to warn of the risks of harm and dangerous propensities of a product and to instruct for safe use of a product. Miller v. Bock Laundry Mach. Co., 568 S.W.2d 648 (Tex. 1977); Shop Rite Foods, Inc. v. Upjohn Co., 619 S.W.2d 574, 578 (Tex. Civ. App.—Amarillo 1981, writ ref'd n.r.e.); Rawlings Sporting Goods Co. v. Daniels, 619 S.W.2d 435 (Tex. App.—Waco 1981, writ ref'd n.r.e.); Dover Corp. v. Perez, 587 S.W.2d 761 (Tex. Civ. App.—Corpus Christi 1979, writ ref'd n.r.e); Lopez v. Aro Corp., 584 S.W.2d 333 (Tex. Civ. App.—San Antonio 1979, writ ref'd n.r.e.); Hamilton v. Motor Coach Indus. Inc., 569 S.W.2d 571 (Tex. Civ. App.—Texarkana 1978, no writ); Ethicon, Inc. v. Parten, 520 S.W.2d 527 (Tex. Civ. App.—Houston [14th Dist.] 1975, no writ).

322. It is the objectively foreseeable use and unintended use of a product that imposes the duty. Pavlides v. Galveston Yacht Basin, Inc. 727 F.2d 330 (5th Cir. 1984); Blackwell Burner Co., Inc. v. Cerda, 644 S.W.2d 512 (Tex. App.—San Antonio 1982, writ ref'd n.r.e.); Pearson v. Hevi-Duty Elec. Co., 618 S.W.2d 784 (Tex. App.—Houston [1st Dist.] 1981, writ ref'd n.r.e.); Dover Corp. v. Perez, 587 S.W.2d 761 (Tex. Civ. App.—Corpus Christi 1979, writ ref'd n.r.e.).

323. *See e.g.*, Brech v. J. C. Penny Co. 698 F.2d 332 (8th Cir. 1983) (danger of exposing cotton nightgown directly to an open flame); Bridges v. Chemex Speciality Coatings, Inc., 704 F.2d 175 (5th Cir. 1983) (risk of harm created by a series of interdependent conditions not perceived to be within the realm of foreseeability); Harms v. Bell Helicopter Tex-

transformed into an insurer.[324]

The third condition that mandates a warning of dangerous propensities or risks of harm associated with use of a product involves a product that may be used safely by a majority of the intended users, but a small class possesses an unusual susceptibility or allergic reaction to the product. The *Restatement* provides that a product supplier is not required to warn of allergic reactions or side effects of products that affect only a few persons possessing an unusual susceptibility or allergy.[325]

The Texas courts have rejected the *Restatement* position regarding idiosyncratic reactions and risks of harm. In *Crocker v. Winthrop Laboratories*,[326] the Texas Supreme Court declared that an appropriate warning of adverse reactions to patients possessing an idiosyncratic reaction to the drug Talwin was required.[327] The court imposed a duty to warn even though the potential plaintiffs

---

tron, 567 F. Supp. 28 (E.D. Ill. 1982) (objectively unreasonable to foresee that user would employ one ton clevis to lift a 10 weight); Landrine v. Mego Corp., 95 A.D.2d 759, 464 N.Y.S.2d 516 (App. Div. 1983) (danger of a child swallowing a balloon). In *Rego Co. v. Brannon*, the court concluded that the manufacturer of a valve for a propane gas cylinder was liable in strict tort liability for failure to warn. The valve was equipped with a safety release mechanism, and as a result of the release of propane gas plaintiff was injured when he ignited a match in the car where the cylinders had been stored. Though the cylinder itself contained a warning that it should not be stored in warm areas, the court concluded that the valve manufacturer had an independent duty to warn: "The evidence introduced at trial established the necessity for an adequate warning affixed to the valve assembly, and it also established the responsibility of the component manufacturer. . .to ensure the effective transmission of that warning." 682 S.W.2d 677, 680 (Tex. Civ. App.—Houston [1st Dist.] 1984).

324. Strict tort liability was not designed to create absolute liability or to impose insurer status on a product supplier. Hagans v. Oliver Mach. Co., 576 F.2d 97 (5th Cir. 1978); Simien v. S.S. Kresge Co., 566 F.2d 551 (5th Cir. 1978); Henderson v. Ford Motor Co., 519 S.W.2d 87 (Tex. 1974); McCants v. Salameh, 608 S.W.2d 304 (Tex. Civ. App.—Waco 1980, writ ref'd n.r.e.); Bell Helicopter Co. v. Bradshaw, 594 S.W.2d 519 (Tex. Civ. App.—Corpus Christi 1979, writ ref'd n.r.e.); Failure to provide a warning cannot be a cause in fact of an injury when the warning is deemed to be adequate as a matter of law. (court determined that an additional warning by the manufacturer would not have prevented driver's negligent act in starting the standard transmission car while in reverse gear without disengaging clutch) Conti v. Ford Motor Co., 743 F.2d 195 (3d Cir. 1984).

325. RESTATEMENT (SECOND) OF TORTS, § 402A, comment j (1965). This provision provides in pertinent part: "The seller may reasonably assume that those with common allergies, as for example to eggs or strawberries, will be aware of them, and he is not required to warn against them." Several jurisdictions have adopted the RESTATEMENT position. *See e.g.*, Presbrey v. Gillette Co., 105 Ill. App. 3d 1082, 435 N.E.2d 513 (1982); Tiderman v. Fleetwood Homes, 102 Wash. 2d 334, 684 P.2d 1302 (1984).

326. 514 S.W.2d 429 (Tex. 1974).

327. *Id.* at 432-33.

constituted only a small group who possessed an unusual idiosyncratic reaction to Talwin. The duty to warn applies even under circumstances where the product is dangerous to a very limited number of individuals when compared to the total number of users of the product.[328]

The majority of jurisdictions have either expressly rejected or simply ignored the *Restatement* limitation relating to allergic or idiosyncratic reaction.[329] The avowed rationale for imposing a duty to warn is the fact that the condition of the product and not the conduct of the product supplier determines liability under Section 402A. Even if only a few individuals are subject to a significant risk of harm or a dangerous propensity, the product supplier is obligated to furnish an adequate warning of the risks of harm.[330]

The last category that requires the product supplier to provide an adequate warning and instruction for safe use involves the unavoidably unsafe product. Unavoidably unsafe products are products that can justifiably be manufactured, notwithstanding the risk involved, because the benefits to society outweigh the risks of harm.[331] The *Restatement* provides that "such a product, properly prepared, accompanied by proper directions and warning, is not defective, nor is it unreasonably dangerous."[332] Thus, a product supplier is not strictly liable in tort for the unfortunate consequences associated with the use of a product that is unavoidably

---

328. *Id.* at 432.

329. *See* Robbins v. Alberto Culver Co., 210 Kan. 147, 499 P.2d 1080, 1086 (Kan. 1972) (two complaints per million bottles presented jury issue whether product supplier could reasonably foresee the number of people might sustain harm); Erny v. Revlon, Inc., 459 S.W.2d 261, 264 (Mo. 1970) (danger of side effect to one person in 50,000 was sufficient to require supplier to provide warning of the risk). *See also* Basko v. Sterling Drug, Inc., 416 F.2d 417 (2d Cir. 1969); Davis v. Wyeth Laboratories, Inc., 399 F.2d 121, 129 (9th Cir. 1968); John Norton Farms v. Todagco, 124 Cal. App.3d 149, 177 Cal.Rptr. 215, 228 (1981); Tomer v. American Home Products Corp., 170 Conn. 681, 368 A.2d 35 (1976); Cooley v. Carter-Wallis, Inc., ____ N.Y.S.2d ____ (1984); Tiderman v. Fleetwood Homes, 102 Wash.2d 334, 684 P.2d 1302 (Wash. 1984).

330. As noted by the Texas Supreme Court in Crocker v. Winthrop Laboratories, 514 S.W.2d 429, 432 (Tex. 1974), "the failure to warn of a danger cannot always be excused by the mere fact that the potentially endangered users are few in number." The adoption of a duty to warn of idiosyncratic reaction overrules earlier Texas decision to the contrary. *See e.g.*, Alberto-Culver Co. v. Morgan, 444 S.W.2d 770, 776 (Tex. App.—Beaumont 1969, writ ref'd n.r.e.); Cudmore v. Richardson-Merrell, Inc., 398 S.W.2d 640, 644 (Tex. Civ. App.—Dallas 1965, writ ref'd n.r.e.).

331. Restatement (Second) of Torts, Section 402A, Comment k (1965).

332. *Id.*

dangerous, provided the product is accompanied by an adequate warning of the risks. Under these circumstances, the user makes an informed judgment to use the product notwithstanding the potential for harm inherent in the product.[333]

The determination of whether a product is unavoidably unsafe within the contemplation of the *Restatement* requires the court to determine whether marketing the product under any circumstances renders it unreasonably dangerous *per se*.[334] A determination that a particular product is unreasonably dangerous *per se* is warranted only when the harmful affects of the product both qualitatively and quantitatively substantially outweigh any beneficial effects to the public.[335] If the court determines that the product is not unreasonably dangerous *per se*, then, in effect, the product may be marketed provided the product supplier furnishes an adequate warning of the risks of harm involved in its anticipated and

---

333. *Id. See generally*, Reyes v. Wyeth Laboratories, Inc., 498 F.2d 1264, 1276 (5th Cir. 1974), *cert. denied*, 419 U.S. 1096 (1974) (possible effect of contracting polio from Sabin polio vaccine); Borel v. Fibreboard Paper Products Corp., 493 F.2d 1076, 1088 (5th Cir. 1973), *cert. denied*, 419 U.S. 869 (1974) (possible contraction of asbestosis from exposure to asbestos); Bristol-Myers Co. v. Gonzales, 561 S.W.2d 801, 804 (Tex. 1978) (side effects of antibiotic Kantrex). *See generally*, Needham v. White Laboratories, Inc., 639 F.2d 394, 400 (7th Cir. 1981); Borchu v. Ortho Pharmaceutical Corp., 642 F.2d 652, 657 (1st Cir. 1981); Lindsay v. Ortho Pharmaceutical Corp., 637 F.2d 87, 90 (2d Cir. 1980); Werner v. Upjohn Co., 628 F.2d 848, 858 (4th Cir. 1980); Davis v. Wyeth Laboratories, Inc., 399 F.2d 121, 131 (9th Cir. 1968).

334. *See generally*, Sales, *The Duty to Warn and Instruct for Safe Use in Strict Tort Liability*, 13 St. Mary's L. J. 521, 539 (1982); Keeton, *Product Liability and the Meaning of Defect*, 5 St. Mary's L.J. 30, 37 (1973); Keeton, *Product Liability - Inadequacy of Information*, 48 Tex. L. Rev. 398, 406 (1970).

335. The Fifth Circuit in Reyes v. Wyeth Laboratories, 498 F.2d 1264 (5th Cir. 1974), *cert. denied*, 419 U.S. 1096 (1974), discussed the issue of the unreasonably dangerous nature of Sabin polio vaccine. Recognizing that the Restatement provides for unavoidably unsafe products that are accompanied by appropriate warnings, the Fifth Circuit noted:

> Rather, in evaluating the possible liability of a manufacturer for injuries caused by his inevitably hazardous products, a two-step analysis is required to determine first, whether the product is so unsafe that marketing it at all is 'unreasonably dangerous per se' and, if not, whether the product has been introduced into the stream of commerce without sufficient safeguards and is thereby "unreasonably dangerous as marketed." In either case, the applicable standard as formulated in the Restatement, is as follows: In terms of the user's interest, a product is "unreasonably dangerous" only when it is 'dangerous to an extent beyond that contemplated by the ordinary consumer'; or, to phrase it in terms of the seller's responsibility, 'so dangerous that a reasonable man would not sell the product if he knew the risk involved.' (See Borel v. Fibreboard Paper Products Corp., (5th Cir. 1973), 493 F.2d 1076, 1088; Helene Curtis Industries, Inc. v. Pruitt, 385 F.2d at 850; Wade, *Strict Tort Liability of Manufacturers*, 19 Sw. L.J. 5, 15 (1965).

foreseeable use.[336] The failure to provide an adequate warning, even for an unavoidably unsafe product, renders the product unreasonably dangerous and imposes strict tort liability on the supplier.[337]

Generally, a distinction exists between the supplier of highly beneficial drugs and the supplier of drugs possessing lesser medical significance. For example, an anti-rabies vaccine that possesses significant side effects is not unreasonably dangerous when marketed with an adequate warning of the risk of harm involved in its use.[338] An experimental drug[339] or a product that is highly dangerous and for which a safer substitute exists may not relieve the product supplier of strict tort liability despite an adequate warning of the risk of harm attendant to its use.[340]

---

336. 498 F.2d at 1274. In determining whether the product is unreasonably dangerous or unavoidably unsafe, the court notes that "obviously, use of an unavoidably unsafe product always presents at least a minimal danger of harm, but only if the potential harmful effects of the product — both qualitative and quantitative — outweigh the legitimate public interest in its availablilty will it be declared unreasonably dangerous per se and the person placing it on the market held liable." Applying this standard here, the scales must tip in favor of availability. The evil to be prevented — poliomyelitis, and its accompanying paralysis — is great. Although the danger that vaccines may contract polio is qualitatively devastating, it is statistically miniscule. On balancing, marketing the vaccine is justified despite the danger." *Id.* at 1274. This approach is adopted by the Seventh Circuit in Needham v. Wyeth Laboratories, Inc., 639 F.2d 394, 401 (7th Cir. 1981). *See also* Borel v. Fibreboard Paper Products Corp., 493 F.2d 1076 (5th Cir. 1973), *cert. denied*, 419 U.S. 869 (1974).

337. *See* Reyes v. Wyeth Laboratories, 498 F.2d 1264, 1275 (5th Cir. 1974), *cert. denied*, 419 U.S. 1096 (1974); Ford Motor Co. v. Russell & Smith Ford Co., 474 S.W.2d 549 (Tex. Civ. App.—Houston [1st Dist.] 1971, no writ); Rumsey v. Freeway Manor Minimax, 423 S.W.2d 387, 393 (Tex. Civ. App.—Houston [1st Dist.] 1968, no writ); RESTATEMENT (SECOND) OF TORTS, § 402A, comment h provides in pertinent part that "where, however, he has reason to anticipate that danger may result from a particular use, as where a drug is sold which is safe only in limited doses, he may be required to give adequate warning of the danger and a product sold without such warning is in a defective condition."

338. *See* Reyes v. Wyeth Laboratories, 498 F.2d 1264, 1274 (5th Cir. 1974), *cert. denied*, 419 U.S. 1096 (1974) (Sabin polio vaccine); Bristol-Myers Co. v. Gonzales, 561 S.W.2d 801 (Tex. 1978) (antibiotic Kantrex).

339. *See e.g.*, Gaston v. Hunter, 121 Ariz. 33, 588 P.2d 326 (1978).

340. *See e.g.*, Filler v. Rayex Corp., 435 F.2d 336, 338 (7th Cir. 1970) (baseball sunglasses that would shatter into sharp splinters when hit by baseball were unreasonably dangerous); Racer v. Johnson & Johnson, 629 S.W.2d 387 (Mo. App. 1981) (disposable surgical drape). As stated by the Colorado Supreme Court in Belle Bonfils Memorial Blood Bank v. Hanson, 195 Colo. 529, 579 P.2d 1158 (Colo. 1983) (en banc) involving a blood serum that caused viral hepatitis, to envoke Comment k of the RESTATEMENT the product's utility must greatly outweight the risk created by its use, the risk must be a known one, the product's benefits must not be achievable in another manner, and the risk must be unavoidable under the present state of scientific knowledge.

Some controversy exists whether commercially distributed blood represents a product that invokes Section 402A. When used for transfusion, blood presents a serious danger of transmitting serum hepatitis. Adhering to the landmark case of *Perlmutter v. Beth Davis Hospital*,[341] most jurisdictions have declined to impose strict tort liability on blood suppliers for post transfusion hepatitis. The rationale is premised on the fact that the use of blood for transfusion is unavoidably unsafe but is critical to the administration of appropriate medical treatment to patients.[342] Texas, like a number of other states, has enacted statutory legislation exempting blood suppliers from liability for the transmission of hepatitis through blood serum.[343]

c. *Basis of a Marketing Defect.* The marketing defect is essentially comprised of: (1) a failure to provide any warning of the risk of harm or dangerous propensities of a product; (2) the failure to provide an adequate warning of the risk of harm or dangerous propensities of a product; (3) the failure to provide any instructions for the safe use of a product to avoid the dangers and risk attendant to the use of the product; and (4) the failure to provide adequate instructions for safe use of a product.[344] An appropriate warning is required under Section 402A for products that present unreasonable risks of harm and unreasonably dangerous propensities when used for their intended and reasonably foreseeable uses. Under these circumstances, an adequate warning is required to be communicated to the ultimate user of the risk of harm or dangerous propensities presented by the product.[345] Knowledge of the dangerous propensities must be known or knowable to the product supplier at the time the product is marketed to impose a duty to warn.[346] The vast majority of marketing defect cases involve the adequacy of existing product warnings rather than the absence of any warning of risks of harm. Either a diluted or overly broad warning of the risks of harm exists, but the warning allegedly fails

341. 308 N.Y. 100 123 N.E.2d 792 (1954).

342. *Id.* at 795.

343. *See* TEX. REV. CIV. STAT. ANN. art. 4590-3 (Vernon 1976). *See generally*, Sales, *The Service-Sales Transaction: A Citadel Under Assault*, 10 ST. MARY'S L. J. 13 (1978)

344. *See generally*, Sales, *The Duty to Warn and Instruct for Safe Use in Strict Tort Liability*, 13 ST. MARY'S L. J. 521, 547-57 (1982); Keeton, *Products Liability—Inadequacy of Information*, 48 TEX. L. REV. 398 (1970).

345. RESTATEMENT (SECOND) OF TORTS, § 402A, comments h and j (1965).

346. Refer to note 279 *supra*.

to focus on the precise nature of the danger or risk involved in the injury producing event.[347]

The failure to adequately warn of a risk of harm or an unreasonably dangerous propensity of a product, otherwise free of defects, renders it unreasonably dangerous.[348] The ultimate user must be afforded a fair opportunity to make an informed election whether the utility of the product outweighs the risk of harm involved in its intended use.

Generally, an adequate warning must communicate with a degree of intensity that would cause a reasonable person to exercise for his own safety caution commensurate with the potential danger.[349] Moreover, an adequate warning must be calculated to bring home to a reasonably prudent user the nature and extent of the danger involved in the use of the product.[350] As declared in *Lopez v. Aro Corp.*,[351] "whether a warning is legally sufficient depends upon the language used and the impression that such language is calculated to make upon the minds of the users of the product."[352]

---

347. *See* Keeton, *Products Liability—Inadequacy of Information*, 48 TEX. L. REV. 399, 406 (1970).

348. Reyes v. Wyeth Laboratories, 498 F.2d 1264 (5th Cir. 1974), *cert. denied*, 419 U.S. 1096 (1974); Borel v. Fibreboard Paper Products Corp., 493 F.2d 1076 (5th Cir. 1973), *cert. denied*, 419 U.S. 869 (1974); Horne v. Liberty Furniture Co., 452 So.2d 204 (La. App. 1984); Technical Chem. Co. v. Jacobs, 480 S.W.2d 602 (Tex. 1972).

349. Shop-Rite Foods, Inc. v. Upjohn Co., 619 S.W.2d 574 (Tex. App.—Amarillo 1981, writ ref'd n.r.e.); Lopez v. Aro Corp., 584 S.W.2d 333 (Tex. Civ. App.—San Antonio 1979, writ ref'd n.r.e.); Bituminous Casualty Corp. v. Black & Decker Mfg. Co., 518 S.W.2d 868 (Tex. Civ. App.—Dallas 1974, writ ref'd n.r.e.). Warnings must be expressed with an intensity proportionate to the risk. Ducote v. Liberty Mutual Ins. Co., 451 So.2d 1211 (La. App. 1984).

350. The court in Bituminous Casualty Corp. v. Black & Decker Mfg. Co., 518 S.W.2d 868, 873 (Tex. Civ. App.—Dallas 1974, writ ref'd n.r.e.), outlined the essential prerequisities of an adequate warning: (1) it must be in such form that it could reasonably be expected to catch the attention of a reasonably prudent man in the circumstances of its use; and, (2) the content of the warning must be of such a nature as to be comprehensible to the average user and to convey a fair indication of the nature and extent of the danger to the mind of a reasonably prudent person. Pavlides v. Galveston Yacht Basin, Inc., 727 F.2d 330 (5th Cir. 1984); Doss v. Apache Powder Co., 430 F.2d 1317 (5th Cir. 1970); Ford Motor Co. v. Nowak, 638 S.W.2d 582 (Tex. App.—Corpus Christi 1982, writ ref'd n.r.e.).

351. 584 S.W.2d 333 (Tex. Civ. App.—San Antonio 1979, writ ref'd n.r.e.).

352. *Id.* at 335 (quoting Green, *Strict Liability Under Sections 402A and 402B: A Decade of Litigation*, 54 TEX. L. REV. 1185, 1200 (1976)). The court in Pearson v. Hevi-Duty Elec. 618 S.W.2d 784 (Tex. App.—Houston [1st Dist.] 1981, writ ref'd n.r.e.), notes that "warnings must be adequate as to both form and content. The warnings must warn and not just instruct the user. . . .The adequacy of a warning cannot be evaluated apart from the knowledge and expertise of those who may reasonably be expected to use the product. (Cites

Adequacy depends on the warning communicating with clarity to the user the particular risk of harm or dangerous propensity associated with the product. This includes dangers inherent in the products or the reasonably foreseeable use of the product in its anticipated environment of use.[353]

The third aspect of a marketing defect involves the failure to provide any or providing inadequate instruction for safe and effective use of a product. Mere directions for proper use of a product that fail to warn of specific dangers and risks of harm if the directions are not followed do not satisfy the marketing requirement.[354] Conversely, the mere fact that the product supplier communicates to the user the particular risk of harm associated with use of the product is insufficient if directions for safe use to avoid the risk of harm is not provided.[355]

Directions for use are distinct from and serve different purposes than warnings. Directions basically instruct the user of the product in the proper and efficient use of the product and the appropriate manner to avoid unsafe use.[356] Warnings, on the other

---

cases)." *Id.* at 787.

An adequate warning may, under certain circumstances, require a pictorial warning to foreseeable users. (see discussion of dissent in *Campos v. Firestone Tire and Rubber Co.*, 469 A.2d 943 (N.J. 1984). Likewise, an adequate warning may require that the warning be embossed or placed on the product itself (radial tire should be embossed not to be mixed with non-radial tires, per decision of the court) Dambacher v. Mallis, 485 A.2d 408 (Pa. Super. 1985), CCH PLR ¶10,370.

353. Pavlides v. Galveston Yacht Basin, Inc., 727 F.2d 330, 338 (5th Cir. 1984); Reyes v. Wyeth Laboratories, 498 F.2d 1264, 1274 (5th Cir. 1974), *cert. denied*, 419 U.S. 1096 (1974); Borel v. Fibreboard Paper Products Corp., 493 F.2d 1076, 1106 (5th Cir. 1973), *cert. denied*, 419 U.S. 869 (1974). As noted by the Fifth Circuit in Pavlides, *supra*, "in assessing what hazards are foreseeable, a manufacturer is held to the status of an expert." 727 F.2d at 338. Concerning the warning, the court observed that:

> A warning must (1) be designed so it can reasonably be expected to catch the attention of the consumer; (2) be comprenhensible and give a fair indication of the specific risk involved with the product; (3) be of an intensity justified by the magnitude of the risk. *Id.* at 338.

354. Pavlides v. Galveston Yacht Basin, Inc., 727 F.2d 330, 338 (5th Cir. 1984); Kritser v. Beech Aircraft Corp., 479 F.2d 1089 (5th Cir. 1973); Bituminous Casualty Corp. v. Black & Decker Mfg., 518 S.W.2d 868 (Tex. Civ. App.—Dallas 1974, writ ref'd n.r.e.); Helicoid Gage Div. of American Chain & Cable Co. v. Howell, 511 S.W.2d 573, 577 (Tex. Civ. App.—Houston [14th Dist.] 1974, writ ref'd n.r.e.); Eddleman v. Scalco, 484 S.W.2d 122 (Tex. Civ. App. - Beaumont 1972, writ ref'd n.r.e.); Rumsey v. Freeway Manor Minimax, 423 S.W.2d 387, 394 (Tex. Civ. App.—Houston [1st Dist.] 1968, no writ).

355. *See generally*, Dillard & Hart, *Products Liability: Directions for Use and Duty to Warn*, 41 VA. L. REV. 145 (1955).

356. *See e.g.*, Bituminous Casualty Corp. v. Black & Decker Mfg., 518 S.W.2d 868, 873

hand, communicate the dangers inherent in the use of the product. Stated differently, warnings focus on risks inherent in the use of a product while instructions seek to insure that the user will employ the product in a safe and appropriate manner.[357] For example, in *Schmidt v. Plains Electric, Inc.*,[358] the manufacturer's instructions booklet accompanying its electric wall heater furnished information that to obtain maximum efficiency and economy for operation it was important not to block the air inlet or outlet. These instructions, however, related merely to attaining optimum and efficient operation of the product and failed to warn the user of the potential fire hazard created by installing an electric heater behind fabric drapes.[359] Again, in *Kerns v. Engelke*,[360] plaintiff was struck in the eye while assisting and setting up a forage blower powered by a power take-off (PTO) attached at one end of the forage blower and, at the other, to the power take-off on the tractor. An instruction manual accompanying the blower contained pictures that depicted the forage blower with the PTO removed. The court rejected the contention that the picture provided an adequate warning of the danger in setting up the forage blower without detaching it from the PTO and stated "At most, however, the pictures merely informed the reader of the manual that the PTO *could* be removed, not that the failure to do so was dangerous."[361]

Instructions for safe handling and use are necessary to all users reasonably expected to utilize or handle the product. The product supplier is obligated to provide instructions for the safe and proper use of a product not only for the intended and foreseeable uses, but for objectively foreseeable misuses.[362] In essence, the

---

(Tex. Civ. App.—Dallas 1974, writ ref'd n.r.e.), (in which the court held that an instruction to use a protective shield on a high speed grinder was inadequate to warn the user of the danger in failing to follow the directions for use.) The effect of directions for safe use and the distinction between directions and warnings is discussed in Dillard & Hart, *Product Liability: Directions for Use and the Duty to Warn*, 41 VA. L. REV. 145, 172 (1955).

357. Pavlides v. Galveston Yacht Basin, Inc., 727 F.2d 330 (5th Cir. 1984); Lopez v. Aro Corp., 584 S.W.2d 333 (Tex. Civ. App.—San Antonio 1979, writ ref'd n.r.e.).

358. 281 N.W.2d 794 (N.D. 1979).

359. *Id.* at 800.

360. 54 Ill. App.3d 323, 369 N.E.2d 1284 (5th dist. 1977), *aff'd as modified*, 76 Ill.2d 154, 390 N.E.2d 859 (1979).

361. *Id.* at 1291.

362. Howard v. General Cable Corp., 674 F.2d 351, 356 (5th Cir. 1982) (using aerial lift bucket in proximity to energized electrical wires in contravention of instruction); Miller v. Bock Laundry Machine Co., 568 S.W.2d 648 (Tex. 1977) (introduction of an operator's arm

duty to provide instructions for safe use is required for the product in its reasonable environment of use.[363] In the absence of an adequate instruction that would insure the safe use of an otherwise dangerous product, strict tort liability is established.[364]

d. Prerequisites of an Adequate Warning and Instruction for Safe Use. The elements essential for an adequate warning or instruction for safe use are articulated in *Bituminous Casualty Corp. v. Black & Decker Manufacturing Co.*[365] Plaintiff was injured while using a cuprock grinder without a protective shield. A notice on the grinder advised the user to install a protective shield on the grinder before use but the label contained no warning of the risks presented if the cuprock ruptured while in use without the protective shield. Concluding that the instruction for use of the shield did not constitute an adequate warning, the court outlined the prerequisites for adequacy. The court notes that an adequate warning or instruction is one that: (1) would reasonably be expected to catch the attention of a reasonably prudent person in the circumstances of its use and (2) would be understandable in content and convey a fair indication of the nature and extent of the danger to the reasonably prudent person.[366] The sufficiency of a

---

into the rotating spindryer of an industrial laundry machine); Blackwell Burner Co. v. Cerda, 644 S.W.2d 512 (Tex. App.—San Antonio 1982, writ ref'd n.r.e.) (city worker attempting to utilize grass burner with the nozzle and hose connected to the pressure vessel by bailing wire); Pearson v. Hevi-Duty Electric Co., 618 S.W.2d 784 (Tex. Civ. App.—Houston [1st Dist.] 1981, writ ref'd n.r.e.) (electrician attempting to work on electric switch gear with fuse in the open position).

363. Environment of use may differ from reasonably foreseeable use or intended use. *See e.g.*, Russell v. G.A.F. Corp., 422 A.2d 989, 994 (D.C. 1980); Fiorentino v. A.E. Staley Mfg. Co., 416 N.E.2d 998, 1002 (Mass. App. Ct. 1981); Shop Rite Foods, Inc. v. Upjohn Co., 619 S.W.2d 574, 578 (Tex. App.—Amarillo 1981, writ ref'd n.r.e.).

364. Gross v. Black & Decker, 695 F.2d 858 (5th Cir. 1983); Pearson v. Hevi-Duty Electric Co., 618 S.W.2d 784 (Tex. App.—Houston [1st Dist.] 1981, writ ref'd n.r.e.) (instruction not to work on electrical switch gear with the fuse in the open position); Lopez v. Aro Corp., 584 S.W.2d 333 (Tex. Civ. App.—San Antonio 1979, writ ref'd n.r.e.) (instruction for use of grinder); Bituminous Casualty Corp. v. Black & Decker Mfg. Co., 518 S.W.2d 868, 873 (Tex. Civ. App.—Dallas 1974, writ ref'd n.r.e.) (instructions to use protective shield on high speed grinder). But instructions to use a product with certain safety equipment may relieve the manufacturer of liability. Quattelbaum v. Hy-Reach Equip., 453 So.2d 578 (La. Ct. App. 1984).

365. 518 S.W.2d 868 (Tex. Civ. App.—Dallas 1974, writ ref'd n.r.e.).

366. *Id.* at 872-73. Some courts enumerate slightly different standards. As articulated in Richards v. Upjohn Co., 95 N.M. 675, 625 P.2d 1192, 1196 (N.M. Ct. App. 1980):

(1) the warning must adequately indicate the scope of the danger;

warning is dependent upon both "the language used and the impression that the language is calculated to make upon the mind of the average user of the product."[367]

Adequacy of warning or adequacy of instruction generally presents a fact issue to be resolved by the trier of fact.[368] As noted by the courts, the unique circumstances of each case involving adequacy of warning and instructions for safe use is best reserved for determination by the jury.[369]

A number of important considerations directly affect the adequacy of a warning or the instruction for safe use. For example, the warning or instruction must be conspicuous and prominent on the product. Normally, the warning or instruction must be printed on the label in a manner designed to attract the user's attention.[370] A warning contained in the body of other information of the same

---

(2) the warning must reasonably communicate the extent or seriousness of the harm that could result from misuse;

(3) the physical aspects of the warning must be adequate to alert a reaasonably prudent person to the danger;

(4) a simply directive warning may be inadequate when it fails to indicate the consequences that might result from failing to follow it; and

(5) the means to convey the warning must be adequate to bring home the warning.

367. 518 S.W.2d at 873.

368. Adequacy is generally acknowledged to constitute an issue to be resolved by the jury. Pavlides v. Galveston Yacht Basin, Inc. 727 F.2d 330, 338 (5th Cir. 1984); Howard v. General Cable Corp., 674 F.2d 351, 356 (5th Cir. 1982); Harrison v. Flota Mercante Grancolombiana S.A., 577 F.2d 968 (5th Cir. 1978); Bristol-Myers Co. v. Gonzales, 561 S.W.2d 801 (Tex. 1978); Miller v. Bock Laundry Machine Co., 568 S.W.2d 648 (Tex. 1977); Dixon v. Van Waters & Rogers, 674 S.W.2d 479 (Tex. App.—Fort Worth 1984, no writ); Ford Motor Co. v. Nowak, 638 S.W.2d 582 (Tex. App.—Corpus Christi 1982, writ ref'd n.r.e.); Pearson v. Hevi-Duty Electric Co., 618 S.W.2d 784 (Tex. App.—Houston [1st Dist.] 1981, writ ref'd n.r.e.); Shop Rite Foods, Inc. v. Upjohn Co., 619 S.W.2d 574 (Tex. App.—Amarillo 1981, writ ref'd n.r.e.); Lopez v. Aro Corp., 584 S.W.2d 333 (Tex. Civ. App.—San Antonio 1979, writ ref'd n.r.e.).

369. *See* Dougherty v. Hooker Chemical Corp., 540 F.2d 174, 179 (3d Cir. 1976); Spruill v. Boyle-Midway, Inc., 308 F.2d 79, 87 (4th Cir. 1962); Shell Oil Co. v. Gutierrez, 119 Ariz. 426, 581 P.2d 271, 281 (Ariz. Ct. App. 1978); Miller v. Bock Laundry Machine Co., 568 S.W.2d 648 (Tex. 1977); Pearson v. Hevi-Duty Electric, 618 S.W.2d 784 (Tex. Civ. App.—Houston [1st Dist.] 1981, writ ref'd n.r.e.); Lopez v. Aro Corp., 584 S.W.2d 333 (Tex. Civ. App.—San Antonio 1979, writ ref'd n.r.e.); Rindlisbaker v. Wilson, 95 Idaho 752, 519 P.2d 421, 428 (1974).

370. In Ziglar v. E. I. Du Pont de Nemours & Co., 53 N.C. App. 147, 280 S.E.2d 510 (1981) (use of the words "dangerous-—poison" accompanied by red skull and crossbones symbols placed on a container of clear liquid crop poison that was similar in appearance to water was not adequate warning as a matter of law. The court noted that the manufacturer should have added a coloration to the poisor to distinguish it from water.) *Id.* at 515-16.

size and color generally is deemed inadequate.[371]

In certain circumstances, words may be inadequate to communicate the warning or instruction. Certain products are unusually dangerous or hazardous for their intended and foreseeable uses. In these instances, symbols such as skull and crossbones, or the symbol for fire or explosion, may be necessary to constitute an adequate warning when the written word alone would be incomprehensible or inadequate to communicate with the intensity required by the risk of harm presented.[372] For example, products anticipated to be used by children or individuals in areas in which English may not be spoken or read might raise an issue on adequacy.[373]

Perhaps the most important factor in an adequate warning is the communication of the specific risk of harm or dangerous propensities associated with the product. The warning must be qualitatively sufficient to convey to the user the particular risk of harm associated with use of the product. In *Fiorentino v. A. E. Staley Manufacturing Co.*,[374] plaintiffs, carpenters, were burned in a flash fire while using a contact adhesive to install formica in a kitchen. Vapors from the adhesive, which were heavier than air, moved along the kitchen floor and were ignited by a closed oven pilot light. A label on the adhesive mixture contained a warning: "Caution: Flammable Mixture. Do Not Use Near Fire Flame". The

---

371. *See, e.g.*, Gasque v. Heublein Inc., 281 S.C. 278, 315 S.E.2d 556 (S.C. App. 1984). *See also* Westerman v. Sears, Roebuck & Co., 577 F.2d 873 (5th Cir. 1978) (in strict liability action for wrongful death in automobile accident allegedly caused by defective tire manufactured by defendant, question of whether owner's manual supplied adequate warnings of dangers of underinflation was for jury).

In *Dixon v. Van Waters and Rogers*, the Texas Supreme Court affirmed a judgment for the manufacturer of hydrocholoric acid, accused of having inadequate warning of danger on the acid container. Parents filed a products liability action for damages relating to the death of their son, whose death was allegedly brought about by the inhalation of hydrochloric acid fumes. The Supreme Court held that the trial court properly instructed the jury that the product supplier was not obligated to warn a user who possesses knowledge concerning the dangerous characteristics of a product if the risks are actually known to the user. Dixon v. Van Waters and Rogers, 674 S.W.2d 479 (Tex. App.—Fort Worth, 1984), *aff'd per curiam*, 682 S.W.2d 533 (Tex. 1985).

372. *Compare* Hubbard-Hall Chemical Co. v. Silverman, 340 F.2d 402, 405 (1st Cir. 1965) *with* Pierluisi v. E.R. Squibb & Sons, Inc., 440 F. Supp. 691, 695 (D. P.R. 1977).

373. *See* Hubbard-Hall Chemical Co. v. Silverman, 340 F.2d 402, 405 (1st Cir. 1965); Ziglar v. E. I. Du Pont de Nemours & Co., 280 S.E.2d 510 (N.C. Ct. App. 1981); Campos v. Firestone Tire & Rubber Co., 469 A.2d 943 (N.J. 1984).

374. 11 Mass. App. Ct. 428, 416 N.E.2d 998, 1002 (1981).

court noted that the warning was inadequate to alert even professional users of the danger of using a flammable adhesive near a closed and concealed pilot light.[375]

Similarly, in *Eddleman v. Scalco*,[376] plaintiffs were injured when carbide exploded. The label on the product indicated that the product was flammable but did not warn of any explosive characteristics. The court noted that the warning was inadequate to communicate the particular risk of harm involved in a foreseeable use of the product.[377]

Another aspect of inadequate warning involves its location. Products presenting high risk of harm may require an understandable warning on the product itself either by label or other device.[378] In *Stapleton v. Kawasaki Heavy Industries, Ltd.*,[379] plaintiff was injured when he accidentally tipped over his motorcycle while cleaning it in the basement of his home. The fuel switch had not been turned to the off position. As a consequence, gas leaked from the tank and was ignited by a nearby pilot light.[380] Plaintiff contended that the motorcycle was defective by reason of the failure to adequately warn of the danger of failing to turn off the fuel switch on the motorcycle. The Fifth Circuit noted that:

> The manual containing the warning was in evidence, and the jury could determine whether putting the warning on P. 13 in ordinary type was an adequate effort and whether the warning so located was sufficient to warn user of the danger. There is no merit to the assertion that the evidence does not support a finding of failure to warn.[381]

---

375. *Id.* at 1001-04.

376. 484 S.W.2d 122 (Tex. Civ. App.—Beaumont 1972, writ ref'd n.r.e).

377. *Id.* at 126-27. (court remanded on the question of adequacy)

378. Stapleton v. Kawaswaski Heavy Industries, Ltd., 608 F.2d 571 (5th Cir. 1979) (warning to shut off fuel line should be on motorcycle and not in accompanying manual); Miller v. Bock Laundry Mach. Co., 568 S.W.2d 648 (Tex. 1977) (warning not to place hand in rotating industrial dryer should be affixed to the dryer and not to an accompanying manuel); Blackwell Burner Co. v. Cerda, 644 S.W.2d 512 (Tex. App.—San Antonio 1982, writ ref'd n.r.e.) (warning on use should be attached to pear burner); Air Shields, Inc. v. Spears, 590 S.W.2d 574 (Tex. Civ. App.—Waco 1979, writ ref'd n.r.e.) (warning of dangers of oxygen in incubator should be placed on the product). *See also* Griggs v. Firestone Tire & Rubber Co., 513 F.2d 851, 855 (8th Cir. 1975), *cert. denied*, 423 U.S. 865 (1975); Ilosky v. Michelin Tire Corp., 307 S.E.2d 603 (W. Va. 1983).

379. 608 F.2d 571 (5th Cir. 1979).

380. *Id.* at 572.

381. *Id.* at 573.

Some products, however, simply are incapable of carrying an individualized warning. In *Scott v. Black & Decker, Inc.*,[382] plaintiff was injured when a band saw that he was using to cut pipe sparked, causing gas in the pipe to ignite and severely burn him. The manual accompanying the saw contained twenty specific safety precautions. A label affixed to the saw suggested the user read the owner's manual before utilizing the tool. Affirming a directed verdict for the manufacturer, the Fifth Circuit noted: "In this case, the injury was caused by explosion, but it could just as easily have been caused by failure to observe any of the other nineteen safety precautions. To require one explicit warning to be placed on the saw would be to require all twenty."[383]

When the magnitude of the danger is severe, adequacy of warning or instructions for safety use may require that the warning be contained on the product rather than in an accompanying manual or information pamphlet. The Texas Supreme Court considered this issue in *Miller v. Bock Laundry Machine Company.*[384] Plaintiff was injured when he opened the lid of a rotating industrial dryer and placed his hand in the dryer capsule. The court held that the warning contained in the manual that accompanied the dryer was inadequate to communicate the risk of harm to the ultimate user. The court noted that the manufacturer could reasonably foresee that an industrial dryer would be used in public laundries and that the manual would become detached and be unavailable to the user.[385]

Another factor in establishing sufficiency and adequacy of warning is the type of language used to communicate the risk of harm. Adequacy of warning is dependent, in large measure, on the language used and the impression that such language is calculated to make upon the mind of the average user of the product. This necessarily involves questions of display, syntax and emphasis.[386]

---

382. 717 F.2d 251 (5th Cir. 1983).

383. *Id.* at 254.

384. 568 S.W.2d 648 (Tex. 1977).

385. *Id.* at 652.

386. *See* Stapleton v. Kawasaki Heavy Industries, Ltd., 608 F.2d 571, 573 (5th Cir. 1979); D'Arienzo v. Clairol, Inc., 125 N.J. Super. 224, 310 A.2d 106, 110 (N.J. Super. Law. Div. 1973). In essence, the warning must communicate with clarity and bring home to the user the particular danger or risk of harm presented in connection with use of the product. As noted by the Fifth Circuit in Pavlides v. Galveston Yacht Basin, Inc., 727 F.2d 330, 338 (5th Cir. 1984), "Where, however, the product is marketed to the general public, the manu-

The warning must be neither ambiguous nor vague in content. For example, in *Harrison v. Flota Mercante Grancolombiana S.A.*,[387] the word "prolong" and the phrase "avoid prolonged breathing" of vapors was deemed ambiguous. Similarly, a warning to use Kantrex on a one-time basis only for post surgical irrigation was not sufficiently clear to communicate the hazard that repeated use of the drug could cause an ototoxic condition.[388] Essentially, an adequate warning must bring home to the user the specific danger or risk of harm that is presented by the product in its foreseeable environment of use.[389] A corollary of a clear and unambiguous warning is a necessity to avoid overly broad or unduly narrow warnings and instructions for use.[390]

Finally, it is important that the warnings of risk of harm or dangerous propensities of a product are not subsequently diluted by representations of or advertising by the product supplier.[391] Overpromotion of certain products designed to induce purchase which have the effect of nullifying or significantly diluting the dangers and risks inherent in the use of the product may negate an otherwise adequate warning.[392] Advertising promotions relating to the safety aspects of a product are particularly relevant on the issue of adequacy.[393]

---

facturer must tailor the warning to the man-in-the-street."

387. 577 F.2d 968 (5th Cir. 1978). The use of the word "prolonged" in connection with instructions to an operator of an aircraft to "prevent fuel flow interruption, avoid prolonged operation in slip or skid attitude under low fuel conditions" was deemed ambiguous. Kritser v. Beech Aircraft Corp., 479 F.2d 1089 (5th Cir. 1973).

388. Bristol-Myers Co. v. Gonzales, 561 S.W.2d 801 (Tex. 1978).

389. *See e.g.*, Bristol-Myers v. Gonzales, 561 S.W.2d 801 (Tex. 1978); Ford Motor Co. v. Nowak, 638 S.W.2d 582 (Tex. App.— Corpus Christi 1982, writ ref'd n.r.e.); Blackwell Burner Co. v. Cerda, 644 S.W.2d 512 (Tex. App.— San Antonio 1982, writ ref'd n.r.e.); Lopez v. Aro Corp., 584 S.W.2d 333 (Tex. Civ. App.—San Antonio 1979, writ ref'd n.r.e.); Schering Corp. v. Giesecke, 589 S.W.2d 516 (Tex. Civ. App.— Eastland 1979, writ ref'd n.r.e.); Bituminous Casualty Corp. v. Black & Decker Mfg. Co., 518 S.W.2d 868 (Tex. Civ. App.— Dallas 1974, writ ref'd n.r.e.).

390. *See* Brownlee v. Louisville Varnish Co., 641 F.2d 397 (5th Cir. 1981); Johnson v. Husky Industries, Inc., 536 F.2d 645, 648 (6th Cir. 1976); Schering Corp. v. Giesecke, 589 S.W.2d 516, 518 (Tex. App.—Eastland 1979, writ ref'd n.r.e.).

391. *See e.g.*, Salmon v. Parke, Davis & Co., 520 F.2d 1359 (4th Cir. 1975).

392. Stevens v. Parke, Davis & Co., 9 Cal. 3d 51, 107 Cal.Rptr. 45, 53, 507 P.2d 653, 661 (Cal. 1973).

393. *See e.g.*, American Optical Co. v. Weidenhamer, 404 N.E.2d 606, 617 (Ind. Ct. App. 1980); (For example, advertising safety glasses as "sure-guard" and "super armour plate" represented to the user that the glasses offered the highest degree of protection and offset a miniscule that "lenses are impact resistent but not unbreakable.") *Id.* at 617.

e. Persons to Whom a Duty is Owed to Warn and Provide Instructions for Safe Use. The duty to warn extends to and must be reasonably calculated to reach the ultimate user and consumer of the product.[394] The class of users to whom the duty of warning extends are those individuals reasonably expected to come in contact with the product as it proceeds to its ultimate destination and while it is used in its anticipated environment.[395] The duty to warn corresponds to the knowledge of the danger possessed by the product supplier relative to the ultimate user of that product. The duty generally arises when there is unequal knowledge between the product supplier and the user. This is illustrated in *Rawlings Sporting Goods Company v. Daniels.*[396] The manufacturer and supplier of football helmets used by high school players was held strictly liable in tort for failure to warn that the helmet would not protect against head injuries. The court reasoned that the manufacturer possessed considerably greater knowledge of the limitations on the helmet's protective ability than the plaintiff who was utilizing the helmet in football practice.[397]

The distributive chain of product supply affects the duty to warn. The duty to warn is imposed on the intermediate distributor or user who is expected to supervise the ultimate use of the product. As an example, the manufacturer of an aircraft is not required to warn passengers of the aircraft, the ultimate consumers, concerning overload potential of the aircraft. This duty is discharged by warning the pilot and owner of the aircraft.[398]

Situations arise in which the duty to warn is properly allo-

Berkebile v. Brantly Helicopter Corp., 462 Pa. 83, 337 A.2d 893, 903 (1975).

394. Pavlides v. Galveston Yacht Basin, Inc., 727 F.2d 330 (5th Cir. 1984); Harrison v. Flota Mercante Grancolombiana S.A., 577 F.2d 968 (5th Cir. 1978); Reyes v. Wyeth Laboratories, 498 F.2d 1264 (5th Cir. 1974), *cert. denied*, 419 U.S. 1096 (1974); Lopez v. Aro Corp., 584 S.W.2d 333 (Tex. Civ. App.—San Antonio 1979, writ ref'd n.r.e.); Miller v. Boch Laundry Mach. Co., 568 S.W.2d 648 (Tex. 1977); Rourke v. Garza, 530 S.W.2d 794 (Tex. 1975). *See also* Whitehead v. St. Joe Lead Co., 729 F.2d 238 (3d Cir. 1984); Hopkins v. Chip-In-Saw, Inc., 630 F.2d 616 (8th Cir. 1980).

395. In Harrison v. Flota Mercante Grancolombiana S.A., 577 F.2d 968 (5th Cir. 1978), the Fifth Circuit concluded that the warning extended to any class or group of persons reasonably expected to contact the product as it proceeded to its ultimate destination. In this particular case, it included stevedores expected to handle the product in transit.

396. 619 S.W.2d 435 (Tex. Civ. App.—Waco 1981, writ ref'd n.r.e.).

397. *Id.* at 439.

398. Stevens v. Cessna Aircraft Co., 115 Cal.App.3d 431, 170 Cal.Rptr. 925 (1981). This concept is predicated on the learned intermediary exception to the general rule of furnishing a warning to the ultimate user of the product.

cated to the intermediate employer who purchases the product and uses it in the normal course of his business. This is particularly apropos to a supplier of basic construction materials who possess no control over the manner in which his materials are used.[399] In this situation, the product supplier generally is not obligated to warn the ultimate user of the danger of using these materials without proper safeguards. The duty to warn appropriately rests with the experienced contractor who utilizes the materials in the course of his business.[400]

Jurisdictions are divided on the duty to warn of risk of harm or dangerous propensities involved in the use of industrial equipment. Some jurisdictions conclude that an adequate warning communicated to the owner-employer of the industrial equipment discharges the duty of warning required under strict tort liability.[401] These jurisdictions note that the employer occupies the most advantageous position to ensure that proper warnings are communicated and that appropriate instruction is given to the employee-users of the industrial equipment.[402]

Other jurisdictions reject any limitation on the duty to warn.

---

399. The court recognizes that a manufacturer may under appropriate circumstances rely on the employer-purchaser of a product to supervise its employees in the proper and safe use of the proper. *See e.g.*, Adams v. Union Carbide Corp., 737 F.2d 1453 (6th Cir. 1984) *cert. denied*, ___ U.S. ___ (1984); Marshall v. H. K. Ferguson & Co., 623 F.2d 882, 886 (4th Cir. 1980); McWaters v. Steel Service Co., 597 F.2d 79 (6th Cir. 1979); Schmeiser v. Trus Joist Corp., 273 Or. 120, 540 P.2d 998 (1975); Reed v. Pennwalt Corp., 22 Wash. App. 718, 591 P.2d 478 (1979).

400. In Shanks v. A.F.E. Industries, Inc., 403 N.E.2d 849 (Ind. Ct. App. 1980), the court held that the grain elevator employer was obligated to instruct and properly warn employees since the employer controlled the work space, the employment and placement of personnel as well as the operation of the grain dryer which was involved in the accident. Similarly, in McWaters v. Steel Service Co., 597 F.2d 79 (6th Cir. 1979), the circuit court held that a construction company that possessed and operated control over basic construction materials and over the manner in which the materials were used, rather than the product supplier, was obligated to provide appropriate warnings and instructions for safe use of the product. Other jurisdictions adopt the view that the product supplier must provide warnings to the ultimate user. *See, e.g.*, Whitehead v. St. Joe Lead Co., Inc., 729 F.2d 283 (3d Cir. 1984); Hopkins v. Chip-In-Saw, Inc., 630 F.2d 616 (8th Cir. 1980); Kozlowski v. John E. Smith's Sons Co., 87 Wis. 2d 882, 275 N.W.2d 915 (Wis. 1979).

401. Jones v. Meat Packers Equip. Co., 723 F.2d 370 (4th Cir. 1983); McWaters v. Steel Service Co., 597 F.2d 79, 80 (6th Cir. 1979); Reed v. Pennwalt Corp., 22 Wash. App. 718, 591 P.2d 478 (1979).

402. Sales, *The Duty to Warn and Instruct for Safe Use in Strict Tort Liability*, 13 St. Mary's L. J. 521, 568 (1982). *See generally*, Adams v. Union Carbide Corp., 737 F.2d 1453 (6th Cir. 1984); Cook v. Branick Mfg. Inc. 736 F.2d 1442 (11th Cir. 1984); Cruz v. Texaco, Inc., 589 F. Supp. 777 (S.D. Ill. 1984).

These jurisdictions declare that a manufacturer who can reasonably foresee that adequate warnings relating to the use of a product may not be communicated to the ultimate users of that equipment owes a duty to warn the ultimate users actually endangered by the equipment.[403] Warnings provided to the purchaser-employer do not necessarily insulate the product supplier from liability for appropriate warning, especially when the danger is latent in nature.[404]

The duty to warn ultimate users extends even to maintenance and repair personnel who may work on the equipment.[405] The product supplier is obligated to provide an adequate warning of the risk of harm and any unusually dangerous propensities of a product to repairmen and maintenance personnel employed to perform reasonably anticipated services on the product.[406] For example, the manufacturer of a transformer is obligated to warn of the danger of substituting fuses in the product sufficient to reach an

---

403. Whitehead v. St. Joe Lead Co., 729 F.2d 238 (3d Cir. 1984); Hopkins v. Chip-In-Saw, Inc., 630 F.2d 616 (8th Cir. 1980); Billiar v. Minnesota Mining & Mfg. Co., 623 F.2d 240 (2d Cir. 1980). In a 1984 decision, the Sixth Circuit in *Grover Hill Grain Co. v. Baughman-Oster, Inc.* considered whether the manufacturer of an unassembled grain bin could be held strictly liable when the dealer for the manufacturer caused the defect by overtorquing the bolts during construction. The court concluded that the inadvertent or negligent overtorquing of the bolts by the dealer constitutes an intervening proximate cause of the collapse under Ohio law, sufficient to break the chain of causation between the manufacturer's failure to warn of dangers in overtorquing. The case was remanded on a question of agency. 728 F.2d 784, 792 (6th Cir. 1984).

404. The Texas view favors imposing a duty on the product supplier to provide an adequate warning to the ultimate user under most circumstances. Pearson v. Hevi-Duty Electric, 618 S.W.2d 784 (Tex. App.—Houston [1st Dist.] 1981, writ ref'd n.r.e.); Lopez v. Aro Corp., 584 S.W.2d 333 (Tex. Civ. App.—San Antonio 1979, writ ref'd n.r.e.); Hamilton v. Motor Coach Indus. Inc., 569 S.W.2d 571 (Tex. Civ. App.—Texarkana 1978, no writ); Bituminous Casualty Corp. v. Black & Decker Mfg. 518 S.W.2d 868 (Tex. App.—Dallas 1974, writ ref'd n.r.e.). In *Avery v. Maremont Corp.*, the Fifth Circuit held that, in an accident involving shock absorbers which had been improperly installed by an intermediary, the manufacturer was obligated to warn the ultimate consumer. Because the shock absorber manufacturer failed to provide an adequate warning and instruction for installation, the manufacturer was not entitled to contribution from the installer. Avery v. Maremont Corp., 628 F.2d 441 (5th Cir. 1980).

405. *See e.g.*, Pearson v. Hevi-Duty Electric, 618 S.W.2d 784 (Tex. App.—Houston [1st Dist.] 1981, writ ref'd n.r.e.) (electrician repairing electric switch gear); Shop Rite Foods, Inc. v. Upjohn Co., 619 S.W.2d 574 (Tex. App.—Amarillo 1981, writ ref'd n.r.e.) (welder working on repair of building); Hamiton v. Motor Coach Indus. Inc., 569 S.W.2d 571 (Tex. Civ. App.—Texarkana 1978, no writ) (mechanic working on product containing a compressed spring).

406. Pearson v. Hevi-Duty Electric, 618 S.W.2d 784 (Tex. App.—Houston [1st Dist.] 1981, writ ref'd n.r.e.).

electrician employed by the purchaser of the transformer.[407]

Bulk suppliers of products present a unique problem.[408] Normally, products supplied in bulk are transported by railroad car or large containers. An adequate warning of the risk of harm in the intended and reasonable foreseeable use of bulk products is furnished to the initial purchaser by informational sheets and pamphlets. The product supplier reasonably expects that the intermediary will package the product in smaller containers for ultimate sale to the public.[409] Realistically, it is impossible to affix a label or to provide any accompanying documentation that would follow the product to its ultimate destination and, therefore, reach the ultimate user. In this particular circumstance, the intermediate distributor occupies a strategic position in the distributive chain of bulk products. Most jurisdictions recognize that an adequate warning provided by the bulk supplier to the intermediate seller satisfies the duty of providing an adequate warning required under strict tort liability.[410] These jurisdictions recognize that the product will be repackaged and sold in different containers and that the original supplier possesses neither the right nor discretion to control the manner and method of intermediate distribution.[411] Several jurisdictions, however, have held that the duty to provide an adequate warning of the risk of harm must be provided to the ultimate user irrespective of bulk sale.[412] This view, of course, ignores the realities of the sale and the transfer of bulk products.

Prescriptive drugs and apparatuses, such as prescriptive medical devices and appliances, provide an exception to the general

---

407. *Id.*

408. *See generally*, Sales, *The Duty to Warn and Instruct for Safe Use in Strict Tort Liability*, 13 St. Mary's L. J. 521, 570 (1982).

409. *See e.g.*, Manning v. Ashland Oil Co., 721 F.2d 192 (7th Cir. 1983).

410. Manning v. Ashland Oil Co., 721 F.2d 192 (7th Cir. 1983); Doss v. Apache Powder Co., 430 F.2d 1317 (5th Cir. 1970); Groll v. Shell Oil Co., 148 Cal. App. 3d 444, 196 Cal. Rptr. 52 (1983); Jones v. Hittle Service, Inc. 219 Kan. 627, 549 P.2d 1383 (1976); Younger v. Dow Corning Corp., 202 Kan. 674, 451 P.2d 177 (1969).

411. The duty to warn is not imposed on bulk suppliers simply because the supplier is not in a position to control or govern the middleman's packaging and labeling. Manning v. Ashland Oil Co., 721 F.2d 192 (7th Cir. 1983); E. I. DuPont de Nemours v. McCain, 414 F.2d 369 (5th Cir. 1969); Groll v. Shell Oil, 148 Cal. App. 3d 444, 196 Cal.Rptr. 52 (1983); Shell Oil Co. v. Harrison, 425 So.2d 67 (Fla. Dist. Ct. App. 1982).

412. Bryant v. Technical Research Co., 654 F.2d 1337 (9th Cir. 1981); Pepper v. Selig Chemical Ind., 161 Ga. App. 548, 288 S.E.2d 693 (1982); Seibel v. Symons Corp., 221 N.W.2d 50 (N.D. 1974).

principle that the product supplier must provide an adequate warning of the risk of harm and unreasonably dangerous propensities of a product to the ultimate user. It is universally recognized that the duty to warn is satisfied when the products' supplier adequately warns the medical profession of the dangers associated with the drug or the medical device.[413] The duty to warn, of course, must be adequate and reasonable under the circumstances.[414] This

---

413. The Texas rule contemplates that the physician is a learned intermediary who knows the patient and is the party best qualified to make an informed choice after weighing the utility and benefits of the drug or medical device and therefore an adequate warning to the physician satisfies the duty of warning. Reyes v. Wyeth Labs, Inc., 498 F.2d 1264 (5th Cir. 1974), *cert. denied*, 419 U.S. 1096 (1974); Bristol-Myers Co. v. Gonzales, 561 S.W.2d 801 (Tex. 1978); Gravis v. Parke-Davis & Co., 502 S.W.2d 863, 870 (Tex. Civ. App. Corpus Christi—1973, writ ref'd n.r.e.). The vast majority of jurisdictions adhere to the rule that a warning to the physician satisfies the obligation on the part of the product supplier. Stanback v. Parke, Davis Co., 657 F.2d 642 (4th Cir. 1981); Lindsay v. Ortho Pharmaceutical Corp., 637 F.2d 87 (2d Cir. 1980); Basko v. Sterling Drug, Inc., 416 F.2d 417 (2d Cir. 1969); Buckner v. Allergen Pharmaceuticals, Inc., 400 So.2d 820 (Fla Dist. Ct. App. 1981); Smith v. E. R. Squibb & Sons, Inc., 69 Mich. App. 375, 245 N.W.2d 52 (1976), *affirmed*, 475 Mich. 79, 273 N.W.2d 476 (Mich. 1979); McDaniel v. McNeil Labs, Inc., 196 Neb. 190, 241 N.W.2d 822 (1976); McKee v. Moore, 648 P.2d 21 (Okla. 1982); Ross v. Jacobs, 684 P.2d 1211 (Okla. Ct. App. 1984); McEwen v. Ortho Pharmaceutical Corp., 270 Or. 375, 528 P.2d 522 (1974); Terhune v. A. H. Robbins Co., 90 Wash.2d 9, 577 P.2d 975 (1978). The duty to provide an adequate warning to the physician is likewise applicable to medical appliances. Air Shields, Inc. v. Spears, 590 S.W.2d 574 (Tex. Civ. App.—Waco 1979, writ ref'd n.r.e.); Brooks v. Medtronic, Inc., 750 F.2d 1127 (4th Cir. 1984) (the learned intermediary applies to medical appliances such as cardiac pacemaker). Warning of a medical appliance that is designed to be prescribed and used by a physician need only extend to the physician and not to the patient (warning that extensive X-ray treatment given for acne might lead to skin cancer adequate when given to the physician). However, a recent opinion by the Massachusetts Supreme Court holds that warning of prescriptive contraceptive pills must be designed to reach the ultimate user even though the pills must be prescribed by a learned intermediary such as a physician. MacDonald v. Ortho Pharmaceutical Corp., 475 N.E.2d 65 (Mass. 1985). *Accord*, Stevens v. G.D. Searle Co., 602 F. Supp. 379 (D.C. Mich. 1985).

414. *See generally* Bryant v. Technical Research Co., 654 F.2d 1337 (9th Cir. 1981); Reyes v. Wyeth Laboratories, 498 F.2d 1264 (5th Cir. 1974), *cert. denied*, 419 U.S. 1096 (1974); Reeder v. Hammond, 125 Mich. App. 223, 336 N.W.2d 3 (1983); Gravis v. Parke-Davis & Co., 502 S.W.2d 863 (Tex. Civ. App. Corpus Christi 1973, writ ref'd n.r.e.). In some instances the supplier of a medical product must warn physicians not only of adverse reactions known to the manufacturer but also of the possible insufficiency of the manufacturer's knowledge. In *Hawkinson v. A. H. Robins Co.*, the court determined that the manufacturer of an IUD called the Dalkon Shield could be held liable under RESTATEMENT Section 402B. The company engaged in an extensive marketing campaign but failed to adequately warn physicians of the small amount of testing done with the new design the Dalkon Shield incorporated. Later testing demonstrated that users of the shield confronted an increased risk of septic abortion if they became pregnant while the shield was in place. The court noted:

> Robins was negligent in its failure to warn adequately of the possible risks involved with use of the Dalkon Shield and its failure to disclose its lack of knowl-

exception to the general rule is predicated on the rationale that the physician is a learned intermediary who knows the patient and is the party best qualified to make an informed choice after weighing the utility and benefits of the drug or medical device against the risk of harm inherent in its use.[415] The manufacturer of prescriptive drugs is absolved of liability as a matter of law upon establishing that adequate warnings of the risks of harm and dangerous side effects of a drug are communicated in a meaningful fashion to the prescribing physician.[416] This exception applies even though the product supplier may foresee that physicians occasionally elect not to provide the patient with a warning of the particular side effects or risks of drugs or medical appliances. A physician's duty to warn the patient of all possible side effects of a drug or the effect of a medical appliance is not an absolute duty.[417] The extent of disclosure of risks rests in the exercise of reasonable medical judgment, and a physician's failure to communicate a particular warning of an adverse side effect or risk of harm to the patient does not translate into liability on the product supplier.[418]

The product supplier who fails to adequately warn the physician of the risk and harm associated with prescriptive or ethical drugs incurs strict tort liability to the patient who is injured by the prescribed drug as well as incurring liability to the prescribing physician for liability incurred in prescribing the drug.[419] Some courts have concluded that a physician is entitled to protection against foreseeable harm he may suffer because of the prescription of a particular drug without adequate warning of potential harm to

---

> edge. It can be said that the warnings and cautions given in Robins' product information to the physicians was representative of what the defendant knew about its product at the time, but the warnings were insufficient because the defendant did not disclose the depth of its ignorance . . . . The medical profession was not made aware of Robins' lack of knowledge about this new product it was touting to them.

Hawkinson v. A. H. Robins Co., 595 F. Supp. 1290, 1294 (D. Colo. 1984).

415. Refer to note 413 *supra*.

416. Refer to note 413 *supra*.

417. Buckner v. Allergan Pharmaceuticals, Inc., 400 So.2d 820, 822 (Fla. Dist. Ct. App. 1981); Seley v. G.D. Searle & Co., 67 Ohio St.2d 192, 423 N.E.2d 831, 840 (Ohio 1981).

418. *Id.*

419. In Oksenholt v. Lederle Laboratories, 51 Or. App. 419, 625 P.2d 1357 (1981) the physician who had been sued by a patient for loss of vision following use of a drug prescribed by the physician filed suit against the drug manufacturer for failure to provide adequate warnings of side effects of the particular drug. The Oregon court concluded that the physician was entitled to protection against foreseeable harm that he might sustain because of prescribing a particular drug without full awareness of its potential harmful effects.

the patient.[420]

The prescriptive drug exception is inapplicable where drugs are sold over the counter without prescription or where prescriptive or ethical drugs may be dispensed in mass immunization without the intervention of a learned intermediary such as a physician.[421] Use of a drug beyond the limitations of a prescription or without a prescription, of course, forecloses any basis to establish lack of adequate warning as the basis of liability against the product supplier.[422]

Whether the duty to warn extends to all individuals who may foreseeably come in contact with the product so as to include trespassers and criminal intervention is not entirely clear.[423] Essentially, the duty of a product supplier is to provide an adequate warning of the risks of harm and the reasonably dangerous propensities of a product to all reasonably foreseeable users and handlers of the product in its intended and reasonably foreseeable use.[424] It is less than clear whether this duty would extend to a thief en-

---

420. *Id.*

421. Petty v. U.S., 740 F.2d 1428 (8th Cir. 1984); Reyes v. Wyeth Laboratories, 498 F.2d 1264, 1276 (5th Cir. 1974), *cert. denied*, 419 U.S. 1096 (1974); Torsiello v. Whitehall Laboratories, 165 N.J. Super. 311, 398 A.2d 132 (1979).

422. *See e.g.*, Ortho Pharmaceutical Corp. v. Chapman, 180 Ind. App. 33, 388 N.E.2d 541, 557 (Ind. App. 1977).

423. *Compare* Barnes v. Litton Industrial Products, Inc., 555 F.2d 1184 (4th Cir. 1977), in which the court held prison inmates illegally obtaining alcohol for consumption entitled to warning of the danger under strict tort liability, *with* Helene Curtis Industries, Inc. v. Pruitt, 385 F.2d 841 (5th Cir. 1967), *cert. denied*, 391 U.S. 913 (1968) *and* Winnett v. Winnett, 57 Ill.2d 7, 310 N.E.2d 1 (Ill. 1974), in which the court held that individuals illegally obtaining or improperly using a product are not foreseeable users entitled to a warning of dangers under strict tort liability.

424. The duty certainly extends to all users of the product as it proceeds along its distributive chain. Miller v. Bock Laundry Mach. Co., 568 S.W.2d 648 (Tex. 1977) (commercial user of industrial equipment); Rourke v. Garza, 530 S.W.2d 794 (Tex. 1975) (employee of lessee of equipment); Rawlings Sporting Goods Co., Inc. v. Daniels, 619 S.W.2d 435 (Tex. App.—Waco 1981, writ ref'd n.r.e.) (high school athlete using football helmet at school); Pearson v. Hevi-Duty Electric, 618 S.W.2d 784 (Tex. App. - Houston [1st Dist.] 1981, writ ref'd n.r.e.) (repairman working on electrical switch gear); Hamilton v. Motor Coach Indus., Inc., 569 S.W.2d 571 (Tex. App.—Texarkana 1978, no writ) (repairman working on product); Ethicon, Inc. v. Parten, 520 S.W.2d 527 (Tex. Civ. App.—Houston [14th Dist.] 1975, no writ) (patient of doctor using medical equipment in hospital surgery); Helicoid Gage, Div. of American Chain & Cable Co. v. Howell, 511 S.W.2d 573 (Tex. Civ. App.—Houston [14th Dist.] 1974, writ ref'd n.r.e.) (employee of purchaser). But, an employee of a smelting plant who inhaled lead fumes while removing lead from used batteries is not entitled to maintain a strict tort liability action against the battery manufacturer. Johnson v. Murph Metals, Inc., 562 F. Supp. 246 (N.D. Tex. 1983).

gaged in stealing a particular product and who is injured in the course of the theft.[425]

f. Limitations on Duty to Warn. There is no duty to warn users of products of dangers that are open and obvious.[426] The purpose of a warning is to communicate information of hazards to afford the user an opportunity to weigh the risk of harm against the utility of the product.[427] When the danger of a product is obvious and apparent, even to the most uncaring, the need to warn simply is unnecessary.[428] A warning is an unnecessary redundancy. For ex-

---

425. Arguably, a thief stealing a product is not an objectively and reasonably foreseeable user of the product. Moreover, criminal intervention effectively interrupts the duty owed by a product supplier to an ultimate user. *See* Bennet v. Cincinnati Checker Cab Co., 353 F. Supp. 1206 (E.D. Ky. 1973); Adkinson v. Rossi Arms Co., 659 P.2d 1236 (Alaska 1983); Baldwin v. Zoradi, 123 Cal. App. 3d 275, 176 Cal.Rptr. 809 (1981); Hulsman v. Hemmeter Dev. Corp., 65 Hawaii 58, 647 P.2d 713 (1982); Thomas v. Bokelman, 86 Nev. 10, 462 P.2d 1020 (1970); Hulsebosch v. Ramsey, 435 S.W.2d 161 (Tex. Civ. App.—Houston [14th Dist.] 1968, writ ref'd n.r.e.).

426. Scott v. White Trucks, 699 F.2d 714 (5th Cir. 1983); Hagans v. Oliver Mach. Co., 576 F.2d 97, 101 (5th Cir. 1978) (obvious danger posed by multifunctional industrial table saw with unprotective circular blade spinning at 3600 revolutions per minute). Brech v. J. C. Penney Co., 698 F.2d 332 (8th Cir. 1983) (flammability of cotton fannel nightgown exposed to open flames); Holecek v. E-Z Just, 124 Ill.App.3d 251, 464 N.E.2d 696 (1984) (danger of flying model airplane near energized electrical wires carrying 340,000 volts); American Optical Co. v. Weidenhammer, 457 N.E.2d 181 (Ind. 1983) (risk of safety glasses being shattered by a large wooden projectile); Height v. Kawasaski Heavy Indus., Ltd., 190 N.J. Super. 7, 461 A.2d 757 (1983) (danger of collision with another vehicle rupturing gas tank and causing operator to be engulfed in flame); Landrine v. Mergo Corp., 95 App.Div.2d 759 (N.Y. 1983) (danger of small child swallowing balloon); Pemberton v. American Distilled Spirits Co., 664 S.W.2d 690 (Tenn. 1984) (risk of drinking half a fifth of 190 proof grain alcohol). *See also* Wood v. Stihl, Inc., 705 F.2d 1101 (9th Cir. 1983); Marshall v. H. K. Ferguson Co., 623 F.2d 882 (4th Cir. 1980); Sowles v. Urschel Labs, Inc., 595 F.2d 1361 (8th Cir. 1979); Carlson v. American Safety Equip. Corp., 528 F.2d 384 (1st Cir. 1976); Zidek v. General Motors Corp., 66 Ill. App. 3d 982, 384 N.E.2d 509 (1978); Maldonado v. Thompson National Press Co., 389 Mass. App. Ct. 911, 449 N.E.2d 1229 (1983). The "no duty" concept was recently discussed in Dixon v. Van Waters and Rogers, 682 S.W.2d 533, 534 (Tex. 1984). Earlier, the Texas Supreme Court abolished the "no duty" concept in negligence actions. Parker v. Highland Park, Inc., 565 S.W.2d 512 (Tex. 1978). But, as the court noted: "A plaintiff does not have the burden to prove and obtain findings that he lacked knowledge and appreciation of a danger; he must, however, prove the defendant *had a duty and breached it.*" (emphasis added). 682 S.W.2d at 534.

427. Hagans v. Oliver Machine Co. 576 F.2d 97 (5th Cir. 1978); Reyes v. Wyeth Labs, Inc., 498 F.2d 1264 (5th Cir. 1974) *cert. denied* 419 U.S. 1096 (1974); Borel v. Fibreboard Paper Prod. Corp., 493 F.2d 1076 (5th Cir. 1973), *cert. denied* 419 U.S. 869 (1974).

428. The purpose of a warning is to apprise the user of a product of the specific risk of danger or danger of propensity of a product. If the particular risk of harm or danger of propensity is open, obvious and apparent even to the most uncaring, obviously a warning constitutes a mere redundancy. *See e.g.*, Campos v. Firestone Tire & Rubber Co., 192 N.J.

ample, in *Hagan v. Oliver Machinery Company*,[429] plaintiff was injured when his hand was caught in an unprotected saw blade. The Fifth Circuit concluded that a warning of the hazard posed by the unprotected saw blade was unnecessary since the condition of the product and the hazard associated with the product was fully obvious and completely appreciated by the user.[430]

The nature and degree of the risk of harm must be open and fully appreciated. Though a warning of danger is not required when the user possesses a knowledge of the danger, a user's belief that a product may cause some injury or may injure the product is ineffectual as a limitation where the full nature of the risk is not appreciated.[431] For example, the danger of storing combustibles in

---

Super. 251, 469 A.2d 943 (1984); Pemberton v. American Distilled Spirits Co. 664 S.W.2d 690 (Tenn. 1984); Davis v. Globe Machine Mfr. Co. 102 Wash.2d 68, 684 P.2d 692 (Wash. 1984).

429. 576 F.2d 97 (5th Cir. 1978).

430. *Id.* at 102-03. *See also* Pressley v. Sears Roebuck & Co., 738 F.2d 1222 (11th Cir. 1984); Holezek v. E-Z Just, 124 Ill. App. 3d, 464 N.E.2d 696 (Ill. App. Ct.— 1984). Various jurisdictions have dealt with the question of an open and obvious danger: Whitehead v. St. Joe Lead Co. 729 F.2d 238 (3d Cir. 1984) (in case of employee's contamination by lead particles, liability of supplier constitutes a fact issue concerning manufacturer's warning to employee and employee's own knowledge of the risk of exposure to lead); Breazeale v. B. F. Goodrich Co., 564 F. Supp. 1541 (E.D. La. 1983) (in action against manufacturer of agricultural tire which exploded, killing repairman as he was filling it with air, court held that manufacturer was not liable when he established that tire did not explode from any internal weakness but due to overinflation. Overinflation was deemed an obvious danger to an ordinary workman); Patricia R. v. Sullivan, 631 P.2d 91 (Ala. 1981) (in case of injuries from electric baseboard heater, the court held that jury instruction should note that product is only required to have warnings as to those hazards or dangers that would not be readily recognized by ordinary users of the product); Brown v. Sears, Roebuck & Co., 136 Ariz. App. 556, 667 P.2d 750 (1983) (in a death involving an electrical extension cord used to power an electric saw, the court held that the manufacturer had no duty to warn of the danger of electrical shock which could result if the cord were cut or frayed, because a product containing an obvious hazard is generally considered neither defective nor unreasonably dangerous); Perez v. National Presto Indus. Inc., 431 So.2d 667 (Fla. Dist. Ct. App. 1983) (manufacturer not liable in pressure cooker explosion where user was aware that cooker parts wore out and needed to be replaced periodically. Here, accident occurred with third-party user 23 years after manufacture); Giordano v. Ford Motor Co., 165 Ga. App. 644, 299 S.E.2d 897 (1983) (fact issue existed as to whether priming a carburetor with gas was foreseeable use, and whether danger of fuel explosion was obvious or generally known); Walker v. Maxwell City, Inc., 117 Ill. App. 3d 571, 453 N.E.2d 917 (1983) (retailer and importer-wholesaler of motorcycle safety helmet not liable in strict liability where the lack of facial protection of the helmet was an open and obvious condition).

431. As noted by the Court in Trujillo v. Uniroyal Corp. 608 F.2d 815 (10th Cir. 1979) plaintiff, a repairman, attempting to mount a 16-inch tire on a 16.5-inch rim was injured when the tire exploded. Though recognizing the general rule that a warning is not required when the user possesses knowledge of the risk of harm or danger of propensities, the Tenth

close proximity to gas-fired appliances that possess a constant pilot light may not be so open and obvious as to obviate an adequate warning.[432] Some courts have imposed strict tort liability for failure to adequately warn of this danger on the basis that a pilot light that is generally out of sight and hidden from view and often forgotten is not an open and obvious condition that limits the product supplier's duty to warn.[433]

A second limitation on the duty to warn involves dangers that are commonly known and appreciated by the general public.[434] The rationale for this limitation is based on the reasonable expectation of the consumer possessing the ordinary knowledge of a product's characteristics, common to the community.[435] For example, common knowledge of the flammability of gasoline forecloses the necessity of the manufacturer providing a warning to a user that dried paint should not be removed by gasoline near an open flame.[436] Likewise, everyone knows the dangers of overextended

---

Circuit noted that "a belief that it should not be done because it may hurt the tire, or even that it may cause injury is different from knowing that there is a risk of explosion, of serious or even fatal bodily harm. Not merely some risk but the nature and degree of the risk must be appreciated." *Id.* at 819. *See also*, Rhodes v. Interstate Battery Systems of America, 722 F.2d 1517 (11th Cir. 1984); Jiminez v. Dreis & Krump Mfg. 736 F.2d 51 (2d Cir. 1984); McGowne v. Challenge-Cook Bros. Inc., 672 F.2d 652 (8th Cir. 1982); Franchetti v. Intercole Automation, Inc., 529 F. Supp. 533 (D. Del. 1982).

432. Harris v. Karri-On Campers, Inc., 640 F.2d 65, 76 (7th Cir. 1981); Hohllenkamp v. Rheem Mfg. Co., 123 Ariz. App. 535, 601 P.2d 298 (1979).

433. In Murray v. Wilson Oak Flooring Co. 475 F.2d 129 (7th Cir. 1973), warning not to use an adhesive near an open flame was deemed too vague to convey warning to remain a reasonably safe distance from an enclosed pilot light.

434. Dougherty v. Santa Fe Marine, Inc., 698 F.2d 232 (5th Cir. 1983) (no duty to warn of risk of releasing wench while boat from an offshore drilling platform is being lowered); Inomar Compania Naviere, S.A. v. Olin Corp., 666 F.2d 897 (5th Cir. 1982) (no duty to warn stevedores of hazards that constitute common knowledge on the docks); Blackwell Burner Co. v. Cerda, 644 S.W.2d 512 (Tex. App.—San Antonio 1982, writ ref'd n.r.e.) (danger of using kerosine in proximity to an open flame); *see also* Garrison v. Heublein, Inc., 673 F.2d 189 (7th Cir. 1982); Burton v. L. O. Smith Foundry Prod. 529 F.2d 108 (7th Cir. 1976); Posey v. Clark Equip. Co. 409 F.2d 560 (7th Cir.), *cert denied*, 396 U.S. 940 (1969). Harms v. Bell Helicopters Textron, 567 F. Supp. 28 (E.D. Ill. 1983); Garman v. American Clipper Corp. 117 Cal. App. 3d 634, 173 Cal. Rptr. 20 (1981); Bojorquez v. House of Toys, Inc. 62 Cal. App. 3d 930, 133 Cal. Rptr. 483 (1976); Vance v. Miller-Taylor Shoe Co. 148 Ga. App. 812, 251 S.E.2d 52 (1978); Fanning v. Lemay, 38 Ill.2d 209, 230 N.E.2d 182 (1967); Berry v. Eckhardt Prosche Audi, Inc., 578 P.2d 1195 (Okla. 1978); Menard v. Newhall, 135 Vt. 53, 373 A.2d 505 (1977).

435. Restatement (Second) of Torts § 402(a) comment i (1965).

436. Johnson v. Jones-Blair Paint Company, 607 S.W.2d 305 (Tex. Civ. App. — Eastland 1980, writ ref'd n.r.e)

use of alcoholic beverages.[437]

While certain general dangers may be matters of common knowledge, for which there is no duty to warn, other dangers related to the general danger compel a warning.[438] As an illustration, while the danger of explosion associated with dynamite is commonly known, the latent danger in lighting the dynamite safety fuse may mandate a warning of the danger involved in such use.[439] A particular hazard associated with a product must be analyzed to determine whether the particular danger, indeed, is obvious and commonly known and appreciated by the general public.[440]

A third limitation involves the class possessing a special knowledge, sophistication or expertise in the dangerous characteristics of a product.[441] Generally, a product supplier is not obligated to provide a warning of the risk of danger or the dangerous propensities associated with the use of a product that is utilized by a class or group possessing a special knowledge, expertise or sophistication about the product and its particular hazards.[442] As an

---

437. Pemberton v. American Distilled Spirits Co. 664 S.W.2d 690 (Tenn. 1984).

438. Cooley v. Quick Supply Co. 221 N.W.2d 763, 771 (Iowa 1974).

439. *See* Littlehale v. E. I. Dupont de Nemours & Co., 268 F. Supp. 791 (S.D.N.Y. 1966), *aff'd*, 380 F.2d 274 (2d Cir. 1967); Cooley v. Quick Supply Co., 221 N.W.2d 763 (Iowa 1974) (safety fuse); Hercules Inc. v. Coto, 434 So.2d 4 (Fla. Dist. Ct. App. 1983) (blasting cap); *Cf* Hercules Powder Co. v. Calcote, 161 Min. 860, 138 So. 583 (1932); Huffstutler v. Hercules Powder Co., 305 F.2d 292 (5th Cir. 1962).

440. *See* Sales, *The Duty To Warn And Instruct For Safe Use In Strict Tort Liability*, 13 St. Mary's L. J. 521, 579 (1982).

441. Scott v. White Truck, 699 F.2d 714 (5th Cir. 1983) (driver of large trucks aware of front end impact of certain designed vehicles); Hagen v. E-Z Mfg. Co., 674 F.2d 1047 (5th Cir. 1982) (industrial saw operators familiar with danger of uncovered saw blades); Guidry v. Kem Mfg. Co. 693 F.2d 426 (5th Cir. 1982)(industrial applicators familiar with chemical qualities of drain solvents); Smith v. Borg-Warner Corp. 626 F.2d 384 (5th Cir. 1980) (chemical plant workers familiar with the explosive nature of ABS); Martinez v. Dixie Carriers, Inc., 529 F.2d 457 (5th Cir. 1976) (Longshoreman familiar with toxic qualities of Hytrol-d); Ragsdale Bros., Inc. v. Margo, ___ S.W. 2d ___ (Tex. App.—San Antonio 1985, no writ) (seller's duty to warn limited where ultimate consumer possesses special knowledge or expertise).

442. *See, e.g.*, Strong v. E. I. Dupont de Neumours Co., 667 F.2d 682, 687 (8th Cir. 1981); Martinez v. Dixie Carriers, Inc., 529 F.2d 457, 464 (5th Cir. 1976). Of course, the mere fact that an individual is a member of a special group does not necessarily establish the sophisticated user exception. Each individual must be evaluated in light of the training, education, experience and environment of use of the product. Ionmar Compania Naveria S.A. v. Olin Corp., 666 F.2d 897, 904 (5th Cir. 1982); Hamilton v. Motor Coach Indus. 569 S.W.2d 571 (Tex. Civ. App. — Texarkana 1978, writ ref'd n.r.e.); Mckay v. Upson-Walton Co., 317 F.2d 826 (7th Cir. 1963); Loughan v. Firestone Tire & Rubber Co., 749 F.2d 1519 (11th Cir. 1985).

example, in *Martinez v. Dixie Carriers, Inc.*,[443] the Fifth Circuit concluded that a warning of a danger commonly known by the trade of which the plaintiff was a member was unnecessary. The court declared that the chemical, Hytrol-D, was distributed only to industrial users and the manufacturer was entitled to rely on the professional knowledge and expertise of those reasonably expected to use the product.[444] Knowledge of the danger and the risks of harm that would be communicated by an adequate warning is imputed to the knowledgeable and sophisticated user.[445]

The mere fact, however, that the ultimate user possesses a generalized expertise or classification as an expert is not necessarily determinative. The knowledgeable and sophisticated user exception is inapplicable where the particular risk or danger posed by the product is generally unknown to the class or group of which the plaintiff is a member.[446] The sophisticated user exception cannot be evaluated in a vacuum. As an example, in *Pearson v. Hevi-Duty Electric*,[447] the deceased electrician was fatally electrocuted while testing a 7200 volt transformer. This system on the transformer was energized when the fuse was in an open position. The original manufacturer of the component had attached an adhesive label to the fuse which stated: "Warning: Fuse or switch may be live in open position." The defendant, the assembler-manufacturer of the transformer, removed the adhesive and attached a warning: "High Voltage, Do Not Touch" and "High Voltage, Remove With Hot Sticks."[448] Recognizing the duty of the assembler-manufacturer to provide an adequate warning to the experienced electrician, the court noted that a sophisticated electrical specialist, such as the decedent, would normally perceive a fuse switch to be live when in the closed position rather than in the open position.[449] Consequently, a specific warning in clear language was mandated

443. 529 F.2d 457 (5th Cir. 1976).

444. *Id.* at 463-64.

445. *Id.* at 464-65. *See also* Ducote v. Liberty Mutual Ins. Co., 451 So.2d 1211 (La. Ct. App. 1984).

446. *See* Pearson v. Hevi-Duty Electric, 618 S.W.2d 784 (Tex. App. — Houston [1st District] 1981 writ ref'd, n.r.e.); Hamilton v. Motor Coach Indus. Inc., 569 S.W.2d 571 (Tex. Civ. App. — Texarkana 1978, writ ref'd, n.r.e.). *See also*, Billiar v. Minnesota Mining & Mfg. Co., 623 F.2d 240 (2d Cir. 1980); Fiorentino v. A. E. Staley Mfg. Co., 416 N.E.2d 998 (Mass. App. 1981); Prince v. Parachutes, Inc., 685 P.2d 83 (Alaska 1984).

447. 618 S.W.2d 784 (Tex. App. — Houston [1st Dist.] 1981 writ ref'd, n.r.e.)

448. *Id.* at 785.

449. *Id.* at 786-87.

to apprise the experienced electrician of the highly dangerous condition that confronted him with a fuse that was energized in an open position.[450] Similarly, the repairman unfamiliar with a particular danger posed in repairing components within a product is entitled to an adequate warning.[451]

The fourth limitation on the duty to warn involves substantial alteration or modification of the original product.[452] It is generally well-established that the product supplier is not obligated to warn that a redesign or replacement of an integral and ultimately dangerous component of a product will destroy the original design and produce an essentially different product with new dangerous propensities.[453] There is no duty to warn of dangers that may be created when a supplier's product is utilized as a mere foundation from which a redesigned product is produced and, which in turn, creates unforeseen and highly dangerous propensities.[454]

The duty to warn may be precipitated if the manufacturer or product supplier can reasonably anticipate that a product will change and become unreasonably dangerous through predictable deterioration on normal use.[455] Thus, an obligation is imposed on the product supplier to know and reasonably anticipate the use and environment of use of products marketed to the public.[456] As a concomitant concept, a product supplier's duty to warn of dangers inherent in any product may extend to removal and replacement of

---

450. *Id.* at 788-89. But in Loughan v. Firestone Tire & Rubber Co., 749 F.2d 1519 (11th Cir. 1985), the manufacturer was not obligated to provide a warning to a mechanic of the dangers and risks of harm in attempting to assemble mismatched tire rim components.

451. Hamilton v. Motor Coach Indus., Inc. 569 S.W. 2d 571 (Tex. Civ. App.—Texarkana 1978, writ ref'd n.r.e.).

452. Elliott v. Century Chevrolet Co., 597 S.W.2d 563 (Tex. Civ. App. — Fort Worth 1980, writ ref'd, n.r.e.); Talley v. City Tank Corp., 158 Ga. App. 130, 279 S.E.2d 264 (1981); Temple v. Wean United, Inc., 50 Ohio St. 2d 317, 364 N.E.2d 267 (Ohio 1977); Shawver v. Roberts Corporation, 90 Wis.2d 672, 280 N.W.2d 226 (Wis. 1979).

453. *See e.g.*, Talley v. City Tank Corp., 158 Ga. App. 130, 279 S.E.2d 264 (1981). *See also*, Rodriguez v. Besser Co. 115 Ariz. App. 454, 565 P.2d 1315, 1320 (1977); Barnes v. Vega Indus. Inc., 234 Kan. 1012, 676 P.2d 761 (1984); Thornhill v. Black Sivalls & Bryson, Inc., 394 So.2d 1189, 1192 (L.A. 1981).

454. Grover Hill Grain Co. v. Baughman-Oster, Inc., 728 F.2d 784 (6th Cir. 1984); Rodriguez v. Besser Co. 115 Ariz. App. 454, 565 P.2d 1315, (Ariz. Ct. App. 1977); Hill v. General Motors Corp. 637 S.W.2d 382 (Mo. Ct. App. 1982); Shawver v. Roberts Corp. 90 Wis.2d 672, 280 N.W.2d 226 (Wis. 1979).

455. *See*, E. G. Hamilton v. Motor Coach Indus., Inc. 569 S.W.2d 571, 576 (Tex. Civ. App. — Texarkana 1978, writ ref'd, n.r.e.).

456. *Id.*

component parts as part of regular maintenance and servicing of the product.[457] Under these circumstances, the product supplier may be obligated to provide clear and adequate warnings on the equipment advising maintenance personnel as well as other users concerning the consequences of improper maintenance that creates an unreasonably dangerous risk of harm.[458] Excessive dangers of significant magnitude preventable by appropriate warnings or instructions for safe use determine the parameters of a product supplier's duty.[459]

4. *Defect as Basis of a Negligence Action.* A negligence action based on a product-related injury requires different proof than a strict tort liability action. Though negligence and strict tort liability share common elements, each represents a separate theory of recovery.[460] Even if the basis of the claim involves a defective design, a cause of action based on strict tort liability does not necessarily include a claim for negligence.

The submission of strict tort liability for a defectively designed product, therefore, does not justify excluding submission of the elements of a negligence action. When evidence adduced at trial warrants, the failure to submit a negligence claim along with a strict tort liability action may constitute error.[461]

---

457. Stewart v. Scott-Kitz Miller Co. 626 P.2d 329 (Okla. Ct. App. 1981); Bich v. General Electric Co. 27 Wash. App. 25, 614 P.2d 1323 (Wash. App. 1980).

458. In Bich v. General Electric Company, 27 Wash. App. 25, 614 P.2d 1323, 1328 (1980), plaintiff, an electrician, replaced a GE fuse housed in a GE transformer with a fuse manufactured by Westinghouse. Plaintiff was injured when the Westinghouse fuse exploded because it was slightly larger in diameter and there was no warning not to substitute one manufacturer's fuse with another. The Court observed that "[i]t would have been a simple and inexpensive matter for GE to have included on its fuses a warning not to substitute fuses or to have given information regarding the time-delay characteristics of its fuses." *Id.* at 1328. An almost identical approach was adopted by the Houston court in Pearson v. Hevi-Duty Electric Co. 618 S.W.2d 784 (Tex. Civ. App. — Houston [1st Dist.] 1981, writ ref'd, n.r.e.).

459. *See generally*, Hill v. General Motors Corp., 637 S.W. 382 (Mo. Ct. App. 1981).

460. Syrie v. Knoll Int'l, 748 F.2d 304 (5th Cir. 1984); Foster v. Ford Motor Co., 616 F.2d 1304 (5th Cir. 1980); Gonzales v. Caterpillar Tractor Co., 571 S.W.2d 867 (Tex. 1978); Rourke v. Garza, 530 S.W.2d 794 (Tex. 1975).

461. In Syrie v. Knoll Int'l, 748 F.2d 304 (5th Cir. 1984) plaintiff was injured when the back of a teller stool on which she was seated fell and the stool rolled out from under her. The plaintiff asserted that the chair was defectively designed. The court submitted strict tort liability but refused to submit negligence. In reversing the trial court judgment for failure to submit negligence despite a jury finding of no defect, the Fifth Ciruit stated that, "[w]e hold that the issue of Knoll's conduct was raised, that the proffered evidence should

B. *Unreasonably Dangerous*

An essential element of a strict tort liability action is proof that the defective condition of the product rendered it unreasonably dangerous.[462] Texas courts have emphasized the need to establish that the defective condition rendered the condition unreasonably dangerous as a separate element of proof.[463] It is essentially impossible, however, to delineate unreasonableness of the danger from the defective nature of the product. Any analysis of the unreasonable danger produced by the defective condition necessarily requires analysis of a specific type of defect involved.

In cases involving a manufacturing defect in a product, the unreasonably dangerous requirement is separable from proof of the defect. Defect is equated with failure of the product to conform to the design specification of the manufacturer.[464] The unreasonableness of the danger, however, depends on other factors, including the reasonable expectations of the consumer possessing knowledge of the characteristics common to the product in the community as well as the expectation of the manufacturer.[465] Thus, in cases involving flaws, the two elements of defect and unreasonable danger are capable of individualized proof. Surprisingly, the unreasonably dangerous element has all but been ignored in the manufacturing defect cases.[466] Generally, the danger is readily apparent in a product containing a manufacturing flaw. In these type cases, the manufacturer has simply failed to comply with even its own standards and such failure subsequently causes harm to the ultimate user of

---

have been admitted, and that a negligence instruction was justified." *Id.* at 309.

462. Reyes v. Wyeth Labs, Inc., 498 F.2d 1264, 1273 (5th Cir. 1974), *cert. denied*, 419 U.S. 1096 (1974); Borel v. Fibreboard Paper Prods. Corp., 493 F.2d 1076, 1083 (5th Cir. 1973), *cert. denied*, 419 U.S. 869 (1974); Acord v. General Motors Corp. 669 S.W.2d 111 (Tex. 1984); Turner v. General Motors Corp. 584 S.W.2d 844 (Tex. 1979); Armstrong Rubber Co. v. Urguidez, 570 S.W. 374 (Tex. 1978); Miller v. Bock Laundry Machine Co. 568 S.W.2d 648 (Tex. 1977).

463. *See, e.g.*, Eli Lilly & Co. v. Casey, 472 S.W.2d 598, 599 (Tex. Civ. App. — Eastland 1971, writ ref'd, n.r.e.).

464. *See generally*, Holford, *The Limits Of Strict Liability For Product Design and Manufacture*, 52 TEX. L. REV. 81, 82 (1973).

465. RESTATEMENT (SECOND) OF TORTS § 402A (1965).

466. *See, e.g.*, Crump v. Clark Equip. Co., 481 F.2d 667 (5th Cir. 1973); Darryl v. Ford Motor Co. 440 S.W.2d 630 (Tex. 1969); Bell Aerospace Corp. v. Anderson, 478 S.W.2d 191 (Tex. Civ. App. — El Paso 1972, writ ref'd, n.r.e.); Barnett v. Ford Motor Co. 463 S.W.2d 33 (Tex. Civ. App. — Waco 1970, no writ).

the product.[467]

Defectively designed products involve a different consideration. Proof of defective design necessarily involves proof that the product is unreasonably dangerous.[468] This is clearly articulated by the Texas Supreme Court in the landmark opinion of *Turner v. General Motors Corporation.*[469] In *Turner*, the Texas Supreme Court declared that defectively designed means unreasonably dangerous and defined unreasonably dangerous to mean "a product that is unreasonably dangerous as designed, taking into consideration the utility of the product and the risk involved in its use."[470] The risk versus utility balancing test for a defective design was reaffirmed by the Texas Supreme Court in *Acord v. General Motors Corporation.*[471] Essentially, the defective condition of the design and the unreasonable danger presented by that defect are synonymous and are evaluated as one element. Articulated differently, a design cannot be considered defective unless it renders the product unreasonably dangerous. The courts have repeatedly reflected the perspective that the defective condition of product is not separable from its unreasonably dangerous condition.[472]

Defective marketing likewise is essentially an issue of the unreasonableness of the danger posed by the failure to warn or provide instructions for safe use. In *Reyes v. Wyeth Laboratories, Inc.*,[473] which involved the marketing of a drug, the Fifth Circuit

---

467. *See, e.g.*, McKisson v. Sales Affiliates, Inc., 416 S.W.2d 787 (Tex. 1967); Shamrock Fuel and Oil Sales, Co. v. Tunks, 416 S.W.2d 779 (Tex. 1967); Waller v. Coca Cola Bottlers Ass'n. 523 S.W.2d 306, 308 (Tex. Civ. App. — Houston [1st Dist.] 1975, no writ); Coca Cola Bottling Co. v. Hobart, 423 S.W.2d 118, 122 (Tex. Civ. App. — Houston [14th Dist.] 1967, writ ref'd, n.r.e.).

468. *See, e.g.*, Rourke v. Garza, 530 S.W.2d 794, 799 (Tex. 1975); Mitchell v. Fruehauf Corp., 568 F.2d 1139 (5th Cir. 1978); Turner v. General Motors Corp., 584 S.W.2d 844 (Tex. 1979).

469. 584 S.W.2d 844 (Tex. 1979).

470. *Id.* at 846-47 n.l.

471. 669 S.W.2d 111 (Tex. 1984).

472. Webb v. Rodgers Mach. Mfg. Co., 750 F.2d 368 (5th Cir. 1985); Davidson v. Stanadyne, Inc., 718 F.2d 1334 (5th Cir. 1983); Carter v. Massy-Ferguson, Inc., 716 F.2d 344 (5th Cir. 1983); Acord v. General Motors Corp., 669 S.W.2d 111 (Tex. 1984); Duncan v. Cessna Aircraft Co., 665 S.W.2d 414 (Tex. 1984); Fleishman v. Guadiano, 651 S.W.2d 730 (Tex. 1983); Kindred v. Con/Chem Inc., 650 S.W.2d 61 (Tex. 1983); Boatland of Houston, Inc. v. Bailey, 609 S.W.2d 743 (Tex. 1980); Turner v. General Motors Corp., 584 S.W.2d 844 (Tex. 1979) *See also*, Arthur v. Avon Inflatables, Ltd., 156 Cal. App. 3d 401, 203 Cal. Rptr. 1 (1984).

473. 498 F.2d 1264 (5th Cir. 1974), *cert. denied*, 419 U.S. 1096 (1974).

concluded that "defective condition has no meaning independent of 'unreasonably dangerous'; the two terms are essentially synonymous."[474]

The *Restatement* defines unreasonably dangerous as "dangerous to an extent beyond what which would be contemplated by the ordinary consumer who purchases the product with the ordinary knowledge common to the community as to its characteristics."[475] This standard for "unreasonably dangerous" has been adopted in Texas as a standard for manufacturing defects and marketing defect cases. The reasonable consumer expectation test has been rejected in the design defect cases in favor of a balancing of the risk against utility standard.[476] This differentiation in standards between design defects and other defects under strict tort liability is attributable to the fact that the average layman possesses little or no expectation regarding design configuration of products. For this reason, the unreasonably dangerous element of the *Restatement* assumes a significant importance in the strict tort liability doctrine as applied in Texas.

Some jurisdictions have abrogated the requirement of establishing that a defective condition rendered the product unreasonably dangerous.[477] This is illustrated in the landmark opinion of *Cronin v. J.B.E. Olson Corp.*[478] In this case, a bread delivery truck collided with another vehicle and, as a result, an aluminum safety hasp designed to hold the bread trays broke and caused the trays to fly forward into the driver. The California court concluded that the element of unreasonably dangerous defect was not a prerequisite under the *Greenman* rationale.[479] The California court further noted that by requiring the plaintiff to establish that the defect rendered the product unreasonably dangerous integrated the flavor

---

474. *Id.* at 1272.

475. RESTATEMENT (SECOND) OF TORTS, § 402A (1965).

476. There exists no reasonable consumer expectation with respect to the design of a product. Consequently, the Texas Supreme Court formulated the risk versus harm balancing standard for evaluating design defect. Turner v. General Motors Corp., 584 S.W.2d 844 (Tex. 1979). This has been reaffirmed in Acord v. General Motors Corp., 669 S.W.2d 111 (Tex. 1984); Kindred v. Con/Chem, Inc. 650 S.W.2d 61 (Tex. 1983); Boatland of Houston v. Bailey, 609 S.W.2d 743 (Tex. 1980).

477. *See, e.g.,* Cronin v. J. B. E. Olson Corp., 8 Cal.3d 121, 501 P.2d 1153, 104 Cal. Rptr. 433 (1972); (overruled) (1973); Berkebile v. Brantly Helicopter Corp., 462 Pa. 83, 337 A.2d 893, 898 (1975).

478. 8 Cal. 3d 121, 501 P.2d 1153, 1162, 104 Cal. Rptr. 433 (1972).

479. 501 P.2d at 1162.

of negligence was integrated into a strict tort liability action. The overwhelming number of jurisdictions, however, have adopted the *Restatement* elements of a strict tort liability action.[480] An essential element, therefore, is proof that the defective condition of a product rendered the product unreasonably dangerous to the user.[481] These jurisdictions recognize that proof of the unreasonably dangerous element is essential to preclude the imposition of insurer status on the product supplier.[482] Contrary to the California concern that the unreasonably dangerous requirement resurrects the shadow of negligence, the element merely acknowledges that the product possesses potential for harm that exceeds society's normal and reasonable expectations.

C. Causation

In any action under Section 402A, the defective and unreasonably dangerous condition of a product must constitute a producing cause of the injury.[483] Circumstantial evidence is sufficient to establish causation.[484] Producing cause is defined to mean "an efficient, exciting, contributing cause which, in a natural sequence, produced the injuries or damages complained of, if any."[485] Proximate cause, on the other hand, adds the additional element of foreseeability—a negligence concept.[486] Manufacturing and design de-

480. *See generally*, Wade, *On Product Design Defects and Their Actionability*, 33 VAND. L. REV. 551 (1980); Birmbaun, *Unmasking the Test for Design Defect: From Negligence [to Warranty] to Strict Liability to Negligence*, 33 VAND. L. REV. 593 (1980); Edgar, *Product Liability in Texas*, 11 TEX. TECH. L. REV. 23 (1979).

481. Reyes v. Wyeth Labs, Inc., 498 F.2d 1264, 1273 (5th Cir. 1974); Borel v. Fibreboard Paper Prod. Corp., 493 F.2d 1076, 1087 (5th Cir. 1973), *cert. denied*, 419 U.S. 869 (1974); Matthews v. Campbell Soup Co., 380 F. Supp. 1061, 1063 (S.D. Tex. 1974); Helicoid Gage Div. of Am. Chain & Cable Co. v. Howell, 511 S.W.2d 573, 577 (Tex. Civ. App.—Houston [14th Dist.] 1974, writ ref'd n.r.e.); Carroll v. Ford Motor Co., 462 S.W.2d 57, 61 (Tex. Civ. App.—Houston [14th Dist.] 1970, no writ); Coca-Cola Bottling Co. v. Hobart, 423 S.W.2d 118, 123 (Tex. Civ. App.—Houston [14th Dist.] 1967, writ ref'd n.r.e.).

482. *Id.*

483. C.A. Hoover & Son v. O. M. Franklin Serum Co., 444 S.W.2d 596, 598 (1969). Producing rather than proximate cause is prescribed by RESTATEMENT (SECOND) OF TORTS, Section 402A (1965).

484. *See* Morgan v. Compugraphic Corp., 675 S.W.2d 729 (Tex. 1984).

485. This definition of producing cause was approved in Rourke v. Garza, 530 S.W.2d 794, 801 (Tex. 1975). It continues as the appropriate test in strict tort liability. *See* Acord v. General Motors Corp., 669 S.W.2d 111 (Tex. 1984); Kindred v. Con/Chem, Inc., 650 S.W.2d 61 (Tex. 1983); Boatland of Houston, Inc. v. Bailey, 609 S.W.2d 743 (Tex. 1980).

486. Reyes v. Wyeth Labs, Inc., 498 F.2d 1264, 1280 (5th Cir. 1974), *cert. denied*, 419

fect cases require producing cause rather than proximate cause.[487] Though marketing defect is also submitted in terms of producing cause, the additional element of foreseeability of the specific risks of harm as a predicate to a duty to warn or provide instructions for safe use inculcates a form of foreseeability into the cause of action.[488]

The issue of causation is generally a question for the trier of fact.[489] A fact issue on causation is established when: (1) general experience and common sense enable a layman fairly to determine the causal relationship between the event and the condition; (2) when scientific principles, established by expert testimony, prove a traceable nexus of causation between the defective condition and the injury producing event; and (3) when probable causal relationship is established by expert testimony.[490] As an example, in *Travenol Labs, Inc. v. Bandy Labs, Inc.*,[491] the plaintiff instituted a strict tort liability action against the manufacturer and seller of

---

U. S. 1096 (1974); Rourke v. Garza, 530 S.W.2d 794 (Tex. 1975); Technical Chem. Co. v. Jacobs, 480 S.W.2d 602, 604 (Tex. 1972), noted in 50 TEX. L. REV. 577 (1972); C. A. Hoover & Son v. O. M. Franklin Serum Co., 444 S.W.2d 596, 598 (Tex. 1969); Helicoid Gage Div. of Am. Chain & Cable Co. v. Howell, 511 S.W.2d 573, 575 (Tex. Civ. App.—Houston [14th Dist.] 1974, writ ref'd n.r.e.); Procter & Gamble Mfg. Co. v. Langley, 422 S.W.2d 773, 778 (Tex. Civ. App.—Dallas 1967, writ dism'd).

487. Rourke v. Garza, 530 S.W.2d 794, 801 (Tex. 1975); Turner v. General Motors Corp., 584 S.W.2d 844 (Tex. 1979).

488. As a predicate to a duty to provide a warning or instruction for safe use, plaintiff must establish that the product supplier knew or, by the application of reasonably available scientific information, should have known of the risk of harm and provided a warning. Reyes v. Wyeth Laboratories, 498 F.2d 1264 (5th Cir,. 1974), *cert. denied*, 419 U.S. 1096 (1974); Borel v. Fibreboard Paper Products, Inc., 493 F.2d 1076 (5th Cir. 1973), *cert. denied*, 419 U.S. 869 (1974); Bristol-Myers Co. v. Gonzales, 561 S.,W.2d 801 (Tex. 1978); RESTATEMENT (SECOND) OF TORTS, Section 402A, comment j (1965). Blockwell Burner Co. v. Cerda, 664 S.W. 2d 512 (Tex. App.—San Antonio 1982 writ ref'd n.r.e.); Ragsdale Bros., Inc. v. Margo — S.W. 2d — (Tex. App.—San Antonio 1985, no writ) (strict liability does not excuse proof that the defect caused the injury).

489. Davidson v. Stanadyne, Inc., 718 F.2d 1334 (5th Cir.1983); Page v. Barko Hydraulics, 673 F.2d 134 (5th Cir. 1982); Acord v. General Motors Corp., 669 S.W.2d 111 (Tex. 1984); Turner v. General Motors Corp., 584 S.W.2d 844 (Tex. 1978); Pearson v. Hevi-Duty Electric, 618 S.W.2d 784 (Tex. Civ. App.—Houston [1st Dist.] 1981, writ ref'd n.r.e.).

490. Travenol Labs, Inc. v. Bandy Labs, Inc., 608 S.W.2d 308 (Tex. Civ. App.—Waco 1980, writ ref'd n.r.e.). There must be a causal nexus between the failure to warn and the accident. *See, e.g.*, Bragg v. Foretravel Inc., 652 F.2d 39 (10th Cir. 1981) (applying Texas law); Gross v. Black & Decker, 695 F.2d 858 (5th Cir. 1983); Conti v. Ford Motor Co., 743 F.2d 195 (3d Cir. 1984); Johnson v. Jones-Blair Paint Co., 607 S.W.2d 305 (Tex. Civ. App. - Eastland 1980, writ ref'd n.r.e.). *But see* Omark Indus. Inc. v. Alewine, 171 Ga. App. 207, 319 S.E.2d 24 (1984).

491. 608 S.W.2d 308 (Tex. Civ. App.—Waco 1980, writ ref'd n.r.e.).

the gloves for bacterial contamination which occurred when rabies vaccine passed through the gloves into the hands of the plaintiff administering the vaccine. Concluding that causation depended upon whether the pinholes in the glove caused the contamination, the court observed:

> The necessary evaluation of scientific principles and problems related to the processing of plaintiff's vaccine and the nature and origin of the contaminants made the case a proper one for the reception of explanations and opinions of experts on the issue of causation.[492]

In marketing cases (failure to warn or to instruct in safe use) a presumption is created that the ultimate user would have read and heeded the warning related to the risk of harm involved in use of the product.[493] This presumption is rebuttable.[494] Conversely, an adequate warning creates a presumption that the product user will heed and comply with all reasonable warnings and instructions for safe use.[495]

The failure to warn must be causally related to the accident that occurred.[496] The failure of the plaintiff to establish a causal

---

492. *Id.* at 312.

493. Restatement (Second) of Torts, § 402A, comment j (1965). *See generally*, Webb v. Rodgers Mach. Mfg. Co., 750 F.2d 368 (5th Cir. 1985); Technical Chemical Co. v. Jacobs, 480 S.W.2d 602 (Tex. 1972). *See also* Ragsdale Bros., Inc. v. Margo ___ S.W. 2d ___ (Tex. App.—San Antonio 1985, no writ); Rawlings Sporting Goods Co. v. Daniels, 619 S.W.2d 435 (Tex. App.—Waco 1981, writ ref'd n.r.e.); Petty v. U.S. 740 F.2d 1428 (8th Cir. 1984); Williams v. Lederle Laboratories, 591 F. Supp. 381 (S.D. Ohio 1984); Nissen Trampoline Co. v. Terre Haute First Nat'l Bank, 332 N.E.2d 820, 826 (Ind. App. 1975), *rev'd on other grounds*, 265 Ind. 457, 358 N.E.2d 974 (1976); Wolfe v. Ford Motor Co., 6 Mass. App. 346, 376 N.E.2d 143 (Mass. App. 1978); Menard v. Newhall, 135 Vt. 53, 373 A.2d 505 (1977).

494. In Technical Chemical Co. v. Jacobs, 480 S.W.2d 602, 606 (Tex. 1972), the Texas Supreme Court noted the presumption that an adequate warning would have averted the injury producing event may be rebutted by evidence that the user was blind, illerate, intoxicated at the time of use, lax in judgment, or totally irresponsible. *Accord* Ragsdale Bros., Inc. v. Margo ___ S.W. 2d ___ (Tex. App.—San Antonio 1985, no writ).

495. Restatement (Second) of Torts, Section 402A, comment j (1965); Grover Hill Grain Co. v. Baughman-Oster Inc. 728 F.2d 784 (6th Cir. 1984); Harrison v. Flota Mercante Grancolombiana, S.A., 577 F.2d 968 (5th Cir. 1978); Cobb Heating and Air Condition Co. v. Hertron Chem. Co., 139 Ga. App. 803, 229 S.E.2d 681 (1976). Morever, evidence that demonstrates that notwithstanding the absence of a warning, the user would still have purchased or used the product nullifies a causal relationship between breach of the duty to warn and the resulting injury. American Motors Corp. v. Ellis, 403 So.2d 459 (Fla. Dist. Ct. App. 1981); Dugan v. Sears, Roebuck & Co., 454 N.E.2d 64 (Ill. App. 1983).

496. *See, e.g.*, Greiner v. Volkswagenwerk, A.G., 429 F. Supp. 495 (E.D. Pa. 1977) (plaintiff required to establish he would not have purchased car in the face of a warning of

nexus between the failure to warn and the injury-prodcing event is fatal to recovery.

1.02 Section 402B

A. Background and General Basis for Section 402B

Undoubtedly one of the most misunderstood concepts of tort liability involves the noncontractual public express warranty characterized as innocent misrepresentation. Perhaps much of the underlying confusion and misunderstanding has been precipitated by the characterization of an essentially *ex contractu* cause of action as *ex delicto* in nature.[497]

Relying on the concept of noncontractual warranty, the American Law Institute in 1965 formulated Section 402B of the *Restatement (Second) Of Torts*[498] Section 402B provides that a seller of chattels, who makes to the public a misrepresentation of a material fact concerning the character or quality of a chattel, is liable for physical harm to a consumer caused by his justifiable reliance

---

the propensity of the vehicle to overturn in a sharp steering maneuver); Rogers v. Unimac Co., 115 Ariz. 304, 565 P.2d 181 (1977) (plaintiff admitted that if the brake on the washer basket had worked properly, even though no warning was attached, he would not have attempted to stop the spinning basket with his hand); Cunningham v. Charles Pfizer & Co., 532 P.2d 1377 (Okla. 1975) (15-year-old child who contracted polio after taking Type I vaccine would still have taken the vaccine with knowledge of the dangers that would have been communicated by an adequate warning of the potential side effects); Salk v. Alpine Ski Shop, Inc., 115 R.I. 309, 342 A.2d 622 (1975) (plaintiff was required to establish that he would not have purchased the particular skis that were involved in the accident if he had been warned of the propensity of the binders not to release under certain conditions); Johnson v. Jones-Blair Paint Co., 607 S.W.2d 305 (Tex. Civ. App.—Eastland 1980, writ ref'd n.r.e.) (product supplier not liable for failing to warn where evidence demonstrated that the paint was not the product that exploded and caused injury).

497. *See generally*, Sales, *The Innocent Misrepresentations Doctrine: Strict Tort Liability Under Section 402B*, 16 Hous. L. Rev. 239 (1979).

498. Restatement (Second) of Torts, § 402B (1965), provides that:

One engaged in the business of selling chattels who, by advertising, labels, or otherwise, makes to the public a misrepresentation of a material fact concerning the character or quality of a chattel sold by him is subject to liability for physical harm to a consumer of the chattel caused by justifiable reliance upon the misrepresentation, even though

(a) it is not made fraudulently or negligently, and

(b) the consumer has not bought the chattel from or entered into any contractual relations with the seller.

In Nugent v. Utica Cutlery Co., 636 S.W.2d 805, 808 (Tex. App.—San Antonio 1982, writ dism'd) the court outlined the elements of a § 402B cause of action. The court enumerated six separate elements that comprise a § 402B action.

upon the misrepresentation, even though the misrepresentation was not made fraudulently or negligently and the consumer was not in contractual privity with the seller.[499]

Though strict tort liability imposed on sellers for innocent misrepresentation of material facts constitutes a corollary of the strict tort liability doctrine promulgated in Section 402A, this doctrine presents a unique and totally distinct cause of action.[500] While Section 402A imposes liability on suppliers of defective products unreasonably dangerous for their intended or reasonably foreseeable use,[501] in contrast, the representational theory of Section 402B requires neither a defective product nor a product that is unreasonably dangerous.[502] Under Section 402B, an individual need merely establish that a product supplied under a misrepresentation of a material fact relied upon by the purchaser or user caused physical harm to the consumer.[503]

The development of a cause of action for recovery against a seller based on the noncontractual express warranty of innocent misrepresentation has been engulfed in unnecessary confusion and misunderstanding. Much of the confusion has evolved from the

---

499. Colorado recently adopted Section 402B in American Safety Equip. Corp., v. Winkler, 640 P.2d 216, 220 (Colo. 1982) (en banc).

500. As noted in American Safety Equip. Corp. v. Winkler, 640 P.2d 216 (Colo. 1982) (en banc), "Section 402A imposes liability on the supplier or manufacturer of a defective product which is unreasonably dangerous for its intended or reasonably foreseeable uses to the user or consumer. . . . In contrast, the representational theory of Section 402B requires neither a defective product nor one that is unreasonably dangerous." *Id.* at 219.

501. RESTATEMENT § 402A provides in pertinent part that "[o]ne who sells any product in a defective condition unreasonably dangerous to the user or consumer or to his property is subject to liability for physical harm thereby caused to the ultimate user or consumer or to his property . . . ." *See generally*, Greenman v. Yuba Power Products, Inc., 59 Cal.2d 57, 377 P.2d 897, 27 Cal.Rptr. 697 (1962). *See also*, Suvada v. White Motor Co. 32 Ill.2d 612, 210 N.E.2d 182 (1965); Shamrock Fuel & Oil Sales Co. v. Tunks, 416 S.W.2d 779, 781 (Tex. 1967); McKisson v. Sales Affiliates, Inc., 416 S.W.2d 787, 788-89 (Tex. 1967). Some jurisdictions have abrogated the unreasonably dangerous requirement of the RESTATEMENT. *See, e.g.*, Cronin v. J.B.E. Olson Corp., 8 Cal.3d 121, 501 P.2d 1153, 104 Cal. Rptr. 433 (1972).

502. American Safety Equip. Cor. v. Winkler, 640 P.2d 216, 219 (Colo. 1982) (en banc); Ford Motor Co. v. Lonon, 217 Tenn. 400, 398 S.W.2d 240, 250 (1966). Some jurisdictions refuse to acknowledge this critical distinction. In Bristol-Myers Co. v. Gonzales, 548 S.W.2d 416, 428 (Tex. Civ. App.—Corpus Christi 1976, *rev'd on other grounds*, 561 S.W.2d 801 (Tex. 1978), the court declared that Section 402B was adopted to protect persons injured by defective products. *See also*, Hawkensen v. A. H. Robbins Co., 595 F. Supp. 1290, 1301 (D. Colo. 1984).

503. Nugent v. Utica Cutlery Co., 636 S.W.2d 805, 809 (Tex. App.—San Antonio 1982, writ dism'd) "[M]aterial fact and justifiable reliance are essential issues within a series of interdependent issues . . ." *Id.* at 809.

form of warranty that underlies the basis for recovery under Section 402B.

The concept of a representational cause of action emerged in the late 1600s. Relying on a trespass on the case characterization, the English Courts declared that an action existed for breach of an express warranty of a material fact, relied upon in the purchase of a chattel, that later proved to be false.[504] Consequently, a species of strict liability evolved based on an express warranty of the quality and condition of chattels.[505] Tort, rather than contract, constituted the basis of the warranty action.[506] Later, however, the courts perceived that breach of an express warranty rising from a personal contract of sale really represented a cause of action based on assumpsit.[507] Thus, during the following century, breach of warranty, whether express or implied in law, legally supported an action sounding in contract.[508] The tort character of express warranty, both figuratively and literally, was obliterated.[509]

The concept of a representational tort based on express assurances of quality in a product was finally conceptualized and given legitimacy in several landmark decisions, the seminal case being *Baxter vs. Ford Motor Company*.[510] Relying on a representation by the manufacturer that all new Ford vehicles were fabricated with shatterproof glass windshields, plaintiff purchased a new Ford from the retail dealer.[511] While plaintiff was operating the vehicle, a pebble struck and shattered the windshield, causing plaintiff blindness in one eye. In the original appeal, the Washington Supreme Court concluded that the plaintiff was entitled to rely on

504. Medina v. Stoughton, 1 Lord Raym. 593, 91 Eng. Rep. 1297 (Ex. 1700).

505. Cross v. Garnet, 3 Mod. 261, 87 Eng. Rep. 172 (Ex. 1689). The court in Beck v. Spindler, 256 Minn. 543, 560, 99 N.W.2d 670, 681 (1959), stated that it was only an accident that led to the classification of breach of warranty as a contract action.

506. Cross v. Garnet, 3 Mod. 261, 87 Eng. Rep. 172 (Ex. 1689).

507. Stuart v. Wilkins, 1 Dougl. 18, 99 Eng. Rep. 15 (Ex. 1778).

508. *See, e.g.*, Rasmus v. A.O. Smith Corp., 158 F. Supp. 70, 78 (N.D. Iowa 1958); Salvadore v. Atlantic Steel Boiler Co., 457 Pa. 24, 319 A.2d. 903 (1974).

509. The court in Markovich v. McKesson & Robbins, Inc., 106 Ohio App. 265, 149 N.E.2d 181 (1958), acknowledging the tort nature of noncontractual warranties authorized recovery for loss of plaintiff's hair following use of a home permanent solution that was represented to be totally safe. Similarly, in Hansen v. Firestone Tire & Rubber Co., 276 F.2d 254, 257 (6th Cir. 1960), the Sixth Circuit emphasized that at common law an action predicated on breach of warranty sounded in tort rather than contract.

510. 168 Wash. 456, 12 P.2d 409, *adhered to on rehearing*, 168 Wash. 465, 15 P.2d. 1118 (1932), *on second appeal*, 179 Wash. 123, 35 P.2d. 1090 (1934).

511. 168 Wash. at 457, 12 P.2d. at 410.

the manufacturer's representations notwithstanding lack of privity between them.[512] By this action, the Court formulated a doctrine that proved to be the harbinger of Section 402B.[513] The Court declared that a seller who misrepresented a material fact concerning a product relied upon by the purchaser was strictly liable for injuries by the failure of the product to conform to the represented facts.[514] The same Court, on a second appeal, stated in pertinent part that, "[i]f a person states as true material facts susceptible of knowledge to one who relies and acts thereon to his injury, if the representations are false, it is immaterial that he did not know they were false, or that he believed them to be true."[515]

The conceptual characterization formulated in *Baxter* was adopted by the Ohio Supreme Court in *Rogers vs. Toni Home Permanent Co.*[516] Plaintiff purchased a home permanent set based on representations contained in advertisements that the product was "safe" and "harmless".[517] When the plaintiff applied the permanent lotion, her hair began falling out and she developed severe scalp irritation. The Ohio Supreme Court imposed liability on the manufacturer for misrepresentations of the performance capabilities of the home permanent. The Court observed that, "[t]he warranties made by the manufacturer in his advertisements and by the labels on his products are inducements to the ultimate consumers, and the manufacturer ought to be held to strict accountability to any consumer who buys the product in reliance on such representations . . . . "[518]

The last of the landmark decisions pioneering strict tort liability for noncontractual warranties is *Randy Knitwear Inc. v. American Cyanamid Co.*[519] Randy Knitwear, a manufacturer of children's clothing, purchased large quantities of the fabric that had

---

512. *Id.* at 463, 12 P.2d at 412.

513. RESTATEMENT, § 402B, comment c, acknowledges that *Baxter* established the theory of strict liability for public misrepresentations concerning the character or quality of a product designed to induce the public to purchase the seller's product.

514. 168 Wash. at 462, 12 P.2d at 412.

515. 179 Wash. at 125, 35 P.2d at 1092. *See also* Bahlman v. Hudson Motor Car Co., 290 Mich. 683, 288 N.W. 309 (1939), in which a vehicle represented to possess "a seamless safety top" actually contained jagged seams that injured the plaintiff during the course of an overturn.

516. 167 Ohio St. 244, 147 N.E.2d 612 (1958).

517. *Id.* at 245, 147 N.E.2d at 614.

518. *Id.* at 249, 147 N.E.2d at 615-16.

519. 11 N.Y.2d 5, 181 N.E.2d 399, 226 N.Y.S.2d 363 (1962).

been treated with a chemical known as Cyana manufactured by American Cyanamid Company. Cyana was advertised in trade journals and phamplets as a chemical that would prevent shrinkage or stretching of fabrics from normal washing.[520] When the fabric treated with Cyana was manufactured into garments, ordinary washing caused the clothing to lose shape and shrink. Adopting the *Baxter* rationale, the New York Court of Appeals imposed strict liability on the manufacturer for material public representations which were relied upon by the ultimate consumer and which proved to be false.[521]

The courts in *Baxter*, *Rogers*, and *Randy Knitwear* acknowledged that the world of merchandising had progressed technologically, thus being transformed from a personal contractual relationship into an impersonal world of mass advertising, labeling, and impersonal communications touting the excellent qualities and superlative characteristics of various products.[522] Under these circumstances, the courts deemed as anachronistic the characterization of an innocent misrepresentation inducing the purchase of a product as sounding in contract. The modern approach to merchandising precipitated judicial rejection of the contractual trappings of the express warranty and a recharacterization of publicly communicated innocent misrepresentations as tortious in nature.[523]

It was inevitable that, with the development and evolution of

---

520. *Id.* at 10, 181 N.E.2d at 400, 226 N.Y.2d at 365.

521. *Id.* at 14, 181 N.E.2d at 404, 226 N.Y.S.2d at 369.

522. Randy Knitwear, Inc. v. American Cyanamid Co., 11 N.Y.2d 5, 12, 181 N.E.2d 399, 402, 226 N.Y.S.2d 363, 367 (1962); Rogers v. Toni Home Permanent Co., 167 Ohio St. 244, 248, 147 N.E.2d. 612, 615 (1958); Baxter v. Ford Motor Co., 168 Wash. 456, 462, 12 P.2d 409, 412, (1932). The court in *Randy Knitwear* noted that:

> Manufacturers make extensive use of newspapers, periodicals and other media to call attention, in glowing terms, to the qualities and virtues of their products, and this advertising is directed at the ultimate consumer or at some manufacturer or supplier who is not in privity with them. Equally sanguine representations on packages and labels frequently accompany the article throughout its journey to the ultimate consumer and, as intended, are relied upon by remote purchasers. Under these circumstances, it is highly unrealistic to limit a purchaser's protection to warranties made directly to him by his immediate seller. The protection that he really needs is against the manufacturer whose published representations caused him to make the purchase. 11 N.Y.2d at 12-13, 181 N.E.2d at 402, 226 N.Y.S.2d at 367.

523. 168 Wash. at 462-63, 12 P.2d at 412. Strict liability for misrepresentation of material facts concerning the quality and condition of products is neither designed to nor does it preempt a warranty provided by the law of sales. Benco Plastics, Inc. v. Westinghouse Electric Corp., 387 F. Supp. 772, 785 (E.D. Tenn. 1974).

today's merchandising techniques, theories of liability would evolve to accommodate the harm produced by the system. As small manufacturers developed, refined technology, and expanded into national suppliers, the direct contractual relationship with purchasers disappeared and a wholly new and totally different concept of merchandising developed to deliver products from the manufacturer to the ultimate consumer.[524] Mass advertising assumed an uncommonly important role in influencing public interest in the purchase of products.[525] Marketing rather than engineering departments assumed responsibility for assuring the public of the wonderful qualities of a particular product.[526] Promotional endeavors all too frequently assured qualities not possessed by the product. The ultimate result has been the judicial imposition of strict liability for publicly disseminated innocent misrepresentations ultimately memoralized in Section 402B.

B. Distribution between §402B and Strict Tort Liability under §402A

The landmark decision of *Baxter vs. Ford Motor Company*,[527] and its progeny mark the initial movement that was destined to lead inexorably to the formation of a tort cause of action for innocent public misrepresentation made by sellers of products. The doctrine was promulgated in Section 402B of the *Restatement*:

> One engaged in the business of selling chattels who, by advertising, labels, or otherwise, makes to the public a misrepresentation of a material fact concerning the character or quality of a chattel sold by him is subject to liability for physical harm to a

---

524. *See generally* Klages v. General Ordinance Equipment Co., 240 Pa.Super. 356, 367 A.2d. 304 (1976); Ford Motor Co. v. Lonon, 217 Tenn. 400, 398 S.W.2d. 240 (1966). For a general discussion of the effects of merchandising techniques on children, *see* Philips, *Product Liability for Personal Injury to Minors*, 56 VA. L. REV. 1223, 1237-38 (1970).

525. As stated in American Safety Equip. Corp. v. Winkler, 640 P.2d 216, 221 (Colo. 1982) (en banc), "a manufacturer intends to reap economic benefit from the public representations it makes regarding the character and quality of its products, and must assume the economic consequences for physical harm resulting from misrepresentations it has made about its products." *Id.* at 221.

526. Materiality envisages "a fact which if it [has] been correctly stated or disclosed would have deterred or tended to deter the average [person] from purchasing the [product]." Escott v. Barchris Constr. Corp., 283 F. Supp. 643, 681 (S.D. N.Y. 1968).

527. 168 Wash. 456, 12 P.2d 409, *adhered to on rehearing*, 168 Wash. 465, 15 P.2d 1118 (1932), *on second appeal*, 179 Wash. 123, 35 P.2d 1090 (1934).

> consumer of the chattel caused by justifiable reliance upon the misrepresentation even though (a) it is not made fraudulently or negligently, and (b) the consumer has not bought the chattel from or entered into any contractual relation with the seller.[528]

The essence of Section 402B is a noncontractual and nonconsentual representation possessing a tort nature.[529] The representational doctrine as articulated in the *Restatement* reflects a hybrid doctrine described as a noncontractual express warranty,[530] a concept that has confused both courts and commentators. This representational theory of strict tort liability is predicated on tort as distinguished from contract. To the extent the cause of action reflects contractual warranty features, it is noticeably different from the warranty defined in the law of sales.[531] The usual trappings of a contractual transaction in which a sale is consummated and a product is exchanged are totally absent as well as irrelevant to liability.

Strict tort liability for innocent misrepresentation is totally distinct from the strict tort liability imposed by Section 402A.[532] Under Section 402A, liability depends upon whether a product is defective and unreasonably dangerous,[533] while Section 402B prescribes only that the injured party establish the misrepresenta-

---

528. RESTATEMENT, § 402B. *See generally*, Phillips, *Products Misrepresentation and the Doctrine of Causation*, 2 HOFSTRA L. REV. 561 (1974); Sales, *The Innocent Misrepresentation Doctrine: Strict Tort Liability Under Section 402B*, 16 HOUS. L. REV. 239 (1979).

529. For a general discussion of the nature of this tort, *see*, Hill, *Damages for Innocent Misrepresentation*, 73 COLUM. L. REV. 679, 745 (1973).

530. In Sales, *An Overview of Strict Tort Liability in Texas*, 11 HOUS. L. REV. 1043, 1072 (1974), the author observes that liability is imposed on the basis of noncontractual express warranty.

531. RESTATEMENT, § 402B, *comment d*, provides:

> The difficulties attending the use of the word "warranty" are the same as those involved under § 402A, and comment m under that section is equally applicable here so far as it is pertinent. The liability stated in this Section is liability in tort, and not in contract; and if it is to be called one of "warranty", it is at least a different kind of warranty from that involved in the ordinary sale of goods from the immediate seller to the immediate buyer, and is subject to different rules.

The Illinois Supreme Court in Rozny v. Marul, 43 Ill.2d 54, 250 N.E.2d 656, 660 (1969), noted that this type warranty is a different warranty from that between immediate contracting parties.

532. RESTATEMENT (SECOND) OF TORTS, § 402A, (1965).

533. *See, e.g.*, O.S. Stapley Co. v. Miller, 103 Ariz. 556, 447 P.2d. 248 (1968); Hiigel v. General Motors Corp., 190 Colo. 57, 544 P.2d 983 (1975); Suvada v. White Motor Co., 32 Ill.2d 612, 210 N.E.2d 182 (1965); Webb v. Zern, 422 Pa. 424, 220 A.2d 853 (1966); Rourke v. Garza, 530 S.W.2d 794, 798 (Tex. 1975).

tion of a material fact.[534] Consequently, Section 402B neither focuses nor depends on a defective product, and the fact a product incidentally may be defective or unreasonably dangerous is wholly immaterial to liability.[535] On the other hand, a product, though perfectly designed and manufactured, may create liability if the representation of its quality or condition prove to be inaccurate or untrue. The public assurance of quality in merchandising is the quintessential factor that supports the judicial formulation of liability under Section 402B.[536]

C. Entities to Whom §402 to be Applied

Section 402B extends only to individuals engaged in the regular business of marketing chattels.[537] It is not, however, limited solely to manufacturers. Strict accountability, as envisioned by Section 402B, includes wholesalers, retailers and others in the distributive chain of marketing who are involved in introducing products into the stream of commerce.[538] Therefore, anyone involved in marketing a product is subject to strict liability for public misrepresentations that induce the purchase of a product.

---

534. RESTATEMENT (SECOND) OF TORTS, § 402B, comment b, declares that "the rule stated in this section differs from the rule of strict liability stated in Section 402A, which is a special rule applicable only to sellers of products for consumption and does not depend upon misrepresentation." *Id.* Unfortunately, some courts fail to perceive the distinction that characterizes these two doctrines. *See, e.g.*, Bristol-Myers Co. v. Gonzales, 548 S.W.2d. 416, 428, (Tex. Civ. App.—Corpus Christi 1976), rev'd on *other grounds*, 561 S.W.2d 801 (Tex. 1978). *See also*, Ford Motor Co. v. Lonon, 217 Tenn. 400, 398 S.W.2d 240, 250 (1966).

535. *See* Green, *Strict Liability Under Sections 402A and 402B: A Decade of Litigation*, 54 TEX. L. REV. 1185, 1214 (1976).

536. The court in Klages v. General Ordinance Equip. Corp., 240 Pa. Super. 356, 367 A.2d 304, 310 (1976), compared the similarity of Sections 402A and 402B noting that "[b]oth provisions, therefore, are concerned with the manufacturer's express statement about his product and whether the product in fact conforms to that representation. Once noncompliance is demonstrated, both sections, in effect, impose liability without fault on the manufacturer." *Id.*

537. RESTATEMENT (SECOND) OF TORTS, § 402B, comment e, provides: "The rule stated applies, however, only to those who are engaged in the business of selling such chattels. It has no application to anyone who is not so engaged in business. It does not apply, for example, to a newspaper advertisement published by a private owner of a single automobile who offers it for sale." Thus it seems clear that a private sale between two individuals or an individual's public sale of a single product does not establish liability under Section 402B. Jasper Aviation, Inc. v. McCollum Aviation, Inc., 497 S.W.2d 240, 242 (Tenn. 1972); Ford Motor Co. v. Russell & Smith Ford Co., 474 S.W.2d 549, 559 (Tex. Civ. App.—Houston [14th Dist.] 1971, no writ).

538. RESTATEMENT (SECOND) OF TORTS, § 402B, comment e, (1965).

The marketing requirement implies that the seller, whether manufacturer, retailer or wholesaler, who is to be held strictly accountable actually author or adopt the public misrepresentation that is relied upon by the purchaser. Though it is suggested that sellers in the marketing chain are vicariously liable for public misrepresentations of the manufacturer, the extension of strict liability to a seller in a marketing chain for the unadopted misrepresentations of others is legally and rationally insupportable. Unlike the socioeconomic rationale that undergirds Section 402A, the risk distribution policy for defective products is totally absent in the context of the innocent misrepresentation concept. The product marketed is nondefective and not unreasonably dangerous. The sole basis for imposing strict accountability is a public reliance on an innocently disseminated misrepresentation of a material fact.[539] Consequently, the imposition of strict liability upon the retailer or wholesaler for the unadopted misrepresentation of the manufacturer is illogical and irrational.[540] The mere sale of a product does not imply adoption of the public advertisements and representations made by the manufacturer of the product.

It appears that strict tort liability as defined by Section 402B is extended to encompass a broad category of suppliers such as lessors, bailors, and home developers, provided that (1) the individuals are regularly engaged in the business of supplying products into the channels of commerce and (2) the individuals author or adopt the misrepresentation that induced purchase of the product in the first instance. It is inappropriate, however, to extend strict liability to suppliers who neither issue nor adopt the misrepresentations of others.[541] Though strict tort liability for innocent misrepresentation clearly does not extend to suppliers of services, at least one

---

539. Sales, *The Innocent Misrepresentation Doctrine: Strict Tort Liability Under Section 402B*, 16 Hous. L. Rev. 239, 252 (1979).

540. Ford Motor Co. v. Lonon, 217 Tenn. 400, 398 S.W.2d. 240 (1966), recognized this limitation in affirming the judgment against the manufacturer and in favor of the retailer of a tractor. The court noted that "the jury might reasonably have found that the representations contained in the manufacturer's sales literature were more extensive and detailed than those made by the retailer, and that it was reliance on more complete representations in the sales literature, rather than the oral representations by the retailer, that induced the plaintiff to purchase the defective tractor." 398 S.W.2d at 251. *But see*, Myers v. United States Auto Club, 281 F. Supp. 48 (E.D. Tenn. 1968).

541. 217 Tenn. 400, 398 S.W.2d 240, 251 (1966). In Times Mirror Co. v. Sisk, 122 Ariz. 174, 593 P.2d 924 (Ct. App. 1978), the court noted that the preparer of flight charts showing terrain near an airport was not a product supplier under Section 402B.

decision has suggested that the concept is applicable to professional service providers. In *Rozny v. Marnul*,[542] a surveyor was deemed strictly liable for supplying an inaccurate survey with the notation "[t]his plat of survey carries our absolute guarantee for accuracy."[543] This aberrational decision may be justified on the basis of demonstrated negligence on the part of the surveyor in the preparation of the plat.[544]

D. *Elements of a Cause of Action for §402B*

Strict tort liability formulated by Section 402B involves a misrepresentation of a material fact that justifiably induces the purchase of a product. In the commentary of the *Restatement*, the authors assert that Section 402B applies only to misrepresentations of material facts concerning the quality or character of a product.[545] Statements of opinion, particularly general praise of goods commonly characterized as "sales talk" or "puffery" are not contemplated by Section 402B.[546] This type statement regarding a product is not a material fact within the ambit of Section 402B.[547] Additionally, broad assurances of good quality and general impressions of durability represent a form of loose sales talk and merchandising that does not qualify as a material fact within the intendment of Section 402B.[548] The factual representations contemplated under Section 402B involve significant product characteristics and performance capabilities rather than mere state-

542. 43 Ill.2d 54, 250 N.E.2d 656 (1969).

543. *Id.* at 58, 250 N.E.2d at 658.

544. *Id.* at 66, 250 N.E.2d at 662.

545. RESTATEMENT (SECOND) OF TORTS, § 402B, comment g.

546. RESTATEMENT (SECOND) OF TORTS, § 402B, comment g, states:

> It does not apply to statements of opinion, and in particular, it does not apply to the kind of loose general praise of wares sold which, on the part of the seller, is considered to be 'sales talk,' and is commonly called 'puffing' - as, for example, a statement that an automobile is the best on the market for the price. . . In addition, the fact misrepresented must be a material one, of importance to the normal purchaser, by which the ultimate buyer may justifiably be expected to be influenced in buying the chattel. *Id.*

547. Grinnell v. Charles Pfizer & Co., 274 Cal. App. 2d 424, 79 Cal. Rptr. 369, 378 (1969).

548. Adkins v. Ford Motor Co., 446 F.2d 1105, 1108 (6th Cir. 1971); Heaton v. Ford Motor Co., 248 Or. 467, 435 P.2d 806, 810 (1967); Ford Motor Co. v. Lonon, 217 Tenn. 400, 398 S.W.2d 240, 247 (1966). A simple statement that a product represents the best is nothing more than puffery. Thompson Farms, Inc. v. Corno Feed Prods. 173 Ind. App. 682, 366 N.E.2d 3, 18 (1977); Brown v. Globe Laboratories, 165 Neb. 138, 84 N.W.2d 151, 161 (1957).

ments of opinion and loose general praise.[549]

Specific representations about product defectiveness and performance capability are generally construed as material facts that are calculated to influence purchase of the product. In *Crocker v. Winthrop Laboratories*,[550] the decedent became addicted to the drug known as "Talwin" which had been represented to be non-addictive in nature. The decedent developed a severe addiction to Talwin and was able to obtain prescriptions from several doctors both in Texas and across the Mexican border for this particular drug. As a consequence of prolonged addiction, a subsequent injection of Demorol, as part of the decedent's treatment, caused his death. The manufacturer circulated materials relating to the non-addictive qualities of Talwin but provided no warning of the possibilities of idiosyncratic addiction. It also represented in the *Physician's Desk Reference Book* the "[a]bsence of addiction liability."[551] Affirming liability under Section 402B, the Texas Supreme Court noted that:

> [w]hatever the danger and state of medical knowledge, and however rare the susceptibility of the user, when the drug company positively and specifically represents its products to be free and safe from all dangers of addiction, and when the treating physician relies upon that representation, the drug company is liable when the representation proves to be false and harm results.[552]

The determination of whether a fact is material involves an objective assessment of the nature of the representation. Clearly factual statements that assure a particular characteristic or define the capability and performance limits of a product are material.[553]

---

549. *Compare* Hauter v. Zogarts, 14 Cal. 3rd 104, 534 P.2d 377, 382, 120 Cal. .Rptr. 681, 686 (1975) (representation of the golf training device was completely safe - ball will not hit player - deemed material) *with* Berkebile v. Brantly Helicopter Corp., 462 Pa. 83, 337 A.2d 893, 903 (1975) (representation that a helicopter was "easy to operate" and "you are assured of a safe, dependable helicopter" characterized as general puffery). *See also* Community Television Servs. Inc. v. Dresser Indus. Inc., 586 F.2d 637, 640 (8th Cir. 1978), *cert. denied* 441 U.S. 932 (1979).

550. 514 S.W.2d 429 (Tex. 1974).

551. *Id.* at 430.

552. *Id.* at 433 (*citing* Randy Knitwear, Inc. v. American Cyanamid Co., 11 N.Y.2d 5, 226 N.Y.S.2d 363, 181 N.E.2d 399 (1962), Brown v. Globe Laboratories, 165 Neb. 138, 84 N.W.2d 151 (1957), *and* Rogers v. Toni Home Permanent Co., 167 Ohio St. 244, 147 N.E.2d 612 (1958)).

553. *See, e.g.*, Mannsz v. Machwhyte Co., 155 F.2d 445, 451 (3rd Cir. 1946) (statement

Conversely, assertions of general safety and dependability, and declarations that a product is the best or as good as any other similar product on the market or that a product is easy to use merely represent loose general praise and puffery that does not satisfy the materiality requirement of Section 402B.[554]

The material facts must be express representations; implied representations relating to the quality or condition of a product are not encompassed within the ambit of Section 402B. In *Franks v. National Dairy Products, Corp.*,[555] plaintiff was injured when Red Label shortening manufactured by the defendant exploded as he attempted to drain used grease from a cooker. The plaintiff permitted the cooker to cool before attempting to drain the grease into an empty Red Label shortening can. Though the defendant directed brochures at users suggesting the manner in which the shortening could be used, none of the brochures represented that the product could be used safely without explosion. The plaintiff asserted that under Section 402B, the mere distribution of a product implied that a product would perform its intended and foreseeable uses in a safe manner.[556] Concluding that implied representation is not embraced by Section 402B, the Court observed that:

---

in manual declaring tinsel strength of rope); Hauter v. Zogarts, 14 Cal. 3rd 104, 534 P.2d 377, 120 Cal. Rptr. 861 (1975) (golf training device was "completely safe - ball will not hit player"); Hamon v. Digliani, 148 Conn. 710, 174 A.2d. 294 (1961) (a detergent was "safe for all household tasks"); Bahlman v. Hudson Motor Car Co., 290 Mich. 683, 288 N.W. 309 (1939) (a vehicle possessed a "seamless safety top"); Rogers v. Toni Home Permanent Co., 167 Ohio St. 244, 147 N.E.2d 612 (1958) (a permanent wave solution was "safe and harmless for use"); Klages v. Gen. Ordinance Equip. Corp., 240 Pa. Super 356, 367 A.2d 304 (1976) (mace weapon would "instantly stop assailants in their tracks"); Bristol-Myers Co. v. Gonzales, 561 S.W.2d 801 (Tex. 1978) (the drug Kantrex "in concentrations of 0.25% has been used satisfactorily as an irrigating solution in abscess cavities"); Crocker v. Winthrop Laboratories 514 S.W.2d 429 (Tex. 1974)(Talwin was "nonaddictive" and as harmless as "aspirin"); Baxter v. Ford Motor Co., 168 Wash. 456, 12 P.2d 409 (1932) (windshield was "shatter-proof" glass).

554. *See* Restatement (Second) of Torts, § 402B, comment g. *See also* Hoffman v. A. B. Chance Co., 339 F. Supp. 1385 (N.D. Pa. 1972) (a hydraulic aerial platform offered "unprecedented safety"); Steen v. Southern Cal. Supply Co., 74 Cal. App. 265, 239 P. 1098 (1925) (a caramel dressing was "just as good or perhaps better than any"); Olson v. A. W. Chesterton Co., 256 N.W.2d 530 (N.D. 1977) (a belt dressing was "easy to use"); Silverman v. Samuel Mallinger Co., 375 Pa. 422, 100 A.2d 715 (1953) (glassware is "as good as any one else's ware"); Jack Roach-Bisonnett, Inc. v. Puskar, 417 S.W.2d 262 (Tex. 1967) (a car with power steering and power brakes would "have safe steering and full control" in the event of loss of power).

555. 282 F. Supp. 528 (W.D. Tex. 1968), *aff'd*, 414 F.2d 682 (5th Cir. 1969).

556. *Id.* at 533.

> The language in the Restatement of Torts, particularly in comment "h" to Section 402B, directs our attention to what we normally denominate as express representations, either oral or written. While the illustrations in the section were certainly not intended to be exhaustive, nevertheless, they speak only in terms of express representations.[557]

The rationale for rejecting implied representations for liability under Section 402B is readily apparent. If the presence of a product in the channels of commerce implies a guarantee of absolute safety, then the doctrine of strict tort liability under Section 402A for a defective and unreasonably dangerous product is unnecessary for a recovery. Obviously when strict liability is predicated on an innocent misrepresentation and the misrepresentation is implied merely by the sale of a product, then Section 402B effectively transforms all suppliers into insurers against product caused injuries.[558]

Justifiable reliance on the misrepresentation constitutes the second critical element of a strict liability claim under Section 402B. Unless the misrepresentation of a particular fact reasonably influences the purchase of the product, it is insufficient to impose liability on the maker of the statement.[559] Subjective intent of the seller in making the representation is irrelevant. It is the reasona-

---

557. *Id.*

558. In Frank's v. Nat'l Dairy Prods. Corp., 282 F. Supp. 528, 533-34 (W.D. Tex. 1968), *aff'd*, 414 F.2d 682 (5th Cir. 1969), the court observed that:

> If one adopts the plaintiff's contention that implicit in the presence of a product in the marketplace is the implied guarantee that it will safely do the jobs for which it was intended, then the section 402A requirement that a product not only be dangerous (i.e. unsafe) but unreasonably so has been redefined in terms solely of a representation of safe use; and the section 402A requirement of proof (by direct or circumstantial evidence) of "defective conditions" has been effectively extinguished. At that point, we may well have reached the age in which, at least as to safe use to prevent physical harm to consumers, we have made manufacturers absolute insurers.

559. RESTATEMENT (SECOND) OF TORTS, Section 402B, comment j (1965) declares that:

> The rule here stated applies only where there is justifiable reliance upon the misrepresentation of the seller, and physical harm results because of such reliance, and because of the fact which is misrepresented. It does not apply where the misrepresentation is not known, or there is indifference to it, and it does not influence the purchase or subsequent conduct. At the time, however, the misrepresentation need not be the sole inducement to purchase, or to use the chattel, and it is sufficient that it has been a substantial factor in that inducement.

Unsupportable subjective reliance is inadequate. American Safety Equip. Corp. v. Winkler, 640 P.2d 216, 223 (Colo. 1982) (en banc).

ble objective belief of the purchaser that determines justifiable reliance.[560] Of course, a purchaser's actual knowledge of the quality or condition of a product, though contrary to the representations of the seller, totally nullifies justifiable reliance.[561] Similarly, a purchaser totally unaware of representations contained in advertising materials cannot, as a matter of law, justifiably rely on the misrepresentation to establish liability under Section 402B.[562]

In construing the justifiable reliance requirement, the courts have declared that the requirement is satisfied when a member of the user's immediate family relies upon the material misrepresentations in purchasing the product. For example, in *Hauter v. Zogarts*,[563] plaintiff's mother purchased a golf training device for him. The son relied on representations made by the manufacturer that the device was "Completely Safe. Ball Will Not Hit Player."[564] The court concluded that the son's reliance on the material misrepresentation satisfied the requirement of Section 402B.[565] This requirement may likewise be satisfied when the product was purchased by the employer for the use of an employee,[566]

---

560. Grinnell v. Charles Pfizer & Co., 274 Cal. App. 2d 424, 79 Cal. Rptr. 369 (1969); American Safety Equip. Corp. v. Winkler, 640 P.2d 216, 223 (Colo. 1982) (en banc); Arrow Transp. Co. v. A. O. Smith Co., 75 Wash.2d 843, 454 P.2d 387 (1969);

561. Harris v. Belton, 258 Cal. App. 2d 565, 65 Cal. Rptr. 808 (1968). A purchaser's or user's actual knowledge of the quality or condition of a product, even though contrary to the representation of the seller, totally nullifies any justifiable reliance. American Safety Equip. Corp. v. Winkler, 640 P.2d 216, 222 (Colo. 1982) (en banc).

562. In Arrow Transp. Co. v. A. O. Smith Co., 75 Wash.2d 843, 454 P.2d 387, 390 (1969), though the seller of fifth-wheels represented certain material facts in its brochure and other literature, neither plaintiff nor anyone related to the plaintiff was aware of or read any of the literature prior to the failures. It is arguable, therefore, that an assumption of the risk by the purchaser merely refutes the fact of justifiable reliance. For example, in a prescriptive drug or even an ordinary product purchased by an individual other than the actual user, it is logical to assume that failure of the physician or purchaser to read or even be aware of the misrepresentation precludes liability under Section 402B. *See* Crocker v. Winthrop Laboratories, 514 S.W.2d 429 (Tex. 1974). It has been urged that prior awareness of the representation is necessary so long as representation constitutes a substantial part of the consideration of the bargain. *See* Phillips, *Product Misrepresentation and the Doctrine of Caustion*, 2 Hofstra L. Rev. 561, 579 (1974); Sales, *The Innocent Misrepresentation Doctrine: Strict Tort Liability Under Section 402B*, 16 Hous. L. Rev. 239 (1979).

563. 14 Cal. 3d 104, 534 P.2d 377, 120 Cal. Rptr. 681 (1975).

564. *Id.* at 108, 543 P.2d at 379, 120 Cal. Rptr. at 683.

565. *Id.* at 114, 543 P.2d at 383, 120 Cal. Rptr. at 684. Restatement (Second) of Torts, § 402B, comment j, specifically declares that the wife of a purchaser is entitled to the benefit of the purchaser husband's reliance on the misrepresentation.

566. Peterson v. Lamb Rubber Co., 54 Cal. 2d 339, 353 P.2d 575, 5 Cal. Rptr. 863 (1960); Wagner v. Larson, 257 Iowa 202, 136 N.W.2d 312 (1965); Divello v. Gardner Mach.

or by an agent for the use of another.[567]

Justifiable reliance by a physician responsible for prescribing ethical drugs satisfies the reliance requirement of Section 402B. In *Crocker v. Winthrop Laboratories*,[568] plaintiff underwent surgery for a hernia and for amputation of several fingers on one hand. The treating physician prescribed Talwin for pain which the plaintiff tolerated better than Demoral. The treating physician continued to prescribe Talwin on the basis of representations in the PDR and other advertising literature that the drug possessed no addicting side effects.[569] The decedent developed an addiction from the continued use of Talwin and ultimately died of a weakened condition caused by the detoxification. The Supreme Court noted that when the treating physician relies upon the representation of the drug company, the company is liable to the patient when the representation proves to be false and harm results.[570]

Similarly, in *Bristol-Myers Co. v. Gonzales*,[571] plaintiff developed deafness as a side effect from the injection of Kantrex. The treating physician irrigated the plaintiff's hip following surgery by repeated use of Kantrex based on representations in the PDR that Kantrex injection in concentrations of 0.25 percent has been used satisfactorily as an irrigating solution in abscess cavities.[572] The Texas Supreme Court determined that the misrepresentation of material facts relied upon by the treating physician entitled the patient to maintain an action under Section 402B.[573]

Justifiable reliance, of course, contemplates the reasonable exercise of knowledge and intelligence in assessing the represented facts. Insupportable subjective reliance does not satisfy the re-

---

Co., 46 Ohio Op. 161, 102 N.E.2d 289 (Ct. of Common Pleas. 1951). This likewise includes a guest of the purchaser's household. Tomczuk v. Town of Cheshire, 26 Conn. Supp. 219, 217 A.2d 71 (1965); McBurnette v. Playground Equip. Corp., 137 So.2d 563 (Fla. 1962).

567. *See* Restatement (Second) of Torts, § 402B, comment i. *See also*, Ruberoid Co. v. Briscoe, 293 F.2d 712 (5th Cir. 1961); Jacquot v. William Filene's Sons Co., 337 Mass. 312, 149 N.E.2d 635 (1958); Greenberg v. Lorenz, 9 N.Y.2d 195, 173 N.E.2d 773, 213 N.Y.S.2d 39 (1961).

568. 514 S.W.2d 429 (Tex. 1974).

569. *Id.* at 430.

570. *Id.* at 433.

571. 548 S.W.2d 416 (Tex. Civ. App.— Corpus Christi 1976), *rev'd on other grounds*, 561 S.W.2d 801 (Tex. 1978).

572. *Id.* at 423.

573. *Id.* at 425. *See generally*, Comment, *Warnings and the Pharmaceutical Companies: Legal Status of the Package Insert*, 16 Hous. L. Rev. 140 (1978).

quirement. A representation that a product used in prescribed manner is safe, however, entitles the user to rely on the stated procedure.[574] Nevertheless, if information or knowledge is acquired that a particular representation is inaccurate or untrue, the user may not ignore a reality and rely on the representation made.[575]

E. Damages Recoverable Under Section 402B

Section 402B imposes liability for physical harm to the consumer of the chattel.[576] Though the parameters of recovery are defined in the *Restatement* the effect of the provision is embroiled in legal controversy. The principal area of controversy focuses on whether pecuniary and economic losses are recoverable, despite the seemingly clear provisions of Section 402B limiting recovery to damages for physical harm.[577] Contrary to parallel provisions in Section 402A, the physical harm alluded to in Section 402B is limited to the user or consumer of the chattel and does not extend to the user's property.[578]

Recovery for physical harm to a user or consumer caused by innocent misrepresentation includes the general elements of damages for personal injury. This includes, of course, medical expenses, physical pain and mental anguish, physical impairment and disfigurement, loss of earnings and earning capacity, emotional distress and other related elements.[579]

Perhaps the area representing the most perplexing difficulty focuses on damage to property and consequential economic loss.

---

574. *See* Franks v. National Dairy Prods. Corp., 282 F. Supp. 528, 533 (W.D. Tex. 1968), *aff'd*, 414 F.2d 682 (5th Cir. 1969); Bristol-Myers Co. v. Gonzales, 548 S.W.2d 416, 425 (Tex. Civ. App.— Corpus Christi 1976), *rev'd on other grounds*, 561 S.W.2d 801 (Tex. 1978).

575. Ford Motor Co. v. Russell & Smith Ford Co., 474 S.W.2d 549, 558-60 (Tex. Civ. App.— Houston [14th Dist.] 1971, no writ). The dealer acquired knowledge that representations that a 1965 Ford Econoline with a 240 engine would solve problems previously experienced with overheating when air conditioning units were installed proved to be false. The dealers' continuing installation of the air conditioning in the Econoline after obtaining this knowledge was unjustified as a matter of law. *Id.* at 560. *See also* American Safety Equip. Corp. v. Winkler, 640 P.2d 216, 222 (Colo. 1982) (en banc).

576. RESTATEMENT (SECOND) OF TORTS, § 402B (1965).

577. *Id.*

578. *See* RESTATEMENT (SECOND) OF TORTS, § 402B, comment i. *See also* Walker Truck Contractors, Inc. v. Crane Carrier Co., 405 F. Supp. 911, 912 (E.D. Tenn. 1975).

579. *See, e.g.*, Bristol-Myers Co. v. Gonzales, 548 S.W.2d 416, 433 (Tex. Civ. App.—Corpus Christi 1976), *rev'd on other grounds*, 561 S.W.2d 801 (Tex. 1978).

The doctrine of strict tort liability as articulated in Section 402B constricts recovery to physical harm to the user or consumer caused by the chattel,[580] while completely omitting any reference to recovery of damage to property or other pecuniary loss.[581] Several jurisdictions, ignoring the limitation incorporated in Section 402B, have sanctioned recovery of economic and pecuniary loss.[582] In *Westric Battery Company v. Standard Electric Company*,[583] the court, without analysis, approved the extension of strict liability under Section 402B to include property damage. The court permitted recovery for out-of-pocket expense, loss of net profits, and capital loss caused by misrepresentation of the condition of batteries that caused failures in golf carts manufactured by the plaintiff.[584] On the other hand, other jurisdictions following the literal provision of Section 402B refuse to legitimize recovery of pecuniary loss.[585]

At least one jurisdiction has authorized recovery of pecuniary loss based on adoption of the parallel, but as yet unadopted, Section 552D of the *Restatement*, In *Ford Motor Co. v. Lonon*,[586] plaintiff purchased a Ford tractor relying on brochures and sales literature stating the tractor had power takeoff and power steering. Several days after purchase, plaintiff attempted to use the tractor only to find the power equipment inoperative. Despite efforts to remedy the deficiency, the tractor continued to operate without any power takeoff or power steering as represented in the sales literature. The Tennessee Supreme Court, adopting the provisions of Section 402B and, in addition, adopting proposed Section 552D of the *Restatement*,[587] noted that:

---

580. RESTATEMENT (SECOND) OF TORTS, § 402B (1965).

581. Walker Truck Contractors, Inc. v. Crane Carrier Co., 405 F. Supp. 911, 912 (E.D. Tenn., 1975). *See also* Randy Knitwear, Inc. v. American Cyanamid Co., 11 N.Y.2d 5, 15, 181 N.E.2d 399, 404, 226 N.Y.S.2d 363, 369 (1962).

582. *Randy*, 181 N.E.2d at 404.

583. 482 F.2d 1307 (10th Cir. 1973).

584. *Id.* at 1316-18. One commentator has suggested that it is difficult to justify denial of recovery for pecuniary loss irrespective of whether the user sustained personal injury or property damage. Hill, *Damages for Innocent Misrepresentation*, 73 COLUM. L. REV. 679, 475 n. 83 (1973).

585. Walker Truck Contractors, Inc. v. Crane Carrier Co., 405 F. Supp. 911, 912 (E.D. Tenn. 1975); Alfred N. Koplan & Co. v. Chrysler Corp., 49 Ill. App. 3d 194, 364 N.E.2d 100, 104 (1977).

586. 217 Tenn. 400, 398 S.W.2d 240 (1966).

587. *Id.* at 246.

> One engaged in a business of selling chattels who, by advertising, labels or otherwise, makes to the public a misrepresentation of a material fact concerning the character or quality of a chattel sold by him is subject to liability for pecuniary loss caused to another by his purchase of the chattel in justifiable reliance upon the misrepresentation, even though it is not made fraudulently or negligently.

The *Lonon* decision, predicated on the yet unadopted proposal of the *Restatement*, implicitly acknowledges that Section 402B alone does not support recovery for pecuniary loss.[588]

Until recently, the extraordinary sanction of punitive damages was unknown in product liability cases. A trend has emerged, however, reflecting increased activity and effort to pursue punitive awards in product cases. This remedy, initially adopted in England and integrated into the common law in 1763,[589] was designed to provide civil punishment for egregiously outrageous conduct rather than serve as compensation to an injured party.[590] Punitive damages in a civil action are awarded for wanton, reckless and grossly negligent conduct of the type that merits punishment. The type of conduct necessary to justify a punitive award must constitute an entire want of care which would raise the belief that the act or omission complained of was a result of a conscious indifference to the rights or welfare of the person or persons to be affected by it.[591]

---

588. *Id.*

589. Huckle v. Money, 2 Wils. K. B. 205, 95 Eng. Rep. 768 (1763). For a comprehensive discussion of the historical evolution of punitive damages, see generally: Sales & Cole, *Punitive Damages: A Relic That Has Outlived Its Origins*, 37 VAND. L. REV. 1117, 1119 (1984); Sales, *The Emergence of Punitive Damages in Product Liability Actions: A Further Assault on the Citadel*, 14 ST. MARY'S L. J. 351 (1983); Owen, *Punitive Damages in Product Liability Litigation*, 74 MICH. L. REV. 1257 (1976); Owens, *Problems in Assessing Punitive Damages Against the Manufacturers of Defective Products*, 49 U. CHI. L. REV. 1 (1982); Ellis, *Fairness & Efficiency in the Law of Punitive Damages*, 56 S. CAL. L. REV. 1 (1982).

590. Three theories have been formulated to justify application of punitive damages in the tort reparations system. One theory postulates that the courts used the concept of punitive damages in early English law to justify otherwise excessive jury verdicts rendered by knights who acted as jurors and provided the only testimony at trial. A second concept envisioned punitive damages as compensation for elements of damage that were not recognized as compensable in the early common law. A third justification envisioned that punitive damages satisfied a void created by the inequitable chasm between severe criminal penalities for wrongs to property and lesser criminal penalties for invasions of personal rights. *See* Sales & Cole, *Punitive Damages: A Relic That Has Outlived Its Origins*, 37 VAND. L. REV. 1117, 1120-24 (1984).

591. Maxey v. Freightliner Corp., 665 F.2d 1372, 1369 (5th Cir. 1982), *aff'd en banc*, 722 F.2d 1238, 1242 (5th Cir. 1984); Burk Royalty Co. v. Walls, 616 S.W.2d 911, 920 (Tex.

Under Section 402B, liability is not predicated on the conduct of the product supplier but upon innocent misrepresentations inducing the purchase of a product. It is critically important to emphasize that the misrepresentation precipitating strict liability is neither negligently nor fraudulently and deceitfully conceived.[592] Clearly, a fraudulent or deceitful misrepresentation that influences the purchase of a product would justify the imposition of punitive damages. To establish a cause of action for fraud or deceit, it is essential to prove that the representation was made with knowledge of its falsity, a requirement that is totally irrelevant and immaterial to liability under Section 402B. By definition, Section 402B presupposes that the conduct of the seller is wholly innocent and that the representation is neither negligently nor deceitfully contrived and disseminated to the public. It is axiomatic that the very nature of an action for innocent misrepresentation contradicts the underlying basis of a punitive damage claim, i.e, punishment and deterrence of outrageous conduct.

F. *Related Matters Governing Section 402B Actions*

Manufacturers and sellers of products may endeavor to limit liability by means of exculpatory clauses in contracts of sale. Contractual limitations, generally classified as disclaimers, are creatures of contract and, as a consequence, their operative effect is uniformly rejected in tort actions. Contractual limitations or disclaimers are disregarded in strict tort liability actions based on Section 402A,[593] and are equally ineffectual in limiting liability for innocent misrepresentation under Section 402B.[594]

Since traditional concepts of contract law are inapplicable to tort causes of action, it is inevitable that disclaimers seeking to limit strict tort liability are invalid.[595] It is equally evident that

---

1981); Southern Cotton Press & Mfg. Co. v. Bradley, 52 Tex. 587, 600 (1880).

592. Nugent v. Utica Cutlery Co., 636 S.W.2d 805, 808 (Tex. App.—San Antonio 1982, writ dism'd).

593. Vandermark v. Ford Motor Co., 61 Cal. 2d 256, 263, 391 P.2d 168, 172, 37 Cal. Rptr. 896, 900 (1964); Henningsen v. Bloomfield Motors, Inc., 32 N.J. 358, 161 A.2d 69, 95 (1960).

594. Walker Truck Contractors, Inc. v. Crane Carrier Co., 405 F. Supp. 911, 915 (E.D. Tenn. 1975); Grinnell v. Charles Pfizer & Co., 274 Cal. App. 2d 424, 433, 79 Cal. Rptr. 369, 380 (1969); Ford Motor Co. v. Taylor, 60 Tenn. App. 271, 446 S.W.2d 521, 532 (1969).

595. Sterner Aero AB v. Page Airmotive, Inc., 499 F.2d 709, 713 (10th Cir. 1974); Vandermark v. Ford Motor Co., 61 Cal. 2d 256, 263, 391 P.2d 168, 172, 37 Cal. Rptr. 896, 900

since privity is not a requirement for strict liability based on innocent misrepresentations, contractual limitations do not bind remote purchasers and users of the product.[596] Of course, any limitation in the advertising literature that specifically limits the affirmative statement and assurance of quality and condition of a product curtails the material facts that may justifiably influence purchase of a product under Section 402B.[597]

Liability predicated on innocent misrepresentation constitutes a viable and effective doctrine in the products arena. The innocent misrepresentation doctrine is particularly significant since it does not depend on negligence or fraud and, unlike its counterpart, does not rely on a defective condition that renders the product unreasonably dangerous. In reality, Section 402B authorizes recovery for breach of a contractual warranty without any of the impediments of contract.

1.03 Implied Warranties Under the Uniform Commercial Code

A. Basis for remedy of implied warranties of merchantability and fitness for a particular purpose

In 1967 the Texas legislature enacted the Uniform Commercial Code as a comprehensive and integrated act to facilitate the continued expansion of commercial practice. As part of the comprehensive provisions of the Code, remedies are provided for breach of implied warranties. Breach of the U.C.C. implied warranties has been judicially construed as an alternative remedy for the recovery of damages resulting from product-caused accidents.[598]

Article 2.314 expressly provides that a warranty that goods shall be merchantable is implied in a contract for their sale if the sellers are merchants with respect to the goods of that kind.[599] Es-

---

(1964).

596. *Id.*

597. Harris v. Belton, 258 Cal. App. 2d 595, 606, 65 Cal. Rptr. 808, 816 (1968); Reliance on a misrepresentation theory predicated upon the manufacturer's advertising is precluded when the warning is actually given and read by the injured party.

598. Garcia v. Texas Instruments, Inc., 610 S.W.2d 456, 462 (Tex. 1980); Signal Oil & Gas Co. v. Universal Oil Prods. 572 S.W.2d 320, 326-27 (Tex. 1978).

599. Tex. Bus. & Comm. Code Ann. § 2.314 (Vernon 1968). This section specifically provides that for goods to be merchantable they must be:

> (1) pass[ed] without objection in the trade under the contract description; and

sentially breach of an implied warranty of merchantability occurs when the product is not fit for the ordinary purposes for which it is sold or used.[600]

A second implied warranty involves fitness for particular purposes. Under §2.315, when the seller has reason to know of the particular purposes for which goods are required and that the buyer is relying on the seller's skill or judgment to select or furnish suitable goods, an implied warranty of fitness for a particular purpose arises under the Uniform Commercial Code.[601] To impose on the product supplier a duty to supply a product that is fit for a particular purpose, two requirements are essential: (1) the product seller must be made aware at the time of the purchase that the product will be used for a particular purpose or in a particular manner; and (2) the product supplier must realize that the purchaser is relying on the supplier's skill and judgment in selecting and furnishing the specific product for the requested use.[602]

B. *Elements affecting warranty actions*

The Code does not limit the definition of seller to the immediate seller of the product. Rather, seller is defined as "a person who sells or contracts to sell goods."[603] Under the Code, a manufacturer

---

(2) in the case of fungible goods, are of fair average quality within the description; and

(3) are fit for the ordinary purposes for which such goods are used; and

(4) run, within the variations permitted by the agreement, of even kind, quality and quantity within each unit and among all units involved; and

(5) are adequately contained, packaged, and labeled as the agreement may require; and

(6) conform[ed] to the promises or affirmations of fact made on the container or label if any.

See, Garcia v. Texas Instruments, Inc., 610 S.W.2d 456, 459 (Tex. 1980).

600. TEX. BUS. & COMM. CODE ANN. at § 2.314(b)(3) (Vernon 1968). Two Rivers Co. v. Curtiss Breeding Service, 624 F.2d 1242, 1251 (5th Cir. 1980), *cert. denied*, 450 U.S. 920 (1981). As emphasized by the Texas Supreme Court in Nobility Homes Inc. v. Shivers, 557 S.W.2d 77 (Tex. 1977), "If the goods are employed for a purpose other than 'the ordinary purposes for which such goods are used,' the manufacturer is not liable." *Id.* at 82. Moreover, breach of implied warranty requires that the goods be unmerchantable on the date of delivery. Fitzgerald v. Caterpillar Tractor Co., 683 S.W.2d 162 (Tex. App.—Fort Worth 1985).

601. TEX. BUS. & COMM. CODE ANN. § 2.315 (Vernon 1968). These prerequisites are emphasized in Two Rivers Co. v. Curtiss Breeding Serv. 624 F.2d 1242, 1252 (5th Cir. 1980), *cert. denied*, 450 U.S. 920 (1981).

602. TEX. BUS. & COMM. CODE ANN. § 2.315, comment 1 and 2 (Vernon 1968).

603. TEX. BUS. & COMM. CODE. ANN. § 2.103(4) defines seller as "a person who sells or

is deemed to be a seller.[604]

Unlike strict tort liability under §402A or 402B, an implied warranty of merchantability or suitability for a particular purpose may be excluded or modified either by words or conduct that negate or limit the warranty.[605] To exclude or modify an implied warranty of merchantability, the exclusionary language must specifically mention merchantability and, in the case of a writing, must be conspicuous.[606] In excluding or modifying an implied warranty of suitability for a particular purpose, the exclusionary language must be in writing and must be conspicuous.[607] To exclude an implied warranty of fitness for a particular purpose, wording that "there are no warranties which extend beyond the description on the face hereof" satisfies the requirements of §2.316.[608] Moreover, all implied warranties are excluded by such exclusionary phrases as "as is," "with all faults," or other similar language.[609]

Until recently, breach of an implied warranty cause as a remedy for personal injury ostensibly had been rejected as an alternative remedy for strict tort liability.[610] The rationale underlying this view was predicated on the contractual nature of the warranty remedies. In *Garcia v. Texas Instruments, Inc.*, the Texas Supreme Court ignored its earlier announced distinction and declared that strict tort liability does not constitute the exclusive remedy for personal injury in the products liability area.[611] Plaintiff, an

---

contracts to sell goods."

604. Nobility Homes of Texas, Inc. v. Shivers, 557 S.W.2d 77, 80 (Tex. 1977). An assembler of a completed product likewise is characterized as a seller under the Code. In Signal Oil & Gas v. Universal Oil Products, 572 S.W.2d 320, 330 (Tex. 1978), the court observes, "In order for the finished product to be merchantible or fit for its intended purposes, it must possess suitable component parts, as well as the proper arrangement assembly, or combination of such parts. Consequently, the assembler constitutes an essential link in the chain of distribution."

605. Tex. Bus. & Comm. Code Ann. § 2.316(a) (Vernon 1968).

606. Tex. Bus. & Comm. Code Ann. § 2.316(b) (Vernon 1968).

607. Tex. Bus. & Comm. Code Ann. § 2.316(b) (Vernon 1968).

608. *Id.* An example of an effective disclaimer is illustrated in Two Rivers Co. v. Curtiss Breeding Serv. 624 F.2d 1242, 1252 (5th Cir. 1980), *cert. denied*, 450 U.S. 920 1981).

609. Tex. Bus. & Comm. Code Ann. § 2.316(c)(1) (1967). The validity of the "as is" disclaimer to nullify an implied warranty in the sale of a used aircraft was confirmed by the Texas Supreme Court in Mid-Continent Aircraft Corp. v. Curry County Spraying Serv., Inc., 572 S.W.2d 308, 313 (Tex. 1978).

610. Mid-Continent Aircraft Corp. v. Curry County Spraying Serv., Inc., 572 S.W.2d 308, 311-13 (Tex. 1978); Nobility Homes, Inc. v. Shivers, 557 S.W.2d 77, 79-80 (Tex. 1977).

611. Refer to notes 430-31 *supra* and accompanying test.

employee of a buyer of sulfuric acid, instituted suit against the seller to recover damages for acid burns sustained when the container of acid broke. Plaintiff alleged that the acid was not adequately contained and, therefore, was not merchantable.[612] Suit was commenced three years and eight months after the accident.[613] Concluding that the Uniform Commercial Code breach of implied warranty would sustain a cause of action seeking damages for personal injuries, the court applied the Code's four year statute of limitations.[614]

C. *Recovery Authorized Under Implied Warranties*

The Texas Supreme Court reasoned that judicial adoption of § 402A, strict tort liability for product defects, does not negate Uniform Commercial Code sections providing a remedy for personal injury based on breach of implied warranty. Moreover, the court concluded that unlike the two year statute of limitations that governs strict tort liability, the four year U.C.C. statute applies to breach of warranty actions.[615]

The court further noted that privity between the plaintiff and the manufacturer does not constitute a requirement.[616] In abrogating the privity requirement, the court noted it was exercising the discretion reserved by the U.C.C. with respect to whether privity would be required.[617] Abrogation of the privity requirement in breach of implied warranty actions was reaffirmed by the Texas

---

612. 610 S.W.2d at 457.

613. *Id.* The statute of limitations is deemed to occur when tender of delivery is accomplished. Fitzgerald v. Caterpillar Tractor Co., 683 S.W.d 162 (Tex. App.—Fort Worth 1985, no writ) (citing cases).

614. Defendant filed a motion for summary judgment alleging that plaintiff's lawsuit was barred by Tex. Rev. Civ. Stat. Ann. Art. 5526(4) (Supp. 1980) which provides for a two year statute of limitations for personal injuries in tort. Plaintiff argued that his suit was not barred by limitations because his suit was based on breach of an implied warranty governed by the Texas Business & Commerce Code Ann. § 2.725(a), which provides a four-year statute of limitations for breach of contract. *Garcia*, 610 S.W.2d at 457-58, 465.

615. The court explained: "Our adoption of Section 402A of the Restatement(Second) of Torts cannot be held to repeal the Code sections providing redress for personal injury based on a breach of implied warranty as such would be an invasion of the legislative field." Garcia, 610 S.W.2d at 462.

616. The court declared: "We hold that privity of contract is not a requirement for a Uniform Commercial Code implied warranty action for personal injuries." *Id.* at 465.

617. *Id.* at 464-65.

Supreme Court in *Gupta v. Ritter Homes, Inc.*[618] in which the builder of a home was deemed liable to subsequent purchasers based on breach of an implied warranty.[619] In addition the implied warranty that a building is constructed in a good workmanlike manner also includes an implied warranty that the building is habitable.[620]

The Texas Supreme Court distinguished *Garcia* from its earlier decisions.[621] In *Nobility Homes of Texas, Inc. v. Shivers*,[622] the court earlier observed that in the absence of personal injuries, an action for economic loss was maintainable on the basis of a breach of warranty as provided for by the Uniform Commercial Code.[623] The scope and purpose of the Uniform Commercial Code are not nullified by substituting strict tort liability when the parties have contracted otherwise.[624] The Supreme court in *Garcia* painstakingly explained that its earlier decisions were not meant to denominate the strict tort liability remedy as mutually exclusive of the breach of warranty remedies.[625] Both the *Restatement* and the Texas Business and Commercial Code[626] constitute mutually compatible remedies for personal injuries resulting from defective products. The court observed that any conceptual difficulties in-

618. 646 S.W.2d 168 (Tex. 1983).

619. *Id.* at 169.

620. Evans v. Stiles, 689 S.W.2d 399, 28 Tex. Sup. Ct. J. 329, 330 (March 27,1985).

621. *Garcia*, 610 S.W.2d 456 (Tex. 1980). The court noted that:

> The trio of decisions by this Court, *Nobility Homes*, *Mid Continent*, and *Signal Oil*, exploring the distinction between contract and tort theories of warranty have sparked considerable discussion by Texas commentators. *See generally*, Keeton, *Annual Survey of Texas Law, Torts*, 33 Sw. L.J. 1, 1-14 (1979); Keeton, *Annual Survey of Texas Law, Torts*, 32 Sw. L.J. 1, 3-9 (1978); Winship, *Annual Survey of Texas Law, Commercial Transactions*, 33 Sw. L.J. 203, 208 (1979); Comment, *Economic Loss, 402A, and an Unreasonably Dangerous Product: Can* Mid Continent Aircraft, Signal Oil *and* Nobility Homes *be Reconciled?* 10 St. Mary's L. J. 569 (1979).

Id. at 461 n.10.

622. Nobility Homes, Inc. v. Shivers, 557 S.W.2d 77 (Tex. 1977); Tex. Bus. & Com. Code Ann. §§ 2.314, 2.315 (Tex. UCC) (Vernon 1968).

623. Mid Continent Aircraft Corp. v. Curry County Spraying Serv., Inc., 572 S.W.2d 308, 313 (Tex. 1978).

624. See *Garcia*, 610 S.W.2d at 461. The court stated: "In *Signal Oil and Gas Co. v. Universal Oil Prods.*, 572 S.W.2d 320, 326 (Tex. 1978) we recognized that defective product remedies are provided by both the Restatement (Second) of Torts and the Texas Business and Commerce Code. 572 S.W.2d at 326." *Id.* at 461.

625. *Id.*

626. Restatement (Second) of Torts, §§ 402A, 402B (1965); Tex. Bus. & Com. Code Ann. § 2.725(a) (Vernon 1968).

herent in applying Code remedies to personal injury claims were easily resolved.[627]

Other jurisdictions differ in their approach to applying the remedies of the Uniform Commercial Code to product-related claims.[628] Some jurisdictions which have adopted the Texas view, declare that a cause of action maybe based either on breach of U.C.C. implied warranty or strict tort liability.[629] Thus, the generally longer statute of limitations of the U.C.C. applies to actions for personal injuries based on breach of an implied warranty. Other jurisdictions, representing the majority view, have determined that the U.C.C. provisions apply only when a buyer-seller relationship exists.[630] These jurisdictions refuse to intertwine contractual principles with tort principles. Some jurisdictions simply

---

627. The court stated: "[T]he Code establishes an alternative remedy to strict liability in tort with respect to injuries suffered from a defective product." *Garcia*, 610 S.W.2d at 462. *Accord* Hiigel v. General Motors Corp., 190 Colo. 57, 544 P.2d 983, 990 (1975); West v. Caterpillar Tractor Co., 336 So.2d 80, 88 (Fla. 1976); Berry v. Searle, & Co. *supra*, 309 N.E.2d at 554; Colvin v. FMC Corp., *supra*, 604 P.2d at 160; Pearson v. Franklin Laboratories, *supra*; 254 N.W.2d at 138-39; Layman v. Keller Ladders, Inc., 224 Tenn. 396, 455 S.W.2d 594, 596 (1970). *Contra*, Austin v. Ford Motor Co., *supra*, 273 N.W.2d at 240.

628. *See generally* Dickerson, *The ABC's of Products Liability—With a Close Look at Section 402A and the Code*, 36 Tenn. L. Rev. 439 (1969); Franklin, *When Worlds Collide: Liability Theories and Disclaimers in Defective Product Cases*, 18 Stan. L. Rev. 974 (1966); McGuire & Wade, *Products Liability, The Commercial Code and the Practitioner*, 31 Tex. B. J. 107 (1968); Rapson, *Products Liability Under Parallel Doctrines: Contrasts Between The Uniform Commercial Code and Strict Liability in Tort*, 19 Rutgers L. Rev. 692 (1965); Shanker, *Strict Tort Theory of Products Liability and the Uniform Commercial Code: A Commentary on Jurisprudential Eclipses, Pigeonholes and Communication Barriers*, 17 Case W. Res. 5 (1965); Titus, *Restatement (Second) of Torts, Section 402A and the Uniform Commercial Code*, 22 Stan. L. Rev. 713 (1970); Wade, *Is Section 402A of the Second Restatement of Torts Preempted by the Uniform Commercial Code and Therefore Unconstitutional?*, 42 Tenn. L. Rev. 123 (1974). *See also* Annot., 20 A.L.R. 4th 915 (1983).

629. *E.g.* Roberts v. General Dynamics, Convair Corp., 425 F. Supp. 688, 691 (S.D. Tex. 1977) (interpreting Texas law); Simmons v. Clemco Indus., 368 So.2d 509, 513 (Ala. 1979); Commercial Truck & Trailer Sales Inc. v. McCampbell, 580 S.W.2d 765, 773 (Tenn. 1979). Both Alabama and Tennessee have abolished by statute privity as a prerequisite to the maintenance of personal injury action. *See also* Moody v. Sears, Roebuck & Co., 324 F. Supp. 844, 845 (S.D. Ga. 1971) (interpreting Georgia law) (citing the Georgia version of the UCC and holding, without further discussion, that an implied warranty action based on personal injuries must be brought within four years.).

630. *E.g.* Reid v. Volkswagen of American, Inc., 575 F.2d 1175, 1176 (6th Cir. 1978) (interpreting Michigan law); Heavner v. Uniroyal, Inc., 63 N.J. 130, 305 A.2d 412, 426-27 (1973); Martin v. Julius Dierck Equip. Co., 43 N.Y.2d 583, 374 N.E.2d 97, 100, 403 N.Y.S.2d 185, 188 (1978); Lee v. Wright Tool & Forge Co., 48 Ohio App. 2d 148, 356 N.E.2d 303, 306 (1975); Colvin v. GMC Corp., 43 Or. App. 709, 604 P.2d 157, 160 (1979); Plouffe v. Goodyear Tire & Rubber Co., 118 R.I. 228, 373 A.2d 492, 495 (R.I. 1977).

declare that the U.C.C. remedies are inapplicable to claims seeking damages for personal injuries arising from product-related accidents.[631] The issue continues to engender an unnecessary degree of confusion and misunderstanding.[632]

1.04 Conclusion

The essential elements of a § 402A strict tort liability cause of action include: (1) proof of a defect; (2) proof that the particular defect existed at the time the product left the possession and/or control of the manufacturer or seller; (3) proof that the defect rendered the product unreasonably dangerous for its intended or reasonably foreseeable uses; and (4) proof that the unreasonably dangerous condition of the product caused the injury to the user. The three types of defects—manufacturing, design and marketing—are conceptually different elements that underlie § 402A strict liability. Recovery for personal injuries in products liability cases likewise is available in Texas under theories of § 402B (innocent misrepresentation), breach of the implied warranties prescribed by the Uniform Commercial Code, and the traditional negligence doctrine.

---

631. *E.g.* Maynard v. General Elec. Co., 486 F.2d 538, 540 (4th Cir. 1973) (interpreting West Virginia law); Tyler v. Street & Co., 322 F. Supp. 541, 543 (E.D. Va. 1971) (interpreting Virginia law); Becker v. Volkswagen of America, Inc., 52 Cal. App. 3d 794, 802, 125 Cal. Rptr. 326, 331 (Ct.App. 1975); Abate v. Barkers of Wallingford, Inc., 27 Conn. Supp. 46, 229 A.2d 366, 369 (1967).

632. *See, e.g.,* Sinka v. Northern Commercial Co., 491 P.2d 116, 118 (Alaska 1971)(holding UCC statute of limitations applicable to breach of warranty action for personal injuries betweeen parties in privity; no subsequent Alaska decision involving parties not in privity). *Compare* Salvador v. Atlantic Steel Boiler Co., 256 Pa. Super. 330, 389 A.2d 1148, 1151 (1978) (holding that tort statute of limitations should be applied to all third party personal injuries arising from a defective product) *with* Gardiner v. Philadelphia Gas Works, 413 Pa. 415, 197 A.2d 612, 614 (1964) (U.C.C. limitations provision governed personal injury claim based on breach of warranty) *and* Salvador v. Atlantic Steel Boiler Co., 457 Pa. 24, 319 A.2d 903, 907 (1974) (neither lack of horizontal nor lack of vertical privity barred personal injury suit premised on breach of warranty); *Compare* Berry v. G.D. Searle & Co., 56 Ill. 2d 548, 309 N.E.2d 550, 556 (1974) (holding that U.C.C. limitations provision applied to breach of warranty action for personal injuries and privity between injured user and manufacturer of contraceptive was not required) *with* Knox v. North American Car Corp., 80 Ill. App. 3d 683, 399 N.E.2d 1355, 1360 (1980) (in absence of vertical privity of horizontal privity within the parameters of the Illinois version of U.C.C. § 2-318, tort statute of limitations governed personal injury claim based on breach of implied warranty).

CHAPTER II. PROOF OF CAUSES OF ACTION*

---

* Rhonda Rhodes Wile coauthored this chapter.

2.00 INTRODUCTION

"Strict liability eliminates both privity and negligence; but it still does not prove the plaintiff's case."[1]

To recover under the theory of strict tort liability, the plaintiff must establish the elements enumerated in Section 402A of the *Restatement (Second) of Torts*.[2] These elements, as developed in

---

1. Prosser, *The Fall of the Citadel (Strict Liability to the Consumer)*, 50 MINN. L. REV. 791, 840 (1966).

2. RESTATEMENT (SECOND) OF TORTS § 402A (1965). In 1967, Texas adopted § 402A as the law governing strict liability of suppliers of defective products. Section 402 states:

> (1) One who sells any product in a defective condition unreasonably dangerous to the user or consumer or to his property is subject to liability for physical harm thereby caused to the ultimate user or consumer, or to his property, if
>
> (a) the seller is engaged in the business of selling such a product, and
>
> (b) it is expected to and does reach the user or consumer without substantial change in the condition in which it is sold.
>
> (2) The rule stated in Subsection (1) applies although
>
> (a) the seller has exercised all possible care in the preparation and sale of his product, and
>
> (b) the user or consumer has not bought the product from or entered into any contractual relation with the seller.

See McKisson v. Sales Affiliates, Inc., 416 S.W.2d 787, 789 (Tex. 1967); Shamrock Fuel & Oil Sales Co. v. Tunks, 416 S.W.2d 779, 783 (Tex. 1967).

case law, require proof: (1) that the product contained a defect; (2) that the defect existed at the time the defendant relinquished possession or control of the product; (3) that the defect rendered the product unreasonably dangerous[3] for its intended and reasonably foreseeable uses; and (4) that the unreasonably dangerous condition of the product caused the injury.[4] It must also be established that the product causing the injury or damage was actually introduced into the channels of commerce.[5]

The elements of a strict tort liability action may be established by direct evidence, expert testimony, circumstantial evidence, or any combination of these methods of proof.[6] Of course, the standard and the amount of proof required vary with the circumstances of each case and, more importantly, with the type of

---

3. Refer to notes 25-32 *infra* and accompanying text. Texas adheres to the RESTATEMENT and follows the overwhelming majority view that requires proof that the product is unreasonably dangerous. *See, e.g.*, Martinez v. Dixie Carriers, Inc., 529 F.2d 457, 465 (5th Cir. 1976); Turner v. General Motors Corp., 584 S.W. 2d 844, 851 (Tex. 1979); Acord v. General Motors Corp., 669 S.W. 2d 111, 114-15 (Tex. 1984). Rourke v. Garza, 530 S.W.2d 794 (Tex. 1975); Henderson v. Ford Motor Co., 519 S.W.2d 87, 92 (Tex. 1974); Darryl v. Ford Motor Co., 440 S.W.2d 630, 633 (Tex. 1969). *Contra* Cronin v. J.B.E. Olson Corp., 8 Cal. 3d 121, 134-35, 501 P.2d 1153, 1163, 104 Cal. Rptr. 433, 443 (1972) (plaintiff who proves that the product contained a defect that proximately caused his injuries need not prove that "such defective condition made the product unreasonably dangerous.").

4. *See, e.g.*, Syrie v. Knoll Int'l, 748 F.2d 304, 306 (5th Cir. 1984); Miller v. Bock Laundry Mach. Co., 568 S.W.2d 648, 650 (Tex. 1977); General Motors Corp. v. Hopkins, 548 S.W.2d 344, 352 (Tex. 1977); Ford Motor Co. v. Stead, 574 S.W.2d 226, 228-29 (Tex. Civ. App.—Waco 1978, no writ); Hamilton v. Motor Coach Indus., Inc., 569 S.W.2d 571, 575 (Tex. Civ. App.—Texarkana 1978, no writ); Gravis v. Parke-Davis & Co., 502 S.W.2d 863, 868 (Tex. Civ. App.—Corpus Christi 1973, writ ref'd n.r.e.).

5. *See, e.g.*, Gardner v. Chevron U.S.A., Inc., 675 F.2d 658, 661 (5th Cir. 1982) (oil well constructed by owner is not a product introduced into stream of commerce). Armstrong Rubber Co. v. Urquidez, 570 S.W.2d 374, 375-76 (Tex. 1978) (test tire used on test car is not introduced into channels of commerce); *see also* Smith v. Borg-Warner Corp., 626 F.2d 384, 386 (5th Cir. 1980) (court acknowledged but did not expressly address whether an employee seriously burned while processing plastic powder for a subcontractor at defendant's manufacturing facility was injured by product introduced into stream of commerce). Merely because a product is *in* the channels of commerce, however, does not mean that the product has been *introduced* into the stream of commerce for purposes of invoking the doctrine of strict tort liability. Thate v. Texas & P. Ry., 595 S.W.2d 591, 598 (Tex. Civ. App.—Dallas 1980, no writ) (defective railroad car which was being repaired by railroad company employee was not a product introduced into the stream of commerce).

6. *See, e.g.*, Darryl v. Ford Motor Co., 440 S.W.2d 630, 632 (Tex. 1969) (circumstantial evidence); Mahan v. Volkswagen, Inc. v. Hall, 648 S.W.2d 324 (Tex. App.—Houston [1st Dist.] 1982, writ ref'd n.r.e.) (direct, circumstantial, and expert evidence); Thiele v. Chick, 631 S.W.2d 526, 530 (Tex. App.—Houston [1st Dist.] 1982, writ ref'd n.r.e.) (expert and circumstantial evidence). *See also* Rheingold, *Proof of Defect in Product Liability Cases*, 38 TENN. L. REV. 325, 326-27 (1971).

defect involved.[7] Because the product involved in the incident is often lost or destroyed, the courts sanction a rather liberal application of the rules of evidence to prove a defective condition.[8]

Texas recently adopted the *Texas Rules of Evidence* for civil proceedings,[9] which in many ways affects the litigation of strict tort liability cases. For example, under Rule 407(a),[10] Texas joins a minority of jurisdictions allowing evidence of subsequent remedial measures in strict tort liability actions, though not admitting such proof under other theories of product liability actions.[11] Rule 407(b)[12] provides definitive standards to govern the admissibility of recall letter evidence, an issue currently unresolved in federal courts.[13] The use of expert testimony under the Texas Rules of Evidence has undergone some modifications from its common law antecedents. Under Rule 703,[14] an expert can now base his opinion entirely on hearsay.[15] Rule 704 allows testimony embracing an ultimate issue to be resolved by the trier of fact.[16] This rule will affect strict tort liability litigation only if it is interpreted more broadly than an earlier Texas case that sired this rule.[17]

This chapter, in outlining the elements of proof for a strict tort liability case, analyzes Texas and federal cases. The types of product defects are discussed as they relate to each aspect of proof.

---

7. Product defects are categorized as manufacturing, design, and marketing defects. Refer to chapter 1 for a discussion of these categories.

8. RHEINGOLD, *supra* note 6, at 343.

9. The Supreme Court of Texas promulgated these rules on November 23, 1982, and the rules became effective on September 1, 1983. Amendments to the rules became effective on November 1, 1984.

10. TEX. R. EVID. 407(a).

11. Refer to text accompanying notes 311-453 *infra*.

12. TEX. R. EVID. 407(b). Refer to note 479 *infra* for the statement of the rule.

13. Refer to text accompanying notes 454-480, *infra*.

14. FED. R. EVID. 703; TEX. R. EVID. 703. Refer to note 213 *infra* for the statement of the rule.

15. Refer to text accompanying notes 213-43, *infra*.

16. FED. R. EVID. 704; TEX. R. EVID. 704. Refer to note 244 *infra* for the statement of the rule.

17. *See* Carr v. Radkey, 393 S.W.2d 806, 810 (Tex. 1965) (Questions presented to experts that involve ultimate issues are often necessary and are generally admissible). Refer to text accompanying notes 244-66, *infra*.

2.01 Proof of Defect

A. *Nature of the Proof Required*

1. Manufacturing Defects. In a manufacturing defect case (involving a flaw in the product), the elements of strict tort liability may be difficult to establish because the product has frequently been discarded or severely damaged in the accident on which the lawsuit is based.[18] This creates difficulties in ascertaining whether the alleged defect caused the accident or merely resulted from the accident.[19] Though specific proof of a manufacturing defect is often impossible, proof of the mere occurrence of an injury-producing incident is inadequate to satisfy the burden of proof.[20] Proof that a defect existed in the product at the time possession was relinquished by the product supplier, as well as at the time of the accident, is critical;[21] however, it is not essential to prove the specific cause that renders the product defective.[22] Circumstantial evi-

---

18. *See, e.g.*, Revlon, Inc. v. Hampton, 551 S.W.2d 121, 122 (Tex. Civ. App.—Beaumont 1977, no writ) (circumstantial evidence must be such that it can properly be inferred that the accident was caused by a defect in the product); Alberto-Culver Co. v. Morgan, 444 S.W.2d 770, 775 (Tex. Civ. App.—Beaumont 1969, writ ref'd n.r.e.); Proctor & Gamble Mfg. Co. v. Langley, 422 S.W.2d 773, 777 (Tex. Civ. App.—Dallas 1967, writ dism'd).

19. *See, e.g.*, Barnett v. Ford Motor Co., 463 S.W.2d 33, 34-35 (Tex. Civ. App.—Waco 1970, no writ) (electrical wiring underneath an automobile instrument panel was consumed by fire).

20. *See, e.g.*, Carroll v. Ford Motor Co., 462 S.W.2d 57, 61 (Tex. Civ. App.—Houston [14th Dist.] 1970, no writ); (failure to prove defect of braking system in automobile); Alberto Culver Co. v. Morgan, 444 S.W.2d 770, 775 (Tex. Civ. App.—Beaumont 1969, writ ref'd n.r.e.) (plaintiff allergic or hypersensitive to hair coloring but failed to show product was defective, because of her failure to prove that she was part of appreciable class of persons to whom harm could be foreseen; thus, no duty to warn); *see also* Simien v. S.S. Kresge Co., 566 F.2d 551, 556 (5th Cir. 1978) ("it is incumbent upon the plaintiff to establish evidence on the critical issue of a 'defect' in the product"); Fort Worth Steel & Mach. Co. v. Norsworthy, 570 S.W.2d 132, 136 (Tex. Civ. App.—Tyler 1978, writ dism'd w.o.j.) (failure to prove any causal link between the design defect and the injuries is fatal); *But see* Revlon Inc. v. Hampton, 551 S.W.2d 121, 122 (Tex. Civ. App.—Beaumont 1977, no writ). (Jury did not find that dye contained thallium which causes hair loss, but still found that dye was defective).

21. *See, e.g.*, Quinn v. Southwest Wood Prods., 597 F.2d 1018, 1019-24 (5th Cir. 1979) (meager evidence did not support verdict that ladder was defectively designed); Dr. Pepper Co. v. Crow, 621 S.W.2d 464, 465 (Tex. App.—Waco 1981, no writ) (insufficient evidence that bottle was defective when it left the manufacturer); Coca Cola v. Hobart, 423 S.W.2d 118, 125 (Tex. Civ. App.—Houston [14th Dist.] 1967, writ ref'd n.r.e.) (proof insufficient to establish defect in bottle when bottler relinquished product to the retailer).

22. *See, e.g.*, Franks v. Nat'l Dairy Prods. Corp., 414 F.2d 682-87 (5th Cir. 1969)

dence suffices to raise an issue that a product is defective.[23]

2. *Design Defects.* In design defect cases, as in manufacturing defect cases, the product is often discarded or destroyed. Salvage of the particular product, however, is not critical, because the defective condition in a design defect case is incorporated in an entire line of products. A defectively designed product conforms precisely to the manufacturer's blueprints and specifications, but some aspect of the design configuration is defective and renders the product unreasonably dangerous.[24] Therefore, establishing the physical properties of the particular injury-producing product is not as critical.

The principal requirement in the proof of a design defect case involves establishing that the design rendered the product unreasonably dangerous[25] for its intended and reasonably foreseeable uses.[26] Not all jurisdictions consider the concept of "unreasonably dangerous" as an essential component for a strict tort liability action; those jurisdictions that disallow the "unreasonably dangerous" requirement perceive it as interjecting negligence into the concept.[27] The vast majority of jurisdictions, however, follow the

---

(plaintiff is not obligated to establish a specific defect to prove that an explosion was caused by defect in the product); V. Mueller & Co. v. Corley, 570 S.W.2d 140, 144 (Tex. Civ. App.—Houston [1st Dist.] 1978, writ ref'd n.r.e.) (failure of a prosthesis after careful surgical implantation constituted circumstantial evidence of a defect).

23. *See, e.g., Franks*, 414 F.2d at 686-87 (circumstantial evidence of defective shortening); Mahan Volkswagen v. Hall, 648 S.W.2d 324, 328 (Tex. App.—Houston [1st Dist.] 1982, no writ) (circumstantial evidence of latent defect in braking system).

24. *See* Keeton, *Product Liability and the Meaning of Defect*, 5 St. Mary's L.J. 30 (1973); Powers, *The Persistence of Fault in Products Liability*, 61 Tex. L. Rev. 777 (1983). The distinction between flaw and design is noted in Ford Motor Co. v. Pool, 688 S.W.2d 879 (Tex. App.—Texarkana 1985, no writ).

25. *See, e.g.*, Davidson v. Stanadyne, Inc., 718 F.2d 1334, 1338 (5th Cir. 1983); Acord v. General Motors Corp., 669 S.W.2d 111, 113 (Tex. 1984); Turner v. General Motors Corp., 584 S.W.2d 844, 851 (Tex. 1979); Gonzales v. Caterpillar Tractor Co., 571 S.W.2d 867, 872 (Tex. 1978); *Miller*, 568 S.W.2d 648, 650; *Hopkins*, 548 S.W.2d 344, 352; Rourke v. Garza, 530 S.W.2d 794, 800 (Tex. 1975).

26. *See, e.g.*, Daberko v. Heil Co., 681 F.2d 445, 450 (5th Cir. 1982) (manufacturer not required to have foreseen and guard against deviation in use of acid-hauling trailer as a sulphur trailer); Helene Curtis Indus., Inc. v. Pruitt, 385 F.2d 841, 855 (5th Cir. 1967), *cert. denied*, 391 U.S. 913 (1968); (application of a mixture of two cosmetic bleaching products not an intended use).

27. *See, e.g.*, Butaud v. Suburban Marine & Sporting Goods, Inc., 543 P.2d 209, 214 (Alaska 1975), *modified*, 555 P.2d 42 (Alaska 1976); Azzarello v. Black Bros. Co., 480 Pa. 547, 554, 391 A.2d 1020, 1027 (1978).

mandate of *Restatement (Second) of Torts* § 402A and require that the defect render the product unreasonably dangerous, thus preventing a product supplier from assuming the unintended status of an insurer.[28] Texas has adhered to the majority position since adoption of the strict tort liability concept in 1967.[29]

In Texas, "defectively designed" is defined as "a product that is unreasonably dangerous as designed, taking into consideration the utility of the product and the risk involved in its use."[30] Essentially, the standard for a defective design is evaluated in relation to available safer design alternatives.[31] Included in the test of a defectively designed product is the consideration of whether additional safety features would significantly increase the cost while diminishing the utility of the product.[32] A manufacturer is not required to destroy the utility of his product to make it safe,[33] and the possibility that the manufacturer might have designed the product with greater safety does not necessarily imply that the product design actually utilized was unreasonably dangerous.[34] Factors that assist in determining the adequacy of a product design include:

1. The usefulness and desirability of the product;
2. The availability of other and safer products to meet the

---

28. *See, e.g.*, Potthoff v. Alms, 41 Colo. App. 51, 583 P.2d 309, 311 (1978); Aller v. Rodgers Mach. Mfg. Co., 268 N.W.2d 830, 834 (Iowa 1978); Rourke v. Garza, 530 S.W.2d 794, 798 (Tex. 1975).

29. *See, e.g.*, Hagans v. Oliver Mach. Co., 576 F.2d 97 (5th Cir. 1978); Acord v. Gen. Motors Corp., 669 S.W.2d 111, 113 (Tex. 1984); *Rourke*, 530 S.W.2d at 798; *Turner*, 584 S.W.2d at 842; *Miller*, 568 S.W.2d at 650; *Hopkins*, 548 S.W.2d at 351; Darryl v. Ford Motor Co., 440 S.W.2d 630 (Tex. 1969).

30. *Turner*, 584 S.W.2d 844, 851. *See, e.g.*, Carter v. Massey-Ferguson, Inc., 716 F.2d 344, 348 (5th Cir. 1983); Accord v. Gen. Motors Corp., 669 S.W.2d 111, 116 (Tex. 1984); *Kindred*, 650 S.W.2d 61, 62; Boatland of Houston, Inc. v. Bailey, 609 S.W.2d 743, 746 (Tex. 1980); Ford Motor Co. v. Pool. 688 S.W.2d 879 (Tex. App.—Texarkana 1985).

31. *See, e.g.*, Shipps v. Gen. Motors Co., 750 F.2d 418, 423 (5th Cir. 1985) (feasibility of safer alternative to Trans Am roof); Davidson v. Stanadyne, Inc., 718 F.2d 1334, 1338 (5th Cir. 1983) (feasibility of scald guards on bathtub shower faucet); Kindred v. Con/Chem, Inc., 650 S.W.2d 61, 62 (Tex. 1983) (different primer base in primer); Boatland of Houston, Inc. v. Bailey, 609 S.W.2d 743, 746 (Tex. 1980) (availability of bass boat kill switch).

32. *See* Helicoid Gage Div. of Am. Chain & Cable Co. v. Howell, 511 S.W.2d 573, 577 (Tex. Civ. App.—Houston 1974, writ ref'd n.r.e.). But the element of increased cost is not a required element of proof. *See* Kindred v. Con/Chem Inc., 650 S.W.2d 61 (Tex. 1983).

33. *See* Hagans v. Oliver Mach. Co., 576 F.2d 97, 101 (5th Cir. 1978); Henderson v. Ford Motor Co., 519 S.W.2d 87, 92 (Tex. 1974).

34. *See* Syrie v. Knoll Int'l., 748 F.2d 304, 307 (5th Cir. 1984); Carter v. Massey-Ferguson, Inc., 716 F.2d 344, 347 (5th Cir. 1983); Daberko v. Heil Co., 681 F.2d 445, 448 (5th Cir. 1982); Hagans v. Oliver Mach. Co., 576 F.2d 97, 100 (5th Cir. 1978); Acord v. General Motors Corp., 669 S.W.2d 111, 113 (Tex. 1984); *Henderson*, 519 S.W.2d 87, 93.

same need;

3. The likelihood of injury and its probable seriousness;

4. The obviousness of the danger;

5. Common knowledge and normal public expectation of the danger;

6. The avoidability of injury by care and use of the product (including the effect of instructions or warnings); and

7. The ability to eliminate the danger without seriously impairing the usefulness of the product or making it unduly expensive.[35]

Though evidence relevant to these elements that constitute the balancing criteria should be overtly advanced by both parties, the jury is prohibited from receiving any instruction on these factors.[36]

3. Marketing Defects. A marketing defect claim; that is, a claim of the absence or inadequacy of any warning or instruction accompanying the product, is established in a manner similar to negligence actions. The plaintiff initially is obligated to establish that the defendant had a duty to warn.[37] This involves establishing that the manufacturer either knew or should have known of the danger or risk of harm inherent in the intended or reasonably anticipated uses of the product.[38] Next, the plaintiff must establish

---

35. Dean Wade, *Strict Tort Liability of Manufacturers*, 19 Sw. L.J. 5, 17 (1965). *See Oliver Mach. Co.*, 576 F.2d 97; Weakley v. Fischbach & Moore, Inc., 515 F.2d 1260, 1267-69 (5th Cir. 1975); Acord v. General Motors Corp., 669 S.W.2d 111, 116 (Tex. 1984); Boatland of Houston, Inc. v. Bailey, 609 S.W.2d 743, 746 (Tex. 1980); Turner v. General Motors Corp., 584 S.W.2d 844, 851 (Tex. 1979).

36. *Turner*, 584 S.W.2d 844, 849; *see* Kindred v. Con/Chem, Inc. 650 S.W.2d 61 (Tex. 1983); *Acord*, 669 S.W.2d at 113; Shipp v. General Motors Corp; 750 F.2d 418, 421 (5th Cir. 1985). *But see* Burks v. Firestone Tire & Rubber Co., 633 F.2d 1152 (5th Cir. 1981) (decided prior to *Acord*, holding that the balancing instruction which included feasibility of the alternative design of a tire rim was properly submitted to the jury). *See generally* Birnbaum, *Unmasking the Test for Design Defect: From Negligence [to Warranty] to Strict Liability to Negligence*, 33 VAND. L. REV. 593, 633 (1980).

37. *See* Borel v. Fibreboard Paper Prods. Corp., 493 F.2d 1076, 1088 (5th Cir. 1973), *cert. denied*, 419 U.S. 869 (1974) (interpreting Texas law). *See generally* Sales, *The Duty to Warn and Instructions for Safe Use in Strict Tort Liability*, 13 ST. MARY'S L.J. 521, 524 (1981); Comment, *Products Liability in Texas: Foreseeability and Warnings*, 58 TEX. L. REV. 1323 (1980) [hereinafter cited as Comment, *Products Liability*].

38. *See, e.g.*, Pavlides v. Galveston Yacht Basin, Inc., 727 F.2d 330, 338-39 (5th Cir. 1984); Scott v. Black & Decker, Inc., 717 F.2d 251, 253 (5th Cir. 1983); *Borel*, 493 F.2d at 1088 ("The requirement of foreseeability coincides with the standard of due care in negligence cases, . . . "); Bristol-Myers Co. v. Gonzales, 561 S.W.2d 801, 804 (Tex. 1978). Pearson v. Hevi-Duty Elec., 618 S.W.2d 784, 787 (Tex. App.—Houston [1st Dist.] 1981, writ

that the product was defective and unreasonably dangerous for its intended and reasonably foreseeable uses in the absence of an adequate warning or instructions for safe use.[39] A defectively marketed product is a product that is unreasonably dangerous; that is, dangerous to an extent beyond that which would be contemplated by the ordinary user of the product, with the ordinary knowledge common to the community of such users as to the product's characteristics.[40] The lack of an adequate warning must also be a producing cause of the plaintiff's injuries.[41] A presumption exists that an adequate warning would have been read and heeded.[42]

Many cases involve the potential for both a design and a marketing defect.[43] Proof of a marketing defect is generally less complex than proof of a design defect, and it is generally easier for the jury to comprehend the need for better warnings or instructions than to comprehend a complex design.[44] The adequacy of a warning or instruction for safe use generally is considered to be an issue for the trier of fact.[45]

---

ref'd n.r.e.); Rawlings Sporting Goods Co. v. Daniels, 619 S.W.2d 435, 439 (Tex. App.—Waco 1981, writ ref'd n.r.e.). *See generally* Sales, *The Duty to Warn and Instructions for Safe Use in Strict Tort Liability*, 13 St. Mary's L.J. 521, 524 (1982).

39. *See, e.g.*, Pavlides v. Galveston Yacht Basin Inc., 727 F.2d 330, 338 (5th Cir. 1984); Gross v. Black & Decker (U.S.) Inc., 695 F.2d 858, 866 (5th Cir. 1983); *Borel*, 493 F.2d 1076, 1089; *Bristol-Myers Co.*, 561 S.W.2d 804.

40. Restatement (Second) of Torts § 402A comment i (1965). *See generally*, Sales, *supra* note 38.

41. *See, e.g.*, Borel v. Fibreboard Paper Prod. Corp., 493 F.2d 1076, 1094 (5th Cir. 1973), *cert. denied*, 419 U.S. 869 (1974); Bristol-Myers Co. v. Gonzales, 561 S.W.2d 801, 804 (Tex. 1978); Travenol Labs., Inc. v. Bandy Labs., Inc., 608 S.W.2d 308 (Tex. Civ. App.—Waco 1980, writ ref'd n.r.e.). The failure to demonstrate that the accident could have been avoided by an adequate warning negates causation. *See, e.g.*, Guidry v. KEM Mfg. Co., 693 F.2d 426, 430-31 (5th Cir. 1982); Hagan v. EZ Mfg. Co., 674 F.2d 1047, 1052 (5th Cir. 1982). Blackwell Burners, Inc. v. Cerda, 644 S.W.2d 512 (Tex. App.—San Antonio 1982, writ ref'd n.r.e.)

42. Technical Chem. Co. v. Jacobs, 480 S.W.2d 602, 606 (1972). *See generally* Comment, *Products Liability*, *supra* note 37, at 1326.

43. *See, e.g.*, Harrison v. Flota Mercante Grancolombiana, S.A., 577 F.2d 968 (5th Cir. 1978); *Giesecke*, 589 S.W.2d 516; *Lopez*, 584 S.W.2d 333; *Bristol-Myers*, 561 S.W.2d 801; Ethicon, Inc. v. Parten, 520 S.W.2d 527 (Tex. Civ. App.—Houston [14th Dist.] 1975, no writ); *Helicoid*, 511 S.W.2d at 576.

44. Noel, *Products Defective Because of Inadequate Directions or Warnings*, 23 Sw. L.J. 256, 260-61 (1969).

45. *Pavlides*, 727 F.2d 330, 338-39; Shop Rite Foods, Inc. v. Upjohn Co., 619 S.W.2d 574, 579 (Tex. App.—Amarillo 1981, writ ref'd n.r.e); Pearson v. Hevi-Duty Elec. Co., 618 S.W.2d 784, 787 (Tex. Civ. App.—Houston [1st Dist.] 1981, writ ref'd. n.r.e.); Lopez v. ARO Corp., 584 S.W.2d 333, 336-337 (Tex. Civ. App.—San Antonio 1979, writ ref'd n.r.e.).

4. *Summary.* The methods of proof utilized in a strict tort liability action are determined by the type of defect alleged. When the case involves a manufacturing defect, circumstantial evidence may be especially important if the product has been destroyed. In a design defect case, evidence of the particular product involved in the accident is not as critical, since the alleged design defect appears in the entire line of that particular product. A number of factors are weighed in determining whether the design is unreasonably dangerous. The marketing defect involves a failure to warn or to instruct for safe use and is akin to a negligence action. Under the marketing defect theory, the plaintiff must prove that the manufacturer had a duty to warn, and that the product was rendered unreasonably dangerous in the absence of a warning or instruction for safe use.

B. *Relevancy: Federal Rules of Evidence 401-403; Texas Rules of Evidence 401-403*

The admissibility of evidence, whether direct, expert or circumstantial, is dependent on relevancy. Relevancy, under both the Federal and Texas Rules of Evidence, is defined to mean "evidence having any tendency to make the existence of any fact that is of consequence to the determination of the action more probable or less probable than it would be without the evidence."[46] Under both the Federal and Texas rule, all relevant evidence is admissible except as provided by statute or by the rules of evidence.[47] Irrelevant evidence, of course, is inadmissible, whether direct, expert or circumstantial.[48]

Evidence, though relevant, may be excluded under provisions of both the Federal and Texas rules. Specifically, Federal Rule 403 provides that evidence may be excluded "if its probative value is

---

46. FED. R. EVID. 401 provides, " 'Relevant evidence' means evidence having any tendency to make the existence of any fact that is of consequence to the determination of the action more probable or less probable than it would be without the evidence.' " This rule is identical to TEX. R. EVID. 401 (1984).

47. FED. R. EVID. 402 provides, "All relevant evidence is admissible, except as otherwise provided by the Constitution of the United States, by Act of Congress, by these rules, or by other rules prescribed by the Supreme Court pursuant to statutory authority. Evidence which is not relevant is not admissible." TEX. R. EVID. 402 adopts verbatim the text of this rule.

48. The common law rule excluding irrelevant evidence is specifically codified in FED. R EVID. 402 and TEX. R. EVID. 402.

substantially outweighed by the danger of unfair prejudice, confusion of the issues, or misleading the jury, or by considerations of undue delay, waste of time, or needless presentation of cumulative evidence."[49] Essentially, the trial court must balance the effect of relevant probative evidence against the danger that unfair prejudice and confusion will unduly and improperly affect the jury.

In determining unfair prejudice under Rule 403, the court must determine that the probative value of the challenged evidence is substantially outweighed by the unfairness of the prejudice that it engenders.[50] Thus, a slight danger that the admission of relevant evidence will cause unfair prejudice is ignored.[51] In essence, the evidence must be more than damaging to the adverse party; it must be "unfairly prejudicial."[52] Unfair prejudice as contemplated by Rule 403 is not equated with testimony that is simply adverse to the opposing party; virtually all evidence is prejudicial or it simply is not material to any issue in the case. The prejudice must rise to the degree of basic "unfairness."[53] As noted by the Fifth Circuit in *Gross v. Black & Decker, (U.S.), Inc.*,[54] "[p]robative evidence will frequently be prejudicial to a party, but that does not mean that it will cause a fact finder to ground a decision on an emotional basis."[55] The Fifth Circuit fashioned a two-prong test by which to weigh the probative value against unfair prejudice: (1) the necessity for and probative effect of the proffered evidence; and (2) whether the same facts can be established by other less prejudicial evidence.[56] After weighing relevancy against

---

49. Fed. R. Evid. 403. *See* Gideon v. Johns-Manville Sales Corp., 761 F.2d 1129 (5th Cir. 1985).

50. *See, e.g.*, Jackson v. Johns-Manville Sales Corp., 750 F.2d 1314, 1319 (5th Cir. 1985) (en banc); Gross v. Black & Decker (U.S.), Inc., 695 F.2d 858, 863 (5th Cir. 1983).

51. *See, e.g.*, United States v. Hearod, 499 F.2d 1003, 1004 (5th Cir. 1974) (the judge must balance probative value against undue prejudice to the objecting party).

52. *See* Soden v. Freightliner Corp., 714 F.2d 498, 509 (5th Cir. 1983) (the Fifth Circuit noted that a limited instruction given by the judge "properly made clear the hearsay, unsworn and a self-serving nature of the other complaints, and specified exactly what consideration the allegations in the other lawsuits were and were not to be given, and mitigated the danger of any unfair prejudice." citing United States v. Moore, 522 F.2d 1068, 1079 (9th Cir. 1975), *cert. denied*, 423 U.S. 1049 (1976).); Koloda v. General Motors Corp., 716 F.2d 373, 378 (6th Cir. 1983); Dollar v. Long Mfg., N.C., Inc., 561 F.2d 613, 618 (5th Cir. 1977), *cert. denied*, 435 U.S. 996 (1977).

53. Gross v. Black & Decker (U.S.), Inc., 695 F.2d 858, 863 (5th Cir. 1983).

54. *Id.*

55. *Id.*

56. *Id.*

unfair prejudice, the court must then determine whether a limiting instruction would defuse such improper influence. Generally, the determination by the trial court that relevant evidence is admissible, even without a limiting instruction, will not be disturbed on appeal absent a clear showing of abuse.[57]

For example, the court considered the admissibility of cancer evidence in *Jackson v. Johns Manville Sales Corp.*,[58] a suit based on strict tort liability against the manufacturer of asbestos products seeking damages for increased risk of contracting cancer and for mental anguish for the fear of contracting cancer. The Fifth Circuit noted that though cancer evidence is relevant to the issue of the manufacturer's liability, its admissibility is unfairly prejudicial under Rule 403 unless Mississippi law allows recovery of damages for either fear of cancer or for the possibility of contracting cancer in the future from exposure to asbestos products[59] If the possibility of contracting future cancer constitutes a recoverable element of damages, only then would the probative value of this prejudicial evidence be sufficiently relevant to be admissible.[60] Similarly, in *Shipp v. General Motors Corp.*,[61] the trial court refused to permit the manufacturer to introduce demonstrative evidence in the form of a film demonstrating occupant movement in a rollover accident. The court noted that the demonstrative film of a rollover accident involved multiple rather than single revolutions, involved a different vehicle with substantially different roof and passenger compartment features, and occurred under somewhat different circumstances.[62] After balancing the acknowledged relevance of the out-of-court experiment against the danger that its admission would mislead, confuse, or prejudice the jury, the trial

---

57. Shipp v. Gen. Motors Corp., 750 F.2d 418, 427 (5th Cir. 1984); *see* FED. R. EVID. 403 advisory committee notes ("In reaching a decision whether to exclude on grounds of unfair prejudice, consideration should be given to the probable effectiveness or lack of effectiveness of a limiting instruction.").

58. 750 F.2d 1314 (5th Cir. 1985) (en banc).

59. *Id.* at 1321 (A trial court's determination under Rule 403, however, will not be reversed absent a finding of an abuse of discretion). *Id. See, e.g.*, Shipp v. General Motors Corp., 750 F.2d 418, 427 (5th Cir. 1984) (Rule 403 determinations are often inextricably bound with the facts of a particular case and thus will not be disturbed absent a showing of clear abuse.); Wright v. Hartford Accident & Indem. Co., 580 F.2d 809, 810 (5th Cir. 1978). *See also*, Jon-T Chems. Inc. v. Freeport Chem. Co., 704 F.2d 1412, 1417 (5th Cir. 1983).

60. 750 F.2d at 1321.

61. 750 F.2d 418 (5th Cir. 1985).

62. *Id.* at 427.

court, under Federal Rule of Evidence 403, excluded the film. The Fifth Circuit affirmed the trial court action holding that "Rule 403 determinations are often inextricably bound with the facts of a particular case and thus will not be disturbed absent a showing of clear abuse."[63]

The Texas rule of relevancy parallels the federal rule. Essentially, relevant evidence may be excluded only when its probative value is substantially outweighed by unfair prejudice. In reality, the rule reflects a codification of decisional law that the court should not exclude relevant evidence without "very good cause."[64] For instance, in *Ford Motor Co. v. Pool,*[65] plaintiff's wife offered evidence of loss of consortium resulting from plaintiff's injuries. The trial court refused defendant's rebuttal evidence to establish that plaintiff's wife had filed for divorce prior to the lawsuit, and had sought a restraining order prohibiting plaintiff's mother from interfering with their marriage. The court held that the trial court erroneously excluded defendant's rebuttal evidence because it was a relevant response to plaintiff's cause of action and would not have opened up new areas of inquiry or injected substantially prejudicial facts.[66]

It is abundantly clear, therefore, that relevant evidence is sanctioned under both the Federal and Texas Rules of Evidence. Relevant evidence should be excluded only upon a showing by the opponent that the prejudicial effect of such evidence substantially outweighs the probative value of such evidence.[67] In making its determination, the court should first determine whether the relevant evidence is necessary and has a probative effect on significant issues involved in the lawsuit and, secondly, whether the issues involved in the lawsuit can be established by other evidence possessing a less prejudicial effect on a jury.[68] A decision by the trial court to admit relevant evidence under Rule 402[69] will not be reversed in the absence of a showing that the probative value of the challenged

---

63. *Id.* Ballou v. Henri Studies, Inc., 656 F.2d 1147, 1153 (5th Cir. 1981); King v. Ford Motor Co., 597 F.2d 436, 445 (5th Cir. 1979); Wright v. Hartford Accident & Indem. Co., 580 F.2d 809, 810 (5th Cir. 1978).

64. Ford Motor Co. v. Pool, 688 S.W.2d. 879 (Tex. App.—Texarkana 1985, no writ).

65. *Id.* at 882.

66. *Id. See also* Davis v. Davis, 521 S.W.2d 603, 607 (Tex. 1975).

67. Fed. R. Evid. 403; Tex. R. Evid. 403.

68. Gross v. Black & Decker (U.S.), Inc., 695 F.2d 858, 863 (5th Cir. 1983).

69. Fed. R. Evid. 402; Tex. R. Evid. 402.

evidence was substantially outweighed by its "unfair prejudice" on the jury.

C. *Direct Evidence*

To fully understand the meaning of direct evidence, the broader category of demonstrative evidence must first be defined. Demonstrative evidence is generally any evidence that the trier of fact experiences firsthand through sensory perception.[70] This broad definition is subdivided into the two categories: real evidence and a more narrow category of demonstrative evidence.[71] The real evidence category includes the production of the product that was actually involved in the injury-producing event as well as an exhibition of the parts of the body injured in the incident.[72] Real evidence includes under its aegis both direct and circumstantial evidence. Direct evidence, the subject of this section, is employed when the condition of the object itself is an issue, such as in exploding bottle cases.[73] Circumstantial evidence includes such evidence as, for example, a piece of burned clothing near the scene of a car that exploded.[74] Demonstrative evidence is distinguished from real evidence because it is not directly involved in the injury-producing event. Rather, demonstrative evidence is merely illustrative and functions as an aid to the jury's understanding of other evidence.[75] Examples of demonstrative evidence include models, maps, photographs, and drawings.[76]

In a strict tort liability action, direct evidence produces a major impact on the jury. When the product is available for examination after the accident, direct evidence consisting of chemical anal-

---

70. *See generally* C. McCormick, Handbook of the Law of Evidence § 212, at 524-28 (2d ed. 1972); Michael & Adler, *Real Proof*, 5 Vand. L. Rev. 344 (1952).

71. M. Graham, Handbook of Federal Evidence § 401.2 (1981).

72. *Id.*

73. *Id. See, e.g.*, Pittsburg Coca-Cola Bottling Works v. Ponder, 443 S.W.2d 546 (Tex. 1969).

74. *Id. See, e.g.*, Franks v. National Dairy Prods. Corp., 414 F.2d 682 (5th Cir. 1969); Caldwell v. United States, 338 F.2d 385 (8th Cir. 1964), *cert. denied*, 380 U.S. 984 (1965); Rawlings Sporting Goods Co. v. Daniels, 619 S.W.2d 435 (Tex. App.—Waco 1981, writ ref'd n.r.e.).

75. *Id. See* Howard v. Faberge, Inc., 679 S.W.2d 644, 648 (Tex. App.—Houston [1st Dist.] 1984, no writ) (in-court demonstrations of cologne's nonflammability throughout the stages of evaporation); *see also* C. McCormick, *supra* note 70.

76. *See* C. McCormick, *supra* note 70.

ysis, visual observations, tests, and court experiments are available to establish an existing defect.[77] Because a jury undoubtedly is greatly influenced by such evidence, the jury may occasionally be misled or confused on the issues.[78] The danger of confusion is minimized by Rule 403,[79] which requires the court to balance all factors before admitting such evidence.[80]

As a general rule, direct evidence must be authenticated.[81] Under Texas Rule 901, "[t]he requirement of authentication or identification as a condition precedent to admissibility is satisfied by evidence sufficient to support a finding that the matter in question is what its proponent claims."[82] Usually, authentication of direct evidence is accomplished by the testimony of a witness connecting the evidence to a relevant issue in the case.[83]

Experiments are admissible to illustrate characteristics of the defective product, cause and effect, and the manner in which a particular event occurred.[84] Because of variations in conditions, courts require that experimental conditions be substantially simi-

---

77. *See, e.g., Faberge*, 679 S.W.2d 644, 648 (demonstrations and tests of nonflammability of cologne); McKisson v. Sales Affiliates, Inc., 416 S.W.2d 787, 792 (Tex. 1967) (chemical test of a permanent wave solution conclusively established that the constituent elements of the solution separated and made the product defective); Shamrock Fuel & Oil Sales Co. v. Tunks, 416 S.W.2d 779, 781 (Tex. 1967) (test of kerosene established that it was adulterated by gasoline); Bell Helicopter Co. v. Bradshaw, 594 S.W.2d 519, 527 (Tex. Civ. App.—Corpus Christi 1979, writ ref'd n.r.e.) (examination of a failed helicopter tail rotor blade disclosed a fatigue fracture); F.M.C. Corp. v. Burns, 444 S.W.2d 315, 318 (Tex. Civ. App.—San Antonio 1969, no writ.).

78. *See, e.g.*, Howard v. Faberge, Inc., 679 S.W.2d 644, 649-50 (Tex. Civ. App.—Houston [1st Dist.] 1984, no writ.) (Trial court committed prejudicial error in allowing defense counsel, during closing argument, to perform an unauthorized demonstration. Counsel, in arguing against the flammability of defendent's manufacturing cologne, poured it on his arm, lit a match, and urged God to burn him if he was wrong.); Turner v. General Motors Corp., 584 S.W.2d 844, 852 (Tex. 1979) (approved trial court exclusion of out-of-court experiments demonstrating effect of roof crush) *See generally*, Ft. Worth & Denver Ry. v. Williams, 375 S.W.2d 279, 282 (Tex. 1964); Kirk v. Bennett, 456 S.W.2d 191, 194 (Tex. Civ. App.—Waco 1970, writ ref'd n.r.e.).

79. TEX. R. EVID 403; FED. R. EVID. 403.

80. *See, e.g.*, Shipp v. General Motors Corp., 750 F.2d 418, 427 (5th Cir. 1985) (excluding defendant's film demonstrating occupant movement in a rollover accident because the purported differences between plaintiff's accident and the accident depicted in the film would mislead, confuse, or prejudice the jury).

81. 2 R. RAY, TEXAS LAW OF EVIDENCE 1451 (Texas Practice 3d ed. 1980).

82. TEX. R. EVID. 901(a).

83. 2 R. RAY, *supra* note 81.

84. M. GRAHAM, *supra* note 71 § 401.10. *See, e.g., Shipp*, 750 F.2d at 427 (drop test of TransAm relevant to roof strength).

lar to the actual conditions of the accident.[85]

The requirement of substantial similarity is emphasized in *Barnes v. General Motors Corp.*[86] Plaintiff alleged that his car crashed because of a malfunctioning accelerator pedal. The plaintiff contended, among other things, that the accelerator pedal stuck because of the defective design of the accelerator linkage, spark plug wire bracket, and engine mounts.[87] Plaintiff theorized that the left engine mount separated prior to the accident, and that the engine acceleration was sufficient to cause the engine to lift, thus binding the accelerator linkage with the spark plug wire bracket. Plaintiff's expert testified about the results of tests he performed on another automobile of the same model. Because the engine mounts on the test car had been removed by the owner and bolted directly onto the frame, the roll-top feature of plaintiff's automobile could not be tested to determine whether that feature would prevent the engine from binding the accelerator. Therefore, plaintiff's expert removed the left bolt and loosened the right bolt of the engine of the test car to simulate actual conditions. In the test, the engine lifted, binding the accelerator.[88]

The admission of the results of this experiment constituted reversible error.[89] The court acknowledged that the trial court possesses considerable discretion to admit evidence of out-of-court experiments conducted under substantially similar conditions.[90] The court further noted that the burden is upon the proponent of out-of-court experiments to establish a proper foundation by demonstrating a substantial similarity of the product, the circumstances, and the existing conditions.[91] Because of the danger of misleading the jury, who may attach exaggerated significance to such tests,[92] the court required that the conditions of the experiment be "so nearly the same in substantial particulars as to afford a fair com-

---

85. *See, e.g.*, Turner v. General Motors Corp., 584 S.W.2d 844 (Tex. 1979) (experiments involving crush tests on car roof).

86. 547 F.2d 275, 277 (5th Cir. 1977). *See also Shipp*, 750 F.2d at 427.

87. 547 F.2d at 276.

88. *Id.* at 277.

89. *Id.*

90. *Id.* (citing Booth v. Garan, Inc., 476 F.2d 591 (5th Cir. 1973); Council v. Duprel, 250 Miss. 269, 165 So.2d 134 (1964); Building Insulators, Inc. v. Stuart, 243 Miss. 287, 136 So. 2d 613 (1962)). *See also F.M.C.*, 444 S.W.2d 315.

91. *Id.* (citing Navajo Freight Lines v. Mahaffy, 174 F.2d 305, 310 (10th Cir. 1949)).

92. *Id.* (citing C. McCormick, *supra* note 70 § 202).

parison in respect to the particular issue to which the test is directed."[93] The court concluded that the test was not conducted under substantially similar circumstances from those admittedly existing at the time of the accident.[94]

Experiments may be conducted in or out of court, though generally they are conducted *out* of court and reported in court.[95] The admissibility of experimental evidence, however, remains within the sound discretion of the trial court and will usually not be disturbed on appeal.[96] Whether to allow the experiment to be performed in court is likewise a matter of trial court discretion.[97]

Viewing the product may be helpful to the jury in a products liability case. "A view may be appropriate to the jury where, for example, the witness can assume his actual position as he operated a piece of machinery."[98] Even if the product has changed, the jury may be permitted to view it if the change is irrelevant or explained.[99] Texas generally permits the common law practice of a jury view.[100]

D. *Expert Testimony*

1. Introduction. The testimony of an expert witness is particularly crucial in strict tort liability actions.[101] Unlike an observer, who testifies based on firsthand knowledge of the facts, an expert draws inferences from the facts that would be difficult or

---

93. *Id.* (quoting Ill. Cent. Gulf R.R. v. Ishee, Miss., 317 So.2d 923, 926 (Miss. 1975)).

94. *Id. See* FMC Corp. v. Burns, 444 S.W.2d 315, 322 (Tex. Civ. App.—San Antonio 1969, no writ); Pitcock v. B & W Inc., 476 S.W.2d 83, 95 (Tex. Civ. App.—Houston [1st Dist.] 1971, writ ref'd n.r.e.); Standard Motor Co. v. Blood, 380 S.W.2d 651, 655 (Tex. Civ. App.—Houston [1st. Dist.] 1964, writ dism'd by agr.); Kainer v. Walker, 377 S.W.2d 613, 616 (Tex. 1964) (absence of substantial similarity); Ft. Worth & Denver Ry. v. Williams, 375 S.W.2d 279, 283 (Tex. 1964) (absence of substantial similarity of conditions).

95. M. Graham, *supra* note 71, § 401.10. *See, e.g.*, Shipp, 750 F.2d at 427.

96. *See Shipp*, 750 F.2d at 427; Wright v. Redman Mobile Homes, Inc., 541 F.2d 1096, 1097-98 (5th Cir. 1976); Continental Bus System, Inc. v. Biggers, 322 S.W.2d 1, 10 (Tex. Civ. App.—Houston [1st. Dist.] 1959, writ ref'd n.r.e.).

97. *See* Fed. R. Evid. 403; Tex. R. Evid. 403. *See generally* Schleunes v. American Casualty Co., 528 F.2d 634, 637-38 (5th Cir. 1976).

98. M. Graham, *supra* note 71, § 401.11.

99. *Id.*

100. *See* 2 R. Ray, *supra* note 81, at 1464 (development of Texas law with respect to "jury view").

101. *See* Henderson v. Ford Motor Co., 519 S.W.2d 87, 92 (Tex. 1974), in which the failure of an expert to identify a design defect and provide an alternative design was deemed fatal.

impossible for a jury to determine.[102] In product liability cases, expert testimony is admissible to establish that a product is defective or unreasonably dangerous,[103] to explain the probable cause of the accident,[104] and to establish a duty to warn.[105]

Rules 702 through 706 of the Federal Rules of Evidence,[106] enacted by Congress in 1975, establish the parameters of admissibility of expert testimony in federal courts. The codified Texas Rules of Evidence 702 through 705[107] correspond to the Federal Rules, except that Texas has not adopted the equivalent of Rule 706 of the Federal Rules relating to court-appointed expert witnesses.[108]

2. *Expert Testimony Generally.* An expert witness must possess special skills, knowledge, training, experience, or education with respect to the subject matter involved, as a predicate for expressing an opinion.[109] Since the proponent of the expert opinion has the burden of demonstrating that the witness qualifies as an expert,[110] the qualification of a witness to express an expert opin-

---

102. C. McCormick, *supra* note 70, at § 13.

103. *See, e.g.*, Kindred v. Con/Chem Inc., 650 S.W.2d 61, 63 (Tex. 1983) (composition of a primer); Sharp v. Chrysler Corp., 432 S.W.2d 131, 137 (Tex. Civ. App.—Houston [14th Dist.] 1968, writ ref'd n.r.e.)(defect in brake cylinder); Davidson v. Stanadyne, Inc., 718 F.2d 1334, 1338 (5th Cir. 1983) (defective design in failing to include scald guard); Gonzales v. Caterpillar Tractor Co., 571 S.W.2d 867, 871 (Tex. 1978)(defective design of step-down from loader); Rourke v. Garza, 530 S.W.2d 794, 799 (Tex. 1975). (defective design in failing to install cleats on scaffolding)

104. *See, e.g.*, General Motors Corp. v. Hopkins, 548 S.W.2d 244, 348-49 (Tex. 1977); Ford Motor Co. v. Bland, 517 S.W.2d 641, 643-44 (Tex. Civ. App.—Waco 1974, writ ref'd n.r.e.).

105. *See, e.g.*, Borel v. Fibreboard Paper Prods. Corp., 493 F.2d 1076, 1092-93 (5th Cir. 1973), *cert. denied*, 419 U.S. 869 (1974); Pavlides v. Galveston Yacht Basin Inc., 727 F.2d 330, 335 (5th Cir. 1984); Bristol-Myers Co. v. Gonzales, 561 S.W.2d 801, 804 (Tex. 1978); Pearson v. Hevi-Duty Electric Co., 618 S.W. 2d 784 (Tex. App.—Houston [1st Dist.] 1981, writ ref'd n.r.e.)

106. Fed. R. Evid. 702-706.

107. Tex. R. Evid. 702-705.

108. *See* Black, *The Texas Rules of Evidence—A Proposed Codification*, 31 Sw. L.J. 969, 995-96 (1977) (stating that Fed. R. Evid. is undesirable and inconsistent with Texas law).

109. *See* Daberko v. Heil Co., 681 F.2d 445, 450 (5th Cir. 1982) (expert opinion); Hutchins v. Humble Oil & Ref. Co., 161 S.W.2d 571, 573 (Tex. Civ. App.—Galveston 1942, writ ref'd w.o.m.) (trial court properly excluded geologist's opinion because it was not demonstrated that he possessed a higher degree of knowledge as to the particular matter which constituted the subject of inquiry); Tokio Marine & Fire Ins. Co. v. Aldridge, 21 S.W.2d 547, 551 (Tex. Civ. App.—Amarillo 1929, writ ref'd) (experienced contractor's testimony relating to cause of damage to a house was admissible).

110. *See* International Sec. Life Ins. Co. v. Beauchamp, 464 S.W.2d 679, 681 (Tex. Civ.

ion must be established prior to rendition of any opinion.[111] Opposing counsel is entitled to cross-examine an expert witness on his qualifications prior to the proffer of an expert opinion.[112]

The determination of whether an expert witness is qualified to render an opinion rests in the trial court's discretion.[113] *Kettle v. Smircich*,[114] an action for personal injuries against a driver of an automobile by a passenger in another automobile, addressed the issue of expert witness qualifications. The appellate court concluded the trial court did not abuse his discretion because the expert's educational background and practical experience concerning the subject under inquiry was sufficient to permit the expression of an expert opinion.[115] The court noted that the defendant failed to properly object to the use of estimated weights of the vehicles.[116]

Even in the absence of a formal education, a witness may qualify as an expert based solely on experience and training. The qualification of a witness may be based on a personal study of technical works, but a degree is not essential.[117] An expert may state an opinion based on personal observation of the facts, on competent evidence in the case, on assumed facts supported by the

---

App.—Amarillo 1971, no writ) (failure of a witness to qualify as an expert renders testimony on "reasonable" medical expenses reversible error); Woods v. Rustay, Martin & Vale, 430 S.W.2d 543, 546 (Tex. Civ. App.—Houston [14th Dist.] 1968, writ ref'd n.r.e.) (testimony of a witness who fails to qualify as an expert must be excluded).

111. *See* J.P. Watkins Land Mortgage Co. v. Campbell, 98 Tex. 372, 84 S.W. 424, 425 (1905); Hugh Cooper Co. v. American National Exchange Bank, 30 S.W.2d 364, 370 (Tex. Civ. App.—Dallas 1930, no writ).

112. *See* Texas Employers' Ins. Ass'n v. Garza, 557 S.W.2d 843, 846 (Tex. Civ. App.—Corpus Christi 1977, writ ref'd n.r.e.); French v. Brodsky, 521 S.W.2d 670, 675 (Tex. Civ. App.—Houston [1st Dist.] 1975, writ ref'd n.r.e.).

113. *See* Simien v. S. S. Kresge Co., 566 F.2d 551, 558 (5th Cir. 1978) (expert opinion too facile for credibility); Perkins v. Volkswagen of America, 596 F.2d 681, 682 (5th Cir. 1979); Page v. Barko Hydraulics, 673 F.2d 134, 139 (5th Cir. 1982) (since the expert did not duplicate the actual mechanics involved in the fire-producing accident, and the testimony could thus have been more confusing than helpful, the trial court did not abuse its discretion).

114. 415 S.W.2d 935 (Tex. Civ. App.—Corpus Christi 1967, no writ).

115. *Id.* at 938.

116. *Id.* at 939.

117. Beard Drilling, Inc. v. Steeger, 361 S.W.2d 888, 896 (Tex. Civ. App.—Houston [1st. Dist.] 1962), *aff'd in part, rev'd in part*, 371 S.W.2d 684 (Tex. 1963) (though exclusion of proffered expert testimony did not constitute an abuse of discretion, the court acknowledged that an expert may be qualified by either study *or* experience); Lone Star Gas Co. v. Thomas, 345 S.W.2d 844, 846-47 (Tex. Civ. App.—Fort Worth 1961, writ ref'd n.r.e.) (a practicing veterinarian authorized to express an expert opinion involving the effect of chemicals on cattle).

evidence, or on a combination of facts within his own knowledge and facts established by the testimony of others.[118] An expert opinion may be based on all previous unconflicting testimony without a recitation of that testimony.[119]

In forming hypothetical questions, an attorney may utilize only facts which the evidence fairly tends to prove and the reasonable inferences that may be deduced from those facts.[120] Hypothetical questions need not be based on all the relevant facts and evidence, but sufficient facts must be included for the witness to form an intelligent decision.[121] Furthermore, facts on which a hypothetical question is based may be proved at a later stage.[122]

---

118. *See* Carter v. Massey Ferguson, Inc., 716 F.2d 344, 349-50 (5th Cir. 1983) (expert may base his opinion that a skidder was defectively designed solely from evidence presented at trial); Zippo Mfg. Co. v. Rogers Imports, Inc., 216 F. Supp. 670, 680-81 (S.D.N.Y. 1963) (expert testimony based on opinion survey); Upjohn Co. v. Rachelle Laboratories, Inc., 661 F.2d 1105, 1111-1112 (6th Cir. 1981) (expert testimony based on survey of salesmen's time in recall campaign).

119. *See* St. Louis Southwestern Ry. Co. of Texas v. Hall, 81 S.W. 571, 572 (Tex. Civ. App. 1904), *rev'd on other grounds*, 98 Tex. 480, 85 S.W. 786 (1905) (prior evidence that was not conflicting authorized expert testimony based on that unrecited evidence).

120. *See* Southwest Texas Methodist Hosp. v. Mills, 535 S.W.2d 27, 31 (Tex. Civ. App.—Tyler 1976, writ ref'd n.r.e.) (hypothetical question based on assumption that injury was not caused by trauma, in the absence of any evidence to support such assumption and where the other possible causes were not negated, was improper).

121. *See* Aetna Casualty & Surety Co. v. Scruggs, 413 S.W.2d 416, 422 (Tex. Civ. App.—Corpus Christi 1967, no writ) (coronary occlusion hypothetical); Jefferson Chemical Co. v. Forney Engineering Co., 466 S.W.2d 361, 364-65 (Tex. Civ. App.—Houston [1st Dist.] 1971, writ dism'd) (if all facts in a hypothetical question are uncontroverted or inferable from the testimony, it is reversible error to exclude the question even if all facts and evidence are not included); Burns v. Bridge Eng. Corp., 465 S.W.2d 427, 432 (Tex. Civ. App.—Houston [14th Dist.] 1971, writ ref'd n.r.e.) (hypothetical question need not be based on facts proven with mathematical certainty; it may include inferences reasonably drawn from other facts proved and consistent with the theory of the party propounding the question); Buchanan v. Central Freight Lines, Inc., 462 S.W.2d 391, 395 (Tex. Civ. App.—Dallas 1970, writ ref'd n.r.e.) (on cross-examination, a different set of facts or additional facts may be incorporated into the original hypothetical question).

122. *See* J. Weingarten, Inc. v. Tripplett, 530 S.W.2d 653, 656 (Tex. Civ. App.—Beaumont 1975, writ ref'd n.r.e.) (proper to admit hypothetical question with the provision that counsel later connect up the facts supported by evidence); Sabelli v. Security Ins. Co., 372 S.W.2d 348, 350-51 (Tex. Civ. App.—Austin 1963, writ ref'd n.r.e.) (improper to admit expert's opinion where medical expert was asked to assume facts that were part of a medical report not in evidence and the doctor who prepared the report was not subsequently called as a witness); John Hancock Mut. Life Ins. Co. v. Stanley, 215 S.W.2d 416, 421 (Tex. Civ. App.—Fort Worth 1948, writ ref'd n.r.e.) (when testimony is not later introduced to support the hypothetical question, then the trial court may protect the rights of the parties by making such ruling as it deems necessary).

An expert witness may not testify to questions of law.[123] Likewise, an expert opinion that is conjectural or speculative in nature is inadmissible.[124] Because an expert opinion must be predicated on facts in the record, an opinion lacking a factual basis possesses no probative value.[125]

3. *Expert Testimony in Products Liability Cases.* Expert testimony is indispensable in strict tort liability cases because such actions usually involve products that are technically complex. A legitimate expert assists the trier of fact in drawing reasonable inferences from the available facts.[126] The expert is particularly necessary to evaluate whether a particular product is defective.[127]

Testimony of qualified experts that a particular design is defective and that feasible alternative designs are available without adversely affecting the utility of the product is mandatory for establishing a defective design.[128] For instance, in *General Motors v.*

---

123. *See* Carr v. Radkey, 393 S.W.2d 806, 813 (Tex. 1965) (expert witness may not be asked whether testator had mental capacity to make a will); Zenith Radio Corp. v. Matsushita Elec. Indus. Co. Ltd., 505 F. Supp. 1313, 1332 (E.D. Pa. 1980) (legal conclusions are never appropriate subjects of expert testimony); United States v. Milton, 555 F.2d 1198, 1203 (5th Cir. 1977) (an expert witness may not substitute for the court in charging the jury regarding applicable law).

124. *See* Galveston, H & S.A. Ry. Co. v. Powers, 101 Tex. 161, 105 S.W. 491 (1907); Brandt v. French, 638 F.2d 209, 212 (10th Cir. 1981) (expert's accident reconstruction theory was not speculative and unsupported); Polk v. Ford Motor Co., 529 F.2d 259, 271 (8th Cir.) *cert denied*, 426 U.S. 907 (1976). (there must be sufficient facts in evidence or disclosed by the witness as a result of his testimony to take such testimony out of the realm of guesswork and speculation).

125. *See* Simien v. S.S. Kresge Co., 566 F.2d 551, 558 (5th Cir. 1978) (expert's facile observation, without more, does not support a finding); Texas & Pac. Ry. v. Meeks, 338 S.W.2d 169, 174 (Tex. Civ. App.—Eastland 1960, writ ref'd n.r.e.) ("The value of a conclusion or of opinion evidence is no stronger than the facts upon which it is based"). *See also* Horton v. W. T. Grant Co., 537 F.2d 1215 (4th Cir. 1976).

126. Defense Research Institute, Products Liability Trial Notebook 167. (1981)

127. *See, e.g.*, Davidson v. Stanadyne, 718 F.2d 1334, 1338 (5th Cir. 1983).

128. *See* Pizza Inn v. Tiffany, 454 S.W.2d 420 (Tex. Civ. App.—Waco 1970, no writ) (testimony of available hand guards on pizza dough machine); General Motors Corp. v. Hopkins, 548 S.W.2d 344, 348-49 (Tex. 1977) (redesign of a lock out lever on a quadrojet carburetor to prevent a lockup condition); Carter v. Massey Ferguson, Inc., 716 F.2d 344, 349-50 (5th Cir. 1983) (expert testimony that a back-up alarm could have been installed on skidder); Mitchell v. Fruehauf Corp., 568 F.2d 1139, 1145 (5th Cir. 1978) (expert evidence that installation of partitions in meat trailers would prevent hanging meat from swinging back and forth while the trailer negotiated sharp curves and causing an overbalance of the trailer); Gonzales v. Caterpillar Tractor Co., 571 S.W.2d 867, 871 (Tex. 1978) (testimony that a stepdown from a caterpillar tractor loader could be relocated away from the treads of the tractor and anti-skid material applied); Dover Corp. v. Perez, 587 S.W.2d 761, 765 (Tex.

Grizzle,[129] the jury found that a design defect in the left rear brake assembly of a vacuum truck was the producing cause of a head-on collision.[130] Two experts testified that the lateral movement of the lower brake shoe was the principal cause of the accident, and that this movement rendered the vehicle unreasonably dangerous. Moreover, the experts expressed the opinion that this defect could have been easily eliminated. The court concluded that this expert testimony constituted sufficient probative evidence of a defective condition in the product.[131]

An examination by an expert of the product and the circumstances surrounding the accident is generally essential to qualify the expert to express an opinion on the condition of the product. Expert testimony, coupled with circumstantial evidence surrounding the accident, is sufficient to establish a defective condition.[132] In *Kindred v. Con/Chem, Inc.*,[133] plaintiffs sustained severe burns when primer they were applying inside a beer storage tank ignited. Plaintiffs instituted suit against the manufacturer of the primer, based on strict tort liability for defective design of the primer formula. An environmental chemist testified that the primer should have been designed with a water base instead of the alcohol base that comprised 90 percent of the formula. The court recognized that when evidence offered in proof of a vital fact is no more than surmise, "the evidence is no more than a scintilla and, in legal effect, is no evidence."[134] The Texas Supreme Court concluded, however, that the environmental chemist's testimony "was more

---

Civ. App.—Corpus Christi 1979, writ ref'd n.r.e.) (expert testimony of mismatching vent hood with a particular heater); General Elec. Co. v. Schmal, 623 S.W.2d 482, 484-85 (Tex. App.—Texarkana 1981, writ ref'd n.r.e.) (expert testimony that control system was improperly designed); Thiele v. Chick, 631 S.W.2d 526, 528 (Tex. App.—Houston [1st Dist.] 1982, writ ref'd n.r.e.) (expert testimony relating to boomer chain swivels).

129. 642 S.W.2d 837 (Tex. App.—Waco 1982, writ dism'd).

130. *Id.* at 841.

131. *Id.* at 843.

132. *See generally* F.M.C. Corp. v. Burns, 444 S.W.2d 315, (Tex. Civ. App.—San Antonio 1969, no writ); Ford Motor Co. v. Bland, 517 S.W.2d 641 (Tex. Civ. App.—Waco 1974, writ ref'd n.r.e.); Thiele v. Chick, 631 S.W.2d 526 (Tex. App.—Houston [1st Dist.] 1982, writ ref'd n.r.e.).

133. 650 S.W.2d 61 (Tex. 1983). Refer to text accompanying notes 290-91, *infra*, for the facts of the case.

134. *Id.* at 63 (citing Seideneck v. Cal Bayreuther Assoc., 451 S.W.2d 752, 755 (Tex. 1970); Joske v. Irvin, 91 Tex. 574, 581-82, 44 S.W.1059, 1062 (1898). *See* Calvert, *"No Evidence" and "Insufficient Evidence" Points of Error*, 38 TEX. L. REV. 361 (1960); 5 W. DORSANEO, TEXAS LITIGATION GUIDE § 122.03(2)(a) (1983).

than a scintilla because it furnished a reasonable basis for differing conclusions concerning the existence of a design defect . . . ."[135]

An expert opinion is insufficient to establish a defective condition where the qualifications of the expert are inadequate or the examination and resulting opinion are cursory. Under these circumstances, the expert opinion constitutes nothing more than bare criticism.[136] The Fifth Circuit in *Simien v. S.S. Kresge Co.*[137] confronted the issue of unqualified expert opinions. In *Simien*, plaintiff sustained injuries when his jacket ignited from a nearby campfire.[138] Plaintiff's expert, a professor of textiles, testified that "the fabric [was] highly dangerous once it [was] ignited."[139] The expert failed to explain this conclusion, to relate his finding to the issue of defective fabrics, or to establish the existence of a safer alternative fabric. The expert's facile observation, without more, was wholly ineffective to establish that the fabric was unreasonably dangerous for use as jacket material.

A corollary to the general rule that bare criticism is inadequate to establish a defective design is the rule that mere unctuous criticism or testimony that a product could have been designed with greater safety is likewise inadequate.[140] The Supreme Court of Texas in *Henderson v. Ford Motor Co.*,[141] considered the testimony of an expert that the design of the carburetor assemblage could have been better. In reversing a judgment for the plaintiff, the court addressed the issue of expert witness criticism: "One witness says that the design could be better . . . . Liability is not predicated upon such bare criticism. The same statements could be made about reasonably safe products . . ."[142] In *Daberko v. Heil*,[143] plaintiff was injured when he fell from the top of a large cylindrical

---

135. 650 S.W.2d at 63.

136. *See* Daberko v. Heil Co., 681 F.2d 445, 450 (5th Cir. 1982) (expert testimony evaluated to be virtually useless); *But see* Ellis v. K-Lan Co., 695 F.2d 157, 160-62 (5th Cir. 1983) (upholding expert testimony).

137. 566 F.2d 551 (5th Cir. 1978).

138. *Id.* at 553-54.

139. *Id.* at 558.

140. *See* Scott v. White Trucks, 699 F.2d 714, 720 (5th Cir. 1983); Simien v. S.S. Kresge Co., 566 F.2d at 558 (5th Cir. 1978); Carter v. Massey Ferguson, Inc., 716 F.2d 344, 347 (5th Cir. 1983); Davidson v. Stanadyne, Inc., 718 F.2d 1334, 1339 (5th Cir. 1983).

141. 519 S.W.2d 87 (Tex. 1974).

142. *Id.* at 93. *Cited in Simien*, 566 F.2d at 558.

143. 681 F.2d 445 (5th Cir. 1982).

trailer-truck while unloading sulphur.[144] The plaintiff's expert testified that the trailer was unreasonably dangerous because an operator standing on the side catwalk was likely to position his face over the domed lid, inhale toxic fumes, stumble backwards and fall. He concluded that the catwalk should have been located on top of the trailer.[145] On cross-examination, however, the expert acknowledged that he had not seen the trailer, that he had never designed a trailer, that he had never loaded a trailer, nor had he observed a trailer being loaded, and that he had merely guessed that the domed lid would be too difficult to open from the side catwalk. Finally, the expert conceded that it might be safer to unload the trailer from the ground rather than from the top.[146] The Fifth Circuit concluded that the expert's testimony was "virtually disintegrated" and could not under any conceivable circumstances establish a defectively designed trailer.[147]

Expert testimony also assumes a significant factor in establishing defective marketing. The duty to warn is critically dependent on establishing that the product is unreasonably dangerous in the absence of a warning of the danger or risk of harm or instructions for safe use.[148] Therefore, expert testimony of the nature of the risk of harm and the fact that such risk was known or knowable is critical.[149] Nine expert witnesses testified regarding the drug Kantrex in *Bristol-Myers Co. v. Gonzales*.[150] Excess administration of the drug, Kantrex, to treat a pain in plaintiff's leg, and then to

---

144. *Id.* at 446, 447.

145. *Id.* at 450.

146. *Id.*

147. *Id.*

148. Refer to text accompanying notes 37-68, *supra*. *See generally Borel*, 493 F.2d 1076; Bristol-Myers Co. v. Gonzales, 561 S.W.2d 801 (Tex. 1978); Sales, *The Duty to Warn and for Safe Use In Strict Tort Liability*, 13 St. Mary's L.J. 521 (1982).

149. *See* Harrison v. Flota Mercante Grancolombiana, S.A., 577 F.2d 968, 978 (5th Cir. 1978) (expert testimony that failure to warn that inhalation of IBA fumes could cause pulmonary fibrosis); *Borel*, 493 F.2d 1076, 1093 (expert testimony of danger of inhaling asbestos dust and the recognition of this danger at the time the product was placed in the stream of commerce was sufficient evidence to demonstrate a foreseeable danger from inhaling asbestos dust); Pearson v. Hevi-Duty Elec., 618 S.W.2d 784, 788 (Tex. App.—Houston [1st Dist.] 1981, writ ref'd n.r.e.) (expert testimony of fuse manufacturer engineer that a special warning was required on an electrical switchgear fuse); Ford Motor Co. v. Nowak, 638 S.W.2d 582, 587 (Tex. App.—Corpus Christi 1982, writ ref'd n.r.e.) (expert testimony that vehicle might self-shift from park to reverse); *Dover*, 587 S.W.2d 761, 765 (expert testimony on the effect of improperly vented fumes from a heater).

150. 561 S.W.2d 801 (Tex. 1978).

irrigate the surgical area, caused the plaintiff to develop deafness.[151] Expert testimony established the defendant's knowledge of the ototoxic side effects of the drug and the need for a warning to the physician that significant amounts of the drug could be absorbed into the body, and that the patient's hearing and kidney functions should be tested to determine a safe dosage.[152]

Expert testimony is not only important in proof of the defective condition of a product; it is equally important to establish whether a condition detected in a product existed at the time the product was manufactured or supplied. To prove that the defective condition existed when the product left the manufacturer's control, the expert may rely on circumstantial evidence.[153] In *Crump v. Clark Equipment Co.*,[154] metallurgical experts relied on direct and circumstantial evidence to express opinions relating to the origin and duration of the defective product, and the operational relationship between earlier occurrences and the product's failure nine years later.[155] Acknowledging that the evidence was not overwhelming, the court concluded that the experts' testimony was predicated on sufficient probative factual data.[156]

Expert testimony may also establish causation,[157] as illustrated in *Jack Roach-Bissonnet, Inc. v. Puskar.*[158] The purchaser of an automobile instituted an action against the dealer and manufacturer for injuries resulting from a one-car accident allegedly caused by the failure of power brake and power steering systems. Three expert witnesses testified, and all agreed that the facts as related by the plaintiff suggested that the engine had not ceased operation.[159] Though the court inferred that the engine stopped, the court was unable to conclude from the expert testimony that engine failure was the cause of plaintiff's inability to stop or turn

---

151. *Id.* at 803.

152. *Id.*

153. *See, e.g.*, Darryl v. Ford Motor Co., 440 S.W.2d 630, 632 (Tex. 1969). "To exclude circumstantial evidence that the product was defective at the time of sale would frustrate the beneficial purposes of the doctrine [of strict liability]." *Id.* at 632.

154. 481 F.2d 667 (5th Cir. 1973).

155. *Id.* at 668.

156. *Id.*

157. *See* Carter v. Massey-Ferguson, Inc., 716 F.2d 344, 349-50 (5th Cir. 1983) (expert opinion on causation of injuries from log-moving device).

158. 417 S.W.2d 262 (Tex. 1967).

159. *Id.* at 265.

the vehicle.[160]

4. *Rule 702*

a. Federal. Federal Rule 702[161] articulates the qualifications of an expert. Rule 702 embodies the criteria of the common law that the expert must be competent and his testimony helpful, but the scope of these requirements has been considerably expanded.[162] The standard formulated by Rule 702, that the expert testimony "assist the trier of fact to understand the evidence or to determine a fact in issue," was recognized prior to the promulgation of the codified Rules.[163] Courts frequently relied, however, on the more stringent rule that expert testimony was unnecessary unless the issue was "not within the common knowledge of the average layman."[164] The admissibility of expert testimony under current federal rules is liberally interpreted.[165] If the subject matter requires special expertise to comprehend it, then the testimony of an expert is admissible.[166]

In determining the preliminary issue of the admissibility of expert testimony, the court must rely on Rule 104(a).[167] First, the court determines whether the testimony assists the fact finder in

---

160. *Id.* at 265-66.

161. FED. R. EVID. 702. Rule 702 states: "If scientific, technical, or other specialized knowledge will assist the trier of fact to understand the evidence or to determine a fact in issue, a witness qualified as an expert by knowledge, skill, experience, training, or education, may testify thereto in the form of an opinion or otherwise." *Id.*

162. DEFENSE, *supra* note 106, at 126. *See* 3 J. WEINSTEIN & M. BERGER, WEINSTEIN'S EVIDENCE § 702 [01] (1982).

163. "On *this subject* can a jury from *this person* receive appreciable help?" 7 J. WIGMORE, EVIDENCE § 1923, at 29 (Chadbourn rev. 1978). *See* Zenith Radio Corp. v. Matsushita Elec. Industrial Co., Ltd., 505 F. Supp. 1313 (E.D. Pa. 1980) (Rule 702 expands the practice in most jurisdictions by permitting expert testimony when helpful to the jury). *See Gideon*, 761 F.2d 1129.

164. *See generally*, 3 J. WEINSTEIN & M. BERGER, *supra* note 162, § 702[02].

165. *See* Mannino v. International Harvester Co., 650 F.2d 846, 849 (6th Cir. 1981); Knight v. Otis Elevator Co., 596 F.2d 84, 87 (3d Cir. 1979).

166. *See* Randolph v. Collectramatic, Inc., 590 F.2d 844, 848 (10th CIr. 1979); Gisriel v. Uniroyal, Inc., 517 F.2d 699, 702 (8th Cir. 1975); Smith v. Ford Motor Co., 626 F.2d 784, 788 (10th Cir. 1980), *cert. denied* 450 U.S. 918 (1981).

167. FED. R. EVID. 104(a). Rule 104(a) states: "(a) Questions of admissibility generally. Preliminary questions concerning the qualification of a person to be a witness, the existence of a privilege, or the admissiblity of evidence shall be determined by the court, subject to the provisions of the subdivision (b). In making its determination it is not bound by the rules of evidence except those with respect to privileges."

understanding the evidence or determining a fact in issue.[168] Second, the court scrutinizes the qualifications of the witness to determine whether the witness is qualified to give the expert opinions.[169] Whether a witness qualifies as an expert rests within the sound discretion of the trial court.[170] Even if a witness qualifies as an expert, his testimony may be excluded under Rule 403 on the basis of unfair prejudice and waste of time.[171]

In *Mannino v. International Manufacturing Co.*,[172] the court recognized the principle that, unless the trial court erred or abused its discretion, the admission of expert testimony is not subject to appellate review.[173] The court emphasized, however, that once the trial court errs in excluding expert testimony, "appellate courts will not hesitate to step in."[174] The court continued: "[W]hile it is not the province of appellate courts to review the discretion of trial courts if exercised within legal bounds, it is the duty and right of appellate courts to determine whether, in the exercise of the discretion committed to it, the trial judge applied correct legal standards."[175] The *Mannino* court recognized that Rule 702 is liberally interpreted.[176]

Weinstein has delineated three intertwined questions that the

---

168. M. GRAHAM, *supra* note 71, at 612, *citing* Holmgren v. Massey-Ferguson, Inc. 516 F.2d 856, 858 (8th Cir. 1975) (the trial judge must decide "whether his knowledge of the subject matter is such that his opinion will most likely assist the trier of fact in arriving at the truth."); Goldwater v. Ginzburg, 414 F.2d 324, 343-44 (2d Cir. 1969), *cert. denied* 396 U.S. 1049, *reh'g denied* 397 U.S. 978 (1970) ("[W]ithin discretion of the trial court, expert opinion is always appropriate where the jury would benefit from technical assistance.").

169. M. GRAHAM, *supra* note 71, at 612.

170. *See* Shipp v. General Motors Corp., 750 F.2d 422 (5th Cir. 1985); Ellis v. K-Lan Co., Inc., 695 F.2d 157, 162 (5th Cir 1983); Perkins v. Volkswagen of America, 596 F.2d 681, 682 (5th Cir. 1979); Robert v. Conti Carriers & Terminals, Inc., 692 F.2d 22, 26 n. 8 (5th Cir. 1982); Page v. Barko Hydraulics, 673 F.2d 134, 139 (5th Cir. 1982); Dunn v. Sears, Roebuck & Co., 639 F.2d 1171, 1174 (5th Cir.), *modified*, 645 F.2d 511 (1981). *See also* Mitchell v. Freuhauf Co., 568 F.2d 1139, 1147 (5th Cir. 1978).

171. *See* Gross v. Black & Decker (U.S.) Inc., 695 F.2d 858, 863 (5th. Cir. 1983); Marx & Co., Inc. v. Diners Club, Inc., 550 F.2d 505, 511 (2d Cir.) *cert. denied* 434 U.S. 861 (1977) (opinion of expert, though relevant, was "prejudicial overweight"). *See also* Herman Schwabe, Inc. v. United Shoe Mach. Corp., 297 F.2d 906, 912 (2d Cir. 1960), *cert. denied* 369 U.S. 865 (1962), *reh'd denied* 370 U.S. 920 (1962). ("[T]he leap required to derive any rational conclusion from the expert's data was too great to allow a jury to take."); United States v. Milton, 555 F.2d 1198, 1203 (5th Cir. 1977).

172. 650 F.2d 846 (6th Cir. 1981).

173. *Id.* at 849.

174. *Id.*

175. *Id.*

176. *Id.*

court should consider to determine whether expert testimony will assist the trier of fact. First, will the expert testimony aid the jury in resolving a controverted issue? Second, is this specialized knowledge of the type that will enhance the jury's understanding of the issues? Third, does the particular expert possess sufficient knowledge to assist the jurors in the case?[177]

The first inquiry focuses on the requirement of Rule 702 that the testimony assist the trier of fact. This requirement necessarily involves the issue of relevancy and must proceed on a case-by-case basis.[178] The court is compelled to evaluate the state of knowledge as currently developed by the evidence already introduced.[179]

The second issue addresses cases in which the expert opinion evidence has not received judicial notice.[180] Prior to the promulgation to the Federal Rules, many courts relied on the test enunciated in *Frye v. United States*.[181] *Frye* declared that, before scientific evidence was admissible, it must have gained general acceptance in its particular scientific field.[182] McCormick decried the *Frye* standard, stating, "Any relevant conclusions which are supported by a qualified expert witness should be received unless there are other reasons for exclusion."[183] Because of the failure of Rule 702 to allude to these standards either in the rule or in the Advisory Committee notes, it is unclear whether either test is now codified.[184]

The third issue involves the qualifications of the expert. Federal courts apply Rule 702 broadly, adhering to the advisory committee's recommendations that an expert "should not be required to satisfy an overly narrow test of his own qualifications."[185] To qualify as an expert, a witness may satisfy the requirements of the

---

177. 3 J. Weinstein & M. Berger, *supra* note 162, § 702[01] (1982).

178. *Id.* at § 702[02].

179. *Id.*

180. *Id.* at § 702[03].

181. 293 F.2d 1012 (D.C. Cir. 1923).

182. *Id.* at 1014.

183. C. McCormick, *supra* note 70, § 203.

184. S. Saltzburg & K. Redden, Federal Rules of Evidence Manual 452 (3d ed. 1982). *But see* 3 J. Weinstein & M. Berger, *supra* note 162, § 702[03] ("The silence of the [*Frye*] rule should be regarded as tantamount of an abandonment of the general acceptance standard.").

185. Fed. R. Evid. 702 advisory committee note. *See* United States v. Barker, 553 F.2d 1013, 1024 (6th Cir. 1977); Gardner v. General Motors Corp., 507 F.2d 525, 528 (10th Cir. 1974).

rule by knowledge, experience, training or education, or by any combination of these factors.[186] The type of expert qualified to proffer expert opinions varies from one with a specific degree, a certificate of training, or membership in a professional organization,[187] to a "skilled expert," such as a banker or a landowner testifying as to land value.[188] Though no specific requirement of expert testimony appears in the Rules, where the topic requires special experience, only the testimony of a witness possessing that experience will be received.[189]

Though the key experts of an industry are normally available to the defendant, an industry's lack of willing experts represents a consideration in assessing the qualifications of an expert. This issue was addressed in *Trowbridge v. Abrasive Company*[190] in which the court stated:

> If we were to declare as a rule of law that one must actually have practical experience in a given industry in order to qualify as an expert in litigation involving its products, we might very well place an onerous burden on plaintiffs in some cases. Where the industry is small and tightly knit, it may be difficult for the plaintiff to obtain the services of an expert currently employed therein, and it might be equally very difficult to find someone who was formerly employed in the industry.[191]

---

186. *Gardner*, 507 F.2d at 528. "Where an expert has the education or background to permit him to analyze a given set of circumstances, he can through reading, calculations, and reasoning process from known scientific principles make himself very much expert in the particular product even though he has not had actual practical experience in its manufacture."; United States v. Viglia, 549 F.2d 335, 337 (5th Cir.) *cert. denied*, 434 U.S. 834 (1977) (doctor permitted to give expert testimony as to obesity even though he did not treat obesity). *See generally* M. Graham, *supra* note 71, § 702.2.

187. *See Barker*, 553 F.2d at 1024. *But see* Tank v. Commissioner, 270 F.2d 477, 486 (6th Cir. 1959) ("The absence of certificates, memberships, and the like, . . . does not in and of itself detract from competency which otherwise exists. . .").

188. Fed. R. Evid. 702 advisory committee notes; *See* La Combe v. A-T-O, Inc., 679 F.2d 431, 434-36 (5th Cir. 1982) (homeowner is automatically qualified to give expert testimony as to the value of his property, regardless of whether his opinion is based in part on hearsay); South Cent. Livestock Dealers, Inc. v. State Bank, 614 F.2d 1056, 1061 (5th Cir. 1980) (financial owner of feedlot was qualified, just as owner would have been qualified, to testify about the feedlot assets).

189. Randolph v. Collectramatic, Inc., 590 F.2d 844, 846 (10th Cir. 1979) (testimony of qualified engineer required when feasibility of protective shields on bottom of pressure cooker at issue).

190. 190 F.2d 825 (3d Cir. 1951).

191. *Id.* at 829 n.9.

The focus of expert testimony is technical, rather than legal expertise. In *Ellis v. K-Lan Co.*[192] the plaintiff instituted suit for strict tort liability to recover damages for chemical burns sustained when his child opened a container of acid-based drain declogger. Plaintiff's expert testified that the container was defectively designed because of the absence of an effective child-proof cap. The court disregarded the contention that an expert witness is disqualified from expressing an expert opinion relating to product defectiveness merely because of an unfamiliarity with standards or definitions set by statutes or regulations that regulate the product.[193] The court then stated:

> Rule 702, Fed. R. Evid. provides that a witness who seeks to testify as an expert must first be found qualified as such 'by knowledge, skill, experience, training, or education.' The failure of the expert to be familiar with a statutory definition or standard affects his credibility, not his qualifications to testify.[194]

The court observed that although K-Lan's counsel exposed the expert's unfamiliarity with governing statutes, the jury elected to accept his testimony over the defendant's expert who testified that the product was not defective.[195] The evidence was deemed legally sufficient to sustain the verdict.

Rule 702, in addition to expanding the common law requirements of expert testimony, also advances the common law practice that an expert need not express opinions in response to hypothetical questions; the advisory committee sanctions an expert's dissertation or exposition of principles related to the case.[196] The trial court, in determining admissibility, appraises the qualifications of the expert, the uniqueness of the evidence, and the extent to which the testimony will assist the trier of fact. These decisions rest within the sound discretion of the trial court.

---

192. 695 F.2d 157 (5th Cir. 1983).

193. *Id.* at 161.

194. *Id.*, citing N.V. Maatschappij Voor Industriele Waarden v. A.O. Smith Corp., 590 F.2d 415, 419 (2d Cir. 1978) (". . . proper focus of expert testimony is technical, rather than legal . . .").

195. *Id.*

196. FED. R. EVID. 702 advisory committee note. *See* S. SALTZBURG & K. REDDEN, *supra* note 184, at 451.

b. Texas. Under Rule 702[197] Texas codified, with some modification, its common law practice of allowing an expert to express opinions and to offer explanatory testimony.[198] Prior to the promulgation of Rule 702, an expert's opinion was admissible only if the testimony assisted the trier of fact and involved matters beyond the understanding of the average layman.[199] Rule 702, however, requires only that the expert's testimony assist the trier of fact.[200]

Rule 702 does not prescribe the minimum requirements for an expert witness; whether an expert is qualified to express an opinion is a matter of degree.[201] Moreover, Rule 702 also does not identify the type of knowledge that an expert must possess. The phrase requiring an expert to possess "knowledge, skill, experience, training, or education" is particularly broad and unfettered.[202] It authorizes as an expert not only one with a formal education, such as a scientist or a physician, but also the "skilled witness" who received more pragmatic training, such as the farmer, banker, technician, or mechanic.[203] Prior to codification of Rule 702, Texas recognized both professional and pragmatic types of expertise.[204]

The proponent of the expert witness must demonstrate to the court that the witness qualifies as an expert.[205] A challenge by op-

---

197. TEX. R. EVID. 702. Refer to note 161, *supra* for a statement of FED. R. EVID. 702, which is identical to the Texas rule.

198. *See* H. WENDORF & D. SCHLUETER, TEXAS RULES OF EVIDENCE MANUAL 145 (1983).

199. *See* Barker v. Dunham, 551 S.W.2d 41, 44 (Tex. 1977) (experts are considered to possess a special knowledge not generally possessed by jurors); Shelley v. City of Austin, 74 Tex. 608, 609, 12 S.W. 753, 754 (1889) (expert testimony that a certain bridge was dangerous was inadmissible). *See also* 2 RAY, *supra* note 81, § 1400; TAURMAN, EXPERT TESTIMONY UNDER THE RULES OF EVIDENCE 40 (1984).

200. TAURMAN, *supra* note 199.

201. STATE BAR OF TEXAS, EVIDENCE F-11 (1983). *See* Houston Lighting & Power Co. v. Dickinson Indep. School Dist., 641 S.W.2d 302, 309-10 (Tex. App.—Houston [14th Dist.] 1982, writ ref'd n.r.e.) (whether an individual qualifies as an expert is a question to be determined by the trier of fact).

202. STATE BAR OF TEXAS, EVIDENCE F-11 (1983).

203. *Id.* at 12; H. WENDORF & D. SCHLUETER, *supra* note 198, at 145. *See, e.g.*, Warren v. Hartnett, 561 S.W.2d 860, 863 (Tex. Civ. App.—Dallas 1977, writ ref'd n.r.e.) (nonphysician may qualify as medical expert based on experience); Sharp v. Chrysler Corp., 432 S.W.2d 131, 137, (Tex. Civ. App.—Houston [14th Dist.] 1968, writ ref'd n.r.e.) (brake repairman). Refer to note 91 *supra*.

204. *See generally* W. WEIR., THE NEW RULES OF EVIDENCE AND DISCOVERY FOR TEXAS 134-36 (1984).

205. H. WENDORF & D. SCHLUETTER, *supra* note 196, at 146 citing Trick v. Trick, 587 S.W.2d 771 (Tex. Civ. App.—El Paso 1977, writ dism'd). *See* Ford Motor Co. v. Bland, 517

posing counsel to an expert's qualifications generally affects the weight, but not the admissibility of the expert's testimony.[206]

Product liability cases are usually technically complex and generally require expert testimony.[207] An expert's opinion may be based, in whole or in part, on inadmissible evidence.[208] This rule mirrors prior decisional law,[209] despite some decisions to the contrary.[210] By using inadmissible evidence to interpret points at issue, the expert witness serves as a fact finder for the jury, though the courts have been appropriately reluctant to recognize this role.[211]

5. *Rule 703*

a. Federal. Rules 703 and 705 codify the approach of the Fifth Circuit and other circuits that permit the disclosure of otherwise hearsay evidence for the purpose of illustrating the basis of the expert witness opinion.[212] Rule 703[213] addresses the bases upon

---

S.W.2d 641, 644 (Tex. Civ. App.—Waco 1974, writ ref'd n.r.e.) citing City of Teague v. Stiles, 263 S.W.2d 623, 628 (Tex. Civ. App.—Waco 1953, writ ref'd n.r.e.); Louis v. Parchman, 493 S.W.2d 310, 321 (Tex. Civ. App.—Fort Worth 1973, writ ref'd n.r.e.)

206. Ford Motor Co. v. Bland, 517 S.W.2d 641 (Tex. Civ. App.—Waco 1974, writ ref'd n.r.e.); Louis v. Parchman, 493 S.W.2d 310 (Tex. Civ. App.—Fort Worth 1973, writ ref'd n.r.e.).

207. *See* Hoppe v. Hughes, 577 S.W.2d 773, 776 (Tex. Civ. App. —Amarillo 1979, writ ref'd n.r.e.) (sometimes expert testimony is not only permitted, but required).

208. Sutton, *Article VII: Opinions and Expert Testimony*, 20 Hous. L. Rev.. 445, 457 (1983 Tex. R. Evid. Handbook); Tex. R. Evid. 703.

209. Ortiz v. Allergan Pharmaceuticals, 489 S.W.2d 135, 140 (Tex. Civ. App.—Houston [14th Dist.] 1972, writ ref'd n.r.e.) (expert testimony of pharmaceutical's doctor, based in part on tests and reports of others, is admissible); Bell Aerospace Corp. v. Anderson, 478 S.W.2d 191, 198 (Tex. Civ. App.—El Paso 1972, writ ref'd n.r.e.) (expert testimony relating to cause of a helicopter crash, based in part on conversations with others, is admissible at trial court's discretion).

210. *See* Calhoun v. United States Fire Ins. Co., 489 S.W.2d 359, 360 (Tex. Civ. App.—Amarillo 1972, writ ref'd n.r.e.) (expert testimony of contractor relating to cost of repairs was inadmissible because his opinion was based on a list of repairs by an architect who did not testify as to repairs); Reed v. Barlow, 157 S.W.2d 933, 935 (Tex. Civ. App.—San Antonio 1941, writ ref'd) (testimony of geologist based on records and reports of others not authenticated nor offered into evidence is inadmissible).

211. *Cf.* Columbia Engineering Int'l v. Dorman,, 602 S.W.2d 72, 77 (Tex. Civ. App.—Beaumont 1980, writ ref'd n.r.e.) (expert opinion proper to and in the construction of a written document).

212. B.Bryan v. John Bean Div. of FMC Corp., 566 F.2d 541, 545 (5th Cir. 1978).

213. Fed. R. Evid. 703. Rule 703 states:

> The facts or data in the particular case upon which an expert bases an opinion or inference may be those perceived by or made known to him at or before the hear-

which opinion testimony may be predicated. Rule 703 makes available to the expert all the sources usually relied on by an expert in formulating his opinion, without requiring that it be admissible.[214] In addition to scientific, technical, and other specialized knowledge itemized under Rule 702, an expert may base his opinion upon any one or more of three sources. First, the expert may base his opinion on first-hand observation.[215] Second, the expert is entitled to express an opinion predicated on the factual testimony at trial[216] or on hypothetical questions. These two formulations of expert testimony represent a codification of the traditional common law.[217] Third, the expert may formulate and express an opinion based on "the presentation of data to the expert outside of court and by his own perception."[218] This last basis marks a severe departure from prior practice in many jurisdictions by broadening the foundation for expert opinions and thus ostensibly bringing "the judicial practice in line with the practice of the experts themselves when not in court. . . ."[219]

Under Rule 703, an expert is allowed significant latitude in determining the basis of the proffered opinions.[220] The expert is permitted to base opinions on hearsay.[221] This purposeful broadening of prior law is designed to align the law with the realities of professional life. Thus, the expert may express an opinion based on the same data normally used in forming an opinion in this area of

---

ing. If of a type reasonably relied upon by experts in the particular field in forming opinions or inferences upon the subject, the facts or data need not be admissible in evidence. *Id.*

214. *See* Soden v. Freightliner Corp., 714 F.2d 498, 502 (5th Cir. 1983); Zenith Radio Corp. v. Matsushita Electric Industrial Co., 505 F. Supp. 1313, 1322 (E.D. Pa. 1980).

215. Mannino v. International Mfg. Co., 650 F.2d 846, 851 (6th Cir. 1981) ("[T]hrough Rule 703, the law is catching up with the realities of professional life").

216. *See* Carter v. Massey-Ferguson, Inc., 716 F.2d 344, 350 (5th Cir. 1983) (plaintiff's expert based his testimony on plaintiff's account of the accident).

217. *See* 3 J. Weinstein & M. Berger, supra note 162 § 703 [01].

218. Fed. R. Evid. 703 advisory committee note.

219. *Id. See* Soden v. Freightliner Corp., 714 F.2d 498, 502 n.4 (5th Cir. 1983) (citing cases illustrating the variety of contexts in which Rule 703 has been used to allow the admission of expert opinions based on sources not themselves admissible or offered into evidence); Frazier v. Continental Oil Co., 568 F.2d 378, 383 (5th Cir. 1978) (the Federal Rules contemplate the admission of opinion testimony by experts based upon materials not necessarily admissible in evidence).

220. *Mannino*, 650 F.2d at 853.

221. *Id.*

expertise.[222]

An expert's testimony may be based on facts, data and conclusions of other experts.[223] There is a distinction, however, between an expert formulating his opinion on another expert's opinions and simply reciting another expert's testimony.[224] This distinction is illustrated in *Barris v. Bob's Drag Chutes & Equipment*.[225] Plaintiff instituted a strict tort liability action against the manufacturer and retailer of a shoulder harness installed in a sprint car. Plaintiff alleged that her husband was fatally injured by a defective shoulder harness he was wearing at the time of his collision.[226] The plaintiff's expert sought unavailingly to introduce into evidence a second expert's report. The court concluded that the second expert's report, an analysis of the fibers of the shoulder harness webbing, did not form the basis in whole or in part of the expert's testimony, and therefore, the facts and data from the nontestifying expert were wholly inadmissible.[227]

Whether the opinion, facts, or data are of a type reasonably relied upon by an expert witness represents a matter of sound judicial discretion.[228] The court considers whether the information is actually relied upon by experts in the field and whether the information is trustworthy enough to justify the expert's reliance.[229] However, the proper role of the trial court, in determining whether an expert reasonably relies on this data remains unclarified.[230]

---

222. *Id.* Miller v. Universal City Studios, Inc., 650 F.2d 1365, 1374 (5th Cir. 1981); Georgia Kaolin Int'l v. M/V Grand Justice, 644 F.2d 412 (5th Cir. 1981); Bauman v. Center Corp., 611 F.2d 1115, 1120 (5th Cir. 1980); Frazier v. Continental Oil Co., 568 F.2d 378, 383 (5th Cir. 1978); U.S. v. Williams, 447 F.2d 1285 (5th Cir. 1971), (*en banc*), *cert denied*, 405 U.S. 754 (1972).

223. Soden v. Freightliner Corp., 714 F.2d 498, 502 (5th. Cir. 1983). United States v. Hill, 655 F.2d 512, 516 (3d Cir. 1981) *cert denied*, 104 S.Ct. 699 (1984). Seese v. Volkswagenwerk, A.G., 648 F.2d 833, 844 (3d Cir.), *cert. denied*, 454 U.S. 867 (1981).

224. *Barris*, 685 F.2d at 101 n.10.

225. *Id.*

226. *Id.* at 96.

227. *Id.* at 101 n.10.

228. *See Soden*, 714 F.2d 498, 503 ("A trial court's inquiry into whether this standard is satisfied must be made on a case-by-case basis and should focus on the reliability of the opinion and its foundation rather than merely on the fact that it was based, technically speaking, upon hearsay."); *Seese*, 648 F.2d 833, 844 ("we recognize that the admission of expert testimony rests within the sound discretion of the district court and that the district court will be reversed only for an abuse of that discretion"); Bauman v. Centex Corp., 611 F.2d 1115, 1120 n. 5 (5th Cir. 1980).

229. M. Graham, *supra* note 71, at § 703.1. *See Soden*, 714 F.2d 498, 502-03.

230. 3 J. Weinstein & M. Berger, *supra* note 162, § 703[03].

b. Texas. Texas Rule of Evidence 703[231] enumerates the permissible bases of an expert's opinion. Though generally consistent with earlier Texas law, Rule 703 alters the common law by authorizing expert testimony based solely on hearsay.[232] Rule 703 authorizes an expert to base an opinion on: (1) personal observation; (2) admissible facts or data made known to the expert at or before trial; and (3) inadmissible evidence reasonably relied on by experts in the field.[233]

The first source of an expert's opinion, personal observation, assists the jury because of the education or training of the witness.[234] To formulate opinions based on personal knowledge, the witness examines the defective product or the injured party. This source of an expert's opinion was permissible in Texas before codification of the Texas Rules.[235] The second source of an expert's testimony, facts or data the expert did not personally perceive but which were made known to him at or before the trial, likewise reflects prior Texas law. Prior to adoption of the codified rules, the court possessed discretion to authorize an expert to express an opinion based on facts that were never introduced into evidence;[236] under Rule 703, the data relied on by the expert need only be admissible. The underlying data represented by this second source is usually presented by a hypothetical question. Prior to the adoption of the Texas Rules, the hypothetical format did not require that all relevant facts be included in the question; the proponent could assume or infer some facts supported by the evidence.[237]

---

231. TEX. R. EVID. 703. Refer to note 191, *supra*, for a statement of FED. R. EVID. 703, which is identical to the Texas rule.

232. *See* Moore v. Grantham, 599 S.W.2d 287, 289 (Tex. 1980) (statements, if solely hearsay, are inadmissible). *See generally* Sutton, *supra* note 208, at 462-68.

233. *See generally* D. LOUISELL & C. MUELLER, FEDERAL EVIDENCE § 389 (1979).

234. *Sutton, supra*, note 208 at 462.

235. *Id. See, e.g.*, Southwestern Bell Tel. Co. v. Sims, 615 S.W.2d 858 (Tex. Civ. App.—Houston [1st Dist.] 1981, no writ); Hilliard v. State, 87 Tex.Crim. 15, 18, 218 S.W. 1052, 1054 (1920); A. Cohen & Co. v. Rittimann, 139 S.W. 59, 62 (Tex. Civ. App.—San Antonio 1911, writ dism'd); St. Louis & S.F. RR v. Kiser, 136 S.W. 852, 856 (Tex. Civ. App. 1911, writ ref'd). *Id.*

236. Sutton, *supra* note 208, at 463. *See, e.g.*, Geochemical Surveys v. Dietz, 340 S.W.2d 114, 118 (Tex. Civ. App. - Austin 1960, writ ref'd n.r.e.); John Hancock Mut. Life Ins. Co. v. Stanley, 215 S.W.2d 416, 421 (Tex. Civ. App.—Fort Worth 1948, writ ref'd n.r.e.).

237. *See, e.g.*, Cooper v. Bowser, 610 S.W.2d 825, 830 (Tex. Civ. App.—Tyler 1980, no writ); Roth v. Law, 579 S.W.2d 949, 954 (Tex. Civ. App.—Corpus Christi 1979, writ ref'd n.r.e.); J. Weingarten, Inc. v. Tripplett, 530 S.W.2d 653, 655-56 (Tex. Civ. App.—Beaumont 1975, writ ref'd n.r.e.); Mobil Oil Co. v. Dodd, 528 S.W.2d 297, 304 (Tex. Civ. App.—Corpus

Though the first two sources of information do not alter prior Texas law, the third source does. The second sentence of Rule 703, which states that an expert may base his testimony on inadmissible information reasonably relied upon by experts in the expert's field, rejects earlier well-defined decisional law that an expert opinion was inadmissible if based solely on hearsay not in evidence.[238] This rule was reaffirmed as late as 1980 in *Moore v. Grantham*.[239] Prior to codification, Texas allowed an expert to rely *partly* on outside sources that were customarily relied on by other experts.[240] Under Rule 702, an expert is now authorized to base his opinion *entirely* on outside sources of information.[241] Under Rule 703, however, these underlying hearsay statements are admissible only for the limited purpose of demonstrating the foundation of the expert's opinion, but are not otherwise admissible evidence possessing probative value.[242] The admissibility of hearsay for certain limited purposes coincides with the interpretation of the federal rule.[243] There exists a significant degree of skepticism whether this third basis for an expert opinion will truly enhance the probative value of such opinions and assist the trier of fact in ascertaining the truth.

6. *Rule 704*

a. Federal. Rule 704[244] abolishes the "ultimate issue" prohi-

---

Christi 1975, writ ref'd n.r.e.); Gray v. Bird, 380 S.W.2d 908, 913 (Tex. Civ. App.—Tyler 1964, writ ref'd n.r.e.). *See generally* H. Wendorf & D.A. Schlueter, *supra* note 198, at 149-153.

238. *See, e.g.*, Simms v. Southwest Methodist Hosp., 535 S.W.2d 192, 199 (Tex. Civ. App.—San Antonio 1976, writ ref'd n.r.e.).

239. 599 S.W.2d 287, 289 (Tex. 1980).

240. *See, e.g.*, Slaughter v. Abilene State School, 561 S.W.2d 789, 790 (Tex. 1977); Lewis v. Southmore Sav. Ass'n, 480 S.W.2d 180, 186 (Tex. 1972); Lister v. Employers Reinsurance Corp., 590 S.W.2d 803, 806 (Tex. Civ. App.—Houston [14th Dist.] 1979, writ ref'd n.r.e.).

241. It can be argued that an expert may rely on data and facts reasonably relied upon by other experts even though they have not been generally accepted, under the test of Frye v. United States, 293 F. 1013, 1014 (D.C. Cir. 1923).

242. *See, e.g.*, Lewis v. Southdown Sav. Ass'n, 480 S.W.2d 180, 186 (Tex. 1972).

243. *See, e.g.*, Baumholser v. Amax Coal Co., 630 F.2d 550, 553 (7th Cir. 1980). *See generally* Sutton, *supra* note 208, at 465.

244. Fed. R. Evid. 704. Rule 704 states: "Testimony in the form of an opinion or inference otherwise admissible is not objectional because it embraces an ultimate issue to be decided by the trier of fact." *Id.*

bition and sanctions opinion testimony on ultimate issues.[245] The rule prohibiting witnesses from expressing opinions on ultimate issues was deemed "unduly restrictive, difficult of application, and generally served only to deprive the trier of fact of useful information."[246] Thus, the argument that such an expert opinion usurps the province of the jury is no longer valid.[247] Of course, all expert opinions are not admissible; an expert opinion must still qualify under Rules 701 and 702 and the testimony must be relevant under Rule 403.[248] The improper effect on a jury of a very broad opinion is minimized by Rule 705, which compels a preliminary disclosure of the underlying data.[249] The disclosure of underlying data is critical, and the courts should be chary of expert opinions dispensed before juries without an initial disclosure of the basis upon which the opinions rest.

An opinion phrased in terms of a legal standard is inadmissible.[250] Legal language in an expert's opinion is not helpful to the jury, and may also be misleading, especially when a legal term conveys a different meaning to the expert, than does the proper legal definition.[251] Because of the danger that jurors will look to the expert instead of the court for guidance in applying the law, only a few courts admit the testimony with appropriate instructions, while most courts totally eschew such testimony as calculated to produce an unfair result.[252]

The standard for lay and expert opinions is "to admit them

---

245. FED. R. EVID. 704 advisory committee note. *See, e.g.*, United States v. McCoy, 539 F.2d 1050, 1063 (5th Cir. 1976), *cert. denied*, 431 U.S. 919 (1977); United States v. Milton, 555 F.2d 1198, 1203 (5th Cir. 1977) (mere fact that an expert's conclusion trenches upon a jury issue does not compel its exclusion).

246. FED. R. EVID. 704 advisory committee note, (*citing* 7 J. WIGMORE, *supra* note 163, §§ 1920, 1921; C. MCCORMICK, *supra* note 70, § 12).

247. FED. R. EVID. 704 advisory committee note. *See, e.g.*, United States v. Morgan, 554 F.2d 31, 33 (2d Cir.) *cert. denied*, 434 U.S. 965 (1977).

248. FED. R. EVID. 704 advisory committee note. *See, e.g.*, United States v. Milton, 555 F.2d 1198, 1203 (5th Cir. 1977).

249. 3 J. WEINSTEIN & M. BERGER, *supra* note 162, § 704[02].

250. 3 J. WEINSTEIN & M. BERGER, *supra* note 162 § 704 [02]; M. GRAHAM, *supra* note 45, § 704.1.

251. *Cf.* United States v. Johnson, 637 F.2d 1224, 1246-47 (9th Cir. 1980) (court draws a distinction between legal terms reasonably clear to laymen and those that are not).

252. *Compare* United States v. Fogg, 652 F.2d 551 (5th Cir. 1981), *cert denied*, 456 U.S. 905 (1982) *with* Owen v. Kerr-McGee Corp., 698 F.2d 236, 240 (5th. Cir. 1983) *and* Strong v. E.I. DuPont de Nemours Co., Inc., 667 F.2d 682 (8th. Cir. 1981).

when helpful to the trier of fact."[253] An opinion is helpful when it reflects an expression of the knowledge of the witness that can be communicated in no other understandable form.[254] Another example of helpfulness involves the witness who is unable to account for all the details upon which his opinion is based.[255] An opinion may aid the trier of fact where the total impression of the expert witness cannot be conveyed by simply recounting details.[256] Elimination of the rule excluding opinions on the ultimate issue purportedly permits an expert witness to testify in a more natural manner and permits the jury to receive the full benefit of the witness' impression.[257]

b. Texas. Because Texas law recognizes that testimony should not be excluded simply because it incidentally embraces an ultimate issue, or may technically invade the province of the jury, Rule 704[258] does not constitute a major change in Texas law.[259] Rule 704 does represent, however, a clarification of the prior common law rule, since many courts were indefinite on this issue.[260]

The "ultimate issue" rule was confronted in 1965 by the Texas Supreme Court in *Carr v. Radkey*.[261] In *Carr*, the court declared that "[t]he witness could not invade the province [of the jury] if he wanted to, since the jury could disbelieve anything it wanted to."[262] With the clarification introduced by *Carr*, recent decisions have adhered to this principle.[263]

---

253. FED. R. EVID. 704 advisory committee note.

254. M. GRAHAM, *supra* note 71, § 704.1.

255. *Id.*

256. *Id.*

257. *See, e.g.*, United States v. Smith, 550 F.2d 277 (5th. Cir.) *cert. denied sub nom*, Wallace v. United States, 434 U.S. 841 (1977).

258. TEX. R. EVID. 704. Refer to note 244, *supra* for a statement of FED. R. EVID. 704, which is identical to the Texas rule.

259. *See, e.g.*, Scalf v. Collin County, 80 Tex. 514, 516, 16 S.W. 314, 315 (1891); Hooten v. Dunbar, 347 S.W.2d 775, 777-78 (Tex. Civ. App.—Beaumont 1961 writ ref'd. n.r.e.).

260. *See, e.g.*, Loper v. Andrews, 404 S.W.2d 300, 305 (Tex. 1966) (a witness' opinion may not invade the province of the trier of facts).

261. 393 S.W.2d 806 (Tex. 1965).

262. *Id.* at 812. *See generally* Norvell, *Invasion of the Province of the Jury*, 31 TEX. L. REV. 731 (1953).

263. *See, e.g.*, Bounds v. Caudle, 549 S.W.2d 438, 445-46 (Tex. Civ. App.—Corpus Christi no writ), *rev'd on other grounds*, 560 S.W.2d 925 (Tex. 1977); Horace Mann Mut. Ins. Co. v. Estate of Andress, 525 S.W.2d 47, 50 (Tex. Civ. App.—Amarillo 1975, no writ);

In Texas, as in the federal courts, a witness is proscribed from expressing an expert opinion relating to legal terminology.[264] If the expert's opinion relates to foreign law, however, then it is not necessarily excludable.[265] Though expert opinion may embrace an ultimate issue, the extent of such opinions are governed by Rules 702 and 403.[266]

7. *Rule 705*

a. Federal. Rule 705[267] eliminates the requirement that an expert express an opinion only in response to hypothetical questions in the absence of personal knowledge of the material facts.[268] Prior to adoption of the Rules, the hypothetical question was necessary to expose all facts upon which an expert relied in formulating his opinion.[269] The hypothetical question was essential because an expert was prohibited from expressing an opinion based on matters personally perceived by him until the specific facts on which the expert relied were factually established in the record.[270] But Rule 705, "while continuing the often-criticized use of hypothetical questions, removes the need for the expert to make elaborate disclosures of the bases of his opinion."[271]

Rule 705 incorporates the approach suggested by Wigmore:

By exempting the offering party from the *requirement* of using

---

Adams v. Smith, 479 S.W.2d 390, 396 (Tex. Civ. App.—Amarillo 1972, no writ).

264. *See, e.g.*, Snow v. Bond, 438 S.W.2d 549, 550 (Tex. 1969); Carr v. Radkey, 393 S.W.2d 806, 812 (Tex. 1965); Speck v. Speck, 588 S.W.2d 853, 854 (Tex. Civ. App.—Houston [14th Dist.] 1979, no writ).

265. *See, e.g.*, Hunt v. Coastal States Gas Prod. Co., 583 S.W.2d 322, 327 (Tex.), *cert. denied*, 444 U.S. 992 (1979).

266. Taurman, *Expert Testimony Under the Rules of Evidence*, THE HOUS. LAWYER 40, 41, (1984). Refer to note 161, *supra*, for a statement of FED. R. EVID. 702. Rule 403 states: "Although relevant, evidence may be excluded if its probative value is substantially outweighed by the danger of unfair prejudice, confusion of the issues, or misleading the jury, or by considerations of undue delay, waste of time, or needless presentation of cumulative evidence." *Id.*

267. FED. R. EVID. 705. Rule 705 states: "The expert may testify in terms of opinion or inference and give his reasons therefor without prior disclosure of the underlying facts or data, unless the court requires otherwise. The expert may in any event be required to disclose the underlying facts or data on cross-examination." *Id.*

268. FED. R. EVID. 705 advisory committee note.

269. 3 J. WEINSTEIN & M. BERGER, *supra* note 162, § 705[01].

270. *Id.*

271. *Bryan*, 566 F.2d at 545 (expert relied on facts and data of other testifying experts).

> the hypothetical form; by according him the *option* of using it; - both of these to be left to the trial court's *discretion*; and by permitting the opposing party on *cross-examination*, to call for a hypothetical specification of the data which the witness has used as the basis of the opinion. The last rule will give sufficient protection against a misunderstanding of the opinion, when any actual doubt exists.[272]

Additionally, Rule 705 adopts Wigmore's proposal that, unless the court requires otherwise, preliminary disclosure of the underlying facts are optional when the expert bases his opinion on first-hand observation.[273] Wigmore suggests altering the treatment of expert opinion because "[t]he hypothetical question, misused by the clumsy and abused by the clever, has in practice led to intolerable obstruction of truth."[274]

Even though disclosure of facts, data, or opinions is not required on direct examination, it is, of course, permitted and will be utilized for tactical reasons.[275] On cross-examination, information not revealed on direct examination may be extracted from the witness.[276] Correcting, discovering, or amplifying facts during cross-examination is greatly aided by Rule 26(b)(4).[277] The expert's opinion may later be stricken if cross-examination demonstrates that it is based upon conjecture or speculation.[278] The court should, in the exercise of its sound discretion, require that a full foundation be established on direct examination as a predicate for

---

272. 2 J. WIGMORE EVIDENCE § 686 at 813. (Chadbourn rev. 1978).

273. *Id.* Rules 703 and 705 codify the approach that "permits the disclosure of otherwise hearsay evidence for the purpose of illustrating the basis of the expert witness' opinion." *Bryan*, 566 F.2d at 545 (citing examples of cases in various jurisdictions that followed this approach prior to the Rules). *See generally* 3 J. WEINSTEIN & M. BERGER, *supra* note 162, § 705[01].

274. 2 J. WIGMORE, *supra* note 163, § 686 at 812.

275. *See, e.g.* Carter v. Massey-Ferguson, Inc., 716 F.2d 344, 350 (5th Cir. 1983); *Bryan*, 566 F.2d at 545.

276. *Carter*, 716 F.2d 344, 350. *See, e.g.*, *Bryan*, 566 F.2d at 545 ("Additionally, the Advisory Committee Note to Rule 705 explicitly contemplates that in attempting to impeach the opinion the cross-examiner will elicit information concerning the basis of the opinion unfavorable to the opinion itself."); Polk v. Ford Motor Co., 529 F.2d 259, 271 (8th Cir. 1976), *cert denied*, 426 U.S. 907 (1977). ("The weakness in the underpinnings of such opinions may be developed upon cross-examination and such weakness goes to the weight and credibility of the testimony").

277. FED. R. CIV. P. 26(b)(4).

278. M. GRAHAM *supra* note 71 § 705.1.

an expert witness' expression of an opinion.[279]

b. Texas. Under Rule 705,[280] an expert is not required to disgorge the factual basis of his opinion unless the trial judge directs otherwise.[281] Rule 705 constitutes a major change in Texas; prior law compelled the use of hypothetical questions as the basis for an expert opinion.[282] The purpose of the hypothetical question is (1) to inform the jury of the underlying facts on which the opinion is based, and (2) to prevent the use of information not in evidence.[283] Though the justification for the hypothetical question survived codification of the rules, the second justification is rendered invalid by the provisions of Rule 703.[284] In *Burns v. Bridge Engineering Corp.*,[285] the court enumerated a number of standards that still apply whenever a hypothetical question is utilized pursuant to Rule 705:

> The trial court in ruling on the propriety of the hypothetical question has "considerable latitude" in determining whether it is based upon a fair assumption of facts in evidence. [citations omitted]. It is not necessary to the propriety of such a question that it include a reference to all of the relevant facts in evidence nor that it be confined to facts proven with mathematical certainty. It may include inferences reasonably drawn from other facts proved and consistent with the theory of the party propounding the question. [citations omitted].[286]

---

279. *Id.*

280. Tex. R. Evid. 705. The original Texas rule was identical to the Federal rule (refer to note 267, *supra*), but the rule was amended, effective Nov. 1, 1984, to read:

> The expert may testify in terms of opinion or inference and give his reasons therefor without prior disclosure of the underlying facts or data, unless the court requires otherwise. The expert may in any event disclose on direct examination, or be required to disclose on cross-examination the underlying facts or data. *Id.*

281. H. Wendorf & D. Schlueter, *supra* note 198 at 156.

282. Fed. R. Evid. 705 advisory committee note. *Compare* Mobil Oil Co. v. Dodd, 528 S.W.2d 297, 304 (Tex. Civ. App.—Corpus Christi 1975, writ ref'd n.r.e.) *with* Gulf, C & S.F Ry. v. Downs, 70 S.W.2d 318, 322 (Tex. Civ. App.—Dallas 1934, writ ref'd).

283. Sutton, *supra* note 208, at 470-71.

284. Tex. R. Evid. 703 states in part: "If on a type reasonably relied upon by experts in the particular field in forming opinions or inferences on the subject, the facts or data need not be admissible in evidence."

285. 465 S.W.2d 427 (Tex. Civ. App.—Houston [14th Dist.] 1971, writ ref'd n.r.e.).

286. *Id.* at 431-32, (citing Foreman v. Texas Employers' Ins. Ass'n, 150 Tex. 468, 474-75, 241 S.W.2d 977, 980 (1951); Aetna Casualty & Sur. Co. v. Scruggs, 413 S.W.2d 416 (Tex. Civ. App.—Corpus Christi 1967, no writ)).

A proponent of opinion testimony under Rule 705 may elect to enhance the expert's credibility by establishing the basis of his opinion; however, this is no longer required.[287] Abandonment of this requirement is based on the supposition that with the growth of discovery practice, opposing counsel is usually familiar enough with the expert's sources to eliminate the necessity for such a disclosure.[288] This supposition may be lacking in substance and may, unwittingly, further erode the legitimacy of expert opinions expressed in the courtroom.

E. *Circumstantial Evidence*

Circumstantial evidence plays a pivotal role in the proof of a strict tort liability case. Because the product has frequently been discarded or severely damaged, it may be impossible to establish the elements of a strict tort liability action by direct evidence. Circumstantial evidence, however, is sufficient to establish the defective condition of the product.[289]

The use of circumstantial evidence is illustrated in a number of strict tort liability cases. In *Kindred v. Con/Chem, Inc.*,[290] plaintiffs were applying a paint primer inside a beer storage tank when the primer ignited and a fire occurred. The Texas Supreme Court acknowledged the absence of direct evidence that the paint primer was the producing cause of the fire, and held that the jury was justified in basing its decision on circumstantial evidence.[291]

---

287. Tex. R. Evid. 705. Refer to note 280 *supra* for the statement of the rule.

288. Houdaille Indus. v. Cunningham, 502 S.W.2d 544, 548 (Tex. 1973); Tenngasco Gas Gathering Co. v. Fisher, 624 S.W.2d 301, 304 (Tex. Civ. App.—Corpus Christi 1981, writ ref'd n.r.e.).

289. General Motors Corp. v. Hopkins, 548 S.W.2d 344, 348-49 (Tex. 1977); Darryl v. Ford Motor Co., 440 S.W.2d 630, 632 (Tex. 1969) *See, e.g.*, Theile v. Chick, 631 S.W.2d 526, 530 (Tex. App.—Houston [1st Dist.] 1982, writ ref'd n.r.e.) ("Circumstantial evidence is probative evidence as to whether a product was defectively manufactured"); Mahan Volkswagen v. Hall, 648 S.W.2d 324, 328 (Tex. App.—Houston [1st Dist.] 1982, no writ); Rawlings Sporting Goods Co. v. Daniels, 619 S.W.2d 435, 438 (Tex. App.—Waco 1981, writ ref'd n.r.e.).

290. 650 S.W.2d 61 (Tex. 1983).

291. *Id.* at 63 (circumstantial evidence by expert testimony that a safer alternative was feasible), (citing General Motors v. Hopkins, 548 S.W.2d 344 (Tex. 1977); Birmingham v. Gulf Oil Corp., 516 S.W.2d 914 (Tex. 1974); Darryl v. Ford Motor Co., 440 S.W.2d 630 (Tex. 1969); V. Mueller & Co. v. Corley, 570 S.W.2d 140 (Tex. Civ. App.—Houston [1st Dist.] 1978, writ ref'd n.r.e.)).

In *Thiele v. Chick*,[292] a truck loaded with pipe overturned, killing the driver. Plaintiffs contended that the load of pipe collapsed because the boomer holding the pipe was defective. The jury found that the boomer was not defectively designed or marketed, but did find that it was defectively manufactured.[293] The court noted that the circumstantial evidence warranted a finding that the boomer was defective.[294] The court relied on *Darryl v. Ford Motor Co.*,[295] in which the Texas Supreme Court announced:

> To exclude circumstantial evidence that the product was defective at the time of the sale would frustrate the beneficial purposes of the doctrine. It would be equally difficult, if not impossible, for the plaintiff to rebut by direct evidence all of the conceivable possibilities (sic) which would account for the defective condition other than the existence of the defect at the time of the sale. Such direct evidence should not be required, particularly when dealing with a latent defect.[296]

The circumstantial evidence in *Thiele* suggesting no change in the condition of the boomer established that the defect existed at the time the boomer left the manufacturer.[297]

Circumstantial evidence was critical in *Mahan Volkswagen, Inc. v. Hall*.[298] A woman was killed when her car suddenly swerved to the left on a two-lane road, struck a culvert, and then hit a utility pole broadside. The brake system was determined to be defective when the vehicle was examined. A critical issue was whether this defect existed when the car left the manufacturer, whether it resulted from the dealer's repair work, or whether the accident occurred because of decedent's misuse.[299] The jury determined the brake system was defectively designed.[300] In analyzing the manufacturer's liability, the court acknowledged that despite strong evidence to the contrary, the jury was entitled to infer from all the

---

292. 631 S.W.2d 526 (Tex. App.—Houston [1st Dist.] 1982, writ ref'd n.r.e.).
293. *Id.* at 529.
294. *Id.* at 530.
295. 440 S.W.2d 630 (Tex. 1969).
296. *Id.* at 632.
297. 631 S.W.2d at 531 (citing *Darryl*, 440 S.W.2d at 632).
298. 648 S.W.2d 324 (Tex. App.—Houston [1st Dist.] 1982, writ ref'd n.r.e.).
299. *Id.* at 327. The defendants were the manufacturer, American Motors Sales Corp., the franchise dealer who sold the car, Astro/AMC Jeep, Inc. and the dealer who bought the car from previous owner, Mahan Volkswagen, Inc.
300. *Id.*

circumstances that the producing cause of the accident was the defective condition of the brakes at the time the car was sold.[301]

An expert witness is particularly important in a case based on circumstantial evidence. An examination of the product and the circumstances surrounding the accident qualifies the expert to express an opinion on the condition of the product.[302] An expert opinion, coupled with the circumstantial evidence surrounding the accident, is sufficient to establish a defective product.[303]

Evidence of subsequent remedial measures and evidence of recall letters constitute forms of circumstantial proof.[304] If the manufacturer is afforded the opportunity of adopting a safer design, this fact constitutes circumstantial evidence to prove a defective design.[305] A safer alternative design may be demonstrated if the manufacturer presently or, in the past, produced a safer product or if other manufacturers of identical products utilize a safer design.[306] State of the art at the time the product was manufactured is critical in a strict tort liability case.[307] Evidence of other accidents, incidents, or claims involving an identically designed or marketed product likewise comprises another type of circumstantial evidence.[308] When a plaintiff negates all other possible causes of the accident except for a defective condition, a defective product may be circumstantially proved.[309] Finally, evidence of state and federal regulations governing design and warnings, as well as evidence of industry standards, represent admissible circumstantial evidence.[310]

---

301. *Id.* at 328.

302. Refer to notes 101-288 *supra* and accompanying text.

303. *See, e.g.*, Shipp v. General Motors Corp., 750 F.2d 418 (5th Cir. 1985); *Kindred*, 650 S.W.2d at 62; General Motors Corp. v. Hopkins, 548 S.W.2d 344, 348-49 (Tex. 1977); *Theile*, 631 S.W.2d at 529; Ford Motor Co. v. Bland, 517 S.W.2d 641, 644 (Tex. Civ. App.—Waco 1974, writ ref'd n.r.e.); F.M.C. Corp. v. Burns, 444 S.W.2d 315, 322 (Tex. Civ. App.—San Antonio 1969, no writ).

304. Refer to notes 311-480 *infra* and accompanying text.

305. *Id.*

306. Refer to notes 481-500 *infra* and accompanying text.

307. Refer to notes 501-542 *infra* and accompanying text.

308. Refer to notes 543-568 *infra* and accompanying text.

309. Refer to notes 569-578 *infra* and accompanying text.

310. Refer to notes 579-611 *infra* and accompanying text.

F. *Subsequent Remedial Measures*

1. *Generally.* In a products case, the admissibility of remedial measures[311] taken by a defendant after the accident is quintessentially important.[312] Normally, a remedial measure is defined to mean action that, if taken before the accident, would have reduced the likelihood of the event occurring.[313] The argument that subsequent remedial measures constitute an admission of prior negligence, however, has been categorically rejected.[314] The admissibility of subsequent remedial measures has engendered considerable controversy throughout the jurisdictions.[315]

Courts articulate two principal reasons for excluding evidence of subsequent remedial measures as an admission of fault.[316] First, conduct subsequent to the accident possesses little relevance to the issue of antecedent negligence.[317] Post-accident changes may represent a response to the occurrence of an accident or may be in response to the plaintiff's own contributory negligence.[318] Evidence

---

311. *See generally* Kobayashi, *Products Liability Lawsuits - Part I*, 1981 TRIAL LAW GUIDE 297, 303 (defining "remedial measures" as a phrase covering virtually any postaccident change, repair, precautionary or corrective measure and citing cases in support of this broad interpretation).

312. *Id.* at 299.

313. Blakely, *Article IV: Relevancy and Its Limits*, 20 HOUS. L. REV. 151, 313 (1983 TEX. R. EVID. HANDBOOK).

314. *See, e.g.*, Werner v. Upjohn Co., 628 F.2d 848, 856 (4th Cir. 1980), *cert. denied*, 449 U.S. 1080 (1981); Bauman v. Volkswagenwerk, A.G., 621 F.2d 230, 233 (6th Cir. 1980); Knight v. Otis Elevator Co., 596 F.2d 84, 91-92 (3d Cir. 1979); Ellis v. Galconda Corp., 352 So. 2d 1221, 1224 (Fla. Dist. Ct. App. 1977); Moldovan v. Allis Chalmers Mfg. Co., 83 Mich. App. 373, 268 N.W.2d 656, 660 (1978), *cert. denied*, 444 U.S. 1034 (1980); Lavin v. Fauci, 170 N.J. Super. 403, 406, 406 A.2d 978, 981 (N.J. (App. Div. 1979); Haysom v. Coleman Lantern Co., 89 Wash. 2d 474, 573 P.2d 785, 790-91 (1978). *See generally* Comment, *Federal Rule of Evidence 407 and Its State Variations: The Courts Perform Some "Subsequent Remedial Measures" of their Own in Products Liability Cases*, 49 UMKC L. REV. 338, 338 (1981) [hereinafter cited as Comment, *Federal Rule*].

315. *See, e.g.*, Farner v. Paccar, Inc., 562 F.2d 518, 528 (8th Cir. 1977); Burke v. Almaden Vineyards, Inc., 86 Cal. App. 3d 768, 774, 150 Cal. Rptr. 419, 422 (1978); Rucker v. Norfolk & W. Ry., 64 Ill. App. 3d 770, 381 N.E.2d 715, 725 (1978), *rev'd on other grounds*, 77 Ill. 2d 434, 436, 396 N.E.2d 534, 536 (1979).

316. *See generally* FED. R. EVID. 407 ADVISORY COMMITTEE NOTE.

317. *See, e.g.*, Marshal v. Joske's, Inc., 581 S.W.2d 192, 195 (Tex. Civ. App.—San Antonio 1979, no writ) (negligence actions for injuries sustained in store *citing* J. Weingarten, Inc. v. Standefer, 490 S.W.2d 941, 946 (Tex. Civ. App.—Beaumont 1973, writ ref'd n.r.e.) ("For aught that appears, defendant may have simply rearranged the store as a housewife frequently rearranges her furniture"). *See generally* H. WENDORF & D. SCHLEUTER, *supra* note 198.

318. FED. R. EVID. 407 advisory committee note. *See generally* W. PROSSER, HANDBOOK

of post-accident changes is per se highly prejudicial. Jurors tend to construe subsequent remedial measures as an admission of guilt.[319] Pragmatically, evidence of subsequent remedial measures is generally determinative in persuading a jury to assess liability.

The second and most important reason for the exclusion of evidence of subsequent remedial measures is the public policy rationale.[320] The public policy of encouraging, or at least not discouraging, persons from undertaking post-accident safety measures is of paramount concern for the good of public safety.[321] The underlying rationale for this policy is that if the evidence of subsequent remedial measures is admissible, a defendant would be unwilling to make any improvements to his product, because such action would be used as an admission that the product as previously designed was unsafe.[322] Because evidence of subsequent remedial measures can be so effective for plaintiffs, efforts have been mounted against the general rule.[323]

Admissibility of post-accident repairs is dependent upon the specific purpose for which the evidence is offered. The general rule excludes subsequent remedial measures as evidence of negligence or culpable conduct.[324] There are several exceptions, however, to this general rule.[325] For example, jurisdictions admit evidence to rebut the contention that the condition or product could not be feasibly altered or redesigned,[326] to show the condition of the

---

OF THE LAW OF TORTS § 31 (4th ed. 1971) (an actor's conduct for subsequent acts may be completely unrelated to negligence).

319. Low, *Federal Rule of Evidence 407 and Strict Products Liability - The Rule Against Subsequent Repairs Lives On*, 48 J. OF AIR L. & COM. 887, 894 (1983); 2 J. WIGMORE, A TREATISE ON THE ANGLO-AMERICAN SYSTEM OF EVIDENCE IN TRIALS AT COMMON LAW § 283(4), at 151 (3d ed. 1940).

320. *See, e.g.*, Simms v. Southwest Texas Methodist Hosp., 535 S.W.2d 192, 199 (Tex. Civ. App.—San Antonio 1976, writ ref'd n.r.e.) (subsequent warning of risk presented by powder on surgical gloves); Louisville & Nashville Ry. v. Williams, 370 F.2d 839, 844 (5th Cir. 1966).

321. FED. R. EVID. 407 advisory committee note. *See* Roosth & Genecov Prod. Co. v. White, 152 Tex. 619, 629, 262 S.W.2d 99, 104-05 (1953).

322. *See Roosth*, 262 S.W.2d at 105. *See generally*, J. WIGMORE, *supra* note 319.

323. *See* Kennelly, *Postaccident Remedial Measures (Federal Rule of Evidence 407) - Suggested Discovery and Methods to Establish Admissibility*, 1977 TRIAL LAW GUIDE 61, 70.

324. FED. R. EVID. 407 advisory committee note.

325. *See* KOBAYASHI, *supra* note 311, at 300.

326. *See, e.g.*, Boeing Airplane Co. v. Brown, 291 F.2d 310, 315 (9th Cir. 1961).

premises or product as it existed at the time of the accident,[327] and to identify the party possessing control of the premises or product.[328] Courts apply the exclusionary rule not only to post-accident repairs, but to other situations including changes in company rules,[329] discharge of employees,[330] and installation of safety devices.[331]

2. *Federal Rule 407.* The generally accepted common law rule excluding evidence of subsequent remedial measures has been codified in Federal Rule of Evidence 407.[332] Rule 407 governs admissibility of evidence of post-accident changes in strict tort liability actions, though the rule does not expressly identify strict tort liability.[333] Rule 407 prohibits the admission of evidence of subsequent remedial measures to prove negligence or culpable conduct,[334] but authorizes admission of this evidence to prove owner-

---

327. *See, e.g.*, Steele v. Wiedemann Mach. Co., 280 F.2d 380, 382 (3d Cir. 1960); *see* Howard v. Faberge, 679 S.W.2d 644, 647 (Tex. App.—Houston [1st. Dist.] 1984, writ ref'd n.r.e.).

328. *See, e.g.*, Houston Lighting & Power Co. v. Taber, 221 S.W.2d 339, 343 (Tex. Civ. App.—Galveston 1949, writ ref'd n.r.e.).

329. *See, e.g.*, Ware v. Boston & M.R.R., 92 N.H. 373, 31 A.2d 58, 60 (1943) (evidence excluded of defendant railroad adopting a traffic regulation limiting the speed at which its trains may cross intersections).

330. *See, e.g.*, Armour & Co. v. Skene, 153 F. 241, 245 (1st Cir.), *cert. denied*, 206 U.S. 562 (1907) ("a hundred things may have happened during the year to cause the discharge".)

331. *See, e.g.*, Hatcher v. Globe Union Mfg. Co., 170 Wash. 494, 16 P.2d 824, 826 (1932) (error to admit evidence that defendant installed a blower to alleviate a lead poisoning problem).

332. FED. R. EVID. 407. Rule 407 states:

> When, after an event, measures are taken which, if taken previously, would have made the event less likely to occur, evidence of the subsequent measures is not admissible to prove negligence or culpable conduct in connection with the event. This rule does not require the exclusion of evidence of subsequent measures when offered for another purpose, such as proving ownership, control, or feasibility of precautionary measures, if controverted, or impeachment.

Id. See 2 J. WEINSTEIN AND M. BERGER, *supra* note 162, § 407[01] at 407-5, which states: "Rule 407 codifies the almost uniform practice in American courts of excluding evidence of subsequent remedial measures as proof of an admission of fault. The use of the phrase: "Remedial Measures" is designed to bring within the scope of the rule any post-accident change, repair of precaution." *Id.*

333. *See generally* Comment, *Federal Rule 407 supra* note 332.

334. *Compare* Grenada Steel Indus. v. Alabama Oxygen Co., 695 F.2d 883 (5th Cir. 1983); *Knight*, 596 F.2d 84; *Upjohn*, 628 F.2d 848; *Bauman*, 621 F.2d 230; Roy v. Star Chopper Co., Inc., 584 F.2d 1124 (1st Cir. 1978), *cert. denied*, 440 U.S. 916 (1979), *and* Cann v. Ford Motor Co., 658 F.2d 54 (2d Cir. 1981), *cert. denied*, 456 U.S. 960 (1982), *with Farner*, 562 F.2d 518; Moe v. Avions Marcel Dassault Brequet Aviation, 727 F.2d 917 (10th Cir.

ship, control, or feasibility of precautionary measures, if controverted, or impeachment.[335] The congressional intent in codifying Rule 407 was to establish a single rule embodying the common law doctrine of subsequent remedial measures.[336] Congress intended, however, for the common law to both complement and supplement the federal rule.[337]

The scope of Federal Rule 407 is limited by the requirements that the remedial measures must be post-accident, made by a party to the suit, and made in response to the accident. The requirement that the subsequent remedial measure constitute a response to an accident was addressed in *Rozier v. Ford Motor Co.*[338] Plaintiff's decedent was a passenger in a Ford automobile that was struck from behind by another vehicle. The impact ruptured the fuel tank, causing fire to engulf the car and fatally burn the decedent.[339] The plaintiff instituted suit based on defective design of the fuel tank. After a judgment for the defendant and during pendency of the appeal, plaintiff's counsel learned of the existence of a Trend Cost Estimate prepared by Ford before the accident but after the manufacture of the automobile in question. The report indicated that Ford planned to utilize a new fuel tank in anticipation of a new safety standard for rear-end collisions.[340] The Fifth Circuit concluded that Rule 407 did not preclude admission of the Trend Cost Estimate for several reasons: (1) the document was not a subsequent remedial measure; (2) the document was authored before the accident; (3) the social policy of encouraging repairs was inapplicable because the design change was required by the Na-

---

1984), *cert. denied*, 53 U.S.L.W. 3239 (1985). *See also* Hallmark v. Allied Prod. Corp., 132 Ariz. 434, 646 P.2d 319 (Ariz. App. 1982).

335. Refer to note 332, *supra*. FED. R. EVID. 407 advisory committee notes. The list of exceptions to Rule 407 is not exhaustive, but merely illustrative. *See also* Low, *supra* note 286, at 900. The phrase "if controverted" could be read as applying only to the "feasibility" exception or to all of the preceding exceptions. Commentators interpret the phrase to apply to all of the exceptions. H. WENDORF & D. SCHLEUTER, *supra* note 175, at 49 (citing S. SALTZBURG & K.R. REDDEN, FEDERAL RULES OF EVIDENCE MANUAL 178 (3d ed. 1982)).

336. Low, *supra* note 319 at 899; FED. R. EVID. 407 advisory committee note.

337. *See Upjohn*, 628 F.2d at 856 (noting that Congress did not intend to eliminate years of common law development, but instead intended that courts rely on common law to answer unsolved questions of Rule 407).

338. 573 F.2d 1332 (5th Cir. 1978).

339. *Id.* at 1337.

340. *Id.* at 1340. If the subsequent alterations are made by a third party, the rule of exclusion under Rule 407 is inapplicable. Dixon v. International Harvestor Co., 754 F.2d 573, 583 (5th. Cir. 1985).

tional Traffic Safety Administration; and (4) even if the report could be characterized as a subsequent remedial measure, it was admissible under an exception to Rule 407.[341]

Arceneaux v. Texaco, Inc.[342] also illustrates the requirement that subsequent remedial measures must be made after an event and in response to it. The occupants of a pickup truck suffered serious burns when a service station attendant lit a cigarette, igniting gasoline. When the attendant jerked the nozzle out of the gas tank, he sprayed the flaming gasoline into the cab of the truck.[343] Plaintiffs instituted suit against General Motors Corporation for defectively designing the gas tank too close to the cab of the truck. The trial court excluded evidence of a change in location of the gas tank made after the model year of the truck, but before the accident.[344] The Fifth Circuit concluded that the trial court improperly excluded this evidence under Rule 407, because the design changes *were not* made in response to this particular event. Realizing the highly prejudicial effect of this type of evidence, the court affirmed exclusion of the evidence because of its prejudicial nature far outweighed its relevancy under Rules 401 and 402.[345]

The limitation that the subsequent remedial measures must have been made by a party to qualify as inadmissible evidence under Rule 407 is generally accepted.[346] Even though evidence of remedial measures undertaken by third parties is deemed admissible under 407, it is usually excluded on such bases as relevancy.[347]

Lolie v. Ohio Brass Co.[348] involved the admissibility of non-

---

341. 573 F.2d at 1343. *See also* Lindsay v. Ortho Pharmaceuical Corp., 481 F. Supp. 314 (E.D. N.Y. 1979).

342. 623 F.2d 924 (5th Cir. 1980), *cert denied*, 450 U.S. 928 (1981).

343. *Id.* at 925.

344. *Id.* at 928.

345. *Id.* This issue was addressed at length by the Fifth Circuit in Jackson v. Johns Mansville Sales Corp., ____ F.2d ____ (5th Cir. 1985) (en banc). The Fifth Circuit noted that evidence of the cancer-causing characteristics of asbestos is relevant to the manufacturer's liability. Standing alone, it is insufficient under Federal Rule of Evidence 403 to qualify for admission. The court concluded that if cancer evidence is relevant only to liability, the danger of unfair prejudice outweighs its probative value. *Id.*

346. *Compare* Louisville & N. RR. v. Williams, 370 F.2d 839, 844 (5th Cir. 1966) (since evidence of subsequent repairs made by muncipality had no bearing on defendant's negligence, it was admissible) *and* Dixon v. International Harvestor Co., 754 F.2d 573, 578 (5th. Cir. 1985) *with* Farner v. Paccar, Inc., 562 F.2d 518, 528 n. 20 (8th Cir. 1977) (policy behind the exclusionary rule would not be served if the rule were not applied to third persons).

347. *Id. See generally* FED. R. EVID. 401-403.

348. 502 F.2d 741 (7th Cir. 1974).

party subsequent remedial measures. In *Lolie*, the power cable attached to the roof of a mine was struck by a steel rail and the metal clips holding the cable in place were dislodged. As a result, the cable collapsed and fatally injured a coal miner. Plaintiff instituted suit against the manufacturer of the clips based on defective design.[349] After the accident, the mine operator, a nonparty, was directed by the state mine inspector to add support to the cable. The trial court excluded evidence of this subsequent modification and the jury returned a verdict for the manufacturer.[350] The court reasoned that this evidence was admissible, noting that the social policy of encouraging remedial measures "clearly has no application when the evidence is offered against a party . . . which did not make the changes."[351] The court held, however, that the exclusion of evidence of the subsequent remedial measures was not reversible error because the trial court possessed discretion to balance its relevancy against the severe prejudicial harm caused by its admission.[352]

Rule 407 prescribes certain exceptions that dilute the vitality of the general exclusionary rule.[353] Rule 407 states in part: "This rule does not require the exclusion of evidence of subsequent measures when offered for another purpose, such as proving ownership, control, or feasibility of precautionary measures, if controverted, or impeachment."[354] The exceptions articulated in Rule 407 are not exhaustive; other exceptions are applicable.

The most controversial exception provided for in Rule 407 involves admission of evidence of subsequent remedial measures to prove the feasibility of precautionary measures when the feasibility of alternative design features is controverted.[355] Because the feasi-

---

349. *Id.* at 743.

350. *Id.*

351. *Id.* at 744. *See also* Steele v. Wiedemann Mach. Co., 280 F.2d 380, 382 (3d Cir. 1960) (nonparty owner-employer made repair); Wallner v. Kitchens of Sara Lee, Inc., 419 F.2d 1028, 1032 (7th Cir. 1969) (policy of encouraging repairs not applicable to manufacturer, who did not make repairs, so could not invoke Rule 407); Brown v. Quick Mix Co., 75 Wash. 2d 833, 454 P.2d 205, 210 (1969) (upheld admission of repair evidence because the defendant had not made the repair).

352. 502 F.2d at 744.

353. Refer to note 332 *supra*. "The ingenuity of counsel in suggesting other purposes has made substantial inroads upon the general rule of exclusion." C. McCormick, *supra* note 70, § 275 at 667.

354. Fed. R. Evid. 407.

355. Caterpillar Tractor Co. v. Boyett, 674 S.W.2d 782, 790 (Tex. App.-Corpus Christi

bility of an alternative safety feature must be denied by the defendant as a predicate to admissibility, the evidence must often be fully developed before a determination of this issue is possible.[356] The scope of the feasibility exception includes subsequent alterations in labels and warnings.[357]

Under the impeachment exception to Rule 407, admission of evidence may take several forms. A defendant may put into issue the nature of the product's condition at the time of the incident, or the feasibility of further improvements. These issues are raised when, for example, the defendant asserts that he used all reasonable care or that he did not own or control the product. These positions sanction admissibility of subsequent remedial measures not only to impeach the defendant, but also to rebut defendant's claims.[358]

When evidence is admitted for a limited purpose under one of the exceptions to Rule 407, a very significant danger exists that it might be interpreted by the jury as an admission of defendant's fault.[359] The court, in its discretion, must consider the danger that the jury might improperly infer negligence or fault to determine whether the subsequent changes are admissible. Rule 403 autho-

---

1984, writ granted) (design changes after accident admissible to show feasibility of safar alternative available at time of accident.) Boeing Airplane Co. v. Brown, 291 F.2d 310, 315 (9th Cir. 1961) ("In our opinion an admission that unspecified "changes" would have been feasible and were actually made does not render irrelevant evidence as to specific changes subsequent to the accident when offered for the limited purpose of proving the feasibility of such changes to correct the specific defects in issue".)

356. Evidence of a subsequent repair cannot be admissible on the premise of feasibility if the defendant stipulates that a certain change was feasible, because the requirement that the feasibility be controverted is not then met. *See, e.g.*, Burks v. Firestone Tire & Rubber Co., 633 F.2d 1152, 1153 (5th Cir. 1981) (noting that defendants stipulated feasibility to gain the benefit of Rule 407). *But see Quick Mix*, 75 Wash. 2d 833, 454 P.2d at 210 (holding that evidence of subsequent remedial measures is admissible regardless of which party raises the issue of precautionary measures). *See* Simms v. Southwest Texas Methodist Hospital, 535 S.W.2d 192, 199 (Tex. Civ. App.—San Antonio 1976, writ ref'd n.r.e.) (warning added to surgical gloves after operation should have been excluded, but since eliminating defect was found feasible, the error was harmless.)

357. *See* Edwards v. Sears, Roebuck & Co., 512 F.2d 276, 284 n.9 (5th Cir. 1975) (tire retailer's owners' manuals withdrawn from market after accident).

358. *See, e.g.*, American Airlines, Inc. v. United States, 418 F.2d 180, 196 (5th Cir. 1969) (evidence of subsequent remedial measures used to impeach early testimony that the changes were not feasible and to rebut the defendant's testimony that the original altimeter was safe and needed no change).

359. *See* Low, *supra* note 319, at 901. *See also* Russell v. Page Aircraft Maintenance, Inc., 455 F.2d 188, 191 (5th Cir. 1972) (such proof is "liable to an overemphasis by the jury").

rizes the court to exclude evidence if the probative value of the evidence is outweighed by the danger of unfair prejudice.[360] If such evidence is admitted, the defendant should request a limiting instruction under Rule 105 to minimize the effect of the evidence on the jury's perception of fault.[361] Though evidence of subsequent remedial measures is inadmissible, Rule 407 does not foreclose pretrial discovery of such information.[362]

Though all jurisdictions have applied Rule 407 in products liability cases based on negligence, there is less consistency in the exclusion of evidence of subsequent remedial measures in cases based on strict tort liability.[363] The majority of circuit courts view Rule 407 as excluding evidence of subsequent remedial measures taken after an accident is irrespective of whether the cause of action predicated on negligence or strict tort liability.[364] Only the Eighth

---

360. FED. R. EVID. 403 states: "Although relevant, evidence may be excluded if its probative value is substantially outweighed by the danger of unfair prejudice, confusion of the issues, or misleading the jury, or by considerations of undue delay, waste of time, or needless presentation of cumulative evidence." The advisory committee note to Rule 403 states, in part: "In reaching a decision whether to exclude on grounds of unfair prejudice, . . . [t]he availability of other means of proof may . . . be an appropriate factor [to consider]." The Fifth Circuit employs a two prong test to aid in deciding whether to exclude evidence: (1) the necessity and probative effect of the evidence, and (2) whether the same facts could be proved by other evidence. Gross v. Black & Decker (U.S.), Inc., 695 F.2d 858, 863 (5th Cir. 1983). *See also* Jackson v. Johns Manville Sales Corp., 757 F.2d 614 (5th Cir. 1985) (en banc). *See generally* Comment, *Fed. Rule*, *supra* note 314, at 341.

361. *See generally* Note, *Products Liability and Evidence of Subsequent Repairs*, 1972 DUKE L.J. 837, 850. A jury should not be permitted to find the defendant liable on evidence of subsequent remedial measures alone; it must not disregard the material elements of proximate cause, legal defectiveness of the product, and control by the defendant. *Id.* "The court must ensure that the plaintiff has introduced independent evidence for all material elements of his case, that a factual dispute exists for jury resolution, and that the jury is properly instructed to restrict its use of the evidence of subsequent repairs to the issues of defectiveness and control." *Id.* In the absence of these constraints, the per se highly prejudicial effects of evidence and subsequent remedial measures ensures liability against the product supplier.

362. *See* FED. R. CIV. P. 26(b)(1), stating the relevancy standard of discovery as "reasonably calculated to lead to the discovery of admissible evidence."

363. *See* P. ROTHSTEIN, RULES OF EVIDENCE FOR THE UNITED STATES COURTS AND MAGISTRATES (1984).

364. *See* Roy v. Star Chopper Co., 584 F.2d 1124 (1st Cir. 1978) *cert. denied* 440 U.S. 916 (1979); Cann v. Ford Motor Co., 658 F.2d 54 (2d Cir. 1981) *cert. denied* 456 U.S. 960 (1982); Josephs v. Harris Corp., 677 F.2d 985 (3d Cir. 1982); Werner v. Upjohn Co., 628 F.2d 848 (4th Cir. 1980) *cert denied*, 449 U.S. 1080 (1981); Grenada Steel Industries, Inc. v. Alabama Oxygen Co., 695 F.2d 883 (5th Cir. 1983); Hall v. American Steamship Co., 688 F.2d 1062 (6th Cir. 1982); Flaminio v. Honda Motor Co., 733 F.2d 463 (7th Cir. 1984); Longenecker v. General Motors Corp., 594 F.2d 1283 (9th Cir. 1979).

and Tenth Circuits specifically construe Rule 407 as allowing evidence of subsequent remedial measures in strict tort liability cases.[365]

In *Meller v. Heil Co.*,[366] plaintiff's husband was fatally injured when the dump bed of a dump truck on which he was working was accidentally lowered on top of him. The trial court permitted plaintiff to introduce evidence of a subsequent change in the design of the bed of the truck.[367] In *Meller*, the Tenth Circuit backed off slightly from its earlier position in *Hernon v. Seven Bar Flying Service, Inc.*,[368] which rejected the majority view and categorically stated that Rule 407 sanctioned the admissibility of subsequent remedial measures in strict tort liability actions simply based on that characterization.[369] The court appears to have adopted a balancing test in determining whether the evidence is admissible. The Tenth Circuit stated:

> An application of Rule 407 does not end our inquiry; the challenged evidence must pass muster under other rules of evidence as well. Heil claims that the evidence should have been excluded under Rule 403 because it was unfairly prejudicial. . . . We conclude that any such tendency in this case was eliminated by the court's instruction to the jury, cautioning it to consider the evidence only with respect to the feasibility of alternatives. We hold that Rule 403 did not bar admission of the evidence.[370]

A few jurisdictions rationalize several distinctions to exist between strict product liability actions and negligence actions in relation to the admissibility of subsequent remedial measure evidence. The first distinction presupposes that in negligence actions evidence of post-accident remedial measures is prejudicial on the issue of antecedent breach of duty.[371] These jurisdictions rationalize

---

365. *See* Farner v. Paccar, Inc., 562 F.2d 518 (8th Cir. 1977); Moe v. Avions Marcel Dassault-Breguet Aviation, 727 F.2d 917 (10th Cir.) *cert. denied*, 105 S. Ct. 176 (1984) Herndon v. Seven Bar Flying Service, Inc., 716 F.2d 1322 (10th Cir. 1983) *cert denied*, 104 S. Ct. 2170 (1984). *Accord* Roth v. Black & Decker U.S., 737 F.2d 779 (8th Cir. 1984).*But see* DeLuryea v. Winthrop Labs, 697 F.2d 222 (8th Cir. 1983) (rule limiting the exclusion of subsequent remedial measures in strict tort liability is inapplicable in cases predicted on a marketing (warning) defect.

366. 745 F.2d 1297 (10th Cir. 1984).

367. *Id.* at 1299.

368. 716 F.2d 1322 (10th Cir. 1983)

369. *Id.* at 1329.

370. 745 F.2d at 1301.

371. Refer to notes 317-19 *supra* and accompanying text.

that strict liability focuses not on the conduct of defendant, but solely on the condition of the product.[372] According to these critics, foreseeability, which is essential to establish negligence, is not an issue in a strict liability case.[373]

The second distinction urged between the two causes of action is that the public policy of encouraging post-accident changes and improvements has applicability to negligence actions but not to strict tort liability.[374] Controversy continues as to whether admission of post-accident remedial measures frustrates this public policy consideration in the strict tort liability context. Admitting evidence of subsequent remedial measures rather clearly contravenes the public policy rationale of encouraging precautionary measures; corporate mass producers are discouraged from making repairs by the threat of creating highly prejudicial evidence. A few jurisdictions myopically perceive that the public policy is not frustrated because manufacturers still have more to gain by correcting the defect and preventing future law suits.[375] But in *Cann v. Ford Motor Co.*,[376] the Second Circuit forcefully repudiated this unrealistic approach, noting:

> Since the policy underlying Rule 407 not to discourage persons from taking remedial measures is relevant to defendants sued under either theory, we do not see the significance of the distinction. A potential defendant must be equally concerned regardless of the theoretical rubric under which this highly prejudicial and extremely damaging evidence is admitted. [citation omitted].[377]

A 1975 California Supreme Court decision is the progenitor for rejection of the exclusionary rule in strict tort liability cases. *Ault v. International Harvester Co.*[378] has been influential in federal and state courts in construing Federal Rule 407 or state

372. *See, e.g.*, Shaffer v. Honeywell, Inc., 249 N.W.2d 251, 257 n.7 (S.D. 1976). *See generally* Costello and Weinberger, *The Subsequent Repair Doctrine and Products Liability*, 51 N.Y. St. B.J. 463, 465-495 (1979).

373. *See, e.g.*, Ault v. International Harvester, 13 Cal. 3d 113, 528 P.2d 1148, 117 Cal. Rptr. 812 (1975)

374. Refer to notes 320-23, *supra* and accompanying text. *See, e.g.*, Phillips v. J. L. Hudson Co., 79 Mich. App. 425, 426, 263 N.W.2d 3, 4 (1977).

375. *See, e.g.*, *Farmers Union*, 552 F.2d 788. *See generally* Costello and Weinberger, *supra* note 372 at 464-65.

376. 658 F.2d 54 (2d Cir. 1981).

377. *Id.* at 60.

378. 13 Cal. 3d 113, 528 P.2d 1148, 117 Cal. Rptr. 812 (1975).

equivalents.[379] In *Ault*, plaintiff, a passenger in a Jeep Scout, was injured when the Jeep left the road and plunged to the bottom of a deep canyon. The plaintiff contended that the gearbox failed because the aluminum alloy from which the gearbox was fabricated suffered metal fatigue, causing the Jeep to travel out of control. The plaintiff produced evidence that three years after the accident, the manufacturer substituted malleable iron for the aluminum alloy in the manufacture of the gearbox. The California Supreme Court authorized admission of evidence of the subsequent modification.[380] The court's rationale for admitting the evidence was that culpability is not an element of proof in a strict liability action.[381] The court totally disavowed the public policy reasons for the exclusionary rule when applied to strict liability:[382]

> The contemporary corporate mass producer of goods, the normal products liability defendant, manufactures tens of thousands of units of goods; it is manifestly unrealistic to suggest that such a producer will forego making improvements in his product, and risk innumerable additional lawsuits and the attendant adverse effect upon its public image, simply because evidence of adoption of such improvement may be admitted in an action founded on strict liability for recovery on an injury that preceded the improvement.[383]

The court, citing Illinois authority, noted that "policy considerations are involved which shift the emphasis from the defendant manufacturer's conduct to the character of the product."[384]

The federal courts have struggled with construction of Rule 407 in strict tort liability cases.[385] The *Ault* holding remains the clear minority view; only the Eighth and Tenth Circuits have construed Rule 407 in line with the *Ault* rationale.[386] The Eighth Cir-

---

379. The California rule relied on in *Ault* was very similar to FED. R. EVID. 407, and, in fact, was used as a model in drafting FED. R. EVID. 407. FED. R. EVID. 407 advisory committee note. *See* CAL. EVID. CODE § 1151 (West 1968).

380. 13 Cal. 3d at 114, 528 P.2d at 1149, 117 Cal. Rptr. at 814.

381. *Id.* at 117, 528 P.2d at 1150, 117 Cal. Rptr. at 814.

382. *Id.* at 118-20, 528 P.2d at 1151-52, 117 Cal. Rptr. at 814-15.

383. *Id.* at 120, 528 P.2d at 1152, 117 Cal. Rptr. at 816.

384. *Id.* at 121, 528 P.2d at 1152, 117 Cal. Rptr. at 816. (*citing* Sutkowski v. Universal Marion Corp., 5 Ill. App. 3d 313, 281 N.E.2d 749 (1972)).

385. Refer to notes 364-69 *supra*.

386. Refer to note 369 *supra* and accompanying text.

cuit reaffirmed its view in *Unterburger v. Snow Co.*[387] A grain elevator employee's arm became entangled in the main drive shaft of a grain auger.[388] The Eighth Circuit concluded that the instruction and parts list illustrating a newer model of the auger was admissible since Rule 407 was inapplicable to strict liability.[389]

The Tenth Circuit, in *Herndon v. Seven Bar Flying Service, Inc.*,[390] following the Eighth Circuit in *Unterburger* and the Wisconsin Supreme Court in *D.L. by Friederichs v. Huebner*,[391] aligned itself with the minority view. In deeming admissible an airplane manufacturer's service bulletins issued more than a year after the accident which instructed owners to modify the pitch trim switch, the court stated that where any reason exists for use of the evidence other than to establish defendant's negligence, Rule 407 is inapplicable.[392]

The overwhelming majority view emphasizes that the rule excluding subsequent remedial measures applies with equal force and vitality to strict tort liability actions.[393] The Fourth Circuit in *Werner v. Upjohn Co.*[394] confronted the applicability of the exclusionary rule in strict tort liability actions. The manufacturer of Cleocin, a substitute for penicillin, significantly expanded its warning of possible side effects after the plaintiff developed pseudomembranous colitis, a condition mentioned in the original warning.[395] The court perceived no difference in the policy argument of not discouraging subsequent repairs whether applied to

---

387. 630 F.2d 599 (8th Cir. 1980).

388. *Id.* at 601, 602.

389. *Id.* at 603. The court does not address the issue that modification of the auger was a subsequent remedial measure, since the change was made before the accident, and not in response to the accident. Consequently the Court was not truly addressing the factual issue of a subsequent change. Moreover, the Eighth Circuit has limited its holding to design cases but not warning cases. See Kehm v. Proctor & Gamble Mfg. Co., 724 F.2d 613 (8th Cir. 1984); Roth v. Bloch & Dicken U.S., 737 F.2d 779 (8th Cir. 1984).

390. 716 F.2d 1322 (10th Cir. 1983).

391. 110 Wis. 2d 581, 329 N.W.2d 890, 903 (1983).

392. 716 F.2d at 1331. The court also stated, "Where there is no issue of culpability the jury's focus is only on the existence of a defect. Where plaintiffs assert both the manufacturer was negligent and, alternatively, that strict liability standards should apply, the trial court upon request can fashion appropriate limiting instructions." *Id. See also* United States v. Poe, 713 F.2d 579 (10th Cir. 1983), *cert denied*, 104 S. Ct. 1907 (1984).

393. Refer to notes 364-68 *supra* and accompanying text.

394. 628 F.2d 848 (4th Cir. 1980), *cert. denied*, 449 U.S. 1080 (1981).

395. *Id.* at 853.

negligence or to strict tort liability.[396] Under either theory, the manufacturer is discouraged from undertaking subsequent remedial measures when evidence of such repairs is admitted.[397]

The exclusionary provisions of Rule 407 were comprehensively analyzed and reviewed by the Seventh Circuit in *Flamino v. Honda Motor Co., Ltd.*[398] Plaintiff was injured when a Honda motorcycle which he was riding apparently wobbled, causing him to swerve off the road and strike a fixed object, resulting in paraplegia. The trial court excluded evidence that subsequent to the accident the manufacturer changed the design of the forkstem of the cycle. After a review of all circuit court decisions involving construction of Rule 407, the Seventh Circuit adopted the majority view and affirmed the trial court ruling.[399] The Seventh Circuit observed:

> In any event, we agree with the majority view that the rule does apply to strict liability cases. We are not persuaded by the purely semantic argument to the contrary that since 'culpable conduct' is not the issue in such a case—defendant is liable, at least prima facie, even if he is not blameworthy in the sense of being willful or negligent, provided that he caused the plaintiff's injury—the rule is inapplicable by its own terms. Wisconsin law rejects this argument in holding that a defendant's blameworthiness must, under the state's comparative-negligence statute, be compared with the plaintiff's blameworthiness in strict liability cases, even though the defendant was not blameworthy in a negligence sense. [citation omitted][400]

The Fifth Circuit in *Grenada Steel Industries v. Alabama Oxygen Co.*,[401] joined the First, Second, Third, Fourth, Sixth, Seventh and Ninth Circuits in construing Rule 407 to apply to strict tort liability actions.[402] The court recognized the public policy rationale

---

396. *Id.* at 857.

397. *Id.* "It makes no difference to the defendant on what theory the evidence is admitted; his inclination to make subsequent improvements will be similarly repressed." *Id.*

398. 733 F.2d 463 (7th Cir. 1984).

399. *Id.* at 469.

400. *Id.*

401. 695 F.2d 883 (5th Cir. 1983).

402. *Id.* at 888. The Fifth Circuit, in *Foster*, 621 F.2d at 721, avoided confronting the issue of the applicability of FED. R. EVID. 407 to strict tort liability actions. In *Foster*, the evidence of subsequent design changes was excluded where the manufacturer conceded the feasibility of the changes. *Id.* at 721. *See also* Cook v. McDonough Power Equip. Co., Inc., 720 F.2d 829 (5th Cir. 1983).

of encouraging subsequent remedial improvements, but based its decision in large measure on the more significant issue of relevance and prejudice.[403] The court stated:

> We cannot really know why changes are made by industry generally or why a change was made in a particular product in the absence of evidence on the question . . . . The real question is whether the product or its design was defective at the time the product was sold . . . . The introduction of evidence about subsequent changes in the product or its design threatens to confuse the jury by diverting its attention from whether the product was defective at the relevant time to what was done later. [citation omitted] . . . Interpreted to require the evidence to focus on the time when the product was sold, Rule 407 would conform to the policy expressed in Rule 403, the exclusion of relevant information if its probative value is substantially outweighed by the danger of confusion. [citation omitted][404]

The Fifth Circuit view announced in *Grenada* was reaffirmed in *Cook v. McDonough Power Equipment, Inc.*.[405] The court reiterated the *Grenada* interpretation of Rule 407 as "not to limit evidence bearing on the manufacturer's knowledge of defect, but to *focus the evidence to that most relevant to proving defect at the time the product was sold.*" (emphasis added)[406]

In the few federal and state jurisdictions that admit evidence of subsequent remedial measures in strict tort liability cases, complications arise when plaintiffs base their causes of action on both negligence and strict tort liability, since evidence of subsequent remedial measures is admissible in these limited jurisdictions under strict liability, but not under negligence.[407] A limiting instruction provided for under Rule 105 provides the only legal remedy.[408]

Related to the controversy of admissibility of evidence of post-accident repairs is the issue of the admissibility of evidence that the existing design or warning complied with, substantially exceeded, or failed to meet *subsequently* enacted state and federal regulations. Generally, such evidence is inadmissible.[409] In *Cover v.*

---

403. *Foster,* 621 F.2d at 721.
404. *Id.* at 888.
405. 720 F.2d 829 (5th Cir. 1983).
406. *Id.* at 831.
407. *See, e.g., Cann,* 658 F.2d at 60. *See generally* Blakely, *supra* note 313, at 313.
408. *See* Blakely, *supra* note 313, at 219.
409. *See, e.g.,* Turner v. General Motors Corp., 584 S.W.2d 844 (Tex. 1979); Rexrode v.

Cohen,[410] plaintiff instituted suit against General Motors, the manufacturer of a car that traveled out of control as a result of a faulty accelerator.[411] The trial court admitted evidence that a different accelerator spring was prescribed by the Federal Motor Vehicle Safety Standard for later model cars.[412] General Motors conceded that the spring required by the subsequent standard was feasible at the time it manufactured the car in question.[413] The appellate court concluded that the agency-proposed change established only that a better design was possible, not that the existing design was not reasonably safe.[414] As a consequence, the court ruled that admission of the post-manufacture standard constituted prejudicial error.[415]

3. *State Views.* State jurisdictions generally adhere to the uniform rule that excludes evidence of subsequent remedial measures as an admission of fault.[416] Several states have adopted a rule

---

American Laundry Press Corp., 674 F.2d 826 (10th Cir. 1982), *cert. denied*, 103 S. Ct. 137 (1982).

410. 61 N.Y.2d 261, 461 N.E.2d 864 (1984).

411. *Id.* 461 N.E.2d at 867.

412. *Id.* at 869.

413. *Id.* at 866.

414. *Id.* at 869.

415. *Id.* at 870. The court stated that the relevant date for applying the exclusionary rule was the date of marketing, not the date of the accident, since strict tort liability focuses on the condition of the product at the time of manufacture. 461 N.E.2d at 866, 868. *But see* Stonehocker v. General Motors Corp., 587 F.2d 151, 157 (4th Cir. 1978) (subsequently enacted federal safety standard admissible as evidence of manufacturer's due care).

416. *See, e.g.*, Sullins v. Third & Catalina Constr. Partnership, 124 Ariz. 114, 602 P.2d 495 (1979); Gist v. Meredith Marine Sales & Serv., 272 Ark. 489, 615 S.W.2d 365 (1981); Martinez v. Atlas Bolt & Screw Co., 636 P.2d 1287 (Colo. Ct. App. 1981); Grochowski v. Stewart, 53 Del. 330, 169 A.2d 14 (1961); Hartman v. Opelika Mach. & Welding Co., 414 So. 2d 1105 (Fla. Dist. Ct. App. 1982); Chastain v. Fuqua Indus., 156 Ga. App. 719, 275 S.E.2d 679 (1980); City of Indianapolis v. Swanson, 436 N.E.2d 1179 (Ind. Ct. App. 1982); Huxol v. Nickell, 205 Kan. 718, 473 P.2d 90 (1970); Cox v. City of Louisville, 439 S.W.2d 51 (Ky. Ct. App. 1969); Givens v. De Soto Bldg. Co., 100 So. 534 (La. 1924); Esta v. Dover Corp., 385 So. 2d 439 (La. Ct. App. 1980); Fiorentino v. A.E. Staley Mfg. Co., 11 Mass. App. Ct. 428, 416 N.E.2d 998 (1981); Smith v. Squibb & Sons, Inc. 405 Mich. 79, 273 N.W.2d 476 (1979); Moldovan v. Allis- Chalmers Mfg. Co., 83 Mich. App. 373, 268 N.W.2d 656 (1978), *cert. denied*, 444 U.S. 1034 (1979); Faber v. Roelofs, 298 Minn. 16 212 N.W.2d 856 (Minn. 1973); Diversified Metals Corp. v. Aaron Ferer & Sons, Inc., 498 S.W.2d 783 (Mo. 1973); O'Neal v. F. W. Woolworth Co., 109 N.H. 197, 247 A.2d 183 (N.H. 1968); Shatz v. TEC Technical Adhesives, 174 (N.J. Super 135, 415 A.2d 1188 1980); Price v. Buckingham Mfg. Co., 110 N.J. Super. 462, 266 A.2d 140 (N.J. Super. App. Div. 1970); La Monica v. Outboard Marine Corp., 355 N.E.2d 533 (Ohio Ct. App. 1976); Mobberly v. Sears, Roebuck & Co., 48 Ohio App.2d 43, 211 N.E.2d 839 (1965); Fields v. Volkswagen of America, Inc., 555 P.2d 48 (Okla.

patterned on Federal Rule of Evidence 407 or on a variation of the rule.[417] Several other states have proposed similar statutes. Various state jurisdictions are currently struggling with the issue of whether the rule excluding evidence of subsequent remedial measures applies in a strict tort liability case.[418] Some jurisdictions have adopted the *Ault* rationale that evidence of subsequent remedial measures is admissible in strict tort liability actions.[419] Other jurisdictions have applied the exclusionary rule equally to negligence and strict liability actions.[420] These jurisdictions acknowledge that the public policy of encouraging remedial measures is furthered whether the cause of action is based on negligence or strict tort liability. Several jurisdictions in fact consider that the public policy rationale of encouraging repairs possesses an even stronger basis in strict tort liability actions, since many strict tort liability claims involve mass production of the identically designed product and liability is imposed in the absence of any tortious or

---

1976); Phipps v. Air King Mfg. Corp., 263 Or. 141, 501 P.2d 790 (Or. 1972); O'Malley v. Peerless Petroleum, Inc., 283 Pa. Super 272, 423 A.2d 1251 (1980); Lapierre v. Greenwood, 85 R.I. 484, 133 A.2d 126, *aff'd*, 135 A.2d 269 (1957); Turner v. General Motors Corp., 584 S.W.2d 844 (Tex. 1979); Turner v. Manning, Maxwell & Moore, Inc., 216 Va. 863, 217 S.E.2d 863 (1975); Mabe v. Huntington Coca-Cola Bottling Co., 145 W. Va. 712, 116 S.E.2d 874 (1960).

417. These states include Alabama, Arizona, Arkansas, California, Colorado, Delaware, Florida, Hawaii, Kansas, Michigan, Minnesota, Montana, Nebraska, Nevada, New Jersey, New Mexico, North Dakota, Ohio, Oklahoma, Oregon, South Dakota, Utah, Virginia, Washington, Wisconsin and Wyoming.

418. *See generally* DEFENSE RESEARCH INSTITUTE, *supra* note 126 at 19, 21-29.

419. *See, e.g.*, Caterpillar Tractor Co. v. Beck, 624 P.2d 790 (Alaska 1981); Roberts v. May, 41 Colo. App. 82, 583 P.2d 305 (Colo. 1978); Good v. A. B. Chance Co., 39 Colo. App. 70, 78-80, 565 P.2d 217, 224 (1977); Sutkowski v. Universal Marion Corp., 5 Ill. App. 3d 313, 281 N.E.2d 749 (1972); Siruta v. Hesston Corp., 232 Kan. 654, 659 P.2d 799, 808-09 (1983) (evidence of subsequent precautions not offered to prove negligence admissible in products liability cases); Carey v. General Motors Corp. 377 Mass. 736, 387 N.E.2d 583, 587-88 (1979) (postaccident automobile recall letter admissible); Ginnis v. Mapes Hotel Corp., 86 Nev. 408, 416-17, 470 P.2d 135, 140 (1970)); Shaffer v. Honeywell, Inc., 249 N.W.2d 251 (S.D. 1976); Caprara v. Chrysler Corp., 417 N.E.2d 545 (N.Y. 1981) D.L. by Friederichs v. Huebner, 110 Wis. 2d 581, 329 N.W.2d 890 (1983); Caldwell v. Yamaha Motor Co., 648 P.2d 519, 523 (Wyo. 1982) (evidence of postaccident design change admissible).

420. *See, e.g.*, Hallmark v. Allied Prod. Corp., 132 Ariz. 434, 646 P.2d 319 (1982); Otts v. Brough, 92 Idaho 124, 409 P.2d 95 (1965); Moldovan v. Allis Chalmers Mfg. Co., 83 Mich. App. 373, 268 N.W.2d 656 (Mich. App. 1978), *cert. denied*, 444 U.S. 1034 (1979); Haysom v. Coleman Lantern Co., 89 Wash.2d 474, 573 P.2d 785 (1978); *See also Grenada*, 695 F.2d at 886-87 nn.2-3 and accompany text for a discussion and list of state cases addressing the admissibility of evidence of subsequent remedial measures.

wrongful conduct by the product supplier.[421]

4. Texas. In Texas, evidence of subsequent remedial measures is governed by Texas Rule of Evidence 407(a). The state has avoided the *Ault* controversy[422] by adopting one significant addendum to Federal Rule 407: "Nothing in this rule shall preclude admissibility [of evidence of subsequent remedial measures] in products liability cases based on strict liability."[423] This statement by the Texas Supreme Court indicates that it will follow the minority of jurisdictions that do not apply this exclusionary rule in strict tort liability cases.[424]

The rule excluding evidence of subsequent remedial measures in warnings or instructions should *not* be affected by the last sentence of Rule 407(a).[425] Unlike design cases, the duty to warn under strict tort liability both under the *Restatement* and Texas law requires that the product supplier know or should have known of the risk of harm or danger *at the time the product is marketed.*[426] The admission of changed warnings based on knowledge

---

421. *See, e.g.*, Ortho, 338 N.E.2d 541 (rejecting evidence that the manufacturer changed the warning accompany the prescriptive medication after the injury-producing incident on the basis of contravention of public policy).

422. Refer to notes 378-86 *supra* and accompanying text.

423. Tex. R. Evid. 407(a). Prior to promulgation of Rule 407a, Texas clearly adhered to the majority view excluding evidence of subsequent remedial measures in both negligence and strict tort liability actions. Simms v. Southwest Texas Methodist Hosp., 535 S.W.2d 192 (Tex. Civ. App.—San Antonio 1976, writ ref'd nr.e.); McCants v. Salameh, 608 S.W.2d 304 (Tex. Civ. App.—Waco 1980, writ ref'd n.r.e.); Caterpillar Tractor Co. v. Boyett, 674 S.W.2d 782 (Tex. App.—Corpus Christi 1984, writ granted); *Cf.* Turner v. General Motors Corp., 584 S.W.2d 844 (Tex. 1979).

424. *See, e.g.*, Caterpillar Tractor Co. v. Beck, 624 P.2d 790, 794 (Alaska 1981); Roberts v. May, 41 Colo. App. 82, 89, 583 P.2d 305, 309 (1978); Sutkowski v. Universal Marion Corp., 5 Ill. App. 3d 313, 321, 281 N.E.2d 749, 758 (1972); Ginnis v. Mapes Hotel Corp., 86 Nev. 408, 416-17, 470 P.2d 135, 140 (1970); *Caprara*, 52 N.Y.2d at 126, 417 N.E.2d at 551, 436 N.Y.S.2d at 257; *Honeywell*, 249 N.W.2d 251, 257 n.7; Chart v. General Motors Corp., 80 Wis.2d 91, 98, 258 N.W.2d 680, 683 (1977). *See generally* Blakely, *supra* note 313, at 218.

425. *See* Howard v. Faberge, 679 S.W.2d 644, 647 (Tex. App.—Houston [1st Dist.] 1984, writ ref'd n.r.e.), where the subsequent placing of a warning on a bottle of men's cologne indicating its flammability was found to fall within the exception of rebutting testimony concerning the product's flammability to the general rule excluding evidence of subsequent remedial measures; *Simms*, 535 S.W.2d at 192.

426. Restatement (Second) of Torts, § 402A (1965). Texas early adopted and reaffirmed that the duty to warn requires, as a predicate, that the danger of unreasonable harm either be *known* or *reasonably knowable* by the product supplier *at the time* of marketing. *See* Pavlides v. Galveston Yacht Basin, Inc., 727 F.2d 330 (5th Cir. 1984); Bridgers v. Chemrex Specialty Coatings, Inc., 704 F.2d 175 (5th Cir. 1983); Carter v. Johns-Manville

acquired *subsequent* to the marketing of a product nullifies and emasculates this critical element of a cause of action for a marketing defect. Moreover, the Eighth Circuit, which is only one of two federal circuits that construe Rule 407 to admit evidence of subsequent remedial measures, excludes evidence of subsequent changes in warnings in defective warning and instruction cases.[427]

Even prior to the adoption of the Texas Rules of Evidence, Texas recognized the general rule of exclusion of evidence of subsequent remedial measures when offered to prove negligence or culpable conduct.[428] For example, in *Turner v. General Motors Corp.*,[429] the Texas Supreme Court noted that, as a rule, evidence of compliance with post-accident enacted regulations are inadmissible.

5. *Federal Diversity Jurisdiction.* Some states have adopted a rule that admits evidence of subsequent remedial measures in strict tort liability actions,[430] a position contrary to the overwhelm-

---

Sales Corp., 557 F. Supp. 1317 (E.D. Tex. 1983); Hagans v. Oliver Mach. Co., 576 F.2d 97 (5th Cir. 1978); Reyes v. Wyeth Laboratories, Inc., 498 F.2d 1264 (5th Cir. 1974), *cert. denied*, 419 U.S. 1096 (1974); Borel v. Fibreboard Paper Products Co., 493 F.2d 1076 (5th Cir. 1973), *cert. denied*, 419 U.S. 869 (1974); Rawlings Sporting Goods Co., Inc. v. Daniels, 619 S.W.2d 435 (Tex. Civ. App.—Waco 1981, writ ref'd n.r.e.); Pearson v. Hevi-Duty Electric Co., 618 S.W.2d 784 (Tex. Civ. App.—Houston [1st Dist.] 1981, writ ref'd n.r.e.); Schering Corp. v. Giesecke, 589 S.W.2d 516 (Tex. Civ. App.—Eastland 1979, writ ref'd n.r.e.); Bristol-Meyers Co. v. Gonzales, 561 S.W.2d 801 (Tex. 1978); Ethicon v. Parten, 520 S.W.2d 527 (Tex. App.—Houston [14th Dist.] 1975, no writ); Crocker v. Winthrop Laboratories, Div. of Sterling Drug, Inc., 514 S.W.2d 429 (Tex. 1974).

427. *See, e.g.*, Roth v. Black & Decker, U.S., 737 F.2d 779 (8th Cir. 1984); Kehm v. Proctor & Gamble Mfg. Co., 724 F.2d 613 (8th Cir. 1983); DeLuryea v. Winthrop Laboratories, 697 F.2d 222 (8th Cir. 1983).

428. *See* Texas Trunk R.R. v. Ayres, 83 Tex. 268, 18 S.W. 684 (1892); Roosth & Genecov Production Co. v. White, 152 Tex. 619, 262 S.W.2d 99 (1953); Marshall v. Joske's, Inc., 581 S.W.2d 192, 195 (Tex. Civ. App.—San Antonio 1979, no writ); Hopper v. J.C. Penney Co., 371 S.W.2d 750 (Tex. Civ. App.—Fort Worth 1963, writ ref'd n.r.e.); S. Blickman, Inc. v. Chilton, 114 S.W.2d 646 (Tex. Civ. App.—Austin 1938, no writ); *But see* Bell Helicopter v. Bradshaw, 594 S.W.2d 519, 530 (Tex. Civ. App.—Corpus Christi 1980, writ ref'd n.r.e.) (holding that the fact that Bell Helicopter Co. had designed a safer and longer lasting rotor blade than the one actually installed on the helicopter involved in the accident supported a finding of a design defect); Howard v. Faberge, Inc., 679 S.W.2d 644, 648 (Tex. App.—Houston [1st Dist. 1984] writ ref'd n.r.e.) *See generally* Black, *The Texas Rules of Evidence—A Proposed Codification*, 31 Sw. L.J. 969 (1977); 1A R. RAY, TEXAS LAW OF EVIDENCE, § 1151 (Supp. 1982).

429. 584 S.W.2d 844 (Tex. 1979).

430. Refer to note 424 *supra* and accompanying text.

ing majority view of the federal circuits.[431] Most product liability cases in federal court are based on diversity jurisdiction; therefore, the substantive law of the forum state applies.[432] When federal and state procedural rules conflict, it is well established that the federal rule governs.[433] State procedural rules govern only in the absence of a federal rule or when the state rule is "intimately bound up with the state right or obligation."[434] Prior to congressional promulgation of the Federal Rules of Evidence, admissibility of evidence in federal courts was generally governed by state law.[435] With congressional promulgation of the Federal Rules of Evidence, federal law controls evidentiary issues unless the rule of evidence states otherwise.[436]

The governing effect of the congressionally mandated Federal Rules of Evidence in diversity cases was expressly recognized by the Seventh Circuit in the recent case of *Flaminio v. Honda Motor Co.*[437] Plaintiff was injured when a Honda motorcycle which he was riding apparently wobbled, causing him to lose control and strike a fixed object on the roadway. Plaintiff instituted a strict tort liability action against the manufacturer of the motorbike in federal court based on diversity jurisdiction. The trial court excluded evidence of subsequent design changes under the Seventh Circuit's interpretation of Rule 407. In affirming the verdict for the manufacturer, the Seventh Circuit expressly rejected the holding in *Moe v. Avions-Marcel Dassault Breguet Aviation.*[438] Concluding that the Federal Rules of Evidence governed in a diversity action because of the congressional enactment of such rules, the circuit court noted:

> But Rule 407 is not based on substantive considerations only. An important though not the primary reason for the rule was distrust

431. Refer to note 364 *supra* and accompanying text.

432. Erie R.R. v. Tompkins, 304 U.S. 64, 78 (1938).

433. *See* Hanna v. Plumer, 380 U.S. 460 (1965).

434. Szantay v. Beech Aircraft Corp., 349 F.2d 60, 63-64 (4th Cir. 1965).

435. *See* Baird v. Koerner, 279 F.2d 623, 627 (9th Cir. 1960).

436. *See* Grenada Steel Indus. v. Alabama Oxygen Co., 695 F.2d 833, 885 (5th Cir. 1983); Rabon v. Automatic Fasteners, Inc., 672 F.2d 1231, 1238 n.14 (5th Cir. 1982); Pollard v. Metropolitan Life Ins. Co., 598 F.2d 1284, 1286 (3d Cir.), *cert. denied*, 444 U.S. 917, *reh'g denied*, 444 U.S. 985 (1979); Johnson v. William C. Ellis & Sons Iron Works, 609 F.2d 820, 821 (5th Cir. 1980).

437. 733 F.2d 463, 469 (7th Cir. 1984).

438. 727 F.2d 917, 932 (10th Cir.) *cert. denied*, 105 S. Ct. 176 (1984).

> of juries' ability to draw correct inferences from evidence of subsequent remedial measures. Although it was a mild distrust, as shown by the exceptions built into the rule, it is enough to establish the rule's constitutionality in diversity cases.[439]

In another strict tort liability action based on diversity jurisdiction, the Seventh Circuit had presaged its holding in *Flaminio* by suggesting that the Federal Rules of Evidence, rather than contradictory state rules of evidence, governed actions based on diversity of jurisdiction.[440]

The controlling effect of the Federal Rules of Evidence in diversity actions appears well established in the Fifth Circuit. In *Carter v. Massey-Ferguson, Inc.*,[441] the Fifth Circuit, adhering to the Supreme Court decision in *Hanna v. Plumber*,[442] observed "Under federal rules of evidence, all relevant evidence is admissible, unless there are sound reasons to exclude it. Fed. R. Evid. 402. Although this case is based upon diversity jurisdiction, federal rules of evidence apply."[443]

A contrary view is expressed in *Moe v. Avions Marcel Dassault Breguet Aviation.*[444] The trial court excluded evidence of subsequent warning under Federal Rule 407.[445] The plaintiff urged that Colorado followed *Ault* in holding that subsequent warnings were admissible in a strict tort liability action.[446] The Tenth Circuit concluded that the purpose of Rule 407 was not to seek the truth or to expedite trial proceedings, but to promote state policy in a substantive law area.[447] Confronted with a conflict between Federal Rule of Evidence 407 and the Colorado rule of evidence, the Tenth Circuit ruled that the state rule should control.[448] The Tenth Circuit attempted to circumvent the mandate of *Hanna v. Plummer*[449] by holding that the state rule in the area of product liability established state public policy. Ignored by the Tenth Cir-

---

439. 733 F.2d at 472.
440. Oberst v. International Harvester Co., 640 F.2d 863 (7th Cir. 1980).
441. 716 F.2d 344, 347 (5th Cir. 1983).
442. 380 U.S. 460 (1965).
443. 716 F.2d at 347.
444. 727 F.2d 917 (10th Cir.) *cert. denied*, 105 S. Ct. 176 (1984).
445. *Id.* at 931.
446. *Id.*
447. *Id.* at 932.
448. *Id.*
449. 380 U.S. 460 (1965). Refer to text accompanying note 143.

cuit is the well-established rule that since Congress mandated the Federal Rules of Evidence, that rule controls in all diversity jurisdiction cases.[450]

The majority view that the Federal Rules of Evidence govern in diversity actions when the state rule is contrary appears to rest on solid logic. The fact that the Federal Rules of Evidence were codified and enacted by Congress to establish a uniform set of rules of evidence in all circuits demonstrates a congressional intent that the rules be accorded preference over state rules. This intent is buttressed by the Federal Rules of Evidence. For example, Federal Rule of Evidence 302 (presumptions), Rule 502 (privileges) and Rule 601 (competency of witnesses) specifically provide that state law governs when contrary to the federal rule.[451] Federal Rule 407 contains no similar provision. In enacting the Federal Rules of Evidence, Congress accorded considerable deference to state evidentiary practice in matters that Congress deemed warranted.[452] Unlike the deference accorded state law in certain designated Federal Rules of Evidence, Congress did not defer to state law in enacting Federal Rule 407 excluding evidence of subsequent remedial measures.

Despite the aberration of the Tenth Circuit, the Fifth Circuit, under current decisions, will likely apply the Federal Rules of Evidence.[453] Applying state procedural rules in federal court would

---

450. *See* Carter v. Massey-Ferguson, 716 F.2d 344 (5th Cir. 1984).

451. FED. R. EVID. 302 provides: "In civil actions and proceedings, the effect of a presumption respecting a fact which is an element of a claim or defense as to which State law supplies the rule of decision is determined in accordance with State law." FED. R. EVID. 501 provides, in pertinent part: "However, in civil actions and proceedings, with respect to an element of a claim or defense as to which State law supplies the rule of decision, the privilege of a witness, person, government, State or political subdivision thereof shall be determined in accordance with State law." FED. R. EVID. 601 provides: "Every person is competent to be a witness except as otherwise provided in these rules. However, in civil actions and proceedings with respect to an element of a claim or defense as to which state law supplies the rule of decision, the competency of a witness shall be determined in accordance with State law."

452. In Rioux v. Daniel International Corp., 582 F. Supp. 620 (D. Maine 1984), the Court noted that the Federal Rule of Exclusion rather than the State of Maine rule of admission controlled. The Court observed that "Because the Rules of Evidence were enacted directly by Congress, their validity *vis-a-vis* state law and the principles of the *Erie* doctrine stand on even firmer ground than that of the Rules of Civil Procedure." (quoting C. WRIGHT, A. MILLER & E. COOPER, 19 FEDERAL PRACTICE AND PROCEDURE, § 4512 at 192-93 (1982) (footnotes omitted).

453. *See Id. See also* Johnson v. William C. Ellis & Sons Iron Works., 609 F.2d 820 (5th Cir. 1980).

undoubtedly reduce forum shopping in the federal courts.

G. *Recall Campaigns*

Closely related to the issue of the admissibility of evidence of subsequent remedial measures is the admissibility of evidence of recall campaigns. The frequency of product recalls has increased in recent years.[454] Mandatory recall campaigns have been prescribed by federal acts and ordered by governmental agencies.[455] Vehicles especially are the subject of recall letters under the notice provision of the National Traffic and Motor Vehicle Safety Act.[456] Voluntary campaigns have likewise increased because of the manufacturer's awareness of potential future liability.[457]

The obligation to recall products that have been found defective is essentially an expansion of a manufacturer's duty to warn.[458] The manufacturer's duty varies according to the age of the product at the time of recall, the categorization of a product as a necessity, the number of products to be recalled, and the commonness of an identical defect in all of the recalled items.[459]

The potential for extreme prejudice of recall letters weighed against the probative value of such evidence under Rule 403 is particularly pertinent.[460] A jury is greatly influenced by evidence of

---

454. *See generally* Ramp, *The Impact of Recall Campaigns on Products Liability*, 44 Ins. Couns. J. 83 (1977).

455. Smith, *Recall Campaigns: A Possible Defense to Products Liability,* 42 Ins. Couns. J. 77, 78 (1975).

456. Act of September 9, 1966, Pub. L. No. 89-563, 80 Stat. 718, 15 U.S.C. §§ 1381-1431 (1982).

457. Of course, though the voluntary recall campaign will help the manufacturer's avoidance of liability in the long run by preventing accidents, the evidence of the voluntary recall campaign will most probably be used in any suits that do arise. *See* Vockie v. General Motors Corp., Chevrolet Div., 66 F.R.D. 57, 60-61 (E.D. Pa.), *aff'd without op.*, 523 F.2d 1052 (3rd Cir. 1975) (an admission "is not of sufficient probative weight to be competent unless it is voluntary.")

458. *Ramp, supra* note 454, at 83. A serious issue involves a continuing duty to warn of learned dangers. *Compare* Cover v. Cohen, 61 N.Y.2d 261, 461 N.E.2d 864, 473 N.Y.S. 2d 378 (1984), Gracyalny v. Westinghouse Elec. Corp., 723 F.2d 1311 (7th Cir. 1983), *and* LaBelle v. McCauley Ind. Corp., 649 F.2d 46 (1st Cir. 1981), *with* Bly v. Otis Elevator, 713 F.2d 1040 (4th Cir. 1983); Syrie v. Knoll Int'l, 67 Cal. App. 3d 221, 748 F.2d 304 (5th Cir. 1984); Price v. Niagara Mach. Co., 67 Cal App.3d 221, 136 Cal. Rptr. 535 (1977), *and* Bell Helicopter v. Bradshaw, 594 S.W.2d 519 (Tex. Civ. App.—Corpus Christi 1979, writ ref'd n.r.e.).

459. *Id.*

460. Refer to text accompanying note 360.

recall letters and normally translates such evidence into an admission of a defect.[461] A recall, pragmatically, represents a form of subsequent remedial measure. Recall letters, even if admissible, do not necessarily establish a defective condition. The standard for compelling a recall of a product is substantially less than the standard for establishing a defective condition under strict tort liability.[462]

Recall letters often identify a potential defect that appears in only a very small percentage of the product line recalled.[463] Therefore, the plaintiff must establish that the product involved in the accident is actually one of the products manifesting the defect that is the subject of recall.[464] In fact, it is well recognized that recall letters are admissible only when the plaintiff has *independently proved* or established as a predicate by expert or other testimonial evidence that the defect that is the subject matter of the recall letter existed in the particular product involved in the lawsuit.[465] The absence of evidence to establish that the conditions outlined in the recall letter existed by independent evidence renders the recall letter inadmissible.[466]

Besides carrying the potential for prejudice, recall campaign evidence is a form of hearsay.[467] Recall evidence may represent an

461. *See* Rockwood Ins. Co. v. Clark Equipment Co., 713 F.2d 577, 578-79 (10th Cir. 1983) (Rule 403 justified exclusion of recall letter) *But see* Barry v. Manglass, 55 App.Div.2d 1, 389 N.Y.S.2d 870 (1976) (prejudice of jury should be minimized by warning jury that recall letters do not establish that the defect was present in a particular vehicle.)

462. 2 L. Frumer & M. Friedman, Products Liabiilty, § 17A.05(1) (1980).

463. *See* Vockie v. General Motors Corp., Chevrolet Div., 66 F.R.D. 57 (E.D. Pa.), *aff'd without op.*, 523 F.2d 1052 (3d Cir. 1975)(recall letters not admissible to show a particular vehicle contained a defect; direct evidence is still required).

464. *See* Glynn Plymouth, Inc. v. Davis, 120 Ga. App. 475, 170 S.E.2d 848 (1969), *aff'd*, 226 Ga. 221, 173 S.E.2d 691 (1970); Kane v. Ford Motor Co., 450 F.2d 315 (3d Cir. 1971); Fields v. Volkswagen, 555 P.2d 48 (Okla. 1976); Muniga v. GMC; 102 Mich. App. 755, 302 N.W.2d 565 (1980).

465. *See* Harley-Davidson Motor Co. v. Carpenter, 350 So.2d 360, 361 (Fla. Dist. Ct. App. 1977); Landry v. Adam, 282 So.2d 590 (La. Ct. App. 1973); Holmquist v. Volkswagen of America, 261 N.W.2d 516 (Iowa App. 1977); Carey v. General Motors Corp., 377 Mass. 736, 387 N.E.2d 583, 587-88 (1979); Barry v. Manglass, 55 A.D.2d 1, 7, 389 N.Y.2d 870, 876 (1976).

466. In *Calhoun v. Honda Motor Co., Ltd.*, 738 F.2d 126 (6th Cir. 1984) plaintiff struck a stopped truck while operating his motorcycle because of alleged defective brakes. Rejecting admissibility of the recall letter the Sixth Circuit noted "Calhoun never submitted evidence independent of the recall letter or campaign which would have established the existence of a defect." Id. at .

467. *See* W. Louisell & B. Mueller, Federal Evidence § 167 (Supp. 1984)

exception to the hearsay rule because it arguably constitutes an admission against interest.[468] Under common law, however, a mandatory recall letter, because of its involuntary nature, is not considered an admission.[469] Under the admission exception, a recall letter is admissible only against the manufacturer because it is the party making the statement; it is not admissible against the retailer or any other parties.[470]

Recall letters are utilized not only by the plaintiff, but also by the defendant. By issuing a recall letter, however, whether mandatory or voluntary, a manufacturer does not necessarily escape liability.[471] Evidence of a recall letter supports the fact that the recipient was apprised of the alleged defective condition and nevertheless proceeded to use the product with subjective knowledge of its condition.[472] Moreover, such evidence supports the position that use of the product with knowledge of a defective condition establishes that the user assumed the risk of harm from such known condition.[473] It certainly satisfies the traditional elements for assumption of the risk.[474] Because a recall campaign generally involves a large number of products in a particular line, of which only a few manifest the potential defect, it is particularly difficult to establish that the plaintiff actually knew and appreciated the risk involved in the product.[475] Recall letters, therefore, are effective notice to the consumer when the campaign is extensive, involving personal contact, and when the situation involves only a limited number of products in the line with the potential for defects being extremely great.[476]

---

468. *See* Farner v. Paccar, 562 F.2d 518, 526-27 (8th Cir. 1977).

469. *See Id.*; Millette v. Radosta, 404 N.E.2d 823, 834-35, 84 Ill. App. 3d 5 (1980) (not voluntary but mandated by federal statute).

470. *See* Higgins v. General Motors Corp., 250 Ark. 551, 465 S.W.2d 898, 900 (1971) (no showing that recall letters sent by manufacturer were binding to dealer-seller)

471. *Smith, supra* note 455, at 78.

472. *Id. See* Restatement (Second) of Torts § 402A, comment *n* at 354 (1965). It may also constitute contributory negligence. See Duncan v. Cessna Aircraft Corp., 665 S.W.2d 414 (Tex. 1984).

473. Ford Motor Co. v. Wagoner, 183 Tenn. 392, 192 S.W.2d 840 (1946); Rekab v. Hrubetz & Co; 261 Md. 141, 274 A.2d 107, 111 (1971).

474. *Smith, supra* note 455, at 78.

475. *Id.* at 446. *See, e.g.*, Balido v. Improved Mach., Inc., 29 Cal. App. 3d 633, 105 Cal. Rptr. 890, 898 (1972); Rekab, Inc. v. Frank Hrubetz & Com 261 Md. 141, 274 A.2d 107, 109 (1971).

476. *See, e.g.*, Balido v. Improved Mach., Inc., 29 Cal. App. 3d 633, 644, 105 Cal. Rptr. 890, 898 (1972); Rekab, Inc. v. Frank Hrubetz & Co., 261 Md. 141, 274 A.2d 107, 109 (1971).

The majority of jurisdictions authorize the admission of recall letter evidence, at least for limited purposes.[477] This type of evidence is admissible in strict tort liability solely to prove that the defect existed at the time it left the manufacturer's control.[478] The Federal Rules of Evidence do not address the admissibility of recall letters. Texas, however, by promulgating Texas Rule of Evidence 407(b),[479] has taken the position that recall evidence is admissible against the manufacturer. Though Texas courts have not yet addressed the admissibility of recall letters, Rule 407(b) appears to resolve the issue. Of course, plaintiff is still obligated to establish by *independent evidence* a defect in the product that is the subject of the recall campaign *as a predicate* to the admission of the recall letter.[480]

H. *Availability of Alternative Safer and Inexpensive Design*

1. Generally. Presenting evidence that a product could be inexpensively redesigned to significantly eliminate the dangerous condition constitutes proof that the existing design is defective.[481]

---

477. Evidence of recall campaigns is usually admissible to prove that the defect existed at the time it was manufactured. *See e.g.*, Nevels v. Ford Motor Co., 439 F.2d 251, 258 (5th Cir. 1971) ("evidence relevant . . . to plaintiff's contention of negligent assembly in the manufacturing process.")

478. Kane v. Ford Motor Co., 450 F.2d 315, 316 (3d Cir. 1971) (per curiam); Carey v. General Motors Corp., 377 Mass. 736, 387 N.E.2d 583; Manieri v. Volkswagenwerk A.G., 151 N.J. Super. 422, 376 A.2d 1317, 1322 (App. Div. 1977); Iadicicco v. Duffy, 60 A.D.2d 905, 401 N.Y.S.2d 557, 559-60 (App. Div. 1978); Barry v. Manglass, 55 A.D.2d 1, 389 N.Y.S.2d 870, Fields v. Volkswagen of America, Inc., 555 P.2d 48 (Okla. 1976).

479. TEX. R. EVID. 407(b). Rule 407(b) states: "(b) Notification of defect. A written notification by a manufacturer of any defect in a product produced by such manufacturer to purchasers thereof is admissible against the manufacturer on the issue of existence of the defect to the extent that it is relevant."

480. *See generally* Blakely, *supra* note 313, at 220.

481. *See* Mitchell v. Freuhauf Corp., 568 F.2d 1139, 1144-45 (5th Cir. 1978) (alternative design of trailers to transport meat other than by hanging it from the trailer roof); Gonzales v. Caterpillar Tractor Co., 571 S.W.2d 867, 872 (Tex. 1978) (relocating stepdown from caterpillar tractor loader and placing antiskid material on the step); Miller v. Bock Laundry Mach Co., 568 S.W.2d 648, 651 (Tex. 1978) (use of neopreme pads rather than rubber pads to support a safety device in an oily environment); General Motors Corp. v. Grizzle, 642 S.W.2d 837, 843 (Tex. App. —Waco 1982, writ dism'd); International Harvester Co. v. Zavala, 623 S.W.2d 699, 706-07 (Tex. App.—Houston [1st Dist.] 1981, writ ref'd n.r.e.) (design tractor with shielding between the operator and the gas tank); Lubbock Mfg. Co. v. Perez, 591 S.W.2d 907, 917 (Tex. Civ. App.—Waco 1979, no writ) (use of an alternative design for an LP gas transport trailer to lower its center of gravity); Helicoid Gage Div. of Am. Chain & Cable Co. v. Howell, 511 S.W.2d 573, 577 (Tex. Civ. App.—Houston [14th

As stated in *Davidson v. Stanadyne*,[482] "We note that Texas has held that a relatively obvious and/or common lack of a simple safety device in an ordinary product may be found by the jury to constitute a design defect."[483]

Proof that a safer design alternative was available, however, does not per se establish that the existing design was defective.[484] Manufacturers and other product suppliers are not required to design the best or safest products possible.[485] A jury may not be instructed on these principles. In *Acord v. General Motors Corp.*,[486] the trial court instructed the jury in a defective design case that "[a] manufacturer is not an insurer of the product he designs, and it is not required that the design adopted be perfect, or render the product accident proof, or incapable of causing injury, nor is it necessary to incorporate the ultimate safety features in the product."[487] Though recognizing that these instructions correctly stated general legal principles, the Texas Supreme Court declared that, "[t]he jury need not and should not be burdened with surplus instructions."[488]

In *Mitchell v. Fruehauf Corp.*,[489] the existence of feasible alternative designs was significant. A hanging meat trailer overturned as a result of the swinging motion of the meat carcasses, and the driver of the other vehicle involved in the accident initi-

---

Dist.] 1974, writ ref'd n.r.e.) (high pressure gauges sold without inexpensive and available shatterproof glass or safety shield options were defective); Hartzell Propeller Co. v. Alexander, 485 S.W.2d 943, 946 (Tex. Civ. App.—Waco 1972, writ ref'd n.r.e.).

482. 718 F.2d 1334 (5th Cir. 1983).

483. *Id.* at 1338. *See, e.g.*, Gonzales v. Caterpillar Tractor Co., 571 S.W.2d 867 (Tex. 1978) (absence of adhesive or antiskid material on tractor step); Rourke v. Garza, 530 S.W.2d 794, 799 (Tex. 1976) (absence of cleats on scaffold boards). *See also* Bailey v. Boatland of Houston, Inc., 585 S.W.2d 805, 811 (Tex. Civ. App.—Houston [1st Dist.] 1979), *rev'd on other grounds*, 609 S.W.2d 743 (Tex. 1980) (absence of "kill switch" to cut off outboard motor when operator falls out of boat).

484. Daberko v. Heil Co., 681 F.2d 445, 448 (5th Cir. 1982); Henderson v. Ford Motor Co., 519 S.W.2d 87, 93 (Tex. 1974); *McCants*, 608 S.W.2d 304, 307.

485. Carter v. Massey-Ferguson, Inc., 716 F.2d 344, 347 (5th Cir. 1984); Hagans v. Oliver Mach. Co., 576 F.2d 97, 100 (5th Cir. 1978); Weakley v. Fischbach & Moore, Inc., 515 F.2d 1260, 1267 (5th Cir. 1975); Henderson v. Ford Motor Co., 519 S.W.2d 87, 93 (Tex. 1974); General Elec. Co. v. Schmal, 623 S.W.2d 482, 486 (Tex. App.—Texarkana 1981, writ ref'd n.r.e.); *McCants*, 608 S.W.2d at 304; *Bell Helicopter Co.*, 594 S.W.2d at 530.

486. 669 S.W.2d 111 (Tex. 1984).

487. *Id.* at 113.

488. *Id.* at 116.

489. 568 F.2d 1139 (5th Cir. 1978).

ated suit against the trailer manufacturer.[490] The plaintiff offered several alternative designs for hanging the meat, including installing partitions to restrict the swinging motion of the meat and tying the meat to the floor. Defendant failed to rebut either of these alternative designs as being neither feasible nor economically appropriate.[491] The Fifth Circuit concluded that the alternative design configuration demonstrated that the meat trailer was defectively designed.[492]

2. *Present or Previous Design of a Safer Product and Other Manufacturers' Designs.* Evidence that a manufacturer presently designs a safer product creates an inference that a safer design was feasible and that the existing design is defective.[493] For example, the feasibility of a safer design may be inferred by demonstrating that the product was manufactured with inexpensive options which contributed to the product's potential for causing harm.[494] If the manufacturer previously manufactured a safer similar product, this evidence creates an inference that a safer design is feasible.[495]

Evidence that other manufacturers and suppliers of a similar product utilize a design configuration that renders the product significantly safer for its intended and foreseeable uses likewise represents evidence that the existing design is defective.[496] In *Rourke v.*

---

490. *Id.* at 1144-1145.

491. *Id.* at 1141.

492. *Id.* at 1145. Alternative feasible design is critical in a defective design case. *See* Turner v. General Motors Corp. 584 S.W.2d 844 (Tex. 1979); Boatland of Houston, Inc. v. Bailey, 609 S.W.2d 743 (Tex. 1983); Kindred v. Con/Chem, Inc., 650 S.W.2d 61 (Tex. 1983); Davidson v. Stanadyne, Inc., 718 F.2d 1334 (5th Cir. 1983); Shipp v. General Motors Co., 750 F.2d 418 (5th Cir. 1984).

493. *See Nowak*, 638 S.W.2d 582 (automatic transmission lever that could hang between "Park" and "Reverse" when another design would prevent this phenomena); *Bell Helicopter*, 594 S.W.2d 519, 530 (tail rotor blade that was capable of operating safely in excess of the 600 hours rather than the particular design rotor blade with more limited durability on the helicopter); Helicoid Gage Div. of Am. Chain & Cable Co. v. Howell, 511 S.W.2d 573, 576-77 (Tex. Civ. App.—Houston [14th Dist.] 1974, writ ref'd n.r.e.) (use of safety lens in high pressure industrial system). *See generally* Black, *Optional Safety Devices: How Strict the Liability?*, 8 N.M. L. Rev. 191 (1978); Wade, *On Product "Design Defects" and Their Actionability*, 33 Vand. L. Rev. 551 (1980).

494. *Helicoid*, 511 S.W.2d at 576-77.

495. *See, e.g.*, Williams v. General Motors Corp., 501 S.W.2d 930, 936 (Tex. Civ. App.—Houston [1st Dist.] 1973, writ ref'd n.r.e.) (steering shaft couplings that lacked previous model design that would prevent uncoupling).

496. *But see* Shipp v. General Motors Corp., 750 F.2d 418, 423 (5th Cir. 1985) ("That no other passenger car employed this design will not alone defeat recovery.")

Garza,[497] an action by a welder for injuries sustained from a fall off a scaffold, the jury found that the scaffold boards were defectively designed and unreasonably dangerous.[498] The scaffold boards were customarily furnished with cleats, unlike the scaffold delivered to plaintiff's employer. Equipped with cleats, the scaffold boards could not slip off the frames, but in the absence of cleats, the scaffold was dangerous.[499] The Texas Supreme Court noted that cleats are inexpensive and do not impair the usefulness of the boards. Because cleats do not place an unreasonable burden on scaffold suppliers and the use of cleats avoids a substantial risk of harm, the failure to incorporate cleats into the boards rendered the scaffold unreasonably dangerous.[500]

3. *State of the Art.* The term "state of the art" implies that "the product was as safe as scientific knowledge could possibly make it."[501] State of the art evidence is determinative to a design or marketing case, though it is irrelevant in a manufacturing defect (flaw) situation.[502] Manufacturers frequently utilize state of the art as a defense or as rebuttal to evidence that the product could be made safer under the current state of human knowledge.[503] Plaintiffs often invoke state of the art as evidence establishing that a product is defective.[504]

Courts and commentators use the term "state of the art" in ways that often create confusion. Each case must be analyzed to determine the connotation.[505] Three main categories of state of the

---

497. 530 S.W.2d 794 (Tex. 1975).

498. *Id.* at 799.

499. *Id.*

500. *Id.*

501. Dreiling v. General Elec. Co., 511 F.2d 768, 776 (5th Cir. 1975); Boatland of Houston, Inc. v. Bailey, 609 S.W.2d 743 (Tex. 1983).

502. *See* Spradley, *Defensive Use of State of the Art Evidence In Strict Products Liability*, 67 MINN. L. REV. 343, 350-355, 412-16 (1982). If evidence of custom or feasibility in manufacturing defect cases based on strict liability was conclusive, "there would be a complete return to negligence standards and a complete effacement of strict liability." *Id.* at 355 and 416.

503. *See* Karasik, *"State of the Art or Science": Is it a Defense to Products Liability?* 60 ILL. B.J. 348, 350 (1972); Murray, *The State of the Art Defense in Products Liability*, 57 MARQ. L. REV. 649, 653 (1974).

504. *See, e.g.*, Moren v. Samuel Langston Co., 96 Ill. App. 2d 133, 237 N.E.2d 759, 762-66 (1968); *Henderson*, 519 S.W.2d at 93.

505. *See* Spradley, *supra* note 502, at 343-47.

art evidence exists.[506] The first category is the technical environment in which the product is manufactured. Feasibility under this category means either that the highest level of technical and scientific knowledge was used or that the defendant could not have known of the danger inherent in the defective product.[507] The second category is evidence of the commercial or economic environment in which the product is manufactured. This involves a cost versus utility analysis as well as consideration of the commercial availability of alternate designs.[508] The final category is evidence demonstrating the normal business practice of an industry, including government and business standards.[509]

The concept of "state of the art" was first utilized in negligence cases to establish that a manufacturer's conduct was reasonable.[510] State of the art evidence creates confusion when applied in a strict tort liability case, because reasonableness is irrelevant in strict tort liability.[511] This confusion is compounded by the uncertainty of the meaning of "state of the art."

Texas has recently clarified and defined state of the art in the area of strict tort liability. Prior to the landmark case of *Turner v. General Motors Corp.*,[512] the law was, at best, inconsistent. *General Motors Corp. v. Hopkins*,[513] decided two years before *Turner*, seemed to denigrate state of the art evidence in strict tort liability.[514] One year after *Hopkins*, in *Gonzales v. Caterpillar Tractor Co.*,[515] the Texas Supreme Court observed that only the condition of the product and not the conduct of the manufacturer is relevant for the imposition of strict tort liability.[516]

In *Turner v. General Motors Corp.*,[517] the Texas Supreme Court adopted a test of balancing the utility of the existing design against the risk of injury resulting from the product's use to deter-

---

506. *See* Comment, *Use of "State of the Art" Evidence in Strict Liability Claims: The New Texas Standards*, 33 Baylor L. Rev. 165, 167-68 (1981).

507. *Id.* at 168.

508. *Id.* at 167.

509. *Id.*

510. Spradley, *supra* note 502, at 347.

511. *Id.* at 347, 348.

512. 584 S.W.2d 844 (Tex. 1979).

513. 548 S.W.2d 344 (Tex. 1977).

514. *Id.* at 351. *See* Comment, *supra* note 506, at 172.

515. 571 S.W.2d 867 (Tex. 1978).

516. *Id.* at 871.

517. 584 S.W.2d 844 (Tex. 1979).

mine whether the product is unreasonably dangerous.[518] The court indicated that state of the art evidence is relevant to the application of this balancing test.[519] *Turner* is interpreted as recognizing state of the art to the extent that it refers to the commercial environment or the technical environment in which the product was designed.[520] Because the *Gonzales* approach of examining only the condition of the product technically contradicts the *Turner* balancing test, it is arguable that the *Turner* decision overruled *Gonzales sub silentio*.[521] Although *Turner* clarified to some extent the application of the state of the art concept, the law after *Turner* remained uncertain.

Amidst this uncertainty, *Boatland of Houston, Inc. v. Bailey*[522] was decided. *Boatland* involved a wrongful death action against the seller of a bass boat. Plaintiffs' decedent was fatally injured by the rotating propeller when the boat struck a partially submerged tree stump and, with its motor still operating, turned and circled back sharply. Plaintiffs alleged that the boat was defectively designed because of the absence of any device that would automatically kill the engine if the operator was ejected from the boat. The plaintiffs introduced evidence of the scientific and economic feasibility of such a device. Evidence was admitted that rebutted plaintiffs' evidence of feasibility. Kill switch devices were not commercially available at the time of the manufacture and sale of this boat and it was not customary to place kill switches on bass boats.[523] The court of appeals viewed the issue of state of the art evidence as one of first impression and held that state of the art evidence was not admissible because the evidence was irrelevant in a strict tort liability case.[524]

518. *Id.* at 849.

519. *Id.* at 851. Among the factors the court enumerated to be considered in the balancing process was the manufacturer's "ability to eliminate the risk without seriously increasing the product's usefulness or cost." *Id.* at 846. Another indication for possible support for the introduction of state of the art evidence was the court's approval of the submission of a special issue relating to the product's defectiveness at the time of manufacture. *Id.* at 847. *See* Comment, *supra* note 506, at 172-73.

520. Comment, *supra* note 506, at 173 & 173 n.55.

521. This is doubtful, though, because the same justice authored both opinions.

522. 585 S.W.2d 805 (Tex. Civ. App.—Houston [1st Dist.] 1979), *rev'd*, 609 S.W.2d 743 (Tex. 1982).

523. *Id.* at 807. The defendant's evidence was not that kill switches were new, but that they were not "commercially available" at the time the boat was sold. *Id.* at 808.

524. *Id.* at 810.

The Texas Supreme Court reversed the decision and affirmed the judgment of the trial court.[525] The supreme court declared that defective design was determined in relation to safer design alternatives and noted that "the fact that [the product's] risks could be diminished easily or cheaply may greatly influence the outcome of a case."[526] The court emphatically announced that "whether a product was defectively designed must be judged against the technological context existing at the time of its manufacture."[527] Feasibility was defined by the court as "the capacity to provide the feature without greatly increasing the product's cost or impairing usefulness," and was considered "a relative, not an absolute concept."[528]

The court acknowledged two forms of evidence of feasibility for the plaintiff. First, evidence of feasibility is admissible to demonstrate that a safer alternative was in actual use, was available, or was known at the time of manufacture by the defendant or by others.[529] Second, feasibility evidence is admissible to show the scientific and economic capacity to develop the safer design alternative.[530] In contrast, a manufacturer's strongest rebuttal evidence is that a particular design alternative was impossible because of the state of the existing art, though the defendant is also entitled to rebut the plaintiff's state of the art evidence with evidence of limitations of feasibility.[531] As an example, an alternative design feature may have been discovered but time constraints inhibited installation of the design alternative on a particular model.[532] Moreover, a design alternative may be impractical because of excessive cost or impairment of the product's utility.[533] Defining state of the art, the court observed:

> The state of the art with respect to a particular product refers to the technological environment at the time of its manufacture. This technological environment includes the scientific knowledge, economic feasibility, and the practicalities of implementation

525. 609 S.W.2d 743 (Tex. 1980).
526. *Id.* at 745, 746.
527. *Id.* at 743.
528. *Id.*
529. *Id.* at 746, 748.
530. *Id.* at 746.
531. *Id.* at 748.
532. *Id.*
533. *Id.* at 748, 749.

> when the product was manufactured. Evidence of this nature is important in determining whether a safer design was feasible. The limitations imposed by the state of the art at the time of manufacture may affect the feasibility of a safer design.[534]

The court minimized the awkwardness of applying a negligence concept to strict liability. The court stated, "Considerations such as the utility and risk of the product in question and the feasibility of safer alternatives are presented according to the facts as they are proved to be, not according to the defendant's perceptions."[535] Even if the defendant exercised due care, the court noted, his product may be found defective.[536]

The court concluded that the manufacturer of the bass boat was entitled to rebut plaintiffs' evidence that a safer design alternative was feasible by demonstrating that kill switches were not technologically feasible or commercially available.[537] The *Boatland* court held that scientific knowledge, the practicalities of implementation of the proposed design alternatives, and economic considerations are distinguishable from and not equated with industry custom or practice. The court refused to address the issue of industry custom, which it carefully distinguished from state of the art evidence.[538] Thus, Texas has expressly excluded the third general type of state of the art evidence, that of industry custom, from its definition of state of the art. Technological feasibility and commercial practicality, however, constitute viable state of the art evidence.

McCants v. Salameh[539] was decided shortly after *Boatland*. Plaintiff was injured when his hand became caught in a meat grinder while he was working in a grocery store. The grinder had been manufactured by defendant in 1948 and was later modified in 1968. Relying on *Boatland*, the court stated that the design of products manufactured at the same time as the allegedly defective product is relevant to establish the technology existing at the time of manufacture, but evidence of a major modification twenty years later was not indicative of the design capabilities existing at the

---

534. *Id.* at 748.
535. *Id.* at 749.
536. *Id.*
537. *Id.*
538. *Id.* at 748, 749.
539. 608 S.W.2d 304 (Tex. Civ. App.—Waco 1980).

time of manufacture of the earlier design.[540]

In *Kindred v. Con/Chem, Inc.*,[541] the Texas Supreme Court emphasized the relationship between *feasibility* of an alternative safer design and a design defect in a product. Reaffirming *Boatland*, the court declared that expert testimony relating to the feasibility of a safer alternative is "some evidence" of a design defect, and therefore admissible.[542]

I. Other Accidents, Incidents, and Claims

Evidence of similar accidents or claims involving an identically designed or marketed product is generally admissible in strict tort liability cases to establish defective design.[543] This type of evidence supports the allegation that the manufacturer possessed notice of the product's defective condition,[544] that the product was defective,[545] or that a causal nexus existed between the condition of the product and the accident.[546] Of course, whether this evidence is admissible is dependent on its relevancy.[547]

---

540. *Id.* at 308.

541. 650 S.W.2d 61 (Tex. 1983). Refer to text accompanying notes 290-91, *supra*, for a recitation of facts.

542. *Id.* at 63.

543. Evidence of other accidents occurring under substantially similar circumstances and involving identical products may constitute evidence of an inadequate and defective design. *See* Soden v. Freightliner Corp., 714 F.2d 498, 507-8 (5th Cir. 1983) (evidence of five other lawsuits and three complaints relating to placement of tractor saddle tanks admissible for design defect); Mitchell v. Freuhauf Corp., 568 F.2d 1139, 1147 (5th Cir. 1978) (this case involved the testimony of other truck drivers involving identically designed meat trailers that their trucks would overturn under identical traveling conditions); McInnes v. Yamaha Motor Corp., U.S.A., 659 S.W.2d 704, 709-10 (Tex. App.—Corpus Christi 1983), *aff'd*, 673 S.W.2d 185, (Tex. 1984) (evidence of motorcycle wobble complaints at high speeds admissible on issue of defect and unreasonably dangerous condition); Rush v. Bucyrus-Erie Co., 646 S.W.2d 298, 302 (Tex. App.—Tyler 1983, writ ref'd n.r.e.) (evidence of two boom failures on the identically designed crane was admissible on the issue of defective design); Magic Chef, Inc. v. Sibley, 546 S.W.2d 851 (Tex. App.—San Antonio 1977, writ ref'd n.r.e.).

544. *See* Rucker Co. v. Shell Oil Co., 449 U.S. 1112 (1981); Soden v. Freightliner Corp., 714 F.2d 498, 508 (5th Cir. 1983); Ramos v. Liberty Mut. Ins. Co., 615 F.2d 334, 339 (5th Cir. 1980), *cert. denied* 449 U.S. 1112 (1981); Mitchell v. Freuhauf Corp., 568 F.2d 1139 (5th Cir. 1978).

545. Magic Chef, Inc. v. Sibley, 546 S.W.2d 851, 855 (Tex. App.—San Antonio 1977, writ ref'd n.r.e.). *See* Gall v. Union Ice Co., 108 Cal. App. 2d 303, 239 P.2d 48, 58 (1951).

546. *See Gall*, 239 P.2d at 58; Becker v. American Airlines, 200 F. Supp. 243, 245-46 (S.D.N.Y. 1961).

547. *See* Fed. R. Evid. 401; Tex. R. Evid. 401. *See also*, Gross v. Black & Decker (U.S.) Inc., 695 F.2d 858 (5th Cir. 1983) (evidence admitted relating to the negligence of plaintiff's employer).

Relevancy of the proffered evidence is dependent upon establishing that the other accidents or complaints occurred under the same or identically similar circumstances[548] and involved the same or identically similar product.[549] The substantial similarity requirement contemplated "reasonably similar but not necessarily identical circumstances."[550] The plaintiff must also establish the identical nature of the products,[551] though the product supplier often sustains the real burden of proof. Though a variation in the *circumstances* of other similar accidents is not invariably fatal, a variation in the *type* of product involved in the other accidents is clearly fatal to admissibility.[552]

In *Soden v. Freightliner Corp.*,[553] a truck driver was fatally injured in a post-collision fuel fire, and his widow and children instituted a strict tort liability action against the manufacturer. The Fifth Circuit concluded that the admission of evidence of five other similar lawsuits and three informal complaints involving post-collision fuel-fed fires with the identical tractor-trailer was permissible. The court stated:

---

548. *See* Jones & Laughlin Steel Corp. v. Matherne, 348 F.2d 394, 400 (5th Cir. 1965); Shofner v. Ill. Cent. R. Co., 302 F.2d 266, 267 (5th Cir. 1962); *But see* Rush v. Bucyrus-Erie Co., 646 S.W.2d 298, 301 (Tex. App.—Tyler 1983, writ ref'd n.r.e.) in which the court held that the trial court committed reversible error in excluding evidence of two prior fatal accidents involving substantially similar incidents with the identical product, and McInnes v. Yamaha Motor Corp., 659 S.W.2d 704 (Tex. App.—Corpus Christi 1983), *affirmed*, 673 S.W.2d 185, (Tex. 1984) in which the court noted that the requisite degree of similarity is not as high in product cases. *Accord* Warsham v. A. H. Robins Co., 734 F.2d 676, 689 (11th Cir. 1984) (evidence of other accidents involving I.U.D.'s).

549. *See, e.g.*, Bailey v. Kawasaki-Kisen, K.K., 455 F.2d 392 (5th Cir. 1972); Barnes v. General Motors Corp., 547 F.2d 275, 277 (5th Cir. 1977); Hale v. Firestone Tire & Rubber Co., 756 F.2d 1322, 1332 (8th Cir. 1985); Ford Motor Co. v. Nowak, 638 S.W.2d 582, 590 (Tex. App.—Corpus Christi 1982, writ ref'd n.r.e.); Magic Chef, Inc. v. Sibley, 546 S.W.2d 851, 873 (Tex. Civ. App.—San Antonio 1977, writ ref'd n.r.e.).

550. M-K-T Ry. Co. v. May, 600 S.W.2d 755, 756 (Tex. 1980); Rush v. Bucyrus Erie Co., 646 S.W.2d 298, 301 (Tex. App.—Tyler 1983, writ ref'd n.r.e.).

551. *See* Annot., 42 A.L.R.3D 780 (1972 & Supp. 1982). *See, e.g.*, McKinnon v. Skil Corp., 638 F.2d 270, 277 (1st Cir. 1981); Shaffer v. Honeywell, Inc., 249 N.W.2d 251 (S.D. 1976).

552. Rush v. Bucyrus-Erie Co., 646 S.W.2d 298 (Tex. App.—Tyler 1983, writ ref'd n.r.e.); Barnes v. General Motors Corp., 547 F.2d 275, 277 (5th Cir. 1977); Magic Chef, Inc. v. Sibley, 546 S.W.2d 851 (Tex. Civ. App.—San Antonio 1977, writ ref'd n.r.e.); *Fruehauf*, 568 F.2d at 1147 ("The requisite degree of similarity is plainly not very high, as the only significant shared characteristics were the brand of the range and the inadventure of ignition.").

553. 714 F.2d 498 (5th Cir. 1983).

> In a products liability case based on defective design, evidence of the defendant's knowledge of other accidents may be relevant to its notice or knowledge of the defect, if the accidents occurred under substantially similar circumstances. [citation omitted]. Such evidence is relevant because it makes more probable "a fact that is of consequence to the determination of the action" - in this case Freightliner's knowledge of the defective design of its fuel system, which was a required element in the appellee's claim for exemplary damage. [citation omitted].[554]

Because allegations in complaints in other lawsuits may not only be unsubstantiated, but may also constitute hearsay, the court noted that allegations of defective design arising out of other accidents are admissible only after the trial court exercises caution and sensitivity in examining the other complaints.[555] The court recognizes, however, that allegations alone may have some probative value on the *limited issue* of notice.[556]

McInnes v. Yamaha Motor Corp.[557] involved a motorcycle accident that rendered the plaintiff a quadriplegic. The trial court rejected evidence that Yamaha received numerous complaints of front wheel wobble at speeds greater than 40 miles per hour, but the court allowed evidence of complaints related to lower speeds on the basis that plaintiff contended he was traveling at 40 miles per hour at the time of the accident.[558] The appellate court noted that evidence of other accidents is admissible in a strict tort liability case to demonstrate the product's dangerous nature, provided the other accidents involved the identical product under the same or substantially similar conditions as those involved in plaintiff's accident.[559] The court commented that, "[I]n addition to showing a dangerous or defective condition, evidence of similar accidents should also be admitted to show that the alleged injury was caused by that condition."[560]

---

554. *Id.* (*citing* Maxey v. Freightliner Corp., 665 F.2d 1367 (5th Cir. 1982)). *See* Burk Royalty Co. v. Walls, 616 S.W.2d 911 (Tex. 1981).

555. *Soden*, 714 F.2d at 508.

556. *Id.*

557. 659 S.W.2d 704 (Tex. App.—Corpus Christi 1983), *affirmed* 673 S.W.2d 185 (Tex. 1984).

558. *Id.* at 709.

559. *Id.* at 710 (*citing Magic Chef*, 546 S.W.2d at 855). *See* Davis, *Evidence of Post-Accident Failures, Modifications and Design Changes in Products Liability Litigation*, 6 St. Mary's L.J. 92, 96 (1975).

560. *McInnes*, 659 S.W.2d at 710. (*citing* Ginnes v. Mapes Hotel, Corp., 86 Nev. 408,

Evidence of the *absence* of other accidents involving the identical product is generally admissible in strict tort liability cases. Although evidence of the absence of accidents is not usually as persuasive as is proof of the occurrence of other accidents, this difference affects only the weight and not the admissibility of this evidence.[561] The underlying rationale supporting the admissibility of evidence of the absence of other accidents involving the same product is noted with a simplistic candor: "It would seem that if other accidents and injuries are admissible where circumstances are similar . . . then logically it would follow that proof of the absence of accidents during a period of similar exposure and experience, would generally be receivable to show the nonexistence of these facts."[562]

Another type of circumstantial evidence is proof that a large number of persons suffered a common injury from using an identical product. This proof constitutes more than a mere showing of product malfunction; it represents credible circumstantial evidence of a product defect.[563] Mere evidence, however, that other similar products possessed a significant number of similar flaws is not admissible.[564] Complaints of prior similar accidents are not admissible when the similarity of such accidents do not coincide with the plaintiff's allegation of the type defect that caused his accident and resulting injury.[565] For example, in *Kontz v. K-Mart Corp.*,[566]

---

470 P.2d 135, 139 (1970)). *See also* Zenkel v. Onerda County Creameries Co., 104 Misc. 251, 171 N.Y.S. 676, 677 (1918), *aff'd*, 188 A.D. 905, 176 N.Y.S. 927 (1919).

561. C. McCormick, *supra* note 70 § 200.

562. *Id. See* Minichello v. U.S. Industries, Inc., 756 F.2d 26 (6th Cir. 1985); Leischner v. Dure & Co., 127 Ill. App.3d 175, 468 N.E.2d 182 (1984); Walker v. Trico Mfg. Co., 487 F.2d 595 (7th Cir. 1973), *cert. denied*, 415 U.S. 978 (1974); Johnson v. Amerco, Inc., 409 N.E.2d 299 (Ill. App. 1980); Darrough v. White Motor Co., 393 N.E.2d 122, 126 (Ill. App. 1979); Belfry v. Anthony Pools, 262 N.W.2d 909, 912 (Mich. App. 1977); Herman v. Midland AG Serv., 264 N.W.2d 161, 173 (Neb. 1978); Williams v. Laurence-David, Inc., 534 P.2d 173 (Or. 1975); Reiger v. Toby Enters., 609 P.2d 402, 403 (Or. App. 1980); Stolz v. McKowen, 545 P.2d 584, 587 (Wash. App. 1976); City of Franklin v. Badger Ford Truck Sales, 207 N.W.2d 866 (Wis. 1973).

563. *See* C. A. Hoover & Son v. O. M. Franklin Serum Co., 444 S.W.2d 596 (Tex. 1969) (one hundred percent adverse reaction to a cattle serum); Herbert v. Loveless, 474 S.W.2d 732 (Tex. App.—Beaumont 1971), writ ref'd n.r.e.) (large number of customers eating the same type of food at a particular restaurant on the same date becoming ill).

564. *See, e.g.*, Hiller v. Kawasaki Motors Corp., U.S.A., 671 P.2d 369 (Alaska 1983) (evidence that two percent of some model snowmobiles had cracked seats).

565. *See* Gumbs v. International Harvester Inc., 718 F.2d 88, 97-98 (3d Cir. 1983) (U.S. D.O.T. complaints of U-bolt failure related accidents).

566. 712 F.2d 1302 (8th Cir. 1983).

plaintiff was injured when a folding beach chair in which she was seated suddenly collapsed. The plaintiff sought to introduce evidence of a Consumer Products Safety Commission Study revealing that approximately 8,000 injuries per year resulted from these mishaps.[567] The court observed that the trial court properly excluded this evidence in the absence of proof of similarity of circumstances.[568]

J. *Negating Other Possible Causes*

An alternative method to establish the existence of a defect is to negate all other possible causes of the accident or injuries except a defect in the product.[569] However, as stated in *Bell Aerospace Corp. v. Anderson*,[570] "[i]f there is no direct evidence as to the existence of an ultimate fact and the evidence presented be consistent with either of two theories and there is nothing to show that one rather than the other is proven, then neither is proven."[571] In *Bell*, a wrongful death action, experts agreed that the helicopter explosion in mid-air was caused by either a mechanical failure (defective wire drive) or pilot error.[572] The main rotor detached in flight and cut into the helicopter, causing the explosion and resulting crash. Some of the evidence included an eyewitness account of the slow rate at which the helicopter was flying, and testimony by defendant's employees that if the aircraft was level, it would be almost impossible for the pilot to sever the mast.[573] This circum-

---

567. *Id.* at 1304.

568. *Id.*

569. The doctrine of *res ipsa loquitur* in negligence cases incorporates this theory. *See* Franks v. National Dairy Products Corp., 414 F.2d 682 (5th Cir. 1969); Marathon Oil Co. v. Sterner, 632 S.W.2d 571, 573 (Tex. 1982); Pittsburg Coca-Cola Bottling Works v. Ponder, 443 S.W.2d 546, 548-49 (Tex. 1969). *See also* Shipp v. General Motors Corp., 750 F.2d 418, 423 (5th Cir. 1985) (defense attempted to prove that plaintiff's injuries were not caused by crush of Trans Am roof, but by falling out of her seat and onto the roof of her car during the rollover.)

570. 478 S.W.2d 191 (Tex. Civ. App.—El Paso 1972, writ ref'd n.r.e.).

571. *Id.* at 196-197 (*citing* Republic Nat. Life Ins. Co. v. Bullard, 399 S.W.2d 376 (Tex. Civ. App.—Houston 1966, writ ref'd n.r.e.)). The *Bell* court continued: "A verdict may be based on inferences fairly drawn from the facts in evidence. An inference cannot be based on surmise or speculation and is without probative force if inconsistent with undisputed or clearly established facts." *Id.* Firestone v. Sims 174 S.W.2d 279 (Tex. Civ. App.—Fort Worth, 1943, writ ref'd n.r.e.).

572. *Bell Aerospace*, 478 S.W.2d at 196.

573. *Id.* at 195.

stantial evidence was sufficient to establish a defect in the helicopter.[574]

The mere fact that an accident occurs involving a particular product does not constitute evidence of a defective product.[575] The Texas Supreme Court in *General Motors Corp. v. Hopkins*,[576] however, suggested that a product malfunction may constitute some, though not conclusive, circumstantial proof of a defective condition.[577] The *Hopkins* court noted that a mere malfunction as evidence of an original defect is supported or defeated by the age and use of that product during the time interval between the purchase and the malfunction.[578]

K. *State and Federal Regulations and Industry Standards*

Failure of a product design to comply with state or federal regulations or with industry standards is generally relevant but not conclusive evidence that the design is defective.[579] Though no rule explicitly addresses the admissibility of safety standards, Rule 403 of both the Federal and Texas rules governs whether the standards are relevant. Because strict tort liability does not encompass the issue of conduct, it has been argued that evidence of compliance or noncompliance with safety standards is not relevant.[580] In Texas, however, evidence of both compliance and noncompliance with standards and regulations is admissible in strict tort liability actions.[581]

---

574. *Id.* at 197.

575. *See* Simien v. S.S. Kresge Co., 566 F.2d 551, 557 (5th Cir. 1978); Helene Curtis Indus., Inc. v. Pruitt, 385 F.2d 841, 849 (5th Cir. 1967), *cert. denied*, 391 U.S. 913 (1968); Jack Roach-Bissonnet, Inc. v. Puskar, 417 S.W.2d 262, 266 (Tex. 1967); Proctor & Gamble Mfg. Co. v. Langley, 422 S.W.2d 773, 778 (Tex. Civ. App.—Dallas 1967, writ dism'd).

576. 548 S.W.2d 344 (Tex. 1977).

577. *Id.* at 349-50.

578. *Id.* at 350. *See also* Simien v. S.S. Kresge Co., 566 F.2d 551, 559 (5th Cir. 1978); Caterpillar Tractor Co. v. Beck, 593 P.2d 871, 879 (Alaska 1979); Barrett v. Atlas Powder Co., 86 Cal. App. 3d 560, 565, 150 Cal. Rptr. 339, 342 (1978); Holloway v. General Motors Corp., 403 Mich. 614, 271 N.W.2d 777, 780 (1978).

579. Rexrode v. American Laundry Press Co., 674 F.2d 826, 831 (10th Cir. 1982), *cert denied*, 103 S. Ct. 137 (1982); *Simien*, 566 F.2d 551; McGee v. Cessna Aircraft Co., 139 Cal. App. 3d 179, 187, 188 Cal. Rptr. 542, 547 (Cal. App. 1983); *Rourke*, 530 S.W.2d 794, 799.

580. Raney v. Honeywell, Inc., 540 F.2d 932, 937-38 (8th Cir. 1976).

581. *See* Shipp v. General Motors Corp., 750 F.2d 418 (5th Cir. 1985); *Rourke*, 530 S.W.2d at 799; *Turner*, 514 S.W.2d at 506-07.

Rexrode v. American Laundry Press Co.[582] addressed the issue of whether industry standards are relevant in strict tort liability. Plaintiff was injured when a laundry press she was operating closed on her hand. Plaintiff introduced evidence of a 1941 nonmandatory safety standard by the American National Standards Institute (ANSI) and a 1972 Occupational Safety Health Association (OSHA) regulation.[583] The defendant contended that the 1941 standard was actually beyond the state of the art at the time the press was manufactured in 1941, and attempted unsuccessfully to introduce the less stringent 1972 OSHA standard.[584] The Tenth Circuit distinguished between utilizing safety standards to demonstrate the manufacturer's duty of care and using such evidence to establish feasibility of design.[585] Because conduct is not relevant in strict tort liability, evidence of the manufacturer's compliance with industry standards was irrelevant.[586] The court noted that such evidence would be extremely relevant if related to the feasibility of design. The court stated, "Manufacturers are not to be held strictly liable for failure to design safety features, if the technology to do so is unavailable at the time the product is made."[587] In this case, however, the court concluded that the 1972 OSHA standards actually mandated the same protection as the 1941 standard.[588]

Even if the manufacturer complies with state or federal regulations or industry standards, this does not establish as a matter of law that the design is not defective.[589] In *Shipp v. General Motors*

---

582. 674 F.2d 826 (10th Cir. 1982), *cert. denied*, 459 U.S. 862 (1982).

583. *Id.* at 831.

584. *Id.* Defendant contended that it should have been permitted to introduce this standard to prove that "the machine was in full compliance with the more recent standards, and to demonstrate that the earlier standards were an inaccurate reflection of the state of the industry." *Id.* (quoting defendant's challenge).

585. *Id.* at 831-32.

586. *Id.* (*citing Raney*, 540 F.2d at 937-38).

587. *Id.* at 832 (*citing* Annot., 96 A.L.R.3D 22, 35-40 (1980)).

588. *Id.* Other reasons given by the court were that the defendant marketed a safety device to bring it into compliance with the OSHA standard, which negated the nonfeasibility argument; and that the 1972 ANSI standard was only remotely relevant to the 1941 ANSI standard of 1959.

589. *See* Page v. Barko Hydraulics, 673 F.2d 134, 138 (5th Cir. 1982); Foster v. Caterpillar Tractor Co., 714 F.2d 654, 656 (6th Cir. 1983); Simien v. S.S. Kresge Co., 566 F.2d 551, 557 (5th Cir. 1978); Lubbock Mfg. Co. v. Perez, 591 S.W.2d 907, 914-15 (Tex. Civ. App.—Waco 1979, no writ); *Turner*, 584 S.W.2d 844; Bristol-Myers Co. v. Gonzales, 548 S.W.2d 416, 423 (Tex. Civ. App.—Corpus Christi 1976), *rev'd on other grounds*, 561 S.W.2d 801, 804 (Tex. 1978); Rumsey v. Freeway Manor Minimax, 423 S.W.2d 387, 394 (Tex. Civ.

Corp.,[590] defendant General Motors contended that the appellate court should apply a stricter standard of review of the jury's finding of liability since the vehicle's roof satisfied the only governmental standard relating to roof strength. The Fifth Circuit rejected this contention, stating that: "[w]hile compliance is evidence, albeit persuasive and contradictory to plaintiff's proof, it is only a piece of the evidentiary puzzle."[591] The court continued, "compliance with such minimum safety standards does not exempt or immunize a manufacturer from common law strict liability."[592]

As illustrated in *Simien v. S.S. Kresge Co.*,[593] however, evidence that the design specifications of a product substantially exceeded the specifications of a federal statute constitutes substantial evidence that a product is not unreasonably dangerous for its intended and foreseeable use.[594] Plaintiff's jacket ignited while the plaintiff was starting an outdoor fire using an open-mouthed container of gasoline.[595] The plaintiff suffered severe burns on his neck and face. The manufacturer established through expert testimony that the jacket satisfied and even greatly exceeded the requirements of the federal Flammable Fabrics Act and Commercial Standard 191-53.[596] The Fifth Circuit noted that "[c]ompliance with these federal statutory safety requirements and industry standards is evidence that a product is not defective."[597] The instruction to the jury that compliance with the statute would be evidence that the product *was* defective was held to be blatant error that

---

App.—Houston [1st Dist.] 1968, no writ).

590. 750 F.2d 418 (5th Cir. 1985).

591. *Id.* at 421.

592. *Id.*

593. 566 F.2d 551, 557 (5th Cir. 1978).

594. *See* Dorsey v. Honda Motor Co., Ltd., 655 F.2d 650, 656 (5th Cir. 1981), *cert. denied*, 103 S. Ct. 177 (1982); Quinn v. Southwest Wood Prod., 597 F.2d 1018 (5th Cir. 1979); Hagans v. Oliver Mach. Co., 576 F.2d 97 (5th Cir. 1978). *See also* Burch v. Amsterdam Corp., 366 A.2d 1079 (D.D.C. 1976); Moehle v. Chrysler Motors Corp., 443 N.E.2d 575 (Ill. 1982); Wilson v. Piper Aircraft Corp., 282 Or. 61, 577 P.2d 1322 (1978); Bunn v. Caterpillar Tractor Co., 415 F. Supp. 286 (W.D. Pa. 1976), *aff'd*, 556 F.2d 564 (3d Cir. 1977), *cert. denied*, 434 U.S. 875 (1977).

595. 566 F.2d at 554.

596. *Id.* (*citing* 15 U.S.C.A. § 1191 *et. seq*).

597. *Id.* (*citing* United States v. Estremera, 531 F.2d 1103 (2d Cir. 1976) (a fabric "normally flammable" under the Flammable Fabrics Act is evidence that the fabric is not unreasonably dangerous)); *cf.* Muncie Aviation Corp. v. Party Doll Fleet, Inc., 519 F.2d 1178 (5th Cir. 1975) (Federal Aviation Administration advisory circulars are admissible as bearing on the standard of care in determining negligence).

merited reversal.[598] The court noted that other jurisdictions did not consider evidence of exceeding set standards to be conclusive.[599] It stated, "If the plaintiff produces substantial expert or lay evidence that a fabric which complies with the federal standard is nevertheless unreasonably dangerous for normal use, the plaintiff is entitled to a jury determination."[600]

Besides evidencing a design defect, the failure to comply with industry standards or governmental regulations may constitute evidence of an inadequate warning or instruction.[601] Compliance with industry or governmental standards, however, does not necessarily establish that a warning accompanying a product was adequate and therefore not defective.[602] In *Bristol Myers Co. v. Gonzales*,[603] a patient who suffered deafness as a result of the administration of drugs instituted a strict tort liability action against the drug manufacturer. The drug was required to have a package insert approved by the Food and Drug Administration, describing both the drug and its use. The insert was published annually in the Physician's Desk Reference (PDR).[604] The jury found that the 1970 PDR issued by Bristol-Myers failed to give the physician adequate warnings and instructions with respect to the drug, Kantrex.[605] The Texas Supreme Court acknowledged that the mere fact that the package insert had been approved by the FDA did not relieve Bristol-Myers of its obligation to communicate an adequate warning.[606] The court then stated:

> The fact that the approved insert did not adequately warn of potential dangers to the users of this drug was known to the proper officials of Bristol-Myers long before the inadequacy became known to the government officials and a change in the warnings and instructions was required in the package insert.[607]

---

598. *Id.* at 554.

599. *Id.* (*citing* Raymond v. Riegel Textile Corp., 484 F.2d 1025 (1st Cir. 1973); La Gorga v. Kroger Co., 275 F. Supp. 373 (W.D. Pa. 1967)).

600. *Id.*

601. Bristol-Meyers Co. v. Gonzales, 561 S.W.2d 801 (Tex. 1978).

602. *Simien*, 566 F.2d 551; *Perez*, 591 S.W.2d 907; Ellis v. K-Lan Co., Inc., 695 F.2d 157 (5th Cir. 1983). *See also Raymond*, 484 F.2d 1025.

603. 561 S.W.2d 801 (Tex. 1978).

604. *Id.* at 803.

605. *Id.* at 803-04.

606. *Id.*

607. *Id.*

Evidence that a warning complies with government regulations is not conclusive on the adequacy of the warning.[608] Of course, neither is the failure to comply determinative of inadequacy of the warning.

Evidence of the absence of governmental standards is inadmissible to establish that the product is safe or that a warning is not necessary.[609] In *Howard v. Faberge, Inc.*,[610] defendant sought to persuade the jury that, because of the absence of any governmental warnings about flammability of cosmetics, Brut cologne was not flammable. Since the jury could only speculate about the absence of any standards, the court concluded that it was error to prove through these means that the product was safe.[611]

2.02 PROOF THAT THE DEFECT EXISTED WHILE UNDER DEFENDANT'S CONTROL

The second basic element of a plaintiff's case in a strict tort liability action is that the defect existed in the product at the time it left the possession or control of the manufacturer or supplier.[612] In a marketing or design case, once it is proved that the defect existed at the time of the injury or damage, establishing that the

---

608. *See, e.g.*, McEwen v. Ortho Pharmaceutical Corp., 270 Or. 375, 528 P.2d 522, 534 (1974) (warnings given by ethical drive manufacturer may be inadequate even though all governance regulations have been met.

609. Howard v. Faberge, Inc., 679 S.W.2d 644, 648-49 (Tex. App.—Houston [1st Dist.] 1984, writ ref'd n.r.e.).

610. *Id.* at 644.

611. *Id.* at 648-49.

612. RESTATEMENT (SECOND) OF TORTS § 402A, comment g at 350 (1965). It is not necessary for the defect to exist in its ultimate form when the product leaves the defendant's control. If change will occur or can be anticipated to occur that will result in a product failure, the defendant will be liable. Sharp v. Chrysler Corp., 432 S.W.2d 131, 136 (Tex. Civ. App.—Houston [14th Dist.] 1968, writ ref'd n.r.e.). *See* Barrett v. Atlas Powder Co., 86 Cal. App. 3d 560, 150 Cal. Rptr. 339 (1978) (court acknowledged that if plaintiff had established a claim of possession from the manufacturer to himself of exploding blasting cap manufactured thirty years earlier, then a manufacturing defect might have been established). *See also* Gray v. Ensearch, Inc., 665 S.W.2d 601, 605 (Tex. App.—Fort Worth 1984, writ ref'd n.r.e.) (strict product liability will not apply against a utility when the product delivered by the utility is not defective); Holloway v. General Motors Corp., 403 Mich. 614, , 271 N.W.2d 777, 780 (1978); Stuckey v. Young Exploration Co., 586 P.2d 726, 730 (Okla. 1978); Seeborg v. General Motors Corp., 284 Or. 695, 588 P.2d 1100, 1103 (1978); V. Mueller & Co. v. Corley, 570 S.W.2d 140, 143 (Tex. Civ. App.—Houston [1st Dist.] 1978, writ ref'd n.r.e.) (jury can conclude product underwent no change from time it left manufacturer when prosthesis passed from the manufacturer to the distributor to the physician in a sealed sterilized container and was not damaged during surgery).

defect existed while under the defendant's control is generally not an issue.[613] The defective condition exists as an integral part of the manufacturing process in design and marketing cases.[614] As stated in *Reyes v. Wyeth Laboratories*[615] regarding marketing defects, "failure to warn by the manufacturer is by definition the *manufacturer's* dereliction."[616] In design defect cases, however, frequently the design has been substantially changed by an intermediate party.[617] In manufacturing cases, where proof that a defect was present does not necessarily imply that it existed while under the defendant's control, this element is often established concomitantly with proof of the existence of a defective condition.

Proof that the defect was present when it left the manufacturer's control can be established by circumstantial evidence.[618] In

---

613. *See* Howard v. Faberge, Inc., 679 S.W.2d 644, 647 (Tex. Civ. App.—Houston [1st Dist.] 1984, writ ref'd n.r.e.) (In addressing question of whether cologne was unreasonably dangerous without a warning concerning flammability, court stated that one of the major issues was whether the seller introduced into commerce a non-defective product that he could anticipate would undergo change, and become unreasonably dangerous if the seller warned the consumer of such change) *citing* Hamilton v. Motor Coach Industries, Inc., 569 S.W.2d 571, 575 (Tex. Civ. App.—Texarkana 1978, no writ); Blackwell Burner Co. v. Cerda, 644 S.W.2d 512 (Tex. App.—San Antonio 1982, writ ref'd n.r.e.).

614. *See* Reyes v. Wyeth Labs, 498 F.2d 1264, 1272 (5th Cir. 1974) *cert. denied* 419 U.S. 1096 (1974)(no tracing requirement in marketing cases). There are a few design cases in which there is an issue as to whether a design has been substantially changed by an intermediate party. Rourke v. Garza, 530 S.W.2d 794, 800 (Tex. 1975) (erection of scaffolding found not to be substantial change in design of scaffolding boards); Ford Motor Co. v. Russell & Smith Ford Co., 474 S.W.2d 549, 558 (Tex. Civ. App.—Houston [14th Dist.] 1971, no writ) (installation of an inappropriate model air conditioner deemed not a substantial change in automobile).

615. 498 F.2d 1264 (5th Cir. 1974), *cert. denied*, 419 U.S. 1096 (1974).

616. *Id.* at 1272.

617. Rourke v. Garza, 530 S.W.2d 794, 800 (Tex. 1975) (erection of scaffolding found not to be substantial change in design of scaffolding boards); *Russell & Smith*, 474 S.W.2d at 558 (installation of air conditioner found not to be substantial change in design of automobile).

618. Darryl v. Ford Motor Co., 440 S.W.2d 630, 632 (Tex. 1969). The court stated:

To exclude circumstantial evidence that the product was defective at the time of sale would frustrate the beneficial purposes of the doctrine. It would be equally difficult, if not impossible, for the plaintiff to rebut by direct evidence all of the conceivable possibilities which would account for the defective condition other than the existence of the defect at the time of the sale. Such direct evidence should not be required, particularly when dealing with a latent defect. *Id.* at 632. *See also* Pittsburg Coca Cola Bottling Works v. Ponder, 443 S.W.2d 546 (Tex. 1969); Dr. Pepper Co. v. Crow, 621 S.W.2d 464 (Tex. App.—Waco 1981, no writ); Olavirez v. Broadway Hardware, Inc., 564 S.W.2d 195 (Tex. Civ. App.—Corpus Christi 1978, writ ref'd n.r.e.); Coca-Cola Bottling Co. v. Hobart, 423 S.W.2d 118 (Tex. Civ. App.—Houston [14th Dist.] 1967, writ ref'd n.r.e.).

General Motors Corp. v. Hopkins,[619] the court observed that the defect may be established by circumstantial evidence of a malfunction.[620] The court then noted, "The age and use of that product during the time intervening between the purchase and malfunction will tend to support or defeat the circumstantial weight of the malfunction as proof of original defect."[621]

In *Martin v. Chesebrough-Pond's, Inc.*,[622] plaintiff's eye was severely injured when a bottle of cologne exploded while located in her automobile on a hot summer day.[623] Expert testimony established that the pressure within the bottle on that particular day would elevate to between 43 and 52 psi.[624] The manufacturer tested the bottles at 87 psi prior to shipping to the bottler. The bottler then tested each bottle at 85 psi before crimping the cap on the bottle, but at only 32 psi afterwards.[625] The evidence of the lower testing by the bottler circumstantially established that the bottler damaged the bottle in the crimping stage of its operation.[626] Therefore the bottler, not the manufacturer, was liable.

Negating misuse of the product supports an inference that the product is defective and that the defect existed at the time of delivery of the product.[627] An integral aspect of negating misuse is that of "tracing" the product defect back to the manufacturer.[628] Tracing as an element of negating substantial alteration is similar to the requirement of exclusive control necessary to invoke the doctrine of *res ipsa loquitur* in negligence actions.[629]

The lapse of time between manufacture of the product and the

---

619. 548 S.W.2d 344 (Tex. 1978).

620. *Id.* at 350. *See also V. Mueller*, 570 S.W.2d at 144 (concerning an allegedly defective silicone breast prosthesis, the court stated, "Although there was no direct evidence tracing the defect to the manufacturer, the fact that the product failed to function properly after being implanted in the plaintiff's body was a matter which the jury could consider as circumstantial proof of an original defect").

621. *Id.* at 350.

622. 614 F.2d 498 (5th Cir. 1980).

623. *Id.* at 499-500.

624. *Id* at 500.

625. *Id.*

626. *Id.* at 500-501.

627. *V. Mueller*, 570 S.W.2d 140; *Ponder*, 443 S.W.2d 546.

628. Note, *Products Liability: Methods of Pleading and Proof for the Plaintiff*, 49 N.D.L. Rev. 105, 124 (1972).

629. *See* Harmon v. Sohio Pipeline Co., 623 S.W.2d 314 (Tex. 1981) (*res ipsa loquitur* would establish a failure in a pipeline gasket, even in the absence of a specific evidence of a defect or failure).

resulting injury does not exonerate the manufacturer of liability. The time factor, however, constitutes some evidence to establish a strict tort liability case.[630] Prosser expressed the importance of time in tracing:

> Tracing the defect in the product into the hands of the defendant confronts the plaintiff with greater difficulties. There is first of all the question of lapse of time and long continued use. This in itself is not enough, even when it has extended over a good many years, to defeat the recovery where there is satisfactory proof of an original defect; but when there is no definite evidence, and it is only a matter of inference from the fact that something broke or gave way, the continued use prevents the inference that the thing was more probably than not defective when it was sold.[631]

The fact that only a short interval of time elapsed between delivery of the product and the accident circumstantially supports the allegation that the product was not altered or misused and that an existing defect caused the accident.[632]

Evidence of complaints prior to the accident represents another approach to tracing a defect. An identical complaint about the same product made prior to the injury represents circumstantial evidence of a defect in the product at the time the manufacturer or supplier relinquished control of the product.[633]

Another factor, that affects tracing is intermediate meddling or handling of the product. Plaintiff must establish that the product was not substantially altered while under an intermediary's control.[634] Intervening mishandling that creates the defective con-

---

630. *See generally* Comment, *Substantial Change: Alteration of a Product as a Bar to a Manufacturer's Strict Liability*, 80 DICK. L. REV. 245, 258-60 (1976).

631. Prosser, *supra* note 1, at 844-45.

632. Barnett v. Ford Motor Co., 463 S.W.2d 33, 35 (Tex. Civ. App.—Waco 1970, no writ) (accident occuring one week after purchase of vehicle). *See* Codling v. Paglia, 298 N.E.2d 622 (N.Y. 1973).

633. Ford Motor Co. v. Ted Arendale Ford Sales, Inc., 447 S.W.2d 744 (Tex. Civ. App.—Fort Worth 1969, no writ). Plaintiff was injured when the tailpipe of his automobile fell under the wheels. *Id.* at 775. He experienced the same rattling on the day of the accident that he had previously reported. This evidence supported the reasonable inference that the tailpipe was defective at the time it left the defendant's control. *Id.* at 776.

634. *See* McLain v. Hodge, 474 S.W.2d 772, 775 (Tex. Civ. App.—Waco 1971, writ ref'd n.r.e.) (defect in seven-year-old rifle was traced to the manufacturer by testimony of previous owner that he learned of the rifle malfunction shortly after purchasing it from the defendant, that it never left his control while he owned it, and that it had never been abused or repaired). Pittsburgh Coca-Cola Bottling Works of Pittsbugh v. Ponder, 443 S.W.2d 546 (Tex. 1969).

dition exonerates the manufacturer of liability.[635]

Negating intervening substantial change may be established by demonstrating that the product came in a sealed container. A product marketed in a sealed container logically reaches the consumer without any substantial change from the condition that existed when it was originally relinquished by the manufacturer.[636]

In *V. Mueller & Co. v. Corley*,[637] the sealed container doctrine was applied in a personal injury action based on negligence and strict liability against the manufacturer and distributor of a silicone breast prosthesis that was surgically implanted in plaintiff. Plaintiff's breast failed to heal properly, and a subsequent surgical procedure revealed a tear in the envelope of the prosthesis. The court noted that plaintiff was impressed with the burden under either negligence or strict tort liability to demonstrate that the defective condition of the product existed when it left the manufacturer's control.[638] It was not essential that the plaintiff identify the specific cause of the defect. Rather, the court stated it was essential that the plaintiff trace the defect to the manufacturer.[639] In affirming judgment for plaintiff, the court stated:

> Although there was no direct evidence tracing the defect to the manufacturer, the fact that the product failed to function properly after being implanted in the plaintiff's body was a matter which the jury could consider as circumstantial proof of an original defect. [citation omitted] A product defect may be established by circumstantial evidence. [citation omitted][640]

The court continued:

> Based upon the testimony that the prosthesis left the manufac-

---

635. *Hobart*, 423 S.W.2d 118, 124-25 (Tex. App.—Houston [14th Dist.] 1967, writ ref'd n.r.e.).

636. The tracing method was originally articulated, and the sealed container doctrine adopted, in McKisson v. Sales Affiliates, Inc., 416 S.W.2d 787, 792 (Tex. 1967) (sealed bottle of hair lotion). *See* Sharp v. Chrysler Corp., 432 S.W.2d 131, 136 (Tex. Civ. App.—Houston [14th Dist.] 1968, writ ref'd n.r.e) (automobile brake drum inferred to be sealed based on testimony from mechanics involved that the brake drum was never invaded to make repairs).

637. 570 S.W.2d 140 (Tex. Civ. App.—Houston [14th Dist.] 1978, writ ref'd n.r.e.).

638. *Id.* at 143 (*citing* Jack Roach-Bissonnet, Inc. v. Puskar, 417 S.W.2d 262 (Tex. 1967); Bass v. General Motors Corp., 491 S.W.2d 941 (Tex. Civ. App.—Corpus Christi 1973, writ ref'd n.r.e.)).

639. *Id.* (*citing* Bell Aerospace Corp. v. Anderson, 478 S.W.2d 191 (Tex. Civ. App.—El Paso 1972, writ ref'd n.r.e.)).

640. *Id.* (*citing Hobart*, 423 S.W.2d 118).

> turer and passed from the distributor to the physician in a sealed and sterilized container and that it was handled with care and was not damaged during the surgical procedure, the jury could have concluded that the product underwent no change from the time it left the control of the manufacturer until the surgery was completed.[641]

As illustrated in *V. Mueller*, expert testimony is helpful to establish that the defective condition existed in the product at the time of sale. Defendant introduced evidence that though the surgeon had performed at least 400 surgical procedures involving the implant, he had never experienced a spontaneous rupture in a seamless implant such as the one inserted in the plaintiff.[642] Plaintiff's expert stated that an implant could be ruptured during the wound closing process even when the surgeon used a shield or retractor.[643]

Tracing the product to the manufacturer or supplier is essential to establish that the product has not been misused or mishandled by the injured party or any intermediate parties. Factors important in establishing tracing include showing that: (1) the product is not mishandled by an intermediate party; (2) control of the product has been relinquished by the defendant only for a short period of time; (3) the user experiences similar problems with the product prior to the accident; and (4) the user purchases the product in a sealed container.

2.03 Proof of Causation

A. *Generally*

A concomitant requirement of proof of the existence of a defect and that the defect existed at the time it left the defendant's control is prima facie proof that the defect caused the injury or damage.[644] As with other elements of a strict tort liability action,

---

641. *Id.* at 144. (*citing Hopkins*, 548 S.W.2d at 349-50; *Darryl*, 440 S.W.2d 630).

642. *Id.*

643. *Id.* at 143. *See also* Martin v. Chesebrough-Ponds, Inc., 614 F.2d 498, 500 (5th Cir. 1980) (plaintiff's expert testified that he believed the crimping process used in securing cap on cologne bottle caused stress on the bottle which ultimately resulted in its failure).

644. Restatement (Second) of Torts § 402A (1965). *See* Houdaille Indus., Inc. v. Edwards, 374 So. 2d 490, 493 (Fla. 1979); Bell Helicopter Co. v. Bradshaw, 594 S.W.2d 519, 532-33 (Tex. Civ. App.—Corpus Christi 1979, writ ref'd n.r.e.).

causation may be established by circumstantial evidence.[645] The law "only demands the best proof of a transaction that it is susceptible of, and when that is produced then it becomes a question whether or not its probative force is such as to establish its existence."[646]

The case of *McInnes v. Yamaha Motor Corp.*[647] clarifies the criteria for a prima facie case. The plaintiff was rendered a quadriplegic when his motorcycle left the roadway and collided with a guardrail. Plaintiff contended that the motorcycle developed an uncontrollable wobble at speeds of at least 40 miles per hour. The jury found that the vehicle was defective, but that the defect was not the producing cause of the accident. Plaintiff's failure to keep a proper lookout was the proximate cause of the accident.[648] In affirming judgment for defendant, the court relied on *Salazar v. Hill*:[649] " 'The jury's failure to find those facts . . . vital to the appellant's recovery need not be supported by affirmative evidence.' "[650]

In *Morgan v. Compugraphic Corp.*[651] a secretary alleged that she suffered serious health problems as a result of inhaling noxious fumes emitted from a typesetting machine recently installed in her office.[652] Plaintiff's testimony constituted the only evidence of the facts.[653] The Texas Supreme Court noted that lay testimony may be adequate to prove causation, and that, generally, "lay testimony establishing a sequence of events which provides a strong, logically traceable connection between the event and the condition is suffi-

---

645. *See* Birmingham v. Gulf Oil Corp., 516 S.W.2d 914 (Tex. 1974); Dr. Pepper Co. v. Crow, 621 S.W.2d 464 (Tex. App.—Waco 1981, no writ); Travenol Laboratories, Inc. v. Bandy Laboratories, Inc., 608 S.W.2d 308 (Tex. App.—Waco 1981, writ ref'd n.r.e.). *See also* Morgan v. Compugraphic Co., 675 S.W.2d 729, 733 (Tex. 1984) ("Lay testimony is adequate to prove causation in those cases in which general experience and common sense will enable a layman to determine, with reasonable probability, the causal relationship between the event and the condition.")

646. Miller v. Fleming, 149 Tex. 368, 233 S.W.2d 571, 575 (1950) (citing Wright v. Giles, 129 S.W. 1163 (Tex. Civ. App. 1910, writ ref'd)).

647. 659 S.W.2d 704 (Tex. App.—Corpus Christi 1983), *aff'd* 673 S.W.2d 185 (Tex. 1984).

648. *Id.* at 707.

649. 551 S.W.2d 518 (Tex. Civ. App.—Corpus Christi 1977, writ ref'd n.r.e.).

650. 659 S.W.2d at 708, *aff'd* 673 S.W.2d 185 (Tex. 1984).

651. 675 S.W.2d 729 (Tex. 1984).

652. *Id.* at 730.

653. *Id.* at 731.

cient to prove causation."[654] The court stated that a plaintiff must establish two "causal nexuses" in order to recover: (a) a causal nexus between the defendant's conduct and the event sued upon (related to liability); and (b) a causal nexus between the event sued upon and the plaintiff's injuries (related to damages).[655] Since plaintiff presented some competent evidence, the sequence of events was established without the aid of expert medical testimony.[656]

B. *Manufacturing Defects*

Producing cause (actual cause) governs manufacturing defect cases as distinguished from proximate cause, which involves the additional element of foreseeability.[657] Producing cause was defined by the Texas Supreme Court in *General Motors Corp. v. Hopkins*.[658] The definition of producing cause submitted and approved by the Supreme Court prescribes that the defective product be " 'an efficient, exciting or contributing cause, which in a natural and continuous sequence, caused in whole or in part the occurrence or injuries, if any, in question, and but for said cause the occurrence or injuries would not have occurred.' "[659]

Circumstantial evidence supports both the inferences of a defective product and of producing cause.[660] For example, negating all other possible causes simultaneously establishes both the defect and causation.[661] Similarly, circumstantial evidence that a large number of users suffered identical injuries or illnesses constitutes evidence for both requirements in a strict tort liability action.[662] Expert testimony that an alleged defect probably caused the acci-

---

654. *Id.* at 733.

655. *Id.* at 731, 732.

656. *Id.* at 733.

657. *See, e.g.*, C.A. Hoover & Son v. O.M. Franklin Serum Co., 444 S.W.2d 596 (Tex. 1969); Herbert v. Loveless, 474 S.W.2d 732, 739 (Tex. Civ. App.—Beaumont 1971, writ ref'd n.r.e.)

658. 548 S.W.2d 344 (Tex. 1977).

659. *Id.* at 351 n.3.

660. Sharp v. Chrysler Corp., 432 S.W.2d 131, 135-36 (Tex. Civ. App.—Houston [14th Dist.] 1968, writ ref'd n.r.e.). *See* Mahan Volkswagen, Inc. v. Hall, 648 S.W.2d 324, 328 (Tex. App.—Houston [1st Dist.] 1982, writ ref'd n.r.e.).

661. *See, e.g.*, Franks v. National Dairy Prod. Corp., 414 F.2d 682, 687 (5th Cir. 1969); Bell Aerospace Corp. v. Anderson, 478 S.W.2d 191, 197 (Tex. Civ. App.—El Paso 1972, writ ref'd n.r.e.).

662. *See, e.g.*, *Herbert*, 474 S.W.2d at 738-39.

dent likewise provides evidence of the existence of the defect and that the defect caused the accident.[663] Though evidence of a defective condition is often relevant to prove causation, proof of a defective condition alone does not necessarily establish causation.[664]

C. *Design Defects*

As in manufacturing defect cases, producing cause, not proximate cause, governs design defect cases.[665] Causation is established by many of the methods of proof utilized in manufacturing defect cases. Both expert testimony[666] and circumstantial evidence[667] are utilized to fashion an inference that the defective design caused the injury or damage.[668]

Expert and lay testimony were critical to establish causation in *Magic Chef, Inc. v. Sibley*.[669] A young girl was severely burned when she stood on a chair next to a gas-fueled stove and leaned against the burner valve while reaching for fudge. Testimony of lay witnesses relating to similar accidents, coupled with expert testimony of the slight torque necessary to activate the burner valve on the stove, established that the range was defectively designed and that the defective design was a producing cause of the occurrence of the minor plaintiff's injuries.[670]

It is not necessary in either a design or manufacturing case to establish that the design defect was the sole producing cause of the

---

663. *See, e.g.*, McKisson v. Sales Affiliates, Inc., 416 S.W.2d 787, 792 (Tex. 1967); McLain v. Hodge, 474 S.W.2d 772, 774-75 (Tex. Civ. App.—Waco 1971, writ ref'd n.r.e.).

664. *See, e.g.*, Jack Roach-Bissonnet, Inc. v. Puskar, 417 S.W.2d 262, 266-67 (Tex. 1967).

665. *See* Shipp v. General Motors Corp., 750 F.2d 418, 425 (5th Cir. 1985) ("We see no retreat in Texas from its rule that a defect need only be a "producing cause" of injury and that there may be more than one such cause.") Turner v. General Motors Corp., 584 S.W.2d 844 (Tex. 1979); General Motors Corp. v. Hopkins, 548 S.W.2d 344 (Tex. 1977); Rourke v. Garza, 530 S.W.2d 794, 801 (Tex. 1975).

666. *See, e.g.*, Williams v. General Motors Corp., 501 S.W.2d 930, 936-37 (Tex. Civ. App.—Houston [1st Dist.] 1973, writ ref'd n.r.e.); General Motors v. Grizzle, 642 S.W.2d 837, 843 (Tex. Civ. App.—Waco 1982, no writ) (evidence including the testimony of two experts was more than a scintilla of evidence for the jury to find a design defect in the brake as the producing cause of the accident).

667. *See, e.g.*, Shipp v. General Motors Corp., 750 F.2d at 422-23.

668. *See, e.g.*, Mitchell v. Fruehauf Corp., 568 F.2d 1139, 1142-43 (5th Cir. 1978); *Hopkins*, 548 S.W.2d at 349; Pizza Inn, Inc. v. Tiffany, 454 S.W.2d 420, 422-23 (Tex. Civ. App.—Waco 1970, no writ).

669. 546 S.W.2d 851 (Tex. Civ. App.—San Antonio 1977, writ ref'd n.r.e.).

670. *Id.* at 855.

accident.[671] In *General Motors Corp. v. Hopkins*,[672] the jury determined two producing causes for an automobile accident: the manufacturer's design of the lock-out lever on the carburetor and the plaintiff's misuse of the vehicle.[673] The combination of a defectively designed carburetor coupled with the substantial misuse by the plaintiff merely established concurring causes of the accident and resulting injury.[674]

In *Scronce v. Howard Brothers Discount Stores, Inc.*,[675] plaintiff was injured when a rifle exploded at a shooting range. Plaintiff instituted a strict tort liability suit against the seller, manufacturer, and importer of the rifle. The trial court directed a verdict for all of the defendants.[676] Affirming the trial court, the Fifth Circuit noted:

> All that is certain is that the accident cannot have come about as Mr. Scronce said it did; . . . Even if the bolt design was a design defect, it is well settled that a plaintiff must prove that the defect produced his injuries. [citations omitted] Failure on a plaintiff's part to produce credible evidence of causation makes a directed verdict in favor of defendant proper. Here Scronce failed to prove that a defect in the bolt design was responsible for the explosion. The evidence showed that the accident could not have happened in the way in which Scronce testified it did; our inquiry necessarily ends there. [Citation omitted].[677]

As *Scronce* illustrates, even though plaintiff proves a defective design and an injury, he has not necessarily satisfied the burden of proof for causation.

In *Curtis v. General Motors Corp.*,[678] a crashworthiness case, the Tenth Circuit declared that the burden of proof is imposed on the plaintiff to establish that "but for" an alleged defective design,

---

671. *See, e.g.*, *Shipp*, 750 F.2d at 425 (defining producing cause as "an efficient, exciting, or contributing cause, which in a natural and continuous sequence in connection with any other cause or causes, produced the injuries."). *See, e.g.*, Ford Motor Co. v. Russell & Smith Ford Co., 474 S.W.2d 549, 577 (Tex. Civ. App.—Houston [14th Dist.] 1971, no writ) (the court recognized two producing causes for the overheating of a van, so the dealer and manufacturer were held jointly liable).

672. 548 S.W.2d 344 (Tex. 1977).

673. 535 S.W.2d at 881, 887.

674. *Id.* at 889.

675. 679 F.2d 1204 (5th Cir. 1982) (applying Texas law).

676. Id. at 1205.

677. Id. at 1206.

678. 649 F.2d 808 (10th Cir. 1981).

certain additional injuries sustained by the plaintiff would not have occurred. The court recognized that the plaintiff is obligated to demonstrate that the defective design caused some specific part or all of the injury sustained in an accident not caused initially by a defect in the product.[679]

D. *Marketing Defects*

Even though the product is faultlessly manufactured and designed, a manufacturer may be found liable if the product is unreasonably dangerous or likely to harm the user if used improperly and is not accompanied by an adequate warning.[680] Proof of causation in a marketing defect case differs from the causation issue in manufacturing or design cases. The defect in a marketing case is not in the product itself, but is in the failure to warn of risks of harm or to provide adequate instructions for the safe use of the product.[681] The failure to warn must represent a causative nexus between the absence of a warning and the resulting injury sustained by the user.[682] Unlike manufacturing and design defect cases, the risk of harm must be known or reasonably foreseeable by the manufacturer or product supplier as a predicate to the duty to provide a warning or instructions for safe use.[683]

---

679. *Id.* at 813.

680. Blackwell Burner Co. v. Cerda, 644 S.W.2d 512, 516 (Tex. App.—San Antonio 1982, writ ref'd n.r.e.).

681. *See, e.g., Id.* at 515; Stapleton v. Kawasaki Heavy Industries Ltd., 608 F.2d 571, 573 (5th Cir. 1979), *modified* 612 F.2d 905 (5th C. 1980) (adequacy of warning "depends upon the language used and the impression that it is calculated to make upon the mind of the average use of the product); Technical Chem. Co. v. Jacobs, 480 S.W.2d 602, 605 (Tex. 1972); (a product is unreasonably dangerous or defective when an ordinary man would not have marketed the product without "supplying warnings as to risks and dangers involved in using the product as well as instructions as to how to avoid those risks and dangers."); Pearson v. Hevi-Duty Elec., 618 S.W.2d 784, 788 (Tex. Civ. App. —Houston [1st Dist.] 1981, writ ref'd n.r.e.); *Bell Helicopter*, 594 S.W.2d at 530; Bituminous Casualty Corp. v. Black & Decker Mfg. Co., 518 S.W.2d 868, 873 (Tex. Civ. App.—Dallas 1974, writ ref'd n.r.e.)("Implicit in the duty to warn is the duty to warn with a degree of intensity that would cause a reasonable man to exercise for his own safety precaution commensurate with the potential dangers.") *See also* Howard v. General Cable Corp., 674 F.2d 351, 354-57 (5th Cir. 1982).

682. *See Bell Helicopter*, 594 S.W.2d at 533-34; Menking v. Bishman Mfg. Co., 496 S.W.2d 762, 765 (Tex. App.—Corpus Christi 1973, no writ); Blackwell Burner Co. v. Cerda, 664 S.W.2d 512 (Tex. App.—San Antonio 1982, writ ref'd); Ragsdale Brothers, Inc. v. Margo, ____ S.W.2d ____ (Tex. App.—San Antonio 1985, no writ).

683. *See* Pavlides v. Galveston Yacht Basin, Inc., 727 F.2d 330, 338 (5th Cir. 1984); Borel v. Fibreboard Paper Prod. Co., 493 F.2d 1076, 1090 (5th Cir. 1973), *cert. denied*, 419

The existence of a dangerous condition or risk of harm in the use of the product creates a rebuttable presumption that an adequate warning would be read and heeded.[684] This presumption may be rebutted by evidence that the user would not have read the warning even if it had been given.[685] Similarly, the fact that an adequate warning has been given creates a rebuttable presumption that if the user had read and heeded the warning the accident would not have occurred and, therefore, the product is not defective.[686]

In *Technical Chemical Co. v. Jacobs*,[687] a can of Freon exploded. The cause of action was based solely on the manufacturer's failure to admonish the user against the danger of connecting the can to the high pressure side of the compressor. The failure of the plaintiff to read the label on the can warranted a jury finding that any warning provided would have been ignored or disregarded.[688] Evidence that users would not read the warning rebuts the presumption of causation.[689] Failure to read a warning because of ignorance, intoxication, physical impediments, or other reasons rebuts the presumption that the warning would be read.

In *Pearson v. Hevi Duty Electric*,[690] an electrician was electrocuted as he attempted to repair a transformer. The court addressed the issue of whether a general warning of danger was adequate where the undisputed evidence revealed that a specific warning would have focused the user's attention to the danger of the live fuse in the open position.[691] The absence of an adequate warning created a rebuttable presumption that a specific warning would have enabled the plaintiff to avoid the particular risk of

---

U.S. 860 (1974); Carter v. Johns-Manville Sales Corp., 557 F. Supp. 1317, 1319 (E.D. Tex. 1983); Bristol-Myers Co. v. Gonzales, 561 S.W.2d 801 (Tex. 1978); Crocker v. Winthrop Laboratories, Division of Sterling Drug Co., 514 S.W.2d 429, 433 (Tex. 1974); Lopez v. Aro Corp., 584 S.W.2d 333, 335 (Tex. Civ. App.—San Antonio 1979, writ ref'd n.r.e.).

684. *Jacobs*, 480 S.W.2d at 606.

685. *Id.* at 606.

686. Reyes v. Wyeth Laboratories, 498 F.2d 1264, 1281 (5th Cir. 1974), *cert. denied*, 419 U.S. 1096 (1974); *Bell Helicopter*, 594 S.W.2d 519, 534; RESTATEMENT (SECOND) OF TORTS § 402A, comment j (1965).

687. 480 S.W.2d 602 (Tex. 1972).

688. *Id.* at 606.

689. *Id.*

690. 618 S.W.2d 784 (Tex. Civ. App.—Houston [1st Dist.] 1981, writ ref'd n.r.e.).

691. *Id.* at 785, 788.

harm.[692] The causative nexus was established by the rebuttable presumption.[693]

Similarly, in *Rawlings Sporting Goods Co., Inc. v. Daniels*,[694] plaintiff sustained a subdural hematoma as the result of head-on contact with another football player. Plaintiff instituted a strict tort liability action based on a defective warning that his football helmet would not protect him against subdural hematomas if he collided with another player. Plaintiff's father testified that he would not have allowed his son to participate in football had he been aware that the helmet would not protect against potential brain injuries.[695] The court stated:

> We think liability arises when a product is manufactured and marketed for protection of the consumer, the consumer buys the product, relying on it for his protection; while engaged in a generally dangerous activity, the manufacturer fails to warn of known limitations in the protective abilities of its product with which the user is not equally familiar, and as a result, the consumer is injured while using the product.[696]

Evidence that proves a defective warning may also establish causation since causation is rebuttably presumed in the absence of an adequate warning.

E. Conclusion

Causation is established in manufacturing or design cases by expert testimony or various methods of circumstantial proof. In marketing cases, the plaintiff is not required to establish affirmatively that the marketing defect caused the injury or damage. Causation in a marketing case is rebuttably presumed in the absence of an adequate warning or instructions for safe use. In cases involving inadequacy of warning or instruction, however, the plaintiff must establish a causative nexus between the absence of a different warning or instruction and the injuries sustained in the use of the product.

---

692. *Id.* at 788.
693. *Id.*
694. 619 S.W.2d 435 (Tex. Civ. App.—Waco 1981, writ ref'd n.r.e.).
695. *Id.* at 439.
696. *Id.*

CHAPTER III. DEFENSES*

3.00 GENERALLY

The adoption of section 402A of the *Restatement (Second) of Torts* introduced a new and unique conceptual doctrine into Texas jurisprudence. Under this novel doctrine of strict tort liability, one who sells any product in a defective condition unreasonably dangerous to the user is subject to liability for harm or injury caused by the product.[1] Several socioeconomic rationale underlie the strict tort liability concept. Initially it is assumed that injured users rely on the implied representation that the product is safe from defects. Most importantly, judicially formulated social policy determines that sellers and suppliers are considered to be the appropriate parties to bear the risk of loss as between the party supplying the product and deriving economic benefit and the injured user.

With the adoption of section 402A, one of the most significant problems that emerged has been the application of defenses to this new doctrine. The effect of the user's conduct with respect to the product and issues concerning contribution and indemnity have historically generated confusion about the nature, scope and

---

* Paul Cauley coauthored this chapter.

1. RESTATEMENT (SECOND) OF TORTS § 402A (1965) [hereinafter cited as section 402A or § 402A].

proper use of defenses. Most recently, these areas have undergone considerable change in Texas in the context of strict tort liability actions. Unique problems have also surfaced concerning contractual disclaimers, limitations, offensive collateral estoppel, and the impact of governmental immunities.

This chapter analyzes and reviews defenses to actions predicated on strict tort liability. It discusses the effects of procedure, policy, and conduct of the user or third parties that may affect the plaintiff's recovery. Particular emphasis is placed on basic tort principles and traditional legal distinctions that are affected by the policy factors underlying the doctrine of strict tort liability.

3.01 Historical Development of Defenses

A. *Contributory Negligence*

The *Restatement (Second) of Torts* section 402A provides that contributory negligence is not a defense to strict tort liability when such negligence consists of a failure to exercise reasonable care to discover the defect or to gaurd against the possible existence of a defect.[2] Texas was one of the early jurisdictions to adopt the *Restatement* position in *Shamrock Fuel and Oil Sales, Inc. v. Tunks,*[3] and *McKisson v. Sales Affiliates, Inc.*[4] Contributory negligence in the form of subpar conduct after the plaintiff has discovered the defect was addressed in *Henderson v. Ford Motor Co.*[5] The plaintiff in *Henderson* intentionally drove into a light pole after an alleged carburetor malfunction caused her vehicle to accelerate out of control.[6] The court rejected the argument that the plaintiff was contributorily negligent in failing to turn off the ignition, shift the transmission to neutral or apply the brakes properly.[7] The court specifically declared that contributory negligence was not a viable defense concerning subpar conduct of the plaintiff im-

---

2. § 402A comment n.
3. 416 S.W.2d 779 (Tex. 1967).
4. 416 S.W.2d 787 (Tex. 1967). *See* Rourke v. Garza, 530 S.W.2d 794, 800 (Tex. 1975) (reaffirming contributory negligence is no defense).
5. 519 S.W.2d 87, 89 (Tex. 1974), *overruled in part*, Turner v. General Motors Corp., 584 S.W.2d 844, 851 (Tex. 1979), *overruled in part*, Duncan v. Cessna Aircraft Corp., 665 S.W.2d 414 (Tex. 1984).
6. *Id.* at 88-89.
7. *Id.* at 89.

mediately following the discovery of the defect.[8]

A plaintiff's conduct in knowingly using a product after the defect has been discovered was acknowledged to consitiute a defense to a strict tort liability action. This conduct, however, was characterized as assumption of the risk.[9] Therefore, the *Henderson* decision effectively eliminated contributory negligence as a legally cognizable defense to strict liability. While Texas recognized contributory negligence as a defense to claims based on negligence[10] or breach of implied warranty,[11] in strict tort liability causes of action, the user's conduct was a defense only if it could be characterized as assumption of the risk or misuse.[12]

B. *Assumption of the Risk*

While the *Restatement (Second) of Torts* rejects contributory negligence as a defense, it does recognize the defense of assumption of the risk.[13] This defense, as formulated and adopted by the *Restatement* requires that the plaintiff actually know of the defect and be aware of the danger, and then proceed voluntarily and *unreasonably* to encounter the danger or risk of harm.[14]

Historically in Texas, assumption of the risk has not included the requirement of unreasonableness in proceeding to encounter a known risk.[15] In *Henderson v. Ford Motor Co.*,[16] the Texas Su-

---

8. *Id.* at 89-90.

9. Refer to notes 13-23 *infra* and accompanying text.

10. Contributory negligence is a partial defense to recovery in negligence actions under TEX. REV. CIV. STAT. ANN. art. 2212a (Vernon Supp. 1985) [hereinafter referred to and cited as Article 2212a]. *See* Farley v. M M Cattle Co., 529 S.W.2d 751, 758 (Tex. 1975).

11. Where a buyer's negligence is a proximate cause of the damages incurred, his recovery is reduced by the percentage which was caused by his negligence. Signal Oil & Gas Co. v. Universal Oil Prods., 572 S.W.2d 320, 329 (Tex. 1978).

12. *See generally* Sales, *Assumption of the Risk and Misuse in Strict Tort Liability—Prelude to Comparative Fault*, 11 TEX. TECH L. REV. 729 (1980); Edgar, *Products Liability in Texas*, 11 TEX. TECH L. REV. 23 (1979).

13. § 402A comment n.

14. *Id. See* Culp v. Rexnord & Booth-Rouse Equip. Co., 38 Colo. Ct. App. 1, 553 P.2d 844, 845 (1976); Brooks v. Dietz, 218 Kan. 698, 545 P.2d 1104, 1110 (1976); Johnson v. Clark Equip. Co., 274 Or. 403, 547 P.2d 132, 138 (1976).

15. *See* J & W Corp. v. Ball, 414 S.W.2d 143, 146 (Tex. 1967); Halepeska v. Callihan Interests, Inc., 371 S.W.2d 368, 379 (Tex. 1963); Biscayne Tex. Properties v. Miner, 502 S.W.2d 225, 228 (Tex. Civ. App.—El Paso 1973, writ ref'd n.r.e.).

16. 519 S.W.2d 87 (Tex. 1974), *overruled in part*, Turner v. General Motors Corp., 584 S.W.2d 844, 851 (Tex. 1979), *overruled in part*, Duncan v. Cessna Aircraft Corp., 665 S.W.2d 414 (Tex. 1984).

preme Court rejected the *Restatement* position in favor of Texas' traditional theory of assumption of the risk.[17] As enunciated by the Texas Supreme Court, assumption of the risk requires (1) subjective knowledge of the particular dangerous condition of the product; (2) subjective appreciation of the nature of the danger; and (3) voluntary use of the product or otherwise voluntarily encountering the known danger.[18] The effect of establishing the three elements of assumption of the risk constituted an absolute bar to recovery by the plaintiff.[19]

Underlying rejection of the reasonableness standard was the courts' desire to maintain assumption of the risk and contributory negligence as separate doctrines.[20] The *Restatement* view was perceived as a merging of the two doctrines and creating a special, higher level or standard of contributory negligence.[21] For example, a car owner aware that the brakes are defective but who drives his injured son to the hospital, under Texas law, has assumed the risk.[22] Under the *Restatement*, the conduct of the vehicle operator would present a fact issue whether he acted unreasonably in driving the car under the circumstances.[23]

Knowledge of general hazards was deemed insufficient to satisfy the assumption of the risk defense: actual knowledge of the specific defective condition of the product was required.[24] Though

---

17. *Id.* at 90-91. The court expressly repudiated the Fifth Circuit prediction that Texas would adopt § 402A comment n of the RESTATEMENT in Messick v. General Motors Corp., 460 F.2d 485 (5th Cir. 1972). *See* Williams v. Brown Mfg. Co., 45 Ill. 2d 418, 261 N.E.2d 305 (1970) (rejecting RESTATEMENT view).

18. *See* Rourke v. Garza, 530 S.W.2d 794 (Tex. 1975); Caterpillar Tractor Co. v. Gonzales, 599 S.W.2d 633 (Tex. Civ. App.—El Paso 1980, writ ref'd n.r.e.); Bell Helicopter Co. v. Bradshaw, 594 S.W.2d 519 (Tex. Civ. App.—Corpus Christi 1979, writ ref'd n.r.e.); Howard v. General Cable Corp., 674 F.2d 351, 357 (5th Cir. 1982); Maxey v. Freightliner Corp., 450 F. Supp. 955 (N.D. Tex. 1978), *aff'd*, 623 F.2d 395 (5th Cir. 1980), *aff'd in part and rev'd on other grounds on reh'g*, 665 F.2d 1367 (5th Cir. 1982).

19. Farley v. M M Cattle Co., 529 S.W.2d at 758; *Shamrock Fuel & Oil Sales*, 416 S.W.2d at 785. As a result of the comparative negligence statute in Texas, assumption of the risk is eliminated as a defense to a negligence cause of action. *Farley*, 529 S.W.2d at 758.

20. Henderson v. Ford Motor Co., 519 S.W.2d at 90.

21. *Id. See generally* Sales, *supra* note 12, at 748-49 (discussing confusion surrounding RESTATEMENT view).

22. *See* Henderson v. Ford Motor Co., 519 S.W.2d at 90-91 (hypothetical example of Reavley, J.)

23. § 402A comment n. *See* Henderson v. Ford Motor Co., 519 S.W.2d at 90-91. Refer to note 14 *supra.*

24. *Maxey*, 450 F. Supp. at 959-60. The plaintiff must have known and appreciated that if his truck turned over, the fuel tanks would contact the ground, that the tanks were

not obligated to demonstrate that the plaintiff actually knew of the specific defective component, the defendant was obligated to prove that the plaintiff was aware of the specific potential danger presented by the defective condition of the product.[25] Factors such as the injured party's age, intelligence, experience and judgment could be considered in evaluating the user's knowledge and appreciation of danger.[26] Knowledge of the dangerous condition would not be imputed to the user of the product unless the condition was patent, open, or obvious.[27]

The requirement of voluntarily encountering a known dangerous condition necessarily implied that the encounter was the result of a free and intelligent choice.[28] Encounters with dangerous conditions resulting from inattention, inadvertence or momentary distraction failed to satisfy the "voluntary" requirement.[29] For instance, a reflex action in an attempt to push spilling trash back into a garbage truck would not be a voluntary act.[30]

The defense generally applied not only to users or consumers, but also to bystanders, who voluntarily proceeded to encounter a known risk.[31] To establish that the plaintiff assumed the risk, the

---

defective because they would not sustain a reasonable impact, and that they lacked proper safety mechanisms. *Id.* at 960. *See* Caterpillar Tractor Co. v. Gonzalez, 599 S.W.2d at 638; *Bell Helicopter*, 594 S.W.2d at 534; Heil Co. v. Grant, 534 S.W.2d 916, 921-22 (Tex. Civ. App.—Tyler 1976, writ ref'd n.r.e.); Blackwell Burner Co. v. Cerda, 644 S.W.2d 512 (Tex. App.—San Antonio 1982, writ ref'd n.r.e.).

25. General Elec. Co. v. Schmal, 623 S.W.2d 482 (Tex. App.—Texarkana 1981, writ ref'd n.r.e.); Caterpillar Tractor Co. v. Gonzalez, 599 S.W.2d at 638.

26. *See* Ellis v. Moore, 401 S.W.2d 789, 794 (Tex. 1966); Dee v. Parish, 160 Tex. 171, 174, 327 S.W.2d 449, 452 (1959); Heil Co. v. Grant, 534 S.W.2d at 922.

27. Rourke v. Garza, 530 S.W.2d at 800. *See* Blackwell Burner Co. v. Cerda, 644 S.W.2d 512, 518 (Tex. App.—San Antonio 1982, writ ref'd n.r.e.). Texas courts appear reluctant to impute knowledge to a plaintiff in this situation. *See* Caterpillar Tractor Co. v. Gonzalez, 599 S.W.2d at 638. *Cf.* Blackwell Burner Co. v. Cerda, 644 S.W.2d at 518.

28. *See e.g.*, Henderson v. Ford Motor Co., 519 S.W.2d at 91; Halepeska v. Callihan Interests, Inc., 371 S.W.2d 368, 379 (Tex. 1963).

29. McAdams v. Pak-Mor Mfg. Co., 602 S.W.2d 374, 381-82 (Tex. Civ. App.—Waco 1980, writ ref'd n.r.e.).

30. *Id.* Likewise, confronting a dangerous condition as a requirement of employment did not satisfy the voluntary factor. *See* Green v. Edmands 639 F.2d 286, 290 (5th Cir. 1981).

31. Baker v. Chrysler Corp., 55 Cal. App. 3d 710, 719, 127 Cal. Rptr. 745, 751 (1976); Auburn Mach. Works Co. v. Jones, 366 So. 2d 1167, 1171-72 (Fla. 1979); Jones v. White Motor Corp., 61 Ohio App. 2d 162, 401 N.E.2d 223, 230-31 (1978). *See* West v. Caterpillar Tractor Co., 336 So. 2d 80, 90 (Fla. 1976). *But see* Barr v. Rivinius, Inc. , 58 Ill. App. 3d 121, 373 N.E.2d 1063, 1068 (1978) (dicta).

However, where a user has assumed the risk or acted negligently, an injured bystander

defendant was impressed with the extremely difficult burden of proving that the plaintiff possessed actual knowledge of the particular defective condition of the product and that he possessed a full appreciation of the nature of the particular danger presented by that defective condition. Though viewed as an emasculated defense, assumption of the risk represented the principal defense to a strict tort liability action until the Texas Supreme Court judicially promulgated the comparative causation doctrine in *Duncan v. Cessna Aircraft Corp.*[32]

C. *Misuse*

Not only does the *Restatement (Second) of Torts* provide for assumption of the risk, it also recognizes the defense of product misuse.[33] Comment *h* of section 402A specifically provides that "[a] product is not in a defective condition when it is safe for normal handling and consumption. If the injury results from abnormal handling . . . or abnormal preparation for use . . . the seller is not liable."[34] This defense was recognized in Texas in the landmark decision of *Shamrock Fuel & Oil Sales Co. v. Tunks*[35] which adopted the *Restatement* theory of strict tort liability as embodied in section 402A.[36]

The precise elements of the defense were refined in the seminal case of *General Motors Corp. v. Hopkins.*[37] Misuse, to constitute a defense, obligated the defendant to establish (1) that the particular misuse was neither intended nor reasonably foreseeable by the manufacturer; (2) that the product user could reasonably foresee injury resulting from a misuse of the product; and (3) the

---

is not barred from recovery due to the user's conduct. *See* Mitchell v. Fruehauf Corp., 568 F.2d 1139, 1146 (5th Cir. 1978); South Austin Drive-In Theatre v. Thomison, 421 S.W.2d 933, 951 (Tex. Civ. App.—Austin 1967, writ ref'd n.r.e.) (user misuse).

32. 665 S.W.2d 414 (Tex. 1984). Comparative causation is discussed in the following section, 3:02. For an extensive review of the assumption of the risk defense, see generally Sales, *supra* note 12, at 738-49; Edgar, *supra* note 12, at 41-46.

33. § 402A comment h.

34. *Id.*

35. 416 S.W.2d 779 (Tex. 1967).

36. *Id.* at 785. *See* Rourke v. Garza, 530 S.W.2d at 799; General Motors Corp. v. Hopkins, 548 S.W.2d 344 (Tex. 1977), *overruled in part*, Turner v. General Motors Corp., 584 S.W.2d 844, 847 (Tex. 1979), *overruled in part*, Duncan v. Cessna Aircraft Corp., 665 S.W.2d 414 (Tex. 1984).

37. 548 S.W.2d 344 (Tex. 1977).

percentage that the misuse proximately contributed to the accident which caused the injury.[38] The *Hopkins* court declared that when an unreasonably dangerous product defect and an unforeseeable product misuse by the consumer concur to produce the injury, the plaintiff's total recovery should be reduced only by the percentage of causation attributable to the misuse.[39]

The misuse defense required the injury to be foreseeable by the user as well as unforeseeable by the manufacturer or supplier. Use of a product in a nonprescribed or unintended manner was often irrelevant since the use was also required to be unforeseeable from the perspective of the manufacturer.[40] For example, a helicopter manufacturer was deemed to foresee that an experienced pilot would use the helicopter's tail rotor blade beyond the manufacturer's prescribed maximum hour limits.[41] At some point, however, failure to maintain and service the product would be objectively unforeseeable and constitute misuse.[42] Also, violation of a safety statute enacted to afford protection against the particular hazard involved could constitute misuse.[43] The failure to follow and heed adequate warnings or instructions for safe use likewise represented misuse.[44]

---

38. *Id.* at 351-52. *See* Allied Indus. Int'l, Inc. v. Placencio, 685 S.W.2d 364, 371 (Tex. App.—San Antonio 1984, no writ); *Bell Helicopter,* 594 S.W.2d at 534; Southwestern Bell Tel. Co. v. Griffith, 575 S.W.2d 92, 104 (Tex. Civ. App.—Corpus Christi 1978, writ ref'd n.r.e.); Magic Chef, Inc. v. Sibley, 546 S.W.2d 851, 856 (Tex. Civ. App.—San Antonio 1977, writ ref'd n.r.e.).

39. General Motors Corp. v. Hopkins, 548 S.W.2d at 351. *See* General Elec. Co. v. Schmal, 623 S.W.2d at 487. *Cf.* Mahan Volkswagen, Inc. v. Hall, 648 S.W.2d 324, 333 (Tex. App.—Houston [1st Dist.] 1982, writ ref'd n.r.e.). Comparative causation principles were later judicially adopted in regard to a plaintiff's contributory negligence in a breach of implied warranty action. *Signal Oil & Gas Co.,* 572 S.W.2d at 329.

40. *Bell Helicopter,* 594 S.W.2d at 534; *Southwestern Bell Tel. Co.,* 575 S.W.2d at 104-05; *Magic Chef, Inc.,* 546 S.W.2d at 856. *Cf.* Allied Indus. Int'l, Inc. v. Placencio, 685 S.W.2d 364 (Tex. App.—San Antonio 1984, no writ).

41. *Bell Helicopter,* 594 S.W.2d at 534.

42. *See* Mitchell v. Ford Motor Co, 553 F.2d 19 (1st Cir.), *cert. denied,* 429 U.S. 871 (1976); Bond v. Transairco Co., 514 F.2d 642 (5th Cir. 1975); Edwards v. Sears, Roebuck & Co., 512 F.2d 276, 279 (5th Cir. 1975) (applying Mississippi law); Sun Valley Airlines, Inc. v. Avco-Lycoming Corp., 411 F. Supp. 598, 602-03 n.4 (D. Idaho 1976).

43. *See* Ruiz v. Flexonics, 517 S.W.2d 853, 860 (Tex. Civ. App.—Corpus Christi 1974, writ ref'd n.r.e.). *Cf.* Martinez v. Martinez, 553 S.W.2d 211, 214 (Tex. Civ. App.—Tyler 1977, no writ).

44. *See, e.g.,* Harville v. Anchor-Wate Co., 663 F.2d 598, 603 (5th Cir. 1981); McDevitt v. Standard Oil of Texas, 391 F.2d 364, 370 (5th Cir. 1968); Temple v. Zimmer U.S.A., Inc., 678 S.W.2d 723, 725 (Tex. App.—Houston [14th Dist.] 1984, no writ); Wenzel v. Rollins Motor Co., 598 S.W.2d 895, 900 (Tex. Civ. App.—El Paso 1980, writ ref'd n.r.e.); Proctor &

Commentators suggested that the element requiring the particular misuse to be unforeseeable by the product supplier significantly emasculated the defense in Texas.[45] Courts likewise criticized the standards for the misuse defense because of the difficult, if not impossible, burden imposed on the defendant.[46] However, prior to *Duncan v. Cessna Aircraft Corp.*,[47] Texas continued to adhere to the defense of misuse as formulated by the Texas Supreme Court in *General Motors Corp. v. Hopkins*.

3.02 Comparative Causation

Strict tort liability produced some unique and confusing concepts pertaining to defenses in Texas. For example, assumption of the risk represented a complete bar to recovery,[48] while misuse was a partial defense[49] and contributory negligence was no defense.[50] Many commentators urged that some form of comparative apportionment should be adopted as an alternative solution to the problems and inconsistencies surrounding strict tort liability.[51] Some of the state's judiciary also suggested that a method to simplify defenses to strict tort liability was essential to provide for a

---

Gamble Mfg. Co. v. Langley, 422 S.W.2d 773, 780 (Tex. Civ. App.—Dallas 1967, writ dism'd). *Cf.* Helene Curtis Indus. v. Pruitt, 385 F.2d 841, 856 (5th Cir. 1967), *cert. denied*, 391 U.S. 913 (1968).

45. Sales, *supra* note 12, at 756-58.

46. Wenzel v. Rollins Motor Co., 598 S.W.2d 895, 900 (Tex. Civ. App.—El Paso 1980, writ ref'd n.r.e.) ("The fact that the conduct must be an unforeseeable use does not simplify the matter for either the trial court or the appellate court. From a practical standpoint, that requirement almost totally abolishes the defense of misuse."); Boatland of Houston, Inc. v. Bailey, 609 S.W.2d 743, 751 (Tex. 1980) (Pope, J., concurring).

47. 665 S.W.2d 414 (Tex. 1984).

48. Farley v. M M Cattle Co., 529 S.W.2d at 758; *Shamrock Fuel & Oil Sales*, 416 S.W.2d at 785.

49. General Motors Corp. v. Hopkins, 548 S.W.2d at 351.

50. Henderson v. Ford Motor Co., 519 S.W.2d at 89; *Shamrock Fuel & Oil Sales*, 416 S.W.2d at 783-85; *McKisson*, 416 S.W.2d at 790.

51. *See* Sales, *supra* note 12, at 773-78; Edgar, *supra* note 12, at 49-50; Sales, *Contribution and Indemnity Between Negligent and Strictly Liable Tortfeasors*, 12 St. Mary's L.J. 323, 357-65 (1980) [hereinafter cited as Sales, *Contribution and Indemnity*]; Special Project, *Texas Tort Law in Transition*, 57 Tex. L. Rev. 381, 491-95 (1979); Wade, *Product Liability and Plaintiff's Fault - The Uniform Comparative Fault Act*, 29 Mercer L. Rev. 373, 376-81, 391 (1978); Feinberg, *The Applicability of a Comparative Negligence Defense in a Strict Products Liability Suit Based on Section 402A of the Restatement of Torts 2d (Can Oil and Water Mix?)*, 42 Ins. Counsel J. 39, 52-53 (1975); Schwartz, *Strict Liability and Comparative Negligence* 42 Tenn. L. Rev. 171, 178-81 (1974).

manageable and equitable apportionment of damages.[52]

Other jurisdictions likewise struggled with formulation of meaningful defenses in strict tort liability actions. In response to mounting criticism, an increasing number of jurisdictions elected to adopt a system of comparative negligence or comparative fault.[53] Comparative fault contemplates that the plaintiff's negligent conduct will be compared directly with the manufacturer's fault in supplying a defective product. Some jurisdictions characterized strict liability as a form of negligence *per se* and applied existing comparative negligence statutes to actions predicated on strict tort liability.[54] Courts in other jurisdictions have not recognized strict liability as negligence *per se*, but have paralleled comparative negligence statutes in formulating a common law comparative fault doctrine applicable to strict tort liability actions.[55]

In other jurisdictions the courts have also judicially formulated a comparative fault doctrine applicable to strict tort liability without reliance upon any comparative negligence statute.[56] In *Daly v. General Motors Corp.*,[57] the California Supreme Court confronted the three basic arguments asserted by opponents of comparative fault. The court considered the purported semantic

---

52. Boatland of Houston, Inc. v. Bailey, 609 S.W.2d at 751 (Pope, J., concurring); Wenzel v. Rollins, 598 S.W.2d at 900-01.

53. Woods, *Product Liability: Is Comparative Fault Winning the Day?*, 36 ARK. L. REV. 360, 360-362 (1983). *See, e.g.*, notes 54-56 *infra*. *But cf.* Kinard v. Coats Co., 37 Colo. App. 555, 553 P.2d 835 (1976); Kirkland v. General Motors Corp., 521 P.2d 1353 (Okla. 1974); Carreia v. Firestone Tire & Rubber Co., 388 Mass. 342, 446 N.E.2d 1033 (1983).

54. Dippel v. Sciano, 37 Wis. 2d 443, 155 N.W.2d 55, 64 (1967); Sun Valley Airlines, Inc. v. Avco-Lycoming Corp., 411 F. Supp. 598, 603 (D. Idaho 1976); Austin v. Raybestos-Manhattan, Inc., 471 A.2d 280, 285 (Me. 1984); Busch v. Busch Constr., Inc., 262 N.W.2d 377, 393 (Minn. 1977); West v. Caterpillar Tractor Co., 336 So.2d 80 (Fla. 1976).

55. W.M. Bashlin Co. v. Smith 277 Ark. 406, 643 S.W.2d 526 (1983); Murray v. Fairbanks Morse, 610 F.2d 149, 157-63 (3d Cir. 1979); Hardin v. Manitowoc-Forsythe Corp., 691 F.2d 449, 454-55 (10th Cir. 1982) (applying Kansas law); Kennedy v. City of Sawyer, 228 Kan. 439. 452, 618 P.2d 788, 798 (1980); Bell v. Jet Wheel Blast, 462 So.2d 166 (La. 1985); Thibault v. Sears, Roebuck & Co., 118 N.H. 802, 395 A.2d 843, 848-49 (1978); Sandford v. Chevrolet Div. of General Motors, 292 Or. 590, 595-98, 642 P.2d 624, 626-28 (1982); Fiske v. MacGregor, Div. of Brunswick, 464 A.2d 719 (CR.I. 1983).

56. Daly v. General Motors Corp., 20 Cal. 3d 725, 742, 575 P.2d 1162, 1172, 144 Cal. Rptr. 380, 390 (1978); Edwards v. Sears, Roebuck & Co., 512 F.2d 276, 290 (5th Cir. 1975) (appling Mississippi law); Butaud v. Suburban Marine & Sporting Goods, Inc., 555 P.2d 42, 45-46 (Alaska 1976); Star Furniture v. Pulaski Furniture Co., 297 S.E.2d 854, 861-62 (W. Va. 1982).

57. 20 Cal. 3d 725, 575 P.2d 1162, 144 Cal. Rptr. 380 (1978). *See* Wade, *supra* note 51, at 376-81.

inconsistencies between the theories of negligence, breach of warranty, and strict tort liability significantly less important than the countervailing policy consideration of just and equitable apportionment of fault.[58] The court noted that comparative fault would not lessen the manufacturer's incentive to produce safe products, but would merely reduce its exposure to liability by the percentage of fault that the user's conduct contributed to his injuries.[59] Finally, the court perceived no problems for the trier of fact in comparing fault, noting the absence of any noteworthy difficulties under the "unseaworthiness" doctrine, a form of strict liability.[60]

Strict tort liability was never designed to transform a manufacturer into an insurer for injuries resulting from use of its product.[61] It is generally recognized that comparative fault provides a simpler, more understandable, and more equitable means of allocating the risk of loss, and provides protection for innocent consumers against payment of the added cost of injuries attributable not to a defective product, but to subpar conduct of plaintiffs.[62] Despite increasing criticism of the existing system, prior to 1984 Texas continued its allegiance to the essentially meaningless defenses of assumption of the risk and unforeseeable product misuse.[63] In 1984 the Texas Supreme Court, in an effort to remedy the unfairness and economic inefficiency created by the existing situation, adopted a system of pure comparative causation for strict tort liability in *Duncan v. Cessna Aircraft Co.*.[64]

In *Duncan*, the plaintiff, Carolyn Parker Duncan, instituted a

---

58. 20 Cal. 3d at 736, 575 P.2d at 1168, 144 Cal. Rptr. at 386.

59. *Id.* at 737-38, 575 P.2d at 1169, 144 Cal. Rptr. at 387.

60. *Id.* at 738-39, 575 P.2d at 1170, 144 Cal. Rptr. at 388.

61. *See* Borel v. Fibreboard Paper Prods. Corp., 493 F.2d 1076, 1087 (5th Cir. 1973), *cert. denied*, 419 U.S. 869 (1974); McDevitt v. Standard Oil Co., 391 F.2d 364, 370 (5th Cir. 1968); Helene Curtis Indus., Inc. v. Pruitt, 385 F.2d 841, 863 (5th Cir. 1967); West v. Caterpillar Tractor Co., 336 So. 2d 80, 90 (Fla. 1976); Timsah v. General Motors Corp., 225 Kan. 305, 591 P.2d 154, 162 (1979); Micallef v. Miehle Co., 39 N.Y.2d 376, 386, 348 N.E.2d 571, 578, 384 N.Y.S.2d 115, 121-22 (1976) (breach of implied warranty); Moss v. Polyco, Inc., 522 P.2d 622, 627 (Okla. 1974); Henderson v. Ford Motor Co., 519 S.W.2d at 93; *Shamrock Fuel & Oil Sales*, 416 S.W.2d at 785; McCants v. Salameh, 608 S.W.2d 304, 307 (Tex. Civ. App.—Waco 1980, writ ref'd n.r.e.).

62. Wade, *supra* note 51, at 379.

63. Refer to note 12 *supra* and accompanying text. Although comparative causation applying to misuse was adopted in *General Motors Corp. v. Hopkins*, the element of unforeseeability of the misuse remained. 548 S.W.2d at 351-52. *See Signal Oil & Gas Co.*, 572 S.W.2d at 329 (comparative causation applicable to breach of warranty actions).

64. 665 S.W.2d 414 (Tex. 1984).

wrongful death action against Cessna Aircraft for the death of her husband who was killed when the aircraft in which he was a passenger crashed.[65] Mrs. Duncan alleged that the aircraft seats were defectively designed and manufactured, and as a result of which her husband sustained fatal injuries.[66] Responding to Mrs. Duncan's complaint, Cessna asserted a counterclaim[67] for contribution against the estate of Benjamin Smithson, the pilot, claiming that his negligence had caused the crash.[68] Mrs. Duncan had previously filed a separate lawsuit against Smithson's estate and his employer, the owner of the aircraft.[69] That suit was settled for $90,000 and Mrs. Duncan executed a general release specifically mentioning the employer and Smithson's estate.[70]

After determining that Cessna was not released in the agreement executed by Mrs. Duncan, the court framed the issue to be resolved: should contributory negligence constitute a defense in a strict tort liability action. Contributory negligence was defined as conduct representing something more than a mere failure to discover a product defect but less than the conduct required for assumption of risk or unforeseeable misuse.[71] The court recognized that a scheme of equitable and rational risk distribution repre-

---

65. *Id.* at 417.

66. *Id.* at 418. James Parker, husband of the plaintiff, was a passenger in an aircraft piloted by Benjamin Smithson who was employed as an instructor pilot by Air Plains West, Inc. At the time of the accident, Smithson was giving flying lessons to Mr. Parker. *Id.*

67. Mrs. Smithson also instituted a wrongful death action against Cessna and the actions were tried together.

68. *Id.* The trial court struck the counterclaim from the lawsuit disallowing the issue of Smithson's negligence. *Id.*

69. *Id.*

70. *Id.* The trial court granted Cessna's motion for judgment *non obstante veridicto* on the ground that the release executed by Mrs. Duncan also discharged Cessna. *Id.* at 419. The first issue addressed by the supreme court was the effect of the general release. The court held that "the mere naming of a general class of tortfeasors in a release does not discharge the liability of each member of that class." *Id.* at 419-20. Only where a tortfeasor is specifically named, or is described in such a way so his identity or connection to the event is not in doubt, does the release apply to him. *Id.* at 420.

71. *Id.* at 422. Assumption of the risk and misuse defenses require more than proving that the plaintiff failed to act as a reasonably prudent person. To prove the plaintiff assumed the risk, it is necessary to establish that he possessed subjective knowledge of the particular dangerous condition as well as subjective appreciation of the nature of the danger. Refer to notes 15-19 *supra* and accompanying text. A plaintiff does not misuse a product by using it negligently, but must use it in a manner which is unforeseeable to the manufacturer and produce an injury foreseeable by the plaintiff. Refer to notes 37-43 *supra* and accompanying text.

sented a fundamental policy for adoption of the strict tort liability doctrine.[72] Consequently, an equitable mechanism to compare causation attributable to the various parties was necessary to maintain the socioeconomic underpinnings of the doctrine.[73] Further, the existing apportionment system in Texas was viewed as unfair, unbalanced and failed to allocate accident costs in proportion to each party's relative ability to prevent or reduce those costs.[74] Following the New Hampshire Supreme Court in *Thibault v. Sears, Roebuck & Co.*,[75] the court promulgated a system of pure comparative causation to be applied in all cases involving a product related accident in which at least one defendant is determined to be liable on a theory other than negligence.[76]

Under comparative causation, the award of damages is reduced by the percentage of harm caused by plaintiff's own conduct, irrespective of the percentage of negligence that contributes to the injury producing event.[77] The relative fault of the parties is not compared. Rather, the harm caused by the defective product is compared with the harm caused by the plaintiff's conduct as well as the conduct of third parties.[78] Conduct by the plaintiff to be considered in making this comparison encompasses contributory negligence, assumption of the risk, misuse, failure to mitigate, and failure to avoid damages (avoidable consequences).[79] Since the or-

---

72. McDevitt v. Standard Oil Co., 391 F.2d 364, 370 (5th Cir. 1968); Helene Curtis Indus. v. Pruitt, 385 F.2d 841, 862 (5th Cir. 1967); Butaud v. Suburban Marine & Sporting Goods, Inc., 555 P.2d 42, 44 (Alaska 1976); Greenman v. Yuba Power Prods., 59 Cal. 2d 57, 377 P.2d 897, 901, 27 Cal. Rptr. 697, 701 (1963); Micallef v. Miehle Co., 39 N.Y.2d 376, 386, 348 N.E.2d 571, 578, 384 N.Y.S.2d 115, 122 (1976).

73. 665 S.W.2d at 425. A similar rationale was used by the Fifth Circuit in adopting a form of comparative causation for maritime torts in defective products cases. Lewis v. Timco, Inc., 716 F.2d 1425, 1432-33 (5th Cir. 1983) (en banc). *See* Butaud v. Suburban Marine & Sporting Goods, Inc., 555 P.2d 42, 46 (Alaska 1976) (comparative negligence is not incompatable with strict liability because manufacturer is still responsible for all harm caused by defective product).

74. *Duncan*, 665 S.W.2d at 424-25. *See* Wade, *supra* note 51, at 379-81 (consumers are forced to pay costs attributable to users' negligence); Special Project, *supra* note 51, at 485-86 (current system is economically inefficient in forcing manufacturer to make unjustified safety improvements).

75. 118 N.H. 802, 395 A.2d 843 (1978).

76. *Duncan*, 665 S.W.2d at 429. *Cf.* Day v. General Motors Corp., 345 N.W.2d 349, 353-57 (N.D. 1984) (adopting comparative causation).

77. 665 S.W.2d at 429. The court opted for pure comparative causation to avoid the inefficiency and "reduced deterrent effect" of a modified system. *Id. Cf.* Article 2212a.

78. *Duncan*, 665 S.W.2d at 427.

79. *Id.* at 428. The court stated the suit may combine theories of crashworthiness,

dinary care standard for negligence represents a lesser standard than required by misuse and assumption of risk, for all practical purposes, misuse and assumption of the risk are eliminated and are subsumed under contributory negligence.[80]

Negligence in the form of a failure to discover or guard against the possibility of a product defect does not qualify as contributory negligence in a strict tort liability action.[81]

Any other form of subpar or negligent conduct by the plaintiff after discovery of the defect, however, qualifies as contributory negligence.[82] Further, under the *Duncan* rationale, negligent conduct, independent or irrespective of knowledge of the defect, also constitutes contributory negligence.[83] Examples of negligence *independent* of a failure to discover or gaurd against the defect would include operating a vehicle at an excessive speed, failing to maintain a proper lookout, driving while intoxicated,[84] disregarding

---

strict products liability, breach of warranty or negliglence. *Id.*

80. *Id.* The only possible application would be in extremely rare situations where (1) a plaintiff voluntarily assumes the risk of a dangerously defective condition but under the circumstances it was reasonable, or (2) an unintended and unforeseeable use is made of a product but the use was reasonable under the circumstances. It is not certain whether the defenses would continue to apply in these situations. *See id.* (overruling *Henderson v. Ford Motor Co.* and *General Motors Corp. v. Hopkins*). *Cf.* National Marine Serv., Inc. v. Petroleum Serv. Corp., 736 F.2d 272, 276-77 (5th Cir. 1984) (maritime law).

81. *See Duncan*, 665 S.W.2d at 422; *Shamrock Fuel & Oil Sales*, 416 S.W.2d at 784; *McKisson*, 416 S.W.2d at 790. *See also* Star Furniture v. Pulaski Furniture Co., 297 S.E.2d at 862-63.

82. *See Duncan*, 665 S.W.2d at 422, 428 (overruling *Henderson v. Ford Motor Co.*). *See also* Flaminio v. Honda Motor Co., 733 F.2d 463, 465 (7th Cir. 1984); Peterson v. Lebanon Mach. Works, 61 Or. App. 258, 656 P.2d 323, 324-25 (1982).

83. Jurisdictions applying comparative principles have stated subpar conduct of the plaintiff may be contributory negligence even where the defect was not known to exist. *See e.g.*, Edwards v. Sears, Roebuck & Co., 512 F.2d 276, 290 (5th Cir. 1975) (dicta); Conti v. Ford Motor Co., 578 F. Supp. 1429, 1435 (E.D. Pa. 1983) (dicta); Lenherr v. NRM Corp., 504 F. Supp. 165, 176 (D. Kan. 1980); Deere & Co. v. Brooks, 250 Ga. 517, 299 S.E.2d 704, 706 (1983); Alden Wells Veterinarian Clinics, Inc. v. Wood, 324 N.W.2d 181, 184 (Minn. 1982) (dicta); Busch v. Busch Constr. Inc., 262 N.W.2d 377, 394 (Minn. 1977) (all types of consumer conduct may be compared other than failure to discover the defect); Sandford v. Chevrolet Div. of Gen. Motors, 292 Or. 590, 610-11, 642 P.2d 624, 635-36 (1982).

84. *E.g.*, Ford Motor Co. v. Pool, 688 S.W.2d 879, 883 (Tex. App.—Texarkana 1985, no writ); Edwards v. Sears, Roebuck & Co., 512 F.2d 276, 290 (5th Cir. 1975) (excessive speed while intoxicated) (dicta); Conti v. Ford Motor Co., 578 F. Supp. at 1435 (grossly excessive speed) (dicta); Sandford v. Chevrolet Div. of Gen. Motors, 292 Or. at 610, 642 P.2d at 635 (operating fully loaded vehicle with little experience and excessive speed under the circumstances). *See* Boatland of Houston, Inc. v. Bailey, 609 S.W.2d at 749-50; Maxey v. Freightliner Corp., 450 F. Supp. at 960. *Boatland* and *Maxey* are pre-*Duncan* cases yet their fact situations would exemplify the type of conduct likely to constitute negligence under com-

available warnings or accessible instructions,[85] or removing safeguards or otherwise altering the product.[86]

The court in *Duncan* expressly adopted comparative causation in crashworthiness cases in which a defective condition of the vehicle neither causes nor contributes to cause the accident but after the accident occurs it is alleged that the design defect causes or enhances the injuries.[87] Arguably the doctrine includes cases in which the plaintiff's conduct enhances the injuries but does not cause the accident.[88] The *Duncan* court suggested that comparative causation authorizes the trier of fact to consider the plaintiff's "failure to mitigate or avoid damages . . . whether the suit combines crashworthiness or other theories. . . . "[89] Though the conduct of the plaintiff in *Duncan* was alleged to have contributed to the accident, the court has declared that failure to mitigate or avoid damages is to be considered in the comparative causation calculation.

Prior to *Duncan*, in non-product negligence cases, Texas courts refused to consider plaintiff's failure to mitigate or avoid damages in applying statutory comparative negligence. Defendants were not entitled to submit special issues on mitigation of damages and were entitled only to an instruction to limit plaintiff's recovery

---

parative causation.

85. *See generally* Pearson v. Heavi-Duty Elec., 618 S.W.2d 784, 789-90 (Tex. App.—Houston [1st Dist.] 1981, writ ref'd n.r.e.); Bell Helicopter Co. v. Bradshaw, 594 S.W.2d at 534-35. These cases were decided prior to *Duncan* but the conduct involved in each would likely exemplify negligence under the comparative causation scheme.

86. Foster v. Ford Motor Co., 616 F.2d 1304, 1307, 1311 (5th Cir. 1980); Helene Curtis Indus. v. Pruitt, 385 F.2d 841, 860-61 (5th Cir. 1967); Blackwell Burner Co. v. Cerda, 644 S.W.2d at 517-18; Bell Helicopter Co. v. Bradshaw, 594 S.W.2d at 534.

87. *Duncan*, 665 S.W.2d at 428. *See* Trust Corp. v. Piper Aircraft Corp., 506 F. Supp. 1093, 1098-99 (D. Mont. 1981), *aff'd*, 701 F.2d 85 (9th Cir. 1983). *Cf.* McGee v. Cessna Aircraft Corp., 139 Cal. App. 3d 179, 184 188 Cal. Rptr. 542, 545 (1983); Austin v. Ford Motor Co., 86 Wis. 2d 628, 273 N.W.2d 233, 236-37 (1979).

88. *Duncan*, 665 S.W.2d at 428. *See* Day v. General Motors Corp., 345 N.W.2d 349, 358 (N.D. 1984) (injury enhancing fault of plaintiff is relevant evidence). *Cf.* Mauch v. Manufacturers Sales & Serv., 345 N.W.2d 338, 347 (N.D. 1984) (fault must be misuse or assumption of risk).

89. 665 S.W.2d at 428. Conduct of the plaintiff classified as failure to mitigate damages is that which occurs after the injury producing event but enhances the plaintiff's injuries. Avoidable damages or avoidable consequences are distinguished as those resulting from plaintiff's conduct prior to the injury producing event constituting not a cause of the accident but enhancement of the injuries. *See generally* Wade, *supra* note 51, at 385-86; Sales, *Limitations on Recovery of Damages in Personal Injury Actions*, 18 S. Tex. L.J. 217, 254 (1976).

for failure to exercise reasonable care in mitigating injuries.[90] In *Kerby v. Abilene Christian College*,[91] the court refused to permit the driver's negligence, in operating his truck with the door open, to reduce or bar recovery from the negligent defendant which collided with him.[92] The supreme court seemingly reaffirmed its position regarding avoidable consequences in *Carnation Co. v. Wong*.[93] In *Wong*, the plaintiffs were injured in an automobile accident and their failure to wear seatbelts was found to have contributed to 50% of the husband's injuries and to 70% of those of the wife.[94] The appellate court reversed reduction of the plaintiffs' recovery and the supreme court refused defendant's writ of error because " persons whose negligence did not *contribute to an automobile accident* should not have the damages awarded to them reduced . . . because of their failure to wear available seat belts."[95]

Other jurisdictions which apply comparative apportionment principles have determined that the injury enhancing conduct of the plaintiff should reduce recovery. Wisconsin, which articulated the concept of comparative apportionment,[96] recently determined that failure to wear available safety belts constitutes a form of contributory fault. In *Foley v. City of West Allis*,[97] the plaintiff's negligence in failing to use available seat belts caused 70% of her injuries.[98] The court emphasized that the plaintiff could only recover damages caused by the defendant. Significantly, the court recognized that the defendant should not be liable for incremental injuries avoidable by the plaintiff.[99]

---

90. Moulton v. Alamo Ambulance Serv., Inc., 414 S.W.2d 444, 450 (Tex. 1967). *See* Whitman v. Campbell, 618 S.W.2d 935, 937 (Tex. Civ. App.—Beaumont 1981, no writ); Armellini Express Lines of Florida, Inc. v. Ansley, 605 S.W.2d 297, 309 (Tex. Civ. App.—Corpus Christi 1980, writ ref'd n.r.e.).

91. 503 S.W.2d 526 (Tex. 1973).

92. *Id.* at 528.

93. 516 S.W.2d 116 (Tex. 1974).

94. *Id.*

95. *Id.* at 117 (emphasis added). It should be noted that the underlying rationale for these decisions focused on the fact that conduct of the plaintiff that did not contribute to the accident producing event was irrelevent.

96. *See* Dippel v. Sciano, 37 Wis. 2d 443, 155 N.W.2d 55 (1967).

97. 113 Wis. 2d 475, 335 N.W.2d 824 (1983).

98. *Id.* at 480, 335 N.W.2d at 827. *Accord*, Insurance Co. of North America v. Pasakarnis, 451 So. 2d 447, 453-54 (Fla. 1984).

99. 113 Wis. 2d at 489, 335 N.W.2d at 831. RESTATEMENT (SECOND) OF TORTS, § 286 (1965), specifically provides that:

> The court may adopt as a standard of conduct of a reasonable man the re-

Similarly, in *Halvorson v. Voeller*,[100] the plaintiff was found to be contributorily negligent for failing to wear a helmet while operating a motorcycle.[101] As a result, the plaintiff's recovery was reduced by the 8% fault attributable to his failure to avoid consequential injury from the motorcycle accident.[102] Under the *Halvorson* formulation, the defendant is required to prove "(1) that a reasonably prudent person would have worn a safety helmet and (2) that the plaintiff's failure to wear a helmet increased his injuries."[103] Because of the equitable apportionment policy underlying Texas' adoption of *comparative causation*, Texas would appear compelled to apply the current doctrine in a comparable fashion.[104]

Recent legislation to restrict use of evidence of a failure to use

---

> quirements of a legislative enactment or an administrative regulation whose purpose is found to be exclusively or in part (a) to protect a class of persons which includes the one whose interest is invaded, and (b) to protect the particular interest which is invaded, and (c) to protect that interest against the kind of harm which has resulted, and (d) to protect that interest against the particular hazard from which the harm results.

Comment (i) of the *Restatement* specifically provides that:

> A statute or ordinance may be construed as intended to protect all persons or a particular class of persons against a more or less narrowly restricted type of hazard. If so, the violation of the enactment will not be negligence unless the harm which results to another is caused by his exposure to the hazard from which it was the purpose of the enactment to protect him.

In Texas the violation of statutory enactment constitutes negligence or negligent conduct when the purpose of the statute is to guard against a particular course of conduct or a particular type of hazard or harm to one for whose benefit it was enacted. *See generally* East Texas Motor Freight Lines v. Loftis, 148 Tex. 242, 223 S.W.2d 613 (1949); Alpine Telephone Corp. v. McCall, 143 Tex. 335, 184 S.W.2d 830, 833 (Tex. 1944); Rudes v. Gottschalk, 159 Tex. 552, 324 S.W.2d 201 (1959); Parrott v. Garcia, 436 S.W.2d 897, 899 (Tex. 1969); Castro v. Hernandez-Davila, No. 13-84-393-CV slip op. at 4-5 (Tex. App.—Corpus Christi April 25, 1985); Martinez v. Martinez, 553 S.W.2d 211, 214 (Tex. App.—Tyler 1977, no writ). The purpose of seat belt legislation is to protect occupants of automobiles from enhanced or more severe injury than would occur in the absence of seat belt use.

100. 336 N.W.2d 118 (N.D. 1983).

101. *Id.* at 121. *Accord* Day v. General Motors Corp., 345 N.W.2d 349, 358 (N.D. 1984).

102. 336 N.W. at 119.

103. *Id.* at 121. The court stressed that there must be competent evidence that the negligence of the plaintiff caused a portion of the injuries sustained. *Id. But cf.* Mauch v. Manufacturers Sales & Serv., 345 N.W.2d 338, 347 (N.D. 1984) (fault must be misuse or assumption of risk).

104. *See Duncan*, 665 S.W.2d at 424-25. *See also* Hermann v. General Motors Corp., 720 F.2d 414, 415 (5th Cir. 1983) (applying Louisianna law); Caiazzo v. Volkswagenwerk, A.G., 647 F.2d 241, 251-52 (2d Cir. 1981). *But cf.* Burgstahler v. Fox, 290 Minn. 495, 186 N.W.2d 182, 183 (1971).

safety restraints in civil actions undoubtedly complicates the issue and may prevent such conduct from qualifying as contributory negligence.[105] Irrespective of the legislative proscription, the fact that comparative causation in strict tort liability cases is a judicially formulated doctrine could possibly prevail over any legislative enactments not specifically directed to this doctrine. Certainly, in a crashworthiness context, the failure to wear available safety restraints represents the quintessential avoidable consequence, since the supplier's product did not cause the accident-producing event.

It is less than clear whether any defendant may invoke comparative causation by obtaining findings of strict liability or breach of warranty against a third party defendant, or whether only the plaintiff must plead and obtain the necessary findings to invoke comparative causation.[106] In negligence cases governed by Article 2212a, any party is entitled to submit issues seeking an allocation of negligence attributable to all tortfeasors.[107] Application of this rationale suggests that negligent defendants may invoke pure comparative causation by pleading and obtaining findings of strict tort liability or breach of warranty against either a third party not joined by the plaintiff or against a settling product supplier.[108]

This issue was partially addressed by the Texas Supreme Court in *Acord v. General Motors Corp.*[109] The court announced that the defendant is entitled to submit issues to the jury concerning the liability of the settling party.[110] Though General Motors

---

105. Tex. S.B. 500, 69th Leg. (1985) (amending Tex. Rev. Civ. Stat. art. 6701d (Vernon Supp. 1985).

106. The *Duncan* court stated that Article 2212a would apply where the *plaintiff* failed to obtain findings of strict liability or breach of warranty against a product supplier who had been joined with a negligent defendant. 665 S.W.2d at 429. If this statement is interpreted literally, a negligent defendant could not invoke comparative causation against a settling product supplier and the case would be governed by Article 2212a.

107. Cypress Creek Util. Serv. Co. v. Muller, 640 S.W.2d 860, 865-66 (Tex. 1982).

108. A nonsettling negligent defendant may not wish to join a settling product supplier thereby avoiding "pure" comparative causation if the defendant concludes that the plaintiff may be more than 50% contributorily negligent. *See* Article 2212a(1); *Duncan*, 665 S.W.2d at 429 (Article 2212a continues to govern negligence cases). In this case the defendant would risk the settlement dollar credit, as opposed to a percentage credit, for the amount paid by the settling product supplier. Article 2212a(2)(d). *See generally* Comment, *Multiple Party Litigation in Comparative Negligence: Incomplete Resolution of Joinder and Settlement Problems*, 32 Sw. L.J. 669, 680-81 (1978).

109. 669 S.W.2d 111 (Tex. 1984).

110. *Id.* at 117 ("General Motors will be entitled to submit [the settling party's] causa-

was authorized to submit issues concerning comparative causation of a third party, the plaintiff had alleged that General Motors was strictly liable in tort. Therefore, a finding of strict tort liability against General Motors necessarily invokes the *Duncan* comparative causation.[111]

Thus *Acord* may not represent a definitive resolution of the issue of a defendant triggering application of pure comparative causation by pleading and obtaining a finding of strict liability against a settling product supplier. A contrary result, however, would necessarily emasculate the rationale postulated by the supreme court in promulgating the comparative causation doctrine.[112]

The *Duncan* decision has effectuated profound changes in strict tort liability. It recognizes that manufacturers and other sellers are not absolute insurers of their products. Accordingly, it establishes a system of risk allocation or risk apportionment that is consistent not only with the policies underlying the adoption of strict tort liablility but also with protecting product suppliers and innocent consumers from absorbing the costs of injuries directly attributable to subpar conduct of the plaintiff and other third persons.

3.03 Contribution and Indemnity

Contribution is defined as the payment of a tortfeasor's proportionate share of the plaintiff's damages to a tortfeasor who has paid more than his proportionate share.[113] Contribution among

---

tion to the jury so that its own liability to Acord, if any, may be reduced by the share of causation assigned to [the settling party]").

111. *Id.* at 113-14.

112. Cypress Creek Util. Serv. Co., v. Muller, 640 S.W.2d at 865-66. In addition to the *Cypress Creek* decision regarding Article 2212a, the supreme court has announced its preference for pure comparative apportionment over a modified or partial bar approach. *Duncan*, 665 S.W.2d at 428-29. It appears the Texas Supreme Court would avoid application of Article 2212a except where expressly mandated by the statute. *Id.*

113. General Motors Corp. v. Simmons, 558 S.W.2d 855, 859 (Tex. 1977), *overruled in part*, Duncan v. Cessna Aircraft Corp., 665 S.W.2d 414, 427 (Tex. 1984); International Harvester Co. v. Zavala, 623 S.W.2d 699, 702 (Tex. App.—Houston [1st Dist.] 1981, writ ref'd n.r.e.); Hodges, *Contribution and Indemnity Among Tortfeasors*, 26 Tex. L. Rev. 150, 150-51 (1947). *See* Caterpillar Tractor Co. v. Boyett, 674 S.W.2d 782, 794 (Tex. App.—Corpus Christi 1984, no writ) (settling party must be adjudged a tortfeasor); UMC, Inc. v. Coonrod Elec. Co., 667 S.W.2d 549, 555 (Tex. App.—Corpus Christi 1983, writ ref's n.r.e.) (contribution not allowed if party not a joint tortfeasor). *See generally* Sales, *Contribution and In-*

multiple tortfeasors is premised on the concept that the tortfeasors are in *pari delicto* and thus should share in compensating the injured party.[114] On the other hand, indemnity provides that one tortfeasor is entitled to total reimbursement from another tortfeasor for all damages paid to the plaintiff.[115] Indemnity shifts the ultimate responsibility for loss from one tortfeasor to another.[116] As between two tortfeasors, indemnity therefore involves an all or nothing concept as distinguished from contribution which involves a concept of sharing or apportioning the plaintiff's damages.[117]

Contribution did not exist at common law. It is a doctrine created by statute.[118] In *General Motors Corp. v. Simmons*,[119] the Texas Supreme Court determined that the contribution statute, as reflected in Article 2212, rather than the comparative negligence statute embodied in Article 2212a, governed actions involving a strictly liable tortfeasor and a negligent third party.[120] Though noting that some jurisdictions did not apply contribution in similar situations, the court determined that pro rata contribution should apply in Texas because a strictly liable manufacturer is no more culpable than a negligent third party.[121] The court emphasized

---

demnity, *supra* note 51, at 326-31.

114. *See Simmons*, 558 S.W.2d at 859; Austin Road Co. v. Pope, 147 Tex. 430, 434-35, 216 S.W.2d 563, 565 (1949); Heil Co. v. Grant, 534 S.W.2d 916 (Tex. Civ. App.—Tyler 1976, writ ref'd n.r.e.).

115. *See* Austin Road Co. v. Pope, 147 Tex. at 435, 216 S.W.2d at 565; Strakos v. Gehring, 360 S.W.2d 787, 797 (Tex. 1962); International Harvester Co. v. Zavala, 623 S.W.2d at 702; B & B Auto Supply, Sand Pit & Trucking Co. v. Central Freight Lines, Inc., 603 S.W.2d 814, 816 (Tex. 1980); Richards Mfg. Co. v. Aspromonte, 557 S.W.2d 543, 552 (Tex. Civ. App.—Houston [1st Dist.] 1977, no writ); Hodges, *supra* note 113, at 151.

116. International Harvester Co. v. Zavala, 623 S.W.2d at 702. For a discussion of the conceptual framework of contribution and indemnity, see Sales, *Contribution and Indemnity*, *supra* note 51, at 326-31; Hodges, *supra* note 113, at 160-61.

117. *See generally* Sales, *Contribution and Indemnity*, *supra* note 51, at 326; Hodges, *supra* note 113, at 150-51. Contribution and indemnity are alternative remedies. *See* Sales, *Contribution and Indemnity*, *supra* note 51, at 340.

118. TEX. REV. CIV. STAT. ANN. art. 2212 (Vernon 1971) [hereinafter cited as Article 2212]. *See* Harville v. Anchor-Wate Co., 663 F.2d 598, 604 (5th Cir. 1981); Foster v. Ford Motor Co., 616 F.2d 1304, 1308 (5th Cir. 1980); Austin Road Co. v. Pope, 147 Tex. at 434, 216 S.W.2d at 564-65.

119. 558 S.W.2d 855 (Tex. 1977).

120. *Id.* at 862. *Accord* Foster v. Ford Motor Co., 616 F.2d at 1308; Pyramid Derrick Equip Co. v. Mason, 617 S.W.2d 727, 729 (Tex. Civ. App.—Beaumont 1981, writ ref'd n.r.e.).

121. 558 S.W.2d at 861.

that Article 2212a, the comparative negligence statute,[122] would continue to govern contribution when only negligent tortfeasors are involved.[123]

Article 2212 requires a tortfeasor to satisfy three prerequisites to be entitled to contribution from another. The tortfeasor seeking contribution must first discharge the other tortfeasor's liability to the plaintiff.[124] Second, the tortfeasor must be established as a judgment debtor through the rendition of either a contested or an agreed judgment.[125] Though an agreed judgment pursuant to a settlement becomes a final judgment, the plaintiff's claim against any non-settling tortfeasors must be released in the settlement agreement or the judgment.[126] Third, the damages paid by the tortfeasor seeking contribution must have been disproportionate to his share of the plaintiff's damages.[127] A tortfeasor seeking contribution and satisfying these three requirements is entitled to a pro rata contribution from another tortfeasor.[128]

---

122. Article 2212a. The statute provides for percentage contribution between negligent defendants. *Id.* at § (2)(b).

123. *Simmons*, 558 S.W.2d at 862; General Elec. Co. v. Schmal, 623 S.W.2d 482, 487 (Tex. App.—Texarkana 1981, writ ref'd n.r.e.); *B & B Auto Supply*, 603 S.W.2d at 816-17.

124. Iowa Mfg. Co. v. Weisman Equip. Co., 667 S.W.2d 209, 212 (Tex. App.—Austin 1983, writ ref'd n.r.e.); Lubbock Mfg. Co. v. International Harvester Co., 584 S.W.2d 908, 911 (Tex. Civ. App.—Dallas 1979, writ ref'd n.r.e.); Callihan Interests, Inc. v. Duffield, 385 S.W.2d 586, 587 (Tex. Civ. App.—Eastland 1964, writ ref'd).

125. *Iowa Mfg. Co.*, 667 S.W.2d at 212-13; Lubbock Mfg. Co. v. International Harvester Co., 584 S.W.2d at 911; Lower Neches Valley Auth. v. City of Beaumont, 392 S.W.2d 733, 736 (Tex. Civ. App.—Beaumont 1965, writ ref'd n.r.e.).

126. *See Lubbock Mfg. Co.*, 584 S.W.2d at 911-12 (contribution not allowed where non-settling party was not released from liability); Callihan Interests, Inc. v. Duffield, 385 S.W.2d at 586 (in an agreed judgment, the plaintiff released all claims against non-party joint tortfeasors). *See also* Beaumont Coca Cola Bottling Co. v. Cain, 673 S.W.2d 338, 339 (Tex. App.—Beaumont 1984, no writ) (settlement must be signed by trial court or reduced to a judgment).

127. *Iowa Mfg. Co.*, 667 S.W.2d at 212; *Lubbock Mfg. Co.*, 584 S.W.2d at 911; *Callihan Interests, Inc.*, 385 S.W.2d at 587.

128. Article 2212. Contribution could only be recovered from a party actually adjudicated as a tortfeasor. Caterpillar Tractor Co. v. Boyett, 674 S.W.2d 782, 794 (Tex. App.—Corpus Christi 1984, no writ); UMC, Inc. v. Coonrod Elec. Co., 667 S.W.2d 549, 555 (Tex. App.—Corpus Christi 1983, writ ref'd n.r.e.). Under pro rata allocation, the total amount of the plaintiff's damages is divided by the number of tortfeasors to determine each party's share of liability. For example, if three defendants are found liable to the plaintiff for damages, each defendant's pro rata share is one-third. Article 2212; Sales, *Contribution and Indemnity*, *supra* note 51, at 347-48. *Cf.* Singleton v. New York Underwriters Ins. Co., 739 F.2d 198, 200 (5th Cir. 1984) (elements also apply to contribution under Article 2212a).

In *Duncan v. Cessna Aircraft Co.*,[129] however, for any case in which at least one tortfeasor is liable under strict tort liability or for breach of warranty, the supreme court announced that comparative contribution based on each defendant's percentage share of causation rather than pro rata contribution governs.[130] The court rejected application of Article 2212 in cases involving strict tort liability.[131] The court reasoned that pro rata allocation is inconsistent with comparative causation principles.[132] Also, since Article 2212 was enacted fifty years prior to Texas' adoption of strict tort liability,[133] the legislature could not have intended for Article 2212 to apply to cases involving strict tort liability.[134] Therefore, the court expressly overruled *General Motors Corp. v. Simmons*,[135] to the extent it declared Article 2212 was applicable to strict tort liability cases.[136]

Now, in products liability cases, when at least one defendant (or perhaps a third-party defendant) is found liable on a theory other than negligence, each tortfeasor's share of liability is to be determined by the percentage of fault attributable to that tortfeasor.[137] It is the injury caused by the tortfeasor's unreasonably dangerous product, breach of warranty, or negligent conduct that is compared.[138] Under comparative causation, the trier of fact first determines the total amount of the plaintiff's injuries, and then apportions liability to each party based on the percentage of

---

129. 665 S.W.2d 414 (Tex. 1984).

130. *Id.* at 427. The court had also adopted the concept of percentage comparative causation in regard to comparing plaintiff's conduct in a case predicated on strict products liability. *Id.* For a discussion of this issue and other details of the case, refer to notes 64-86 *supra* and accompanying text.

131. 665 S.W.2d at 427.

132. *Id.*

133. The legislature enacted Article 2212 in 1917. Act of March 30, 1917, ch. 152, 1917 Tex. Gen. Laws 360. *See Duncan*, 665 S.W.2d at 427. Texas did not adopt the doctrine of strict tort liability until 1967. *Shamrock Fuel & Oil Sales*, 416 S.W.2d at 783-84; *McKisson*, 416 S.W.2d at 789.

134. *Duncan*, 665 S.W.2d at 427.

135. 558 S.W.2d 855 (Tex. 1977).

136. *Duncan*, 665 S.W.2d at 427.

137. *Id. See* Richardson v. Volkswagenwerk, 552 F. Supp. 73, 88 (W.D. Mo. 1982) (comparative fault contribution). Comparative causation is not invoked simply because the plaintiff pleads and submits issues against one or more defendants on a theory of strict liability or breach of warranty. To avoid application of Article 2212a, the plaintiff *must obtain* a finding of liability based on strict liability or breach of warranty. *Duncan*, 665 S.W.2d at 427.

138. 665 S.W.2d at 427.

the injuries which it caused.[139] Each tortfeasor is liable according to the percentage of the plaintiff's injury caused by the defective product or negligent conduct.[140] One tortfeasor is not liable for the percentage of harm caused by other tortfeasors.[141]

Despite adoption of pure comparative causation, each defendant remains jointly and severally liable for the entire amount to which the plaintiff is entitled.[142] By retaining joint and several liability, the percentage of causation attributed to the insolvent defendant is shifted to the remaining solvent defendants.[143] The court in *Duncan* justified this holding on three policy considera-

---

139. *Id.* at 427 n.8. A settling tortfeasor need not be joined as a party for purposes of determining its percentage share of causation. Acord v. General Motors Corp., 669 S.W.2d 111, 117 (Tex. 1984). Further, one Texas appellate court has suggested that under *Duncan*, misuse of a non-joined third party may also be considered in apportioning damages. Caterpillar Tractor Co. v. Boyett, 674 S.W.2d 782, 794 (Tex. App.—Corpus Christi 1984, no writ).

140. For example, the trier of fact determines the plaintiffs injuries to be $ 100,000 and apportions causation as follows:

Plaintiff 30 %
Strictly liable manufacturer 30 %
Retailer - breach of warranty 25 %
Negligent third party 15 %

The plaintiff will receive an award of damages for $ 70,000. Defendants are liable to the plaintiff accordingly: manufacturer $ 30,000, retailer $ 25,000, and negligent third party $ 15,000.

141. However, where one defendant is insolvent, the other defendants are liable for his share. Should one solvent tortfeasor pay more than his share, a right to contribution would exist against the other tortfeasors. *Duncan*, 665 S.W.2d at 429. Refer to notes 142-146 *infra* and accompanying text.

142. 665 S.W.2d at 429. *See* American Motorcycle Assn. v. Superior Court, 20 Cal. 3d 578, 588-90, 578 P.2d 899, 905-06, 146 Cal. Rptr. 182, 188-89 (1978); Dunham v. Kampman, 37 Colo. App. 233, 547 P.2d 263, 266 (1975), *aff'd*, 192 Colo. 448, 560 P.2d 91 (1977); Tucker v. Union Oil Co., 100 Idaho 590, 603 P.2d 156, 164 (1979); Seattle First Nat'l Bank v. Shoreline Concrete Co., 91 Wash. 2d 230, 588 P.2d 1308, 1313 (1978); Fitzgerald v. Badger State Mutual Cas. Co., 67 Wis. 2d 321, 227 N.W.2d 444, 449 (1975). *Cf.* Artice 2212a (2)(c) (joint and several liability applies to negligence actions except as to tortfeasors whose negligence was less than that of the plaintiff).

143. 665 S.W.2d at 429. When an insolvent defendant exists, it is unclear if a nonsettling defendant that has paid the insolvent party's share of liability may proceed against a settling defendant for contribution. *See* Palestine Contractors, Inc. v. Perkins, 386 S.W.2d 764, 771 (Tex. 1964) (stating that under Article 2212 a nonsettling defendant may seek contribution against a settling defendant). *Cf.* Cypress Creek Util. Serv. Co. v. Muller, 640 S.W.2d 860, 862 (Tex. 1982) (stating Article 2212 is silent as to contribution claims against settling tort fensors).

Since most settlement releases state that the plaintiff will "indemnify and hold harmless" the settling party, contribution against the settling party would indirectly be contribution against the plaintiff. However, in *Duncan*, the Texas Supreme Court elected not to impose on the plaintiff any of the liability attributable to an insolvent defendant. 665 S.W.2d at 429.

tions. First, the defendant's product, breach of warranty, or negligence endangered others while the plaintiff's conduct endangered only himself.[144] Second, the plaintiff is seeking recovery for physical injuries while the defendant is seeking contribution for economic loss.[145] Lastly, a solvent manufacturer is better able to spread the liability or indebtedness of the insolvent tortfeasor than is the plaintiff.[146]

In Texas, several limitations apparently foreclose submission of issues against certain parties whose conduct caused or contributed to cause the plaintiff's injuries. Generally, the negligence of the plaintiff's employer may be submitted to determine his share of liability.[147] When the plaintiff's claim arises out of an injury covered by worker's compensation insurance, it is not clear whether the employer's negligence may be considered under comparative causation.

In *Varela v. American Petrofina Co. of Texas, Inc.*,[148] the Texas Supreme Court concluded that in comparative negligence cases under 2212a, the employer's negligence could not be included in the apportionment of damages.[149] Under the Texas Worker's Compensation statute,[150] an employee is deprived of all common law rights of action against his employer.[151] The court reasoned that the exclusivity of worker's compensation precluded defen-

---

144. 665 S.W.2d at 429.

145. *Id.*

146. *Id.*

147. Foster v. Ford Motor Co., 616 F.2d 1304, 1308-09 (5th Cir. 1980); Farley v. M M Cattle Co., 529 S.W.2d 751, 754 (Tex. 1974).

148. 658 S.W.2d 561 (Tex. 1983)

149. *Id.* at 562-63. *Accord* Teakell v. Perma Stone Co., 658 S.W.2d 563, 563 (Tex. 1983); Charter Builders v. Durham, 683 S.W.2d 487 (Tex. App.—Dallas 1984, no writ); Blackwell Burner Co. v. Cerda, 644 S.W.2d 512, 520-21 (Tex. App.—San Antonio 1982, writ ref'd n.r.e.); Houston Lighting and Power Co. v. Eller Outdoor Advertising Co., 635 S.W.2d 133, 135 (Tex. App.—Houston [1st Dist.] 1982, writ ref'd n.r.e.); Texas Indus., Inc. v. Lucas, 634 S.W.2d 748, 756-57 (Tex. App.—Houston [14th Dist.] 1982), *aff'd in part and rev'd in part on other grounds*, No. C-1238 slip op. (Tex. July 11, 1984); Grove Mfg. Co. v. Cardinal Constr. Co., 534 S.W.2d 153, 156 (Tex. Civ. App.—Houston [14th Dist.] 1976, writ ref'd n.r.e.).

150. Tex. Rev. Civ. Stat. Ann. art. 8306 (Vernon Supp. 1985).

151. Paradissis v. Royal Indemnity Co., 507 S.W.2d 526, 528-29 (Tex. 1974); Bell v. Humble Oil & Refining Co., 142 Tex. 645, 647-48, 181 S.W.2d 569, 569-70 (1944); Hedgeman v. Berwind Ry. Serv. Co., 512 S.W.2d 827, 829 (Tex. Civ. App.—Houston [14th Dist.] 1974, writ ref'd n.r.e.). *See* Houston Lighting & Power Co. v. Eller Outdoor Advertising Co., 635 S.W.2d 133, 134 (Tex. App.—Houston [1st Dist.] 1982, writ ref'd n.r.e.); Cohn v. Spinks Indus., 602 S.W.2d 102, 103-04 (Tex. Civ. App.—Dallas 1980, writ ref'd n.r.e.).

dants from seeking contribution from the employer.[152] In *Foley v. Cox*,[153] a Texas appellate court declared that the rationale in *Varela* applies equally to claims for contribution under Article 2212 in a strict tort liability action. The court emphasized that a defendant's contribution claim is derivative of the plaintiff's right to recover from the employer.[154]

As an alternate approach, the compensation payment by the employer is the equivalent of a settlement and thus the employer is viewed as a settling tortfeasor for purposes of allocating damages.[155] This approach was rejected by the *Varela* court which refused to classify payment of a worker's compensation claim as a form of settlement.[156] In a strict tort liability context, however, a federal district court in *Erickson v. Harvey Hubbell, Inc.*,[157] determined that comparative causation applies to an employer covered by worker's compensation insurance.[158] In refusing to extend *Varela* to insulate submission of an employer's liability in a strict liability action, the court noted that the Texas Supreme Court in *Duncan* promulgated comparative causation to achieve efficient and even handed loss allocation. Since the most equitable solution involves a consideraton of all actors who contribute to plaintiff's injuries, the employer is considered a settling tortfeasor and his conduct is submitted to the jury.[159] Absent a Texas Supreme Court pronouncement, it is not certain whether the *Varela* rationale will be extended to the comparative causation doctrine in strict tort liability actions.

A similar issue regarding immunity of a tortfeasor is whether a defendant may seek contribution against a negligent spouse of the plaintiff. Interspousal immunity precludes one spouse from suing the other for premarital torts[160] or torts committed during mar-

---

152. 658 S.W.2d at 562-63. It was argued that allowing contribution against the employer would be forbidding a direct action by the plaintiff yet permitting an indirect one through the "back door". *But cf.* Powers, *Torts-Personal*, 38 Sw. L.J. 1, 21-24 (1984).

153. 679 S.W.2d 58 (Tex. App.—Houston [14th Dist.] 1984, no writ).

154. *Id.* at 7. *See* Thompson v. Stearns Chemical Corp., 345 N.W.2d 131, 135-36 (Iowa 1984).

155. Erickson v. Harvey Hubbell, Inc., 593 F. Supp. 1319, 1320 (N.D. Tex. 1984); Powers, *supra* note 152, at 121-24. Refer to notes 176-189 *infra* concerning settlement.

156. 658 S.W.2d at 562.

157. 593 F. Supp. 1319 (N.D. Tex. 1984).

158. *Id.* at 1320.

159. *Id.*

160. Latiolais v. Latiolais, 361 S.W.2d 252, 253 (Tex. Civ. App.—Waco 1962, writ ref'd

riage.[161] Since one spouse is precluded from suing the other, it would appear that a defendant is precluded from seeking contribution against the tortfeasor spouse.[162] There are two instances, however, when the negligence of one spouse will reduce the recovery of the injured spouse. One exception is presented when the injury occurs while an agency or joint enterprise relationship exists between the spouses. In such cases, the negligence of one spouse may be imputed to the other.[163] The second exception is applicable when the plaintiff's recovery is classified as community property. The contributory negligence of the other spouse, under these circumstances, is imputed to the plaintiff.[164] Contribution would be unnecessary because the negligence of one spouse is imputed to the injured spouse thereby reducing the defendant's liability in the form of contributory negligence.[165]

Likewise, submission of comparative causation is foreclosed by governmental immunities where the plaintiff is precluded from initiating suit against a governmental agency.[166] A tortfeasor may not seek contribution or indemnity against the United States when, for example, the plaintiff is a serviceman who is precluded from as-

---

n.r.e.).

161. Turner v. Turner, 385 S.W.2d 230, 232-33 (Tex. 1964); Nickerson v. Nickerson, 65 Tex. 281, 283 (1886). Interspousal immunity does not exist where one spouse allegedly injured the other willfully or intentionally. Bounds v. Caudle, 560 S.W.2d 925, 927 (Tex. 1977).

162. Patterson v. Tomlinson, 118 S.W.2d 645, 646 (Tex. Civ. App.—Austin 1938, writ ref'd). Interspousal immunity was incorporated into the limitations of the guest statute. TEX. REV. CIV. STAT. ANN. art. 6701 (b)(1)(a) (Vernon 1977 & Supp. 1985). *See* Pomerantz v. Rosenberg, 593 S.W.2d 815, 817 (Tex. Civ. App.—Houston [1st Dist.] 1980, no writ); Patterson v. Tomlinson, 118 S.W.2d at 646. *But see* Whitworth v. Bynum, 28 Tex. Sup. Ct. J. 549, 551 (July 10, 1985) (holding guest statute unconstitutional).

163. Wilkinson v. Stevison, 514 S.W.2d 895, 897-98 (Tex. 1974). *Cf.* Satterfield v. Satterfield, 448 S.W.2d 456, 458-60 (Tex. 1969) (application of guest statute to non-spouses).

164. Graham v. Franco, 488 S.W.2d 390, 397 (Tex. 1972); Wilkinson v. Stevison, 500 S.W.2d 549, 551 (Tex. Civ. App.—Beaumont 1973), *aff'd*, 514 S.W.2d 895 (Tex. 1974). Community property recovery would include costs of medical expenses and lost earnings, but would not include damages for pain and suffering. 488 S.W.2d at 397; Wilkinson v. Stevison, 500 S.W.2d at 551. *See generally* Ellis v. K-Lan Co., 695 F.2d 157, 162 n.7 (5th Cir. 1983).

165. *See Duncan*, 665 S.W.2d at 429.

166. City of Houston v. Selph, 356 S.W.2d 850, 851 (Tex. Civ. App.—Houston 1962, no writ). Texas governmental agencies are immune from liability except as waived by the Texas Tort Claims Act. TEX. REV. CIV. STAT. ANN. art. 6252-19 (Vernon 1970 & Supp. 1985). *See generally* Lowe v. Texas Tech Univ., 540 S.W.2d 297 (Tex. 1976). Similarly, the United States is immune from suit except as waived by the Federal Tort Claims Act. 28 U.S.C. § 1346, 2671-80 (1982) [hereinafter cited as FTCA). *See* Feres v. United States, 340 U.S. 135, 146 (1950).

serting an action under the Federal Tort Claims Act (FTCA).[167] Similarly, when the plaintiff is a longshoreman, the defendant-shipowner is precluded from seeking contribution against the United States.[168] While the particular issue has not been addressed by the Texas Supreme Court, Texas courts have consistently denied contribution against a third party otherwise immune from suit by the plaintiff.[169] Immunity differs from an employer who is a subscriber under the worker's compensation act since the plaintiff is entitled to monetary payments in the form of a settlement from the employer's insurance carrier.

When the government is sued for negligence under the FTCA, another potential problem is presented. For example, a motorist injured in a collision by an allegedly defective automobile driven by a government employee may sue the government for negligence and the vehicle manufacturer under strict tort liability. An action against the United States under the FTCA must be tried to the court[170] but the vehicle manufacturer possesses a constitutional right to trial by jury.[171] Generally this type of procedural dilemma can be remedied by a joint trial which permits the jury to decide those issues against the party possessing a right to trial by jury and the non-jury issues to be resolved by the court.[172] Under comparative causation, however, the relative percentages of causation must be assigned to each party and cannot be apportioned by both the court and the jury. Either the trial judge or the jury must make

---

167. Stencel Aero Eng'g Corp. v. United States, 431 U.S. 666, 673 (1977).

168. *See, e.g.*, Freeborn v. Upper Lakes Shipping, Ltd., 541 F. Supp. 1099, 1102-03 (W.D. Mich. 1982).

169. *E.g.*, *Varela*, 658 S.W.2d at 563; Hunter v. Fort Worth Capital Corp., 620 S.W.2d 547, 552-53 (Tex. 1981); Brown & Root, Inc. v. Rust Eng'g, 679 S.W.2d 576, 578 (Tex. App.—Texarkana 1984, writ ref'd n.r.e.); Patterson v. Tomlinson, 118 S.W.2d at 646. Refer to note 151 *supra*.

170. 28 U.S.C. § 2402 (1982). *See* United States v. Nuestadt, 366 U.S. 696, 701 n.10 (1961); Moffitt v. United States, 430 F. Supp. 34, 38-39 (E.D. Tenn. 1976); Glasspool v. United States, 190 F. Supp. 804, 807 (D. Del. 1961); Honeycutt v. United States, 19 F.R.D. 229, 230-31 (W.D. La. 1956). *See also* O'Connor v. United States, 269 F.2d 578, 585 (2d Cir. 1959). *See generally* 9 C. Wright & A. Miller, Federal Practice and Procedure § 2314 (1971) (trial must be to the court when the United States is a party).

171. *In re* N-500L Cases, 691 F.2d 15, 20-21 (1st Cir. 1982); Palmer v. United States, 652 F.2d 893, 896 (9th Cir. 1981). *See generally* 35 Tex. Jur. 2d *Jury* § 18-19, 28 (1962).

172. United States v. Yellow Cab Co., 340 U.S. 543, 555-57 (1951); Simon v. Lovgren, 368 F. Supp. 265, 269-70 (D.V.I. 1973); Englehardt v. United States, 69 F. Supp. 451, 452-53 (D. Md. 1947). *See generally* 9 C. Wright & A. Miller, Federal Practice and Procedure § 2337 (1971) (trial by court and by jury).

the ultimate determination.

In *Palmer v. United States*,[173] the plaintiff was struck by a government automobile while directing traffic around a car which was wrecked on the side of the road. The plaintiff instituted suit against the United States under the FTCA and the United States joined the driver of the wrecked car seeking indemnity.[174] The liability of the parties was to be determined in accordance with the California comparative negligence doctrine and, recognizing that contribution constituted a legal and not an equitable right, the court determined that the third party defendant was entitled to a jury trial on this issue.[175] Though the Ninth Circuit did not specifically outline the mechanics for trial, it would appear that the jury must apportion liability to uphold the defendant's right to a jury trial.

Another factor concerning contribution among tortfeasors involves the settlement by one or more tortfeasors with the plaintiff. Prior to *Duncan v. Cessna Aircraft Co.*,[176] a settling tortfeasor later adjudicated to be a joint tortfeasor in *pari delicto* with the non-settling defendant precipitated a pro rata reduction in plaintiff's recovery in proportion to the total number of tortfeasors.[177] By allowing this reduction, potential collusive settlements between the plaintiff and a single tortfeasor were deterred.[178] To prevent a

---

173. 652 F.2d 893 (9th Cir. 1981).

174. *Id.* at 895.

175. *Id.* at 896. *Accord In re* N-500L Cases, 691 F.2d 15, 20-21 (1st Cir. 1982). *Cf.* Dawson v. Contractors Transport Corp., 467 F.2d 727, 729-31 (D.C. Cir. 1972) (contribution characterized as an equitable doctrine).

176. 665 S.W.2d 414 (Tex. 1984).

177. General Motors Corp. v. Simmons, 558 S.W.2d at 861-62; Palestine Contractors, Inc. v. Perkins, 386 S.W.2d 764, 773-74 (Tex. 1964); General Elec. Co. v. Schmal, 623 S.W.2d at 487-88; Lubbock Mfg. Co. v. Perez, 591 S.W.2d 907, 923 (Tex. Civ. App.—Waco 1979, no writ); Bell Helicopter Co. v. Bradshaw, 594 S.W.2d at 535. *See* Caterpillar Tractor Co. v. Boyett, 674 S.W.2d 782, 794 (Tex. App.—Corpus Christi 1984, no writ) (settling party must be adjudicated as a tortfeasor). *Cf.* Petco Corp. v. Plummer, 392 S.W.2d 163, 166-67 (Tex. Civ. App.—Dallas 1965, writ ref'd n.r.e.). For example, if one of four defendants settle with the plaintiff but all are deemed tortfeasors, the plaintiff's recovery would be reduced 25%. *See* Armstrong v. Chambers & Kennedy, 340 F. Supp. 1220, 1248-49 (S.D. Tex. 1972), *aff'd in part and reversed in part*, 499 F.2d 263 (5th Cir. 1974), *cert. dismissed sub nom.* Monk v. Chambers & Kennedy, 423 U.S. 886 (1975). *See generally* Sales, *Contribution and Indemnity*, *supra* note 51, at 346-50.

178. In *Palestine Contractors*, the plaintiff settled with one tortfeasor for $1. The plaintiff was initially awarded a judgment of $25,500 but the amount was reduced pro rata and the non-settling tortfeasor was liable for $13,250. 386 S.W.2d at 772. *See Duncan*, 665 S.W.2d at 430.

plaintiff from recovering more than once for the same injuries,[179] however, the non-settling tortfeasors were authorized to elect a dollar credit for any settlements entered into by the plaintiff.[180] To forestall plaintiff from recovering more than the total amount of the damage award, the settling parties were not required to be adjudged tortfeasors for the dollar credit to be taken.[181]

In *Duncan v. Cessna*, the Texas Supreme Court rejected pro rata and dollar credits in favor of a percentage credit.[182] Under this approach the total judgment awarded by the jury is reduced by the percentage of causation allocated to the settling party, regardless of the amount of the settlement.[183] The pro rata credit was determined to be inconsistent with the objectives of a pure comparative apportionment system because under the pro rata scheme each party paid in proportion to the number of parties rather than on the percentage of the injury caused by each tortfeasor.[184]

The practice of credit for settlements was also viewed to be inconsistent with the theory underlying the comparative system of apportionment as the non-settling defendant's liability fluctuates according to the amount of settlement, rather than according to the percentage of injury caused.[185] Allowing a dollar credit, however, insured that a plaintiff did not receive more than one recovery.[186] Because the concept of dollar credit conflicted with the phi-

---

179. Bradshaw v. Baylor Univ., 126 Tex. 99, 104, 84 S.W.2d 703, 705 (1935), *overruled*, Duncan v. Cessna Aircraft Corp., 665 S.W.2d 414 (Tex. 1984).

180. Lubbock Mfg. Co. v. Perez, 591 S.W.2d at 923; Schering Corp. v. Giesecke, 589 S.W.2d 516, 519 (Tex. Civ. App.—Eastland 1979, writ ref'd n.r.e.); Richards Mfg. Co. v. Aspromonte, 557 S.W.2d at 549-50. *But see* Lynn v. Southwestern Elec. Power Co., 453 F. Supp. 599, 603-04 (E.D. Tex. 1978).

181. Payne v. Gould, Inc., 503 F. Supp. 1060, 1061-64 (E.D. Tex. 1980); Migues v. Nicolet Indus., 493 F. Supp. 61, 63-65 (E.D. Tex. 1980), *rev'd on other grounds*, 662 F.2d 1182 (5th Cir. 1982); Caterpillar Tractor Co. v. Boyett, 674 S.W.2d 782, 794 (Tex. App.—Corpus Christi 1984, no writ). *Cf.* Columbia Eng'g, Int'l Ltd. v. Dorman, 602 S.W.2d 72, 79 (Tex. Civ. App.—Beaumont 1980, writ ref'd n.r.e.) (discussing Article 2212a), *overruled*, Cypress Creek Util. Serv. Co. v. Muller, 640 S.W.2d 860, 866 (Tex. 1982).

182. *Duncan*, 665 S.W.2d at 430.

183. *Id. See* Acord v. General Motors Corp., 669 S.W.2d at 117 (joinder of settling party not necessary for his share of liability to be determined).

184. 665 S.W.2d at 430. The court noted that the rationale for adopting pro rata credit remained valid in so much as it deterred collusive settlements and also allowed for finality of settlement without prejudicing the rights of the non-settling defendant. *Id.* at 429-30. As noted by the court in *Duncan*, this rationale was first adopted by the court in *Palestine Contractors Inc.*, 386 S.W.2d at 772.

185. 665 S.W.2d at 430.

186. Refer to notes 179-80 *supra*.

losophy of comparative causation, the court expressly abrogated the longstanding one recovery concept in Texas.[187] A non-settling tortfeasor may no longer elect to take a dollar credit under any circumstances against the plaintiff's judgment.[188] As a result, the plaintiff benefits from a good settlement and suffers from a bad one.[189]

Indemnity, as distinguished from contribution, represents an all or nothing concept which provides that one tortfeasor is entitled to recoup from another tortfeasor any money previously paid to the plaintiff.[190] At common law, a tortfeasor was entitled to indemnity in three situations.[191] First, when one tortfeasor breached a higher degree of care than the other, he was entitled to indemnity from the tortfeasor breaching the lesser degree of care.[192] For example, in a wreck in which a common carrier breached the high degree of care owed to its passengers, and a truck driver breached his duty of reasonable care, the common carrier was entitled to obtain indemnity from the truck driver.[193] Second, a party liable under principles of respondeat superior was entitled to indemnity from his employee or servant.[194] Third, when one tortfeasor breached a duty not only to the plaintiff but also to a second

---

187. 665 S.W.2d at 430-32. The court reasoned that since the plaintiff bore the risk of bad settlements, he should likewise receive the benefit of a good settlement. Also, the non-settling tortfeasor's liability should not be affected by the settlement. Finally, the court noted that settlement dollars were not the same as damages but represented an estimate of liability with risk avoidance, trial expense, and adverse publicity being considered. *Id.* The one recovery rule was earlier abandoned in cases governed by Article 2212a. Cypress Creek Util. Serv. Co. v. Muller, 640 S.W.2d at 866-67.

188. 665 S.W.2d at 432. This may pose serious difficulties for a defendant where plaintiff pleads both negligence and strict tort liability and the jury finding is limited to negligence. Under negligence, Article 2212a governs, and defendant may elect to either submit percentage of fault or to take a credit.

189. *Id.* at 430-32.

190. *See* Austin Road Co. v. Pope, 147 Tex. at 435, 216 S.W.2d at 565; International Harvester Co. v. Zavala, 623 S.W.2d at 702; Richards Mfg. Co. v. Aspromonte, 557 S.W.2d at 551-52; Strakos v. Gehring, 360 S.W.2d at 797.

191. *See generally* Sales, *Contribution and Indemnity, supra* note 51, at 326-31.

192. Wheeler v. Glazer, 137 Tex. 341, 343-45, 153 S.W.2d 449, 451 (1941). *See* Knutson v. Morton Foods, Inc., 603 S.W.2d 805, 806 (Tex. 1980).

193. *See, e.g.*, Wheeler v. Glazer, 137 Tex. at 344, 153 S.W.2d at 451.

194. San Antonio v. Smith, 94 Tex. 266, 271-72, 59 S.W. 1109, 1111 (1900); Frantom v. Neal, 426 S.W.2d 268, 272 (Tex. Civ. App.—Fort Worth 1968, writ ref'd n.r.e.). *See* Coastal States Crude Gathering Co. v. Williams, 476 S.W.2d 339, 350 (Tex. Civ. App.—Corpus Christi 1971, writ ref'd n.r.e.) (using active-passive test). *But see* General Motors v. Simmons, 558 S.W.2d at 860 (rejecting active-passive test).

tortfeasor, the second tortfeasor was entitled to indemnity.[195] For instance, a truck owner who negligently allowed a repairman to work on a defective truck would be entitled to indemnity from the manufacturer who breached a duty to provide safe products to both the repairman and the owner.[196]

The right of common law indemnity was abrogated in cases involving multiple negligent tortfeasors under Article 2212a, by the recent case of *B & B Auto Supply, Sand Pit, & Trucking Co. v. Central Freight Lines, Inc.*[197] In *B & B*, the plaintiff was injured when Central's truck jackknifed on some clay left on the highway by B & B. Both defendants were found negligent.[198] Noting that Article 2212a was designed to apportion fault comparatively and to avoid the all or nothing result of indemnity, the court eliminated common law indemnity in cases governed by article 2212a.[199] The court, however, expressed no opinion regarding common law indemnity in strict liability cases.[200]

A tortfeasor is currently entitled to indemnity in only two situations: when the party is vicariously liable[201] and when an innocent retailer merely distributes a defective product.[202] In *Bonniwell v. Beech Aircraft Corp.*,[203] the Texas Supreme Court stated that:

> [o]nly a vestige of common law indemnity remains. In *B & B*

195. Austin Road Co. v. Pope, 147 Tex. at 435, 216 S.W.2d at 565; Bell Helicopter v. Bradshaw, 594 S.W.2d at 535; Heil Co. v. Grant, 534 S.W.2d at 927; Air Shields, Inc. v. Spears, 590 S.W.2d 574, 582 (Tex. Civ. App.—Waco 1979, writ ref'd n.r.e.); Atchison, Topeka and Sant Fe Ry. Co. v. Smith, 563 S.W.2d 660, 668 (Tex. Civ. App.—Waco 1978, writ ref'd n.r.e.). Texas courts used an "imaginary lawsuit" test where the party seeking indemnity becomes an imaginary plaintiff in a fictitous action against the other tortfeasor. *See Austin Road*, 147 Tex. at 434-35, 216 S.W.2d at 565; Foster v. Ford Motor Co., 616 F.2d at 1308; Harris v. Atchison, Topeka & Santa Fe R.R., 538 F.2d 682, 690 (5th Cir. 1976); Butler v. Henry, 589 S.W.2d 190, 193 (Tex. Civ. App.—Waco 1979, writ ref's n.r.e.).

196. Heil Co. v. Grant, 534 S.W.2d at 926.

197. 603 S.W.2d 814 (Tex. 1980). *See Cypress Creek Util. Serv. Co.*, 640 S.W.2d at 864; Thiele v. Chick, 631 S.W.2d 526, 533 (Tex. Civ. App.—Houston [1st Dist.] 1982, writ ref'd n.r.e.). In *B & B*, the court reasoned that where both tortfeasors were found negligent, the comparative aspects of Article 2212a rendered common law indemnity no longer reasonable. 603 S.W.2d at 817.

198. 603 S.W.2d at 815-16.

199. *Id.* at 817.

200. *Id.* at 818.

201. Refer to note 194 *supra* and accompanying text. *See generally* Sales, *Contribution and Indemnity*, *supra* note 51, at 327-28.

202. Indemnity would also apply to any other member of the marketing chain which merely distributed the product and was not otherwise liable. *Duncan*, 665 S.W.2d at 432.

203. 663 S.W.2d 816 (Tex. 1984).

> *Auto Supply*, we recognized the survival of common law indemnity with respect to liability of a purely vicarious nature. An analogous indemnity right survives in products liability cases to protect the *innocent* retailer in the chain of distribution. Essentially, this is all that remains of the common law doctrine of indemnity.[204]

The adoption of comparative causation does not affect the innocent retailer's right to receive indemnity from the manufacturer of the defective product when the retailer is "merely a conduit for the defective product and is not independently culpable."[205]

If the retailer or other member of the marketing chain is liable for an independent act, the retailer or other member may only seek contribution and is precluded from indemnification.[206] A retailer's right to indemnification, therefore, is dependent on establishing that it merely delivered into commerce a product that was defectively designed or manufactured by another.[207] For example, in a action by a plaintiff for injuries sustained in an automobile accident due to faulty brakes, an innocent seller would be entitled to indemnity from the mechanic or repair shop which negligently serviced the brakes, and from the strictly liable manufacturer of the defective brake system.[208]Consequently, comparative contribution applies between joint tortfeasors except when one tortfeasor is vicariously liable or was merely a conduit for the defective product.

3.04 Sole Cause

In negligence cases, the act of a codefendant, a third party, or some condition existing at the time of the accident may be asserted as the sole cause[209] of the plaintiff's injuries.[210] Sole cause

---

204. *Id.* at 819-20.

205. *Duncan*, 665 S.W.2d at 432.

206. *Id.*; Ford Motor Co. v. Russell & Smith Ford Co., 474 S.W.2d 549, 561-62 (Tex. Civ. App.—Houston [14th Dist.] 1971, no writ); International Harvester v. Zavala, 623 S.W.2d at 704; United Tractor, Inc. v. Chrysler Corp., 563 S.W.2d 850, 851 (Tex. Civ. App.—El Paso 1978, no writ).

207. Mahan Volkswagen v. Hall, 648 S.W.2d 324, 335 (Tex. App.—Houston [1st Dist.] 1982, writ ref'd n.r.e.); Thiele v. Chick, 631 S.W.2d at 532-33. *But see* Lubbock Mfg. Co. v. Perez, 591 S.W.2d at 912-913. *Cf.* United Tractor, Inc. v. Chrysler Corp., 563 S.W.2d at 851.

208. *Mahan Volkswagen*, 648 S.W.2d at 335.

209. Texas courts generally refer to this concept as "sole proximate cause" when asserted in cases predicated on negligence. When discussed in terms of all types of tort actions, this defense is more accurately charaterized as the "sole cause" defense. Refer to note

does not undertake to circumvent a defendant's duty to exercise ordinary or reasonable care; rather, the defendant introduces evidence that demonstrates that the injury producing event is solely attributable to another party's conduct or condition of the premises.[211] Since the defendant seeks to disprove causation, an essential element of the plaintiff's case, sole cause is characterized as an inferrential rebuttal defense.[212] Further, when a third party is alleged to be the sole cause of the plaintiff's injuries, the party need not be joined in the action for evidence to be admitted because the defendant is not endeavoring to impose liability on the third party.[213] This defense may not be asserted against the plaintiff;[214] and therefore, its application is limited to cases in which the sole cause is claimed to be an act of a third party or some extraneous event or condition.[215]

The defendant must plead and introduce evidence demonstrating a prima facie case of sole causation against another defendant, third party, or condition.[216] Sole cause may be asserted or pleaded by a general denial. To establish a prima facie case, the defendant must present evidence establishing a causal connection between the act of the third party or condition, and the plaintiff's

---

227 *infra.*

210. Gross v. Black & Decker, Inc., 695 F.2d 858, 861 (5th Cir. 1983); Deal v. Madison, 576 S.W.2d 409, 423 (Tex. Civ. App.—Dallas 1978, writ ref'd n.r.e.), *overruled on other grounds*, Cypress Creek Util. Serv. Co. v. Muller, 640 S.W.2d 860, 866 (Tex. 1982); Dallas Ry. & Terminal Co. v. Tucker, 207 S.W.2d 937, 938 (Tex. Civ. App.—Dallas 1948, no writ).

211. *See, e.g.*, Pride of Dallas Taxicab Co. v. Lawrence, 277 S.W.2d 169 (Tex. Civ. App.—Amarillo 1953, writ ref'd n.r.e.); Dallas Ry. & Terminal Co. v. Tucker, 207 S.W.2d 937 (Tex. Civ. App.—Dallas 1948, no writ). *Cf.* Gross v. Black & Decker, Inc., 695 F.2d at 862.

212. *See* Scott v. Atchison, Topeka and Santa Fe Ry. Co., 572 S.W.2d 273, 279 (Tex. 1978) ("act of God"); American Jet, Inc. v. Leyendecker, 683 S.W.2d 121, 126 (Tex. App.—San Antonio 1984, no writ). Transport Ins. Co. v. Liggins, 625 S.W.2d 780, 784 (Tex. App.—Fort Worth 1981, writ ref'd n.r.e.) ("act of God" and "greater hazard"). *See generally* G. Hodges, *Special Issue Submission in Texas* § 19, at 50 (1959) (sole proximate cause).

213. *See* Gross v. Black & Decker, Inc., 695 F.2d at 861; Deal v. Madison, 576 S.W.2d at 423.

214. Perma Stone Co. v. Teakell, 653 S.W.2d 483, 489 (Tex. App.—Corpus Christi), *rev'd on other grounds*, 658 S.W.2d 563 (Tex. 1983); American Jet, Inc. v. Leyendecker, 683 S.W.2d 121, 126 (Tex. App.—San Antonio 1984, no writ). Panhandle & Santa Fe Ry. Co. v. Ray, 221 S.W.2d 936, 941 (Tex. Civ. App.—Austin 1949, writ ref'd n.r.e.).

215. The proper defense concerning conduct of the plaintiff is contributory negligence. Evidence that the plaintiff caused the injury is admissible to rebut the plaintiff's proof of causation. The defendant need not assert the defense to introduce this evidence.

216. Eastman Kodak Co. v. Martin, 362 F.2d 684, 686-87 (5th Cir. 1966); Hicks v. Brown, 136 Tex. 399, 403-04, 151 S.W.2d 790, 792-93 (1941).

injury.[217]

Once the defendant has established a prima facie case, the burden of persuasion shifts to the plaintiff.[218] As an inferrential rebuttal defense, the defendant is not entitled to submission of a special issue but is entitled to a jury instruction concerning sole cause.[219] Since causation is an element of the plaintiff's cause of action, the defendant is relieved of the burden of persuasion as to sole cause.[220] The plaintiff must negate by a preponderance of the evidence that the act of a third party or an extraneous condition was not the sole cause of his injuries.[221] If the plaintiff succeeds in carrying the burden of persuasion, he has disproved any allegation of "sole cause".[222]

The Fifth Circuit, in *Gross v. Black & Decker, Inc.*,[223] was the first court to apply the sole cause defense in a strict liablility context. In *Gross*, the plaintiff's fingers were amputated upon accidental contact with an unprotected radial arm saw.[224] The plaintiff asserted liability against the manufacturer based on negligence and

---

217. *See* Hicks v. Brown, 136 Tex. at 403, 151 S.W.2d at 793; Martin v. Texaco, Inc., 726 F.2d 207, 212 (5th Cir. 1984); Webb v. Western Casualty & Surety Co., 517 S.W.2d 529, 530 (Tex. 1974). *See also* Pride of Dallas Taxicab Co. v. Lawrence, 277 S.W.2d 169, 171 (Tex. Civ. App.—Amarillo 1953, writ ref'd n.r.e.) (citing *Hicks v. Brown*) [hereinafter cited as *Pride of Dallas*].

218. *Eastman Kodak*, 362 F.2d at 686-87; *Pride of Dallas*, 277 S.W.2d at 170-71; Dallas Ry. & Terminal Co. v. Tucker, 207 S.W.2d at 938; *Hicks*, 136 Tex. at 403, 151 S.W.2d at 793.

219. *See* Scott v. Atchison, Topeka and Santa Fe Ry. Co., 572 S.W.2d 273, 279 (Tex. 1978); Select Ins. Co. v. Boucher, 561 S.W.2d 474, 479-80 (Tex. 1978); Tex. R. Civ. P. 277. *See generally* Pope and Lowerre, *The State of the Special Verdict—1979*, 11 St. Mary's L.J. 1, 20-36 (1979). A sample instruction following the submission of causation is:

> There may be more than one proximate cause of an occurrence, but there can be only one sole proximate cause. If an act or omission of any person was the sole proximate cause of an occurrence, then no act or omission of any other person could have been a proximate cause.

Texas Pattern Jury Charges 3.04 (Supp. 1973).

220. *See Dallas Ry.*, 207 S.W.2d at 938; *Pride of Dallas*, 277 S.W.2d at 171; *Hicks*, 136 Tex. at 403, 151 S.W.2d at 793.

221. *See Eastman Kodak*, 362 F.2d at 687.

222. While there can be several proximate, or producing, causes of a plaintiff's injuries, there can obviously be only one sole cause. *Pride of Dallas*, 277 S.W.2d at 171. If the plaintiff proves, as he is required, that the defendant's conduct was a proximate, or producing, cause, the defense of "sole cause" must fail. Placing the burden of proof on the defendant would serve no purpose since he will not be liable if the plaintiff fails to prove proximate, or producing, cause.

223. 695 F.2d 858 (5th Cir. 1983).

224. *Id.* at 860.

strict tort liability for failing to provide an anti-kickback device on the saw and for failing to notify users of its availability.[225] The manufacturer rebutted the claim by asserting that the sole cause of the plaintiff's injury was her employer's failure to provide or warn of the optional anti-kickback device.[226] Noting that Texas permitted the "sole proximate cause" defense in negligence actions, the court extended application of sole cause to strict products liability actions.[227]

In negligence actions, the negligence of an employer-subscriber under the Texas Worker's Compensation Act,[228] may not be submitted when the plaintiff is an employee seeking recovery for a "covered" injury.[229] In *Varela v. American Petrofina Co.*,[230] a negligent defendant was denied submission of the employer's negligence and was precluded from seeking contribution from the employer.[231] The Fifth Circuit concluded, however, that a product supplier may allege that an act of the employer constituted the *sole cause* of the employee's injuries.[232] The court reasoned that when a defendant undertakes to rebut that its product was a contributing cause of plaintiff's injuries and does not seek contribution or indemnity from the employer, the employer's immunity and the exclusivity aspects of the Worker's Compensation Act are immaterial to application of the "sole cause" issue.[233]

---

225. *Id.* at 860-61.

226. *Id.* at 861.

227. *Id.* at 861-62. The court referred to this concept as "sole cause" as opposed to "sole proximate cause" as used in negligence actions. A probable reason is that the proper causation standard in strict tort liability actions is *producing* cause, which does not require the element of foreseeability. *See* General Motors Corp. v. Hopkins, 548 S.W.2d 344, 351 (Tex. 1977), *overruled on other grounds*, Duncan v. Cessna Aircraft Corp., 665 S.W.2d 414 (Tex. 1984); Rourke v. Garza, 530 S.W.2d 794, 801 (Tex. 1975); C. A. Hoover & Son v. O. M. Franklin Serum Co., 444 S.W.2d 596, 596 (Tex. 1969); Bell Helicopter Co. v. Bradshaw, 594 S.W.2d 519, 532-33 (Tex. Civ. App.—Corpus Christi 1979, writ ref'd n.r.e.).Therefore, even if a third party is determined to be the sole proximate cause of the plaintiff's injury, the manufacturer's product may still have been a producing cause. This would necessitate a showing that an extraneous condition or act of a third party constituted the sole producing cause of the plaintiff's injury in a strict liability action.

228. Tex. Rev. Civ. Stat. Ann. art. 8306 (Vernon 1967 & Supp. 1985).

229. Varela v. American Petrofina Co. of Texas, Inc., 658 S.W.2d 561, 562-63 (Tex. 1983); Teakell v. Perma Stone Co., 658 S.W.2d 563 (Tex. 1983); Foley v. Cox, 679 S.W.2d 58, 63-64 (Tex. App.—Houston [14th Dist.] 1984, no writ).

230. 658 S.W.2d 561 (Tex. 1983).

231. *Id.* at 562-63.

232. Gross v. Black & Decker, Inc., 695 F.2d at 862.

233. *Id.* The *Varela* court had reasoned that since an employer subscribing to Workers

In *Herrera v. FMC Corp.*,[234] the court of appeals acknowledged that evidence of an employer's conduct was admissible when such conduct was alleged to be the sole cause of the employee's injuries.[235] The court stated that evidence was properly admitted which demonstrated that the employer's misuse and improper installation of a rotation swivel on a drilling unit was the sole cause of plaintiff's injuries.[236] After analyzing Texas cases which immunize employer-subscribers from contribution and indemnity, the court discussed no logical basis for excluding the sole cause defense in strict tort liability.[237]

In *First International Bank v. Roper*,[238] however, the Texas Supreme Court declined to follow the Fifth Circuit decision in *Gross v. Black & Decker, Inc.*,[239] and declared that an instruction on sole cause in an action based on strict liability constitutes reversible error.[240] In *Roper*, a three year old child was injured when she placed her hand into the "grass-catcher" opening of a lawn mower left operating by her father.[241] The manufacturer attempted to rebut causation by claiming that the father's negligence constituted the sole cause of the child's injuries.[242]

The sole cause instruction given by the trial court[243] was perceived as not only superfluous but, more importantly, it was deemed to focus undue attention or emphasis on the negligence of

---

Compensation Insurance is immune from suit by the employee, the defendant could not indirectly seek to recover through contribution. 658 S.W.2d at 563. In *Gross*, the Fifth Circuit stated that the defendant was not seeking to prove concurrent liability, but only to establish that the conduct of another party had been the sole proximate cause of the plaintiff's injuries. 695 F.2d at 862.

234. 672 S.W.2d 5 (Tex. App.—Houston [14th Dist.] 1984, no writ).

235. *Id.* at 7-8.

236. *Id.*

237. *Id.* at 8.

238. 686 S.W.2d 602 (Tex. 1985).

239. 695 F.2d 858 (5th Cir. 1983). Refer to notes 223-227 *supra* and accompanying text.

240. 686 S.W.2d at 605. *But see* Woods v. Crane Carrier Co., Inc., 28 Tex. Sup. Ct. j. 583, 585.

241. *Id.* at 285-86.

242. *Id.* at 286.

243. The instruction submitted to the jury was as follows:

> There may be more than one cause of an occurrence, but there can be only one sole cause. If an act or omission of any person not a party to the suit was the sole cause of the occurrence, then no act, omission, or product of any party to the suit could have been a cause of the occurrence.

686 S.W.2d at 603.

the parents.[244] The supreme court emphasized its approval of a single special issue concerning design defects and the accompanying instruction defining producing cause. It further stated that additional instructions which single out competing factors are tantamount to improper comments on the case.[245]

Notwithstanding *Roper*, it appears that sole cause remains a viable inferrential rebuttal defense in negligence cases.[246] It is therefore unclear whether an instruction on sole cause may be given in an action encompassing both the theories of negligence and strict products liability. This uncertainty exists because the court in *Roper* distinguished *Gross* on the basis that it was grounded both on negligence and strict products liability.[247]

Though the *Roper* opinion fails to address the effect of comparative causation, it appears that the rationale would likewise apply in a strict tort liability action governed by comparative causation.[248] The court stressed its adherence to its adopted special issue and instruction regarding producing cause, implying that the instruction will not change with the implementation of comparative causation, thereby rendering any sole cause instruction harmful error.[249] Currently, it is less than clear whether submission of a

---

244. *Id.* at 603-04. The trial was conducted prior to Duncan v. Cessna Aircraft Corp., 665 S.W.2d 414 (Tex. 1984). In cases decided subsequent to *Duncan*, parental negligence would be a defense and would entitle the defendant to a special issue regarding the conduct of the parents. Refer to subchapter 3:02 *supra*.

245. *Id.* The court relied on earlier Texas cases which held that superfluous instructions concerning defective design would be impermissible. Acord v. General Motors Corp., 669 S.W.2d 111, 113 (Tex. 1984); Fleishman v. Guadiano, 651 S.W.2d 730, 731 (Tex. 1983). Neither of these cases involved instructions concerning inferrential rebuttal defenses. The *Roper* court did not address sole cause as an inferrential rebuttal defense, but only in the context of a definitional instruction. 686 S.W.2d at 603-04.

246. *See* Brown v. Goldstein, 685 S.W.2d 640, 642-43 (Tex. 1985) (suggesting continued viability of "unavoidable accident" and "sudden emergency" in a pre-*Roper* negligence action).

247. *Roper*, 686 S.W.2d at 605. According to the court's reasoning any inferrential rebuttal instruction is superfluous and harmful error when submitted in conjunction with a definition of producing cause. Following would be the proposition that an inferrential rebuttal instruction may likewise be harmful error if submitted with a definition of proximate cause in negligence cases. This dilemma is partially created by the court's failure to address sole cause as an inferential rebuttal defense in the *Roper* opinion. *See* Brown v. Goldstein, 685 S.W.2d 640, 642-43 (Tex. 1985) (suggesting viability of inferential rebuttal instructions in a pre-*Roper* negligence action).

248. Refer to note 244 *supra*.

249. *See Roper*, 686 S.W.2d at 603-04. It should be noted that if Varela v. American Petrofina, Inc., 658 S.W.2d 561 (Tex. 1983) is extended to cases predicated on strict products liability, the conduct of an employer could not be submitted to the jury in either the

sole cause instruction when a defendant is alleged to be negligent will also constitute harmful error. It is difficult to perceive the manner in which a sole cause inferential rebuttal issue impinges on the standard definition and instruction for a defective product.[250]

3.05 CONTRACTUAL DEFENSES

A manufacturer or seller often includes, in a contract for the sale of a product a disclaimer of any warranties, express or implied, or a clause limiting or waiving certain designated remedies.[251] The issue generally presented is whether a contractual disclaimer or an exculpation clause is legally cognizable as a defense for the seller in an action based on strict tort liability.[252] Disclaimers and exculpation clauses are contractual, or *ex contractu*, in nature while strict tort liabilty is *ex delicto*.[253] The *Restatement (Second) of Torts* rejects the validity of contractual disclaimers and exculpation clauses in strict tort liability actions.[254] The *Restatement* provides:

> The consumer's cause of action does not depend upon the validity of his contract with the person from whom he acquires the product, and it is not affected by any disclaimer or other agreement, whether it be between the seller and his immediate buyer, or attached to and accompanying the product into the consumer's hands.[255]

---

form of a special issue or an instruction. Refer to subchapter 3:03, notes 147-159 *supra* and accompanying text.

250. It could be argued that sole cause could be submitted by allowing the jury to allocate causation to all causes supported by evidence. If 100% fault was not allocated to the third party deemed to be the sole cause, then the percentage would be disregarded similar to insolvent defendants. Refer to notes 142-43 *supra* and accompanying text.

However, such an approach may be viewed as inconsistent with the traditional classification of sole cause as an inferential rebuttal defense. Refer to note 219 *supra* and accompanying text.

251. For a distinction between these two contractual defenses, see Comment, *Consumer Claims for Personal Injuries Under the Texas UCC Implied Warranties - Defenses*, 16 HOUS. L. REV. 165, 188-191 (1978).

252. *See generally* Comment, *supra* note 251, at 165-66; Parker, *The Warranty Disclaimer v. Manufacturer's Products Liability*—Sterner Aero AB v. Page Airmotive, Inc.: *Did the Tenth Circuit Bury the Disclaimer Alive?*, 10 TULSA L.J. 612 (1975).

253. *Ex contractu* actions are those arising from a contract, while *ex delicto* actions arise from a tortious act. BLACK'S LAW DICTIONARY 508, 509 (5th ed. 1979).

254. § 402A comment m.

255. *Id.*

In the landmark case of *Vandermark v. Ford Motor Co.*,[256] the California Supreme Court addressed the applicability of contractual defenses in a strict tort liability context.[257] In *Vandermark*, the plaintiff initiated suit against the seller based on strict tort liability for injuries sustained when the brakes on her automobile malfunctioned.[258] The seller asserted that the warranty clause in the contract of sale limited the seller's liability.[259] Recognizing that contractual liability and strict tort liability are distinct actions,[260] the court concluded that the contractual limitation was immaterial. A seller is subject to strict tort liability based not on contract, but on the socioeconomic policy of risk distribution.[261]

The Texas Supreme Court has not specifically addressed whether contractual disclaimers constitute a defense to strict products liability.[262] The issue was addressed by an intermediate appellate court in *McMillen Feeds, Inc. v. Harlow*.[263] The plaintiff sought to recover damages for the death of a flock of turkeys caused by unwholesome feed.[264] The plaintiff's cause of action was based on strict liability for breach of an implied warranty of fitness.[265] The court, relying on the *Vandermark* rationale, rejected

256. 61 Cal. 2d 256, 391 P.2d 168, 37 Cal. Rptr. 896 (1964).

257. *Id.* at 263, 391 P.2d at 172, 37 Cal. Rptr. at 900.

258. *Id.*

259. *Id.*

260. *Id. Vandermark* implicitly supports the division of strict liability as *ex delicto* and disclaimers as *ex contractu* in nature.

261. *Id. See* Dement v. Olin-Mathieson Chemical Corp., 282 F.2d 76, 81 (5th Cir. 1960). Policy differences have not prevented the applicability of disclaimers and exculpatory provisions which attempt to limit liability in negligence actions. *See, e.g.*, Jig The Third Corp. v. Puritan Marine Ins. Underwriters Corp., 519 F.2d 171, 176 (5th Cir. 1975); Southwest Forest Indus. v. Westinghouse Elec. Corp., 422 F.2d 1013, 1020 (9th Cir.), *cert. denied*, 400 U.S. 902 (1970); Allright, Inc. v. Elledge, 515 S.W.2d 266, 268 (Tex. 1974); Sherwin-Williams Co. v. Perry Co., 424 S.W.2d 940, 948-51 (Tex. Civ. App.—Austin), *writ ref'd n.r.e. per curiam*, 431 S.W.2d 310 (Tex. 1968). However, these clauses are strictly construed. *See Jig The Third Corp.*, 519 F.2d at 177; Fireman's Fund Ins. Co. v. Commercial Standard Ins. Co., 490 S.W.2d 818, 822-23 (Tex. 1972). *See* K & S Oil Well Serv. v. Cabot Corp., 491 S.W.2d 733, 737-39 (Tex. Civ. App.—Corpus Christi 1973, writ ref'd n.r.e.). The clauses will not be allowed where the parties are in unequal bargaining positions. Allright, Inc. v. Elledge, 515 S.W.2d at 268; Crowell v. Housing Authority ,495 S.W.2d 887, 889 (Tex. 1973).

262. *See* Mid Continent Aircraft Corp. v. Curry County Spraying Serv., 572 S.W.2d 308, 310 (Tex. 1978) (dicta) (contractual disclaimers are enforced less readily in cases predicated on strict tort liability).

263. 405 S.W.2d 123 (Tex. Civ. App.—Austin 1966, writ ref'd n.r.e.).

264. *Id.* at 125.

265. *Id.* This theory was the predecessor to strict tort liability adopted in *Shamrock Fuel & Oil Sales*, 416 S.W.2d at 783-85, and *McKisson*, 416 S.W.2d at 789. *See* Greenman v.

the defendant's argument that the contractual disclaimer of warranties barred recovery, reiterating that strict liability is not affected by contractual defenses.[266] The invalidity of contractual disclaimers in actions predicated on strict tort liability reflects the prevailing view today.[267]

While contractual disclaimers and exculpation clauses are not valid defenses to strict tort liability actions, they are valid in limiting claims based on breach of a contractual warranty.[268] A disclaimer may be valid as a defense when it is made in writing or in the form of an "as is" sale.[269] To be effective, the disclaimer must be disclosed to the plaintiff, and when communicated in a writing, it must be conspicuous.[270] It also appears that to disclaim a particular warranty, the type of warranty disclaimed must be referred to specifically.[271]

Since economic loss is generally governed by the Uniform Commercial Code[272] and product related personal injury actions by strict tort liability,[273] the characterization of the type of loss incurred by the plaintiff directly affects the availability of contrac-

---

Yuba Power Prods, 59 Cal. 2d 57, 60-61, 377 P.2d 897, 900-01, 27 Cal. Rptr. 697, 700-01 (1963). *See generally* Putman v. Erie City Mfg. Co., 338 F.2d 911 (5th Cir. 1964) (discussing predicted transition from warranty of fitness implied by law to strict tort liability).

266. 405 S.W.2d at 137.

267. *See, e.g.*, Sterner Aero AB v. Page Airmotive, Inc., 499 F.2d 709, 713 (10th Cir. 1974); Diedrich v. Wright, 550 F. Supp. 805, 809 (N.D. Ill. 1982); *Vandermark*, 61 Cal. 2d at 263, 391 P.2d at 172, 37 Cal. Rptr. at 900; Sipari v. Villa Olivia Country Club, 63 Ill. App. 3d 985, 380 N.E.2d 819, 823 (1978). *Cf.* Airlift Int'l, Inc. v. McDonnell Douglas Corp., 685 F.2d 267, 269-70 (9th Cir. 1982).

268. Two Rivers Co. v. Curtiss Breeding Serv., 624 F.2d 1242, 1252 (5th Cir. 1980), *cert. denied*, 450 U.S. 920 (1981); *Mid Continent Aircraft Corp.*, 572 S.W.2d at 313. However, a limitation for personal injuries under the U.C.C. is "prima facie unconscionable." TEX. BUS. & COM. CODE ANN. § 2.719(c) (Tex. UCC) (Vernon 1968). For an overview of the application of these defenses in breach of warranty actions, see generally Comment, *supra* note 251, at 188-89; Weintraub, *Disclaimer of Warranties and Limitation of Damages for Breach of Warranty Under the UCC*, 53 TEX. L. REV. 60, 65-67 (1974).

269. *Two Rivers Co.*, 624 F.2d at 1252; *Mid Continent Aircraft Corp.*, 572 S.W.2d at 313.

270. *See Two Rivers Co.*, 624 F.2d at 1252; Willoughby v. Ciba-Geigy Corp., 601 S.W.2d 385, 388 (Tex. Civ. App.—Beaumont 1979, no writ).

271. 624 F.2d at 1252. *See* Walter Baxter Seed Co. v. Rivera, 677 S.W.2d 241, 245 (Tex. App.—Corpus Christi 1984, writ ref'd n.r.e.). The *Two Rivers* court stated that in order to disclaim an implied warranty of merchantability, the disclaimer must refer specifically to merchantability. *Id. See* TEX. BUS. & COM. CODE ANN. §§ 2.314, 2.316 (Tex. UCC) (Vernon 1968).

272. Nobility Homes of Texas, Inc. v. Shivers, 557 S.W.2d 77, 79-80 (Tex. 1977).

273. *See* § 402A.

tual defenses.[274] In *Two Rivers Co. v. Curtiss Breeding Service*,[275] the Fifth Circuit recognized four separate and distinct types of property loss in Texas. A user or consumer may seek recovery for (1) personal injury to the user or damage to the user's property; (2) economic loss caused by the defective product; (3) economic loss limited to damage to the product itself; or (4) damage to the product itself but also involving damage to other property.[276]

The Texas Supreme Court announced that strict tort liability is not appropriate as a cause of action seeking damages to the product itself,[277] or economic loss caused by the defective product, including consequential damages.[278] On the other hand, injury to the ultimate user or his property is clearly under the aegis of strict tort liability.[279] In *Signal Oil & Gas Co. v. Universal Oil Products*,[280] the Texas Supreme Court confronted a hybrid situation in which a plaintiff suffered damage to the product itself as well as physical damage to his other property.[281] A fire generated by a defective heater spread and damaged other surrounding property of the plaintiff.[282] Noting that section 402A specifically established a

---

274. *Mid Continent Aircraft Corp.*, 572 S.W.2d at 310-311. Refer to notes 268-271 *supra* and accompanying text.

275. 624 F.2d 1242 (5th Cir. 1980), *cert. denied*, 450 U.S. 920 (1981).

276. *Id.* at 1245-47. The plaintiff was seeking recovery for the reduction in market value of his herd due to defective bull semen. Only 22 of the 98 calves were actually inseminated with the defective semen. Because the losses incurred to the herd were considered economic, the doctrine of strict tort liability was declared inapplicable. *Id.* at 1247. *Cf.* Edgar, *Product Liability in Texas*, 11 TEX. TECH L. REV. 23, 33-41 (1979).

277. 572 S.W.2d at 311-13. *See* Delta Air Lines, Inc. v. Douglas Aircraft Co., 238 Cal. App. 2d 95, 103, 47 Cal. Rptr. 518, 523-24 (1965). *See also* Airlift Int'l, Inc. v. McDonnell Douglas Corp., 685 F.2d at 269.

278. Nobility Homes of Texas, Inc. v. Shivers, 557 S.W.2d at 79-80. *See* Alaska v. Tyonek Timber, Inc., 680 P.2d 1148, 1151-52 (Alaska 1982) (economic loss not recoverable in strict tort liability); Hawkins Constr. Co. v. Matthews Co., 190 Neb. 546, 209 N.W.2d 643, 653 (1973), *overruled in part*, National Crane Corp. v. Ohio Steel Tube Co., 213 Neb. 782, 332 N.W.2d 39, 43-44 (1983). *Cf.* Garcia v. Texas Instruments, Inc., 610 S.W.2d 456, 462-63 (Tex. 1980) (consequential damages recoverable when classified as personal injuries). Economic loss may be described as that loss which is not physical damage to property or person. Two Rivers Co. v. Curtiss Breeding Serv., 624 F.2d at 1246. As defined by the Texas Supreme Court, economic loss encompasses damage based on insufficient product value, including out of pocket expenses, loss of the bargain, and indirect loss, such as loss of profits. Nobility Homes of Texas v. Shivers, 557 S.W.2d at 78 n.1 (quoting Note, *Economic Loss in Products Liability Jurisprudence*, 66 COLUM L. REV. 917, 918 (1966)).

279. § 402A. *See McKisson*, 416 S.W.2d at 789-90 (adopting § 402A).

280. 572 S.W.2d 320 (Tex. 1978).

281. *Id.* at 324-25.

282. *Id.* at 322-23, 325.

remedy for damage to the consumer's other property, the court concluded that strict tort liability was applicable to this type of damage.[283] Further, damage to the product itself is considered property damage under strict tort liability rather than economic loss governed by the *U.C.C.*, when the defective product also causes collateral property damage.[284]

Other contractual defenses of notice and privity simply are inapplicable in a strict tort liability context;[285] nor are they defenses to U.C.C. actions bases on breach of implied warranty to recover economic losses.[286] Strict tort liability in the guise of a breach of warranty implied by operation of law was first enumerated in Texas as a matter of public policy.[287] Under this progenitor of strict tort liability, privity of contract was rejected as a valid limitation.[288] These defenses are rejected primarily because their origin is contractual in nature which is entirely distinct from the *ex delicto* nature of strict tort liability.[289] It appears, therefore, that the contractual defenses of disclaimer of warranties and limitation of remedies, are inapplicable to actions in which the plaintiff seeks recovery for personal injuries or damage to property.[290] These limitations retain their validity in actions seeking recovery of economic

---

283. *Id.* at 325.

284. *Id.*

285. McLain v. Hodge, 474 S.W.2d 772, 776 (Tex. Civ. App.—Waco 1971, writ ref'd n.r.e.); Procter & Gamble Mfg. Co. v. Langley, 422 S.W.2d 773, 779 (Tex. Civ. App.—Dallas 1967, writ dism'd). *See* Fisher v. Gate City Steel Corp., 190 Neb. 699, 211 N.W.2d 914, 917 (1973). *See also* Garcia v. Texas Instruments, Inc., 610 S.W.2d 456, 465 (Tex. 1980) (privity not required for personal injury action based on breach of implied warranty). *See generally* Comment, *supra* note 251, at 187-93 (discussing application to action for breach of implied warranty).

286. Nobility Homes of Texas, Inc. v. Shivers, 557 S.W.2d 77, 81 (Tex. 1977). Privity of contract is a defense to an action based on breach of express warranty. Texas Processed Plastics, Inc. v. Gray Enters., Inc., 592 S.W.2d 412, 415 (Tex. Civ. App.—Tyler 1979, no writ).

287. Jacob E. Decker & Sons, Inc. v. Capps, 139 Tex. 609, 612-22, 164 S.W.2d 828, 829-34 (1942). *Accord* Putman v. Erie City Mfg. Co., 338 F.2d 911, 912 (5th Cir. 1964); Dement v. Olin-Mathieson Chem. Corp., 282 F.2d 76, 81 (5th Cir. 1960).

288. 139 Tex. at 620-21, 164 S.W.2d at 831-32; Putman v. Erie City Mfg. Co., 338 F.2d at 912. *See* Fisher v. Gate City Steel Corp., 190 Neb. 699, 211 N.W.2d 914, 917 (1973).

289. Fisher v. Gate City Steel Corp., 211 N.W.2d at 917; McCormack v. Hankscraft Co., 278 Minn. 322, 340, 154 N.W.2d 488, 500 (1967); *see* Vandermark v. Ford Motor Co., 61 Cal. 2d at 263, 391 P.2d at 172, 37 Cal. Rptr. at 900.

290. Simply because a plaintiff has suffered this type of loss, his cause of action is not limited to strict liability. *See* Garcia v. Texas Instruments, Inc., 610 S.W.2d at 461-62. *See also Two Rivers Co.*, 624 F.2d at 1247; *Signal Oil & Gas Co.*, 572 S.W.2d at 325.

loss, including damage only to the product itself.

Product suppliers, particularly lessors, frequently seek to obtain a contractual indemnity from the purchaser or lessee indemnifying the product supplier against any liability resulting from or arising out of the use of a defective product. Such an agreement which provides that the purchaser or user will indemnify and hold harmless the seller is generally valid if it specifies that the indemnity is for a defective product.[291] For example, a lease provision which provides that the lessee agrees to pay for all claims and damages arising from equipment *defects* is sufficient to indemnify the lessor.[292]

When a product supplier seeks a contractual indemnity from strict tort liability actions, it is vital that the agreement specifically provide for indemnity caused by or resulting from product defects.[293] In *UMC, Inc. v. Coonrod Electric Co.*,[294] a strictly liable seller of a defective conveyor system sought contractual indemnity from a subcontractor which had performed the electrical wiring.[295] The court refused to enforce the indemnity agreement since it only provided for indemnity against negligence and did not provide for indemnity against defects in the product.[296] Similarly in *Southwestern Electric Power Co. v. Martin Equipment Co.*,[297] an agreement to indemnify the seller against damages arising on account of personal injuries was insufficient because it failed to specifically include a provision covering strict liability for a defective product.[298]

---

291. Safway Scaffold Co. v. Safway Steel Prods., Inc., 570 S.W.2d 225, 227-28 (Tex. Civ. App.—Houston [1st Dist.] 1978, writ ref'd n.r.e.); Garcia v. Sky Climber, Inc., 470 S.W.2d 261, 269-70 (Tex. Civ. App.—Houston [1st Dist.] 1971, writ ref'd n.r.e.). *See* Air & Pump Co. v. Almaquer, 609 S.W.2d 309, 313 (Tex. Civ. App.—Corpus Christi 1980, no writ). If properly drafted it would appear that a product supplier could contractually preclude indemnity to an innocent retailer. Foley v. Cox, 679 S.W.2d 58, 63 (Tex. App.—Houston [14th Dist.] 1984, no writ).

292. Garcia v. Sky Climber, Inc., 470 S.W.2d at 269-70.

293. UMC, Inc. v. Coonrod Elec. Co., 667 S.W.2d 549, 555 (Tex. App.—Corpus Christi 1983, writ ref'd n.r.e.); Air & Pump Co. v. Almaquer, 609 S.W.2d 309, 313 (Tex. Civ. App.—Corpus Christi 1980, no writ) (dicta); Southwestern Elec. Power Co. v. Martin Equip. Co., 593 S.W.2d 428, 430 (Tex. Civ. App.—Dallas 1980, no writ); Rourke v. Garza, 511 S.W.2d 331, 341 (Tex. Civ. App.—Houston [1st Dist.] 1974), *aff'd*, 530 S.W.2d 794 (Tex. 1975); Garcia v. Sky Climber, Inc., 470 S.W.2d at 269-70.

294. 667 S.W.2d 549 (Tex. App.—Corpus Christi 1983, writ ref'd n.r.e.).

295. *Id.* at 552.

296. *Id.* at 555.

297. 593 S.W.2d 428 (Tex. Civ. App.—Dallas 1980, no writ).

298. *Id.* at 430.

Since indemnity agreements are used by a seller to avoid future potential payment of damages for which it is liable, the provisions are strictly construed.[299] To be effective, the provisions must be clear and unequivocal.[300] Further, the provision must be sufficiently conspicuous in the purchase or lease agreement to place the indemnitor on fair notice of his obligation to indemnify the seller or lessor.[301] Also, the indemnity agreement must be executed by the purchaser or a duly authorized representative, and the agreement to indemnify must be based on actual negotiations and discussions between the contracting parties.[302]

3.06 Limitations

Another area of defense involves statutory limitations on the time for instituting suit in actions predicated on strict tort liability. Generally tort actions in Texas are governed by the two-year statute of limitations.[303] It appears that this statute governs actions predicated on strict tort liability.

In *Puretex Lemon Juice, Inc. v. S. Riekes & Sons of Dallas*,[304] a Texas appellate court declared that the two-year statute of limitations applied to actions based on breach of implied warranty of suitability,[305] a progenitor of the current strict tort liability action

---

299. K & S Oil Well Serv. v. Cabot Corp., 491 S.W.2d 733, 737 (Tex. Civ. App.—Corpus Christi 1973, writ ref'd n.r.e.). *See* Rourke v. Garza, 530 S.W.2d 794, 804 (Tex. 1975) (contracts indemnifying one against distribution of defective products should be scrutinized in the same manner as those indemnifying one against his own negligence).

300. Fireman's Fund Ins. Co. v. Commercial Standard Ins. Co., 490 S.W.2d 818, 822 (Tex. 1972); Safway Scaffold Co. v. Safway Steel Prods., 570 S.W.2d 225, 228 (Tex. Civ. App.—Houston [1st Dist.] 1978, writ ref'd n.r.e.); K & S Oil Well Serv. v. Cabot Corp., 491 S.W.2d at 737.

301. Goodyear Tire & Rubber Co. v. Jefferson Constr. Co., 565 S.W.2d 916, 919-20 (Tex. 1978); Safway Scaffold Co. v. Safway Steel Prods., 570 S.W.2d at 228; Rourke v. Garza, 511 S.W.2d at 342; K & S Oil Well Serv. v. Cabot Corp., 491 S.W.2d at 738. *See* Air & Pump Co. v. Almaquer, 609 S.W.2d 309, 313 (Tex. Civ. App.—Corpus Christi 1980, no writ) (dicta).

302. Rourke v. Garza, 530 S.W.2d at 804-05; Haws & Garrett Gen. Contractors, Inc. v. Gorbett Bros. Welding Co., 480 S.W.2d 607, 610 (Tex. 1972).

303. Tex. Rev. Civ. Stat. Ann. art. 5526(4) (Vernon Supp. 1985). The statute provides in pertinent part: "There shall be commenced and prosecuted within two years after the cause of action shall have accrued, and not afterward, all actions or suits in the court of the following description: . . . 4. Action for injury done to the person of another." *Id.*

304. 351 S.W.2d 119 (Tex. Civ. App.—San Antonio 1961, writ ref'd n.r.e.).

305. *Id.* at 120.

in Texas.[306] After Texas adopted section 402A, the Fifth Circuit applied the Texas two-year statute of limitations to a strict tort liability action in *Roman v. A. H. Robins, Co.*[307] The plaintiff instituted suit against a drug manufacturer more than two years after his eye condition initially developed. The court affirmed an instructed verdict for the manufacturer on the basis that the action was barred by the Texas two-year statute of limitations.[308]

Adoption of the U.C.C. in Texas presented an additional statute of limitations for actions predicated on breach of contractual implied warranties.[309] Prior to 1968, Texas courts applied the two-year statute of limitations to actions seeking recovery for injuries caused by breach of implied warranty.[310] The applicability of the U.C.C. to actions seeking recovery for product-related injuries was first addressed in *Morton v. Texas Welding and Manufacturing Co.*[311] In *Morton*, employees of the purchaser sued the seller of a propane truck for injuries incurred when the truck exploded.[312] The court noted that the U.C.C. contemplated recovery for personal injury for breach of implied warranty[313] and concluded that Texas would apply the four year limitation prescribed in section 2.725 to such actions.[314]

The Texas Supreme Court addressed the issue of whether the U.C.C. applied to personal injury actions in *Garcia v. Texas Instruments, Inc.*[315] The plaintiff, an employee of the purchaser of

---

306. *See Shamrock Fuel & Oil Sales*, 416 S.W.2d at 783-85; *McKisson*, 416 S.W.2d at 789. *Cf.* Greenman v. Yuba Power Prods., 59 Cal. 2d 57, 63, 377 P.2d 897, 900-01, 27 Cal. Rptr. 697, 700-01 (1962). *See generally* Putman v. Erie City Mfg. Co., 338 F.2d 911 (5th Cir. 1964) (discussing predicted transition from warranty of fitness implied by law to strict tort liability).

307. 518 F.2d 970, 971 (5th Cir. 1975).

308. *Id. See* Timberlake v. A. H. Robins Co., 727 F.2d 1363, 1366 (5th Cir. 1984); Cleveland v. Square-D Co., 613 S.W.2d 790, 792 (Tex. Civ. App.—Houston [14th Dist.] 1981, no writ).

309. Tex. Bus. & Com. Code Ann. § 2.725 (Tex. UCC) (Vernon 1968).

310. Metal Structures Corp. v. Plains Textiles, Inc., 470 S.W.2d 93, 98 (Tex. Civ. App.—Amarillo 1971, writ ref'd n.r.e.); Richker v. United Gas Corp., 436 S.W.2d 215, 218 (Tex. Civ. App.—Houston [1st Dist.] 1968, writ ref'd n.r.e.); Thrift v. Tenneco Chemicals, Inc., 381 F. Supp. 543, 546-47 (N.D. Tex. 1974).

311. 408 F. Supp. 7 (S.D. Tex. 1976).

312. *Id.* at 8-9.

313. Section 2.715 provides that consequential damages may include "injury to person or property proximately resulting from any breach of warranty". Tex. Bus. & Com. Code Ann. § 2.715(b)(2) (Tex. UCC) (Vernon 1968).

314. 408 F. Supp. at 11.

315. 610 S.W.2d 456, 462 (Tex. 1980).

sulfuric acid, sustained personal injuries when a container of the acid fractured.[316] The court determined (1) that a cause of action for personal injuries resulting from a breach of implied warranty is provided by the U.C.C.[317] and (2) that privity is not required to maintain the cause of action.[318]

The court determined that since the Code authorized recovery of consequential damages caused by the seller's breach of warranty including "injury to person or property proximately resulting from any breach of warranty," the Code's four-year limitation period applied.[319] Despite the necessity of separating strict liability from *ex contractu* actions under the Code,[320] the court announced that the two theories were not mutually exclusive and both were applicable in an action seeking damages for personal injuries.[321] The court also noted that a majority of jurisdictions apply section 2.725 to breach of warranty actions for personal injuries.[322]

It is generally recognized that the two-year statute of limitations commences when the plaintiff discovers or in the exercise of reasonable care should have discovered his injury.[323] In *Puretex*

---

316. *Id.* at 457.

317. *Id.* at 461-62.

318. *Id.* at 465.

319. *Id. See* Rothe v. Ford Motor Co., 531 F. Supp. 189, 193-94 (N.D. Tex. 1981); Cleveland v. Square-D Co., 613 S.W.2d 790, 791-92 (Tex. Civ. App.—Houston [14th Dist.] 1981, no writ).

320. *See* Nobility Homes of Texas, Inc. v. Shivers, 557 S.W.2d 77, 80 (Tex. 1977); Mid Continent Aircraft Corp. v. Curry County Spraying Serv., 572 S.W.2d 308, 312 (Tex. 1978).

321. *Garcia*, 610 S.W.2d at 461. *See* Two Rivers Co. v. Curtiss Breeding Serv., 624 F.2d 1242, 1247 (5th Cir. 1980) (dicta), *cert. denied*, 450 U.S. 920 (1981); Signal Oil and Gas Co. v. Universal Oil Prods., 572 S.W.2d 320, 325 (Tex. 1978); Hawkeye Security Ins. Co. v. Ford Motor Co., 199 N.W.2d 373, 381-82 (Iowa 1972); Redfield v. Mead, Johnson, & Co., 266 Or. 273, 512 P.2d 776, 777-778 (1973); Williams v. West Penn Power Co., 467 A.2d 811, 818 (1983). The *Garcia* court rejected defendant's arguments that at common law personal injury actions for breach of warranty lie in tort, strict liability in tort eliminated the need for resort to breach of warranty causes of action, and that strict liability abrogated the cause of action because common law and Code remedies are identical. 610 S.W.2d at 458. *Contra* Austin v. Ford Motor Co., 86 Wis. 2d 628, 273 N.W.2d 233, 240 (1979) ("It is inappropriate to bring an action for breach of warranty where a tort remedy is sought").

322. 610 S.W.2d at 460. *See e.g.*, Ayala v. Joy Mfg. Co., 580 F. Supp. 521, 524 (D. Colo. 1984); Berry v. G. D. Searle & Co., 56 Ill. 2d 548, 309 N.E.2d 550, 556 (1974); Williams v. West Penn Power Co., 467 A.2d at 818. *Cf.* Reid v. Volkswagen of America, Inc., 575 F.2d 1175, 1176 (6th Cir. 1978) *But Cf.* Thomas v. Heinrich Equip. Corp., 563 F. Supp. 152, 156 (D. Kan. 1983); Smith v. Cessna Aircraft Co., 571 F. Supp. 433, 436-37 (M.D.N.C. 1983).

323. Timberlake v. A. H. Robins Co., 727 F.2d 1363, 1364-65 (5th Cir. 1984); Fusco v. Johns-Manville Prods. Corp., 643 F.2d 1181, 1183 (5th Cir. 1981); Roman v. A. H. Robins Co., 518 F.2d at 971-72; Strickland v. Johns-Manville Int'l Corp., 461 F. Supp. 215, 217-18

Lemon Juice, Inc. v. S. Riekes & Sons of Dallas,[324] the plaintiff sought to recover for damage to its lemon juice which was contaminated by defective bottle caps.[325] However, the action was commenced more than two years after the sale of the bottle caps.[326] The court of appeals held that in a strict liability action for breach of an implied warranty, the statute of limitations commenced when the buyer either discovered or should have discovered the injury caused by the defective bottle caps.[327]

After Texas adopted section 402A, several Fifth Circuit cases recognized that the discovery rule applies in actions based on strict tort liability.[328] In *Roman v. A. H. Robins Co.*,[329] the court concluded that the statute of limitations commenced when the plaintiff discovered or should have discovered her injuries were caused by the allegedly defective drug.[330] The plaintiff had been informed by the attending physician almost five years prior to instituting suit that her eye difficulties were probably caused by an allergic reaction to the drug she was taking.[331] Though the action would have been barred irrespective of the discovery rule, the Fifth Circuit emphasized that discovery of the injury was the critical inquiry for commencement of limitations.[332]

In *Timberlake v. A. H. Robins Co.*,[333] the plaintiff instituted an action predicated partly on strict tort liability against the manufacturer of an intrauterine device (IUD) for injuries allegedly caused by the device.[334] The suit was instituted more than three years after her doctor had informed her that her problems were

---

(S.D. Tex. 1978); Allen v. Ortho Pharmaceutical Corp., 387 F. Supp. 364, 366 (S.D. Tex. 1974); Puretex Lemon Juice, Inc., v. S. Riekes & Sons of Dallas, Inc., 351 S.W.2d at 121-22. *But see* Metal Structures Corp. v. Plains Textiles, Inc., 470 S.W.2d at 98.

324. 351 S.W.2d 119 (Tex. Civ. App.-San -Antonio 1961, writ ref'd n.r.e.).

325. *Id.* at 120.

326. *Id.* at 121.

327. *Id.* at 121-22.

328. Timberlake v. A. H. Robins Co., 727 F.2d at 1365; Fusco v. Johns-Manville Prods. Corp., 643 F.2d at 1183; Roman v. A. H. Robins Co., 518 F.2d at 971-72.

329. 518 F.2d 970 (5th Cir. 1975).

330. *Id.* at 971.

331. *Id.*

332. *Id.* The court relied on Texas malpractice cases in determining that Texas would apply the discovery rule. *Id. See* Nichols v. Smith, 507 S.W.2d 518 (Tex. 1974); Hays v. Hall, 488 S.W.2d 412 (Tex. 1972); Gaddis v. Smith, 417 S.W.2d 577 (Tex. 1967).

333. 727 F.2d 1363 (5th Cir. 1984).

334. *Id.* at 1364.

caused by the IUD.[335] Since the doctor had informed the plaintiff of the cause of her injuries, the statute of limitations barred both the plaintiff's claims based on negligence and strict tort liability.[336] The court concluded that the plaintiff's cause of action accrued when she discovered or should have discovered the injury and its cause in fact.[337] Once the plaintiff discovered that the defendant's product caused her injuries, the court specifically refused to toll the limitations period until the plaintiff further discovered, or should have discovered, that the defendant's conduct may have been wrongful.[338]

Similarly, in *Mann v. A. H. Robins Co.*,[339] the plaintiff used an IUD for a year and a half until 1972 when she was diagnosed to have endometriosis which necessitated undergoing a total hysterectomy. Plaintiff claimed that she did not discover that the defendant's product caused her injuries until 1982.[340] Reaffirming its earlier position in *Timberlake*, the Fifth Circuit concluded that the discovery rule applies to toll the statute of limitations until the cause of action accrued, which was when the plaintiff discovered or reasonably should have discovered the *cause in fact* of her injury.[341] Likewise a significant majority of jurisdictions apply the discovery rule in actions based on strict tort liability.[342]

---

335. *Id.* The plaintiff was fitted with the IUD in May of 1974 and wore the device four years before experiencing adverse effects in 1978. At that time the device was removed and plaintiff underwent a hysterectomy as a result of an acute pelvic inflammatory disease. *Id. Cf.* Hines v. Tenneco Chemicals, Inc., 546 F. Supp. 1229, 1234-35 (S.D. Tex. 1982), *aff'd*, 728 F.2d 729 (5th Cir. 1984) (plaintiff must have discovered or had an opportunity to discover the particular injury which was the subject of the lawsuit).

336. 727 F.2d at 1366. *See* Fusco v. Johns-Manville Prods. Corp., 643 F.2d at 1183-84.

337. 727 F.2d at 1365. *Accord* Woodruff v. A. H. Robins Co., 742 F.2d 228, 229-230 (5th Cir. 1984); Mann v. A. H. Robins Co., 741 F.2d 79, 81-82 (5th Cir. 1984). For cases addressing applicability of a worker's compensation statute to toll limitations, *compare* Strickland v. Johns-Manville Int'l Corp., 461 F. Supp. at 218 (state worker's compensation) *with* Fusco v. Johns-Manville Prods. Corp., 643 F.2d at 1184 (federal worker's compensation claim).

338. 727 F.2d at 1365. The plaintiff had argued that, although her physician had informed her that the IUD caused her injuries, she did not learn until four months prior to instituting suit that the defendant may have been negligent in its manufacture and sale of the IUD. *Id.* at 1364.

339. 741 F.2d 79 (5th Cir. 1984).

340. *Id.* at 80.

341. *Id.* at 81-82. *Accord* Woodruff v. A. H. Robins Co., 742 F.2d at 229-30.

342. *See generally*, Comment, *The Last Vestige of the Citadel—Products Liability: Accrual Time of Statutes of Limitation Under Strict Liability in Tort and Under the Uniform Commercial Code*, 2 HOFSTRA L. REV. 721, 744-45 (1974).

Commencement of the U.C.C. statute of limitations presents a more difficult problem.[343] Section 2.725 provides that "[a] cause of action accrues when the breach occurs, regardless of the aggrieved party's lack of knowledge of the breach. A breach of warranty occurs when tender of delivery is made . . ."[344] While the language of section 2.725 ostensibly rejects the discovery rule, some jurisdictions have suggested that limitations should not commence at the time of delivery in an action for personal injuries.[345] The first court to address this issue in Texas was the United States District Court in *Morton v. Texas Welding & Manufacturing Co.*[346] The plaintiff was injured when a truck, owned by his employer, exploded.[347] The plaintiff instituted his cause of action more than four years after the truck was sold to his employer but less than four years after he sustained an injury.[348] The court reaffirmed that the discovery rule was based on sound policy and unchanged by the U.C.C. Following the rationale of *Puretex*, the court held that the statute commenced when the injury occurred.[349]

The Texas Supreme Court has not yet been confronted with this issue. In *Garcia v. Texas Instruments, Inc.*,[350] the supreme court alluded in an ambiguous manner to the commencement provision of section 2.725(b).[351] The plaintiff instituted suit approximately three years and eight months after sustaining an acid burn *injury* in the course of his employment.[352] The court specifically mentioned the date of injury and the date on which Garcia filed

---

343. *See generally* Comment, *The UCC Statute of Limitations' Conflict with the Equitable Rule of Discovery in Texas*, 15 TEX. TECH L. REV. 417 (1984); Note, *Garcia v. Texas Instruments: Another Hybrid Child is Born*, 34 BAYLOR L. REV. 67 (1982).

344. U.C.C. § 2.725(b).

345. *See* Parish v. B. F. Goodrich Co., 395 Mich. 271, 235 N.W.2d 570, 573 (1975); Mendel v. Pittsburgh Plate Glass Co., 25 N.Y.2d 340, 346-47, 253 N.E.2d 207, 211, 305 N.Y.S.2d 490, 495-96, (1969) (dissenting opinion). *Cf.* Victorson v. Bock Laundry Mach. Co., 37 N.Y.2d 395, 399-400, 335 N.E.2d 275, 276, 373 N.Y.S.2d 39, 40-41 (1975) (overruling *Mendel* as to strict liability only). Under the U.C.C., the limitation period could run before a plaintiff ever possessed a cause of action. *Id.* Some jurisdictions have legislatively changed the tender of delivery rule in cases of personal injury. *See* ALA. CODE § 7-2-725(2) (1975); ME. REV. STAT. ANN. tit. 11, § 2-725 (1964 & West Supp. 1983-84).

346. 408 F. Supp. 7 (S.D. Tex. 1976).

347. *Id.* at 8-9.

348. *Id.* at 10.

349. *Id.* at 11.

350. 610 S.W.2d 456 (Tex. 1980).

351. *See generally* Note, *supra* note 343, at 77.

352. 610 S.W.2d at 457.

suit, but the date for sale varied from eighteen days to six months prior to the date of injury.[353] After first determining that a cause of action for personal injuries existed under the U.C.C., the court declared that the action was not time barred, noting that Garcia filed suit approximately three years and eight months after the *sale* of the acid to his employer.[354] Because the court never specifically identified the date of sale, it is impossible to determine which date was considered critical to commencement of the limitations period.

Several other courts have concluded that the four-year statute of limitations commences on *tender of delivery*.[355] In *Clark v. DeLaval Separator Corp.*,[356] the Fifth Circuit, following the literal language of section 2.725, declared that the statute of limitations accrues upon tender of delivery, regardless of the plaintiff's lack of knowledge.[357] *Clark* involved not a claim for personal injuries but one for economic losses sustained by the plaintiff in his dairy business.[358] In *Southerland v. Northeast Datsun,*[359] a Texas appellate court, however, endorsed the Fifth Circuit interpretation reflected in *Clark*.[360]

Recently, in *Timberlake v. A. H. Robins Co.*,[361] the Fifth Circuit applied the tender of delivery rule to bar a claim for personal injuries allegedly caused by a defective IUD.[362] Relying on the ambiguous dictum in *Garcia v. Texas Instruments*, the court con-

---

353. *Id.*

354. *Id.* at 465.

355. *Timberlake*, 727 F.2d at 1367; Clark v. DeLaval Separator Corp., 639 F.2d 1320, 1324-25 (5th Cir. 1981); Ayala v. Joy Mfg. Co., 580 F. Supp. at 524; Tolen v. A. H. Robins Co., 570 F. Supp. 1146, 1153 (N.D. Ind. 1983); Mendel v. Pittsburgh Plate Glass Co., 25 N.Y.2d 340, 344-45, 253 N.E.2d 207, 209-10, 305 N.Y.S.2d 490, 493-94 (1969), *overruled in part*, Victorson v. Bock Laundry Mach. Co., 37 N.Y.2d 395, 399-400, 335 N.E.2d 275, 276, 373 N.Y.S.2d 39, 40-41 (1975) (only as to actions in strict tort liability); Williams v. West Penn Power Co., 460 A.2d 278, 284, *aff'd in part and rev'd in part*, 467 A.2d 811 (1983); Southerland v. Northeast Datsun, Inc., 659 S.W.2d 889, 892 (Tex. App.—El Paso 1983, no writ).

356. 639 F.2d 1320 (5th Cir. 1981).

357. *Id.* at 1324-25. An exception is where a warranty explicitly extends to future performance of the product. In such cases, the discovery rule applies. U.C.C. § 2.725(b). *See* Iowa Mfg. Co. v. Joy Mfg. Co., 669 P.2d 1057, 1060 (Mont. 1983). An implied warranty cannot "explicitly" extend to the products future performance. Clark v. DeLaval Separator Corp., 639 F.2d at 1325; Southerland v. Northeast Datsun, Inc., 659 S.W.2d at 892.

358. 639 F.2d at 1322.

359. 659 S.W.2d 889 (Tex. App.—El Paso 1983, no writ).

360. *Id.* at 892.

361. 727 F.2d 1363 (5th Cir. 1984).

362. *Id.* at 1367.

cluded that Texas adheres to the tender of delivery rule for U.C.C. breach of implied warranty actions.[363] Under the tender of delivery rule, the statute of limitations would apparently commence no later than upon insertion of the IUD or purchase by the initial retail consumer.[364]

Still another Texas appellate court has held that Section 2.725 commences with tender of delivery. In *Fitzerald v. Caterpillar Tractor Co.*,[365] a plaintiff sued the seller and manufacturer of a forklift over six years after the forklift had been sold to the plaintiff's employer.[366] Though suit had been filed within four years of the injury, the Court stated that the express language of Section 2.725 must be followed as any other interpretation would alter or add a meaning not included by the legislature.[367] Currently, because *Southerland* and *Fitzgerald* represent the only Texas court pronouncements on this issue, it is not completely clear whether Texas will apply the the tender of delivery rule for commencing the U.C.C. statute of limitations.

Some jurisdictions have enacted statutes of repose in the area of tort liability.[368] Statutes of repose are similar to statutes of limitations but differ in that a statute of repose commences when the product is manufactured or sold.[369] Therefore, a statute of repose provides an ultimate cutoff date for instituting suit. Since a statute of repose may commence prior to the date of injury, a plaintiff's

---

363. *Id.* Refer to notes 350-355 *supra* and accompanying text. *Cf.* Nelson v. Krusen, 678 S.W.2d 918, 922-23 (Tex. 1984) (limiting application of discovery rule unconstitutional violation of open courts provision). However, in non-malpractice personal injury actions, section 2.725 is not the only statute of limitations. *See* TEX. REV. CIV. STAT. ANN. art. 5526(4) (Vernon Supp. 1985).

364. *See, e.g., Timberlake*, 727 F.2d at 1364, 1367; O'Brien v. Eli Lilly & Co., 668 F.2d 704, 711 (3d Cir. 1981); Tolen v. A. H. Robins Co., 570 F. Supp. 1146, 1153 (N.D. Ind. 1983); Patterson v. Her Majesty Indus., 450 F. Supp. 425, 428-31 (E.D. Pa. 1978).

365. 683 S.W.2d 162 (Tex. App.—Fort Worth 1985, no writ).

366. *Id.* at 163.

367. *Id.* at 166.

368. *E.g.*, ARIZ. REV. STAT. ANN. § 12-551 (West 1982); CONN. GEN. STAT. ANN. § 52-577 (West Supp. 1984); FLA. STAT. ANN. § 95.031(2) (1982); IND. CODE § 33-1-1.5-5 (Supp. 1981); OR. REV. STAT. § 30.905(1) (1977); UTAH CODE ANN. § 78-15-3 (1977).

369. *See* McGovern, *The Variety, Policy and Constitutionality of Product Liability Statutes of Repose*, 30 AM. U.L. REV. 579, 586-87 (1981). For an overview of varying definitions of a statute of repose, see *id.* at 582-87. *See generally* Phillips, *An Analysis of Proposed Reform of Products Liability Statutes of Limitations*, 56 N.C.L. REV. 663 (1978); Massery, *Date-of-Sale Statutes of Limitation—A New Immunity for Product Suppliers*, 1977 INS. L.J. 535.

cause of action conceivably could be barred before it actually accrues.[370]

Two principle rationales have been advanced in support of statutes of repose. The first is the lack of reliability and availability of evidence after an extended period of time.[371] The other recognizes that individuals must be permitted to plan their affairs with a degree of certainty unfettered by the disruptive burden of unknown potential liability after expiration of an unreasonably extended period of time.[372]

Many jurisdictions have enacted statutes of repose covering medical malpractice and architectural liability, as well as products liability.[373] Texas has not yet adopted a statute of repose applicable to strict tort liability. The legislature, however, has enacted a ten-year statute of repose for actions instituted against registered or licensed engineers or architects involved in designing, planning or inspecting of construction.[374]

3.07 Offensive Collateral Estoppel

Generally, collateral estoppel is characterized as issue preclusion, barring relitigation of an ultimate issue of fact that has been actually litigated in a prior suit and which was essential to the judgment in the prior suit.[375] Collateral estoppel is distinguished from res judicata on the basis that res judicata bars claims that were or should have been brought in the previous cause of action,

---

370. *See* Dworkin, *Product Liability of the 1980s: "Repose is Not the Destiny" of Manufacturers*, 61 N.C.L. Rev. 33, 43 (1982); McGovern, *supra* note 368, at 586-87; McGovern, *The Status of Statutes of Limitations and Statutes of Repose in Product Liability Actions: Present and Future*, 16 Forum 416, 418 (1980). *Cf.* Nelson v. Krusen, 678 S.W.2d 918, 922-23 (Tex. 1984) (medical malpractice).

371. Johnson v. Star Mach. Co., 270 Or. 694, 700-01, 530 P.2d 53, 56 (1974). *See* Prokolkin v. General Motors Corp., 170 Conn. 289, 365 A.2d 1180, 1186 (1976).

372. Johnson v. Star Mach. Co., 270 Or. at 701, 530 P.2d at 56.

373. McGovern, *supra* note 369 at 587-88. Concerning the constitutionality of statutes of repose, see Dworkin, *supra* note 370, at 53-64; McGovern, *supra* note 369, at 600-02.

374. Tex. Rev. Civ. Stat. Ann. art. 5536a (Vernon Supp. 1985). For cases upholding the validity of art. 5536a, see Brown v. M. W. Kellogg Co., 743 F.2d 265, 268-69 (5th Cir. 1984); Hill v. Forest & Cotton, Inc., 555 S.W.2d 145 (Tex. Civ. App.—Eastland 1977, writ ref'd n.r.e.).*Cf.* Nelson v. Krusen, 678 S.W.2d 918, 922-23 (Tex. 1984).

375. Bonniwell v. Beech Aircraft Corp., 663 S.W. 816, 818 (Tex. 1984); Van Dyke v. Boswell, O'Toole Davis, & Pickering, 28 Tex. Sup. Ct. J. 457, 459 (June 5, 1985); Wilhite v. Adams, 640 S.W.2d 875 (Tex. 1982); Benson v. Wanda Petroleum Co., 468 S.W.2d 361, 362 (Tex. 1971).

while collateral estoppel precludes relitigation of specific issues determined in a different cause of action.[376]

Collateral estoppel may not be asserted against anyone who was not a party, or in privity with a party, to the prior suit in which the issue of fact was determined.[377] Further, some jurisdictions adhere to a rule that the party asserting collateral estoppel must have been a party to the prior suit. This requirement is characterized as mutuality of parties.[378] Where the mutuality requirement has been completely abrogated,[379] a plaintiff may assert as offensive collateral estoppel a finding obtained in a prior suit by a different plaintiff against the same defendant.[380]

Collateral estoppel assumes a significant posture in strict tort liability cases when the plaintiff is authorized to assert as conclusive a prior finding against a product supplier.[381] For example, if a plaintiff establishes that defendant's product as designed or marketed is unreasonably dangerous, and this issue is essential to the final adjudication of the suit, plaintiffs in other actions may, under limited circumstances, prevent the manufacturer from relitigating

---

376. Parklane Hosiery Co. v. Shore, 439 U.S. 322, 326 n.5 (1979); Van Dyke v. Boswell, O'Toole Davis & Pickering, 28 Tex. Sup. Ct. J. at 459; Bonniwell v. Beech Aircraft Corp., 663 S.W.2d 816, 818 (Tex. 1984). *See* Comment, *The Future of Offensive Collateral Estoppel in Texas*, 35 BAYLOR L. REV. 291, 292-93 (1983).

377. Blonder-Tongue Laboratories, Inc. v. University of Ill. Found., 402 U.S. 313, 328-29 (1971); Benson v. Wanda Petroleum Co., 468 S.W.2d at 363; Windmill Dinner Theatre of Dallas, Inc. v. Hagler, 582 S.W.2d 585, 586-87 (Tex. Civ. App.—Dallas 1979, writ dism'd); Olivarez v. Bradway Hardware, Inc., 564 S.W.2d 195, 198-99 (Tex. Civ. App.—Corpus Chrisit 1978, writ ref'd n.r.e.).

378. *E.g.*, Goodson v. McDonough Power Equip., Inc., 2 Ohio St. 3d 193, 443 N.E.2d 978, 987 (1983).

379. Parklane Hosiery Co. v. Shore, 439 U.S. 322, 327-31 (1979); Blonder Tongue Laboratories, Inc. v. University of Ill. Found., 402 U.S. at 325-27.

380. Walsh v. United States, 520 F. Supp. 377, 381 (N.D. Tex. 1981) (tax proceedings). *See* Sun Towers, Inc. v. Heckler, 725 F.2d 315, 322 n.7 (5th Cir. 1984), *cert. denied*, 105 S. Ct. 100 (1985); Charles J. Arndt, Inc. v. City of Birmingham, 748 F.2d 1486, 1494 n.9 (11th Cir. 1984) (eminent domain); RESTATEMENT (SECOND) OF JUDGMENTS § 29 comment *d*, illustration 2 (1982). *See generally* Comment, *The Impacts of Defensive and Offensive Assertion of Collateral Estoppel by a Nonparty*, 35 GEO. WASH. L. REV. 1010, 1032-49 (1967); Note, *Collateral Estoppel: The Demise of Mutuality*, 52 CORNELL L.Q. 724, 724 (1967).

381. The two most noteworthy areas where the issue of offensive collateral estoppel has arisen involves suits against drug and asbestos manufacturers. *See generally*, Erlenbach, *Offensive Collateral Estoppel and Products Liability: Reasoning with the Unreasonable*, 14 ST. MARY'S L.J. 19, 33-49 (1982). Collateral estoppel may also be invoked offensively in jurisdictions requiring mutuality of parties. In this situation, the doctrine does not have the far reaching effect of non-mutual offensive collateral estoppel because both plaintiff and defendant were parties to the prior action.

the issue of whether the product design or marketing is unreasonably dangerous.[382]

In evaluating the legal impact of offensive collateral estoppel, federal common law must be separated from the law in Texas. Federal courts sitting in diversity cases apply the federal law of collateral estoppel when the prior judgment was in a federal court.[383] Likewise, under the *Erie* doctrine, a federal court will apply state law when the prior judgment was rendered by a state court.[384] Under Texas law, the plaintiff must establish three elements to invoke collateral estoppel. The plaintiff must establish that: (1) the identical fact issue presented in the subsequent action was fully and fairly litigated in the prior action; (2) the fact issue sought to be precluded was essential to the original judgment; and (3) the parties litigating the issue were "cast" as adversaries in the original action.[385] Texas courts have emphasized that the issues in the two suits must be identical.[386] Though Texas courts have not

---

382. *See, e.g.*, Flatt v. Johns Manville Sales Corp., 488 F. Supp. 836 (E.D. Tex. 1980); Mooney v. Fibreboard Corp., 485 F. Supp. 242 (E.D. Tex. 1980).

383. Seven Elves, Inc. v. Eskenazi, 704 F.2d 241, 243 (5th Cir. 1983); Hardy v. Johns-Manville Sales Corp., 681 F.2d 334, 337-38 (5th Cir. 1982); Southern Pacific Transp. Co. v. Smith Material Corp., 616 F.2d 111, 115 (5th Cir. 1980); Aerojet-General Corp. v. Askew, 511 F.2d 710, 716-17 (5th Cir.), *cert. dismissed*, 423 U.S. 908 (1975); Mooney v. Fibreboard Corp., 485 F. Supp. at 245-46. *See* Flatt v. Johns Manville Sales Corp., 488 F. Supp. at 839; RESTATEMENT (SECOND) OF JUDGMENTS § 87 (1982). *But see* Amader v. Johns-Manville Corp., 541 F. Supp. 1384, 1385 (E.D. Pa. 1982); McCarty v. Johns-Manville Sales Corp., 502 F. Supp. 335, 338-39 (S.D. Miss. 1980).

384. *See* Lee v. City of Peoria, 685 F.2d 196, 198-99 (7th Cir. 1982); Kuehn v. Garcia, 608 F.2d 1143 (8th Cir. 1979), *cert. denied*, 445 U.S. 943 (1980). *See generally* RESTATEMENT (SECOND) OF JUDGMENTS § 86 comment c (1982).

385. *Bonniwell*, 663 S.W.2d at 818; Van Dyke v. Boswell, O'Toole, Davis, & Pickering, 28 Tex. Sup. Ct. J. at 459 (June 5, 1985); Benson v. Wanda Petroleum Co., 468 S.W.2d at 362. *See* Wilhite v. Adams, 640 S.W.2d at 876; Gilbert v. Fireside Enter., 611 S.W.2d 869, 871 (Tex. Civ. App.—Dallas 1980, no writ). *See also Bonniwell*, 663 S.W.2d at 820-21 (McGee J., dissenting) (agreeing as to "elements" of collateral estoppel). *See generally* RESTATEMENT (SECOND) OF JUDGMENTS § 38 comment a (1982) (codefendants may be considered as adversaries)

386. *See* Martin v. United States Trust Co., 690 S.W.2d 300, 308 (Tex. App. ___ Dallas 1985, no writ) (accuracy of accounts); Tobbon v. State Farm Mut. Auto. Ins. Co., 616 S.W.2d 243, 246-47 (Tex. Civ. App.—San Antonio 1981, writ ref'd n.r.e.) (misrepresentation in release). *See also* Drescher v. Hoffman Motor Corp., 585 F. Supp. 555, 558 (D. Conn. 1984) (issue of plaintiff's contributory negligence not precluded because second case involved different legal standards). *Compare* Williams v. Laurence-David, Inc., 271 Or. 712, 723, 534 P.2d 173, 177-78 (1975) (no evidence presented to show product came from same case or lot) *with* Flatt v. Johns Manville Sales Corp., 488 F. Supp. at 841 (applying federal law) (any product containing asbestos is defective whether it is a cement pipe or insulation).

determined the extent to which the issues must be identical in a strict tort liability action, it appears the same rationale applies so that the defect at issue in the later action must be identical in nature, character, and time to the defect in the identical product in the prior action.[387] Further, it appears that to preclude relitigation of causation, it must be established that the defect caused the same type of injury and in the same manner that was found in the prior action.[388] Even when the issues are the same, some jurisdictions have concluded that if newly discovered evidence is presented, collateral estoppel should be disallowed because it would frustrate a full and fair litigation of the issue.[389]

While the issue presented in both cases may have been resolved in the prior action, the plaintiff must establish that the resolution of the issue was essential to the prior judgment.[390] In *Bonniwell v. Beech Aircraft Corp.*,[391] defendant Beech Aircraft (Beech) sought indemnity against codefendants Metroflight, Inc. (Metro) and Shawnee Airlines Inc. (Shawnee).[392] In a prior action against these three defendants, the jury had apportioned comparative negligence 75% to Metro and 25% to Shawnee.[393] Arguing that this finding was conclusive on its claim for indemnity, Beech sought to assert collateral estoppel against Metro and Shawnee based on the jury finding of negligence in the previous action.[394] The Texas Supreme Court rejected Beech's claim for indemnity on the basis that the determination of the comparative negligence issue was not essential to the prior judgment.[395] The court stated

---

387. *See generally* Erlenbach, *supra* note 381, at 27-28.

388. *See* Vincent v. Thompson, 50 A.D.2d 211, 377 N.Y.S.2d 118, 125-26 (1975). *See also* Amader v. Johns-Manville Corp., 541 F. Supp. at 1386-87 (applying Pennsylvania law).

389. Ezagui v. Dow Chemical Corp., 598 F.2d 727, 732 (2d Cir. 1979); United States v. United Air lines, Inc., 216 F. Supp. 709, 728 (E.D. Wash. 1962); Vincent v. Thompson, 377 N.Y.S.2d at 127.

390. *Bonniwell*, 663 S.W.2d at 818; Benson v. Wanda Petroleum Co., 468 S.W.2d at 362; Van Dyke v. Boswell, O'Toole, Davis & Pickering, 28 Tex. Sup. Ct. J. at 460.

391. 663 S.W.2d 816 (Tex. 1984).

392. *Id.* at 817. Metro was the owner and operator of the airplane which crashed, fatally injuring the plaintiff's husband. The airplane was manufactured by Beech and sold to Metro by Shawnee. *Id.*

393. *Id.* In the prior action, the jury found Beech free from liability for negligence or strict liability. While the comparative negligence of Shawnee and Metro was submitted to the jury, Beech was denied contribution or indemnity since the issues were moot due to the absence of Beech's liability. *Id.*

394. *Id.* Note that Beech was attempting to assert *offensive* collateral estoppel.

395. *Id.* at 817-18.

that the only essential determination in the prior action was the absence of Beech's liability to the plaintiff.[396] Since Beech could not seek contribution under the comparative negligence statute,[397] the issue comparing Beech's negligence was not essential to the determination of comparative negligence for contribution purposes.[398]

Collateral estoppel may not be asserted against anyone not a party, or in privity with the party to the previous action.[399] Generally, a party is in privity with another who was party to the prior judgment if the parties "have such an identity of interest that the party to the [prior] judgment represented the same legal right."[400] Courts have recognized, however, that a blackletter definition or absolute standard of privity does not automatically apply in cases involving collateral estoppel.[401] For instance, in actions based on strict tort liability, a retailer is not in privity with a manufacturer when the only relationship involves the retailer's sale of the identical product in the chain of distribution.[402] Privity requires more than an interest in the outcome of the litigation; the second party's interest must be fully and adequately represented by the party to the first action.[403]

Despite Texas' adherence to the privity requirement, mutuality of parties is no longer necessary to invoke defensive collateral

---

396. *Id.* at 818. The court stressed that Beech's negligence had not been considered in a comparative negligence context since Beech was not found to be a joint tortfeasor. *Id.* Collateral estoppel could not be applied against Bonniwell who was not a party to the prior action. *Id.* at 819.

397. Article 2212a.

398. *Id.* at 818-19. The dissenting judge disputed this part of the majority's opinion. He acknowledged that collateral estoppel could not be applied against Bonniwell, but felt that the determination of liability as between the defendants had been fully and fairly litigated. *Id.* at 822 (McGee J., dissenting). *Cf.* RESTATEMENT (SECOND) OF JUDGMENTS § 38 comment a, illustration 2 (1982).

399. *Id.* at 818; Benson v. Wanda Petroleum Co., 468 S.W.2d at 363; Windmill Dinner Theater Inc. v. Hagler, 582 S.W.2d at 586-87. This requirement is based on a due process rationale that a party is entitled to his day in court before a previous judgment may operate against him. *Benson*, 468 S.W.2d at 363.

400. *Benson*, 468 S.W.2d at 363; Olivarez v. Broadway Hardware, Inc., 564 S.W.2d at 199.

401. 468 S.W.2d at 363.

402. *See, e.g.*, Olivarez v. Broadway Hardware, Inc., 564 S.W.2d at 199-200.

403. *Benson*, 468 S.W.2d at 363. *See Bonniwell*, 663 S.W.2d at 819; Hardy v. Johns-Manville Sales Corp., 681 F.2d at 340 (approving of *Benson* view of privity) (federal law). *See also* Olivarez v. Broadway Hardware, Inc., 564 S.W.2d at 199 (dicta) (suggesting participation in defense of prior action may constitute privity).

estoppel.[404] In *Hardy v. Fleming*,[405] a doctor was allowed to assert a plea of collateral estoppel against the plaintiff, even though the doctor was not a party to the previous judgment against the plaintiff.[406] This position has been consistently reaffirmed by Texas courts.[407] It is unclear, however, whether collateral estoppel may be asserted offensively. In *Bonniwell v. Beech Aircraft Corp.*,[408] a Texas appellate court allowed the first offensive use of collateral estoppel between parties to the prior action.[409] The supreme court determined, however, that the issue decided was not essential to the prior judgment.[410] Since the court did not reverse the use of offensive collateral estoppel, the issue of whether Texas courts will permit parties to assert collateral estoppel offensively remains unanswered.[411]

While Texas courts have been reluctant to apply offensive collateral estoppel, the doctrine has been applied with frequency by federal courts. In *Parklane Hosiery Co. v. Shore*,[412] the United

---

404. Hardy v. Fleming, 553 S.W.2d 790, 792 (Tex. Civ. App.—El Paso 1977, writ ref'd n.r.e.); Tobbon v. State Farm Mut. Auto. Ins. Co., 616 S.W.2d at 246; Windmill Dinner Theater v. Hagler, 582 S.W.2d at 586; Olivarez v. Broadway Hardware, Inc., 564 S.W.2d at 198-99.

405. 553 S.W.2d 790 (Tex. Civ. App.—El Paso 1977, writ ref'd n.r.e.).

406. *Id.* at 792-93. *See Benson*, 468 S.W.2d at 363-64. In *Benson*, the court disallowed collateral estoppel against a non-party to the prior action, making no mention of any mutuality requirement. *Id. Cf.* Standage Ventures, Inc. v. State, 114 Ariz. 480, 562 P.2d 360, 364 (1977) (defensive collateral estoppel); Ryan v. New York Tel. Co., 62 N.Y.2d 494, 467 N.E.2d 487, 493, 478 N.Y.S.2d 823, 829 (1984) (defensive collateral estoppel).

407. *See* Tobbon v. State Farm Mut. Auto. Ins. Co., 616 S.W.2d at 246; Windmill Dinner Theater v. Hagler, 582 S.W.2d at 586; Olivarez v. Broadway Hardware, Inc., 564 S.W.2d at 198-99.

408. 633 S.W.2d 553 (Tex. App.—Houston [14th Dist.] 1982), *rev'd on other grounds*, 663 S.W.2d 816 (Tex. 1984).

409. *Id.* at 558. The decision of the appellate court was originally affirmed by the Supreme Court. Bonniwell v. Beech Aircraft Corp., 26 Tex. Sup. Ct. J. 259 (March 16, 1983), *withdrawn*, 663 S.W.2d 816 (Tex. 1984). No Texas court has allowed the use of *non-mutual* offensive collateral estoppel.

410. *Bonniwell*, 663 S.W.2d at 818-19. Refer to notes 391-98 *supra* and accompanying text.

411. In *Bonniwell*, Beech was a party to the previous action and therefore was accorded its "day in court". 663 S.W.2d at 817. No Texas court has addressed the issue of offensive collateral estoppel where the plaintiff was a non-party. Two federal district courts have stated that they believe Texas would allow offensive collateral estoppel. Hardy v. Johns-Manville Sales Corp., 509 F. Supp. 1353, 1361 (E.D. Tex. 1981), *rev'd*, 681 F.2d 334 (5th Cir. 1982); Mooney v. Fibreboard Corp., 485 F. Supp. 242, 248 (E.D.Tex. 1980). *See* Hossler v. Barry, 403 A.2d 762, 766 (Me. 1979) (allowing offensive collateral estoppel); Beall v. Doe, 315 S.E.2d 186, 187-90 (S.C. 1984) (allowing offensive collateral estoppel).

412. 439 U.S. 322 (1979).

States Supreme Court first recognized the offensive use of collateral estoppel.[413] The court declared that collateral estoppel was applicable where the defendant was afforded a "full and fair opportunity" to litigate its claims.[414] Federal law continues to require that the party against whom collateral estoppel is asserted must have been a party, or in privity with a party, to the previous judgment.[415] The doctrine of offensive collateral estoppel has had an important effect in the area of products liability, particularly in asbestos and drug related litigation.[416]

With the exception of privity, federal law governing collateral estoppel requires three elements. The party seeking to invoke collateral estoppel must establish that "(1) the issue to be concluded is identical to that involved in the prior action; (2) in the prior action the issue was actually litigated'; and (3) the determination made of the issue in the prior action must have been necessary and essential to the resulting judgment."[417] These requirements have been specifically adopted by the Fifth Circuit[418] and are very similar to those required under Texas law with the exception that the federal rule does not require parties to be "cast" as adversaries.[419]

Undoubtedly, identity of issues has generated the most controversy in the application of offensive collateral estoppel. While federal law has clearly established that the issue to be precluded in

---

413. *Id.* at 332-33. The Supreme Court had previously abandoned the requirement of mutuality in Blonder-Tongue Laboratories, Inc. v. University of Ill. Found., 402 U.S. at 349-50 (defensive use of collateral estoppel). Nonmutual offensive collateral estoppel cannot be asserted against the government. United States v. Mendoza, 104 S. Ct. 568, 574 (1984). *See* Sun Towers, Inc. v. Heckler, 725 F.2d 315, 322 (5th Cir. 1984), *cert. denied*, 105 S. Ct. 100 (1985) (citing *Mendoza*). *Cf.* United States v. Stauffer Chemical Co., 104 S. Ct. 575, 579-80 (1984) (permitting mutual defensive collateral estoppel).

414. 439 U.S. at 332-33.

415. Blonder-Tongue Laboratories, Inc. v. University of Ill. Found., 402 U.S. at 328-29; Flatt v. Johns Manville Sales Corp., 488 F. Supp. at 841.

416. Refer to note 381 *supra*.

417. Hardy v. Johns-Manville Sales Corp., 681 F.2d at 341. *Cf.* Vincent v. Thompson, 377 N.Y.S.2d at 124.

418. Hibernia Nat'l Bank v. United States, 740 F.2d 382, 387 (5th Cir. 1984) (taxation); Holmes v. Jones, 738 F.2d 711, 713 (5th Cir. 1984); Seven Elves, Inc. v. Eskenazi, 704 F.2d at 244; Hardy v. Johns-Manville Sales Corp., 681 F.2d at 341. *See* Flatt v. Johns Manville Sales Corp., 488 F. Supp. at 839. *See also* Cotton States Mut. Ins. Co. v. Anderson, 749 F.2d 663, 666 (11th Cir. 1984). *Cf.* Oldham v. Pritchett, 599 F.2d 274, 279 (8th Cir. 1979).

419. *See* Scooper Dooper, Inc. v. Kraftco Corp., 494 F.2d 840, 845 (3d Cir. 1974); Oldham v. Pritchett, 599 F.2d at 279. *Cf. Bonniwell*, 663 S.W.2d at 818.

the second action must be "substantially identical",[420] this determination is particularly troublesome.[421] In strict tort liability cases, the defect alleged in the second action must be identical to the defect found to exist in the prior action.[422] If an asbestos product produced by a manufacturer is found in an earlier action to be defective, another plaintiff may invoke collateral estoppel to preclude relitigation of the issue of whether the product is defective.[423] When a prior decision involves a determination that asbestos is defective and unreasonably dangerous based on a failure to warn, this finding may not be conclusive in a subsequent action against the same manufacturer.[424] In *Hardy v. Johns-Manville Sales Corp.*,[425] the Fifth Circuit rejected use of offensive collateral estoppel on the specific basis that it was impossible to determine when the duty to warn attached.[426] The court explained that whether a product is so hazardous as to require a warning depends on the knowledge available to the manufacturer at the time the product was sold.[427]

The general rationale for applying offensive collateral estoppel presupposes that a party who has been afforded a day in court should not be entitled to relitigate a particular issue, simply because the party seeking to assert collateral estoppel and to avoid costly litigation was not a party to the first suit.[428] In *Parklane*

420. Montana v. United States, 440 U.S. 147, 155 (1979). *Accord* Zdanok v. Glidden Co., 327 F.2d 944, 955 (2d Cir.), *cert. denied*, 377 U.S. 934 (1964); Seven Elves, Inc. v. Eskenazi, 704 F.2d at 244; Hardy v. Johns-Manville Sales Corp., 681 F.2d at 341.

421. *See, e.g.*, Starker v. United States, 602 F.2d 1341, 1344-50 (9th Cir. 1979).

422. *See* Erlenbach, *supra* note 381, at 27-28.

423. *See, e.g.*, Flatt v. Johns Manville Sales Corp., 488 F. Supp. at 841; Mooney v. Fibreboard Corp., 485 F. Supp. at 249-50. *But see* Williams v. Laurence-David, Inc., 271 Or. at 723, 534 P.2d at 177-78.

424. *See* Hardy v. Johns-Manville Sales Corp., 681 F.2d at 344-45.

425. 681 F.2d 334 (5th Cir. 1982).

426. *Id.* at 344-45. The plaintiff sought to apply collateral estoppel based on the decision on Borel v. Fibreboard Paper Prods. Corp., 493 F.2d 1076 (5th Cir. 1973), *cert. denied*, 419 U.S. 869 (1974). After *Borel*, several plaintiffs sought to invoke collateral estoppel on the basis of that decision. *See, e.g.*, Flatt v. Johns Manville Sales Corp., 488 F. Supp. at 838; Mooney v. Fibreboard Corp., 485 F. Supp. at 244; Amader v. Johns-Manville Corp., 541 F. Supp. at 1385; Migues v. Fibreboard Corp., 662 F.2d 1183 (5th Cir. 1981). *See generally* Erlenbach, *supra* note 380, at 46 (*Hardy* renders offensive collateral estoppel a "dead letter").

427. 681 F.2d at 344.

428. Bernhard v. Bank of America National Trust & Savings Ass'n, 19 Cal. 2d 807, 813, 122 P.2d 892, 894 (1942). *See* Blonder-Tongue Laboratories, Inc. v. University of Ill. Found., 402 U.S. at 328-29; Oldham v. Pritchett, 599 F.2d at 278.

Hosiery Co. v. Shore,[429] the Supreme Court emphasized that parties should not be allowed to repeatedly litigate the identically same issue, once fairly resolved, against a host of unrelated parties.[430] The court recognized that offensive collateral estoppel does not provide the judicial economy that defensive collateral estoppel provides because plaintiffs are encouraged to avoid joining an ongoing suit to await the outcome.[431] In *Parklane* the court, recognizing that offensive collateral estoppel potentially creates unfairness for defendants, suggested strongly that trial courts must exercise utmost caution in their "broad discretion" before applying the doctrine.[432]

Because the potential for gross unfairness to defendants is quite significant, many courts, including the Supreme Court in *Parklane*, state that the application of offensive collateral estoppel should be restricted to situations where the defendant has had a "full and fair opportunity" to litigate the issue. It is not entirely clear whether the party asserting collateral estoppel must establish the issue was fully and fairly litigated in the prior action or whether the defending party is obligated to establish a lack of a full and fair opportunity to litigate the issue. It appears that some courts place the burden of establishing the elements of the defense[433] on the party asserting offensive collateral estoppel and the party to be bound must establish the lack of a full and fair litigation of the issue.[434] Yet, because of the significant opportunity for

---

429. 439 U.S. 322 (1979).

430. *Id.* at 326.

431. *Id.* at 330. *See* Hunter v. City of Des Moines, 300 N.W.2d 121, 126 (Iowa 1981); Hossler v. Barry, 403 A.2d 762, 769 (Me. 1979). *See generally* Flanagan, *Offensive Collateral Estoppel: Inefficiency and Foolish Consistency*, 45 ARIZ. ST. L.J. 45 (1982).

432. *Parklane*, 439 U.S. 331. *See* Cotton States Mut. Ins. Co. v. Anderson, 749 F.2d 663, 666 (11th Cir. 1984); Hossler v. Barry, 403 A.2d at 769; Williams v. Laurence-David, Inc., 534 P.2d at 177-78; Note, *supra* note 380, at 728-29. *See also* Vincent v. Thompson, 377 N.Y.S.2d at 129-30 (approvingly quoting *Williams*). For discussions, both pro and con, concerning offensive collateral estoppel compare Flanagan, *supra* note 431, *with* Note, *Applying Offensive Collateral Estoppel to Asbestos Cases: A Viable Alternative*, 16 SUFFOLK U.L. Rev. 705 (1982).

433. Refer to note 417 *supra* and accompanying text.

434. Kearney & Trecker Corp. v. Cincinnati Milacron, Inc., 403 F. Supp. 1040, 1046 (S.D. Ohio 1975), *aff'd*, 562 F.2d 365 (6th Cir. 1977)); Ryan v. New York Tel. Co., 62 N.Y.2d 494, 467 N.E.2d 487, 491, 478 N.Y.S.2d 823, 827 (1984); Schwartz v. Public Adm'r of Bronx, 24 N.Y.2d 65, 73, 246 N.E.2d 725, 730, 298 N.Y.S.2d 955, 962 (1969). *See* Blonder-Tongue Laboratories, Inc. v. University of Ill. Found., 402 U.S. at 332-33; Consolidated Express, Inc. v. New York Shipping Assoc., 602 F.2d 494, 504-05 (3d Cir. 1979), *vacated on other grounds*,

denial of a full and fair opportunity to the constitutionally mandated day in court, other jurisdictions have imposed on the party seeking the benefits of offensive collateral estoppel the burden to establish that the issue to be precluded was fully and fairly litigated in the prior suit.[435]

Irrespective of which party bears the burden of proof, several factors establish the absence of a full and fair adjudication of the issue in the prior action.[436] To reduce the temptation for plaintiffs to "wait and see" the outcome of prior litigation, the *Parklane* court stated that as a general rule, a plaintiff should not be permitted to invoke collateral estoppel if he could have easily joined in the prior action.[437] The court also suggested that when the second action presents procedural opportunities different from those of the first action which could cause a different result, offensive collateral estoppel is inapplicable.[438] One example which has been suggested occurs when discovery would be available in the second action which was not available to the party in the prior action.[439] Similarly, where the plaintiff's choice of the forum may unfairly prejudice the defendant, offensive collateral estoppel should not be allowed.[440]

Another limitation arises when prior inconsistent judgments involving the defendant have been rendered concerning the same issue the plaintiff seeks to assert as the basis for collateral estoppel.[441] In such a case the plaintiff is prohibited from employing of-

---

448 U.S. 902 (1980).

435. Jetro Cash and Carry Enter. v. Food Distrib. Center and Philadelphia Fresh Food Terminal Corp., 569 F. Supp. 1404, 1417 (E.D. Pa. 1983) (applying Pennsylvania law); Bonniwell v. Beech Aircraft Corp., 663 S.W.2d 816, 818 (Tex. 1984).

436. *See* Ryan v. New York Tel. Co., 467 N.E.2d at 491, 478 N.Y.S.2d at 827 ("nature of the forum and the importance of the claim in the prior litigation, the incentive and initiative to litigate and the actual extent of litigation, the competence and expertise of counsel, the availability of new evidence, the differences in the applicable law and the foreseeability of future litigation"). *See generally* RESTATEMENT (SECOND) OF JUDGMENTS § 29 (1982).

437. *Parklane*, 439 U.S. at 331. *Accord* Charles J. Arndt, Inc. v. City of Birmingham, 748 F.2d 1486, 1494 (11th Cir. 1984).

438. *Parklane*, 439 U.S. at 331.

439. *Id.* (dicta). *See* Consolidated Express, Inc. v. New York Shipping Assoc., Inc., 602 F.2d 494, 504-05 (3d Cir. 1979) (dicta) (citing *Parklane*), *vacated on other grounds*, 448 U.S. 902 (1980).

440. Zdanok v. Glidden Co., 327 F.2d 944, 956 (2d Cir.), *cert. denied*, 377 U.S. 934 (1964); Ryan v. New York Tel. Co., 467 N.E.2d at 491, 478 N.Y.S.2d at 827.

441. *Parklane*, 439 U.S. at 330-31; Hardy v. Johns-Manville Sales Corp., 681 F.2d at 345-46; Amader v. Johns-Manville Corp., 541 F. Supp. at 1385-86.

fensive collateral estoppel. For instance, when a plaintiff seeks to invoke collateral estoppel on the issue of a defective product previously resolved against a manufacturer of asbestos, prior judgments in favor of the manufacturer suggesting that the asbestos was not defective forecloses the plaintiff from invoking offensive collateral estoppel.[442] Inherent in this limitation is a balancing of the desire to prevent unfairness to the defendant with the desire to encourage judicial economy in mass tort litigation.[443]

Finally, courts generally disallow offensive collateral estoppel when in a prior action the defendant possessed little incentive to vigorously defend the action.[444] This situation most often arises when the amount in controversy in the prior action was relatively small, while an unforeseen and potentially large liability lurks in the background.[445] In *Hardy v. Johns-Manville Sales Corp.*,[446] the court recognized that though a $68,000 judgment was not a small amount, it was inconsequentially small in comparison to the significant potential liability then facing the defendant.[447] The court concluded that the "staggering potential liability" to the defendants could not have been foreseen during litigation of the prior action.[448]

3.08 GOVERNMENT CONTRACT DEFENSE

Contractors performing work pursuant to government contracts possess two defenses to tort causes of action. These are the contract specification defense and the government contract defense.[449] The contract specification defense provides that a con-

---

442. *See, e.g.*, Setter v. A. H. Robins Co., 748 F.2d 1328, 1330 (8th Cir. 1984); Hardy v. Johns-Manville Sales Corp., 681 F.2d at 345-46. *Cf.* Flatt v. Johns Manville Sales Corp., 488 F. Supp. at 841; Mooney v. Fibreboard Corp., 485 F. Supp. at 247-48.

443. *Compare* Amader v. Johns-Manville Corp., 541 F. Supp. at 1385 *with* Mooney v. Fibreboard Corp., 485 F. Supp. at 248.

444. *Parklane*, 439 U.S. at 330-31; Hardy v. Johns-Manville Sales Corp., 681 F.2d at 346-47. *See* Occidental of Umm Al Qaywayn, Inc. v. Cities Serv. Oil Co., 396 F. Supp. 461, 467 (W.D. La. 1975).

445. *Parklane*, 439 U.S. at 330-31; *Hardy*, 681 F.2d at 347.

446. 681 F.2d 334 (5th Cir. 1982).

447. *Id.* at 347. The district court's order involved 58 pending cases with some plaintiffs seeking damages of as much as $ 2.5 million. *Id.*

448. *Id.* at 347.

449. *In re* "Agent Orange" Product Liability Litigation, 580 F. Supp. 690, 701 (E.D.N.Y. 1984) [hereinafter cited as Agent Orange IV]; Johnston v. United States, 568 F. Supp. 351, 353-54 (D. Kan. 1983). *See generally* Comment, *The Government Contract De-*

tractor is not liable unless the specifications provided by the government are so dangerous or defective that a reasonably prudent contractor would have realized the danger.[450] Since this defense is based on ordinary negligence principles, it applies equally to private contracts as well as government contracts.[451] It appears, however, that this defense is not applicable to actions predicated on strict tort liability.[452]

Currently, Texas courts have not addressed this issue. The Fifth Circuit has predicted that Texas would not allow a contractor to rely on contract specifications as a defense to an action predicated on strict tort liability. In *Challoner v. Day & Zimmermann, Inc.*,[453] an injured serviceman and the estate of a deceased serviceman sued the manufacturer of a howitzer round which exploded prematurely causing the injuries and death.[454]

The court determined that a manufacturer could not escape liability by claiming that a reasonably prudent manufacturer would not have recognized the defective design furnished by the government.[455] Since strict tort liability is dependent on the sale of a defective product and not negligent conduct, the manufacturer's claim that it was not negligent in failing to detect design defects is essentially a moot issue.[456] Significantly, however, liability was ac-

---

fense: Sharing the Protective Cloak of Sovereign Immunity After McKay v. Rockwell International Corp., 37 BAYLOR L. REV. 181, 183-84 (1985); Note, *Liability of a Manufacturer for Products Defectively Designed by the Government*, 23 B.C.L. REV. 1025, 1031-32 (1982).

450. 580 F. Supp. at 701; *Johnston*, 568 F. Supp. at 354; Note, *supra* note 449, at 1032-33. *See* McClish v. Niagara Mach. & Tool Works, 266 F. Supp. 987, 992 (S.D. Ind. 1967); Davis v. Henderlong Lumber Co., 221 F. Supp. 129, 134 (N.D. Ind. 1963); Bush v. Albert D. Wardell Contractor, Inc., 165 Mont. 312, 528 P.2d 215, 217-18 (1974); Ryan v. Feeney & Sheehan Building Co., 239 N.Y. 43, 46, 145 N.E. 321, 321-22 (1924); Benson v. Ames, 604 P.2d 927, 929-30 (Utah 1979).

451. *See, e.g.*, Spangler v. Kranco, Inc., 481 F.2d 373 (4th Cir. 1973). *See generally* Agent Orange IV, 580 F. Supp. at 701 (discussing the contract specification defense); *Johnston*, 568 F. Supp. at 354 (discussing the contract specification defense); Note, *supra* note 449, at 1032-39.

452. Challoner v. Day & Zimmermann, Inc., 512 F.2d 77, 82-83 (5th Cir.), *vacated on choice of law grounds*, 423 U.S. 3 (1975); *Johnston*, 568 F. Supp. at 354; Lenherr v. NRM Corp., 504 F. Supp. 165, 174 (D. Kan. 1980); Michalko v. Cooke Color and Chem. Corp., 91 N.J. 386, 451 A.2d 179, 183-84 (1982). *But see* Union Supply Co. v. Pust, 196 Colo. 162, 170-71, 583 P.2d 276, 281-82 (1978); Spangler v. Kranco, Inc., 481 F.2d at 375 n.2 (dicta).

453. 512 F.2d 77, 82-83 (5th Cir. 1975), *vacated on choice of law grounds*, 423 U.S. 3 (1975).

454. *Id.* at 78.

455. *Id.* at 83.

456. *Id.* at 82-83.

tually premised on improper adherence to the government specifications.

The government contract defense is generally considered an affirmative defense which protects a government contractor from liability arising out of the contractor's compliance with government specifications.[457] It differs from the contract specification defense in that the government contractor is allowed to "share" the government's *immunity* from suit on public policy grounds.[458] While limited to government contractors, the government contract defense is noticeably broader in scope than the contract specification defense.[459] This protection, however, is not extended to situations in which the product defect is due to a manufacturing flaw or error.[460]

The government contract defense traditionally applied to prevent actions against the contractor performing public works projects.[461] The contractor is generally considered an agent or of-

---

457. McKay v. Rockwell Int'l Corp., 704 F.2d 444, 448 (9th Cir. 1983), *cert. denied*, 104 S. Ct. 711 (1984); Hubbs v. United Technologies, 574 F. Supp. 96, 98 (E.D. Pa. 1983); Merritt, Chapman & Scott Corp. v. Guy F. Atkinson Co., 295 F.2d 14, 16 (9th Cir. 1961). *See generally* Comment, *The Government Contract Defense: An Overview*, 27 How. L.J. 275 (1984); Note, *supra* note 449, at 1048-64.

458. *See* Comment, *supra* note 449, at 183-84; Comment, *supra* note 457, at 282-87; Note, *supra* note 449, at 1049.

459. *See* Note, *supra* note 449, at 1055. According to one view, the general contractor would be entitled to immunity from suit along with the government even though the contractor was negligent. *Id.*; *Johnston*, 568 F. Supp. at 354-56; Casabianca v. Casabianca, 104 Misc. 2d 348, 350, 428 N.Y.S.2d 400, 402 (Sup. Ct. 1980). The elements of the defense suggest that a contractor could be negligent in design where the government is as knowledgeable as the contractor. Refer to note 477 *infra* and accompanying text. The contract specification defense would be available where the government was not immune, but the claim against the contractor must be based on negligence and not strict liability. *Johnson* 568 F. Supp. at 354.

460. *See* Brown v. Caterpillar Tractor Co., 696 F.2d 246, 253 (3d Cir. 1982) (dicta); Foster v. Day & Zimmermann, Inc., 502 F.2d 867, 874 n.5 (8th Cir. 1974). This assumes that the manufacturer exercises control over its own manufacturing process. *See* Montgomery v. Goodyear Tire & Rubber Co., 231 F. Supp. 447, 451 (S.D.N.Y. 1964). *See generally* Note, *supra* note 449, at 1055-56.

461. *See, e.g.*, Yearsley v. W. A. Ross Constr. Co., 309 U.S. 18 (1940) (dike construction); Myers v. United States, 323 F.2d 580 (9th Cir. 1963) (road construction); Merritt, Chapman & Scott Corp. v. Guy F. Atkinson Co., 295 F.2d 14 (9th Cir. 1961) (cofferdam construction); Green v. ICI America, Inc., 362 F. Supp. 1263 (E.D. Tenn. 1973) (operation of TNT plant); Dolphin Gardens, Inc. v. United States, 243 F. Supp. 824 (D. Conn. 1965) (dredging operations); Jemison v. The Duplex, 163 F. Supp. 947 (S.D. Ala. 1958) (dredging operations); Hunt v. Blasius, 55 Ill. App. 14, 370 N.E.2d 617 (1977), *aff'd*, 74 Ill. 2d 203, 384 N.E.2d 368 (1979) (street sign construction).

ficer of the government and therefore acting pursuant to governmental authority.[462] Most recently, the defense has been asserted in cases concerning defectively designed military products.[463] These cases generally adopt the position that a contractor should not be liable for design defects in government contracts over which it exercised no discretion. This matter is generally considered by the courts as best left to the military.[464]

The doctrine of sovereign immunity prohibits suits by private citizens against the United States without its consent.[465] Conceptually, the government contract defense authorizes a contractor as an agent of the United States, to share the government's immunity from suit.[466] Though the federal government has waived its immunity from suits for certain negligent torts,[467] the government continues to possess immunity in a variety of situations.[468] For instance, the government is immune from suits by military

---

462. *Yearsley*, 309 U.S. at 21-22. *See generally* Note, *supra* note 449, at 1050.

463. *See, e.g.*, McKay v. Rockwell Int'l Corp., 704 F.2d 444 (9th Cir. 1984), *cert. denied*, 104 S. Ct. 711 (1984); Tillett v. J.I. Case Co., 756 F.2d 591 (7th Cir. 1985); Koutsoubos v. Boeing Vertol, 755 F.2d 352 (3d Cir. 1985); Sanner v. Ford Motor Co., 144 N.J. Super 1, 364 A.2d 43 (1976), *aff'd*, 154 N.J. Super 407, 381 A.2d 805 (1977), *cert. denied*, 75 N.J. 616, 384 A.2d 846 (1978); Casabianca v. Casabianca, 104 Misc. 2d 348, 428 N.Y.S.2d 400 (Sup. Ct. 1980). *See also* Littlehale v. E. I. DuPont de Nemours & Co., 268 F. Supp. 791 (S.D.N.Y. 1966). *But see* O'Keefe v. Boeing Co., 335 F. Supp. 1104 (S.D.N.Y. 1971).

464. Sanner v. Ford Motor Co., 364 A.2d at 46; *Casabianca*, 104 Misc. 2d at 350, 428 N.Y.S.2d at 402. *See Littlehale*, 268 F. Supp. at 802-03.

465. Cohens v. Virginia, 19 U.S. (6 Wheat) 120, 184 (1821). *Accord* Feres v. United States, 340 U.S. 135, 139 (1950); Gibbons v. United States, 75 U.S. (8 Wall.) 269, 275-76 (1868); Hill v. United States, 50 U.S. (9 How.) 409, 412-13 (1850).

466. *See McKay*, 704 F.2d at 450-51; *In re* "Agent Orange" Products Liability Litigation, 506 F. Supp. 762, 792 (E.D.N.Y. 1980) [hereinafter cited as Agent Orange I], *continued*, 534 F. Supp. 1046 (E.D.N.Y. 1982) [hereinafter cited as Agent Orange II], *continued*, 565 F. Supp. 1263 (E.D.N.Y. 1983) [hereinafter cited as Agent Orange III], *continued*, 580 F. Supp. 690 (E.D.N.Y. 1984). *See generally* Comment, *supra* note 449, at 184-87; Comment, *supra* note 457, at 277-82; Note, *supra* note 449, at 1049.

467. Federal Tort Claims Act, 28 U.S.C. § 1346(b), 2671-80 (1982). For a historical perspective of the evolution of sovereign immunity, see Comment, *The Effect of the Feres Doctrine on Tort Actions Against the United States by Family Members of Servicemen*, 50 FORDHAM L. REV. 1241, 1241-46 (1982).

468. *See* Comment, *supra* note 449, at 185; Comment, *supra* note 467, at 1243-44. The immunity waived by the FTCA applies only to negligent acts by the United States. 28 U.S.C. § 1346(b). As a result, the United States is immune from suits predicated on strict liability for engaging in ultrahazardous activities or owning inherently dangerous property. Laird v. Nelms, 406 U.S. 797, 802-03 (1972); Dalehite v. United States, 346 U.S. 15, 45 (1953). Further, the government cannot be held liable for defectively designed products. Watson v. Alexander, 532 F. Supp. 1004, 1006-07 (E.D. Tex. 1982).

servicemen for injuries sustained in the course of their service.[469] When the government is immune from suit, the government is likewise immune from claims for contribution asserted by third parties liable to servicemen for accidents arising from their military service.[470] The rationale for the government contract defense is the government's immunity from suit.[471]

Since the sovereign immunity of the federal government is often involved in litigation in which the defense is asserted, confusion has emerged as to whether state or federal common law applies. In diversity actions, federal courts generally adopt the conflicts-of-law rules of the forum state.[472] These rules require that the law of the jurisdiction which has the "most significant relationship" to the action should control the substantive law.[473] Federal law may apply, however, in special circumstances, such as a large class action suit against several manufacturers involving the substantive law of several states.[474] Regarding state substantive law,

---

469. Feres v. United States, 340 U.S. at 146.

470. Stencel Aero Eng'g Corp. v. United States, 431 U.S. 666, 673 (1977). *See* Starr v. United States, 393 F. Supp. 1359, 1363 (N.D. Tex. 1975) (contribution against City of Dallas not allowed).

471. *McKay*, 704 F.2d at 451; Tillett v. J.I. Case Co., 756 F.2d at 596-98; Koutsoubos v. Boeing Vertol, 755 F.2d at 354; Agent Orange I, 506 F. Supp. at 792. *But cf.* Jemison v. The Duplex, 163 F. Supp. 947, 950-51 (S.D. Ala. 1958); Note, *supra* note 449, at 1051 n.136 (suggesting that governmental immunity may not be required as an element of the defense).

472. Klaxon Co. v. Stentor Elec. Mfg. Co., 313 U.S. 487, 496 (1941). *Accord* Day & Zimmermann, Inc. v. Challoner, 423 U.S. 3, 4-5 (1975); *In re* "Agent Orange" Products Liability Litigation, 635 F.2d 987, 993 (2d Cir. 1980), *cert. denied sub nom.* Chapman v. Dow, 454 U.S. 1128 (1981). In *Agent Orange*, the Second Circuit reversed application of federal common law in a diversity based class action suit because no significant conflict existed between between federal policy and state substantive law. The court first held that no federal interest in uniformity was present since no government rights or duties depended on the outcome. Competing government interests in the welfare of its veterans and in procurement of materials for the military were recognized. 635 F.2d at 993-94. However, since the exact interest had not been identified, the conflict posed by state law could not be determined. *Id.* at 995.

473. Gutierrez v. Collins, 583 S.W.2d 312, 318-19 (Tex. 1979); Houston North Hosp. Properties v. Telco Leasing, Inc., 688 F.2d 408, 409 (5th Cir. 1982); Crim v. International Harvester Co., 646 F.2d 161, 163 (5th Cir. 1981); Hines v. Tenneco Chemical, Inc., 546 F. Supp. 1229, 1232-33 (S.D. Tex. 1982), *aff'd*, 728 F.2d 729 (5th Cir. 1984); TEX. REV. CIV. STAT. ANN. art. 4678 (Vernon Supp. 1985). *Cf.* Challoner v. Day & Zimmermann, Inc., 546 F.2d 26 (5th Cir. 1977) (on remand); Boeing Airplane Co. v. Brown, 291 F.2d 310, 313 (9th Cir. 1961).

474. Agent Orange IV, 580 F. Supp. 690, 703 (E.D.N.Y. 1984). *Compare* McLaughlin v. Sikorsky Aircraft, 148 Cal. App. 3d 203, 195 Cal. Rptr. 764, 768 (1983) (federal law applies to government contract defense) *with* Brown v. Caterpillar Tractor Co., 696 F.2d 246, 248-49 (3d Cir. 1982) (liability of government contractor to serviceman not governed by federal

Texas courts have neither expressly accepted nor rejected this defense. Most often, the government contract defense has arisen in the federal courts, and while certain aspects of the defense are consistently applied, not all courts have agreed on the specific elements of the defense.

Recently, in *In re "Agent Orange" Product Liability Litigation*,[475] the United States District Court articulated three principle elements as a prerequisite for invoking the defense.[476] It must be proven that (1) the government established the specifications; (2) the product satisfied the government specifications in all material respects; and (3) the government knew as much or more than did the product supplier.[477] As to each element of the defense, courts have placed the burden of proof on the defendant.[478]

These criteria were also outlined by the Ninth Circuit in *McKay v. Rockwell International Corp.*[479] *McKay* involved the death of two navy pilots allegedly caused by a defective ejection system.[480] Since the deaths were incident to the pilots' military service, the United States was immune from suit.[481] In allowing defendant to assert the defense, the court emphasized that the defense applied only when the United States is immune from suit under the *Feres* and *Stencel* doctrines.[482]

---

law), *cert. denied sub nom.* Diamond Shamrock Chem. Co. v. Ryan. 104 S.Ct. 1417 (1984).

475. 534 F. Supp. 1046 (E.D.N.Y. 1982).

476. *Id.* at 1055. This litigation involved a class action on the part of several Vietnam veterans and members of their families against several chemical companies for injuries resulting from exposure to herbicides used in Vietnam. Agent Orange I, 506 F. Supp. at 768-69.

477. Agent Orange II, 534 F. Supp. at 1055. *Accord* Shaw v. Grumman Aerospace Corp., 593 F. Supp. 1066, 1074 (S.D. Fla. 1984); *In re* All Maine Asbestos Litigation, 575 F. Supp. 1375, 1377 (D. Me. 1983); Hubbs v. United Technologies, 574 F. Supp. 96, 98 (E.D. Pa. 1983); Tillett v. J.I. Case Co., 756 F.2d 591 (7th Cir. 1985); Koutsoubos v. Boeing Vertal, 755 F.2d 352 (3d Cir. 1985); Tefft v. A.C. & S., Inc., No. C80-924M (W.D. Wash., Sept. 15, 1982).

478. McKay v. Rockwell Int'l Corp., 704 F.2d 444, 451 (9th Cir. 1983), *cert. denied*, 104 S. Ct. 711 (1984); Shaw v. Grumman Aerospace Corp., 593 F. Supp. 1066, 1074 (S.D. Fla. 1984); Hubbs v. United Technologies, 574 F. Supp. 96, 98 (E.D. Pa. 1983); Agent Orange II, 534 F. Supp. at 1055.

479. 704 F.2d 444, 451 (9th Cir. 1983), *cert. denied*, 104 S. Ct. 711 (1984).

480. *Id.* at 449.

481. The sovereign immunity of the United States is not waived with respect to injuries incurred by servicemen incident to their military service. Feres v. United States, 340 U.S. 135, 146

482. *McKay*, 704 F.2d at 451. Refer to notes 469-70 *supra* and accompanying text. *See generally* Note, *The Government Contractor Defense and Manufacturers of Military*

Though the government must prescribe the specifications, participation by the defendant in designing the product does not defeat applicability of the defense.[483] Evidence of the defendant's participation is relevant, however, to determine whether the government actually participated in the design the specifications.[484] If the contractor establishes the specifications and the government merely furnishes its approval, the defense is inapplicable.[485] Assuming that the government does actually provide the contract specifications, it appears that the specifications must be reasonably precise, thereby limiting the design discretion attributable to the contractor.[486]

Further, specifications made by the government are limited to those describing a particular product, and may not specify performance requirements. Design specifications entail precise measurements, tolerance levels, materials, and quality control requirements. In contrast, performance requirements may only specify that the product should withstand certain speeds or altitudes, and necessarily imply that the actual design is not that of the government, but rather, reflect the design of the contractor.[487] If the court determines that the contract specified only performance requirements, the defense fails.[488] One court has even stated that where the performance specification could be satisfied by only one product then available, a performance specification does not transform into one of design.[489]

Equipment: McKay v. Rockwell International Corporation, 21 Hous. L. Rev. 855 (1984).

483. Koutsoubos v. Boeing Vertol, 755 F.2d at 355; Tellett v. J.I. Case Co., 756 F.2d at 597; Agent Orange II, 534 F. Supp. at 1056.

484. *Koutsoubos*, 755 F.2d at 355, Agent Orange II, 534 F. Supp. at 1056. *See* Shaw v. Grumman Aerospace Corp., 593 F. Supp. at 1073.

485. Shaw v. Grumman Aerospace Corp., 593 F. Supp. at 1074; Schoenborn v. Boeing Co., 586 F. Supp. 711, 717 (E.D. Pa. 1984). *See* Hubbs v. United Technologies, 574 F. Supp. at 99.

486. *McKay*, 704 F.2d at 451.

487. Tefft v. A.C. & S., Inc., No. C84-154M slip op. (W.D. Wash. Oct. 12, 1984).

488. *Id.*; Agent Orange II, 534 F. Supp. at 1056. *See* Shaw v. Grumman Aerospace Corp., 593 F. Supp. at 1073.

489. Tefft v. A.C. & S., Inc., No. C84-154M slip op. ("heat resisting compounds suitable for the temperature conditions and purposes intended" was not a requirement specifying asbestos). The court placed great emphasis on the Navy's process of creating performance specifications for the purpose of encouraging improvement within the industry and the development of new products. *Id. But cf. Johnston*, 568 F. Supp. at 355-56 (summary judgment denied because defendant failed to demonstrate product used was the only one available).

The product supplied by the contractor must comply with the government specifications without any material discrepencies.[490] In determining whether the product complies with the contract specifications, the *Agent Orange II* court stated that the specifications must be compared with the characteristics and quality of the product supplied by the contractor.[491] In *Johnston v. United States*,[492] the government contract specified that the aircraft should contain self-luminous instrument dials.[493] The court denied summary judgment to the defendant because of the failure to demonstrate that no other substance could have been used that would have prevented plaintiff's injuries.[494] It should be noted that if a substance other than radium could have been used, the specification requiring the dials to be self-luminous would represent a performance specification that would prevent application of the defense.[495]

Some courts confronting the government contract defense have not required the contractor to warn the government of patent errors in design.[496] Other courts, however, have declared that a contractor must inform the government of these errors.[497] Still others merely require the defendant to demonstrate that it knew of no hazards which if known by the government would have altered the government's decision to use the product.[498] Evidence concerning foreseeability, the state of the art, and patent defect were considered relevant by the *Agent Orange II* court in its formulation of

---

490. Tefft v. A.C. S., Inc., No. C84-154m slip op.; Agent Orange II, 534 F. Supp. at 1057. *See Koutsoubos*, 755 F.2d at 355.

491. Agent Orange II, 534 F. Supp. at 1057.

492. 568 F. Supp. 351 (D. Kan. 1983).

493. *Id.* at 355. The plaintiff's alleged that the radium used by the contractor was the cause of their injuries. *Id.* at 353.

494. *Id.* at 355-56. *Cf.* Nobriga v. Raybestos-Manhattan, Inc., 683 P.2d 389, 392 (Haw. 1984) (where specified materials are inherently dangerous defect is not in design therefore government contract defense does not apply).

495. Refer to notes 487-88 *supra* and accompanying text.

496. Casabianca v. Casabianca, 104 Misc. 2d at 350, 428 N.Y.S.2d at 402 (complete defense even if design is faulty); Sanner v. Ford Motor Co., 144 N.J. Super. at 8-9, 364 A.2d at 46-47 (applied defense without mentioning knowledge of contractor).

497. *McKay*, 704 F.2d at 451; Shaw v. Grumman Aerospace Corp., 593 F. Supp. at 1074. The *McKay* court stated that such an application would apply to patent errors known by the supplier and not by the government. *Id. Cf. Casabianca*, 104 Misc. 2d at 350, 428 N.Y.S.2d at 402.

498. Hubbs v. United Technologies, 574 F. Supp. at 100; *Koutsoubos*, 553 F. Supp. at 344.

the defense.[499] At a later stage of the litigation, the court granted summary judgment to defendants who possessed no knowledge of the product's harmful effects or knew less than the government.[500] Summary judgment was denied, however, to those defendants possessing knowledge comparable to that of the government.[501]

The government contract defense is based on several considerations. Courts have consistently recognized that judicial second-guessing of military decisions poses a serious detrimental effect on national security.[502] This consideration is particularly important when the military occupies a better position to ascertain its needs than the manufacturer.[503] Further, in the military context, a supplier or contractor incurs risks much higher than acceptable for consumer goods in order to press technology toward its outer limits in support of the defense effort.[504]

Courts have also recognized the unequitability of imposing liability on a government contractor when the contractor is compelled to follow government design specifications.[505] This is especially pertinent when the products are manufactured during time of war and the contractor is obligated to follow the government's specifications.[506] Certain courts and commentators have stated that government compulsion is required before the contractor is entitled to the defense.[507] Underlying this requirement is the concept that a

---

499. Agent Orange II, 534 F. Supp. at 1057.

500. Agent Orange III, 565 F. Supp. at 1272-74.

501. *Id.* at 1266-72.

502. *See McKay*, 704 F.2d at 449; Johnston v. United States, 568 F. Supp. at 357; Agent Orange II, 534 F. Supp. at 1054-55; Agent Orange I, 506 F. Supp. at 771; Comment, *supra* note 449, at 187-88. In *Agent Orange I*, the court noted that if the civil courts were required to "examine and pass upon the propriety of military decisions[,] [t]he security and common defense of the country would quickly disintegrate under such meddling." *Id. But cf.* Comment, *Strict Product Liability Suits for Design Defects in Military Products: All the King's Men; All the King's Privileges?*, 10 DAYTON L.R. 117, 140-41 (1984).

503. Agent Orange II, 534 F. Supp. at 1054-55; Sanner v. Ford Motor Co., 144 N.J. Super. at 9, 364 A.2d at 47. One court has commented that this rationale should only apply to the design of new and technically complex products. *Johnston*, 568 F. Supp. at 357. *Cf.* Shaw v. Grumman Aerospace Corp., 593 F. Supp. at 1074; Note, *supra* note 449, at 1071-73.

504. *McKay*, 704 F.2d at 449-50; Hubbs v. United Technologies, 574 F. Supp. at 98; Note, *supra* note 449 at 1073.

505. *McKay*, 704 F.2d at 450; Merritt, Chapman & Scott Corp. v. Guy F. Atkinson Co., 295 F.2d at 16; *Johnston*, 568 F. Supp. at 357-58; Agent Orange I, 506 F. Supp. at 794.

506. *Casabianca*, 104 Misc. 2d at 350, 428 N.Y.S.2d at 402.

507. *Merritt, Chapman & Scott Corp.*, 295 F.2d at 16; *Johnston*, 568 F. Supp. at 357-58; *McKay*, 704 F.2d at 458 (dissenting opinion); Note, *supra* note 449, at 1053; Note, *supra* note 482, at 868. *But see McKay*, 704 F.2d at 450-51, Agent Orange II, 534 F. Supp. at 1055.

contractor, if not compelled, can refuse to manufacture defectively designed products or those which are perceived as dangerous to the public.[508] However, several courts have rejected government compulsion as a prerequisite for the government contract defense.[509]

Other rationale have been advanced which apply to situations involving government contracts other than military supply contracts.[510] It has been suggested that foreclosing the government contractor from sharing the government's immunity from suit, would eventually transfer significantly higher costs to the government in the form of higher prices.[511] Allowance of the defense provides an incentive for the manufacturer to work with the government in the design and manufacture of the products.[512] At least one commentator has argued that these rationale do not support applicatioin of the defense when the government contract is not one for supplying military products.[513] It is argued that even when the government is immune from suit it must shoulder increased costs inherent with existing tort liability including liability for manufacturing defects, and the threat of increased costs does not justify absolving the contractor of liability for design defects.[514]

While both courts referred to government compulsion as a rationale, neither court required government compuslion to exist before the defense could apply. 704 F.2d at 451; 534 F. Supp. at 1055.

508. *Johnston*, 568 F. Supp. at 357-58. *See* Note, *supra* note 449, at 1053 n.146.

509. *E.g.*, *McKay*, 704 F.2d at 451; Brown v. Caterpillar Tractor Co., 696 F.2d 246, 253-54 (3d Cir. 1982); *Koutsoubos*, 755 F.2d at 355. Tillett, 756 F.2d at 597-98; Agent Orange II, 534 F. Supp. at 1054-55; Sanner v. Ford Motor Co., 144 N.J. Super. at 8-9, 364 A.2d at 46-47. For an overview of underlying rationale and policy concerning this defense, see generally Comment, *supra* note 449, 186-92.

510. For cases suggesting that this theory may apply to non-military contracts, see Price v. Tempo, Inc., No. 83-0006 (E.D. Pa. March 18, 1985); Tefft v. A.C. & S., Inc., No. C80-924M (W.D. Wash. Sept. 15, 1982).

511. *See McKay*, 704 F.2d at 449; *Johnston*, 568 F. Supp. at 357 (rationale is inapplicable to manufacturing defects); *Casabianca*, 104 Misc. 2d at 350, 428 N.Y.S.2d at 402. *See also* Dolphin Gardens, Inc. v. United States, 243 F. Supp. at 827.

512. *See McKay*, 704 F.2d at 450. Theoretically the contractor would share its knowledge regarding the product with the government, thereby insuring the government knows as much as the contractor. *See* Agent Orange II, 534 F. Supp. at 1055 (the government must know as much or more than the contractor). *Cf.* Comment, *supra* note 502, at 142. For an extensive discussion of policy considerations for the defense in a strict liability context, see Comment, *supra* note 457, at 292-99.

513. Note, *supra* note 449, at 1070-71.

514. *Id.* at 1071. *Cf.* Note, *supra* note 482, at 866. One theory for imposition of strict liability is based on a policy of compensating victims, placing the risk of loss on the party best able to insure against the loss, or prevent the loss. *See* Comment, *supra* note 457, at 294-95. *Cf. Johnston*, 568 F. Supp. at 357 (increased cost rationale applies to design defects

Virtually all courts applying the government contract defense have done so in connection with products manufactured for the military.[515] It is well established that the defense applies to all theories of liability, including strict tort liability and breach of warranty.[516] It is not completely clear, however, whether courts will allow contractors to share the government's immunity when the defectively designed products are not supplied pursuant to a contract with the military.[517]

3.09 Conclusion

Strict liability in tort is premised on a policy that product suppliers are the appropriate parties to bear the risk of loss attributable to defective products as opposed to injured users relying on the safety of the product. One justification for this fundamental policy is that a supplier is generally in a superior position to prevent risk of injury when a product is used properly. While recognizing this underlying rationale of strict tort liability, courts have consistently declared that product suppliers are not to be insurers of their products.

For this policy of risk distribution to be satisfied in an equitable fashion, each party's relative ability to prevent risk of harm should be considered. Recognizing the need for a rational system of risk distribution, the Texas Supreme Court adopted comparative causation whereby all the parties whose conduct or product which may have caused the plaintiff's injuries are to be considered. Accordingly, the resulting liability attributed to each party is allocated on a percentage basis in proportion to the percentage of the

---

but not manufacturing defects).

515. *See, e.g., McKay*, 704 F.2d at 446; *Johnston*, 568 F. Supp. at 353; *Koutsoubos*, 553 F. Supp. at 341; Agent Orange I, 506 F. Supp. at 768-69; Sanner v. Ford Motor Co., 364 A.2d at 43-44; *Casabianca*, 428 N.Y.S.2d at 401. *See generally* Comment, *supra* note 457, at 282-92; Comment, *The Government Contract Defense in Strict Liability Suits for Defective Design*, 48 U. Chi. L. Rev. 1030 (1981); Note, *supra* note 449, at 1055-64.

516. *See McKay*, 704 F.2d at 447 (strict products liability); Agent Orange II, 534 F. Supp. at 1055-56 (all theories); Sanner v. Ford Motor Co., 364 A.2d at 806 (strict products liability); *Casabianca*, 104 Misc. 2d at 350, 428 N.Y.S.2d at 402 (all theories); Hunt v. Blasius, 370 N.E.2d at 620-22 (strict liability).

517. *See McKay,* 704 F.2d at 458-59 (dissenting opinion); Note, *supra* note 448, at 1071-73. *Contra* Price v. Tempo, No. 83-0006 (E.D.Pa. March 18, 1985); Tefft v. A.C. & S., Inc., No. C80-924M (W.D. Wash. Sept. 15, 1982). *See generally* Comment, *supra* 457, at 289-90.

injuries caused by that party. It appears that this system better allocates responsibility for resulting injuries to the party in the best position to have prevented them.

Due to the magnitude and ramifications of the doctrine of strict tort liability, other emerging defensive issues have been generated. Recognizing important national security interests, several courts have permitted government contractors to share the government's immunity from suit when plaintiffs are injured by defectively designed products supplied to the military. This defense is also based partially on a rationale that suppliers should not pay for faulty government designs.

Strict tort liability has also generated significant confusion in litigation concerning large scale defective products such as drugs, chemicals, and insulation materials. The application of collateral estoppel offers judicial economy in preventing repeated litigation of identical issues and also offers a possible defense for products involved in catastrophic accidents.

CHAPTER IV. ENTITIES SUBJECT TO STRICT TORT LIABILITY*

4.00 GENERALLY

The *Restatement (Second) of Torts* § 402A imposes strict tort liability on sellers of defective products that are unreasonably dangerous and cause damage to a user, consumer or his property.[1] Section 402A was officially adopted by the Texas courts in 1967.[2] The

---

* Catherine Graubart coauthored this chapter.

1. RESTATEMENT (SECOND) OF TORTS § 402A (1965).

2. McKisson v. Sales Affiliates, Inc., 416 S.W.2d 787, 788-90 (Tex. 1967); Shamrock Fuel & Oil Sales Co. v. Tunks, 416 S.W.2d 779, 784 (Tex. 1967).

policy reasons underlying the concept of strict tort liability embodied in Section 402A are essentially socioeconomic:

> [T]he seller, by marketing his product for use and consumption, has undertaken and assumed a special responsibility toward any member of the consuming public who may be injured by it; that the public has the right to and does expect, in the case of products which it needs and for which it is forced to rely upon the seller, that reputable sellers will stand behind their goods; that public policy demands the burden of accidental injuries caused by products intended for consumption be placed upon those who market them, and be treated as a cost of production against which liability insurance can be obtained; and that the consumer of such products is entitled to the maximum protection at the hands of someone, and the proper persons to afford it are those who market the products.[3]

Under Section 402A, a supplier of products is subject to strict tort liability if it is engaged in the regular business of selling products, and one of the products that it sells is defective and unreasonably dangerous. The requirement that the seller be regularly engaged in such business was adopted primarily to exclude from liability the occasional seller of a product.[4] Necessarily, a seller within the contemplation of Section 402A must be regularly engaged in the sale of "products" that reach the ultimate user or consumer in essentially the same condition that existed at the time possession of the product was relinquished by the product supplier. Because the term "product" has not been defined under the Restatement, decisional law has struggled to define the parameters of tangible goods that qualify as products. For example, navigational charts prepared and designed for mass production and marketing are deemed products,[5] as well as unprocessed substances

---

3. RESTATEMENT (SECOND) OF TORTS § 402A comment c (1965).

4. *Id.* Section 402A(1)(a), Comment *f*, states: "The rule does not, however, apply to the occasional seller of food or other such products who is not engaged in that activity as a part of his business." *See* Bailey v. ITT Grinnell Corp., 536 F. Supp. 84, 89 (N.D. Ohio 1982); Goetz v. Avildsen Tool & Mach. Co., 82 Ill.App.3d 1054, 403 N.E.2d 555, 561-62 (1980); Allen v. Nicole, Inc., 172 N.J. Super. 442, 412 A.2d 824, 825-26 (1980); Bevard v. Ajax Mfg. Co., 473 F. Supp. 35, 38 (D.C. 1979); Bruce v. Martin-Marietta Corp., 544 F.2d 442, 448-49 (10th Cir. 1976). Additionally, a purchaser-owner of a product is not a seller within the meaning of Section 402A. Foster v. Ford Motor Co., 616 F.2d 1304, 1312 (5th Cir. 1980). *See* Galendo v. Precision American Co., 754 F.2d 1212, 1221 (5th Cir. 1985) (enumerating the standard for evaluating the regular business of a product supplier).

5. Brocklesby v. United States, 753 F2d. 794 (9th Cir. 1985); Saloomey v. Jeppesen &

such as raw asbestos.[6] Conversely, a fabricated guardrail incorporated as an indivisible part of an entire building structure is not considered an independent product within the contemplation of Section 402A.[7] The contents of books supplied by book publishers generally are not considered products.[8] Similarly, a multi-level open air parking garage is not characterized as a product for purposes of strict tort liability.[9]

The term "seller" of defective products under Section 402A has been substantially expanded to include many nonselling entities that are considered an integral part of the distributing or marketing chain engaged in the regular introduction of products into the channels of commerce.[10] Notwithstanding expansion of the term "seller" to include non-selling entities, the party sought to be held strictly liable must be regularly engaged in the business of

---

Co., 707 F.2d 671, 676-77 (2d Cir. 1983), (navigational charts a product); Halstead v. United States, 535 F. Supp. 782, 790 (D. Conn. 1982) (navigational charts deemed a product).

6. Hammond v. North American Asbestos Corp., 97 Ill.2d 195, 454 N.E.2d 210, 216 (Ill. 1983)(natural unprocessed asbestos is characterized as a product because the policy underlying strict tort liability is furthered by such characterization).

7. Walker v. Shell Chem., Inc., 101 Ill.App.3d 880, 428 N.E.2d 943, 946 (1981); Chicago Heights Venture v. Dynamit Nobel of America, 575 F. Supp. 214, 218 (N.D. Ill. 1983).

8. *See* Walter v. Bauer, 109 Misc.2d 189, 439 N.Y.S.2d 821 (1981), *modified on other grounds*, 451 N.Y.S.2d 533 (1982); Cardozo v. True, 342 So.2d 1053 (Fla. App.), *cert. denied*, 353 So.2d 674 (Fla. 1977). *But see* Sears Roebuck & Co. v. Employers Ins. Co. of Wausau, 585 F. Supp. 739 (N.D. Ill. 1984).

9. Lowrie v. City of Evanston, 50 Ill.App.3d 376, 365 N.E.2d 923, 928-29 (1977). *See also* Immergluck v. Ridgeview House, Inc., 53 Ill.App.3d 472, 368 N.E.2d 803, 804-06 (1977)(sheltered care medical facility is not considered a product within Section 402A) Likewise, though electricity may constitute a product, strict tort liability is inapplicable to transmission lines installed and maintained to transmit the electrical power. Erwin v. Guadalupe Valley Elec. Co-op, 505 S.W.2d 353, 355 (Tex. Civ. App.—San Antonio 1974, writ ref'd n.r.e.). Moreover, strict tort liability does not extend to a utility when the product delivered is not defective. Gray v. Enserch, Inc., 665 S.W.2d 601, 605 (Tex. App.—Ft. Worth 1984, writ ref'd n.r.e) Even though electricity is a product the transmission of electricity is not encompassed by strict tort liability. *See* Smith v. Home Light & Power Corp., 695 P.2d 788 (Colo. App. 1984).

10. Armstrong Rubber Co. v. Urquidez, 570 S.W.2d 374 (Tex. 1978); CNG Producing Co. v. Columbia Gulf Transmission, 709 F.2d 959 (5th Cir. 1983); Gardner v. Chevron U.S.A., Inc., 675 F.2d 658 (5th Cir. 1982); Thate v. Texas & Pacific Ry.Co., 595 S.W.2d 591 (Tex. Civ. App.—Dallas 1980, writ dism'd); Hernandez v. Southern Pacific Transportation Company, 641 S.W.2d 947 (Tex. App.—Corpus Christi 1982, no writ); Foster v. Ford Motor Co., 616 F.2d 1304 (5th Cir. 1980); Watson v. Alexander, 532 F. Supp. 1004 (E.D. Tex. 1982). Recently, in Smith v. Borg-Warner Corp., 626 F.2d 384 (5th Cir. 1980), the Fifth Circuit noted that where a product was in the process of manufacture when it exploded and injured an employee of a company which had subcontracted the work that resulted in the accident, the product was not legally introduced into the stream of commerce.

introducing products into the channels of commerce for use by the public.[11] "Channels of commerce" implies that a product is placed into the stream of commerce for sale to or use by the consuming public.[12] The determination of when a product has been introduced into the stream of commerce by a product supplier was addressed by the Texas Supreme Court in *Armstrong Rubber Co. v. Urquidez*.[13] The deceased driver, who was employed by Armstrong to test tires on a test track owned by his employer, was operating a truck equipped with both test and "noninterest" tires.[14] The noninterest tires were never actually sold by Armstrong, though they were identical to the quality of the other tires distributed by the company.[15] The fatal accident occurred when one of the noninterest tires blew out, causing the test vehicle to overturn and fatally injure the driver. The imposition of strict tort liability on the tire manufacturer was denied on the basis that the specific tire that failed was never introduced or placed into the stream of commerce.[16] The Texas Supreme Court observed that application of strict tort liability does not necessarily depend upon the sale of a product but that, at a minimum, the product must be released into the stream of commerce in some fashion.[17] The court emphasized that "the Restatement does not make a manufacturer an insurer of every person who is injured by one of its products.[18] To invoke the provisions of Section 402A, it is imperative to establish that the product supplier is engaged in the regular business of supplying

---

11. RESTATEMENT (SECOND) OF TORTS, Section 402A(1)(a), Comment *f* (1965). As noted by the Texas Supreme Court in Armstrong Rubber Co. v. Urquidez, 570 S.W.2d 374, 375 (Tex. 1978), "[i]t is not necessary that the defendant actually sell the product but only that he be engaged in the business of introducing the product into channels of commerce."

12. *See, e.g.*, Armstrong Rubber Co. v. Urquidez, 570 S.W.2d 374 (Tex. 1978); Foster v. Ford Motor Co., 616 F.2d 1304 (5th Cir. 1980); Thate v. Texas & Pacific Ry.Co., 595 S.W.2d 591 (Tex. Civ. App.—Dallas 1980, writ dism'd).

13. 570 S.W.2d 374 (Tex. 1978).

14. *Id.* at 375.

15. *Id.* at 376.

16. *Id.*

17. *Id.*

18. *Id.* at 376. Texas law adopts the principle that a manufacturer is not an insurer of the product and does not guarantee that no harm will result from use of a product. Syrie v. Knoll Int'l, 748 F.2d 304 (5th Cir. 1984); Acord v. General Motors Corp., 669 S.W.2d 111, 113 (Tex. 1984); Shamrock Fuel & Oil Sales Co. v. Tunks, 416 S.W.2d 779 (Tex. 1967); Henderson v. Ford Motor Co., 519 S.W.2d 87 (Tex. 1974); Martinez v. Dixie Carriers, Inc., 529 F.2d 457 (5th Cir. 1976).

products into the stream of commerce for sale or use.[19] For instance, the mere loan of a product to a customer[20] or simply providing a product for use by a customer in a store does not constitute introducing the product into the stream of commerce as contemplated by Section 402A.[21] The introduction of a product into the stream of commerce represents the quintessential requirement for invoking the strict tort liability doctrine.

Often, the imposition of strict products liability hinges upon whether one is a seller regularly engaged in the business of selling or an occasional seller of products. The court of appeals for the Fifth Circuit recently dealt with this issue in *Galindo v. Precision American Corporation*.[22] The plaintiff in *Galindo* was severely injured while operating a sawmill trimmer. Defendant Georgia-Pacific Corporation operated a number of sawmills and sold the trimmer to a used products supplier after it became obsolete. The supplier subsequently sold the trimmer to the plaintiff's employer.

The district court granted summary judgment in favor of Georgia-Pacific on the basis that the corporation was not engaged in the business of selling sawmill trimmers.[23] The court made an *Erie* guess that Texas courts would:

> determine that sales of depreciated owner-user equipment, *even when such sales are quite numerous*, will not remove the seller from the category "occasional seller" [and place him in the category of one "engaged in the business of selling"] . . . , if the sales are of equipment used by the seller in its business and not otherwise any part of a line of products or goods sold by the seller in its ordinary course of business.[24]

The court classified Georgia-Pacific as an occasional seller irrespec-

---

19. 570 S.W.2d at 376. The mere introduction of similar products into the stream of commerce is insufficient; rather, the specific product causing injury must enter the stream of commerce. *Id.*

20. A tire company that merely loans a spare tire to a customer is not considered as introducing a product into the stream of commerce for sale or use. Browning-Ferris Industries, Inc. v. Baden Tire Center, Inc., 536 S.W.2d 203 (Mo. Ct. App. 1976).

21. In Keen v. Dominick's Finer Foods, Inc., 49 Ill.App.3d 480, 364 N.E.2d 502 (1977), a grocery store providing carts for shoppers in the store does not qualify as a product supplier of grocery carts within the ambit of Section 402A. *Accord*, Katz v. Slade, 460 S.W.2d 608 (Mo. 1970).

22. Galindo v. Precision American Corp., 754 F.2d 1212 (5th Cir. 1985).

23. 754 F.2d at 1215.

24. *Id.*

tive of its sales efforts or the regularity of the transactions.[25]

The Fifth Circuit rejected the trial court characterization.[26] The basis of the court's action was the belief that there was a material issue of fact as to whether the defendant was an occasional seller and therefore immune from strict products liability. The court stated that "there may well exist circumstances in which, because of the number of sales or the extent of sales activities, a seller of depreciated equipment would fit squarely within the rationale for imposition of strict liability."[27] Relying on comment *c* to section 402A of the *Restatement*, the court declared that strict liability would be justified when it could be concluded that: (1) he [the seller] has undertaken a special responsibility for product safety; (2) the public has a right to expect that he will stand behind the product; and (3) as between the consumer and the seller, it is equitable to impose upon the seller the loss caused by the product and the burden of spreading that loss as a cost of doing business.[28]

A defective and unreasonably dangerous product manufactured and used by a party does not ipso facto transform that party into a seller within the expanded meaning of Section 402A. In *Gardner v. Chevron U.S.A., Inc.*,[29] plaintiff's husband was fatally injured when excessive pressure precipitated a disruption of an oil flow line causing hot oil to spray back and ignite the burners on the hot oil truck in which the decedent was located.[30] Recognizing that strict tort liability was not applicable to Chevron, the Fifth Circuit observed that "strict liability does not apply to entities like Chevron which had merely constructed an item when those entities were not engaged in the business of selling such items. . . . Although it is not necessary that the defendant actually sell the product, the defendant must be engaged in the business of introducing the product into the channels of commerce."[31]

---

25. *Id.* at 1217-18.
26. *Id.* at 1223.
27. *Id.* at 1220-21.
28. *Id.* at 1221.
29. 675 F.2d 658, 660 (5th Cir. 1982).
30. *Id.* at 660.
31. The court observed that "Chevron did not manufacture, lease or sell nipples of the type that failed. Chevron did construct the well, but it was not sold, leased or placed in any way in the stream of commerce. Rather, Chevron designed the well and constructed it in the field of Sherman, Texas, for its own use. On that basis, the trial court properly determined

Similarly, in *CNG Producing Co. v. Columbia Gulf Transmission*,[32] plaintiff was injured while on an offshore oil platform when vented gases accumulated underneath an overhanging heliport and ultimately ignited causing an extreme explosion. The Fifth Circuit observed that the owner and operator of the offshore platform was not subject to strict tort liability. The court noted that "[i]f the defendant has not offered a product for sale, but kept it for its own purposes, then the justification for strict tort liability does not apply."[33]

Limitations exist even on product suppliers who may supply products as a promotional feature in the operation of their regular business. For example, in *Gobhai v. K-L-M Royal Dutch Airlines*,[34] plaintiff's son sustained injuries when he slipped and fell while wearing a pair of K-L-M slippers in a noncarpeted area of his apartment. In denying liability based on Section 402A, the court observed that K-L-M neither manufactured, designed nor sold the defective footwear.[35] Rather, distribution of the slippers by K-L-M was incidental to the service provided by the airline and the slippers were furnished to its customers for in-flight use.[36] Promoting air flight service by providing footwear for the flight did not transform K-L-M into a seller regularly engaged in the business of supplying slippers into the stream of commerce for sale to or use by the consuming public.[37]

The production and marketing of products generally involves four basic legal entities: the component-part manufacturer, the

---

that, as a matter of law, strict tort liability did not apply." *Id.* at 661.

32. 709 F.2d 959, 961 (5th Cir. 1983).

33. The Fifth Circuit, in discussing the basis for the requirement observed that "The rationale for this rule is easily explained by the policy behind the imposition of product liability on manufacturers. As Justice Traynor explained in Greenman, 'The purpose of such liability is to insure that the cost of injuries resulting from defective products are borne by the manufacturers that put such products on the market rather than by the injured persons who are powerless to protect themselves.' . . . In the case at bar, Columbia Gulf kept the station for its own purposes and did not inject it into the stream of commerce. Plaintiff's product liability claim fails." *Id.* at 963.

34. 85 A.D.2d 566, 445 N.Y.S.2d 445 (1981) *affirmed* 57 N.Y.2d 837, 442 N.E.2d 61, 455 N.Y.S.2d 839 (1982).

35. *Id.* at 447.

36. *Id.*

37. *Id. See generally*, Armstrong Rubber Co. v. Urquidez, 570 S.W.2d 374 (Tex. 1978); Hernandez v. Southern Pacific Transportation Co., 641 S.W.2d 947 (Tex. App.—Corpus Christi 1982, no writ); Thate v. Texas & Pacific Ry.Co., 595 S.W.2d 591 (Tex. App.—Dallas 1980, writ dism'd).

manufacturer and/or assembler, the distributor and/or wholesaler, and the retailer. Though § 402A imposes strict tort liability on any manufacturer/assembler, wholesaler/distributor, or retailer in the distributive chain, the *Restatement* expresses no opinion about the liability of component-part manufacturers.[38]

4.01 Sellers of Defective Products

A. *Component Part Manufacturers and Suppliers*

Most jurisdictions have extended strict tort liability to manufacturers of defective component parts.[39] The socioeconomic concept of risk distribution and reliance on product integrity provide the rationale for extending strict tort liability to suppliers of component parts.[40] Liability is also predicated on a recognition of the indisputable fact that the component part supplier constitutes an integral part of the distributive marketing chain.[41]

The imposition of strict tort liability on component part suppliers is noticeably more restrictive than the imposition of similar liability on other parties in the marketing chain. As a general principle, when the component part is integrated into a larger unit for distribution to the public, strict tort liability for the component part is limited.[42] For example, in *Haupt v. Atwood Oceanics,*

---

38. Restatement (Second) of Torts § 402A comment *q* (1965) provides in pertinent part: "It is no doubt to be expected that where there is no change in the component part itself, but it is merely incorporated into something larger, the strict liability will be found to carry through to the ultimate user or consumer. But in the absence of a sufficient number of decisions on the matter to justify a conclusion, the Institute expresses no opinion on the matter."

39. City of Franklin v. Badger Ford Truck Sales, Inc., 58 Wis.2d 641, 207 N.W.2d 866, 870 (1973); Burbage v. Boiler Eng'r & Supply Co., 433 Pa. 319, 249 A.2d 563, 566 (1969); Barth v. B. F. Goodrich Tire Co., 265 Cal.App.2d 228, 71 Cal.Rptr. 306, 315, (1968); Michalko v. Cooke Color Chemical Corp., 91 N.J. 386, 451 A.2d 179, 183 (1982).

40. *See,. e.g.*, Rourke v. Garza, 511 S.W.2d 331, 336 (Tex. App.—Houston [1st Dist.] 1974), *aff'd*, 530 S.W.2d 794 (Tex. 1975); Haupt v. Atwood Oceanics, Inc., 681 F.2d 1058, 1061 (5th Cir. 1982).

41. Putman v. Erie City Mfg. Co., 338 F.2d 911 (5th Cir. 1964); Michalko v. Cooke Color Chem. Co., 91 N.J. 386, 451 A.2d 179 (1982).

42. Wright v. Federal Machine Co., 535 F. Supp. 645 (E.D. Pa. 1982) (component supplier of rollers sold to an employer as a replacement part to be assembled on a press from which the owner had previously removed safety guards); Klein v. Continental-Emsco, 445 F.2d 629 (5th Cir. 1971) (air valve installed in a console on a drilling rig); Hebel v. Sherman Equip. Co., 92 Ill.2d 368, 442 N.E.2d 199 (Ill. 1982) (manufacturer of drive train asssembly installed in a carwash is not subject to strict tort liability); Bennett v. Span Indus. 628 S.W.2d 470 (Tex. Civ. App.—Texarkana 1981, writ ref'd n.r.e.) (concrete sections to be in-

Inc.,[43] plaintiff, a derrickman on an offshore oil rig, was injured while working on the rig floor. When he slipped and fell on some muddy pipe, he instinctively grabbed for a tensioner system with his hand. A tensioner applies a variable pressure to a riser pipe to offset movement of the offshore vessel by the movement of the sea. Plaintiff's hand became caught in an unguarded pulley over which the tensioner cable was placed.[44] The Fifth Circuit affirmed a directed verdict for the supplier of the tensioner component. The court noted that "any danger posed by these component parts was a function not only of the design and installation of the tensioner system itself, but also a function of the location of the work place on the rig. Proof showed that all of these were unforeseeable elements of which Shaffer [the defendant] had neither responsibility nor control."[45]

A corollary of the limitation governing component part suppliers' liability is the supply of a component pursuant to a purchaser's specifications for integration into a completed product.[46] When the components are integrated or assembled into a larger product in accordance with the design specifications of the purchaser, the supplier of the component part is relieved of responsibility.[47] In *Bennett v. Span Industries, Inc.*,[48] an employee of a subcontractor was seriously injured when he fell through an opening in a concrete roof system manufactured by the defendant and installed by the subcontractor. The plaintiff instituted suit against the supplier of the concrete roof panelings based on strict tort liability. In refusing to impose strict tort liability on the supplier of the component roof system, the court noted that the supplier simply manufactured and sold concrete sections of roofing which were then installed on a building according to the design plans and

---

stalled on a roof deck); Riggins v. Ford Motor Co., 596 F. Supp. 1379 (E.D. La. 1984) (manufacturer of chassis upon which was installed on garbage compactor manufactured by another).

43. 681 F.2d 1058 (5th Cir. 1982).

44. *Id.* at 1059.

45. *Id.* at 1060.

46. Lesnefsky v. Fischer & Porter Co., 527 F. Supp. 951 (E.D.Pa. 1982); Orion Ins. Co., Ltd. v. United Technologies Corp., 502 F. Supp. 173, 175-78 (E.D.Pa. 1980); Moon v. Winger Boss Co., Inc., 205 Neb. 292, 287 N.W.2d 430 (1980). *Contra*, Michalko v. Cooke Chem. Co., 91 N.J. 386, 451 A.2d 179, 183 (1982).

47. Haupt v. Atwood Oceanics, Inc., 681 F.2d 1058, 1060 (5th Cir. 1982); Bennett v. Span Industries, 628 S.W.2d 470 (Tex. Civ. App.—Texarkana 1981, writ ref'd n.r.e.).

48. 628 S.W.2d 470 (Tex. Civ. App.—Texarkana 1981, writ ref'd n.r.e.).

specifications of the contractor-owner.[49]

Merely manufacturing a component part according to another's specifications, however, does not per se limit the potential strict tort liability of the component supplier. Public policy protects the supplier of component parts from strict tort liability for supplying specialized parts of highly technical machinery created in accordance with the design, plans and specifications of the manufacturer-assembler of the product. Despite this, strict tort liability may ensue where the design specifications provide for an obviously or patently defective and unreasonably dangerous product.[50]

A product involving multiple components provides yet another limitation on component part supplier liability. This is particularly apropos when a product involves the assembly of safety devices or features designed to render the ultimately assembled product safe for use, and the assembly of the product involves a number of parties other than the component supplier.[51] When a component device is intended to be installed into an assembled product at a later stage, the determination of potential strict tort liability on the supplier of the component part is dependent on (1) the stage at which the safety device reasonably ought to be installed on the completed product; (2) the expertise of the various parties in the distributive chain for installing safety devices; and (3) the general custom in industry for installing safety devices on the assembled product.[52]

In *Elliott v. Century Chevrolet Co.*,[53] plaintiff was injured when a beer truck backed up and crushed him against a fixed object. Plaintiff instituted a strict tort liability action against the manufacturer of the truck chassis based on the manufacturer's failure to install a backup buzzer on the chassis. In rejecting the imposition of strict tort liability on the manufacturer of the chassis, the court observed that the installer of the beer storage unit on the chassis, not the chassis manufacturer, possessed the expertise and the opportunity to install appropriate safety devices that would

49. *Id.* at 472-73.

50. Jenkins v. Whittaker, 551 F. Supp. 110, 114-15 (D. Hawaii 1982); Christopherson v. Hyster Co., 374 N.E.2d 858, 872 (Ill. App. 1978); Michalko v. Cook Color Chem. Co., 91 N.J. 385, 451 A.2d 179, 183 (N.J. 1982).

51. *Id.*

52. *See* Verge v. Ford Motor Co., 581 F.2d 384, 386 (3d Cir. 1978); Taylor v. Paul O. Abbe Inc., 516 F.2d 145, 147 (3d Cir. 1975); Bexiga v. Havir Mfg. Co., 60 N.J. 402, 290 A.2d 281, 285 (1972); Smith v. Ford Motor Co., 59 Ohio App.2d 41, 392 N.E.2d 1287, 1293 (1978).

53. 597 S.W.2d 563 (Tex. Civ. App.—Fort Worth 1980, writ ref'd n.r.e.).

have prevented the assembled vehicle from becoming unreasonably dangerous.[54]

Concomitantly, the failure to establish that a particular component installed into an assembled product was defective and unreasonably dangerous at the time it left the component supplier's possession presents yet another limitation on the imposition of strict tort liability. In *Klein v. Continental-Emsco*,[55] plaintiff instituted suit based on strict tort liability to recover damages from the manufacturer of air valves and pneumatic controls installed on a drilling rig. The traveling block on a drilling rig fell unexpectedly, causing extensive damage to the rig. Because the air valve was enclosed in a sealed container, the plaintiff contended that the court inferred it was defective when it left the possession of the component manufacturer. Rejecting the imposition of strict tort liability, the Fifth Circuit concluded that the particular valve was integrated into the console by the assembler and therefore the console, not the air valve, constituted the sealed container.[56] In the absence of proof that the component valve was defective before its installation into the console, liability could not be extended to the component part supplier.[57]

B. *Manufacturers and/or Assemblers*

The Supreme Court of Texas adopted § 402A of the *Restatement (Second) of Torts*, which provides that the manufacturer of a defective and unreasonably dangerous product is strictly liable for personal injury or property damage caused by the defect irrespective of whether contractual privity exists between the injured per-

---

54. The court noted that "there would clearly be no duty on Century to install one [backup buzzer] since the dealership sold the truck chassis with no knowledge of what purpose the truck chassis was to serve after its sale." *Id.* at 565. In Grover Hill Grain Co. v. Baughman-Oster, Inc., 728 F.2d 784 (6th Cir. 1984), the Sixth Circuit refused to apply strict tort liability to the supplier of component parts for a large grain bin. The court noted that "It is clear. . .a manufacturer who markets a product in an unassembled state knowing that a third party will complete the assembly process, cannot be strictly liable for a defect introduced by that third party." *Id.* at 789. *See also* Riggins v. Ford Motor Co. 596 F. Supp. 1379, 1380 (E.D. La. 1984); Cunningham v. Lynch-Davidson Motors, 425 So.2d 131 (Fla. App. 1982).

55. 445 F.2d 629 (5th Cir. 1971).

56. *Id.* at 631.

57. *Id.*

son and the manufacturer.[58] One of the principal policy reasons supporting the imposition of strict tort liability is the manufacturer's exercise of control over production and marketing, thereby controlling the safety and quality of the product.[59] A second rationale is the socioeconomic policy that the commercial entity responsible for placing the product into the marketplace is best situated to distribute to the purchasing public the individual and social costs of injuries sustained by consumers of its product.[60] Under the socioeconomic rationale, the manufacturer, aware of the potential risk, may procure liability insurance as protection and distribute the cost to the public by increasing the price of its products.[61]

The first Texas case to impose a form of strict tort liability on a manufacturer arose prior to the formulation and adoption of § 402A of the *Restatement*. In *Jacob E. Decker & Sons, Inc. v. Capps*,[62] the court imposed strict liability as a matter of public policy on the processor of contaminated sausage. The court reasoned:

> A party who processes a product and gives it the appearance of being suitable for human consumption, and places it in the channels of commerce, expects someone to consume the food in reliance on its appearance that it is suitable for human consumption. . . . [H]e uses the newspapers, magazines, billboards, and the radio to build up the psychology to buy and consume his products. . . . The mere fact that a manufacturer . . . may thus induce the public to consume unwholesome food evidences the soundness of the rule which imposes a warranty, as a matter of public policy on the sale of food or other products intended for human consumption.[63]

---

58. Darryl v. Ford Motor Co., 440 S.W.2d 630, 633 (Tex. 1969).

59. Shamrock Fuel & Oil Sales, Inc. v. Tunks, 416 S.W.2d 779, 785-86 (Tex. 1967); Rourke v. Garza, 530 S.W.2d 794, 798 (Tex. 1978); Giberson v. Ford Motor Co., 504 S.W.2d 8, 10 (Mo. 1974); Codling v. Paglia, 32 N.Y.2d 330, 341, 298 N.E.2d 622, 627-28, 345 N.Y.S.2d 461, 468-69 (1973).

60. Greenman v. Yuba Power Prods., Inc., 59 Cal.2d 57, 377 P.2d 897, 27 Cal. Rptr. 697 (1962); Codling v. Paglia, 32 N.Y.2d 330, 298 N.E.2d 622, 528, 345 N.Y.S.2d 461 (1973).

61. Restatement (Second) of Torts § 402A comment *c* (1965) provides, in pertinent part: "that public policy demands that the burden of accidental injuries caused by products intended for consumption be placed upon those who market them, and be treated as a cost of production against which liability insurance can be obtained."

62. 139 Tex. 609, 164 S.W.2d 828 (1942).

63. *Id.* at 832-33.

The Fifth Circuit extended the *Decker* rationale employing a warranty implied by law to nonfood products prior to adoption of § 402A by the Texas Supreme Court.[64] Since adoption of § 402A, Texas courts have upheld causes of action in strict tort liability against a wide range of manufacturers.[65]

---

64. Putman v. Erie City Mfg. Co., 338 F.2d 911, 914-15 (5th Cir. 1964). The plaintiff was injured when his wheelchair collapsed due to a defective fork stem. The court noted that wheelchairs are medical appliances utilized by the old, the sick, and the infirm, who all require special protection. *Id.* at 914-15. Thus, strict tort liability was extended to the manufacturer of the fork stem as well as to the assembler of the wheelchair. *Id.* at 915.

65. (A) Chemical Products and Harmful Substances: Jackson v. Johns-Manville Sales Corp., 727 F.2d 506 (5th Cir. 1984) (asbestos product); Kindred v. Con/Chem Inc., 650 S.W.2d 61 (Tex. 1983) (chemical primer); Bristol-Myers Co. v. Gonzales, 561 S.W.2d 801 (Tex. 1978) (drug for surgical irrigation); C. A. Hoover & Son v. O.M. Franklin Serum Co., 444 S.W.2d 596 (Tex. 1969) (cattle serum); Shamrock Fuel & Oil Sales Co. v. Tunks, 416 S.W.2d 779 (Tex. 1967) (kerosene); Tide Prods., Inc. v. Browning, 493 S.W.2d 654 (Tex. Civ. App.—Amarillo 1973, no writ) (crop pesticide); Monsanto Co. v. Thrasher, 463 S.W.2d 25 (Tex. Civ. App.—Amarillo 1970, writ dism'd) (weed killer); Geigy Chem. Corp. v. Hall, 449 S.W.2d 115 (Tx. Civ. App.—Amarillo 1969, no writ) (weed killer).

(B) Motor Vehicles: Acord v. General Motors Corp., 669 S.W.2d 111 (Tex. 1984) (design of automobile); Turner v. General Motors Corp., 584 S.W.2d 844 (Tex. 1979) (roof of vehicle); Messick v. General Motors Corp., 460 F.2d 485 (5th Cir. 1972) (steering and suspension); Darryl v. Ford Motor Co., 440 S.W.2d 630 (Tex. 1969) (brakes); Mahan Volkswagen, Inc. v. Hall, 648 S.W.2d 324 (Tex. Civ. App.—Houston [1st Dist.] 1982, writ ref'd n.r.e.) (vehicle brakes); General Motors Corp. v. Hebert, 501 S.W.2d 950 (Tex. Civ. App.—Houston [1st Dist.] 1973, writ ref'd n.r.e.) (steering system); Sharp v. Chrysler Corp., 432 S.W.2d 131 (Tex. Civ. App.—Houston [14th Dist.] 1968, writ ref'd n.r.e.) (brakes).

(C) Working Equipment: Rourke v. Garza, 530 S.W.2d 794 (Tex. 1975) (industrial scaffolding); Fleishman v. Guadiano, 651 S.W.2d 730 (Tex. 1983) (ladder); Crump v. Clark Equip. Co., 481 F.2d 667 (5th Cir. 1973) (per curiam) (ladders); Garcia v. Sky Climber, Inc, 470 S.W.2d 261 (Tex. Civ. App.—Houston [1st Dist.] 1971, writ ref'd n.r.e.) (scaffolding).

(D) Processing Machinery: Gross v. Black & Decker, 695 F.2d 858 (5th Cir. 1983) (industrial saw); Hagans v. Oliver Mach. Co., 576 F.2d 97 (5th Cir. 1978) (industrial saw); Pizza Inn, Inc. v. Tiffany, 454 S.W.2d 420 (Tex. Civ. App.—Waco 1970, no writ) (pizza dough rollers); F.M.C. Corp. v. Burns, 444 S.W.2d 315 (Tex. Civ. App.—San Antonio 1969, no writ (cucumber wax).

(E) Medical Supplies: Bristol Myers v. Gonzales, 561 S.W.2d 801 (Tex. 1978) (drug Kantrex); Crocker v. Winthrop Labs, 514 S.W.2d 429 (Tex. 1974) (drug Talwin); Vergott v. Deseret Pharm. Co., 463 F.2d 12 (5th Cir. 1972) (hypodermic needles); Olsen v. Royal Metals Corp., 392 F.2d 116 (5th Cir. 1968) (hospital bed).

(F) Heavy Duty Equipment: Howard v. General Cable Corp., 674 F.2d 351 (5th Cir. 1982) (aerial cable bucket); Gonzales v. Caterpillar Tractor Co., 571 S.W.2d 867 (Tex. 1978) (industrial loader); John Deere Co. v. Ramirez, 503 S.W.2d 382 (Tex. Civ. App.—Amarillo 1973, writ dism'd) (farm combines); K & S Oil Well Serv., Inc. v. Cabot Corp., 491 S.W.2d 733 (Tex. Civ. App.—Corpus Christi 1973, writ ref'd n.r.e.) (oil drilling rig).

(G) Aviation Equipment: Duncan v. Cessna Aircraft Corp., 665 S.W.2d 414 (Tex. 1984) (aircraft seat supports); Bell Helicopter Co. v. Bradshaw, 594 S.W.2d 519 (Tex. Civ. App.—Corpus Christi 1979, writ ref'd n.r.e.) (helicopter rotor blades); Hartzell Propeller Co. v. Alexander, 485 S.W.2d 943 (Tex. Civ. App.—Waco 1972, writ ref'd n.r.e.) (airplane pro-

In *Duncan v. Cessna Aircraft Co.*,[66] decedent, a student pilot, was killed during a flying lesson in a Cessna aircraft. His widow brought a wrongful death action against the manufacturer of the aircraft, alleging that defective design of the cockpit seat leg supports caused the supports to collapse during the crash, resulting in the student pilot's death.[67] The Texas Supreme Court held the manufacturer strictly liable in tort, concluding that the defect in the cockpit seat supports rendered the seats unreasonably dangerous.[68] Significantly, the *Duncan* court adopted comparative causation as a means to allocate damages in strict tort liability cases.[69]

The Supreme Court of Texas in *Miller v. Bock Laundry Machine Company*,[70] concluded that a manufacturer of a centrifugal extractor clothes dryer was strictly liable in tort for placing a defectively designed product into the stream of commerce.[71] The extractor was equipped with a safety device to prevent the lid from being opened while the basket inside was spinning. The safety device failed to operate as an eleven-year-old boy attempted to remove a load of laundry from the machine. The boy's arm became ensnared in the extractor and was severed at the shoulder. The court concluded that the safety device on the extractor which was defective at the time of the accident was the producing cause of the injury.[72] The court emphasized that "a defect in a product at the time of an accident is not alone enough to render the manufacturer strictly liable."[73] The product must be defective at the time it leaves the possession of the manufacturer to impose strict tort

---

pellers); Bell Aerospace Corp. v. Anderson, 478 S.W.2d 191 (Tex. Civ. App.—El Paso 1972, writ ref'd n.r.e.) (helicopters).

(H) Military Ammunition: Challoner v. Day & Zimmermann, Inc., 512 F.2d 77 (5th Cir.), *vacated on choice of law grounds*, 423 U.S. 3 (1975) (howitzer shell).

66. 665 S.W.2d 414 (Tex. 1984). The companion case of the pilot's claim is Smithson v. Cessna Aircraft Corp., 665 S.W.2d 439 (Tex. 1984).

67. 665 S.W.2d at 418.

68. *Id.* at 434.

69. *Id.* at 434. The court, in effect, rejected the earlier decision of assumption of the risk and misuse. *See, e.g.*, Rourke v. Garza, 530 S.W.2d 794 (Tex. 1975); General Motors Corp. v. Hopkins, 548 S.W.2d 344 (Tex. 1977).

70. 568 S.W.2d 648 (Tex. 1978).

71. The court noted that a manufacturer was liable for a dangerous product, "whether designed defectively and manufactured perfectly, or whether designed perfectly but defectively manufactured." *Id.* at 650.

72. *Id.* at 650.

73. *Id.*

liability on the manufacturer.[74] Expert testimony established that the extractor was defectively designed by the manufacturer;[75] thus, strict tort liability was established.[76]

In *Borel v. Fibreboard Paper Products Corp.*,[77] plaintiff, an asbestos insulation worker for more than thirty-three years, was exposed to and inhaled large amounts of asbestos dust from products manufactured by at least six different manufacturers. As a result, he contracted asbestosis and mesothelioma which caused his death prior to trial. Plaintiff sued the manufacturers of the asbestos insulation materials for injuries caused by defendant's failure to warn of the dangers involved in handling asbestos. In imposing liability on the manufacturers, the court noted that the failure to warn of the risks of harm from exposure to asbestos rendered the insulation materials unreasonably dangerous to foreseeable users of the product.[78] Liability was imposed on all the manufacturers of the asbestos products without requiring the plaintiff to prove the extent of injury attributable to each individual manufacturer.[79] The court noted that a manufacturer is liable to the *ultimate* user or consumer of its products for failure to warn, and the presence of an intermediate party[80] does not relieve the manufacturer of this duty.[81]

C. *Distributors and/or Wholesalers*

In Texas, wholesalers and distributors of defective and unreasonably dangerous products are subject to strict tort liability to the same extent as the manufacturer of the product.[82] Though not re-

---

74. *Id.*

75. Experts testified that the safety device failed as the result of a deterioration or shrinking of a rubber pad. The witnesses were of the opinion that the design was defective because a prudent manufacturer at the time would have made the pads out of neophrene or chloroprene. *Id.* at 651.

76. *Id.* at 653.

77. 493 F.2d 1076 (5th Cir. 1973), *cert. denied*, 419 U.S. 869 (1974).

78. *Id.* at 1088.

79. *Id.* at 1094.

80. The manufacturers claimed that the insulation contractors were obligated to warn of any possible danger. *Id.* at 1091.

81. *Id.* at 1088.

82. Bryan v. John Bean Div. of F.M.C. Corp., 566 F.2d 541, 544 n.3 (5th Cir. 1978) (designer - distributor of a cast iron automotive tool); McKisson v. Sales Affiliates, Inc., 416 S.W.2d 787, 790 n.3 (Tex. 1967) (distributor of permanent wave solution); Shamrock Fuel & Oil Sales Co. v. Tunks, 416 S.W.2d 779, 785-86 (Tex. 1967) (distributor of kerosene).

sponsible for the manufacture and production of the product, wholesalers and distributors occupy a position in the distributive chain of marketing. The imposition of strict tort liability is premised on the policy rationale that the distributor, by virtue of his position in the marketing process, possesses the ability to exert pressure on the manufacturer to enhance the quality and safety of the product.[83] In addition, the wholesaler or distributor who does not create the defective condition in the product is entitled to seek indemnity from the manufacturer responsible for creating the defective condition.[84]

In *McKisson v. Sales Affiliates, Inc.*,[85] the Texas Supreme Court imposed strict tort liability on the distributor of a defective permanent wave solution which caused the plaintiff to lose her hair.[86] The product was distributed as an advertising sample to beauty shops without charge.[87] The expectation of future sales resulting from distribution of the samples effectively transformed the distributor into a member of the marketing chain involved in the introduction of products into the channels of commerce. Strict tort liability for the distribution of products was extended to claims seeking property damages in *O.M. Franklin Serum Co. v. C.A. Hoover & Son.*[88] The doctrine of strict tort liability was imposed on the distributor of a defective animal serum that caused plaintiff's cattle to develop a severe reaction and die.[89]

D. *Retailers*

Retailers are subject to strict tort liability for defective prod-

---

83. Restatement (Second) of Torts, Section 402A, comment *f* (1965) provides in pertinent part that "It [Rule 402A] therefore applies to any manufacturer of such a product, to any wholesale or retail dealer or distributor . . ."

84. In Duncan v. Cessna Aircraft Corp., 665 S.W.2d 414, 432 (Tex. 1984), the Texas Supreme Court declared that "comparative causation does not affect the right of a retailer or other member of the marketing chain to receive indemnity from the manufacturer of the defective product when the retailer or other member of the marketing chain is merely a conduit for the defective product and is not independently culpable." *See also* Thiele v. Chick, 631 S.W.2d 526 (Tex. App.—Houston [1st Dist.] 1982, writ ref'd n.r.e.).

85. 416 S.W.2d 787 (Tex. 1967).

86. *Id.* at 792.

87. The court noted that "one who delivers an advertising sample to another with the expectation of profiting therefrom through future sales is in the same position as one who sells the product." *Id.* at 792.

88. 418 S.W.2d 482 (Tex. 1967) (per curiam).

89. *Id.*

ucts notwithstanding that they are not responsible for creating the defective condition in the retailed product.[90] The policy reasons advanced for imposing strict tort liability on retailers are enumerated in the landmark California decision of *Vandermark v. Ford Motor Co.*[91] Justice Traynor observed:

> Retailers like manufacturers are engaged in the business of distributing goods to the public. They are an integral part of the overall producing and marketing enterprise that should bear the cost of injuries resulting from defective products. . . . In some cases the retailer may be the only member of that enterprise reasonably available to the injured plaintiff. In other cases the retailer himself may play a substantial part in ensuring that the product is safe or may be in a position to exert pressure on the manufacturer to that end; the retailer's strict liability thus serves as an added incentive to safety. Strict liability on the manufacturer and retailer alike affords maximum protection to the injured plaintiff and works no injustice to the defendants, for they can adjust the costs of such protection between them in the course of their continuing business relationship.[92]

The imposition of liability on the retailer is based primarily on the rationale that the retailer is entitled to indemnity from the manufacturer. Indemnity is not automatic, however, because the retailer must establish that the defective condition of the product existed at the time the product left the possession and/or control of the manufacturer.[93] The crucial nature of this requirement is illustrated in *Coca-Cola Bottling Co. v. Hobart.*[94] Plaintiff was injured when a Coca-Cola bottle exploded in her hands. Though the retailer and the bottler were determined to be jointly and severally liable, the trial court awarded the retailer indemnity against the

---

90. *See* RESTATEMENT (SECOND) OF TORTS, Section 402A, comment *f* (1965).

91. 61 Cal.2d 256, 391 P.2d 168, 37 Cal.Rptr. 896 (1964).

92. 391 P.2d at 171-72. *See generally*, Note, *Strict Products Liability for Retailers*, 45 WASH. L. REV. 431 (1970) (discussion of policy reasons for extending strict tort liability to retailers).

93. Coca-Cola Bottling Co. v. Hobart, 423 S.W.2d 118 (Tex. Civ. App.—Houston [14th Dist.] 1967, writ ref'd n.r.e.); Sharp v. Chrysler Corp., 432 S.W.2d 131 (Tex. Civ. App.—Houston [14th Dist.] 1968, writ ref. n.r.e.); *But see* United Tractor Co. v. Chrysler Corp., 563 S.W.2d 850 (Tex. Civ. App.—El Paso 1978, no writ) (manufacturer-assembler denied indemnity from manufacturer of component part where assembler discovered the defect but failed to take corrective action).

94. 423 S.W.2d 118 (Tex. Civ. App.—Houston [14th Dist.] 1967, writ ref'd n.r.e.).

bottler.[95] In denying indemnity to the retailer, the appellate court underscored the absence of sufficient evidence that the bottle, though defective when sold to the plaintiff, was in that same defective condition when it left the bottler's control.[96]

Retailer indemnity is significantly more accessible when the product involves a design as distinguished from a manufacturing defect.[97] For instance, in *Turner v. General Motors Corp.*,[98] plaintiff suffered paralysis when the roof of his vehicle collapsed in the course of an overturn. Plaintiff sought recovery based on strict tort liability against the manufacturer and the retailer of the automobile on the theory that the vehicle was not crashworthy. Though the retailer was deemed strictly liable in tort for selling a defectively designed automobile that enhanced the extent of plaintiff's injuries, the retailer was granted indemnity.[99] Similarly, in *Williams v. General Motors Corp.*[100] the court awarded indemnity to the automobile dealer against the manufacturer.[101] The court implicitly concluded that the manufacturer's design of the steering mechanism, and not any concurring acts or conduct of the dealer, rendered the vehicle unreasonably dangerous.[102]

Of course, if the retailer is deemed independently liable for causing or contributing to the cause of plaintiff's injuries, comparative liability rather than indemnity applies. In *Ford Motor Co. v. Russell & Smith Ford Co.*,[103] indemnity was denied to the retailer. Plaintiff was injured by steam and hot water emitted from a split radiator hose in his van. The jury determined that the van's cooling system was defectively designed and that the design defect was a producing cause of the injury. The jury also found that the dealer installed a size and type of air conditioner in the van which

---

95. *Id.* at 120.

96. *Id.* at 125.

97. Turner v. General Motors Corp., 584 S.W.2d 844 (Tex. 1979) (design of vehicle roof); Duncan v. Cessna Aircraft Corp., 665 S.W.2d 414 (Tex. 1984) (support for aircraft seats); Williams v. General Motors Corp., 501 S.W.2d 930, 931 (Tex. Civ. App.—Houston [1st Dist.] 1973, writ ref'd n.r.e) (steering system).

98. 584 S.W.2d 844 (Tex. 1979).

99. *Id.* at 848.

100. 501 S.W.2d 930 (Tex. App.—Houston [1st Dist.] 1973, writ ref'd n.r.e.).

101. *Id.* at 931.

102. *Id.* at 938. In International Harvester Co. v. Zavala, 623 S.W.2d 699, 704 (Tex. App.—Houston [1st Dist.] 1981, writ ref'd n.r.e.), indemnity was rejected based on defendants' independent fault in contributing to the accident.

103. 474 S.W.2d 549 (Tex. Civ. App.—Houston [14th Dist.] 1971, no writ).

aggravated the cooling system problem. Though the manufacturer never warned retailers against the installation of air conditioners in such vans, the retailer was aware of the adverse effect caused by installation of this type air conditioner on similar vans. The retailer's argument for indemnity was rejected on the basis that the defective condition of the product was attributable to both the retailer and the manufacturer.[104]

A potential sale by the retailer rather than an actual sale and transfer of the product is sufficient to invoke the doctrine of strict tort liability. In *Davis v. Gibson Products Co.*,[105] the plaintiff suffered a severe cut while examining a machete on display in the defendant's self-service store. Notwithstanding the absence of any sale of the product, the court concluded that "strict liability rests on foreseeability, and not on esoteric concepts relating to transfer or delivery of possession."[106] The concept of strict tort liability was imposed on the retailer because the retail outlet displayed the machetes with the expectation that people would examine, handle, and purchase them.[107]

Similarly, in *Shoppers World v. Villarreal*,[108] the plaintiff slipped on some soap leaking from a split in a plastic bottle of liquid soap which she had placed in her shopping cart. Though no sale actually occurred, the retailer was held strictly liable in tort because the container of soap reached a potential customer in an unreasonably dangerous condition.[109]

Retailers do not occupy the status of insurers that their goods will not cause injuries.[110] The court in *Moore v. J. Weingarten, Inc.*[111] refused to extend the doctrine of strict tort liability to com-

---

104. *Id.* at 561-62. As the Texas Supreme Court in Duncan v. Cessna Aircraft Corp., 655 S.W.2d 414 (Tex. 1984) notes, indemnity for the retailer applies only when the retailer acts "merely as a conduit for the defective product and is not independently culpable."

105. 505 S.W.2d 682 (Tex. Civ. App.—San Antonio 1973, writ ref'd n.r.e.), *per curiam*, 513 S.W.2d 4 (Tex. 1974).

106. 505 S.W.2d at 691.

107. *Id.* at 691-92.

108. 518 S.W.2d 913 (Tex. Civ. App.—Corpus christi 1975, writ ref'd n.r.e.).

109. *Id.* at 919-20.

110. Acord v. General Motors Corp., 669 S.W.2d 111, 113 (Tex. 1984); Henderson v. Ford Motor Co., 519 S.W.2d 87 (Tex. 1974); General Motors Corp. v. Hopkins, 548 S.W.2d 344 (Tex. 1977). Syrie v. Knoll Int'l., 748 F.2d 304 (5th Cir. 1984). Nor is the retailer an insurer of the safety of customers who enter the store to shop. Bosquez v. H.E. Butt Grocery Co., 586 S.W.2d 680 (Tex. Civ. App.—Corpus Christi 1979, writ ref'd n.r.e.).

111. 523 S.W.2d 445 (Tex. Civ. App.—Beaumont 1975, writ ref'd n.r.e.).

pensate an employee injured when he slipped on a grape near the produce counter where grapes were displayed for sale.[112] The presence on the floor of a single grape on which the plaintiff slipped simply did not constitute a defective product.[113]

Municipalities may qualify under certain limited circumstances as retailers for purposes of the doctrine of strict tort liability.[114] In *Moody v. City of Galveston*,[115] the city operated a water supply system which supplied the plaintiff with water adulterated with flammable gas. Strict tort liability was imposed on the city because it sold a product that was defective and unreasonably dangerous to the consumer.[116] The sale of water by the city was deemed a *proprietary* as distinguished from a *governmental* function to circumvent an immunity against liability arising from the performance of governmental functions.[117]

4.02 Suppliers of Defective Products

Though strict tort liability initially was applied to *sellers* in the traditional sense, i.e., manufacturers, wholesalers, distributors, and retailers, evolution of the doctrine quickly expanded to encompass entities not normally characterized as product suppliers. These entities include, among others, used-product sellers, building contractors, lessors, bailors, certifiers, endorsers, licensors and franchisors.

A. *Sellers of Used Products*

Section 402A of the *Restatement* expresses no opinion on whether strict tort liability applies to a seller of a defective used product.[118] Because the *Restatement* employs the broad term *products*,[119] some jurisdictions have concluded that the strict tort

---

112. *Id.* at 449.

113. *Id.* at 449-50. The court relied on concepts adopted in Technical Chemical Co. v. Jacobs, 480 S.W.2d 602, 605 (Tex. 1972).

114. Moody v. City of Galveston, 524 S.W.2d 583 (Tex. Civ. App.—Houston [1st Dist.] 1975, writ ref'd n.r.e.).

115. 524 S.W.2d 583 (Tex. Civ. App.—Houston [1st Dist.] 1975, writ ref'd n.r.e.).

116. *Id.* at 588-89.

117. *Id.* at 588.

118. Restatement (Second) of Torts § 402A (1965).

119. Restatement (Second) of Torts § 402A (1)(a) (1965) provides that "the seller is engaged in the business of selling such a product."

liability doctrine embraces used products.[120] The minority of jurisdictions that extend the applicability of strict tort liability to sellers of used products articulate several policy reasons in justification of such an extension. Dealers in used products, just as manufacturers and retailers, introduce products into the stream of commerce.[121] The imposition of strict tort liability purportedly encourages dealers marketing used products to inspect and repair their products to ensure the quality and safety of products for the benefit of the public.[122] A second policy rationale proffered in support of the application of strict tort liability presumes that sellers of used products can distribute the costs caused by the imposition of strict tort liability by increasing the price of other used products and by obtaining insurance.[123]

The overwhelming number of jurisdictions exclude sellers of used products from the ambit of strict tort liability.[124] Significant

---

120. Kodiak Elec. Ass'n. v. De Laval Turbine, Inc., 694 P.2d 150, 154 n.6 (Alaska 1984). Josephs v. Harris Corp., 677 F.2d 985, 988 (3d Cir. 1982); Jordan v. Sunnyslope Appliance, Propane & Plumbing Supplies Co., 135 Ariz. 309, 660 P.2d 1236, 1242 (Ct. App. 1983); Peterson v. Lou Backrodt Chevrolet Co. 17 Ill.App.3d 690, 307 N.E.2d 729, 731 (1974), *rev'd on other grounds*, 61 Ill.2d 17, 329 N.E.2d 785 (1975); Turner v. International Harvester Co., 133 N.J. Super. 277, 336 A.2d 62, 67 (1975); Realmuto v. Straub Motors, Inc., 65 N.J. 336, 322 A.2d 440, 444 (1974). *Compare* Note, *Protecting the Buyer of Used Products: Is Strict Liability for Commercial Sellers Desirable*?, 33 Stan. L. Rev. 535 (1981), *with* Note, *Sales of Defective Used Products: Should Strict Liability Apply?*, 25 S. Cal. L. Rev. 805 (1979).

121. Peterson v. Lou Backrodt Chevrolet Co., 17 Ill.App.3d 690, 307 N.E.2d 729, 731 (1974), *rev'd on other grounds*, 61 Ill.2d 17, 329 N.E.2d 785 (1975).

122. 307 N.E.2d at 732. In Realmuto v. Straub Motors, Inc., strict tort liability was extended to a used car dealer but the defect in the vehicle was actually created by the dealer. 65 N.J. 335, 322 A.2d 440 (1974).

123. 307 N.E.2d at 734.

124. Sell v. Bertsch & Co., 577 F. Supp. 1393, 1399 (D.C. Kan. 1984); Bruce v. Martin-Marietta Corp., 544 F.2d 442 (10th Cir. 1976); Rix v. Reeves, 23 Ariz.App. 243, 532 P.2d 185, 186-87 (1975); La Rossa v. Joe Clar & Sons, 122 Cal.App.3d 746, 176 Cal.Rptr. 224, 236-37 (1981); Wilkinson v. Hicks, 126 Cal.App.3d 515, 179 Cal.Rptr. 5 (1981); Tauber-Arons v. Superior Court, 101 Cal.App.3d 268, 161 Cal.Rptr. 789, 797 (1980; Masker v. Smith, 405 So.2d 432, 434 (Fla. App. 1981); Peterson v. Lou Backrodt Chevrolet Co., 61 Ill.2d 17, 329 N.E.2d 785 (1975); Pridgett v. Jackson Iron & Metal Co., 253 So.2d 837, 844 (Miss. 1971); Tillman v. Vance Equip. Co., 286 Or. 747, 596 P.2d 1299, 1303-04 (Or. 1979); Burrows v. Follett & Leach, Inc., 115 Wisc. 2d 272, 340 N.W.2d 485, 488-92 (1983). *See* Christiansen, *Used Products and Strict Liability: A Practical Approach to a Complex Problem,* 81 B.Y.U. L. Rev. 154 (1981). An occasional seller of used machines previously used in its own manufacturing business likewise is not subject to strict tort liability. Bailey v. I.T.T. Grinnell Corp., 536 F. Supp. 84, 87-88 (N.D. Ohio 1982); La Rosas v. Superior Court 122 Cal.App.3d 741, 176 Cal.Rptr. 224, 234-36 (1982).

policy considerations support the majority position.[125] In *Wilkinson v. Hicks*,[126] the California court explained the refusal to extend strict tort liability to a seller of used machinery:

> To impose such liability would as a practical matter require all dealers in used goods routinely to dismantle, inspect for latent defects, and repair or condition their products. Such a rule would affect a radical change in the nature of the used product market, which would deprive that market of . . . desirable flexibility. It would in effect render used goods dealers as insurers against defects which came into existence after the original chain of distribution and while the product was under the control of previous consumers.[127]

In *Sell v. Bertsch & Co.*,[128] the seller of used machinery was not subject to strict tort liability for defects in the machinery that existed at the time of the original manufacture.[129] Plaintiff was injured while using a sixty-year-old steel rolling mill. The court declared strict tort liability was totally inappropriate as a remedy against the seller of the used mill.[130] The court refused to extend strict tort liability to the seller of the used product. The court emphasized that the entity in the distributive chain of marketing that creates the risk and reaps the profits should bear the loss resulting from a defective product.[131]

Similarly, in *Tillman v. Vance Equipment Co.*,[132] claimant instituted suit against the seller of a used crane based on strict tort liability. After reviewing prior Texas decisions the Oregon Supreme Court concluded that the Texas rationale was fallacious and inapplicable to justify extension of strict tort liability to the supplier of used products. The Oregon Supreme Court elaborated:

> As to the risk reduction aspect of strict products liability, the position of the used goods dealer is normally entirely outside the original chain of distribution of the product. As a consequence,

---

125. *Sell*, 517 F. Supp. 1393.
126. 126 Cal.App.3d 515, 179 Cal.Rptr. 5 (1981).
127. 179 Cal. Rptr. at 8.
128. 577 F. Supp. 1393 (D.C. Kan. 1984).
129. *Id.* at 1399.
130. *Id.* at 1397.
131. *Id.* at 1399. As noted by the court, "This used product seller was so far removed from the initial chain of distribution that it could not have discouraged the production and manufacturing of a defective product."
132. 286 Or. 747, 596 P.2d 1299 (1979).

> we conclude, any risk reduction which would be accomplished by imposing strict liability on the dealer in used goods would not be significant enough to justify taking that step. The dealer in used goods generally has no direct relationship with either manufacturers or distributors. Thus, there is no ready channel of communication by which the dealer and the manufacturer can exchange information about possible dangerous defects in particular product lines or about actual and potential liability claims . . . We believe, however, that the influence of this possibility as a practical factor and risk prevention is considerably diluted where used goods are involved due to such problems as statute of limitation and the increasing difficulty as time passes of locating a still existing and solvent manufacturer.[133]

A further policy rationale for refusing to extend strict tort liability to sellers of used products is that when purchasing a worn and perhaps damaged product in an "as is" condition,[134] the consumer neither expects nor actually pays as much as he would if the product were new.[135] In the absence of an express or implied representation of the quality or safety of the product by the seller, the consumer of a used product reasonably expects and contemplates that the product may be worn, broken, or defective.

Two Texas appellate court decisions ostensibly expand strict tort liability to include sellers of used products, though the policy reasons for its imposition are not addressed.[136] In *McLain v. Hodge*,[137] the plaintiff was injured when a used gun that he had purchased from the defendant prematurely fired. The defendant, a seller of new and used guns, sold the gun when it was new, repur-

---

133. 596 P.2d at 1304.

134. In Burrows v. Follett & Leach, Inc., 115 Wisc.2d 272, 340 N.W.2d 485 (1983), the plaintiff suffered amputation of his leg after it became caught in the unguarded power take-off shaft of a corn picker. The defendant dealer sold the corn picker as a used product in an "as is" condition. The Wisconsin Supreme Court concluded that the seller of a used product is not subject to strict tort liability under section 402A. The court reasoned that strict tort liability was inapplicable because (1) the seller made no express representation about the corn picker's safety and the danger of the unguarded take-off was obvious to everyone; (2) the imposition of liability would not achieve any risk reduction; and (3) compensation for injuries would be more served by negligence principles.

135. Rix v. Reeves, 23 Ariz. App. 243, P.2d 185, 187 (1975).

136. *See* Galindo v. Precision American Corp., 754 F.2d 1212 (5th Cir. 1985) for a discussion of the relationship between strict products liability for used products and the classification of an entity as an occassional seller or one regularly engaged in the business of selling. Refer to notes 13-18, *supra*.

137. 474 S.W.2d 772 (Tex. Civ. App.— Waco 1971, writ ref'd n.r.e.).

chased it, and later sold it to the plaintiff in a used condition.[138] The appellate court determined that the gun was defective when new and that this same original defect caused the injuries suffered by the plaintiff.[139] Because the gun was defective when new and the same dealer sold the gun both as a new and a used product, the policy considerations for expanding strict tort liability to used product dealers were not technically involved.

In *Hovenden v. Tenbush*,[140] a seller of new and used bricks sold some used bricks to the plaintiff for use on a commercial building. After the building was completed, the walls began to deteriorate and crumble. The court simply declared that strict tort liability applied to the seller irrespective of whether the bricks sold were new or used.[141] The court relied on and interpreted *McLain* to support the principle that strict tort liability applies to a defective product despite its used condition.[142] The *Hovenden* court totally ignored the significant policy rationale against extension of strict tort liability to used product dealers. Significantly, the court misinterpreted the basis on which the *McLain* court imposed strict tort liability.

Related to the issue of extending strict tort liability to sellers of used products is the potential liability of intermediate sellers of used products. The rationale and policy considerations against imposing strict tort liability on the intermediate seller of used products are equally, and probably more compelling, for intermediate owners and sellers of used products. In *Bruce v. Martin-Marietta Corp.*,[143] the Tenth Circuit Court refused to extend strict tort liability to the intermediate seller of an aircraft. The seller was neither a manufacturer, wholesaler, distributor, nor retailer of the aircraft.[144] The court concluded that there was no sound rationale for imposing strict tort liability on intermediate sellers of used products.[145] Intermediate sellers possess neither the opportunity nor ability to inspect, repair, and rework used products distributed in the marketing chain of used articles. More importantly, inter-

---

138. *Id.* at 774.
139. *Id.* at 775.
140. 529 S.W.2d 302 (Tex. Civ. App.—San Antonio 1975, no writ).
141. *Id.* at 306.
142. *Id.* at 307.
143. 544 F.2d 442 (10th Cir. 1976).
144. *Id.* at 448-49.
145. *Id.* at 449.

mediate sellers of used products are deprived of distributing the increased costs to a large purchasing public.

Sellers of reconditioned used products may be held strictly liable in tort based on the theory that reconditioning consciously raises the reasonable expectations of the consumer concerning the quality and condition of the product. In *Crandell v. Larkin & Jones Appliance Co.*,[146] plaintiff purchased a used clothes dryer which was displayed as quality reconditioned, tag tested, and guaranteed. Upon first use of the machine, the clothing in the dryer caught fire. As the fire spread, it totally destroyed the plaintiff's home.[147] Extending the concept of strict tort liability to the reconditioner, the Court noted: "We believe. . . . that those used product merchants who rebuild or recondition goods are subject to the strict liability doctrine. The application of strict liability to sellers of used products, who rebuild or recondition those products, helps to protect the reasonable expectations of consumers."[148]

The court explained that strict tort liability should not be imposed on sellers of used products because the reasonable expectations of consumers of used products contemplate that the product is worn and probably afflicted with numerous defects.[149] Purchasers of reconditioned used products, on the other hand, reasonably expect and contemplate that the product has been reconditioned to a quality level that insures against the usual defects expected and usually existent in an unworked used product. The "raised expectations" of consumers of reconditioned used products, therefore, provide a legitimate basis for the imposition of strict tort liability on sellers of such products. In fact, reconditioning constitutes a form of representational pronouncement that the product possesses the usual quality that insures users they may rely on its safe and normal performance.[150]

---

146. 334 N.W.2d 31 (S.D. 1983). The identical rationale was employed in Fugate v. AAA Mach. & Equip. Co., 593 F. Supp. 392, 393 (E.D. Tenn. 1984) to impose strict tort liability. *See* Gentile v. MacGregor Mfg. Co., ____ A.2d ____ (N.J. Super. Ct. Law Div.) (No. 1-75952-80).

147. 334 N.W.2d at 34. Similarly in Bailey v. Montgomery Ward & Co., 690 P.2d 1280 (Colo. App. 1984) installation of a used tube in a new tire purchased by plaintiff subjected the seller to strict tort liability for a failure to warn of the danger of such matching.

148. 334 N.W.2d at 34.

149. *Id.*

150. This theory "protects the reasonable expectations of consumer." *Id.*

B. *Lessors and Bailors*

Lessors and bailors of products are not addressed in the *Restatement*. The *Restatement* expressly provides for strict tort liability against "sellers" of products who are regularly engaged in the business of selling or supplying such products.

Texas case law has established, however, that the lessor or bailor of a defective product that is unreasonably dangerous is strictly liable for injuries or damages caused by the leased or bailed product.[151] The rule is limited to lessors and bailors who lease products as a *regular* part of their business and who constitute an integral part of the regular commercial marketing enterprise.[152] Further, liability only extends to those lessors and bailors engaged in regularly releasing products into the channels of commerce.[153]

The Supreme Court of Texas in the landmark case of *Rourke v. Garza*[154] was confronted with the applicability of the strict tort liability doctrine to a lessor of products. The defendant, who was engaged in the business of renting scaffolding equipment, leased unassembled scaffolding to plaintiff's employer. The scaffold boards were leased unassembled and without cleats. Once assembled and placed into use, the scaffold boards slipped off their frames, due to the absence of cleats, causing plaintiff to fall and sustain injuries.[155] Concluding that strict tort liability extends to lessors, the Supreme Court refused to distinguish between the lessor of a product and a seller. The court emphasized that "where one is engaged in the business of introducing products into the channels of commerce, he will be subject to strict liability for physical harm caused by such products if they are unreasonably dangerous to the user or consumer whether he sells or leases his products."[156]

---

151. Rourke v. Garza, 530 S.W.2d 794, 800 (Tex. 1975). A mere gratuitous loan of a defective product does not invoke the doctrine of strict tort liability. Gilliland v. Rothermel, 83 Ill. App. 3d 116, 403 N.E.2d 759, 761 (1980); Brimbau v. Ausdale Equip. Rental Corp., 440 A.2d 1291 (R.I. 1982); Dewberry v. LaFollette, 598 P.2d 241, 242 (Okla. 1979).

152. Rourke v. Garza, 530 S.W.2d 794 (Tex. 1975). *But see* Torres v. Southern Pacific Transp. Co., 584 F.2d 900 (9th Cir. 1978).

153. Freitas v. Twin Cities Fisherman's Coop. Ass'n., 452 S.W.2d 931, 937 (Tex. Civ. App.—Corpus Christi 1970, writ ref'd n.r.e.).

154. 530 S.W.2d 794 (Tex. 1975).

155. *Id.* at 797.

156. *Id.* at 800.

In *Thate v. Texas & Pacific Railway Co.*,[157] the plaintiff was injured when he jumped to the ground from a flatbed railroad car to avoid a falling stanchion. Plaintiff instituted a strict tort liability action against the railroad company under the *Rourke* rationale that one who introduces a defective and unreasonably dangerous product into the stream of commerce is liable for any injury or damage caused by the product. The application of strict tort liability was rejected on the basis that the railroad car had not been introduced into the channels of commerce.[158] A significant distinction exists between a product *employed* in interstate commerce and one *introduced* into the *channels of commerce*:

> Channels of commerce implies that a product is placed for use by or sale to the consuming public, while interstate commerce is a term used for purposes of determining the scope of federal regulation. Merely because a product is employed in interstate commerce does not necessarily mean that it is in the channels of commerce.[159]

Essentially, a bailment is insufficient if it is not consummated by a release of the product to a user or consumer in the regular stream of commerce.[160] Under Section 402A, a lessor engaged in isolated or only occasional leasing of products is excluded from liability.[161] The emphasis is on "the regular business of leasing."[162] Obviously, a mere gratuitous lease of a defective product is insufficient to invoke strict tort liability.[163]

The case of *Freitas v. Twin Cities Fisherman's Cooperative Association* [164] illustrates a further limitation on the applicability of strict tort liability to lessors and bailors of products. Plaintiff

---

157. 595 S.W.2d 591 (Tex. Civ. App.—Dallas 1980, writ dism'd).

158. *Id.*

159. *Id.*

160. *Id.* at 599. *See also* Hernandez v. Southern Pacific Transp. Co., 641 S.W.2d 947 (Tex. App.—Corpus Christi 1982).

161. Browning-Ferris Industries, Inc. v. Baden Tire Center, Inc., 536 S.W.2d 203 (Mo. App. 1976); Smith v. Nick's Catering Service, 549 F.2d 1194 (8th Cir. 1977).

162. *See, e.g.*, Price v. Shell Oil Co. 2 Cal.3d 245, 254, 466 P.2d 722, 728, 85 Cal. Rptr. 178, 184 (1970). For example, in Edwards v. Neely Oil, Inc., 556 S.W.2d 114 (Tex. Civ. App.—Amarillo 1977, writ ref'd n.r.e.), the lessor of a service station was held not subject to strict tort liability for an explosion precipitated by a defect in the heating system of the leased building.

163. Gilliland v. Rothermel, 83 Ill.App.3d 116, 403 N.E.2d 759, 761 (1980); Keen v. Dominick's Finer Foods Inc., 49 Ill. App. 3d 480, 364 N.E.2d 502, 504 (1977).

164. 452 S.W.2d 931 (Tex. Civ. App.—Corpus Christi 1970, writ ref'd n.r.e.).

fell from an oil tank platform when the ladder that he was climbing suddenly and unexpectedly detached from the oil tank. The defendant had leased the tank for storage of its petroleum products. Defendant claimed it was not a "seller engaged in the business of selling platforms and/or ladders and that the case [did] not involve a product in commerce."[165] The court acknowledged that § 402A extended only to persons or concerns engaged in the business of selling products.[166] Because defendant was in the business of selling petroleum products, and not leasing platforms and ladders, strict tort liability was inapplicable.[167]

A lessee of products, as distinguished from a lessor of products, is not encompassed by Section 402A of the *Restatement*. The lessee essentially occupies the position of a user or consumer of products. For instance, in *Hernandez v. Southern Pacific Transportation Co.*,[168] a railroad employee was injured when a stanchion collapsed and fell on his leg. The defendant-employer occupied the status of a mere lessee of the railroad car. In rejecting the imposition of liability under § 402A, the court observed that "[t]he railroad merely leased the stanchion from Trail Train Corp. and, through persons such as the appellant, used it for its intended purpose. We have found no case in which strict liability has been imposed upon a lessee, and we decline to do so here."[169]

Though Texas has not determined specifically whether strict tort liability extends to motor vehicle rental companies, the majority of jurisdictions have extended the doctrine to these leasing entities.[170] The Supreme Court of New Jersey in the seminal case of

---

165. *Id.* at 935.

166. *Id.* at 937.

167. *Id.* at 938.

168. 641 S.W.2d 947 (Tex. App.—Corpus Christi 1982, no writ).

169. *Id.* at 952.

170. Bachner v. Pearson, 479 P.2d 319, 327-28 (Alaska 1979) (leased airplane); Stewart v. Budget Rent-A-Car Corp., 52 Hawaii 71, 75, 470 P.2d 240, 243 (1970) (leased automobile); Galluccio v. Hertz Corp., 1 Ill.App.3d 272, 274 N.E.2d 178, 183 (1971) (leased van); Stang v. Hertz Corp., 83 N.M. 739, 497 P.2d 732, 737 (1972) (leased automobile); Coleman v. Hertz Corp., 534 P.2d 940, 944-45 (Okla. Ct. App. 1975) (leased milk truck); Francioni v. Gibsonia Truck Corp., 472 Pa. 362, 372 A.2d 736, 739 (1977) (leased truck); Martin v. Ryder Truck Rental, Inc. 353 A.2d 581 (Del. 1979) (leased truck); Gilbert v. Stone City Const. Co., 171 Ind. App. 418, 357 N.E.2d 738, 742 (1976) (leased machinery); Hawkins Constr. Co. v. Matthews Co., 190 Neb. 546, 209 N.W.2d 643, 654 (1973) (leased scaffolding); Brimbau v. Ausdale Equip. Rental Corp., 440 A.2d 1292, 1298 (R.I. 1982)(leased backhoe).

Cintrone v. Hertz Truck Leasing & Rental[171] explained that a bailor of motor vehicles, as part of its regular business, introduces its vehicles into the stream of commerce for the use of the public. In furtherance of the socioeconomic rationale underlying strict tort liability, the bailor occupies a better position to detect and eliminate defects than the bailee. The court reasoned:

> The operator of the rental business must be regarded as possessing expertise with respect to the service life and fitness of his vehicles for use. That expertise ought to put him in a better position than the bailee to detect or anticipate flaws or defects or fatigue in his vehicles. Moreover, as between bailor for hire and bailee the liability for flaws or defects not discoverable by ordinary care in inspecting or testing ought to rest with the bailor . . .with respect to failure of a rented vehicle from fatigue, since control of the length of the lease is in the lessor, such risk is one which, in the interest of the consuming public as well as of the members of the public traveling the highways, ought to be imposed on the rental business.[172]

The extension of the doctrine of strict tort liability to lessors regularly engaged in the business of leasing products to the consuming public is uniquely parallel to the application of the doctrine to sellers of new products.[173] An analysis of the lessor's involvement in the introduction of products into the channels of commerce demonstrates that (1) the lessor, like the seller, may be the only member in the marketing chain available to the injured party for redress; (2) as in the case of the seller, strict tort liability imposed on the lessor provides an incentive for furnishing safe products; (3) the lessor occupies a better position than the consumer to prevent introduction of defective products into the public domain; and (4) the lessor can distribute the cost of injuries resulting from defective products by adjusting the rental terms of the product or procuring appropriate insurance coverage.[174] Perhaps most significant in extending strict tort liability to the lease trans-

---

171. 45 N.J. 434, 212 A.2d 769 (1965). Plaintiff instituted suit against the truck rental company on the theory of breach of warranty. The plaintiff was injured as a result of brake failure on a truck that had been leased to his employer.

172. 212 A.2d at 778.

173. Francioni v. Gibsonia Truck Corp., 472 Pa. 362, 372 A.2d 736 (1977).

174. See Francioni v. Gibsonia Truck Corp., 472 Pa. 362, 372 A.2d 736 (1977); Bachner v. Pearson, 479 P.2d 319 (Alaska 1970); Ettin v. Ava Truck Leasing, Inc., 100 N.J. Super. 515, 242 A.2d 663 (App. Civ. 1986); Stang v. Hertz Corp., 83 N.M. 730, 497 P.2d 732 (1972).

action is the lessee's lack of opportunity for inspection of the leased product compared to the lessor's opportunity for inspection and repair and the implied representation of the lessor that the product is safe for normal use.

C. *Endorsers, Testers and Certifiers*

The testing and certification of products by independent agencies has assumed an increasingly important role in the overall marketing scheme of products. Both the consumer and manufacturer frequently rely on these independent agencies for evaluations and evolvement of the product—the consumer for selecting a particular product and the manufacturer for promoting consumer demand for its products.

Generally, agencies which merely approve or certify products are deemed beyond the reach of § 402A strict tort liability.[175] Jurisdictions that extend liability to the certifier or tester rely on the theory of negligence as articulated in § 324A of the *Restatement (Second) of Torts*:

> One who undertakes, gratuitously or for consideration, to render services to another which he should recognize as necessary for the protection of a third person or his things, is subject to liability to the third person for physical harm resulting from his failure to exercise reasonable care to protect his undertaking, if
> (a) his failure to exercise reasonable care increases the risk of such harm, or
> (b) he has undertaken to perform a duty owed by the other to the third person, or
> (c) the harm is suffered because of reliance of the other or the third person upon the undertaking.[176]

Liability is predicated solely on the basis of negligence. Thus far, no jurisdiction has sanctioned liability on endorsers or certifiers based on a concept of strict tort liability.[177]

---

175. Refer to notes 139-145 *infra* and accompanying text. *See generally*, Babij, *Liability of a Product Endorser of Certifier: A Tort Whose Time Has Come and Gone*, 20 TRIAL 38-40 (April 1984).

176. RESTATEMENT (SECOND) OF TORTS § 324A (1965).

177. *See*, Note, *Liability of Certifiers of Quality to Ultimate Consumers*, 36 NOTRE DAME LAW 176 (1961); Comment, *Potential Liability of Non-Manufacturer Certifiers of Quality*, 10 VILL. L. REV. 708 (1965). In *Benco Plastics, Inc. v. Westinghouse Electric Corp.*, 387 F. Supp. 772 (E.D. Tenn., 1974), the plaintiff sought to impose liability on Underwrit-

Several policy reasons argue persuasively against the extension of strict tort liability to endorsers and certifiers. These parties do not occupy a position in the distributive or marketing chain of products. A fortiori, these agencies are precluded from spreading the increased cost of strict tort liability by seeking indemnity from others in the distributive chain. Additionally, the extent of an endorser's or tester's potential liability is substantially greater and more encompassing than the liability of individual manufacturers. If the strict tort liability doctrine applied, the tester or certifier would be burdened with liability for injuries produced by defects in multiple lines of products of different manufacturers rather than a single line attributable to a single manufacturer.[178] Further, the prospect of obtaining sufficient insurance to protect against liability is remote, while the cost of distributing this additional cost burden to the subscribing manufacturer would be prohibitive. Therefore, "the extension of strict tort liability to the tester or certifier would have the effect of eliminating certifiers and testers as viable business entities."[179]

Another consideration against imposing strict tort liability is the fact that the tester and the certifier merely furnish a service and not a product. If strict liability focuses solely on the condition of the product and not the conduct of the party associated with the product, then certifiers and testers, by definition, necessarily fall outside the aegis of strict tort liability.[180]

As a final policy consideration, endorsers, testers, and certifiers possess little or no control over the production and marketing process and, therefore, cannot ensure increased quality or protection of the product. Usually, the tester or certifier merely tests a product on a sample basis to determine the product's performance

---

ers' Laboratories (U.L.) for misrepresenting the quality and character of a lampholder U.L. listed and represented to be suitable for outdoor use. The court considered (1) the degree of closeness between the injured party and the endorser; (2) the nature of plaintiff's injury; (3) the causal connection between plaintiff's injury and the endorser's representation; (4) the evidence of reliance on the endorser's representations; (5) the moral culpability attached to the endorser's conduct; (6) the policy of preventing future harm; and (7) the nature of the endorser's business. Balancing these factors, the court refused to hold U.L. liable under a theory of strict liability for misrepresentation.

178. *See* Note, *Liability of Certifiers of Products for Personal Injuries to the User or Consumer*, 56 CORNELL L. REV. 132, 141-44 (1970).

179. *See generally* Sales, *The Service - Sales Transaction: A Citadel Under Assault*, 10 ST. MARY'S L.J. 13, 23 (1978).

180. *Id.* at 23.

capability and its durability. The tester or certifier is afforded, at best, little if any opportunity for input into the design of the manufacturer's products.[181]

The landmark case considering strict tort liability in the context of a certifier is *Hanberry v. Hearst Corp.*[182] Plaintiff sustained injuries when she slipped and fell on a vinyl floor as a result of a defectively designed shoe which carried the Good Housekeeping seal of approval. Rejecting the imposition of strict tort liability on the certifier, the court noted:

> [The plaintiff] does not contend . . . it examined or tested the particular pair of shoes involved. The most that can be implied . . . is that it has examined or tested samples of the product and found the general design and materials used to be satisfactory. Application of . . . strict liability in tort would subject [the defendant] to liability even if the general design and materials used in making this brand of shoe were good, but the particular pair became defective through some mishap in the manufacturing process. We believe this kind of liability for individually defective items should be limited to those directly involved in the manufacturing and supplying process. . . ."[183]

In any event, liability, if imposed, would arise only in instances of inadequate design.[184] Because the testing is restricted to samples, the certification of quality can only refer to the design and construction of the particular samples under review and not to the construction of the specific injury-causing product.[185] Any effort to extend strict tort liability to agencies engaged in testing, certifying and inspecting products would contravene the concept of Section 402A strict tort liability. Further, such an extension would be economically destructive because of the absence of the ability to equalize the burden by distributing increased costs to the marketing public that is afforded other product suppliers.

---

181. *Id.* at 23-24.

182. 276 Cal. App. 2d 680, 81 Cal. Rptr. 519 (1969).

183. 81 Cal. Rptr. at 524. *See also* Hempstead v. General Fire Extinguisher, 269 F.Supp 109, 118 (D. Del. 1967) (endorser liable only under negligence).

184. 81 Cal. Rptr. at 522.

185. *See* Hanberry v. Hearst Corp., 276 Cal. App. 2d 680, 687, 81 Cal. Rptr. 519, 524 (1969); Post v. Alameda Amusement Co., 117 Cal. App. 2d 588, 590, 256 P.2d 580, 581 (1953) (involving seal by Underwriter's Laboratories, Inc.). *See generally* Note, *Liability of Certifiers of Products for Personal Injuries to the User or Consumer*, 56 CORNELL L. REV. 132 (1970).

D. *Licensors and/or Franchisors*

The application of strict tort liability under Section 402A to licensors and franchisors developed and evolved much later than application of the doctrine to the more traditional suppliers occupying a position in the regular marketing chain.[186] Like distributors and wholesalers, franchisors and licensors participate in the distributive chain, albeit more peripherally, by encouraging the introduction of products into the stream of commerce for use by the public. Liability is predicated on a form of sponsorship of the product; the licensor and franchisor imply to the consumer or user that they stand behind the product.[187]

A number of policy reasons support extension of strict tort liability to entities occupying the legal status of licensor or franchisor.[188] The usual rationale underlying application of the doctrine include (1) the risk that the franchisor creates by approving an unsafe product for distribution; (2) the franchisor's ability and opportunity to eliminate the unsafe character of the product and prevent loss; (3) the consumer's lack of any knowledge of the danger in the sponsored product; and (4) the consumer's reliance on the trade name which gives the intended impression that the franchisor is responsible for and stands behind the product.[189]

The imposition of strict tort liability on licensors and franchisors was explored in *Connelly v. Uniroyal, Inc.*[190] Plaintiff instituted a strict tort liability action against Uniroyal for a defec-

---

186. Kosters v. Seven-Up Co., 595 F.2d 347, 353 (6th Cir. 1979); Carter v. Joseph Bancroft & Sons Co., 360 F. Supp. 1103, 1106-09 (E.D.Pa. 1973); Kasel v. Remington Arms Co., 24 Cal.App.3d 711, 101 Cal.Rptr. 314 (1972); City of Hartford v. Associated Const. Co., 34 Conn.Supp. 204, 384 A.2d 390 (1978); Connelly v. Uniroyal, Inc., 75 Ill.2d 393, 389 N.E.2d 155 (Ill. 1979), *cert. denied*, 444 U.S. 1060 (1980); Wojciuk v. United States Rubber Co., 13 Wis.2d 173, 108 N.W.2d 149 (1961), *modified*, 19 Wis.2d 235, 122 N.W.2d 737 (1963).

187. *See, e.g.*, Taylor v. General Motors Corp., 537 F. Supp. 949 (E.D. Ky. 1982). (General Motors Corporation deemed to sponsor a fan blade installed in its vehicle even though manufactured by an independent company).

188. Kosters v. Seven Up Co., 595 F.2d 347, 353 (6th Cir. 1979). The plaintiff was injured when a bottle of Seven-Up exploded after it slipped from the carton and fell on the floor. Since the carton was packaged and distributed by a franchisee of the defendant bottler, the court extended strict tort liability to the franchisor.

189. *Id.* at 353. *See* Wise v. Kentucky Fried Chicken Corp., 555 F. Supp. 991, 996 (D.N.H. 1982) (franchisor selection of equipment for its franchisee). *Cf* Franchisor disharges its duty under strict tort liability by informing franchisee of the product's dangerous propensities. See Cook v. Branick Mfg. Inc., 736 F.2d 1442, 1446 (11th Cir. 1984)

190. 75 Ill.2d 393, 389 N.E.2d 155 (1979), *cert. denied*, 444 U.S. 1060 (1980).

tive tire on his vehicle that blew out and caused his accident. The tire manufacturer was a nonexclusive licensee of Uniroyal. Imposing strict tort liability on the licensor, the court emphasized that socioeconomic considerations require that anyone who, for consideration, authorizes use of a trademark on a defective product is subject to strict tort liability.[191]

The sponsorship rationale underlying the application of strict tort liability to a licensor was liberally extended in *Taylor v. General Motors Inc.*[192] Plaintiff was fatally injured when stabbed by a detached fan blade as he leaned into the engine compartment of his car attempting to correct an engine malfunction. Though the blade was fabricated by Hayes-Albion Company, ninety-nine percent of Hayes-Albion fans were installed in defendant's vehicles while the remaining one percent were installed in Checker cabs.[193] Plaintiff was unable to establish whether the faulty fan was obtained from a GMC or a Checker cab. Evidence established that defendant supplied the drawings and specifications for the fan, furnished orders to stop work on or destroy fan blades that it did not need, approved and accepted the fan blade design, and suggested the sale of fans to Checker Cab Company. Concluding that General Motors was strictly liabile in tort, the court noted that General Motors exercised control over the design of the product and decided that the fan should be designed to resist stresses encountered in only a few model cars when, with slight additional expense, it could have insured safety for use in any passenger vehicle.[194] Any entity which forms an integral part of the business enterprise responsible for placing a defective product into the channels of commerce, in essence, assumes a position in the marketing chain and, therefore, is strictly liable in tort for the defective product.[195]

Franchisor liability for defective equipment prescribed for its franchisee was considered in *Wise v. Kentucky Fried Chicken Corp.*[196] An employee of the franchisee was burned by hot cooking oil from an allegedly defective pressure fryer. The fryer was pur-

---

191. 389 N.E.2d at 163.
192. 537 F. Supp. 949 (E.D.Ky. 1982).
193. *Id.* at 950.
194. 537 F. Supp. at 954.
195. *See* Kosters v. Seven Up Co., 595 F.2d 347 (6th Cir. 1979).
196. 555 F. Supp. 991 (D.N.H. 1982).

chased from an approved supplier, as determined by the franchisor. The manufacturer notified the franchisor of defects in the fryer and suggested it notify all of its franchisees of the problem. The franchisor failed to warn its franchisees of the defect and failed to require a modification of the fryers. Strict tort liability resulted because the franchisor failed to warn its franchisees of the defect.[197]

The concept of sponsorship underlies the application of strict tort liability to licensors and franchisors of defective products. Clearly, any agency placing into the stream of commerce a defective product under its auspices invites liability under Section 402A.

4.03 Providers of Services

Perhaps the most controversial issue presently under debate involves the extension of strict tort liability to providers of services. The nature and the type of service provided often influences the issue of liability. Strict tort liability is more likely to attach when a defective product is provided as part of a service than to a defectively performed service.[198] If the product is adulterated food, however, the restaurateur, as a provider of services, is subject to strict tort liability.[199]

Texas is reluctant to extend strict tort liability to providers of services.[200] Strict tort liability has been imposed, however, on restaurateurs.[201] There is an indication that in some circumstances, strict tort liability may be extended even to medical professional and nonprofessional sales-service providers.[202] The extension of

---

197. *Id.* at 996.

198. *See generally* Sales, *The Service-Sales Transaction: a Citadel Under Assault*, 10 St. Mary's L.J. 13 (1978); Powers, *Distinguishing Between Products & Services in Strict Tort Liability*, 62 N.C.L. Rev. 415 (1984); Note, *Products and the Professional: Strict Liability in the Sale-Service Hybrid Transaction*, 24 Hastings L.J. 111 (1972). Note, *Strict Liability in Hybrid Cases*, 32 Stan. L. Rev. 391 (1980). *See, Application of Rule of Strict Liability in Tort to Person Rendering Service*, 29 ALR.3d 1425 (1970).

199. Restatement (Second) of Torts, § 402A comment *f* (1965) limits application to "any person engaged in the business of *selling products.*" This necessarily excludes service agencies who sell primarily services and not products.

200. Refer to notes 204-06 *infra* and accompanying text.

201. Hebert v. Loveless, 474 S.W.2d 732, 738 (Tex. Civ. App.—Beaumont 1971, writ ref'd n.r.e.).

202. *See, e.g.,* Thomas v. St. Joseph's Hosp., 618 S.W.2d 791 (Tex. Civ. App.—Houston [1st Dist.] 1981, no writ); Providence Hosp. v. Truly, 611 S.W.2d 127 (Tex. Civ. App.—Waco 1980, writ dism'd). *But see* Neveaux v. Park Place Hospital, Inc., 656

strict liability to these entities represents a recent and rather unprecedented deviation from previously well established Texas decisional law.

A. *Pure Service Transactions*

The rule that strict tort liability does not extend to the providers of services is well entrenched in the jurisprudence of almost all jurisdictions.[203] When service constitutes the essence of a transaction, the focus for consideration is the conduct of the service provider. The consumer possesses reasonable expectations that the service provider will perform the services with reasonable care, competence, and skill.[204] When the issue involves the potential liability of the service provider, strict tort liability is inapplicable because strict liability under § 402A focuses solely on the condition of a *product*; it is not concerned with the conduct of the service provider.[205]

A significant reason for rejecting the imposition of strict tort liability in the service provider context is the total absence of any mass production of services.[206] Consequently, there is neither a middleman nor members of a distributive chain to disseminate the costs of liability.[207] The imposition of strict tort liability, therefore,

---

S.W.2d 923 (Tex. App.—Beaumont 1983, writ ref'd n.r.e.).

203. Winans v. Rockwell International Corp., 705 F.2d 1449, 1452-53 (5th Cir. 1983); Johnson v. William C. Ellis & Sons Iron Works, Inc., 604 F.2d 950, 955 (5th Cir. 1979); Lemley v. J & B Tire Co., 426 F. Supp. 1376, 1378 (W.D. Pa. 1977); Raritan Trucking Corp. v. Aero Commander, Inc., 458 F.2d 1106, 1113 (3d Cir. 1972); Swenson Trucking & Excavating, Inc. v. Truckweld Equip. Co., 604 P.2d 1113, 1116-17 (Alaska 1980); Times Mirror Co. v. Sisk, 122 Ariz. 174, 593 P.2d 924, 928 (Ct. App. 1978); Endicott v. Nissan Motor Corp., 73 Cal.App.3d 917, 930, 141 Cal. Rptr. 95, 103 (1977); Pena v. Sita World Travel, Inc., 88 Cal. App. 3d 642, 152 Cal. Rptr. 17 (1978); Castaldo v. Pittsburgh-Des Moines Steel Co., 376 A.2d 88, 91 (Del. 1977); Hinojasa v. Automatic Elevator Co., 92 Ill. App. 3d 351, 416 N.E.2d 45, 47 (1980); Hunt v. Guaranty Elect. Co. 667 S.W.2d 9, 12 (Mo. Ct. App. 1984); Siciliano v. Capitol City Shows, Inc., 124 N.H.719, 475 A.2d 19, 25 (1984); Bolduc v. Herbert Schneider Corp., 117 N.H. 566, 374 A.2d 1187, 1189, (1977); Steckal v. Haughton Elevator Co., 59 N.Y.2d 628, 629, 463 N.Y.S.2d 186, 186-87, 449 N.E.2d 1264 (1983); Nickel v. Hyster Co., 97 Misc.2d 770, 412 N.Y.S.2d 273, 276 (Sup. Ct. 1978), Hoover v. Montgomery Ward & Co., Inc., 270 Or. 498, 528 P.2d 76, 78 (1974); Klein v. Council of Chem. Assoc., 587 F. Supp. 213, 223 (E.D.Pa. 1984). For a thorough discussion of pure service transactions, see Sales, *The Service-Sales Transaction: A Citadel Under Assault*, 10 St. Mary's L.J. 13, 18-25 (1978).

204. Sales, *The Service-Sales Transaction: A Citadel Under Assault*, *supra* note 179 at 18.

205. *Id.*

206. *Id.*

207. *Id.* at 19.

would jeopardize the viability of service providers.[208] Moreover, because service transactions represent a face-to-face relationship, and consumers reasonably expect and contemplate skilled and competent service, liability based on negligence represents an effective remedy of reason.[209]

B. *Restaurateurs*

Restaurateurs provide a service to their patrons by preparing and serving food. While providers of services generally are beyond the ambit of strict tort liability, most jurisdictions impose strict tort liability on restaurateurs based on an implied warranty of fitness for human consumption.[210] The *Restatement* suggests that strict tort liability applies to restaurateurs on the theory that restaurateurs, in reality, are sellers of food products for consumption.[211] Patrons of restaurants reasonably expect and contemplate edible food for human consumption. Service is merely incidental to the purchase of the product. This is reflected in the fact that waiters, the true service providers, are remunerated primarily by tipping.[212]

Several policy reasons underlie the imposition of liability on restaurateurs.[213] While restaurateurs provide a service, they are, in fact, sellers of food products.[214] The patron reasonably contemplates that the food will be wholesome and fit for consumption, and relies on the skill of the restaurateur in selecting and preparing edible and non-adulterated food.[215] As an additional consideration, the restaurateur is entitled to indemnification from the sup-

---

208. *Id.*

209. *Id.* at 18.

210. *See, e.g.*, F.W. Woolworth Co. v. Garza, 390 S.W.2d 90 (Tex. Civ. App.—San Antonio 1965, writ ref'd n.r.e.); Brumit v. Cokins, 281 S.W.2d 154, 157 (Tex. Civ. App.—Galveston 1955, writ ref'd n.r.e.); Cushing v. Rodman, 82 F.2d 864, 871 (D.C. Cir. 1936); Cliett v. Lauderdale-Biltmore Corp., 39 So.2d 476, 478 (Fla. 1949); Levy v. Paul, 207 Va. 100, 147 S.E.2d 722, 726 (1966).

211. Restatement (Second) of Torts § 402A, comment *f* (1965) provides, in part: "The rule stated in this Section applies to any person engaged in the business of selling products for use or consumption. It therefore applies to any manufacturer of such a product, to any wholesale or retail dealer or distributor, and to the operator of a restaurant."

212. Wachtel v. Rosol, 159 Conn. 496, 271 A.2d 84, 86-87 (1970); Hebert v. Loveless 474 S.W.2d 732, 738 (Tex. Civ. App.—Beaumont 1971, writ ref'd n.r.e.).

213. Cushing v. Rodman, 82 F.2d 864 (D.C. Cir. 1936).

214. *Id.* at 866.

215. *Id.* at 867-69.

plier for the unwholesome condition of the food not created by the independent culpable acts of the restaurateur.[216] The single most important factor is the socioeconomic rationale that the restaurateur may distribute the costs of liability through increased prices while securing protection from liability with insurance.[217]

Since the 1930's, Texas courts have imposed on restaurateurs a form of strict liability sounding in warranty that the food dispensed is fit for human consumption.[218] In the early case of *Brumit v. Cokins*,[219] plaintiff was injured by glass in a milkshake served at defendant's restaurant. Liability based on breach of an implied warranty of fitness for human consumption was imposed on the restaurant.[220] The warranty emanates from a public policy that food sold for immediate consumption must be wholesome and is implied to protect and preserve the health of members of the public.[221]

In *Hebert v. Loveless*,[222] plaintiff became ill after consuming impure ice at the defendant's restaurant. The restaurateur was deemed strictly liable in tort for injuries caused by food determined to be unfit for human consumption.[223] Refusing to permit indemnity against the ice manufacturer, the court observed that the failure to establish that the product is defective or unfit for consumption when delivered by the manufacturer precludes indemnity.[224]

Many jurisdictions have struggled with differentiating liability for food rendered unwholesome because of a foreign particle indigenous to the product, i.e., pits in peaches, and particles not reasonably contemplated in the food, i.e., bone in "boneless" chicken or fish.

---

216. *Id.* at 867-68.

217. *Id.* at 869-70.

218. *See* F.W. Woolworth Co. v. Garza, 390 S.W.2d 90, 91 (Tex. Civ. App.—San Antonio 1965, writ ref'd n.r.e.); Brumit v. Cokins, 281 S.W.2d 154, 157 (Tex. Civ. App.—Galveston 1955, writ ref'd n.r.e.); S.H. Kress & Co. v. Ferguson, 60 S.W.2d 817, 821 (Tex. Civ. App.—Beaumont 1933, writ dism'd). *See also* Truitt v. Shamrock Hotel, 143 F. Supp. 376, 380 (S.D. Tex. 1956).

219. 281 S.W.2d 154 (Tex. Civ. App.—Galveston 1955, writ ref'd n.r.e.).

220. *Id.* at 157.

221. *Id.*

222. 474 S.W.2d 732 (Tex. Civ. App.—Beaumont 1971, writ ref'd n.r.e.).

223. *Id.* at 737.

224. *Id.* at 739.

In *Jim Dandy Fast Foods, Inc. v. Carpenter*,[225] plaintiff was injured when a piece of bone in a portion of a boneless chicken breast lodged in his throat. The jury determined that the chicken served to the plaintiff "was in a defective and unreasonably dangerous condition, making it unfit for human consumption,"[226] and that the defective and unreasonably dangerous condition of the chicken proximately caused plaintiff's injuries.[227] Adopting strict tort liability for food containing substances not reasonably contemplated by the consumer, the court concluded that public policy mandated liability for food not suitable for human consumption.[228]

The underlying basis for the imposition of strict tort liability is enumerated in the *Restatement*.[229] A restaurant that provides food impliedly represents to the consuming public that it is properly prepared and is fit for human consumption.[230]

C. *Medical Professionals*

A majority of jurisdictions recognize that the doctrine of strict tort liability does not extend to those individuals in the medical profession who provide services to patients, notwithstanding that a defective product may be provided or utilized in performing the service or administering the medical treatment.[231] The policy rationale constraining the application of strict tort liability to medical professionals is discussed in *Magrine v. Krasnica*.[232] The medi-

---

225. 535 S.W.2d 786 (Tex. Civ. App.—Houston [1st Dist.] 1976, no writ).

226. *Id.* at 788.

227. *Id.*

228. *Id.* at 789.

229. RESTATEMENT (SECOND) OF TORTS §402A, comment *f* states, in part, that: The rule stated in this section applies to any person engaged in the business of selling products for use or consumption. It therefore applies to any manufacturer of such a product, to any wholesale or retailer dealer or distributor, and to the operator of a restaurant.

230. Shaffer v. Victoria Station, Inc., 91 Wash. 2d 295, 588 P.2d 233, 236 (1978) (the container in which food is served integral part of the product purchased).

231. Vergott v. Deseret Pharm. Co., 463 F.2d 12, 16 (5th Cir. 1972); Barbee v. Rogers, 425 S.W.2d 342, 346 (Tex. 1968); Nevauex v. Park Place Hosp., Inc., 656 S.W.2d 923, 926 (Tex. App.—Beaumont 1983, writ ref'd n.r.e.); Shivers v. Good Shepherd Hosp., Inc., 427 S.W.2d 104, 107 (Tex. Civ. App.—Tyle 1968, writ ref'd n.r.e.), 100 A.L.R.3D 1205 (1980). A pharmacist's role is inextricably intertwined with that of the prescribing physician and, therefore, he is immune from strict tort liability. Murphy v. E.R. Squibb & Sons, 156 Cal. App. 3d 589, 202 Cal.Rptr. 802 (1984). Ingram v. Hooks Drugs, Inc., ____ N.E.2d ____ (Ind. App. 1984).

232. 94 N.J. Super. 228, 227 A.2d 539 (Hudson County Ct. 1967), *aff'd sub. nom.* Magrine v. Spector, 100 N.J. Super. 223, 241 A.2d 637 (App. Div. 1968), *aff'd*, 53 N.J. 259,

cal professional may secure only limited protection against liability for defective products incidentally used in the treatment of patients. Even when liability insurance is available, the medical professional necessarily is required to distribute the risk by raising fees that are already inordinately high.[233] Because the public must be provided access to *affordable* medical services, the usual policy of risk distribution is inapplicable to medical professionals. Unlike the sale of most products, the availability of affordable medical services is critical to the public welfare.

Contrary to the rationale that product suppliers control the quality of their products, medical professionals occupy no superior position than their patients to discover defects in products incidentally employed in administering treatment. The patient's reasonable expectation regarding medical treatment neither contemplates nor focuses on a guarantee by the physician that the instrumentalities utilized in performing medical services are non defective. The patient anticipates that the physician will perform necessary medical treatment in a skillful and competent manner; the sale of products is not even remotely contemplated. Additionally, the medical professional is not engaged in the business of selling or promoting the sale of medical products in the channels of commerce.[234] Texas earlier adhered to the well established majority rule that strict tort liability is not applicable to medical professionals. Two recent decisions, ostensibly ignoring earlier decisional authority, recently imposed strict tort liability on medical professionals for defective products incidentally used in the administration of medical treatment.[235]

---

250 A.2d 129 (1969). The court held that a dentist was not strictly liable in tort for personal injuries caused by the breaking of a defective hypodermic needle in the patient's jaw. The court noted that a professional essentially offers a service. Further, to supply or use a product in the performance of a service is merely incidental and not the true essence of the transaction. *Id.* at 546. *Accord*, Carmichael v. Reitz, 17 Cal. App. 3d 958, 978-79, 95 Cal. Rptr. 381, 392-93 (1971); Hoven v Kelble, 79 Wis.2d 444, 256 N.W.2d 379, 392 (1977).

233. 227 A.2d at 543-46. *See* Sales, *The Sales-Service Transaction: A Citadel Under Assault*, 10 ST. MARY'S L.J. 13, (1978).

234. *But see*, Thomas v. St. Joseph's Hosp., 618 S.W.2d 791 (Tex. Civ. App.—Houston [1st Dist.] 1981, writ ref'd n.r.e.) and Providence Hosp. v. Truly, 611 S.W.2d 127, 132 (Tex. Civ. App.—Waco 1980, writ dism'd), extending strict tort liability for defective medication and medical garments supplied by a health care facility.

235. Thomas v. St. Joseph's Hospital, 618 S.W.2d 791 (Tex. App.—Houston [1st Dist.] 1981, writ ref'd n.r.e.); Providence Hospital v. Truly, 611 S.W.2d 1227 (Tex. Civ. App.—Waco 1980, writ dism'd).

The Texas Supreme Court in *Barbee v. Rogers*[236] refused to impose strict liability in tort on an optometrist for injuries caused by improperly fitted contact lenses. The court concluded that the lenses were not defective: "The miscarriage, if such there was, [rested] in the professional acts of [the defendants] and not in the commodity they prescribed, fitted, and sold."[237] While the court characterized the transaction as a hybrid between a professional service and merchandising, such characterization did not justify imposing strict tort liability.[238]

Subsequently, in *Vergott v. Deseret Pharmaceutical Co.* [239] plaintiff was injured during the course of medical treatment due to the breakage of a needle in her vein. The doctrine of strict tort liability under § 402A was deemed inapplicable.[240] Hospitals are not perceived as sellers engaged in the business of introducing needles into the stream of commerce.

The same rationale was reaffirmed in *Shivers v. Good Shepherd Hospital, Inc.*[241] Though recognizing that strict tort liability in Texas applies to manufacturers and distributors of medical products, the court concluded that the doctrine should not be extended to hospital suppliers.[242]

More recently, the plaintiff in *Providence Hospital v. Truly* [243]instituted suit against the hospital under the Deceptive Trade Practices Act alleging a breach of implied warranty of fitness of goods sold for a particular purpose. Plaintiff was injured when contaminated Miochol was injected in her eye during cataract surgery. Ignoring the pronouncement of *Barbee* and its progeny, the court concluded that the hospital and physicians were "sellers" of Miochol and, therefore, liable for breach of implied warranty.[244] This aberration was essentially adopted without review of professional medical considerations in *Thomas v. St. Joseph's Hospital.*[245] Plaintiff's husband died after suffering burns over a substantial

---

236. 425 S.W.2d 342 (Tex. 1968).
237. *Id.* at 346.
238. *Id.*
239. 463 F.2d 12 (5th Cir. 1972).
240. *Id.* at 16 n. 5.
241. 427 S.W.2d 104 (Tex. Civ. App.—Tyler 1968, writ ref'd n.r.e.).
242. *Id.* at 107.
243. 611 S.W.2d 127 (Tex. Civ. App.—Waco 1980, writ dism'd).
244. *Id.* at 131.
245. 618 S.W.2d 791 (Tex. Civ. App.—Houston [1st Dist.] 1981, writ ref'd n.r.e.).

portion of his body when his hospital gown ignited when he dropped a lighted match in an oxygenated environment. The trial court refused to submit any issues on strict tort liability based on a defective hospital gown. The appellate court concluded that strict tort liability applied to a defective hospital gown provided by the hospital as part of its medical services.[246] Struggling to distinguish earlier decisional law, the court reasoned that strict tort liability applied because the hospital released an unreasonably dangerous product into the stream of commerce: "It is true that the essence of the relationship between a physician and his patient relates to the professional services and skill he offers and the patient purchases. Where, as here, a hospital apparently supplies a product unrelated to the essential professional relationship, we hold that it cannot be said that as a matter of law the hospital did not introduce the harmful product into the stream of commerce."[247]

Most recently, in *Nevauex v. Park Place Hospital*,[248] the court returned to the traditional rule that strict tort liability does not apply to providers of services in which a defective product may incidentally be involved. Plaintiff sustained radiation burns from cobalt therapy administered for treatment of uterine bleeding. Refusing to impose strict tort liability on either the hospital or treating physicians, the court noted that even if radiation therapy constituted a product, strict tort liability was inapplicable because it was "intimately and inseparably" connected with the professional services rendered.[249] Neither the hospital nor the technician administering the radiation qualified as a merchant introducing cobalt radiation into the channels of commerce and, therefore, no liability existed for defective cobalt application.[250]

A central consideration when determining whether a physician or health care facility is strictly liable in tort for a defective product incidentally employed in administering medical treatment is the reasonable expectation of the patient. Patients seek medical assistance performed in a skillful and competent manner. The fact that a defective product may incidentally be used for that treatment does not alter the patient's expectations. Equally important,

---

246. *Id.* at 797.
247. *Id.* at 796-97.
248. 656 S.W.2d 923 (Tex. App.—Beaumont 1983, writ ref'd n.r.e.).
249. *Id.* at 926.
250. *Id.*

of course, is the absence of the two principal rationales that support strict tort liability: (1) the physician and medical facility are not engaged in the business of marketing products and therefore, do not impliedly represent the quality of the product; and (2) risk distribution to a large purchasing public by increased pricing is not available to the physician and medical facility.

D. *Nonmedical Professionals*

Nonmedical professionals, like other service providers, generally are outside the scope of strict tort liability.[251] The policy rationale for refusing to extend liability stems from the reasonable expectation of the user that the professional will provide competent, skillful and non-negligent service. Neither the consumer nor user of professional services relies on the quality or condition of products incidentally used in the performance of the service.[252] Additionally, there exists no mass production of goods or a large body of distant consumers to enable the nonmedical professional to distribute the risk.[253]

In the landmark case of *Gagne v. Bertran*,[254] the California Supreme Court rejected application of strict tort liability and breach of warranty to a soil tester because he provided a service, as distinguished from promoting goods for sale.[255] Liability, if any, is dependent on establishing negligence or intentional misconduct in

---

251. K-Mart Corp. v. Midcon Realty Group Ltd., 489 F. Supp. 813, 819 (D. Conn. 1980)(architect); Raritan Trucking Corp. v. Aero Commander, Inc., 458 F.2d 1106, 1115 (3d Cir. 1972) (airplane servicer); La Rossa v. Scientific Design Co., 402 F.2d 937, 943 (3d Cir. 1968) (design engineer); Del Mar Beach Club Owners Ass'n v. Imperial Contracting Co., 123 Cal. App. 3d 898, 914, 176 Cal. Rptr. 886, 894 (1981) (architects, engineers); Swett v. Gribaldo, Jones & Associates, 40 Cal. App. 3d 573, 576, 115 Cal. Rptr. 99, 101 (1974) (soil engineer); Stuart v. Crestview Mut. Water Co., 110 Cal.Rptr. 543, 549 (Ct. App. 1973) (water engineer); Gagne v. Bertran, 43 Cal.2d 481, 275 P.2d 15 (1954) (soil tester); Castaldo v. Pittsburg-Des Moines Steel Co., 376 A.2d 88 (Del. 1977) (engineer); Mechanical Rubber & Supply Co. v. Caterpillar Tractor Co., 399 N.E.2d 722 (Ill. 1980) (engineer-designer); Lowrie v. City of Evanston, 50 Ill.App.3d 376, 365 N.E.2d 923 (1977) (engineer); Board of Trustees v. Kennerly, Slomanson & Smith, 167 N.J. Super. 311, 490 A.2d 850 (Law Div. 1979); Hall v. State, 106 Misc. 2d 860, 435 N.Y. S.2d 663 (1981) (bridge designer).

252. *See generally* Sales, *The Service-Sales Transaction: A Citadel Under Assault*, 10 St. Mary's L.J. 13 (1978).

253. *See id. See also* La Rossa v. Scientific Design Co., 402 F.2d 937, 942-43 (3d Cir. 1968).

254. 43 Cal. 2d 481, 275 P.2d 15 (1954).

255. 275 P.2d at 20.

performing the contracted for services.[256] The court pointedly noted:

> The services of experts are sought because of their special skill. They have a duty to exercise the ordinary skill and competence of members of their profession, and a failure to discharge that duty will subject them to liability for negligence. Those who hire such persons are not justified in expecting infallability, but can expect only reasonable care and competence. They purchase service, not insurance.[257]

The policy rationale articulated in *Gagne* continues to represent the predominant basis for rejecting strict tort liability in the service-oriented area.[258]

The Third Circuit in *La Rossa v. Scientific Design Co.*,[259] considered the applicability of strict tort liability to an engineering company that designed, engineered, and supervised construction of a chemical plant.[260] Plaintiff contended that her husband died as a result of throat cancer caused or activated by inhaling chemical dust while working as an employee of the plant. The court refused to extend liability to the professional service provider on the basis that professional services do not ordinarily lend themselves to the doctrine of strict tort liability.[261] Essentially, there is no mass production of goods or a body of distant consumers for whom it would be unfair to require tracing the article along the channels of commerce to the original manufacturer to establish negligence.[262]

One of the early justifications advanced in support of a strict tort liability doctrine involved the perceived difficulty of an injured party to prove negligence against the remote manufacturer or product supplier. As noted by the *LaRossa* court, this difficulty is non-existent in connection with an identifiable professional engaged to perform a service for a consumer.

The Texas Supreme Court in *Langford v. Kraft* [263] acknowledged the exemption of the professional service provider from

---

256. *Id.*
257. *Id.* at 21.
258. Refer to note 252 *supra*.
259. 402 F.2d 937 (3d Cir. 1968).
260. *Id.* at 938-39.
261. *Id.* at 942.
262. *Id.*
263. 551 S.W.2d 392 (Tex. Civ. App.—Beaumont 1977), *aff'd*, 565 S.W.2d 223 (Tex. 1978).

strict tort liability. The defendant, a professional engineer, designed a drainage system for a new subdivision. This system interrupted the natural flow of surface waters, resulting in excess water flow onto plaintiff's property. Relying on the theory of trespass articulated in § 822 of the *Restatement of Torts*,[264] the court concluded that the engineer, acting in the capacity of an independent contractor for the developer, was strictly liable for *trespass* to another's property caused by the diversion of surface waters.[265] In distinguishing the trespass from strict tort liability under § 402A, the court emphasized the absence of any "sale" incident to the performance of professional services as reflected in *Barbee*.[266]

Presently, computer programmers are legally insulated from strict tort liability, [267]though the increasing importance and prevalence of computers in both business and domestic areas may prompt the courts to reconsider the existing rationale. Strict tort liability under § 402A applies only when a product causes physical injury to the plaintiff or damage to his property. Economic loss alone does not trigger the doctrine of strict tort liability. Physical injury has resulted from computer program errors, however, in such diverse areas as medical monitoring and diagnosis, production control, control of aircraft flight, and security systems.[268]

More problematic is the unassailable requirement that strict tort liability applies only to products introduced into the channels of commerce. As reflected in decisional authority, courts are often confronted with identifying the narrow but very significant distinction between a product and personal services. The distinction between products and services is especially difficult for computer

264. RESTATEMENT OF TORTS § 822 (1939). The court extended the provision of § 822 to the defendant engineer based on RESTATEMENT OF TORTS § 834 comment *d* (1939) which provides that an individual participates in "an activity that either directly or through the creation of a physical condition causes an invasion of another's interest in the use and enjoyment of land, not only when he acts for his own benefit, but also when he acts in the capacity of . . . independent contractor." Langford v. Kraft, 551 S.W.2d 392, 395 (Tex. App.—Beaumont 1977), *aff'd*, 565 S.W.2d 223 (Tex. 1978).

265. 551 S.W.2d 395.

266. *Id.* at 396. The court further noted that La Rossa v. Scientific Design Co., 402 F.2d 937 (3d Cir. 1968) was distinguishable because it did not involve the theory of trespass. 551 S.W.2d at 397.

267. *See generally*, Note, *Strict Products Liability and Computer Software: Caveat Vendor*, 4 COMPUTER L.J. 373 (1983); COMMENT, *Computer Software and Strict Products Liability*, 20 SAN DIEGO L. REV. 439 (1983).

268. 4 COMPUTER L.J. at 375.

software programs.

Computer software may be characterized as a product which is mass produced, mass marketed, and reaches the consumer through the distributive chain.[269] Examples of mass marketed computer software include computer games, computer word processing programs, and computerized business and accounting software. Several reasons have been suggested by commentators for extending strict tort liability to mass produced and mass distributed computer programs. First, manufacturers of mass produced computer software are better able to discover defects in their products than the consumer.[270] Second, the socioeconomic rationale of risk distribution underlying strict tort liability appears applicable to manufacturers of mass produced computer software. Manufacturers purportedly can distribute the increased cost of liability through increased prices to their customers and by obtaining insurance protection against liability.[271] While mass produced computer programs may be characterized as products, strict tort liability is not applicable in the absence of physical injury or damage to the property. Considering the nature of mass produced software, it is unlikely that physical injury will result. Manufacturers and distributors of mass produced computer programs, therefore likely will remain beyond the reach of the strict tort liability doctrine.

Some forms of computer software necessarily are characterized as services provided by the computer company. When software is customized for individual customer needs, the essence of the transaction clearly qualifies as a service because the customer relies upon the skill and expertise of the programmer.[272] The policy reasons that exempt professional service providers from strict tort liability apply with equal relevance and vigor to computer software providers.[273]

The advent of the electronic age certainly involves computer programmers in the inevitable process of litigation. It is not totally illogical, considering judicial expansion of the literal meaning of "product" in § 402A, that the courts may ultimately classify computer programmers of mass produced and mass distributed

---

269. *Id.* at 393.
270. *Id.* at 395.
271. 20 San Diego L. Rev. at 448.
272. 4 Computer L.J. at 398.
273. See notes 216 to 227 *supra* and accompanying text.

software programs as manufacturers of products. Once characterized in this manner, strict tort liability would quickly encompass manufacturers for computer programs that cause physical harm to a user or consumer or to his property. Programmers who customize software programs for individual customers should remain insulated from strict tort liability since the essence of their work is a service. In this latter situation, the customer possesses a reasonable expectation that the computer programmer will design a program with the requisite skill and competence of a professional.

E. *Nonprofessionals and the Sales-Service Hybrid*

A significant lack of unanimity exists among the jurisdictions as to whether strict tort liability applies to nonprofessional service-sale providers. Some jurisdictions hold that a nonprofessional service provider who incidentally provides a product in connection with performing a service is subject to strict tort liability to the same extent as any other product supplier.[274] These jurisdictions equate an individual engaged primarily in providing a service but who furnishes a product ancillary to performing the service with a retailer or other entity in the distributive chain.[275] Under this hypothesis, the nonprofessional service provider who sells a defective product presumably is entitled to seek indemnification from the ultimate manufacturer or distributor of the product.[276]

This issue was addressed by the New Jersey Supreme Court in *Newmark v. Gimble's, Inc.*[277] Plaintiff was injured when a beauty parlor employee applied a defective permanent wave solution to her hair. The trial court refused to apply strict tort liability on the basis that no sale had occurred.[278] The New Jersey Supreme Court rejected the sales-service distinction as artificial, observing that if the defendant had sold the solution to the plaintiff for home appli-

---

274. Newmark v. Gimble's, Inc., 54 N.J. 585, 258 A.2d 697 (1969); Carpenter v. Best's Apparel, Inc, 4 Wash. App. 439, 481 P.2d 924 (1971).

275. Saloomey v. Jeppesen & Co., 707 F.2d 671 (2d Cir. 1983) (preparation and sale of navigational charts). Sears Roebuck & Co. v. Employers Ins. of Wausau, 585 F. Supp. 739 (N.D. Ill. 1983) (books). Halstead v. United States, 535 F. Supp. 782 (D. Conn. 1982), *aff'd*, 707 F.2d 671 (2d Cir. 1983); Aetna Casualty & Sur. Co. v. Jeppesen & Co., 642 F.2d 339 (9th Cir. 1981) (supply of navigational charts);

276. 642 F.2d 339 (9th Cir. 1981); 54 N.J. 585, 258 A.2d 697 (1969).

277. 54 N.J. 585, 258 A.2d 697 (1969).

278. 258 A.2d at 700.

cation, an implied warranty would arise.[279] As perceived by the court, the transaction was, in reality, a hybrid performance of a service coupled with a furnishing of goods for consideration.[280] Since the beautician was regularly engaged in and operated as a commercial enterprise, she occupied the legal status of a retailer.[281] In support of extending strict tort liability to the beautician, the potential availability of indemnification from the party that created the defective product constituted an important consideration.[282]

Even the service-sale dichotomy provokes a blurred and incomprehensible distinction. For instance, when does a service metamorphize into a product for purposes of strict tort liability? In *Halstead v. United States*[283] the court was obligated to characterize a navigational chart either as a product or the performance of a service. Plaintiff's husband was fatally injured when the aircraft he was piloting crashed into a mountain ridge. The plaintiff contended that the defendant furnished the pilot with an incorrect and defective navigational chart. Rejecting the contention that the defendant performed a service rather than sold a product, the court imposed strict tort liability:

> The fact that a customer purchases a plan, design, or map to obtain the information contained therein does not render the essence of the transaction a service outside the ambit of Section 402A. If suitable for mass marketing, the information is in some sense a fungible good for which the manufacturer placing it on the market must assume responsibility. . . .[284]

The majority of jurisdictions currently refuse to extend strict tort liability to a nonprofessional service provider who incidentally provides a product in connection with the performance of a ser-

---

279. *Id.*

280. *Id.* at 701.

281. *Id.* at 702.

282. *Id.* at 702-05.

283. 535 F. Supp. 782 (D. Conn. 1982).

284. *Id.* at 791. *See also* Saloomey v. Jeppesen & Co., 707 F.2d 671 (2d Cir. 1983). In *Saloomey*, a designer of navigational charts was held strictly liable in tort for selling a defective product. The court followed the rationale of *Halstead*, adding that the burden of accidental injury was a cost of production to be covered by liability insurance. *See also* Sears Roebuck & Co. v. Employers Ins. of Wausau, 585 F. Supp. 739 (N.D. Ill. 1983) (information contained in a book).

vice.[285] Initially, acknowledging that the service provider does not endeavor to promote products in connection with performing its service rebuts one of the principal rationales undergirding the strict tort liability doctrine. Further, the mere incidental use of a product in the course of performing a contractual service does not ipso facto transform the service supplier into a member of the product's marketing chain. Perhaps most importantly, the fact that the service provider operates beyond the parameters of the marketing chain irrefutably rebuts any control he may exercise over the production of the product to ensure product quality and safety. Quality control of a product represents one of the three most reiterated rationales to support the doctrine of strict tort liability. Lastly, the service provider basically provides a service and is obligated to charge a premium for his time, skill, and experience. Consequently, the ability to distribute the risk which is the predominant socioeconomic rationale underlying strict tort liability is denied the service provider.[286] A customer who employs an individual to provide a service has the reasonable expectation that the serviceman will perform the service in a competent, skillful and reasonable manner.[287]

An example of a service provider who incidentally furnishes a product as part of the performance of a service is a franchise dealer who performs recall work on a tractor.[288] Strict tort liability is inapplicable because an agreement for repair constitutes a service contract despite the incidental use of property in performing the service.[289]

---

285. Stafford v. International Harvester Co., 668 F.2d 142 (2d Cir. 1981); Times Mirror Co. v. Sisk, 122 Ariz. 174, 593 P.2d 924 (1978); Epstein v. Giannattasio, 25 Conn.Sup. 109, 197 A.2d 342 (1963); Van Iderstine v. Lane Pipe Corp., 89 App. Div.2d 459, 455 N.Y.S.2d 450 (1982); De Loach v. Whitney, 275 S.C. 543, 273 S.E.2d 768 (1981); Delta Refining Co. v. Procon, Inc., 552 S.W.2d 387 (Tenn. App. 1976). *Cf.* Chicago Heights Venture v. Dynamit Nobel of Am., 575 F. Supp. 214 (N.D. Ill. 1983) (dismissing strict liability count for failure of roofing material); Gobhai v. KLM Royal Dutch Airlines, 85 App. Div. 2d 566, 445 N.Y.S.2d 445 (1981), *aff'd*, 455 N.Y.S. 2d 762, 442 N.E.2d 61 (1982) (dismissing strict liability suit for slippers supplied to passengers).

286. *See generally* La Rossa v. Scientific Design Co., 402 F.2d 937 (3d Cir. 1968). *But see* Southwestern Bell Telephone Co. v. Griffith, 575 S.W.2d 92 (Tex. Civ. App.—Corpus Christi 1978, writ ref'd n.r.e.).

287. *See* Sales, *The Sales-Service Tranaction: A Citadel Under Assault*, 10 St. Mary's L.J. 13, 18 (1978).

288. Stafford v. International Harvester Co., 668 F.2d 142 (2d Cir. 1981).

289. *Id.* at 147.

In *Siciliano v. Capitol Shows, Inc.*,[290] plaintiff's children were fatally injured in an amusement ride accident. Plaintiffs instituted suit against the amusement park based on strict tort liability for a defective and unreasonably dangerous amusement ride. Rejecting strict tort liability, the court noted that, "The defendant. . . . does not sell or supply a product. It provides persons with a service, namely, a ride on a machine."[291]

Decisional law in Texas is noticeably silent on whether strict tort liability applies to a nonprofessional sales-service provider. In *Thomas v. St. Joseph Hospital*,[292] strict tort liability was imposed on the hospital for fatal burns sustained by plaintiff's husband when his hospital gown ignited after he dropped a lighted match in an oxygenated environment.[293] Ignoring earlier precedent, the appellate court concluded that a medical professional service provider is strictly liable in tort for a defective product that is incidentially utilized in connection with performing a medical service.[294] To the extent that *Thomas* truly represents the current status of Texas law, then it is logical to conclude that strict tort liability necessarily extends to a nonprofessional sales-service provider.[295] Extension of strict tort liability to the service provider hybrid, as was done in *Thomas*, ignores the safeguards established in formulating strict tort liability under Section 402A. Neither risk distribution nor quality control of products underlies extension of strict tort liability to service providers.

4.04 Home Builders and Building Contractors

Some jurisdictions have extended strict liability to builders of homes and building contractors for constructing defective and unreasonably dangerous structures or for installing defective and un-

---

290. 475 A.2d 19 (N.H. 1984). The court relied on its earlier decision in Bolduc v. Herbert Schneider Corp., 117 N.H. 566, 374 A.2d 1187 (1977).

291. 475 A.2d at 25.

292. 618 S.W.2d 791 (Tex. Civ. App.—Houston [1st Dist.] 1981, writ ref'd n.r.e.).

293. Refer to notes 248-50, *supra* and accompanying text.

294. 618 S.W.2d at 796. The rationale of *Thomas* represents a deviation in earlier well established Texas Supreme Court decisions, and it was expressly repudiated by another appellate court in Neveaux v. Park Place Hospital, Inc, 656 S.W.2d 923 (Tex. App.—Beaumont 183, no writ).

295. *See generally*, Sales, *The Service-Sales Transaction: A Citadel Under Assault*, 10 St. Mary's L.J. 13 (1978). *See also* dicta used by the court in Signal Oil & Gas Co. v. Universal Oil Prod., 572 S.W.2d 320 (Tex. 1978).

reasonably dangerous products in buildings.[296] Undoubtedly the landmark case extending strict tort liability to builders is *Schipper v. Levitt & Sons, Inc.*[297] The court noted that purchasers of mass constructed and mass developed homes possess a reasonable expectation that the house is fit and safe for human habitation.[298] Moreover, the contractor responsible for constructing the house occupies a much better position than the vendee to discover and correct defects in the building.[299]

The Texas courts sanction recovery against builders of mass-produced homes based on a theory of breach of implied warranty.[300] Texas has not yet extended the doctrine of strict tort liability to home builders; however, the cases suggest a predisposition to extending the doctrine. In *Melody Home Manufacturing Co. v. Morrison*,[301] strict tort liability was imposed on the manufacturer of mass produced mobile homes for personal injuries caused by a harmful foreign substance contained in the water system of the

---

296. Del Mar Beach Club Owners Ass'n. v. Imperial Contracting Co., 123 Cal. App. 3d 898, 176 Cal.Rptr. 886 (1981); Avner v. Longridge Estates, 272 Cal. App.2d 607, 615, 77 Cal. Rptr. 633, 639 (1969) (building contractor and soil engineers held liable for defective compaction of soil on lot which resulted in the settling and partial collapses of the lot); Kriegler v. Eichler Homes, Inc., 269 Cal. App.2d 224, 229, 74 Cal. Rptr. 749, 753 (1969) (building contractor held liable for defective heating unit that corroded); State Stove Mfg. Co. v. Hodges, 189 So.2d 113, 123 (Miss. 1966), *cert. denied*, 386 U.S. 912 (1967) (contractor held liable for installing defective water heater that exploded); Schipper v. Levitt & Sons, Inc., 44 N.J. 70, 207 A.2d 314, 329-30 (1965) (contractor held liable for installing defective water heater that produced excessively hot water). *See generally* Valore, *Product Liability for A Defective House*, 18 CLEV.-MAR. L. REV. 319, 326-31 (1969). Other jurisdictions have refused to extend strict tort liability to home builders. *See* De Matteo v. White, 233 Pa. Super. 339, 336 A.2d 355 (1975). The marketing and sale of condominium units may invoke strict tort liability. Towers Tenant Ass'n v. Towers Ltd. Partnership, 563 F. Supp. 566 (D.C. 1983).

297. 44 N.J. 70, 207 A.2d 314 (1965).

298. 207 A.2d at 325-26. In Delmar Beach Club Owners Association, Inc. v. Imperial Contracting Co., 123 Cal.App.3d 898, 176 Cal. Rptr. 886 (1981), a developer of 192 units located in 27 residential buildings was deemed subject to strict tort liability.

299. 176 Cal. Rptr. at 893.

300. Gupta v. Ritter Homes, Inc., 646 S.W.2d 168 (Tex. 1983); Woods v. Littleton, 554 S.W.2d 662 (Tex. 1977); Humber v. Morton, 426 S.W.2d 554 (Tex. 1968); Holifield v. Coronado Bldg., Inc., 594 S.W.2d 214 (Tex. Civ. App.—Houston [14th Dist.] 1980, no writ); Young v. De Guerin, 591 S.W.2d 296 (Tex. Civ. App.—Houston [1st Dist.] 1979, no writ); Rogowicz v. Taylor & Gray, Inc., 498 S.W.2d 352 (Tex. Civ. App.—Tyler 1973, writ ref'd n.r.e.); Moore v. Werner, 418 S.W.2d 918 (Tex. Civ. App.—Houston [14th Dist.] 1967, no writ). The implied warranty includes both habitability and good workmanship. Evans v. Stites, ____ S.W.2d ____, 28 Tex. Sup. Ct. J. 329, 330 (March 27, 1985).

301. 468 S.W.2d 505 (Tex. Civ. App.—Houston [1st Dist.] 1971, no writ).

home.[302] Breach of warranty, however, formed the basis of liability in *Humber v. Morton* [303] in which plaintiff's home was partially destroyed by a fire attributable to an improperly constructed fireplace and chimney. The contractor was in the business of assembling houses on his own property and then selling the houses and the lots. Under these circumstances, the builder was viewed as impliedly warranting that his homes were constructed in a good workmanlike manner and were suitable for human habitation.[304] Significantly, the court noted: "[T]he notion of implied warranty [in Texas] arising from sales is considered to be a tort rather that a contract concept."[305] The characterization of warranty as ex delicto presages expansion of strict tort liability to home builders. This expansion probably will be limited to builders and sellers of *mass-produced* homes, and not to builders of customized homes that are individually planned, designed, and supervised by architects or other independent agents selected by the purchaser. In the latter instance, the purchaser relies on and expects building services that are skillful and competent.

Recently, the Texas Supreme Court in *Gupta v. Ritter Homes, Inc.*[306] declared that the builder of a home remained liable on a breach of implied warranty theory to *subsequent purchasers* for latent defects not discoverable by a reasonably prudent inspection at the time of sale.[307] The plaintiff, a second owner of the house, sued the builder for damages precipitated by a defective slab foundation. The Texas Supreme Court concluded that the warranty of habitability and good workmanship implicit in the contract between the builder and the original purchaser automatically transferred to the subsequent purchaser.[308]

4.05 LANDLORDS

Only a very limited number of jurisdictions impose strict tort liability on landlords of apartments and homes for injuries resulting from defects in the premises. Landlords who are engaged in the

---

302. *Id.* at 506.
303. 426 S.W.2d 554 (Tex. 1968).
304. *Id.* at 555.
305. *Id.* at 556.
306. 646 S.W.2d 168 (Tex. 1983).
307. *Id.* at 169.
308. *Id.*

regular business of leasing apartments and commercial buildings are strictly liable in tort for defective furniture, appliance, and appurtenances attached to the realty that cause injury or damage to property.[309] For instance, in *Becker v. IRM Corp.*,[310] plaintiff was severely injured when he slipped and fell against an untempered glass shower door in his apartment. Strict tort liability was extended to anyone engaged in the business of distributing goods to the public as an integral part of the overall producing and marketing enterprise.[311] The rationale underlying extension of the strict tort liability was based on the perceived ability of a landlord to distribute the cost of injury by purchasing insurance.[312] More importantly the landlord's control of the premises enables him to eliminate or reduce defects existing on the premises.[313]

The landlord, under these circumstances, is equivalent to and treated as a lessor of products.[314] This application represents a novel and unprecedented liberal extension of strict tort liability since it ignores the traditional and long standing common law principles governing landlord-tenant relationships.

Most jurisdictions, including Texas, have refused to extend the strict tort liability doctrine to landlords.[315] These jurisdictions decline to impose liability in the absence of an agreement or covenant to repair, fraud, or a duty to repair or maintain. As an illustration, in *Morton v. Burton-Lingo*,[316] plaintiff's decedent was fatally injured when he fell due to a defect in the porch at the top of

---

309. Golden v. Conway, 55 Cal. App.3d 948, 128 Cal.Rptr. 67 (1976); Fakhoury v. Magner, 25 Cal.App.3d 58, 101 Cal.Rptr. 473 (1972).

310. 144 Cal. App.3d 321, 192 Cal. Rptr. 570 (1983), *vacated*, 38 Cal. 3d 454, 213 Cal. Rptr. 213, 698 P.2d 116 (1985).

311. *Id.* at 576-77.

312. *Id.* at 577.

313. *Id.*

314. *Id.* at 576.

315. Morton v. Burton-Lingo, 136 Tex. 263, 150 S.W.2d 239 (1941); Perez v. Raybaud, 76 Tex. 191, 13 S.W. 177 (1890); Vanderburg v. Drake, 518 S.W.2d 285 (Tex. Civ. App.—Eastland 1974, writ dism'd); Wallace v. Horn, 506 S.W.2d 325 (Tex. Civ. App.—Corpus Christi 1974, writ ref'd n.r.e.); Daniels v. Shell Oil Co., 485 S.W.2d 948 (Tex. Civ. App.—Fort Worth 1972, writ ref'd n.r.e.). In Livingston v. Begay, 98 N.M. 712, 652 P.2d 734 (1982), plaintiff's husband was fatally asphyxiated by carbon monoxide which apparently escaped from a disconnected exhaust vent attached to a gas space heater located in his hotel room. The New Mexico Supreme Court refused to extend strict tort liability to the hotel operator. The court held that strict tort liability under § 402A was never intended or fashioned to apply to landlords or others involved in a real estate setting. *Id.* at 738.

316. 136 Tex. 263, 150 S.W.2d 239 (1941).

the stairs of his apartment. The landlord was exonerated of any liability because of the absence of any agreement to repair the premises.[317] Similarly, in *Vanderburg v. Drake*[318] a guest in an apartment was injured as a result of a defective chair. The landlord was not held liable because the tenant who rented the apartment had knowledge of the defect that injured his guest.[319] Additionally, the absence of any fraud, concealment, or agreement to repair effectively shields the landlord from any liability.[320]

4.06 Financial Brokers

The same policy considerations that govern sellers of defective products and providers of services apply to financial brokers. In *Abco Metals Corp. v. Equico Lessors, Inc.*,[321] plaintiff was injured while using a wire chopping machine. Arrangements for manufacture of and specifications for the machine were supplied by Abco Metals Corporation. The financial lessor, Equico, entered into the transaction wholly unable to influence or control the earlier bargain between Abco and the manufacturer, and possessed no right to interfere in the production or marketing of the machine. Under these circumstances, a financial lessor who merely provides financing and is not part of the marketing and production chain of a product is not subject to strict tort liability.[322] The inapplicability of strict tort liability rests on the acknowledged fact that financial lessors are afforded neither the means nor the opportunity to ensure the quality and safety of the product.[323]

In *Nath v. National Equipment Leasing Corporation*[324] plaintiff's hand was caught in a wire and cable stripping machine that was designed without a protective hand guard. Plaintiff's employer obtained the machine from Rigby Manufacturing Company and financing for the purchase was provided by National Equipment Leasing Corporation. National borrowed money from a bank to fi-

---

317. 150 S.W.2d 239, 241 (1941).
318. 518 S.W.2d 285 (Tex. Civ. App.—Eastland 1974, writ dism'd).
319. *Id.* at 286.
320. *Id.*
321. 721 F.2d 583 (7th Cir. 1983). *See generally*, Snell, *Finance Lessor Liability Under Section 402A*, Restatement (Second) of Torts, 7 Am.J. Trial Advocacy 155-66 (Fall 1983).
322. 721 F.2d at 584-86.
323. *Id.* at 585.
324. 497 Pa. 126, 439 A.2d 633 (1981).

nance the purchase and assigned its lease schedule to the bank as security on the loan. The court resolved that § 402A was inapplicable to financial lessors under a secured transaction financing device.[325]

The policy considerations for extending strict tort liability to a commercial or true lessor are absent where the lessor neither markets nor supplies the product but is merely a secured party or a financier.[326] Section 402A was never intended to apply to transcactions designed solely for financing.[327] As the court in *Nath* perceptively commented: "[T]he financier is not supplying the chattel but rather is offering the use of money."[328] Financial institutions possess neither the means to pass upon the quality of the products they finance, nor do they possess a relationship with the manufacturer so as to exercise any form of quality control.[329]

The issue of financiers occupying a status outside the usual marketing chain was addressed by the court in *Wright v. Newman.*[330] Plaintiff's decedent was fatally injured when a vehicle being towed by the defendant detached from its tow chain, travelled into the opposing lane and crashed into the vehicle operated by the decedent.[331] Plaintiff filed a strict tort liability action against GMC Corporation, which financed the hauling of the vehicle under a contract between the owner and GMC. Rejecting strict tort liability, the Eighth Circuit noted that "The focus is thus on whether the commercial entity is in the chain of distribution that provides a product to the consumer. Finance companies have the mere tangential function of providing money to make the purchase of a product possible."[332]

4.07 Dual Employers

A distinct minority of jurisdictions recognize two separate and independent bases for recovery of damages for product-related accidents that occur in the course and scope of an employee's em-

---

325. 439 A.2d 633, 634-35 (1981).
326. *Id.* at 635.
327. *Id.*
328. *Id.* at 636.
329. *Id.*
330. 735 F.2d 1073 (8th Cir. 1984).
331. *Id.* 1074.
332. *Id.* at 1078.

ployment. Under the "dual capacity" doctrine,[333] an employee otherwise covered by worker's compensation may contemporaneously maintain a cause of action against the employer based on strict tort liability. *Douglas v. E. & J. Gallo Winery*[334] pioneered the concept that an employee is entitled to maintain a cause of action based on strict tort liability for a defective and unreasonably dangerous product, provided the product involved is manufactured by the employer for sale to the public rather than for the sole use of the employer.[335] The mere fact that an employer manufactures products for sale to the general public ostensibly overrides the legislative policy that worker's compensation furnishes the exclusive remedy to an injured employee.[336]

The few jurisdictions that have promulgated the dual capacity doctrine distinguish the exclusivity provisions of the Worker's Compensation acts as affecting only those employees' causes of action in existence at the time the worker's compensation laws were enacted.[337] Because strict tort liability represents a relatively new cause of action, the exclusive remedy of worker's compensation is rejected in these jurisdictions.[338] Some courts even declare that a corporation should be foreclosed from merging into an employer status to thereby preclude an employee's recovery for injuries caused by the employer-corporation's products.[339] Significantly, California, which pioneered the dual capacity doctrine, has now

---

333. Under this doctrine, an employer normally shielded from tort liability by the exclusivity remedy of Worker's Compensation may become strictly liable in tort to his own employee if he occupies, in addition to his capacity as employer, a second capacity that confers on him obligations independent of those imposed on him as an employer. The decisive dual-capacity test is not concerned with how separate or different the second function of the employer is from the first but whether the second function generates obligations unrelated to those flowing from the first, that of employer. A. Larson, 2A?? *The Law of Workmen's Compensation* §72.80, at 14-228 (1983). *See generally*, 23 A.L.R.4TH 1152 (1983); Liebo, *Dual Capacity Doctrine and Employer's Products*, 25 FOR THE DEF. 6-7 (Jan. 1983).

334. 69 Cal. App. 3d 103, 137 Cal. Rptr. 797 (1977).

335. 137 Cal. Rptr. at 799.

336. *See* Reed v. S.S. Yaka, 373 U.S. 410 (1963); Siva v. General Tire & Rubber Co., 146 Cal. App. 3d 152, 194 Cal. Rptr. 51 (1983); Bell v. Industrial Vangas, Inc., 30 Cal. 3d 268, 637 P.2d 266, 179 Cal. Rptr. 30 (1981); Quinn v. National Gypsum Co., 469 A.2d 1368 (N.H. 1983); Mercer v. Uniroyal Corp., 49 Ohio App.2d 279, 361 N.E.2d 492 (1976); Chaddock v. Johns-Manville Sales Corp., 599 F. Supp. 204 (S.D. Ohio 1984).

337. 137 Cal. Rptr. at 802.

338. *Id.*

339. *Id.* at 801-03.

legislatively repudiated the doctrine.[340]

The overwhelming majority of the jurisdictions have categorically rejected the dual capacity concept on the basis that the employee's claim arises from the employer-employee relationship and is appropriately handled by worker's compensation.[341] These jurisdictions view worker's compensation as the injured employee's statutory and exclusive remedy. Texas adheres to the majority view, rejecting any vestige of the dual capacity remedy in a product-related accident.[342]

The court in *Cohn v. Spinks Industries, Inc.*[343] explained the basis of its refusal to sanction the dual capacity doctrine. Plaintiff's decedent was fatally injured when the helicopter he was piloting in the course of his employment crashed. The court reaffirmed that the worker's compensation law in Texas provides the exclusive means of compensation for injuries arising from employment.[344] According to the court, the law "provides an employee a prompt and sure form of remuneration without proof of his employer's negligence, but this is in lieu of and in derogation of his common law causes of action."[345] While an employer "may have more than one function, it nonetheless remains an employer within the terms

---

340. CAL. LABOR CODE Section 3602 (West Supp. 1985): "Where the conditions of compensation set forth in Section 3600 concur, the right to recover such compensation is, except as specifically provided in this Section and Sections 3706 and 4558, the sole and exclusive remedy of the employer or his or her dependents against the employer, and the fact that either the employer or the employer also occupied another or dual capacity prior to, or at the time of, the employee's industrial injury shall not permit the employee or his or her dependents to bring an action at law for damages against the employee." *Id.* at § 3602(a).

341. *See, e.g.*, Horne v. General Elec. Co., 716 F.2d 253 (4th Cir. 1983); Kohr v. Raybestos-Manhattan, Inc., 522 F. Supp. 1070 (E.D. Pa. 1981); Toth v. Westinghouse Elevator Co., 114 Ill. App. 3d 925, 449 N.E.2d 1005 (120 Wis. 2d 344, 1983); Goetz v. Aveldsen Tool & Mach. Inc., 82 Ill. App. 3d 1054, 403 N.E.2d 555 (1980); Longever v. Revere Copper & Brass, Inc., 381 Mass. 221, 408 N.E.2d 857 (1980); Billy v. Consolidated Mach. Tool Corp., 71 App. Div. 2d 796, 419 N.Y.S.2d 29 (1979); Latendresse v. Preskey, 290 N.W.2d 267 (N.D. 1980). This rule does not necessarily encompass the narrower concept of "dual persona." *See* Schweiner v. Hartford Accident & Indemnity Co., 354 N.W. 2d 767 (Wis. App. 1984). *But See* Silkwood v. Kerr-McGee Corp., 667 F.2d 908 (10th Cir. 1983), *rev'd* 464 U.S. 238, 104 S. Ct. 615 (1984).

342. Mott v. Mitsubishi Int'l Corp., 636 F.2d 1073 (5th Cir. 1981); Cohn v. Spinks Indus. Inc., 602 S.W.2d 102 (Tex. Civ. App.—Dallas 1980, writ ref'd n.r.e.). *See generally* Kelly, *Workmen's Compensation and Employer Suability: The Dual Capacity Doctrine*, 5 ST. MARY'S L.J. 818 (1974). *See also* Paradissis v. Royal Indem. Co., 507 S.W.2d 526 (Tex. 1974).

343. 602 S.W.2d 102 (Tex. Civ. App. — Dallas 1980, writ ref'd n.r.e.).

344. *Id.* at 103.

345. *Id.*

of the worker's compensation laws."[346]

4.08 Successor Corporations to Entities Subject to Strict Tort Liability

The mere sale of corporate property does not impose liability on the purchaser-successor for the torts of the selling corporation.[347] Despite the general rule, the courts recognize four exceptions to the rule of nonliability. Under these exceptions, the successor corporation may be subject to strict tort liability for a defective and unreasonably dangerous product that was manufactured and sold by the predecessor corporation prior to the purchase agreement between the successor and the original manufacturer.[348]

One exception to the general rule of nonliability involves an agreement pursuant to which the successor corporation contractually assumes the tort liabilities of the predecessor corporation.[349] The provisions of the agreement are crucial in determining whether the successor corporation did, in fact, assume the predecessor's tort liabilities. Merely assuming enumerated debts and liabilities of the predecessor corporation does not imply an assumption of tort liability for the predecessor's defective products,[350] while assumption of the predecessor's product liability is suffi-

---

346. *Id.* at 104. *See also* State v. Purdy, 601 P.2d 258 (Alaska 1979); Lewis v. Gardner Eng. Corp., 254 Ark. 17, 491 S.W.2d 778, 779-80 (1973); Rosales v. Verson Allsteel Press Co., 41 Ill. App. 3d 787, 354 N.E.2d 553, 555-56 (1976); Hudson v. Allen, 11 Mich. App. 511, 517-18, 161 N.W.2d 596, 598-99 (1968).

347. *See generally* Travis v. Harris Corp., 565 F.2d 443 (7th Cir. 1977); Bazan v. Kux Machine Co., 358 F. Supp. 1250 (E.D. Wis. 1973); Shane v. Hobam, Inc., 332 F. Supp. 526 (E.D. Pa. 1971); Johnson v. Marshall & Huschart Mach. Co., 66 Ill. App. 3d 766, 384 N.E.2d 141 (1978); *Cf.* Western Resources Life Ins. Co., v. Gerhardt, 553 S.W.2d 783 (Tex. Civ. App.—Austin 1977, writ ref'd n.r.e.).

348. *See generally* Cyr v. B. Offen & Co., Inc., 501 F.2d 1145 (1st Cir. 1974); Knapp v. North Am. Rockwell Corp., 506 F.2d 361 (3d Cir. 1974), *cert. denied*, 421 U.S. 965 (1975); Manh Hung Nguyen v. Johnson Mach. & Press Corp., 104 Ill. App. 3d 1141, 1143-44, 433 N.E.2d 1104, 1106 (1982); McKee v. Harris-Seybold Co., 109 N.J. Super. 555, 264 A.2d 98 (1970), *aff'd per curiam*, 118 N.J. Super. 480, 288 A.2d 585 (1972). *But see* Reed v. Armstrong Cork Co., 577 F. Supp 246 (E.D. Ark. 1983).

349. *See* Fenton Area Pub. Schools v. Sorenson-Gross Const. Co., 124 Mich. App. 631, 335 N.W.2d 221 (1983); Downtowner, Inc. v. Acrometal Prod., Inc., 347 N.W.2d 118, 122 (N.D. 1984).

350. Kloberdanz v. Joy Mfg. Co., 288 F. Supp. 817 (D. Colo. 1968); Southwestern Gas, Light & Power Co. v. Jay, 275 S.W. 735 (Tex. Civ. App.—El Paso 1924, writ ref'd).

cient.[351] An assumption of the undetermined liabilities and commitments entered into in the regular course of business may constitute evidence of an assumption of such liability of the predecessor corporation.[352] Expressly refusing to assume the tort liabilities of the predecessor, however, clearly precludes imposition of liability on a successor corporation.[353]

A second exception to the general principle of nonliability involves a transaction that essentially amounts to a merger of the predecessor corporation with or into the successor corporation. The method of merger and business activity after the merger represent factors that determine whether the successor corporation is liable for its predecessor's defective products. Some jurisdictions, and at least one Texas court prior to the recent amendment of the Texas Business Corporation Act, distinguish between a de facto merger and a bona fide sale.[354] In a de facto merger, liability for the predecessor's torts apparently attaches to the successor, while in a bona fide sale the purchaser is immunized from liability for the acts and products of its predecessor.[355] The cash purchase of assets ostensibly eliminates any continuation of control by the predecessor corporation.[356] Another factor considered in determining whether the successor corporation is subject to liability involves the period of time during which the predecessor remains in business after consummation of the sale.[357]

A third exception imposes liability when the successor corporation constitutes a mere continuation of the predecessor corporation. The purchase of the predecessor corporation's stock, employ-

---

351. Rivers v. Stihl, Inc., 434 So. 2d 766, 772 (Ala. 1983).

352. Bouton v. Litton Indus. 423 F.2d 643 (3d Cir. 1970).

353. Dayton v. Peck, Stow & Wilcox, No. 78-273-5 (D. Mass. Apr. 27, 1983), *aff'd*, 739 F. 2d 690 (1st Cir. 1984).

354. A de facto merger is where the purchaser pays the seller in stock. When the purchaser pay the seller in cash, the transaction is deemed a bona fide sale.

355. Travis v. Harris Corp., 565 F.2d 443 (7th Cir. 1977); R. J. Enstrom Corp. v. Interceptor Corp., 555 F.2d 277 (10th Cir. 1977); Leannais v. Cincinnati Inc., 565 F.2d 437 (7th Cir. 1977); Menacho v. Adamson United Co., 420 F. Supp. 128 (D.N.J. 1976); Shannon v. Samuel Langston Co., 379 F. Supp. 797 (W.D. Mich. 1974); Gonzalez v. Rock Wool Eng. & Equip. Co., 117 Ill.App.3d 435, 453 N.E.2d 792 (1983); Western Resources Life Ins. Co. v. Gerhardt, 553 S.W.2d 783 (Tex. Civ. App.—Austin 1977, writ ref'd n.r.e.).

356. Cowan v. Harris Corp., No. 80-4134 (P. Kan. 1982).

357. Travis v. Harris Corp., 565 F.2d 443 (7th Cir. 1977); R. J. Enstrom Corp. v. Interceptor Corp., 555 F.2d 277 (10th Cir. 1977); Holloway v. John E. Smith's Sons Co., 432 F. Supp. 454 (D.S.C. 1977); Bazan v. Kux Machine Co., 358 F. Supp. 1250 (E.D. Wis. 1973).

ment of its employees, and assumption of its liabilities does not establish a continuation.[358] A continuation is generally established when there is continuity of management and purchase of assets by the successor, assumption of business related liabilities by the successor, and successor utilization of the predecessor's good will.[359] If the successor corporation continues doing business in the same manner as the predecessor and has merely changed hats, there is an indicia of continuation for which liability probably attaches.[360] The continuation of the same business rule applies irrespective of whether the predecessor is a sole proprietorship, partnership, or corporation.[361]

The fourth exception contemplates liability in the event the transaction between the successor and the predecessor corporation constitutes a fraudulent effort to escape liability for the predecessor's acts and/or products. In large measure, a determination of fraud depends on an analysis of the transaction. The payment of totally inadequate consideration for the predecessor's assets circumstantially evidences a fraudulent transaction.[362] The absence of good faith in the transaction coupled with the transfer of the predecessor corporation's assets without adequate consideration to protect creditors of the predecessor represents even stronger evidence of a fraudulent transaction.[363]

---

358. Menacho v. Adamson United Co., 420 F. Supp. 128 (D.N.J. 1976); Kelly v. Am. Precision Indus. Inc., 438 So.2d 29 (Fla. App. 1983); Downtowner, Inc. v. Acrometal Prod. Inc., 347 N.W.2d 118 (N.D. 1984); Southwestern Gas, Light & Power Co. v. Jay, 275 S.W. 735 (Tex. Civ. App.—El Paso 1924, writ ref'd).

359. Fenton Area Publ. Schools v. Sorenson-Gross Const. Co., 124 Mich. App. 631, 335 N.W.2d 221 (1983). *See generally*, Liebo, *Products: Successor Liaiblity; Continuity*, 26 For Def. 7-9 (Feb. 1984).

360. Bonee v. L & M Const. Chem., 518 F. Supp. 375 (M.D. Tenn. 1981); Leannais v. Cincinnati Inc., 565 F.2d 437 (7th Cir. 1977); Manh Hung Nguyen v. Johnson Mach. & Press Co., 104 Ill. App. 3d 1141, 433 N.E.2d 1104 (1982); Turner v. Bituminous Casualty Co., 397 Mich. 405, 244 N.W.2d 873 (Mich. 1976); Tift v. Forage King Indus., 108 Wis.2d 72, 322 N.W.2d 14 (1982). A new plant with a different set of directors and lack of identity of shareholders are important considerations. Weaver v. Nash Int'l Inc., 562 F. Supp. 860 (S.D. Iowa 1983), *aff'd* 730 F.2d 547 (8th Cir. 1984).

361. Tift v. Forage King Indus., 108 Wis.2d 72, 322 N.W.2d 14 (1982).

362. Cowan v. Harris Corp., No. 80-4134 (D. Kan. 1982); Fehl v. S.W.C. Corp., 433 F. Supp. 939 (D. Del. 1977); Menacho v. Adamson United Co., 420 F. Supp. 128 (D.N.J. 1976); Forest Laboratories, Inc. v. Pillsbury Co., 452 F.2d 621 (7th Cir. 1971); McKee v. Harris-Seybold Co., 109 N.J. Super. 555, 264 A.2d 98, 107 (1970), *aff'd per curiam*, 118 N.J. Super. 480, 288 A.2d 585 (1972); Southwestern Gas, Light & Power Co. v. Jay, 275 S.W. 735 (Tex. Civ. App.—El Paso 1924, writ ref'd).

363. Schwartz v. McGraw-Edison Co., 14 Cal. App. 3d 767, 781, 92 Cal. Rptr. 776, 784

Some jurisdictions reject the general rules governing successor liability and have formulated a new rule to impose strict tort liability on the successor corporation. This unique concept is generally characterized as the "product line" theorem.[364] The concept is predicated on the socioeconomic theory that the successor corporation is a better risk distributor than the injured party.[365] Moreover, the existence of several successor corporations does not militate against the imposition of strict tort liability when predicated on the "product line" doctrine.[366] In *Amader v. Pittsburg Corning Corp.*,[367] the court enumerated the factors governing successor corporation liability: "(1) the virtual destruction of the plaintiff's remedies against the original manufacturer caused by the successor's acquisition of the business; (2) the successor's ability to assume the original manufacturer's risk spreading role; and (3) the fairness of requiring the successor to assume a responsibility for defective products that was a burden necessarily attached to the original manufacturer's good will being enjoyed by the successor in the continued operation of that business."[368]

The majority of jurisdictions which have been confronted with the "product line" doctrine have expressly repudiated the concept.[369] For instance, the court in *Jones v. Johnson Machine &*

(1971); 109 N.J. Super. 555, 264 A.2d 98, 106-07 (1970), *aff'd per curiam*, 118 N.J. Super. 480, 288 A.2d 585 (1972).

364. Ray v. Alad Corp., 19 Cal.3d 22, 560 P.2d 3, 136 Cal.Rptr. 574 (1977); Martin v. Abbott Laboratories, 102 Wash. 2d 581, 689 P.2d 368 (1984) Amader v. Johns-Manville Corp., 541 F. Supp. 1384 (E.D.Pa. 1982); Rawlings v. D.M. Oliver, Inc., 159 Cal.Rptr. 119, 97 Cal.App.3d 890 (1979); Ramirez v. Amstead Indus., Inc., 86 N.J. 332, 431 A.2d 811 (1981); Hickman v. Thompson Co., 592 F. Supp. 1282 (D. Colo. 1984). *See generally*, Snell, *Successor Corporation's Liability for Defective Products of Its Transferor—The Product Line Exception*, 4 J.L. & Com. 65-89 (Summer 1984). The Washington supreme court appears to repudiate its earlier adoption of the product line in Martin v. Abbott Labs. *See* Hall v. Armstrong Cork, Inc., 103 Wash.2d 258, 692 P.2d 787 (1984).

365. Ray v. Ala. Corp., 19 Cal.3d 22, 136 Cal. Rptr. 574, 560 P.2d 3 (1977) ("The cost of an injury and the loss of time or health may be an overwhelming misfortune to the person injured, and a needless one, for the risk of injury can be insured by the manufacturer and distributed among the public as a cost of doing business." (*quoting* Escola v. Coca Cola Bottling Co., 24 Cal.2d 453, 462, 150 P.2d 436, 441) [concurring opinion]).

366. Nieves v. Bruno Sherman Corp., 86 N.J. 361, 431 A.2d 826 (1981).

367. 546 F. Supp. 1033 (E.D.Pa. 1982).

368. *Id.*

369. Weaver v. Nash Int'l Inc., 562 F. Supp. 860 (S.D. Iowa 1983) *aff'd*, 730 F.2d 547 (8th Cir. 1984) ; Cowan v. Harris Corp., No. 80-4134 (D. Kan. 1982); Rhynes v. Branick Mfg. Corp., 629 F.2d 409 (5th Cir. 1980); Travis v. Harris Corp., 565 F.2d 443 (7th Cir. 1977); Bernard v. Kee Mfg. Co., 409 So.2d 1047 (Fla. 1982); Gonzales v. Rock Wool Eng. & Equip.

Press Co.[370] explained:

> The public policy considerations which motivate imposition of strict liability on those who create risk and obtain profit by placing defective products in the stream of commerce do not necessarily apply equally to successor corporations. To paraphrase the language of several courts, the corporate asset purchaser, as a successor of the manufacturer of a defective product, cannot be said to have created the risk of a product manufactured by its predecessor, and except in a very remote way, does not realize a profit for the sale of a predecessor's product. Generally speaking, the successor corporation has neither invited use of its predecessor's product nor represented to the public that the product is safe and suitable for use.[371]

Rejection of the product line doctrine for imposing strict tort liability on a successor corporation is based on the successor's lack of ability to influence the safety of a predecessor's product.[372]

Recent Texas decisions and an amendment of the Texas Business Corporations Act have significantly affected the exceptions to the general principle of nonliability of a successor corporation. The Texas Supreme Court in *Hunter v. Fort Worth Capital Corporation*[373] construed Tex. Bus. Corp. Act Ann., Article 7.12 (Vernon's 1980) as a bar to the trust fund theory of recovery, which precludes an injured party from prosecuting a claim against the assets of a dissolved corporation responsible for manufacturing the product involved in the injury-producing event.[374] More significantly, Article 5.10(B)(2) of the Texas Business Corporation Act[375] appears to exclude any liability for a successor corporation in the absence of an express assumption of liability or fraud. Article 5.10(b)(2) (1980) provides in pertinent part as follows:

Co., 117 Ill. App. 3d 435, 453 N.E.2d 792 (1983); Hernandez v. Johnson Press Corp., 70 Ill.App.3d 664, 388 N.E.2d 778 (1979); Ostrowski v. Hydra-Tool Corp., 479 A.2d 126 (Vt. 1984).

370. 211 Neb. 724, 320 N.W.2d 481 (1982).

371. 320 N.W.2d at 484.

372. Ostrowski v. Hydra-Tool Corp., 479 A.2d 126 (Vt. 1984).

373. 620 S.W.2d 547 (Tex. 1981).

374. *See also* Henry I. Siegel Co. v. Holliday, 663 S.W.2d 824 (Tex. 1984). In *Siegel* the court said that the trust fund doctine provides no bases for personal liability of directors. "It only allows corporate creditors to follow the corporate assets and to subject those assets to the payment of their claim". *Id.* at 827.

375. Tex. Bus. Corp. Act, Art. 5.10(B)(2) (Vernon's 1980).

> A disposition of all, or substantially all, of the property and assets of a corporation requiring the special authorization of the shareholders of the corporation under Section A of this article:
> (1) is not considered to be a merger or consolidation pursuant to this Act or otherwise; and
> (2) except as otherwise expressly provided by another statute, does not make the acquiring corporation responsible or liable for a liability or obligation of the selling corporation that the acquiring corporation did not expressly assume.[376]

It therefore appears doubtful that the Texas courts will impose strict liability on an acquiring successor corporation for the defective and unreasonably dangerous products manufactured and sold by its predecessor. The only exceptions contemplated are an express contractual assumption of liabilities by the successor or a demonstration of fraud between the successor and the predecessor corporation.[377]

The issue of successor liability in Texas was directly addressed in the recent case of *Griggs v. Capitol Machine Works, Inc.*[378] Plaintiff sustained an injury while using a product manufactured by an earlier dissolved corporation. The defendant, Capitol Machine Works, Inc., possessed the same name as the corporation that had voluntarily dissolved in 1979 after manufacturing and selling the particular product that caused plaintiff's injury. Plaintiff contended that the defendant succeeded to the liabilities of the dissolved corporation and, therefore, was subject to strict tort liability for the defectively designed product manufactured and sold by the predecessor corporation. Though plaintiff urged that the court to adopt the "product line" doctrine, the court, after analyzing the product line decisions, concluded that this doctrine "merely declared a result."[379] As the court noted,

> the liability they find simply floats between earth and sky, buoyed perhaps by the salutary policy that one should have reparation for his injuries but disregarding nevertheless the fundamental proposition that there is no preexisting legal principle declaring that liability for such reparation shall descend and fasten

---

376. *Id.*
377. *See generally* Castilla v. Trinity Indus., Inc., 626 S.W.2d 798 (Tex. Civ. App.—San Antonio 1981, writ dism'd) (concurring opinion).
378. 690 S.W.2d 287 (Tex. App.—Austin 1985, no writ).
379. *Id.*

> upon a purchasing corporation, as opposed to any other person in the universe. Recognizing the want of legal precedent, they embrace but find rejection in § 402A of the Restatement. We find in such decisions a patently insufficient analysis and justification for the raw judicial legislation they illustrate so vividly.[380]

The court seemingly ignored the provisions of Article 5.10(b)(2) of the Texas Business Corporation Act as they may apply to this type of action. Rather, relying on the early decision of *Mexican National Construction Co. v. Middlegge*,[381] the court concluded that strict tort liability applies to a successor corporation only when such successor specifically assumes the liabilities of the predecessor or participates with the predecessor in the commission of a fraud.[382] Significantly, contractual assumption of predecessor liability and fraud represent the only exceptions to the rule that a sucessor corporation is not liable for its predecessor's torts.[383] Though the court does not allude to the Texas Business Corporation Act provisions, its decision, in practical effect, adopts the statutory posture of that act.

The court emphasizes that the rationale underlying the "product line" theory is founded on public policy and "implies in the strongest possible terms that the proper province for dealing with any underlying policies is in the legislative department of government and not the judicial, particularly since other 'public policies' of equal importance are involved and must be accommodated or adjusted in the process, a task for which the judicial department is uniquely ill-suited for a multitude of reasons."[384] The court, in a footnote, declares that the product line theory raises extraordinary and unsettling questions relative to:

> (a) the reality of the consent by which a business is purchased if the buyer is faced with startlingly new and enormous obligations to injured persons that he had no reason to anticipate in settling upon a price he would pay; (b) the fairness and justice of a catch all statute of limitations, in light of the purposes of statutes of limitation, when the buyer may be held liable for injuries occurring as much as 27 years after the product was sold by the

380. *Id.*
381. 13 S.W.2d 257 (Tex. 1890).
382. *Id.*
383. *Id.*
384. *Id.*

> prececessor corporation, as happened in one case; (c) the possible 'annihilation of small businesses,' as pointed out in another case; (d) the unfairness of giving 'notice' to purchasers of going businesses in the form of a new liability imposed by a judicial decision in a particular case, rather than by statute, precluding the possibility of protective action being taken by the class of persons made subject to the new exposure; (e) the consideration and working out of a rational basis for the treatment of 'successor corporations' differently from partnerships or natural persons who purchase the assets in a going business of another, so that the different treatment may be constitutionally justified; (f) the working out of the standards by which it may be held that a purchaser is indeed continuing the same 'product line' as the predecessor corporation; and, of course, (g) there is a question of whether the new liability actually reflects the reality of the 'social policies' upon which it is said ultimately to rest. These are not the only 'social policies' affected by the 'product line' theory, and the legislature itself would face an enormous task in formulating and adjusting all of the logically relevant polices. [385]

4.09 Conclusion

Since the initial adoption of § 402A of the *Restatement* in Texas, the law of strict tort liability has expanded and adapted to meet the changing reality of modern business relations. The term seller has been liberalized to include entities that extend well beyond that contemplated by Section 402A. The definition of "product" has been expanded as the courts have struggled to distinguish between products and services. As the metamorphosis of the application of strict tort liability continues, issues on whether the doctrine will be extended further than its current liberal boundaries remain for further judicial clarification.

---

385. *Id.*

processes or compositions as suggested in one case; (e) the possible [illegible] design of small businesses, as opposed [illegible] enterprise; (f) the [illegible] matter [illegible] business [illegible] a judicial decision in a particular case rather than by [illegible] the [illegible] bility of protective action being [illegible] the [illegible] subject to [illegible] and working out of a rational base for the [illegible] of the [illegible] for [illegible] differently from [illegible] persons who [illegible] the [illegible] business of another [illegible] that different treatment may be [illegible] (i) the [illegible] of the standards by which [illegible] is [illegible] the same [illegible] corporations and, [illegible] (j) there is a question of [illegible] the [illegible] which [illegible] points upon which [illegible] and [illegible] are not the only social policies [illegible] by the [illegible] theory and its [illegible] of the [illegible] relevant [illegible]

4.20 CONCLUSION

Since the initial adoption of § 402A of the *Restatement* in Texas, the law of strict tort liability has expanded and adapted to meet the changing reality of modern [illegible]. The [illegible] has been [illegible] to include [illegible] beyond that contemplated by [illegible] § 402A. The [illegible] has been expanded [illegible] to distinguish between [illegible] and services. [illegible] of the [illegible] and whether the [illegible] will be [illegible] boundaries remains for further judicial clarification.

CHAPTER V. INDUSTRY-WIDE STRICT TORT LIABILITY*

5.00 INTRODUCTION

The concept of industry-wide liability is designed to impose strict tort liability for a defective product in the absence of plaintiff's ability to identify the specific manufacturer of the injury-causing product. The theory evolved only recently as a result of the unique difficulty confronted in identifying the specific manufacturer in certain types of product caused injuries. Industry-wide liability represents a marked departure from traditional tort principles that require the plaintiff in a product liability action to identify the specific manufacturer of the particular injury producing product.[1]

---

* Therese Hartwell coauthored this chapter.

1. Under traditional tort law the party asserting a claim is obligated to prove that the

Under the industry-wide liability theorem, the plaintiff is relieved of the traditional burden of identifying the specific product supplier where the plaintiff is unable to trace the supplier through no fault of his own. Confronted with this unusual situation, some jurisdictions have refashioned traditional tort concepts to shift to the defendant the burden of negating that it supplied the product involved in the litigation.[2] Absent proof by the manufacturer that it did not supply the particular product, liability is imposed on manufacturers who represent an integral part of the industry that formulated, designed and introduced generically identical products into the stream of commerce.

The public policy consideration underlying industry-wide liability envisages that the plaintiff, who is unable to identify the manufacturer that actually supplied the product causing the injury, should not be required to bear the unfortunate consequences of a product related injury. Additionally, the fact that manufacturers presumably occupy a better position than the plaintiff to bear the cost of injuries resulting from a product furnishes the socioeconomic rationale for the theory.[3] An added basis for imposing industry-wide liability is predicated upon the judicial presumption that the imposition of liability on industry members promotes safety by providing an incentive for manufacturers to discover and guard against product defects and to warn of potentially harmful

---

defendant supplied the product which caused the injury. *See, e.g.* Layton v. Blue Giant Equip. Co. 599 F. Supp. 93 (E.D. Pa. 1984)(lift jacks). Bradley v. Firestone Tire & Rubber Co., 590 F. Supp. 1177 (D.S.D. 1984) (multipiece tire rim); Morton v. Abbott Laboratories, 538 F. Supp. 593 (M.D. Fla. 1982) (DES supplier); Starling v. Seaboard Coast Line R.R. Co., 533 F. Supp. 183 (S.D. Ga. 1982) (supplier of asbestos products); Prelick v. Johns-Manville Corp., 531 F. Supp. 96 (W.D. Pa. 1982) (asbestos supplier); Ryan v. Eli Lilly & Co., 514 F. Supp. 1004 (D.S.C. 1981) (DES supplier); Gray v. United States, 445 F. Supp. 337 (S.D. Tex. 1978) (DES supplier); Wetzel v. Eaton Corp., 62 F.R.D. 22 (D. Minn. 1973) (tractor component supplier); Centrone v. C. Schmidt & Sons, Inc., 114 Misc.2d 840, 452 N.Y.S.2d 299 (1982) (beer bottle supplier). *Cf.* Lillage v. Johns-Manville Corp., 602 F. Supp. 855 (E.D. Wisc. 1985).

2. Comment, *DES and a Proposed Theory of Enterprise Liability*, FORDHAM L. REV. 963 (1978); Comment, *The Market Share Theory: Sindell's Contribution to Industry Wide Liability*, 19 HOU. L. REV. 107 (1982); Comment, *Texas Asbestos Claims and Market Share Liability: New Remedy for an Old Tort*, 13 ST. MARY'S L.J. 957 (1982); Comment, *Industry Wide Liability*, 13 SUFFOLK U.L. REV. 980 (1979). *See also* Mizell v. Eli Lilly & Co., 526 F. Supp. 589, 595 (D.S.C. 1981).

3. *Compare* Sindell v. Abbott Laboratories, 26 Cal. 3d 588, 607 P.2d 924, 163 Cal. Rptr. 132, *cert. denied*, 449 U.S. 912 (1980) *with* Payton v. Abbott Laboratories, 512 F. Supp. 1031 (D. Mass. 1981), Gray v. United States, 445 F. Supp. 337 (S.D. Tex. 1978), *and* Zafft v. Eli Lilly & Co., 676 S.W.2d 241 (Mo. 1984).

or dangerous risks associated with a product.

Adoption of industry-wide liability expands rather significantly the scope of strict tort liability as formulated in Section 402A of the *Restatement*. A number of courts have expressed serious concern that adoption of industry-wide liability essentially imposes insurer status on manufacturers for *all* generic products manufactured and marketed within the same industry.[4] In addition, industry's continued ability to absorb the costs of injuries under expanding theories of product liability is less than clear.[5] Moreover, the increasing frequency with which liability is imposed on suppliers of certain beneficial products, including drugs, undoubtedly leads to a dampening effect on pioneering research and production of useful and beneficial products because of increasing preoccupation with absolute safety.[6] In addressing the issue of industry-wide liability, the courts have struggled, unavailingly, to balance the legitimate public policy of both the manufacturers and the consumers.

The principal application of industry-wide liability to date involves diethylstilbestrol (DES) litigation. DES is a synthetic estrogen compound that was marketed for three decades by virtually all major United States drug firms. It was marketed generically rather than as a brand name drug of the manufacturer. Many years after it was initially marketed, the drug was determined to cause vaginal and cervical cancer in a small percentage of daughters of women who consumed the drug during pregnancy.[7] Varying approaches to industry-wide liability in DES cases evolved because of

---

4. *See, e.g.*, Starling v. Seaboard Coast Line R.R. Co., 533 F. Supp. 183 (S.D. Ga. 1982) (market share liability); Ryan v. Eli Lilly & Co., 514 F. Supp. 1004 (D.S.C. 1981) (market share liability); Sindell v. Abbott Laboratories, 26 Cal. 3d 588, 607 P.2d 924, 163 Cal. Rptr. 132, *cert. denied*, 449 U.S. 912 (1980) (enterprise liability); Namm v. Charles E. Frosst & Co., 178 N.J. Super. 19, 427 A.2d 1121 (1981) (alternative liability). *See generally*, Kroll, *Intra-Industry Joint Liability: The Era of Absolute Products Liability*, 687 INS. L.J. 185 (April 1980).

5. *See* Starling v. Seaboard Coast Line R.R. Co., 533 F. Supp. 183, 190 (S.D. Ga. 1982). *See also* Comment, *Market Share Liability for Defective Products: An Ill-Advised Remedy for the Problem of Identification*, 76 NW. U.L. REV. 300, 321-23 (1981).

6. *See* Sheffield v. Eli Lilly & Co., 144 Cal. App. 3d 583, 597, 192 Cal. Rptr. 870, 878-79 (1983). *See also*, Comment, *supra* note 5 at 317-21; Comment, *Products Liability - An Analysis of Market Share Liability*, 34 VAND. L. REV. 1623, 1650-53 (1982).

7. Note, *A Remedy for the "DES Daughters": Products Liability Without the Identification Requirement*, 42 U. PITT. L. REV. 669, 670 (1981). The DES identification problem was initially identified and discussed in Comment, *DES and A Proposed Theory of Enterprise Liability*, 46 FORDHAM L. REV. 963 (1978).

the difficulty in identifying the particular manufacturer who supplied the injury-causing DES. These theories have been expanded to include cases involving injuries related to asbestos exposure. This acceptance and further expansion of industry-wide liability in DES and asbestos litigation suggests the possibility of its application to future product liability litigation involving silicosis from exposure to silica, leukemia from exposure to by-products of the petro-chemical industry and other product-related injuries. The primary theories of industry-wide liability that have been developed include: (1) market share liability; (2) alternative liability; (3) concert of action; (4) enterprise liability; (5) risk contribution; (6) market share alternate liability; (7) aiding and abetting; (8) joint venture; and (9) conspiracy.

5.01 Historical Background

Diethylstilbestrol (DES) was first developed as a synthetic estrogen in the late 1930's in England. Used in the treatment of female hormonal disturbances, DES presented a highly desirable alternative to the more costly natural estrogen. Moreover, DES possessed the advantage of oral administration, whereas natural estrogen was administered only by painful injection.[8]

In 1939, the United States drug industry sought to introduce DES into the market. In accordance with the requirements of the Food and Drug Administration (FDA), the initial drug company filed a New Drug Application (NDA) detailing information concerning the drug's chemical composition, its safety, efficacy and proposed uses.[9] By the end of the following year, ten additional manufacturers seeking to market the drug likewise filed NDAs with the FDA. To expedite processing the applications, the FDA in 1940 formally requested that the drug companies pool their respective clinical data and jointly submit a master file on DES.[10] The FDA considered individual NDAs filed by various drug companies insufficient to enable proper evaluation of both the safety and effi-

---

8. Payton v. Abbott Laboratories, 512 F. Supp. 1031, 1032 (D. Mass. 1981); Ferrigno v. Eli Lilly & Co., 175 N.J. Super. 551, 420 A.2d 1305, 1310 (1980).

9. The evolution of DES and its approval for marketing in the United States is chronicled in more detail in the Comment, *DES and a Proposed Theory of Enterprise Liability*, 46 Fordham L. Rev. 963 (1978) and, Note, *Market Share Liability: An Answer to the DES Causation Problems*, 94 Harv. L. Rev. 668 (1981).

10. Payton v. Abbott Laboratories, 512 F. Supp. 1031, 1033 (D. Mass. 1981).

cacy of DES. The pooled information was deemed necessary to cure this deficiency. In response to the FDA's request, the "small committee" was formed to coordinate the "pooling" of data. This committee consisted of representatives from the firms that had previously filed NDAs. In addition to pooling data, the drug manufacturers acceded to the FDA's request to standardize both the drug and method of marketing. This involved establishing common chemical standards for the drug and uniformity of labeling the drug regarding indications for use, recommended dosage and warnings of potential risks. Most of the drug manufacturers also agreed to include a permission clause in their NDAs authorizing the FDA to use this data in considering any other NDAs that might be filed for DES.[11]

The initial FDA approval for DES was granted in 1941 for purposes unrelated to miscarriage prevention.[12] Application and subsequent FDA approval for use of the drug during pregnancy occurred in 1947. Each individual manufacturer obtained approval for use in the prevention of problems during pregnancy by filing individual supplemental NDAs for this particular use. Most applicants relied on published studies by independent researchers on the safety and efficacy of DES for problems of pregnancy.[13] Few drug processors conducted their own tests.[14] While the supplemental NDAs did not refer to the "master file" submitted in 1941, the FDA considered this data as the basis for approval.[15] Between 1947 and 1971, DES was produced and marketed by approximately 150

---

11. *Id.* This conduct was judicially declared to constitute conscious parallelism sufficient to establish concert of action upon which liability was predicated by at least one court. Bichler v. Eli Lilly & Co., 55 N.Y.2d 571, 584, 436 N.E.2d 182, 188, 450 N.Y.S.2d 776, 782, (1982). Six of the companies on the "small committee" refused to include the permission clause in their N.D.A.'s. *Payton*, 512 F. Supp. at 1033.

12. These purposes include the treatment of menopausal symptoms, senile and gonorrheal vaginitis and the suppression of lactation. Lyons v. Premo Pharmaceutical Labs, Inc. 170 N.J. Super. 183, 406 A.2d 185, 189 (App. Div. 1979).

13. The drug law in the U.S. prior to 1962 did not require a showing of effectiveness. Federal Food, Drug, and Cosmetic Act of 1938, ch. 675, Sec. 505(b), 52 Stat. 1052 (1983). Therefore, a University of Chicago Study in 1951-52 showing that DES failed to reduce the incidence of spontaneous abortions did not preclude FDA approval of the drug for that purpose. Dieckmann, *Does Administration of Diethylstilbestrol During Pregnancy Have Therapeutic Value?*, 66 Am. J. Obstet. & Gynecol. 1062, 1074 (1953). See Comment, *The Market Share Theory: Sindell's Contribution to Industry Wide Liability*, 19 Harv. L. Rev. 107 (1981).

14. *Id.*

15. *Payton*, 512 F. Supp. at 1034.

to 300 companies.[16] Some firms marketed DES under a trade name, while others marketed it generically. Because all products were identical in composition, pharmacies filled prescriptions on the basis of whichever manufacturer's product was available.[17] Eli Lilly & Company constituted the single largest supplier of DES, possessing an estimated 45% of the market. The next five largest producers, considered together with Eli Lilly, marketed approximately 90% of all DES.[18]

In 1971, medical research linked cancer in young women with DES ingested by their mothers during pregnancy.[19] The inherent latent period between maternal exposure to DES and contraction of cancer by the offspring rendered earlier discovery of this causal link impossible. In 1972, the FDA banned further sale of DES for miscarriage prevention although it continues to be sold for other purposes.[20] Between 1947 and 1971, DES was ingested by several million women whose daughters developed cancer at a rate ranging from 1 in 250 to 1 in 10,000.[21]

The theory of industry-wide liability has also been proposed for cases involving injuries attributable to asbestos exposure. Exposure to asbestos dust may produce two diseases: asbestosis and

---

16. *See* Payton v. Abbott Laboratories, 512 F. Supp. 1031, 1034 (D. Mass. 1981) (150 manufacturers); Ryan v. Eli Lilly & Co., 514 F. Supp. 1004, 1011 (D.S.C. 1981) (300 companies); Sindell v. Abbott Laboratories, 26 Cal. 3d 588, 602, 607 P.2d 924, 931, 163 Cal. Rptr. 132, 139 *cert. denied*, 449 U.S. 912 (1980) (200 companies); Abel v. Eli Lilly & Co., 94 Mich. App. 59, 289 N.W.2d 20 (1979), *aff'd*, 418 Mich. 311, 343 N.W.2d 164 (1984) (300 companies); Namm v. Charles E. Frosst & Co., 178 N.J. Super. 19, 427 A.2d 1121, 1124 (1981) (300 companies).

17. Payton v. Abbott Laboratories, 512 F. Supp. 1031, 1034 (D. Mass. 1981). This practice was known by manufacturers and the FDA.

18. Bichler v. Eli Lilly & Co., 79 A.D.2d 317, 436 N.Y.S.2d 625, 627 (1981), *aff'd*, 55 N.Y.2d 571, 436 N.E.2d 182, 450 N.Y.S.2d 776 (1982); Comment, *DES and A Proposed Theory of Enterprise Liability*, 46 FORDHAM L. REV. 963, 977 (1978).

19. *See* Comment, *DES and a Proposed Theory of Enterprise Liability*, 46 FORDHAM L. REV. 963, 964 n. 5 (1978), *citing* Greenwald, Barlow, Nasca & Burnett, *Vaginal Cancer After Maternal Treatment with Synthetic Estrogens*, 285 N. ENG. J. MED. 390 (1971); Herbst, Ulfelder & Poskanzer, *Adenocarcinoma of the Vagina*, 284 N. ENG. J. MED. 878 (1971). *See generally* Sindell v. Abbott Laboratories, 26 Cal. 3d 588, 594, 607 P.2d 924, 925, 163 Cal. Rptr. 132, 133, *cert. denied*, 449 U.S. 912 (1980).

20. 26 Cal. 3d at 594, 607 P.2d at 925, 163 Cal. Rptr. at 133. For an explanation of the uses of DES which are still allowed see Comment, *DES and A Proposed Theory of Enterprise Liability*. 46 FORDHAM L. REV. 963, 963 n. 2 (1978).

21. Comment, *supra* note 20 at 965 n. 7. *See generally* Sindell v. Abbott Laboratories, 26 Cal. 3d 588, 607 P.2d 924, 163 Cal. Rptr. 132, *cert. denied*, 449 U.S. 912 (1980).

mesothelioma.[22] The asbestos industry purportedly knew, or should have known, of this danger since the mid-1930's.[23] Both diseases involve a rather lengthy latent period between initial exposure and apparent effect, usually as long as ten to twenty-five years. In addition, each exposure to asbestos dust may cause additional tissue changes by reason of its cumulative effect. Mesothelioma may, however, result from a single exposure to asbestos dust or fibers. Because of these factors a determination of which exposure or exposures to asbestos dust caused the disease is rather difficult.[24]

5.02 Theories Of Industry-Wide Liability

A. *Alternative Liability*

The theory of alternative liability authorizes recovery by a plaintiff unable to identify which of two or more negligent tortfeasors caused the injury.[25] Under this theory, the burden of disproving tortious conduct shifts to the defendants upon a showing that *all potential tortfeasors are joined as defendants. Summers v. Tice*[26] first articulated this concept of alternative liability. In *Summers*, plaintiff was injured while hunting when two fellow hunters simultaneously and negligently discharged their rifles in his direction. Because the plaintiff was unable to prove which shot actually caused the injury, the court determined that the legal cause was the negligence of both defendants.[27] Under this tradi-

---

22. *See* Borel v. Fibreboard Paper Products Corp., 493 F.2d 1076, 1083-85 (5th Cir. 1973), *cert. denied*, 419 U.S. 869 (1974) for a comprehensive discussion on the discovery of the dangers of asbestos exposure. *See also* Migues v. Fibreboard Corp., 662 F.2d 1182 (5th Cir. 1981); Karjala v. Johns-Manville Prod. Corp., 523 F.2d 155 (8th Cir. 1975); Flatt v. Johns-Manville Corp., 488 F. Supp. 836 (E.D. Tex. 1980).

23. Hardy v. Johns-Manville Sales Corp., 509 F. Supp. 1353, 1355 (E.D. Tex. 1981), *rev'd on other grounds*, 681 F.2d 334 (5th Cir. 1982).

24. *Id.*

25. The principle, embodied in the Restatement (Second) of Torts, §433(B)(3) (1979) provides:

> Where the conduct of two or more actors is tortious, and it is proved that harm has been caused to the plaintiff by only one of them, but there is uncertainty as to which one has caused it, the burden is upon each such actor to prove that he has not caused the harm.

26. 33 Cal.2d 80, 199 P.2d 1 (1948). The *Summers* court recognized the use of the concert of action concept to reach the same result in earlier cases. *Id.* at 84-85, 199 P.2d at 3.

27. *Id.* at 84, 199 P.2d at 2-3.

tional alternative liability theory, liability is joint and several.[28] Almost all strict tort liability claims premised on alternative liability have been rebuffed because of the failure to join all potential tortfeasors in the action.[29] A cause of action under alternative liability, however, has been approved in several DES cases. In *Abel v. Eli Lilly & Co.*,[30] plaintiff was unable to identify the specific supplier of DES. In reversing a summary judgment for the defendant, the court adopted the alternative liability theory based on plaintiff's allegation that the defendants constituted *all known manufacturers* of DES whose products were distributed in Michigan during the relevant time period.[31] By joining all possible defendants, plaintiff actually satisfied the requirements prescribed by the alternative liability concept. The court concluded that liability was joint and several.[32]

Though the Michigan Supreme Court affirmed the intermediate appellate court decision, the court noted several significant differences between DES litigation and the traditional alternative liability theory postulated in *Summers v. Tice*.[33] The most important difference involves the relationship of the parties. In *Summers*, each defendant was negligent toward *the* plaintiff; in *Abel*, each defendant was negligent toward *a* user; yet, each defendant was not negligent toward *the* plaintiff.[34] Despite this rather significant

---

28. *See* Starling v. Seaboard Coast Line R.R. Co., 533 F. Supp. 183, 188 (S.D. Ga. 1982) in which the court notes that the market share liability theory espoused in *Sindell v. Abbott Laboratories*, 26 Cal. 3d 588, 607 P.2d 924, 163 Cal. Rptr. 132 (1980), *cert. denied*, 449 U.S. 912 (1980) replaces joint and several damage liability with a percentage apportionment based on the defendant's share of the market.

29. *See, e.g.*, Ryan v. Eli Lilly & Co., 514 F. Supp. 1004, 1016-17 (D.S.C. 1981); Gray v. United States, 445 F. Supp. 337, 338 (S.D. Tex. 1978); Sindell v. Abbott Laboratories, 26 Cal. 3d 588, 602-03, 607 P.2d 924, 930-31, 163 Cal. Rptr. 132, 138-39, *cert. denied*, 449 U.S. 912 (1980); Zafft v. Eli Lilly & Co., 676 S.W.2d 241, 244 (Mo. 1984) (en banc); Namm v. Charles E. Frosst & Co., 178 N.J.Super. 19, 32-33, 427 A.2d 1121, 1128 (1981); Martin v. Abbott Laboratories, 689 P.2d 368, 375 (1984); Mason v. Spiege, ___ F. Supp. ___ (D.C. Minn. 1984); *See also* Bradley v. Firestone Tire & Rubber Co., 590 F. Supp. 1177, 1179 (D.S.D. 1984), in which the court notes, "This theory [alternative liability] is inapplicable in this case because each of the defendants must have acted tortiously. Here only one defendant made the rim in question." *Cf.* Layton v. Blue Giant Equip. Co. 599 F. Supp. 93, 95 N.4 (E.D. Pa. 1984).

30. 94 Mich. App. 59, 289 N.W.2d 20 (1980), *aff'd*, 418 Mich. 311, 343 N.W.2d 164 (1984).

31. *Id.* at 73-76, 289 N.W.2d at 25-26.

32. *Id.*

33. 33 Cal. 2d 80, 199 P.2d 1 (1948).

34. Abel v. Eli Lilly & Co., 418 Mich. 311, 343 N.W.2d 164, 172-73 (1984); *Accord*,

difference, the Michigan Supreme Court concluded that the alternative liability theory could be tailored to accommodate DES cases. By restructuring the critical elements of the concept, the court acknowledged that its decision not only extended the policy of traditional alternative liability, but in fact, created a modified version of alternative liability designed specifically for DES cases.[35] The court enunciated the criteria that the plaintiff must satisfy to shift the burden of proof to the defendants: (a) that all defendants acted tortiously; (b) that plaintiffs were harmed by the conduct of one of the defendants; (c) that all possible defendants were joined in the action; and (d) that plaintiffs were unable to identify the specific defendant who actually caused the injury.[36] The court restricted the use of alternative liability to actions based on negligence and not breach of warranty or strict tort liability.[37]

The Ohio Supreme court in *Minnich v. Ashland Oil Co., Inc.*[38] adopted the concept of alternative liability. Plaintiff, an employee of a printing company was injured when some ethyl acetate supplied by two different manufacturers exploded as he was cleaning a chain in the press. In outlining the elements of the doctrine, the Ohio Supreme Court declared that "plaintiff must still prove (1) that two or more defendants committed tortious acts, and (2) that plaintiff was injured as a proximate result of the wrongdoing of one of the defendants."[39]

Cousineau v. Ford Motor Co., 363 N.W.2d 721 (1985) (multiple tire rim assembly; concert of action applicable).

35. *Abel*, 418 Mich. 311, 343 N.W.2d 164, 173.

36. *Id.* The court noted that the plaintiffs must be unable to identify the specific defendant through no fault of their own. In addition, the plaintiffs must make a good faith effort at identification measured by a due diligence standard. *Contrast*, Collins v. Eli Lilly & Co., 116 Wis. 2d 166, 342 N.W.2d 37, 50 (1984), where the court, with regard to identification, required only that a plaintiff commence suit against a defendant who produced or marketed the same type of DES taken by the plaintiff's mother. If the plaintiff cannot prove the type of DES the mother took, the plaintiff is merely required to allege and prove that the defendant drug company produced or marketed DES for the purpose of preventing miscarriage. The Wisconsin Supreme Court does not appear to require that the plaintiff make any real attempt to prove the *specific* manufacturer responsible for producing the injury-causing DES. Refer to text accompanying notes 255-264 *infra*.

37. 418 Mich. 311, 343 N.W.2d 164, 173 (1984). Contrast the contention in *Starling v. Seaboard Coast Line R.R. Co.*, 533 F. Supp. 183, 188 n. 5 (1982) that the *Sindell* language suggests the market share liability theory can apply to strict liability as well as negligence.

38. 15 Ohio St. 3d 396, 473 N.E.2d 1199 (1984).

39. *Id.* at 1200. The court emphasizes that alternative liability is inapplicable in cases "where there is no proof that the conduct of more than one defendant has been tortious." *Id.*

Unlike *Abel* where the Michigan court required that all potential suppliers of the product be identified and joined, the New Jersey Court applied alternative liability absent a complete joinder. In *Ferrigno v. Eli Lilly & Co.*,[40] the court announced that alternative liability represented a valid theory although the plaintiff was unable to identify the actual manufacturer and all potential suppliers of the product were not joined.[41] Relying on its interpretation of *Anderson v. Somberg*,[42] the *Ferrigno* court concluded that plaintiff's cause of action was not subject to dismissal merely because of the possibility that the defendants did not include the party who caused the actual injury. While recognizing that Anderson differed factually from cases involving DES, the court focused on the parallels between the cases. The strong policy [in New Jersey] which favors recovery by all injured parties who could not otherwise recover because of an inability to identify the source of their injuries represented the overriding consideration.[43]

In accepting the alternative liability theory, the *Ferrigno* court rejected the *Sindell v. Abbott Laboratories*[44] requirement that *all parties* who could have been responsible for the plaintiff's injury should be joined as parties. The court, however, elected to adopt the *Sindell* market share concept of damages[45] on the basis that market share percentage allocation was more appropriate in DES

---

40. 175 N.J. Super. 551, 420 A.2d 1305 (1980).

41. 420 A.2d at 1313.

42. 67 N.J. 291, 338 A.2d 1, (1975) *cert. denied*, 423 U.S. 929 (1975). Plaintiff sustained injuries when a piece of a rongeur broke off while it was being manipulated in his spinal canal during a back operation. The plaintiff initiated an action against the surgeon, the hospital, the manufacturer and the supplier of the rongeur, though he was unable to determine the actual cause of the failure. 338 A.2d at 3. The court held that where an unconscious or helpless patient suffers an injury not reasonably foreseeable nor related to the surgery, the burden shifts to those who owed the patient a duty of care to prove their nonculpability. 338 A.2d at 7. The court noted that while such a shift is not normally available against multiple defendants, in the absence of evidence of which one of several defendants is culpable, the shift in the burden of proof is appropriate because of a special responsibility each defendant owes to the plaintiff. 338 A.2d at 6-7. The court acknowledged the possibility that the defendants joined did not include the actual cause of the broken rongeur. However, there was no evidence to support such a possibility and, thus, it was "pure and undisguised speculation." 338 A.2d at 8.

43. 175 N.J. Super. 551, 420 A.2d 1305, 1314 (1984). *See* Lyons v. Premo Pharmaceutical Labs, Inc., 170 N.J. Super. 183, 192-193, 406 A.2d 185, 190, (1979) *cert. denied*, 82 N.J. 167, 412 A.2d 774 (1979).

44. 26 Cal. 3d 588, 602, 603, 607 P.2d 924, 930-31, 163 Cal. Rptr. 132, 138-39 *cert. denied*, 449 U.S. 912 (1980).

45. Refer to text accompanying notes 125-149 *infra*.

cases than joint and several liability.[46] The results in *Sindell* and *Ferrigno* are essentially identical, even though *Ferrigno* expressly adopts alternative liability while *Sindell* expressly rejects the theory. Perhaps the major difference is that *Sindell* requires joinder of a substantial percentage of the DES market while *Ferrigno* imposes no such requirement. Under *Ferrigno*, a plaintiff is entitled to maintain a cause of action by joining only one DES manufacturer and still recover damages, albeit damages limited to the percentage of defendant's share of the market.

The decision in *Ferrigno* may, however, lack precedential value because it was expressly disapproved by the New Jersey Superior Court in *Namm vs. Charles E. Frosst & Co.*[47] In *Namm*, plaintiff sued forty-four DES manufacturers and suppliers. Affirming a summary judgment for the defendants, the court categorically rejected alternative liability. The court reaffirmed the fundamental principle of strict tort liability: the plaintiff is required to identify the supplier who actually produced and marketed the injury causing product.[48] The court observed that alternative liability shifts the burden of proof when the actual wrongdoer is unknown.[49] The court distinguished *Anderson* on the basis that *all potential tortfeasors* were defendants in the litigation.[50] Additionally, the court emphasized that the mere fact that plaintiff confronted difficulties in identifying the particular tortfeasor did not

---

46. 175 N.J. Super. 551, 420 A.2d 1305, 1316 (1980).

47. 178 N.J. Super. 19, 427 A.2d 1121 (1981).

48. 427 A.2d at 1125. W. Prosser, Law of Torts § 41 (5th ed. 1984) defines the burden of proof as follows:

> [A plaintiff] must introduce evidence which affords a reasonable basis for the conclusion that it is more likely than not that the conduct of the defendant was cause in fact of the result. A mere possibility of such causation is not enough, and when the matter remains one of pure speculation or conjecture, or the probabilities are at best evenly balanced, it becomes the duty of the court to direct a verdict for the defendant.

See, e.g., Morton v. Abbott Laboratories, 538 F. Supp. 593, 599 (M.D. Fla. 1982); Ryan v. Eli Lilly & Co., 514 F. Supp. 1004, 1018 (D.S.C. 1981); Gray v. United States, 445 F. Supp. 337, 338 (W.D. Tex. 1978).

49. *Namm*, 427 A.2d at 1127.

50. It is interesting to note that the decisions in both *Namm* and *Ferrigno*, 175 N.J. Super. 531, 420 A.2d 1305 (1980) relied on *Anderson v. Somberg* to support their respective decisions. The court in *Namm* interpreted *Anderson* to require that all possible defendants must be joined for the burden of proof to shift. The court in *Ferrigno* interpreted the holding by the *Anderson* court as an indication that all possible defendants are not required to be joined.

justify shifting the burden of proof to the defendants.[51] The court observed that the defendants, individually or as a group, occupied no superior position and possessed no special ability greater than the plaintiff in identifying the supplier of the DES.[52]

Alternative liability for unidentified suppliers of identical products was also rejected for public policy reasons: it would result in the named defendants paying damages caused by only one defendant or by another party unknown to the defendants and "over whom they have no control or even any meaningful contact"[53] any extensive policy shifts properly should be deferred to the state's highest court or the legislature.[54] In the absence of a decision by the New Jersey Supreme Court, the rule declared in *Namm* adhering to traditional requirements of complete joinder, constrains the use of alternative liability.[55]

The expansion of alternative liability to strict tort liability liti-

---

51. *Namm*, 178 N.J. Super. 427 A.2d 1121, 1127 (1981).

52. Courts vary their approach to the requirement that the defendant occupy a superior position to that of the plaintiff to identify the tortfeasor who actually caused the injury. *See, e.g.*, Sindell v. Abbott Laboratories, 26 Cal. 3d 588, 602, 607 P.2d 924, 930, 163 Cal. Rptr. 132 (1980), *cert. denied*, 449 U.S. 912 (1980) (the fact that defendants were not in a better position to identify the specific manufacturer causing injury does not prevent *per se* the application of alternative liability); Abel v. Eli Lilly & Co., 418 Mich. 311, 343 N.W.2d 164, 174 (1984) (this issue is irrelevant); Cousineau v. Ford Motor Co., 363 N.W.2d 721, (1984); Zafft v. Eli Lilly & Co., 676 S.W.2d 241, 244, (Mo. 1984) (en banc) (this requirement is not necessary but is important to the theory because in DES cases, the passage of time impairs efforts of plaintiffs and defendants alike); Namm v. Charles E. Frosst & Co., 178 N.J. Super. 19, 427 A.2d 1121, 1127-28 (1981) (alternative liability rejected in part because the defendant occupies no better position than the plaintiff to make identification); Collins v. Eli Lilly & Co., 116 Wis. 2d 166, 342 N.W.2d 37, 46 (1984) (alternative liability is rejected in part because plaintiff and defendants were equally unable to identify the responsible defendant); Mason v. Spiegel, ____ F. Supp. ____ (D.C. Minn. 1984); RESTATEMENT (SECOND) OF TORTS § 433 (B)(3) (1979) requires "that defendants be either (a) in a superior position to offer evidence of identification, or (b) responsible for plantiff's inability to identify the supplier of the drug."

53. *Namm*, 178 N.J. Super 19, 427 A.2d 1121, 1128. The court in Sheffield v. Eli Lilly & Co., 144 Cal. App. 3d 583, 608, 192 Cal. Rptr. 870, 886 (1983) observes, however, that this is "overly strong" in that it fails to recognize that all the manufacturers are tortfeasors. Of course, the court simply issued a judicial characterization of all DES suppliers as tortfeasors without any legal analysis.

54. 178 N.J. Super. 19, 427 A.2d 1121, 1128 (1981).

55. *See* Pipon v. Burroughs-Wellcome Co., 532 F. Supp. 637, 639 (D.N.J. 1982) where plaintiffs requested that the case be placed on a "reserve calendar" based on their belief that the New Jersey Supreme Court would, at the first opportunity, reverse the identification requirement. Plaintiffs claimed that the *Namm* court suggested such a result but the *Pipon* court rejected this argument.

gation was recently rejected in *Ryan v. Eli Lilly & Co.*[56] The court noted that alternative liability, as embodied in the *Restatement*,[57] requires as essential elements: (1) that all possible suppliers of the product are before the court as defendants, and (2) that defendants be either (a) in a superior position to offer evidence of identification, or (b) responsible for plaintiff's inability to identify the supplier of the drug.[58] Only when the plaintiff has demonstrated that the particular party responsible for causing the harm is joined as a defendant does the burden shift to the defendants to disprove culpability.[59] The court further observed that though the *Restatement* recognizes modification of the rule where one of the actors is not, or cannot be joined, the *Restatement* does not suggest a total abandonment of the requirement that all conceivable defendants be joined. Relying on the traditional doctrinal principles embodied in the *Restatement*, the court concluded that plaintiff's suit against only seven of 118 DES manufacturers was insupportable. No evidence existed that one of the defendant's products was ingested by her mother or caused plaintiff's injuries.[60] The court stressed the remoteness of the possibility that one of the seven named defendants supplied the particular injury producing DES. The court concluded that it was inherently unfair to require a few manufacturers, representing only a minimal share of the market, to disprove culpability.[61]

The court in *Martin v. Abbott Laboratories*[62] also rejected al-

---

56. 514 F. Supp. 1004 (D.S.C. 1981).

57. Restatement (Second) of Torts § 433(B)(3) (1979).

58. *Ryan*, 514 F. Supp. at 1016.

59. Restatement (Second) of Torts § 433(B)(3) comment *h* (1979) states:

> [I]t is possible that cases may arise in which some modification of the rule stated may be necessary because of complications arising from the fact that one of the actors involved is not or cannot be joined as a defendant, or because of the effect of lapse of time, or because of substantial differences in the character of the conduct of the actors or the risks which they have created. Since such cases have not arisen, and the situations which might arise are difficult to forecast, no attempt is made to deal with such problems in this Section. The rule stated in Subsection (3) is not intended to preclude possible modifications if such situations call for it.

Contrast McElhaney v. Eli Lilly & Co., 564 F. Supp. 265, 270 (D.S.D. 1983) which construes comment "h' as allowing a shift in the burden of proof even though all possible tortfeasors may not be joined.

60. *Ryan*, 514 F. Supp. at 1017.

61. *Id.*

62. 689 P.2d 368 (1984).

ternative liability on the basis that it does not "provide a fair way to apportion damages among the defendants."[63] Under alternative liability, "defendants that produced or marketed small amounts of DES and those that produced or marketed large amounts would be equally liable."[64]

Alternative liability may be applied under the traditional doctrine when *all potential tortfeasors are joined as parties.* When alternative liability is expanded to product liability cases, an individual defendant may escape liability only by demonstrating that it neither manufactured nor marketed the particular injury-producing product. Alternative liability at best possesses questionable applicability when there is an incomplete joinder of all possible producers of the product. Alternative liability involves an individual tort based on the independent tortious act of each manufacturer in producing and marketing the product. Some courts hold that unless the plaintiff can demonstrate that one or more defendants occupy a superior position in identifying the particular product which caused the injury, there is simply no justification for extending the alternative liability concept. Otherwise, product suppliers are metamorphosized into insurers.

B. *Concert of Action*

Concert of action is predicated on the tortious conduct of all defendants which produces plaintiff's harm. Under this concept, multiple tortfeasors who participate in a joint endeavor are jointly and severally liable for the injuries arising from the joint endeavor.[65] Liability is imposed on all defendants because each breaches a duty of care to the plaintiff. Concert of action, as embodied in the *Restatement*, provides:

> For harm resulting to a third person from the tortious conduct of another, one is subject to liability if he (a) does a tortious act in concert with the other or pursuant to a common design with him, or (b) knows that the others' conduct constitutes a breach of duty and gives substantial assistance or encouragement to the other so to conduct himself, or (c) gives substantial assistance to the other in accomplishing a tortious result and his own conduct, separately

---

63. 689 P.2d at 377.
64. *Id.*
65. *See* note 21, *supra.*

considered, constitutes a breach of duty to the third person.[66]

The *Restatement* cautions that a mere common plan, design or even an express agreement does not constitute sufficient conduct for concert of action liability; the defendants must engage in acts of a tortious character to execute the plan or agreement.[67] Some commentators denigrate the *Restatement* postulation for concert of action liability. As viewed by Dean Prosser, concert of action encompasses in its application "all those who, in pursuance of a common plan or design to commit a tortious act, actively take part in it, or further it by cooperation or request, or lend aid or encouragement to the wrongdoer, or ratify and adopt his acts done for their benefit . . . . "[68] Prosser further suggests that the theory does not require an express agreement; a mere tacit understanding by and among its perpetrators suffices.[69]

The classic example of concert of action involves a bystander injured by a car participating in a drag race.[70] Even though only one vehicle actually strikes the injured party, all participants in the race are not acting independently but rather are jointly engaged in a common tortious endeavor that causes the plaintiff's injury.[71]

Concert of action has been expanded to product related injuries in two jurisdictions.[72] In *Bichler v. Eli Lilly & Co.*,[73] plaintiff

---

66. RESTATEMENT (SECOND) OF TORTS § 876 (1979).

67. RESTATEMENT (SECOND) OF TORTS § 876 comment b (1979). In the case of *In Re Related Asbestos Cases*, 543 F. Supp. 1152 (N.D. Cal. 1982), the court recognized the potential applicability of concert of action in a suit seeking damages for asbestosis. The court declared that the plaintiff "must tend to establish that defendants, in pursuance of a common plan or design to commit a tortious act, actively took part in the act, or furthered it by cooperation or request, or lent aid or encouragement to a wrongdoer, or ratified and adopted wrongful acts done for their benefit." *Id.* at 1159.

68. W. PROSSER W. KEETON, LAW OF TORTS § 46 (5th ed. 1984).

69. *Id.*

70. *See, e.g.*, Finn v. Morgan, 46 A.D.2d 229, 362 N.Y.S.2d 292, 297 (1974); Lemons v. Kelly, 239 Or. 354, 397 P.2d 784, 785 (1964); Skipper v. Hartley, 242 S.C. 221, 130 S.E.2d 486, 488-89 (1963); *cf.* Parrott v. Garcia, 436 S.W.2d 897, 900 (Tex. 1969) (a willing participant or principal in the race cannot recover).

71. Morton v. Abbott Laboratories, 538 F. Supp. 593, 596 (M.D. Fla. 1982); Hall v. E.I. DuPont De Nemours & Co., 345 F. Supp. 353, 371 (E.D.N.Y. 1972).

72. Bichler v. Eli Lilly & Co., 79 A.D.2d 317, 436 N.Y.S.2d 625 (1981), *aff'd* 55 N.Y.2d 571, 436 N.E.2d 182, 450 N.Y.S.2d 776 (1982). Concert of action, though not applied, was approved as a potential cause of action in *Abel v. Eli Lilly & Co.*, 94 Mich. App. 59, 289 N.W.2d 20, 25 (1980). In *Abel*, plaintiff alleged that all the potential suppliers of the involved product were joined as parties and the recovery was really based on alternative liabil-

asserted a claim for injuries resulting from her mother's ingestion of DES based on defendant's concert of action in obtaining approval for and marketing DES without adequately testing the drug.[74] Eli Lilly, the sole defendant, was deemed jointly and severally liable for the total damage award. The trial court determined that Eli Lilly acted in concert with the original twelve companies seeking FDA approval for DES in the United States. Moreover, Eli Lilly had been the most prominent proponent for approval. The original manufacturers, allegedly with the organizational impetus provided by Eli Lilly, cooperated with one another by: (1) pooling information and clinical data, (2) agreeing on the same basic chemical formula, and (3) adopting Eli Lilly's literature as a model for package inserts destined for joint submission to the FDA in 1941. These activities were construed as an express agreement.[75] Further, the court concluded that the acts of the twelve companies represented all DES manufacturers because these acts established the pattern for subsequent approval and marketing.[76] The drug industry members who later sought FDA approval of DES for use in miscarriage prevention engaged in activity that was consciously parallel by relying on the data contained in the original application for DES usage.[77] This parallel activity ostensibly established an inference of a tacit agreement.[78]

---

ity. Indeed, if all possible suppliers of DES during the relevant time period and in the particular geographic area were joined as defendants, the alternative liability concept of *Summers v. Tice*, 33 Cal. 2d 80, 199 P.2d 1 (1948) applied. *See also* Cousineau v. Ford Motor Co., 363 N.W.2d 721 (Mich. App. 1984).

73. 79 A.D.2d 317, 436 N.Y.S.2d 624 (1981), *aff'd*, 55 N.Y.2d 571, 436 N.E.2d 182, 450 N.Y.S.2d 776 (1982).

74. For a description of the state of scientific knowledge at the time that drug companies applied to the FDA for the use of DES in miscarriage prevention and during the following years *see* Bichler v. Eli Lilly & Co., 29 A.D.2d 317, 436 N.Y.S.2d 625, 629-30 (1981), *aff'd*, 55 N.Y.2d 571, 436 N.E.2d 182, 450 N.Y.S.2d 776 (1982).

75. The court reached this unusual conclusion notwithstanding the fact that such cooperation was first invited by the FDA.

76. *Bichler*, 436 N.Y.S.2d at 633.

77. *Id. But see,* Morton v. Abbott Laboratories, 538 F. Supp. 593, 597 (M.D. Fla. 1982), where the court in analyzing the factual basis upon which the *Bichler* court predicated a conscious parallellism, noted "These actions [pooling of information and using a model package insert] cannot lead to a finding of tacit agreement in a DES case." *Accord*, In Re Related Asbestos Cases, 543 F. Supp. 1152, 1159 (N.D. Cal. 1982).

78. *Bichler*, 436 N.Y.S.2d at 633. In determining whether tacit as opposed to express agreement was sufficient to support a concert of action theory, the trial court in *Bichler* stated that the case "was not being tried under the classic version of concerted action, but rather a modified version. . . expanded to adapt to the exigencies of trying a case in the

In affirming the trial court's decision, however, the appellate court observed that evidence of collaboration with other drug manufacturers in 1941 to secure the initial FDA approval was unrelated to defendants' concerted action regarding the supplemental application in 1947.[79] These applications relied substantially on the same studies and requested approval to market the same dosage (which was five times more powerful than the maximum dosage approved in 1941). On the basis of this closely parallel conduct, the court concluded that the jury could infer that the conduct was conscious or that Eli Lilly's participation in the filings substantially encouraged the other companies who ultimately marketed DES for pregnancy-related purposes.[80]

Eli Lilly's argument that it was unfairly singled out by the imposition of joint and several liability for 100% of the damages was summarily rejected. Eli Lilly argued that the pharmacist who filled the prescription stocked DES from four or five different suppliers, any one of which could be responsible for the DES ingested by plaintiff's mother. The court declared that the imposition of liability on Eli Lily was not unfair because the plaintiff possessed the option to proceed against any joint tortfeasor participating in the concerted action.[81]

Typically, concert of action is applied in situations where the particular tortfeasor has been identified, but the plaintiff seeks to extend liability to those acting in league with that defendant.[82] The court in *Bichler*, however, perceived that an expansion of concert of action to the DES cases was appropriate to solve the difficult identification problem confronted by plaintiffs. The rationale for the adoption of concert of action seemingly is a perception that the plaintiff should not be penalized for identification problems

---

rapidly developing area of the law of strict products liability." 436 N.Y.S.2d at 630-31. Further, the court states that even with the classic usage of concerted action, Dean Prosser's view that only tacit understanding, not express agreement, is required would apply. Of course, this application expressly contravenes the very foundation of concert of action promulgated in RESTATEMENT (SECOND) OF TORTS § 876 (1979). *See supra* note 68 and accompanying text.

79. Bichler v. Eli Lilly & Co., 55 N.Y.2d 571, 584 n. 7, 436 N.E.2d 182, 188 n. 7, 450 N.Y.S.2d 776, 782 n.7 (1982). It is important to remember that the 1941 application made no mention of the use of DES by pregnant women.

80. *Id.* at 585, 436 N.E.2d at 188-89, 450 N.Y.S.2d at 782-83.

81. Bichler v. Eli Lilly & Co., 436 N.Y.S.2d at 633-34; *See also*, Cousineau v. Ford Motor Co., 363 N.W.2d 721 (1984).

82. *See, e.g.*, Collins v. Eli Lilly & Co., 116 Wis. 2d 166, 342 N.W.2d 37, 47 (1984).

caused by the industry's generic marketing technique.[83] The decision, in essence, is predicated on the socio-economic concept that whenever someone is injured there must be someone also answerable in damages.[84]

Concert of action was also approved in *Cousineau v. Ford Motor Co.*[85] Plaintiff instituted a cause of action for the wrongful death of her son caused by a defective three piece wheel rim. The manufacturer of the rim could not be determined despite distinctive identifying marks on the rim, because the rim had been lost. Plaintiff therefore sued various manufacturers of identically designed wheels alleging that the injury occurred due to negligent wheel design, failure to adequately warn and failure to provide safety devices by the defendant manufacturers.[86] The court observed that under a concert of action claim it was unnecessary for the party actually causing the injury to be joined since both named and unnamed defendants who acted in concert are jointly and severally liable for all harm.[87] Concert of action was predicated on a tacit understanding among the defendant manufacturers to refrain from making the multi-piece tire rims safer.[88]

Most jurisdictions that have considered concert of action have summarily rejected its application. The California Supreme Court in the seminal case of *Sindell v. Abbott Laboratories*[89] disapproved application of concert of action because of the customary accepted practice of manufacturer reliance upon the experience of others producing the same product. Such conduct cannot be construed as even a tacit understanding among the manufacturers to engage in tortious activity.[90] The court observed that application of the concept of concert of action to this situation would expand the doctrine far beyond its intended scope and would render virtually any manufacturer liable for the defective products of an entire indus-

---

83. *Bichler*, 436 N.Y.S.2d at 632.

84. The distortions of traditional tort doctrines to provide a basis for recovery to anyone who is injured is disclosed in *Martin v. Harrington & Richardson, Inc.*, 743 F.2d 1200 (7th Cir. 1984) (attempt to extend strict tort liability to manufacturer of a handgun used by a criminal to kill plaintiff's husband).

85. 363 N.W.2d 721 (1984).

86. *Id.*

87. *Id.*

88. *Id.*

89. 26 Cal. 3d 588, 607 P.2d 924, 163 Cal. Rptr. 132, *cert. denied*, 449 U.S. 912 (1980).

90. *Id.* at 605, 607 P.2d at 933, 163 Cal. Rptr. at 141.

try, even if it could be demonstrated that the product which caused the injury was not made by the defendant.[91]

Similarly in *Payton v. Abbott Laboratories*,[92] the court refused to adopt concert of action. Plaintiff contended that an agreement not to test the drug properly and not to warn of the carcinogenic danger could be inferred from the consciously parallel behavior of the drug companies.[93] The court concluded that the plaintiffs failed to satisfy the burden of establishing that an agreement, either express or tacit, existed among the defendants.[94] Moreover, the court refused to recognize any connection between the collaboration in the application procedures in 1941 and the subsequent NDA's for DES use in miscarriage prevention.[95] The suggestion of a collaborative effort in 1947 was rejected because the drug companies acted independently in collecting data for approval of DES to prevent miscarriage.[96]

The court in *Ryan v. Eli Lilly & Co.*[97] likewise rejected concert of action based on the plaintiff's failure to demonstrate that the DES manufacturers agreed not to adequately test the drug for use during pregnancy and not to warn of knowable risks of harm. Evidence of parallel conduct alone is simply insufficient to support the imposition of liability based on concert of action.[98]

Other courts similarly have rejected concert of action as a basis for the imposition of liability on manufacturers of DES.[99] Con-

---

91. *Id.*

92. 512 F. Supp. 1031 (D. Mass. 1981). *But see*, Payton v. Abbott Labs, 386 Mass. 540, 437 N.E.2d 171, 190 (1983) suggesting Massachusetts, under proper circumstances, might consider relaxation of the traditional identification requirement.

93. *Payton*, 512 F. Supp. at 1037.

94. *Id.* at 1038. The drug companies collaborated in gathering clinical data, already amassed by the individual drug companies, for joint submission to the FDA. This collaboration was achieved through the central organizing effort of a small committee of companies formed at the request of the FDA. The committee, however, performed no administrative functions and in no way regulated the testing conducted by the manufacturers.

95. *Id.* Any and all cooperation by the drug companies in submitting clinical data in 1941 was directed only at obtaining approval for DES uses unrelated to problems of pregnancy. The court acknowledged that the 1947 NDAs were supplemental to the 1941 NDAs and that the FDA may have considered clinical data submitted in 1941 in passing on the 1947 applications. Nonetheless, the 1947 applications were supported by new scientific studies and did not refer to the clinical data submitted in 1941.

96. *Id. Accord*, Zafft v. Eli Lilly & Co, 676 S.W.2d 241, 245 (Mo. 1984)(en banc).

97. 514 F. Supp. 1004 (D.S.C. 1981).

98. *Id.* at 1016. *Accord* Payton v. Abbott Laboratories, 512 F. Supp. 1031, 1037 (D. Mass. 1981); In Re Related Asbestos Cases, 543 F. Supp. 1152, 1159 (N.D. Cal. 1982).

99. *See* Morton v. Abbott Laboratories, 538 F. Supp. 593, 596 (M.D. Fla. 1982); Zafft

cert of action was formulated and designed to punish anti-social conduct rather than to provide a cause of action for plaintiffs unable to identify the manufacturer of a product allegedly causing an injury. For example, in *Collins v. Eli Lilly & Co.*[100] the court rejected the theory on the basis that the parallel action between the drug companies was simply too insubstantial to establish that a tacit agreement existed between them. The court emphasized that the concert factor presupposes that a particular tortfeasor is already identified and the plaintiff desires to extend liability to those acting in league with that tortfeasor.[101] The theory clearly is not designed to impose liability when the actual manufacturer of the particular product causing plaintiff's injury is unidentified.

In summary, concert of action imposes liability by reason of a party's involvement or participation in a joint tortious endeavor. Unlike market share and alternative liability, concert of action is not predicated on the individual acts of the parties but rather, on joint activity. As applied to product litigation, the tortious act is not the manufacture of the product but consists of the conduct of all the manufacturers in jointly marketing the product in a manner that breaches a duty owed to consumers. Liability is deemed joint and several and, as applied in *Bichler v. Eli Lilly & Co.*,[102] may be imposed against a single defendant. The fact that the plaintiff has not joined all potential defendants, which is fatal in the traditional alternative liability cause of action, is immaterial under concert of action. Once tortious conduct is established, liability is imposed on any defendant participating in that conduct, even if the defendant did not market the product involved in the particular injury.[103] Liability is imposed because all defendants theoretically have joined in breaching their duty of care and the plaintiff was injured as a result. The *Bichler* court simply did not address the implicit requirement of the *Restatement* that the manufacturer of the product causing plaintiff's injury must be identified.

---

v. Eli Lilly & Co., 676 S.W.2d 241, 245 (Mo. 1984) (en banc); Lyons v. Premo Pharmaceutical Laboratories, Inc., 170 N.J. Super. 183, 406 A.2d 185, 190 (1970), *cert. denied*, 82 N.J. 267, 412 A.2d 774 (1979); Payton v. Abbott Labs, 386 Mass. 540, 437 N.E.2d 171, 190 (1983); Martin v. Abbott Laboratories, 689 P.2d 368, 379 (1984).

100. 116 Wis. 2d 166, 342 N.W.2d 37 (1984).

101. 342 N.W.2d at 46-47.

102. 79 A.D.2d 317, 436 N.Y.S.2d 625, 634 (1981), *aff'd*, 55 N.Y.2d 571, 436 N.E.2d 182, 450 N.Y.S.2d 776 (1982).

103. Collins v. Eli Lilly & Co., 116 Wis. 2d 166, 342 N.W.2d 37, 47 (1984).

C. Enterprise Liability

Under enterprise liability each manufacturer is deemed liable because of adherence to an industry-wide standard. This adherence constitutes the legal cause of injury and defendants who participate in perpetuating the standard are deemed to have contributed to and are liable for plaintiff's injury.[104] This theory resembles concert of action, though the degree and amount of proof required under enterprise liability are noticeably less than that required under concert of action. Rather than proving a joint tortious activity as required in concert of action, the plaintiff need only establish an adherence to and consequent encouragement of an inadequate industry standard. Each defendant unable to satisfy the burden of disproving causation is presumed liable.[105] One rationale for the imposition of such liability is based on the perception that:

> [W]here an entire industry, engaged in a particularly dangerous enterprise and following similar safety practices, places an identically defective product in the stream of commerce, the industry rather than the individual manufacturer should be the focal point for liability because it can best allocate risk, distribute cost and take preventative measures.[106]

The enterprise liability concept was originally formulated in *Hall v. E. I. DuPont de Nemours & Co., Inc.*[107] Defendants were blasting cap manufacturers who placed their products on the market with insufficient warnings. Following an explosion of a cap that injured the plaintiff, suit was instituted against the six manufacturers that comprised virtually the entire United States market and the industry's trade association.[108] The plaintiff was unable to identify which of the six manufacturers actually produced the defective blasting cap. The court concluded that the entire industry

---

104. Hall v. E. I. DuPont De Nemours & Co., 345 F. Supp. 353, 379 (E.D.N.Y. 1972).

105. *Id.*

106. Comment, *DES and A Proposed Theory of Enterprise Liability*, 46 FORDHAM L. REV. 963, 1002 (1978). *See also*, Bradley v. Firestone Tire & Rubber Co., 590 F. Supp. 1177, 1181 (D.S.D. 1984), where the court rejected enterprise liability for an allegedly defective multipiece tire rim. The court noted that plaintiff failed to establish that all multipiece tire rims were defective. *Id.* at 1181; Lillage v. Johns-Manville Corp., 602 F. Supp. 855, 856 (E.D. Wisc. 1985).

107. 345 F. Supp. 353 (E.D.N.Y. 1972).

108. *Id.* at 359.

was liable for the harm caused by the operation of the trade association.[109] As a predicate for liability, the court determined that the plaintiff is obligated to prove that the defendants were jointly aware of the risks and possessed a joint capacity to significantly reduce or totally eliminate the risks.[110] The plaintiff is *not* required to identify the particular defendant responsible for manufacturing the cap involved in the accident. The plaintiff is only obligated to demonstrate that it is more probable than not that one of the joined defendants manufactured the cap. The burden of proof then shifts to the defendants to individually exculpate themselves.[111]

The court expressly limited this theory of liability to specific cases which involve only a small number of manufacturers in a highly centralized industry. Enterprise liability, the court noted, is manifestly unreasonable when applied to a large, decentralized industry.[112] In *Sindell v. Abbott Laboratories*, the court relied upon this distinction in rejecting enterprise liability.[113]

Enterprise liability was likewise rejected in *Namm v. Eli Lilly & Co.*[114] The court determined that this theory ignores the well-established principle that the plaintiff is obligated to identify the actual manufacturer of the injury-producing product.[115] Further, the imposition of enterprise liability would require a completely new method of assessing and apportioning damages among defendants.[116] The court acknowledged that the extensive policy shifts necessary to adopt enterprise liability should be accomplished, if at all, by the state's highest court or the state legislature.[117] Similarly,

---

109. *Id.*

110. *Id.* at 378.

111. *Id.* at 379-80.

112. *Id.* at 378.

113. 26 Cal. 3d 588, 609, 607 P.2d 924, 935, 163 Cal. Rptr. 132, 143 *cert. denied*, 449 U.S. 912 (1980).

114. 178 N.J. Super. 19, 427 A.2d 1121, 1129 (1981).

115. *See* Ryan v. Eli Lilly & Co., 514 F. Supp. 1004 (D.S.C. 1981). The court comments that, "The expansive motion of vicarious liability represented by the enterprise concept - which would render every manufacturer an insurer not only of the safety of its own products, but of all generically similar products made by others - is repugnant to the most basic tenets of tort law." *Id.* at 1017.

116. 427 A.2d at 1129.

117. *Id. Accord*, Starling v. Seaboard Coast Line R.R. Co., 533 F. Supp. 183, 186 (S.D. Ga. 1982) (deferring to the legislature to evaluate the competing public policy considerations involved is consistent with the policy of judicial restraint). *Contrast*, Collins v. Eli Lilly & Co., 116 Wis. 2d 166, 342 N.W.2d 37, 52 N. 12 (1984) where the court regarded their duty "to modify the existing common law if that becomes necessary to promote justice under the

in *Morton v. Abbott Laboratories*[118] the court rejected the theory based on the large number of manufacturers of DES as compared to only six manufacturers of the blasting caps involved in *Hall.* The manufacturers of DES had not delegated safety functions to a manufacturers' controlled trade association as was done by the limited number of manufacturers of blasting caps.[119] Likewise, in *Collins v. Eli Lilly & Co.*[120] enterprise liability was rejected because so many drug companies had entered and departed the DES marketplace that the assumption that the defendants jointly controlled product safety functions was too weak, tenuous and speculative to lend any credence to this theory.[121]

In *Davis v. Yearwood,*[122] plaintiffs sought damages for injuries resulting from a fire that ignited in a jail cell. Suit was instituted against the suppliers of all materials present in the cell. The court perfunctorily rejected application of any enterprise form of liability, noting the number of different types of product manufacturers involved in the case.[123] The court also distinguished the case from *Hall* on the basis that the blasting caps industry is generally subject to strict, if not absolute, liability for engaging in an ultrahazardous activity.[124]

D. *Market Share Liability*

Market share liability was first enunciated by the California Supreme Court in *Sindell v. Abbott Laboratories.*[125] California formulated the novel and unique concept of market share liability to apportion responsibility for a DES related injury.[126]

The facts of *Sindell* are typical of DES cases. Plaintiff insti-

---

law."

118. 538 F. Supp. 593 (N.D. Fla. 1982). *Accord* Zafft v. Eli Lilly & Co., 676 S.W.2d 241 (Mo. 1984) (en banc) in which the court notes, "This court agrees with the majority of courts which reject industry-wide liability in DES cases because of the large number of drug manufacturers involved, the lack of evidence of delegation of responsibility for safety standards to a trade association, and the pervasive role of the FDA in setting industry-wide standards." *Id.* at 245.

119. *Morton,* 536 F. Supp. at 598.

120. 116 Wis. 2d 166, 342 N.W.2d 37 (1984).

121. 342 N.W.2d at 47.

122. 612 S.W.2d 917 (Tenn. App. 1980).

123. *Id.* at 920.

124. *Id.*

125. 26 Cal. 3d 588, 607 P.2d 924, 163 Cal. Rptr. 132, *cert. denied,* 449 U.S. 912 (1980).

126. *Id.* at 612-13, 607 P.2d at 937, 163 Cal. Rptr. at 145.

tuted suit individually and as a class representative for those female residents of California who had been exposed to DES prior to birth. Named as defendants in the lawsuit were eleven of approximately 200 DES manufacturers.[127] Plaintiffs alleged that the defendants, without conducting adequate testing or providing warnings of the drug's dangers, manufactured, marketed and promoted DES as a safe and effective drug to prevent miscarriage. Further, plaintiffs asserted that the defendants: (1) collaborated in marketing and testing the drug; (2) relied on each other's testing; (3) adhered to an industry-wide standard; (4) produced DES from a common and mutually agreed upon formula; and (5) either knew or should have known that their product was sold generically rather than by actual brand name, a fact that rendered positive identification of the actual manufacturer virtually impossible.[128] In addition to negligence, plaintiffs asserted causes of action predicated on strict tort liability, warranty, conspiracy, and lack of consent. Joint and several liability was alleged under each of the causes of action based on the defendants' concert of action in the development, marketing and testing of DES.

The trial court dismissed all of plaintiff's allegations for failure to identify the particular manufacturer whose product was ingested by the plaintiff's mother.[129] The California Supreme Court reversed, adopted market share liability and rejected several other potential bases for imposing liability.[130] The rejected theories included alternative liability, concert of action and enterprise or industry-wide liability. The court distinguished each doctrine and determined that each was inapplicable in the circumstances of the case.[131] First, alternative liability was summarily rejected because all potential defendants were not joined.[132] Secondly, the court rejected concert of action because of the absence of parallel or imitative conduct sufficient to constitute a tacit agreement among the drug manufacturers. The California Supreme Court recognized the common and approved practice of drug producers to utilize and

---

127. *Id.* at 593-94, 607 P.2d at 925-26, 163 Cal. Rptr. at 133-34.

128. *Id.* at 595, 607 P.2d at 926, 163 Cal. Rptr. at 134.

129. *Id.* at 595-96, 607 P.2d at 926, 163 Cal. Rptr. at 134.

130. *Id.* at 614, 607 P.2d at 938, 163 Cal. Rptr. at 134.

131. It has been suggested that *Sindell v. Abbott Laboratories supra*, "is as remarkable for what it rejects as for what it proposes." Comment, *The Market Share Theory: Sindell's Contribution to Industry-Wide Liability*, 19 Hous. L. Rev. 107, 141 (1981).

132. 26 Cal. 3d at 602-03, 607 P.2d at 930-31, 163 Cal. Rptr. at 138-39.

rely upon the experiences and techniques of others. [133] The court concluded that expansion of concert of action to DES litigation would extend the concept significantly beyond its intended scope and render virtually every manufacturer liable for the defective products of an entire industry.[134] Third, the court rejected the enterprise liability theory articulated in *Hall v. E. I. DuPont de Nemours & Co., Inc.*[135] on the basis that *Hall* involved a very limited number of manufacturers who utilized a centralized marketing plan and who delegated all safety functions to a trade association they controlled.[136] The court acknowledged that the standards for marketing utilized by drug manufacturers are largely suggested, if not actually compelled, by the FDA. Thus, the imposition of liability on a manufacturer of drugs it did not supply merely because it adhered to the standards of the industry was clearly inappropriate and unfair.[137]

After rejecting the more traditional tort doctrines, the California Supreme Court expressed a reluctance to foreclose recovery by the plaintiffs.[138] The court undertook, to formulate a unique remedy for plaintiffs injured by the acts of an unknown and unidentified tortfeasor operating within an identifiable industry. The court judicially proclaimed that liability would be imposed on the defendants based on each defendant's share of the total relevant DES market.[139]

Market share liability, in essence, evolved from the concept of alternative liability earlier adopted by California in *Summers v. Tice.*[140] While refusing to apply alternative liability because all po-

---

133. *Id.* at 605, 607 P.2d at 932-33, 163 Cal. Rptr. at 140-41. In addition, the court questioned whether liability under concert of action may even be predicated upon tacit understanding, or whether direct encouragement or assistance is required. *Id.*

134. *Id. Accord,* Morton v. Abbott Laboratories, 538 F. Supp. 593, 597, (M.D. Fla. 1982); Starling v. Seaboard Coast Line R. Co., 533 F. Supp. 183, 190 (S.D. Ga. 1982); Payton v. Abbott Laboratories, 512 F. Supp. 1031, 1035 (D. Mass. 1981); Lyons v. Premo Pharmaceutical Labs, Inc., 170 N.J. Super. 1983, 406 A.2d 185, 190 (1979), *cert. denied,* 82 N.J. 267, 412 A.2d 774 (1979); Zafft v. Eli Lilly & Co., 676 S.W.2d 241, 245 (Mo. 1984) (en banc). A contrary view has been adopted by New York in *Bichler v. Eli Lilly & Co.,* 79 A.D.2d 317, 436 N.Y.S.2d 625 (1981), *aff'd,* 55 N.Y.2d 571, 436 N.E.2d 182, 450 N.Y.S.2d 776 (1982).

135. 345 F. Supp. 353 (E.D. N.Y. 1972). Refer to text accompanying notes 104-124.

136. 26 Cal. 3d at 608-10, 607 P.2d at 934-35, 163 Cal. Rptr. at 142-43.

137. *Id.* at 609-10, 607 P.2d at 935, 163 Cal. Rptr. at 143.

138. *Id.* at 610-11, 607 P.2d at 936, 163 Cal. Rptr. at 144.

139. *Id.* at 611-13, 607 P.2d at 937, 163 Cal. Rptr. at 145.

140. 33 Cal. 2d 80, 199 P.2d 1 (1948). See notes 25-28 *supra* and accompanying text.

tential defendants were not joined, the California court restructured the concept by abandoning the joinder requirement.[141] Under the market share doctrine, the plaintiff who is unable to identify the actual manufacturer of the defective product causing the injury need only join a "substantial percentage" of the manufacturers within the industry.[142] Once the plaintiff establishes that she contracted DES related cancer and that her mother ingested DES during pregnancy, the burden of proof shifts to the defendants. Assuming that a substantial percentage of the manufacturers of DES have been joined as defendants, each defendant is obligated to exculpate itself from liability.[143] The judicially perceived likelihood that the manufacturer of the injury-causing product is joined as a party prompted the court to shift the burden of proof.[144]

In addition, the court in *Sindell* fashioned an equally unique method of apportioning damages based on market share. The court rejected the rule of joint and several liability traditionally applied with alternative liability. Instead, it declared that liability is based on each defendant's percentage share of the DES market.[145] The court observed that the probability that any defendant supplied the product which actually injured the plaintiff was in direct proportion to that defendant's percentage share of the total market.[146] While recognizing that market share cannot be calculated precisely, the court determined that this difficulty did not preclude its use.[147]

In its decision to impose a new form of liability, the California Supreme Court relied entirely on public policy. The court declared:

> In our contemporary complex industrialized society, advances in science and technology create tangible goods which may harm

---

141. The court noted that the RESTATEMENT (SECOND) OF TORTS § 433(B)(3), comment *h* (1979) allows for a modification of the *Summers* rationale which requires all potential defendants be joined. *Contrast* Ryan v. Eli Lilly & Co., 514 F. Supp. 1004 (D.S.C. 1981).

142. 26 Cal. 2d at 612, 607 P.2d at 937, 163 Cal. Rptr. at 145. As one commentator notes: "The most significant omission from the *Sindell* majority opinion is a definition of the phrase 'substantial percentage.'" Comment, *Texas Asbestos Claims and Market Share Liability: A New Remedy for an Old Tort*, 13 ST. MARY'S L.J. 957, 973 (1982).

143. 26 Cal. 3d at 612, 607 P.2d at 937, 163 Cal. Rptr. at 145.

144. *Id.*

145. 26 Cal. 3d at 611-12, 607 P.2d at 934, 163 Cal. Rptr. at 145.

146. *Id.* at 612, 607 P.2d at 934, 163 Cal. Rptr. at 145.

147. *Id.*

> consumers and which cannot be traced to any specific producer. The response of the courts can be either to adhere rigidly to prior doctrine, denying recovery to those injured by such products, or to fashion remedies to meet these changing needs . . . . The most persuasive reason for finding plaintiff states a cause of action is that advanced in Summers: as between an innocent plaintiff and negligent defendants, the latter should bear the cost of the injury.[148]

The court further based its decision on the rationale that the manufacturer occupies a superior position to bear the cost of the injury. Additionally, the imposition of liability presumably creates an incentive for manufacturers to provide safer drugs or to refrain from producing any drugs.[149]

While the *Sindell* decision heralded market share liability as a solution specially tailored to the peculiar problems of proof posed by DES litigation, it is unlikely that the court intended that this newly devised theory of liability should be restricted to DES cases. Rather, the court suggests an extension of market share liability to other areas of product liability litigation.[150]

Texas ostensibly has rejected the market share liability rationale, though not yet directly considering application of this unique form of liability. In *Gray v. United States*,[151] plaintiff instituted suit against Eli Lilly & Co., although she could not establish that DES ingested by her mother was, in fact, manufactured by Eli Lilly. The United States District Court granted summary judgment for the defendant, holding that: "it is a fundamental principle of products liability law that a plaintiff must prove, as an essential element of his case, that a defendant manufacturer actually made the particular product which caused injury."[152]

More recently, in *Hardy v. Johns-Manville Sales Corp.*,[153] an-

---

148. *Id.* at 610-11, 607 P.2d at 936, 163 Cal. Rptr. at 144.

149. *Id.*

150. The law review article which first promoted the concept of market share liability stated that "[t]he DES cases are only the tip of an iceberg." Comment, *DES and A Proposed Theory of Enterprise Liability*, 46 FORDHAM L. REV. 963, 1007 (1978). *See* Note, *Market Share Liability: An Answer to the DES Causation Problem*, 94 HARV. L. REV. 668, 677-79 (1981); Comment, *The Market Share Theory: Sindell's Contribution to Industry Wide Liability*, 19 HOUS. L. REV. 107, 138-41 (1981).

151. 445 F. Supp. 337 (S.D. Tex. 1978).

152. *Id.* at 338.

153. 509 F. Supp. 1353 (E.D. Tex. 1981), *rev'd on other grounds*, 681 F.2d 334 (5th Cir. 1982).

other United States District Court wholly ignored *Gray* and speculated that Texas would adopt the *Sindell* approach. In *Hardy* the lawsuits of 57 or more plaintiffs with asbestos related claims against numerous asbestos manufacturers were consolidated for pretrial discovery purposes. Plaintiffs had worked over the course of several years in the asbestos industry and each claimed either pulmonary asbestosis or mesothelioma caused by the exposure. Relying on *Sindell v. Abbott Laboratories*,[154] the court adopted the market share liability scheme to apportion liability and the attendant damages among the numerous defendants.[155] The court concluded that similarity in proof problems common to the DES and asbestos plaintiffs compelled this result.[156] In both instances, the lapse of time between exposure and injury[157] rendered it virtually impossible for the plaintiff to identify the specific manufacturer of the asbestos product that caused the injury.[158] In addition, the court concluded that a form of market share liability had been imposed in asbestos cases since the *Borel*[159] decision.[160] The decision, formulated under the court's *Erie*[161] powers, was also based on the

---

154. 26 Cal. 3d 588, 607 P.2d 924, 163 Cal. Rptr. 132, *cert. denied*, 449 U.S. 912 (1980).

155. 509 F. Supp. at 1359.

156. *Id.* at 1358.

157. The particular identification problem with mesothelioma is attributable to its long latency period. Asbestosis, on the other hand, is a cumulative progressive disease and may, therefore, lack a precise causative agent. The seminal case discussing the historical background of the relationship between mesothelioma and asbestosis and the exposure to asbestos products is *Borel v. Fibreboard Paper Prods. Corp.*, 493 F.2d 1076 (5th Cir. 1973), *cert. denied*, 419 U.S. 869 (1975). *See also* Migues v. Fibreboard Corp., 662 F.2d 1182 (5th Cir. 1981); Karjala v. Johns-Manville Corp., 523 F.2d 155 (8th Cir. 1975); Flatt v. Johns-Manville Corp., 488 F. Supp. 836 (E.D. Tex. 1980).

158. *Contra*, Starling v. Seaboard Coast Line R.R. Co., 533 F. Supp. 183 (S.D. Ga. 1982).

159. Borel v. Fibreboard Paper Prods. Corp., 493 F.2d 1076 (5th Cir. 1973), *cert. denied*, 419 U.S. 869 (1974).

160. Hardy v. Johns-Manville Sales Corp., 509 F. Supp. 1353, 1358 (E.D. Tex. 1981), *rev'd on other grounds*, 681 F.2d 334 (5th Cir. 1982). *Contrast*, Prelick v. Johns-Manville Corp., 531 F. Supp. 96, 98 (W.D. Pa. 1982) (*Sindell* theory does not apply where plaintiff is able to identify at least one manufacturer or supplier whose product caused the injury).

161. Erie Railroad Co. v. Tompkins, 304 U.S. 64 (1938). The District Court in *Hardy* noted that it faced an issue which had not yet been adjudicated in Texas courts. All the relevant asbestos law had been made in federal court. Therefore, the court concluded that under the *Erie* doctrine it was compelled to analyze the indications and determine what action the state's highest court would take. 509 F. Supp. at 1356-57. Significantly, the court ignored the earlier decision in *Gray v. United States,* 445 F. Supp. 337 (S.D. Tex. 1978) which rejected recovery in the absence of plaintiff establishing the identity of the DES manufacturer.

fact that Texas has adopted alternative liability,[162] the progenitor of the *Sindell* genre of liability. Therefore, the court rationalized, Texas would presumably adopt the *Sindell* concept of market share liability.[163] The court noted that since Texas was moving toward a form of comparative fault in strict liability, the only true means of achieving an allocation of fault for asbestos-related cases was adoption of enterprise liability of which market share apportionment is an integral part.[164]

After adopting the market share concept and thereby relieving the plaintiff of the critical identification burden, the court discussed the relative merits of joint and several liability versus market share apportionment of damages. The court opined that the current *pro rata* approach to apportionment under joint and several liability was unfair to all concerned because small manufacturers would be required to bear costs disproportionate to their culpable conduct and the large manufacturers, relieved of accountability for the full extent of their activity, would receive a windfall.[165] The court therefore embraced market share liability as the most equitable means of curing this perceived problem.[166]

The viability of the market share concept adopted in *Hardy* is uncertain and rather dubious. The decision was formulated under the court's *Erie* powers and has not received the imprimatur of the Texas Supreme Court. The validity of the decision is further limited because appeal to the Fifth Circuit was interlocutory. The issue of market share liability was before the court on pretrial discovery motions and, therefore was not a final adjudication of the applicability of market share liability.[167] A quintessential element for recovery in strict tort liability in Texas is proof by the plaintiff that the defendant supplied a defective product.[168] Absent proof

---

162. *See* Landers v. East Texas Salt Water Disposal Co., 151 Tex. 251, 248 S.W.2d 731 (1952). Note the reliance on *Landers* by the court in *Borel v. Fibreboard Paper Prods. Corp.*, 493 F.2d 1076, 1095 (5th Cir. 1973), *cert. denied*, 419 U.S. 869 (1974).

163. 509 F. Supp. at 1359.

164. *Id.*

165. *Id.* at 1358.

166. Id. at 1358-59. *See generally*, Note, *The Market Share Liability: An Answer to the DES Causation Problems*, 94 HARV. L. REV. 668 (1981).

167. The Fifth Circuit, on appeal, deferred resolution of this issue because it was not properly raised and preserved as a point on appeal. 681 F.2d 334 (5th Cir. 1982).

168. Syrie v. Knoll Int'l, 748 F.2d 304 (5th Cir. 1984); Davidson v. Stanadyne, Inc., 718 F.2d 1334 (5th Cir. 1983); Rourke v. Garza, 530 S.W.2d 794 (Tex. 1975); Turner v. General Motors Corp., 584 S.W.2d 844 (Tex. 1979).

that the defendant supplied the product and that it was defective at the time it left the possession of the manufacturer, strict tort liability is inapplicable.

Market share liability was also recognized in *Copeland v. Celotex Corp.*[169] The court noted that: "[T]raditional theories of causation may not be realistic in light of contemporary advances in science and technology and the complexity of an industrialized society, such as ours, which creates harmful products that cannot be traced to a specific producer."[170]

The court, however, rejected the *Sindell* extension of the alternative liability theory embodied in Section 433(B)(3) of the *Restatement (Second) of Torts*.[171] Under alternative liability, only one tortfeasor causes the injury. Thus, the theory is inapplicable to asbestosis cases where the injury generally results from the cumulative exposures often caused by multiple manufacturers of asbestos products.[172] The court, instead, based its formulation of market share liability on section 443(B)(2) of the *Restatement* which states that:

> Where the tortious conduct of two or more actors has combined to bring about harm to the plaintiff, and one or more of the actors seeks to limit his liability on the ground that the harm is capable of apportionment among them, the burden of proof as to the apportionment is upon each such actor.[173]

The court notes that *comment d* to Section 433(B)(2) of the *Restatement* renders inappropriate the application of the theory when it involves a large number of tortfeasors, each of whom contributed a small part to the total harm.[174] The court concluded, however, that this obstacle is circumvented by market share apportionment of damages.[175]

The overwhelming majority of courts hold that where the

---

169. 447 So. 2d 908 (Fla. Dist. Ct. App. 1984), *rev'd*, ____ So. 2d ____ (Fla. Sup. 1985) (No. 65, 124) (rejects market share liability in asbestos related cases).

170. *Id.* at 913.

171. Refer to note 25, *supra*.

172. 447 So. 2d at 916.

173. Restatement (Second) of Torts § 433(B)(2) (1979). But see the dissenting opinion which points out that this section places the burden of proof on the defendants as to apportionment of damages rather than constituting a determination of liability. Copeland v. Celotex Corp., 447 So. 2d 908, 919 (Fla. Dist. Ct. App. 1984) (Nesbitt, J., dissenting).

174. Restatement (Second) of Torts § 433(B)(2), comment d (1979).

175. 447 So. 2d at 916.

plaintiff possesses the ability to identify at least one manufacturer or supplier of the product causing the injury, enterprise liability is inapplicable.[176] The entire rationale of shifting the burden of proof vanishes when the plaintiff can prove at least one defendant's culpability.[177]

In *Starling v. Seaboard Coast Line R. R. Co.*[178] the court rejected market share liability in an asbestos case.[179] Recognizing an emerging trend toward recovery by plaintiffs unable to recover under traditional tort principles, the court expressed concern that market share liability would result in imposing insurer status on product manufacturers.[180] Moreover, the court observed that market share apportionment precipitates undesirable social and economic effects and questioned the continued ability of asbestos manufacturers to spread the loss through insurance.[181] Finally, the court decreed the inherent unfairness of imposing market share liability in asbestos cases.[182] As the court recognized, injuries caused by asbestos may be caused by other products as well. Of importance is the fact that some asbestos products are more harmful than others,[183] and therefore, a close correlation between the total volume of asbestos produced and the injuries caused probably does not exist. The companies' market share, however, is not adjusted to take into consideration these circumstances. Additionally, the court noted that the plaintiff in an asbestos case is not required to prove definitively which producer's asbestos caused the injury so long as proof exists that he was exposed on at least one occasion to the defendant's products.[184]

---

176. In Re Related Asbestos Cases, 543 F. Supp. 1152, 1158 (N.D. Cal. 1982); Prelick v. Johns-Manville Corp., 531 F. Supp. 96 ,97 (W.D. Pa. 1982); Hannon v. Waterman Steamship Corp., 567 F. Supp. 90, 93 (E.D. La. 1983).

177. *See* Lyons v. Premo Pharmaceutical Labs, Inc., 170 N.J. Super. 1983, 406 A.2d 185, *cert. denied*, 82 N.J. 267, 412 A.2d 774 (1979) in which the court rejected application of alternative liability because plaintiffs had identified the company which had manufactured the DES taken by her mother and had reached a settlement with the company.

178. 533 F. Supp. 183 (S.D. Ga. 1982).

179. *Id.* at 191.

180. *Id.* at 190.

181. *Id.*

182. *Id.* at 190-91.

183. *Id.*

184. *Id.* at 191 *citing* Borel v. Fibreboard Paper Prods. Corp., 493 F.2d 1076, 1094 (5th Cir. 1973), *cert. denied*, 419 U.S. 869 (1974). In most asbestos cases, the plaintiff has been exposed to the product of various manufacturers over a period of time. Plaintiff must only prove that the defendant was one of those manufacturers. As the court in *Collins v. Eli*

Market share liability likewise was soundly rejected in *Ryan v. Eli Lilly & Co.*[185] Initially the court noted that the plaintiff failed to adhere to the *Sindell* requirement that the defendants constitute a "substantial share" of the DES market.[186] More importantly, the court concluded that even if plaintiff had correctly adhered to the requirement of market share liability, South Carolina simply was not prepared to disregard traditional tort law to adopt the *Sindell* approach. The court noted that abandoning the fundamental concept that the plaintiff sustain the burden of proving proximate cause, "would violate established public policy and fundamental principles of tort law and procedure in this state in a variety of ways."[187] Similarly, in *Collins v. Eli Lilly & Co.*[188] the court declined to adopt market share liability. The practical difficulty in defining and approving market share simply creates a waste of judicial resources.[189]

The Supreme Court of Missouri, *Zafft v. Eli Lily & Co.*,[190] likewise repudiated market share liability as contravening fundamental principles of tort law and the public policy of the state. The court found that the theory was unfair because it involves the risk that the actual wrongdoer is not before the court and exposes those defendants who are joined to liability "greater than their responsibility."[191] The court also rejected a theory developed and proposed by the trial court. Under the trial court's theory of market share liability plaintiffs may recover damages if they can prove: (1) traditional elements of a products liability action; (2) that defendants knew that the product would be sold and used in a way

---

Lilly, 116 Wis. 2d 166, 342 N.W.2d 37 (1984) points out, the plaintiff in a DES case may also have been exposed to the products of different manufacturers because her mother's prescription may have been refilled with DES produced by several different drug companies.

185. 514 F. Supp. 1004 (D.S.C. 1981).

186. *Id.* at 1018.

187. *Id.* at 1018-19. *Accord*, Morton v. Abbott Laboratories, 538 F. Supp. 593, 599 (M.D. Fla. 1982) (DES); Starling v. Seaboard Coast Line R.R. Co., 533 F. Supp. 183, 186 (S.D. Ga. 1982) (asbestosis). *See* Mizell v. Eli Lilly & Co., 526 F. Supp. 589, 596-97 (D.S.C. 1981) where the district court refused to apply California law though the injury occurred in California, because the *Sindell* theory was so antithical to South Carolina public policy.

188. 166 Wis. 2d 166, 342 N.W.2d 37 (1984).

189. *Id.* at 342 N.W.2d at 48. *Contra*, Martin v. Abbott Laboratories, 689 P.2d 368 (Wash. 1984) where the court concluded that the market share theory distorts liability by requiring defendants to pay 100 percent of the plaintiff's damages though the defendants may represent less than 100 percent of the market.

190. 676 S.W.2d 241, 245-47 (Mo. 1984)(en banc).

191. *Id.* at 246.

that would render identification with a particular manufacturer impossible; (3) that plaintiffs are unable, through no fault of their own, to identify the manufacturer of the product causing the injury.[192]

The Missouri Supreme Court likewise rejected this theory, which assumed that the drug manufacturers accelerated the marketing of their products in generic form to render identification impossible.[193] While sympathizing with innocent plaintiffs who are seriously injured, the court found that "Missouri law does not guarantee relief to every deserving plaintiff."[194] Nor did the adoption of strict products liability and comparative negligence in Missouri require the court to eliminate the traditional causation requirement.[195] In fact, the court emphasized:

> To shift the burden of proof on causation to [defendants] substantially alters the existing rights and liabilities of the litigants . . . . There is insufficient justification at this time to support abandonment of so fundamental a concept of tort law as the requirement that a plaintiff prove, at a minimum, some nexus between wrongdoing and injury.[196]

The court expressed serious concern that imposing liability would discourage desired pharmaceutical research and development without the concomitant benefit of an incentive to produce safer products, since all manufacturers would be subject to liability irrespective of their efforts.[197] Such socially and economically devastating consequences would extend beyond the drug industry to other areas of product manufacture.

Market share liability, even in California, is inapplicable when a product is not defective. In *Sheffield v. Eli Lilly & Co.*[198] a young girl suffered permanent disability as a result of defective Salk antipolio vaccine. Plaintiff was unable to identify the manufacturer of the particular vaccine received by the child. Unlike *Sindell*, the injuries were not caused by the use of a drug generally defective

---

192. 676 S.W.2d at 246.

193. *Id.*

194. *Id. Citing* O'Neill v. Claypool, 341 S.W.2d 129 (Mo. 1960).

195. 676 S.W.2d at 246.

196. *Id.* at 246-47.

197. *Id.* at 247. "Strict liability in tort continues to provide a remedy to those plaintiffs who satisfy the identification requirement"

198. 144 Cal.App. 3d 583, 192 Cal. Rptr. 870 (1983).

when used for the purpose for which it was marketed. Rather, the Salk vaccine in *Sheffield* which caused the injury was generally safe but this particular dosage of vaccine was adulterated.[199] The delay in discovering the cause of the injury was not related to the nature of the defective product or any other act or ommission of the defendant.[200] The rationale for market share liability is that "each manufacturer's liability would approximate its responsibility for the injuries caused by its products."[201] Such approximation does not occur where only one manufacturer has marketed a defective i.e., *flawed* product, but other innocent manufacturers of the same product are required to share in the liability.[202] Obviously, if the "deep pocket" theory is applied to careful and careless manufacturers alike, it fails to act as an incentive for product safety. Rather it may result in keeping highly beneficial but potentially dangerous products off the market.[203]

Similarly, in *Bradley v. Firestone Tire & Rubber Co.*[204] plaintiff was injured while workong on a multi-piece tire rim. The rim was lost and plaintiff instituted suit against all manufacturers of that type of rim. Rejecting market share liability, the court stated that "[i]n *Sindell*, all of the manufacturers of DES produced a defective product because DES itself was found to be harmful. The plaintiff has failed to show that all multi-piece tire rims of the LB or LW type were defective."[205]

1. *What is Market Share?* Market share liability which requires that the plaintiff join a substantial share of the appropriate or relevant market lacks precision. The *Sindell* court failed to define or clarify the standard other than to suggest that 90% of the relevant market certainly satisfied the "substantial share" requirement.[206] Left unanswered is whether the standard prescribed is less

---

199. *Id.* at 594, 192 Cal. Rptr. at 876.

200. *Id.* at 594, 192 Cal. Rptr. at 877.

201. Sindell v. Abbott Laboratories, 26 Cal. 2d 588, 612, 607 P.2d 924, 937, 163 Cal. Rptr. 132, 145, *cert. denied*, 449 U.S. 912 (1980).

202. 144 Cal. App.3d at 594, 192 Cal. Rptr. at 876-77.

203. *Id.* at 597, 192 Cal. Rptr. at 878-79.

204. 590 F. Supp. 1177 (D.S.D. 1984).

205. *Id.* at 1181.

206. *See* Comment, *The Market Share Theory: Sindell's Contribution to Industry Wide Liability*," 19 Hous. L. Rev. 107, 128 (1981) in which the commentator states "The decision indicates that 90% of the market is clearly sufficient to rank as a substantial share. Whether a lesser percentage would also constitute a substantial share is left unanswered by

stringent than the 75-80% standard suggested in the law review article[207] which is the genesis of *Sindell* market share liability.[208] Clearly the meaning of "substantial percentage," as currently defined, lacks any degree of legitimacy.[209]

2. *What is Relevant Market?* The *Sindell* court also left unclarified the meaning of "relevant market." That ambiguity creates significant uncertainty whether the relevant market is based on a specific geographical area, or the national or international market. Similarly unclear is whether the relevant market contemplates a specific time period during which the plaintiff was exposed to the product, or whether it encompasses defendant's total production of the product during the entire manufacturing period.[210] Also unanswered is whether different definitions govern different cases or whether one rule governs all cases.[211] Either choice leads to inconsistent and conflicting decisions.[212]

3. *What is Defendant's Percentage Liability?* The *Sindell* court left unclear whether the named defendants are required to pay 100% of the plaintiff's damage though the defendants represent less than 100% of the market. If 100% liability is imposed, each defendant's liability is apportioned based on the defendant's *relative* share of the market.[213] The alternative interpretation is

---

Sindell."

207. Comment, *DES and A Proposed Theory of Enterprise Liability*, 46 FORDHAM L. REV. 963, 996 (1978).

208. *See* Sindell v. Abbott Laboratories, 16 Cal. 2d at 612, 607 P.2d at 937, 163 Cal. Rptr. at 145. *cf.* Note, *Refining Market Share Liability: Sindell v. Abbott Labs*, 33 STAN. L. REV. 937 (1981) (*Sindell* rejects the seventy-five to eighty percent standard) with Comment, *The Market Share Theory: Sindell's Contribution to Industry Wide Liability*, 19 HOUS. L. REV. 107, 128-29 (1981) (the *Sindell* court did not intend to reject the *Fordham* standard but rather to leave flexibility in its theory regarding the definition of a substantial share under the circumstances).

209. *See, e.g.*, Zafft v. Eli Lilly & Co., 676 S.W.2d 241, 246 (Mo. 1984) (en banc).

210. *See id.* at 248 which suggests that plaintiffs would have a cause of action under traditional alternative liability if the market could be limited enough geographically and temporally and if a finite number of possible manufacturers could be joined. *See also* Kroll, *Intra-Industry Joint Liability: The Era of Absolute Products Liability*, 687 INS. L.J. 185, 193 (1980) which notes "Anyone who has had any contacts with the antitrust field knows full well the difficulties which can be encountered in attempting to define the 'market', let alone 'market share.' " *See also*, Fischer, *Product Liability — An Analysis of Market Share Liability*, 34 VAND. L. REV. 1623 (1981).

211. Comment, *Products Liability - An Analysis of Market Share Liability*, 34 VAND. L. REV. 1623, 1643 (1981).

212. *Id.* at 1643-44.

213. 607, P.2d.

that each defendant's liability is limited to its *actual* percentage share of the DES market.[214] Though the opinion is not entirely clear, it appears that the court intended each defendant to be liable for its market share percentage of the total damages. If market share liability is construed to impose 100% liability on existing defendants, the impact of the percentage required for joinder of a substantial share of the market is even greater. Only if the substantial share approaches the total market will each defendant's liability reflect its actual share of the damage.[215]

In addition to the ambiguities inherent in market share liability, other aspects of the concept portend a disproportionate share of liability for certain defendants.[216] First, while drug companies are liable for their market share, they may also be liable in other cases for full damages if identified as the actual cause of a plaintiff's injury. Thus a company could conceivably be exposed to double liability.[217] Second, if market share is accepted in one or two jurisdictions, liability will be disproportionately placed on those manufacturers amenable to suit in those states.[218] Third, the market share concept translates into selective industry liability because only those within the industry who are selected by the plaintiff are subject to liability.[219] If unnamed in the lawsuit, the manufacturer of the defective product that caused the injury totally eludes responsibility for its product. A corollary problem involves the substantial likelihood that some manufacturers will be joined

---

214. *See* Copeland v. Celotex Corp., 447 So. 2d 908, 914 (Fla. Dist. Ct. App. 1984) where the court stated that by joining less than 100% of the market plaintiff limited his recovery to less than 100% of total damages. *See also*, Comment, *The Market Share Theory: Sindell's Contribution to Industry Wide Liability*, 19 Hous. L. Rev. 107, 131-32 (1981); Note, *Refining Market Share Liability: Sindell v. Abbott Labs*, 33 Stan. L. Rev. 937, 941-42 (1981); Comment, *supra* note 211, at 1645-46.

215. Comment, *The Market Share Theory: Sindell's Contribution to Industry Wide Liability*, 19 Hous. L. Rev. 107, 131-32 (1981).

216. *See* Martin v. Abbott Laboratories, 689 P.2d 368, 380-81 (1984).

217. *See* Note, *Refining Market Share Liability: Sindell v. Abbott Labs*, 33 Stan. L. Rev. 937, 942 (1981) which suggests that if market share liability is to be applied, plaintiffs should not also be allowed to identify a particular defendant as the cause of injury. *See also*, Note, *Market Share Liability: An Answer to the DES Cauation Problems*, 94 Harv. L. Rev. 668, 676 (1981).

218. Comment, *supra* note 211, at 1647-48,& n. 152 *citing* Sindell v. Abbott Laboratories, 26 Cal. 3d 588, 617, 607 P.2d 924, 940, 163 Cal. Rptr. 132, 148 (Richardson, J., dissenting), *cert. denied*, 449 U.S. 912 (1980).

219. *See*, Copeland v. Celotex Corp., 447 So. 2d 908, 919 (Fla. Dist. Ct. App. 1984) (Nesbitt, J.dissenting).

in every lawsuit and will be obligated to pay each time. Conversely, manufacturers enjoying only a small percentage of the market generally will not be joined as defendants. For example, Eli Lily & Co., with an estimated 45% of the DES market represents an obvious target, particularly if 55% of the DES market is deemed sufficient under the substantial percentgage requirement.[220]

The market share theory also raises serious constitutional problems.[221] The lack of statistical or mathematical assurance that any named defendant undoubtedly caused plaintiff's injury may constitute a taking of property without due process of law.

4. Proof of Market Share. Difficulties also exist regarding proof of market share. The court in *Collins v. Eli Lilly Co.*[222] rejected market share liability because of the practical difficulty of defining and proving market share. The court noted that in many cases the records necessary to establish market share may not exist. Further, even if such records are available, accurate assessment of the total market is probably impossible because of market fluidity.[223]

The court in *In Re Related Asbestos Cases*[224] rejected market share liability for asbestos cases because of the difficulty in determining market share. Several factors deemed to be particularly troubling include: (1) the varieties of asbestos fibers, each used in varying quantities in defendant's products and each differing in its harmful effects; (2) the numerous uses for asbestos and the fact that some of the products to which plaintiffs are exposed are probably purchased out of state prior to plaintiff's exposure; and (3) exposure of some plaintiffs to asbestos over many years, during which time some defendants began or discontinued making asbestos products.[225]

Similarly the court in *Starling v. Seaboard Coast Line R. Co.*[226] questioned the fairness of applying market share liability in

---

220. *See e.g.*, Bichler v. Eli Lilly & Co., 79 A.D.2d 317, 436 N.Y.S.2d 625 (1981), *aff'd* 55 N.Y.2d 571, 436 N.E.2d 182, 450 N.Y.S.2d 776 (1982).

221. Tidler v. Eli Lilly & Co., 95 F.R.D. 332 (D.C. 1982).

222. 116 Wis. 2d 166, 342 N.W.2d 37, 48 (1984).

223. *Id.*

224. 543 F. Supp. 1152 (N.D. Cal. 1982).

225. *Id.* at 1158. *See also*, Copeland v. Celotex Corp., 447 So.2d 908, 920 (Fla. Dist. Ct. App. 1984) (Nesbitt J., dissenting).

226. 533 F. Supp. 183 (S.D. Ga. 1982).

asbestos cases. The court noted that asbestos products are not fungible commodities and the injuries caused by the products are also caused by other sources. Many products contain varying degrees of asbestos and thus are not uniformly harmful. A manufacturer's market share, however, would not be adjusted for the relative harmfulness of its products or the harmful effect of non-asbestos products. Additionally, the court notes that manufacturers have different market shares for different types of asbestos products.[227]

E. *Risk Contribution Theory*

Yet another theory has been postulated to authorize an injured party to recover damages when identification of the manufacturer of the product that causes injury is difficult. This is the concept of risk contribution fashioned by the Wisconsin Supreme Court in *Collins v. Eli Lilly Co.*[228] While rejecting theories of alternative liability,[229] concert of action,[230] enterprise liability,[231] civil conspiracy[232] and market share liability,[233] the court concluded that the manufacturer of DES should bear the cost of injury. The court, therefore, fashions its own unique "risk contribution" theory of recovery for plaintiffs in DES cases.[234] This theory requires that plaintiff institute suit against only one defendant.[235] After considering proposals that the plaintiff join a "substantial share" of the market or a "reasonable number" of defendants, the court rejected each alternative.[236] Because of the problem in defining these terms and the resultant waste of judicial resources, the court elected to require suit against only one identifiable manufacturer. According to perhaps overly simplistic logic, the court perceives that the defendant occupies a superior position to that of the plaintiff to iden-

---

227. *Id.* at 191. *See* Celotex Corp. v. Copeland, *supra* note 169.

228. 116 Wis. 2d 166, 342 N.W.2d 37 (1984).

229. Refer to notes 25-64 *supra* and accompanying text.

230. Refer to notes 65-103 *supra* and accompanying text.

231. Refer to notes 104-24 *supra* and accompanying text.

232. Refer to notes 262-268 *infra* and accompanying text.

233. Refer to notes 125-205 *supra* and accompanying text.

234. 342 N.W.2d at 49. The court also indicated that it would apply the theory to other factually similar situations.

235. 342 N.W.2d at 50.

236. Refer to notes 206-227 *supra* and accompanying text for a discussion of the difficulties in determining a "substantial share" of the market.

tify other drug manufacturers who should be joined.[237] The defendant need only implead other manufacturers who are potentially liable. The Wisconsin Supreme Court combined selected fragments of alternative liability, concert of action, and market share liability in allowing the plaintiff to proceed against a single manufacturer.[238] The plaintiff must allege as elements: (a) that the plaintiff's mother took DES; (b) that DES caused the plaintiff's subsequent injuries; (c) that the defendant produced or marketed the type of DES taken by the plaintiff's mother; and (d) that the defendant's conduct in producing or marketing the DES constituted a breach of a legally recognized duty to the plaintiff.[239]

If the plaintiff is unable to determine the type of DES ingested by the mother, then the plaintiff need only prove that the defendant produced or marketed DES for miscarriage prevention.[240] The plaintiff has then established a prima facie case based either on negligence or strict tort liability. The burden then shifts to the defendant to prove by a preponderance of the evidence that it did not produce or market DES for the prevention of miscarriage during the relevant time period or in the relevant geographical market area.[241] If the plaintiff sues only one defendant, that defendant is liable for all damages awarded.[242] If more than one defendant is joined by the plaintiff (or if the named defendants implead other manufacturers) the damages are apportioned on the basis of the jury's assessment of liability under comparative negligence.[243] This statute apportions damage based on the percentage of causal negligence attributable to each defendant.[244] The court enumerates the various factors which the jury may consider in assigning the percentage of liability.[245]

---

237. 342 N.W.2d at 50-51.

238. Alternative liability usually requires the joinder of all potential defendants. Market share liability requires joinder of a "substantial share" of the market.

239. 342 N.W.2d at 50.

240. *Id.*

241. *Id.* at 52.

242. *Id.*

243. *Id.* at 52.

244. *Id.* at 50.

245. *Id.* at 53. These factors include:

1) Whether the drug company conducted tests on DES for safety and efficacy in uses for pregnancies;

2) To what degree the company took a role in gaining FDA approval of DES for use in pregnancies;

Adoption of the risk contribution theory is predicated on judicially structured public policy. Each defendant producing or marketing DES for use in pregnancy contributed to the risk of injury to the public and, therefore, to individual plaintiffs.[246] Perhaps more importantly to the ultimate decision is the candid acknowledgemnt by the court that the manufacturer occupies a better position to absorb the cost of injury.[247] Finally, the court rationalized that drug companies would be motivated by the cost of damage awards to adequately test all drugs before marketing.[248]

Risk contribution differs from every other form of industrywide liability. This concept, combining selected fragments of alternative liability, concert of action and market share liability, essentially imposes an insurer status on manufacturers of generic type products. Risk contribution as formulated by Wisconsin extends far beyond the limits established for strict tort liability under Section 402A.

---

3) Whether the company had a small or large market share in the relevant area;

4) Whether the company took the lead or merely followed the lead of others in producing or marketing DES;

5) Whether the company issued warnings about the dangers of DES;

6) Whether the company produced or marketed DES after it knew or should have known of the possible hazards DES presented to the public; and

7) Whether the company took any affirmative steps to reduce the risk of injury to the public.

The court did not consider this list of factors exclusive.

246. 342 N.W.2d at 49. *See* Robinson, *Multiple Causation in Tort Law: Reflections on the DES Cases*, 68 VA. L. REV. 713 (1982) in which the author proposes adoption of a "risk contribution" theory in DES cases. The author argues that liability should be based not on the actual occurrence of an injury but rather on the creation of an unreasonable risk of such an occurrence. While agreeing with this concept in theory, the court in *Collins* concluded that the concept was not a sufficient basis for liability absent an additional showing that the defendant drug company reasonably could have contributed to the actual injury. Collins v. Eli Lilly Co., 116 Wis. 2d 155, n.10, 342 N.W.2d 37, 49, n.10 (1984).

247. *Cf.* Starling v. Seaboard Coast Line R. R. Co., 533 F. Supp. 183, 190 (S. D. Ga. 1982) where the court questions the ability of the asbestos industry to continue to spread the loss. The court suggests that the balancing of the economic and social ramifications involved in fashioning remedies for asbestos victims should occur in the legislature. Compare, Zafft v. Eli Lilly & Co., 676 S.W.2d 241, 246 (Mo. 1984) (en banc), in which the court emphasized a salient but conveniently overlooked theorem that "Missouri law does not guarantee relief to every deserving plaintiff."

248. 342 N.W.2d at 49 & n.11. Significantly, DES has been off the market for treatment of problem pregnancies. It is difficult to perceive how ruinous damage awards will affect testing of a drug use that has long been discontinued for problem pregnancies. Punishment and deterrence retroactively suggests a contradiction in the very purpose of the doctrine.

F. Market Share Alternate Liability

In *Martin v. Abbott Laboratories*,[249] the court rejected theories of alternative liability,[250] concert of action,[251] enterprise liability[252] and market share liability.[253] The court, however, fashioned a new concept reflecting some similarity to risk contribution.[254] Characterizing this doctrine as market share-alternate liability, the court notes it is presented with a conflict between the familiar principle that a tortfeasor may be held liable only for damage that it has caused and the sense of justice which urges that the victims of this tragedy should not be denied compensation because of the impossibility of identifying the individual manufacturer of these generic tablets if their manufacture and distribution were otherwise culpable.[255]

The court concludes that because all the manufacturers and distributors contributed to the risk of injury to consumers from DES, they all share the culpability in producing or marketing DES.[256] The court, parallelling the philosophy of the Wisconsin court, judicially postulates that manufacturers are in a better position than the injured plaintiffs to absorb the costs of injuries.[257] Under this theory, the plaintiff is authorized to initiate suit against only one manufacturer, alleging precisely the same elements as required for the risk contribution theory.[258] The plaintiff is not required to prove that the defendant produced or marketed the particular DES ingested by the plaintiff's mother. Unlike risk contribution, however, market share alternate liability requires the plaintiff to prove that the defendant produced or marketed the *type* of DES ingested by plaintiff's mother.[259] Individual defen-

---

249. 689 P.2d 368 (1984).

250. 689 P.2d at 377. Refer to notes 25-64 *supra*.

251. 689 P.2d at 379. Refer to notes 65-103 *supra*.

252. 689 P.2d at 380. Refer to notes 104-24 *supra*.

253. 689 P.2d at 381. Refer to notes 125-205 *supra*.

254. Refer to notes 228-248 *supra*.

255. 689 P.2d at 381.

256. 689 P.2d at 382.

257. 689 P.2d at 382. The drug companies could insure against the loss, absorb the loss or pass the cost along to consumers. As a practical matter, all costs are passed on to the consumers. When a company no longer is able to pass on the costs to all consumers it soon confronts the inevitable bankruptcy.

258. 689 P.2d at 382-83.

259. Refer to note 240 *supra* and accompanying text.

dants may exculpate themselves from liability by establishing that they did not produce the DES ingested by plaintiff's mother. If defendants do not exculpate themselves they are designated members of the plaintiff's DES market. These defendants are initially presumed liable for equal shares of the market. Each defendant may then reduce its potential liability by proving its respective *actual market* share of DES in the plaintiff's *particular geographic market*. The defendant is ultimately liable only for its share of the market as it relates to the total judgment. Those defendants who fail to establish their actual market share have their presumed market share adjusted to account for 100% of the market. Defendants may also implead additional manufacturers of the product. If all defendants establish their respective actual market shares and the total of those shares is less than 100%, then the plaintiff recovers less than 100%.[260]

Market share alternate liability represents the latest judicial attempt to compensate plaintiffs who are injured by inherently dangerous drugs which cannot be traced to the actual manufacturer. Like risk contribution, the theory is based on the rationale that each industry member contributed to the consumer's risk of injury through the manufacture and distribution of an inherently defective generic product. While risk contribution apportions damages on the basis of comparative fault, market share alternate liability apportions damages on the basis of a modified market share liability.

The *Washington* court, like its counterpart the Wisconsin Supreme Court, judicially melded fragments of alternative liability, concert of action, and market share liability in formulating a doctrine of recovery.[261] The melding of portions of each of these three unique tort doctrines, while selectively omitting legal principles basic to each, creates a doctrine that virtually imposes insurer states on manufacturers of generic type products. Shifting the burden of proof constitutes a significant departure from the traditional tort doctrine that the plaintiff has the burden of proving that a manufacturer's product caused his injury.

---

260. 689 P.2d at 382.

261. *Compare* notes 214-215 *supra* and accompanying test.

G. Other Liability Theories

1. Conspiracy. Conspiracy, which has been proposed unsuccessfully in DES litigation, is closely related to concert of action. Conspiracy, however, requires much more stringent proof. In *Ryan v Eli Lilly & Co.*,[262] the plaintiff asserted a cause of action against eight defendants premised on civil conspiracy. The court rejected the conspiracy claim on the basis that the plaintiff neither alleged nor offered proof of any of the four essential elements of conspiracy. These elements, as enumerated by the court, include: (1) an agreement between the party who actually committed the wrongful act and the defendant; (2) the agreement to do an unlawful act or to do a lawful act in an unlawful manner (conspiracy to commit negligence or to fail to exercise due diligence does not exist); (3) the plaintiff is injured by an unlawful overt act performed by one of the participants; and (4) the injury-producing wrongful act is done by one or more of the conspirators pursuant to the common scheme and in furtherance of the common object.[263]

The pooling of DES information in a master file for the initial new drug application (NDA's) in 1941 by the twelve original manufacturers constituted mere compliance with an FDA directive. In conspiracy cases, "[l]iability cannot flow from compliance with a legal requirement."[264] Furthermore, the 1941 filings, even if they constituted evidence of an agreement, bore no relation to subsequent use of the drug during pregnancy. Because DES was still a "new drug"[265] the 1941 NDA's could not have been used as a basis for the 1947 supplemental NDA's.[266] The court noted that in 1947 Eli Lilly acted independently in seeking FDA permission to market DES for the treatment of problem pregnancies. The absence of any evidence of cooperation, coordination, consultation or even communication between Eli Lilly and other drug companies regarding

---

262. 514 F. Supp. 1004 (D.S.C. 1981).

263. *Id.* at 1012.

264. *Id.* at 1014.

265. Though a drug has gained FDA approval for specified uses, it is considered "new" when it is "recommended for a different indication or condition, to affect another structure or function of the body or because of the newness of the dosage, method or duration of administration." *Id.* at 1011, n.3. Such a "new" drug requires submission and approval of a new NDA before it can be marketed for the new indication or use.

266. *Id.* at 1013. *Accord* Lyons v. Premo Pharmaceutical Labs, Inc., 170 N.J. Super. 183, 192-93, 406 A.2d 185, 190, *cert. denied*, 82 N.J. 267, 412 A.2d 774 (1979).

the manufacture and marketing of DES for this purpose totally negated any possible agreement to act in an unlawful manner.[267]

In *Collins v. Eli Lilly & Co.*,[268] the court also rejected a conspiracy claim. The court emphasized the absence of any tacit or express agreement between the defendants and noted that many drug companies entered the DES market well after FDA approval of the drug.

2. *Aiding and Abetting.* A majority of jurisdictions consider aiding and abetting a subspecies of concert of action. Unlike concert of action, however, aiding and abetting does not require an agreement between the parties. In *Payton v. Abbott Labs*,[269] plaintiff unsuccessfully argued that the defendants were aiding and abetting in the manufacture and marketing of DES. Massachusetts considers aiding and abetting a distinct cause of action.[270] The courts recognize the *Restatement* position requiring that: (a) the defendant give substantial assistance or encouragement to the other party, and (b) the defendant know that the other party is breaching a duty and intend to assist that other party.[271] The court summarily rejected plaintiff's claim after failing to find even a remote suggestion that the drug companies aided and abetted each other in marketing DES.[272]

3. *Joint Venture.* In *Payton v. Abbott Labs*,[273] the court addressed the issue of whether the DES manufacturer could be liable on the basis of a joint venture concept, which Massachusetts has failed to define. The court noted several important elements established by decisional law: (1) an agreement binding the defendants to associate themselves in a business activity; (2) a sharing by the defendants in the profits and losses of the venture; (3) joint control of the objectives of the undertaking and of the means of achieving those objectives; and (4) jointly held assets contributed to by all the defendants.[274] Joint venture, it appears, is wholly inappropriate to industry-wide product litigation, because none of these re-

---

267. 514 F. Supp. at 1014.
268. 116 Wis. 2d 166, 342 N.W.2d 37, 47-48.
269. 512 F. Supp. 1031 (D. Mass. 1981).
270. *Id.*
271. RESTATEMENT (SECOND) OF TORTS § 876 comment *b* (1979).
272. 512 F. Supp. at 1039.
273. *Id.* at 1031.
274. *Id.* at 1036.

quired factors are present in industry-wide product cases.[275]

In summary, the courts have struggled to provide injured plaintiffs with a vehicle to recover damages for injuries caused by generic type products when the plaintiff is unable to identify the manufacturer of the product that actually caused injury. Most courts adhere to the fundamental tort doctrine that the plaintiff is legally obligated to prove the identity of the manufacturer of the product that actually caused plaintiff's injuries. A number of jurisdictions, however, have endeavored to circumvent this traditional tort requirement by restructuring a variety of existing tort concepts. These burden-shifting theories include alternative liability, concert of action, enterprise liability, market share liability, risk contribution, and market share alternate liability. The effect of utilizing any of these doctrines to impose liability on an unidentified manufacturer of a product, is to transform strict tort liability for a defective product into absolute liability. The manufacturer is thus cast in the role of an insurer of products that in many instances it neither manufactured nor supplied to the plaintiff. Underlying this effort is the perception that for every injury there is someone who must be answerable in damages. This expansion of strict tort liability appears to extend beyond the established boundaries of Section 402A.

The concept that for every injury there must be redress against someone contradicts a fundamental premise of the tort reparations system. Yet, the imposition of liability on a manufacturer based solely on the fact that the manufacturer is engaged in supplying identical type products pragmatically guarantees relief to every plaintiff.

5.03 Punitive Damages

Industry-wide liability provides a means by which plaintiffs who cannot identify the specific cause of their injury may nevertheless recover compensatory damages. The imposition of this type of liability, however, raises the issue of whether punitive damages may appropriately be awarded in such situations.

In *Morris v. Parke, Davis & Co.*,[276] plaintiff's child suffered

---

275. *Id.*

276. 573 F. Supp. 1324 (C.D. Cal. 1983); *contra*, Magallanes v. Superior Court, County of Los Angeles, ____ Cal. Rptr. ____ (Cal. App. 2d No. B006504) (no punitive damages).

irreversible brain damage as a result of receiving a diptheria, pertussis and tetanus (DPT) vaccine.[277] Defendants allegedly manufactured a substantial share of the vaccine at the time of the child's injury.[278] Because the drug was marketed generically, the plaintiff could not identify the specific manufacturer of the vaccine administered to the child. Therefore, the plaintiffs relied on market share liability espoused in *Sindell*.[279] In overruling the manufacturer's motion to strike the plaintiff's prayer for punitive damages, the court concluded:

> If plaintiffs are able to establish that their injuries were caused by DTP, and can further show that one or more of the defendants marketed the drug with conscious disregard for the health of consumers, they will be entitled to recover punitive damages from each such defendant. This view is not only consistent with *Sindell* but also comports with the venerable line of authority recognizing that punitive damages are an indispensable deterrent to conduct that would endanger the public health.[280]

The court emphasized that the perceived social goals of punishment and deterrence form the basis of punitive damages under California law. Accordingly, these goals apply with special force in the area of strict tort liability because of potential for harm created by a manufacturer who knowingly markets a defective product. The court concluded that in the absence of a punitive damage remedy, manufacturers would find it more profitable to risk paying compensatory damages than to incur the cost of remedying defective products.[281]

---

277. *Id.* at 1324.

278. *Id.* at 1324-25.

279. *Id.* at 1325.

280. *Id. Compare,* Jackson v. Johns-Manville Sales Corp., 727 F.2d 506 (5th Cir. 1984), *rev'd,* ____ F.2d ____ (5th Cir. 1985) (en banc) (compensatory damages in asbestos cases sufficient to deter unsafe conduct).

281. 573 F. Supp. at 1327. Interestingly, the court cites *Owen* in support of its position, Owen, *Punitive Damages in Products Liability Litigation,* 74 MICH. L. REV. 1258, 1291 fn. (1976). The court does not cite the subsequent article by Owen in which the author significantly amended his earlier position. Owen, *Problems In Assessing Punitive Damages Against Manufacturers of Defective Products,* 49 U. CHI. L. REV. 1 (1982). The court totally denigrates an article authored by Priest, *Punitive Damages and Enterprise Liability,* 56 S. CAL. L. REV. 123 (1982) appearing in the same footnote. The court observes: "Where economic analysis is used to produce nonsensical results, the courts had best turn a deaf ear to commentators and follow the dictates of common sense." Priest argues that in products liability compensation damages are sufficient to deter corporate misconduct.

Once the court presumed the applicability of the punitive damages doctrine, it shifted its focus to the particular problems presented by *Sindell* market share. Utilizing the analogy of a corporate employer who is deemed liable for punitive damages for the egregious conduct of its employee, the court declared that recovery of punitive damages does not require a showing that the defendant personally participated in the injurious conduct.[282] Where a number of manufacturers act with conscious disregard for human safety, the court concluded they should not be allowed to escape punitive damages simply because the plaintiff is unable to identify the responsible party. The court further concluded that the need to safeguard the public health outweighs the difficulty of measuring and apportioning punitive damages under market share liability.[283] While market share liability apportions compensatory damages on the basis of market share liability, punitive damages are apportioned on the basis of traditional yardsticks such as the wealth of the individual defendants[284] and the relative blameworthiness of their conduct.[285] This conclusion was based on the rationale that the purpose of punitive damages is to punish and deter rather than to compensate the plaintiff. Therefore, punitive damages need not bear a relationship to the fact that defendants particular product may not have caused the plaintiff's injuries.[286] The court however emphasized that to recover punitive damages

---

282. *Id.* at 1328. California utilizes the *respondeat superior* doctrine to impose damages on a corporate employer. Texas rejects the *respondeat superior* doctrine in favor of the complicity doctrine embodied in RESTATEMENT (SECOND) OF TORTS, § 907 (1979). *See* Fort Worth Elevators Co. v. Russell, 123 Tex. 128, 70 S.W.2d 397, 405 (1934); Fisher v. Carrousel Motor Hotel, Inc., 424 S.W.2d 627 (Tex. 1967) (offender was manager of the club); Martin v. Texaco, Inc., 726 F.2d 207 (5th Cir. 1984) (applying Texas law).

283. *Morris,* 573 F. Supp. at 1329.

284. The court acknowledged defendant's contention that considering the wealth of the defendants in measuring punitive damages may result in an award completely disproportionate to the harm suffered. However, the court stated that the problem is not limited to cases involving market share liability and summarily dismissed the argument. *Id.* at 1329-30. Texas excludes evidence of the wealth of a defendant for purposes of punitive damages. *See,* Texas Public Utils. Corp. v. Edwards, 99 S.W.2d 420, 427 (Tex. Civ. App.—Austin 1936, writ dism'd).

285. *Morris,* 573 F. Supp. at 1329-30. The court declared: "[d]efendants are all culpable regardless of their market shares, and the court need not look to market share in apportioning punitive damages among them . . . Certainly it [apportionment] does not outweigh the policy favoring punitive damages where defendants have acted with conscious disregard for human safety." *Id.* at 1330.

286. *Id.* at 1329.

the plaintiff was required to establish liability under *Sindell* market share and prove that one or more of the defendant's marketed DPT with a conscious disregard for human safety.[287]

The abrogation of the fundamental tort concept requiring the plaintiff to establish that a defendant's conduct or defective product caused the injury is a significant and dramatic departure from existing law. The abrogation of the burden to establish that defendant's conduct or defective product caused the injury for purposes of imposing large awards of punitive damages represents a dramatic and unprecedented extension of the basic doctrine of punitive damages.[288]

Some courts have authorized punitive damages in asbestos cases in which the manufacturer of the generic product has been properly identified by the plaintiff.[289] For example, in *Moran v. Johns-Manville Sales Corp.*,[290] the court rejected the argument that the punishment and deterrence goals are not served by punitive damages.[291] The award of punitive damages was based on deterrence as a general rather than specific goal. Defendant's prior cessation of the activity apparently is irrelevant to the deterrence rationale underlying the punitive damage doctrine. Significantly,

---

287. *Morris*, 573 F. Supp. at 1330. California statutorily authorizes punitive damages for fraud, oppession, or malice. Cal. Civ. Code, § 3294(a) (West Supp. 1983). The decision of the court is astonishing, particularly in the absence of any direct causal nexus between the defendant's conduct or product and plaintiff's injury. Morever, liability is predicated on the unidentified manufacturer for the condition of a generic product and not on the conduct of the manufacturer toward the plaintiff. *See*, Sales, *The Emerging of Punitive Damages in Product Liability Actions: A Further Assault on the Citadel*, 14 ST. MARY'S L.J. 351, 388-403 (1983); Sales & Cole, *Punitive Damages: A Relic That Has Outlived Its Origins*, 37 VAND. L. REV. 1117, 1141 (1984).

288. As the Missouri Court in *Zafft v. Eli Lilly & Co.*, 676 S.W.2d 241, 246 (Mo. 1984) (en banc) notes, "[m]arket share liability continues the risk that the actual wrongdoer is not among the named defendants and exposes those pined to greater liability than their responsibility . . . [l]iability will discourage desired pharmaceutical research and development while adding little incentive to production of safe products, for all companies face potential liability regardless of their efforts. Id. at 247. If the Missouri court correctly perceived this untoward effect of compensatory damages under market share liability, then the imposition of punitive damages which is based on "malice" on unidentified manufacturers of generic products represents the ultimate irresponsible act.

289. *See* Neal v. Carey Canadian Mines, Ltd., 548 F. Supp. 357 (E.D. Pa. 1982); Froud v. Celotex Corp., 107 Ill. App. 3d 654, 437 N.E.2d 910 (1982), *rev'd on other grounds*, 456 N.E.2d 131 (1983); Fischer v. Johns-Manville Corp., 193 N.J. Super. 113, 472 A.2d 577 (1984).

290. 691 F.2d 811 (6th Cir. 1982).

291. *Id.* at 816.

the fact that persons responsible for the tortious activity of a corporation who no longer are agents of the corporation does not foreclose a punitive award.[292] Nor did the court express concern about the effect of a punitive award on admittedly innocent shareholders of a manufacturing company. As an abstract legal principle, unrelated to the practicalities of the real world, punitive liability purportedly compels innocent shareholders to invest in responsible corporations that select only responsible managers, directors and engineers, chemists, etc.[293] The court did not consider it appropriate to relieve a company of punitive damages because it was confronted with repeated awards of punitive damages for marketing a single product line.[294] If relief is to be granted, the court declared such relief rested in the province of the state or federal legislature.[295] The court either overlooked or rejected the fact that strict tort liability in products litigation is a judicially formulated and adopted doctrine and, therefore, its structure, including the requirements for recovery, available defenses, applicable limitations, and the nature of recoverable damages are subject to judicial restructuring.[296] Consequently, no barriers exist to providing rational guidelines for and limitations on the strict tort liability doctrine.

In *Martin v. Johns-Manville Corp.*,[297] the court approved an award of punitive damages. The court rejected the argument that the prospect of repeated large compensatory damages and injury to the manufacturer's reputation was sufficient to deter unsafe prac-

---

292. *Id.* at 816-17.

293. *Id.* at 817.

294. *Accord* Froud v. Celotex Corp., 107 Ill. App. 3d 654, 657, 437 N.E.2d 910, 913 (1982), *rev'd on other grounds*, 456 N.E.2d 131 (1983) ("Such a rule would encourage wrongdoers to continue their misconduct because if they kept it up long enough to injure a large number of people they could escape all liability for punitive damages"); Neal v. Carey Canadian Mines, Ltd., 548 F. Supp. 357, 376-77 (E.D. Pa. 1982); Fischer v. Johns-Manville Corp., 193 N.J. Super. 113, 472 A.2d 577 (1984).

295. 691 F.2d at 817.

296. For example, in 1967 the Texas Supreme Court, adopted strict tort liability in *Shamrock Fuel & Oil Sales, Inc. v. Tunks*, 416 S.W.2d 779 (Tex. 1967). Then, in *Henderson v. Ford Motor Co.*, 519 S.W.2d 87 (Tex. 1974) the Texas Supreme Court rejected contributory negligence as a defense in favor of assumption of the risk and misuse. Ten years later, in *Duncan v. Cessna Aircraft Corp.*, 665 S.W.2d 414 (Tex. 1984), the Supreme Court rejected *Henderson* and its progeny and rejected misuse and assumption of the risk as a defense in favor of pure comparative causation in which contributory negligence constitutes the only defense. Yet, TEX. REV. CIV. STAT. ANN. art. 2212a, continues to govern all other tort actions in Texas.

297. 332 Pa. Super. 348, 469 A.2d 655 (1984).

tices.[298] Since punitive damages increase the number of suits instituted by plaintiffs, the threat of increased litigation ostensibly serves as a deterrent to bad business practices.[299] The court summarily rejected the arguments that: (1) the availability of insurance eliminates the deterrent effects of punitive damages awards,[300] (2) "innocent shareholders" are punished, and[301] (3) bankruptcy of the defendant inevitably results.[302] The court concluded that the possibility of the defendant's bankruptcy is: "[N]either unique to products liability actions nor sufficient to persuade us that defendants in products liability actions should enjoy a windfall while potential plaintiffs suffer the deprivation of a right to which they would otherwise be entitled."[303]

The applicability of punitive damages in industry-wide liability is a matter of serious concern. Jurisdictions adopt a variety of approaches to the issue. Most courts declare that the deterrent effect of punitive damages is appropriate in strict tort liability involving industry-wide litigation. Consequently most courts that impose punitive damages accord little weight to the economic impact on business enterprises perpetrated by the multitude of product liability actions.[304] The expansion of strict tort liability to un-

---

298. 469 A.2d at 662; *Accord* Thiry v. Armstrong World Industries, 661 P.2d 515 (Okla. 1983).

299. 469 A.2d at 663.

300. 469 A.2d at 663-64.

301. 469 A.2d at 664-65. *But see* Sales & Cole, *Punitive Damages: A Relic That Has Outlived Its Origins*, 37 VAND. L. REV. 1117 (1984).

302. 469 A.2d at 665-66.

303. 469 A.2d at 666. *Accord* Fischer v. Johns-Manville Corp., 193 N.J. Super. 113, 472 A.2d 577 (1984). *Cf.* Thiry v. Armstrong World Indus. 661 P.2d 515, 518 (Okla. 1983) ("punitive damages should not primarily be used to obtain a windfall for the individual plaintiff.").

304. For example in Acosta v. Honda Motor Co., 717 F.2d 828, 838 (3d Cir. 1983), the Third Circuit observed that, "[i]t is, of course, possible that 'a sufficiently egregious error as to one product' could result in the demise of its manufacturer, but such a result is not inevitable." In a supporting footnote, the court further observed, "[N]or is such a result necessarily untenable." *Id.* at N. 15. More recently, in *Martin v. Johns-Manville Corp.*, 469 A.2d 655, 665 (Pa. Super. 1983), *appeal filed*, April 2, 1984, the court, in an equally offhanded manner, commented that, "if the defendant's conduct was so reckless and injured so many people, that the effect of the damages awarded against it is bankruptcy, we are hard pressed to understand why that defendant should not be required to live with the consequences of its actions." A similar view has been expressed by the Oregon court in *State ex rel Young v. Crookham*, 290 Or. 61, 618 P.2d 1268 (1980). And, in Fischer v. Johns-Manville Corp., 193 N.J. Super. 113, 472 A.2d 577, the state court echoed the importance of exacting a pound of flesh from reckless defendants in its statement demanding "the ultimate protection which punitive damages afford." Id. at 585. The courts likewise have rejected applica-

identified product suppliers under any form of market share liability forecasts serious economic problems. The award of punitive damages against unidentified manufacturers of generic type products foreshadows a form of "economic overkill" that may well jeopardize certain industries.[305]

The only jurisdiction that has undertaken to impose punitive damages upon all unidentified manufacturers of a generic product that causes an injury is California.[306] Not only is the punitive damage doctrine imposed, but the court has suggested that each manufacturer, even though all may be totally innocent of supplying the generic product, is subject to punitive damage liability under market share liability. This raises the following concerns: (1) the imposition of punitive damages on a party not even identified as a tortfeasor: (2) the imposition of punitive damages on every member of the industry which could include as many as 300 members; and (3) the imposition of punitive damages on each defendant as a grossly negligent tortfeasor based on membership in a particular industry and measured by each member's financial worth.[307] The

---

tion of the double jeopardy principle to foreclose repeated punitive damage awards from identical product design defects. *See* Hansen v. Johns-Manville Prods. Corp., 734 F.2d 1036 (5th Cir. 1984) U.S. appeal pending.

305. Owen, *Problems in Assessing Punitive Damages Against Manufacturers of Defective Products*, 49 U. Chi. L. Rev. 1, 6 (1981); *See* Roginsky v. Richardson-Merrell, Inc., 378 F.2d 832, 841 (1967)(the impracticality of imposing an effective ceiling on punitive awards in hundreds of cases against a single manufacturer, when added to large compensatory damages, could lead to catastrophic awards). *See also*, Note, *Mass Liability and Punitive Damages Overkill*, 30 Hastings L.J. 1797 (1979).

306. Morris v. Parke, Davis & Co., 573 F. Supp. 1324 (C.D. Cal. 1983).

307. *Id.* at 1329. The court rather casually observes:

> Compensatory damages are intended to compensate the plaintiff for injuries actually suffered—medical expenses, lost earning, and so forth. By apportioning the judgment among the defendants according to their market shares, the *Sindell* court ensured that every defendant would compensate the plaintiff in an amount related to the statistical likelihood that it had caused the injuries actually suffered. This approach makes much less sense in the case of punitive damages. Punitive damages are not intended to compensate the plaintiff for his injuries, but rather to punish the defendant and deter others from engaging in similar conduct. It is thus unnecessary that punitive damages be apportioned according to the likelihood that any particular defendant caused plaintiff's injuries. *Id.* at 1329.
>
> If plaintiff's succeed in establishing liability under the market share theory of *Sindell*, and can further show that one or more of the defendants marketed DPT with conscious disregard for human safety, they will be entitled to recover punitive damages from each such defendant. *Id.* at 1330.

Essentially, the court approves punitive awards against each manufacturer that is a member of a particular industry producing a generic type product on each occasion that a

abrogation of fundamental tort principles to accomplish these results raises serious legal questions.

Strict tort liability was adopted to transfer the costs of product-related injuries to the product suppliers based on the socioeconomic "deep pocket" theory that the supplier is better able to absorb the costs of injuries than the injured plaintiffs. The transfer of costs to unidentified product suppliers simply because of membership in the industry that produces the generic product raises concern that liability is extended significantly beyond the ambit of Section 402A. The imposition of individual punitive awards, on each unidentified manufacturer of a generic product that causes injury suggests clear disregard for the principles underlying the concept of strict tort liability. If such severe legal remedies are to be sanctioned, then this approval should emanate from society through its elected Congress and State Legislatures.

5.04 Collateral Estoppel

Collateral estoppel is a doctrine designed to preclude relitigation of issues and matters previously decided. Unlike *res judicata*, which forecloses relitigation of an entire cause of action,[308] collateral estoppel precludes relitigation of specific issues litigated in an earlier cause of action.[309]

Traditionally collateral estoppel was limited by the doctrine of mutuality of parties. Under this doctrine, neither party could use a prior judgment to estop the other unless both parties were bound by the judgment.[310] The court in *Blonder-Tongue Laboratories,*

---

strict tort liability lawsuit is filed under market share liability as if each member actually committed malice (under California law) against the plaintiff. Yet the underlying rationale of *Sindell* market share liability is that plaintiff cannot prove the actual manufacturer of the product that caused the injury and the court apportions liability to every manufacturer based only on a statistical percentage likelihood that it was each manufacturer's particular product that caused plaintiff's injury.

308. *See, e.g.*, Bonniwell v. Beech Aircraft Corp., 663 S.W.2d 816, 818 (Tex. 1984). Peterson v. Peterson, 548 S.W.2d 83 (Tex. Civ. App.—Tyler 1977, no writ): Masters v. Stair, 518 S.W.2d 439 (Tex. Civ. App.—San Antonio 1975, no writ).

309. *See* Parklane Hosiery Co. v. Shore, 439 U.S. 322, 326 (1979) *citing* 1B J. Moore, Moore's Federal Practice §0.405[1], at 178 n. 1 (2d ed. 1974); Bonniwell v. Beech Aircraft Corp., 663 S.W.2d 816 (Tex. 1984); Benson v. Wanda Petroleum Co. 468 S.W.2d 361, 363 (Tex.1971); Franklin v. Rainey, 556 S.W.2d 583 (Tex. Civ. App.—Dallas 1977, no writ).

310. *See, e.g.*, Buckeye Powder Co. v. E. I. DuPont de Nemours Powder Co., 248 U.S. 55, 63 (1918); Bigelow v. Old Dominion Copper Mining and Smelting Co., 225 U.S. 111, 127 (1912).

Inc. v. University of Illinois Foundation[311] rejected the mutuality requirement in defensive collateral estoppel cases which precluded the plaintiff from relitigating issues previously determined against another defendant. The mutuality doctrine, as a prerequisite for invoking offensive collateral estoppel, was clearly repudiated in *Parkline Hosiery Co. v. Shore.*[312] Utilizing offensive collateral estoppel, plaintiff sought to estop a defendant from relitigating issues which the defendant previously litigated against another plaintiff. The court in *Parklane* concluded that the use of offensive collateral estoppel rested in the broad discretion of the trial court.[313] *Parklane* provides, however, that offensive collateral estoppel is inapplicable where the plaintiff could easily have joined the defendant in the earlier action or where estoppel would be unfair to the defendant.[314] To determine the fairness of utilizing offensive collateral estoppel, the court must ascertain: (a) whether or not the defendant had an incentive to defend the previous suit; (b) whether or not the judgment relied on for collateral estoppel is inconsistent with any prior decision; and (c) whether or not the defendant has procedural advantages available to him in the second suit which were not available to him in the first suit which may have led to a different result.[315] The Supreme Court determined that the fact that the first suit was tried non-jury and that the second suit will be tried by a jury does not effect application of the collateral estoppel doctrine.[316]

Under industry-wide liability, offensive collateral estoppel may be applicable, under certain limited circumstances, in subsequent litigation involving identical claims against the same product manufacturers. Once liability is determined, collateral estoppel may possibly preclude relitigation of certain issues in subsequent lawsuits. It appears doubtful that offensive collateral estoppel could be utilized to preclude a manufacturer from litigating the many and varied issues in unidentified product supplier cases.

Collateral estoppel appears appropriate only under the follow-

---

311. 402 U.S. 313 (1971); *Accord* Benson v. Wanda Petroleum Co., 468 S.W.2d 361 (Tex. 1971).

312. 439 U.S. 322 (1979).

313. *Id.* at 331.

314. *Id.*

315. *Id.* at 329-31.

316. *Id.* at 335.

ing circumstances: (1) when a party has been afforded a full and fair opportunity to litigate the issue, (2) when preclusion will not work unfairness to the parties, and (3) when the interests of judicial economy will be served.[317] Several prerequisites must be satisfied: (a) the party against whom collateral estoppel is asserted must have been a party, or in privity with a party, in the prior action;[318] (b) the prior adjudication must have ended in a final judgment on the merits;[319] (c) the party against whom collateral estoppel is asserted must have been afforded a "full and fair opportunity" to litigate the issue in question;[320] (d) the issue to be precluded in the subsequent lawsuit must have been necessary to the prior judgment;[321] (e) the issue to be precluded must have been foreseeably important in potential future litigation of the issue;[322] (f) the issue to be precluded must be identical or substantially identical to the issue involved in the prior case and must have actually been litigated in the earlier case;[323] and (g) the parties to the subsequent lawsuit need not have been adversaries in the prior action.[324]

The preclusive effect of collateral estoppel was applied in as-

---

317. Parklane Hosiery Co. v. Shore, 439 U.S. 322 (1979); Montana v. United States, 440 U.S. 147 (1970).

318. Blonder-Tongue Laboratories, Inc. v. University of Illinois Found. 402 U.S. 313, 320-21 (1971); Kuehn v. Garcia, 608 F.2d 1143 (8th Cir. 1979), *cert. denied*, 445 U.S. 943 (1980); Bonniwell v. Beechnut Aircraft Corp., 663 S.W.2d 816 (Tex. 1984); Benson v. Wanda Petroleum Co., 468 S.W.2d 361 (Tex. 1971); Gilbert v. Fireside Enter., 611 S.W.2d 869 (Tex. Civ. App.—Dallas 1980, no writ).

319. Seaboard Coast Line R.R. Co. v. Union Camp Corp., 613 F.2d 604, 607 (5th Cir.), *cert. denied*, 449 U.S. 835 (1980); Shimman v. Frank, 625 F.2d 80 (6th Cir. 1980); Bonniwell v. Beechnut Aircraft Corp., 663 S.W.2d 816 (Tex.1984).

320. Parklane Hosiery v. Shore, 439 U.S. 322, 328 (1970). This forms the basis for the New York court rejecting offensive collateral estoppel against Eli Lilly based on the finding of liability under a concert of action theory for DES related injuries in *Bichler v. Eli Lilly & Co.*, 79 A.D.2d 317, 435 N.Y.S.2d 625, *aff'd*, 55 NY.2d 571, 450 N.Y.S.2d 776, 436 N.E.2d 182 (1982). *See* Kaufman v. Eli Lilly & Co., 99 A.D.2d 695, 471 N.Y.S.2d 830 (1984), *leave to app. granted*, 474 N.Y.S.2d 415 (1984) *See also*, Bonniwell v. Aircraft Corp., 663 S.W.2d 816 (Tex. 1984).

321. Southern Pacific Transportation Co. v. Smith Material Corp., 616 F.2d 111, 115 (5th Cir. 1980).

322. United States v. Standefer, 610 F.2d 1076, 1092-93 (3d Cir. 1979), *aff'd*, 447 U.S. 10 (1980).

323. Parklane Hosiery Co. v. Shore, 439 U.S. 322, 327 (1970); Lindsay v. Ortho Pharmaceutical Corp., 637 F.2d 87 (2d Cir. 1980); Oldham v. Pritchett, 599 F.2d 274, 279 (8th Cir. 1979); Starker v. U.S., 602 F.2d 1341, 1344 (9th Cir. 1979).

324. Oldham v. Pritchett, 599 F.2d 274, 278 (8th Cir. 1979).

bestos litigation in *Flatt v. Johns-Manville Sales Corp.*[325] Relying on *Borel v. Fibreboard Paper Products Corp.*,[326] the court determined that litigation of whether asbestos products are defective because of an inadequate warning was precluded. The *Flatt* court determined that in a diversity action federal law controls collateral estoppel, based on the rationale of *Aerojet-General Corp. v. Askew.*[327] The *Aerojet* holding that federal law determines the res judicata effect of a prior diversity judgment applied equally to the issue of collateral estoppel. The enumerated three requirements for application of collateral estoppel are: (a) the issue must be identical to the one involved in prior action; (b) the issue must have been actually litigated in the prior action; and (c) the determination made of the issues in the prior action must have been necessary and essential to the resulting judgment.[328]

The court concluded these traditional requirements were satisfied. Notwithstanding that the case involved cement pipe containing abestos, unlike *Borel* which involved asbestos insulation products,[329] the differences between the two products, including the end uses, the percentage of asbestos content of the products, and the environmental conditions present when the products were used were not sufficient to exclude offensive collateral estoppel. The court determined that these differences related to the issue of sufficient exposure to asbestos dust rather than liability.[330] The court also concluded that the collateral estoppel effet of *Borel* relates to all products containing asbestos.[331] Finally, the court indicated that collateral estoppel could be appropriately applied notwith-

---

325. 488 F. Supp. 836 (E.D. Tex. 1980).

326. 493 F.2d 1076 (5th Cir. 1973), *cert. denied*, 419 U.S. 869 (1974). In *Borel*, manufacturers of asbestos insulation products were held strictly liable to an insulation worker who developed asbestosis and mesothelioma. The Fifth Circuit in *Borel* affirmed a jury finding that insulation containing asbestos was an unreasonably dangerous product. As a competent producing cause of asbestosis and mesothelioma, asbestos insulation products required an adequate warning of the risks and dangers involved. On the basis of a finding that the asbestos insulation industry provided no warning whatsoever during the relevant time period, the Fifth Circuit sustained liability predicated on a marketing defect theory.

327. 511 F.2d 710 (5th Cir. 1975).

328. 488 F. Supp. at 839, *citing* James Talcott, Inc. v. Allahabad Bank, Ltd., 444 F.2d 451, 458-59 (5th Cir. 1971).

329. 493 F.2d 1076 (5th Cir. 1973), *cert. denied*, 419 U.S. 869 (1974).

330. 488 F. Supp. at 840.

331. *Id.* at 841.

standing prior decisions in favor of the defendants.[332] The prior decisions favorable to the defendants were distinguished on the basis that they involved insufficient exposure to asbestos or that the injured party failed to contract asbestosis or mesothelioma.

The collateral estoppel doctrine was applied in *Hardy v. Johns-Manville Sales Corp.*[333] The court determined that *Borel* collaterally estopped relitigation of two issues: (1) whether asbestos causes mesothelioma or asbestosis and (2) whether asbestos products are defective.[334] The court reaffirmed its former declaration in *Flatt v. Johns-Manville Corp.*, that offensive collateral estoppel precluded suppliers of asbestos products from relitigating these issues.[335] Defendants who were not parties in *Borel* disputed the binding effect of the prior adjudication. The court determined that under federal law strict mutuality of parties is not required.[336] Even if state law applied, however, the court concluded that Texas law does not require the defendant to be a party to the prior action, provided the defendant was in privity with a party involved in the prior adjudication. Privity, for collateral estoppel purposes, is perceived to mean an identity of interest.[337] The court concluded that the non-*Borel* defendants shared sufficient identity of interest to establish the required privity. The court, therefore, held that *Borel* collaterally estopped the issue that asbestos is a competent producing cause of asbestosis and mesothelioma.[338] The court recognized however, that the standard of conduct for warnings on asbestos insulation materials may differ from other products containing asbestos. The court determined that the *Borel* decision collaterally estopped the issue of the duty to warn for insulation and non-insulation products.[339] Because of the potential difference in standards, the issue of adequacy of warnings would be estopped in insulation cases only.[340]

---

332. *Id.*

333. 509 F. Supp. 1353 (E.D. Tex. 1981), *rev'd*, 681 F.2d 334 (5th Cir. 1982). Refer to text accompanying note 153 *supra*.

334. 493 F.2d 1076 (5th Cir. 1973, *cert. denied*, 419 U.S. 869 (1974).

335. 509 F. Supp. at 1363.

336. *Id.* at 1360 *citing* Aerojet-General Corp. v. Askew, 511 F.2d 710 (5th Cir.) *appeal dismissed*, 423 U.S. 908 (1975).

337. 509 F. Supp. at 1361 *citing* Olivarez v. Broadway Hardware, Inc., 564 S.W.2d 195 (Tex. Civ. App.—Corpus Christi 1978, writ ref'd n.r.e.).

338. 509 F. Supp. at 1362.

339. 509 F. Supp. at 1362.

340. 488 F. Supp. 836 (E.D. Tex. 1980).

The Fifth Circuit reversed the decision of the District Court relating to collateral estoppel.[341] Though holding that the District Court appropriately applied federal law as opposed to state law,[342] the Fifth Circuit determined that while mutuality is not an essential element of collateral estoppel, privity is required.[343] The Fifth Circuit defined privity to mean that the parties estopped must have been afforded a prior "full and fair' opportunity to litigate their claims."[344]

The absence of privity between the *Borel* and non-*Borel* defendants foreclosed the use of collateral estoppel even though all parties manufactured products containing asbestos.[345] The court noted that privity does not exist merely because the persons involved are interested in the same questions or set of facts.[346] Collateral estoppel, therefore, could not be appropriately applied against non-*Borel* defendants. Additionally, the court concluded that even the *Borel* defendants could not be collaterally estopped. While *Borel* conclusively established that manufacturers of asbestos-containing insulation products had a duty to warn of its dangers, the court left unanswered *when* that duty attached.[347] This factor was crucial to the issue of whether the defendant knew or should have known of the danger when it marketed asbestos. The court stated:

> Since we cannot say that *Borel* necessarily decided as a matter of fact, that all manufacturers of asbestos containing insulation products knew or should have known of the dangers of their particular products at all relevant times, we cannot justify the trial court's collaterally estopping the defendants from presenting evi-

---

341. Hardy v. Johns-Manville, 681 F.2d 334 (5th Cir. 1982).

342. *Id.* at 337 *citing* Aerojet-General Corp. v. Askew, 511 F.2d 710 (5th Cir.), *appeal dismissed*, 423 U.S. 908 (1974). *Cf.* McCarty v. Johns-Manville Sales Corp., 502 F. Supp. 335, 338-39 (S.D. .Miss. 1980)(applying state law). *See also* Bertrand v. Johns-Manville Sales Corp., 529 F. Supp. 539, 542-43, n. 3 (D. Minn. 1982) (Minnesota law and federal law essentially identical on the issue precluding the need to choose between the two).

343. 681 F.2d at 338. Texas likewise rejects mutuality of parties in favor of privity between the parties. *See generally,* Hardy v. Fleming, 553 S.W.2d 790 (Tex. Civ. App.—El Paso 1977, writ ref'd n.r.e.); Olivarez v. Broadway Hardware Inc., 564 S.W.2d 195 (Tex. Civ. App.—Corpus Christi 1978, writ ref'd n.r.e.).

344. *Id. citing* Parklane Hosiery Co. v. Shore, 439 U.S. 322 (1979).

345. 681 F.2d at 339.

346. *Id.* at 340 *citing* Bensen v. Wanda Petroleum Co., 468 S.W.2d 361, 363 (Tex. 1971).

347. 681 F.2d at 343-44.

dence as to the state of the art.[348]

The Fifth Circuit also denied collateral estoppel because of the existence of prior favorable judgments for the defendants.[349] Since these verdicts were inconsistent with *Borel*, the court concluded that the imposition of collateral estoppel is arbitrary and "undermines the premise that different juries reach equally valid verdicts."[350]

Finally, the court determined that application of collateral estoppel to *Borel* defendants would be unfair.[351] It is doubtful that the defendants could have foreseen that their liability in *Borel* would foreshadow multimillion dollar asbestos liabilities.

The Fifth Circuit found the application of collateral estoppel equally inappropriate to preclude litigating whether asbestos is always a competent producing cause of mesothelioma and asbestosis.[352] The court based this decision on the finding that *Borel* did not conclude that because asbestos dust and fibers are dangerous, then "all products containing asbestos—in whatever quantity or however encapsulated—are hazardous."[353] Defendants must be allowed to present evidence relating to the dangerousness of their particular product rather than being subjected to a presumption that all products containing asbestos produce cancer.[354]

The Fifth Circuit once again considered collateral estoppel in *Migues v. Fibreboard Corp.*[355] The court declined, however, to determine whether the defendant could be collaterally estopped from litigating the unreasonably dangerous nature of its asbestos products.[356] The Fifth Circuit interpreted the trial court's Partial Summary Judgment Order as precluding such litigation by the appellant on the basis of *stare decisis*[357] rather than collateral estoppel.[358] Therefore, the issue of collateral estoppel was not presented to the court on appeal. Thus, defendants who were par-

---

348. *Id.* at 345.
349. *Id.* at 345-46. *Accord*, Setter v. A. H. Robbins Co., 748 F.2d 1328 (8th Cir. 1984).
350. 488 F. Supp. 836 (E.D. Tex. 1980).
351. 681 F.2d at 346.
352. *Id.*
353. *Id.* at 347.
354. *Id.*
355. 662 F.2d 1182 (5th Cir. 1981).
356. *Id.* at 1185.
357. *Id.*
358. 662 F.2d at 1185.

ties to *Borel* were estopped from relitigating the issue, whereas the non-party defendants were not.[359] The Fifth Circuit limited its holding to the *stare decisis* effect of *Borel*, and expressly declined to consider the collateral estoppel issue.[360]

Under Texas law, plaintiff is obligated to establish three basic elements to trigger collateral estoppel. Plaintiff must demonstrate that: (1) the identical fact issue in the later action was fully and fairly litigated; (2) the issue to be precluded was necessary to the original judgment; and (3) the parties litigating the issue occupied an adversial posture to one another.[361] Inherent in the doctrine is the need for identity of parties or those in privity with the parties in the prior action. A party is in privity with a party to a prior action if the party "has such an identity of interest that the party to the [prior] judgment representeed the same legal right.[362] Whether the Texas courts would authorize the use of offensive collateral estoppel is less than clear despite the more liberal interpretation adopted by the federal courts.[363]

5.05 Conclusion

Industry-wide liability involves the imposition of liability on manufacturers of generic type products where the injured party is frequently unable to prove the identity of the particular product supplier. Though some courts have restructured traditional tort principles to impose liability, a majority of jurisdictions have rejected the imposition of strict tort liability on unidentified manufacturers of products that may be involved in accidents.

Jurisdictions that impose industry-wide liability necessarily

---

359. *Id.* at 1186, nn. 6-7.

360. *Id.* at 1187.

361. *See*, Bonniwell v. Beechnut Aircraft Corp., 663 S.W.2d 816 (Tex. 1984); Benson v. Wanda Petroleum Co., 468 S.W.2d 361 (Tex. 1971); Olivarez v. Broadway Hardware Inc., 564 S.W.2d 195 (Tex. Civ. App.—Corpus Christi 1978, writ ref'd n.r.e.).

362. Bonniwell v. Beechnut Aircraft Corp., 663 S.W.2d 816 (Tex 1984); Benson v. Wanda Petroleum Co., 468 S.W.2d 361 (Tex. 1971); Windmill Dinner Theater v. Hazler, 582 S.W.2d 585 (Tex. Civ. App.—Dallas 1979, writ dism'd).

363. The Texas courts have not addressed the issue of offensive collateral estoppel. The federal court in *Hardy v. Johns Manville Sales Corp.*, 509 F. Supp. 1353, 1361 (E.D. Tex. 1981), *rev'd* 681 F.2d 334 (5th Cir. 1982) suggested Texas would recognize offensive collateral estopel. It is significant, however, that in diversity jurisdiction, the federal courts apply federal rather than state procedural law. *See*, Aerojet Gen. Corp. v. Askew, 511 F.2d 710 (5th Cir.1975).

confront the thorny issue of ascertaining an evenhanded method for apportionment of damages. Alternative liability, concert of action and enterprise liability impose joint and several liability. Market share liability allocates damages based on the manufacturer's percentage share of the market. Numerous problems however, plague market share liability. "Risk contribution" apportions damages based on causative fault, while market share alternate liability employs a modification of market share apportionment.

Other issues effect industry-wide liability. The award of punitive damages under a market share concept raises a potentially explosive issue. Likewise, the doctrine of offensive collateral estoppel when applied to industry-wide litigation poses further legal entanglements. Considerable litigation remains in this new and novel area of strict tort liability.

CHAPTER VI. PROSPECTIVE PLAINTIFFS*

6.01 Introduction

Strict tort liability, as enunciated under Section 402A of the *Restatement (Second) of Torts*[1], provides a remedy for any user who sustains an injury while using a defective and unreasonably dangerous product. The class of individuals entitled to assert strict tort liability is therefore limited by the judicial interpretation of the term "user" under Section 402A. When a plaintiff sues a manufacturer of a defective product under the doctrine of strict tort liability, it is imperative for the plaintiff to qualify as a "user" of that product within the contemplation of Section 402A.[2] This chapter addresses the issue of the extent to which strict tort liability is expanded to include individuals who technically are neither users or consumers of the product.

A strict tort liability cause of action suggests a commercial relationship or involvement with a supplier who is regularly engaged in commerce;[3] however, when a cause of action is based upon the doctrine of strict tort liability, the ultimate consumer or user of the product need not be in privity of contract with the supplier.[4]

---

* Barbara Paulissen coauthored this chapter.

1. Restatement (Second) of Torts § 402A (1965).

2. *Id.*

3. Refer to text accompanying notes 25-30 *infra*.

4. *See* McKisson v. Sales Affiliates, Inc., 416 S.W.2d 787, 791-92 (Tex. 1967) (privity of contract not required when defective product sample was given to plaintiff by sales representative with expectation of future sales); Bernard Johnson, Inc. v. Continental Constructors, Inc., 630 S.W.2d 365, 369-70 (Tex. App.—Austin 1982, writ ref'd n.r.e.) (appellant owed no contract based duty to appellee but might owe a duty based in common law); Texas

The landmark case of *Jacob E. Decker & Sons, Inc. v. Capps*[5] established the rule in Texas that "in a food case privity of contract is not a prerequisite to recovery for breach of a manufacturer's warranty of fitness for human consumption".[6] Breach of a warranty implied by law constituted the precursor of the current strict tort liability doctrine.[7] The court in *Putman v. Erie City Manufacturing Co.*[8] confronted the issue of whether privity of contract constituted a prerequisite to recovery in "nonfood" cases. In *Putman*, a defective fork stem utilized to connect the wheel to a wheelchair which had been rented by the plaintiff caused injuries to the plaintiff when the stem fractured and caused the wheelchair to collapse. The plaintiff initiated an action against the assembler of the wheelchair and the manufacturer of the fork stem. The court determined that a manufacturer of a defective product that is unreasonably dangerous to the user is subject to strict tort liability for any injury resulting from the defect, even in the absence of privity of contract between the user and the manufacturer.[9] Privity is, therefore, rejected as a prerequisite for an action based on strict tort liability.[10]

With the relegation of privity to obscurity, attention quickly focused on the outer limits of the new doctrine's applicability. Considering the socioeconomic rationale underlying strict tort liability, it was inevitable that the doctrine's scope would be virtually limitless.

In *Darryl v. Ford Motor Co.*[11] the plaintiff instituted a strict tort liability action against a manufacturer for injuries suffered when his vehicle was struck from the rear by a truck allegedly equipped with defective brakes. Confirming that privity no longer constituted a relevant consideration for a strict tort liability action,

---

Processed Plastics, Inc. v. Gray Enterprises, Inc., 592 S.W.2d 412, 415 (Tex. Civ. App.—Tyler 1979, no writ) (privity of contract not required when cause of action grounded in strict liability).

5. 139 Tex. 609, 164 S.W.2d 828 (1942).

6. Putman v. Erie City Mfg. Co., 338 F.2d 911, 912 (5th Cir. 1964) (commenting on the significance of *Jacob*).

7. *Id.*

8. 338 F.2d 911 (5th Cir. 1964).

9. *Id.* at 912.

10. Restatement (Second) of Torts § 402A (2)(b) (1965). Strict tort liability applies "although . . . the user or consumer has not bought the product from or entered into any contractual relation with the seller." *Id.*

11. 440 S.W.2d 630 (Tex. 1969).

the court noted that "[a] manufacturer who places in commerce a product rendered dangerous to life or limb by reason of some defect is strictly liable in tort to one who sustains injury because of the defective condition."[12]

Almost from adoption of Section 402A, privity has been repudiated as a relevant element for a cause of action seeking damages for injuries resulting from product-caused incidents.[13] As a consequence, the parameters for the class of individuals authorized to assert a strict tort liability action expanded significantly and quickly. Currently, the class of individuals authorized to assert a strict tort liability action appears to be limited only by the standard of reasonable foreseeability in the manner of use and environment of use.[14]

Foreseeability as a limiting factor was initially recognized by the Fifth Circuit in *Helene Curtis Industries, Inc. v. Pruitt*.[15] The plaintiff sustained chemical burns to her scalp and ear when she applied a mixture of two products designed for bleaching hair. Though the products were purchased from a beauty parlor, the plaintiff instituted suit against the manufacturers of the chemicals. The court noted that "these products were intended to be used by a professional beautician," and since the maker is only liable to those whom it can reasonably expect to use its product, Mrs. Pruitt could not recover.[16] Of the reasons enumerated by the court for denying the plaintiff recovery, the court focused on the foreseeability of the plaintiff's use of the product as the critical element.[17] The court essentially employed the "reasonably intended or foreseeable use doctrine" as the basis for limiting recovery. The reasonably intended or foreseeable use doctrine constitutes an acknowledgment that individuals injured as the consequences of abnormal handling, substantial alteration, or use of a product in an unintended environment are foreclosed from recovery of damages

---

12. *Id.* at 633.

13. *See* McKisson v. Sales Affiliates, Inc., 416 S.W.2d 787 (Tex. 1967); Daryl v. Ford Motor Co., 440 S.W.2d 630 (Tex. 1969): Metal Window Prods. v. Magnusen, 485 S.W.2d 355 (Tex. Civ. App.-Houston [14th Dist.] 1972, writ ref'd n.r.e.)

14. Refer to notes 15-21 *infra* and accompanying text.

15. 385 F.2d 841 (5th Cir. 1967), *cert. denied*, 391 U.S. 913 (1968).

16. *Id.* at 857.

17. *Id.* at 863. The court was attempting "to confine the scope of liability to the zone of danger which could reasonably have been foreseen before these products were sold." *Id.*

for product related accidents.[18]

In *Davis v. Gibson Products Co.*[19] the court reaffirmed the reasonably intended or foreseeable use doctrine. The court noted that "[t]he scope of responsibility under Section 402A is limited by the 'intended use' doctrine, which requires consideration of the defendant's marketing scheme and the foreseeability of harm."[20] It appears, therefore, that the doctrine of strict tort liability does not extend to the unforeseeable user or to individuals using a product in an unintended and unforeseeable environment.[21]

Perhaps the most definitive enunciation of the reasonably foreseeable use standard to define the class of individuals who may maintain a strict tort liability action against the manufacturer of a product is encapsulated in the recent Texas Supreme Court case of *Colvin v. Red Steel Co.*[22] Plaintiff, an ironworker, was injured when an overhead iron purlin manufactured by the defendant gave way as he grasped the purlin in an attempt to raise himself to an upright position. The purlin manufactured and furnished by the defendant was significantly shorter and weighed less than stated in specifications dictated by the architect and general contactor. The court concluded that the plaintiff was not entitled to maintain a strict tort liability action against the supplier of the shorter than specified purlins. The court observed:

> An essential element of Colvin's strict liability cause of action is a finding that the product was not fit for its intended or reasonably foreseeable use at the time it left the manufacturer. The purlins were intended to be welded to the top of the trusses and were to serve as spacers between the trusses and the roof material. . . . . The question remaining is whether Red Steel reasonably could have foreseen that the purlins would be placed atop the trusses, left there unattached, violating the safety standards of the Associated General Contractors of America, Inc., and then

---

18. *Id.* at 855-56.

19. 505 S.W.2d 682 (Tex. Civ. App.—San Antonio 1973, writ ref'd n.r.e.).

20. *Id.* at 691. The court stated: "[T]he liability created by the doctrine of strict liability rests on foreseeability." *Accord* Harrison v. Flota Mercante Grancolombiana, S.A, 577 F.2d 968, 977 (5th Cir. 1978); Winnett v. Winnett, 57 Ill. 2d 7, 12-13, 310 N.E.2d 1, 4-5 (1974); Williams v. RCA Corp., 59 Ill. App. 3d 299, 376 N.E.2d 37, 38-39 (1978) (an intervening criminal act that is foreseeable does not break the causal chain).

21. *See* Helene Curtis Indus. v. Pruitt, 385 F.2d 841, 861-62 (5th Cir.), *cert. denied*, 391 U.S. 913 (1968).

22. 682 S.W.2d 243 (Tex. 1984).

> used by a skilled ironworker to pull himself upright. Red Steel could not reasonably have foreseen such a use. The purlins were used for the intended purpose and there is no evidence of any other intended or foreseeable use. The dangerous condition which contributed to Colvin's fall was created on the job site not by Red Steel, but by Colvin, his fellow employees and McKee.[23]

The *Colvin* court verbalized succinctly the governing standards for measuring whether a party injured in a product-related accident is entitled to initiate a strict tort liability action against the product supplier. Reinforcing earlier decisions, the Supreme Court clearly delineated that strict tort liability extends to an injured party only when the product is used for its reasonably intended purposes and in a reasonably foreseeable manner. The reasonably intended use and reasonably foreseeable environment of use is governed by the objective standard of reasonable foreseeability and not by the anticipation of the bizarre or the aberrational.

6.02 PURCHASERS

Section 402A expressly provides that purchasers of products are entitled to maintain a strict tort liability action.[24] The rule that a purchaser may assert a strict tort liability action, however, is not without limitations. It is essential that the purchaser obtain the defective product from a party who is regularly engaged in the business of supplying the type of product that caused the accident.[25] For example, in *Freitas v. Twin City Fisherman's Cooperative Association*,[26] the plaintiff, a fuel deliveryman, sustained injuries when a ladder attached to a large fuel tank on which he was perched suddenly detached. The ladder had been constructed by a contractor and furnished by an oil company to a shrimp boat service cooperative that the plaintiff was servicing. The inapplicability of strict tort liability was predicated on the fact that the defendant was not regularly engaged in the business of selling tanks, ladders or platforms.[27] The court interpreted Section 402A:

---

23. *Id.* at 246.

24. RESTATEMENT (SECOND) OF TORTS § 402A(1) (1965) refers to the liability of "[o]ne who *sells* any product . . . to the user or consumer . . ." (emphasis added).

25. RESTATEMENT (SECOND) OF TORTS § 402A comment f (1965).

26. 452 S.W.2d 931 (Tex. Civ. App.—Corpus Christi 1970, writ ref'd n.r.e.).

27. *Id.* at 938. *Accord* Goetz v. Avildsen Tool & Mach., Inc., 82 Ill. App. 3d 1054, 403 N.E.2d 555, 561 (1980).

> Comment f indicates that the drafters of Section 402A assumed that one who manufactures a product is also normally a seller of that product. As we construe the rule and the comments, the rule of strict liability does not apply to persons who merely construct items but are not engaged in the business of selling such items.[28]

The court emphasized the necessity of a sale or an introduction of products into the stream of commerce as a predicate for the imposition of strict liability under Section 402A.[29] The mere gratuitous furnishing of a product for an individual's use simply does not satisfy this fundamental requirement.[30]

A purchaser's or user's ability to maintain a strict tort liability action against a manufacturer is dependent on the product being introduced into the stream of commerce.[31] In *Armstrong Rubber Co. v. Urquidez*[32] the court confronted, for the first time, the issue of "whether the doctrine of strict liability in tort applies where the product has not entered the stream of commerce and where there has been no sale of the product by the manufacturer but a bailment for mutual benefit."[33] The beneficiaries of a test car driver initiated a strict tort liability action against a tire manufacturer to recover for the driver's death. The manufacturer supplied, in addition to the tires being tested, other tires mounted on the vehicle used during testing. One of the tires not being tested failed and precipitated the crash in which the driver was fatally injured. Because the tire was never introduced into the stream of commerce, the doctrine of strict liability was viewed as inapplicable against the tire manufacturer.[34]

It is neither essential nor necessary that the injured party ac-

---

28. *Id.* at 937.

29. *Id. Cf.* Rourke v. Garza, 530 S.W.2d 794, 800 (Tex. 1975) (strict liability extended to include persons engaged in the business of leasing products to third parties); Hernandez v. S. Pac. Trans. Co., 641 S.W.2d 947, 952 (Tex. App.—Corpus Christi 1982, no writ) (strict liability not applicable when defendant was not engaged in releasing product into stream of commerce).

30. *See* text accompanying notes 35-37.

31. Refer to notes 32-39 *infra* and accompanying text.

32. 570 S.W.2d 374 (Tex. 1978).

33. *Id.* at 375.

34. *Id.* at 377. *Accord* Thomas v. St. Joseph Hosp., 618 S.W.2d 791, 796-97 (Tex. Civ. App.—Houston [1st Dist.] 1981, writ ref'd n.r.e.) (hospital gown introduced into stream of commerce because the manufacturer was engaged in a bailment for mutual benefit involving the sale of hospital services).

tually purchase the product; it is sufficient if "the transaction by which the product is transmitted into the stream of commerce is 'essentially commercial' in character."[35] In *McKisson v. Sales Affiliates, Inc.*,[36] the plaintiff, a beauty shop operator, was injured by a free sample of permanent wave solution. Concluding that Section 402A extended to the supplier of the product, the Texas Supreme Court observed that "[o]ne who delivers an advertising sample to another with the expectation of profiting therefrom through future sales is in the same position as one who sells the product."[37]

Similarly, in *Malinak v. Firestone Tire & Rubber Co.*[38] the plaintiff desired to purchase new tires for his vehicle. A service station ordered the tires from a Firestone outlet, but the plaintiff picked up and paid for the tires on the basis of a dealer discount price. The service station operator then mounted the tires for a service charge. The court, acknowledging the applicability of Section 402A to the station operator, stated: "[t]he transaction was essentially commercial in that by reason of appellant's purchase [the service station operator] received compensation for mounting the tires. . ."[39]

Potential purchasers of products likewise are encompassed by Section 402A.[40] A customer shopping in a retail store who is injured by a defective product displayed in the store is entitled to maintain a cause of action based on strict tort liability. For example, in *Davis v. Gibson Products Co.*,[41] plaintiff cut his hand while examining a machete displayed in a self-service outlet. Though the plaintiff admitted that he did not plan to purchase the machete during his patronage of the store, the court nevertheless concluded that a potential customer merely browsing through a store was enshrouded in the protective embrace of the strict tort liability doctrine.[42] Similarly, a customer who slips on liquid soap leaking from

---

35. Hill, *How Strict is Strict?*, 32 Tex. B.J. 759, 767 (1969).
36. 416 S.W.2d 787 (Tex. 1967).
37. *Id.* at 792.
38. 436 S.W.2d 210 (Tex. Civ. App.—Houston [1st Dist.] 1968, writ ref'd n.r.e.).
39. *Id.* at 212-13. Defendant was engaged in the service station business, which included the sale of tires.
40. Restatement (Second) of Torts § 402A(2)(b) (1965).
41. 505 S.W.2d 682 (Tex. Civ. App.—San Antonio 1973, writ ref'd n.r.e.).
42. *Id.* at 691-92. The element of foreseeability constituted a significant factor in the court's decision:

> The liability . . . rests on foreseeability, and not on esoteric concepts relating to transfer or delivery of possession. . . . In this case, injury to a person in [the

a defective container in her shopping basket qualifies as a purchaser within the intendment of Section 402A.[43]

6.03 CONSUMERS AND USERS

Section 402A of the *Restatement* expressly applies to all consumers and users. The comment to the *Restatement* defines customers as those who either consume a product or prepare it for consumption.[44] More importantly, the term "consumption" includes all reasonably intended uses of the product.[45] Since consumers are defined in terms of use, the terms "consumers" and "users" are essentially synonymous.[46]

Prior to the adoption of strict tort liability in Texas, the absence of privity between the consumer or user created an undesirable impediment to recovery against product suppliers.[47] Abrogation of privity under strict tort liability therefore unleashed the fetters that earlier constrained consumers and users from asserting a cause of action for product-caused accidents.[48] The terms "user" and "consumer" have received liberal judicial interpretation and include the broadest possible spectrum of injured parties. Unfettered by literal interpretation, "consumer" or "user" has been expanded to include family members,[49] employees,[50] and guests and

---

> plaintiff's] position was clearly foreseeable by defendant. It is undisputed that defendant foresaw that persons in the store . . . would handle the machetes and, in the process of examining them, would remove the machete from the sheath . . . .

Id. at 691.

43. Shoppers World v. Villarreal, 518 S.W.2d 913, 917 (Tex. Civ. App.—Corpus Christi 1975, writ ref'd n.r.e.) (item is sold when consumer picks it up for handling or purchase).

44. RESTATEMENT (SECOND) OF TORTS § 402A, comment l (1956).

45. *Id.*

46. Helicoid Gage Div. of Am. Chain & Cable Co. v. Howell, 511 S.W.2d 573, 578 (Tex. Civ. App.—Houston [14th Dist.] 1974, writ ref'd n.r.e.), (employee of purchaser).

47. Refer to notes 4-12 *supra* and accompanying text.

48. *See, e.g.,* Gonzales v. Caterpillar Tractor Co., 571 S.W.2d 867, 871 (Tex. 1978) (user of a caterpillar tractor front-end loader); Miller v. Bock Laundry Mach. Co., 568 S.W.2d 648, 649 (Tex. 1977) (user of industrial dryer); Blackwell Burner Co. v. Cerda, 644 S.W.2d 512, 515 (Tex. Civ. App.—San Antonio 1982, writ ref'd n.r.e.) (employees of purchaser, The State Highway Department); Rawlings Sporting Goods Co. v. Daniels, 619 S.W.2d 435, 437 (Tex. Civ. App.—Waco 1981, writ ref'd n.r.e.) (user of a football helmet at school).

49. *See, e.g.,* Miller v. Bock Laundry Mach. Co., 568 S.W.2d 648, 649 (Tex. 1977) (son of customer at laundromat); Magic Chef, Inc. v. Sibley, 546 S.W.2d 851, 853 (Tex. Civ. App.—San Antonio 1977, writ ref'd n.r.e.) (child injured in baby-sitter's apartment).

50. *See, e.g.,* Daberko v. Heil Co., 681 F.2d 445, 446 (5th Cir. 1982) (chemical company employee injured on tank truck); Howard v. General Cable Corp., 674 F.2d 351, 354 (5th

donees [51] of the purchaser.

For example, in *Helicoid Gage Division of American Chain & Cable Co. v. Howell*[52] the court accepted the *Restatement* view that a "user or consumer" contemplates an employee of the ultimate purchaser. In the industrial context, the user rarely occupies the status of a purchaser."[53] Workers employed to fabricate goods from raw asbestos materials are deemed "users" of the product.[54]

In *Guidry v. KEM Manufacturing Co.*[55] the plaintiff was hired by a church to work as an operating engineer, a position that included maintaining the kitchen sinks in the church's rectory. When the sinks would clog, plaintiff utilized Drano to unclog the sinks. Electing to substitute a different product, and being aware of the danger in mixing chemicals, plaintiff refrained from using the substitute product until he was confident all traces of Drano were removed. When informed that the kitchen sink was again clogged, he used the new product unaware that Drano had been recently used by someone else. The mixture of the two chemicals generated an explosion that seriously injured the plaintiff. As an employee of the purchaser, plaintiff was deemed a user entitled to

---

Cir. 1982); Foster v. Ford Motor Co., 616 F.2d 1304, 1307 (5th Cir. 1980) (tractor-operator injured by hayfork and front end loader); Litton Industrial Prods., Inc. v. Gammage, 668 S.W.2d 319, 321 (Tex. 1984); Rourke v. Garza, 530 S.W.2d 794, 795-96 (Tex. 1975) (construction worker injured by rented equipment); Pearson v. Hevi-Duty Elec., 618 S.W.2d 784, 785 (Tex. Civ. App.—Houston [1st Dist.] 1981, writ ref'd n.r.e.) (an employee working on a product which incorporates product components manufactured by others is also a user); Lopez v. Aro Corp., 584 S.W.2d 333, 334 (Tex. Civ. App.—San Antonio 1979, writ ref'd n.r.e.) (employee of purchaser); Hamilton v. Motor Coach Indus., Inc. 569 S.W.2d 571, 576 (Tex. Civ. App.—Texarkana 1978, no writ) (a mechanic working on or repairing a product is regarded as a user under Section 402A); Helicoid Gage Div. of Am. Chain & Cable Co. v. Howell, 511 S.W.2d 573 (Tex.Civ.App.—Houston [14th Dist.] 1974, writ ref'd n.r.e.) (oil field worker injured by pressure gauge).

51. *See, e.g.*, Wagner v. Coronet Hotel, 10 Ariz. App. 296, 458 P.2d 390, 392-395 (1969) (hotel guest injured by defective bathmat); Tomczuk v. Cheshire, 26 Conn. Sup. 219, 217 A.2d 71, 73 (Sup. Ct. 1965) (injured bike rider was guest in buyer's home); McKisson v. Sales Affiliates, Inc., 416 S.W.2d 787, 790 (Tex. 1967) (beautician injured by sample of permanent wave solution); Metal Window Prods. Co. v. Magnusen, 485 S.W.2d 355, 356 (Tex.Civ.App. —Houston [14th Dist.] 1972, writ ref'd n.r.e.) (recovery by lessee's guest who collided with glass door denied on other grounds). *See also* RESTATEMENT (SECOND) OF TORTS § 402A, comment l (1965).

52. 511 S.W.2d 573 (Tex. Civ. App.—Houston [14th Dist.] 1974, writ ref'd n.r.e.).

53. *Id.* at 578.

54. *See*, Borel v. Fibreboard Paper Prods. Corp., 493 F.2d 1076 (5th Cir. 1973) *cert. denied*, 419 U.S. 869 (1974) (duty to warn extends to all foreseeable users).

55. 693 F.2d 426 (5th Cir. 1982).

maintain an action based on strict tort liability.[56]

The expanded reach of "consumer" is exemplified in *Ethicon, Inc. v. Parten*,[57] Plaintiff was injured when a surgical needle fractured during the course of an abdominal operation. The manufacturer contended that the patient qualified as neither a consumer nor a user of the surgical needle. In denominating the plaintiff as a user and consumer, the court observed:

> Comment l of [Section] 402A recognizes that to be a user or consumer, one need not have purchased the product. Especially applicable is the illustration . . . that . . . the customer in a beauty shop to whose hair a permanent wave solution is applied by the shop is a consumer. Appellants attempt to convince us that Dr. Chambler was the sole user or consumer, but it is obvious that [Section] 402A also contemplates Mrs. Parten as a consumer.[58]

The plaintiffs in *Bell Helicopter Co. v. Bradshaw*[59] were passengers aboard a helicopter that crashed due to a defective rotor blade. They instituted a strict tort liability action naming the manufacturer-seller of the helicopter as one of the defendants. The court declared that passengers were, indeed, users of a product.[60] Most jurisdictions extend strict liability to passengers traveling in defective vehicles.[61]

Despite the expansive interpretation accorded users and consumers, the application of strict tort liability to this group is not totally unqualified. An illegal user or consumer may be foreclosed from asserting a strict tort liability action.[62] As a general principle, the product supplier is liable only to that class of individuals who are reasonably likely to use the product, and to those individuals

---

56. *Id.* (recovery denied on other grounds).

57. 520 S.W.2d 527 (Tex. Civ. App.—Houston [14th Dist.] 1975, no writ).

58. *Id.* at 533, (quoting RESTATEMENT (SECOND) OF TORTS § 402A (1965)). *See also* Otis Elevator Co. v. Wood, 436 S.W.2d 324, 328 (Tex. 1968) (one who leans across a moving escalator to save a falling child is a "user" of the escalator).

59. 594 S.W.2d 519 (Tex. Civ. App.—Corpus Christi 1979, writ ref'd n.r.e.).

60. *Id.*

61. *See, e.g.*, Higginbotham v. Ford Motor Co., 540 F.2d 762, 770 (5th Cir. 1976) (passenger in automobile); McKee v. Brunswick Corp., 354 F.2d 577, 582 (7th Cir. 1965) (passenger of a vessel); Hacker v. Rector, 250 F. Supp. 300, 301-02, (W.D. Mo. 1966) (automobile passenger); Ulmer v. Ford Motor Co., 75 Wash 2d 522, 452 P.2d 729 (Wash. 1969) (passenger in automobile).

62. *Cf.* Davis v. Gibson Prods. Co., 505 S.W.2d 682, 685 (Tex. Civ. App.—San Antonio 1973, writ ref'd n.r.e.).

injured within the reasonably foreseeable environment of the product's use.[63] Reasonable foreseeability contemplates that which is objectively expected or contemplated; it does not include the bizarre, unusual, or the exceptional.

A thief who steals a product or a trespasser on property where the defective equipment is operating is not a user or consumer of a product as contemplated by the *Restatement*. The thief or a trespasser simply is not objectively perceived as a forseeable user of a product.[64] However, in *Barnes v. Litton Industrial Products, Inc.*[65] prison inmates working as dental assistants in the prison dental office improperly and illegally obtained burning alcohol for consumption and were acknowledged to possess a cause of action under strict tort liability for inadequate warning.[66]

The class of users authorized to initiate a strict tort liability action may also be limited by the type of use for which a particular product is employed. In *Johnson v. Murph Metals, Inc.*[67] employees of lead smelting companies instituted suit against automobile battery manufacturers. Plaintiffs inhaled fumes and particles emitted during the process of smelting lead from the manufacturers' recycled automobile batteries. Although acknowledging the broad class encompassed within the ambit of "users" by Section 402A,[68] the court concluded that the plaintiffs were not "users" of the battery manufacturers' products within the purview of Section 402A.[69]

6.04 Employees

The dual capacity doctine is a recent concept developed in an effort to provide an employee injured by a defective product in the course and scope of his employment with a strict tort liability

---

63. *See* Helene Curtis Indus., Inc. v. Pruitt, 385 F.2d 841, 863 (5th Cir. 1967), *cert. denied*, 391 U.S. 913 (1968).

64. *But see* Pegg v. General Motors Corp., 258 Pa. Super 59, 391 A.2d 1074, 1081-82 (1978) (fact that plaintiff stole the product was not a sufficient reason to deny recovery).

65. 555 F.2d 1184 (4th Cir. 1977).

66. *Id.* at 1188.

67. 562 F. Supp. 246 (N.D. Tex. 1983).

68. *Id.* at 249. "[E]ven an accidental contact with the product, after it has passed through many hands, can constitute 'use' of the product." *Id.*

69. *Id.* at 249. "To hold that Plaintiffs are 'users' of Defendants' product would expand the concept of products liability far beyond its existing boundaries . . . it would be untenable to find that the creation of dangerous gases due to the smelting of scrap metal is a 'use' of Defendants' automotive batteries." *Id.*

cause of action against the employer.[70] The dual capacity doctrine contemplates that an employer possessing an immunity from tort liability by reason of the exclusive remedy of the Workers' Compensation Act[71] may become strictly liable in tort for product related injuries to his own employee.[72] If the employer occupies, in addition to his capacity as employer, a second capacity that confers on him obligations to the employee independent of those imposed on him as employer, the employee may, in a minority of jurisdictions, maintain a strict tort liability action for a product caused accident.[73]

In the landmark case of *Douglas v. E. & J. Gallo Winery*,[74] plaintiff, an employee of the defendant, sustained injuries when an elevator scaffolding device on which he was working collapsed. The employer-defendant manufactured and sold similar scaffolding devices to the public. The court concluded that the employee was entitled to maintain a strict tort liability cause of action against the employer because "the product involved is manufactured by the employer for sale *to the public* rather than being manufactured for the sole use of the employer".[75] The California court determined that the employer-manufacturer is not relieved of tort liability when products it manufactures and sells to the public injure an employee in the course and scope of his employment for the employer-manufacturer.[76] The dual capacity doctrine applies, however, only if the product causing the injury is one manufactured for sale to the public rather than one used by the employee in performing duties for the employer.[77]

Occasional disconnected sales, however, do not invoke the dual capacity doctrine and the concommitant liability to the employee.[78] The employer-defendant who manufactures a product for his own use and thereafter sells a similar product to another busi-

---

70. 2a LARSON, THE LAW OF WORKMEN'S COMPENSATION 72.80 at 189 (Supp. 1981).
71. *Id. See also* TEX. REV. CIV. STAT. ANN. arts. 8306, 8307 (1967).
72. Refer to notes 73-86 *infra* and accompanying text.
73. *See* Mercer v. Uniroyal Corp., 49 Ohio App. 2d 279, 361 N.E.2d 492 (1976); Quinn v. National Gypsum Co., 469 A.2d 1368 (N.H. 1983).
74. 69 Cal. App. 3d 103, 137 Cal. Rptr. 797 (1977).
75. *Id.* at 107, 137 Cal. Rptr. at 799 (emphasis in original).
76. *Id.*, at 137 Cal. Rptr. at 802. *Accord* Reed v. The Yaka, 373 U.S. 410, 415-16 (1963); Mercer v. Uniroyal, Inc., 49 Ohio App. 2d 279, 361 N.E.2d 492, 496 (1976).
77. 137 Cal. Rptr. at 799.
78. 137 Cal. Rptr. at 803.

ness is not subject to strict tort liability when an employee is injured using the retained product.[79] The *Douglas* court declared that the dual capacity doctrine applies only when the employer-defendant is engaged in manufacturing to an extent that justifies the conclusion that "it is part and parcel of an activity which occupies the effort, attention and time of the defendant for the purpose of possible profit on a continuing basis".[80] Dual capacity therefore, is limited to manufacturers engaged in manufacturing products for sale to the general public.[81]

The overwhelming majority of jurisdictions have categorically rejected the dual capacity concept.[82] Texas adheres to the majority view, rejecting an employee's dual capacity as the basis for an employee to maintain a strict tort liability action.[83] In *Cohn v. Spinks Industries, Inc.*[84] the deceased was fatally injured when a helicopter purchased, rebuilt, and maintained by the defendant-employer crashed. The helicopter was leased to Helix Air Transport, Inc., a wholly owned subsidiary of the employer, and the decedent was employed to serve as a helicopter pilot for Helix. The trial court granted a summary judgment for the defendant-employer.[85] After reviewing the conflicting approaches to the dual capacity concept, the appellate court concluded:

> We find the arguments against adoption of the dual capacity doctrine to be more compelling under the state of the law as it exists in Texas today. The intent of the legislature in enacting

---

79. *Id.*

80. *Id.*

81. *Id.*

82. *See,* Billy v. Consolidated Mach. Tool Corp., 71 A.D.2d 796, 797, 419 N.Y.S. 2d 29, 30 (App. Div. 1979) (not rejecting the dual capacity doctrine but reserving acceptance of it to the Court of Appeals). *But see,* Goetz v. Avildsen Tool & Mach., Inc., 82 Ill. App. 3d 1054, 403 N.E.2d 555, 560 (1980) (accepting dual capacity doctrine but holding the doctrine inapplicable on the facts of the case); Longever v. Revere Copper & Brass, Inc., 381 Mass. 221, 408 N.E.2d 857 (1980) (accepting dual capacity doctrine but holding that separate divisions in a company are insufficient to establish dual capacity); Latendresse v. Preskey, 290 N.W.2d 267 (N.D. 1980) (accepting doctrine but holding that it is inapplicable because product not sold to public). *Cf.* DePaolo v. Spaulding Fibre Co., 119 N.H. 89, 397 A.2d 1048 (1979) (employee could not recover from manufacturer when product was not sold to the public).

83. Cohn v. Spinks Indus., Inc., 602 S.W.2d 102 (Tex. Civ. App.—Dallas 1980, writ ref'd n.r.e.); *accord* Mott v. Mitsubishi Int'l Corp., 636 F.2d 1073 (5th Cir. 1981) (applying Texas law and following *Cohn*).

84. 602 S.W.2d at 102.

85. *Id.*

> our workers' compensation law appears to be unequivocal; this law represents the exclusive remedy an employee has against his employer unless other remedies are expressly provided. To adopt the dual capacity doctrine would do considerable violence to the statutory language. Further, while some authorities have termed the result we reach a simplistic response to a complex question, we do not believe that the creation of a new ground of recovery for employees covered by a workers' compensation law is a proper judicial function.[86]

The exclusivity of workers' compensation stands in stark contradiction to the dual capacity doctrine. The trade off of absolute liability for scheduled compensation benefits underlies the entire system of workers' compensation. Dual capacity was a conscious legislative decision to implement a compensation system between employers and injured employees.

6.05 Bystanders

Initially, an innocent bystander was not perceived as a party protected by strict tort liability law.[87] As a consequence, the applicability of strict tort liability to injured bystanders received limited consideration.[88] Though Section 402A adopts a neutral position on bystander recovery,[89] a majority of jurisdictions rather quickly extended the doctrine to bystanders.[90]

Perhaps one of the first cases to extend strict tort liability to bystanders is *Elmore v. American Motors Corp.*[91] Plaintiff was injured when his vehicle was struck by a Rambler station wagon. The station wagon began fishtailing when a defective drive shaft detached from the vehicle causing the operator to lose control. The manufacturer maintained that the injured bystander was not entitled to institute a strict tort liability action. Rejecting any effort to limit the applicability of the strict tort liability doctrine, the California Supreme court noted that:

---

86. *Id.* at 104.

87. Prosser, *The Assault Upon the Citadel*, 69 Yale L. J. 1099, 1142-43 (1960).

88. *See* Mitchell v. Miller, 26 Conn. Sup. 142, 214 A.2d 694, 698-99 (Super. Ct. 1965); Piercefield v. Remington Arms Co., 375 Mich. 85, 93, 133 N.W.2d 129, 132 (1965).

89. Restatement (Second) of Torts § 402A caveat 1 and comment o (1965).

90. Jentz & Collins, *Extension of Strict Liability to All Third Persons*, 12 Am. Bus. L. J. 231, 240-41 (1975); Noel, *Defective Products: Extension of Strict Liability to Bystanders*, 38 Tenn. L. Rev. 1,4-13 (1970).

91. 70 Cal. 2d 578, 451 P.2d 84, 75 Cal. Rptr. 652 (1969).

> If anything, bystanders should be entitled to greater protection than the consumer or user where injury to bystanders from the defect is reasonably foreseeable. Consumers and users, at least, have the opportunity to inspect for defects and to limit their purchases to articles manufactured by reputable manufacturers and sold by reputable retailers, whereas the bystander . . . is in greater need of protection from defective products which are dangerous, and if any distinction should be made between bystanders and users, it should be made, contrary to the position of defendants, to extend greater liability in favor of the bystanders.[92]

Within two years after adoption of strict tort liability in Texas, the Texas Supreme Court extended the application of Section 402A to bystanders. In *Darryl v. Ford Motor Co.*,[93] plaintiff was injured when his vehicle was struck from the rear by an allegedly defective Ford truck. In expanding the reach of Section 402A to include bystanders, the Texas Supreme Court noted:

> We hold that recovery under the strict liability doctrine is not limited to users and consumers . . . [t]here is no adequate rationale or theoretical explanation why non-users and non-consumers should be denied recovery against the manufacturer of a defective product. The reason for extending the strict liability doctrine to innocent bystanders is the desire to minimize risks of personal injury and/or property damage. A manufacturer who places in commerce a product rendered dangerous to life or limb by reason of some defect is strictly liable in tort to one who sustains injury because of the defective condition.[94]

The extension of recovery to bystanders is premised on the concept that while actual purchasers are protected even though they are afforded the opportunity to inspect the product and thereby protect themselves, bystanders are not afforded a similar opportunity to inspect the product. Consequently, bystanders occupy a more innocent status than do purchasers. Further, the courts emphasize that the socio-economic theory of risk distribution which undergirds strict tort liability should protect wholly innocent parties from the costs of injuries caused by defective

---

92. *Id.* at 586, 451 P.2d at 89, 75 Cal. Rptr. *Accord*, Osborne v. International Harvester, Inc., 688 P.2d 390 (Ore. 1984).
93. 440 S.W.2d 630 (Tex. 1969).
94. *Id.* at 633.

products.[95]

Whether an individual qualifies as an innocent bystander is dependent on the manufacturer's ability to reasonably foresee such a class or group of persons occupying a zone of danger in connection with the use and operation of the product.[96] For example, in *Winnett v. Winnett*[97] plaintiff, a four-year-old child, injured her hand on the open conveyor belt of a forage wagon operated by her grandfather. The court rejected characterizing the plaintiff as either a user or consumer of the product and, instead, considered her an unforeseeable bystander. Concluding that the doctrine of strict tort liability did not extend to this class of bystanders, the Illinois Supreme Court noted:

> In our judgment the liability of a manufacturer properly encompasses only those individuals to whom injury from a defective product may reasonably be foreseen and only those situations where the product is being used for the purpose for which it was intended or for which it is reasonably foreseeable that it may be used. Any other approach to the problem results in making the manufacturer and those in the chain of product distribution virtual insurers of the product.
>
> It cannot, in our judgment, fairly be said that a manufacturer should reasonably foresee that a four-year-old child will be permitted to approach an operating farm forage wagon or that the child will be permitted to place her fingers in or on the holes in its moving screen.[98]

The foreseeable bystander concept was considered in *Jackson v. Johns-Manville Sales Corp.*[99] A former shipyard worker initiated a strict liability action against asbestos manufacturers and sellers of asbestos products for injuries caused by the defendants' failure to warn plaintiff of the hazards of exposure to asbestos products. The manufacturers contended that strict liability in tort was inapplicable because the plantiff did not qualify as a "user or consumer" of their asbestos products. The court determined that the manufacturer owed a duty "to those persons whom it should

95. Refer to notes 90-92 *supra* and accompanying text.

96. Jackson v. Johns-Manville Sales Corp., 727 F.2d 506, 514 (5th Cir. 1984). Refer to notes 98-99 *infra* and accompanying text.

97. 57 Ill. 2d 7, 310 N.E.2d 1 (1974).

98. *Id.* at 11, 13, 310 N.E.2d at 4-5, (referring to *Suvada v. White Motor Co.*, 32 Ill. 2d 612, 210 N.E.2d 182 (1965).

99. 727 F.2d 506 (5th Cir. 1984).

reasonably foresee would likely use such products or who are likely to come into contact with the danger, if any, inherent in the use of its product or products."[100]

The extension of strict tort liability to innocent bystanders appears to be well established. It is evident, therefore, that the class of individuals reasonably expected to use a product or any individual who is foreseeably in the environment of the product's intended use is accorded the benefits of strict tort liability under Section 402A.[101]

6.06 Rescuers

Though characterized as a type of bystander, rescuers occupy a slightly altered status. In *Court v. Grzelinski*,[102] a fireman fighting an automobile fire was injured when the gas tank exploded. The fireman instituted a strict tort liability suit against the dealer and the manufacturer for defective design of the vehicle's gas tank. In recognizing the fireman's right to maintain a strict tort liability action, the court noted that: "to the extent a fireman is a person to whom injury from the product may reasonably be foreseen, he may recover in products liability, even though his injury was incurred while fighting a fire in the course of his employment."[103]

Fedorchick v. Massey Ferguson, Inc.[104] involved an action brought against the manufacturer of a crawler loader. The plaintiff, an employee of the lessee of the loader, sustained injuries when he attempted to prevent a fellow employee from being struck by the runaway loader. While attempting to disengage the loader's

---

100. *Id.* at 514.

101. The plaintiff in a strict liability case based upon a design defect must establish that a defect exists, that the defect makes the product unreasonably dangerous, and that the defect is a producing cause of the injury. *See* Restatement (Second) of Torts § 402A (1965); *see also* Carter v. Massey-Ferguson, Inc., 716 F.2d 344 (5th Cir. 1983) (plaintiff sued the manufacturer of a motorized log-moving device that backed into him); Mitchell v. Fruehauf Corp., 568 F.2d 1139 (5th Cir. 1978) (plaintiff injured in a collision with a defective meat truck); Lubbock Mfg. Co. v. Perez, 591 S.W.2d 907 (Tex. Civ. App.—Waco 1979, writ dism'd by agr.) (plaintiffs were bystanders when a LP gas trailer overturned, struck a concrete culvert, and exploded); Dover Corp. v. Perez, 587 S.W.2d 761 (Tex.Civ.App.—Corpus Christi 1979, writ ref'd n.r.e.) (plaintiff was a tenant in an apartment in which a defective heating unit had been installed); *See generally* Turner v. General Motors Corp., 584 S.W.2d 844 (Tex. 1979).

102. 72 Ill.2d 141, 379 N.E.2d 281 (1978).

103. 379 N.E.2d at 285.

104. 438 F. Supp. 60 (E.D. Pa. 1977).

control, the plaintiff was struck by the runaway loader. The court declared the employee was entitled to maintain a strict tort liability action against the loader manufacturer.[105] The manufacturer asserted that the plaintiff was not within the loader's "orbit of danger"; rather, the plaintiff "placed himself in the path of the runaway loader," thereby elminating his status as an "innocent bystander."[106] Rejecting the argument, the court noted that "as a matter of law [the] plaintiff was an innocent bystander."[107] The court seemingly ignored the issue of foreseeability in characterizing the plaintiff as an innocent bystander. Arguably, under the rescue doctrine, the plaintiff might foreseeably have been considered within the environment of the product's use.[108] More likely, the court deemed the policy of encouraging bystander assistance to be a predominant consideration.[109]

In *Guarino v. Mine Safety Appliance Co.*[110] plaintiffs asserted an action against the manufacturer of malfunctioning oxygen masks. The plaintiffs alleged that death and serious injuries were sustained by individuals who sought to rescue workers stricken by lethal sewer gas because their masks failed to supply oxygen. The court adopted the "danger invites rescue" doctrine[111] as the basis for imposing liability on the supplier of defective face masks. The rescue doctrine is a well recognized doctrine in negligence actions; however, convinced that the doctrine should apply irrespective of the type of action involved, the *Guarino* court stated: "[w]e do not believe that the theory of the action, whether it be negligence or breach of warranty is significant where the doctrine of 'danger invites rescue' applies . . . We conclude that a person who by his culpable act, whether it stems from negligence or breach of warranty, places another person in a position of imminent peril, may be held liable for any damages sustained by a rescuer in his attempt to aid the imperilled victim."[112]

---

105. *Id.* at 61.
106. *Id.* at 64.
107. *Id.*
108. *Id.*
109. *Id.* at 63.
110. 25 N.Y.2d 460, 255 N.E.2d 173, 306 N.Y.S.2d 942 (1969).
111. *Id.* at 464, 255 N.E.2d at 175, 306 N.Y.S.2d at 944. "The doctrine has been most frequently applied when a defendant through his negligence either injured or imperilled another and a third person was injured in attempting to rescue the person in jeopardy." *Id.*
112. *Id.* at 465-66, 255 N.E.2d at 175-76, 306 N.Y.S.2d at 944-46.

6.07 Plaintiffs Not Directly Injured By The Defective Product

The expansion of strict tort liability to innocent bystanders[113] and ultimate consumers and users,[114] based on foreseeability[115] has precipitated plaintiffs increasingly to utilize strict tort liability as a basis to recover for injuries not directly caused by the defective product. This category of prospective plaintiffs, as distinguished from the bystander category,[116] envisions the class of individuals who are not physically injured by the product but nevertheless suffer in some way because of a defective product.

In *Gnirk v. Ford Motor Co.*,[117] the mother of an infant automobile passenger instituted an action against the manufacturer seeking compensatory damages for emotional distress suffered while witnessing the death of her child. Characterizing the mother as a "user" of the automobile, rather than as a "bystander,"[118] the court concluded that: "[b]y virtue of her status as the user of the Ford car involved, at the time involved, Ford, under 402A, owed to plaintiff an independent legal duty not to harm her."[119] Relying on decisions that emotional injury is closely related to physical injury[120] the court determined that the plaintiff was authorized to assert a strict tort liability action against the manufacturer for emotional distress.[121] Significantly, the plaintiff was within the foreseeable environment of use of the vehicle.

In *Portee v. Jaffee*,[122] a mother was authorized to recover damages for mental and emotional distress sustained when she observed her seven-year-old son die when he became trapped in a defective elevator. Recovery was permitted notwithstanding the fact that the mother was not personally subjected to any risk of

---

113. Refer to notes 87-101 *supra* and accompanying text.

114. Refer to notes 44-69 *supra* and accompanying text.

115. Refer to notes 14-21 *supra* and accompanying text.

116. Refer to notes 87-101 *supra* and accompanying text.

117. 572 F. Supp. 1201 (D.S.D. 1983).

118. *Id.* at 1202.

119. *Id.* at 1203 (citing Shaffer v. Honeywell, Inc., 249 N.W.2d 251 (S.D. 1976)); Engberg v. Ford Motor Co., 87 S.D. 196, 205 N.W.2d 104 (1973).

120. 572 F. Supp. at 1204, citing one Texas case: Haught v. Maceluch, 681 F.2d 291, 299 n.9 (5th Cir. 1982) (applying Texas law; depression, nervousness, weight gain and nightmares are equivalent to physical injury).

121. *Id.* at 1205.

122. 84 N.J. 88, 417 A.2d 521 (1980) (negligence action).

physical harm.[123]

Spouses of injured parties represent yet another class of persons who may assert strict tort liability action against suppliers of defective products. In *Whittlesey v. Miller*,[124] the wife of the injured party initiated a negligence action to recover damages for loss of her husband's consortium. The court determined that "either spouse has a cause of action for loss of consortium that might arise as a result of any injury caused to the other spouse by a third party tortfeasor's negligence."[125] Though predicated on negligence, the *Whittlesey* decision may well be extended to include strict tort liability.

A plaintiff may also maintain an action against a manufacturer of a defective product if the defect caused injury to and consequently the wrongful death of a family member or spouse. Article 4671[126] provides a cause of action "[w]hen an injury causing the death of any person is caused by the wrongful act . . . of another. . . . [127] Article 4675[128] applies to the institution of the wrongful death action: "[a]ctions for damages arising from death shall be for the sole and exclusive benefit of and may be brought by the surviving husband, wife, children, and parents of the person whose death has been caused or by either of them for the benefit of all."[129]

Article 4675 also provides that the executor or administrator of the deceased may prosecute the action if none of the enumerated parties commence a suit in three calendar months.[130]

In *Dover Corp. v. Perez*[131] the decedent's wife recovered damages for the wrongful death of her husband caused by a defective wall heater which emitted an excessive amount of carbon monoxide. The court acknowledged a spouse's right to maintain a strict tort liability action as a beneficiary under the Wrongful Death

---

123. 417 A.2d at 526-28.

124. 572 S.W.2d 665 (Tex. 1978).

125. *Id.* at 668. *See also* DePaolo v. Spaulding Fibre Co., 119 N.H 89, 397 A.2d 1048, 1049 (1979) (wife can maintain action against husband's employer for loss of consortium).

126. TEX. REV. CIV. STAT. ANN. art. 4671 (Vernon 1979).

127. *Id.*

128. TEX. REV. CIV. STAT. ANN. art. 4675 (Vernon 1979).

129. *Id.*

130. *Id.*

131. 587 S.W.2d 761 (Tex. Civ. App.—Corpus Christi 1979, writ ref'd n.r.e.).

Act.[132]

A person injured by a defective product who dies prior to the institution of a strict tort liability action against the manufacturer of the defective product, or who dies prior to the adjudication of such suit, enables the decedent's heirs or beneficiaries to maintain an action for the benefit of the estate.[133] This legislative authorization provides:

> All causes of action upon which suit has been or may hereafter be brought for personal injuries . . . shall not abate by reason of the death of the [plaintiff], . . . but . . . all such causes of action shall survive to and in favor of the heirs and legal representatives and estate of such injured party . . . and may be instituted and prosecuted as if such person or persons against whom same accrued were alive.[134]

A cause of action under Article 5525 represents a "separate and distinct" cause of action from a wrongful death action.[135]

In *Mahan Volkswagen, Inc. v. Hall*[136] the plaintiff instituted a products liability action against the manufacturer, dealer, and distributer of an automobile to recover for fatal injuries sustained by the plaintiff's decedent when her car suddenly left the road and hit a utility pole. Because the decedent pursued a cause of action for damages prior to her death,[137] the cause of action survived to her beneficiaries under Article 5525.[138]

6.08 Conclusion

The courts are increasingly expanding the class of individuals authorized to maintain a strict tort liability claim. Prospective

---

132. *Id. See also* Howard v. General Cable Corp., 674 F.2d 351, 354 (5th Cir. 1982); Pearson v. Hevi-Duty Elec., 618 S.W.2d 784 (Tex. Civ. App.—Houston [1st Dist.] 1981, writ ref'd n.r.e.).

133. Tex. Rev. Civ. Stat. Ann. art. 5525 (Vernon 1958).

134. *Id.*

135. Theobold v. Pate, 542 S.W.2d 460, 465 (Tex. Civ. App.—Tyler 1976, writ dism'd) (plaintiff had capacity to sue under survival statute although they could not maintain wrongful death action).

136. 648 S.W.2d 324 (Tex. App—Houston [1st Dist.] 1982, no writ).

137. *Id.* at 332.

138. *Id.* at 333. *See also* Castleberry v. Goolsby Bldg. Corp., 617 S.W.2d 665, 666 (Tex. 1981); Mitchell v. Akers, 401 S.W.2d 907, 909 (Tex. Civ. App.—Dallas 1966, writ ref'd n.r.e.); Norman v. Valley Gin Co., 99 S.W.2d 1065, 1066-67 (Tex. Civ. App.—Beaumont 1936, writ ref'd).

plaintiffs now include, in addition to consumers and users, the class of individuals characterized as bystanders, rescuers, employees, passengers, purchasers, potential purchasers, and individuals not even directly injured by the defective product. The class of individuals authorized to maintain a strict tort liability action is limited primarily by the standard of reasonable foreseeability. If an individual is a reasonably foreseeable user of a product, or is an individual who may reasonably be foreseen to be in the environment of the product's use, Section 402A applies; otherwise, the individual is precluded from maintaining a strict tort liability action.

CHAPTER VII. DAMAGES*

7.00 GENERALLY

The *Restatement (Second) of Torts* imposes strict liability for "physical harm . . . caused to the ultimate user or consumer or to his property" by a defective product.[1] Though the nature of the recovery is clearly delineated in the *Restatement*, the outer parameter of recoverable damages is the subject of continuous controversy and legal refinement. The principal areas of controversy have focused upon recovery for enhanced injuries in a crashworthiness context, physical injury to bystanders, emotional distress sustained by bystanders and others witnessing product related accidents, and the applicability of punitive damages in strict tort liability cases. This chapter analyzes the current Texas view on the spectrum of damages recoverable under the doctrine of strict tort liability.

7.01 DAMAGES FOR PERSONAL INJURY

A. *Bodily Injury*

The courts adopted strict tort liability as a vehicle preferable

---

* Debbie Crupain coauthored this chapter.

1. RESTATEMENT (SECOND) OF TORTS 402A(1) (1966).

to the unwieldly doctrine of implied warranty sounding in tort which had been used in cases of product related injuries. The concepts of privity and disclaimer, applicable to warranty actions in the commercial sphere, were simply unworkable when applied to actions seeking damages for injuries caused by defective products; more often than not, the injured person was a remote party, not in privity with the seller or manufacturer, and neither a user nor consumer of the defective product.

Strict tort liability was initially formulated to impose liability upon a non-negligent manufacturer of contaminated food. In *Jacob E. Decker & Sons v. Capps*,[2] the Texas Supreme Court imposed a form of strict liability on a food manufacturer for a consumer's injuries attributable to adulterated meat. Though the court characterized the action as a breach of implied warranty, the court explained that it "[was] not the more modern contractual warranty, but . . . an obligation imposed by law . . . [where liability was] not dependent upon any provision of the contract."[3] The court emphasized that this cause of action required neither privity nor proof of negligence.[4] Despite the "implied warranty" label, the court applied a form of strict liability against the manufacturer based on considerations of public policy. The action was characterized as "ex delicto" as opposed to "ex contractu" in nature.

In *McKisson v. Sales Affiliates, Inc.*,[5] the Texas Supreme Court adopted the concept of strict tort liability articulated initially in Section 402A of the *Restatement (Second) of Torts* to encompass non-foodstuffs. Plaintiff sustained chemical burns to her face and scalp as a result of a defective permanent wave solution applied to her hair. In applying *Restatement* Section 402A, the court observed:

> We are further of the opinion that as a logical proposition, the rule stated in *Decker* should be held applicable to defective products which cause physical harm to persons. As pointed out by the concurring justice in the Court of Civil Appeals, no sound distinc-

---

2. 139 Tex. 609, 164 S.W.2d 828 (1942).
3. *Id.* at 616, 164 S.W.2d at 831-32.
4. *Id.* at 620-21, 164 S.W.2d at 833.
5. 416 S.W.2d 787 (Tex. 1967). The supreme court also decided the case of *Shamrock Fuel & Oil Sales Co. v. Tunks*, which recognized a strict tort liability action against a distributor and owner of a gas station for burns sustained as the result of adulterated kerosene that ignited. 416 S.W.2d 779 (Tex. 1967).

tion can be drawn between the use of an eye-wash solution that impairs or destroys vision and a foodstuff which causes illness.[6]

This landmark decision marked the formal judicial adoption of the doctrine of strict tort liability which had been pioneered in the seminal case of *Greenman v. Yuba Power Products, Inc.*.[7] After *Greenman*, the authors of the *Restatement* incorporated this innovative concept into the now well established Section 402A of the *Restatement (Second) of Torts.*

Damages recoverable for injuries caused by a defective product include the usual elements of past and future physical pain and mental anguish, past and future medical expenses, past loss of earnings, impairment of future earning capacity, disfigurement, and past and future physical impairment.[8] Disfigurement and physical impairment are generally considered separate elements of recovery.[9] Physical impairment and loss of future earning capacity, however, may constitute a double recovery under certain circumstances.[10] When physical impairment and loss of earning capacity create a double recovery an appropriate cautionary instruction alleviates the duplication.[11]

---

6. 416 S.W.2d at 789.

7. 59 Cal. 2d 57, 377 P.2d 897, 27 Cal. Rptr. 697 (1963). The California Supreme Court sanctioned the imposition of a form of strict liability for personal injuries caused by a defective lathe.

8. *See* McKisson v. Sales Affiliates, Inc., 416 S.W.2d 787 (Tex. 1967); Rourke v. Garza, 530 S.W.2d 794 (Tex. 1975) (defective scaffolding collapsed and injured an employee-user); Rawlings Sporting Goods Co., Inc. v. Daniels, 619 S.W.2d 435 (Tex. Civ. App.—Waco 1981, writ ref'd n.r.e.) (defective football helmet resulted in head injury); Caterpillar Tractor Co. v. Gonzales, 599 S.W.2d 633 (Tex. Civ. App.—El Paso 1980, writ ref'd n.r.e.) (defective caterpillar tractor step); Bell Helicopter v. Bradshaw, 594 S.W.2d 519 (Tex. Civ. App.—Corpus Christi 1979, writ ref'd n.r.e.) (defective helicopter rotor blades caused a crash); Lubbock Mfg. Co. v. Perez, 591 S.W.2d 907 (Tex. Civ. App.—Waco 1979, no writ) (defective design of liquefied petroleum gas transport vehicle caused an overturn); Ethicon Inc. v. Parten, 520 S.W.2d 527 (Tex. Civ. App.—Houston [14th Dist.] 1975, no writ) (surgical needle fractured in patient's body).

9. Though separate elements, an instruction is appropriate to insure that a double recovery does not occur. *See* Mikell v. La Beth, 344 S.W.2d 702, 708 (Tex. Civ. App.—Houston 1961, writ ref'd n.r.e.); French v. Grigsby, 567 S.W.2d 604, 608 (Tex. Civ. App.—Beaumont), *writ ref'd*, 571 S.W.2d 867 (Tex. 1978).

10. *See, e.g.*, Charles T. Picton Lumber Co. v. Redden, 452 S.W.2d 713 (Tex. Civ. App.—Corpus Christi 1970, writ ref'd n.r.e.); Green v. Baldree, 497 S.W.2d 342 (Tex. Civ. App.—Houston [14th Dist.] 1973, no writ). *Contra* Browning v. Paiz, 586 S.W.2d 670 (Tex. Civ. App.—Corpus Christi 1979, writ ref'd n.r.e.).

11. *See, e.g.*, Mikell v. La Beth, 344 S.W.2d 702 (Tex. Civ. App.—Houston 1961, writ ref'd n.r.e.); City of Houston v. Riggins, 568 S.W.2d 188 (Tex. Civ. App.—Tyler 1978, writ

B. *Loss of Consortium*

Consortium is defined as "the mutual right of the husband and wife to that affection, solace, comfort, companionship, society, assistance, and sexual relations necessary to a successful marriage."[12] Loss of consortium differs from "loss of services". Loss of services represents an element of damages recoverable by the community due to the inability of the injured spouse to perform household and domestic duties.[13] Historically, loss of consortium was recoverable by husbands due to injuries negligently inflicted upon their wives. Wives, on the other hand, were generally barred from recovery.[14] Finally, in 1950, the U.S. Court of Appeals for the District of Columbia acknowledged a wife's separate cause of action for loss of consortium.[15] The court concluded that the wrongs committed against the wife by her husband's injury were equivalent to those of the husband resulting from the wife's injury and thus, the remedy should likewise extend to the wife.[16] The Texas Supreme Court, in 1978, recognized for the first time that either spouse is entitled to maintain a separate cause of action for loss of consortium against a negligent tortfeasor.[17]

In *Whittlesey v. Miller*,[18] plaintiff instituted suit to recover for loss of consortium after her husband settled with the negligent tortfeasor for injuries he sustained in an automobile accident.[19] After reviewing an earlier decision rejecting a cause of action for the wife's loss of consortium, the court acknowledged the need for change.[20] The court observed that "Providing either spouse with a

---

ref'd n.r.e.).

12. Whittlesey v. Miller, 572 S.W.2d 665, 666 (Tex. 1978).

13. *Id.* at 666 n.2. *See also* El Paso City Lines Inc. v. Dudney, 280 S.W.2d 303, 306 (Tex. Civ. App.—El Paso 1955, writ ref'd n.r.e.).

14. *See, e.g.*, Hitaffer v. Argonne Co., 183 F.2d 811, 812-16 (D.C. Cir.), *cert. denied*, 340 U.S. 852 (1950). The court enumerated several reasons which had traditionally been used to deny a wife's recovery: (1) a wife possessed no right to a husband's services and thus was denied a cause of action when he was injured; (2) loss of consortium constituted a double recovery to the wife since the husband recovered for his injuries; (3) the wife's injuries were too remote to be compensated; and (4) the common law simply did not recognize this right in a wife.

15. *Id.*

16. *Id.* at 816.

17. Whittlesey v. Miller, 572 S.W.2d 665 (Tex. 1978).

18. 572 S.W.2d 665 (Tex. 1978).

19. *Id.* at 665-66.

20. *Id.* at 668. The court disapproved of *Garrett v. Reno Oil Co.*, 271 S.W.2d 764 (Tex.

cause of action for loss of consortium would allow us to keep pace with modern society by recognizing that the emotional interests of the marriage relationship are. . .worthy of protection from negligent invasion . . ."[21] Despite the prior settlement by the husband, the wife was entitled to recover damages based on this separate cause of action.[22]

Loss of consortium applies whether the incident causes injury or death to a spouse. For example, in *Missouri Pacific Railroad v. Dawson*,[23] plaintiff instituted suit under both the Texas Wrongful Death Statute and the Texas Survival Statute. In authorizing a separate recovery for loss of consortium under the Wrongful Death Act, the court recognized the incongruity of permitting recovery if one spouse suffers a total paralysis and lives, but denying recovery if death occurs.[24] The court pointedly noted that, "We can find no logic in a rule of law which terminates a spouse's independent cause of action simply because a tortious act was committed with deadly efficiency."[25] While *Whittlesey* recognizes the wife's right to recover damages for loss of consortium, a spouse is foreclosed from recovering damages for loss of consortium if the injured party possesses no independent cause of action for his injuries.[26] In *Copelin*,[27] the husband's injuries sustained in the course and scope of his employment were covered by worker's compensation, thereby effectively precluding suit for common law negligence against the employer. The supreme court concluded that since the wife's cause of action was derivative in nature, a bar to the husband's cause of action likewise barred the spouse's claim for loss of consortium.[28]

A cause of action for loss of consortium currently is available in negligence actions. Whether recovery of damages for loss of consortium is authorized in a strict tort liability action is not totally

---

Civ. App.—Fort Worth 1954, writ ref'd n.r.e.).

21. *Id.*

22. *Id.* at 669.

23. 662 S.W.2d 740 (Tex. App.—Corpus Christi 1983, writ ref'd n.r.e.).

24. *Id.* at 742. *See also* Stanford v. McLean Trucking Co., 506 F. Supp. 1252, 1258 (E.D. Tex. 1981) ("The time has come . . . for there to be recovery in Texas for damages for loss of love and affection and for loss of consortium in a wrongful death case."); Air Florida Inc. v. Zondler, 683 S.W.2d 769 (Tex. App.—Dallas 1984, no writ).

25. 662 S.W.2d at 742.

26. Reed Tool Co. v. Copelin, 610 S.W.2d 736 (Tex. 1980).

27. *Id.*

28. *Id.* at 739. The wife could recover damages for loss of consortium if the husband's injuries were intentionally inflicted.

clear at this time. The basis for recovery of damages for loss of consortium is the actor's negligent or intentional acts which cause the spouse's injury. While both negligence and strict tort liability are "ex delicto" in nature, they involve two separate and wholly independent theories of recovery.[29] Negligence evaluates the *conduct* of the wrongdoer while strict liability focuses solely upon the *condition* of the product and not the supplier's conduct.[30] Strict tort liability is predicated on the socioeconomic theorem of risk distribution for product related accidents. Recovery for loss of consortium based on strict tort liability would appear to require a judicial extension of the socioeconomic underpinnings of this doctrine. Nevertheless, it seems rather clear that loss of consortium will be embraced within the elements of demages recoverable under Section 402A.

C. *Wrongful Death*

Under the common law, no cause of action existed for wrongful death because all causes of action were deemed extinguished upon the death of the injured party.[31] In 1846, the English Parliament enacted Lord Campbell's Act which altered the existing common law by providing for recovery of damages for wrongful death.[32] Since Texas adopted the common law prior to enactment of Lord Campbell's Act, a cause of action for wrongful death was not recognized as part of English common law as adopted in Texas. In 1860, Texas enacted its first wrongful death statute when the legislature enacted the progenitor of current Article 4671.[33] This statue has been periodically revised by amendments and is now embodied in Article 4671. The Wrongful Death Act authorizes recovery of damages sustained by the surviving spouse, children or parents for death of another.[34] Recovery of damages is predicated

---

29. Gonzales v. Caterpillar Tractor Co., 571 S.W.2d 867, 871 (Tex. 1978); Rourke v. Garza, 530 S.W.2d 794, 800 (Tex. 1975).

30. 571 S.W.2d at 871.

31. *See* Marmon v. Mustang Aviation, Inc., 430 S.W.2d 182, 186 n.4 (Tex. 1968).

32. 9 & 10 Vict. Ch. 93 (1846).

33. TEX. REV. CIV. STAT. ANN. art. 4671-78 (Vernon 1952). This act was originally enacted as Acts 1860, 8th Leg. Ch. 35, 4 H. GAMMELL, LAWS OF TEXAS 1394 (1898).

34. TEX. REV. CIV. STAT. ANN. art. 4671 (Vernon 1952). Under the Survival Statute, Tex. Rev. Civ. Stat. Ann. art. 5525 (Vernon 1958), a decedent's cause of action obtained prior to his death passes to his heirs, legal representatives or estate after his death. *See* Tarrant County Hosp. Dist. v. Jones, 664 S.W.2d 191 (Tex. App.—Fort Worth 1984, no

on the wrongful death "caused by the wrongful act, neglect, carelessness, unskillfulness or default of another."[35] Strict tort liability under Section 402A of the *Restatement* is not premised upon an individual's act, neglect, carelessness, unskillfulness or default; rather, it is solely predicated upon a product's defective condition.[36] Notwithstanding the literal language of the statute, the Wrongful Death Act has been extended to strict tort liability actions in Texas.[37]

The application of the wrongful death action to a strict tort liability action was initially confronted in *General Motors Corp. v. Herbert*.[38] The deceased was fatally injured in an automobile accident allegedly caused by a defective steering mechanism. In extending the wrongful death remedy to strict tort liability actions, the court rationalized the injustice of permitting only nonfatal accidents to form the basis of recovery under strict tort liability.[39] The court concluded that the "plaintiff is permitted to assert any basis for recovery that the decedent could have asserted if he were alive."[40] A plethora of decisions have applied the Wrongful Death Act to strict tort liability actions without further discussion or analysis of the contradiction between the underlying basis of strict tort liability and the literal terminology of the statute which focuses solely on specified wrongful conduct of a tortfeasor.[41]

---

writ).

35. TEX. REV. CIV. STAT. ANN. art. 4671 (Vernon Supp. 1985). The Wrongful Death Statute provides in part: "When an injury causing the death of any person, occurring either within or without this state, is caused by the wrongful act, neglect, carelessness, unskillfulness, or default of another person . . . such persons . . . shall be liable in damages for the injuries causing such death."

36. Gonzales v. Caterpillar Tractor Co., 571 S.W.2d 867 (Tex. 1978); Rourke v. Garza, 530 S.W.2d 794 (Tex. 1975).

37. General Motors Corp. v. Herbert, 501 S.W.2d 950 (Tex. Civ. App.—Houston [1st Dist.] 1973, writ ref'd n.r.e.).

38. *Id.*

39. *Id.* at 959.

40. *Id.* (citing Vasallo v. Nederl-Amerik Stoomv Maats Holland, 162 Tex. 52, 56, 344 S.W.2d 421, 423 (1961)).

41. *See* Acord v. General Motors Corp., 669 S.W.2d 111 (Tex. 1984) (fatal multicar accident); Duncan v. Cessna Aircraft Co., 665 S.W.2d 414 (Tex. 1984) (fatal aircraft crash); Smithson v. Cessna Aircraft Co., 665 S.W.2d 439 (Tex. 1984) (fatal aircraft crash); Boatland of Houston, Inc. v. Bailey, 609 S.W.2d 743 (Tex. 1980) (fatal bass boat accident); General Motors Corp. v. Grizzle, 642 S.W.2d 837 (Tex. App.—Waco 1982, writ dism'd) (fatal vehicle crash); Dover Corp. v. Perez, 587 S.W.2d 761 (Tex. Civ. App.—Corpus Christi 1979, writ ref'd n.r.e.) (fatal heating ventilator accident); Lubbock Mfg. Co. v. Perez, 591 S.W.2d 907 (Tex. Civ. App.—Waco 1979, no writ) (fatal accident involving an overturned liquefied pe-

Commentators have observed that the literal provisions of the Wrongful Death Statute simply do not justify a cause of action predicated on strict tort liability.[42] Most Wrongful Death Acts specifically authorize recovery for *conduct* that is deemed wrongful, negligent, careless or unskillful. Since strict tort liability eschews conduct and focuses solely on the product's condition, this cause of action is not contemplated by the literal language of the Act.[43] However, Texas courts have and undoubtedly will continue to authorize recoveries under the Wrongful Death Statute without further addressing or acknowledging this contradiction.[44]

For more than a hundred years, Article 4671 was judicially interpreted as limiting the measure of damages to pecuniary loss sustained by the designated beneficiaries.[45] As recently as 1980, the Texas Supreme Court reaffirmed and applied the literal provisions of Article 4671 in a case involving the death of a minor.[46] Under the well established interpretation of pecuniary loss, a surviving parent was entitled to recover as actual damages for the child's death the pecuniary value of the child's services until majority, less the costs and expenses of the child's care, support, and maintenance. In addition, the parent was entitled to recover such amounts as could reasonably be expected after the child reached majority.[47] In 1983, the Texas Supreme Court in *Sanchez v. Schin-*

---

troleum gas truck); Bell Aerospace Corp. v. Anderson, 478 S.W.2d 191 (Tex. Civ. App.—El Paso 1972, writ ref'd n.r.e.) (fatal helicopter crash); Hartzell Propeller Co. v. Alexander, 485 S.W.2d 943 (Tex. Civ. App.—Waco 1972, writ ref'd n.r.e.) (fatal aircraft crash).

42. *See* Note, *Wrongful Death Action May Not Be Maintained Under Strict Liability Statute*, 29 MERCER L. REV. 649 (1978). *Cf.* Higginbotham v. Ford Motor Co., 540 F.2d 762, 768 (5th Cir. 1976) (Georgia Wrongful Death Statute possesses more restrictions than the provisions in the statutes of some states, requiring a criminal or negligent act).

43. *See, e.g.*, General Motors v. Simmons, 558 S.W.2d 855 (Tex. 1977) in which the Texas Supreme Court declared that Article 2212a governing comparative negligence does not encompass strict tort liability since negligence involves a tortfeasor's conduct and is not the equivalent of strict tort liability. The same literal interpretation was reaffirmed by the Texas Supreme Court in *Duncan v. Cessna Aircraft Co.*, 665 S.W.2d 414 (Tex. 1984), yet, Article 4671 specifically refers to the conduct of the actor as the basis of recovery.

44. Refer to note 41 *supra* and accompanying text.

45. *See, e.g.*, St. Louis Southwestern Ry. v. Shiflett, 98 Tex. 102, 81 S.W. 524 (1904); Taylor, B & H Ry. v. Warner, 84 Tex. 122, 19 S.W. 449 (1892); Houston City St. Ry. v. Sciacca, 80 Tex. 350, 16 S.W. 31 (Tex. 1891).

46. Bedgood v. Madalin, 600 S.W.2d 773, 775 (Tex. 1980).

47. *Id. See also* Houston City St. Ry. v. Sciacca, 80 Tex. 350, 16 S.W. 31 (1891); Galveston, H. & N. Ry. v. Olds, 112 S.W. 787 (Tex. Civ. App.—1908, no writ). Under this rule the jury could find that the cost of support and maintenance exceeded the value of the child's services and contributions and could return a verdict of no damages. *See* Rishworth

dler[48] overruled numerous of its prior decisions that limited damages under Article 4671 to the pecuniary loss sustained by the statutory beneficiaries.

In *Sanchez v. Schindler*,[49] plaintiff's son was severely injured in a motorcycle - pick-up truck collision and died several hours later. Despite a finding of the absence of any pecuniary loss, the jury awarded $102,500 for the mental anguish suffered by the parents.[50] The trial court disregarded the jury's award on the basis that only pecuniary losses were recoverable under the Wrongful Death Act.[51] The Texas Supreme Court reversed the judgment and judicially reinterpreted Article 4671 to authorize the recovery of non-pecuniary damages. The court declared:

> In the past, a surviving parent's damages in an action for the death of a child under the Texas Wrongful Death Act have been limited to the pecuniary value of the child's services and financial contributions, minus the cost of his care, support and education. The Texas Statute does not expressly limit recovery to pecuniary loss . . . Article 4677 provides that [t]he jury may give such damages as they may think proportionate to the injury resulting from such death . . . . [The] parent's recovery under the Wrongful Death Statute includes the mental anguish suffered as a result of the child's wrongful death.[52]

The Supreme Court therefore rejected the pecuniary loss limitation and declared that a statutory beneficiary was authorized to recover damages for mental anguish resulting from the death of a child.[53] The decision indirectly suggested that the surviving parents likewise would be entitled to recover damages for loss of society and companionship.[54]

In *Madisonville Independent School District v. Kyle*,[55] the

---

v. Moss, 191 S.W. 843, 852 (Tex. Civ. App.—San Antonio 1916), *aff'd*, 222 S.W. 225 (Tex. Comm'n App. 1920, holding approved).

48. 651 S.W.2d 249 (Tex. 1983).

49. 626 S.W.2d 871 (Tex. Civ. App.—Corpus Christi 1981), *rev'd in part on other grounds*, 651 S.W.2d 249 (Tex. 1983) (6-3 opinion).

50. 651 S.W.2d at 250.

51. *Id.* at 251.

52. *Id.* at 251-53.

53. *Id. See* Stanford v. McLean Trucking Co., 506 F. Supp. 1252 (E.D. Tex. 1981)(predicting eventual change by the Texas Supreme Court); Bedgood v. Madalin, 600 S.W.2d 773 (Tex. 1980) (concurring opinion).

54. 651 S.W.2d at 253.

55. 658 S.W.2d 149, 150 (Tex. 1983) (Parents "may recover for loss of companionship

Supreme Court, without discussion, ostensibly approved recovery for both loss of companionship and society under the Wrongful Death Act. The pecuniary loss authorized under Article 4671 apparently now includes damages for both mental anguish as well as the loss of companionship and society caused by the destruction of the parent-child relationship.[56] The issue of duplicative recovery was directly addressed in *Gulf States Utilities Co. v. Reed.*[57] Plaintiff, the mother of a deceased minor son, instituted suit under the Wrongful Death Act. Plaintiff's son was electrocuted when he crawled underneath a building to retrieve an errant frisbee. Defendant contended that recovery for loss of society and mental anguish constituted a double recovery for identical elements of damage.[58] The appellate court affirmed recovery of damages for both elements stating, "[W]e feel. . .it clear that recovery would be allowed under the wrongful death statute for *both* mental anguish and loss of companionship and society."[59] In a forceful dissent, Chief Justice Brown asserted: " 'Mental anguish' and 'loss of society' constitute *emotional distress* which should constitute one element of damages in a wrongful death case . . . [These] elements of damage . . . should not be separately submitted so as to invite, if not compel, a double recovery."[60] Recent decisions also recognize the right of parents to recover damages for both mental anguish and loss of society for the death of adult children.[61] Similarly adult children may recover these same elements for the wrongful death of their parents.[62]

---

and society and mental anguish.").

56. Viewing *Sanchez v. Schindler*, 651 S.W.2d 249 (Tex. 1983), *Bedgood v. Madalin*, 600 S.W.2d 773 (Tex. 1980) (concurring opinion), and *Madisonville I.S.D. v. Kyle*, 658 S.W.2d 149 (Tex. 1983) as a triumvirate of landmark decisions reinterpreting the Wrongful Death Act, it appears that both mental anguish and loss of companionship constitute separate and independent elements of recovery.

57. 659 S.W.2d 849 (Tex. App.—Houston [14th Dist.] 1983, writ ref'd n.r.e.).

58. *Id.* at 853.

59. *Id.* (emphasis added). This interpretation is followed in *Williams v. Steves Inds. Inc.*, 678 S.W.2d 205 (Tex. App.—Austin 1984, no writ), approving a mother's recovery of $87,500 for loss of companionship and $150,000 for mental anguish because of the death of her child in a rear end auto-truck collision.

60. *Id.* at 856. (Brown, C.J., dissenting)(emphasis in original).

61. Air Florida Inc. v. Zondler, 683 S.W.2d 769, 772 (Tex. App.—Dallas 1984, n.w.h.).

62. Cavnar v. Quality Control Parking, Inc., 678 S.W.2d 548 (Tex. App.—Houston [1st Dist.] 1984), *aff'd in part, rev'd in part,* 28 Tex. Sup. Ct. J. 468 (June 8, 1985); Air Florida Inc. v. Zondler, 683 S.W.2d 769 (Tex. App.—Dallas 1984, n.w.h.); Malone & Hyde Inc. v. Hobrecht, 685 S.W.2d 739 (Tex. App.—San Antonio 1985, n.w.h.).

In *Cavnar*,[63] decedent's adult children were allowed to recover for loss of companionship and mental anguish resulting from the death of their mother. Most significantly, rejecting earlier decisions, the court also awarded prejudgment interest. The rationale announced by the court was that failure to include prejudgment interest would frustrate the primary objective of compensating injured plaintiffs.[64] The court reasoned that the availability of such interest recoveries would expedite both settlements and trials.[65] The court adopted the following method for determining the amount of prejudgment interest: (1) in wrongful death and non-death personal injury cases, interest shall begin to accrue on both pecuniary and non-pecuniary damages from a date six months after the occurrence of the incident giving rise to the cause of action; (2) in survival actions, decedent's estate is entitled to prejudgment interest either from the date of death or six months after the injury-causing incident occurred, whichever yields the larger interest award.[66] Prejudgment interest, however, will not be awarded on future damages nor on punitive damages.[67]

More than a mere familial relationship, however, must exist to justify recovery.[68] The courts are less than precise regarding the

---

63. 28 Tex. Sup. Ct. J. 468 (June 8, 1985).

64. *Id.* The court stressed that adequate compensation includes the ability to invest and earn interest on the amount of damages between the time of occurrence and the time of judgment.

65. *Id.* Significantly, there exists no incentive for the plaintiff to accept a settlement. Unless a countervailing penalty is imposed on the plaintiff for failure to accept a good faith reasonable settlement, the court's rationale is meaningless judicial rubric.

66. *Id.* The time periods set for accrual of prejudment interest may prove to be unjustly harsh on defendants. For instance, in an asbestos case, the occurrence of the incident giving rise to the cause of action may translate into the period when plaintiff was first exposed. Six months after this exposure prejudgment interest accrues even though it may be thirty years before any injury manifests. The statute of limitations only commences when the plaintiff knows or should have known, i.e., the disease becomes apparent. Thus, plaintiff is allowed to wait and file suit when injuries appear and, in the meantime, is accruing interest for thirty years since six months after the exposure or other occurrence giving rise to the present cause of action. The same problem exists when a young child is injured but a lawsuit is not filed until two years after the child reaches majority.

67. A submission of both past and future pain and suffering in one special issue will necessarily void any hopes at prejudgment interest since any jury award on the dual issue will be incapable of apportionment between past damages, which permit prejudgment interest, and future damages which deny prejudgment interest recoveries.

68. *See* Moore v. Lillebo, 674 S.W.2d 474 (Tex. App.—El Paso 1984, no writ). *See, e.g.*, Cantu v. Southern Pac. Ry., 166 S.W.2d 963 (Tex. Civ. App.—Amarillo 1942, writ ref'd) (natural mother denied recovery where care, custody, and responsibility of child relinquished to others). But, every class of beneficiary under the Wrongful Death Action may

nature of proof essential to recover for both mental anguish and loss of society. It has been suggested that five elements constitute the essential basis to recover for loss of society: (1) the existence of a familial relationship; (2) a continuous living together; (3) the fact that the deceased was not absent from the home for extended periods of time; (4) a family relationship that was harmonious; and (5) the existence of common interests.[69] Because loss of society and mental anguish are viewed as independent elements of recoverable damages, separate proof for each element appears necessary.[70]

D. *Second Impact - Crashworthiness*

A unique aspect of damages involves cases in which the product neither causes nor contributes to cause the accident or mishap, but rather, an alleged defective design of the product increases or enhances the injury after the initial accident occurs. These cases are generally identified as "second impact" or "crashworthiness" cases. As a general rule, an injured party is entitled to maintain a strict tort liability action to recover damages that are attributable to or enhanced by a defective design after the accident-producing event has occurred.[71] Two major problems arise, however: identification of the portion of the injury attributable to the second impact and determination of the party possessing the burden of proof to apportion the injury.

Apportionment of injuries attributable to the second impact requires, essentially, a divisible injury. A divisible injury is one that is subject to reasonable apportionment between two or more separate events. Crashworthiness cases contemplate recovery only for the injuries produced as a result of a defective design configur-

---

recover damages for mental anguish. Missouri Pacific Railroad Co. v. Vlach, 687 S.W.2d 414 (Tex. App.—Houston [14th Dist.] 1985, n.w.h.).

69. 674 S.W.2d at 477. *See also* 4 P.O.F. 147 (1960) which lists elements that establish loss of comfort, society, protection, and companionship. Other jurisdictions utilize these and other factors in awarding damages for loss of companionship and society. *See* Jones v. Carvell, 641 P.2d 105 (Utah 1982) (kindly demeanor between family members); Curry v. Fruin-Colnon Contracting Co., 202 So. 2d 345 (La. Ct. App. 1967) (degree of love and affection and closeness of ties considered).

70. 674 S.W.2d at 477.

71. *See, e.g.*, Shipp v. General Motors Corp., 750 F.2d 418 (5th Cir. 1985); Acord v. General Motors Corp., 669 S.W.2d 111 (Tex. 1984); Duncan v. Cessna Aircraft Co., 665 S.W.2d 414 (Tex. 1984); Turner v. General Motors Corp., 584 S.W.2d 844 (Tex. 1979).

ation of a vehicle arising after the initial accident has occurred.[72]

Apportionment in a crashworthiness context is easily accomplished when an injury is divisible in nature. In *Turner v. General Motors Corp.*,[73] plaintiff sustained a severe neck injury rendering him a quadriplegic when a 1969 Chevrolet he was driving overturned as he swerved into a ditch to avoid colliding with another vehicle. When the vehicle overturned, the roof above the driver's compartment collapsed and deformed inward. The plaintiff alleged that the roof was defectively designed and unreasonably dangerous in overturn accidents. The court extended the doctrine of strict tort liability to crashworthiness cases in which the plaintiff sustains injuries after the original accident has occurred.[74]

The issue of apportionment assumes significant proportions in successive traumatic events.[75] Jurisdictions are divided on whether the plaintiff or defendant is obligated to apportion injuries in a crashworthiness case. In the landmark case of *Huddell v. Levin*,[76] the court declared that the plaintiff was obligated to sustain the burden of apportionment.[77] The deceased was fatally injured when his vehicle was struck from the rear. As a result of the impact, the deceased was thrown backward, striking his head against the seat headrest. Decedent subsequently died as a result of a fractured skull. The jury concluded that his death was proximately caused by a defectively designed headrest.[78] Reversing the trial court's judgment for the plaintiff, the Third Circuit observed that a plaintiff must satisfy three critical elements of proof: (1) that a safer alternative design exists that is practicable under the circumstances; (2) that no injury or fewer injuries would have resulted

---

72. Liability only for injuries received over and above those produced by the original accident represent the quintessence of the crashworthiness doctrine. *See, e.g.*, Larsen v. General Motors Corp., 391 F.2d 495 (8th Cir. 1968); Huddell v. Levin, 537 F.2d 726 (3d Cir. 1976); Caiazzo v. Volkswagenwerk A.G., 647 F.2d 241 (2d Cir. 1981).

73. 584 S.W.2d 844 (Tex. 1979). *See also* General Motors Corp. v. Simmons, 558 S.W.2d 855 (Tex. 1977), in which plaintiff's injuries resulted solely from an allegedly defective window glass that exploded into slivers when the automobile was hit, causing permanent eye injury.

74. 584 S.W.2d at 848.

75. *See generally* Sales, *Limitations on Recovery of Damages in Personal Injury Actions*, 18 S. TEX. L.J. 217, 256-65 (1977) (discussing the distinctions between divisible and indivisible injuries in analyzing crashworthiness cases).

76. 537 F.2d 726 (3d Cir. 1976).

77. *Id.* at 740.

78. *Id.* at 731.

had the alternative safer design been utilized; and (3) that some method exists to establish the extent to which the injuries were enhanced by the defective design over and above the injuries sustained in the original accident.[79] Thus, before a duty to design a crashworthy vehicle is imposed upon a defendant, the plaintiff must establish that *but for* a defective design, the injury received in the initial accident would have been identifiably less or nonexistent.[80] The failure of the plaintiff to establish the specific injury attributable to the alleged defective design is fatal.[81]

Other jurisdictions express a reluctance to impose upon the plaintiff the difficult, if not insurmountable burden of proving that portion of the injury enhanced by the defective product in cases where the nature of the accident or injury makes apportionment difficult.[82] In *Mitchell v. Volkswagenwerk A.G.*,[83] the Eighth Circuit specifically rejected the rule enunciated in *Huddell* — that the plaintiff is required to apportion the injuries enhanced by the second collision. Instead, the Eighth Circuit fashioned the principle that the plaintiff need only prove that a defective design constitutes a "*substantial factor* in producing damages over and above those which were *probably caused* [by] the original impact . . ."[84] If the defective vehicle is determined to be a substantial producing cause and the injury is essentially indivisible, then the manufacturer is deemed a joint tortfeasor.[85] Under this criteria, joint and several liability is imposed on the manufacturer notwithstanding that the alleged defective design configuration neither caused nor contributed to cause the original accident. The plaintiff's burden of

---

79. *Id.* at 737-38.

80. *Accord.* Curtis v. General Motors Corp., 649 F.2d 808 (10th Cir. 1981); Caiazzo v. Volkswagenwerk, A.G., 647 F.2d 241 (2d Cir. 1981); Jeng v. Witters, 452 F. Supp. 1349, 1360 (N.D. Pa. 1978), *aff'd*, 591 F.2d 1335 (3d Cir. 1979); Fox v. Ford Motor Co., 575 F.2d 774 (10th Cir. 1978); Knippen v. Ford Motor Co., 546 F.2d 993 (D.C. Cir. 1976). These cases adopt the rule that the manufacturer's liability is limited to injuries caused by the defect, if determinable, and that the manufacturer is not jointly liable.

81. Refer to Sales, note 75 *supra*.

82. *See* Jeng v. Witters, 452 F. Supp. 1349, 1360 (M.D. Pa. 1978), *aff'd*, 591 F.2d 1335 (3d Cir. 1979). *See also* Caiazzo v. Volkswagenwerk, A.G., 647 F.2d 241, 251 (2d Cir. 1981) ("We realize that a plaintiff's burden of offering evidence. . .will be heavy in some instances and perhaps impossible in others."). In the seminal case of *Larsen v. General Motors Corp.*, 391 F.2d 495, 503 (8th Cir. 1968) the court noted that "[t]he obstacles of apportionment are not insurmountable".

83. 669 F.2d 1199 (8th Cir. 1982).

84. *Id.* at 1206 (emphasis added).

85. *Id.* at 1208.

proof is significantly ameliorated because the plaintiff need only establish that one or more defects exist and that the defective condition constitutes a substantial factor in producing injuries after the initial impact.[86] The burden of apportionment is imposed on the defendant; the failure of the defendant to establish a divisible injury invokes joint and several liability.[87]

Texas adheres neither to the *Huddell* nor the *Mitchell* apportionment rules in a crashworthiness context.[88] Prior to the adoption of comparative causation in 1984, when at least one defendant was strictly liable in tort or breach of warranty and at least one was negligent,[89] Texas utilized the concurrent (joint) tortfeasor rationale. This joint tortfeasor concept was originally promulgated in *Landers v. East Texas Saltwater Disposal Co.*[90] Plaintiff's property was polluted by salt water and oil escaping from nearby pipelines owned by the defendants. The plaintiff established that the negligence of each of the various defendants proximately caused the harm.[91] The burden of proof then shifted to the defendants to apportion liability. The court declared, "Where the tortious acts of two or more wrongdoers join to produce an indivisible injury, that is, an injury which from its nature cannot be apportioned with reasonable certainty to the individual wrongdoers, all of the wrongdoers will be held jointly and severally liable for the entire damages . . ."[92]

In a crashworthiness case, however, the manufacturer is strictly liable in tort only to the extent of the injuries sustained by

86. *Id.* at 1206. Significantly, the Court was confronted with paraplegia which was an indivisible injury caused by ejection from the vehicle and clearly was not capable of apportionment. The court acknowledged that the arm injury was a divisible injury.

87. *See* McLeod v. American Motors Corp., 723 F.2d 830, 833-34 (11th Cir. 1984) (applying Florida law) (defendant has burden of proof in crashworthiness cases); Mitchell v. Volkswagenwerk, A.G., 669 F.2d 1199, 1209-10 (8th Cir. 1982) ("[P]araplegic injury was an indivisible one and. . .the harm could not be apportioned. . .the manufacturer and driver [are] jointly and severally liable for damages. . ."); Smith v. Fiat-Roosevelt Motors, Inc., 556 F.2d 728, 729 (5th Cir. 1977) ("In Florida, where an injury is indivisible and apportionment impossible, plaintiff may recover his entire damages from either tortfeasor."); Fouche v. Chrysler Motors Corp., 103 Idaho 249, 646 P.2d 1020, 1024 (Idaho App. 1982) (defendants have burden of proving apportionment and if apportionment cannot be achieved, then joint and several liability results).

88. *See* Duncan v. Cessna Aircraft Co., 665 S.W.2d 414 (Tex. 1984).

89. *See, e.g.*, General Motors Corp. v. Simmons, 558 S.W.2d 855 (Tex. 1977).

90. 151 Tex. 251, 248 S.W.2d 731 (1952).

91. 248 S.W.2d at 734.

92. *Id.*

the plaintiff over and above the injuries attributable to the original accident. Strict tort liability is imposed because of the defective nature of the product, and not because of the culpability, fault or conduct of the manufacturer.[93] It is illogical to equate a manufacturer with a concurrent tortfeasor when the alleged defective product neither causes nor contributes to cause the original accident and resulting injury. A concurrent tortfeasor is jointly and severally liable with the other tortfeasor who caused the accident. The manufacturer in a crashworthiness context, on the other hand, is strictly liable only to the extent that the defective design of the product *enhances* the injury caused by the original accident.

Apportionment of liability for injuries caused in a crashworthiness context has been resolved very recently by the doctrine of comparative causation judicially formulated in *Duncan v. Cessna Aircraft Co.*[94] The deceased was fatally injured when an aircraft in which he was riding as a passenger crashed into a mountain. The plaintiffs originally alleged that though negligence caused the initial crash, the collapse of the defectively designed seats upon impact produced the fatal injuries.[95] The Texas Supreme Court, utilizing this appeal to restructure defenses in strict tort liability actions, fashioned a comparative causation concept to allocate liability for injuries sustained by the plaintiff in strict tort liability cases.[96] Articulating the application of comparative causation, the Supreme Court noted:

> The trier of fact is to compare the harm caused by the defective product with the harm caused by the negligence of the other defendants, any settling tortfeasors and the plaintiff. The fault or conduct of the products defendant is not at issue . . . .[97] Comparative causation is especially appropriate in crashworthiness cases where the product defect causes or enhances injuries but does not cause the accident. The conduct which actually caused the accident, on the other hand, would not cause the same degree of harm if there were no product defect. Rather it is a combination of factors that causes plaintiff's injuries. The jury is asked to apportion responsibility between all whose actions or products

93. Gonzales v. Caterpillar Tractor Co., 571 S.W.2d 867 (Tex. 1978).
94. 665 S.W.2d 414 (Tex. 1984).
95. 632 S.W.2d 375, 378 (Tex. App.—Austin 1982, writ granted).
96. 665 S.W.2d at 427.
97. *Id.*

combined to cause the entirety of the plaintiff's injuries.[98]

Though not involving the precise issue of comparative causation allocation, the general matter of comparative causation in a crashworthiness context was considered by the Fifth Circuit in *Shipp v. General Motors Corp.*[99] Plaintiff was injured when she lost control of her 1976 Pontiac Trans Am while navigating a severe curve, causing the vehicle to leave the roadway and overturn. During the rollover, the roof over the driver's compartment collapsed inward and plaintiff sustained a severely fractured back in the accident. The jury awarded the plaintiff $750,000 based on defective design of the roof. The Fifth Circuit, conceding that plaintiff's case as to "design defect and producing cause was not compelling and GM [had] dealt it hard blows,"[100] affirmed the trial court judgment based essentially on the fact that the jury had spoken. In discussing the issue of causation, the Fifth Circuit acknowledged the conflict in jurisdictions between the *Huddell v. Levin*[101] rule imposing on the plaintiff the burden to establish the nature and extent of the enhanced injury attributable to the defective design in a crashworthiness context, and the rule in *Mitchell v. Volkswagenwerk A.G.*,[102] declaring that plaintiff is obligated only to establish that the design defect constituted a *substantial factor* in producing damages over and above those that were caused in the original impact.[103] The court notes at the outset of its analysis that there was but one liability producing cause on which to "cast responsibility."[104] The Fifth Circuit then observes that Texas ad-

98. *Id.* at 428.

99. 750 F.2d 418 (5th Cir. 1985).

100. *Id.* at 427.

101. 537 F.2d 726 (3d Cir. 1976).

102. 669 F.2d 1199 (8th Cir. 1982).

103. 750 F.2d at 1206. Cases adhering to the *Huddell v. Levin* rule include Barris v. Bob's Drag Shutes & Safety Equip., Inc., 685 F.2d 94, 99 (3d Cir. 1982), Caiazzo v. Volkswagenwerk A.G., 647 F.2d 241, 250 (2d Cir. 1981); Seese v. Volkswagenwerk A.G., 648 F.2d 833, 843 (3d Cir.), *cert. denied*, 454 U.S. 867 (1981), Dawson v. Chrysler Corp., 630 F.2d 950, 960 (3d Cir. 1980), *cert. denied*, 450 U.S. 959 (1981); Stonehocker v. General Motors Corp., 587 F.2d 151, 158 (4th Cir. 1978). Cases following the liberal rule of *Mitchell v. Volkswagenwerk* include McLeod v. American Motors Corp., 723 F.2d 830, 834 (11th Cir. 1984); Smith v. Fiat-Roosevelt Motors, Inc., 556 F.2d 728, 729 (5th Cir. 1977); Richardson v. Volkswagenwerk A.G., 552 F. Supp. 73, 80-83 (W.D. Mo. 1982); Lahocki v. Contee Sand & Gravel Co., 41 Md. App. 579, 398 A.2d 490, 501 (Md. Ct. Spec. App. 1979), *rev'd on other grounds sub. nom.*, General Motors Corp. v. Lahocki, 286 Md. 714, 410 A.2d 1039 (1980); Sumnicht v. Toyota Motor Sales U.S.A., 360 N.W.2d 2 (Wis. 1984).

104. 750 F.2d at 425.

heres to the tenet of concurrent causation which contemplates, "if two or more causes produce a single injury and each is an efficient cause without which the damage would not have occurred, the injury may be attributed to any or all of the causes."[105] The court emphasized that since the defect in a crashworthiness case combines with other forces to produce plaintiff's single injury, the entire injury could be attributed solely to the defect. Upon this basis, the Fifth Circuit stated: "We are persuaded that Texas courts would conclude that it would be illogically harsh to force a plaintiff to segregate causation in crashworthiness cases, where 'the collision, the defect and the injury are intradependent and . . . viewed as a combined event.' "[106]

The doctrine of crashworthiness contemplates that a design configuration of a vehicle neither causes nor contributes to cause the original accident but, rather, produces an enhancement of the injury after the original accident has occurred. The duty to adopt an alternative safer design is wholly dependent on establishing that an enhancement of an injury has occurred.[107] Application of strict tort liability based on a design defect in a crashworthiness context necessarily requires an enhancement of injury over and above the injury caused in the original accident; the product supplier is not a joint tortfeasor in the traditional manner. Rather, the crashworthiness case is analogous to that of the plaintiff who sustains an injury in an accident and later physician malpractice enhances the nature and character of the injury. Under these circumstances, the physician is liable only for the injuries that the plaintiff establishes were enhanced by the malpractice.[108]

This distinction was originally articulated in the seminal case that established the doctrine of crashworthiness. In *Larson v. General Motors Corp.*,[109] the Eighth Circuit specifically noted that "[a]ny design defect not causing the accident would not subject the manufacturer to liability for the entire damage, but the manufac-

---

105. *Id.* (emphasis in original).

106. *Id.* at 426. *See also* Turner v. General Motors Corp., 584 S.W.2d 844, 848 (Tex. 1979); Huff v. White Motor Corp., 656 F.2d 104, 109 (7th Cir. 1977).

107. *See, e.g.*, Larson v. General Motors Corp., 391 F.2d 495, 503 (8th Cir. 1968); Huddell v. Levin, 537 F.2d 726 (3d Cir. 1976); Ciazzo v. Volkswagenwerk A.G., 647 F.2d 241, 249 (2d Cir. 1981).

108. *See, e.g.*, Schering v. Giesecke, 589 S.W.2d 516 (Tex. App.—Eastland 1979, writ ref'd n.r.e.). Refer to Sales, *supra* note 75 at 261.

109. 391 F.2d 495, 503 (8th Cir. 1968).

turer should be liable for that portion of the damage or injury caused by the defective design *over and above the damage or injury that probably would have occurred as a result of the impact or collision, absent the defective design.*"[110] Rejecting the contention that the obstacles of apportionment were insurmountable, the Circuit Court observed that "it is done with regularity in those jurisdictions applying comparative negligence statutes and in other factual situations as condemnation cases, where in some jurisdictions the jury must assess the value of the land before and after a taking and then assess a special benefit accruing to the remaining property of the condemnee."[111]

Under *Duncan v. Cessna Aircraft Co.*,[112] the Texas Supreme Court adopted comparative causation of injury pursuant to which the jury assesses the percentage of responsibility of each tortfeasor for the injury caused by a tortfeasor's conduct and/or a defective product. The allocation by the jury of the percentage that a product defect in a crashworthiness context contributes to the injury sustained by the plaintiff establishes precisely the apportionment that was alluded to in *Larson.* It also satisfies the divisibility of injury mandated by those jurisdictions holding that a product manufacturer is jointly and severally liable for indivisible injuries attributable to a design defect that enhances injury in a crashworthiness context.[113] Unlike jurisdictions utilizing comparative fault, comparative negligence or other concepts, Texas allocates injury based upon a precise percentage of causation as distinguished from allocating fault.[114] The interpretation in *Shipp* implies that comparative causation is a form of comparative fault. On the contrary, comparative causation is designed for percentage allocation of the injury caused by a defective product or other tortious conduct, not the fault in causing the accident or occurrence. This is the essence of measuring divisibility of injury. Since the

---

110. *Id.* at 503 (emphasis added).

111. *Id.* at 504.

112. 665 S.W.2d 141 (Tex. 1984).

113. *See, e.g.*, Mitchell v. Volkswagenwerk A.G., 669 F.2d 1199, 1206 (8th Cir. 1982); McLeod v. American Motors Corp., 723 F.2d 830, 833 (11th Cir. 1984).

114. The Texas Supreme Court in *Duncan v. Cessna Aircraft Co.*, 665 S.W.2d 141 (Tex. 1984), specifically notes that the manufacturer is liable only for "that portion of the damage or injury caused by the defective design over and above the damage or injury that probably would have occurred as a result of the impact or collision, absent the defective design."

quintessential element of strict tort liability in a crashworthiness context is liability for injuries that are caused *over and above* those that were caused in the original accident, the allocation of comparative causation defines the exact contours of a divisible injury. Since divisibility of injury was not an issue in *Duncan*, the Texas Supreme Court did not address the fact that cases of strict tort liability for crashworthiness rest on a different basis than strict tort liability for design defects that cause or contribute to cause the accident-producing event. The product supplier in a crashworthiness context simply is not a joint tortfeasor under Section 433B of the *Restatement (Second) of Torts.*[115] The very essence and legal justification for imposing liability in a crashworthiness context is the "excess" or "enhanced" amount of injury.

Comparative causation enables the trier of fact to identify and allocate divisibility, i.e., the percentage of injury over and above that caused by the original accident attributable to the product defect in a crashworthiness context. Consequently, it would seem legally incongruous to impose joint and several liability on a product supplier in *a crashworthiness context* under the comparative causation doctrine when the trier of fact has allocated or apportioned that percentage of plaintiff's injuries caused by the product defect.[116] To hold otherwise eviscerates the crashworthiness doctrine and the concept of enhancement. When that portion of the injury has been properly apportioned by the trier of fact under pure comparative causation, the traditional rule of joint and several liability logically should not apply.

7.02 Bystander Recovery For Emotional Distress

The doctrine of bystander recovery for emotional distress is a relatively new, but rapidly evolving damage concept.[117] Early com-

---

115. Restatement (Second) of Torts § 433B(2) provides as follows:

> Where the tortious conduct of two or more actors has combined to bring about harm to the plaintiff, and one or more of the actors seeks to limit his liability on the ground that the harm is capable of apportionment among them, the burden of proof as to apportionment is upon each such actor.

116. The Texas Supreme Court in *Duncan v. Cessna Aircraft Corp.* did not specifically address this issue. Unfortunately, the court made a generalized statement that joint and several liability was retained. *Id.* at 429. Whether this generalization applies to the precise issue of liability only for the enhancement of an injury in a crashworthiness context remains unclear.

117. *See generally*, Annot., 31 A.L.R. 4th 162 (1984).

mon law prohibited bystander recovery of damages in the absence of some contemporaneous injury or impact attributable to the tortious acts committed by the defendant against a third party. This basic approach to bystander claims, denoted as the "impact rule", is currently followed by only a minority of courts.[118]

A second view of bystander recovery is represented by the "zone of danger" rule.[119] The zone of danger rule contemplates that the bystander be within the zone of probable harm and suffers emotional injury as a direct result of concern for his own safety. For example, in *Houston Electric Co. v. Dorsett*,[120] plaintiff was walking across the street when a bus narrowly missed striking her. Though the bus did not physically strike her, it was necessary for plaintiff to jump from its path to elude injury. The court recognized a right to recover based on plaintiff's position within the zone of danger. This "zone of danger" rationale was reaffirmed in *Dave Snelling Lincoln-Mercury v. Simon*,[121] in which the plaintiff's child fell from a moving vehicle. Though the parent was not physically injured, she was entitled to recover for emotional distress because she was physically located within the zone of danger.

A growing number of jurisdictions have adopted foreseeability of injury as the basis of bystander recovery.[122] In the landmark case of *Dillon v. Legg*,[123] plaintiff, mother of the injured child, witnessed her daughter's fatal injury when she was struck by a vehicle negligently operated by the defendant. The court declared that

---

118. *See, e.g.*, Little v. Williamson, 441 N.E.2d 974 (Ind. App. 1982); Champion v. Gray, 420 So. 2d 348 (Fla. App. 1982) (follows the rule but discusses the reasons for abandoning it).

119. *See* Rickey v. Chicago Transit Authority, 98 Ill. 2d 546, 457 N.E.2d 1 (1983); Stadler v. Cross, 295 N.W.2d 552 (Minn. 1980); Whetham v. Bismarck Hosp., 197 N.W.2d 678 (N.D. 1972); Shelton v. Russell Pipe & Foundrey Co., 570 S.W.2d 861 (Tenn. 1978). *See also* Restatement (Second) of Torts § 313(2) comment d (1966) (The rule "has no application where the emotional distress arises solely because of harm or peril to a third person, and the negligence of the actor has not threatened the plaintiff with bodily harm in any other way.").

120. 145 Tex. 95, 194 S.W.2d 546 (1946). *See also* H.E. Butt Grocery Co. v. Perez, 408 S.W.2d 576 (Tex. Civ. App.—San Antonio 1966, no writ).

121. 508 S.W.2d 923 (Tex. Civ. App.—Houston [1st Dist.] 1974, no writ).

122. Dillon v. Legg, 68 Cal. 2d 728, 441 P.2d 912, 69 Cal. Rptr. 72 (1968); Haught v. Maceluch, 681 F.2d 291 (5th Cir. 1982); Paugh v. Hanks, 6 Ohio St. 3d. 72, 451 N.E.2d 759 (1983); Culbert v. Sampson's Supermarkets, Inc., 444 A.2d 433 (Me. 1982); Barnhill v. Davis, 300 N.W.2d 104 (Iowa 1981); Walker v. Clark Equipment Co., 320 N.W.2d 561 (Iowa 1982); Portee v. Jaffee, 84 N.J. 88, 417 A.2d 521 (1980).

123. 68 Cal. 2d 728, 441 P.2d 912, 69 Cal. Rptr. 72 (1968).

plaintiff was entitled to recover for the mental anguish in witnessing her child's fatal accident. The court concluded that the defendant could have reasonably foreseen injury to parents from witnessing a fatal injury inflicted on their child. Foreseeability as formulated by the court is determined on the basis of three primary factors: (1) the proximity of the plaintiff to the scene of the accident; (2) the manner in which the plaintiff learns of the accident; and (3) the relationship between the plaintiff and the victim.[124] Essentially, foreseeability rests upon establishing (1) that the plaintiff is located near the scene of the accident as distinguished from a plaintiff located a significant distance away; (2) that the emotional shock is directly produced by a sensory perception and contemporaneous observation of the accident as distinguished from learning of the accident from others after its occurrence; and (3) that the plaintiff and the victim were familially related as distinguished from the absence of any familial ties.

The concept of foreseeability is uniquely different from that of the zone of danger. The distinction is critically important because the mental trauma results from the sensory perception of an injury inflicted on another party and not mental anguish produced from exposure to the zone of probable harm. Recent Texas decisions apparently have ignored the earlier zone of danger limitation in favor of foreseeability of harm.[125]

---

124. 441 P.2d at 920. California has refused to extend recovery for mental distress to a bystander located beyond the line of perception at the scene. Krouse v. Graham, 19 Cal. 3d 59, 562 P.2d 1022, 137 Cal. Rptr. 863 (1977).

125. *See* Dawson v. Garcia, 666 S.W.2d 254 (Tex. App.—Dallas 1984, no writ) (entire family in car involved in an automobile collision); Genzer v. City of Mission, 666 S.W.2d 116 (Tex. App.—Corpus Christi 1983, writ ref'd n.r.e.) (parents and grandparents witnessed fireworks explosion which killed child); Apache Ready Mix Co. v. Creed, 653 S.W.2d 79 (Tex. App.—San Antonio 1983, n.w.h.) (mother regained consciousness after automobile accident and saw injured child beside her); Bedgood v. Madalin, 589 S.W.2d 797 (Tex. Civ. App.—Corpus Christi 1979), *rev'd on other grounds*, 600 S.W.2d 773 (Tex. 1980) (concurring opinion at 777) (Father, in backyard, heard son scream and seconds later found him injured in the street); Covington v. Estate of Foster, 584 S.W.2d 726 (Tex. Civ. App.—Waco 1979, writ ref'd n.r.e.) (Parents with child at time of automobile collision); Landreth v. Reed, 570 S.W.2d 486 (Tex. Civ. App.—Texarkana 1978, no writ) (infant watched fourteen month old sister drown in day care center's pool). *But see* Sales, *supra* note 75 at 226. The author reviews cases and suggests that the "zone of danger" requirement is essential to establish minimal parameters on the scope of a tortfeasor's liability. Otherwise, a tortfeasor's liability is unlimited and extends to the world. Forseeability is a catchall mechanism that permits courts to achieve result-oriented decisions rather than decisions based on meaningful legal standards.

Jurisdictions remain noticeably divided on whether a bystander who is not injured but who suffers emotional distress as a result of witnessing a product-caused injury to another may recover damages for those injuries.[126] In *Walker v. Clark Equipment Co.*,[127] plaintiff witnessed her brother's death when an allegedly defective forklift overturned. In permitting a recovery for emotional distress premised upon strict tort liability, the Iowa Supreme Court commented, "[W]e see no qualitative difference, once liability is found, between recoveries under theories of negligence, strict liability or warranty. . . We know of no logical way, on the basis of damages, that a line could be drawn between any of the three theories of recovery."[128] Conversely, in *Woodhill v. Parke-Davis*,[129] plaintiff's child was injured when the drug Petocin was administered to the mother during the fetal stage. Rejecting recovery, the Illinois Supreme Court declared, "[S]trict liability should not be extended to include recovery for the plaintiff's emotional distress and mental anguish."[130]

Strict tort liability has been extended by the Texas Supreme Court to bystanders physically injured by a defective product. In *Darryl v. Ford Motor Co.*,[131] plaintiff was injured when a truck with an allegedly defective brake pushrod struck the rear of his car. The Texas Supreme Court stated: "We hold that recovery under the strict liability doctrine is not limited to users and consumers. . .There is no adequate rationale or theoretical explanation why non-users and non-consumers should be denied recovery against the manufacturer of a defective product."[132]

The issue of bystander recovery for emotional distress was addressed in *General Motors Corp. v. Grizzle*.[133] Plaintiff's minor

---

126. *Compare* Cadillac Motor Car Div. v. Brown, 428 So. 2d 301 (Fla. Dist. Ct. App. 1983) and Woodhill v. Parke-Davis, 79 Ill. 2d 26, 402 N.E.2d 194 (1980), which reject liability for bystander injuries suffered from witnessing a product-caused injury to another *with* Kately v. Wilkinson, 148 Cal. App. 3d 576, 195 Cal. Rptr. 902 (1983) and Walker v. Clark Equip. Co., 320 N.W.2d 561 (Iowa 1982), which hold that strict tort liability applied to a bystander who suffered emotional distress from witnessing a product caused injury to another.

127. 320 N.W.2d 561 (Iowa 1982).

128. *Id.* at 563.

129. 402 N.E.2d 194 (Ill. 1980).

130. *Id.* at 200.

131. 440 S.W.2d 630 (Tex. 1969).

132. *Id.* at 633.

133. 642 S.W.2d 837 (Tex. App.—Waco 1982, writ dism'd).

daughters were injured in an accident allegedly caused by a defective vehicle design. Plaintiff arrived at the scene several minutes later and observed her child trapped in the car and screaming. The jury awarded the plaintiff damages for loss of companionship and mental anguish for the death of her daughter. Relying on the *Dillon* concept of foreseeability,[134] and ignoring any reference to the Texas zone of danger rule, the court stated, "the triggering of the mental anguish is not from only perceiving a collision, but from realizing its consequences . . . The realization of the consequences can be produced from the moans and cries of the victim at the accident as well as from the actual observation of the victim."[135] The court thus extended the perception factor to allow recovery where the bystander did not actually observe the accident but did experience almost contemporaneous or experential perception.[136] This decision demonstrates rather graphically the rather limitless nature and character of the foreseeability doctrine.

Whether foreseeability of harm will replace the long established zone of danger limitation awaits ultimate resolution by the Texas Supreme Court. The intermediate appellate courts have sensed a philosophical shift in the Supreme Court and in formulating their decisions the courts have concluded that the Supreme Court undoubtedly will judicially substitute the California rule for the Texas zone of danger rule articulated in *Dorsett* and its progeny in product liability cases.

Under the Wrongful Death Act as interpreted in *Sanchez v. Schindler*,[137] a parent is entitled to recover for the loss of companionship and mental anguish for the wrongful death of a child as elements of statutory pecuniary loss.[138]Bystander recovery for mental and emotional trauma, on the other hand, is independent of the Wrongful Death Act.[139] A bystander who is not a beneficiary

---

134. Refer to notes 123-125 *supra* and accompanying text.

135. 642 S.W.2d at 844. The California Court of Appeals in *Nevels v. Yeager*, 152 Cal. App. 3d 162, 199 Cal. Rptr. 300 (1984), labeled this as "substantially contemporaneous perception" and allowed a mother to recover for her mental anguish when she arrived ten minutes after the accident but saw her bloody daughter screaming.

136. 642 S.W.2d at 844. *See also* Dawson v. Garcia, 666 S.W.2d 254 (Tex. App.—Dallas 1983, no writ).

137. 651 S.W.2d 249 (Tex. 1983).

138. Refer to the discussion on wrongful death, notes 48-54 *supra* and accompanying text.

139. *See* Landreth v. Reed, 570 S.W.2d 486 (Tex. Civ. App.—Texarkana 1978, no writ) (sister allowed recovery).

under the Wrongful Death Act may, under the foreseeability standard, recover damages for emotional distress from witnessing injury or harm to another.

Bystander recovery for emotional distress based on strict tort liability is a recent but increasingly litigated remedy.[140] Except for *Grizzle*,[141] the Texas courts have not directly confronted the issue in a strict tort liability context. Though strict tort liability is liberally construed and applied, it is based solely on the condition of the product and not the conduct of the supplier. Whether this distinction is a limitation on bystander recovery for emotional distress remains unanswered.

Even if the *Dillon* test governs in a strict tort liability action, a critical issue involves the relationship between the bystander and the victim. In negligence cases, siblings[142] and grandparents[143] satisfy this requirement. Bystanders who are unrelated to the victim arguably satisfy the foreseeability standard under the philosophy of the California Courts. Though the issue in Texas remains unresolved, the fact that Texas authorizes bystander recovery based on strict tort liability suggests that any form of injury, even emotional distress, will be recognized.[144]

7.03 Property Damages

The *Restatement* provides that the seller of a product is liable "for physical harm thereby caused to . . . [the user's or consumer's] property . . ."[145] By its literal terms, the *Restatement* expressly authorizes recovery for property damage. Its application to property loss claims, however, has precipitated considerable confusion and misunderstanding. To resolve the confusion it is necessary to distinguish the three types of property loss which may occur: (1)

---

140. *See, e.g.,* Shepard v. Superior Court, 76 Cal. App. 3d. 16, 142 Cal. Rptr. 612 (1977); Barnhill v. Davis, 300 N.W.2d 104 (Iowa 1981); Walker v. Clark Equip. Co., 320 N.W.2d 561 (Iowa 1982).

141. 642 S.W.2d 837 (Tex. App.—Waco 1982, writ dism'd).

142. Landreth v. Reed, 570 S.W.2d 486 (Tex. Civ. App.—Texarkana 1978, no writ) (infant sister observed her 18 month old sister drown).

143. Genzer v. City of Mission, 666 S.W.2d 116 (Tex. App.—Corpus Christi 1983, writ ref'd n.r.e.) (grandparents of decedent); Gulf States Utilities Co. v. Reed, 659 S.W.2d 849 (Tex. App.—Houston [14th Dist.] 1983, writ ref'd n.r.e.) (mother of decedent).

144. *See generally* Annot., 31 A.L.R. 4th 162 (1984); Flannery, *Bystander Recovery in Texas*, 44 Tex. Bar J. 746 (1981); Sales, *supra* note 75, at 226.

145. Restatement (Second) of Torts) § 402A (1966).

damage to the product itself; (2) damage to property other than the product itself; and (3) consequential or economic losses resulting from damage to the product.

A. *Damage to the Product Itself*

Prior to 1970, Texas ostensibly permitted recovery under strict tort liability for damage to the defective product. In *Barnett v. Ford Motor Co.*,[146] a one week old vehicle sustained fire damage caused by defective dashboard wiring. Plaintiff sought the value of the automobile as damages, relying on the doctrine of strict tort liability. The court concluded that upon sufficient proof, the plaintiff was entitled to recover the difference in value of the vehicle before and after the fire.[147] Without addressing the applicability of strict tort liability, the court assumed that damages to the defective product were recoverable based on this theory.

The application of strict tort liability to property damage recoveries was directly addressed and definitively clarified by the Texas Supreme Court in *Mid Continent Aircraft Corp. v. Curry County Spraying Service, Inc.*[148] Plaintiff purchased a rebuilt airplane "as is". When the plane crashed as a result of a defective condition, plaintiff instituted actions based both on strict tort liability and breach of implied warranty to recover damages. Rejecting application of strict tort liability as a basis for recovery of damage to the product itself, the Texas Supreme Court noted:

> The present case does not involve personal injury but concerns only economic loss to the purchased product itself . . . [D]amage to the product itself is essentially a loss to the purchaser of the benefit of the bargain with the seller . . . [and] between a commercial seller and commercial buyer, when no physical injury has occurred to persons or other property, injury to the defective product itself is an economic loss governed by the Uniform Commercial Code.[149]

The rationale of the court is remarkably straightforward. Damage to the product constitutes an economic loss governed by

---

146. 463 S.W.2d 33 (Tex. Civ. App.—Waco 1970, no writ).
147. *Id.* at 34-35.
148. 572 S.W.2d 308 (Tex. 1978).
149. *Id.* at 312-13.

the legislatively promulgated Uniform Commercial Code.[150] As the court observed, there is "no difference between a product that is unusable because of a defect and one that causes physical harm to itself because of a defect."[151]

One commentator has endeavored to distinguish between economic loss and damage to the product itself:

> When the defect causes an accident 'involving some violence or collision with external objects', the resulting loss is treated as property damage [to the product itself]. On the other hand, when the damage to the product results from deterioration, internal breakage, or other non-accidental causes, it is treated as economic loss.[152]

A minority of jurisdictions allow recovery based on strict tort liability for damage to the product resulting from a sudden, violent event, ignoring the rationale that underlies the strict tort liability concept espoused in the *Restatement*. In *Pennsylvania Glass Sand Corp. v. Caterpillar Tractor Co.*,[153] a front end loader was damaged as the result of a sudden and dangerous fire caused by an allegedly defective condition in the product. The Third Circuit, applying Pennsylvania law, sanctioned the application of strict tort liability to recovery damage to the product itself:

> In cases such as the present one where only the defective product is damaged, the majority approach is to identify whether a particular injury amounts to economic loss or physical damage. . .[T]he line between tort and contract must be drawn by analyzing interrelated factors such as the nature of the defect, the type of risk, and the manner in which the injury arose. These factors bear directly on whether the safety-insurance policy of tort law or the expectation-bargain protection policy of warranty law is most applicable to a particular claim.[154]

A similar view is reflected in *National Crane Corp. v. Ohio Steel Tube Co.*[155] Plaintiff initiated an action in strict tort liability

---

150. *Id.*

151. *Id.* at 311. *See also* James v. Bell Helicopter Co., 715 F.2d 166, 170-71 (5th Cir. 1983).

152. Note, *Economic Loss in Products Liability Jurisprudence*, 66 COLUM. L. REV. 917, 918 (1966).

153. 652 F.2d 1165 (3d Cir. 1981).

154. *Id.* at 1173.

155. 213 Neb. 782, 332 N.W.2d 39 (1983).

for losses sustained from retrofitting cranes with new, nondefective replacement parts. The Nebraska Supreme Court concluded that the doctrine of strict tort liability may be extended to allow recovery for physical harm to the product itself where "the damage occurred as a result of a sudden, violent event and not as a result of an inherent defect that reduced the property's value without inflicting physical harm to the product."[156] The court emphasized that it would not permit recovery of economic loss based on strict tort liability.[157] These jurisdictions seemingly ignore the obvious—damage to a product either from deterioration or from a defective condition is still an economic loss.

Strict tort liability does not encompass damage to the product inflicted by the biological combining of two products into a single unit. In *Two Rivers Co. v. Curtiss Breeding Service*,[158] plaintiff purchased semen to artificially inseminate his cattle. The offspring were born diseased. The Fifth Circuit, applying Texas law, declared that the Uniform Commercial Code governs "mere loss of value resulting from the failure of the product to perform according to . . . contractual . . . expectations."[159] The court refused to apply strict liability where the products themselves (cattle) were damaged.

When collateral property damage occurs in addition to damage to the product itself, either strict tort liability, breach of implied warranty, or both, constitute viable causes of action for recovery of damages.[160] The injured party need not be burdened with the obligation to use one theory to recover for personal injuries and a totally different theory for the damaged property in the same lawsuit.

B. *Damage to Property Other than the Product*

It is well established that the doctrine of strict tort liability authorizes the recovery of damage to property other than the de-

---

156. *Id.* at 43. *See also* Fordyce Concrete, Inc. v. Mack Trucks, 535 F. Supp. 118 (D. Kan. 1982); Star Furniture Co. v. Pulaski Furniture Co., 297 S.E.2d 854 (W. Va. 1982); Moorman Mfg. Co. v. National Tank Co., 435 N.E.2d 443 (Ill. 1982).

157. 332 N.W.2d at 44.

158. 624 F.2d 1242 (5th Cir. 1980), *cert denied*, 450 U.S. 920 (1981).

159. *Id.* at 1246.

160. *See* Mercer v. Long Mfg. N.C., Inc., 665 F.2d 61 (5th Cir. 1982); Signal Oil & Gas Co. v. Universal Oil Prods., 572 S.W.2d 320 (Tex. 1978).

fective product itself.[161] Section 402A states that a seller of a defective product is strictly liable when the product causes "physical harm . . . to [the user's or consumer's] property . . ."[162]

In *O.M. Franklin Serum Co. v. C.A. Hoover & Son,*[163] plaintiff's cattle died as a result of an injection of a defective antibiotic serum. In approving recovery based on strict tort liability, the Texas Supreme Court observed that:

> In *McKisson v. Sales Affiliates, Inc.*, . . . we adopted the rule of strict liability in tort with respect to sellers of defective products which cause physical harm to persons. The Court of Civil Appeals has held in the present case that the seller of a defective product is also subject to strict liability for damage caused to the property of the ultimate consumer . . . We are in agreement with this holding . . .[164]

Consistent with the *Restatement* provision as adopted by the Texas Supreme Court, the Fifth Circuit in *James v. Bell Helicopter Co.,*[165] observed that "[P]hysical harm (as contained in Section 402A of the *Restatement (Second) of Torts*) to the . . . [plaintiff's] property *other than the product* is recoverable in a products liability action."[166]

It is abundantly clear that the rule of strict tort liability as enunciated in Section 402A provides an acceptable theory for the recovery of damage to property other than the product itself. Texas, as well as the majority of jurisdictions, adheres to this rule.[167]

---

161. Restatement (Second) Of Torts § 402A (1966).
162. *Id.*
163. 418 S.W.2d 482 (Tex. 1967) (per curiam).
164. *Id.*
165. 715 F.2d 166 (5th Cir. 1983).
166. *Id.* at 170 (emphasis in original).
167. *See* Two Rivers Co. v. Curtiss Breeding Service, 624 F.2d 1242 (5th Cir. 1980), *cert. denied*, 450 U.S. 920 (1981) (semen killed cows); Signal Oil & Gas Co. v. Universal Oil Prods., 572 S.W.2d 320 (Tex. 1978) (defective isomax reactor caused property damage); Tide Prods., Inc. v. Browning, 493 S.W.2d 654 (Tex. Civ. App.—Amarillo 1973, no writ) (chemicals damaged peanut crop); FMC Corp. v. Burns, 444 S.W.2d 315 (Tex. Civ. App.—San Antonio 1969, no writ) (chemicals damaged cucumbers); Dealers Transp. Co. v. Battery Distrib. Co., 402 S.W.2d 441 (Ky. Ct. App. 1965) (acetylene gas tank damaged property); State Stove Mfg. Co. v. Hodges, 189 So. 2d 113 (Miss. 1966), *cert. denied*, 386 U.S. 912 (1967) (hot water heater destroyed home); Bombardi v. Pochel's Appliance & T.V. Co., 9 Wash. App. 797, 515 P.2d 540, *modified*, 10 Wash. App. 243, 518 P.2d 202 (1973) (defective television caused fire to other property).

C. Economic or Consequential Loss Resulting from a Defective Product

Strict tort liability does not extend to or authorize a cause of action to recover economic or consequential loss caused by a defective product.[168] Economic loss has been defined as both direct and consequential damage:

> Direct economic loss may be said to encompass damage based on insufficient product value . . . or "loss of bargain" . . . Direct economic loss also may be measured by costs of replacement and repair. Consequential economic loss includes all indirect loss, such as loss of profits resulting from inability to make use of the defective product.[169]

In *Nobility Homes of Texas, Inc. v. Shivers*,[170] plaintiff initiated suit against the manufacturer to recover damages for a defective mobile home. The trial court found the unit's reasonable market value was $8,750 less than its purchase price.[171] The Texas Supreme Court denominated this loss as economic in nature and stated: "We . . . hold that strict liability does not apply to economic losses. There is no finding . . . that the product was unreasonably dangerous . . . or caused physical harm to [the person] or his property."[172] The court refused to extend Section 402A to a purely economic loss because of the absence of physical harm to the user or his property as prescribed by Section 402A. Plaintiff was permitted to seek recovery, however, based upon breach of the Uniform Commercial Code's implied warranty of merchantability.[173] As the court emphasized appropriate remedies for economic losses have been fashioned by the Legislature under the Uniform Commercial Code.[174]

---

168. *See* James v. Bell Helicopter Co., 715 F.2d 166 (5th Cir. 1983); Mercer v. Long Mfg. N.C., Inc., 665 F.2d 61 (5th Cir. 1982); Signal Oil & Gas Co. v. Universal Oil Prods., 572 S.W.2d 320 (Tex. 1978); Nobility Homes of Texas, Inc. v. Shivers, 557 S.W.2d 77 (Tex. 1977); Lockwood Corp. v. Spencer, 613 S.W.2d 369 (Tex. Civ. App.—Amarillo 1981, writ ref'd n.r.e.).

169. Note, *Economic Loss in Products Liability Jurisprudence*, 66 COLUM. L. REV. 917, 918 (1966). *See also* Mercer v. Long Mfg. N.C., Inc., 665 F.2d 61, 68 (5th Cir. 1982) (the Texas Supreme Court adopted this definition).

170. 557 S.W.2d 77 (Tex. 1977).

171. *Id.* at 78.

172. *Id.* at 80.

173. 557 S.W.2d at 81.

174. *Id. See also* U.C.C. § 2-314 (implied warranty of merchantability) and § 2-315

In *Mid-Continent Aircraft Corp. v. Curry County Spraying Services, Inc.*,[175] damage to an allegedly defective aircraft that crashed was deemed an economic loss. Because the direct loss of value by reason of damage to the property represented an economic loss, strict tort liability was inapplicable.[176]

The majority of jurisdictions that reject the application of strict tort liability for economic losses recognize that the commercial law of sales preempts tort law in economic transactions and provides both an adequate and appropriate remedy.[177] In the landmark case of *Seely v. White Motor Co.*,[178] Chief Justice Traynor emphasized that:

> The law of sales has been carefully articulated to govern the economic relations between suppliers and consumers of goods. The history of the doctrine of strict liability in tort indicates that it was designed, not to undermine the warranty provisions of the sales act of the Uniform Commercial Code but, rather, to govern the distinct problem of physical injuries.[179]

Only a few jurisdictions have ignored the limitations inherent in strict tort liability doctrine and extended the doctrine to include

---

(fitness for a particular purpose).

175. 572 S.W.2d 308 (Tex. 1978).

176. *Id.* at 313.

177. *See* James v. Bell Helicopter Co., 715 F.2d 166 (5th Cir. 1983) (defective clutch in helicopter); Mercer v. Long Mfg. N.C., Inc., 665 F.2d 61 (5th Cir. 1982) (defective peanut combine); Signal Oil & Gas Co. v. Universal Oil Prods., 572 S.W.2d 320 (Tex. 1978) (defective isomax reactor charge heater); County of Suffolk v. Long Island Lighting Co., 728 F.2d 52 (2d Cir. 1984) (allegedly defective nuclear power plant); Southwest Forest Indus., Inc. v. Westinghouse Elec. Corp., 422 F.2d 1013 (9th Cir.), *cert. denied*, 400 U.S. 902 (1970) (defective turbine generator); Noel Transfer & Pkg. Delivery Serv., Inc. v. General Motors Corp., 341 F. Supp. 968 (D. Minn. 1972) (defective diesel truck); Polycon Indus., Inc. v. Hercules Inc., 471 F. Supp. 1316 (E.D. Wis. 1979) (defective plastics blowmolding machines); Morrow v. New Moon Homes, Inc., 548 P.2d 279 (Alas. 1976) (defective mobile home); Beauchamp v. Wilson, 21 Ariz. App. 14, 515 P.2d 41 (1973) (defective diesel truck); Long v. Jim Letts Oldsmobile, Inc., 135 Ga. App. 293, 217 S.E.2d 602 (1975) (defective car); Clark v. International Harvester Co., 99 Idaho 326, 581 P.2d 784, 792 (1978) (defective tractor); Hawkins Constr. Co. v. Matthews Co., 190 Neb. 546, 209 N.W.2d 643 (1973) (defective scaffolding equipment); Price v. Gatlin, 241 Ore. 315, 405 P.2d 502 (1965) (defective tractor); Star Furniture Co. v. Pulaski Furniture Co., 297 S.E.2d 854 (W. Va. 1982) (defective curio clock); Moorman Mfg. Co. v. National Tank Co., 91 Ill. 2d 69, 435 N.E.2d 443 (1982) (grain storage tank cracked); Alaska v. Tyonek Timber Inc., 680 P.2d 1148 (Alas. 1984) Hagert v. Hatton Commodities, Inc., 350 N.W.2d 591 (N.D. 1984); St. Paul Fire & Marine Ins. Co. v. Steeple Jac Inc., 352 N.W.2d 107 (Minn. Ct. App. 1984).

178. 63 Cal. 2d 9, 45 Cal. Rptr. 17, 403 P.2d 145 (1965).

179. 63 Cal. 2d at 15, 45 Cal. Rptr. at 21, 403 P.2d at 149.

economic losses.[180] This extension is premised on the judicially formulated public policy of the jurisdiction, not upon the provisions and rationale of the *Restatement*.

The Texas courts permit recovery for economic losses under the Uniform Commercial Code — not under strict liability.[181] In a suit to recover economic losses based upon Section 2-314 of the U.C.C.[182] (suitability) or Section 2-315 of the U.C.C.[183] (fitness for a particular purpose), the plaintiff is entitled to maintain an action for breach of implied warranty without the necessity of establishing privity of contract.[184] In *Nobility*,[185] the Texas Supreme Court noted that the legislature, in enacting the U.C.C., specifically deferred declaring that privity was required for a cause of action based on contractual warranty, leaving that task to the courts.[186] Consequently, the court elected to abolish the traditional requirement of privity in breach of warranty actions.[187] With the elimination of the privity requirement Texas has, in effect, sanctioned a form of strict tort liability recovery for economic or consequential loss.[188] Of course, the other requirements and limitations of the U.C.C. continue to govern breach of warranty actions.

Strict tort liability is available as a remedy to recover economic loss when the loss is coupled with a product-caused injury to an individual or his property. In *Signal Oil & Gas Co. v. Universal Oil Products*,[189] allegedly defective bolts caused a rupture and resulting fire in a reactor-charged heater at plaintiff's chemical plant.

---

180. *See* ICI Australia Ltd. v. Elliot Overseas Co., 551 F. Supp. 265 (D.N.J. 1982); Santor v. A & M Karagheusian, Inc., 44 N.J. 52, 207 A.2d 305 (1965). *See also* Hales v. Green Colonial, Inc., 490 F.2d 1015 (8th Cir. 1974); Mead Corp. v. Allendale Mut. Ins. Co., 465 F. Supp. 355 (N.D. Ohio 1979); Berg v. General Motors Corp., 87 Wash. 2d 584, 555 P.2d 818 (1976).

181. *See* Nobility Homes, Inc. v. Shivers, 557 S.W.2d 77 (Tex. 1977) (intent is not to undermine the Code).

182. U. C. C. § 2-314 (1983).

183. U. C. C. § 2-315 (1983).

184. *See* Nobility Homes, Inc. v. Shivers, 557 S.W.2d 77 (Tex. 1977).

185. *Id.*

186. *Id.* at 81.

187. *Id.* at 81. *See* Garcia v. Texas Inst. Inc., 610 S.W.2d 456 (Tex. 1980); Ford Motor Co. v. Tidwell, 563 S.W.2d 831 (Tex. Civ. App.—El Paso 1978, writ ref'd n.r.e).

188. *See* Fredonia Broadcasting Corp., Inc. v. RCA Corp., 481 F.2d 781 (5th Cir. 1973), *cert. denied*, 439 U.S. 859 (1978); Pioneer Hi-Bred Int'l Inc. v. Talley, 493 S.W.2d 602 (Tex. Civ. App.—Amarillo 1973, no writ); Eli Lily & Co. v. Casey, 472 S.W.2d 598 (Tex. Civ. App.—Eastland 1971, writ dism'd).

189. 572 S.W.2d 320 (Tex. 1978).

As a result of the fire and a subsequent explosion, damage was inflicted to both the heater and the refinery, producing significant consequential damages attributable to shutdown of the refinery. The court commented:

> Where such collateral property damage exists in addition to damage to the product itself, recovery for such damages are recoverable under Section 402A . . . or under the Texas Business and Commerce Code, Section 2.715 . . . . To the extent that the product itself has become part of the accident risk or the tort by causing collateral property damage, it is properly considered as part of the property damages, rather than as economic loss.[190]

7.04 Punitive Damages

The punitive damage doctrine traces its origins to the Code of Hammurabi in 2000 B.C.[191] Punitory damages appeared in the Hittite law in 1400 B.C. and the Hindu Code of Manu in 200 B.C.[192] Numerous examples of multiple damage remedies are recorded in the Bible for a variety of offenses.[193] English courts before the eighteenth century upheld jury verdicts that exceeded plaintiff's actual compensatory damages.[194] In fact, in 1763, in the case of *Huckle v. Money*, an English court used punitive awards to recognize that a jury could legitimately return a verdict for excessive awards.[195]

A variety of historical justifications have been urged in support of the punitive damage doctrine. The most popular theory advanced perceives that exemplary damages were utilized to justify otherwise excessive jury verdicts.[196] Early English common law juries often consisted of local townspeople who knew more about the facts of cases than did the judges. In some courts, knights acted as

---

190. *Id.* at 325.

191. *See, e.g.*, G. Driver & J. Miles, *The Babylonian Laws*, 500-01 (1952); Sales & Cole, *Punitive Damages: A Relic That Has Outlived Its Origins*, 37 Vand. L. Rev. 1117, 1119 (1984); Owen, *Punitive Damages in Products Liability Litigation*, 74 Mich. L. Rev. 1258, 1260 (1976); Sales, *The Emergence of Punitive Damages in Product Liability Actions: A Further Assault on the Citadel*, 14 St. Mary's L.J. 351, 351 n.l. (1983).

192. K. Redden, *Punitive Damages*, § 2.2(A)(1), at 24 (1980).

193. *See, e.g.*, Exodus 22:1, Exodus 22:9.

194. Refer to K. Redden, note 192 *supra* at 26, § 2.2(A) (2).

195. 2 Wils. K.B. 205, 95 Eng. Rep. 768 (C.P. 1763).

196. Sales & Cole, *supra* note 191, at 1120; Ellis, *Fairness and Efficiency in the Law of Punitive Damages*, 56 S. Cal. L. Rev. 1, 12 (1982).

jurors and also provided the only testimony at trial.[197] The primitive English courts were reluctant to interfere with the decisions reached by these juries, and the punitive damage concept served to justify excessive awards.

Another theory advanced to justify exemplary damages is based on the supposition that the punitive damage award serves as compensation for the ethereal injuries sustained by the plaintiff such as humiliation, wounded dignity, loss of companionship, embarrassment, disfigurement, and mental anguish. During the early stages of the common law, the courts refused to recognize these injuries as worthy of actual compensation.[198] The concept of punitive damages, therefore, performed the task of compensating for elements of harm that, in the early development of the common law, were not recoverable elements of compensatory damages.[199] As the theory of compensatory damages expanded, and recoveries for physical injuries as well as mental anguish, loss of society, emotional distress, and other ethereal injuries were permitted, the rationale for punitive awards as a means of additional compensation ceased to exist. Thus, critics have argued that this evolution of compensatory damages has significantly eroded the rationale undergirding the use of punitive damages.[200]

A third justification for punitive damages perceives that awards in the form of quasi-criminal fines satisfy the inequities between severe criminal penalties for wrongs involving property losses and the lesser criminal penalties for more severe invasions of personal rights.[201] The courts, therefore, employed the punitory awards to punish egregious torts causing personal harm under the rationale that individuals were more likely to institute suits to protect their rights and enforce the civil law if punitive damages provided an economic incentive.[202] With the advent of the significantly enlarged compensatory damage awards to embrace both tangible and intangible injuries, the economic incentive for initiating civil litigation for egregious torts has rapidly supplanted this

---

197. Refer to K. Redden, note 192 *supra* at 26, § 2.2 (A)(2).

198. *Id.* at 28, § 2.2(C). *See also* J. Ghiardi & J. Kircher, *Punitive Damages, Law and Practice* § 1.02 (1984).

199. Refer to Sales, note 191 *supra,* at 354.

200. Refer to Sales & Cole, note 191 *supra.*

201. Freifield, *The Rationale of Punitive Damages,* 1 Ohio St. L. J. 5, 9 (1935).

202. *See, e.g., Special Project, An Analysis of the Legal, Social, and Political Issues Raised by Asbestos Litigation,* 36 Vand L. Rev. 573, 694 (1983).

historical rationale for punitory awards. Arguably, even absent punitive damage awards, the current tort reparations system fulfills the mission of compensating the injured party for all elements of damages.

The majority of jurisdictions, however, continue to recognize the punitive damages doctrine as it existed under the common law.[203] Only a minority of jurisdictions prohibit the recovery of common law punitive damages.[204] Some jurisdictions limit punitive damages to statutorily authorized situations.[205] Several additional jurisdictions either totally or partially prohibit the use of punitive damages in civil cases.[206] Some jurisdictions, despite judicial acknowledgement that punitive damages constitute an integral component of the common law, restrict its scope such that its application essentially constitutes a compensatory award.[207]

Various jurisdictions have adopted differing standards for the award of punitive damages. Some jurisdictions assert that punitive damages are appropriate solely as punishment for a party adjudged guilty of egregious conduct.[208] Other jurisdictions conclude that the single most important basis for justifying punitive damages in a civil context is to deter the wrongdoer and others.[209] A few jurisdictions view punitive damages as additional monetary awards to supplement the compensatory award.[210] Most jurisdictions, including Texas, justify the use of punitive damages on the basis of both punishment and specific deterrence of the wrongdoer and a general deterrence of others from similar egregious conduct.[211] Accord-

---

203. Refer to Sales & Cole, note 191 *supra* at 1124-25.

204. *See, e.g.*, McCoy v. Arkansas Natural Gas Co., 175 La. 487, 143 So. 383, *cert. denied*, 287 U.S. 661 (1932); City of Lowell v. Massachusetts Bonding & Ins. Co., 313 Mass. 257, 47 N.E.2d 265 (1943); Abel v. Conover, 170 Neb. 926, 104 N.W.2d 684 (1960); Kammerer v. Western Gear Corp., 96 Wash. 2d 416, 635 P.2d 708 (1981).

205. The jurisdictions are Louisiana and Massachusetts.

206. *See, e.g.*, Glissman v. Rutt, 175 Ind. App. 493, 372 N.E.2d 1188 (1978); Abel v. Conover, 170 Neb. 926, 104 N.W.2d 684 (1960); Kammerer v. Western Gear Corp., 96 Wash. 2d 416, 635 P.2d 708 (1981).

207. *See* Collens v. New Canaan Water Co., 155 Conn. 477, 234 A.2d 825 (1967); Westview Cemetery, Inc. v. Blanchard, 234 Ga. 540, 216 S.E.2d 776 (1975); Wise v. Daniel, 221 Mich. 229, 190 N.W. 746 (1922).

208. *See, e.g.*, Malcolm v. Little, 295 A.2d 711 (Del. 1972).

209. *See, e.g.*, Jolley v. Puregro Co., 94 Idaho 702, 496 P.2d 939 (1972).

210. *See, e.g.*, Collens v. New Canaan Water Co., 155 Conn. 477, 234 A.2d 825 (1967); Perry v. Melton, 299 S.E.2d 8 (W. Va. 1982).

211. *See, e.g.*, Ratner v. Sioux Natural Gas Corp., 719 F.2d 801 (5th Cir. 1983); Gent v. Collinsville Volkswagen, Inc., 116 Ill. App. 3d 496, 451 N.E.2d 1385 (1983); Miller v. Wat-

ingly, the Texas Supreme Court in *Hofer v. Lavender*,[212] concluded that either punishment of the wrongdoer or deterrence of others against similar conduct, or both, constitutes separate and independent rationales for the imposition of punitive damage awards on wrongdoers. Additionally, the court suggests that punitive damage awards also serve as compensation for elements of damage not otherwise recoverable. It is readily apparent from a review of the historical evolution and from the rationale articulated in support of the punitive damage doctrine that the concept, in today's tort reparations system, has precipitated considerable inquiry into the continued relevancy of the punitive damage doctrine.[213]

The rationale employed by the courts for imposing punitive damages varies in significant degrees. The basis of any punitive award is the wrongdoer's egregious conduct rather than the nature and extent of the harm sustained by the plaintiff.[214] Most commentators acknowledge that the imposition of punitive damages requires more than the mere commission of a tort; defendant's conduct must be characterized as aggravated, outrageous or involving some element of conscious wrongdoing that significantly exceeds mere negligence.[215] Essentially, conduct that is deemed to be conscious, malicious, and intentional in nature supports the impo-

---

kins, 653 P.2d 126 (Mont. 1982); Leimgruber v. Claridge Assocs., Ltd., 73 N.J. 450, 375 A.2d 652 (1977); Newton v. Standard Fire Ins. Co., 291 N.C. 105, 229 S.E.2d 297 (1976); Hofer v. Lavender, 679 S.W.2d 470 (Tex. 1984); Pace v. State, 650 S.W.2d 64 (Tex. 1983); First City Nat'l Bank v. Haynes, 614 S.W.2d 605 (Tex. 1981); Bernal v. Seitt, 158 Tex. 521, 313 S.W.2d 520 (Tex. 1958); Hays v. Houston & G.N.R. R., 46 Tex. 272 (1876); Cole v. Tucker, 6 Tex. 266 (1851); Graham v. Roder, 5 Tex. 141 (1849); Ogden v. Wilson, 649 S.W.2d 780 (Tex. App.—Austin 1983, writ ref'd n.r.e.); General Ins. Corp. v. Harris, 327 S.W.2d 651 (Tex. Civ. App.—Dallas 1959, no writ); J.S. Abercrombie Co. v. Scott, 267 S.W.2d 206 (Tex. Civ. App.—Galveston 1954, writ ref'd n.r.e.). *See also* W. Prosser & W. Keeton, *The Law of Torts*, § 2, at 9 (5th ed. 1984).

212. 679 S.W.2d 470 (Tex. 1984) (Spears' dissent states that punishment and deterrance are separable concepts).

213. Refer to Sales & Cole and to Owen, note 191 *supra*. *See also* Owen, *Problems in Assessing Punitive Damages Against Manufacturers of Defective Products*, 49 U. Chi. L. Rev. 1 (1982); Duffy, *Punitive Damages: A Doctrine Which Should Be Abolished*, Defense Research Institute: *The Case Against Punitive Damages* (Hirsch & Pourous Eds. 1969); Ellis, *Fairness and Efficiency in the Law of Punitive Damages*, 56 S. Cal. L. Rev. 1 (1982).

214. Refer to Sales, note 191 *supra*, at 364. *See also Special Project*, note 202 *supra* at 695.

215. W. Prosser & W. Keeton, *The Law of Torts* § 2 (5th ed. 1984); C. McCormick, *Handbook on the Law of Damages* § 79 at 280 (1935). For example, punitive damages based solely on constructive knowledge of a highly dangerous product is not recoverable. Loney v. Colemon Co. Inc., 758 F.2d 1299, 1305 (8th Cir. 1985).

sition of punitive damages.[216] The lower continuum of conduct that is legally recognized as the basis for imposing punitive damages is gross negligence.[217] Gross negligence, essential to support an award of punitive damages, is defined as "that entire want of care which would raise the belief that the act or omission complained of was the result of a conscious indifference to the rights or welfare of the person or persons to be affected by it."[218]

In wrongful death actions, a punitive damage recovery based on willful acts or gross negligence is authorized by the Texas Constitution.[219] The Texas Constitution authorizes the surviving husband, widow, and heirs of his or her body to recover exemplary damages.[220] This constitutional provision has been construed so that only beneficiaries specifically enumerated are authorized to maintain an action for exemplary damages. Consequently, the surviving spouse and children are authorized to initiate an action for exemplary damages for the death of a deceased spouse and father,[221] but surviving parents are not constitutionally entitled to recover exemplary damages for the wrongful death of their children.[222] The surviving parents may recover exemplary damages,

---

216. *See* Light v. Wilson, 663 S.W.2d 813 (Tex. 1983) (fraud); National Bonding Agency v. Demeson, 648 S.W.2d 748 (Tex. App.—Dallas 1983, no writ) (libel/slander and invasion of privacy); Christopher v. General Computer Systems, Inc., 560 S.W.2d 698 (Tex. Civ. App.—Dallas 1977, writ ref'd n.r.e.) (malicious conversion); K-Mart No. 4195 v. Judge, 515 S.W.2d 148 (Tex. Civ. App.—Beaumont 1974, writ dism'd) (false imprisonment); Frank B. Hall Co. v. Buck, 678 S.W.2d 612 (Tex. App.—Houston [14th Dist.] 1984, n.w.h.) (defamation of character). *See also* Sales & Cole, note 191 *supra*.

217. Maxey v. Freightliner Corp., 665 F.2d 1367 (5th Cir. 1982) (en banc); Schwartz v. Sears, Roebuck & Co., 669 F.2d 1091 (5th Cir. 1982); Putnam v. Missouri Valley, Inc., 616 S.W.2d 930 (Tex. 1981); Burk Royalty Co. v. Walls, 616 S.W.2d 911 (Tex. 1981); Texas Pac. Coal & Oil Co. v. Robertson, 125 Tex. 4, 79 S.W.2d 830 (1935); Missouri Pac. Ry. v. Shuford, 72 Tex. 165, 10 S.W. 408 (1888).

218. Burk Royalty Co. v. Walls, 616 S.W.2d 911, 920 (Tex. 1981); Bennett v. Howard, 141 Tex. 101, 108, 170 S.W.2d 709, 712 (1943); Missouri Pac. Ry. v. Shuford, 72 Tex. 165, 170, 10 S.W. 408, 411 (1888).

219. TEX. CONST., art. 16, section 26 provides:

> Every person, corporation, or company that may commit a homicide, through a willful act, or omission, or gross neglect, shall be responsible, in exemplary damages, to the surviving husband, widow, heirs of his or her body, or such as them as there may be . . .

220. *Id.*

221. *See, e.g.*, Scoggins v. Southwestern Elec. Serv. Co., 434 S.W.2d 376, 380 (Tex. Civ. App.—Tyler 1968, writ ref'd n.r.e.).

222. *See, e.g.*, Gulf, C. & S.F. Ry. v. Compton, 75 Tex. 667, 13 S.W. 667 (1890); Fleming Oil Co. v. Watts, 193 S.W.2d 979 (Tex. Civ. App.—Texarkana 1946, writ ref'd n.r.e.); Smith v. Farrington, 117 Tex. 459, 8 S.W.2d 317 (Tex. Civ. App.—Amarillo 1928, no writ).

however, for the death of a child as beneficiaries of the decedent's estate under the Survival Statute.[223]

Texas currently recognizes punitive damages for gross negligence as authorized by the Texas Constitution. Additionally, Texas recognizes an injured party's common law right to seek punitive damages based either on an intentional act or gross negligence that constitutes an entire want of care that would raise a belief that the act or omission complained of was the result of a conscious indifference to the rights and welfare of the persons affected by it. The mere fact that an act is unlawful, however, does not satisfy the requisite conduct for a punitive award.[224]

Irrespective of the basis upon which punitive damages are premised, the award of punitive damages requires that the plaintiff recover actual compensatory damages.[225] The absence of compensatory damages or the finding of only nominal damages is inadequate to support a punitory award.[226] Significantly, the contributory fault of the injured party may not be utilized to diminish the award of punitive damages based on comparative fault.[227]

The award of punitive damages, however, need not bear a precise ratio to the award of compensatory damages.[228] The Texas Su-

---

223. *See* Hofer v. Lavender, 679 S.W.2d 470 (Tex. 1984). This represents an indirect method to circumvent the literal provisions of the Texas Constitution.

224. Accent Builders Co. v. Southwest Concrete Sys. Inc., 679 S.W.2d 106, 111 (Tex. App.—Dallas 1984, writ ref'd n.r.e.).

225. *See, e.g.*, City Prods. Corp. v. Berman, 610 S.W.2d 446, 450 (Tex. 1980) (absent proof of actual loss, punitive damages could not be awarded); Fort Worth Elevators Co. v. Russell, 123 Tex. 128, 149-50, 70 S.W.2d 397, 409 (1934) (proof of actual damage is a prerequisite to a punitive award); Flanagan v. Womack, 54 Tex. 45, 50 (1880) (vindictive damages not recoverable absent showing of actual injury); Sam Bradley Realty Co. v. McNair, 644 S.W.2d 533, 536 (Tex. App.—Corpus Christi 1982, no writ) ("It is elementary that exemplary damages. . . cannot be recovered unless claimant is shown to have sustained actual damages."); Nutting v. National Home Mfg. Co., 639 S.W.2d 721, 724 (Tex. App.—Austin 1982, no writ) (exemplary damages are dependant upon establishing actual damages); Pan American Petroleum Corp. v. Mitchell, 338 S.W.2d 740, 742-43 (Tex. Civ. App.—El Paso 1960, no writ) ("actual damage must be found, to sustain an award of exemplary damages"). *See generally* W. Prosser & W. Keeton, *The Law of Torts* § 2, at 14-15 (5th ed. 1984) (punitive award predicated on proof of actual damages in most jurisdictions).

226. Fort Worth Elevators Co. v. Russell, 123 Tex. 128, 149-50, 70 S.W.2d 397, 409 (1934); Giraud v. Moore, 86 Tex. 675, 676, 26 S.W. 945, 945-46 (1894).

227. The court in *Anderson v. Trentom*, 685 S.W.2d 712 (Tex. App.—Dallas 1984, writ ref'd n.r.e.) rejected the rule announced in *Pedernales Elec. Coop. Inc. v. Schultz*, 583 S.W.2d 882 (Tex. Civ. App.—Waco 1979, writ ref'd n.r.e.), that reduced the punitive award by the percentage of plaintiff's negligence.

228. *See* Martin v. Texaco, Inc., 726 F.2d 207 (5th Cir. 1984); Alamo Nat'l Bank v. Kraus, 616 S.W.2d 908 (Tex. 1981); Southwestern Inv. Co. v. Neeley, 452 S.W.2d 705 (Tex.

preme Court has articulated several factors to be considered in determining the proportional validity of the punitive to compensatory award. These factors include: (1) the nature of the wrong; (2) the character of conduct involved; (3) the degree of the wrongdoer's culpability; (4) the situation and sensibilities of the concerned parties; and (5) the extent to which the conduct offends the public's sense of justice and propriety.[229]

Punitive damages are also imposed upon corporations for the acts and conduct of their representatives. Many jurisdictions adhere to the doctrine of respondeat superior. Under this concept, an employer is subject to punitive damages when an employee, while operating within the scope of his employment, commits outrageous acts that further the employer's interests.[230] Logically, the imposition of punitive awards vicariously on another does not mesh with the rationale undergirding the objective of punishment and deterrence of a wrongdoer for opprobrious conduct. Punishing the corporation for the opprobrious conduct of its servant based solely on the legal relationship between the offending individual and the corporate employer is insupportable in theory.

Texas, consistent with a majority of jurisdictions, has adopted the complicity rule.[231] The complicity rule governs the imposition

---

1970); Costa v. Storm, 682 S.W.2d 599, 604 (Tex. App.—Houston [1st Dist.] 1984, no writ); North Houston Pole Line Corp. v. McAllister, 667 S.W.2d 829 (Tex. App.—Houston [14th Dist.] 1983, no writ). *See also* Comment, *The Reasonable Ratio Between Exemplary and Actual Damages in Texas*, 10 Hous. L. Rev. 131, 132 (1972). *See, e.g.*, Pinckard v. Dunnavant, 281 Ala. 533, 206 So. 2d 340, 344 (1968) (exemplary award need not be mathematically related to a compensatory award); Ray Dodge, Inc. v. Moore, 251 Ark. 1036, 479 S.W.2d 518, 524 (1972) (other factors should be considered besides a ratio between punitive and actual damages); Lassitter v. International Union of Operating Eng'rs, 349 So. 2d 622, 626 (Fla. 1976) (punitive and compensatory damages are not required to be proportional). *See generally* Leimgruber v. Claridge Assocs., Ltd., 73 N.J. 450, 375 A.2d 652, 656-57 (1977) (discusses the split among the jurisdictions regarding the "ratio rule").

229. *See* Alamo Nat'l Bank v. Kraus, 616 S.W.2d 908, 910 (Tex. 1981). *See also* Martin v. Texaco, Inc., 726 F.2d 207, 213 (5th Cir. 1984) (lists factors for the jury to measure punitive awards under Texas law). These factors were also reaffirmed in *Costa v. Storm*, 682 S.W.2d 599, 604 (Tex. App.—Houston [1st Dist.] 1984, no writ).

230. For an analysis of jurisdictions following the respondeat superior doctrine, see Ellis, *Fairness and Efficiency in the Law of Punitive Damages*, 56 S. Cal. L. Rev. 1 (1982). *See also* J. Ghiardi & J. Kircher, *Punitive Damage Law and Practice* 5.05 at 18 (1984); W. Prosser & W. Keeton, *The Law of Torts* § 2 at 12 (5th ed. 1984).

231. Restatement (Second) of Torts § 909 (1979) provides:

> Punitive damages can properly be awarded against a master or other principal because of an act by an agent if, but only if: (a) the principal authorized the doing and the manner of the act, or (b) the agent was unfit and the principal was reck-

of punitory awards on corporate entities in Texas.[232] The complicity rule limits vicarious liability to situations in which vice principals either commit the egregious act, authorize the act, ratify the egregious act after the fact, or employ an unfit employee who commits the opprobrious act. Essentially, representatives of the corporation who may bind the corporation must occupy the status of vice principals. A vice principal includes corporate officers and agents empowered to employ and discharge employees of the corporation, agents engaged in performance of nondelegable duties, and agents entrusted with the management of a department or a division of the corporation.[233]

Punitive damages are not awarded for breach of contract actions involving breach of express and/or implied warranties.[234] Even where the breach is malicious, intentional or capricious, punitive damages will not be awarded when based solely on breach of contract.[235] However, a contract breach coupled with egregious tortious conduct will support an award of punitive damages.[236] For example, in *Amoco Production Co. v. Alexander*,[237] royalty owners sued an oil company lessee for breach of an implied covenant to protect against field-wide drainage. The denial of exemplary damages was predicated on the fact that a covenant to protect was a

---

> less in employing him, or (c) the agent was employed in a managerial capacity and was acting in the scope of employment, or (d) the principal or a managerial agent of the principal ratified or approved the act.

See also Fort Worth Elevators Co. v. Russell, 123 Tex. 128, 145 70 S.W.2d 397, 406 (1934) (corporation liable for acts of (a) corporate officers; (b) vice principals overseeing employees; (c) agents performing non-delegable duties; and (d) department or division managers).

232. *See* Martin v. Texaco, Inc., 726 F.2d 207 (5th Cir. 1984); Maxey v. Freightliner Corp., 665 F.2d 1367 (5th Cir. 1982) (en banc); Fisher v. Carrousel Motor Hotel, Inc., 424 S.W.2d 627 (Tex. 1967).

233. *See, e.g.,* Martin v. Texaco, Inc., 726 F.2d 207 (5th Cir. 1984); King v. McGuff, 149 Tex. 432, 234 S.W.2d 403 (1950); Morton Salt Co. v. Walls, 123 Tex. 151, 70 S.W.2d 409 (1934); Fort Worth Elevators Co. v. Russell, 123 Tex. 128, 70 S.W.2d 397, 406 (1934).

234. *See, e.g.,* City Prods. Corp. v. Berman, 610 S.W.2d 446 (Tex. 1981); Superior Trucks, Inc. v. Allen, 664 S.W.2d 136, 141 (Tex. App.—Houston [1st Dist.] 1983, writ ref'd n.r.e.); K.W.S. Mfg. Co. v. McMahon, 565 S.W.2d 368 (Tex. Civ. App.—Waco 1978, writ ref'd n.r.e.); McDonough v. Zamora, 338 S.W.2d 507 (Tex. Civ. App.—San Antonio 1960, writ ref'd n.r.e.).

235. *See, e.g.,* Amoco Prod. Co. v. Alexander, 622 S.W.2d 563, 571 (Tex. 1981).

236. *See, e.g.,* Manges v. Guerra, 673 S.W.2d 180 (Tex. 1984); Nelson Cash Register, Inc. v. Data Terminal Sys., 671 S.W.2d 594, 598 (Tex. App.—San Antonio 1984, no writ); Superior Trucks, Inc. v. Allen, 664 S.W.2d 136, 141 (Tex. App.—Houston [1st Dist.] 1983, no writ).

237. 622 S.W.2d 563 (Tex. 1981).

contract action and, absent proof of an independent tort, a punitive recovery was not warranted.[238]

A majority of jurisdictions, excluding Texas, reject recovery of punitive damages against the estate of a deceased wrongdoer.[239] The rationale underlying denial of punitive damages is that a deceased wrongdoer is no longer subject to punishment and specific deterrence by mere mortals.[240] Texas, however, views judicial punishment of decedents as a basis for general deterrence of others. In *Hofer v. Lavender*,[241] the Texas Supreme Court, disapproving earlier decisions, authorized recovery of punitive damages against the estate of a deceased wrongdoer. The court stated: "[W]e conclude that under the Texas Survival Statute there exists a right to collect exemplary damages from the estate of a deceased tortfeasor."[242] The court, in reversing its earlier established rule and joining a minority of three other states,[243] postulated that the purpose for punitive damages was not merely to punish but also to deter others by setting an example.[244] The court further announced that though the Texas Constitution does not enumerate parents as a statutorily designated beneficiary entitled to recover punitive damages under Article XVI, parents may recover punitive damages for their adult children as beneficiaries of the decedent's estate under the Texas Survival Statute.[245] Apparently, "exemplary damages survive to the estate, whoever the beneficiaries of that estate may be."[246]

The dissent concluded that the aim of general deterrence was a wholly insufficient basis for awarding punitive damages.[247] Pun-

---

238. *Id.* at 571.

239. Refer to Sales, note 191 *supra* at 9. *See also* RESTATEMENT (SECOND) OF TORTS § 926(b) (1979). Section 926 provides:

> Under statutes providing for the survival or revival of tort actions, the damages for a tort not involving death for which the tortfeasor is responsible are not affected by the death of either party before or during trial, except that . . . (b) the death of the tortfeasor terminates liability for punitive damages.

240. *See, e.g.*, Allen v. Anderson, 93 Nev. 204, 562 P.2d 487, 489-90 (1977).

241. 679 S.W.2d 470, *rev'g*, 658 S.W.2d 812 (Tex. 1984).

242. *Id.* at 475.

243. Florida, Illinois and West Virginia permit punitive awards in this situation. *See* Johnson v. Rinesmith, 238 So. 2d 659 (Fla. App. 1969); National Bank v. Norfolk & Western Ry. Co., 73 Ill. 2d 160, 383 N.E.2d 919 (1978); Perry v. Melton, 299 S.E.2d 8 (W. Va. 1982). Texas now joins this rather exclusive group.

244. 679 S.W.2d 470 (Tex. 1984) (Justice Spears dissents).

245. *Id.* at 476. *See also* TEX. REV. CIV. STAT. ANN. art. 5525 (Vernon 1958).

246. 679 S.W.2d 470, 476 (Tex. 1984).

247. *Id.*

ishment and deterrence are inseparable, and as the dissent noted, "members of the public are deterred from similar misconduct because they witness the wrongdoer's punishment. When, through death, the tortfeasor is no longer subject to legal punishment, the general deterrent effect likewise is greatly diminished, if not completely frustrated. Effective deterrence cannot be achieved when punishment is impossible."[248] Recognition of deterrence and punishment as separate bases for punitive damages, if considered literally, sanctions a double recovery.[249]

In the majority of jurisdictions, punitive damages have been approved in actions based on strict tort liability cases. Rejecting the rationale that the punitive damage doctrine is predicated upon the outrageous and quasi-criminal conduct of the wrongdoer while strict tort liability is based solely upon the condition of a product,[250] Texas courts have sanctioned the imposition of punitive damages against product manufacturers.[251] Though compensatory damages are recoverable in strict tort liability cases, the courts conclude that gross negligence may be superimposed on this underlying action to justify the award of punitive damages. Under the standard articulated in *Burk Royalty Co. v. Walls*,[252] the jury may consider all the evidence relating to the manufacturer's con-

---

248. *Id.* at 478.

249. *Id.* Justice Spears stated, "The court's reasoning will allow parties to submit one issue seeking damages to punish and deter the tortfeasor and another issue seeking damages as an example to others." *Id.* (Chief Justice Pope and Justices McGee and Barrow joined in the dissent).

250. *See, e.g.,* Turner v. General Motors Corp., 584 S.W.2d 844, 847 (Tex. 1979) (a defect is vital to establish a claim of product liability); Gonzales v. Caterpillar Tractor Co., 571 S.W.2d 867, 871 (Tex. 1978) (care exercised by supplier irrelevant because strict liability concentrates on the product). *See also* RESTATEMENT (SECOND) OF TORTS § 402A (1965) (the supplier of a defective product is strictly liable regardless of the amount of care exercised).

251. Maxey v. Freightliner Corp., 450 F. Supp. 955 (N.D. Tex. 1978), *aff'd,* 623 F.2d 395 (5th Cir. 1980), *rev'd on other grounds,* 665 F.2d 1367 (5th Cir. 1982) (en banc), *aff'd in part, rev'd in part,* 722 F.2d 1238 (5th Cir.), *aff'd,* 727 F.2d 350 (5th Cir. 1984) (manufacturer of tractor); Ford Motor Co. v. Nowak, 638 S.W.2d 582 (Tex. App.—Corpus Christi 1982, writ ref'd n.r.e.) (transmission lever system in an automobile); Rawlings Sporting Goods Co. v. Daniels, 619 S.W.2d 435 (Tex. Civ. App.—Waco 1981, writ ref'd n.r.e.) (a defect in a football helmet manufactured by defendant); Heil Co. v. Grant, 534 S.W.2d 916 (Tex. Civ. App.—Tyler 1976, writ ref'd n.r.e.) (defect in a telescopic sleeve hoist manufactured by defendant). *But see* Newding v. Kroger Co., 554 S.W.2d 15 (Tex. Civ. App.—Houston [14th Dist.] 1977, no writ) (bottler deemed not liable for punitive damages).

252. 616 S.W.2d 911 (Tex. 1981). Refer to notes 94-104 *supra* and accompanying text. The standard for appellate review of punitive awards is specifically outlined in *Dyson v. Olin Corp.,* 28 TEX. SUP. CT. J. 512 (June 19, 1985).

duct to determine whether the conduct is grossly negligent. Gross negligence is defined as a willful or wanton disregard of the rights and welfare of others.[253] Thus the jury evaluates the manufacturer's conduct despite the fact that the underlying basis of strict tort liability is imposed without reference to the supplier's conduct and is based on evidence otherwise inadmissable in a negligence action. In essence, a remedy based on the quasi-criminal conduct of the wrongdoer is pyramided upon evidence relating to and focusing solely on the condition of the product.

Subsequent to *Burk*,[254] the punitive damage doctrine in a strict tort liability action was considered in *Rawlings Sporting Goods Co. v. Daniels*.[255] Plaintiff sustained permanent brain damage when his football helmet deformed inward when he collided with another player. Plaintiff alleged that the manufacturer was liable for punitive damages for failure to warn of the dangers. The jury awarded the plaintiff $750,000 actual and $750,000 punitive damages.[256] The court approved the punitory award based in part on evidence that: (1) the manufacturer's knew that the helmet would not protect against brain injury; (2) the general public was unaware of the potential dangers while wearing a football helmet; and (3) the manufacturer consciously decided not to warn the public that the helmet would not protect against all head injuries under every conceivable circumstance.[257] It has been suggested that if these elements (i.e. failure to warn of potential dangers) constitute willful and wanton misconduct (i.e. an entire want of care) on the part of the manufacturer, then liability for punitive damages is imposed essentially on a negligence standard.[258]

In *Ford Motor Co. v. Nowak*,[259] a punitive award of $4,000,000 was approved for the death of an elderly woman fatally injured by

---

253. The application of punitive damages in a product liability case under the *Burk* standard is exhaustively analyzed, discussed, praised, and criticized in *Maxey v. Freightliner Corp.*, 450 F. Supp. 955 (N.D. Tex. 1978), *aff'd*, 623 F.2d 395 (5th Cir. 1980), *rev'd on other grounds*, 665 F.2d 1367 (5th Cir. 1982) (en banc), *aff'd in part, rev'd in part*, 722 F.2d 1238 (5th Cir.), *aff'd*, 727 F.2d 350 (5th Cir. 1984). *See also* Dyson v. Olin Corp., 28 Tex. Sup. Ct. J. 512 (June 19, 1985).

254. 616 S.W.2d 911 (Tex. 1981).

255. 619 S.W.2d 435 (Tex. Civ. App.—Waco 1981, writ ref'd n.r.e.).

256. *Id.* at 437.

257. *Id.* at 440-41.

258. It should be noted that the elements enumerated to sustain the award have been criticized as "feeble." *See* Sales, note 191 *supra* at 383 and n.164.

259. 638 S.W.2d 582 (Tex. App.—Corpus Christi 1982, writ ref'd n.r.e.).

an alleged design defect in the shift lever of a vehicle's automatic transmission.[260] The award was predicated on the fact that Ford possessed some limited knowledge of a possible design problem in the shift system but failed to take corrective action.[261] The failure of Ford to rectify a known, potentially dangerous problem was deemed sufficient evidence of gross negligence for which punitive damages, in a ratio of ten to one to compensatory damages, were judicially sanctioned.[262]

The dissent criticized approval of the punitive damage award, suggesting that the totality of all the evidence was insufficient even to support a finding that a design defect existed at all.[263] The dissent noted:

> A review of the record as a whole leads me to the conclusion that there is no evidence from which the jury could find that the utility of the transmission was outweighed by the likelihood of and the gravity of injury from its use. Further, there is no evidence that Ford was consciously indifferent to appellees' rights, welfare and safety, so as to justify the award of punitive damages.[264]

Recently, in *International Armament Corp. v. King*,[265] plaintiff was inadvertently injured when a 12 gauge shotgun supplied by the defendant misfired when the receiver was closed by the user. The court found the gun was defectively manufactured and awarded both compensatory and punitive damages. Without any analysis of the applicability of the punitive damage doctrine to a strict tort liability action, the Texas Supreme Court simply observed that "The evidence was sufficient for the jury to infer that Interarms intentionally did not inspect the safety related parts of the guns, but was interested only in the cosmetic appearance of the guns . . ."[266]

Recent decisions have imposed punitive damages on product suppliers based upon strict tort liability, but analysis of the applicability of punitive damages in this context has been rather attenuated. While some jurisdictions question whether the punitive

---

260. *Id.* at 598.
261. *Id.* at 593-95.
262. *Id.* at 593.
263. *Id.* at 602.
264. *Id.*
265. 686 S.W.2d 595 (Tex. 1985).
266. 686 S.W.2d at 599.

damage doctrine is applicable against a manufacturer in actions predicated on strict tort liability, there has been a significant increase in the number of jurisdictions sanctioning punitive damages.[267] Jurisdictions disallowing recovery recognize that the punitive damage doctrine is used to punish egregious conduct whereas strict tort liability is a socioeconomic concept of risk distribution premised upon the product's condition.[268] Some jurisdictions simply disavow punitive damages as an outdated concept.[269]

Some commentators have suggested that application of the punitive damage doctrine in strict tort liability against the manufacturer or supplier of a single product line may constitute a form of overkill. For example, punitive damages assessed against a manufacturer based upon a defectively designed product or defective marketing (failure to warn) typically affects thousands of identically designed products introduced into the stream of commerce. Punitive damages that are repeatedly awarded based upon an identically designed or marketed product may subject the manufacturer or product supplier to economic overkill.[270] While most ju-

---

267. *Compare* Saupitty v. Yazoo Mfg. Co., 726 F.2d 657 (10th Cir. 1984) (design defect in lawn mower); Acosta v. Honda Motor Co., Ltd., 717 F.2d 828 (3rd Cir. 1983) (alleged defect in motorcycle wheel); Dorsey v. Honda Motor Co., Ltd., 655 F.2d 650 (5th Cir. 1981), *cert. denied,* 459 U.S. 880 (1982) (defective automobile); Gillham v. Admiral Corp., 523 F.2d 102 (6th Cir. 1975), *cert. denied,* 424 U.S. 913 (1976) (defective television); Hasson v. Ford Motor Co., 32 Cal. 3d 388, 185 Cal. Rptr. 654, 650 P.2d 1171 (1982), *cert. denied,* 459 U.S. 1190 (1983) (defective brakes); Grimshaw v. Ford Motor Co., 119 Cal. App. 3d 757, 174 Cal. Rptr. 348 (1981) (defective design of Ford Pinto); Toyota Motor Co. v. Moll, 438 So. 2d 192 (Fla. Dist. Ct. App. 1983) (defective gas tank); Gryc v. Dayton-Hudson Corp., 297 N.W.2d 727 (Minn.), *cert. denied,* 449 U.S. 921 (1980) (defective "flannelette" pajamas); Leichtamer v. American Motors Corp., 67 Ohio St. 2d 456, 424 N.E.2d 568 (1981) (defective jeep); Thiry v. Armstrong World Indus., 661 P.2d 515 (Okla. 1983) (defective asbestos product); and Wangen v. Ford Motor Co., 97 Wis. 2d 260, 294 N.W.2d 437 (1980) (defective fuel tank in Ford Mustang) all sanctioning punitive damages *with* Roginsky v. Richardson-Merrell, Inc., 378 F.2d 832 (2d Cir. 1967) (allegedly defective drug); Knippen v. Ford Motor Co., 546 F.2d 993 (D.C. Cir. 1976) (alleged design defect in station wagon); and Drayton v. Jiffee Chem. Corp., 395 F. Supp. 1081 (N.D. Ohio 1975) (defective design of liquid drain cleaner) all denying recovery.

268. *See* Gold v. Johns-Manville Sales Corp., 553 F. Supp. 482 (D.N.J. 1982), *appeal dism'd,* 723 F.2d 1068 (1983) (would not allow punitive damages in action based on strict liability); Wolf v. Proctor & Gamble Co., 555 F. Supp. 613 (D.N.J. 1982) (punitive damages are based on defendant's conduct which is a negligence concept); Butcher v. Robertshaw Controls Co., 550 F. Supp. 692, 705 (D. Md. 1981) (punitive damages are incompatible with the theory of strict tort liability). *Cf.* Sanford v. Celotex Corp., 598 F. Supp. 529 (D.C. Tenn. 1984).

269. *See* Kammerer v. Western Gear Corp., 96 Wash. 2d 416, 635 P.2d 708 (1981).

270. See the discussion in Roginsky v. Richardson-Merrell, Inc., 378 F.2d 832 (2d Cir.

risdictions eschew the concern of economic overkill based upon lack of data,[271] some courts express the concern that punitive damages may pose a threat and should be reviewed by the federal or state legislature.[272]

In *Hansen v. Johns-Manville Products Corp.*,[273] plaintiff's husband died from asbestos-related diseases. Plaintiff instituted suit based on strict tort liability for failure to test, inspect and warn.[274] The jury found the manufacturer strictly liable in tort, and the Fifth Circuit affirmed. Essentially ignoring an analysis of the application of punitive damages in strict tort liability actions, the court, relying on *Heil Co. v. Grant*,[275] observed that "punitive damages may be recovered under Article 16, Section 26 of the Constitution of the State of Texas."[276]

The defendants suggested that repetitive punitive damage awards were unconstitutional and constituted a form of double jeopardy.[277] Moreover, defendants urged that the very real potential of overkill was inconsistent with the underlying policy objectives of both strict tort liability and the punitive damage doctrine.[278] The court found the unique problems presented by mass litigation essentially irrelevant because of Article 16 of the Texas

---

1967). *See also* K. Redden, *Punitive Damages* § 4.7 (A) at 118-19 (1980) (discussing excessive awards that cripple a corporate defendant).

271. *See* Acosta v. Honda Motor Co., Ltd., 717 F.2d 828 (3d Cir. 1983); Martin v. Johns-Manville Corp., 322 Pa. Super. 348, 469 A.2d 655, 665 (1983), *appeal filed*, Apr. 2, 1984 ("if the defendant's conduct was so reckless, and injured so many people, that the effect of the damages awarded against it is bankruptcy, we are hardpressed to understand why that defendant should not be required to live with the consequences of its actions"). A similar view is apparent in *State ex rel. Young v. Crookham*, 290 Or. 61, 618 P.2d 1268 (1980).

272. *See* Moran v. Johns-Manville Sales Corp., 691 F.2d 811, 817 (6th Cir. 1982). *See also* Jackson v. Johns-Manville Corp., 727 F.2d 506 (5th Cir. 1984), *rev'd*, 750 F.2d 1314 (1985) (en banc) (suggesting federal legislation may be appropriate to govern industry-wide litigation to prevent destruction of manufacturers since the issue is not "uniquely federal" and thus insufficient to predicate the imposition of a federal substantive rule).

273. 734 F.2d 1036 (5th Cir. 1984).

274. *Id.* at 1039.

275. 534 S.W.2d 916, 926 (Tex. Civ. App.—Tyler 1976, writ ref'd n.r.e.).

276. 734 F.2d at 1041. *See also* TEX CONST. art. 16, § 26. Article 16, Section 26 provides:

> Every person, corporation, or company that may commit a homicide, through a willful act, or omission, or gross neglect, shall be responsible, in exemplary damages, to the surviving husband, widow, heirs of his or her body, or such as them as there may be . . .

277. 734 F.2d at 1040.

278. *Id.*

Constitution.[279] The court concluded that repetitive punitive awards were not within the purview of the double jeopardy doctrine because such awards were not judicially regarded as criminal fines.[280] It appears, therefore, that the potential for economic overkill is acceptable and poses no impediment to the use of the punitive damage doctrine. Perhaps it is significant that Article 16 of the Texas Constitution was adopted more than a hundred years before the concept of strict tort liability for product related accidents was formulated by the authors of the *Restatement* and adopted by the Texas courts.[281]

Strict liability rests upon the socioeconomic concept of risk distribution. While the supplier is blameless, liability is imposed because the supplier purportedly is best able to absorb the loss by increasing the price of products marketed to the public and by purchasing insurance coverage. A critical issue, therefore, is whether exemplary damages are covered by insurance. The standard insurance policy declares that the insurer shall pay "all sums which the insured shall become legally obligated to pay as damages . . ."[282] Insurance coverage has been extended in negligence cases to grossly negligent operators of motor vehicles.[283] In *Ridgway v.*

---

279. *Id.* at 1041. *But see* Jackson v. Johns-Manville Sales Corp., 750 F.2d 1314 (5th Cir. 1985) (en banc), *rev'g*, 727 F.2d 506 (1984). The court certified the question of damages in a mass tort context to the Mississippi Supreme Court because they were "reluctant to undertake the careful weighing of competing state policies" needed to reach "a principled rather than a conjectural result." *Id.* at 1328. The dissent vehemently opposed certification to the state, desiring instead certification to the United States Supreme Court thereby developing a federal common law rule regarding damages recoverable in mass tort litigation. The dissent emphasized that "an equitable division of any scarce resource between citizens of different states" would be thwarted if conflicting state laws applied. The dissent reasoned that absent Congressional action, the Supreme Court was the only other institution capable of imposing uniformity in this area. *Id.* at 1329.

280. 734 F.2d at 1042. This indeed is an interesting observation. Fines for severe criminal acts such as burglary, robbery, rape, and other less than desirable societal acts are clearly deliniated by a minimum and maximum limit which may only be levied one time rather than being unlimited and imposed repeatedly like punitive damage awards in product liability cases.

281. For example, the Texas Supreme Court in *Sanchez v. Shindler*, 651 S.W.2d 249 (Tex. 1983), abandoned more than 100 years of common law jurisprudence because it was no longer deemed apropos to today's world and society's needs.

282. TEX. REV. CIV. STAT. ANN. art. 6701h, § 21(b) (2) (Vernon Supp. 1985).

283. *See* Home Indem. Co. v. Tyler, 522 S.W.2d 594 (Tex. Civ. App.—Houston [14th Dist.] 1975, writ ref'd n.r.e.); Dairyland County Mut. Ins. Co. v. Wallgren, 477 S.W.2d 341 (Tex. Civ. App.—Fort Worth 1972, writ ref'd n.r.e.).

Gulf Life Ins. Co.,[284] defendant, an insurance company, issued an umbrella liability policy which stated that the company agreed "[t]o indemnify the insured for all sums which the insured shall be obligated to pay by reason of the liability (A) imposed upon the insured by law . . ."[285] The Fifth Circuit construed this provision to "necessarily include both actual and punitive damages."[286] The court summarily rejected the suggestion that permitting insurance to cover punitive damages nullifies the rationale of punishment and deterrence upon which the punitive damage doctrine rests.[287]

Texas courts have not specifically addressed the issue of insurance coverage for punitive damages in a strict tort liability context. Since insurance coverage for gross negligence does not contravene public policy in negligence actions, the courts probably will extend the rationale of these prior decisions to strict tort liability actions. It should be emphasized, however, that punitive damages are designed to "punish and deter." Allowing insurance companies to absorb the impact of punitive awards appears to contradict, as well as frustrate, the punishment and deterrence rationale. Though manufacturers are forced to pay higher premiums, innocent consumers and members of society are likewise penalized by the corresponding rise of insurance premiums. It seems somewhat incongruous to visit punishment upon innocent members of society, but this appears to be the pragmatic effect of levying punitive damage awards and then authorizing insurance coverage. This approach seemingly rests upon the "deep pocket" legal theorem.

7.05 Deceptive Trade Practices Act in Products

The Texas Deceptive Trade Practices - Consumer Protection Act (DTPA)[288] was enacted to provide consumers a remedy for deceptive trade practices without the burden of proof and the numerous defenses encountered in common law fraud or breach of war-

---

284. 578 F.2d 1026 (5th Cir. 1978) (per curiam).

285. *Id.* at 1029.

286. *Id.*

287. *Id.* at 1030. *But see* Northwestern Nat'l Casualty Co. v. McNulty, 307 F.2d 432 (5th Cir. 1962) (Florida law) (punitive damages may not be assessed against the insurer as a matter of public policy); Dorsey v. Continental Casualty Co., 730 F.2d 675 (11th Cir. 1984) (purpose of punitive damages is to punish the wrongdoer-insured, not the insurance company).

288. Tex. Bus. & Comm. Code Ann. § 17.41 *et seq.* (Vernon Supp. 1985).

ranty actions.[289] In strict tort liability, the identical evidence supports a dual cause of action - one sounding in strict tort liability and another under the DTPA.[290]

Under Sec. 17.50 of the DTPA, three types of damages may be awarded: (1) actual damages; (2) statutory damages that are mandatory if actual damages are awarded; and (3) discretionary damages if the defendant's conduct was committed knowingly.[291] Damages for personal injuries as well as attorney's fees also are recoverable.[292]

To recover damages under the DTPA, plaintiff must establish that the alleged deceptive trade practice was the producing cause of his injury.[293] In *Pope v. Rollins Protective Services Co.*,[294] plaintiff leased a burglar alarm system from defendant. Defendant represented that even if the alarm's wires were cut, the alarm would go off and alert the company's "central station."[295] When the plaintiff was robbed at gunpoint and the alarm wires cut, the alarm was deactivated. Moreover, the alarm signals were merely received by defendant's answering service which was not connected to a police station.[296] Plaintiff instituted suit under the DTPA for the product's failure to perform as represented. The trial court awarded plaintiff $150,000 for her resulting mental anguish and, pursuant to 17.50(b) of the DTPA, trebled that amount.[297] The Fifth Circuit approved application of the DTPA remedies because

---

289. *See* Pope v. Rollins Protective Servs. Co., 703 F.2d 197 (5th Cir. 1983).

290. *See* Keller Indus., Inc. v. Reeves, 656 S.W.2d 221 (Tex. App.—Austin 1983, writ ref'd n.r.e.).

291. Martin v. McKee Realtors, Inc., 663 S.W.2d 446 (Tex. 1984). *See also* Jim Walter Homes, Inc. v. Valencia, 690 S.W.2d 239, 241 (Tex. 1985) (achieves three objectives).

292. *See, e.g.*, Cail v. Service Motors, Inc., 660 S.W.2d 814 (Tex. 1983); Pace v. State, 650 S.W.2d 64 (Tex. 1983); Mahan Volkswagen, Inc. v. Hall, 648 S.W.2d 324 (Tex. App.—Houston [1st Dist.] 1982, writ ref'd n.r.e.); Litton Indus. Prods., Inc., v. Gammage, 644 S.W.2d 170 (Tex. App.—Houston [1st Dist.] 1982), *aff'd on other grounds*, 668 S.W.2d 319 (Tex. 1984).

293. American Transfer & Storage Co. v. Brown, 584 S.W.2d 284, 294-96 (Tex. Civ. App.—Dallas 1979), *rev'd on other grounds*, 601 S.W.2d 931 (Tex.), *cert. denied*, 449 U.S. 1015 (1980). Producing cause is distinct from proximate cause; proximate cause involves cause-in-fact and foreseeability. Farley v. M M Cattle Co., 529 S.W.2d 751, 755 (Tex. 1975). Foreseeability, however, is not an element of producing cause. C.A. Hoover & Son v. O.M. Franklin Serum Co., 444 S.W.2d 596, 598 (Tex. 1969).

294. 703 F.2d 197 (5th Cir. 1983).

295. *Id.* at 199-200.

296. *Id.*

297. *Id.* at 206.

defendant's misrepresentations were the producing cause of plaintiff's mental anguish which, in turn, satisfied the "actual damage" requirement of the Act.[298] The court declared that trebling the actual damages was mandatory.[299] This latter holding conflicts with *Martin v. McKee Realtors, Inc.*,[300] in which the Texas Supreme Court specifically declared that the trebling of damages rested in the discretion of the trier of fact, and thus, was not mandatory.[301]

Damages for personal injuries may be trebled when the injury results from a violation of the Act. In *Litton Industrial Products v. Gammage*,[302] plaintiff was injured when a rachet adapter failed. Plaintiff instituted suit against defendant based on negligence, strict tort liability and the DTPA.[303] The trial court trebled the damages under the DTPA and the appellate court affirmed.[304] Though the Texas Supreme Court did not reject prior holdings that personal injuries are recoverable and can be trebled under the DTPA, it reversed the treble award due to lack of evidence that the DTPA had been violated.[305]

Attorney's fees, as well as personal injuries, are recoverable under the DTPA. In *Cail v. Service Motors, Inc.*,[306] plaintiff purchased a pickup truck represented to be a 1978 model but which was, in reality, a combination of damaged 1973 and 1978 trucks. The defendant made a settlement offer that did not include repayment for attorney's fees. Plaintiff instituted suit under the DTPA seeking damages and attorney's fees. Though the jury awarded attorney's fees, the trial court denied the award because the amount was substantially the same as the offer.[307] The Texas Supreme Court declared that the settlement offer was improper absent attorney's fees.[308] While *Cail* involved a settlement offer, Section 17.50(d) of the statute explicitly provides: "Each consumer who prevails shall be awarded court costs and reasonable and necessary

---

298. *Id.* at 202-04.
299. *Id.* at 206-07.
300. 663 S.W.2d 446 (Tex. 1984).
301. *Id.*
302. 644 S.W.2d 170 (Tex. App.—Houston [14th Dist.] 1982), *aff'd on other grounds*, 668 S.W.2d 319 (Tex. 1984).
303. 668 S.W.2d at 319.
304. 644 S.W.2d at 171.
305. 668 S.W.2d at 324.
306. 660 S.W.2d 814 (Tex. 1983).
307. *Id.*
308. *Id.*

attorneys' fees."[309] Under the DTPA, recovery of attorney's fees and applicable penalties under the Act may be recovered in a product liability case involving a violation of this Act.[310]

The recovery of treble damages under the DTPA is considered to be punitive in nature.[311] A plaintiff, therefore, is precluded from recovering both treble and punitive damages based on the same defective product.[312]

7.06 Conclusion

A wide spectrum of damages is authorized in strict tort liability actions. Recovery of damages for bodily injury and/or wrongful death caused by a defective product is indisputably recognized. Loss of consortium appears to be available as a separate recovery in a strict tort liability action. Recovery of damages in second impact cases for enhanced injuries (injuries that have been enhanced as a result of a defective product) may be recovered based on a system of comparative causation.

Recovery of damages to property other than the defective product itself is well established. Recovery of damages to the product itself and economic losses are recoverable under the Uniform Commercial Code but not under strict tort liability. Of course, if economic loss is collaterally involved with personal injury or harm to other property, suit may be brought on either breach of warranty or strict tort liability.

Bystander recovery in Texas and elsewhere has been greatly expanded. The punitive damage doctrine is currently recognized in strict tort liability actions but it has been suggested that the doctrine may be inconsistent with the very underpinnings of strict tort liability. Punitive damages, however, remain a significant factor in damage recoveries obtained from product-related accidents.

---

309. Tex. Bus. & Comm. Code Ann. § 17.50(d) (Vernon Supp. 1985).

310. *See, e.g.*, Pace v. State, 650 S.W.2d 64 (Tex. 1983); American Transfer & Storage Co. v. Brown, 601 S.W.2d 931 (Tex. 1980), *cert. denied,* 449 U.S. 1015 (1980); Keller Indus. Inc., v. Reeves, 656 S.W.2d 221 (Tex. App.—Austin 1983, writ ref'd n.r.e.); Mahan Volkswagen, Inc. v. Hall, 648 S.W.2d 324 (Tex. App.—Houston [1st Dist.] 1982, writ ref'd n.r.e.); Charlie Thomas Courtesy Ford v. Avalos, 619 S.W.2d 9 (Tex. Civ. App.—Houston [1st Dist.] 1981, no writ).

311. Pace v. State, 650 S.W.2d 64, 65 (Tex. 1983).

312. Charlie Thomas Courtesy Ford v. Avalos, 619 S.W.2d 9 (Tex. Civ. App.—Houston [1st Dist.] 1981, no writ); Riverside Nat'l Bank v. Lewis, 572 S.W.2d 553 (Tex. Civ. App.—Houston [1st Dist.] 1978), *rev'd on other grounds,* 603 S.W.2d 169 (Tex. 1980).

CHAPTER VIII. DISCOVERY*

---

* Adam Schiffer coauthored this chapter.

8.01 Introduction

> The purpose of the Discovery Rules is to augment and facilitate the trial process, to narrow as much as possible, the actual issues in dispute, and to change the trial of a lawsuit from a game of chance and surprise, . . . to an orderly process of unclouding matters and uncovering the actual facts involved.[1]

Unlike evidence, pretrial discovery is not limited to matters that will be admissible at trial. Instead, any matter "reasonably calculated to lead to the discovery of admissible evidence" is gen-

1. Pearson Corp. v. Wichita Falls Boys Club Alumni Ass'n, Inc., 633 S.W.2d 684, 686 (Tex. App.—Fort Worth 1982, no writ). *Cf.* West v. Solito, 563 S.W.2d 240, 243 (Tex. 1978) ("Discovery proceedings have as their aim and purpose the administration of justice by allowing the parties to obtain the fullest knowledge of issues and facts prior to trial"); Martinez v. Rutledge, 592 S.W.2d 398, 399 (Tex. Civ. App.—Dallas 1979, writ ref'd n.r.e.) ("The purpose of discovery is to allow the parties to obtain the fullest knowledge of facts and issues prior to trial"); International Sec. Life Ins. Co. v. Maas, 458 S.W.2d 484, 488 (Tex. Civ. App.—Houston [1st Dist.] 1970, writ ref'd n.r.e.) ("the primary purpose of the rule is to simplify trials by eliminating matters about which there is no real controversy, but which may be difficult or expensive to prove"); Gordon v. Blackmon, 675 S.W.2d 790, 793 (Tex. App.—Corpus Christi 1984, no writ)("the ultimate purpose of discovery is to seek the truth, so that disputes may be decided by what the facts reveal, not by what facts are concealed").

erally discoverable.[2] This broad grant is limited, however, by the opposing party's legitimate interest in avoiding overly broad requests for discovery, disclosure of privileged or exempt information, or harassment.[3] Though the concept of relevance is not susceptible to precise definition, "nonetheless, relevance does implicate a balancing of the probative value of the information sought and the burden upon the movant, if discovery is denied, weighed against the burden placed upon the respondent, if discovery is granted."[4] The expansive language incorporated in the rules is consciously designed to encourage the liberal, but relevant, use of pretrial discovery.[5] Recently promulgated Rule 166b[6] establishes the parameters of permissible discovery.[7]

---

2. TEX. R. CIV. P. 166b; Jampole v. Touchy, 673 S.W.2d 569 (Tex. 1984); Fisher v. Continental Ill. Nat'l Bank & Trust Co., 424 S.W.2d 664, 669 (Tex. Civ. App.—Houston [14th Dist.] 1968, writ ref'd n.r.e.) (pretrial procedure has a two-fold purpose: it may be used to develop evidence to be used at trial; and it may be used to develop the facts relating to a claim or a defense in a pending trial).

3. *See* Jampole v. Touchy, 673 S.W.2d 569, 573 (Tex. 1984); General Motors Corp. v. Lawrence, 651 S.W.2d 732 (Tex. 1983); Gordon v. Blackmon, 675 S.W.2d 790, 793 (Tex. App.—Corpus Christi 1984, no writ)

4. Gordon v. Blackmon, 675 S.W.2d 790, 793 (Tex. App.—Corpus Christi 1984, no writ) ("If relevance is shown by this balancing process, the trial judge nonetheless may direct 'that requested discovery not be sought in whole or in part' if the circumstances of the case require.")

5. Martinez v. Rutledge, 592 S.W.2d 398, 399 (Tex. Civ. App.—Dallas 1979, writ ref'd n.r.e.) (the rules pertaining to discovery should be liberally construed); Fisher v. Continental Ill. Nat'l Bank & Trust Co., 424 S.W.2d 664, 669 (Tex. Civ. App.—Houston [14th Dist.] 1968, writ ref'd n.r.e.) (the courts encourage a liberal use of pretrial discovery procedures). *But see* General Motors Corp. v. Lawrence, 651 S.W.2d 732, 734 (Tex. 1983) in which the Texas Supreme Court imposed some measure of limitation on discovery. Where General Motors Corp. was compelled to produce tests on all models of cars, trunks, tanks, trains, or other vehicles ever produced by General Motors Corporation since its incorporation in 1908, court reasoned that these overly broad requests constituted a clear abuse of discovery.

6. TEX. R. CIV. P. 166b.

7. For a further overview of pretrial discovery in Texas see Barrow & Henderson, *1984 Amendments to the Texas Rules of Civil Procedure Affecting Discovery*, 15 ST. MARY'S L.J. 713 (1984); McConnico, *1984 Texas Rules of Civil Procedure Amendments*, 36 BAYLOR L. REV. 73 (1984); Spears, *The Rules of Civil Procedure: 1981 Changes in Pre-Trial Discovery*, 12 ST MARY'S L.J. 633 (1981); Pope & McConnico, *Practicing Law with the 1981 Texas Rules*, 32 BAYLOR L. REV. 457 (1980); Sales, *Pre-Trial Discovery in Texas*, 31 SW. L.J. 1017 (1977); Sales, *Discovery Under the Texas Rules of Civil Procedure: A Supplement*, 38 TEX. B.J. 541 (1975); Sales, *Discovery Under the Texas Rules of Civil Procedure*, 37 TEX. B.J. 39 (1974).

8.02 Rule 166b: Scope of Discovery

Prior to the 1984 amendments, the scope of discovery was defined in several different rules. Under the amended rules, the standards governing the scope of discovery are essentially embodied in Rule 166b.[8]

A. *Forms of Discovery*

Under Rule 166b(1) the permissible forms of discovery include: oral[9] or written depositions[10] of any party or nonparty; written interrogatories to a party;[11] requests of a party for admission of facts and the genuineness or identity of documents and things;[12] requests and motions for production, examination, and copying of documents or other tangible materials;[13] requests and motions for entry upon and examination of real property;[14] and motions for a mental or physical examination of a party.[15]

B. *Scope of Discovery*

Rule 166b provides that parties may obtain discovery regarding any matter that is relevant to any issue in the case.[16] The bur-

---

8. *See* Tex. R. Civ. P. 167 (Vernon 1983) (discovery of documents and things); *Id.* 186a (scope of examination); *Id.* 186b (orders for protection of parties and deponents). *Compare* Tex. R. Civ. P. 166b(2) (documents and tangible things); *Id.* 166b(4) (protective order).

9. *See* Tex. R. Civ. P. 200. Formerly *Id.* 186, 199 (Vernon 1983).

10. Tex. R. Civ. P. 208. Formerly *Id.* 186, 196 (Vernon 1983).

11. Tex. R. Civ. P. 168.

12. Tex. R. Civ. P. 169.

13. Tex. R. Civ. P. 167.

14. Tex. R. Civ. P. 166(2)c. Formerly Rule 167(1)c (Vernon 1983).

15. Tex. R. Civ. P. 167a.

16. Tex. R. Civ. P. 166b(2)a. *See* Carroll Cable Co. v. Miller, 501 S.W.2d 299, 299 (Tex. 1973) (relevancy shown where insurance agreement not available to moving party and that the information was needed to determine settlement and litigation strategy); Narro Warehouse, Inc. v. Kelly, 530 S.W.2d 146, 150 (Tex. Civ. App.—Corpus Christi 1975, writ ref'd n.r.e.) (income tax returns subject to discovery if relevant); Ramsay v. Santa Rosa Medical Center, 498 S.W.2d 741, 744 (Tex. Civ. App.—San Antonio 1973, writ ref'd n.r.e.), *cert denied*, 417 U.S. 938, 94 S. Ct. 3062 (1974) (mental patient's diary relevant to show patient's mental state which was relevant to the main cause); Lower Nueces River Water Supply Dist. v. Sellers, 323 S.W.2d 324, 328 (Tex. Civ. App.—San Antonio 1959, writ ref'd n.r.e.) (information upon which income tax returns are based such as that kept and furnished to a public accountant for the purpose of making the tax returns is admissible if relevant). *But see* Great Am. Ins. Co. v. Murray, 437 S.W.2d 264, 265 (Tex. 1969) (decided prior to the amendment authorizing disclosure of insurance agreements; insurance policy limits were not discoverable because the ability to satisfy a judgment was not material to the issue of liability);

den rests on the moving party to plead and to establish the relevancy of the information sought; a mere conclusion or assertion of relevance is insufficient.[17] As the court in *Durham v. Cannan Communications*[18] noted, despite the liberalization of the rules, discovery rules are not intended to sanction "fishing excursions."[19] The rules are not a vehicle to harass or to impose undue costs, expense, and interruption of a party's business; rather, they provide a means to elicit legitimate relevant facts in a search for the truth.

Though relevancy constitutes the essential element for discovery of information, a conflict immediately arises when relevant personal and private information is sought.[20] In *Maresca v. Marks*,[21] plaintiff attempted to obtain copies of defendant's income tax returns.[22] Plaintiff asserted that the tax returns contained private information which was irrelevant to any issues in the lawsuit. The Texas Supreme Court acknowledged the conflict between discovery of relevant information and the constitutional protection of pri-

---

Dallas Ry. & Terminal Co. v. Oehler, 156 Tex. 488, 491, 296 S.W.2d 757,759 (1956) (the fact that the ends of justice might have been better served by calling all occurrence witnesses, did not, however, make discovery of their names relevant).

17. *See* Durham v. Cannan Communications, Inc. 645 S.W.2d 845, 847 (Tex. App.—Amarillo 1982, writ dism'd); Bryan v. General Elec. Credit Corp., 553 S.W.2d 415, 419 (Tex. Civ. App.—Houston [1st Dist.] 1977, no writ); Texhoma Stores, Inc. v. American Cent. Ins. Co., 424 S.W.2d 466, 472 (Tex. Civ. App.—Dallas 1968, writ ref'd n.r.e.) (sufficient facts should be included to enable the court to evaluate the materiality of the information).

18. 645 S.W.2d 845 (Tex. App.—Amarillo 1982, writ dism'd).

19. *Id.* at 848. *See also* Texhoma Stores, Inc. v. American Cent. Ins. Co., 424 S.W.2d at 472 ("while the spirit of these rules requires liberal construction, it was never intended to revolutionize practice by allowing 'fishing excursions' "). Refer to note 2 *supra* and accompanying text.

20. *See* Automatic Drilling Machs., Inc. v. Miller, 515 S.W.2d 256, 259-60 (Tex. 1974) (trade secrets were not necessarily privileged; yet, it was the duty of the trial judge to examine the documents and determine their relevance and need and the extent to which disclosure should be made); Maresca v. Marks, 362 S.W.2d 299, 300 (Tex. 1962) (income tax returns); Crane v. Tunks, 160 Tex. 182, 191, 328 S.W.2d 434, 440 (1959) (income tax returns); Aztec Life Ins. Co. v. Dellana, 667 S.W.2d 911, 916 (Tex. App.—Austin 1984, no writ) (insurance company's denial journal relevant to prove whether insurance company consistently denied claims without prior investigation. The trial judge was ordered to examine the files to determine which files contained privileged matter); Zenith Radio Corp. v. Clark, 665 S.W.2d 804, 810-11 (Tex. App.—Austin 1983, no writ) (the problem of privacy may best be handled by an in camera inspection and the issuance of a protective order if needed); Texhoma Stores, Inc. v. American Cent. Ins. Co., 424 S.W.2d 466 (Tex. Civ. App.—Dallas 1968, writ ref'd n.r.e.) (income tax returns). *But see* Dallas Ry. & Terminal Co. v. Oehler, 156 Tex. 488, 491, 296 S.W.2d 757, 759 (1956) (list of passengers on a streetcar not discoverable).

21. 362 S.W.2d 299 (Tex. 1962).

22. *Id.* at 300.

vacy.[23] Yet the court ruled that "[s]ubjecting federal income tax returns . . . to discovery is sustainable only because the pursuit of justice between litigants outweighs protection of their privacy."[24] The trial court was mandated to balance and weigh the competing interests of the parties before ordering discovery of income tax return information that was relevant and material to the matters in controversy.[25]

Prior to the 1984 amendments, questions of law and mixed questions of law[26] and fact[27] were not the proper subject of pretrial discovery. Under Rule 166b "[i]t is . . . not ground for objection that an interrogatory [or request for admission] propounded . . . involves an opinion or contention that relates to fact or the application of law to fact."[28] Rule 166b, thus, sanctions the propounding by interrogatory or request for admissions of mixed questions of law and fact.[29] For example, inquiring whether an individual was acting in the course and scope of his employment or acting as agent for another is clearly permissible.

1. *Documents and Tangible Things.* Rule 166b(2)b authorizes a party to obtain discovery of documents and other tangible

---

23. *Id.* at 301. *See also* Texhoma Stores, Inc., 424 S.W.2d at 472 (income tax returns are not wholly privileged, but are discoverable to the extent of relevancy which must be shown. The discovery procedure does not allow the examination of information of a highly personal and private nature not relevant and material to the issues); Crane v. Tunks, 160 Tex. at 191, 328 S.W.2d at 442 (Calvert, J., concurring).

24. 362 S.W.2d at 301.

25. *Id. See also* Crane v. Tunks, 160 Tex. at 192, 328 S.W.2d at 441 (the trial court may order discovery only after a determination and identification of the relevant portions to protect against any disclosure of private matters not relevant).

26. Eskew v. Johnston Printing Co., 615 S.W.2d 287, 289 (Tex. Civ. App.—Dallas 1981, no writ) (defendant was not held to an admission where he did not file a timely answer because the question called for a conclusion regarding the legal effect of the disputed matter rather than a matter of fact); American Title Co. v. Smith, 445 S.W.2d 807, 809-10 (Tex. Civ. App.—Houston [1st Dist.] 1969, no writ). In *American Title*, defendant's voluntary admission of a legal conclusion was not a judicial admission of fact, and did not alleviate the burden of the plaintiff from proving the contract. Answers which merely constitute admissions of law are not binding on the court. *Id.* at 809-10.

27. International Sec. Life Ins. Co. v. Maas, 458 S.W.2d 484, 489 (Tex. Civ. App.—Houston [1st Dist.] 1970, writ ref'd n.r.e.) (where an admission's request was the basic issue of the case, and where its answers involved a mixed question of law and fact, it was not the proper subject for requests for admissions).

28. TEX R. CIV. P. 166b(2)a.

29. *See* Barrow & Henderson, *1984 Amendments to the Texas Rules of Civil Procedure Affecting Discovery*, 15 ST. MARY'S L.J. 713, 717 (1984).

things which constitute or contain matters relevant to the subject matter in the action.[30] The movant is obligated only to establish relevancy as a prerequisite for production of the requested documents.[31] Similar to the general relevancy requirement of Rule 166b(2), a mere conclusory pleading that the documents contain relevant material may not suffice for production.[32]

A party is obligated to produce or disclose relevant material that is in a party's possession, custody, or control.[33] Possession, custody, or control includes constructive possession such that the party need not exercise actual physical possession.[34] To the extent that a party possesses a *superior right* to compel the production of documents from a third party, the individual is deemed to exercise possession, custody or control.[35] The amended rule liberalizes custody and control to include within its definition a superior right to control third parties.[36] Thus, constructive possession has been significantly expanded by redefinition.[37]

The current language of the Rule augments the custody and control guidelines enunciated in *Martinez v. Rutledge*.[38] In *Martinez*, the court determined that the plaintiff in a personal injury

---

30. Tex. R. Civ. P. 166b(2)b.

31. Refer to notes 16-25 *supra* and accompanying text.

32. *Id.*

33. Tex. R. Civ. P. 166b(2)b provides:

> A party may obtain discovery of the existence, description, nature, custody, condition, location & contents of any and all documents, (including papers, books, accounts, drawings, graphs, charts, photographs, electronic or videotape recordings, and any other data compilations from which information can be obtained and translated, if necessary, by the person from whom production is sought, into reasonably usable form) and any other tangible things which constitute or contain matters relevant to the subject matter in the action. A person is not required to produce a document or tangible thing unless it is within the person's possession, custody or control. Possession, custody or control includes constructive possession such that the person need not have actual physical possession. As long as the person has a superior right to compel the production from a third party (including an agency, authority or representative), the person has possession, custody or control.

34. *Id.*

35. *Id.* (emphasis added).

36. *Id. Compare* Tex. R. Civ. P. 167(8) (Vernon 1983) which states, "Possession, custody or control includes constructive possession whereby the Respondent has a right to compel the production of a matter or entrance from a third party."

37. *See* Medenco, Inc. v. Myklebust, 615 S.W.2d 187, 189 (Tex. 1981); Barrow & Henderson, *1984 Amendments to the Texas Rules of Civil Procedure Affecting Discovery*, 15 St. Mary's L.J. 713, 723 (1984).

38. 592 S.W.2d 398 (Tex. Civ. App.—Dallas 1979, writ ref'd n.r.e.).

action possessed custody and control over his medical records.[39] The court emphasized plaintiff's right of control because by either granting or withholding consent, plaintiff determined who would have access to his medical records. The plaintiff could not refuse to produce records merely because they were not in his actual possession unless he could demonstrate that he lacked the means, in the exercise of reasonable diligence, to gain actual possession.[40] Expanding this rationale, discovery may be obtained of a party's bank records that are in the physical possession of the bank.[41] In the absence of either a legal right or the practical ability to obtain the items sought, the requisite constructive possession is not satisfied.[42]

2. *Land.* Rule 166b(2)c governs requests for entry upon land. Relevancy of the particular land to the subject matter,[43] and a superior right of possession[44] are determinative.[45] The right to the inspection of land is not unqualified; land previously inspected need not voluntarily be submitted to unlimited inspections.[46] Inherent in the discovery process is the discretion of the trial court "to protect a party from undue annoyance, embarrassment, oppression, or expense."[47]

3. *Potential Parties and Witnesses.* Rule 166b(2)d provides that a party may obtain discovery of the identity of any potential party or person having knowledge of relevant facts. The term "knowledge" is defined to mean knowledge of any discoverable matter.[48] Though this rule authorizes a party to discover the names and addresses of any persons possessing knowledge of discoverable

---

39. *Id.* at 401.

40. *Id.*

41. Hopkins v. Hopkins, 540 S.W.2d 783, 789 (Tex. Civ. App.—Corpus Christi 1976, no writ).

42. Barrow & Henderson, *supra* note 29, at 724.

43. *See* Vance v. My Apartment Steak House, Inc., 677 S.W.2d 480, 481 (Tex. 1984)(contractor may obtain trial court order to enter owners premises to observe and inspect defects).

44. Refer to notes 33-43 *supra* and accompanying text.

45. Tex. R. Civ. P. 166b(2)c.

46. Day & Zimmerman, Inc. v. Strickland, 483 S.W.2d 541, 547 (Tex. Civ. App.—Texarkana 1972, writ ref'd n.r.e.).

47. *Id.*

48. Tex. R. Civ. P. 166b(2)d.

matters, it leaves unchanged the prohibition against compelling production of the names and addresses of witnesses expected to be called by a party, with the exception of expert witnesses.[49]

The court in *Lopresti v. Wells*[50] confronted the discoverability of fact witnesses to be utilized by a party as trial witnesses.[51] The court, however, failed to resolve the issue.[52] Later, in *Employers Mutual Liability Insurance Co. v. Butler*[53] the court concluded that the rule authorizing discoverability of individuals possessing knowledge of relevant facts, is not designed to compel a party to reveal fact witnesses that party expects to call at trial to prove his cause of action.[54] Obviously the determination of witnesses to be called at trial constitutes the trial strategy of a party's attorney and necessarily must be protected by the work product exerption.

4. Experts and Expert Reports. Rule 166b(2)e provides for the discovery of expert witnesses and expert witness reports. Consistent with the other provisions, this rule mandates that the information sought from experts must be relevant to the subject matter of the pending action.[55] The rule categorizes expert witnesses and expert reports into three basic classes, two of which are discoverable, and one of which is not discoverable.[56] The first category includes the expert who is expected to be called as a witness at the time of trial.[57] The second category involves the consulting but nontestifying expert whose analyses, conclusions, expert reports, and opinions form a basis, either in whole or in part, for the opin-

---

49. Employers Mut. Liab. Ins. Co. v. Butler, 511 S.W.2d 323, 325 (Tex. Civ. App.—Texarkana 1974, writ ref'd n.r.e.); Comment, *Texas Work Product Protection: Time for a Change*, 15 Hous. L. Rev. 112 (1977).

50. 515 S.W.2d 933 (Tex. Civ. App.—Fort Worth 1974, no writ).

51. *Id.* at 936-37. "[T]he inquiry was designed to learn the identity of those witnesses discovered by defendant . . . . These were, or would have been, witnesses developed as a part of the 'work product' and pursuant to incident activities . . . , though, nevertheless, they would undoubtedly also be persons who 'having knowledge of relevant facts . . . are discoverable.' "

52. *Id.* at 937.

53. 511 S.W.2d 323.

54. *Id.* at 325. (In promulgating the final rules, the Supreme Court omitted this provision). *See, e.g.*, W. W. Rodgers & Sons Produce Co. v. Johnson, 673 S.W.2d 291, 294 (Tex. App.—Dallas 1984, no writ)

55. Tex. R. Civ. P. 166b(2)e. Refer to notes 16-25 *supra* and accompanying text.

56. Tex. R. Civ. P. 166b(2)e (experts expected to be called as witnesses are discoverable). *Cf.* Tex. R. Civ. P. 166b(3)c (consulting experts not discoverable).

57. Tex. R. Civ. P. 166b(2)e(1).

ions of an expert who is to be called as a witness.[58] Both classes of experts are subject to discovery. The third category characterizes an expert engaged solely as a consultant. The consulting expert and his report are not discoverable provided his factual observations, opinions, and conclusions do not, either in whole or in part, form the basis of the opinions of an expert expected to be called as a witness.[59] The court is empowered to compel a party to make the determination and disclosure of experts expected to be called as witnesses within a reasonable and specific time before the date of the trial.[60] The latitude entrusted to the trial court rests in the exercise of judicial discretion and will not be interfered with in the absence of an abuse of that discretion.

The expert witness rule evolved over a period of more than ten years.[61] The problem of defining an "expert witness" was initially confronted in *Houdaille Industries, Inc. v. Cunningham.*[62] *Houdaille* involved a suit to recover damages for the negligent performance of a foundation investigation and pavement design.[63] Defendant sought production of the written reports of several experts who had been employed by the plaintiff to examine and evaluate problems with the paving.[64] Plaintiff's attorney responded that the experts were used solely for consultation and would not be called as witnesses, except perhaps for rebuttal purposes.[65] The Texas Supreme Court determined that the report of an expert not intended to be called as a witness at the time of trial is not discoverable.[66] But, the report of an expert whom a party might possibly

---

58. Rule 166b(2)e(1) provides: "The disclosure of the same information concerning an expert used for consultation and who is not expected to be called as a witness at trial is required if the expert's work product forms a basis either in whole or in part of the opinions of an expert who is to be called as a witness."

59. Tex. R. Civ. P. 166b(3)c.

60. Tex. R. Civ. P. 166b(2)e(3). *See, e.g.*, West v. Solito, 563 S.W.2d 240 (Tex. 1978) (time schedule dictated by the Court).

61. *See* Jones & Laughlin Steel, Inc. v. Schattman, 667 S.W.2d 352 (Tex. App.—Fort Worth 1984, no writ); Werner v. Miller, 579 S.W.2d 455 (Tex. 1979); Barker v. Dunham, 551 S.W.2d 41 (Tex. 1977); Allen v. Humphreys, 559 S.W.2d 798 (Tex. 1977); *Ex parte* Shepperd, 513 S.W.2d 813 (Tex. 1974); Houdaille Indust., Inc. v. Cunningham, 502 S.W.2d 544 (Tex. 1973). *See generally* Sales, *Pre-Trial Discovery in Texas*, 31 Sw. L.J. 1017 (1977).

62. 502 S.W.2d 544.

63. *Id.* at 545.

64. *Id.*

65. *Id.* at 548.

66. *Id.*

call for rebuttal or impeachment purposes is discoverable.[67] The conclusions and opinions of experts are protected from discovery only when the experts are not expected to be called as witnesses at the time of trial, whether in chief or otherwise.[68]

Generally, discovery of the records of expert witnesses solely for the purpose of establishing bias or prejudice of the expert is prohibited.[69] That purpose simply does not satisfy the relevancy requirement.[70] Discovery of information, data, reports of experts that are unrelated to transactions or matters involved in the lawsuit is dependent upon a showing of relevancy.[71] In *Ex Parte Shepperd*,[72] for example, condemnees sought the state's appraisers' reports concerning the value of the condemned land involved in the lawsuit as well as the value of the adjacent land tracts not involved in the litigation.[73] The condemnees alleged that the appraisals on adjacent land tracts were relevant to preparation of an effective cross-examination and impeachment of the state's appraisers' valuation of the tract of land involved in the litigation.[74]

---

67. *Id.*

68. *Id.*

69. *See* Russell v. Young, 452 S.W.2d 434,435-3b (Tex. 1970) (records of a physician demonstrating his testifying history not discoverable); W. W. Rodgers & Sons Produce Co. v. Johnson, 673 S.W.2d 291, 294 (Tex. App.—Dallas 1984, no writ) (statements of witnesses may not be discovered for purposes of impeachment). But discovery of records of a witness sought for other purposes, although impeachment may constitute one of the incidental reasons for discovery, is permissable. Kupor v. Solito, 687 S.W.2d 441, 443 (Tex. App.—Houston [14th Dist.] 1985, no writ).

70. Russell, 452 S.W.2d at 437 (pretrial discovery of potential expert's records for impeachment purposes is prohibited. A witnesses' records possess no impeachment value where there is nothing yet to impeach.).

71. *See Ex Parte* Shepperd, 513 S.W.2d at 815. *But see* Russell v. Young, 452 S.W.2d at 437; *Ex Parte* Shepperd, 513 S.W.2d at 817 (Walker, J., dissenting) ("In my opinion these cases should be ruled by *Russell v. Young*."); Zenith Radio Corp. v. Clark, 665 S.W.2d 804, 809 (Tex. App.—Austin 1983, no writ). In *Zenith*, the state brought suit against Zenith claiming that Zenith's defective and unreasonably dangerous television caused the blaze which damaged the East Wing of the Capitol building. Zenith requested that the fire marshal produce investigative reports concerning the fire. The state refused discovery of the report claiming that the fire marshal was a state employee whose investigation was made in connection with the action and thereby privileged. The court disallowed the privilege. The court concluded that, "[i]t does not follow from the fact that the Fire Marshal is a state employee that all information which he obtains while performing his tasks is privileged simply because at some later time the State is, or may become involved in litigation arising from the fire." *Id.* at 809.

72. 513 S.W.2d 813 (Tex. 1974).

73. *Id.* at 814.

74. *Id.* at 815.

Relying on *Russell v. Young*[75] the state contended that the reports of nonparty witnesses which were to be utilized solely for establishing bias or prejudice of the witnesses were protected from discovery.[76] The Texas Supreme Court distinguished *Russell* in evaluating the discoverability of reports regarding adjacent land tracts.[77] The supreme court observed that when expert reports are sought to establish inconsistencies in the appraisal reports,"[a] thorough exploration, on cross-examination and re-direct examination, of any such inconsistencies and the reasons therefor, might well assist the jury in reaching an independent conclusion concerning the fair market value of the subject properties."[78] Expert witness reports involving adjacent land tracts that were either in the negotiation or trial stage, however, are protected from disclosure.[79] Limited by this qualification, the expert appraisers' reports involving adjacent land tracts are peculiarly relevant and discoverable.[80]

Several principles governing production of expert witnesses emerge from these decisions. The personal records of an expert witness sought solely to establish a possible bias or prejudice of the expert is irrelevant to any issue in the lawsuit and is protected from discovery.[81] But expert witnesses' reports that relate to matters other than the specific matters involved in the lawsuit and that are substantially related and material to the opinions and conclusions formulated by the witness establishes the necessary relevancy and are discoverable.[82] In ascertaining whether the other information or reports are discoverable, the court must balance the relevancy against the protection afforded work product in other

---

75. 452 S.W.2d 434.

76. *Id.* at 437. *See also* W. W. Rodgers & Sons Produce Co. v. Johnson, 673 S.W.2d 291, 294 (Tex. App.—Dallas 1984, no writ) (prohibiting discovery of witness statements for the purpose of possible impeachment of the witnesses at the time of trial). *But see*, Kupor v. Solito, 687 S.W.2d 441, 443 (Tex. App.—Houston [14th Dist.] 1985, no writ).

77. 513 S.W.2d at 816.

78. *Id.*

79. *Id.* at 817.

80. *Id.*

81. *See* Sales, *Pre-Trial Discovery in Texas*, 31 Sw. L.J. 1017, 1026 (1977).

In Lindsey v. O'Neill, 689 S.W.2d 400 (Tex. 1985), the Texas Supreme Court further noted that all expert reports of a party were discoverable unless made subsequent to the occurrence giving rise to the claim and made in connection with the prosecution or defense of the claim.

82. *Id.*

unrelated pending or prospective litigation.[83]

The Texas Supreme Court further reviewed the expert issue in *Allen v. Humphreys*.[84] Plaintiff instituted a worker's compensation suit against Safeway, alleging that she had developed lung cancer from exposure to polyvinyl chloride particles released into the air when meat wrapping paper was cut with hot wire while she was working in the scope of her employment with Safeway.[85] Plaintiff sought, among other items, expert surveys and reports not made in connection with her claim regarding the possibility that polyvinyl chloride fumes could cause cancer. The court prohibited the discovery of any expert tests and surveys prepared by experts employed solely for consultation in similar pending lawsuits.[86] Plaintiff was entitled, however, to the production of test and survey results made in connection with her action.[87]

It is important to note that the reports prepared for other pending litigation involved in *Shepperd* were prepared by the experts who were expected to be called as witnesses in the trial of the pending litigation.[88] *Shepperd* did not involve or even consider reports involved in other pending litigation that were prepared by other "consulting experts."[89]

Barker v. Dunham[90] and *Jones & Laughlin Steel, Inc. v. Schattman*[91] acknowledge the absence of any legally significant distinction between an expert who is a regular employee of a party

---

83. *Ex Parte* Shepperd, 513 S.W.2d at 817.

84. 559 S.W.2d 798 (Tex. 1977).

85. *Id.* at 800.

86. *Id.* at 803.

87. *Id.*

88. Sales, *supra* note 81 at 1027.

89. *Id.* "Unquestionably, the evaluations made by an expert witness in other litigation that directly affect opinions and conclusions rendered in pending litigation are extremely pertinent and should not be exempt from discovery, except as limited by the guidelines outlined in *Shepperd*." Rule 166b(2)e appears to cover this consideration. The proviso states that a nontestifying consultant and reports are discoverable if that consultant's opinion forms a basis either in whole or in part of the opinions of an expert who is to be called as a witness. TEX. R. CIV. P. 166b(2)e. Yet, as Rule 166b(3)c connotes, these same considerations are absent when the reports involved in other litigation were prepared by a consulting expert who will not provide any evidence or constitute a factor in the pending litigation. But, as noted in Lindsey v. O'Neill, 689 S.W.2d 400 (Tex. 1985), expert reports not made after an occurrence and in connection with the prosecution or defense of the claim may be discoverable.

90. 551 S.W.2d 41, 43 (Tex. 1977).

91. 667 S.W.2d 352, 356 (Tex. App—Fort Worth 1984, no writ).

and one who is temporarily employed by a party to assist in the preparation of a defense. In *Barker*, plaintiff's husband was fatally injured when a crane boom failed and collapsed.[92] The plaintiff endeavored, through deposition, to elicit the opinion and conclusions of the vice-president of engineering for the manufacturer of the crane. Though the vice-president qualified as a mechanical engineer who had examined the crane and formulated opinions on the cause of the collapse, the defendant asserted that the vice-president occupied the status of a consultant because defendant had not decided whether to use him as a witness.[93] The vice-president was compelled to express his expert opinions because defendant had not unequivocally declared that he would not be called as an expert.[94] An expert who may be an employee, agent, or officer of a party occupies the same legal status, for purposes of pretrial discovery, as any independently employed expert.[95] A definitive, clear disclaimer of any intention to call the employee expert to testify at trial, however, is critical to invoke the "consultant" exemption.[96]

In *Jones & Laughlin*, plaintiff claimed that the defendant supplied him with defective tubing which caused a gas well failure.[97] Plaintiff sought to depose an employee and senior field engineer of technical services of the manufacturer.[98] During the deposition, the expert employee was directed not to answer any questions relating to his investigation.[99] Acknowledging the absence of any

---

92. 551 S.W.2d at 42.
93. *Id.*
94. *Id.* at 44.
95. Sales, *supra* note 81 at 1025. But, as noted by the Texas Supreme Court in Griffin v. Smith, 688 S.W.2d 112, (Tex. 1985), information possessed by an officer or agent of a party which forms the basis of the claim may not necessarily be protected from pre-trial discovery. Discovery is dependent on the information occurring after the transaction upon which suit is based and made in connection with the prosecution or defense of the claim. *Id.* at 114.
96. 551 S.W.2d at 44:

> The expert has something different [from first-hand knowledge] to contribute. This is a power to draw inferences from the facts which a jury would not be competent to draw. To warrant the use of expert testimony, then, two elements are required. First, the subject of the inference must be distinctively related to some science, profession, business or occupation as to be beyond the ken of the average layman, and second, the witness must have skill, knowledge or experience in that field or calling as to make it appear that his opinion or inference will probably aid the trier in his search for truth.

97. 667 S.W.2d at 353.
98. *Id.*
99. *Id.*

distinction between an expert who is a regular employee and one who is temporarily employed to aid in the preparation of a claim, discovery of the expert employee's conclusions and opinions was not allowed because defendant positively declared the expert-employee as a consultant.[100]

Recently the Texas Supreme Court in *Lindsey v. O'Neill*,[101] expanded the permissible scope of discovery of expert opinion testimony. The plaintiff in *Lindsey* brought action against Hermann Hospital and several pharmaceutical companies based upon medical malpractice and products liability causes of action.[102] Accordingly, plaintiff served notice of deposition upon defendant Travenol Labs. This notice requested Travenol to produce individuals for deposition on approximately thirty-nine subject areas.[103] Defendant moved for a protective order on the ground that the subjects called for Travenol to produce expert testimony.[104] Following this motion, the trial court excluded from discovery all of the mental impressions and opinions of experts associated with Travenol without any showing that this information was acquired or developed in anticipation of litgation.[105]

The Texas Supreme Court held that the trial court's ruling conflicted with the Texas Rules of Civil Procedure; and that the trial court had abused its discretion.[106] The Court ruled that,

> Rule 166B-3 does *not* exempt from discovery the mental impressions and opinions of the parties' nontestifying experts when

---

100. *Id.* at 356. The holdings of *Barker* and *Jones* differ regarding "positive averments." In *Barker*, defendant stated under oath that he did not know if the expert employee would appear as a witness in the case, but that he might use him. 551 S.W.2d at 42. No positive averment was made. The court held that where a party does not positively aver that the expert will be used only for consultation, that expert's reports, factual observations, and opinions may be discovered. *Id.* at 44.

On the other hand, the defendant in *Jones* positively averred that the expert employee was a consultant. 667 S.W.2d at 335. The court noted that even though the defendant delayed making the designation until the last possible minute, the averment was no less effective to render the expert employee a consultant and to foreclose both plaintiff's discovery of the expert and defendant's use of the expert as an expert witness at trial. *Id. But see*, Houdaille Indus., Inc. v. Cunningham, 502 S.2d 544 (Tex. 1973) (requiring prompt disclaimer that an expert might be called as a witness).

101. 689 S.W.2d 400 (Tex. 1985).

102. *Id.* at 341.

103. *Id.*

104. *Id.*

105. *Id.* at 342.

106. *Id.*

> those mental impressions and opinions were formulated neither (1) in the course and scope of the "prosecution, investigation or defense" of a claim or transaction or occurrence given rise to a claim or (2) "in anticipation of litigation or preparation for trial."[107]

Thus, before the trial court may hold an entire category of expert opinion evidence exempt from discovery, there must be proof that the opinions were acquired or developed in anticipation of litigation. This Rule ostensibly elaborates on *Ex Parte Shepherd* and *Barker v. Dunham.*

The trial court is accorded significant latitude to designate the precise point during the pretrial stage when experts must be designated.[108] For example, in *Werner v. Miller*, plaintiff sought to recover damages for injuries sustained by his minor daughter when her right leg came in contact with the rotary blade of a lawn tractor allegedly designed, manufactured, and sold by the defendant.[109] Both parties sought unsuccessfully to compel the other to disclose the identity of all expert witnesses.[110] The trial court ordered plaintiff to designate all expert witnesses he anticipated calling thirty days before filing his trial setting. Defendant, within two days after receipt of plaintiff's designation of experts, was ordered to then designate his experts. Experts not designated in accordance with this schedule were declared ineligible to testify at the trial.[111] The trial court properly exercised its discretion in supervising designation of expert witnesses as part of its function in the pretrial process.[112] The court focused on the stage at which parties must "positively aver" that an expert consultant will not be called as a witness: "This declaration . . . should be made in sufficient time to permit the opposing party to discover the reports, factual observations, and opinions of the potential expert witness. On the other hand, the party employing the consultant must be given sufficient time to develop his case so that an intelligent decision can be made regarding the use of the expert."[113]

---

107. *Id.* at 341-42.

108. Werner v. Miller, 579 S.W.2d 455, 456 (Tex. 1979). Refer to note 60 *supra* and accompanying text.

109. 579 S.W.2d at 455.

110. *Id.* at 455-56.

111. *Id.* at 456

112. *Id.*

113. *Id. See* Tex. R. Civ. P. 166b(4)b. This discretion has been significantly eroded in

The appropriate approach in controlling pretrial discovery of expert witnesses has received various comments.[114] One commentator observes that under the amended rules:

> It is contrary to the spirit of the rule for a party to shield information from discovery by having it developed through a consultant who will not testify, but then making it available to the expert who will testify. While maintaining a policy of full disclosure, the rule continues to protect those consultants whose work product actually does not form the basis of another's testimony. The test is: If the work product of the expert in question forms a basis either in whole or in part of the opinions of an expert who is to be called as a witness then you may discover the identity, mental impressions, and opinions of the expert.[115]

In summary, an expert who is expected to be called as a witness at the time of trial clearly is discoverable. If an expert consultant's analyses, conclusions, opinions, or reports form the basis, in whole or in part, of the opinion of an expert expected to be called as a witness, then this class of expert witness likewise is subject to discovery. It is only the expert, employed as a consultant, who will not be called as a witness and whose conclusions, opinions and reports are not relied upon in any manner by an expert expected to be called as a witness that is exempt from pretrial discovery.

5. *Indemnity, Insurance and Settlement Agreements.* The amended rules authorize discovery of the existence and contents of any insurance policy or settlement agreement under which any person engaging in an insurance business may be liable to satisfy either part or all of a judgment.[116] Under the rules that preexisted the amendments, the Texas Supreme Court in *Great American Insurance Co. v. Murray*,[117] addressed the discoverability of policy limits of an insurance policy applicable to the pending action.[118] Defendant insurance company alleged that its policy afforded no

---

Jampole v. Touchy, 673 S.W.2d 569 (Tex. 1984).

114. *See* Barrow & Henderson, *1984 Amendments to the Texas Rules of Civil Procedure Affecting Discovery*, 15 St. Mary's L.J. 713 (1984).

115. *Id.* at 730-31.

116. Tex. R. Civ. P. 166b(2)f.

117. 437 S.W.2d 264 (Tex. 1969).

118. *Id.* at 265.

coverage for the driver of the insured vehicle and refused to divulge the policy limits. The Texas Supreme Court confirmed that the amount of insurance coverage was immaterial to any issue involved in the personal injury lawsuit.[119] Immateriality was premised on the belief that the presence or absence of resources out of which a future judgment may be enforced is not material to the purposes for which discovery may be employed.[120]

After *Murray*, pretrial discoverability of insuring agreements was reconsidered in *Carroll Cable Co. v. Miller*.[121] The court determined that insurance policies, including policy limits, are subject to pretrial discovery upon a showing that the agreement is not otherwise available to the moving party and that the information is needed to determine settlement and litigation strategy.[122]

Rule 166b(2)f represents a significant clarification of earlier pretrial practice. Under the provisions of Rule 166b, the existence and contents of any indemnity, insuring agreement, or settlement agreement is per se discoverable without the necessity of establishing any real or modified good cause.[123] This necessarily includes any Mary Carter agreements or similar indemnifying understandings. Discoverability, however, does not transform discoverable insuring agreements into admissible evidence.

6. *Statements.* Rule 166b(2) expressly declares that any person is entitled to obtain his own statement previously made regarding the subject matter of a lawsuit, which is in the possession, custody, or control of any party.[124] On the other hand, Rule

119. *Id.*

120. *Id.*

121. 501 S.W.2d 299 (Tex. 1973).

122. *Id.* at 299.

123. The progression of change has been evolutionary. Initially, insurance agreements were deemed not relevant under under the trial discovery. Then, under *Carroll Cable Co.*, good cause, which includes relevancy, was noticeably liberalized. The current rule now prescribes the discoverability of such arguments.

124. Tex. R. Civ. P. 166b(2)g provides:

> Any person, whether or not a party, shall be entitled to obtain, upon written request, his own statement previously made concerning the subject matter of a lawsuit, which is the possession, custody, or control of any party. For the purpose of this paragraph, a statement previously made is (a) a written statement signed or otherwise adopted or approved by the person making it, and (b) a stenographic, mechanical, electrical or other type of recording, or any transcription thereof which is a substantially verbatim recital of a statement made by the person and contemporaneously recorded.

166b(3)b reaffirms that written statements of potential parties and witnesses are exempt from pretrial discovery.[125] Though anyone, party or nonparty, is authorized to secure a copy of any statement made to any party in a lawsuit, the statements of any other potential parties or witnesses constitute exempt work product and are insulated from pretrial discovery by the opposing party.[126]

7. *Medical Records and Medical Authorization.* The pretrial discovery of a party's medical records and reports is specifically provided for under the amended rules. Rule 166b(2)h modifies previous Rule 167(7)[127] in several significant respects. Initially, the current rule requires a written request for the disclosure of medical records. The party alleging damages for physical or mental injury is obligated to produce or furnish an authorization permitting the full disclosure of all relevant medical records without the necessity of a formal motion.[128] Unlike its predecessor,[129] Rule 166b(2)h provides that once medical information is made available to a party, the requesting party is responsible for reproducing and furnishing a copy of the records to the party furnishing the authorization.[130] Copies of medical records are no longer required to be provided free of charge to all other parties involved in the litigation. Additionally, Rule 166b extends the time period in which medical records must be made available to the parties to thirty days,[131] rather than the fourteen day period specified under the earlier

---

125. All statements except those specifically excluded by Rule 166b(2)g are exempt, even statements given to an insurance adjuster prior to litigation. *See* Hiebert v. Weiss, 622 S.W.2d 150 (Tex. App.—Fort Worth 1981, writ ref'd n.r.e.).

126. *See* W. W. Rodgers & Sons Produce Co. v. Johnson, 673 S.W.2d 291, 294 (Tex. App.—Dallas 1984, no writ).

127. Tex. R. Civ. P. 166(2)(h) (Vernon 1983).

128. Tex. R. Civ. P. 166b(2)h ("[a]ny party alleging physical or mental injury . . . which is the subject of the case shall be required, upon written request, to produce . . ."). *Compare* Tex. R. Civ. P. 167(7) (Vernon 1983) ("[a]ny party alleging physical or mental injury and damages . . . shall be required, upon request, to produce . . ."). The disclosure must relate to medical records relevant to the injuries involved in the lawsuit. Martinez v. Rutledge, 592 S.W.2d 398 (Tex. Civ. App.—Dallas 1979, writ ref'd n.r.e.).

129. Tex. R. Civ. P. 167(7) (Vernon 1983) ("Copies of all medical . . . shall be furnished without charge to all parties . . .").

130. Tex. R. Civ. P. 166b(2)h ("Copies of all medical . . . shall be furnished . . . without charge, to the party who furnished the authorization . . .").

131. Tex. R. Civ. P. 166b(2)h ("it shall be furnished . . . not less than thirty (30) days prior to trial . . .").

rule.[132] Mailing notice of the availability of the medical records constitutes "making them available."[133]

In *Martinez v. Rutledge*,[134] plaintiff alleged that, as a result of an automobile collision, he suffered back injury.[135] Because plaintiff had been previously hospitalized for back injuries, the defendant requested plaintiff to execute a medical authorization after attempts to secure the prior medical records through normal discovery procedures proved totally unavailing.[136] The trial court dismissed plaintiff's cause of action based on a refusal to either produce his prior medical records or to execute a medical authorization for them.[137] Medical records relating to a prior back injury were clearly relevant to the issue involved in the pending litigation.[138]

8. *Effect of United States Treaties on Pretrial Discovery.* According to Rule 188, "[w]henever the deposition, written or oral, of any person is to be taken in a sister state or a foreign country, or in any other jurisdiction, foreign or domestic, for use in this state, such deposition may be taken . . . (4) pursuant to the means and terms of any applicable treaty or convention."[139] The court in *Goldschmidt v. Smith*[140] considered the effect of the Hague Evidence Convention on pretrial discovery by deposition of employees of a party who is a resident of a signatory country.

Upjohn Corporation instituted suit against Goldschmidt Chemical, alleging that the chemicals purchased from defendant were defective.[141] Upjohn requested leave to depose six West German employees of the defendant and requested documents of the defendant located in West Germany.[142] Goldschmidt urged that pretrial discovery contravened the Multilateral Convention on the

---

132. Tex. R. Civ. P. 167(7) (Vernon 1983) ("it shall be furnished not less than fourteen days prior to trial . . .").
133. Tex. R. Civ. P. 166b(2)h.
134. 592 S.W.2d 398 (Tex. Civ. App.—1979, writ ref'd n.r.e.).
135. *Id.* at 399.
136. *Id.*
137. *Id.* at 400.
138. *Id.* at 400-01.
139. Tex. R. Civ. P. 188(1).
140. 676 S.W.2d 443 (Tex. App.—Houston [1st Dist.] 1984, no writ).
141. *Id.* at 444.
142. *Id.*

Taking of Evidence Abroad in Civil or Commercial Matters.[143] The court determined that the plaintiff in attempting to obtain pretrial discovery from a West German corporation was required to comply with Hague Evidence Convention procedures, at least as an avenue of first resort.[144]

Pursuant to the terms of the Hague Evidence Convention, West Germany will not execute Letters of Request issued for the purpose of obtaining pretrial discovery of documents.[145] The West German government considers the gathering of evidence within its territorial boundaries to be an exclusive function of its judicial system. Any action in disregard of the prescribed procedure is deemed a blatant violation of West German sovereignty.[146]

The *Goldschmidt* court perceived that, as a matter of comity, discovery orders that conflict with reservations under the Convention impinge upon West Germany's sovereignty. Consequently pretrial orders should not be issued in ordinary circumstances, unless a balancing of competing interests clearly demonstrates that an order authorizing actions outside the Convention is imperative to foreclose a total impasse.[147] The fact that Rule 188 authorizes depositions to be taken only according to specified procedures, including the requirement that the taking of depositions be pursuant to "the means and terms of any applicable Treaty or Convention", buttresses the controlling legal effect of terms and limitation of the Hague Convention.[148]

C. *Exemptions*

Rule 166b(3)[149] enumerates specific matters that are exempt from pretrial discovery. These exempt matters include: (1) the work product of an attorney;[150] (2) the written statements of potential witnesses and parties;[151] (3) the identity, mental impressions, and opinions of an expert informally consulted who will not

---

143. *Id.*
144. *Id.* at 445.
145. *Id.* at 444.
146. *Id.* at 445.
147. *Id.*
148. *Id.* at 445-46.
149. Tex. R. Civ. P. 166b(3) supersedes Tex. R. Civ. P. 816a (Vernon 1983).
150. Refer to notes 49-54 *supra* and accompanying text.
151. Refer to notes 48-54 *supra* and accompanying text.

be called as a witness and whose impressions and opinions do not form the basis, in whole or in part, of an expert expected to be called as a witness;[152] (4) communications passing between agents, representatives or employees of any party to the action or, communications between any party and his agents when made subsequent to the occurrence upon which the suit is based, and made in connection with the investigation, prosecution or defense of a claim arising from such occurrence;[153] and, (5) any matter protected from disclosure by a specific privilege.[154]

1. Attorney Work Product. Under former Rule 186a, the work product doctrine was often merged into the "party communication" privilege. Rule 166b(3)a[155] undoubtedly is noticeably influenced by the nearly forty years of federal experience with *Hickman v. Taylor*[156] and its progeny. An analysis of the federal work product doctrine provides meaningful guidance in the future interpretations of Rule 166b(3)a.

In *Hickman v. Taylor*, the United States Supreme Court recognized that a limited or qualified immunity from discovery exists for documents created by an attorney in the course of trial preparations. In recognizing the need for a work product privilege, the court pointedly remarked that the attorney-client privilege does not per se include within its scope the memoranda prepared by an attorney in the course of witness interviews performed in anticipation of litigation.[157] The *Hickman* court recognized that the traditional attorney-client privilege applies neither to documents prepared by the attorney for his own use in prosecuting a client's case, nor to documents which reflect an attorney's mental impressions, conclusions, opinions or legal theories.[158] Cognizant of the impor-

---

152. Refer to notes 55-117 *supra* and accompanying text.

153. *See, e.g.,* West v. Solito, 563 S.W.2d 240 (Tex. 1978), Greenspan v. State, 618 S.W.2d 939, 941 (Tex. App.—Fort Worth 1981, writ ref'd. n.r.e.) (The communication must be made subsequent to the occurrence or transaction that constitutes the lawsuit.); Highway Ins. Underwriters v. Griffith, 290 S.W.2d 950, 953 (Tex. Civ. App.—Austin 1956, writ ref'd. n.r.e.) (statements made before occurrence of transaction upon which suit is based are exempt from discovery).

154. Tex. R. Civ. P. 166b(3)e. *See* Peebles v. Hon. Fourth Supreme Judicial District, ___ S.W.2d ___, 28 Tex. Sup. Ct. J. 539, 540 (July 6, 1985) (four-part test).

155. Tex. R. Civ. P. 166b(3)a.

156. 329 U.S. 495 (1947).

157. *Id.* at 508.

158. *Id.*

tant public policy reasons that exist for preventing "unwarranted inquiries into the files and mental impressions of an attorney,"[159] the *Hickman* court noted that an attorney, as an officer of the court, must "work with a certain degree of privacy, free from unnecessary intrusion by opposing parties and their counsel."[160]

> Proper preparation of a client's case demands that he assemble information, sift what he considers to be the relevant from the irrelevant facts, prepare his legal theories and plan his strategy without undue and needless interference. That is the historical and the necessary way in which lawyers act within the framework of our system of jurisprudence to promote justice and to protect their clients' interest. This work is reflected, of course, in interviews, statements, memoranda, correspondence, briefs, mental impressions, personal beliefs, and countless other tangible and intangible ways—aptly, though roughly termed by the Circuit Court of Appeals in this case as the "work product of the lawyer."[161]

The court recognized the problems which would result if work product materials were generally available to opposing counsel on mere demand.[162] Accordingly, the files and mental impressions of lawyers are not subject to scrutiny by their adversaries.[163] Yet, the work product doctrine is not absolute; relevant and nonprivileged matters that are contained in an attorney's file and that are essential to the preparation of the case may be subject to discovery.[164] In such instances, however, the party seeking access to the materials is impressed with the onerous burden of justifying the invasion into opposing counsel's records.[165] The party seeking the materials must show a substantial need for the materials to prepare his case and establish that he cannot without undue hardship obtain substantial equivalents of such materials.

The federal "work product doctrine" translates into a qualified immunity from discovery for certain materials prepared by an

---

159. *Id.* at 510.

160. *Id.* at 510-11.

161. *Id.* at 511.

162. *Id.* "An attorney's thoughts, heretofore inviolate, would not be his own. Inefficiency, unfairness and sharp practices would inevitably develop in the giving of legal advice and in the preparation of cases for trial. The effect on the legal profession would be demoralizing. And the interests of the clients and the cause of justice would be poorly served."

163. *Id.* at 514.

164. *Id.* at 511.

165. *Id.* at 512.

attorney acting for a client in the anticipation and conduct of litigation.[166] The doctrine is designed primarily to shelter the mental processes, impressions and theories of the attorney.[167] Federal Rule 26(b)3 substantially incorporates the *Hickman* work product doctrine.[168] The work product doctrine incorporated in Rule 26(b)3 ostensibly is narrower in scope than the doctrine as enunciated in *Hickman*. In *Hickman*, plaintiff sought through interrogatories to obtain the mental impressions of an attorney that had not yet been reduced to tangible form.[169] The United States Supreme Court has repeatedly reaffirmed and emphasized the importance of protecting the mental processes and impressions of a party's attorney.[170]

An issue unanswered by *Hickman v. Taylor* relates to the immunity status of materials prepared by an attorney's agent in anticipation of litigation. In *United States v. Nobles*,[171] the Supreme Court addressed this issue. The court acknowledged that the work product immunity rests on the realities of an adversarial litigation system. One of these realities is the reliance by attorneys on the assistance and investigation of agents and representatives.[172] Concluding its analysis, the Supreme Court declared that, "[i]t is therefore necessary that the doctrine protect material prepared by agents for the attorney as well as those prepared by the attorney himself."[173]

---

166. *See* United States v. Nobles, 422 U.S. 225, 237-38 (1975); United States v. Davis, 636 F.2d 1028, 1039-40 (5th Cir. 1981), *cert. denied*, 454 U.S. 862 (1981). In Re Grand Jury Proceedings, 601 F.2d 162, 171 (5th Cir. 1979).

167. *See* United States v. Nobles, 422 U.S. at 238. *See also*, Upjohn Co. v. United States, 449 U.S. 383, 397-402 (1981).

168. Fed. R. Civ. P. 26(b)3.

> (A) party may obtain discovery of documents and tangible things otherwise discoverable under subdivision (b)1 of this rule and prepared in anticipation of litigation or for trial by or for another party or by or for that other party's representative (including his attorney, consultant, surety, indemnitor, insurer, or agent) only upon a showing that the party seeking discovery has substantial need of the materials in the preparation of his case and that he is unable without undue hardship to obtain the substantial equivalent of the materials by other means. In ordering discovery of such materials when the required showing has been made, the court shall protect against disclosure of the mental impression, conclusions, opinions, or legal theories of an attorney or other representative of a party concerning the litigation.

169. *See* Hickman v. Taylor, 329 U.S. at 499.

170. Upjohn Co. v. United States, 449 U.S. 383, 399 (1981)

171. 422 U.S. 225 (1975) (criminal case).

172. *Id.* at 238.

173. *Id.* at 238-39.

2. *Written Communications Made in Connection with the Lawsuit.* Another specific exemption authorized by Rule 166b includes written communication of a party or its agents, representatives or employees subsequent to the occurrence made the basis of the lawsuit and in connection with the investigation, prosecution or defense of such a claim. Though the exemption is specific, the nature and character of the communication possessing an immunity as well as the limitations of the immunity have engendered some confusion. The scope of a written communication was confronted by the Texas Supreme Court in *Houdaille Industries, Inc. v. Cunningham.*[174] Plaintiff filed a motion for defendant to produce various expert witness reports and accompanying photographs. Disavowing the adage that a photograph communicates a thousand words, the Court declared that a photograph was not a written communication.[175] The Court noted, however, that photographs constituting an integral part of an exempt expert's written report assumed the same immunity as the written report.[176] Only written communications qualify as an exemption from pretrial disclosure.

To invoke the immunity from pretrial discovery, the written communication: (1) must be made subsequent to the occurrence or transaction made the basis of the lawsuit; and (2) it must be made in connection with the investigation, prosecution or defense of the suit arising from the occurrence.[177] In *Greenspan v. State*,[178] plaintiff sought to discover the transcript of a proceeding conducted by a grievance committee.[179] The committee originally filed a grievance claim against plaintiff based on a fiduciary misapplication of funds.[180] In rejecting production of the transcript, the court noted that "[i]nasmuch as the transcript of the proceeding before the grievance committee is the written statements of witnesses made subsequent to the occurrence or transaction in question upon which the suit is based and made in connection with the investiga-

---

174. 502 S.W.2d 544 (Tex. 1973).

175. *Id.* at 548-50.

176. *Id.* at 550.

177. Tex. R. Civ. P. 166b(3). The importance of this dual requirement has repeatedly been emphasized by the Texas Supreme Court. See Lindsey v. O'Neill, 689 S.W.2d 400 (Tex. 1985); Griffin v. Smith, 688 S.W.2d 112 (Tex. 1985).

178. 618 S.W.2d 939 (Tex. Civ. App.—Fort Worth 1981, writ ref'd n.r.e.).

179. *Id.* at 940.

180. *Id.*

tion of the claim, . . . the transcript was privileged . . . and therefore not subject to discovery."[181]

In satisfying both aspects of the written communication, the two-prong test cannot be overemphasized. For instance, in *Zenith Radio Corp. v. Clark*,[182] the state instituted suit against the defendant alleging that a defective television precipitated a fire and resulting damage and injuries to the State Capital building.[183] Defendant sought production of the fire marshal's investigation report of the fire.[184] The state endeavored to suppress the report on the basis of a privilege: it was a written report made by a state employee in connection with prosecution of a lawsuit.[185] In conceding that the fire report was a written communication and that the fire marshal was a state employee, the court noted that the fire marshal's status as a state employee does not transform information which he obtains while performing his official duties into privileged matters simply because at some later time the state may be involved in a lawsuit arising from the fire.[186] The exemption may only be invoked where the written communication is specifically *prepared* "in connection" with the defense or prosecution of a lawsuit arising from the occurrence.[187]

Similarly, in *Allen v. Humphreys*,[188] plaintiff filed a motion for the defendant to produce various documents, test data, and written reports relating to the toxicity of polyvinyl chloride wrapping materials. The majority of the matters requested either was not prepared subsequent to the occurrence upon which plaintiff's claim was based or was not made or prepared in the investigation

---

181. *Id.* at 941.

182. 665 S.W.2d 804 (Tex. App.—Austin 1983, no writ).

183. *Id.* at 806.

184. *Id.*

185. *Id.* at 809.

186. *Id.* "It does not follow from the fact that the Fire Marshal is a state employee that all information which he obtains while performing his tasks is privileged simply because at some later time the State is, or may become involved in litigation arising from the fire. The final sub-proviso of Rule 186a can be invoked only when the information sought to be protected was prepared *in connection* with the prosecution or defense of a lawsuit in which the discovery is sought." *Id. See also* Giffin v. Smith, 688 S.W.2d 112 (Tex. 1985).

187. *Id. See also* St. Paul Ins. Co. v. Rahn, 641 S.W.2d 276, 283 (Tex. App.—Corpus Christi 1982, no writ) (privilege can be invoked only when the documents sought to be protected were prepared in connection with the instant lawsuit).

188. 559 S.W.2d 798 (Tex. 1977).

or for defense of plaintiff's claim.[189] In *Giffin v. Smith*[190], the Texas Supreme Court again declared that the communications exemption is dependent upon a showing that the communications were made subsequent to the occurrence giving use to the claim *and* made in connection with the prosecution or defense of such claim.

3. *Trade Secrets.* Trade secrets qualify as a partial privilege in Texas. In *Automatic Drilling Machines, Inc. v. Miller,*[191] plaintiff asserted that defendants wrongfully claimed ownership of plaintiff's patent licenses, trade secrets and design methods. Defendant endeavored to obtain various documents from plaintiff's expert, a pioneer in the field of automatic drilling rigs. At deposition, plaintiff's attorney withdrew from the expert's file material which related solely to new systems and procedures that were designed subsequent to the suit,[192] which were highly confidential, and which were the subject of pending applications for patents.[193] The Texas Supreme Court concluded that, "[t]rade secrets and confidential information are not necessarily 'privileged' matters . . . . If the information is material and necessary to the litigation and unavailable from any other source, a witness may be required to make disclosure."[194] The trade secrets pending patent approval were deemed exempt from discovery because defendant was not entitled to obtain information on every secret process that had been developed subsequent to suit.[195]

The partial privilege of trade secrets is likewise recognized in the newly codified Rules of Evidence.[196] Rule 507 provides that an individual may refuse to disclose and prevent others from disclosing a trade secret unless the allowance of the privilege would con-

189. *Id. See also* Neville v. Brewster, 352 S.W.2d 449, 450-51 (Tex. 1961) (communications made subsequent to an injury and in connection with the suit between plaintiff and his doctors were not privileged).

190. 688 S.W.2d 112 (Tex. 1985).

191. 515 S.W.2d 256 (Tex. 1974).

192. *Id.* at 258.

193. *Id.*

194. *Id.* at 259; Firestone Photographs, Inc. v. Lamaster, 567 S.W.2d 273, 278 (Tex. Civ. App.—Texarkana 1978, no writ).

195. 515 S.W.2d at 260. The court possesses discretion, however, to order an in camera inspection of these type of documents. Finn v. Finn, 658 S.W.2d 735, 746 (Tex. App.—Dallas 1983, no writ).

196. TEX. R. EVID. 507.

ceal a fraud or otherwise work an injustice.[197]

4. *Attorney-Client Privilege.* The attorney-client privilege perhaps represents the most well established and certainly, the most traditional, exemption under Rule 166b(3). Rule 166b(3) specifically provides that the privilege belongs to the client. For instance, documents prepared by an attorney for a decedent possess an attorney-client privilege.[198] Though the attorney-client privilege may exist, any privilege that attaches to the communications is a privilege of the client and not the attorney.[199] The attorney or his representative is presumed to possess authority to claim the privilege, but only on behalf of the client.[200]

The attorney-client privilege for purposes of pretrial discovery[201] is governed by the definition incorporated in the Texas Rules of Evidence. In *Giffin v. Smith,*[202] the Texas Supreme Court adopted Texas Rules of Evidence 503b as delineating the parameters of an attorney-client privilege. The court further noted that a confidential communication between a client and an attorney was one that is "not intended to be disclosed to third persons other than those to whom disclosure is made in furtherance of the rendition of the professional legal services to the client or those reasonably necessary for the transmission of the communication."[203]

In *West v. Solito,*[204] plaintiff alleged a conspiracy among the executors of her husband's estate. Defendants attempted unsuccessfully to take the deposition pursuant to a subpoena duces tecum of plaintiff's counsel who was not a party to the suit.[205] The Texas Supreme Court concluded that the trial court abused its discretion by failing to determine whether defendant's request for discovery violated the attorney-client privilege.[206] Suggesting strongly that the attorney is encouraged to protect legitimate at-

---

197. *Id.*

198. Fisher v. Continental Illinois National Bank & Trust Co., 424 S.W.2d 664, 671 (Tex. Civ. App.—Houston [14th Dist.] 1968, writ ref'd n.r.e.).

199. *Id.*

200. TEX. R. EVID. 503(c).

201. *Id.*

202. 688 S.W.2d 112 (Tex. 1985).

203. *Id.* at 355. The court adapted the confidential communication definition incorporated in Texas Rules of Evidence 503 (a)(5).

204. 563 S.W.2d 240 (Tex. 1978).

205. *Id.* at 242-43.

206. *Id.* at 246.

torney-client privileges, the supreme court noted that, "[t]he purpose of the attorney-client privilege is to promote the unrestrained communication and contact between any attorney and client in all matters in which the attorney's professional advice or services are sought, without fear that these confidential communications will be disclosed by the attorney, voluntarily or involuntarily, in any legal proceeding."[207]

The attorney-client privilege does not terminate with the attorney-client relationship. In *Maryland American General Insurance Co. v. Blackmon*,[208] a bank instituted an action against a customer who drew checks on insufficient funds and who defaulted on several loans. The bank's insurance company, as originator of the fidelity bond for this matter, was joined as a party.[209] The trial court ordered the attorney for the insurance company to produce all investigation and attorney's files pertinent to resolution of the claim.[210] This action in ordering production represented a clear abuse of discretion.[211] The attorney-client privilege necessarily extends to and exempts the attorney's files.[212] More importantly, the attorney-client privilege continues beyond termination of either the attorney-client relationship or the controversy which originally created the need for the attorney-client communications.[213] In fact, the attorney-client privilege even continues after the insurer's liability is established.[214]

The reach of the attorney-client privilege also extends beyond the traditional relationship. For example, in *Hiebert v. Weiss*,[215] defendant gave a statement to his insurance investigator following the occurrence of an accident.[216] The insurance policy issued to the defendant contractually obligated the company to furnish an attor-

---

207. *Id.* at 245.

208. 639 S.W.2d 455 (Tex. 1982).

209. *Id.* at 456.

210. *Id.* at 457.

211. *Id.* at 458.

212. *Id.*

213. *Id.*

214. *Id. Accord*, State Nat'l Bank v. Farah Mfg. Co., 678 S.W.2d 661, 699 (Tex. App.—El Paso 1984, writ dissm'd).

215. 622 S.W.2d 150 (Tex. App.—Fort Worth 1981, writ ref'd n.r.e.). *But see* Highway Ins. Underwriters v. Griffith, 290 S.W.2d 950, 953 (Tex. Civ. App.—Austin 1956, writ ref'd n.r.e.) (where insurance investigator's statements were made prior to the transaction in issue, the statements were not exempt from pretrial discovery).

216. 622 S.W.2d at 151.

ney to defend the insured against all claims.[217] Plaintiff attempted to utilize the statement given by the defendant to his insurance investigator for purposes of impeachment. The court deemed the statement inadmissible on the basis that the attorney-client privilege is created when the defendant gives a statement directly to his attorney.[218] Of necessity, the attorney-client privilege extends to the insurance company which provided the attorney to represent defendant.[219] Obviously, any relationship between the client and his attorney or the attorney's agent creates a privilege.[220] The law encourages the unrestrained communication between a client and his attorney in all matters in which professional services are sought.

There are exceptions to the attorney-client privilege. These exceptions to the privilege include communication between an attorney and client: (1) for the purpose of committing or planning to commit a crime or fraud; (2) relevant to an issue between parties who claim through the same deceased; (3) breach of duty by the lawyer to his client or by the client to his lawyer; (4) an attested document to which the attorney is the attesting witness; and (5) actions between two or more clients where the attorney is retained by all the clients.[221]

5. *Statutory Privilege.* Certain privileges emanate from legislative enactments. For example, Article 5561h[222] provides that communication between a patient-client and a medical professional is confidential.[223] Thus, a party is exempt from responding to pretrial discovery that would disclose either the patient-client identity or patient information.[224]

In *Falkner v. Gibraltar Savings Association,*[225] the court considered the legal effect of Article 1136a-9 which classifies the banking commissioner's records as confidential. The court recognized the validity of this statutory provision which completely forecloses

---

217. *Id.*
218. *Id.*
219. *Id.*
220. TEX. R. EVID. 503(b).
221. TEX. R. EVID. 503(e)(1-5).
222. TEX. REV. CIV. STAT. ANN. art. 5561h (Vernon Supp. 1984).
223. *Id.* 5561(h), [[2(a).
224. Ex Parte Abell, 613 S.W.2d 255, 258 (Tex. 1981).
225. 348 S.W.2d 472 (Tex. Civ. App.—Austin 1961, writ ref'd n.r.e.).

pretrial discovery of the banking commissioner investigator's reports.[226]

6. *Literal Interpretation of Privilege.* Prior to promulgation of Rule 166b, the specific exemptions from discovery were embodied in significant measure in Rule 186a. In *Ex Parte Hanlon,*[227] the Texas Supreme Court early interpreted Rule 186a[228] literally in shielding the deposition of an insurance investigator relating to the results obtained in his investigative work.[229] This interpretation of Rule 186a precluded the plaintiff from obtaining the name of the operator of the vehicle who was involved in the collision and resulting injuries to the plaintiff.[230] Of course, under Rule 166b, the identity of any potential parties is discoverable, though the statements of such parties are exempt from disclosure.

The identity of persons having knowledge of relevant facts of a claim may never be shielded from discovery. In *Giffin v. Smith,*[231] the defendant refused to disclose in response to questions propounded on oral deposition the name and address of all persons possessing knowledge of plaintiff's alleged acceptance of kickbacks while employed by the defendant. In mandating discovery, the court declared that "The plain language of Rule 166b thus makes it clear that information concerning the identity and location of persons having knowledge of relevant facts can never be protected from discovery."[232]

Recently, in *Menton v. Lattimore,*[233] defendant endeavored to compel production of a taped transcript of defendant's interview with his insurance carrier.[234] The court refused production based on the privileged nature of the statement. Disclosure of privileged material subjects a party to irreparable harm,[235] and, communications between an insurer and its insured obligated by contract to provide an attorney to represent the insurer relating to the occur-

226. *Id.* at 476.
227. 406 S.W.2d 204 (Tex. 1966).
228. Refer to note 149 *supra* and accompanying text.
229. 406 S.W.2d at 206.
230. *Id.* at 206-07.
231. 688 S.W.2d 112 (Tex. 1985).
232. *Id.*
233. 667 S.W.2d 335 (Tex. App.—Fort Worth 1984, no writ).
234. *Id.* at 336-37.
235. *Id.* at 338.

rence giving rise to a lawsuit necessarily must be exempt from pretrial discovery.[236] The exemption may be inapplicable, however, when the communication is made in connection with the perpetration of a fraud.[237]

7. *Waiver of Privilege.* A communication that is made subsequent to the occurrence of an event from which the lawsuit arises and that is made in connection with the investigation, prosecution or defense of the suit, is exempt from discovery.[238] A matter other-

---

236. *Id.* at 339.

237. *Id.* TEX. R. EVID. 503e(1) provides that no privilege exists "(1) . . . If the services of the lawyer were sought or obtained to enable or aid anyone to commit or plan to commit what the client knew or reasonably should have known to be a crime or fraud."

238. Refer to notes 174-190 *supra* and accompanying text.

In the recent case of United States v. American Tel. and Tel. Co., 642 F.2d 1285 (D.C. Cir. 1980), the Court of Appeals presented a thorough discussion of the principles underlying both the attorney-client privilege and the work product doctrine, and drew a clear distinction between those types of actions which may waive the protections afforded by each:

> The *attorney-client privilege* exists to protect confidential communications, to assure the client that any statement he makes in seeking legal advice will be kept strictly confidential between him and his attorney; in effect, *to protect the attorney-client relationship.* Any voluntary disclosure by the holder of such a privilege is inconsistent with the confidential relationship and thus waives the privilege. (Footnote omitted).
>
> By contrast, the *work product privilege* does not exist to protect a confidential relationship, but rather to *promote the adversary system by safeguarding the fruits of an attorney's trial preparations from the discovery attempts of the opponent.* (Footnote omitted). The purpose of the work doctrine is to protect information against opposing parties, rather than against all others outside a particular confidential relationship, in order to encourage effective trial preparation. In the leading case on the work product privilege, the Supreme Court stated: "[P]roper preparation of a client's case demands that he assemble information, sift what he considers to be the relevant from the irrelevant facts, prepare his legal theories and plan his strategy without undue and needless interference." (Footnote omitted). A disclosure made in the pursuit of such trial preparation, and not inconsistent with maintaining secrecy against opponents, should be without waiver of the privilege. We conclude, then, that *while the mere showing of a voluntary disclosure to a third person will generally suffice to show waiver of the attorney-client privilege, it should not suffice in itself for waiver of the work product privilege.* *Id.* at 1299. (emphasis in original).

The court then discussed with greater specificity the types of disclosures which either would or would not constitute a waiver of the work product protections:

> The existence of common interests between transferor and transferee is relevant to deciding whether the disclosure is consistent with the nature of the work product privilege. But "common interest" should not be construed as narrowly limited to co-parties. So long as transferor and transferee anticipate litigation against a common adversary on the same issue or issues, they have strong common interests in sharing the fruit of the trial preparation efforts. Moreover, with com-

wise possessing a valid exemption, however, may be waived. In *Dobbins v. Gardner*,[239] plaintiff in a malpractice action sought to discover a written communication between the defendant doctor and his insurance carrier.[240] Defendant sought to quash the communication based on its exempt status since it was a communication made subsequent to the occurrence and was prepared for the defense against plaintiff's claim.[241] Though the court acknowledged the exempt status of the communication, it was, nonetheless, subject to pretrial discovery because of waiver.[242] A party who voluntarily and intentionally discloses the contents of an exempt communication to a third person, not his agent, representative, or party connected with the defense of the claim, impliedly waives the privilege.[243]

The waiver, however, must represent a conscious and intentional disclosure of a privileged communication. In *Gass v. Baggerly*,[244] plaintiff complained that defendant's prior inconsistent statement[245] was admissible.[246] After defendant gave the statement to his insurance agent following the accident,[247] the statement inadvertently, and without defendant's knowledge or consent, was furnished to plaintiff.[248] Immediately upon plaintiff's tender of the statement at trial, defendant moved to suppress.[249] In the absence of a conscious and knowing consent, the inadvertent disclosure to third parties does not rise to the level of a waiver.[250]

---

mon interests on a particular issue against a common adversary, the transferee is not at all likely to disclose the work product material to the adversary. When the transfer to a party with such common interests is conducted under a guarantee of confidentiality, the case against waiver is even stronger. *Id.* at 1299-1300.

239. 377 S.W.2d 665 (Tex. Civ. App.—Houston 1964, writ ref'd n.r.e.).

240. *Id.* at 667.

241. *Id.* at 667-68.

242. *Id.* at 668-69.

243. *Id.* at 668. *But see* Menton v. Lattimore, 667 S.W.2d 335, 342 (Tex. App.—Fort Worth 1984, no writ) (Even where defendant admitted that much of his inquest testimony was false after he had been or would be indicted for aggravated perjury, the court did not agree that the admission freely and intentionally waived the privilege.).

244. 332 S.W.2d 426 (Tex. Civ. App.—Dallas 1960, no writ).

245. *Id.* at 430.

246. *Id.*

247. *Id.*

248. *Id.*

249. *Id.*

250. *Id.*

D. Protective Order

Prior to the promulgation of the amended rules, Rule 186b provided the basic relief to a party against whom inappropriate discovery was requested.[251] Essentially, any discovery that subjects a party to undue annoyance, embarrassment, oppression, or expense is prohibited. Protection requires a timely motion to restrict, limit or otherwise control discovery. As a general principle, the court is compelled to hear arguments or make in camera inspections to define the parameters of requested discovery.

As an example, in *Neville v. Brewster*,[252] the Texas Supreme Court compelled the trial court to examine, in camera, requested documents to ascertain the relevant from the irrelevant material and otherwise private matters.[253] Discovery of private information that is irrelevant in nature is prohibited.[254] Rule 186b requires the movant seeking to foreclose discovery of privileged matters to present a motion for protection to the trial court.[255] Motions for protection encompass matters that are private and otherwise irrelevant or that would result in "undue annoyance, embarrassment, oppression, or expense."[256] In the absence of a motion for protective relief under Rule 186b, a party is precluded from pursuing appellate relief through the original jurisdiction of mandamus.[257] The burden rests on the responding party to clearly identify for the trial court the material which it seeks to protect and to specify with particularity the basis for protecting against disclosure.

The wide latitude accorded trial courts in utilizing protective orders to control pretrial discovery was reaffirmed and emphasized in *Automatic Drilling Machines, Inc. v. Miller*.[258] When plaintiff refused to produce an expert witness' records, defendant filed a motion to compel the witness to comply with the subpoena and to prohibit plaintiff's attorney from interfering with the discovery

---

251. TEX. R. CIV. P. 166b(4) supersedes TEX. R. CIV. P. 186b (Vernon 1983).

252. 352 S.W.2d 449 (Tex. 1962). *See also* Maresca v. Marks, 362 S.W.2d 299 (Tex. 1962) (trial court to examine income tax returns before they were discoverable); Crane v. Tunks, 160 Tex. 182, 328 S.W.2d 434 (1959) (trial court to examine income tax returns to determine which parts relevant and discoverable).

253. 352 S.W.2d at 451.

254. *Id.*

255. *Id.*

256. *Id.* at 451-52.

257. Refer to notes 616-638 *infra* and accompanying text and 352 S.W.2d at 452.

258. 515 S.W.2d 256 (Tex. 1974).

process.[259] At this juncture, plaintiff filed a motion for a protective order under Rule 186b.[260] In reviewing the mandamus application, the supreme court noted the discretion available to the trial court to: (1) examine and determine the material that is relevant and essential to defendant's investigation and development of their case, and or discovery;[261] or (2) defer action on document production until defendant completes his examination of the witness.[262] Responding to the timeliness of a protective motion filed during a witness' deposition, the court commented that a Rule 186b motion was not required to be filed before commencement of discovery.[263]

An in camera inspection of requested documents pursuant to a protective motion was involved in *West v. Solito*.[264] Plaintiff filed a motion under Rule 186b to quash subpoenaed matters based on attorney-client privilege.[265] An attorney is not obligated to produce documents that are denominated as privileged until a trial court reviews the requested materials and determines whether a valid privilege exists.[266]

Protective orders serve various beneficial purposes. For instance, in *Burr v. Shannon*,[267] plaintiff sought a mandamus to mandate that a tape recorded deposition need not be recorded by stenographic means.[268] The Texas Supreme Court, relying on earlier Rule 186b, concluded that the trial court possesses the discretion to issue a protective order to assure that justice is done.[269] A protective order is clearly appropriate to compel stenographic transcription of a nonstenographic deposition.[270]

Motions for a protective order need not be restricted to protection *from* discovery.[271] Rather, as *Sobel v. Taylor*[272] illustrates,

---

259. *Id.* at 258.
260. *Id.* at 259.
261. *Id.* at 260.
262. *Id.*
263. *Id.*
264. 563 S.W.2d 240 (Tex. 1978).
265. *Id.* at 243.
266. *Id.* at 246. *See* Aztec Life Ins. Co. v. Dellana, 667 S.W.2d 911, 916 (Tex. App.—Austin 1984, no writ) (appellate court order that trial court perform an in camera inspection and issue a protective order for privileged matters).
267. 593 S.W.2d 677 (Tex. 1980).
268. *Id.* at 677.
269. *Id.* at 678.
270. *Id.*
271. *See* Sobel v. Taylor, 640 S.W.2d 704 (Tex. App.—Houston [14th Dist.] 1982, no

the trial court ordered plaintiff to return certain documents to defendants after imposing certain controls and restrictions to insure the organization and identity of the documents during the trial.[273] Despite a contention that the protective order as issued constituted a temporary injunction, the order was characterized as a nonappealable pretrial discovery order.[274]

Rule 166b now incorporates the provisions of prior Rule 186b.[275] The current rules suggest that protective orders extend to:

> (a) ordering that requested discovery not be sought in whole or in part, or that the extent or subject matter of discovery . . . be limited, or that it not be undertaken at the time or place specified (b) ordering that the discovery be undertaken only by such method or upon such terms and conditions or at the time and place directed by the court (c) ordering that results of discovery be sealed or otherwise adequately protected; that its distribution be limited; or that its disclosure be restricted.[276]

E. *Duty To Supplement*

Undoubtedly, one of the more significant modifications in Rule 166b involves the duty to supplement. The last section of Rule 166b(5) addresses the duty to supplement.[277] The new rule has been expanded to impose a duty to supplement all forms of discovery, not just interrogatories and depositions.[278] Rule 166b(5) has shortened the time within which a party may supplement a response to thirty days prior to trial.[279] The answering party is obligated to supplement discovery if he obtains information upon the basis of which he ascertains that: (1) the information was incorrect or incomplete when made; or (2) the discovery, though correct and complete when made, is no longer accurate and complete and a

---

writ).

272. *Id.*

273. *Id.* at 708.

274. *Id.* at 707.

275. TEX. R. CIV. P. 166b(4).

276. *Id.*

277. TEX. R. CIV. P. 166b(5).

278. *Id. Compare* TEX. R. CIV. P. 167(7) (Vernon 1983) (duty to supplement limited to interrogatories and depositions).

279. *Compare* TEX. R. CIV. P. 167(7) (Vernon 1983) (interrogatories pertaining to experts had to be supplemented not less than fourteen days (14) days prior to trial).

failure to supplement is, in substance, misleading.[280] Additionally, the amended rule further provides that a party who expects to call an expert witness to testify concerning matters as yet undisclosed to the opponent must supplement the response to an appropriate interrogatory to include the name, address, and telephone number of the expert witness and the substance of the expected testimony within thirty days prior to trial. Court permission is required to extend this time period.[281]

8.03 RULE 167; DISCOVERY AND PRODUCTION OF DOCUMENTS AND THINGS[282]

The production of any designated documents, papers, books, accounts, letters, photographs, objects or other tangible things which constitute or contain, or are reasonably calculated to lead to the discovery of evidence material to any issue is governed by Rule 167.[283] Until the current amendment, the scope of discovery was governed by the provisions of Rule 186a and 186b.[284] Rule 166b now governs the scope of Rule 167 discovery.[285] Former Rule 167 in conjunction with Rule 186a governing production of expert reports,[286] witness statements,[287] injury-damages,[288] and construc-

---

280. TEX. R. CIV. P. 166b(5) provides that,

a. A party is under a duty seasonably to supplement his response if he obtains information upon the basis of which: (1) he knows that the response was incorrect or incomplete when made; (2) he knows that the response though correct and complete when made is no longer true and complete and the circumstances are such that failure to amend the answer is in substance misleading; or

b. If the party expects to call an expert witness when the identity or the subject matter of such expert witness' testimony has not been previously disclosed in response to an appropriate inquiry directly addressed to these matters, such response must be supplemented . . . as soon as is practical, but in no event less than thirty (30) days prior to the beginning of trial except on leave of court.

c. In addition, a duty to supplement answers may be imposed by order of the court or agreement of the parties, or at any time prior to trial through new requests for supplementation of prior answers.

281. *Id.*

282. *See generally* McConnico & Bishop, Practicing Law with 1984 Rules: *Texas Rules of Civil Procedure Amendments* Effective April 1, 1984, 36 BAYLOR L. REV. 73 (1984); Barrow & Henderson, *1984 Amendments to the Texas Rules of Civil Procedure Affecting Discovery*, 15 ST. MARY'S L.J. 713 (1984); Nations, *Discovery: Motions to Produce Under the Texas Rules*, 18 S. TEX. L.J. 49 (1976).

283. TEX. R. CIV. P. 167.

284. *See* commentary TEX. R. CIV. P. 166b.

285. TEX. R. CIV. P. 167(1)a.

286. *Id.* 167(5) (Vernon 1983). Refer to notes 55-115 *supra* and accompanying text.

tion[289] are now embodied in and authorized by Rule 166b. This reorganization collates all matters relating to the scope of discovery in one rule. In addition, earlier Rule 167(3) prescribing sanctions[290] has been integrated into Rule 215.[291]

Rule 167(1)c incorporates several major changes. This rule states that, "[t]he **request** shall set forth the items to be inspected either by individual item or by category, and describe each item and category with reasonable particularity."[292]

Under the current rule, a formal motion for production of documents or things need no longer be filed with the court. Rather, Rule 167(1) provides that a request for production may be served on any other party.[293] This language is adopted from Federal Rule 34,[294] upon which the 1981 revisions to Texas Rule 167 were largely modeled.[295] During the 1981 revision, the "good cause" requirement for production was totally eliminated and the abrogation of the "good cause" requirement continues in the current revisions.

The scope of production has recently undergone significant reassessment. In *General Motors Corp. v. Lawrence*,[296] plaintiff instituted a wrongful death suit claiming strict liability against General Motors Corporation arising from a truck collision.[297] Plaintiff served the defendant with interrogatories and a motion seeking production of all defendant's investigation results of fuel spills caused by damaged filler necks on any vehicle, whether car, truck, locomotive, tank, or other vehicle ever manufactured or sold by defendant from the date of its incorporation in 1908 to the present.[298] Despite written objections under Rule 167 and motions for protection under Rule 186b, the trial court ordered defendant to respond

---

287. Tex. R. Civ. P. 167(6) (Vernon 1983). Refer to notes 30-42 *supra* and accompanying text.

288. Tex. R. Civ. P. 167(7) (Vernon 1983). Refer to notes 127-138 *supra* and accompanying text.

289. Tex. R. Civ. P. 167(8) (Vernon 1983). Refer to notes 30-42 *supra* and accompanying text.

290. Tex. R. Civ. P. 167(3) (Vernon 1983). Refer to § 7.08 *infra*.

291. Tex. R. Civ. P. 215.

292. Tex. R. Civ. P. 167(1)c.

293. Tex. R. Civ. P. 167(1)c.

294. Fed. R. Civ. P. 34.

295. *See* Commentary to Tex. R. Civ. P. 167.

296. 651 S.W.2d 732 (Tex. 1983).

297. *Id.* at 732.

298. *Id.* at 733.

to all interrogatories and to produce all requested documents.[299] The Texas Supreme Court concluded rather decisively that the trial court clearly abused his discretion by ordering overly broad and irrelevant discovery.[300] "Vehicle" includes not only cars and trucks in its definition, but also locomotives, airplanes, submarines, etc.[301] Further, the request was not limited to any relevant time period.[302] The court concluded that discovery should have been limited to records relating to truck model years 1949 through 1972, and should have included all impact test results.[303] The Supreme Court emphasized that discovery and more particularly, pretrial production, is not designed for trial harassment, but rather, represents a search for truth based solely and, only, on "relevant" facts.

The scope and breath of relevant production was again reviewed by the Texas Supreme Court in *Jampole v. Touchy*.[304] The trial court, in the exercise of its discretion, limited plaintiff's request for production of alternative design and assembly documents.[305] Plaintiff alleged that General Motors Corporation manufactured and marketed its 1976 Vega hatchback with a defectively designed gas tank placement.[306] Plaintiff endeavored to discover, among other things, all documents of alternative fuel storage system designs in any model or type vehicle known to the defendant.[307] He also sought all installation and assembly diagrams and specifications for 1971-77 Vegas and their counterpart, Pontiac Astres.[308]

The Supreme Court concluded that these requests for production constituted relevant information under the liberalized interpretation of the current rules and ordered production.[309] The court noted that designs that may have prevented fuel from escaping from the tank were relevant to demonstrate that the Vega tank was unreasonably dangerous;[310] and, documents that showed de-

---

299. *Id.* at 732.
300. *Id.* at 734.
301. *Id.* at 733.
302. *Id.*
303. *Id.* at 734.
304. 673 S.W.2d 569 (Tex. 1984).
305. *Id.* at 573.
306. *Id.* at 572.
307. *Id.* at 573.
308. *Id.* at 572.
309. *Id.* at 573.
310. *Id.*

fendant's knowledge of alternative designs were relevant to demonstrate a conscious indifference that supported plaintiff's gross negligence claim.[311] The court did not consider, as did the trial court which heard three full days of expert testimony from both parties on the relevancy of the documents sought for production, that the requested time period for the vehicle production was overly broad, and that plaintiff failed to limit his request to include only relevant tests on passenger vehicles.[312] The court rather clearly expanded the concept of relevancy in a pretrial context.

Justice Barrow, in a vigorous dissent, discussed the negative precedent of the majority's ruling upon pretrial discovery.[313] Because the 1984 amendments contemplate primary responsibility for controlling discovery abuse upon trial judges, the Supreme Court significantly curtailed the previously recognized broad discretion of the trial court.[314] The fact that the Supreme Court intervened in the pretrial discovery process when the trial court exercised its discretion in strict compliance with the mandate of *Maresca v. Marks* and *Crane v. Tunks* suggests the uninviting prospect of the frequent interruption of orderly discovery through mandamus proceedings.[315]

Objections to request for production must be made in writing to the specific items requested by the opposing party.[316] Either party may request a hearing and the court is authorized to exercise its discretion in ordering or denying the matters requested be produced.[317]

---

311. *Id.*

312. *Id.* at 573.

313. *Id.* at 577 (Barrow, J., dissenting). This case furnishes the court with a unique opportunity to support the efforts of Texas trial judges in curbing discovery abuses. Rather than seizing upon this opportunity and expressing confidence in trial judges, the court has now unnecessarily usurped the discretion of the trial judge. From this decision emanates a signal to the trial judge in contradiction to the court's prior attitude in this context and of the purpose of the amended rules of discovery. *Id.* Discretion to control discovery previously vested in the trial court under Werner v. Miller, 579 S.W.2d 455 (Tex. 1979) has now been severely constrained.

314. *Id.*

315. *Id.*

316. Tex. R. Civ. P. 167(1)(d).

317. Tex. R. Civ. P. 167(3). This discretion has been severely impaired by the decision in Jampole v. Touchy, 673 S.W.2d 569 (Tex. 1984).

8.04 RULE 167a: PHYSICAL AND MENTAL EXAMINATION

Rule 167a addresses the physical and mental examination of a party whose mental or physical condition is in controversy.[318] The examination, unlike a request for production, requires a court order based on a motion for good cause.[319] This provision is patterned, in a large measure, after the Federal Rules of Civil Procedure.[320]

Good cause is a prerequisite for obtaining a physical or mental examination of a party. The term "good cause" requires pleading and proof of both "materiality" and "necessity.[321] A cause of action seeking damages for personal injuries satisfies the "good cause" requirement. In *Schlagenhauf v. Holder*,[322] the United States Supreme Court considered the issue of good cause in connection with a medical examination ordered under Federal Rule 25, the progenitor of the current Rule 34:

> A plaintiff in a negligence action who asserts mental or physical injury . . . places that mental or physical injury clearly in controversy and provides the defendant with good cause for an examination to determine the existence and extent of such asserted injury. This is not only true as to a plaintiff, but applies equally to a defendant who asserts his mental or physical condition as a

---

318. TEX. R. CIV. P. 167a(a) provides: "When the mental or physical condition (including the blood group) of a party, or of a person in the custody or under the legal control of a party, is in controversy, the court in which the action is pending may order the party to submit to a physical or mental examination by a physician or to produce for examination the person in his custody or legal control. The order may be made only on motion for good cause shown and upon notice to the person to be examined and to all parties and shall specify the time, place, manner, conditions, and scope of the examination and the person or persons by whom it is to be made."

Previously, Texas prohibited mental and physical examinations as part of trial discovery. Austin & N.W. Ry. Co. v. Cluck, 97 Tex. 172, 77 S.W. 403 (1903).

319. TEX. R. CIV. P. 167a(a).

320. *See* FED. R. CIV. P. 35 provides: When the mental or physical condition (including the blood group) of a party or of a person in the custody or under the legal control of a party, is in controversy, the court in which the action is pending may order the party to submit to a physician or mental examination by a physician or to produce for examination the person in his custody or legal control. The order may be made only on motion for good cause shown and upon notice to the person to be examined and to all parties and shall specify the time, place, manner, conditions, and scope of the examination and the person or persons by whom it is to be made.

321. *See, e.g.*, Lueg v. Tewell, 572 S.W.2d 97 (Tex. Civ. App.—Corpus Christi 1978, no writ); Irwin v. Basham, 507 S.W.2d 621 (Tex. Civ. App.—Dallas 1974, writ ref'd. n.r.e.).

322. 379 U.S. 104 (1964).

defense to a claim . . .[323]

In addition to the good cause requirement, the movant is obligated to demonstrate that the physical or mental condition of a party is "in controversy."[324] In some instances the pleadings alone are sufficient to satisfy this requirement.[325] A party who asserts a claim or defense based on a mental or physical injury places that issue clearly "in controversy" and provides the other party with good cause for an examination of the asserted injury.[326] For example, in *C.E. Duke's Wrecker Service v. Oakley*,[327] plaintiff's physical condition was directly in dispute when she sued to recover damages for injuries sustained when defendant's truck struck her automobile from the rear.[328]

Conversely, when a defendant places another party's mental or physical condition in issue, the claimants must establish good cause and "in controversy".[329] Any party, even a co-defendant, may be examined upon the motion of any other party upon a showing of "good cause" and "in controversy." The United States Supreme Court commented:

> [t]hey [good cause and controversy] are not met by mere conclusory allegations of the pleadings - nor by mere relevance to the case - but require an affirmative showing by the movant that each condition as to which the examination is sought is really and genuinely in controversy and that good cause exists.[330]

The "in controversy" requirement expresses a judicial concern for the individual's right to the privacy of his person.[331] Yet, even where the "good cause" and "in controversy" requirements are satisfied, the decision to order an examination rests in the sound discretion of the trial court.[332]

The examinee may request and receive a copy of the report of

---

323. *Id.* at 119.
324. *Id.* at 118-19.
325. *Id.* at 119.
326. *Id.*
327. 526 S.W.2d 228 (Tex. Civ. App.—Houston [1st Dist.] 1975, writ ref'd n.r.e.).
328. *Id.* at 234.
329. *See* Schlagenhauf, 379 U.S. at 119.
330. *Id.* at 118-119.
331. *See* Sales, *Pre-Trial Discovery in Texas*, 31 Sw. L.J. 1017, 1034 (1978).
332. Tex. R. Civ. P. 167a(a) ("the court in which the action is pending may order the party to submit to a physical or mental examination . . ."). *See*, Texas Emp. Ins. Ass'n. v. Garza, 675 S.W.2d 245 (Tex.App.—Corpus Christi 1984, no writ)

the examining physician outlining his findings, including the results of all tests, diagnosis and conclusions. The written report, however, does not extend to the physician's office notes.[333] Once an examinee makes a request, the requesting party is obligated to submit a report of the examining physician setting out his findings, including the results of all tests, diagnosis and conclusions. Once an examinee requests a report of the court ordered examination, the party requesting the medical examination is then entitled to all reports of any examinations previously or thereafter made of the same condition.[334]

The party seeking the examination generally is permitted to select the examining physician.[335] The right of the requesting party to select the examining physician, however, is not an absolute right.[336] The final selection of the examining physician is a matter resting within the sound discretion of the trial court.[337] The determination of the number of physicians who may conduct the examination is likewise within the trial court's discretion.[338] Moreover, the manner, conditions and scope of the examinations is governed solely by the discretion of the trial court.[339]

Once a court ordered examination is completed, subsequent examinations may be ordered if (1) a party suffers multiple injuries requiring analysis by several specialists; (2) the condition of the party changes after the initial examination; or (3) the examining physician requires consultation with other physicians.[340]

Unlike its federal counterpart, [341] the Texas rules expressly provide that in the event no examination is requested, either by

---

333. *See* Sales, *supra* note 331 at 1036.

334. *See, e.g.*, Weir v. Simmons, 233 F. Supp. 657 (D. Neb. 1964); Chastain v. Evennou, 35 F.R.D. 350 (D. Utah 1964); Butts v. Sears, Roebuck & Co., 9 F.R.D. 58 (D.D.C. 1949).

335. Liechty v. Terrill Trucking Co., 53 F.R.D. 590 (E.D. Tenn. 1971).

336. *See, e.g.*, Stuart v. Burford, 42 F.R.D. 591 (N.D. Okla. 1967); Gitto v. Societa Anonima Di Navigazion, Genova, 27 F. Supp. 785 (E.D.N.Y. 1939).

337. *See* Leach v. Grief Bros. Cooperage Corp., 2 F.R.D. 444 (S.D. Miss. 1942); Martin v. Superior Court, 104 Ariz 268, 451 P.2d 597 (1969); Timpte v. District Court, 161 Colo. 309, 421 P.2d 728 (1966).

338. Bowing v. Delaware Rayon Co., 38 Del. 111, 188 A. (1937).

339. Klein v. Yellow Cab, 7 F.R.D. 169 (N.D. Ohio 1944); Riss & Co. v. Galloway, 108 Colo. 93, 114 P.2d 550 (1941); Atchinson T.& S.F. Ry. Co. v. Palmore, 68 Kan. 545, 75 P. 509 (1904).

340. *See, e.g.*, Stuart v. Burford, 42 F.R.D. 591 (N.D. Okla. 1967); Hildyard v. Western Fastners, Inc., 33 Colo. App. 396, 522 P.2d 596 (1974).

341. FED. R. CIV. P. 35.

agreement or under the rule, the party whose physical or mental condition is in controversy may not comment to the court or jury on his willingness to submit to an examination; on the right of the other party to request a physical or mental examination; or on the failure of the other party to move or request a physical or mental examination.[342] This prohibition was designed to eliminate the practice of the plaintiff commenting to the jury that he was always ready and willing to submit to a medical examination if the opposing party even remotely contested the extent or nature of his injury. The mandatory nature of Rule 167a(c) was recognized in *C.E. Duke's Wrecker Service, Inc.*[343] Plaintiff testified that she had been willing to be examined by any physician the defendant chose to evaluate her injuries.[344] The court concluded that this testimony and the argument of plaintiff's counsel violated the provisions of Rule 167a(c):

> We do not think the intention of the [Texas] Supreme Court in promulgating this rule was to allow a party whose physical or mental condition is in question to require another party to the suit to have him examined by a physician on the penalty of opening his failure to do so to comment before the jury by merely offering to enter into an agreement to submit to a physical examination.[345]

The philosophy underlying this provision contemplates that the opportunity for an examination offered by Rule 167a is a privilege that may not be exercised; if not exercised, no penalty attaches to a party's failure, for whatever reason, to take advantage of this opportunity.[346]

---

342. Tex. R. Civ. P. 167a(c):

> c. If no examination is sought either by agreement or under the provisions of this rule, the party whose mental or physical condition is in controversy shall not comment to the court or jury on his willingness to submit to an examination, or the right of any other party to request an examination or move for an order, or on the failure of such other party to do so.

343. 526 S.W.2d 228.

344. *Id.* at 231. *See also* Texas Employers' Ins. Ass'n v. Henson, 569 S.W.2d 516, 517 (Tex. Civ. App.—Beaumont 1978, no writ) (the court determined that plaintiff committed reversible error by violating Rule 167a(c) in testifying he was willing to be examined by anyone following the date of the injury).

345. 526 S.W.2d at 232.

346. *Id.*

8.05 Rule 168: Interrogatories To Parties[347]

Rule 168 states that at any time after a party has made an appearance in the cause of action, any other party may serve upon that party written interrogatories.[348] Unlike the earlier practice, a party is limited to two sets of interrogatories and neither set may number more than thirty questions.[349] The two-set limitation may be modified either by agreement or court order.[350] The enlargement of the number of sets of interrogatories or the number of interrogatories may be granted only upon a hearing on a motion for good cause.[351]

The scope[352] and duty to supplement[353] of earlier Rule 168 are now embodied in Rule 166b. Also, the sanctions provided for failure to comply with prior Rule 168(8) are now articulated in Rule 215.[354] Interrogatories are authorized for pretrial discovery purposes only, and may not be utilized for post judgment purposes.[355]

Rule 168(6) provides that a party shall have a minimum of thirty days after interrogatories are served to serve written objections to some or all of the interrogatories.[356] Answers to interrogatories to which an objection has been filed are deferred until the objections are ruled upon and for such additional time as the court

---

347. *See generally* McConnico & Bishop, *Practicing Law with the 1984 Rules: Texas Rules of Civil Procedure Amendments*, Effective April 1,1984, 36 Baylor L. Rev. 73 (1984); Barrow & Henderson, *1984 Amendments to the Texas Rules of Civil Procedure Affecting Discovery*, 15 St. Mary's L.J. 713 (1984); Spears, *The Texas Rules of Civil Procedure: 1981 Changes in Pre-Trial Discovery*, 12 St. Mary's L.J. 633; Comment, *Written Interrogatories and Requests for Admissions*, 19 Baylor L. Rev. 133 (1967); Sales, *supra* note 331 at 1037.

348. Tex. R. Civ. P. 168 provides: At any time after a party has made appearance in the cause, or time therefor has elapsed, any other party may serve upon such party written interrogatories to be answered by the party served, or, if the party served is a public or private corporation or a partnership or association, or governmental agency, by any officer or agent who shall furnish such information as is available to the party.

349. *Id.* 168(5).

350. *Id.*

351. In Heissner v. Koons, 679 S.W.2d 112 (Tex. App.—Dallas 1984, no writ), the court declares that a hearing and a showing of good cause are prerequisite to enlargement of either the number or sets of interrogatories.

352. Tex. R. Civ. P. 186a (Vernon 1983). *Compare* Tex. R. Civ. P. 168(2).

353. Tex. R. Civ. P. 168(7) (Vernon 1983).

354. Refer to § 7.08 *infra*.

355. *See* Ana-Log, Inc. v. Tyler, 520 S.W.2d 819, 824 (Tex. Civ. App.—Tyler 1975, no writ) (in which the court prohibited use of Rule 168 interrogatories in conjunction with a motion for new trial). *See also* Vega v. Royal Crown Bottling Co., 526 S.W.2d 729 (Tex. Civ. App.—Corpus Christi 1975, no writ).

356. Tex. R. Civ. P. 168(6)

directs.[357]

Where the answer to an interrogatory may be ascertained from (a) public records or (b) the business records of the party served, and the burden of finding the answer is substantially the same for the serving party as for the party served, it is sufficient to specify the records from which the answer may be obtained and to afford the serving party an opportunity to examine those records.[358] Compliance requires the answering party to specifically designate where the answers may be obtained and their precise location.[359] Rule 168(2)(b) corresponds with the final sentence of Federal Rule 33(c).[360] The comment to Rule 33(c) states that,

> [a] party who is permitted by the terms of this subdivision to offer records for inspection . . . should offer them in a manner that permits the same direct and economical access that is available to the party. If the information sought exists in the form of compilations, abstracts or summaries then available to the responding party, those should be made available to the interrogating party. The final sentence is added to make it clear that a responding party has the duty to specify, by category and location, the records from which answers to interrogatories can be derived.[361]

When business records are sought, the responding party must specify whether the information sought is in the designated records. If the information sought from the records can be located and identified as readily by the requesting party as the answering party, then the requesting party is obligated to make a search of the records.[362]

The answering party is obligated to supplement answers to interrogatories if he obtains information upon the basis of which he knows: (1) the answer was incorrect or incomplete when made, or (2) the answer, although correct and complete when made, is no longer true and complete and the failure to amend the answer is, in substance, misleading.[363] The current rule also contains a specific

---

357. TEX. R. CIV. P. 168(6).
358. TEX. R. CIV. P. 168(2).
359. TEX. R. CIV. P. 168(2).
360. FED. R. CIV. P. 33(c). *See* Barrow & Henderson, *supra* note 347 at 741.
361. FED. R. CIV. P. 33(c) (advisory committee note to the 1980 amendment).
362. *See* Barrow & Henderson, *supra* note 347 at 741.
363. *See, e.g., Id.*

provision requiring supplementation for expert witnesses. If previously propounded interrogatories inquire about expert witnesses, answers to such interrogatories must be supplemented to include the name, address and telephone number of the expert witness and the substance of the testimony concerning which the expert witness is expected to testify as soon as is practicable and, in no event, less than 30 days prior to the beginning of trial, except by leave of court.[364] The requesting party, to be entitled to supplementation, must direct an interrogatory that specifically requests identification of expert witnesses.[365] Of course, a party also may be obligated to amend or supplement answers to interrogatory pursuant to court order.[366] Under earlier decisions, prior to amendment of the rules, a failure to supplement did not necessarily result in exclusion of the evidence at the time of trial.[367] The revised rules now specifically provide that "a party who fails to supplement reasonably his responses to a request for discovery . . . shall not be entitled to present evidence which the party was under a duty to provide . . . or to offer the testimony of an expert witness or of any other person having knowledge of discoverable matter . . ., unless the trial court finds that good cause sufficient to require admission exists."[368]

Though a party's answers to interrogatories may be changed with court permission, the adverse party may still utilize former answers given in response to interrogatories as a basis for impeach-

364. *See* Tex. R. Civ P. 166b(5)(b). Failure to supplement the identity of expert witnesses warrants exclusion of the experts' testimony at trial. City of Denton v. Page, 683 S.W.2d 180, 203 (Tex. App.—Fort Worth 1985, no writ).

365. *See, e.g.*, Meyerland Co. v. Palais Royal of Houston, Inc., 557 S.W.2d 534 (Tex. Civ. App.—Houston [14th Dist.] 1977, no writ).

366. *See, e.g.*, Werner v. Miller, 579 S.W.2d 455 (Tex. 1979); Texas Employer's Ins. Ass'n. v. Thomas, 517 S.W.2d 832 (Tex. Civ. App.—San Antonio 1974, writ ref'd n.r.e.); Allright, Inc. v. Yeager, 512 S.W.2d 731 (Tex. Civ. App.—Houston [1st Dist.] 1974, writ ref'd n.r.e.).

367. *See* Smithson v. Cessna Aircraft Co., 665 S.W.2d 439 (Tex. 1984); Texas Employer's Ins. Ass'n. v. Thomas, 517 S.W.2d 832 (Tex. Civ. App.—San Antonio 1975, writ ref'd n.r.e.).

368. Tex. R. Civ. P. 215(5). *See, e.g.*, Texas Industries, Inc. v. Lucas, 634 S.W.2d 748 (Tex. App.—Houston [14th Dist.] 1982, *reversed on other grounds*, 27 Tex. Sup. Ct. J. 491 (July 11, 1984); Trubell v. Patten, 582 S.W.2d 606 (Tex. Civ. App.—Tyler 1979, no writ); Texas Employer's Ins. Ass'n. v. Meyer, 620 S.W.2d 179 (Tex. Civ. App.—Waco 1981, no writ). The trial court is mandated to find good cause for late supplementation of experts. Texas Employers Ins. Ass'n v. Garza, 687 S.W.2d 299 (Tex. 1985) writ ref'd per curiam, 675 S.W.2d 245 (Tex. App.—Corpus Christi 1984).

ment.[369] Answers to interrogatories may be used only against the party responding to the interrogatory.[370] Concomitantly, the answering party may not use its answers to another party's interrogatories as probative evidence in support of its own position on motion for summary judgment or any similar motion.[371] Likewise, answers to interrogatories made by one defendant may not be used against a co-defendant.[372] Answers to interrogatories are subject to the general rules of evidence, and unlike responses to requests for admissions, do not necessarily constitute binding judicial admissions.[373] The provisions of Rule 166b and 168 apply with equal force and effect to the State of Texas as to private litigants.[374]

8.06 RULE 169: ADMISSION OF FACTS AND GENUINENESS OF DOCUMENTS[375]

Rule 169, modeled after Federal Rule 36,[376] provides that at

---

369. *See* Thomas v. International Ins. Co., 527 S.W.2d 813 (Tex. Civ. App.—Waco 1975, writ ref'd n.r.e.).

370. *See* Netherland v. Wittner, 624 S.W.2d 685 (Tex. App.—Houston [14th Dist.] 1981, no writ); Duncan v. Horning, 587 S.W.2d 471 (Tex. Civ. App. Dallas 1979, no writ).

371. *See, e.g.*, Thurman v. Frozen Food Express, 600 S.W.2d 369 (Tex. Civ. App.—Dallas 1980, no writ); Holmes v. Canlen Management Corp., 542 S.W.2d 199 (Tex. Civ. App.—El Paso 1976, no writ); Sympson v. Mor-Win Products, Inc., 501 S.W.2d 362 (Tex. Civ. App.—Fort Worth 1973, no writ).

372. *See* United Services Automobile Ass'n v. Ratterree, 512 S.W.2d 30 (Tex. Civ. App.—San Antonio 1974, writ ref'd n.r.e.); Stanfield v. Kroll, 484 S.W.2d 603 (Tex. Civ. App.—Houston [1st Dist.] 1972, writ ref'd n.r.e.).

373. *See, e.g.*, Barnwell v. Fox & Jacobs Construction Co., 469 S.W.2d 199 (Tex. Civ. App.—Dallas 1971, no writ); General Plywood Corp. v. Collins, 414 S.W.2d 224 (Tex. Civ. App.—Amarillo 1967, no writ); Standard Fire Ins. Co. v. Ratcliff, 537 S.W.2d 355 (Tex. Civ. App.—Waco 1976, no writ).

374. *See* Lowe v. Texas Tech Univ., 540 S.W.2d 297 (Tex. 1976); Texas Dep't of Corrections v. Herring, 513 S.W.2d 6 (Tex. 1974); Mokry v. University of Texas Health Sciences Center, 529 S.W.2d 802 (Tex. Civ. App.—Dallas 1975, writ ref'd n.r.e.).

375. *See generally* McConnico, *supra* note 347; Barrow & Henderson, *supra* note 347; Bush, *Rule 169: An Overview*, 44 TEX. B.J. 1049 (1981); *Written Interrogatories and Requests for Admissions*, *supra* note 347; Sales, *supra* note 331 at 1047.

376. FED. R. CIV. P. 36 states: A party may serve upon any other party a written request for the admission, for purposes of the pending action only, of the truth of any matters within the scope of Rule 26(b) set forth in the request that relate to statements or opinions of fact or of the application of law to fact, including the genuineness of any documents described in the request. Copies of documents shall be served with the request unless they have been or are otherwise furnished or made available for inspection and copying. The request may, without leave of court, be served upon the plaintiff after commencement of the action and upon any other party with or after service of the summons and complaint upon that party.

any time after the defendant has made appearance in the cause, a party may serve upon any other party a written request for admissions of fact or the genuineness of documents for purposes of the pending action only.[377] Under prior Rule 169,[378] a party was entitled to a minimum of ten days in which to answer a request for admissions.[379] The revised rule extends the time to thirty days in which a party must either admit or deny the truth of any matter[380] within the scope of discovery.[381] This modification is consistent with the objective of making discovery responses generally due within thirty days.[382] An exception to this time limit occurs when a defendant is served with requests immediately after the filing of a suit. In this specific instance, the answers are due within thirty days after being served or within forty-five days after service of the citation, whichever is longer.[383]

Procedurally, a request must now separately set forth each matter for which an admission is requested.[384] Specific requests avoid the necessity of proving individual facts which are not controverted.[385] Rule 169 does not require that a request for admission be addressed to a specific individual. It requires only delivery to the attorney of record, unless the court orders delivery to the party.[386]

See Comment to TEX. R. CIV. P. 169; Sanders v. Harter, 148 Tex. 593, 596, 227 S.W.2d 206, 208 (1950); Masten v. Masten, 165 S.W.2d 225, 227 (Tex. Civ. App.—Fort Worth 1942, writ ref'd).

377. TEX. R. CIV. P. 169(1); Phillips v. Latham, 433 S.W.2d 775, 777 (Tex. Civ. App.—Eastland 1968, writ ref'd n.r.e.), *cert. denied*, 396 U.S. 830, 90 S. Ct. 82 (1969) (request for admissions and answers in a different lawsuit were inadmissible in the pending action).

378. TEX. R. CIV. P. 169 (Vernon 1983).

379. *Id.*

380. TEX. R. CIV. P. 169.

381. Refer to § 7.02(B) *supra.*

382. *See* Comment to TEX. R. CIV. P. 169.

383. TEX. R. CIV. P. 169(1); Barrow, *supra* note 347 at 742.

384. TEX. R. CIV. P. 169(1).

385. *See* Fireman's Fund Ins. Co. v. Commercial Standard Ins. Co., 490 S.W.2d 818, 825-26 (Tex. 1972); Texas Employers Ins. Ass'n v. Miller, 596 S.W.2d 621, 625 (Tex. Civ. App.—Waco 1980, no writ); Guerra v. Pena, 406 S.W.2d 769, 774 (Tex. Civ. App.—San Antonio 1966, no writ); Gore v. Cunningham, 297 S.W.2d 287, 291 (Tex. Civ. App.—Beaumont 1956, writ ref'd n.r.e.); Caddo Grocery & Ice v. Carpenter, 285 S.W.2d 470, 474 (Tex. Civ. App.—Austin 1955, no writ); Sanchez v. Caroland, 274 S.W.2d 114, 116 (Tex. Civ. App.—Fort Worth 1954, no writ).

386. *See* Fireman's Relief & Retirement Fund Trustees v. Fontenot, 446 S.W.2d 365, 372 (Tex. Civ. App.—Austin 1969, writ ref'd n.r.e.). *But cf.* Krasa v. Derrico, 193 S.W.2d

Rule 169 provides that a party upon whom requests are served must either admit or deny the requests or specify the reason that such requests cannot be answered. Objections to requests for admissions must be stated with specificity.[387] The answer must specifically deny the matter requested to be admitted or elaborate in detail the reasons that the answering party can neither truthfully admit nor deny the matter requested.[388] An answering party may not assert lack of information or knowledge as the basis for a failure to admit or deny unless that party has made a reasonable inquiry and the information that is either known or easily obtainable by him simply is insufficient to either admit or deny a requested matter.[389]

In the absence of a response to requests for admission within the time prescribed, and absent a motion for an extension of time, the matters requested are deemed admitted without the necessity of a court order.[390] The trial court may permit withdrawal or amendment of a response to a request for admission when (1) the presentation of the merits will be subserved thereby and (2) the party who obtained the admission fails to satisfy the court that withdrawal or amendment will prejudice him in maintaining his action or defense on the merits.[391]

Admissions made under Rule 169(2) relate only to the pending

891, 892 (Tex. Civ. App.—San Antonio 1946, no writ) (where requests were addressed only to defendant and her attorney, and were not addressed to defendant in her representative capacities in which she was sued, defendant's failure to answer was not an admission).

387. *See* Hunt v. Mid-West Life & Hosp. Ins. Co., 468 S.W.2d 142, 143 (Tex. Civ. App.—Texarkana 1971, no writ) (requests for admission should either be admitted or denied but if a request can neither be admitted nor denied, the answering party must provide in detail the reason why such requests cannot be either admitted or denied).

388. Tex. R. Civ. P. 169(1).

389. *Id. See also* Watson v. Godwin, 425 S.W.2d 424, 427 (Tex. Civ. App.—Amarillo 1968, writ ref'd n.r.e.) ("a party may not evade the rule by merely saying that he does not have sufficient information to either admit or deny the matters requested when the facts inquired about are reasonably available to him"); McIntire v. Sawicki, 353 S.W.2d 952, 953 (Tex. Civ. App.—Eastland 1962, writ ref'd n.r.e.); McPeak v. Texas Dep't of Public Safety, 346 S.W.2d 138, 140 (Tex. Civ. App.—Dallas 1961, no writ); Taylor v. Owen, 290 S.W.2d 771, 776 (Tex. Civ. App.—San Antonio 1956, writ ref'd n.r.e.); Montgomery v. Gibbens, 245 S.W.2d 311, 315 (Tex. Civ. App.—Eastland 1951, no writ); Durrett v. Boger, 234 S.W.2d 898, 900 (Tex. Civ. App.—Texarkana 1950, no writ).

390. Tex. R. Civ. P. Rule 169. But a request to admit facts within 10 days is defective and, therefore, the trial court may exercise its discretion in deeming unanswered requests as admitted. *See* Boyter v. MCR Const. Co., 673 S.W.2d 938, 939 (Tex.App.—Dallas 1984, no writ).

391. Tex. R. Civ. P. 169(2).

action[392] and do not constitute an admission for any other purpose[393] or in any other proceeding.[394] Moreover, admissions of one party in a lawsuit are not admissible or binding on any other party involved in the same lawsuit.[395] Similarly, an admission of a party acting in one capacity is not binding on the same party occupying other legal capacities in the pending action.[396]

Previously, requests for admission involving a party's contentions or conclusions of fact or law or a combination of fact and law were impermissible in pretrial discovery. Rule 166b specifically states that, "[i]t is also not ground for objection that a request for admission propounded pursuant to Rule 169 relates to statements or opinions of fact or of the application of law to fact or mixed questions of law and fact or that the documents referred to in a request may not be admissible at trial."[397] Consequently, objections that a request for admission or the genuineness of documents calls for ultimate conclusions of law or fact has been eliminated from the rules. Reliance on an objection that a request calls for an ultimate issue of fact or law will result in the request being deemed admitted by operation of law.

8.07 Rules 200-208: Oral and Written Depositions

Rule 200 provides the controlling procedure for oral depositions.[398] This rule outlines with specificity the notice requirements for oral depositions.[399] An oral deposition may be noticed and

---

392. *See* Sprouse v. Texas Employer's Ins. Ass'n., 459 S.W.2d 216 (Tex. Civ. App.—Beaumont 1970, writ ref'd n.r.e.); English Freight Co. v. Preston, 203 S.W.2d 657 (Tex. Civ. App.—Galveston 1947, no writ).

393. *See* Brooks v. Eaton Yale & Towne, Inc., 474 S.W.2d 321 (Tex. Civ. App.—Waco 1971, no writ); Houston Shoe Hosp. v. State, 423 S.W.2d 624 (Tex. Civ. App.—Houston [14th Dist.] 1968, no writ).

394. 423 S.W.2d at 625.

395. *See, e.g.*, Freestone County Title & Abstract Co. v. Johnson, 594 S.W.2d 817, 818 (Tex. Civ. App.—Dallas 1980, no writ).

396. *See* Krasa v. Derrico, 193 S.W.2d 891 (Tex. Civ. App.—San Antonio 1946, no writ).

397. Tex. R. Civ. P. 166b(2)(a).

398. Tex. R. Civ. P. 200. *See also* West v. Solito, 563 S.W.2d 240 (Tex. 1978) (scope of depositions); Automatic Drilling Machs., Inc. v. Miller, 515 S.W.2d 256 (Tex. 1974); Neville v. Brewster, 163 Tex. 155, 352 S.W.2d 449 (1961); Lucas v. Lucas, 365 S.W.2d 372, 375 (Tex. Civ. App.—Beaumont 1962, no writ) (the primary object of judicial inquiry is to seek and establish the relevant facts. One of the most effective means of discovery is by the use of depositions); McConnico, *supra* note 347; Barrow, *supra* note 347.

399. *See* Pouncy v. Gardner, 626 S.W.2d 337, 343-44 (Tex. App.—Tyler 1981, writ

taken after the commencement of any action.[400] If, however, a party seeks to take a deposition prior to defendant's appearance day, leave of court must be obtained.[401] In other words, a trial court, after appropriate consideration, may allow a party to serve notice of an oral deposition prior to the defendant's appearance so long as the actual date of the deposition occurs after appearance day.[402] The deposition may be taken, however, prior to the appearance day of other defendants.[403]

Reasonable notice[404] by a party proposing to take an oral deposition must be served in writing to all attorneys of record for all parties.[405] If the proposed deponent is a corporation, partnership, association, or governmental agency, the party deposing must describe with reasonable particularity the matters on which the examination is requested.[406]

Service of a subpoena and a subpoena duces tecum directs an individual to appear for a deposition and produce items within his possession, custody or control, respectively.[407] When the deponent is a party, service of notice upon an attorney is as effective as actual service of a subpoena upon a nonparty.[408]

The trial court [409] may designate a reasonable time and place

---

ref'd n.r.e.) (trial court properly excluded deposition of a witness, where deposition was taken without notice, and no commission had issued for the deposition of this witness).

400. TEX. R. CIV. P. 200(1).

401. *Id.*

402. *Id.*

403. *Id.*

404. TEX. R. CIV. P. 200(2). *Compare* TEX. R. CIV. P. 200 (Vernon 1983).

405. *Id.* 200(2)(a).

406. *Id.* 200(2)(b). Refer to note 293 *supra* and accompanying text.

407. TEX. R. CIV. P. 201(1), (2). The requesting party must designate the "items to be produced by the deponent either by individual item or by category and which describes each item and category with reasonable particularity."

408. *Id.* 201(3).

409. *See* Munden v. Chambless, 315 S.W.2d 355, 389 (Tex. Civ. App.—Dallas 1958, writ ref'd n.r.e.) (trial court has broad discretion concerning depositions, especially when taken more than one hundred miles from the court). *E.g.*, Fisher v. Continental Illinois Bank & Trust Co., 424 S.W.2d 664 (Tex. Civ. App.—Houston [14th Dist.] 1968, writ ref'd n.r.e.). Defendant sought to depose plaintiff in Harris County where plaintiff's suit was pending. Plaintiff, a resident of Florida, moved to have his deposition changed from an oral deposition to written interrogatories. The motion was quashed on the basis that plaintiff's residence in Florida was not good cause for his failure to appear for deposition. By electing to assert jurisdiction in Harris County, plaintiff was obliged to submit to the procedures of the Texas courts. The court also noted that compared to the amount involved in the litigation, neither plaintiff's expense nor inconvenience would be disproportionate. *Id.* at 670-71.

for a deposition.[410] In *Dresser Industries Inc. v. Solito*,[411] plaintiff served defendant with notice to take oral depositions in Houston of nine of defendant's foreign employees.[412] Defendant moved to quash the depositions; the trial court denied the motion, and ordered defendant to produce the witnesses at its expense.[413] In a second motion, defendant suggested that the depositions be taken alternatively by written questions, by telephone, in London, or in Houston at plaintiff's expense.[414] The trial court again denied this motion.[415] The Texas Supreme Court concluded that the trial court clearly abused its discretion.[416] The trial judge was mandated to be especially sensitive in weighing the actual need for the requested depositions, and in selecting alternative reasonable and less costly means for obtaining the information sought through the depositions.[417]

Rule 202 authorizes any party to record an oral deposition by other than stenographic means.[418] A nonstenographic record, how-

---

410. TEX. R. CIV. P. 201(5).

411. 668 S.W.2d 893 (Tex. App.—Houston [14th Dist.] 1984, no writ).

412. *Id.* at 894.

413. *Id.*

414. *Id.*

415. *Id.*

416. *Id.* at 896.

417. *Id.* at 895. The court agreed with *Hyam v. American Export Lines, Inc.* which reasoned that,

> [N]ot in every case is a party seeking pre-trial discovery entitled as of right to a deposition on oral examination at the situs of the forum. His preference therefore, if opposed . . . , must be weighed both against his actual, . . . need for oral examination at the forum and against the resulting burden to his opponent. . . . [T]he judge . . . may order the deposition to be taken, if not at the forum, at an appropriate distant place under terms whereby the reasonable expense thereof may ultimately be reflected in the taxable costs, or may order that the depositions be taken, . . ., only on written interrogatories.

418. *Id.* at 895. *Compare* Fisher v. Continental, 424 S.W.2d 664. 418 TEX. R. CIV. P. 202(1) provides:

1. NONSTENOGRAPHIC READING. Any party may cause the testimony and other available evidence at a deposition upon oral examination to be recorded by other than stenographic means, including videotape recordings, without leave of court, and the nonstenographic recording may be presented at trial in lieu of reading from a stenographic transcription of the deposition, subject to the following rules:

> a. Any party intending to make a nonstenographic recording shall give five day's notice to all other parties by certified mail, return receipt requested, and shall specify in said notice the type of nonstenographic recording which will be used.
>
> b. After the notice is given, any party may make a motion for relief under Rule 166b. If a hearing is not held prior to the taking of the deposition, the non-

ever, does not dispense with the requirement of a stenographic transcription. A trial court may make such provision as necessary to insure that the recorded testimony will be intelligible, accurate and trustworthy.[419] This rule incorporates the decision rendered in *Burr v. Shannon.*[420] Plaintiff sought to take defendant's oral deposition by use of a tape recorder and to use a secretary-notary public to transcribe the recording for defendant's signature.[421] The Supreme Court declared that when the trial court excuses a transcribed record, the trial court is required to make provisions for the protection of the intelligibility, accuracy, and trustworthiness of the record.[422]

Certification, copies, and the filing of depositions are specifically provided for in Rule 206.[423] An officer must certify on the deposition that the witness was sworn and that the deposition constitutes a true record of the witness' testimony.[424] After payment of reasonable charges, the officer is obligated to furnish a copy of the deposition to any party or to the deponent.[425] Prompt notice of filing the deposition must be communicated to all parties by the party actually filing the deposition.[426] In the absence of compliance with these provisions, the deposition is rendered inadmissible at

---

stenographic recording shall be made subject to the courts ruling at a later time.

c. Any party shall have reasonable access to the original recording and may obtain a duplicate copy at his own expense.

d. The expense of a nonstenographic recording shall not be taxed as costs, unless before the deposition is taken, the parties so agree, or the court so orders on motion and notice.

e. The nonstenographic recording shall not dispense with the requirement of a stenographic transcription of the deposition unless the court shall so order on motion and notice before the deposition is taken, and such order shall also make such provision concerning the manner of taking, preserving and filing the nonstenographic recording as may be necessary to assure that the recorded testimony will be intelligible, accurate and trustworthy. Such order shall not prevent any party from having a stenographic transcription made at his own expense. In the event of an appeal, the nonstenographic recording shall be reduced to writing.

419. *Id.*

420. 593 S.W.2d 677 (Tex. 1980).

421. *Id.* at 677.

422. *Id.* at 678.; Tex. R. Civ. P. 202; *Compare Id.* 215(c) (Vernon 1983) (nonstenographic recording).

423. Tex. R. Civ. P. 206.

424. Tex. R. Civ. P. 206(1).

425. Tex. R. Civ. P. 206(3).

426. Tex. R. Civ. P. 206(4).

trial.[427]

The use of depositions at trial is governed by Rule 207.[428] Any part or all of a deposition, insofar as admissible under the rules of evidence, may be used by any person for any purpose against a deposed party.[429] Moreover, unless a motion and notice to suppress all or a part of the deposition is made and provided to all other parties prior to trial, any error or irregularities in the deposition are waived.[430] Objections to the form of the question and the nonresponsiveness of the answer must be made at the time of taking the deposition.[431] All other substantive objections may be reserved for action of the court in which the case is litigated.

Depositions may also be taken by written questions.[432] A party, after an action commences, may take a deposition upon written questions of any person or party.[433] The party proposing the written deposition must serve the written questions with a written notice ten days before the deposition is to be taken.[434] Cross-questions may be served ten days after the service of direct

---

427. *See* Pouncy v. Gardner, 626 S.W.2d 337, 334-44 (Tex. App.—Tyler 1981, writ ref'd n.r.e.) (trial court properly excluded deposition of a witness where no copy of the notice of filing of the deposition was sent to one of the party's attorneys); Zamora v. Romero, 581 S.W.2d 742, 748 (Tex. Civ. App.—Corpus Christi 1979, writ ref'd n.r.e.) (unless waived, a deposition which is not signed and has not been filed in the court where the cause is docketed is not admissible at trial).

428. Tex. R. Civ. P. 207(1); *See, e.g.*, Spring Branch Bank v. Mengden, 628 S.W.2d 130, 138 (Tex. App.—Houston [14th Dist.] 1981, writ ref'd n.r.e.) (deposition testimony may be read in evidence at trial without the necessity of demonstrating that a witness is unable to testify).

429. Tex. R. Civ. P. 207(1). *But see* Elizondo v. Tavarez, 596 S.W.2d 667, 670 (Tex. Civ. App.—Corpus Christi 1980, writ ref'd n.r.e.) (depositions are inadmissible in evidence against one not a party to the suit at the time the deposition was taken).

430. Tex. R. Civ. P. 207(3); Texas Employers Ins. Ass'n v. Henson, 569 S.W.2d 516, 517 (Tex. Civ. App.—Beaumont 1978, no writ). An objection that an answer in a deposition is unresponsive to the question goes to the manner and form of taking the deposition, and not to the actual substance of the answers. An objection to the manner and form must be made in writing with notice to opposing counsel, if the deposition has been on file with the court for one or more days. *Id.* If this objection is made for the first time at trial, the objection is untimely, and the defect is waived. *Id.*; Victoria Comfort Air Co. v. Alamo Express, Inc., 529 S.W.2d 250, 251-52 (Tex. Civ. App.—Corpus Christi 1975, no writ).

431. Tex. R. Civ. P. 204(4). Any party seeking to assert a Fifth Amendment privilege against self-incrimination must actually appear for the deposition and claim the privilege on a question by question basis. United States v. Davis, 636 F.2d 1028, 1038 (5th Cir. 1981).

432. Tex. R. Civ. P. 208.

433. *Id.* 208(1).

434. *Id. Cf. Id.* 189 (Vernon 1983) (a party proposing to take a deposition upon written questions must serve them with ten days (10) written notice).

questions.[435] Redirect questions may be served five days after the cross-questions are served.[436] And, recross questions may be served three days after the redirect questions are served.[437] Objections to the form of the questions must be made in writing within the prescribed time limits, or the objections are deemed waived.[438] The court may, upon motion and hearing for good cause, lengthen or shorten the time period for filing written objections.[439]

8.08 RULE 215: ABUSE OF DISCOVERY - SANCTIONS[440]

A. *Purpose*

Rule 215 governs all sanctions relating to pretrial discovery.[441] This rule collates all former provisions relating to sanctions for the various discovery violations.[442] Rule 215, as revised, represents an interdependent part of the objectives of discovery.[443] Patterned after Federal Rule 37,[444]

> [it] was designed to give the trial court an expeditious procedure for insuring the effectiveness of pretrial discovery and for dealing with recalcitrant or contumacious parties and witnesses. The authorized sanctions are not intended to be arbitrary and exclusive, but flexible and plural, vesting in the trial court broad discretion to fashion a remedy which will secure compliance with its orders and deter future noncompliance.[445]

The exercise of sanctions rests in the sound discretion of the trial court.[446] To the extent the trial court imposes any of the sanc-

---

435. *Id.* 208(3).

436. *Id.*

437. *Id.*

438. Rule 208(3) specifically provides that "objection to the form of written questions are waived unless served in writing upon the party propounding them within the time allowed for serving the succeeding cross or other questions. . ."

439. *Id.*

440. *See* Kilgarlin & Jackson, *Sanctions of Discovery Abuse Under New Rule 215*, 15 ST. MARY'S L.J. 767 (1984); Sales, *supra* note 331.

441. TEX. R. CIV. P. 215.

442. *See Id.* 167(3); 167a(b); 168(6); 169; 170; 215a; 215b (Vernon 1983).

443. Refer to note 1 *supra* and accompanying text.

444. FED. R. CIV. P. 37.

445. Firestone Photographs, Inc. v. Lamaster, 567 S.W.2d 273, 277 (Tex. Civ. App.—Texarkana 1978, no writ).

446. TEX. R. CIV. P. 215(2)(b) (trial court in which action is pending may impose sanctions). *See* Bosnich v. National Cellulose Corp., 676 S.W.2d 446, 447 (Tex.App.—Houston

tions authorized by Rule 215, such sanctions will not be overruled in the absence of a clear abuse of discretion.[447]

Conflicting views on the purposes of Rule 215 have emerged, especially to the extent the rule authorizes the dismissal of lawsuits.[448] *Bottinelli v. Robinson*[449] and *Lindley v. Flores*[450] reflect these conflicting views. In *Bottinelli*, plaintiff appealed from a trial court order striking his pleadings and dismissing his suit with prejudice for failure to comply with a discovery order.[451] In affirming the dismissal of the suit, the court commented that though sanctions were designed to encourage compliance with discovery, that was not its only function.[452] The trial court must be allowed to apply even the most severe sanctions, " . . . not merely to penalize those whose conduct may be deemed to warrant such a sanction, but to deter those who might be tempted to such conduct in the

---

[1st Dist.] 1984, no writ); Lindley v. Flores, 672 S.W.2d 612, 614 (Tex.App.—Corpus Christi 1984, no writ)

447. *See* Olin Corp. v. Dyson, 678 S.W.2d 650 (Tex. App.—Houston [1st Dist.] 1984 *rev'd on other grounds*, 28 Tex. Sup. Ct. J. ___ (June 19, 1985); Bosnich v. National Cellulose Corp., 676 S.W.2d 446, 447 (Tex. App.—Houston [1st Dist.] 1984, no writ); Alexander v. Barlow, 671 S.W.2d 531 (Tex. App.—Houston [1st Dist.] 1983, writ ref'd n.r.e.); Wiley v. Browning, 670 S.W.2d 729 (Tex. App.—Tyler 1984, no writ); Reyes v. International Metals Supply Co., 666 S.W.2d 622 (Tex. App.—Houston [1st Dist.] 1984, no writ); Illinois Employers Ins. Co. v. Lewis, 582 S.W.2d 242 (Tex. Civ. App.—Beaumont 1979), *writ ref'd*, 590 S.W.2d 119 (Tex. 1979); Lueg v. Tewell, 572 S.W.2d 97 (Tex. Civ. App.—Corpus Christi 1978, no writ); Hankins v. Haffa, 469 S.W.2d 733 (Tex. Civ. App.—Amarillo 1971, writ ref'd n.r.e.); Fisher v. Continental Ill. Nat. Bank & Trust Co., 424 S.W.2d 664 (Tex. Civ. App.—Houston [14th Dist.] 1968, writ ref'd n.r.e.). Refer to § 7.09 *infra*.

448. *See* Aquamarine Operators v. Downer, 689 S.W.2d 472 (Tex. App.—Houston [14th Dist.] 1985, no writ); Phillips v. Vinson Supply Co., 581 S.W.2d 789 (Tex. Civ. App.—Houston [14th Dist.] 1979, no writ) (sanctions are to secure compliance with discovery rules, not to punish erring parties); Smith v. Wilkins, 577 S.W.2d 522 (Tex. Civ. App.—Texarkana 1979, no writ); United States Leasing Corp. v. O'Neill, Price, Anderson & Fouchard, Inc., 553 S.W.2d 11 (Tex. Civ. App.—Houston [14th Dist.] 1977, no writ); Plodzik v. Owens-Corning Fiberglas Corp., 549 S.W.2d 52 (Tex. Civ. App.—Austin 1977, no writ); Young Co. v. Bayou Corp., 545 S.W.2d 901 (Tex. Civ. App.—Beaumont 1977, no writ); Lloyd A. Fry Roofing Co. v. State, 524 S.W.2d 313 (Tex. Civ. App.—Dallas 1976, writ ref'd n.r.e.); Ebeling v. Gawlik, 487 S.W.2d 187 (Tex. Civ. App.—Houston [1st Dist.] 1972, no writ). *But see* Lindley v. Flores, 672 S.W.2d 612 (Tex. App.—Corpus Christi 1984, no writ) (sanctions as a deterrence); Bottinelli v. Robinson, 594 S.W.2d 112 (Tex. Civ. App.—Houston [1st Dist.] 1979, no writ); Southern Pacific Transp. Co. v. Evans, 590 S.W.2d 515 (Tex. Civ. App.—Houston [1st Dist.] 1979, writ ref'd n.r.e.), *cert denied*, 449 U.S. 994 (1980).

449. 594 S.W.2d 112.

450. 672 S.W.2d 612.

451. 594 S.W.2d at 114.

452. *Id.* at 118.

absence of such a deterrence."[453]

The plaintiff in *Lindley* appealed an order that plaintiff pay expenses directly to defendant's attorney for plaintiff's recalcitrance.[454] The appellate court affirmed and noted "[w]hile language in some cases indicates that the purpose of the sanctions is not to punish the disobeying party, but to secure compliance, it is difficult to separate the two concepts realistically. Logically, more frequent punishment for failure to comply would ensure better compliance."[455] Both *Bottinelli* and *Lindley* acknowledge that while discovery sanctions initially serve to encourage discovery compliance, they may be employed for the purpose of deterring the recalcitrant party and other litigants from future abuses of discovery.[456]

B. *Motions For Sanctions*

Rule 215(1) authorizes a party upon reasonable notice to other parties to apply for sanctions, or an order compelling discovery.[457] Under this section, "notice" and "sanctions without a prior court order" are critical.

In *Lueg v. Tewell*[458] the court addressed the issue of notice. The trial court dismissed plaintiff's suit with prejudice after plaintiff failed to comply with orders to produce documents.[459] Plaintiff

---

453. *Id. quoting* National Hockey League v. Metropolitan Hockey Club, Inc., 427 U. S. 639, 642-43 (1976). *Accord*, City of Houston v. Arney, 680 S.W.2d 867 (Tex. App.—Houston [1st Dist.] 1985, no writ); Bosnich v. National Cellulose Corp., 676 S.W.2d 446 (Tex. App.—Houston [1st Dist.] 1984, no writ).

454. 672 S.W.2d at 613-14.

455. *Id.* at 614., *quoting* Spears, *The Rules of Civil Procedure*: 1981 *changes in Pre-Trial; Discovery*, 12 St. Mary's L.J. 633, 651 (1981).

456. *See* 594 S.W.2d at 118.

457. Tex. R. Civ. P. 215(1). Some courts suggest caution in the imposition of harsh sanctions such as a default judgment. In *Aquamarine Operators v. Downer*, 689 S.W. 2d 472, 476 (Tex. App.—Houston [14th Dist.] 1985, no writ), imposition of such harsh sanctions requires movant to demonstrate (1) the individual from whom discovery is sought is either a party or officer (2) clear identification of the party against whom discovery is sought (3) motion and notice of hearing on sanctions.

458. 572 S.W.2d 97 (Tex. Civ. App.—Corpus Christi 1978, no writ). *See also* Sears, Roebuck & Co. v. Hollingsworth, 156 Tex. 176, 293 S.W.2d 639 (1956); Smith v. Wilkins, 577 S.W.2d 522, 524 (Tex. Civ. App.—Texarkana 1979, no writ) (penalties for failure to obey the discovery rules may be imposed only where all parties have been given notice of the motion to compel production, and have had an opportunity to be heard); Plodzik v. Owens-Corning Fiberglas Corp., 549 S.W.2d 52 (Tex. Civ. App.—Austin 1977, writ ref'd n.r.e.); Sherrill v. Plumley, 514 S.W.2d 286 (Tex. Civ. App.— Houston [1st Dist.] 1974, writ ref'd n.r.e.).

459. 572 S.W.2d at 101.

contended that the trial court abused its discretion by ordering the production of documents because of inadequate description of the items requested.[460] Both the motion to produce and the court's order were deemed sufficiently precise to notify the plaintiff of the documents desired.[461] A party must be given notice and a chance to be heard on any motion to impose a sanction for failure to produce documents.[462] "Once these procedural safeguards are met, the imposition of sanctions for failure to comply with discovery is directed to the sound discretion of the trial court."[463]

Conversely, *Ebeling v. Gawlik*[464] concerned the absence of reasonable notice. The trial court ordered plaintiff to make more complete answers to interrogatories.[465] Accordingly, plaintiff supplemented and completed his answers but the defendant contended that plaintiff's answers remained deficient because of his failure to swear that the answers were unqualifiedly true.[466] The plaintiff swore the answers were true and correct to the best of his knowledge.[467] Dismissal of plaintiff's suit based on a failure to properly verify his answers was viewed as an abuse of the trial court's discretion.[468] Neither defendant's motion to answer more fully, nor the trial court order in response to the motion were based upon plaintiff's lack of verification.[469]

A trial court may now impose sanctions against a party even in the absence of a court order compelling compliance with a discovery request.[470] Thus, a party seeking discovery may elect either to seek sanctions immediately, or first obtain an order compelling discovery. The revised rule is similar in nature to the rule announced in *Lewis v. Illinois Employers Insurance Co.*[471] The Supreme Court ruled that, "[w]hen . . . a party wholly fails to answer any of

---

460. *Id.* at 104.
461. *Id.*
462. *Id.*
463. *Id.*
464. 487 S.W.2d 187 (Tex. Civ. App.—Houston [1st Dist.] 1972, no writ).
465. *Id.* at 189.
466. *Id.*
467. *Id.*
468. *Id.*
469. *Id.*
470. Tex. R. Civ. P. 215(1) states that the requesting party "may apply to the court in which the action is pending for the imposition of sanctions . . . without the necessity of first having obtained a court order compelling such discovery."
471. 590 S.W.2d 119 (Tex. 1979).

the interrogatories, the propounding party may immediately move for the imposition of sanctions without first seeking and obtaining an order from the court requiring answers to interrogatories."[472]

Prior to the current revision of Rule 215, the "most severe" sanctions could not immediately be imposed except in instances of a total failure to comply with discovery rules.[473] For example, if some but not all interrogatory answers were filed, a motion and order to compel more complete answers was required as a predicate to the imposition of the more severe sanctions.[474] Moreover, prior to the current amendment, the courts were equally divided whether the trial court was empowered to dismiss a lawsuit with prejudice as one of the available sanctions for failure to make discovery.[475] The change effectuated by the revision of amended Rule 215 is extensively reviewed and analyzed by Justice Kilgarlin.[476] Relying on the commentary to Rule 215, Justice Kilgarlin declares:

> The new Rule 215 is designed to incorporate and extend the holding of Lewis v. Illinois, Employers Insurance Co. In Lewis, the Texas Supreme Court ruled that the trial court's authorization to impose sanctions was dependent on the degree of compliance or noncompliance present. When a party responded to some, but not all, interrogatories, the interrogating party was required to move for an order compelling the interrogated party to answer. If that order was violated, the court had discretion to utilize sanctions. But when the interrogated party made no response, the propounding party could move immediately for sanctions. In this manner, Lewis distinguished between a total failure to answer an entire set of interrogatories and an inadequate or incomplete response to a set of interrogatories.
>
> The Lewis distinction is *not* perpetuated by Rule 215. Rather, the rule applicable to an absolute failure to answer interrogatories under Lewis now obtains for any failure to adequately

---

472. *Id.* at 120.

473. *See* Lewis v. Illinois Employer's Ins. Co., 590 S.W.2d 119 (Tex. 1979).

474. *See* Lewis v. Illinois Employers Ins. Co., 590 S.W.2d 119 (Tex. 1979); Saldivar v. Facit-Addo, Inc., 620 S.W.2d 778, 779 (Tex. App.—El Paso 1981, no writ); Pearson Corp. v. Wichita Falls Boys Club Alumni Ass'n., 633 S.W.2d 684 (Tex. App.—Fort Worth 1982, no writ).

475. *See* Bottinelli v. Robinson, 594 S.W.2d 112 (Tex. App.—Houston [1st Dist.] 1979, no writ). *Compare* Fultz v. Cummins Sales & Service, Inc., 587 S.W.2d 515 (Tex. Civ. App.—Corpus Christi 1979, writ ref'd n.r.e.).

476. *See* Kilgarlin & Jackson, *Sanctions for Discovery Abuse Under New Rule 215*, 15 St. Mary's L.J. 767, 777 (1984).

respond. This treatment is prescribed for all forms of discovery that are initiated by action of the parties independent of the court, except for request for admissions. In other words, if the deposed, interrogated, or requested party does not respond sufficiently to one question or request for production, the discovering party may elect to move immediately for sanctions without first obtaining an order for discovery.[477]

An order for sanctions, with the exception of expenses, cannot be imposed after a party has complied with a discovery order. In *Young Companies, Inc. v. Bayou Corp.*,[478] the trial court abused its discretion by granting a default judgment against defendant on the same day, but *after* defendant had complied with a discovery order.[479] Though extending over a period of five months, defendant's good faith response was finally produced.[480] Defendant could only be taxed with any expense or attorney's fees precipitated by the delay.[481]

The application for sanctions, or an order compelling discovery, must be filed in the appropriate court.[482] For sanctions relating to depositions, application is made to either the court in which the action is pending, or the court where the deposition is to be taken.[483] If the deponent is not a party to the action, application must be made to the court possessing jurisdiction in the district in which the deposition is taken.[484]

Rule 215(1)b(2)a-d outlines situations that allow the movant to obtain an order compelling discovery for failure to comply with the rules of pretrial discovery. Rule 215(1)c states that an evasive or incomplete answer is considered a failure to answer.[485] Therefore, subsection (c) would, in practice, view an evasive or incomplete answer as a subsection (1)b(2)a-d failure to answer.

When a motion to compel discovery is granted, the party or deponent whose conduct necessitated the motion may be ordered

---

477. *Id.* at 777-78.
478. 545 S.W.2d 901 (Tex. Civ. App.—Beaumont 1977, no writ).
479. *Id.* at 902-03.
480. *Id.*
481. *Id.*
482. Tex. R. Civ. P. 215(1)a.
483. *Id.*
484. *Id.*
485. Tex. R. Civ. P. 215(1)(c) states: "for purposes of this subdivision an evasive or incomplete answer is to be treated as a failure to answer."

to pay the reasonable expenses incurred in obtaining the order, including attorney's fees.[486] A court may deny reasonable expenses if the opposition to the motion was "substantially justified" or circumstances make an award of expenses "unjust".[487] Likewise, if a motion is denied, the movant may be required to pay to the opposing party reasonable expenses incurred in defending against the motion.[488]

In *Waguespack v. Halipoto*,[489] plaintiff appealed a trial court order that she pay opposing counsel's attorney fees for failure to comply with discovery.[490] In affirming the award of expenses, the court observed that "a court is now empowered to impose reasonable attorney's fees against a party whose response to a request is unreasonably frivolous or made for the purpose of delay. . . . An unjustified failure to respond which in turn causes delay fits within this rule."[491]

When an individual has requested but not received his own statement,[492] he may obtain an order compelling production of that statement.[493] If the motion is granted, the movant is entitled to recover the expenses incurred in obtaining the order, including reasonable attorney's fees.[494]

C. *Sanctions*

Rule 215(2) governs sanctions for failure to comply with an order or discovery request. [I]t . . . empowers the court to use sanctions to force a person from whom discovery is sought to permit or provide discovery in compliance with the rules."[495]

---

486. Tex. R. Civ. P. 215(1)(d).

487. Tex. R. Civ. P. 215(1)d; Hankins v. Haffa, 469 S.W.2d 733, 738-39 (Tex. Civ. App.—Amarillo 1971, writ ref'd n.r.e.) (trial court did not abuse its discretion where it overruled a motion for discovery. Its order was within the scope and spirit of "such other order . . . as may be just.").

488. Tex. R. Civ. P. 215(1)d.

489. 633 S.W.2d 628 (Tex. App.—Houston [14th Dist.] 1982, writ dism'd).

490. *Id.* at 629-30.

491. *Id.* at 633. *See also*, Lindley v. Flores, 672 S.W.2d 612, 614 (Tex.App.—Corpus Christi 1984, no writ).

492. Refer to § 7.02(B)6 *supra*.

493. Tex. R. Civ. P. 215(1)e. Tex. R. Civ. P. 166b(2)(g) allows any party or other person to obtain a copy of his written statement upon request to the party possessing such statement.

494. *Id.*

495. Kilgarlin, *supra* note 440 at 793.

Rule 215(2)a relates to a deponent's failure to appear for a duly noticed deposition. It authorizes the court in the district where the deposition is taken to hold the recalcitrant party or deponent in contempt.[496] Rule 215(2)(b) enumerates the sanctions available to the court in which the action is pending.[497] The court may impose sanctions upon a party, officer, director or managing agent of a party. Furthermore, the court in which the action is pending may, after due notice and a hearing,[498] enter such orders it deems just for failure to comply with the requested discovery.[499]

In *Firestone Photographs, Inc. v. Lamaster*,[500] the trial court ordered Firestone to pay two hundred-fifty dollars for its failure to appear for a deposition.[501] For each succeeding twenty-day period that the failure continued, Firestone was ordered to pay additional fines of double the amount of the last preceding twenty-day period.[502] Reviewing the trial court sanction order, the appellate court concluded:

> Although the right to impose monetary penalties . . . is not specifically mentioned, it seems that if the court, upon a party's disobedience, is empowered to immediately preclude the presentation of all that party's defenses and enter default judgment against him on the pleadings, it would alternatively have the right to impose periodic monetary penalties for his continuing disobedience, not to exceed the amount for which judgment could have been summarily entered. Such a procedure would appear to be more just and lenient toward the defendant than the immediate entry of a default judgment.[503]

1. *Further Discovery Prohibited.* The trial court may enter an order forbidding a disobedient party from further discovery of

---

496. Tex. R. Civ. P. 215(2)a.

497. *Id.* 215(2)b.

498. Refer to notes 441-456 *supra* and accompanying text.

499. *See* Firestone Photos, Inc. v. Lamaster, 567 S.W.2d 273 (Tex. Civ. App.—Texarkana 1978, no writ) (monetary sanctions were just); Hankins v. Haffa, 469 S.W.2d 733 (Tex. Civ. App.—Amarillo 1971, writ ref'd n.r.e.) (where trial court deemed it just not to impose discovery sanctions). *But see* General Motors v. Lawrence, 651 S.W.2d 732 (Tex. 1983) (compelling discovery of nonrelevant material is not a sanction granted to the trial court by the rules). Refer to Kilgarlin, *supra* note 440 at 796.

500. 567 S.W.2d 273 (Tex. Civ. App.—Texarkana 1978, no writ).

501. *Id.* at 275-76.

502. *Id.* at 276.

503. *Id.* at 277.

any kind or of a particular kind.[504] This is a new sanction incorporated in the Texas Rules of Civil Procedure.[505]

2. *Expenses.* A disobedient party or that party's attorney may be charged for all or any portion of the expenses of discovery or taxable court costs.[506] For example, in *Mims v. Houston Fire & Casualty Insurance Co.*,[507] defendant denied plaintiff's request for admission.[508] The denials were established to represent false responses to relevant facts involved in the suit.[509] Thus, plaintiff was entitled to recover reasonable expenses in proving facts relative to the insurance policy which the insurer had wrongfully denied.[510]

3. *Matters Established.* Matters or any other facts may be designated as established for the purposes of the action in accordance with the claim of the moving party.[511] This sanction is very similar in effect to subsection 4.

4. *Introducing Matters Into Evidence Prohibited.* Under subsection 4 a disobedient party may be precluded from supporting or opposing the designated claims or defenses, or introduce designated matters into evidence for that party's failure to provide discovery of those matters.[512] Therefore, like *Railway Express Agency, Inc. v. Spain*,[513] in which the party failed to produce records in compliance with a prior court order, the trial court is authorized to prohibit those records from being introduced as evidence.[514]

---

504. Tex. R. Civ. P. 215(2)b(1).

505. *Compare* Tex. R. Civ. P. 170, 215a (Vernon 1983).

506. Tex. R. Civ. P. 215(2)b(2); Lindley v. Flores, 672 S.W.2d 612 (Tex. App.—Corpus Christi 1984, no writ); Waguespack v. Halipoto, 633 S.W.2d 628 (Tex. App.—Houston [14th Dist.] 1982, writ dism'd); Tharp v. Blackwell, 570 S.W.2d 154 (Tex. Civ. App.—Texarkana 1978, no writ); Mims v. Houston Fire & Casualty Ins. Co., 362 S.W.2d 880 (Tex. Civ. App.—Texarkana 1962, no writ). Refer to note 483-90 *supra* and accompanying text.

507. 362 S.W.2d 880 (Tex. Civ. App.—Texarkana 1962, no writ).

508. *Id.* at 883.

509. *Id.*

510. *Id.* at 884.

511. Tex. R. Civ. P. 215(2)b(3).

512. *Id.* 215(2)b(4).

513. 249 S.W.2d 644 (Tex. Civ. App.—Austin 1952), *dism'd*, 152 Tex. 198, 255 S.W.2d 509 (1953).

514. *Id.* at 653. *But see* Lloyd A. Fry Roofing Co. v. State, 524 S.W.2d 313, 319-20 (Tex. Civ. App.—Dallas 1975), *aff'd*, 541 S.W.2d 639 (Tex. Civ. App.—Dallas 1976, writ

In *Employers Mutual Liability Insurance Co. v. Butler*,[515] the trial court refused defendant permission to have one of its witnesses testify at the trial.[516] The witness was not included in the list of witnesses which the court had ordered defendant to furnish the plaintiff at trial.[517] The preclusion of a witness from testifying is appropriate only where a party fails to make discovery during the pretrial proceeding.[518] Pretrial discovery sanctions are inapplicable to orders made in the course of the actual trial.[519] Contempt remains the available sanction for inappropriate conduct during trial.[520]

5. Pleadings Stricken, Continuance, Dismissed, Default Judgment. The dismissal of a lawsuit or the entry of a default judgment represents harsh penalties and the trial court is cautioned to use this sanction sparingly.[521] This sanction includes an order striking pleadings or parts of pleadings, or staying further proceedings until a discovery order is obeyed. Dismissal with or without prejudice, or rendering a default judgment against a disobedient party, however, is a viable sanction.[522]

Alexander v. Barlow[523] illustrates the use of this sanction. Defendant initially failed to answer completely four interrogatories

---

ref'd n.r.e) (relevant information may be excluded when the offering party has withheld relevant information that he had a clear duty to produce, and even then the evidence should not always be excluded if the rights of the opposing party can be fully protected).

515. 511 S.W.2d 323 (Tex. Civ. App.—Texarkana 1974, writ ref'd n.r.e.).

516. *Id.* at 326.

517. *Id.* at 324.

518. *Id.* at 325.

519. *Id.*

520. Tex. R. Civ. P. 215(2)(6).

521. Tex. R. Civ. P. 215(2)b(5). *See* Aquamarine Operators v. Downer, 689 S.W.2d 472 (Tex. App.—Houston [14th Dist.] 1985, no writ); Reimer v. Ford Motor Credit Co., 635 S.W.2d 162 (Tex. Civ. App.—Houston [1st Dist.] 1982, no writ); Lueg v. Tewell, 572 S.W.2d 97 (Tex. Civ. App.—Corpus Christi 1978, no writ); Texhoma Stores, Inc. v. American Central Ins. Co., 398 S.W.2d 344 (Tex. Civ. App.—Tyler 1966), *writ ref'd n.r.e.*, 401 S.W.2d 593 (Tex. 1966).

522. Tex. R. Civ. P. 215(2)b(5).

523. 671 S.W.2d 531 (Tex. App.—Houston [1st Dist.] 1983, no writ). *See also* Notgrass v. Equilease Corp., 666 S.W.2d 635, 638 (Tex. App.—Houston [1st Dist.] 1984, no writ) (pleadings struck for failure to answer interrogatories) Nutting v. National Homes Mfg. Co., 639 S.W.2d 721, 723 (Tex. App.—Austin 1982, no writ) (trial court granted default judgment against defendant who disobeyed and reflected conscious indifference towards the requirements of discovery).

and failed to verify his answers.[524] Plaintiff obtained two court orders to compel the defendant to provide more complete answers.[525] Thereafter, plaintiff served defendant with a second set of interrogatories which the defendant failed to answer timely.[526] Upon failure to comply with the trial court's third order, plaintiff filed a motion for sanctions.[527] The trial court ordered that defendant's pleadings be stricken unless he filed answers to the interrogatories within five days.[528] In response, defendant filed unverified and incomplete answers. A motion to strike defendant's pleadings was granted and, after defendant failed to appear for a hearing on motion for judgment, a default judgment was rendered.[529]

Prior to the 1984 amendments, a conflict existed whether a trial court was empowered to dismiss a cause with prejudice.[530] In *Bottinelli v. Robinson*,[531] the trial court struck plaintiff's pleadings and dismissed his action with prejudice for failure to comply with a previous court order to produce certain documents.[532] In affirming the order and discussing the equity in favor of dismissal with prejudice,[533] the court commented:

> [a] default judgment can . . . only be rendered against a defendant, while dismissal of an action or claim, on the other hand, can only be entered against a plaintiff. We agree with the appellee that it undermines even-handed fairness under the discovery rules to hold that a trial court may enter a default judgment

---

524. 671 S.W.2d at 532.
525. *Id.*
526. *Id.*
527. *Id.*
528. *Id.*
529. *Id.*
530. *See* Fultz v. Cummins Sales & Service, Inc., 587 S.W.2d 515 (Tex. Civ. App.—Corpus Christi 1979, writ ref'd n.r.e.) (dismissed without prejudice); Gonzalez v. Mann, 583 S.W.2d 637 (Tex. Civ. App.—Houston [14th Dist.] 1979), *rev'd*, 595 S.W.2d 102 (Tex. 1979) (Dismissal under Rule 170 was limited to dismissal as it was commonly understood. A dismissal is not an adjudication of the rights of parties; it merely places them in the position that existed before the courts jurisdiction was invoked. *Id.* at 640. On the other hand, a dismissal with prejudice constitutes an adjudication of the rights of the parties and, thus, is a much harsher sanction); Phillips v. Vinson Supply Co., 581 S.W.2d 789 (Tex. Civ. App.—Houston [14th Dist.] 1979, no writ); Texhoma Stores, Inc. v. American Central Ins. Co., 398 S.W.2d 344 (Tex. Civ. App.—Tyler 1966), *writ ref'd n.r.e.*, 401 S.W.2d 593 (Tex. 1966). *Contra* Lueg v. Tewell, 572 S.W.2d 97, 101 (Tex. Civ. App.—Corpus Christi 1978, no writ) (within trial court's discretion to dismiss an action with prejudice).
531. 594 S.W.2d 112 (Tex. Civ. App.—Houston [1st Dist.] 1979, no writ).
532. *Id.* at 114.
533. *Id.*

against a recalcitrant defendant, thereby finally disposing of his lability defense, yet may not dismiss with prejudice the action of plaintiff who refuses to permit discovery, leading him to refile the action and avoid the discovery order.[534]

6. *Contempt.* The sanction of contempt[535] is available in addition to or in place of any other sanction. Contempt may not be used, however, as a sanction for failure to submit to a physical or mental examination.[536] Indeed, contempt is a preferable sanction to dismissal. In *Texhoma Stores, Inc. v. American Central Insurance Co.*,[537] plaintiff's suit was dismissed with prejudice because plaintiff's attorney refused to comply with a trial court order directing him to deliver his income tax returns in their entirety.[538] The trial court did not exercise its contempt power;[539] rather, it elected the more drastic order of dismissal.[540] Noting that the trial court abused its discretion, the appellate court declared:

> [t]he trial court had two alternative methods of enforcing the production of the documents, either by contempt or by dismissal . . . . In our view, the appellant should not have been deprived of its privileges as a litigant 'until his contempt has been adjudicated rightfully' . . . . [A] proper exercise of judicial discretion, under the facts and circumstances presented here, would require a determination of the question of contempt before invoking a drastic order which fixes a penalty before a determination of guilt . . . We think the appellant and its officers had a right to rely upon the trial judge to at least make an effort to require obedience to his order before assessing punishment against the corporation.[541]

On the other hand, in *Ramsay v. Santa Rosa Medical Center*,[542] after it was finally determined that plaintiff would not

---

534. *Id.* at 117.

535. Tex. R. Civ. P. 215(2)b(6); *See* Rainwater v. Haddox, 544 S.W.2d 729 (Tex. Civ. App.—Amarillo 1976, no writ).

536. Tex. R. Civ. P. 215(2)(b)(6) provides in pertinent part that "an order treating as a contempt of court the failure to obey any orders except an order to submit to a physical or mental examination."

537. 398 S.W.2d 344.

538. *Id.* at 344.

539. *Id.* at 347.

540. *Id.*

541. *Id.*

542. 498 S.W.2d 741 (Tex. Civ. App.—San Antonio 1973), *cert. denied*, 417 U.S. 938,

produce his personal diary, the trial court dismissed his suit.[543] Despite a failure to employ contempt in the first instance, the court failed to find an abuse of discretion.[544] Because the plaintiff admitted that his diary would not be produced even if contempt was applied, a contempt citation was deemed to possess little value as an effective sanction.[545]

7. *Rule 215(7).* Rule 215 declares that, when a party has failed to comply with a Rule 167a order requiring him to appear or produce another for a physical or mental examination, sanctions outlined in Rule 215(2)b(1), (2), (3), (4), or (5) may be imposed, unless the person failing to comply establishes that he is not able to appear or produce the person for examination.[546]

The court in *Harrell v. Fashing*[547] confronted a party's failure to submit to a medical examination.[548] The trial court ordered a continuance until plaintiff submitted to the examination. Plaintiff contended that a continuance was an impermissible sanction for failure to submit to examination.[549] The appellate court concluded that since Rule 167a failed to provide sanctions for a failure to submit to a court ordered examination, continuance constitutes an appropriate exercise of discretion.[550] Now, however, Rule 215(2)b(7) articulates precise sanctions for a violation of a Rule 167a order.

8. *Substantial Justification For Failure To Obey Discovery Order.* Like its counterpart in Rule 215(a)d,[551] 215(2)b(8)[552] provides for reasonable expenses, including attorney's fees for failure to comply with discovery, unless the failure was substantially justified or that other circumstances make an award of expenses unjust.[553] This rule supports the philosophy that "a party who ob-

94 S. Ct. 3062 (1974).

543. *Id.* at 743.
544. *Id.* at 744.
545. *Id.*
546. Tex. R. Civ. P. 215(2)b.
547. 562 S.W.2d 544 (Tex. Civ. App.—El Paso 1978, writ ref'd n.r.e.).
548. *Id.* at 545.
549. *Id.*
550. *Id.*
551. Tex. R. Civ. P. 215(1)d.
552. *Id.* 215(2)b(8).
553. Refer to notes 441-448 *supra* and accompanying text.

structed discovery should bear the costs of his opponent's efforts."[554]

9. *Nonparty Contempt.* Nonparties who fail to comply with a discovery order are governed by Rule 215(2)(c).[555] If a *nonparty* fails to comply with an order under Rule 167, the court may treat the failure to obey as a contempt of court. In *Barrientos v. Texas Employers' Insurance Association,*[556] the trial court struck plaintiff's pleadings because a witness failed to appear for a deposition.[557] Denominating the sanction as an abuse of discretion, the court reasoned that the trial court may strike pleadings only if a party, after subpoena, fails to appear at for deposition.[558] The failure of a nonparty deponent to appear, however, may be sanctioned only by a contempt order.[559]

D. *Abuse Of Discovery*

When the court determines an abuse of the discovery process, it may impose sanctions.[560] An abuse consists of either seeking or resisting discovery that is unreasonably frivolous, oppressive, or harassing.[561] A response or answer that is unreasonably frivolous or made for purposes of delay may also constitute an abuse of pretrial discovery process.[562]

E. *Failure To Comply With Rule 169*

Unanswered requests for admissions are deemed admitted.[563] An evasive or incomplete answer likewise is viewed as a failure to answer.[564] For example, in *Stewart v. Vaughn,*[565] which involved an action for personal injuries arising out of an automobile accident,

---

554. *See* Lindley v. Flores, 672 S.W.2d 612, 614 (Tex. App.—Corpus Christi 1984, no writ).
555. TEX. R. CIV. P. 215(c).
556. 507 S.W.2d 900 (Tex. Civ. App.—Amarillo 1974, writ ref'd n.r.e.).
557. *Id.* at 903.
558. *Id.*
559. *Id.*
560. TEX. R. CIV. P. 215(3).
561. *Id.*
562. *Id.*
563. TEX. R. CIV. P. 215(4).
564. *Id.*
565. 504 S.W.2d 600 (Tex. Civ. App.—Houston [14th Dist.] 1974, no writ).

defendant responded to a request that he admit colliding with plaintiff's automobile, with the answer that he possessed insufficient knowledge to either admit or deny the request.[566] This response was declared to be clearly evasive. Responses for admissions that are evasive, may be deemed admitted by the trial court.[567] "A party must make an effort to ascertain the facts requested to be admitted."[568]

If no response is made and no motion for an extension is requested within the time prescribed,[569] then the matters requested are conclusively established[570] as to the party making the admission,[571] unless the court on motion permits withdrawal or amendment of the admission.[572] Once admitted, a party cannot introduce

---

566. *Id.* at 602.

567. *Id. See also* Lowe v. Employers Casualty Co., 479 S.W.2d 383, 386 (Tex. Civ. App.—Fort Worth 1972, no writ) (a nonresponsive answer to a request for admissions is not binding on the party making the request. A nonresponsive, or evasive answer is not in compliance with Rule 169); Hill Farm, Inc. v. Hill County, 425 S.W.2d 414 (Tex. Civ. App.—Waco 1968), *aff'd*, 436 S.W.2d 320 (Tex. 1969); Kansas City Title Ins. Co. v. Atlas Life Ins. Co., 336 S.W.2d 204 (Tex. Civ. App.—Texarkana 1960, no writ).

568. 504 S.W.2d at 602.

569. *See* Texas Employers Ins. Ass'n v. Bragg, 670 S.W.2d 712, 716 (Tex. App.—Corpus Christi 1984, no writ) (where answers to requests were not timely filed and motions to permit late filing of answers were not made until the day of trial, the trial court did not abuse its discretion in deeming requests admitted).

570. *See* Reyes v. Int'l Metals Supply Co., 666 S.W.2d 622, 624 (Tex. App.—Houston [1st Dist.] 1984, no writ) (facts admitted are considered to be established as a matter of law); Brooks v. Eaton Yale & Towne, Inc., 474 S.W.2d 321 (Tex. Civ. App.—Waco 1971, no writ); American Title Co. v. Smith, 445 S.W.2d 807 (Tex. Civ. App.—Houston [1st Dist.] 1969, no writ); Thornell v. Equitable Life Assurance Society, 385 S.W.2d 716 (Tex. Civ. App.—Texarkana 1964, no writ); O'Connor v. Dallas, 337 S.W.2d 741 (Tex. Civ. App.—Texarkana 1960, writ dism'd); Masten v. Masten, 165 S.W.2d 225 (Tex. Civ. App.—Fort Worth 1942, writ ref'd).

571. *Compare* Texas Supply Center, Inc. v. Daon Corp., 641 S.W.2d 335, 338 (Tex. App.—Dallas 1982, writ ref'd n.r.e.) (by failing to answer requests for admission, a party has not made a statement that may in turn be imputed to his co-party under a theory of vicarious admissions); Bryant v. Kimmons, 430 S.W.2d 73 (Tex. Civ. App.—Austin 1968, no writ); Davis v. Coastal States Petrochemical Co., 405 S.W.2d 854 (Tex. Civ. App.—Houston 1966, no writ); Trice Contract Carpets & Furniture, Inc. v. Martin, 334 S.W.2d 554 (Tex. Civ. App.—Amarillo 1960, no writ).

572. TEX. R. CIV. P. Rule 169(2) (1984). Johnson v. Americana Motel, 604 S.W.2d 293, 296 (Tex. Civ. App.—San Antonio 1980), *rev'd*, 610 S.W.2d 143 (Tex. 1980) (the trial court under Rule 169 had considerable discretion in refusing or granting a motion to deem admitted the matters requested where there is neither answer nor denial within the time specified in the request); Bynum v. Shatto, 514 S.W.2d 808 (Tex. Civ. App.—Corpus Christi 1974, no writ); Kirby v. Spitzenberger, 514 S.W.2d 95 (Tex. Civ. App.—Eastland 1974, writ ref'd n.r.e.); Schindler v. AG Aero Distrib., Inc., 502 S.W.2d 581 (Tex. Civ. App.—Corpus Christi 1973, no writ).

evidence that contradicts the admitted facts.[573] A litigant is not required to prove any fact admitted to be true by his opponent.[574]

Reyes v. International Metal Supply Co.,[575] involved money damages for the mishandling of a shipment of valves.[576] In response to defendant's request for admission, plaintiff denied handling the shipment.[577] The answers to the requests for admission were neither signed nor sworn.[578] Moreover, plaintiff made no effort to either withdraw or amend his previous responses.[579] The court determined:

> [W]here a party fails to answer a request for admissions within the period set by the court, the facts stated therein will be taken as true, and the courts will not allow evidence to refute or controvert these facts. The requests are likewise deemed admitted when the answers are not properly verified. The facts are considered to be established as a matter of law.[580]

It might be argued that amended Rule 169 is inconsistent with *Reyes*. According to Rule 169, a sworn response is no longer necessary.[581] Yet, the admitting party or his attorney must sign the an-

---

573. *See* American Title Co. v. Smith, 445 S.W.2d at 809 (a party who has formally admitted a fact cannot introduce evidence to the contrary); Hill v. Caparino, 370 S.W.2d 760 (Tex. Civ. App.—Houston 1963, no writ); Cohen v. Vogt, 211 S.W.2d 762 (Tex. Civ. App.—Texarkana 1948, writ ref'd n.r.e.); Billingslea v. Greaves, 196 S.W.2d 945 (Tex. Civ. App.—Amarillo 1946, no writ). *Cf.* Denton Constr. Co. v. Mike's Elec. Co., 621 S.W.2d 846, 848 (Tex. Civ. App.—Fort Worth 1981, writ ref'd n.r.e.) (response to requests for admission may not be used affirmatively by a party upon whom the requests are served); Sympson v. Mor-win Prod., Inc., 501 S.W.2d 362 (Tex. Civ. App.—Fort Worth 1973, no writ); Gravis v. Parke-Davis & Co., 502 S.W.2d 863 (Tex. Civ. App.—Corpus Christi 1973, writ ref'd n.r.e.)

574. *See* Reyes v. International Metals Supply Co., 666 S.W.2d at 625; Red Top Taxi Co. v. Snow, 452 S.W.2d 772, 776 (Tex. Civ. App.—Corpus Christi 1970, no writ) (facts which are admitted under Rule 169 are established as a matter of law and do not require further proof. A litigant is not required to prove the allegation of fact admitted to be true by his adversary).

575. 666 S.W.2d 622 (Tex. App.—Houston [1st Dist.] 1984, no writ).

576. *Id.* at 623.

577. *Id.*

578. *Id.*

579. *Id.*

580. *Id.* at 624. *Accord*, Smith v. Home Indemnity Co., 683 S.W.2d 559, 562 (Tex. App.—Fort Worth 1985, no writ); Henke Grain Co. v. Kennon, 658 S.W.2d 343, 347 (Tex. App.—Corpus Christi 1983, no writ).

581. TEX. R. CIV. P. 169. *See also* Barrow & Henderon, *1984 Amendments to the Texas Rules of Civil Procedure Affecting Discovery*, 15 ST. MARY'S L.J. 713, 714 (1984) (a sworn response is no longer required; a written answer or objection will suffice).

swers.[582] A motion to amend or withdraw a response must be made within the time prescribed for answering.[583]

To avoid the consequences of a failure to answer, a party must establish a legal or equitable excuse.[584] In the absence of a motion to permit late filing of an answer, the trial court is authorized to deem a request to be admitted.[585]

A request for admission may support summary judgment. In *Carpenter v. Globe Leasing, Inc.*,[586] a leasing company sued for truck rentals.[587] Defendant failed to answer the requests for admission. The court ruled that defendant admitted every fact plaintiff pled as to truck rental and damages.[588] These facts were, in turn, sufficient to support plaintiff's summary judgment.[589]

F. Failure To Comply With Rules 166b - Duty To Supplement

In the past, the problem of an appropriate sanction for failure to supplement presented a particularly thorney problem. In *Texas Employers Insurance Association v. Thomas*,[590] defendant filed a motion for mistrial based on plaintiff's failure to supplement written interrogatories timely.[591] Because of the absence of any express sanction for failure to supplement, the issue was whether the trial court abused its discretion in allowing the undisclosed expert witness to testify.[592] On the basis that the medical evidence was fully developed in pretrial discovery and because the undisclosed doctor did not interject any new medical evidence into the case, the trial court did not abuse its discretion in permitting the witness to testify.[593]

---

582. Tex. R. Civ. P. 169(1).
583. Refer to note 569 *supra* and accompanying text.
584. *See* Mathes v. Kelton, 565 S.W.2d 78 (Tex. Civ. App.—Amarillo 1978), *aff'd*, 569 S.W.2d 876 (Tex. 1978); Burnett v. Cory Corp., 352 S.W.2d 502 (Tex. Civ. App.—Dallas 1961, writ ref'd n.r.e.); Lazano v. Kazen, 313 S.W.2d 894 (Tex. Civ. App.—Eastland 1958, no writ).
585. *See* Texas Employer's Ins. Ass'n v. Bragg, 670 S.W.2d at 715.
586. 421 S.W.2d 413 (Tex. Civ. App.—Fort Worth 1967, no writ).
587. *Id.* at 414.
588. *Id.* at 415.
589. *Id.*
590. 517 S.W.2d 832 (Tex. Civ. App.—San Antonio 1975, writ ref'd n.r.e.).
591. *Id.* at 833.
592. *Id.* at 834.
593. *Id.* at 835.

In *Trubell v. Patten*,[594] the trial court attempted to impose sanctions for failure to supplement. Defendant requested the names of all expert witnesses known to plaintiff who might be witnesses, and also asked plaintiff to supplement his answers.[595] Plaintiff responded that he knew of no expert, and that plaintiff would supplement his answer prior to trial if any experts were to be called as witnesses.[596] Plaintiff did not supplement his answer and assured defendant as late as one week prior to trial that he had no expert and did not disclose this fact of an expert witness until the second day of trial.[597] The trial court excluded the expert testimony, and, alluding to the federal rules, held that: "[t]he duty [to supplement a response] will normally be enforced, in those limited instances where it is imposed, through sanctions imposed by the trial courts, including exclusion of evidence, continuance, or other action, as the [trial] court may deem appropriate."[598]

The Texas Rules in 1981 provided sanctions for failure to supplement.[599] The court in *National Surety Corp. v. Rushing*[600] applied the standard. Defendant in a medical malpractice action requested plaintiff to identify each expert witness that she expected to testify at trial.[601] Plaintiff responded that her experts had not yet been determined.[602] Moreover, the interrogatory response was not supplemented or amended before trial.[603] At trial, however, plaintiff tendered an expert.[604] The trial court proposed a continuance to allow defendant an opportunity to depose the witness.[605] Defendant declined the offer, and the trial court admitted the ex-

---

594. 582 S.W.2d 606 (Tex. Civ. App.—Tyler 1979, no writ).

595. *Id.* at 608.

596. *Id.*

597. *Id.* at 607.

598. *Id.* at 611.

599. *See* TEX. R. CIV. P. 167(7) (Vernon 1983) (changed by amendment effective January 1, 1981); National Surety Corp. v. Rushing, 628 S.W.2d 90, 92 (Tex. App.—Beaumont 1981, no writ) (the 1981 amendment corrected the omission regarding sanctions).

600. 628 S.W.2d 90. *See also* Allied Finance Co. v. Garza, 626 S.W.2d 120, 125 (Tex. App.—Corpus Christi 1981, writ ref'd n.r.e.) (trial judge did not abuse his discretion in allowing undisclosed expert to testify where the basis of the witness's testimony was available at all times).

601. 628 S.W.2d at 91.

602. *Id.*

603. *Id.*

604. *Id.*

605. *Id.*

pert's testimony.[606] Though the rule provides a sanction for plaintiff's failure to supplement,[607] the rule also vests the trial court with discretion to determine the sanction; "the mandatory exclusion of the testimony of the unnamed witness was not required."[608]

The Texas Supreme Court considered sanctions for failure to supplement in *Smithson v. Cessna Aircraft Co.*.[609] The trial court admitted that the deposition testimony of plaintiff's expert witness whose identity had not been disclosed in pretrial interrogatories.[610] The Supreme Court concluded that the trial court did not abuse its discretion.[611] The failure to supplement could be mitigated by other alternatives rather than solely by the exclusion of the expert's testimony:[612]

> [w]e cannot endorse such an inflexible restriction on the trial court's ability to fulfill its discretionary duties in conducting a fair trial and administering discovery rules. To conclude that there was only one permissible action available to the trial court is virtually to deny the court any discretion in these instances.[613]

The court acknowledged that though plaintiff's expert surprised defendant, defendant had not requested a continuance and, therefore, could not seek the harsh sanction of excluding the testimony.[614]

Currently, sanctions for failure to supplement are outlined in Rule 215(5): A party who fails to supplement seasonably his response to a request for discovery in accordance with paragraph 5 of Rule 166b shall not be entitled to present evidence which the party was under a duty to provide in a supplemented response or to offer the testimony of an expert witness or of any other person having knowledge of discoverable matter when the information required by Rule 166b concerning the witness has not been disclosed, unless the trial court finds that good cause sufficient to require admission

---

606. *Id.*

607. Tex. R. Civ. P. 167(7) (Vernon 1983) ("if such amendment is not timely made, the testimony of the witness shall not be admitted in evidence unless the trial court finds that good cause sufficient to require the admission exists").

608. 628 S.W.2d at 92.

609. 665 S.W.2d 439 (Tex. 1984).

610. *Id.* at 440.

611. *Id.* at 443.

612. *Id.* (i.e. continuance, or postponement).

613. *Id.*

614. *Id.*

exists.[615]

8.09 REVIEW OF TRIAL COURT DISCOVERY ORDERS[616]

A trial court's order relating to pretrial discovery is reviewed either on appeal,[617] or by mandamus[618] upon grounds of a clear abuse of discretion. Rule 215 specifies the situations in which orders are reviewed only on appeal from a final judgment.

During the course of discovery, when a trial court orders too much or not enough discovery, a party may initiate an original jurisdiction mandamus action to compel the trial court to order or withhold the requested discovery. In *Crane v. Tunks*[619] and *Maresca v. Marks*,[620] the Texas Supreme Court discussed the mandamus remedy relating to pretrial discovery. In both cases, the trial courts ordered complete discovery of plaintiff's income tax returns.[621] In *Crane*, the Supreme Court addressed the appropriate parameters for mandamus.[622] The court noted that discovery was designed to develop evidence to be used in the trial and was not an

---

615. TEX. R. CIV. P. 215(5). But see Holiday Hills Retirement & Nursing Center v. Yeldell, _____S.W.2d_____ (Tex. App.—Ft. Worth 1985) (no duty to supplement an incomplete answer). 2-84-138 CV (slip opinion March 14, 1985).

616. *See generally* Comment, *The Expanding Use of Mandamus to Review Texas District Court Discovery Orders: An Immediate Appeal is Available*, 32 Sw. L.J. 1283 (1979); Sales, *Pre-Trial Discovery in Texas*, 31 Sw. L.J. 1017, 1032 (1977).

617. *See* Lindley v. Flores, 672 S.W.2d 612 (Tex. App.—Corpus Christi 1984, no writ); Reyes v. Int'l Metals Supply Co., 666 S.W.2d 622 (Tex. Civ. App.—Houston [1st Dist.] 1984, no writ); Alexander v. Barlow, 671 S.W.2d 531 (Tex. App.—Houston [1st Dist.] 1983, no writ); Sobel v. Taylor, 640 S.W.2d 704 (Tex. App.—Houston [14th Dist.] 1982, no writ); National Surety Corp. v. Rushing, 628 S.W.2d 90 (Tex. Civ. App.—Beaumont 1981, no writ); Bottinelli v. Robinson, 594 S.W.2d 112 (Tex. Civ. App.—Houston [1st Dist.] 1979, no writ); Firestone Photos, Inc. v. Lamaster, 567 S.W.2d 273 (Tex. Civ. App.—Texarkana 1978, no writ); Ebeling v. Gawlik, 487 S.W.2d 187 (Tex. Civ. App.—Houston [1st Dist.] 1972, no writ); Hankins v. Haffa, 469 S.W.2d 733 (Tex. Civ. App.—Amarillo 1971, writ ref'd n.r.e.); Fisher v. Continental Ill. Nat. Bank & Trust Co, 424 S.W.2d 664 (Tex. Civ. App.—Houston [14th Dist.] 1968, writ ref'd n.r.e.).

618. Jampole v. Touchy, 673 S.W.2d 569 (Tex. 1984); Pope v. Ferguson, 445 S.W.2d 950 (Tex. 1969), *cert. denied*, 397 U.S. 997 (1970); Menton v. Lattimore, 667 S.W.2d 335 (Tex. App.—Fort Worth 1984, no writ); General Motors Corp. v. Lawrence, 651 S.W.2d 732 (Tex. 1983); West v. Solito, 563 S.W.2d 240 (Tex. 1978); Allen v. Humphreys, 559 S.W.2d 798 (Tex. 1977); Barker v. Durham, 551 S.W.2d 41 (Tex. 1977); Maresca v. Marks, 362 S.W.2d 299 (Tex. 1962); Crane v. Tunks, 160 Tex. 182, 328 S.W.2d 434 (1959).

619. 160 Tex. 182, 328 S.W.2d 434.

620. 362 S.W.2d 299.

621. *See* Crane v. Tunks, 160 Tex. 182, 186, 328 S.W.2d 434, 437-38; Maresca v. Marks, 362 S.W.2d at 300.

622. 328 S.W.2d at 438.

end within itself.[623] Second, once relators exposed their papers for inspection in compliance with an erroneous court order the damage was irreparable.[624] An appeal is not an adequate remedy when the privileged matters have been disclosed. In these situations mandamus may issue.[625]

In *Maresca*, mandamus was issued on the basis that the trial court abused its discretion in ordering discovery of relator's income tax records.[626] The Supreme Court held that, "[i]t is self-evident that the maximum protection of privacy is unattainable if trial courts do not exercise their discretion to safeguard from discovery those portions of income tax returns which are irrelevant and immaterial, and it is our view that failure to exercise such discretion is arbitrary action."[627] While *Crane* and *Maresca* were mandamus actions to review affirmative grants of discovery, *Allen v. Humpreys*[628] used mandamus as a remedy where the trial court *denied* discovery.

Pope v. Ferguson[629] contrasts *Allen*. The court in *Pope* maintained that mandamus should never be utilized to correct interlocutory trial court rulings in which the right of appeal exists.[630] The considerations espoused in *Crane* for granting mandamus simply are not present where the trial court denies discovery.

The Texas Supreme Court in *General Motors Corp. v. Lawrence*[631] granted relator's writ of mandamus and instructed the trial judge to limit discovery of defendant's records from "all vehicles for all model years" to records of trucks for relevant years.[632] The court discussed mandamus and concluded that:

> This court had been flooded with mandamus actions to either compel or deny discovery. Although this court has extensively revised the discovery rules to expedite discovery, the revisions have not solved the abuse of the discovery process caused by overly broad requests, delay in production, or production of material in

623. *Id.*
624. *Id.*
625. *Id.*
626. 362 S.W.2d at 301.
627. *Id.*
628. 559 S.W.2d 798 (Tex. 1977).
629. 445 S.W.2d 950 (Tex. 1969), *cert. denied*, 397 U.S. 997 (1970).
630. *Id.* at 953-54.
631. 651 S.W.2d 732 (Tex. 1983).
632. *Id.* at 734.

> a meaningless manner. The discovery rules provide for sanctions which, if used, might possibly discourage these practices . . . . Compelling discovery of nonrelevant material, however, is not one of the available sanctions under our rules.[633]

The 1984 amendments to the Texas Rules of Procedure were partly promulgated to curb discovery abuses at the trial level.[634] However, the Supreme Court's recent grant of mandamus in *Jampole v. Touchy*[635] appears to contravene the stated purpose of the new rules. As the dissent in *Jampole* states,: "[t]hese amendments place upon trial judges the primary responsibility for arresting discovery abuses . . . . [by granting mandamus] the court has now unnecessarily usurped the discretion of the trial judge."[636] Justice Barrow concludes that it is essential that a trial judge be permitted to conduct an orderly pretrial process without interference from the higher courts.[637] The trial court occupies a far superior position to rule upon discovery because the court is confronting the facts directly rather than in an abbreviated and often misleading record. But as Justice Barrow noted, the Supreme Court has now enshrouded itself in the thicket.[638]

8.10 Conclusion

Pretrial discovery lies at the heart of litigation. The rules "change the trial of a lawsuit from a game of chance and surprise . . . to an orderly process of unclouding matters and uncovering the actual facts involved."[639] The newly amended rules are designed to facilitate and improve this process. Only if the Texas Supreme Court accords the trial court appropriate latitude in supervising pretrial discovery can there be hope for insuring that the process will become more effective and more evenhanded.

---

633. *Id.*
634. *See* Jampole v. Touchy, 673 S.W.2d 569 (Tex. 1984) (Barrow, J., dissenting).
635. 673 S.W.2d 569 (Tex. 1984).
636. *Id.* at 465.
637. *Id.*
638. *Id.*
639. *See* Pearson Corp. v. Wichita Falls Boys Club Alumni Ass'n, Inc., 633 S.W.2d 684, 686 (Tex. App.—Fort Worth 1982, no writ). Refer to note 1 *supra* and accompanying text.

CHAPTER IX. JURISDICTION AND VENUE*

9.01 JURISDICTION

A. *Introduction*

The principal jurisdictional problem in the area of products

* Barbara Paulissen coauthored this chapter.

liability arises when the plaintiff has sustained an injury in Texas as a result of the use of a product manufactured by a foreign corporation. The critical issue involves the extent of the personal jurisdiction that a Texas court may exercise over a corporation whose principal connection with the state involves a product that has ended up in Texas. The Texas "Long Arm" Statute[1] constitutes the statutory basis authorizing the exercise of in personam jurisdiction.

Section 1 of Article 2031b[2] relates to a party's failure to appoint an agent and the consequent designation of the Secretary of State as its lawful agent. This statute provides, in pertinent part:

> Section 1. When any foreign corporation, association, joint stock company, partnership, or nonresident natural person, required by any Statute of this State to designate or maintain a resident agent, or any such corporation . . . has not appointed or maintained a designated agent, upon whom service of process can be made, or has one or more resident agents and two (2) unsuccessful attempts have been made on different business days to serve process upon each of its designated agents, such corporation . . . shall be conclusively presumed to have designated the Secretary of State of Texas as their true and lawful attorney upon whom service of process or complaint may be made.[3]

Section 2[4] provides that service may be effectuated on any foreign corporation or person engaging in business in this state when that corporation or person is not required by any statute to appoint an agent. This is accomplished "by serving a copy of the process with the person who, at the time of the service, is in charge of any business in which the defendant or defendants are engaged in this State."[5]

Section 3 of the statute[6] essentially provides for service for any foreign corporation or person engaging in business in Texas that maintains neither a regular place of business nor a designated agent within the state. In this instance, the foreign corporation or

---

1. TEX. REV. CIV. STAT. ANN. art. 2031b (Vernon 1964 & Supp. 1985).
2. *Id.* art. 2031b, § 1.
3. *Id.*
4. *Id.* art. 2031b, § 2.
5. *Id.*
6. *Id.* art. 2031b, § 3.

person is deemed to have appointed the Secretary of State as its agent for service.[7]

Section 4[8] defines "doing business" in Texas. Much of the litigation involving the exercise of in personam jurisdiction focuses on whether the defendant's acts constitute "doing business" in Texas. This section provides:

> For the purpose of this Act, and without including other acts that may constitute doing business, any foreign corporation, joint stock company, association, partnership, or nonresident natural person shall be deemed doing business in this State by entering into contract by mail or otherwise with a resident of Texas to be performed in whole or in part by either party in this State, or the committing of any tort in whole or in part in the State. The act of recruiting Texas residents, directly or through an intermediary located in Texas, for employment inside or outside of Texas shall be deemed doing business in this State.[9]

B. *The Standard of In Personam Jurisdiction.*

Both state and federal courts have struggled to define the prerequisites for and the application of in personam jurisdiction in particular cases. The landmark case of *Pennoyer v. Neff*[10] established the principle that a personal judgment entered against a nonresident of the state who is served by publication of summons instead of by personal service and who makes no appearance violates the due process clause of the Fourteenth Amendment, and is, therefore, void.

Since *Pennoyer v. Neff*,[11] the standard for measuring the extent of the jurisdictional power that a state may exercise over foreign corporations or nonresident persons has been predicated upon such concepts as "domicile,"[12] "consent,"[13] "doing business"[14] and

---

7. *Id.*

8. *Id.* art. 2031b, § 4 (Vernon Supp. 1985).

9. *Id.*

10. 95 U.S. 714 (1877).

11. *Id.*

12. *See, e.g.*, Milliken v. Meyer, 311 U.S. 457, 463 (1940) (domicile is a sufficient basis for extraterritorial service over an absent party).

13. *See, e.g.*, National Equip. Rental v. Szukhent, 375 U.S. 311, 315-16 (1964) (consent by contract); Adam v. Saenger, 303 U.S. 59, 67-68 (1938) (consent by filing suit); Hess v. Pawloski, 274 U.S. 352, 354 (1927) (implied consent by using highway within the state).

14. *See* Old Wayne Mut. Life Ass'n v. Mcdonough, 204 U.S. 8, 22 (1907) (corporation

"presence."[15] The seminal case of *International Shoe Co. v. Washington*,[16] however, promulgated a new standard and expanded the jurisdiction of a state over nonresidents and foreign corporations. The Supreme Court in *International Shoe* declared that a court acquires jurisdiction over a nonresident or foreign corporation without violating the Due Process clause of the Fourteenth Amendment if the nonresident or foreign corporation had certain "minimum contacts" with the forum state.[17] The minimum contacts standard contemplates "that the maintenance of the suit does not offend 'traditional notions of fair play and substantial justice' " when the cause of action arises from such contacts.[18]

The Supreme Court in *McGee v. International Life Insurance Co.*[19] thereafter addressed the nature and character of acts essential to satisfy the "minimum contacts" requirement.[20] The beneficiary named in a life insurance policy issued to a California resident instituted suit against a Texas insurance company which had assumed the obligation owed to the insured by the original insurer. The jurisdiction of the California court was based entirely on a state statute subjecting foreign corporations to suit in California involving insurance contracts with California residents, notwithstanding that the corporations were not amenable to service of process within its borders. Reviewing the constitutionality of the California long-arm statute, the United States Supreme Court acknowledged a trend "toward expanding the permissible scope of state jurisdiction over foreign corporations and other nonresidents."[21] The court decided that "[i]t is sufficient for purposes of due process that the suit was based on a contract which had sub-

---

that does business in state will be presumed to have assented to jurisdiction); Green v. Chicago, Burlington & Quincy Ry. Co., 205 U.S. 530, 532 (1907) (validity of jurisdiction depends on whether corporation was doing business in such a manner and to such an extent as to warrant inference that it was present).

15. *See, e.g.*, Darrah v. Watson, 36 Iowa 116, 121 (1873) (party amenable to service while temporarily within local jurisdiction). *But see* Shaffer v. Heitner, 433 U.S. 186, 209 (1977) (mere presence of property insufficient to constitutionally confer in personam jurisdiction).

16. 326 U.S. 310 (1945).

17. *Id.* at 316.

18. *Id.*

19. 355 U.S. 220 (1957).

20. *Id.* at 223.

21. *Id.* at 222.

stantial connection with that State."[22]

The minimum contacts standard was further refined in *Hanson v. Denckla.*[23] This standard served as the principal basis upon which the Texas Long Arm statute was enacted.[24] In *Hanson v. Denckla,*[25] the defendant possessed only slight contacts with the forum state. Most importantly, the plaintiff's cause of action did not arise from and was unrelated to these insignificant contacts. The United States Supreme Court concluded that the defendant was not amenable to in personam jurisdiction because he did not maintain sufficient "minimum contacts" with the state.[26] Moreover, the cause of action did not arise from the acts performed in the forum state.[27] *Hanson* reaffirmed the basic territorial limitation on the power of a state to subject nonresidents and foreign corporations to in personam jurisdiction and established a standard for determining the existence of "minimum contacts." The Court held that "it is essential in each case that there be some act by which the defendant purposefully avails itself of the privilege of conducting activities within the forum State, thus invoking the benefits and protections of its laws."[28]

In 1959, one year after *Hanson v. Denckla,*[29] the legislature enacted Article 2031b, generally characterized as the Texas Long Arm Statute.[30] The application and reach of Article 2031b was initially considered in *Lone Star Motor Import, Inc. v. Citroen Cars Corp.*[31] The court determined that the "minimum contacts" standard of *International Shoe* governed the outer reach of personal jurisdiction under the statute.[32]

The effect of the "doing business" provision of Article 2031b was considered in *Hearne v. Dow-Badische Chemical Co.*[33] The court was confronted with an attack on in personam jurisdiction in

---

22. *Id.*
23. 357 U.S. 235 (1958).
24. TEX. REV. CIV. STAT. ANN. art. 2301b (Vernon 1964 & Supp. 1985).
25. 357 U.S. 235 (1958)
26. *Id.* at 254-55.
27. *Id.* at 251.
28. *Id.* at 253 (citing International Shoe Co. v. Washington, 326 U.S. 310, 319 (1945).
29. 357 U.S. 235 (1958).
30. TEX. REV. CIV. STAT. ANN. art. 2031b (Vernon 1964 & Supp. 1985).
31. 185 F. Supp. 48 (S.D. Tex. 1960), *rev'd on other grounds,* 288 F.2d 69 (5th Cir. 1961).
32. 288 F.2d at 74.
33. 224 F. Supp. 90 (S.D. Tex. 1963).

an action against a foreign corporation which manufactured a valve in a state other than Texas but shipped it to a corporation in Texas, where it caused an explosion injuring a person. The issue presented was whether the foreign corporation committed a "tort in whole or in part within the State of Texas".[34] The court outlined a two-step inquiry: 1) whether statutory authority exists for the exercise of "long arm" jurisdiction; and 2) whether the jurisdiction, if authorized, satisfies constitutional due process.[35] The court determined that the wording "in part"[36] was clearly intended to include a situation where the operative wrongful act occurs in another state but the injury occurs in Texas.[37] In evaluating whether article 2031b violated the due process clause of the Fourteenth Amendment, the court acknowledged the controlling effect of the "minimum contacts" standard articulated in *International Shoe*[38] and reaffirmed in *Hanson*[39] and *Lone Star Motor Import, Inc.*[40] The court enumerated five factors to measure the sufficiency of "minimum contacts" essential to satisfy due process. These factors are:

> (1) the nature and character of the business;
> (2) the number and type of activities within the forum;
> (3) whether such activities give rise to the cause of action;
> (4) whether the forum has some special interest in granting relief; and
> (5) the relative convenience of the parties.[41]

The court concluded that due process was not violated by Texas' assertion of long-arm jurisdiction when the injury occurred in Texas and the wrongful acts of the defendant occurred outside the

---

34. *Id.* at 93.
35. *Id.*
36. > . . . any foreign corporation, joint stock company, association, partnership, or non-resident natural person shall be deemed doing business in this State by . . . the committing of any tort in whole or in part in this State.

TEX. REV. CIV. STAT. ANN. art. 2031b, § 4 (Vernon Supp. 1985).
37. 224 F. Supp. at 96.
38. 326 U.S. 310 (1945).
39. 357 U.S. 235 (1958).
40. 185 F. Supp. 48 (S.D. Tex. 1960), *rev'd on other grounds*, 288 F.2d 69 (5th Cir. 1961).
41. 224 F. Supp. at 99. This test was adopted by Minnesota in Dent-Air, Inc. v. Beech Mountain Air Serv. Inc., 332 N.W.2d 904, 907 (Minn. 1983) and reaffirmed in Rostad v. On-Deck, Inc., 354 N.W.2d 95, 98 (Minn. Ct. App. 1984).

state.[42]

The Texas Supreme Court in *O'Brien v. Lanpar Co.*[43] adopted a three-part test to determine whether personal jurisdiction over a nonresident defendant satisfied due process:

> (1) The nonresident defendant or foreign corporation must purposefully do some act or consummate some transaction in the forum state;
>
> (2) The cause of action must arise from, or be connected with, such act or transaction; and
>
> (3) The assumption of jurisdiction by the forum state must not offend traditional notions of fair play and substantial justice, consideration being given to the quality, nature and extent of the activity in the forum state, the relative convenience of the parties, the benefits and protection of the laws of the forum state afforded the respective parties, and the basic equities of the situation.[44]

The Texas Supreme Court reaffirmed this three prong test in *U-Anchor Advertising, Inc. v. Burt.*[45] The court, however, failed to delineate the factors necessary to evaluate the "nexus requirement" embodied in the "arise from or be connected with" part of the test in the exercise of general jurisdiction cases.[46]

The question arises whether the nexus requirement is to be treated as a component of due process, or rather, a component of Article 2031b. Despite criticism that the nexus requirement is overly restrictive on due process,[47] Texas courts have continually reaffirmed the nexus requirement under due process consideration.[48]

---

42. 224 F. Supp. at 101. See Union Carbide Corp. v. UGI Corp., 731 F.2d 1186, 1189 (5th Cir. 1984) (tortions interference of contract occurred in Texas and damage likewise occurred). See generally, D.J. Investments v. Metzeler Motorcycle Tire, 754 F.2d 542, 547-48 (5th Cir. 1985).

43. 399 S.W.2d 340 (Tex. 1966).

44. *Id.* at 342 (citing Tyee Constr. Co. v. Dulien Steel Prod., Inc., 62 Wash. 2d 106, 115-16, 381 P.2d 245, 251 (1963)).

45. 553 S.W.2d 760, 762 (Tex. 1977), *cert. denied*, 434 U.S. 1063 (1978).

46. Refer to text accompanying notes 47-52 and notes 79-83 *infra*.

47. Comment, *The Texas Long-Arm Statute, Article 2031b: A New Process is Due*, 30 Sw. L.J. 747, 760 (1976).

48. Wright Waterproofing Co. v. Applied Polymers, 602 S.W.2d 67, 71 (Tex. Civ. App.—Dallas 1980, writ ref'd n.r.e.); Sherman Gin Co. v. Planters Gin Co., 599 S.W.2d 348, 350 (Tex. Civ. App.—Texarkana 1980, writ ref'd n.r.e.); Rosemont Enter., Inc. v. Lummis, 596 S.W.2d 916, 921 (Tex. Civ. App.—Houston [14th Dist.] 1980, no writ); Michigan Gen. Corp. v. Mod-U-Kraf Homes, Inc., 582 S.W.2d 594, 596 (Tex. Civ. App.—Dallas 1979, writ ref'd n.r.e.).

Contrary to state court interpretation, the Fifth Circuit has viewed the nexus requirement simply as a statutory component mandated by Article 2031b.[49] But, in *Product Promotions, Inc. v. Cousteau*,[50] the Fifth Circuit adopted the test articulated in *O'Brien v. Lanpar Co.*,[51] absent the second prong of the test. Significantly, the court perceived that the nexus requirement was irrelevant. As a consequence, the Fifth Circuit recognized in personam jurisdiction in cases in which the nonresident defendant has maintained substantial and continuous contacts with Texas unrelated to the cause of action.[52] Jurisdiction is dependent, therefore, on the nature, quality, and quantity of a party's contacts with the forum state; it purportedly need not constitute the act or activity that gives rise to the asserted claim.

The sufficiency of "minimum contacts" to support in personam jurisdiction in a strict tort liability context was addressed in *Eyerly Aircraft Co. v. Killian*[53] and *Coulter v. Sears, Roebuck & Co.*[54] In *Eyerly*, the plaintiff was injured on an amusement ride manufactured by the defendant. The court stated and answered the question presented: "Our question in this diversity case is whether the Texas 'Long Arm' statute has the stretch, within constitutional permissibility, to embrace the products liability action before us. We find both the stretch and the embrace."[55] Jurisdiction was sustained against constitutional attack on two grounds. First, the defendant maintained direct contacts with the state in the form of substantial and continuous business relationships.[56] Second, the defendant had introduced the defective product into the stream of commerce and could reasonably expect that the product would arrive in the state in which its defective condition caused injury.[57]

---

49. *See* Note, *The Texas Long-Arm Statute After* Hall v. Helicopteros Nacionales de Colombia, S.A.: *Will Texas Become a Magnet Forum?*, 20 HOUS. L. REV. 1221, 1231 (1983). *See also* Prejean v. Sonatrach, Inc., 652 F.2d 1260, 1265 (5th Cir. 1981).

50. 495 F.2d 483 (5th Cir. 1974).

51. 399 S.W.2d 340 (Tex. 1966); Refer to text accompanying note 44 *supra*.

52. *See* Jetco Elec. Indus. Inc. v. Gardiner, 473 F.2d 1228, 1234 (5th Cir. 1973); Eyerly Aircraft Co. v. Killian, 414 F.2d 591, 601 (5th Cir. 1969).

53. 414 F.2d 591 (5th Cir. 1969).

54. 426 F.2d 1315 (5th Cir. 1970).

55. 414 F.2d at 592.

56. *Id.* at 597.

57. *Id.* The stream of commerce approach has received the approval of a number of jurisdictions. *See, e.g.*, DeJames v. Magnificence Carriers, Inc., 654 F.2d 280, 285 (3d Cir.),

In *Coulter,* the "stream of commerce" theory was deemed sufficient to overcome any constitutional objections.[58] The court concluded that the defendant could reasonably expect that its product would be retailed in Texas, and it enjoyed the benefits of the Texas market and the protections of the state laws. Under these circumstances, due process of law was not violated by the exercise of in personam jurisdiction over the defendant.[59]

Subsequently, the United States Supreme Court reentered the much litigated area of in personam jurisdiction. In *World-Wide Volkswagen Corp. v. Woodson,*[60] the plaintiff, a New York resident, was traveling through Oklahoma en route to Arizona when he was involved in an automobile accident. The plaintiff instituted suit in Oklahoma against the automobile's manufacturer, importer, distributor, and dealer, claiming that the severe burns he received in the accident were caused by a defectively designed gas tank. The distributor and the dealer contested jurisdiction on the basis of the absence of any contacts with the state of Oklahoma.[61] The United States Supreme Court, employing the "minimum contacts" standard, determined that Oklahoma was foreclosed from the exercise of in personam jurisdiction over the distributor and the dealer.[62] The Court rejected the argument that jurisdiction can be predicated upon mere foreseeability that a product might migrate into and cause harm in the forum state:[63] "Rather, it is that the defendant's conduct and connection with the forum State are such that he should reasonably anticipate being haled into court there."[64]

The Supreme Court emphasized, in dictum, that:

> [I]f the sale of a product of a manufacturer or distributor . . . is not simply an isolated occurrence, but arises from the efforts of the manufacturer or distributor to serve, directly or indi-

---

cert. denied, 454 U.S. 1085 (1981); Nelson v. Park Indus., Inc., 717 F.2d 1120, 1127 (7th Cir. 1983), *cert. denied, sub nom.* United Garment Mfg. Co. v. Nelson, 104 S.Ct. 1278 (1984).

58. 426 F.2d 1315, 1320 (5th Cir. 1970).

59. *Id.*

60. 444 U.S. 286 (1980).

61. *Id.* at 289.

62. *Id.* at 298. *Accord,* Fidelity and Casualty Co. v. Philadelphia Resins Corp., ____ F.2d ____ (10th Cir. 1985) (No. 83-1362).

63. *Id.* at 295-96.

64. *Id.* at 297 (emphasis added) relying on Kulho v. California Superior Court, 436 U.S. 84 (1978) and Shaffer v. Heitner, 433 U.S. 186 (1977).

> rectly, the market for its product in other States, it is not unreasonable to subject it to suit in one of those States if its allegedly defective merchandise has there been the source of injury to its owners or to others. The forum State does not exceed its powers under the Due Process Clause if it asserts personal jurisdiction over a corporation that delivers its products into the stream of commerce with the expectation that they will be purchased by consumers in the forum State.[65]

Jurisdiction was considered lacking, however, because the only contact by the local retailer and the New York wholesaler with the State of Oklahoma was the single automobile involved in the suit. This "isolated occurrence" did not constitute a sufficient connection with the forum State so that the defendant should "reasonably anticipate being haled into court there."[66]

Thereafter, in *Oswalt v. Scripto, Inc.*,[67] plaintiff instituted a suit against Tokai-Seiki, a Japanese cigarette lighter manufacturer, and its American distributor to recover damages for injuries sustained when one of its lighters allegedly malfunctioned. Unlike the New York retailer and wholesaler in *World-Wide Volkswagen*, whose commercial ties were limited, Tokai-Seiki's distribution of lighters was unlimited within the United States. The Fifth Circuit confirmed in personam jurisdiction, noting that Tokai-Seiki reasonably anticipated that its product would be marketed and sold in Texas.[68] Distinguishing the case from *World-Wide Volkswagen*,

---

65. *Id.* at 297-98.

66. *Id.* at 297. However, when a manufacturer or distributor endeavors to serve directly, or indirectly, the market for its products in all the various states, it is not unreasonable to assert in personam jurisdiction in a state where one of its products has produced an injury. *Id.* at 297. This stream of commerce concept as a basis of jurisdiction is well established. Coulter v. Sears, Roebuck & Co., 426 F.2d 1315, 1319 (5th Cir. 1970).

67. 616 F.2d 191 (5th Cir. 1980).

68. A manufacturer or product supplier intending to serve a broad national market and deriving direct benefits from such a market distribution necessarily subjects itself to a forum's personal jurisdiction. In Nelson v. Park Indus., Inc., 717 F.2d 1120 (7th Cir. 1983), *cert. denied sub. nom.* United Garment Mfg. Co. v. Nelson, 104 S. Ct. 1278 (1984) garment suppliers incorporated under the laws of Hong Kong, who distributed their products through a system of local distributive agents, were deemed subject to in personam jurisdiction. The court noted that "[t]he *World-Wide Volkswagen* Court's recognition of a distinction among the various entites that might compose a distribution system of a product is pivotal to the decision in this case." *Id.* F.2d at 1125; *accord* Crose v. Volkswagenwerk Aktiengesellschaft, 88 Wash. 2d 50, 558 P.2d 764 (1977) (en banc). *But see,* Glater v. Eli Lilly & Co., 744 F.2d 213 (1st Cir. 1984) (defendant's sale of diethylstilbestrol in New Hampshire not sufficient to support the exercise of general jurisdiction).

yet utilizing that court's standard, the Fifth Circuit observed that "Tokai-Seiki's conduct and connection with Texas are such that it should reasonably anticipate being haled into court in Texas."[69] The rationale of the court ostensibly reflected an awareness of the standards enumerated in *World-Wide Volkswagen Corp.* and basically reaffirmed the stream of commerce concept articulated in *Eyerly* and *Coulter.*[70]

C. *Continuation of The "Minimum Contacts" Standard*

The Texas Supreme Court, in 1982, decided *Hall v. Helicopteros Nacionales de Colombia, S.A.*[71] Previously, Texas employed a three pronged test to evaluate in personam jurisdiction. Under this earlier test, the nonresident defendant was required to purposefully perform some act or consummate some transaction in the forum state. In addition, the cause of action was required to arise from, or be connected with that act or transaction. Finally, the assumption of jurisdiction by the forum state could not offend traditional notions of fair play and substantial justice.[72]

One prong of this test is characterized as the "nexus requirement."[73] While the court acknowledged that the nexus requirement must be satisfied when a defendant's contacts with Texas are minimal, the Texas Supreme Court rejected this requirement for cases in which a nonresident defendant's activities within Texas are considered substantial.[74]

In *Hall* the surviving family members of four United States citizens who were killed in a helicopter crash in Peru initiated

---

69. 616 F.2d at 200. A similar analysis and result was reached by the court in Rostad v. On-Deck, Inc., 354 N.W.2d 95, 99 (Minn. Ct. App. 1984).

70. *Coulter* held that a reasonable expectation of distribution in a forum state was sufficient alone to support jurisdiction. This basis for in personam jurisdication was clearly recognized by the Supreme Court in World-Wide Volkswagen Corp. v. Wordson, 444 U.S. 286 (1980). *See also,* Rockwell Int'l Corp. v. Costruzioni Aeronautiche Giovanni Agusta, 553 F. Supp. 328, 334 (E.D. Pa. 1982) (exercise of in personam jurisdiction over nonresident defendant appropriate where the defendant manufactured ball bearings with the knowledge that they would be distributed throughout the United States).

71. 638 S.W.2d 870 (Tex. 1982) *rev'd,* 104 S.Ct. 1868 (1984).

72. O'Brienv. Lanpar Co., 399 S.W.2d 340, 342 (Tex. 1966).

73. Refer to notes 47-52 *supra* and notes 79-83 *infra* and accompanying text.

74. Notes, *The Texas Long-Arm Statute After* Hall v. Helicopteros Nacionales de Colombia, S.A.: *Will Texas Become a Magnet Forum?*, 20 Hous. L. Rev. 1221, 1221 (1983).

wrongful death actions in Harris County, Texas. The defendant owned and operated the helicopter that crashed. The defendant made a special appearance to contest the jurisdiction of the Texas Court[75] on the basis that it did not maintain an office in Texas, it had no designated agent for service of process in Texas, it was not authorized to do business in Texas, it performed no helicopter operations in Texas, and it did not recruit any employees in Texas.[76] In deciding whether the exercise of in personam jurisdiction was consistent with due process under the Fourteenth Amendment,[77] the Court examined the three pronged test adopted in *O'Brien v. Lanpar Co.*[78] The court asserted that the second prong is unnecessary when the nonresident defendant's presence in the forum through numerous contacts is of such nature that it satisfies the demands of due process.[79] The court implied, therefore, that the state's long-arm statute reaches as far as the Due Process Clause of the Fourteenth Amendment permits.[80] After eliminating the nexus requirement, the court applied the "minimum contacts" test to determine whether it was "reasonable . . . to require the corporation to defend the particular suit which is brought there."[81] In a vigorous dissent,[82] Justice Pope emphasized that Article 2031b "expressly requires a nexus between the helicopter crash and the contacts relied upon to justify jurisdiction. The nexus requirement in Texas is found in the clear wording of the statute itself."[83] Justice

---

75. 638 S.W.2d at 871. *See* TEX. R. CIV. P. 120a.

76. 638 S.W.2d at 871. *See* TEX. REV. CIV. STAT. ANN. art. 2031b, § 4, (Vernon Supp. 1985).

77. 638 S.W.2d at 871.

78. 399 S.W.2d 340 (Tex. 1966). Refer to note 44 *supra* and accompanying text.

79. 638 S.W.2d at 872.

80. *Id.* at 872.

81. *Id.* at 873.

82. *Id.* at 877.

83. *Id.* at 877. Section of article 2031b provides:

> Any foreign corporation, association, joint stock company, partnership, or non-resident natural person that engages in business in this State, irrespective of any statute or law respecting designation or maintenance of resident agents, and does not maintain a place of regular business in this State or a designated agent upon whom service may be made *upon causes of action arising out of such business done in this State*, the act or acts of engaging in such business within this State shall be deemed equivalent to an appointment by such foreign corporation . . . of the Secretary of State of Texas as agent upon whom service of process may be made in any action, suit or proceeding *arising out of such business done in this State*, wherein such corporation . . . is a party or is to be made a party.

TEX. REV. CIV. STAT. ANN. art. 2031b, § 3 (Vernon 1964) (emphasis added).

Pope predicted that this case will establish Texas as a "magnet forum, drawing to its courts the trial of any lawsuit involving a defendant who has ever made purchases in Texas." The concern involved marauding tortfeasors seeking a haven of favorable law that would ultimately prove lucrative at the expense of the Texas Court System.[84]

Helicopteros Nacionales de Colombia, S.A. v. Hall[85] was considered by the United States Supreme Court on writ of certiorari in 1984. The United States Supreme Court noted that all the parties conceded that Hall's claim did not arise out of Helicol's activities within Texas. The issue to be decided, therefore, was whether Helicol's contacts with Texas satisfied Due Process.[86] In reversing the Texas Supreme Court decision,[87] the United States Supreme Court concluded that defendant's contacts with the State of Texas were insufficient to satisfy the requirements of the Due Process clause;[88] mere purchases in the forum state are insufficient as a matter of law to warrant a state's assertion of in personam jurisdiction over a nonresident defendant in a cause of action unrelated to those purchase transactions.[89] The Supreme Court did not feel the necessity to determine whether the nexus requirement was essential to in personam jurisdiction over a nonresident engaged in only minimal contacts within the state; the Court deemed the minimal contacts constitutionally insufficient.

The United States Supreme Court noted the distinction between the exercise of personal jurisdiction over a defendant in a suit arising from a defendant's contacts with the forum state and personal jurisdiction over a defendant in a suit that occurs in another state and does not arise out of defendant's contact with the forum state.[90] The exercise of in personam jurisdiction over a defendant in a suit that arises out of and is related to defendant's

---

84. 638 S.W.2d at 883. The consequence of unfettered jurisdiction is illustrated in Holmes. v. Syntex Laboratories, Inc., 156 Cal. App. 3d 372, 202 Cal. Rptr. 773 (1984).

85. ___ U.S. ___ 104 S.Ct. 1868 (1984).

86. *Id.* at 1873.

87. *Id.* at 1874.

88. *Id.*

89. *Id.* The court cited Rosenberg Bros. & Co. v. Curtis Brown Co., 260 U.S. 516 (1923), as establishing the rule that "purchases and related trips, standing alone, are not a sufficient basis for a State's assertion of jurisdiction." The court further noted that the fact of defendant sending its personnel to Texas for training in connection with the purchases of helicopters and equipment did not enhance defendant's contracts with the state of Texas.

90. *Id.* at 1872, n. 8-9.

minimal contacts with the forum state is characterized as "specific jurisdiction."[91] The exercise of in personam jurisdiction over a defendant in a lawsuit that occurs in another state and does not arise from and is not related to a nonresident's minimal contacts with the forum state is characterized as "general jurisdiction."[92] In *Helicopteros Nacionales de Colombia, S.A. v. Hall*,[93] the Texas Courts were confronted with general jurisdiction since the nonresident defendant's minimal contacts with the State of Texas did not give rise to and were not involved in the accident that formed the basis of the lawsuit filed in the state court of Texas; the accident underlying the lawsuit filed in Texas occurred in Peru.

Perhaps the most incisive analysis of the variance in minimal contacts required for general jurisdiction as distinguished from specific jurisdiction is discussed in *Glater v. Eli Lilly & Co.*[94] Plaintiff instituted suit in the United States District Court of New Hampshire against the defendant seeking damages based on strict tort liability for injuries that resulted when her mother ingested DES prescribed by her physician. The incident giving rise to the cause of action occurred in Massachusetts. The plaintiff was not a resident of New Hampshire at the time of filing suit and the defendant was an Indiana corporation engaged in marketing DES nationwide. The evidence indicated that the defendant engaged in limited advertising of its pharmaceutical products in trade journals in New Hampshire, that it employed eight sales representatives to provide information concerning its products to New Hampshire physicians, and three of its representatives were permanent residents of New Hampshire. The defendant neither directly nor indirectly sold its products in New Hampshire but rather distributed its products through wholesale distributors, some of whom were located in New Hampshire. The trial court dismissed plaintiff's cause for lack of personal jurisdiction, and the First Circuit affirmed. Following an analysis of *Worldwide Volkswagen Corp. v. Woodson*,[95] and *Helicopteros Nacionales de Columbia, S.A. v.*

---

91. *Id.* at 1872, n.8. Relying on Von Mehren & Trautman, *Jurisdiction to Adjudicate: A Suggested Analysis*, 79 HARV. L. REV. 1136 (1966) the court defines specific jurisdiction to mean "when a state exercises personal jurisdiction over a defendant in a suit arising out of or related to defendant's contracts with the forum."

92. *Id.* at 1872, n.9.

93. 104 S.Ct. 1868 (1984).

94. 744 F.2d 213 (1st Cir. 1984).

95. 444 U.S. 286 (1980).

Hall,[96] the Court noted that a fundamental consideration was whether the cause of action arose out of or was related to defendant's contacts with the forum state. Significantly, the Court observed that specific jurisdiction may be based on the relationship between the defendant, the forum, and the litigation involved, while general jurisdiction rested on minimal contacts considerably more stringent than those required for specific jurisdiction. The court then noted:

> General jurisdiction may be found in the absence of a relationship between a nonresident defendant's contacts with the forum and the cause of action where the defendant engages in the "continuous and systematic" pursuit of general business activities in the forum state. . . .
>
> Lilly's New Hampshire contacts, which are of primary importance under a general jurisdiction analysis, are indistinguishable from those of the defendant in *Seymour v. Parke, Davis & Co.*, 423 F.2d 584 (1st Cir. 1970). In *Seymour*, a manufacturer and distributor of another drug was sued in New Hampshire for injuries occurring in Massachusetts. The defendant maintained no office and engaged in no manufacturing in New Hampshire; it held no property there; it was not registered to do business there. Its only contacts with New Hampshire consisted of advertising and the activities of a half dozen salesmen, mostly New Hampshire residents, who accepted orders and disseminated product information to New Hampshire physicians, hospitals and retail pharmacies. *Id.* at 585. Noting '[t]he importance of differences,' we expressly distinguished *Perkins* and held that where 'defendant's only activities consist of advertising and employing salesmen to solicit orders, we think that fairness will not permit a state to assume jurisdiction.'[97]

The circuit court acknowledged that in *Helicopteros Nacionales* the United States Supreme Court expressly declined to address the issue whether defendant's minimal contacts would be sufficient to confer specific jurisdiction.[98] Under this analysis, the circuit court concluded that the United States Supreme Court impliedly suggests that the distinction between specific and general jurisdiction is probably dispositive where defendant's contacts with

---

96. 104 S.Ct. 1868 (1984).
97. 744 F.2d 213, 216-17 (1984).
98. *Id.* at 217

the forum state, though judicially cognizable, are minimal.

Despite the declared intent of Article 2031b to expand in personam jurisdiction to the furthest reach permissible under due process, the minimal contacts standard that governs in personam jurisdiction differs in degree depending on whether specific or general jurisdiction is invoked. Specific jurisdiction contemplates that a nonresident defendant's minimal contacts in the forum state form the basis of the cause of action being asserted by the plaintiff against the defendant in that forum. This means, basically, that the lawsuit arises out of or is related to defendant's contacts with the forum state. On the other hand, the assertion of in personam jurisdiction over a nonresident defendant for a claim arising in another state is deemed general jurisdiction and mandates that the minimal contacts be more significant than required for specific jurisdiction.[99] To support the general jurisdiction standard, the minimal contacts of the nonresident defendant must consist of conduct in the forum state that is "continuous and systematic".[100] Defendant's conduct must be such that it should reasonably anticipate being brought into court in the forum state. Irrespective of the provisions of Article 2031b, the minimal contacts standard for due process mandates that the nonresident's contacts constitute continuous and systematic general business contacts with the forum state.[101] Any lesser degree of the minimal contacts fails the due process test prescribed under the Fourteenth Amendment.

The United States Supreme Court in *Helicopteros Nacionales de Colombia v. Hall*[102] restated the longstanding principle that a nonresident defendant is subject to in personam jurisdiction of the forum state when the party engages in certain "minimum contacts" with the forum state "such that the maintenance of the suit does not offend 'traditional notions of fairplay and substantial justice'."[103] The most recent Texas case involving personal jurisdictional reflects adherence to this rule. In *C. W. Brown Machine Shop, Inc. v. Stanley Machinery Corp.*[104] a Texas corporation

---

99. Refer to notes 91-92 *supra* and accompanying text.

100. *See* Perkins v. Benguet Consolidated Mining Co., 342 U.S. 437 (1952); International Shoe Co. v. Washington, 326 U.S. 310 (1945).

101. 342 U.S. at 418; Keeton v. Hustler Magazine, Inc., 104 S.Ct. 1473 (1984).

102. 104 S. Ct. 1868 (1984).

103. International Shoe Co. v. Washington, 326 U.S. 310, 316 (1945).

104. 670 S.W.2d 791 (Tex. App.—Fort Worth 1984, no writ).

sought to recover for an allegedly defective machine it purchased from the defendant. The defendant maintained a place of business in no state other than Massachusetts, had not registered with the Texas Secretary of State, had no registered agent in Texas, maintained no employees in Texas, and had not advertised in Texas telephone directories or publications. The court observed that the mere fact that the defendant had advertised in national publications was insufficient to satisfy the "minimum contacts" standard.[105] Under *Helicopteros Nacionales,* the minimum contacts of a nonresident defendant must give rise to the claim asserted for constitutionally permissible exercise of general jurisdiction.

D. Special Appearance

A nonresident defendant may contest jurisdiction under the provisions of Rule 120a of the Texas Rules of Civil Procedure.[106] Rule 120a permits objection by the defendant to in personam jurisdiction "on the ground that such party . . . is not amenable to process issued by the courts of this State."[107] Rule 120a outlines the procedure by which jurisdiction may be contested.[108] Due order of pleading is critically important because "[e]very appearance, prior to judgment, not in compliance with this rule is a general appearance."[109] The defendant may elect to submit a general denial in the

---

105. *Id.* at 793; *Accord* Southern v. Glenn, 677 S.W.2d 576 (Tex. App.—San Antonio 1984, no writ); Steve Tyrell Prod. Inc. v. Ray, 674 S.W.2d 430 (Tex. App.—Austin 1984, no writ).

106. TEX. R. CIV. P. 120a:

> 1. . . . a special appearance may be made by any party either in person or by attorney for the purpose of objecting to the jurisdiction of the court over the person or property of the defendant on the grounds that such party or property is not amenable to process issued by the courts of this State. . . . Such special appearance shall be made by sworn motion filed prior to motion to transfer venue or any other plea, pleading or motion; provided however that a motion to transfer venue and any other plea, pleading, or motion may be contained in the same instrument or filed subsequent there to without waiver of such special appearance, and may be amended to cure defects. The issuance of process for witnesses, the taking of depositions, the serving of requests for admissions, and the use of discovery processes, shall not constitute a waiver of such special appearance. Every appearance, prior to judgment, not in compliance with this rule is a general appearance.

107. *Id.*

108. *Id.* "Such special appearance shall be made by sworn motion filed prior to motion to transfer venue or any other plea, pleading or motion; . . ."

109. Special appearance pleading is a technical process. For example, the filing of unsworn pleas by nonresident defendants followed by the appearance of counsel in open court

pleading which contains the special appearance. The special appearance, however, must appear at the beginning of the pleading and should be clearly distinguished from the remainder of the pleadings contained in the document. Unlike the motion to transfer venue, the defendant is impressed with the burden of pleading and proving lack of jurisdiction.[110] A decision overruling a defendant's motion to dismiss for want of jurisdictioin may not be reviewed on interlocutory appeal.[111] An appeal for lack of *in personam* jurisdiction requires a final judgment on the merits.[112] If the special appearance is sustained, the cause of action will be dismissed and the plaintiff is entitled to an immediate appeal.[113]

E. A Foreign Forum's Jurisdiction Over a Texas Corporation

When jurisdiction over a Texas corporation is exercised by a foreign forum, the jurisdictional issue must be carefully analyzed in light of that forum's "long-arm" statute. In *Country Clubs, Inc. v. Ward*,[114] a court judgment against a Texas corporation was entered based on a default judgment against the corporation previously entered by a Kentucky court.[115] The court recognized that each state must accord full faith and credit to the judicial proceedings of other states.[116] The court noted, however, that Texas courts must determine whether jurisdiction was properly exercised in the first instance by the foreign state.[117] Plaintiff's failure to comply strictly with the Kentucky "Long-Arm" statute foreclosed the Kentucky court from exercising in personam jurisdiction over the defendant.[118]

---

has been held to constitute a general appearance. *See* Stewart v. Walton Enter., Inc. 496 S.W.2d 956, 959 (Tex. Civ. App.—Austin 1973, writ ref'd n.r.e.).

110. Product Promotions, Inc. v. Cousteau, 495 F.2d 483, 489 (5th Cir. 1974); Tabulating Sys. & Serv., Inc. v. I.O.A. Data Corp., 498 S.W.2d 690, 695 (Tex. Civ. App.—Corpus Christi 1973, no writ).

111. Carpenter Body Works, Inc. v. McCulley, 389 S.W.2d 331, 332 (Tex. Civ. App.—Houston 1965, writ ref'd), *cert. denied*, 382 U.S. 979 (1966).

112. 389 S.W.2d at 332.

113. *See* Bodzin v. Regal Accessories, Inc., 437 S.W.2d 655, 656 (Tex. Civ. App.—Dallas 1969, writ ref'd n.r.e.).

114. 461 S.W.2d 651 (Tex. Civ. App.—Dallas 1970, writ ref'd n.r.e.).

115. *Id.* at 654.

116. *Id.* at 655.

117. *Id.*

118. *Id.* at 656.

In *Delray Beach Aviation Corp. v. Mooney Aircraft, Inc.*,[119] the plaintiff sought damages against Mooney Aircraft, Inc., a Texas corporation, for the loss of its plane which crashed in Florida allegedly due to a manufacturing defect.[120] Though the defendant had notice of the suit brought in Florida, it deliberately ignored the state summons and a default judgment was rendered by the Florida court.[121] The Fifth Circuit concluded that "Mooney Aircraft was engaged in business activity within the State of Florida and therefore [was] amenable to service of process."[122] The Florida default judgment was, therefore, subject to full faith and credit.[123]

F. *Pleading in Default Judgment Situations*

Default judgments against nonresidents raise unique issues. In *McKanna v. Edgar*[124] the Texas Supreme Court judicially declared that the plaintiff's petition did not properly allege the essential facts upon which service of process on the Secretary of State could provide jurisdiction necessary for default judgment. "[J]urisdiction in this type of case must affirmatively appear on the face of the record."[125] Therefore, to invoke Article 2031b, the plaintiff must specifically plead that the nonresident corporation was doing business in Texas and had neither designated an agent for process nor maintained a regular place of business in the state.[126]

The necessity for specificity and particularity in pleading is especially critical in default judgments.[127] A petition which alleges that the defendant is a foreign corporation but fails to allege that the corporation is doing or had done business in Texas, that the corporation is authorized or had a permit to do business in Texas, or that it failed to appoint an agent for the purpose of service, is

---

119. 332 F. 2d 135 (5th Cir.), *cert denied.*, 379 U.S. 915 (1964).

120. *Id.* at 137.

121. *Id.* at 141.

122. *Id.*

123. *Id.* at 144.

124. 388 S.W.2d 927 (Tex. 1965).

125. *Id.* at 930.

126. *Id.* at 929. *See* Tex. Rev. Civ. Stat, art. 2031b(3).

127. Firence Footwear Co. v Campbell, 411 S.W.2d 636 (Tex. Civ. App.—Houston 1967, writ ref'd n.r.e.). (where pleadings allege no facts that authorize service on the secretary of state and where it affirmatively appears that the defendant has not made an appearance, the court lacks jurisdiction to enter a default judgment).

fatal.[128] Plaintiff's petition must allege facts authorizing substituted service on the Secretary of State.[129] Otherwise, service on the Secretary of State is ineffectual to confer jurisdiction upon the trial court, and a default judgment is a nullity.[130]

9.02 VENUE

A. *Introduction*

On September 1, 1983, the Legislature adopted the revised Texas Venue Statute.[131] Critics urged that the earlier statute promoted appeal of venue questions that were consuming a disproportionate amount of appellate court time.[132] Under the amended statute, the venue process is noticeably simplified because the interlocutory appeal has been abolished.[133] A "mini-trial" no longer is necessary to prove that plaintiff possesses a cause of action.[134] A motion to transfer venue substitutes for the previous plea of privilege.[135]

B. *The Revised Texas Venue Statute As Compared With Prior Venue Law*

1. The General Rule. Prior to the September 1, 1983, revision of Article 1995, the general rule governing venue in Texas[136] stated that "[n]o person who is an inhabitant of this State shall be sued

---

128. *Id.* at 637.
129. *Id.* at 638.
130. *Id.*
131. TEX. REV. CIV. STAT. ANN. art. 1995 (Vernon Supp. 1985).
132. Others criticized "the overall vagueness of the statute's terminology and the discrimination between classes of defendants" and the fact that there was "no common principle, rationale, or organization to the venue rules." Price, *New Texas Venue Statute: Legislative History*, 15 ST. MARY'S L.J. 855, 859 (1984).
133. TEX. REV. CIV. STAT. ANN. art. 1995, sec. 4(d) (Vernon Supp. 1985). In an appeal on the merits the appellate court will consider the "entire record, including the trial on the merits." This means that if the venue determination by the trial court was erroneous, then it is a reversible error and the case will have to be tried in the county of proper venue. *See* Morrison v. Williams, 665 S.W.2d 212, 213 (Tex. Civ. App.—San Antonio 1984, no writ) ("Perhaps the most significant change is the elimination of the right to an interlocutory appeal from a venue determination. A court's venue determination may now be challenged only on appeal from a trial on the merits."). For a discussion of the legislative history regarding "Venue Appeal," *See* 15 ST. MARY'S L.J. at 875.
134. Refer to notes 152-53 *infra* and accompanying text.
135. Refer to note 236 *infra* and accompanying text.
136. TEX. REV. CIV. STAT. ANN. art. 1995 (Vernon 1964).

out of the county in which he has his domicile except [under certain exceptions]."[137] The concept of "domicile" referred to both the defendant's actual residence and the residence which he intended to make his home.[138] For venue purposes, therefore, a person could reside and be sued in more counties than just the county of actual residence.[139]

The Texas Supreme Court developed a three-part test[140] for determining whether a second residence had been established: residence was defined as:

> (1) A fixed place of abode within the possession of the defendant;
> (2) occupied or intended to be occupied consistently over a substantial period of time; and
> (3) which is permanent rather than temporary.[141]

Under the amended venue statute,[142] the general rule states that "[a]ll lawsuits, except as provided in Sections 2 and 3 of this article, shall be brought in the county where the cause of action or a part thereof accrued or in the county of defendant's residence if defendant is a natural person."[143]

Though the term "domicile" is not employed, presumably because prior law enabled a nondomiciliary to maintain a Texas residence for venue purposes, the *Snyder* definition of residence remains operative.[144] The addition of "if defendant is a natural person" to the general rule relating to defendant's residence limits the character of defendant covered by the general rule to individuals.[145] The venue rules govern corporations in the exceptions to the

---

137. *Id.*

138. Snyder v. Pitts, 241 S.W.2d 136, 139 (Tex. 1951).

139. *Id.* at 138-39; Covington v. Eskridge, 430 S.W.2d 589 (Tex. Civ. App. — San Antonio, 1968); Ward v. Fairway Operating Co., 364 S.W. 2d 194 (Tex. 1963).

140. Snyder v. Pitts, 241 S.W.2d 136 (Tex. 1951).

141. *Id.* at 140.

142. TEX. REV. CIV. STAT. ANN. art. 1995 (Vernon Supp. 1984).

143. *Id.*

144. Snyder v. Pitts, 150 Tex. 407, 412, 241 S.W.2d 136, 138 (1951). (the word "domicile," as used in the Texas Venue Statute, means a residence which is a lesser included element within the technical definition of domicile). Venue will be proper in the one or more counties where a natural person has a "residence" meeting the *Snyder* test. *See also* Covington v. Eskridge, 430 S.W.2d 589, 590 (Tex. Civ. App.—San Antonio 1968, no writ) (using the rule of Snyder v. Pitts, the court stated that it is possible for a person to have a "domiciliary residence" in Illinois and a second or "venue residence" in Texas.).

145. Although Ward v. Fairway Operating Co., 364 S.W.2d 194, 195 (Tex. 1963), held

general rule.[146]

The principal difference between the newly enacted general rule as compared to the old, however, is that the plaintiff is accorded the additional choice of initiating suit in the "county where the cause of action or a part thereof accrued."[147] Though the earlier venue statute authorized the plaintiff to exercise this option, the rule regarding venue in the county where the cause of action or a part thereof accrued was reflected as an exception to the general rule.[148]

The amended general venue rules effectuate a significant modification of the law. Under the earlier version of article 1995,[149] the plaintiff who asserted venue based on where the cause of action arose was compelled to rely on one of the exceptions to the general rule.[150] Consequently he was required to prove by a preponderance of the evidence that he in fact had a cause of action.[151] A plaintiff asserting venue based on where the cause of action or part thereof accrued was confronted with a "mini-trial" on the merits to establish a cause of action and that venue was proper in the county in which the suit was filed. The current statute eliminates the "mini-trial" by relegating this venue option to the general rule. For venue purposes, plaintiff no longer is obligated to prove a cause of action.[152] This change, therefore, creates a significant procedural

---

that "the place of its designated registered office and agent shall constitute a statutory place of residence of the corporation where it can always be found," it is unlikely that the new Article 1995 General Rule would apply to corporations, partnerships or associations because of the inclusion of the phrase "if defendant is a natural person."

146. TEX. REV. CIV. STAT. ANN. art. 1995, §§ 3(f), 3(g), 3(c) (Vernon Supp. 1985).

147. TEX. REV. CIV. STAT. ANN. art. 1995 § 1 (Vernon Supp. 1985).

148. TEX. REV. CIV. STAT. ANN. art. 1995, subdivs. 23, 27 (Vernon 1964), subdiv. 31 (Vernon Supp. 1976).

149. TEX. REV. CIV. STAT. ANN. art 1995 (Vernon 1964).

150. Refer to note 148 *supra*.

151. *See* Employers Casualty Co. v. Clark, 491 S.W.2d 661, 662 (Tex. 1973) *quoting* Victoria Bank & Trust Co. v. Monteith, 138 Tex. 216, 158 S.W.2d 63 (1941) ("To prove that a cause of action has arisen in his favor a plaintiff must prove that he in fact has a cause of action.").

152. *See* TEX. REV. CIV. STAT. ANN. art. 1995, sec. 4(d) (Vernon Supp. 1985):

> Hearings. (1) In all venue hearings, no factual proof concerning the merits of the case shall be required to establish venue; the court shall determine venue questions from the pleadings and affidavits.

See also TEX. R. CIV. P. 87(2)(b):

> Cause of Action. It shall not be necessary for a claimant to prove the merits of a cause of action, but the existence of a cause of action, when pleaded properly, shall be taken as established as alleged by the pleadings.

modification. If the defendant specifically denies plaintiff's venue allegations, the plaintiff may establish a prima facie proof of venue by affidavit.[153]

Both the earlier general rule and the amended general rule contain exceptions.[154] Under the current statutory scheme, the exceptions are divided into mandatory[155] and permissive exceptions.[156] The mandatory exception provides that the suit "must" or "shall" be brought in a given county. The permissive exception, on the other hand, states that suit "may" be brought in designated counties.

When a plaintiff files suit, the importance of whether the venue choice is mandatory or permissive does not arise unless and until the defendant asserts that venue is improper. Mandatory venue choices necessarily prevail over both permissive venue choices and the option outlined in the general rule. Therefore, when a plaintiff files suit in a proper county under either the general rule[157] or permissive exception,[158] the defendant may only rely on a mandatory exception[159] when filing a motion to transfer venue.[160] This means that the defendant may file a motion to transfer venue only to a county of mandatory venue if plaintiff's venue option is proper, but not mandatory.[161] If the plaintiff filed suit in a county of improper venue, or an "impartial trial cannot be had in the county where the action is pending,"[162] then the defendant may utilize the general rule or any of the mandatory or permissive exceptions when filing a motion to transfer venue to a proper county.[163]

---

153. Refer to text accompanying notes 259-62 *infra*.

154. See discussion of "Venue Choice" in 15 St. Mary's L.J. at 868.

155. Tex. Rev. Civ. Stat. Ann. art. 1995, § 2 (Vernon Supp. 1985).

156. *Id.* art. 1995, § 3.

157. *Id.* art. 1995, § 1.

158. *Id.* art. 1995, § 3.

159. *Id.* art. 1995, § 2.

160. *Id.* art. 1995, § 4(c); Tex. R. Civ. P. 86(3)(b).

161. Tex. R. Civ. P. 86(3)(b), 87(3)(c).

162. Tex. Rev. Civ. Stat. Ann. art. 1995, 4(c)(2) (Vernon Supp. 1985) states that:

> The court, upon motion filed and served concurrently with or before the filing of the answer, shall transfer an action to another county of proper venue where: . . . (2) an impartial trial cannot be had in the county where the action is pending . . .

163. When more than one mandatory provision applies, in other words, if there is an apparent conflict between two provisions of "equal rank," the principal relief sought will most likely control the matter. *See* Brown v. Gulf Television Co., 157 Tex. 607, 611, 306

2. *Exceptions to the General Rule Relating to Products Liability.* When suit is instituted against a defendant under strict tort liability and venue is not based on the general rule, plaintiff must elect venue based on one of the exceptions that apply to a claim relating to strict tort liability.[164] Otherwise, a motion to transfer will be determinative.

a. *Nonresidents; Residence Unknown.* Prior to September 1, 1983, the venue statute incorporated an exception to the general rule which provided that "if one or all of several defendants reside without the State or if their residence is unknown, suit may be brought in the county in which plaintiff resides."[165] Section 3(j)[166] of the current statute is identical to the earlier subdivision 3; therefore, suit may still be brought in the county where the plaintiff resides if one or all of the defendants reside outside of the state.

b. *Suits Against Multiple Parties and Suits Involving Multiple Claims.* Unlike amended section 3(j),[167] which incorporates prior law, section 4(a)[168] substantially alters its earlier counterpart. Under the earlier venue statute, subdivisions 4[169] and 29a[170] governed venue in suits involving multiple defendants. Subdivision 4 of the earlier venue statute stated that "if suit is brought against two or more defendants, suit may be brought in any county where one of the defendants resides."[171] Under subdivision 4, a plaintiff was obligated to prove that (1) one defendant was a resident of the county of suit; (2) the party asserting the plea of privilege was a

---

S.W.2d 706, 708 (1957); Gonzalez v. Texaco, Inc., 645 S.W.2d 324, 327 (Tex. App.—Corpus Christi 1982, no writ). Both cases held that where the venue depends on the nature of the suit, venue is determined by the nature of the principal right asserted.

164. The exceptions applicable to a strict liability suit are found in Tex. Rev. Civ. Stat. Ann. art. 1995, §§ 3(c), 3(f), 3(g) and 3(j) (Vernon Supp. 1985). They are all permissive. Section 4(a), although not an exception, applies to a plaintiff suing two or more defendants.

165. Tex. Rev. Civ. Stat. Ann. art. 1995, subdiv. 3 (Vernon 1964).

166. *Id.* art. 1995, § 3(j) (Vernon Supp. 1985).

167. *Id.* art. 1995, § 3(j).

168. *Id.* art. 1995, § 4(a).

169. *Id.* art. 1995, subdiv. 4 (Vernon 1964).

170. *Id.* art. 1995, subdiv. 29a.

171. *Id.* art. 1995, subdiv 4.

proper party to the claim against the resident defendant;[172] and (3) the plaintiff was asserting a bona fide claim against the resident defendant.[173]

The prior rule enunciated in subdivision 29a[174] of article 1995 stated that "where there are two or more defendants, suit may be maintained against all necessary parties if venue is lawfully maintainable as to any defendant under any other exception of article 1995."[175] In asserting venue under subdivision 29a, the plaintiff was obligated to establish that the defendant asserting the plea of privilege[176] was a necessary party to the action[177] and that venue was maintainable under article 1995 in the county of suit as to a co-defendant.[178]

Under the earlier venue statute, subdivision 29a differed from subdivision 4 in that (1) subdivision 29a was inapplicable if any defendant was a resident of the county of suit,[179] and (2) only necessary parties were allowed to be joined under 29a, provided venue was maintainable against one or more defendants under article

---

172. *See* H. Molsen & Co. v. Williamson, 510 S.W.2d 366, 368-69 (Tex. Civ. App.—Dallas 1974, no writ) ("under subdivision 4 suit may be maintained in the county of the domicile of one defendant against all other defendants not domiciled there who are proper parties.")

173. Chem-Spray Aerosols, Inc. v. Edwards, 576 S.W.2d 478, 479-80 (Tex. Civ. App.—Houston [14th Dist.] 1979, writ dism'd). In order to prove a bona fide claim in strict tort liability against a manufacturer, the plaintiff must show that the manufacturer was "engaged in the business of selling such products at the time of sale; that the product was expected to reach a user or consumer without substantial change in the condition in which it was sold; that the product contained a defect; that the defect existed at the time the [manufacturer] relinquished control of the product; and that the defect was a producing cause of the [plaintiff's] injuries." *Id.* at 480. *See also* Socony Mobil Co. v. Southwestern Bell Tel. Co., 518 S.W.2d 257, 263 (Tex. Civ. App.—Corpus Christi 1974, no writ); Mobile County Mut. Ins. Co. v. Maldonado, 506 S.W.2d 639, 641 (Tex. Civ. App.—San Antonio 1973, no writ); Stockyards Nat'l Bank v. Maples, 127 Tex. 633, 638, 95 S.W.2d 1300, 1302-03 (Comm. App. 1936).

174. TEX. REV. CIV. STAT. ANN. art. 1995, subdiv. 29a (Vernon 1964).

175. *Id.*

176. TEX. R. CIV. P. 86 (Vernon 1979).

177. Schwertner v. Nalco Chem. Co., 615 S.W.2d 263, 266 (Tex. Civ. App.—Tyler 1981, writ dism'd) ("a party is a necessary party under 29a only if complete relief cannot be obtained without the joinder of such party."); *accord* Duval County Ranch Co. v. Wooldridge, 667 S.W.2d 887, 896 (Tex. App.—Austin 1984, no writ); Mote Resources, Inc. v. Northridge Oil Co., 667 S.W.2d 179, 181 (Tex. App.—Texarkana 1983, no writ).

178. White Stores, Inc. v. Fielding, 533 S.W.2d 431, 433 (Tex. Civ. App.—Corpus Christi 1976, no writ).

179. Mobile County Mut. Ins. Co., 506 S.W.2d at 642. *See also* General Motors Corp. v. Brady, 477 S.W.2d 385, 391 (Tex. Civ. App.—Tyler 1972, no writ).

1995.[180] Therefore, subdivision 29a mandated suit against two or more defendants,[181] none of whom could be residents of the county of suit.[182]

Amended section 4(a)[183] eliminates the provisions of these earlier statutory sections governing multiple defendants. It provides that if an action is proper as to one defendant, it is proper as to all other defendants that are properly joined. This provision that the defendants be properly joined eliminates any requirement that they represent necessary parties.

Also under the amended section 4(a),[184] if venue of the action is proper as to one claim in a suit alleging multiple claims, it is proper as to all other claims which are properly joined, unless a mandatory venue exception controls the disposition of one or more of the claims. This provision codifies the longstanding principle characterized as the "Middlebrook Doctrine."[185] In *Middlebrook v. David Bradley Manufacturing Co.*,[186] the court declared that if venue is proper as to one of several claims against the same defendant, the other claims against the same defendant which are properly joined may be tried jointly to avoid a multiplicity of suits.[187] The Middlebrook Doctrine was subject to the limitation that (1) the claim upon which venue is based must be asserted in good faith;[188] (2) a mandatory exception prevails over this doctrine;[189] and (3) the doctrine may not be employed to sustain venue against a defendant who is not a party to the in-county claim or cause of action.[190] The Middlebrook Doctrine and its limitations form the

---

180. 506 S.W.2d at 643.

181. Boyd v. Thompson-Hayward Chem. Co., 450 S.W.2d 937, 946 (Tex. Civ. App.—Tyler 1970, writ dism'd).

182. 506 S.W.2d at 642.

183. TEX. REV. CIV. STAT. ANN. art. 1995, § 4(a) (Vernon Supp. 1985).

184. *Id.*

185. This principle was developed in the case of Middlebrook v. David Bradley Mfg. Co., 86 Tex. 706, 26 S.W. 935 (1894), and it has been applied to sustain venue as to a claim added by an amended pleading.

186. 86 Tex. 706, 26 S.W. 935 (1894).

187. *See* TEX. R. CIV. P. 51.

188. Noel v. Griffin & Brand of McAllen, Inc., 478 S.W.2d 633, 635 (Tex. Civ. App.—Corpus Christi 1972, no writ).

189. Pinkston v. Farmers State Bank, 201 S.W.2d 595, 603 (Tex. Civ. App.—Beaumont 1947, no writ).

190. City of Gilmer v. State, 281 S.W.2d 109, 110-13 (Tex. Civ. App.—Austin 1955, no writ).

basis for the rule incorporated in amended section 4(a).[191]

c. *Suits Against Domestic Corporations.* Before Article 1995 was amended, subdivision 23[192] authorized:

> suits against a private corporation, association or joint-stock company . . . in the county in which its principal office is situated; or in the county in which the cause of action or part thereof arose; or in the county in which the plaintiff resided at the time the cause of action or part thereof arose, provided such corporation, association or company has an agency or representative in such county; or if the corporation . . . had no agency or representative in the county in which the plaintiff resided at the time the cause of action or part thereof arose, then suit may be brought in the county nearest that in which plain tiff resided at said time in which the corporation . . . then had an agency or representative.[193]

This subidivision[194] imposed on the plaintiff the burden of proving the elements of the cause of action alleged in the case.[195] In *Lubbock Manufacturing Co. v. Sames*,[196] plaintiff endeavored to maintain venue under subdivision 23 in the county where the accident occurred. The trial court sustained venue on the basis that the alleged defective product caused damages in the county where suit was instituted. The Texas Supreme Court concluded that the mere occurrence of product-caused harm in the forum county establishes venue under subdivision 23.[197]

In *John Deere Co. v. Ramirez*,[198] the court enumerated the elements required to prove a cause of action based on strict tort liability under subdivision 23:

> (1) The manufacturer sold the product in a defective condition;

---

191. TEX. REV. CIV. STAT. ANN. art. 1995, § 4(a) (Vernon Supp. 1985).

192. *Id.* art. 1995, subdiv. 23 (Vernon 1964).

193. *Id.*

194. White Stores, Inc. v. Fielding, 533 S.W.2d 431 (Tex. Civ. App.—Corpus Christi 1976, no writ).

195. *Id.* at 432. *See also* Ford Motor Co. v. Stead, 574 S.W.2d 226, 229 (Tex. Civ. App.—Waco 1978, no writ).

196. 598 S.W.2d 234 (Tex. 1980); *accord* USLIFE Title Ins. Co. v. Howard, 603 S.W.2d 322, 324-25 (Tex. Civ. App.—Amarillo 1980, no writ).

197. 598 S.W.2d at 236.

198. 503 S.W.2d 382 (Tex. Civ. App.—Amarillo 1974, writ dism'd).

(2) The product reached the plaintiff without substantial change; and

(3) The product caused the injury to the plaintiff.[199]

The amended venue statute virtually duplicates subdivision 23. Amended section 3(f)[200] now includes partnerships as well as corporations, associations, and joint stock companies. Because of the similarity between the earlier and the amended provision regarding venue of domestic corporations, the established decisional law remains operative.[201]

d. Suits Against Foreign Corporations. Previous subdivision 27[202] authorized suits against foreign corporations, private or public, joint stock companies or associations, not incorporated by the laws of Texas, and doing business within Texas:

> in any county where the cause of action or a part thereof accrued, or in any county where such company may have an agency or representative, or in the county in which the principal office of such company may be situated; or, when the defendant corporation has no agent or representative in this State, then in the county where the plaintiffs or either of them, reside.[203]

The court in *John Deere v. Ramirez*[204] enumerated the elements for venue under subdivision 27. Under subdivision 27, the plaintiff was obligated to establish that the defendant:

(a) was a foreign corporation,

(b) was doing business in Texas, and

(c) was maintaining an agent or representative in the county of suit.[205]

A foreign corporation that maintained an agent or representa-

---

199. *Id.* at 384; *accord* Pittsburgh Corning Corp. v. Thomas, 668 S.W.2d 876, 878 (Tex. App.—Houston [14th Dist.] 1984, no writ).

200. TEX. REV. CIV. STAT. ANN. art. 1995, § 3(f) (Vernon Supp. 1985).

201. Lubbock Manufacturing Co. v. Sames, 598 S.W.2d 234 (Tex. 1980); John Deere Co. v. Ramirez, 503 S.W.2d 382 (Tex. Civ. App. — Amarillo 1974, writ dism'd); Pittsburgh Corning Corp. v. Thomas, 668 S.W.2d 876, 878 (Tex. App. — Houston [14th Dist.] 1984, no writ).

202. TEX. REV. CIV. STAT. ANN. art. 1995, subdiv. 27 (Vernon 1964).

203. *Id. See* White Stores, Inc. v. Fielding, 533 S.W.2d 431, 433 (Tex. Civ. App.—Corpus Christi 1976, no writ) (under subdivision 27, the plaintiff had to prove that the defendant was in fact a foreign corporation).

204. 503 S.W.2d 382 (Tex. Civ. App.—Amarillo 1974, writ dism'd).

205. *Id.* at 384.

tive in the county where the suit was instituted eliminated the necessity of proving a cause of action to maintain venue in that county.[206] Proof of a cause of action was necessary, however, to maintain venue against a domestic corporation. Despite foreign and domestic corporations being viewed differently under the earlier venue statute, the constitutionality of subdivision 27 was upheld by the United States Supreme Court.[207]

The amended statute provides for venue against a foreign corporation in section 3(g).[208] This section repeats verbatim earlier subdivision 27. In light of this duplication, it is reasonable to assume that the judicial interpretation of subdivision 27 continues to govern section 3(g).[209]

e. *Suits for Breach of Warranty by a Manufacturer.* The prior venue statute provided, in subdivision 31,[210] that venue in suits for breach of warranty by a manufacturer of consumer goods was proper in the county where the plaintiff resided.[211] This venue provision could not be invoked when the plaintiff failed to introduce evidence that the defendant was, in fact, the manufacturer of the goods.[212]

Under prior subdivision 31, plaintiff was obligated to establish that, (1) suit was for breach of warranty; (2) the defendant was the manufacturer; (3) the product was a consumer good;[213] and (4) the suit was instituted in the county of the plaintiff's residence.[214]

---

206. See Hanover Ins. Co. v. Sanford, 457 S.W.2d 115, 117-18 (Tex. Civ. App.—Beaumont 1970, no writ).

207. American Motorists Ins. Co. v. Starnes, 425 U.S. 637 (1976).

208. Tex. Rev. Civ. Stat. Ann. art. 1995 § 3(g) (Vernon Supp. 1985).

209. Refer to notes 204-07 *supra*.

210. Tex Rev. Civ. Stat. Ann. art. 1995, subdiv. 31 (Vernon Supp. 1976).

211. The other possible places for suit provided by subdivision 31 were already available. *See* 1 R. McDonald, Texas Civil Practice § 4.37.1 (Supp. 1976).

212. Burrows v. Texas Kenworth Co., 554 S.W.2d 300, 304 (Tex. Civ. App.—Tyler 1977, writ dism'd).

213. For cases discussing the definition of "consumer goods" *see* Schwertner v. Nalco Chem. Co., 615 S.W.2d 263, 266 (Tex. Civ. App.—Tyler 1981, writ dism'd) (an agricultural use product is not a consumer good under subdivision 31); Gorman-Rupp Corp. v. Kirk, 601 S.W.2d 49, 50-51 (Tex. Civ. App.—Houston [1st Dist.] 1980, no writ) (Consumer goods are "those goods used or bought for use primarily for personal, family or household use." An industrial water pump is, therefore, not a consumer good.).

214. John Deere Co. v. Whitley, 597 S.W.2d 43, 45 (Tex. Civ. App.—Amarillo 1980, writ dism'd). *See also* Gorman-Rupp Corp. v. Kirk, 601 S.W.2d 49, 50 (Tex. Civ. App.—Houston [1st Dist.] 1980, no writ); Trucker's Equip., Inc. v. Sandoval, 569 S.W.2d

Amended Article 1995 sec. 3(c) governs venue in suits for breach of warranty by a manufacturer:[215]

> Suits for Breach of Warranty by a manufacturer of consumer goods may be brought in any county where the cause of action or a part thereof accrued, or in any county where such manufacturer may have an agent or representative, or in the county in which the principal office of such company may be situated, or in the county where the plaintiff or plaintiffs reside.[216]

Similar to predecessor subdivision 31, amended section 3(c) provides for venue in the county where the plaintiff resides. This provision introduces an additional venue option to the choices already provided for in the exceptions applicable to domestic and foreign corporations.

3. Counterclaims, Cross-Claims and Third Party Claims. Section 4(b)[217] of the amended venue statute states that "[v]enue of the main action shall establish venue of a counterclaim, cross-claim, or third party claim properly joined under the Texas Rules of Civil Procedure."[218] The earlier venue statute[219] contained no provision specifically governing venue for counterclaims,[220] cross-claims[221] and third party actions;[222] therefore, the earlier rules were

---

518, 522 (Tex. Civ. App.—Corpus Christi 1978, no writ).

215. Tex. Rev. Civ. Stat. Ann. art. 1995, § 3(c) (Vernon Supp. 1985).

216. *Id.*

217. *Id.* art. 1995, § 4(b) (Vernon Supp. 1985).

218. *Id.*

219. *Id.* art. 1995 (Vernon 1964).

220. Tex. R. Civ. P. 97(a) and 97(b). *See* Schero V. Manges, 648 S.W.2d 358, 359-61 (Tex. App.—San Antonio 1983, no writ), wherein the court held that:

> a plaintiff who institutes a suit in a county other than that of his residence submits to the jurisdiction of the court of that county as to all matters growing directly out of the subject matter of the suit, and thereby waives his right to insist on his privilege to be sued in the county of his domicile on a cause of action of that character asserted in a cross-action.

Id. at 359.

221. Tex. R. Civ. P. 97(e).

222. *See* Tex. R. Civ. P. 38 and Tex. Rev. Civ. Stat. Ann. art. 2212a, § 2(g) (Vernon Supp. 1985). The case of Union Bus Lines v. Byrd, 142 Tex. 257, 177 S.W.2d 774, 775-76 (1944) stated the rule that in considering venue with regard to a third party defendant, a court must view a third party action as separate and distinct from the principal action. *Accord*, Coquina Oil Corp. v. Sojourner Drilling Corp., 515 S.W.2d 172, 173 (Tex. Civ. App.—Eastland 1974, no writ).

The case of Arthur Brothers, Inc. v. U.M.C., Inc., 647 S.W. 2d 244, 246 (Tex. 1982), however, overruled Union Bus Lines. *Accord* Lane Wood, Inc. v. Grayco Mobile Homes,

governed by the Texas Rules of Civil Procedure and the cases interpreting those rules.[223]

The amended venue statute adopts the established rules of procedure and the existing decisional law governing counterclaims, cross-claims and third party claims.[224] The statute also reflects the decision authored in *Arthur Brothers, Inc. v. U.M.C., Inc.*[225] The court determined that "the purpose of article 2212a, section 2(g)[226] is to avoid separate trials of the plaintiff's claims and contribution claims against several defendants. The purpose of the statute is achieved by maintaining the contribution claims against several defendants in the original suit."[227] *Arthur Brothers*[228] and subsequently, Article 1995 sec. 4(b),[229] creates ancillary venue for all cross-actions.

4. *Procedural Changes*

a. Venue Practice Prior to September 1, 1983. Before article 1995 was amended, a defendant challenged plaintiff's venue by filing a sworn plea of privilge.[230] This plea contained a formal allega-

---

Inc., 668 S.W.2d 892, 893 (Tex. App.—Houston [14th Dist.] 1984, no writ). *But see* Bohnert v. Barbour, 679 S.W.2d 700 (Tex. App.—San Antonio 1984).

223. Refer to notes 218-220 *supra*.

224. Tex. Rev. Civ. Stat. Ann. art. 1995, § 4(b) (Vernon Supp. 1985).

225. 647 S.W.2d 244 (Tex. 1982).

226. Tex. Rev. Civ. Stat. Ann. art. 2212a, § 2(g) (Vernon Supp. 1985) provides: All claims for contribution between named defendants in the primary suit shall be determined in the primary suit, except that a named defendant may proceed against a person not a party to the primary suit who has not effected a settlement with the claimant.

227. 647 S.W.2d at 246.

228. 647 S.W.2d 244 (Tex. 1982).

229. Tex. Rev. Civ. Stat. Ann. art. 1995, § 4(b) (Vernon Supp. 1985).

230. Tex. R. Civ. P. 86 (Vernon 1982):

> A plea of privilege to be sued in the county of one's residence shall be in writing and sworn to, and shall state that the party claiming such privilege was not, at the institution of such suit, nor at the time of the service of process therein, nor at the time of filing such plea, a resident of the county in which suit was instituted, and shall state the county of his residence, and the post office address of himself or his attorney and that "no exception to exclusive venue in the county of one's residence provided by the law exists in said cause."
>
> A plea of privilege to be sued in a county other than the county of one's residence shall be in writing and sworn to and shall state that the party filing the plea is asserting venue under and by virtue of one or more specific statutory provisions which shall be clearly designated or indicated.
>
> When a plea of privilege is filed in accordance with this rule, it shall be prima facie proof of the defendant's right to change of venue; provided that such plea

tion that "no exception to exclusive venue in the county of one's residence provided by law exists in said cause."[231] To maintain venue in the county where suit was brought, plaintiff was compelled to file a controverting plea, under oath, which enumerated the specific grounds upon which venue was predicated.[232]

To determine which party had asserted proper venue, a trial on the venue facts was held[233] in which evidence was introduced.[234] After a ruling on the plea of privilege, either party was authorized to pursue an interlocutory appeal of the decision.[235]

b. Venue Practice After September 1, 1983. Since amendment of article 1995, a defendant no longer challenges venue by filing a plea of privilege. The defendant may properly challenge venue only by filing a motion to transfer venue. The motion must be filed concurrently with or prior to the filing of any other responsive pleading.[236]

Section 4(c),[237] the motion to transfer section of amended Article 1995, provides:

> (c) Transfer. The court, upon motion filed and served concurrently with or before the filing of the answer, shall transfer an action to another county of proper venue where:
>
> (1) the county where the action is pending is not a proper county as provided by this Act; or
>
> (2) an impartial trial cannot be had in the county where the action is pending; or
>
> (3) written consent of the parties to transfer to any other county is filed at any time.[238]

---

shall nor constitute a denial under oath of any allegations of plaintiff's petition required to be denied under oath by Rule 93 unless specifically alleged in such plea.

231. *Id.*

232. *Id.*

233. TEX. R. CIV. P. 87 (Vernon 1982).

234. *See* McElyea V. Bowles, 233 S.W.2d 482 (Tex. Civ. App.—Fort Worth 1950, no writ).

235. Wiley v. Joiner, 223 S.W.2d 539 (Tex. Civ.App.—Fort Worth 1949, no writ).

236. TEX. REV. CIV. STAT. ANN. art. 1995, § 4(c) (Vernon Supp. 1985); TEX. R. CIV. P. 86 states that the motion to transfer must be filed "prior to or concurrently with any other plea, pleading or motion except a special appearance motion provided for in Rule 120a."

237. TEX. REV. CIV. STAT. ANN. art 1995, § 4(c) (Vernon Supp. 1985).

238. *Id. See also* TEX. R. CIV. P. 86. TEX. R. CIV. P. 84, 85, 120a and 527 have been amended by replacing all references to pleas of privilege with references to motions to transfer venue.

A motion to transfer venue must state either that the county where the suit was filed is not a proper county[239] or that mandatory venue of the action in another county is prescribed by statute.[240] If any venue fact is controverted by the defendant, the motion must specifically deny those venue facts; a pleaded venue fact not specifically denied is deemed admitted for venue purposes.[241] The motion to transfer must also request transfer of the case to a specific county where venue is proper under the statute.[242]

Unlike the requirements prescribed by prior law, the motion to transfer venue need not be verified.[243] Merely pleading venue facts establishes those facts for venue purposes, unless specifically denied by the plaintiff. The attachment of affidavits to the motion for transfer of venue constitutes prima facie proof of the essential venue facts.[244]

Texas Rule of Civil Procedure 86(4)[245] prescribes that the plaintiff need not respond to the motion to transfer venue except as provided in Rule 87(3)(a).[246] This rule[247] also provides that "verification of a response is not required."[248] Under Rule 87(3)(a),[249] however, to avoid transfer, the plaintiff must respond to defendant's motion to transfer venue, (1) by supplying prima facie proof of venue facts pleaded by the plaintiff in the original petition and specifically denied by the defendant in the motion to transfer venue,[250] and (2) by specifically denying any venue facts pleaded

---

239. TEX. R. CIV. P. 86(3)(a).

240. TEX. R. CIV. P. 86(3)(b).

241. TEX. R. CIV. P. 87(3)(a) (The particular section of the venue provision must be stated in the motion).

242. TEX. R. CIV. P. 86(3)(b). Defendent may seek transfer to any county that comes under the General Rule of Article 1995, and he may also seek transfer of venue to any county of proper venue as listed in the exceptions in Section 3. (Under the new law corporations no longer have residence under the General Rule—only "natural persons.")

243. TEX. R. CIV. P. 93, before amended, stated that a pleading setting up that "suit is not commenced in the proper county" must be verified. The new Texas Rule of Civil Procedure 93 no longer requires this certain pleading to be verified. Also, Rule 86(3) expressly says that the motion need not be verified.

244. TEX. R. CIV. P. 87(3)(a).

245. TEX. R. CIV. P. 86(4).

246. TEX. R. CIV. P. 87(3)(a).

247. TEX. R. CIV. P. 86(4).

248. *Id.*

249. TEX. R. CIV. P. 87(3)(a).

250. TEX. R. CIV. P. 86(4) and 87(3)(a).

by the defendant to make venue proper in the county to which transfer is sought.[251] The plaintiff must attach affidavits to his response to demonstrate prima facie proof of the venue facts specifically denied by defendant.[252]

A significant difference between the earlier statute and the amended statute is that the plaintiff no longer is obligated to introduce prima facie evidence of the existence of a cause of action, even if the defendant specifically denies the existence of a cause of action.[253] Once the plaintiff specifically denies the venue facts in the motion to transfer venue, the defendant, to preserve the motion, must file a reply to plaintiff's response.[254]

Pursuant to Rule 87(1), the determination of whether to grant defendant's motion to transfer venue is made by the court.[255] The defendant is obligated to request and obtain a hearing.[256] At the hearing, the plaintiff possesses the burden of establishing that the county where the suit is filed is proper.[257] Unlike the earlier discarded venue practice, oral testimony is not presented at the hearing and the court's decision is not subject to interlocutory appeal.[258]

The court examines the original petition to determine whether the plaintiff has properly pleaded the existence of a cause of action and facts sufficient to support venue. If the plaintiff has pleaded properly, the court is obligated to ascertain whether the defendant's motion specifically denies any of the plaintiff's venue facts. If the defendant has not specifically denied plaintiff's venue facts, the court will deny the defendant's motion to transfer venue, provided the court is satisfied (1) that venue is proper where the suit is filed, (2) that the defendant has not asserted mandatory venue, and (3) that the plaintiff has not elected a mandatory venue initially. The defendant's specific denial of plaintiff's venue facts compels the court to examine plaintiff's response to determine

---

251. *Id.*

252. TEX. REV. CIV. STAT. ANN. art. 1995, § 4(d)(1) and TEX. R. CIV. P. 87(3)(a).

253. TEX. R. CIV. P. 87(2)(b).

254. TEX. R. CIV. P. 86(4) and 87(3)(a), TEX. REV. CIV. STAT. ANN. art. 1995, § 4 (Vernon Supp. 1985).

255. TEX. R. CIV. P. 87(1).

256. *Id.* The plaintiff may also request a setting for the hearing, but the duty is on the defendant.

257. TEX. R. CIV. P. 87(3)(b).

258. TEX. R. CIV. P. 87(3)(c).

whether the response contains adequate prima facie proof of the asserted venue facts.[259] The plaintiff's failure to plead facts sufficient to support venue or the plaintiff's failure to establish prima facie proof of the pleaded but specifically denied venue facts mandates that the court sustain defendant's motion to transfer venue. Of course, the defendant must satisfy the burden to either plead sufficient facts to support venue or to provide prima facie proof of the venue facts pleaded but which the plaintiff has specifically denied.[260] Further, the plaintiff will be penalized for selecting a county of improper venue because the trial court is directed to tax against the plaintiff all costs which have accrued until the date the suit is filed in the court to which it has been transferred.[261] An erroneous denial of a motion to transfer venue constitutes reversible error per se and the case will be reversed and relitigated in the proper county.[262]

C. *The Effective Date Problem*

When article 1995 was amended, the effective date for implementation was established as September 1, 1983. Clearly, cases filed after September 1, 1983, are governed by the amended venue statute.[263] The problem has arisen, however, regarding the law applicable to venue questions arising in cases filed prior to September 1, 1983, but heard after that date. The statute[264] fails to provide for venue issues in cases pending in a trial court.[265]

Application of the usual rules of statutory construction appears to dictate that the earlier venue statute governs all cases filed before September 1, 1983. The landmark case of *Baines v. Jemison*[266] established the rule of construction applicable to the "effective date" issue. This case involved a suit to recover for wrongful levy on the plaintiff's property. Suit was filed in March of

---

259. Hazel, *Venue Procedure In The Trial Court*, 1984 TEX. B.J. 625, 627.

260. TEX. R. CIV. P. 87(3)(c).

261. TEX. R. CIV. P. 89.

262. Refer to note 133 *supra*.

263. TEX. REV. CIV. STAT. ANN. art. 1995 (Vernon Supp. 1985).

264. Act of June 17, 1983, ch. 385, §§ 2-3, 1983 Tex. Sess. Law Serv. 2119, 2124-2125 (Vernon).

265. Section 3 of the bill states that "this Act takes effect September 1, 1983, and shall not apply to pending appeals. On venue questions pending prior to September 1, 1983, the former law is continued in effect."

266. 86 Tex. 118, 23 S.W. 639 (Tex. 1893).

1887, and the case was decided in November of 1893. During that time the applicable venue statute was amended twice. The court acknowledged the prerogative of the legislature to make application of the amendments retroactive; however, "its intention would have to be clear before the courts would give the statute such a retroactive effect."[267] The court concluded that "the act in question was intended to apply only to future actions;" therefore, the law existing when the suit was filed controlled.[268]

After *Baines v. Jemison*,[269] the courts have consistently reaffirmed that, when amending a statute, the legislature's intent in providing for an effective date is to govern suits filed prior to the effective date of the existing statute. All suits filed on or after the effective date are governed by the amended statute.[270]

Further, the legislative intent to establish retroactive application must be clear. The court in *Blakely v. Commercial Union Assurance Co.*[271] concluded that an intention to alter the "status of the case as to the court in which it was commenced" will be found only when "plainly manifested" in the language of the statute. It is unclear whether the legislature intended the amended venue statute[272] to apply to actions pending at the trial court stage.

The recent case of *Gonzalez v. H. E. Butt Grocery*[273] defined Section 3[274] to mean that if "there was a *venue question pending* prior to September 1, 1983, . . . the former law is to be applied."[275] The court, therefore, refused to limit the earlier statute's application only to cases in which appeal had been perfected prior to Sep-

---

267. *Id.* at 640.

268. *Id.*

269. 86 Tex. 118, 23 S.W. 639 (1893).

270. *See* General Electric Credit Corp. v. Gutierrez, 668 S.W. 2d 463, 465 (Tex. App.—Corpus Christi 1984, no writ); Cacanay Corp. v. Shepherd, 336 S.W.2d 779, 782 (Tex. Civ. App.—Houston 1960, writ dism'd) ("venue is determined by the law as of the date of filing suit"); Holt v. Wheeler, 301 S.W.2d 678, 680 (Tex. Civ. App.—Galveston 1957, writ dism'd) ("a statute controlling venue and becoming effective between the time that the cause of action arises and the time that suit is filed will control matters of venue in all subsequently filed suits"); Genecov v. Marcus, 285 S.W.2d 872, 873 (Tex. Civ. App.—Dallas 1955, no writ) (The law in effect at the time of institution of action ordinarily controls the venue of the action).

271. 160 S.W. 443 (Tex. Civ. App.—San Antonio 1913, no writ).

272. TEX. REV. CIV. STAT. ANN. art. 1995 (Vernon Supp. 1985).

273. 667 S.W.2d 188 (Tex. App.—Corpus Christi 1983, no writ).

274. Act of June 17, 1983, ch. 385, §§ 2-3, 1983 Tex. Sess. Law Serv. 2124-2125 (Vernon).

275. 667 S.W.2d at 189.

tember 1, 1983.[276]

The legislature created an ambiguity by adding to section 3[277] of the new venue statute the provision regarding use of the former law when addressing "pending appeals": "this Act takes effect September 1, 1983, and shall not apply to pending appeals. On venue questions pending prior to September 1, 1983 the former law is continued in effect."[278] Additionally, this ambiguity makes it difficult to determine the effective date for application of the amended venue statute.[279] The maxim of construction, *expressio unius est exclusio alterius*,[280] indicates that the provision expressly declaring that former law governs pending appeals limits application of former law only to pending appeals.

The court in *State v. Stone*;[281] refused to apply this maxim for two reasons: (1) applying the maxim would thwart legislative intent, and (2) if the legislature had intended the exclusion, it would have used more appropriate language.[282] The majority of recent decisions however, have interpreted section 3[283] as providing retroactive application of the amended venue statute to pending cases. In *Byrd v. Pharris*[284] the court construed section 3[285] to mean that the effective date is inapplicable to "pending appeals on venue questions" only. Essentially, since an interlocutory appeal taken from a

---

276. *Id.* at 189. In the recent case of Voss Int'l, Inc. v. General Portland, Inc., 670 S.W.2d 771 (Tex. App.—Austin 1984), the court acknowledged the *Gonzalez* decision, but instead of holding inconsistently with *Gonzalez,* the court distinguished its case on the facts, and decided that because the appeal was not pending prior to September 1, 1983, the amended statute applied and the interlocutory appeal was disallowed.

277. Act of June 17, 1983, ch. 385, §§ 2-3, 1983 Tex. Sess. Law Serv. 2124-2125 (Vernon).

278. *Id.*

279. The legislature apparently intended that the bill should affect pending plea of privilege hearings at the trial level in order to provide immediate relief to crowded trial and appellate dockets. The Act does not, however, affect pending appeals. 15 St. Mary's L.J. at 880. "Note that a venue matter is not pending on appeal until appellate jurisdiction is perfected, until an appeal bond or affidavit is timely filed or a cash certificate is filed in lieu thereof." *Id.* citing Byrd v. Pharris, 663 S.W.2d 856 (Tex. App.—San Antonio 1983, no writ).

280. 53 Tex. Jur. 2d *Statutes* § 142 (1964) (the express mention of one thing is tantamount to an express exclusion of all others.)

281. 271 S.W.2d 741, 750-751 (Tex. Civ. App.—Beaumont 1954, no writ).

282. *Id.*

283. Act of June 17, 1983, ch. 385, §§ 2-3, 1983 Tex. Sess. Law Serv. 2124-2125 (Vernon).

284. Byrd v. Pharris, 663 S.W.2d 856 (Tex. App.—San Antonio 1983, no writ).

285. Act of June 17, 1983, ch. 385, §§ 2-3, 1983 Tex. Sess. Law Serv. 2119, 2124-2125 (Vernon).

ruling on the venue matter was not pending prior to September 1, 1983, statutory authority does not permit an interlocutory appeal.[286]

Though the effective date provision in the amended venue statute[287] appears ambiguous, recent decisions have disregarded the customary rules of statutory construction in interpreting the provision.[288] The courts have, instead, construed the effective date provision literally and interpreted the provision to mean that the new venue law applies to all venue cases except pending appeals only.[289] Unfortunately this interpretation may lead to an unfair result.[290]

9.03 Conclusion

In personam jurisdiction of Texas courts over a defendant corporation in a strict tort liability action depends upon the interpretations of Article 2031b, the Texas Long Arm Statute. It is well established that a nonresident defendant is subject to in personam jurisdiction of this state when the party engages in certain "minimum contacts" with the state. Under the "minimum contacts" standard, the cause of action must be related to one or more of the minimum contacts. When jurisdiction over a Texas corporation is exercised by a foreign forum, however, the jurisdictional issue is determined based upon that forum's Long Arm Statute.

The venue issue is governed by article 1995, which was amended on September 1, 1983. There are several significant alterations reflected in the new venue statute. Though venue choice has virtually remained intact, venue determination is now simplified by the elimination of the dual-trial requirement. The amended venue statute also eliminates the interlocutory appeal of venue issues.

A plaintiff who institutes suit against a defendant based on strict tort liability may select venue based on the amended general

---

286. 663 S.W.2d at 857.

287. Act of June 17, 1983, Ch. 385, §§ 2-3, 1983 Tex. Sess. Law Serv. 2124-2125 (Vernon).

288. Refer to notes 279-286 *supra* and accompanying text.

289. Refer to notes 279-286 *supra* and accompanying text.

290. *See* Graue-Haws, Inc. v. Fuller, 666 S.W.2d 238, 239 (Tex. App.—El Paso 1984, no writ) (Preslar, J., dissenting).

rule of article 1995, or select venue based on one of the exceptions that apply to a claim relating to strict tort liability.

CHAPTER X. SUBMISSION OF THE PRODUCTS CASE*

10.00 General Considerations
10.01 Plaintiff's Case
- A. *Strict Liability 402A*
  - 1. *Essential Elements*
  - 2. *Submissions to the jury*
    - a. *Special Issues Involving Manufacturing Defects*
    - b. *Special Issues Involving Design Defects*
    - c. *Special Issues Involving Marketing Defects*
      - 1) *Complete Failure to Warn or Instruct*
      - 2) *Inadequate Warnings or Instructions*
      - 3) *Warnings and Instructions for Prescription Drugs*
- B. *Innocent Misrepresentation 402B*
  - 1. *Innocent Misrepresentation Generally*
  - 2. *Innocent Misrepresentation and Prescriptive Drugs*
- C. *Breach of Implied Warranty*
  - 1. *Special Issues for Breach of the Implied Warranty of Merchantability.*
  - 2. *Special Issues for Breach of the Implied Warranty of Fitness for a Particular Purpose.*
- D. *Negligence*

10.02 Defendant's Case
- A. *Defenses Prior to Duncan v. Cessna Aircraft Co.*
- B. *Comparative Causation under Duncan v. Cessna Aircraft Co.*
- C. *Contribution under Duncan and Art. 2212a*
  - 1. *Statutory Contribution*
  - 2. *Duncan and Common Law Contribution*
  - 3. *Partial Settlements*
- D. *Submission of the Issues Under Duncan and Art. 2212a*

---

* Dale Mellencamp coauthored this chapter.

10.00 General Considerations

Prefatory to examining submission of issues in the products case, several general observations merit consideration. In all jury cases the court *may*, or if requested by a party, *shall* submit special issues raised by the written pleadings and the evidence introduced at trial.[1] The court may also, for good cause and subject to review, submit such issues to the jury in a general charge.[2] In either situation, the court possesses discretionary authority in determining whether to submit special issues narrowly, to submit an issue for each element of the cause, or to submit broad issues that include a combination of specific elements or issues.[3]

Whether special issues are submitted broadly or narrowly, the court must include such explanatory instructions and definitions that are both proper and necessary to enable the jury to render a verdict.[4] In submitting explanatory instructions, however, the court may not comment on the weight of the evidence or advise the jury of the effect of its answers.[5] Nor may the Court give in-

---

1. Tex. R. Civ. P. 277.

2. The rule recognizes submission of a general charge on basis of either good cause or on agreement of the parties. Tex. R. Civ. P. 277.

3. *Id.* In *Hernandez v. Montgomery Ward and Co.*, 652 S.W.2d 923, 925-28 (Tex. 1983), the Texas Supreme Court approved a broad single issue submission of damages. The court based its decision on the failure of the trial court to rule on the defendant's objection before submission to the jury; consequently, the objection was not properly presented for appellate review. Though this portion of *Hernandez* was overruled in Acord v. General Motors Corp., 669 S.W.2d 111, 114 (Tex. 1984), the concurring and dissenting opinions in *Hernandez* approving broad submission was not overruled. This suggests that the Court may favor broad submission over narrow submission. *See also*, Members Mutual Insurance Co. v. Muckelroy, 523 S.W.2d 77 (Tex. Civ. App.—Houston [1st Dist.] 1975, writ ref'd n.r.e.) (The court approved a broad single question submission of negligence and proximate cause even though the plaintiffs pleaded specific acts of negligence.) *But see*, Cavnar v. Quality Parking, 28 Tex. Sup. Ct. J. 468 (June 8, 1985) (broad submission of damages issues preclude assessment of prejudgment interest).

4. Tex. R. Civ. P. 277. *See also* Durbin v. American Mfg. Co. 643 S.W.2d 239, 241 (Tex. App.—El Paso 1982, writ ref'd n.r.e.) (recognizing that the trial court possesses considerable discretion under Rule 277 in determining what instructions are necessary and proper). In Bolling v. Baker, 671 S.W.2d 559, 566 (Tex. App.—San Antonio 1984, no writ), the Court declared that instructions which do not aid the jury are not required.

5. *Id. See, e.g.*, Acord v. General Motors Corp., 669 S.W.2d 111 (Tex. 1984). The court determined that the trial court's additional instructions that "General Motors was neither

structions that are unnecessary, improper, or serve only to confuse and distract the jury. In *Fleishman v. Guadiano*,[6] a case involving an allegedly defectively designed ladder, the Texas Supreme Court determined that an instruction requested by the plaintiff that the jury not consider plaintiff's negligence in determining whether the defendant's product was defective constituted a prohibited explanatory instruction.[7] The Court noted that this instruction was not only unnecessary but that it diverted the jury's attention from the real issue of whether the product was defective.[8] This proposed instruction, therefore, failed to satisfy the requirement that instructions "enable the jury to render a verdict" and constituted reversible error.[9]

Fleishman illustrates that compliance with the general rules of submission is as critical in a strict tort liability case as in any other type of case. The unique characteristics of the products liability cases makes proper submission of issues to the jury critical.

10.01 Plaintiff's Case

It is well established that a party injured by a product may seek recovery under one or more of the following theories: Strict tort liability under Sec. 402A; Innocent misrepresentation under Sec. 402B; Breach of implied warranty; or Negligence.[10] Each theory prescribes elements and requirements that differentiate one

---

an insurer nor a guarantor of a perfect accident-proof product . . ." constituted a comment on the case as a whole and thus constituted reversible error. *Id.* at 116. A similar result was mandated in *Fleishman v. Guadiano, 651 S.W.2d 730 (Tex. 1983), in which the Supreme Court rejected as improper an instruction that the jury not consider the contributory negligence of the plaintiff in a strict tort liability action.* Tex. R. Civ. P. 277 provides, however, that the "court's charge shall not be objectionable on the grounds that it incidentally constitutes a comment on the weight of the evidence . . . " *See, e.g.*, Hickey v. Johnson, 672 S.W.2d 33, 34 (Tex. App.—Houston [14th Dist.] 1984, no writ). *But see* First Int'l Bank in San Antonio v. Roper Corp., 686 S.W. 2d 602 (Tex. 1985) (court rejects use of sole cause inferential rebuttal instruction).

6. 651 S.W.2d 730 (Tex. 1983).

7. *Id.* at 731. The instruction proposed: "You are further instructed that in answering this issue you shall not consider any evidence of negligence on the part of Virginia Guadiano, if any, in climbing the ladder in question on the occasion in question."

8. *Id.*

9. *Id.*

10. *See, e.g.*, Signal Oil and Gas Co. v. Universal Oil Prods., 572 S.W.2d 320 (Tex. 1978) (the plaintiff sued the manufacturer in strict tort liability, negligence and breach of implied warranty). In *Syrie v. Knoll Int'l.* 748 F. 2d 304 (5th Cir. 1984), the court emphasized that the plaintiff is entitled to submit both negligence and strict tort liability theories.

theory of recovery from the other. As a result, the manner in which plaintiff's case is submitted is dependent upon the theories under which recovery is sought.

A. Strict Liability: Section 402A

In *McKisson v. Sales Affiliates, Inc.*,[11] and the companion case of *Shamrock Fuel and Oil Sales Co. v. Tunks*,[12] the Texas Supreme Court expressly adopted the doctrine of strict tort liability articulated in Sec. 402A of the *Restatement (Second) of Torts*. Since adoption of Sec. 402A, the courts have formulated varying interpretations that have altered and modified many of the provisions of Sec. 402A in its implementation. The essential elements of the strict tort liability theory, however, have remained essentially unchanged.

1. Essential Elements. The requirements that must be established for submission of strict tort liability under Sec. 402A are:

a. that the product is defective;[13]

b. that the product reaches the user without substantial change in its condition from the time it left the supplier's possession;[14]

---

11. 416 S.W.2d 787 (Tex. 1967).

12. 416 S.W.2d 779 (Tex. 1967).

13. The product must be defective at the time it leaves the supplier's possession. Hagans v. Oliver Mach. Co., 576 F.2d 97, 99 (5th Cir. 1978); Colvin v. Red Steel Co., 682 S.W.2d 243, 246 (Tex. 1984); Miller v. Bock Laundry Mach. Co., 568 S.W.2d 648, 650 (Tex. 1977). It is not necessary, however, to identify the specific engineering or structural cause of the defect. V. Mueller & Co. v. Corley, 570 S.W.2d 140, 143 (Tex. Civ. App.—Houston [1st Dist.] 1978, writ ref'd n.r.e.).

14. Armstrong Rubber Co. v. Urquidez, 570 S.W.2d 374, 375 (Tex. 1978) *citing* RESTATEMENT (SECOND) OF TORTS 402A (1965). The requirement of proving that the product was defective at the time it left supplier's possession applies to each person or legal entity in the distributive chain. Carroll v. Ford Motor Co., 462 S.W.2d 57, 62 (Tex. Civ. App.—Houston [1st Dist.] 1970, no writ); Coca Cola Bottling Co. v. Hobart, 423 S.W.2d 118, 124 (Tex. Civ. App.—Houston [1st Dist.] 1967, writ ref'd n.r.e.). In the absence of evidence of a defect at the time of sale or relinquishment, strict liability does not apply. Martin v. Chesebrough- Pond's Inc., 614 F.2d 498, 500 (5th Cir. 1980); Quinn v. Southwest Wood Prods., Inc., 597 F.2d 1018, 1019-20 (5th Cir. 1979); Revlon, Inc. v. Hampton, 551 S.W.2d 121, 123 (Tex. Civ. App.—Beaumont 1977, no writ). The product must actually be introduced into the stream of commerce for sale or use before strict liability applies. Armstrong Rubber Co., 570 S.W.2d at 376; Hernandez v. Southern Pacific Transp. Co., 641 S.W.2d 947, 952 (Tex. Civ. App.—Corpus Christi 1982, no writ); Thomas v. St. Joseph Hosp., 618 S.W.2d 791, 796 (Tex. Civ. App.—Houston [1st Dist.] 1981, no writ n.r.e.); Thate v. Texas & Pac. Ry, 595 S.W.2d 591, 598 (Tex. Civ. App.—Dallas 1980, no writ).

c. that the defect renders the product unreasonably dangerous for its intended and reasonably foreseeable use;[15] and

d. that the defect caused plaintiff's injury.[16]

Unless otherwise stipulated by the parties, these elements constitute the ultimate issues to be determined by the trier of fact.

2. *Submission to the Jury.* Though the essential elements are identical for all claims predicated on Sec. 402A, the issues and instructions differ considerably depending on whether strict tort liability is based on an alleged manufacturing flaw in the product, defective design, or defective marketing. For instance, the definition of "unreasonably dangerous" that relates to a design defect is inapplicable to a marketing defect. Likewise, foreseeability of a particular risk of harm or danger is critical in a defective marketing case but is entirely immaterial for an alleged manufacturing defect in a product. Thus an understanding of the three types of defects is imperative.

Product defects are classified into three basic categories:

i) Defects in manufacturing[17]

ii) Defects in design[18]

iii) Defects in marketing.[19]

---

15. Daberko v. Heil Co., 681 F.2d 445, 448 (5th Cir. 1982); Hagans v. Oliver Mach. Co., 576 F.2d 97, 99-100, (5th Cir. 1978); Mitchell v. Fruehauf Corp., 568 F.2d 1139, 1147 (5th Cir. 1978); Lubbock Mfg. Co. v. Sames, 598 S.W.2d 234, 236 (Tex. 1980); Turner v. General Motors Corp., 584 S.W.2d 844, 851 (Tex. 1979); Fitzgerald Marine Sales v. LeUnes, 659 S.W.2d 917, 919 (Tex. App.—Fort Worth 1983, writ dism'd).

16. Migues v. Fibreboard Corp., 662 F.2d 1182, 1185 (5th Cir. 1981); Mitchell v. Fruehauf Corp., 568 F.2d 1139, 1142; (5th Cir. 1978); Turner v. General Motors Corp., 584 S.W.2d 844, 848 (Tex. 1979); Gonzales v. Caterpillar Tractor Co., 571 S.W.2d 867, 872 (Tex. 1978); Magic Chef, Inc. v. Sibley, 546 S.W.2d 851, 858 (Tex. Civ. App.—San Antonio 1977, writ ref'd n.r.e.).

17. *See, e.g,.* McNeese v. Reading & Bates Drilling Co., 749 F.2d 270 (5th Cir. 1985); Miller v. Bock Laundry Mach. Co., 568 S.W.2d 648 (Tex. 1977), Fitzgerald Marine Sales v. LeUnes, 659 S.W.2d 917 (Tex. App.—Fort Worth 1983, writ dism'd); Barnes v. General Motors Corp., 653 S.W.2d 85 (Tex. App—San Antonio 1983, writ ref'd n.r.e.).

18. *See, e.g.,* Webb v. Rodgers Machinery Mfg. Co., 750 F.2d 368 (5th Cir. 1985); Acord v. General Motors Corp., 669 S.W.2d 111 (Tex. 1984); Fleishman v. Guadiano, 651 S.W.2d 730 (Tex. 1983); Kindred v. Con/Chem, Inc., 650 S.W.2d 61 (Tex. 1983); Turner v. General Motors Corp., 584 S.W.2d 844 (Tex. 1979), Gonzales v. Caterpillar Tractor Co., 571 S.W.2d 867 (Tex. 1978). When both marketing and design defect issues are submitted, the appropriate definition for a manufacturing and a design flow should be included with each. Ford Motor Co. v. Pool, 688 S.W.2d 879, 882 (Tex. App.—Texarkana 1985, no wirt).

19. *See, e.g.,* Pavlides v. Galveston Yacht Basin Inc., 727 F.2d 330 (5th Cir. 1983); Hagans v. Oliver Mach. Co., 576 F.2d 97 (5th Cir. 1978); Bristol-Myers Co. v. Gonzales, 561

Defects in manufacturing involve flaws, deficiencies, or miscarriages in the preparation assembley or construction of the product. A flawed product is illustrated in *Shamrock Fuel and Oil Sales Co. v. Tunks.*[20] There the product, kerosene, was adulterated with gasoline. The admixture of gas reduced the ignition level of the kerosene and caused it to ignite, explode, and injure the plaintiff.[21]

Design defects involve errors in planning or conceptualization which render the product unreasonably dangerous. In *Carter v. Massey-Ferguson, Inc.*,[22] the failure to equip a log skidder with a back-up alarm rendered the skidder defective as designed.[23] Even though the machine was manufactured and assembled in strict compliance with the blueprints and design specifications, it was defective and unreasonably dangerous due to insufficient planning; a properly designed skidder would have been designed with a back-up alarm.[24]

Marketing defects generally involve a complete failure to warn of dangers or risks of harm in the use of a product, the failure to instruct in the safe use of the product, or a failure to warn or instruct adequately. In *Pittsburgh Corning Corp. v. Thomas*,[25] the court was confronted with a failure to warn of potential risks and dangers. The manufacturer of asbestos insulation failed to provide any warning concerning the carcinogenic risk presented by exposure to asbestos.[26] The failure to warn of known potential hazards rendered the product defective.[27]

Notwithstanding that submission of marketing, design, and manufacturing defects requires individual special issues for each, the causation issue is submitted in the same form regardless of the

---

S.W.2d 801 (Tex. 1978); Technical Chem. Co. v. Jacobs, 480 S.W.2d 602 (Tex. 1972); Allied Industrial Int'l, Inc. v. Placencro, 685 S.W.2d 364 (Tex. App.—San Antonio 1985, no writ); Pittsburgh Corning Corp. v. Thomas, 668 S.W.2d 876, 879 (Tex. App.—Houston [14th Dist.] 1984, no writ); Blackwell Burner Co. v. Cerda, 644 S.W.2d 512 (Tex. App.—San Antonio 1982, writ ref'd n.r.e.); Pearson v. Hevi-Duty Elec., 618 S.W.2d 784 (Tex. Civ. App.—Houston [1st Dist.] 1981, writ ref'd n.r.e.); Bituminous Casualty Corp. v. Black & Decker Mfg. Co., 518 S.W.2d 868 (Tex. App.—Dallas 1974, writ ref'd n.r.e.).

20. 416 S.W.2d 779 (Tex. 1967).
21. *Id.* at 781.
22. 716 F.2d 344 (5th Cir. 1983).
23. *Id.* at 346.
24. *Id.* at 350.
25. 668 S.W.2d 876 (Tex. App.—Houston [14th Dist] 1984, no writ).
26. *Id.* at 879.
27. *Id.*

type of defect involved. In *Rourke v. Garza*,[28] the Texas Supreme Court reaffirmed the principle that producing rather than proximate causation governs strict tort liability submission.[29] The court cited with approval the trial courts definition of producing cause as: "an efficient, exciting, or contributing cause which in a natural sequence produced injuries or damages complained of, if any. There can be more than one producing cause."[30] This definition of producing cause governs in all Sec. 402A actions. The proper submission of each type of defective product under strict tort liability, therefore, requires a customized format.

a. Special Issues Involving Manufacturing Defects (flaws). The term "defect" is defined as a condition that renders the product unreasonably dangerous for its intended or reasonably foreseeable use.[31] The unreasonably dangerous element, therefore, is an integral and unique characteristic of a defective product under Sec. 402A. The standard for measuring whether a defect renders a product unreasonably dangerous in a manufacturing flaw case is noticeably different than the standard in a defective design case. A product is unreasonably dangerous as manufactured when it is:

> dangerous to an extent beyond that which would be contemplated by the ordinary consumer who purchases it with the ordinary knowledge common to the community as to its characteristics.[32]

The following submission typifies the issues and definitions for strict tort liability based on a defectively manufactured product:

Special Issue No. 1

Was the punch press defective at the time it left the possession of

---

28. 530 S.W.2d 794 (Tex. 1975).

29. *Id.* at 801.

30. *Id.*

31. *See* Mitchell v. Fruehauf Corp., 568 F.2d 1139, 1142 n.1 (5th Cir. 1978); Blackwell Burner Co. v. Cerda, 644 S.W.2d 512, 515 (Tex. App.—San Antonio 1982, writ ref'd, n.r.e.).

32. RESTATEMENT (SECOND) OF TORTS § 402A comment i (1965). This definition governs all claims involving manufacturing defects. The risk-utility standard formulated in Turner v. General Motors Corp., 584 S.W.2d 844 (Tex. 1979) applies only to design and not manufacturing defects, *See, e.g,.* Ford Motor Co. v. Pool, 688 S.W.2d 879, 881 (Tex. App.—Texarkana 1985 no writ); Fitzgerald Marine Sales v. LeUnes, 659 S.W.2d 917, 921 (Tex. App.—Fort Worth 1983, no writ); Barnes v. General Motors Corp., 653 S.W.2d 85, 90 (Tex. App.—San Antonio 1983, no writ). *See also* 3 Texas Pattern Jury Charge § 71.01 commentary at 216 (1982).

the Press Forward Co.?

You are instructed that the term "defective" as used in this issue is meant to be a condition of the product that renders it unreasonably dangerous.

You are further instructed that "unreasonably dangerous" as used in this issue is meant to be a product that is dangerous to an extent beyond that which would be contemplated by the ordinary user of the product, with the ordinary knowledge common to the community of such users as to the product's characteristics.

Answer: ____________

Special Issue No. 2 (Predicated)

Was such defect a producing cause of the occurrence in question? You are instructed that the term "producing cause" as used in this issue means an efficient, exciting, or contributing cause which, in a natural sequence, produced the injuries or damages complained of, if any. There can be more than one producing cause.

Answer: ____________

b. Special Issues Involving Design Defects. Strict tort liability based on alleged defective design presents a more formidable problem in submission to a jury than does the manufacturing defect. A manufacturer could conceivably design an absolutely safe product, but the costs involved would undoubtedly be enormous and the utility of the product might be severely compromised. The critical issue, therefore, is "to what extent should suppliers be encouraged to diminish the product's marketability for the sake of safety?" It is axiomatic that the product supplier is not the insurer of the product.[33] Stated differently, a manufacturer simply is not re-

33. *See, e.g.*, Hagans v. Oliver Mach. Co., 576 F.2d 97, 100 (5th Cir. 1978) (The "manufacturer is not an insurer of his product, charged by the law to design every part to be the best that science can produce or to guarantee that no harm will come to the user"); Henderson v. Ford Motor Co., 519 S.W.2d 87, 93 (Tex. 1974) ("manufacturer is not charged by the law nor expected by the purchasing public to design every part to be the best that science can produce or to guarantee that no harm will befall the user"); Miller v. Bock Laundry Mach. Co., 551 S.W.2d 775, 781 (Tex. Civ. App.—Tyler 1977, no writ) (manufacturer is not required to design every part to be the best that science and engineering can produce or to guarantee that no harm will befall the user). *Accord* Acord v. General Motors Corp., 669 S.W.2d 111, 116 (Tex. 1984) (the inclusion of a statement of governing legal principles in the jury charge, "however correctly [it] may state the law . . ." constitutes a comment on the

quired to destroy a product's utility to insure that it is absolutely safe for use under any and all circumstances.[34] This general principle, however, offers scant guidance for evaluating whether a particular design renders the product supplier strictly liable in tort under Sec. 402A. As a consequence, the definition of unreasonably dangerous in the design context has undergone interminable reformulation and refinement.

In *Henderson v. Ford Motor Co.*,[35] the Texas Supreme Court articulated a bifurcated test which defined "unreasonably dangerous," meaning that the product threatened harm either to an extent that it would not be placed in the stream of commerce by a prudent manufacturer aware of the risks it would pose or to the extent that it would not meet the reasonable expectations of the ordinary consumer as to its safety.[36] This formulation was reaffirmed in *General Motors Corp. v. Hopkins*.[37]

Thereafter, in *Turner v. General Motors Corp.*,[38] the Texas Supreme Court reconsidered the bifurcated test for instructing the jury in a defective design case.[39] Plaintiff was severely injured when his vehicle overturned, causing the roof to partially collapse. Plaintiff alleged that the vehicle was defectively designed because it lacked a roll bar or roll cage.[40] The trial court instructed the jury on unreasonably dangerous as designed under the consumer rea-

---

case as a whole that precipitates reversible error). *Cf.* Lemos v. Montez, 680 S.W.2d 798 (Tex. 1984).

34. The courts have consistently held that evidence concerning the manufacturer's ability to eliminate some risk without adversely affecting the usefulness or cost of the product should be submitted to the jury. *See, e.g.*, Daberko v. Heil Co., 681 F.2d 445, 448 (5th Cir. 1982); Hagans v. Oliver Mach. Co., 576 F.2d 97, 101 (5th Cir. 1978); Turner v. General Motors Corp., 584 S.W.2d 844, 846-471 (Tex. 1979); Boatload of Houston, Inc. v. Bailey, 609 S.W.2d 743 (Tex. 1980); Ford Motor Co. v. Nowak, 638 S.W.2d 582, 585-86 (Tex. App.—Corpus Christi 1982, writ ref'd n.r.e.).

35. 519 S.W.2d 87 (Tex. 1974) (overruled in part in Turner v. General Motors Corp., 584 S.W.2d 844 (Tex. 1979)).

36. *Id.* at 92.

37. 548 S.W.2d 344 (Tex. 1977) (overruled in part in Turner v. General Motors Corp., 584 S.W.2d 844 (Tex. 1979)).

38. 584 S.W.2d 844 (Tex. 1978).

39. *Id.* at 846. *See also* Acord v. General Motors Corp., 669 S.W.2d 111 (Tex 1984); Ford Motor Co. v. Pool, 688 S.W.2d 879 (Tex. App.—Texarkana 1985, no writ) (when submitting both a manufacturing flaw-defect and a design defect, the instruction for the manufacturing flaw-defect differs from the design defect and must be submitted in connection with such issue). Refer to notes 220-221 *infra*.

40. *Id.*

sonable expectation standard.[41] The Texas Supreme Court concluded that a risk-utility balancing instruction should have been submitted to the jury rather than the consumer expectation definition as given by the trial court.[42]

The Texas Supreme Court reviewed the evolution of design defect submission in Texas. In addressing the consumer expectation portion of the *Henderson* and *Hopkins* test, the court questioned the assumption that jurors possess ordinary consumer expectations on design configurations of products or that they can apply in a meaningful manner standards that significantly exceed their unsophisticated technical experiences or expectations.[43] Addressing the second prong of the *Henderson* test the Texas Supreme Court acknowledged that the rationale that sired the reasonably prudent manufacturer test no longer justified its use.[44] Accordingly, the court rejected the *Henderson* bifurcated test and declared that in strict tort liability cases based on defective design the appropriate instruction of defective design would contemplate a design that is "unreasonably dangerous as designed taking into consideration the utility of the product and the risk involved in its use."[45]

The manufacturer in *Turner* requested that specific factors be submitted to assist the jury in balancing the utility of the product against the risk involved in its use.[46] The Supreme Court determined that though evidence of such factors should be presented

---

41. *Id.*

42. *Id.* at 847.

43. *Id.* at 851.

44. *Id.*

45. *Id.* at 847 n.1. *Accord* Shipp. v. General Motors Corp., 750 F.2d 418 (5th Cir. 1985); Hagans v. Oliver Mach. Co., 576 F.2d 97, 99 (5th Cir. 1978); Burks v. Firestone Tire & Rubber Co., 633 F.2d 1152, 1155 (5th Cir. 1981); Acord v. General Motors Corp., 669 S.W.2d 111 (Tex. 1984); Fleishman v. Guadino, 651 S.W.2d 730 (Tex. 1983); Kindred v. Con/Chem, Inc., 650 S.W.2d 61 (Tex. 1983); Ford Motor Co. v. Pool, 688 S.W.2d 879, 881 (Tex. App.—Texarkana 1985, no writ).

46. *Turner*, 584 S.W.2d at 849. The factors included: (1) the usefulness and desirability of the product; (2) the availability of other and safer products to meet the same need; (3) the likelihood of injury and its possible seriousness; (4) the obviousness of the danger; (5) common knowledge and normal public expectation of the danger; (6) the avoidability of injury by care in use of the product (including the effect of instructions and warnings); and (7) the ability to eliminate danger without seriously impairing the usefulness of the product or making it unduly expensive. General Motors Corp. v. Turner, 567 S.W.2d 812, 817 n.9 (Tex. Civ. App.—Beaumont 1978) *rev'd* 584 S.W.2d 844 (Tex. 1979), *citing* Wade, *Strict Tort Liability of Manufacturers*, 14 Sw.L.J. 5, 17 (1965).

and argued by the parties, such factors may not constitute a part of the jury instructions.[47] Recent efforts to supplement the *Turner* risk versus utility test have met with similar disapproval. In *Acord v. General Motors Corp.*,[48] a case involving a design defect, the trial court instructed the jury that "A manufacturer is not an insurer of the product he designs, and it is not required that the design adopted be perfect, or render the product accident proof, or incapable of causing injury, nor is it necessary to incorporate the ultimate safety features of the product."[49] Categorically rejecting any further elaboration of the risk versus utility instruction for defective design, the Texas Supreme Court emphasized that additional explanatory instructions on abstract legal principles constitutes an impermissible comment by the trial court.[50] The court then disapproved the instruction stressing that juries "need not and should not be burdened with surplus instructions."[51]

Any submission of design defect issues must incorporate the *Turner* risk versus utility definition of "design defect" with no additions or modifications. The following represents an example of the submission of a strict tort liability action based on a defective design.[52]

Special Issue No. 1

Was the wood shaper defectively designed at the time it was manufactured by the Woodcutter Co.?[53]

---

47. *Turner*, 584 S.W.2d at 849. In Boatland of Houston Inc. v. Bailey, 609 S.W.2d 743, 746 (Tex. 1980), the supreme court again addressed the specific factors in establishing a defective design. The court noted that "[t]he jury may consider many factors . . . [and] [t]heir finding on defectiveness may be influenced by evidence of a safer design that would have prevented the injury." Similarly, in Kindred v. Con/Chem, Inc., 650 S.W.2d 61, 63 (Tex. 1983), the supreme court noted the necessity of the plaintiff establishing the feasibility of developing a safer alternative design.

48. 669 S.W.2d 111 (Tex. 1984).

49. *Id.* at 113.

50. *Id.* at 116.

51. *Id.*

52. *See also* First Int'l Bank in San Antonio v. Roper Corp., 686 S.W.2d 602 (Tex. 1985); Fleishman v. Guadino, 651 S.W.2d 730 (Tex. 1983). *See* Volume II of the TEXAS PATTERN JURY CHARGES 71.02 at 221 (1982). The Court in *Acord* explicitly approved this instruction and disapproved the addition of any other instructions in design defect cases. *Accord*, 669 S.W.2d at 116.

53. In proper cases, this instruction may be altered to read "was the lathe defectively designed at the time it *left the possession* of the Woodcutter Co." 3 TEXAS PATTERN JURY CHARGE § 71.03 commentary at 222. Though the authors of the Pattern Jury Charge do not

You are instructed that a defectively designed product is a product that is unreasonably dangerous as designed, taking into consideration the utility of the product and the risk involved in its use.

Answer: ____________________

Special Issue No. 2 (Predicated)

Was such defective design a producing cause of the occurrence [injury] in question?

You are instructed that the term "producing cause" as used in this issue means an efficient, exciting, or contributing cause which, in a natural sequence produces the injuries or damages complained of, if any. There can be more than one producing cause.

Answer: ____________________

The intermediate appellate court in *Turner* distinguished crashworthiness cases from other design defect cases on the basis that the alleged defective design configuration in crashworthiness cases neither causes nor contributes to cause the accident; rather, it merely enhances injuries over and above the injuries that result from an accident.[54] The Texas Supreme Court rejected this distinction, determining that there is no valid reason for distinguishing between design defects that cause an accident and design defects that cause an injury.[55] The court concluded, therefore, that "there is no rational basis for a difference in the manner of submission of the issues to be determined by the fact finder."[56]

Despite the categorical pronouncement of *Turner* that submission of a crashworthiness case must be submitted in a form identi-

---

define the "proper" case, it is apparent that where the defendant is not a manufacturer but a distributor of the product, such a modification would be appropriate. A more obvious and significant need for the distinction arises where the product is altered or modified by either third parties or the user after the product is marketed. Likewise, subsequent advances in technology would require this modification of the issue. *See e.g.*, Boatland of Houston Inc. v. Bailey, 609 S.W.2d 743, 749 (Tex. 1982); Caterpillar Tractor Co. v. Boyett, 674 S.W.2d 782 (Tex. App.—Corpus Christi 1984, no writ).

54. Turner v. General Motors Corp., 567 S.W.2d 812 (Tex. Civ. App.—Beaumont, 1978), *rev'd*, 584 S.W.2d 844 (Tex. 1979).

55. Turner v. General Motors Corp., 584 S.W.2d 844, 848 (Tex. 1979); Shipp v. General Motors Corp., 750 F.2d 418 (5th Cir. 1985).

56. *Turner*, 584 S.W.2d at 848. *See also* Duncan v. Cessna Aircraft Co., 665 S.W.2d 414, 427 (Tex. 1984) (holding that article 2212a does not apply when strict products liability, *including uncrashworthiness* and breach of warranty, is established.)

cal to those submitted in any other design defect case, the Court focused primarily on whether the enumerated balancing factors should be submitted to the jury.[57] Since *Turner*, commentators have advocated a minor modification in crashworthiness cases; it has been suggested that in crashworthiness cases the issue of causation should focus on causation of the injury rather than causation of the accident. The following issues are suggested for crashworthiness cases.[58]

Special Issue No. 3 (Predicated)

Was the defective design a producing cause of any injuries sustained by the plaintiff?

You are instructed that by the term "producing cause" as used in this issue is meant an efficient, exciting, or contributing cause which in the natural sequence, produces the injuries or damages complained of, if any. There can be more than one producing cause.

Answer: ______________________

c. *Special Issues Involving Marketing Defects.* A product may be designed and manufactured free of any defects and yet still be defective if it is marketed in a manner that makes it unreasonably dangerous.[59] Marketing defects involve either a complete failure to warn or instruct or a failure to warn or instruct adequately of particular dangers or risks of harm.

1. *Complete Failure to Warn or Instruct.* Unlike claims based on defective design or manufacture, a strict tort liability claim for defective marketing necessarily involves questions of duty and foreseeability.[60] Before a product supplier may be subject

---

57. *Turner*, 584 S.W.2d at 848.

58. The adoption of comparative causation clearly compels submitting the issue of causation in terms of injury. *See* Duncan v. Cessna Aircraft Co., 665 S.W.2d 414, 427-28 (Tex. 1984) (emphasizing that comparative causation looks to the cause of injuries rather than the accident).

59. Pavlides v. Galveston Yacht Basin Inc., 727 F.2d 330 (5th Cir. 1984); Pearson v. Hevi-Duty Electric, 618 S.W.2d 784, 788 (Tex. Civ. App.—Houston [1st Dist.] 1981, writ ref'd n.r.e.); Hamilton v. Motor Coach Industries, Inc., 569 S.W.2d 571, 575 (Tex. Civ. App.—Texarkana 1978, no writ); Bituminous Casualty Corp. v. Black & Decker Mfg. Co., 518 S.W.2d 868 (Tex. Civ. App.—Dallas 1974, writ ref'd n.r.e.).

60. *See, e.g.*, Martinez v. Dixie Carriers Inc., 529 F.2d 457, 466 (5th Cir. 1976) (discussing circumstances that relieve the supplier of duty to warn).

to strict tort liability for failure to warn of inherent or reasonably foreseeable risks of harm or instruct for safe use, the plaintiff must establish that the supplier was impressed with a duty to warn or instruct. Under Sec. 402A, the supplier is obligated to warn or instruct only against those dangers and risks of harm of which it knows or should know at the time the product is supplied.[61] For purposes of determining whether a manufacturer is deemed to have foreseen the risk of harm posed by its product, the courts judicially presume that the manufacturers possess the knowledge and skills of an expert. "[A]t a minimum, he must keep abreast of scientific knowledge, discoveries, and advances and is presumed to know what is imparted thereby."[62] If the dangers posed by the product are reasonably unforeseeable even to such an "expert," then the *duty* to warn or instruct is never activated.[63] Nor does a duty to warn or instruct arise where the risk of harm or danger inherent in a product is patently obvious or actually known by the user.[64]

Similarly, the manufacturer or seller is not obligated to warn of the product's inherent dangers when it is marketed to a group of persons possessing special expertise or sophistication in its use or a particular knowledge of its dangerous characteristics.[65] The fact

---

61. Webb v. Rodgers Mach. Mfg. Co., 750 F.2d 368 (5th Cir. 1984); Pavlides v. Galveston Yacht Basin, Inc., 727 F.2d 330, 338 (5th Cir. 1984); Hardy v. Johns-Manville Sales Corp., 681 F.2d 334, 344 (5th Cir. 1982); Reyes v. Wyeth Labs Inc., 498 F.2d 1264, 1274-75 (5th Cir.), *cert. denied*, 419 U.S. 1096 (1974); Borel v. Fibreboard Paper Prods. Corp., 493 F.2d 1076, 1088 (5th Cir. 1973), *cert. denied* 419 U.S. 869 (1974); Bristol Meyers Co. v. Gonzales, 561 S.W.2d 801, 804 (Tex. 1978); Technical Chem. Co. v. Jacobs, 480 S.W.2d 602, 603 (Tex. 1972); Rawlings Sporting Goods Co. v. Daniels, 619 S.W.2d 435, 439 (Tex. Civ. App.—Waco 1981, writ ref'd n.r.e.). Unforeseeable intervening cause may relieve the product supplier of a duty to warn. *See* Martin v. Harrington & Richardson, Inc., 743 F.2d 1200, 1205 (7th Cir. 1984); Daberko v. Heil Co., 681 F.2d 445 (5th Cir. 1982).

62. *Hardy*, 681 F.2d at 344; *Borel*, 493 F.2d at 1089; *Reyes*, 498 F.2d at 1277.

63. *See, e.g.*, Crocker v. Winthrop Labs., 514 S.W.2d 429, 433 (Tex. 1974) (the defendant manufacturer could not be held liable for defective marketing where it was unforeseeable at the time of sale that Talwin would cause drug dependency).

64. Restatement (Second) of Torts, § 402A, comment j (1965). *See generally*, Hagans v. Oliver Mach. Co., 576 F.2d 97, 102 (5th Cir. 1978); Martinez v. Dixie Carriers, Inc., 529 F.2d 457, 466 (5th Cir. 1976); Ragsdale Bros. Inc., v. Magro, ____ S.W.2d ____ (Tex. App.—San Antonio 1985), 04-82-00546-c.v. *See also* Sales, *The Duty To Warn and Instruct For Safe Use in Strict Tort Liability*, 13 St. Mary's L.J. 521 (1983).

65. *See, e.g.*, Guidry v. KEM Mfg. Co., 693 F.2d 426, 430 (5th Cir. 1982) (no duty to warn industrial users of drain cleaners of danger inherent in pouring cleanser into a drain containing another chemical cleaner). Martinez v. Dixie Carriers Inc., 529 F.2d 457, 467 (5th Cir. 1976) (a product supplier is not obligated to warn men of professional expertise who

that only a few users will be adversely affected by a product, however, does not excuse the duty to warn.[66]

Once the plaintiff establishes that the supplier is obligated to warn of the dangers either inherent in the use or the reasonably foreseeable misuse of a product, the plaintiff still must establish that such failure rendered the product unreasonably dangerous.[67] To determine whether the lack of warnings or instructions rendered the product "unreasonably dangerous," it appears that the consumer-expectation definition of "unreasonably dangerous," governs submission of a defective marketing case.[68] Thus, the plaintiff must prove that the product supplier's failure to instruct for safe use or to warn of known or knowable risks and dangers rendered the product dangerous to an extent beyond that which would be contemplated by the ordinary user with the ordinary knowledge common to the community concerning its characteristics.[69]

If the product is found to be unreasonably dangerous, the plaintiff must then, of course, establish causation. Significantly, though the duty to warn or instruct is dependent on foreseeability of the risk of harm or danger, the courts consistently have disavowed proximate cause as a prerequisite for liability in a defective marketing case; producing cause represents the appropriate causation issue.[70] Apparently, though the *duty to warn* of dangers or to instruct for safe use is governed by the standard of foreseeability of the danger, the nexus between the dangerous condition and causation need not be foreseeable; it need only be a cause in fact.[71]

---

know of the dangers inherent in the product).

66. Crocker v. Winthrop Labs., 514 S.W.2d 429, 432 (Tex. 1974). RESTATEMENT (SECOND) OF TORTS, Sec. 402A, comment j (1965) was rejected as a limitation on the duty to warn in Texas.

67. *See, e.g.,* Shop Rite Foods, Inc. v. Upjohn Co., 619 S.W.2d 574, 577-80 (Tex. Civ. App.—Amarillo, 1981, writ ref'd n.r.e.) (acknowledging the necessity to establish that the failure to warn rendered the product unreasonably dangerous).

68. The *Turner* risk-utility balancing test is limited solely to design defect cases and applies neither to marketing defects nor manufacturing defects. *See, e.g.*; Durbin v. American Mfg. Co., 643 S.W.2d 239, 241 (Tex. App.—El Paso 1982, writ ref'd n.r.e.) (giving the ordinary expectation instruction in a post *Turner* defective marketing case). *See also* 3 Pattern Jury Charge § 71.04, Caveat at 238 (1982).

69. *See* RESTATEMENT (SECOND) OF TORTS § 402A comment j (1965): *See generally,* Borel v. Fibreboard Paper Products Co., 493 F.2d 1076 (5th Cir. 1973), *cert. denied*, 419 U.S. 869 (1974). Technical Chem. Co. v. Jacobs, 480 S.W.2d 602 (Tex. 1972); Ragsdale Bros. Inc. v. Magro, -S.W.2d- (Tex. App.—San Antonio 1985) 04-82-00546-c.v.

70. *See Edgar, Products Liability in Texas,* 11 Tex. Tech. L. Rev. 23, 30 (1979).

71. *But see,* Morgan v. Compugraphic Corp., 675 S.W.2d 729, 732 (Tex. 1984). This

The following illustrates broad form submission of issues for a complete failure to warn or to give instructions for safe use.

Special Issue No. 1

Did the Acme Battery Co. know, or by application of reasonably developed human skill and foresight should it have known, at the time it sold the battery that it could explode when exposed to excessive heat?

Answer: ____________________

Special Issue No. 2 (Predicated)

Did the failure of the Acme Battery Co. to warn of this danger or instruct as to safe use render the battery defective as marketed?

You are instructed that by the term "defective" as used in this issue is meant a condition that renders it unreasonably dangerous. You are further instructed that by the term "unreasonably dangerous" as used in this issue is meant a product that is dangerous to an extent beyond that which would be contemplated by the ordinary user of the product with the ordinary knowledge common to the community as to the product's characteristics.

Answer: ____________________

Special Issue No. 3 (Predicated)

Was such failure a producing cause of the occurrence [injury] in question?

You are instructed that the term "producing cause" as used in this issue is meant an efficient, exciting, contributing cause which in a natural sequence produced the injuries or damages complained of, if any. There may be more than one producing cause.

Answer: ____________________

2. *Inadequate Warnings or Instructions*. When the risk of harm is known or is reasonably knowable the manufacturer must not only warn of the dangers and instruct for safe use but the warnings and instructions must be adequate.[72] Adequacy of warn-

---

issue is perceptively analyzed by the court in Conti v. Ford Motor Co., 743 F.2d 195, 197-98 (3rd Cir. 1984).

72. Pearson v. Hevi Duty Elec., 618 S.W.2d 784, 787 (Tex. Civ. App.—Houston [1st

ing or instruction for safe use generally presents a fact issue for determination by the jury.[73] But the courts have established certain standards which must be satisfied. A warning is adequate if it communicates to the average user a fair indication of the nature and extent of the danger.[74] To satisfy the adequacy requirement, the warning must also be in a form expected to catch the attention of a reasonably prudent person in the circumstances of its use, and it must be of a nature that is comprehensible to the average user.[75] Though few cases discuss these prerequisites, the issue of adequacy applies with equal effect to instructions.[76] The following illustrates broad form submission of both allegedly inadequate warnings and instructions for safe use.

Special Issue No. 1

At the time the Ace Tool Company sold the metal griner in question, did it fail to give adequate warnings of the danger of the cup rock exploding when used on heat treated metals? (It has been suggested that a definition of "adequate" should accompany this issue.)[77]

Dist.] 1981, writ ref'd n.r.e.); Bituminous Cas. Corp. v. Black & Decker Mfg. Co., 518 S.W.2d 868, 872-74 (Tex. Civ. App.—Dallas 1974, writ ref'd n.r.e.).

73. Shop Rite Foods, Inc. v. Upjohn Co., 619 S.W.2d 574, 577-78 (Tex. Civ. App.—Amarillo 1981, writ ref'd n.r.e.); Lopez v. Aro Corp., 584 S.W.2d 333, 335 (Tex. Civ. App.— San Antonio 1979, writ ref'd n.r.e.). *See generally*, Sales, *The Duty to Warn and Instruct for Safe Use in Strict Tort Liability*, 13 St. Mary's L.J. 521, 550-53 (1982) (discussing the factual settings of various cases involving adequacy of warnings).

74. Pearson v. Hevi-Duty Elec., 618 S.W.2d 784, 788 (Tex. Civ. App.—Houston [1st Dist.] 1981, writ ref'd n.r.e.); Lopez v. Aro Corp., 584 S.W.2d 333, 335 (Tex. Civ. App.—San Antonio 1979, writ ref'd n.r.e.); Bituminous Cas. Corp. v. Black & Decker Mfg. Co., 518 S.W.2d 868, 873 (Tex. Civ. App.—Dallas 1974, writ ref'd n.r.e.).

75. *Shop Rite Foods Inc.*, 619 S.W.2d at 578; *Lopez*, 584 S.W.2d at 335; *Bituminous Cas. Corp.*, 518 S.W.2d at 872-73.

76. Bitiminous Cas. Corp., 518 S.W.2d at 873; *Shop Rite Foods Inc.*, 619 S.W.2d at 578; *Lopez*, 584 S.W.2d at 336.

77. The following definition has been suggested in 3 Pattern Jury Charge § 71.04 commentary at 238 (1982).

"Adequate warnings and instructions" means warnings and instructions that are given in such form that they could reasonably be expected to catch the attention of the reasonably prudent person in the circumstances of its use; and the content of the warnings and instructions must be of such a nature as to be comprehensible to the average user and to convey a fair indication of the nature and extent of the danger and how to avoid it to the mind of a reasonably prudent person.

For further discussion of the legal meaning of "adequate", *see* Bristol-Myers Co. v. Gonzales, 561 S.W.2d 801, 804 (Tex. 1978); Ford Motor Co. v. Nowak, 638 S.W.2d 582, 592 (Tex.

Answer: ________________

Special Issue No. 2 (Predicated)

Did such failure render the metal grinder defective as marketed?

You are instructed that by the term "defective" as used in this issue is meant a condition that renders it unreasonably dangerous. You are further instructed that by the term "unreasonably dangerous" as used in this issue is meant a product that is dangerous to an extent beyond that which would be contemplated by the ordinary user of the product, with the ordinary knowledge common to the community as to the product's characteristics.

Answer: ____________________

Special Issue No. 3 (Predicated)

Was such failure a producing cause of the occurrence [injury] in question?

You are instructed that by the term "producing cause" as used in this issue is meant an efficient, exciting, contributing cause which, in a natural sequence, produced the injuries or damages complained of, if any. There may be more than one producing cause.

Answer: ________________

3. Warnings and Instructions for Prescription Drugs. Ordinarily, the product supplier's duty to provide adequate warnings and instructions extends beyond the purchaser to the ultimate user.[78] Prescription drugs and certain prescribed medical appliances, however, constitute an exception to this rule. The supplier is, of course, still obligated to provide an adequate warning of any potential risks of harm or danger and to provide adequate instructions for the safe administration of the drug. But the duty is lim-

---

App.—Corpus Christi 1982, writ ref'd n.r.e.); Shop Rite Foods Inc. v. Upjohn Co., 619 S.W.2d 574, 578 (Tex. Civ. App.—Amarillo 1981, writ ref'd n.r.e.); Bituminous Cas. Corp. v. Black & Decker Manufacturing Co., 518 S.W.2d 868, 872-73 (Tex. Civ. App.—Dallas 1974, writ ref'd n.r.e.).

78. Harrison v. Flota Mercante Grancolombina S.A., 577 F.2d 968, 977 (5th Cir. 1978). Reyes v. Wyeth Laboratories, 498 F.2d 1264, 1276 (5th Cir.) *cert. denied*, 419 U.S. 1046 (1974); Technical Chem. Co. v. Jacobs, 480 S.W.2d 602, 603 (Tex. 1972).

ited to providing instructions and warnings adequate for the treating physician.[79] This limitation is predicated on the rationale that the physician is a learned intermediary and is the individual best qualified to make an informed choice for a particular patient after weighing the benefits of a particular drug against the risk of harm posed by its use.[80]

The following illustrates submission of a prescriptive drug case.

Special Issue No. 1

At the time the ACME Company sold the thyroid medication in question, did it fail to give adequate warnings of the dangers of possible blindness to Dr. Easy Prescription? (There is some suggestion that the term "adequate" may require a definition.)[81]

Answer: ________________

Special Issue No. 2 (Predicated)

Did such failure render the medication defective as marketed?

You are instructed that by the term "defective" as used in this issue is meant a condition that renders it unreasonably dangerous. By the term "unreasonably dangerous" as used in this issue is meant a product that is dangerous to an extent beyond that which would be contemplated by the ordinary physician administering the product with the ordinary knowledge common to the community of physicians as to the product's characteristics.

Answer: ________________

Special Issue No. 3 (Predicated)

Was such failure a producing cause of the occurrence [injury] in question?

By the term "producing cause" as used in this issue is meant an efficient, exciting, or contributing cause, which, in a natural sequence, produced the injuries or damages complained of, if any.

---

79. *Reyes*, 498 F.2d at 1276; Cooper v. Bowser, 610 S.W.2d 825, 831 (Tex. Civ. App.—Tyler 1980, no writ); Gravis v. Parke- Davis & Co., 502 S.W.2d 863, 870 (Tex. Civ. App.—Corpus Christi 1973, writ ref'd n.r.e.).

80. *Reyes*, 498 F.2d at 1276; *Gravis*, 502 S.W.2d at 870.

81. Refer to note 77 *supra*.

There can be more than one producing cause.

Answer: ______________

B. Innocent Misrepresentation 402B

A form of strict liability distinct from strict tort liability under section 402A exists under the pseudonym of innocent misrepresentation. This doctrine was formulated by the authors of the Restatement in section 402B.[82] Section 402B provides that:

One engaged in the business of selling chattels who, by advertising, labels, or otherwise, makes to the public a misrepresentation of a material fact concerning the character or quality of a chattel sold by him is subject to liability for physical harm to a consumer of the chattel caused by justifiable reliance upon the misrepresentation, even though a) it is not made fraudulently or negligently, and b) the consumer has not bought the chattel from or entered into any contractual relation with the seller.[83]

1. Innocent Misrepresentation Generally. Significantly, in claims predicated on Sec. 402B, the product need not be defective in any respect; liability is premised on a misrepresentation of a material fact concerning the quality or character of the product that is relied upon and causes the plaintiff's injuries.[84] The representation, however, must be express; implied representations are not encompassed under the aegis of Sec. 402B.[85] Furthermore, mere statements of opinion or general praise of the product, commonly labeled as "sales talk" or "puffing" do not constitute representations of material facts. Section 402B requires factual representations of significant characteristics or performance capabilities of the product.[86]

---

82. Restatement (Second) of Torts § 402B (1965). *See generally* Sales, *The Innocent Misrepresentation Doctrine: Strict Liability under Sec. 402B*, 16 Hous. L. Rev. 239 (1979).

83. *Id.* Failure to request submission of any one of the elements in this section is an incorrect request that constitutes a waiver of any right to complain on appeal that should it have been submitted. Nugent v. Utica Cutlery Co., 636 S.W.2 805, 809 (Tex. App.—San Antonio 1982, writ dism'd).

84. Sales, *supra* note 73 at 252.

85. Franks v. National Dairy Products Corp., 282 F. Supp. 528, 533 (W.D. Tex. 1968), *aff'd*, 414 F.2d 682 (5th Cir. 1969). *See also* Sales, *supra* note 73 at 259.

86. Restatement (Second) of Torts § 402B, comment g (1965) *See also* Sales, *supra* note 73 at 256-57.

Moreover, an express misrepresentation of a material fact alone is insufficient to sustain liability; the misrepresentation must have reasonably influenced the plaintiff's use of the product.[87] In evaluating justifiable reliance, the subjective intent of the seller is immaterial; the user's reasonable objective belief is determinative.[88] Though a user is entitled to rely on a representation that a product is safe when used in a prescribed manner,[89] acquired information or knowledge that the representation is false rebuts the claim that the user justifiably relied on it.[90] Likewise, a user unaware of the misrepresentation at the time of the accident is precluded from later claiming reliance.[91]

The Texas Supreme Court adopted Sec. 402B in *Crocker v. Winthrop Laboratories*.[92] Plaintiff's husband died after becoming addicted to the drug Talwin prescribed by his physician. The manufacturers represented the drug as nonaddictive.[93] The jury determined that the drug was unreasonably dangerous as marketed even though the manufacturer "did not know and could not know of the risk involved."[94] The jury also found that the doctor relied upon the manufacturer's representations concerning the nonaddictive nature of Talwin.[95] Since the danger was neither foreseeable nor known when the product was marketed, the supreme court rejected

---

87. Restatement (Second) of Torts § 402B, comment j declares:

The rule here stated applies only where there is justifiable reliance upon the misrepresentation of the seller, and physical harm results because of such reliance, and because of the fact which is misrepresented. It does not apply where the misrepresentation is not known, or there is indifference to it, and it does not influence the purchase or subsequent conduct. At the same time, however, the misrepresentation need not be the sole inducement to purchase, or to use the chattel, and it is sufficient that it has been a substantial factor in that inducement.

88. American Safety Equip. Corp. v. Winkler, 640 P.2d 216, 222 (Colo. 1982) (en banc), *citing* Sales, *supra* note 73 at 261.

89. *See Franks*, 282 F. Supp. at 533; *Bristol-Myers Co.*, 548 S.W.2d at 425.

90. Ford Motor Co. v. Russell & Smith Ford Co., 474 S.W.2d 549, 559 (Tex. Civ. App.—Houston [14th Dist.] 1971, no writ), involved a dealer who discovered the falseness of representations that the 1965 Econoline Ford with a 240-engine would solve problems previously experienced with overheating when air conditioning units were installed. The dealer's continued installation of the air conditioning in the Econoline after obtaining this knowledge was unjustified as a matter of law. *Id.* at 560.

91. Restatement (Second) of Torts § 402B Comment j (1965); Sales, *supra* note 73 at 261.

92. 514 S.W.2d 429 (Tex. 1974).

93. *Id.* at 429-30.

94. *Id.* at 431.

95. *Id.*

strict tort liability under Sec. 402A for defective marketing.[96] The court, however, imposed strict liability under sec. 402B:

Whatever the danger and state of medical knowledge, and however rare the susceptibility of the user, when the drug company positively and specifically represents its product to be free and safe from all dangers of addiction, and when the treating physician relies upon that representation, the drug company is liable when the representation proves to be false and harm results.[97]

As *Crocker* demonstrates, the plaintiff may recover under Sec. 402B in instances in which recovery under Sec. 402A is foreclosed. Yet, while Sec. 402A offers recovery for injuries to collateral property as well as for personal injuries, recovery under Sec. 402B is limited to personal injury.[98] The two theories of strict tort liability differ not only in their essential elements but in their respective scope of recovery as well. Significantly, however, Sec. 402B parallels Sec. 402A in requiring that the plaintiff establish producing rather than proximate causation.[99]

The following illustrates submission of a Sec. 402B claim.

Special Issue No. 1

Did the Safe Drug Company represent to the public that its "Maximum Strength" aspirin would never cause stomach disorders or irritations?

Answer: ____________________

Special Issue No. 2 (Predicated)

Did the "Maximum Strength" aspirin cause stomach disorders or irritations?

Answer: ____________________

---

96. *Id.* at 433.

97. *Id.*

98. The language in § 402B speaks only of recovery for physical harm to the user or consumer and completely omits any reference to recovery for damages to property or economic loss. *See* Sales, *supra* note 73 at 264.

99. Crocker v. Winthrop Labs., 514 S.W.2d 429, 431 (Tex. 1974); Ford Motor Co. v. Russell & Smith Ford Co., 474 S.W.2d 549, 552 (Tex. Civ. App.—Houston [14th Dist.] 1971, no writ).

Special Issue No. 3 (Predicated)

Did the representation about the "Maximum Strength" aspirin involve a material fact concerning the character or quality of the aspirin in question?

You are instructed that by the term "material fact" is meant a fact that is important to a reasonable purchaser by which the purchaser may justifiably be expected to be influenced in making the decision to purchase the product.

Answer: ____________________

Special Issue No. 4 (Predicated)

Did the plaintiff rely on the representations made by the Safe Drug in purchasing the aspirin in question?

Answer: ____________________

Special Issue No. 5 (Predicated)

Was the failure of the aspirin to conform to representations of the Safe Drug Co. a producing cause of the occurrence [injury]?

You are instructed that by the term "producing cause" is meant an efficient, exciting, or contributing cause which, in the natural sequence, produced the injuries complained of, if any. There may be more than one producing cause.

Answer: ____________________

2. Innocent Misrepresentation and Prescriptive Drugs. As reflected in *Crocker*, the manufacturer of a prescription drug may be strictly liable for the physician's reliance on representations concerning ethical drug propensities.[100] Accordingly, issues for prescriptive drug cases under Sec. 402B require a different submission.

Special Issue No. 1

Did the Acme Drug Company represent to the medical profession that the drug "Good for a Lift" would cause no adverse side

---

100. *Crocker*, 514 S.W.2d at 433. *See also* Bristol Myers Co. v. Gonzales, 548 S.W.2d 416, 425 (Tex. Civ. App.—Corpus Christi 1976), *rev'd on other grounds*, 561 S.W.2d 801 (Tex. 1978). *See generally*, Comment, *Warnings and the Pharmaceutical Companies: Legal Status of the Package Insert*, 16 Hous. L. Rev. 140 (1978).

effect to patients suffering from diabetes?
Answer: ____________________

Special Issue No. 2 (Predicated)

Did the drug "Good for a Lift" cause adverse side effects in patients suffering from diabetes?
Answer: ____________________

Special Issue No. 3 (Predicated)

Did the representation concerning the absence of an adverse side effect involve a material fact concerning the character or quality of the drug in question?

You are instructed that by the term "material fact" is meant a fact that is important to a reasonable physician by which the physician may justifiably be expected to be influenced in making the decision to prescribe the drug for his patients.
Answer: ____________________

Special Issue No. 4 (Predicated)

Did Dr. E. Z. Prescription rely upon the representations made by the defendant in prescribing the drug "Good for a Lift" for the plaintiff?
Answer: ____________________

Special Issue No. 5 (Predicated)

Were the adverse side effects of the drug "Good for a Lift" a producing cause of the injuries sustained by the plaintiff?

You are instructed by the term "producing cause" is meant an efficient, exciting, or contributing cause which, in the natural sequence, produced the injuries complained of, if any. There may be more than one producing cause.
Answer: ____________________

C. *Breach of Implied Warranty*

In 1968, the Texas Legislature adopted the Uniform Commercial Code by enacting the TEXAS BUSINESS AND COMMERCE CODE.[101] The Code provides two types of implied warranty - the implied warranty of merchantability[102] and the implied warranty of fitness for a particular purpose.[103] The implied warranty of merchantability requires that the goods be fit for the ordinary purposes for which such goods are used.[104] The implied warranty of fitness for a particular purpose arises when the seller is cognizant of the particular use for which the goods are required and the buyer relies on the seller to furnish goods suitable for that purpose.[105]

These statutory warranties, unlike Sections 402A and 402B, provide a contractual remedy for recovering economic losses precipitated by unmerchantable products. In *Nobility Homes, Inc. v. Shivers*,[106] for example, plaintiff sought recovery for damage to his mobile home caused by defects in the home itself. In distinguishing

---

101. TEX. BUS. & CODE ANN. (Tex. UCC) (Vernon 1968 & Supp. 1985).

102. TEX. BUS. & CODE ANN. § 2.314 (Tex. UCC) (Vernon 1968).

103. TEX. BUS. & CODE ANN. § 2.315 (Tex. U.C.C.) (Vernon 1968).

104. Section 2.314 provides as follows:

> (a) Unless excluded or modified (Section 2.316), a warranty that the goods shall be merchantable is implied in a contract for their sale if the seller is a merchant with respect to goods of that kind. Under this section the serving for value of food or drink to be consumed either on the premises or elsewhere is a sale.
>
> (b) Goods to be merchantable must be at least such as
>
> (1) pass without objection in the trade under the contract description; and
>
> (2) in the case of fungible goods, are of fair average quality within the description; and
>
> (3) are fit for the ordinary purposes for which such goods are used; and
>
> (4) run, within the variation permitted by the agreement, of even kind, quality and quantity within each unit and among all units involved; and
>
> (5) are adequately contained, packaged, and labeled as the agreement may require; and
>
> (6) conform to the promises or affirmations of fact made on the container or label if any,
>
> (c) Unless excluded or modified (Section 2.316) other implied warranties may arise from course of dealing or usage of trade.

Id. at Section 2.314.

105. Section 2.315 provides as follows:

> Where the seller at the time of contracting has reason to know any particular purpose for which the goods are required and that the buyer is relying on the seller's skill or judgment to select or furnish suitable goods, there is unless excluded or modified under the next section an implied warranty that the goods shall be fit for such purpose.

Id. at Section 2.315.

106. 557 S.W.2d 77 (Tex. 1977).

between physical harm to property and economic loss, the Texas Supreme Court concluded that economic loss was not recoverable under strict tort liability.[107] The plaintiff was entitled, however, to recover for the economic loss to his mobile home under the U.C.C. warranty provisions.[108]

The court later elaborated on *Nobility Homes* in *Mid Continent Aircraft Corp. v. Curry County Spraying Service.*[109] The Court noted that damage to the product itself is essentially a loss of the benefit of the bargain and suggested that this motivated the legislature to provide that parties may rely on sales and contract law as the remedy for economic loss to the product itself.[110] The court stated further that the extension of the strict tort liability doctrine to economic loss would frustrate the legislature's intent that the code fully govern and codify the law of commercial transactions.[111]

Economic losses recoverable under breach of an implied warranty include damage to the product itself,[112] the cost of repair or replacement,[113] and any consequential loss resulting from the loss of the product.[114] Significantly, "consequential damages" as defined by the code includes injury to person or property.[115] A personal injury claim may thus be redressed under breach of an implied warranty as well as under Sec. 402A or Sec. 402B.[116] In the event collateral property is damaged as well as the product itself, the plaintiff may recover damages for both under either breach of implied warranty or under Sec. 402A.[117]

Though privity of contract traditionally is a prerequisite for

---

107. *Id.* at 80.
108. *Id.*
109. 572 S.W.2d 308 (Tex. 1978).
110. *Id.* at 313.
111. *Id.*
112. *Id.*
113. *Nobility Homes, Inc.*, 557 S.W.2d at 78 n.l.
114. Signal Oil & Gas Co. v. Universal Oil Prods., 572 S.W.2d 310 (Tex. 1978).
115. TEX. BUS. & COM. CODE ANN. § 2.715 (Tex. UCC).
116. Garcia v. Texas Instruments, Inc., 610 S.W.2d 456, 462 (Tex. 1980). Breach of implied warranty applies to defects in homes. Humber v. Morton, 426 S.W.2d 554 (Tex. 1968). This warranty action extends to subsequent purchasers of a home for latent defects. Gupta v. Ritter Homes Inc., 646 2d 168 (Tex. 1983). Moreover, the implied warranty encompasses both good workmanship and habitability; Evans v. Stiles, ___ S.W.2d ___, 28 Tex. Sup. Ct. J. 329, 330 (March 27, 1985).
117. *Signal Oil & Gas Co.*, 572 S.W.2d at 328.

actions predicated on breach of an implied warranty the supreme court in *Nobility Homes* repudiated privity as a requirement for actions initiated under the U.C.C.[118] The court stated that to hold otherwise would encourage manufacturers to use "collapsible corporations" to sell inferior products leaving buyers with no one to sue for economic loss.[119] The court summarily rejected the claim that in the absence of a privity requirement manufacturers would be exposed to unlimited and unforeseeable liability, observing that manufacturers and sellers are authorized to restrict their liability by modifying or excluding both implied and express warranties.[120] Accordingly, protection under an implied warranty parallels that of Sections 402A and 402B, extending past the purchaser to the ultimate user.

Unlike claims predicated on Sections 402A or 402B, a plaintiff alleging a breach of implied warranty must establish proximate rather than producing causation.[121] This distinction in the two remedies emanates from the code's definition of "consequential damages" as including injury to person or property "proximately resulting from any breach of warranty."[122] Thus, the plaintiff must not only prove that the breach caused the accident, but that it was

---

118. *Nobility Homes, Inc.* 557 S.W.2d at 81. See also Garcia, 610 S.W.2d at 465.

119. *Nobility Homes Inc.*, 557 S.W.2d at 81.

120. *Id.* Exclusions or modifications of implied warranty are governed by section 2.316 of the Texas Business and Commerce Code. Subsection (b) of this section states:

> To exclude or modify the implied warranty of merchant ability or any part of it the language must mention merchantability and in case of a writing must be conspicuous, and to exclude or modify any implied warranty of fitness the exclusion must be by a writing and conspicuous. Language to exclude all implied warranties of fitness is sufficient if it states, for example, that "There are no warranties which extend beyond the description on the face hereof.

However, subsection (g) of § 2.316 provides that:

> Notwithstanding Subsection (b)
>
> (1) unless the circumstances indicate otherwise, all implied warranties are excluded by expressions like "as is," "with all faults" or other language which in common understanding calls the buyer's attention to the exclusion of warranties and makes plain that there is no implied warranty; and
>
> (2) when the buyer before entering into the contract has examined the goods or the sample or model as fully as he desired or has refused to examine the goods there is no implied warranty with regard to defects which an examination ought in the circumstances to have revealed to him; and
>
> (3) an implied warranty can also be excluded or modified by course of dealing or course of performance or usage of trade.

121. *Signal Oil & Gas Co.*, 572 S.W.2d at 328.

122. *Id.*

reasonably foreseeable that the breach would cause such an accident and resulting injury or damage.

1. Special Issues for Breach of Implied Warranty of Merchantability. The following illustrates a proper submission of issues for breach of implied warranty of merchantability under the Uniform Commercial Code.

Special Issue No. 1

Was the welding mask supplied by the Craftlite Tool Co. unfit for the ordinary purposes for which such masks are used?

Answer: ____________________

Special Issue No. 2 (Predicated)

Was that unfit condition a proximate cause of the occurrence in question?

You are instructed that "proximate cause" means that cause which, in a natural and continuous sequence, produces an event, and without which cause such event would not have occurred; and in order to be a proximate cause the act or omission complained of must be such that a person using ordinary care would have foreseen that the event or some similar event, might reasonably result therefrom. There may be more than one proximate cause of an event.

Answer: ____________________

2. *Special Issues For Breach of Implied Warranty of Fitness for a Particular Purpose.* The following illustrates a proper submission of issues for breaches of implied warranty of fitness for a particular purpose under the Uniform Commercial Code.

Special Issue No. 1

At the time of the contracting, did the Acme Engine Co. know the particular purpose for which the diesel engine was purchased?

Answer: ____________________

Special Issue No. 2 (Predicated)

At the time of the contracting, did Acme Engine Co. have reason to know that the Plaintiff was relying on the company's skill or judgment to select a suitable engine?

Answer: ____________________

Special Issue No. 3 (Predicated)

Was the diesel engine supplied by Acme Engine Co. unfit for the particular purpose for which it was purchased?

Answer: ____________________

Special Issue No. 4 (Predicated)

Was the unfit condition of the engine a proximate cause of the occurrence in question?

You are instructed that "proximate cause" means that cause which, in a natural and continuous sequence, produces an event, and without which cause such event would not have occurred; and in order to be a proximate cause the act or omission complained of must be such that a person using ordinary care would have foreseen that the event or some similar event, might reasonably result therefrom. There may be more than one proximate cause of an event.

Answer: ____________________

D. *Negligence*

The plaintiff in a product case frequently institutes suit against the product supplier based on negligence as well as strict tort liability.[123] This approach may be advantageous under various circumstances. For example, plaintiff may desire to recover damages for economic loss. Under *Nobility Homes*, the plaintiff is precluded from recovering economic damages under Section 402A of the Restatement.[124] Thus, the plaintiff may elect to sue the seller for breach of an implied warranty. Under Section 2.316 of the Texas Business and Commerce Code, however, a seller is author-

---

123. *See, e.g.*, Hagans v. Oliver Mach. Co., 576 F.2d 97, 98 (5th Cir. 1978); *Signal Oil & Gas Co.*, 572 S.W.2d at 323; Durbin v. American Mfg. Co., 643 S.W.2d 239, 240 (Tex. App.—El Paso 1982, writ ref'd n.r.e.); Thomas v. St. Joseph Hospital., 618 S.W.2d 791, 793 (Tex. Civ. App.—Houston [1st Dist.] 1981, no writ). When plaintiff alleges both negligence and strict tort liability, he is entitled to submission of both theories to the jury. Syrie v. Knoll Int'l, 748 F.2d 304, 310 (5th Cir. 1984).

124. Nobility Homes Inc., v. Shivers, 557 S.W.2d 77, 78 (Tex. 1977).

ized to disclaim such warranties pursuant to Section 2.316 of the Code.[125] Confronted with a legally recognizable disclaimer of all warranties, the plaintiff may still recover damages for the economic loss based on negligence.[126] To preserve all options for a complete recovery, the plaintiff should plead negligence as well as breach of implied warranty and strict tort liability.[127]

In other instances, negligence may represent the plaintiff's only cause of action against a particular defendant. Significantly, the U.C.C. warranties apply only to merchants or sellers[128] while the strict tort liability doctrine extends to product suppliers engaged in the regular business of selling or leasing products.[129] To recover against product suppliers that do not qualify under these characterizations, the plaintiff must establish a cause of action based on negligence. As an example, in *Freeman v. United States*,[130] the plaintiff sustained adverse side effects from a vaccination administered under a federal program. Since the United States government qualifies as neither a merchant nor a party regularly engaged in selling vaccine, liability could not be imposed under either the U.C.C. warranty provisions or strict tort liability. Accordingly, the only legally cognizable remedy available to the plaintiff against the government was negligent failure to warn.

As the court in *Freeman* indicates, suits based on negligence must satisfy more stringent requirements than actions predicated on strict tort liability.[131] Negligence requires the plaintiff to establish that the defendant failed to use ordinary care and that such failure was a proximate cause of the event.[132] Absent proof of these essential elements, liability cannot be predicated on negligence.

The following issues and definitions illustrate submission of

---

125. TEX. BUS. & COM. CODE ANN. § 2.316 (Vernon 1968).

126. *Nobility Homes Inc.*, 557 S.W.2d at 78.

127. *Syrie v. Knoll Int'l*, 748 F.2d 304, 306-307 (5th Cir. 1984); Foster v. Ford Motor Co., 616 F.2d 1304 (5th Cir. 1984); Gonzales v. Caterpillar Tractor Co., 571 S.W.2d 867 (1978).

128. TEX. BUS. & COM. CODE ANN. §§ 2.314, 2.315 (Vernon 1968).

129. *See* RESTATEMENT (SECOND) OF TORTS 402A (1965). *See also* Rourke v. Garza, 530 S.W.2d 794, 798 (Tex. 1975) (discussing "seller" under 402A). Seller encompasses any party involved in regularly introducing products into the stream of commerce. *See, e.g.*, Armstrong Rubber Co. v. Urquidez, 570 S.W.2d 374 (Tex. 1978).

130. 704 F.2d 154 (5th Cir. 1983).

131. *See Id.* at 158-159. (Plaintiff failed to meet burden of proving that the side effect was reasonably foreseeable).

132. *See generally* 3 TEXAS PATTERN JURY CHARGE 2.01-02 (1982).

negligence actions.

Special Issue No. 1 (Predicated)

Did defendant fail to warn the plaintiff that the EZ hay bailer could propel objects into the area of the operator?

Answer: ________________

Special Issue No. 2 (Predicated)

Do you find that such failure to warn was negligence?

You are instructed that by the term "negligence" is meant a failure to use ordinary care: that is to say, failure to do that which a person of ordinary prudence would have done under the same or similar circumstances, or doing that which a person of ordinary prudence would not have done under the same or similar circumstances.

Answer:________________

Special Issue No. 3 (Predicated)

Was such negligence a proximate cause of the occurrence in question?

You are instructed that "proximate cause" means that cause which, in a natural and continuous sequence, produces an event, and without which cause such event would not have occurred; and in order to be a proximate cause the act or omission complained of must be such that a person using ordinary care would have foreseen that the event or some similar event, might reasonably result therefrom. There may be more than one proximate cause of an event.

Answer: ________________

10.02 DEFENDANTS CASE

A. Defenses Prior to Duncan v. Cessna Aircraft Co.

Restatement (Second) of Torts expressly rejects contributory negligence in the form of the failure to inspect or the failure to guard against a defect as a defense to strict liability actions.[133] Un-

133. RESTATEMENT (SECOND) OF TORTS § 402A Comment n (1965) states as follows:

til the recent Texas Supreme Court decision in *Duncan v. Cessna Aircraft Co.*,[134] Texas courts scrupulously rejected any form of contributory negligence as a defense to strict tort liability.[135] Even under the Restatement, however, manufacturers and sellers were exonerated from strict tort liability for unforeseeable misuse of the product and assumption of the risk.[136]

Assumption of the risk, though rejected as a defense in negligence actions due to the enactment of Article 2212a,[137] was retained as a defense in strict tort liability actions. Assumption of the risk constituted a complete bar to recovery.[138] To invoke the assumption of the risk defense, the product supplier was required to establish 1) that the plaintiff knew of the particular defective condition that caused his injury, 2) that the plaintiff appreciated the nature and extent of the danger and 3) that the plaintiff acted voluntarily in encountering the dangerous condition of the product.[139] The plaintiff's knowledge and appreciation of the danger was required to be subjective rather than objective.[140] These requirements coupled with the court's hesitancy to completely bar a plaintiff's recovery, effectively emasculated assumption of the risk as a viable defense.[141]

Contributory negligence. Since the liability with which this Section deals is not based upon negligence of the seller, but is strict liability, the rule applied to strict liability cases (see 524) applies. Contributory negligence of the plaintiff is not a defense when such negligence consists merely in a failure to discover the defect in the product, or to guard against the possibility of its existence. On the other hand, the form of contributory negligence which consists in voluntarily and unreasonable proceeding to encounter a known danger, and commonly passes under this Section as in other cases of strict liability. If the user or consumer discovers the defect and is aware of the danger, and nevertheless proceeds unreasonably to make use of the product and is injured by it, he is barred from recovery.

134. 665 S.W.2d 414 (Tex. 1984).

135. The Texas Supreme Court in Shamrock Fuel & Oil Sales v. Tunks, 416 S.W.2d 779 (Tex. 1967), adopted the Restatement position. Later in Henderson v. Ford Motor Co., 519 S.W.2d 87, 89 (Tex. 1974), the Supreme Court rejected any form of contributory negligence as a defense.

136. Refer to note 133 *supra*.

137. Tex. Rev. Civ. Stat. Ann. art. 2212a (Vernon Supp. 1982-83) (comparative negligence statute).

138. Sales, *Assumption of the Risk and Misuse in Strict Tort Liability - Prelude to Comparative Fault*, 11 Tex. Tech. L. Rev. 729, 748 (1980).

139. *See generally* Hagans v. Oliver Mach. Co., 576 F.2d 97, 103 (5th Cir. 1978); Henderson v. Ford Motor Co., 519 S.W.2d 87, 91-92 (Tex. 1974). *See generally* Sales, *supra* note 138 at 741.

140. Sales, *supra* note 138 at 741.

141. *See generally* Caterpillar Tractor Co. v. Gonzales, 599 S.W.2d 633 (Tex. Civ. App.—El Paso 1980, no writ) (operator knowledgeable of the slippery condition of the step

Though not constituting a complete bar to recovery, plaintiff's misuse of the product was recognized as a partial defense to a strict tort liability action. In *General Motors v. Hopkins*[142] the Texas Supreme Court established that recovery would be barred to the extent the plaintiff's misuse proximately caused the damaging event.[143] In theory, *Hopkins* established a system of comparative fault which presumably offered defendant suppliers some minimal relief from the harshness of strict tort liability. As the *Hopkins* court emphasized, however, misuse of the product constituted a defense only to the extent it was unforeseeable from the perspective of the product supplier and then only to the extent that the plaintiff should reasonably have foreseen that the misuse would lead to injury.[144]

The requirement that the misuse be unforeseeable to the supplier successfully eviserated the legal effect of this defense. Arguably, nearly all forms of product misuse are foreseeable, and court decisions confirmed the emasculating effect of the unforeseeable standard.[145] In practice, therefore, the misuse defense was equally as ineffectual as the defense of assumption of the risk.[146]

Recognizing the inadequacies of misuse of the product and assumption of the risk as defenses and the ineluctable need for revision, the Texas Supreme Court reappraised the defenses applicable to breach of implied warranty actions. In *Signal Oil and Gas Co. v. Universal Oil Products,*,[147] the court established contributory negligence as a valid defense to actions predicated on breach of an implied warranty.[148] Moreover, relying on its decision in *Hopkins*,

---

down from the operator's compartment was deemed not to subjectively appreciate the specific danger of slipping); Bell Helicopter v. Bradshaw, 594 S.W.2d 518 (Tex. Civ. App.—Corpus Christi 1979, writ ref'd n.r.e.)(experienced helicopter pilot found not to appreciate the specific condition or the specific danger involved in using rotor blades in excess of 500 hours prescribed in the owners manual).

142. 548 S.W.2d 344 (Tex. 1977).

143. *Id.* at 351.

144. *Id.*

145. *See, e.g.*, Wenzel v. Rollins Motor Co., 598 S.W.2d 895, 900 (Tex. Civ. App.—El Paso 1980, writ ref'd n.r.e.) (stating that unforeseeable use requirement essentially abolishes the defense of misuse). *See also* Sales, *Comparative Causation in Strict Liability: One Perspective of Duncan v. Cessna Aircraft Corp.*, 3 The Advocate, State Bar Litigation section Report No. 2,3,4 (1984).

146. *See generally*, Sales, *Assumption of the Risk and Misuse in Strict Liability - Prelude to Comparative Fault.* 11 Tex. Tech. L. Rev. 729, 752 (1980).

147. 572 S.W.2d 320 (Tex. 1978).

148. *Id.* at 329.

the court judicially promulgated a system of pure comparative fault in determining the product supplier's liability.[149] Accordingly, in suits predicated on breach of an implied warranty the plaintiff's recovery is limited to the extent his own negligence proximately caused his injuries.[150] Only if the plaintiff's contributory negligence constitutes 100% of the cause of his injuries is the plaintiff completely barred from recovery.[151]

During the period in which the courts were evolving defenses to breach of implied warranty and strict tort liability claims, the Texas legislature enacted a comparative negligence system under Article 2212a.[152] Under article 2212a, plaintiff's recovery is reduced by the percentage of the harm attributable to his negligence.[153] The statute closely resembles the common law treatment of unforeseeable misuse in strict tort liability cases and contributory negligence in implied warranty cases. Unlike these common law systems, however, article 2212a imposes a 51% bar that precludes the plaintiff from any recovery when his negligence causes more than 50% of the damages.[154] Undoubtedly influenced by the 51% bar provision, the Texas Supreme Court in *General Motors Corp. v. Simmons*[155] limited Article 2212a to cases involving negligent defendants only.[156] The court recognized the persuasive arguments in favor of comparative fault allocation in strict tort liability cases and urged the legislature to take constructive action.[157]

In 1981, the Texas House of Representatives responded to these urgings, passing a bill which called for the adoption of comparative fault as a defense to strict tort liability actions.[158] The bill

---

149. *Id.*
150. *Id.*
151. *Id.*
152. TEX. REV. CIV. STAT. ANN. art. 2212a § 1 (Vernon Supp. 1982-83):

Section 1. Contributory negligence shall not bar recovery in an action by any person or party or the legal representative of any person or party to recover damages for negligence resulting in death or injury to persons or property if such negligence is not greater than the negligence of the person or party or persons or parties against whom recovery is sought, but any damages allowed shall be diminished in proportion to the amount of negligence attributed to the person or party recovering.

153. *Id.*
154. *Id.*
155. 558 S.W.2d 855 (Tex. 1977).
156. *Id.* at 862.
157. *Id.* at 863.
158. Sales, *Comparative Causation in Strict Tort Liability: One Perspective of Duncan v. Cessna Aircraft Corp.*, 3 THE ADVOCATE, State Bar Litigation Section Report No.

failed in the Senate, however, and the defenses to strict liability remained unchanged.

B. *Comparative Causation under Duncan v. Cessna Aircraft Co.*

After waiting unavailingly for legislative action, the Texas Supreme Court concluded that the time had come for judicial intervention. In *Duncan v. Cessna Aircraft Co.*[159] the court was confronted with a crashworthiness case in which the decedent was fatally injured in the crash of an aircraft in which he was riding as a passenger when the supports on the seat he occupied collapsed upon impact. The manufacturer contended that the pilot's and owner's negligence were either the sole or at least contributing causes of decedent's fatal injuries.[160] Reviewing the painful evolution of products liability defenses, the supreme court concluded that consideration of plaintiff's negligence should no longer be precluded in suits based on strict tort liability.[161] The court then announced that in all cases in which at least one defendant is found liable under a theory other than negligence, the doctrine of comparative causation would apply.[162]

Under comparative causation, assumption of the risk and misuse no longer represent separate defenses but are "subsumed under the more familiar notion of contributory negligence."[163] Plaintiff's conduct, whether characterized as contributory negligence, assumed risk, misuse, failure to mitigate and failure to avoid damages must now be compared with the defendant's conduct or products.[164] Consequently, plaintiff's contributory negligence constitutes a partial bar to recovery based on a pure comparative evaluation.[165] The court reaffirmed, however, that the simple failure to discover or to guard against the possibility of a product defect does not constitute negligence under the comparative causation

---

2, 3, 4 (1984).

159. 665 S.W.2d 414 (Tex. 1984).

160. *Id.* at 418.

161. *Id.* at 423-24.

162. The court stated, "[w]e therefore hold that in products liability cases in which at least one defendant is found liable on a theory other than negligence, the plaintiff's damages shall be reduced only by the percentage of causation attributed to the plaintiff, regardless of how large or small that percentage may be." *Id.* at 429.

163. *Id.* at 428.

164. *Id.* at 427.

165. *Id.* at 429.

doctrine.[166]

The *Duncan* court emphasized that it was establishing a "pure" rather than "modified" system of comparative allocation.[167] In other words, the "51% bar rule" imposed by article 2212a simply does not apply in cases governed by *Duncan*. Thus, even where plaintiff's negligence contributes substantially more than fifty percent of his injuries, the comparative causation doctrine authorizes recovery for that portion of the injuries attributable to defendant's defective product.[168]

This "pure" system of allocating loss is characterized as comparative "causation" rather than comparative "fault."[169] According to the court, causation is a more appropriate concept than fault since negligence has never constituted a requirement for strict tort or breach of warranty liability.[170] Furthermore, the court emphasized that comparative causation contemplates causation of the injury rather than the accident.[171] Thus, this new doctrine is especially appropriate for cases involving crashworthiness in which the defect neither causes nor contributes to cause the accident, but rather, it causes or enhances the injuries over and above the injuries produced by the initial accident.[172]

Prior to *Duncan*, the supreme court determined in two nonproduct negligence cases that a plaintiff's negligence contributing to his injuries but not contributing to the accident producing event was not applicable to limit that plaintiff's recovery.[173] Under the

---

166. *Id.* at 432. The court reaffirmed this provision of § 402A Comment n., citing McKisson v. Sales Affiliates, Inc., 416 S.W.2d 787 (Tex. 1967) and Shamrock Fuel and Oil Sales Co. v. Tunks, 416 S.W.2d 779 (Tex. 1967).

167. *Duncan*, 665 S.W.2d at 424 (Tex. 1984).

168. *Id.* at 428.

169. *Id.* at 427.

170. *Id.*

171. *Id.* at 428.

172. *Id.*

173. In *Kerby v. Abilene Christian College*, 503 S.W.2d 526 (Tex. 1973), the supreme court refused to consider the contributory negligence of a truck driver who left the door of his van open in order to limit the damage caused by the negligent driver who collided with the plaintiff's van. In so refusing, the court fashioned a distinction between negligence that contributes to the accident and negligence that contributes to the plaintiff's injuries. The court further stated that "contributory negligence must have the causal connection with the accident that but for the conduct the accident would not have happened. Negligence that merely increases or adds to the extent of the loss or injury occasioned by another's negligence is not such contributory negligence as will defeat recovery." *Id.* at 528. Similarly in Carnation Co. v. Wong, 516 S.W.2d 116 (Tex. 1974), the court, following its decision in

comparative negligence statute, the court declared that a plaintiff's failure to wear safety belts or otherwise mitigate the injury did not limit his recovery even though such failure unquestionably contributed to his injuries.[174] However, under comparative causation as literally defined in *Duncan*,[175] the plaintiff's recovery should be reduced by the percentage of the injury caused by his failure to avoid the consequences of injury.[176] Thus, when the plaintiff obtains a jury award based on a theory other than negligence, contributory negligence in failing to utilize injury avoidance devices should clearly limit the amount of recovery.

Though the failure to avoid the consequences of injury and the failure to mitigate damages constitute defenses under the pure comparative causation doctrine of *Duncan* such failures apparently are not valid defenses to claims governed by article 2212a.[177] Consequently, when a plaintiff's failure to avoid the consequences of injury-producing events contributes substantially to the injury but not to the accident, it undoubtedly is advantageous for the plaintiff to institute suit against the manufacturer based solely on negligence rather than breach of implied warranty or strict tort liability, thereby bringing article 2212a into play. Likewise, defendant manufacturers in such cases will undoubtedly endeavor to invoke pure comparative causation by instituting a third party action

---

Kerby, concluded that the failure to wear seat belts is not the type of contributory negligence that would limit the plaintiff's recovery since such failure did neither cause nor contribute to the accident. *Id.* at 117.

174. *See* Carnation Co. v. Wong, 516 S.W.2d 116 (Tex. 1974).

175. *Duncan*, 665 S.W.2d at 428.

176. *See, e.g.*, Foley v. City of West Allis, 113 Wis. 2d 475, 335 N.W.2d 824, 830-31 (1983) (where plaintiff was found negligent for failing to use seatbelt, such negligence contributed to 70% of her injuries thus so reducing her recovery); Halvorsen v. Voeller, 336 N.W.2d 118, 121 (N.D. 1983) (failure to wear a motorcycle helmet reduces damages if jury finds that such failure constitutes negligence).

177. The *Duncan* court emphasized that "[i]n cases *not* controlled by Art. 2212a, the system we adopt will allow comparison of plaintiff's conduct, whether it is characterized as assumption of risk, misuse, or *failure to mitigate or avoid damages*, with the conduct or product of a defendant. . ." 665 S.W.2d at 428 (emphasis added). This statement indicates that the court did not intend to alter the law of defenses established under article 2212a, including that law concerning failure to avoid or mitigate injuries. *Refer* to note 173 *supra* for cases holding that failure to avoid or mitigate injuries does not constitute a defense under Article 2212a. It must be noted, however, that the recent amendment to TEX. REV. CIV. STAT. ANN. art. 6701d expressly provides that failure to wear safety belts shall not constitute contributory negligence. Plaintiff's recovery would not be reduced if his negligence was failure to use a safety belt, but should be if, for example, the negligence was failure to wear a motorcycle helmet.

based on either Sections 402A, 402B or breach of an implied warranty.[178] Such "theory shopping" and disparity in treatment, however, may eventually lead the courts to establish one rule for all tort cases regardless of whether *Duncan* or article 2212a govern. It appears that the more uniform and realistic rule fashioned by the supreme court in *Duncan* effectuates an evenhanded allocation of the risk of injury producing events.[179]

C. Contribution Under Duncan *and Article 2212a*

The *Duncan* court addressed the issue "whether comparative contribution among joint tortfeasors is possible when at least one is strictly liable."[180] In answering this question, the court considered the development of two statutory provisions for contribution - Article 2212[181] and Article 2212a.[182]

1. Statutory Contribution. Under article 2212, the original contribution statute, all tortfeasors are jointly and severally liable to the plaintiff. The plaintiff may recover the entire judgment of

---

178. It is not entirely clear whether a negligent defendant can invoke the pure comparative causation doctrine through a third party action against a strictly liable tortfeasor or by submitting issues of an alleged strictly liable settling party's share of causation. In *Acord v. General Motors Corp.*, 669 S.W.2d 111 (Tex. 1984), the court held that a settling party's causation could be considered, without joinder, for the purpose of comparative causation. However, *Acord* is not entirely determinative of the issue since General Motors was found strictly liable and therefore comparative causation already applied before the settling party's causation was submitted. But, in *Cypress Creek Utility Service Co. v. Muller*, 640 S.W.2d 860 (Tex. 1982) the court held that under article 2212a, both the defendant and the plaintiff could submit liability issues for the purpose of seeking an allocation of negligence. Extending the rationale of both *Muller* and *Acord* it appears that the negligent defendant referred to in the text is entitled to invoke comparative causation by obtaining a finding of liability under Sections 402A, 402B or breach of implied warranty against a third party. *See generally*, Sales, *Comparative Causation in Strict Liability: One perspective of Duncan v. Cessna Aircraft Corp.*, 3 THE ADVOCATE, State Bar Litigation Section Report No. 2, 3, 8 (1984). The *Duncan* court demonstrates a clear intent to activate the comparative causation doctrine in as many situations as possible and avoid the 51% bar rate and credit election of article 2212a.

179. *See generally* Note, *An End in Search of a Means: Comparison-Based Defenses in Strict Products Liability in Texas* Duncan v. Cessna Aircraft Co., 21 HOUS. L. REV. 279, 280 (1984) (discussing *Duncan* as an attempt to avoid the inequities present in past decisions).

180. *Id.* at 422. *See also* Smithson v. Cessna Aircraft Co., 665 S.W.2d 439 (Tex. 1984) (companion case).

181. TEX. REV. CIV. STAT. ANN. art. 2212 (Vernon 1971).

182. TEX. REV. CIV. STAT. ANN. art. 2212a (Vernon Supp. 1984).

damages from any one tortfeasor.[183] Under article 2212, however, each tortfeasor possesses the right to seek contribution from nonpaying tortfeasors. Furthermore, joint liability under 2212 is allocated on a pro rata basis.[184] In other words, each tortfeasor owes an equal share of the damages.[185]

Article 2212 existed for more than five decades before another contribution statute was enacted - Article 2212a. Section 2 of article 2212a provides for contribution between joint tortfeasors on a percentage rather than a pro rata basis.[186] Accordingly, under article 2212a each tort feasor's share of the liability is proportionate to the percentage of fault allocated to him by the jury.[187] While article 2212 imposes joint and several liability in all instances, article 2212a provides an exception to defendants found to be less negligent than the plaintiff.[188]

Plaintiffs who are more than 50% at fault in causing the accident are barred from any recovery under article 2212a.[189] All tortfeasors escape liability when the plaintiff is responsible for causing 51% or more of the injuries.

Since the legislature adopted article 2212a without repealing article 2212, the full scope of article 2212a is not entirely clear. The Supreme Court in *General Motors Corp. v. Simmons*,[190] attempted to clarify this issue. In *Simmons*, the court determined that article 2212a was limited entirely to claims predicated on negligence.[191] Consequently, article 2212 was deemed to apply to suits in which

---

183. *See* note 180 *supra*. *See also* Sales, 3 THE ADVOCATE, State Bar Litigation Report No. 2 at 7.

184. TEX. REV. CIV. STAT. Ann. art. 2212 (Vernon 1971).

185. *Id. See* Sales, *Contribution and Indemnity Between Negligence & Strictly Liable Tortfeasors*, 12 ST. MARY'S L.J. 323, 331 (1980).

186. *See* note 182 *supra*.

187. Deal v. Madison, 576 S.W.2d 409, 416 (Tex. Civ. App.—Dallas 1978, writ ref'd. n.r.e.).

188. Subsection (c) of article 2212 § 2 states as follows:

> Each defendant is jointly and severally liable for the entire amount of the judgment awarded the claimant, *except that a defendant whose negligence is less than that of the claimant is liable to the claimant only for that portion of the judgment which represents the percentage of negligence attributable to him.* (emphasis added).

TEX. REV. CIV. STAT. ANN. art. 2212a, § 2(c) (Vernon Supp. 1985). *See also Duncan*, 665 S.W.2d at 429.

189. *Duncan*, 665 S.W.2d at 428.

190. 558 S.W.2d 855 (Tex. 1977).

191. *Id.* at 862.

strict tort liability was asserted against at least one of the defendants.[192] The court recognized, however, the problems inherent in dealing with such liability cases and, therefore, urged the legislature to take remedial action.[193]

2. *Duncan and Common Law Contribution.* Due to the legislature's failure to respond to the court's urging in *Simmons*, the *Duncan* court addressed the issue of contribution in the context of strict tort liability. After reviewing pro rata contribution, the court perceived the concept to be inconsistent with the doctrine of pure comparative causation.[194] Accordingly, the court overruled its prior decision in *Simmons* and declared that article 2212 no longer applied to claims predicated on either strict tort liability or breach of warranty.[195] While rejecting article 2212, the court also refused to embrace article 2212a. Instead, it extended the concept of pure comparative causation to claims for contribution as well as defenses in the primary suits.[196] If a defendant is found liable under Section 402A or Section 402B or for breach of an implied warranty, the doctrine of pure comparative contribution applies.[197] In several respects, *Duncan's* comparative causation doctrine parallels contribution under article 2212a. Primarily, both schemes allocate liability on a percentage rather than a pro rata basis.[198] Each joint tortfeasor is responsible to the other for the percentage of fault allocated. Under pure comparative contribution, however, all defendants remain jointly and severally liable to the plaintiff. The *Duncan* court expressly rejected article 2212a's exception[199] for defendants who are less at fault than the plaintiff.[200] Furthermore, joint tortfeasors are not discharged simply because the plaintiff's contributory fault caused more than 51% of his injuries.[201]

3. *Partial Settlements.* Another area in which pure comparative causation differs significantly from comparative negligence

---

192. *Id.* at 861-62.
193. *Id.* at 862-863. *See also Duncan*, 665 S.W.2d at 424.
194. *Duncan*, 665 S.W.2d at 427.
195. *Id.*
196. *Id.*
197. *Id.*
198. *See Id.* at 428-29 (comparing article 2212a and pure comparative causation).
199. TEX. REV. CIV. STAT. ANN. art. 2212a, § 2(c).
200. *Duncan*, 665 S.W.2d at 429.
201. *Id.* at 429.

under article 2212a involves suits in which at least one alleged tort feasor has settled with the plaintiff. Under article 2212a, a nonsettling defendant possesses the right to reduce liability to the plaintiff by one of two options. When the fault of the settling tortfeasor is submitted to the jury, each nonsettling defendant's liability is reduced in proportion to the percentage of negligence allocated to the settling tortfeasor.[202]

The nonsettling defendant may also reduce the ultimate liability by taking a dollar credit for the settlement.[203] This option exists only where there has been no determination of the settling tortfeasor's percentage of negligence.[204] When applicable, this credit reduces the total judgment by the amount of the settlement and the remaining portion of the judgment is then allocated to each nonsettling defendant in proportion to the percentage of fault assigned by the jury.[205] When the plaintiff makes a settlement which exceeds the total amount of the judgment, all the tortfeasors are exonerated of liability. This results from the one satisfaction rule established in *Bradshaw v. Baylor University*.[206]

In *Duncan* the supreme court considered the *Bradshaw* concept in the context of pure comparative causation.[207] The supreme court observed that the one satisfaction rule was originally adopted because courts could not conceive of allocating liability for indivisible injuries and therefore believed that a settlor could offer pay-

---

202. TEX. REV. CIV. STAT. ANN. art. 2212a, § 2(b) (Vernon Supp. 1985). For discussion of this process of contribution see Cypress Creek Util. Serv. Co. v. Muller, 640 S.W.2d 860, 864 (Tex. 1982).

203. TEX. REV. CIV. STAT. ANN. art. 2212a, § 2(d) (Vernon Supp. 1985). *See also Cypress Creek Util. Serv. Co.*, 640 S.W.2d at 864.

204. *Cypress Creek Util. Serv. Co.*, 640 S.W.2d at 864 (*citing inter alia*, Clemtex v. Dube, 578 S.W.2d 813 (Tex. Civ. App.— Beaumont 1979, writ ref'd n.r.e.); Edgar, *Procedural Aspects of Settlement: An Overview of Texas Law*, 12 ST. MARY'S L.J. 279, 319 (1980); Sales, *Limitations on Recovery of Damages in Personal Injury Actions*, 18 S. TEX. L.J. 217, 269 (1977)).

205. TEX. REV. CIV. STAT. ANN. art. 2212a, § 2(e) (Vernon Supp. 1985); *Cypress Creek Util. Serv. Co.*, 640 S.W.2d at 864.

206. 126 Tex. 99, 84 S.W.2d 703 (Tex. Comm'n App. 1935, opinion adopted) The court held that a plaintiff has no right to recover damages from a non-settling tortfeasor when he has been fully compensated for his injuries in a settlement with another tortfeasor. 126 Tex. at 104, 84 S.W.2d at 705. Significantly, in *Cypress Creek Util. Serv. Co.*, 640 S.W.2d at 864-65, the Texas Supreme Court held that the *Bradshaw* rule was abrogated by article 2212a, § 2(c). Subsection (e) dictates that if a settling party's percentage of fault is established, his settlement acts as a complete release of his liability. *Id.*, at 864-65. Notably the settlement in *Cypress* was beyond the defendant's control yet the dollar credit was still denied.

207. *Duncan*, 665 S.W.2d at 430.

ment only for the whole injury and not just his part.[208] Since comparative causation allows allocation of liability even for indivisible injuries, the *Duncan* court held that the rationale for the one recovery rule no longer applied.[209] The court, therefore, rejected the one satisfaction rule as well as the dollar credit allowed under article 2212a and limited the nonsettling defendant's remedy to reduction of liability based on the percentage of causation assigned by the trier of fact to the settling tortfeasor.

Whether article 2212a or comparative causation governs is often critical. For example, when the plaintiff effectuates a substantial settlement with an alleged strictly liable tortfeasor and then sues a negligent joint tortfeasor, it is significant whether article 2212a or comparative causation applies. If article 2212a applies and no issues are submitted against the settling tortfeasor, the defendant can elect to take a dollar credit for the settlement to reduce the amount of the damage award. [210] If the comparative causation doctrine applies then, of course, the defendant is limited to a proportionate reduction based on the percentage of fault allocated to the settling tortfeasor. Under *Duncan*, comparative contribution applies whenever grounds of recovery other than negligence are established.[211]

The issue of joinder of settling parties arises under partial settlement. The *Duncan* court failed to clarify whether settling parties must be joined before their percentage of causation may be submitted to the jury. Following *Duncan*, it was less than clear whether a defendant could reduce liability by the percentage of causation attributable to the settling tort feasor without instituting a third party action against the settling party.

The supreme court confronted this issue in *Acord v. General Motors Corp.*[212] The court established that joinder was not required to seek and obtain an allocation of a percentage share of causation.[213] In fact, the court emphasized that requiring such joinder would serve "no useful purpose."[214] The defendant is entitled

---

208. *Id.* at 431.
209. *Id.*
210. Refer to note 206 *supra* and accompanying text.
211. *Duncan*, 665 S.W.2d at 429.
212. 669 S.W.2d 111 (Tex. 1984).
213. *Id.* at 117.
214. *Id.*

to submit issues of the settling tortfeasor's percentage share of causation without making the settling tortfeasor a party to the suit. The same rule ostensibly applies to suits predicated on article 2212a.[215]

D. *Submission of the issues under* Duncan *and Art. 2212a*

In *Duncan*, the court attempted to resolve the procedural and substantive problems encountered in product liability suits involving multiple theories of liability. The following illustrates submission of comparative causation in strict tort liability actions.

If in answer to Questions ____, ____, and ____ you have found that more than one party's act(s), omission(s) or product(s) caused the [injury], and only in that event, then answer the following question.

Question

For each party or product found by you to have caused or contributed to cause the plaintiff's injury find from a preponderance of the evidence the percentage of the total injury caused by:

Dangerous Defendant ____%
Product X

[and ABC Company] ____%

Pious Plaintiff ____%
Silent Settlor -—%
TOTAL 100%
The percentage you find must total 100%."

10.03 Plaintiffs' - Defendants' Case Submitted Under Both Negligence and Strict Tort Liability Theories

An obvious problem is presented by the dichotomy in treatment of plaintiff's conduct in the submission issues to the jury when the plaintiff alleges both negligence and strict tort liability against one or more defendants. It is well established that when the plaintiff pleads and introduces evidence on both the theory of negligence and strict tort liability, the trial court is obligated to

---

215. *See, e.g.,,* Deal v. Madison, 576 S.W.2d 409 (Tex. Civ. App.—Dallas 1978, writ ref'd n.r.e.); *See generally*, Sales, *Conribution and Indemniy Between Negligent and Strictly Liable to Tortfeasors* 12 St. Mary's L.J. 323, 348 (1980).

submit both theories to the jury.[216] If the jury finds strict tort liability, the doctrine of comparative causation applies and defenses such as contributory negligence, (except failure to discover a defect or to anticipate a defective condition) mitigation of damage and avoidable consequences attributable to the plaintiff may be considered by the jury in assigning a percentage causation of injury.[217] On the other hand, if the jury fails to find issues that support the strict tort liability theory but finds in favor of the plaintiff on the negligence issues, conduct of the plaintiff constituting failure to discover a defective condition and failure to anticipate the existence of a defective condition, qualifying as contributory negligence for purposes of a defense to the plaintiff's claim. However, avoidable consequences is not a defense and mitigation of damages must be submitted only as an instruction.[218] The negligent failure to discover or to anticipate the presence of a defect in a product which is not a defense under pure comparative causation, however, does constitute contributory negligence for purposes of a negligence action.[219] Consequently, the submission of issues under the dual theories of negligence and strict tort liability present unique and difficult problems in the submission practice.

Perhaps the most viable approach to the submission of issues under dual theories involves submission of detailed issues inquiring about the percentage of plaintiff's injuries caused respectively by a product defect, the negligent defendant, and the contributorily negligent plaintiff. Utilizing an issue predicated on a finding of percentage of causation attributed to the plaintiff's overall con-

---

216. In Syre v. Knoll Int'l., 748 F.2d 304 (5th Cir. 1984), the plaintiff pleaded both negligence and strict tort liability. The trial court submitted the theory of strict tort liability but refused to submit any issues on negligence. After the jury returned a verdict in favor of the manufacturer on strict tort liability, the trial court entered judgment for the defendant. The Fifth Circuit reversed and remanded the case on the basis that despite the finding of no liability under § 402A, the plaintiff was entitled to submission of her negligence theory. 748 F.2d at 310.

217. *Duncan*, 665 S.W.2d at 428.

218. *See, e.g.*, Kerby v. Abilene Christian College, 503 S.W.2d 526 (Tex. 1973) (refusing to permit the use of avoidable consequences as a form of contributory negligence). Carnation Co. v. Wong, 516 S.W.2d 116 (Tex. 1974) (refusing to permit use of avoidable consequences in failing to wear seat belts as a form of contributory negligence).

219. In *Duncan*, 665 S.W.2d at 432, the court "reaffirm[ed] the rule in § 402A comment n of the RESTATEMENT (SECOND) OF TORTS that negligent failure to discover or guard against a product defect is not a defense." Significantly, the court did not attempt to extend this caveat to claims of negligence governed by article 2212a.

tributory negligence, the jury would then be requested to determine the percentage of causation that plaintiff's failure to inspect or failure to guard against the existence of a defect in a product, failure to mitigate damages and failure to avoid the consequences of injury caused the injuries as distinguished from the occurrence.

The following submission illustrates the issues and definitions for the dual submission of a negligence and strict tort liability case:

Special Issue No. 1

On the occasion in question, was Dangerous Defendant driving his vehicle at a greater rate of speed than a person using ordinary care would have driven?

Answer: ______________

You are instructed that by the term "ordinary care" is meant the degree of care which would be used by a person of ordinary prudence under the same or similar circumstances.

Special Issue No. 2 (Predicated)

Was Dangerous Defendant's action a proximate case of the occurrence in question?

Answer: ________________

By the term "proximate cause" is meant that cause which, in a natural and continuous sequence, produces an event, and without which cause such an event would not have occurred; in order to be a proximate cause, the act or omission complained of must be such that a person using ordinary care would have foreseen that the event, or some similar event, might reasonably result there from. There may be more than one proximate cause to an event.

Special Issue No. 3

On the occasion in question, did Silent Settlor fail to keep such lookout as a person using ordinary care would have kept?

Answer: ________________

You are instructed that by the term "ordinary care" is meant that degree of care which would be used by a person of ordinary prudence in the same or similar circumstances.

Special Issue No. 4 (Predicated)

Was such act by Silent Settlor a proximate cause of the occurrence in question?

Answer: ________________

You are instructed that by the term "proximate cause" means that cause which, in a natural and continuous sequence, produces an event, and without which cause such event would not have occurred; in order to be a proximate cause, the act or omission complained of must be such that a person using ordinary care would have foreseen that the event, or some similar event, might reasonably result therefrom. There may be more than one proximate cause of an event.

Special Issue No. 5

On the occasion in question, did Pious Plaintiff fail to apply the brakes on his automobile such as would have been applied by a person using ordinary care would have applied such brakes?

Answer: ________________

You are instructed that by the term "ordinary care" is meant that degree of care which would be used by a person of ordinary prudence under the same or similar circumstances.

Special Issue No. 6 (Predicated on No. 5)

Was Pious Plaintiff's act a proximate cause of the occurrence in question?

Answer: ________________

By the term "proximate cause" is meant that cause which, in a natural and continuous sequence, produces an event, and without which cause such event would have not occurred; and in order to be a proximate cause, the act or omission complained of must be such that a person using ordinary care would have foreseen that the event, or some similar event, might reasonably result therefrom. There may be more than one proximate cause of an event.

Special Issue No. 7

Was the suspension system on the automobile of Pious Plaintiff defective at the time it left the possession of the ABC Manufacturing Company?

Answer: ________________

You are instructed that by the term "defective" as used in this issue is meant a condition of the product that renders it "unreasonably dangerous."

You are further instructed that by the term "unreasonably dangerous" as used in this issue is meant a product that is dangerous to an extent beyond that which would be contemplated by the ordinary user of the product, with the ordinary knowledge common to the community as to the product's characteristics.[220]

Special Issue No. 8 (Predicated on No. 7)

Was such defect a producing cause of the occurrence [injury] in question?

Answer: ________________

You are instructed that by the term "producing cause" as used in this issue is meant an efficient, exciting, or contributing cause which, in a natural sequence, produces the injuries or damages complained of, if any. There can be more than one producing cause.

Special Issue No. 9

Was the roof of Pious Plaintiff's automobile defectively designed at the time it left the possession of the ABC Manufacturing Company?

Answer: ________________

You are instructed that a defectively designed product is a product that is unreasonably dangerous, taking into consideration the utility of the product and the risk involved in its use."[221]

---

220. When submitting both a manufacturing defect and a design defect, both the "ordinary user" instruction appropriate for manufacturing defects and the *Turner* "balancing" instruction appropriate for design defects must be submitted to the jury. *See* Ford Motor Co. v. Pool, 688 S.W.2d 879 (Tex. App.—Texarkana 1985, no writ).

221. An issue inquiring about a design defect, whether it involves a defect causing the accident or simply enhancing injury in a crashworthiness context, must be accompanied by the risk versus utility balancing test. Turner v. General Motors Corp., 584 S.W.2d 844 (Tex. 1979); Acord v. General Motors Corp., 669 S.W.2d 111 (Tex. 1984); Ford Motor Co. v. Pool, 688 S.W.2d 879 (Tex. App.—Texarkana 1985, no writ).

Special Issue No. 10 (Predicated)

Was such defective design a producing cause of any injury sustained by Pious Plaintiff?

Answer: ________________

You are instructed that by the term "producing cause" as used in this issue is meant an efficient, exciting or contributing cause which, in a natural sequence, produces the injuries or damages complained of, if any. There may be more than one producing cause.

Special Issue No. 11

Did the ABC Manufacturing Company fail to use ordinary care in designing the suspension system on Pious Plaintiff's automobile?

Answer: ________________

By the term "ordinary care" is meant that degree of care which would be used by a person of ordinary prudence under the same or similar circumstances.

Special Issue No. 12 (Predicated)

Was such failure a proximate cause of the occurrence in question?

Answer: ________________

By the term "proximate cause" is meant that cause which, in a natural and continuous sequence, produces an event, and without which cause such event would not have occurred; in order to be a proximate cause, the act or omission complained of must be such that a person using ordinary care would have foreseen that the event, or some similar event, might reasonably result therefrom. There may be more than one proximate cause of an event.

Special Issue No. 13

On the occasion in question, was Pious Plaintiff negligent in failing to heed the warnings of mechanic Jones to have the suspension system of his automobile replaced?

Answer: ________________

By the term "negligence" is meant the failure to use ordinary care; that is to say, failure to do that which a person of ordinary prudence would have done under the same or similar circumstances, or doing that which a person of ordinary prudence would not have done under the same or similar circumstances.

Special Issue No. 14 (Predicated)

Was such negligence a proximate cause of any injuries that Pious Plaintiff sustained on the occasion in question?

Answer: ________________

By the term "proximate cause" is meant that cause which, in a natural and continuous sequence, produces an event, and without which cause such event would not have occurred; in order to be a proximate cause, the act or omission complained of must be such that a person using ordinary care would have foreseen that the event, or some similar event, might reasonably result therefrom. There may be more than one proximate cause of an event.

Special Issue No. 15

Was Pious Plaintiff negligent in failing to continue prescribed therapy prescribed by his physician after only one year following the accident in question?

Answer: ________________

Special Issue No. 16

Was such negligence a proximate cause of any injury sustained by Pious Plaintiff?

Answer: ________________

Special Issue No. 17

If in answer to Special Issues No. 2, 4, 6, 8, 10, 12 14 or 16, you have found that more than one party's acts, omissions or products caused the occurrence and injuries, and only in that event, then answer the following issue.

For each party or product found by you to have caused the occurrence in question and injury to Pious Plaintiff, find from a preponderance of the evidence the percentage of the total injury caused by:

Dangerous Defendant ____%

The ABC Manufacturing Co. and its automobile ____%

Silent Settlor ____%
Pious Plaintiff ____%
TOTAL 100%
The total percentage you find must total 100%.

Special Issue No. 18 (Predicated on No. 16)

What percentage of causation assigned by you to Pious Plaintiff in answer to Special Issue No. 16 that you found resulted from his failure to take therapy.

Answer with a percentage: ____%

This proposed submission submits the contributory negligence of the plaintiff, the negligence of the nonsettling tortfeasor, the negligence of the settling tortfeasor, and the negligence and strict tort liability of the product supplier. It likewise submits the contributory negligence of the plaintiff under both the comparative negligence of article 2212a and the *Duncan* pure comparative causation doctrine. In addition, it submits avoidable consequences as negligence of the plaintiff that constitutes a defense under *Duncan* pure comparative causation but which does not constitute contributory negligence under article 2212a.[222] The separate submission of plaintiff's negligence in failing to avoid the consequences of injury enables the court to ascertain the percentage of injury causation attributable to anticipate the effect of a defective condition in a product as distinguished from the negligent conduct of the plaintiff that contributes to the accident.[223]

In the event the jury finds negligence against one or all of the parties but fails to find strict tort liability, then the provisions of article 2212a control the effect of the jury verdict.[224] On the other hand, if the jury finds negligence against one or more of the parties and strict tort liability against the product manufacturer, then the doctrine of pure comparative causation governs rather than the

---

222. Refer to notes 216-218 *supra* and accompanying text.

223. For discussion of the injury versus accident distinction, refer to notes 171-176 *supra* and accompanying text.

224. *Duncan*, 665 S.W.2d at 429. Under article 2212a, the failure of the plaintiff to anticipate the effects of a defective condition in a product would not constitute a form of contributory negligence and the trial court, under this submission, would disregard this percentage finding of the jury for purposes of entering judgment. Likewise, the provisions of article 2212a provide that should plaintiff's negligence exceed 51%, his contributory negligence would totally bar recovery against any defendant.

provisions of article 2212a.[225]

This proposed submission merely illustrates one approach to submitting the negligence and strict tort liability theories. Unquestionably, the dichotomy between article 2212a and the *Duncan* pure comparative causation presents a challenge in formulating appropriate special issue submission.[226] All elements of plaintiff's theory and all elements of defendant's defenses must be submitted in a manner that jeopardizes neither the theories of recovery nor the available defenses.

10.04 Conclusion

Under Texas law an individual injured by a product may seek recovery under any of the following theories: section 402A strict tort liability, section 402B misrepresentation, breach of an implied warranty, and common law negligence. Each theory possesses characteristics or elements which distinguish it from the others. Accordingly, submission of the plaintiff's case varies significantly depending upon the theory under which recovery is sought.

Unlike the plaintiff's case, submission of the defendant's case is generally the same regardless of the theories involved. Under both pure comparative causation and article 2212a comparative negligence, the jury is instructed to determine the percentage of the injuries caused by the plaintiff's actions as well as the defendant's conduct and/or products. Despite this uniformity in submission, however, article 2212a and pure comparative causation differ significantly on several critical issues not determined by the jury.

---

225. *Duncan*, 665 S.W.2d at 424. Under pure comparative causation, the failure of the plaintiff to avoid the consequences of an injury producing event constitutes a form of negligence for allocation of a percentage of causation. Since the jury allocates the percentage causation for avoidable consequences, the manufacturer has been afforded the opportunity to submit all defenses recognized under *Duncan v. Cessna Aircraft Corporation*, 665 S.W.2d 414 (Tex. 1984). Despite the percentage of contributory negligence found by the jury against the plaintiff, the plaintiff necessarily will recover the percentage of causation found by the jury against the nonsettling negligent defendant and the strictly liable in tort manufacturer. The percentage of fault allocated to the settling tortfeasor precludes plaintiff from recovering the percentage of the jury's award.

226. A more difficult problem involves the decision of the defendants to elect either to submit issues of fault against a settling tortfeasor or to take a credit under the provisions of Article 2212a. If plantiff succeeds in obtaining a finding of strict tort liability against at least one defendant, *Duncan* pure comparative causation applies and defendants are precluded from electing to take a credit for a settling tortfeasor. Proper submission of issues to provide for this contingency presents a most difficult challenge.

TABLE OF CASES

C

N

O

P

Q

R

S

T

U

INDEX OF TOPICS

DEFENDANTS

DEFENSES

DEPOSITIONS

DESIGN DEFECTS

EXEMPLARY DAMAGES

EXPERT TESTIMONY

FAILURE TO WARN

FORUM NON CONVENIENS

GOVERNMENT CONTRACT DEFENSE

INDUSTRY-WIDE LIABILITY

INNOCENT MISREPRESENTATION

JURISDICTION

LIABILITY

LIMITATIONS

MANUFACTURING DEFECTS

RELEVANCY

RESTATEMENT (SECOND) OF TORTS

SALES-SERVICE HYBRID

SEALED-CONTAINER DOCTRINE

SECOND IMPACT

SERVICES

SPECIAL ISSUES